University of
Hertfordshire

College Lane, Hatfield, Herts. AL10 9AB

Learning and Information Services
College Lane Campus Learning Resources Centre, Hatfield

For renewal of Standard and One Week Loans,
please visit the web site **http://www.voyager.herts.ac.uk**

This item must be returned or the loan renewed by the due date.
The University reserves the right to recall items from loan at any time.
A fine will be charged for the late return of items.

Neuropsychology:
From theory to practice

David G. Andrewes

Psychology Press
Taylor & Francis Group

HOVE AND NEW YORK

Published 2001 by Psychology Press Ltd
27 Church Road, Hove, East Sussex BN3 2FA

www.psypress.co.uk

Simultaneously published in the USA and Canada
by Taylor & Francis Inc,
29 West 35th Street, New York, NY 10001

First published in paperback 2002 by Psychology Press
27 Church Road, Hove, East Sussex BN3 2FA
29 West 35th Street, New York, NY 10001

Psychology Press is part of the Taylor & Francis Group

British Library Cataloguing in Publication Data
A catalogue record for this book is available from the British Library

Library of Congress Cataloging in Publication Data
Andrewes, David G., 1946–
    Neuropsychology : from theory to practice / David G. Andrewes.
      p. cm.
    Includes bibliographical references and index.
    ISBN 1–84169–103–8
    1. Neuropsychology.   2. Clinical neuropsychology.   I. Title.
  QP360 .A53   2001
  612.8—dc21   2001019340

ISBN 1–84169–103–8 (hbk)
ISBN 1–84169–291–3 (pbk)

Cover design by Jim Wilkie
Half title illustration by Holly Andrewes
Typeset in the UK by RefineCatch Limited, Bungay, Suffolk
Printed and bound in the UK by Bookcraft, Midsomer Norton, UK

About the Author

David Andrewes completed a doctorate in Clinical Neuropsychology at the Institute of Psychiatry, University of London. He also worked there as a lecturer and researcher. In 1984 he was invited to take up a lecturing post in clinical neuropsychology at the University of Melbourne, Australia. He is now a senior lecturer in the Department of Psychology and a Senior Clinical Neuropsychologist with the Royal Melbourne Hospital. His research interests within both clinical and experimental neuropsychology include memory disorders, remediation of memory, and perceptual disorders and problem solving.

To Jenny, Nicholas and Holly, and in loving memory of my mother Jennifer M. Andrewes.

Contents

Preface

This book derives from the author's own teaching to medical students and advanced undergraduate psychology students, and some postgraduate teaching. The chapters have therefore been developed from basic to more advanced levels of teaching. While the student intending to take neuropsychology to a higher level will find this book useful even at an early stage in their undergraduate education, the text is largely aimed at the more advanced student. As the title would suggest, this text may be particularly useful to students who are ultimately considering a clinically oriented career within the health-related sciences or clinicians who wish to "brush up" on their neuropsychology.

Although this text is not a book on clinical neuropsychology, it reflects the author's own background as a researcher and clinician. There are books that cover theoretical issues and books on clinical issues, and this one is an attempt to bring these areas together without compromising a theoretical approach.

This book was developed partly out of the perceived need to bring together topics that have been traditionally treated separately. There is an attempt to provide what the author refers to as a third-generation text in neuropsychology. A first-generation text is seen as one of the traditional type where each chapter was devoted to a differ-

ent lobe of the brain. Such an approach tends to ignore the brain dynamics, the way different brain areas interact to provide function, a feature that is well illustrated by functional neuroimaging studies. A second-generation text discusses neuropsychology in terms of functional topics such as memory or perception, allowing brain dynamics to be described in terms of a particular functional goal. This is an advantage because this approach allows the brain to be viewed as a network of systems, with different brain areas contributing towards a function in concert. However, a third-generation text attempts to show links and a synthesis between these various functional areas. In this way the various overlaps between topics are revealed. Terms like attention and perception are developed by us, and the brain does not recognise the borderlines that we have artificially provided. It is important that a third-generation text recognises that these functions influence each other.

A second theme within this book is to provide a polemic within which to view what is a rapidly changing science. As an educator one of the greatest pleasures is to see a student develop a sense of power as they supply their own interpretations to a set of interesting results. This developing independence is an indication of a style of thinking that promises a development of knowledge long after leaving university. In order to encourage this kind of approach the book sometimes discusses the progression of thinking towards a final conclusion as a way of showing how the detective story of neuropsychology may be logically unravelled.

Finally, it is with some trepidation that the author has produced a book during the first Kuhnian explosion of a new paradigm referred to as *functional imaging*. These new techniques allow the metabolic dynamics of the brain to be inspected while the patient completes a task. A literature search of key words gives an indication of the rapidity with which researchers have embraced this research tool. Since 1990 the number of studies using these techniques has doubled. Even with a healthy degree of scepticism and caution it is easy to see that functional imaging is the most amazing advance in the search for knowledge that neuropsychology has ever seen. The golden age of neuropsychology has arrived and I hope readers will enjoy sharing it with me.

1

An introduction to modern neuropsychology

GENERAL INTRODUCTION

Neuropsychology is the study of the relationship between brain and behaviour. The term behaviour is used here in its broadest sense to include the study of higher mental functions such as memory, language, perception, and attention, but other areas are included such as emotional and physical behaviour (motor movements). All of these areas provide chapter headings within this book that focus on how different brain mechanisms act to support function. Also, and in keeping with the author's clinical research background, there are further chapters that deal with issues regarding the recovery and rehabilitation of brain-damaged patients.

This first chapter is designed to orient the newcomer to neuropsychology. Over the years the author has noted apprehension among some students when they are faced with the many unfamiliar neuroanatomical terms that describe the brain. This task is not nearly so challenging when brain structures are described alongside their functional purpose. Therefore, while it is

assumed that the reader will have access to an additional neuroanatomical text, it is expected that the student will learn much of their working neuroanatomy as this book progresses through the various chapters.

In order to ease the reader into a grasp of basic concepts, this chapter starts with a look at ideas that concern the evolutionary development of the brain and how the human brain compares with other species. There is also a discussion of the main arteries of the brain using the clinical disorder of stroke as a basic exercise. Many of the patients studied in neuropsychology have some form of damage to arterial flow of the brain so this provides information that is of value to research and clinical practice.

In the second half of this chapter there is a brief description of the history of neuropsychology. Here there is an accent on not so much what past researchers have done but on their viewpoints on how brain organisation should be conceived. There is a description ranging from researchers who first introduced the scientific study of neuropsychology, to more recent influences. In the final part of this chapter the discussion focuses on modern neuropsychology and methods of research. In this context, the influence of cognitive neuropsychology with its accent on the analysis of psychological process is discussed, together with the more recent innovations of functional neuroimaging. Also, as an introduction to modern neuropsychology, functional neuroimaging methods are described as a means of observing the activity within the brain during task performance. As will be discussed, this gives enormous advantages to the modern researcher and the description of these methods provides an introduction to the many functional imaging studies that are described in this book.

TABLE 1.1	
Approximate relative brain size compared to body size for a number of species	
Species	**Ratio**
Rat	0.4
Cat	1.0
Rhesus monkey	2.1
Chimpanzee	2.5
Dolphin	6.0
Human	6.3
Adapted from Blinkov and Glesner (1968).	

FUNCTIONAL NEUROANATOMY

Brain evolution and interspecies comparisons.

An exploration of brain evolution and comparison of the structure of our brain with other species reveal certain basic attributes of the human brain. Comparison with other species is also important if only because a great deal of research is conducted with these species and the results of these studies are often used to model human neuropsychology. By reviewing these differences attention is drawn to some basic, but important, features of human development and behaviour.

We will never have a good knowledge of the skills and attributes of early man but archaeological detective work has revealed some interesting explanations for our success as a species.

One of our most basic advantages is the size of our brain. Fossil remains of hominid skulls indicate the way our brain size has increased as we have evolved. This is of interest because our brain, relative to our body size, is larger compared to other species (see Table 1.1). Most of the recorded increases in brain size occurred long after our ancestors became bipeds. Indeed, fossil remains of the skulls of the first upright walking hominids show a brain size similar to that of the modern-day chimpanzee (Lewin, 1993). It is of interest that increased brain size is related, in a broad way, to increased sophistication in terms of both skill development and culture (see Table 1.2), although this remains somewhat controversial. For example, the more robust, larger (and from digit width, arguably less dextrous) Neanderthals had a larger brain than our more direct ancestor *Homo sapiens* and ourselves (Lewin, 1993). Neanderthal man lived alongside our ancestor *Homo sapiens* for some 40,000 years before becoming extinct for reasons not known. However, when brain size according to skull casts is compared to the size of the head of the femoral bone (hip bone), Neanderthals had a smaller encephalisation quotient than those hominids that followed (see Ruff, Trinkaus, & Holliday, 1997, for an argument for this measure).

There is obviously a broad and inexact relationship between the increase in skills and the encephalisation quotient as indicated in Table 1.2. Nevertheless, a similar progressive relationship may be seen with the increased sophistication of tool making. *Homo erectus* used a rough two-headed axe referred to as an Acheulian axe, which was found in France and was named after a village of the same name. Later, some 500,000 years ago, a more sophisticated method of stone splitting was developed by the later *Homo erectus*, while *Homo sapiens* developed a two-process method of making blades. The skill improvements of modern man compared to other hominids are sometimes referred to as a cultural revolution by archaeologists and the turning

TABLE 1.2

Endocranial volumes and skills of the hominids (not indicative of the line of descent)

	Approx. years from present	Skills					Enceph. Quotient
Australopithecines	2–4 million	Biped					
The Habiles	1.7–2 million	Biped	Tools				<3.4
Homo erectus	1.7 million to 250,000	Biped	Tools	Fire			3.5–4.2
Neanderthal man	36,000–150,000	Biped	Tools	Fire	Ceremony		4.8
Modern Man: *Homo sapiens sapiens*	50,000	Biped	Tools	Fire	Ceremony	Art	5.3

Encephalisation quotients are approximate adaptations from Ruff, Trinkaus, and Holliday (1997).
Reprinted with permnission from *Nature, 387*, 173–176. Copyright 1997 Macmillan Magazines Limited.

point for many is the introduction of art. Early art records suggest that art was not merely for spiritual purposes, but was also important for the development of symbolism and reasoning (Delporte, 1995).

It is perhaps not too surprising that there is not a close relationship between relative brain size and skill enhancement of the hominids if one considers the number of unrecorded non-durable ways in which we must have developed during this time (Corballis, 1991). No doubt there have also been other important processes that have encouraged natural selection towards greater brain capacity and one of these may be our apparent predilection for intraspecies competition.

There are also some reasons why brain size or encephalisation quotient may not be the only consideration. There are a number of qualitative features of brain structure that reflect on brain efficiency, most obviously the development of the upper part or surface of the human brain, referred to as the cortex or neocortex. This is the excessively corrugated walnut-like surface of the brain. These corrugations or folds allow a larger surface area of the brain—a surface area that contains most of the brain cell bodies. In this way a maximum number of brain cells can be compressed into a relatively small area. A second important way in which the actual size of the brain may be misleading relates to the function of

the brain areas that have undergone the most development in the human species. There is also a qualitative way in which the brain has developed, which is missed if we merely look at size.

The pertinence of these more specific brain developments becomes clearer when a comparison of our brain is made with those of other related and unrelated species. Such comparisons provide insights into the special attributes and qualities of human behaviour. When comparisons are made between species, it is clear that the neocortex is the area which is most developed in hominids (Stephan & Andy, 1969). However, there are other more subtle distinctions. For example, it can be seen from Figure 1.1 that the overall size is perhaps not as important as the relative size of the different brain areas. It can be seen that, in the rat brain, a proportionally large area is devoted to olfaction (sense of smell). In contrast, the distribution and relative proportion of the sense areas of our cousin the chimpanzee are remarkably similar to our own. The brain of the chimpanzee and the human brain have considerable areas *not* devoted to primary senses. These "non-sensory" areas include the prefrontal cortex, an area that has relevance to our ability to adapt to the environment and solve problems creatively. Other areas that surround the sensory areas are referred to as the "sensory association" areas. Because the sensory association areas are

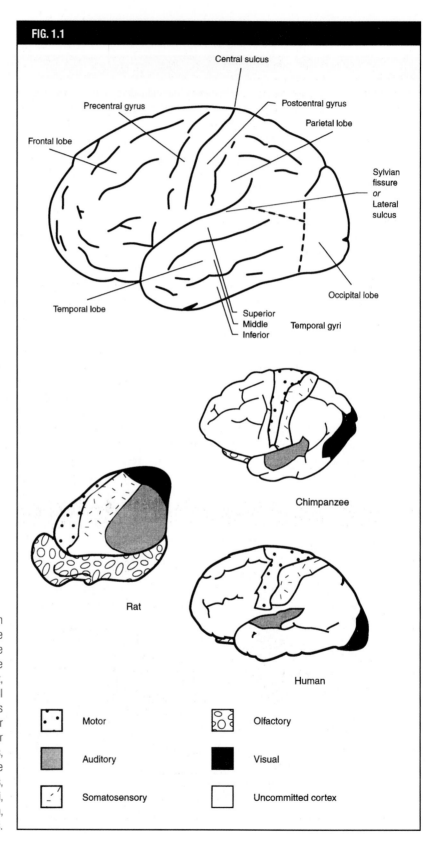

FIG. 1.1

Comparison of the human brain with the chimpanzee and the rat brain. Note the relative area devoted to the sensory system. The cortex, which contains the cell bodies of the neurone, is corrugated to give a greater surface area. The creases or valleys are the sulci (sulcus, singular) and the bumps are referred to as gyri (gyrus, singular). The larger sulci, which divide up the brain, are referred to as fissures.

Central sulcus

Precentral gyrus

Postcentral gyrus

Parietal lobe

Frontal lobe

Sylvian
fissure
or
Lateral
sulcus

Temporal lobe

Superior
Middle
Inferior

Temporal gyri

Occipital lobe

Chimpanzee

Rat

Human

	Motor		Olfactory
	Auditory		Visual
	Somatosensory		Uncommitted cortex

situated in areas bordering areas of sensory input (visual for sight, auditory for hearing, somatosensory for tactile or haptic sense), the position of the association areas allows some integration between these different sensory systems. The association areas are the neutral go-betweens that allow the combined analysis of all the sensory systems of the brain. These association areas are, therefore, broadly important to the analysis of information according to our experience.

Whether or not the frontal areas are relatively larger in humans compared to chimpanzees is a matter of some controversy. Recently, comparisons between humans and apes confirm that we have larger brains, but when compared to chimpanzees our frontal lobes are not relatively larger in contrast to other brain areas (Semendeferi, Damasio, Frank, & Van Hoesen, 1997). However, Rilling and Insell have shown that the human frontal cortex has more and deeper convolutions, suggesting a relatively greater bulk of cortex in this area (Rilling & Insell, 1999).

There are other developments in brain areas that may be seen, even when different hominids are compared. For example, there is an increase in relative skull size in two areas associated with language skills. These protuberances correspond to two areas within the left brain hemisphere. They are referred to respectively as Broca's area and Wernicke's area and are situated in the left frontal lobe and the left parietal cortex respectively (See Figure 1.2). Estimated developments of some form of language may have developed earlier than was originally assumed. Tobias proposes, largely on the basis of the protuberances found in the left cranial area, that some language may have been present in hominids about two million years ago, at the time of the Habiles (Tobias, 1995). The degree of sophistication of our communications at that stage, of course, remains a mystery. One theory is that our estimated pharynx size may have limited the ability to communicate, so that hominids as recent as Neanderthal may have had a severely reduced range of vocalisations (Lenneberg, 1967).

Therefore, there appears to be some evidence of early and specialised brain development within our species that is associated with the faculty of language and communication, which must be seen as one of the cornerstones of our intellectual development and dominance as a species.

However, claims have been made that other structures, such as the hippocampus and the amygdala, within the temporal lobes, are also

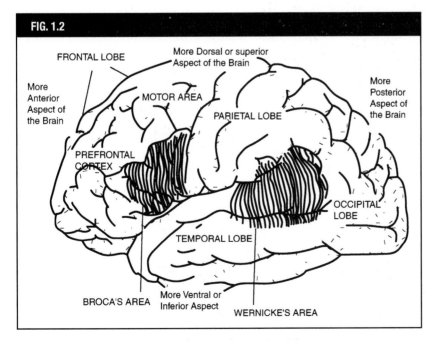

FIG. 1.2

Illustration of the areas of special development in the hominid brain, including the prefrontal area, Broca's and Wernicke's areas, which are responsible for language. This is the lateral aspect of the brain.

developed to an exaggerated degree in humans when compared to other primates and monkeys (Stephan et al., personal communication 1988, cited in Eccles, 1989, p. 105; Semendeferi & Damasio, 2000). The hippocampus and amygdala are structures that make up part of the temporal lobe. These structures are important to the laying down and storage of new memories and the expression of emotion respectively (see Figure 1.3).

Our ability to communicate and remember allows us to pass on information from generation to generation. This has allowed us an extraordinary advantage in interspecies competition. Our quest for increased knowledge does not merely depend on our brain capacity to hold information. We have extended our biological limitations by artificial means, initially by cave drawings, then books and now through CD-ROM and the Internet.

The relative prominence of Broca's area (expressive language) and the temporal lobe with the hippocampus and amygdala (memory and emotion) would seem to suggest something of the adaptive progress of hominids as a species. However, it could be argued that the most crucial marker for our success is our phenomenal ability

to adapt to practically any type of environment. The relative size and complexity of the frontal lobes compared to most other species reflect our adaptive problem-solving abilities. The frontal lobes consist of several areas that are associated with the preparation of motor movements and include an important sub-area referred to as the prefrontal cortex (see Figure 1.2). The prefrontal cortex is associated with functions that give our behaviour organisation, direction, and ingenuity.

This last faculty gives us some flexibility in our adaptation to our environment and enables us to cooperate with others in order to solve problems and achieve goals. It allows us the initiative to use tools that we have to hand in a creative way. For example, given the goal of collecting termites, an anteater will scrape with claws and use its specifically developed and designed snout and tongue. Chimpanzees, however, will have an extended repertoire of skills, which include cleverly prepared twigs that are inserted into the termite mound (Van Lawick-Goodall, 1971). If humans were interested in collecting termites, they would probably produce many more techniques of obtaining the same food source: for example, especially adapted vacuum cleaners. We would probably also set up an association of registered

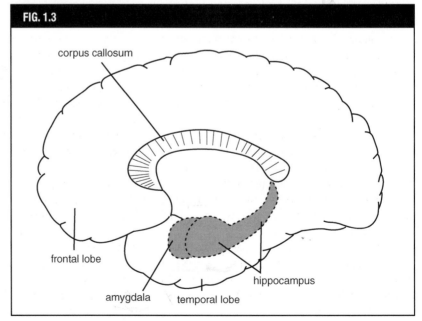

FIG. 1.3

Medial aspect of the brain, as if it had been sliced down the longitudinal fissure. The view is looking at one half of the brain from inside. The hippocampus (important for memory) and the amygdala (important for emotion) are structures that are made up from specialised brain cells beneath the cortex, inside the temporal lobe. These structures are within the medial aspect of the brain (towards the middle of the brain). The corpus callosum is a thick wedge of axons that join the two brain hemispheres and allow intercommunication.

corpus callosum

frontal lobe

amygdala   temporal lobe

hippocampus

collectors to protect our business interests. Something of this ability to be creative, adaptive, and flexible is implied when we talk of the functions of the "executive system", which is most obviously associated with the role of the prefrontal cortex.

Apart from the extension of brain areas that allows us to be more communicative, knowledgeable, and more resourceful compared to rival species, we also have the advantage of an extended infancy and childhood. Other species are more able and well developed at birth. The Australian bush turkey is virtually born running, with behaviours that are largely indistinguishable from the adult. However, we have a rather startling immaturity at birth, to the extent that we are sometimes referred to as being born prematurely. Even compared to the chimpanzee, we have a prodigiously delayed childhood. Following birth we are virtually helpless and dependent for a far longer period, but this immaturity also has some advantage since we have the benefit of being exposed to the environment during a time when our brain is still in rapid development.

Because our brain weight increases roughly fourfold after birth in as many years (Dodgson, 1962), it is just as well that this rapid increase in size takes place *after* birth—if only from the practical point of view of the ease of delivery and the limited size of the adult pelvis (Corballis, 1991, p. 69). However, the increase in size of the brain is very much related to postnatal experience, being associated not with an increase in the number of brain cells, but with the development, maturation and proliferation of connections between neurones (see Figure 1.4).

The features of neuronal development include an increasing arborisation (like the growing branches of a tree) of the neurones. This process involves an increased dendritic growth and an increasing number of connections or synapses with other neurones (synaptogenesis). Studies of animals that have been reared in enriched and stimulating environments show increased neuronal development compared to those reared in impoverished environments (see the Chapter 10 for a more elaborate discussion). As a result, this delayed development offers our species a unique opportunity to be more greatly influenced by our culture and other sources of information that are contrived and newly developed. Because of this, we are less at the mercy of hard-wired instincts and more likely to be able to adapt to changing conditions as they exist at the time of birth. After the number of interconnections between neurones reaches their peak some synaptic connections are then pruned away. In a very real way our brain structure is being moulded by the environment.

There are many novels and films that describe persons being shocked at arriving at a future time after being frozen or put in some form of stasis for hundreds of years. Our prolonged stage of development allows for a kind of 'catch-up' in infancy and childhood. The special features of brain development after birth allow us to adapt to existing conditions in a world of computers and cars. Compared to others species we are not so dependent on the "hard-wired" legacy of evolution.

Essentials elements of brain structure

The basic unit of the brain is the neurone (see Figure 1.4). Neurones include electrically excitable cells that communicate with each other through points of contact referred to as synapses. Transmission between neurones is achieved through the release of a chemical neurotransmitter that travels across the gap (synaptic cleft) between the neurones. The electrochemical transmission travels from the presynaptic terminal to the postsynaptic receptors of the neighbouring neurone. The brain cell body (soma), which contains the brain cell, is located at one end of the neurone. The cell body has the opportunity to send its message over some distance via the axon. The cortex (the upper outer layer of the brain) is made up of the brain cell bodies of the neurones. This is referred to as the grey matter because of its darker colour. As indicated, the axons, with their insulating, white myelin fatty sheath (white matter), are used to carry the messages from one cell to others. Therefore beneath (subcortically) the "grey" cell matter of the cortex is the white matter of the axons. These axons make connections between different brain areas

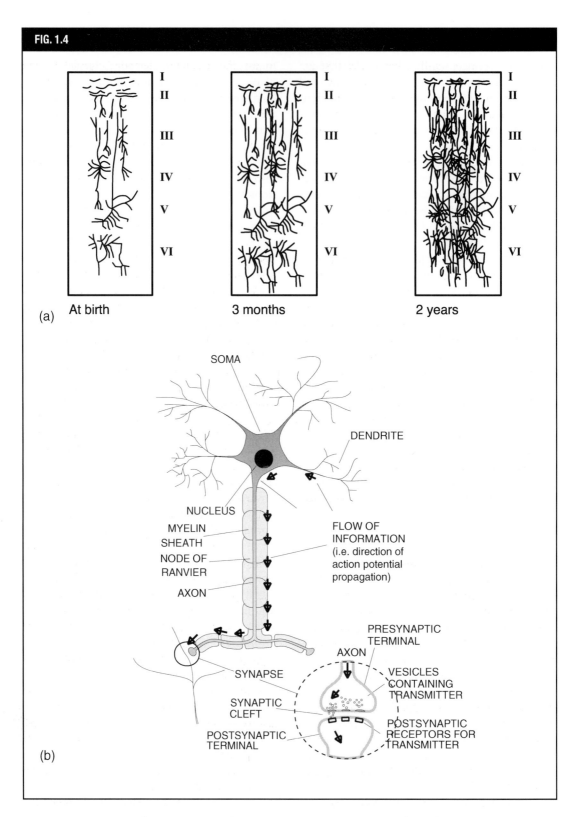

FIG. 1.4

I
II
III
IV
V
VI

(a) At birth

3 months

2 years

SOMA

DENDRITE

NUCLEUS

MYELIN
SHEATH

NODE OF
RANVIER

AXON

FLOW OF
INFORMATION
(i.e. direction of
action potential
propagation)

PRESYNAPTIC
TERMINAL

AXON

VESICLES
CONTAINING
TRANSMITTER

SYNAPSE

SYNAPTIC
CLEFT

POSTSYNAPTIC
TERMINAL

POSTSYNAPTIC
RECEPTORS FOR
TRANSMITTER

(b)

(a) Illustration of increased synaptogenesis and arborisation of brain cells after birth. (b) Illustration of neurone structure (From Barker & Dunnett, 1999, with permission).

within the cortex or with other nuclei that are beneath the cortex. Some areas of the brain such as the internal and external capsules consist of bundles of axons mostly in the same direction, something like a series of super-highways. Some axons are extremely long, going all the way from the motor area in the cortex through the brain stem and spinal cord finally connecting with the peripheral nervous system to allow limb movements. Other neurones have short and stubby axons, adapted to connecting merely with their most immediate neighbours.

The hippocampus and amygdala are structures consisting of "grey matter". There are two other important structures yet to be mentioned: the first is the thalamus, which is discussed in more detail in the next chapter; the second is the basal ganglia, which is discussed in the chapter on movement disorders. The basal ganglia from a collection of structures that also play an important role in preparing and running off sequences of motor movements; it is located in a deep area in each hemisphere and ultimately projects to the cortex, influencing the motor areas shown in Figure 1.6.

Figure 1.4 shows a cross-section of the cortex, which is demarcated into six numbered levels. In this way a cross-section of the cortex reveals a column of cells that have different cell types at the different levels. You would see this if you cut a section out of the cortex, a bit like looking at the layers of a cake. Studies into the processing of sensory information reveal that a particular column of cells may have a single duty, e.g., all concerned with detecting information at a particular visual position on the retina. But the different cell types at the different levels carry out different duties to achieve that goal. In this way some cells may be analysing certain types of visual information such as colour in that area of the retina, while others might be analysing the luminance, whereas still other cells within the column may be transmitting that information to yet other cells. In this way a column may be serving a unified purpose or goal but each level of cells within the column is focused on different sub-tasks to achieve this goal.

As illustrated in Figure 1.1 the cortex (neocortex) of the brain is broadly divided into four lobes: the occipital, temporal, parietal, and frontal lobes. However, a more definitive way of demarcating the various areas of the cortex is to inspect the nature of these cell layers and the predominance of particular cell types. The choice of six levels rather than four is somewhat arbitrary, to the extent that it is dependent on the method of studying and staining the cells (histology) post mortem.

Different brain areas may have a different preponderance of cell types at the various levels. It was Brodmann (1909) who mapped the cortex according these cell profiles in this manner. Brodmann was able to detect changes in the predominance of cell types at the various levels according to the topographical location on the cortex. In other words, depending on the area of the cortex, there is a different prevalence of certain cell types within the different levels. In looking at the different patterns of cell types, he produced a map of the brain according to its cytoarchitecture (cell structure). Some disagreements on the borders of these areas have arisen as different histological techniques have been developed and the functional contributions of different brain areas have become clearer. Although some of his brain areas have since been challenged, Brodmann's areas remain a useful standard providing a reference point that allows communication between scientists.

Cell types vary depending on the area and function of that part of the cortex. For example, when considering brain cell specialisation from a broad perspective the cell type within the visual cortex is quite different from that of the prefrontal cortex. The prefrontal cortex is sometimes referred to as the granular cortex because of the preponderance of granular cells; these cells, such as short stellate cells, allow complex communication within the cortex. The cytoarchitecture in the motor areas is different again, with a preponderance of pyramidal cells. These cells, which are named according to their shape, are designed for transmitting information down long axons: the longest has already been described, leading down through the brain stem eventually to link up with the peripheral nervous system. Brodmann used the evidence of the relative quantity of different cell types at the various levels to map out the areas illustrated below in Figure 1.5.

The cerebral vascular system

A discussion of the brain's vascular system is essential for understanding some of the disorders that will be referred to in this book. Before such a discussion can take place it is important to describe the location and distribution of the main cerebral arteries. These arteries look not unlike the tributaries of a river, although the river is flowing in the opposite direction, from the mouth to the tributaries. At the end of these artery tributaries, the veins emerge to remove the blood on its passage back to the heart. The cerebral arteries supply oxygen and nutrients such as glucose to

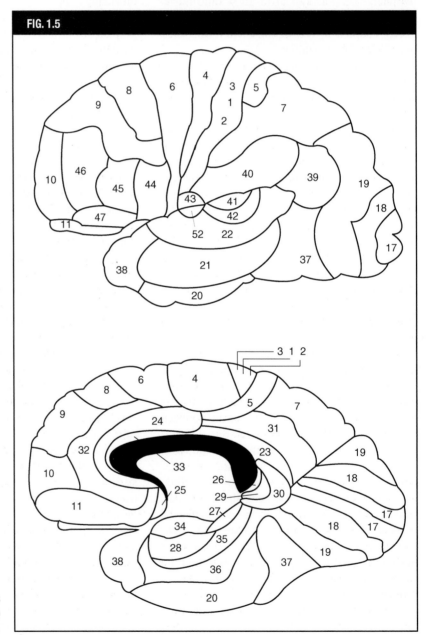

FIG. 1.5

Illustration of Brodmann's areas: (a) lateral and (b) medial brain.

the various areas of the brain. Four main arteries are described at this stage. The middle cerebral arteries supply mainly the temporal lobe, parietal lobe, and some lateral surfaces of the occipital and frontal lobe. The posterior cerebral arteries irrigate mainly the occipital lobe. The anterior cerebral arteries mainly irrigate the medial aspects of the frontal lobes. Finally there is the basilar artery, which irrigates the brain stem (see Figure 1.7). These arteries are supplied by a circular feeder system at the base of the brain called the circle of Willis (Figure 1.7).

In the past neuropsychology studies have often used *stroke* patients because it is a common natural lesion. The term stroke is used to describe two conditions, which are different in the way they arise. A stroke may involve a blockage or a bursting of an artery, usually in an older person. The reader will see the broad areas such strokes may encompass and how it is essential to know which arteries are most affected (Chapter 7 makes specific reference to such lesions). It has to be said, however, that often in cases of stroke there is more than one cerebral artery undermined. In other words the same pathological mechanism that causes a stroke is often affecting the cerebral arterial flow in more than one artery and therefore a right hemisphere stroke affecting one cerebral artery is no guarantee of isolated pathology.

The middle cerebral arteries (left and right) are the most common site for stroke and, as Figure 1.6 reveals, the branches of this artery cover a wide area of the lateral aspect of the brain. A stroke may be associated with either a blockage of a cerebral artery by a blood clot or *embolism* being lodged in an artery (*embolic stroke*) or from rupture in the walls of the cerebral artery (*haemorrhagic stroke*). In both instances areas of the brain may be deprived of the oxygen and nutrients (*ischaemia*), which may cause cell death; this is referred to as an *infarct*. If the heart is not healthy it will produce blood clots (thrombotic embolisms), which may find their way into the cerebral vascular system. The situation may be aggravated by *atherosclerosis* (build-up of plaque on the walls of the arteries) in which the gauge of the cerebral arteries becomes narrowed or sten-

osed (*stenosis*) (see Figure 1.7), thereby increasing the likelihood of embolic stroke, for a blood clot is more likely to be lodged at a point where the artery narrows. To the initiate, the analogy with plumbing is a useful one: The pipe is more likely to get blocked at areas where it has narrowed, and when this narrowing or blockage occurs then pressure builds. As a consequence, as the pressure builds up a burst pipe (artery) may occur if there is a weakness.

Instead of stroke, the term *cerebrovascular accident* (CVA) is also sometimes used, although the term stroke is often preferred since there is usually nothing accidental about the disease process. The process steadily progresses, involving gradual atherosclerosis of the arteries, which includes the steady build-up of plaque material on the inner wall of the artery. This process causes narrowing and reduces the flexibility and resilience of the arteries, making a stroke more likely. Also, as indicated, heart disease may be associated with blood clots forming (thrombosis); these may find their way into the cerebra arteries, causing embolic stroke. Therefore, in one sense at least, there is nothing accidental but rather an insidious onset in which a variety of factors may predispose a person to the likelihood of stroke. The event of the stroke itself, however, is sudden and dramatic in its impact on the patient and therefore the term stroke is apposite, and often preferred (Hachinski & Norris, 1985, p. 3).

The most obvious neuropsychological consequences of stroke relate to whether it occurs in the left or right hemisphere. At an elementary level of discussion a left middle cerebral artery stroke will often involve a number of areas, which may include the areas for language (see Figure 1.6). Therefore the result may be a language disorder referred to as aphasia. A right middle cerebral artery stroke may be more likely to be associated with problems of a visuospatial nature. There may be more problems in tasks that require construction of designs or other copying tests or there may be attentional difficulties. These problems are discussed in more detail in later chapters. It can be seen (Figure 1.6) that the middle cerebral artery feeds the areas necessary for the perception of auditory information (within the temporal lobe area) and the somatosensory area for processing bodily sensations such as touch (within the parietal lobe area). Therefore, depending on the branch involved within the middle cerebral artery, there may be different functional difficulties in these areas. The posterior cerebral artery irrigates the occipital area, more especially within the medial aspect. Therefore a stroke associated with the posterior cerebral artery may result in visual difficulties coinciding with partial destruction of the visual sensory system and possibly perception. In the worst case there might be blindness to visual information opposite to the side of the lesion.

Previously, there has been some discussion of the frontal lobe and a sub-part of this area that is referred to as the prefrontal cortex. As mentioned, this area is important for adaptive and problem-solving behaviour. The anterior branches of the middle cerebral artery and the anterior cerebral artery both irrigate separate areas within the frontal lobe. The middle cerebral artery irrigates the lateral frontal lobe while the anterior cerebral artery irrigates the medial

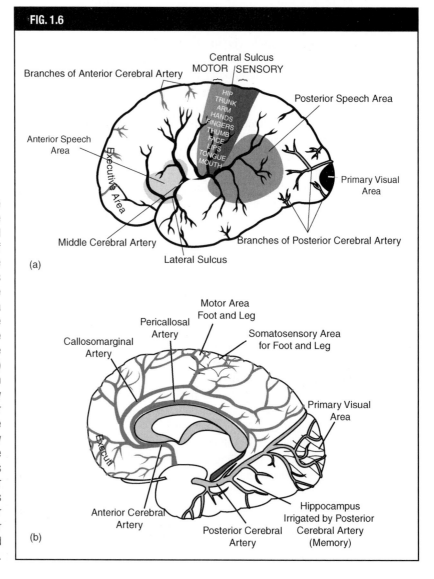

FIG. 1.6

Illustration of the relationship between the cerebral arteries and corresponding areas of functional localisation. The proliferation of arteries has been reduced for the sake of clarity. Often a dysfunction can predict the artery involved and vice versa. The lateral view of the cerebral hemisphere (a) indicates the superior path of the middle cerebral artery as it becomes the anterior rolandic artery irrigating the motor and sensory (somatosensory) areas. The medial view (b) illustrates the passage of the anterior cerebral artery and its relationship to the motor area; also, the posterior cerebral artery (adapted from Petersdorf, 1983).

frontal lobe, sweeping backwards dorsally. Therefore it is not surprising to see different effects on cognition and emotion depending on which cerebral artery is undermined.

In Figure 1.6A the primary motor cortex is illustrated with the primary sensory motor area. They are located in the precentral and postcentral gyrus respectively, either side of the central

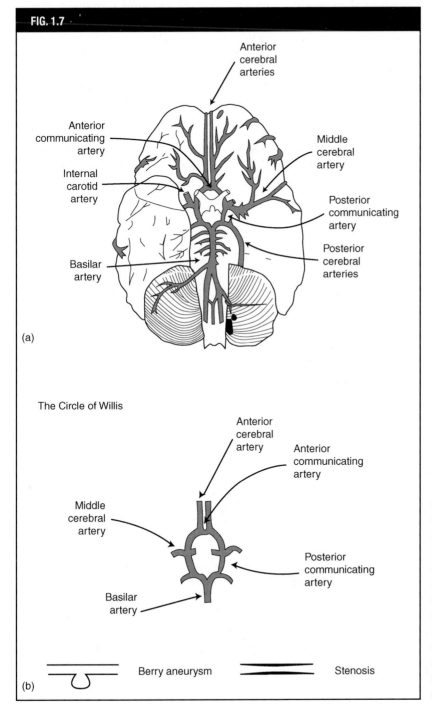

FIG. 1.7

Anterior cerebral arteries

Anterior communicating artery

Internal carotid artery

Middle cerebral artery

Posterior communicating artery

Posterior cerebral arteries

Basilar artery

(a)

The Circle of Willis

Anterior cerebral artery

Anterior communicating artery

Middle cerebral artery

Posterior communicating artery

Basilar artery

Berry aneurysm   Stenosis

(b)

(a) Illustration of the cerebral arteries from a perspective that views the brain at its base. The basilar artery, which irrigates the brain stem, is shown and the various arteries branching off the circle of Willis at the base of the brain. (b) The circle of Willis and illustrations of a berry aneurysm and a stenosis.

sulcus. Destruction of these areas may affect the motor movements on the contralateral side of the body. This is because the long nerve fibres that descend from the brain stem from the primary motor area cross over or *decussate* at an area at the level of the brain stem before they enter the spinal cord.

Stroke often affects limb movements in the form of a hemiparesis (partial or incomplete paralysis of one side). Sometimes one limb on the contralateral side to the lesion is more affected than the other. However, it does depend on which cerebral artery is affected and where in that artery the stroke has occurred. For example, the reader may work out the likely cerebral artery involved if a person has a right paresis of the upper limb and right facial droop. The answer can be worked out using Figure 1.6.[1] A patient with an isolated paresis of the left leg will appear to be swinging his leg forward after each step like a pendulum and is likely to have a stroke involving a different cerebral artery on the other side.[2] Which of these patients is more likely to have a long-standing language disorder?[3]

Finally, on the topic of cerebrovascular disease, the basilar artery may also be associated with obvious clinical symptoms. For example, these patients may suffer from a variety of difficulties involving some motor symptoms since this is the site of the cranial nerves and many of the motor projections pass through this area (see Chapter 8). The brain stem area is also associated with life-preserving characteristics such as respiration, heart rate and also arousal. Patients with brain stem lesions may appear to be very sleepy or have variable levels of arousal. In the worst scenario the patient may go into a coma.

Undue pressure on the brain stem causing a loss of cortical arousal can also occur due to rupture of an aneurysm. In this case, there is a rupture within a circular arterial system called the *circle of Willis* (Figure 1.7). This is a cistern for blood which is fed from the basilar and internal carotid arteries. The circle of Willis allows the blood to be distributed to the various cerebral

arteries of the brain. The blood then travels along the cerebral arteries to the smaller capillaries and even smaller arterioles before being returned to the heart via the cerebral veins. Aneurysms involve a ballooning out of a arterial wall; they may occur anywhere in the circle of Willis and even in the walls of the main arteries branching off the main stems of the cerebral arteries. One of the most vulnerable areas for an aneurysm is the anterior communicating artery. Typically the wall of the artery balloons to form a berry-like shape. This *berry aneurysm* may eventually rupture. Alternatively, slow bleeding may occur, causing gradual symptoms (including drowsiness) may follow. There are treatments for aneurysms, which include surgical repair and the insertion of metal coil within the aneurysm to increase strength and clotting in the area. The worst scenario is that the aneurysm bursts, causing blood to spray out under some considerable pressure within the subarachnoid space. In this case the subarachnoid haemorrhage may cause not only a loss of consciousness (i.e., coma), but also pressure on areas of the brain stem, such as the pons. As the pons serves such vital functions as respiration, emergency surgery may be essential in such a case to relieve the pressure and preserve life.

Although some of the essential brain structures have been discussed there are a number of important areas in neuroanatomy that will be covered in the remainder of this book (see also the appendices for some basic neuroanatomical information). The approach taken here is that neuroanatomy is difficult to learn without some association with function. If the reader is a novice in this area hopefully this information will gradually be learned as this book progresses.

Summary

Humans, compared to other species, tend to have larger brains relative to certain measures of body size. We have a well-developed cortex, which is the upper mantle of the brain that contains much of the brain's nuclei, the parts of the neurone that contain the cell body. The cell body is darker and hence the reference to the cortex as grey matter. The axon or stalk of the neurone has a white fatty myelin sheath, which supports and speeds up the

---

[1] The left middle cerebral artery.
[2] The right anterior cerebral artery.
[3] The patient with the left middle cerebral artery stroke.

transference of the electrochemical impulse; therefore in the area beneath the cortex and between the subcortical nuclei such as the thalamus there are "super-highways" of axons (white matter). These make their passage through brain areas such as the *internal* and *external capsules*.

In the first few months after birth the number of brain cells is almost at its maximum but there is a huge development of the connections or synapses between neurones. The increase in brain size over the first year is related to these increased connections (*synaptogenesis*), but as we develop further some of these interconnections die off and certain patterned connections between cells are encouraged at the expense of others. In this way the infant human brain adapts to environmental demands.

The cortex is more developed in humans than in other species and our behaviour is correspondingly more undermined by injury to this area. Nevertheless, we are more flexible because unlike the lower species we are less specialised to a particular environmental niche. Because of the complexity of our neuronal system within the cortex we have many more options in responding to different stimuli (see Mesulam, 1998, for a further discussion).

The functional significance of different types of neurone was discussed earlier. These were described as showing up at different layers within the cortex and are discernible after certain staining techniques have been applied post mortem. Each layer shows a different configuration or *preponderance* of cell type, depending on the brain area. This pattern of different layers of brain cell is referred to as cytoarchitecture. Different areas have a different cytoarchitecture. This may seem a rather subjective way of demarcating different brain areas; however, this demarcation into Brodmann's areas often usefully reflects the functional significance of these areas. For example, when you move from the premotor area to the primary motor area or motor strip there is a change, with a predominance of Betz cells—those large pyramidal cells that transmit messages to the brain stem and beyond. These changes in the neuronal configuration have been noted and used to demarcate different brain areas by Brodmann.

Controversy surrounds his demarcation and empirical data for some of the areas within the fissures (large sulci) is being researched at the present time. The Brodmann areas remain a useful point of communication between scientists.

Finally in this section there has been an attempt to show some preliminary information concerning the relationship between damage to the cerebral arteries as a consequence of stroke or aneurysm on some areas of functioning. Stroke patients are not uncommonly observed in our daily lives and observation of these patients may give us clues concerning the artery involved and the kinds of neuropsychological dysfunction they may be suffering from. The process of clinical diagnosis is one of deduction and logic, and a knowledge of neuroanatomy is helped by realising the relationship of impaired function to possible causes. Individual differences may undermine expectations but rules that are true more often than not may be learned and applied.

Neurological disorders such as stroke may have a particular profile of symptoms which may give an indication of the underlying physiological mechanism. The probability that language is organised to the left hemisphere, that certain body parts are located in upper or lower areas of the motor strip and the positioning of the various sensory areas all encourage an analysis of the patients lesion even before they go for a brain scan. Throughout this book there will be a further identification of the influence of cerebrovascular damage on function.

AN INTRODUCTION TO HISTORICAL AND MODERN RESEARCH PERSPECTIVES WITHIN NEUROPSYCHOLOGY

Introduction

In many ways the arguments that existed in the past within neuropsychology are still with us. There are still tensions and similar disagreements on how neuropsychology should be researched and modelled. For example, whether the study of single cases can be relied on to illustrate theory or whether modelling of psychological impairment can take place without reference to brain structure are both arguments that have been recycled over the years.

Nevertheless, there have been huge advances with the recent paradigm shift in the use of functional imaging. This has resulted in models that are more dynamic and frequently suggest networks of neuronal connections that interact between brain structures. Functional imaging allows a window into brain metabolism during the time that a task is actually being carried out and therefore allows many insights into how the brain produces function. This area, which is discussed towards the end of the chapter, has revolutionised research into neuropsychology but as will be argued, it does not provide all the answers. Despite these advances in research methods there is still great uncertainty concerning how we should conceptualise the organisation of the brain and how this relates to the way we function. There are still interesting and valid lessons that we can learn from discussing past endeavours in this area and clear historical influences that have helped to shape modern perspectives of neuropsychology.

In this chapter the path is tracked from early to recent approaches to research. Over this time we see a contrast between a dependence on lesion studies in which single patients or groups of patients with damage to specific brain areas have been compared to normal functioning persons. In these lesion studies, the patient(s) will show some impaired performance on some tasks and not others. Such lesion method studies alert the neuropsychologist to the possible function of the damaged area. Today modern studies often use radiological imaging techniques, which track the movement of blood in the brain of a person engaged in a particular task. The challenge to interpretation is somewhat similar. Is the area which has increased blood flow playing a functional role and if so what role?

Here are three possible explanations of such results of a single hypothetical lesion that has resulted in the impairment of a function, e.g. language. In such cases the theoretician has decided what has caused the impairment. Here are some alternatives:

1. One possible explanation is that damage has occurred to a centre for language. This is an extreme localisationist view in which the specific brain area on its own provides the mechanism for the function, e.g. a speech centre. For example, we will learn that bilateral destruction of the hippocampus causes amnesia: the patient is unable to learn new information. The hippocampus is a highly specialised structure that has a role that cannot be easily taken over by other structures.

2. An alternative explanation is that there has been a disconnection between two centres. Here the coordination between two centres is required for the expression of a function. The connections between two centres are damaged, preventing the communication crucial to expression of the function. Patients may not be able to read (dyslexia) because the visual information from the print is not reaching the structures that are important for analysing the meaning of information.

3. Yet another possibility is partial damage to a system or network. Such a system contains a number of interacting components necessary for the expression of the function. This is a more holistic or hierarchical view that proposes that a system is damaged and consequently undermined. For example, a Parkinson patient has a loss of neurotransmitter substance called dopamine. This may undermine the integrity of a group of structures called the basal ganglia deep in the brain. The patient may still be able to walk but motor movements are abnormal.

The appreciation of these possibilities, and a range of others, is essential when considering the difficulties that neuropsychologists face when model making.

If we step inside the shoes of a car mechanic who is trying to diagnose why a car has broken down, the above proposed example 1 might be described by damage within a specific part of the engine which is vital to its running, e.g. a malfunction of an alternator. Continuing with the analogy, example 2 above might be described as a broken fuel-line in a car: the petrol is not getting from the petrol tank to the engine. Example 3 might be described in terms of impure petrol. The car is still functioning but with less efficiency. One should note that both the mechanic and the theorist in neuropsychology are often beset by the problem that the same deterioration in performance can be due to quite different causes. Unlike the motor mechanic, neuropsychological theorists do not have a manual. The manual has to be created.

In the following section we survey some of the early attempts at modelling the brain. This is followed by a more elaborate account of the influence of Alexandra Luria and his contributions, which have strongly influenced contemporary thought in neuropsychology. The discussion will then be brought more up to date by contemplating the influence of cognitive neuropsychology. Cognitive neuropsychology can at once be seen as

an approach to research but can also be seen in its historical context as a movement that has had an impact on modern theory. Finally, the implications of the most recent progress allowed by the functional neuroimaging revolution are discussed. This description of methods will include reference to what these new approaches are measuring, the reliability of these methods and their limitations and advantages.

Early historical perspectives within neuropsychology

Past and present neuropsychology abounds with different descriptions of how the brain processes act on information. Some of these models, which are referred to here as *micro* models, are based on specific aspects of neuropsychological function, e.g. how we recognise faces. In contrast, *macro* models take a broader perspective and attempt to

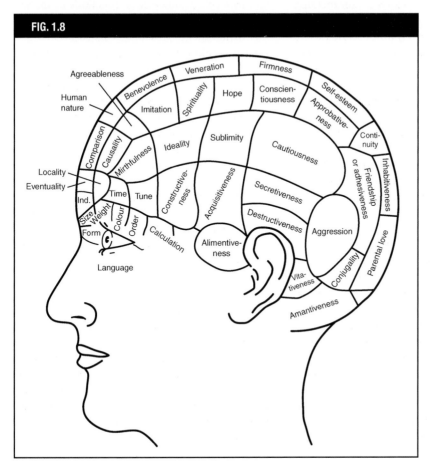

FIG. 1.8

Phrenology and Gall's 27 attributes (adapted from Miller & Buckhout, 1973).

provide an *overview* of how the brain works to process a wide variety of functions. When we review the early history of neuropsychology many of these macro models can be seen to be supportive of either a holistic or localisationist point of view. Broadly, the extreme localisationist position proposes that each part of the brain performs a different and separate function, while the contrasting extreme holistic position sees the whole brain as being involved, with no part operating in isolation to provide a specific function.

The earliest and most extreme localisationist view was put forward by Franz Josef Gall towards the end of the eighteenth century (Boring, 1929). Gall believed that different attributes of personality and intellect were represented by separate centres in the brain (see Figure 1.8). Further, Gall believed that the specific development of a particular centre would push out the cranium to the extent that it would cause a protuberance or bump that could be observed and felt externally. He derived this view from observing classmates at school. He thought, for example, that he noticed those with excellent memories appeared to have protruding orbits around the eyes. While Gall's theory might cause some amusement today, he was not quite as frivolous as he is sometimes portrayed. He was highly respected as a brain anatomist and, among his other achievements, he was also the first person to identify the commissures, e.g. corpus callosum—the dense wedges of axons that allow communication between the two brain hemispheres (see Chapter 6 for diagrams of these interhemispheric connections).

Although Gall's theory was not clearly connected to his anatomical work (Zola-Morgan, 1995, p. 362). It was nevertheless derived upon an empirical basis of sorts. For example, he studied a very large number of skulls and casts of persons of notoriety such as criminals, and those who were particularly gifted, for example Voltaire and Descartes.

In fairness to Gall, he was also suitably cautious about his model of the human mind (Zola-Morgan, 1995). However, his collaborator Johann Gaspard Spurzheim was far more ambitious for this theory and perhaps saw the possi-

bilities of some financial gain. Spurzheim developed the theory of attributes and location into the art of phrenology, which was a method that can basically be described as discovering a person's attributes by feeling the bumps on their head. This early type of personality test was very popular around the turn of the century and it is said that Queen Victoria had all her children assessed by this method. Of course, reading bumps is a very subjective process and cleverly couched interpretations can be made to sound true most of the time. For this reason, like astrology and some psychotherapies, phrenology lasted longer than it should have done.

Gall nevertheless had a positive influence on theoretical thinking for two reasons. Firstly, he drew attention to the possibility that localisation could exist and also observed cases of injury produced by sword injuries—findings that allowed him to localise some verbal functions to the left frontal lobe. This theory was to be developed further by another localisationist called Bouillard, a French neurologist who developed these ideas in the 1860s (Boring, 1929). It is possible that eventually Paul Broca was also directly, or indirectly, influenced by Gall's work. Since Gall located one of the areas of expressive language within the left frontal lobe using sounder principles of research, working from previous results of lesions to the brain following sword duels.

Secondly, Gall's view that the brain was functionally heterogeneous was a push against the rather restrictive religious and philosophical views of the day. These views, at the time, saw the brain as an undifferentiable seat of the soul, a view that lent itself to the ethically dubious proposition that insanity could be seen as a case of "possession by the devil". Phrenology, although it was obviously in error at the time, allowed the proposition that lunacy could be diagnosed by physiological attributes without blame. This helped social reform and the sick patients who needed care rather than exorcism no doubt benefited. Therefore phrenology, unlike some of the more damaging mythologies, was used as a means of diagnosis and a guide to treatment of mental illness in Europe and the United States (Zola-Morgan, 1995).

Following Gall, and in distinct opposition to his views, Flourens espoused a holistic theory of brain function. He suggested that one can remove a rather large part of an animal's brain, either in the "front", or in the "back" or on the "top", without losing any of its faculties (Flourens, 1824). Flourens' methods of research have since been criticised and found wanting but it was not until some 40 years later that the holistic view started to lose ground. In 1861 Paul Broca, an anthropologist and physician, reported on a patient nicknamed "Tan". Tan was named after one of the few expressive sounds this patient could make. Based on the observations of Tan and other patients, Broca proposed that speech was centred in the area which was later to take his name, within the left frontal operculum (the third frontal convolution of the left hemisphere, see Figure 1.3). This was the main site of damage that was found following a post-mortem investigation. While later evidence provided by such researchers as Wernicke proved this to be an oversimplification (Wernicke, 1876), the first foundations of modern theory had, nonetheless, been laid. Carl Wernicke showed that a more posterior area (to the back of the brain, see Figure 1.2) was also important for language, especially for comprehension.

Perhaps it is an illustration of our uncertainty in this area that some of the older models are, on occasions, resurrected and given a fresh airing. For example, Goldstein's holistic model has been referred to as a useful model for describing the processes of recovery from brain damage (Kinsbourne, 1981). Goldstein described the brain in terms of acting as a whole to produce a function (Goldstein, 1942, 1948), with neurones (which include the cell bodies of the brain) acting variously in inhibitory and excitatory ways throughout the brain. In his model the pattern of excitation varies with the functional requirements.

There are other models, which have take a middle road and do not fit into either the holistic or localisationist camp. For example, Hughlings Jackson (Taylor, 1933) had an alternative theory, which was hierarchical in its structure. He is often acknowledged as the father of English neurology and in the latter half of the nineteenth century was noted for his contributions to the understanding of epilepsy. Hughlings Jackson recognised the expertise of Broca and his work in reporting the lateralisation of language to the left, but would not be drawn to supporting a localisationist approach. He was greatly influenced by the writings of a philospher, Herbert Spencer, and the evolutionary view of brain organisation. He proposed that the brain was organised into three levels within a hierarchy according to the assumed phylogenetic evolution of the structures. The earliest and most basic level was thought to be at the level of the spinal cord and cerebellum, the next level including basal ganglia being referred to as a motor region. Finally the highest level was seen as being made up of the prefrontal cortex and sensory cortical areas such as the occipital lobe.

Broadly, Jackson's model predicted certain outcomes which showed the relationship between these levels. For example, if the highest cortical level is damaged then the next level is not contained and therefore behaviour is expressed at the lower, more primitive level. Thus increased speed of reflexes would be expected since the patient would be without cortical control. In keeping with this more subtle approach he proposed that a lesion might result in negative or positive symptoms. This distinction is still popularly used today. Negative symptoms are illustrated by the loss of a function, e.g. loss of language, while positive symptoms are illustrated by aberrant or abnormal behaviour that has occurred since damage, e.g. ataxia (abnormal gait). Positive symptoms may occur when a particular level is damaged and thereby cause an imbalance in the integrity of the overall system.

Jackson reveals a complexity not shared by some other models and provides a view that the dysfunctional effect of lesions is not merely due to the location of the lesion but also to the effect of that lesion on the release or inhibition of other areas. His model has been especially influential within neurology and the clinical analysis of motor disorders.

Alexandra Luria and the functional systems model

A similar sophistication is present in a more comprehensive model devised by a Russian neuropsychologist called Alexandra Luria. This macro model has influenced thinking within neuropsychology for many years and has special relevance for clinicians. This *functional systems model* is outlined by Luria (1973) in his translated book, *The working brain*.

This model proposes that different areas of the brain are specialised to carry out particular roles, but these specialised roles or units are not sufficient on their own to produce a function. Integration is required in this process, whereby different brain modules act in an interdependent manner. Specialised brain areas are reliant on the integrity and efficient functioning of other parts of the brain. This theory gives the impression of different areas working in collaboration or concert to produce behaviour in much the same way that a complete symphony is dependent on the coordinated product of different sections of an orchestra.

Before describing the broad substance of Luria's model, it is important to understand what Luria means by the term *functional systems*. Luria writes that it is entirely correct to use the word function in terms of a function of tissue. He uses an example, in which we might talk about the function of liver, which is to secrete bile, or the function of the pancreas is the secretion of insulin. Luria also points out that we can similarly talk about the function of certain parts of the brain in a similar manner. For example, the function of the Betz cells (a large pyramidal brain cell found in the primary motor cortex or motor strip) is ultimately to generate or execute a motor response. Thus certain parts of the brain appear to have certain specialised functions (Luria, 1973, pp. 27–31). We can therefore talk about certain parts of the brain in the same manner, for example, as one may talk of the functions of the thalamus is to relay sensory information.

However, as Luria points out, there are certain difficulties in talking of some other processes in this same way. He gives the example of the function of respiration. In this case several aspects of

the body and brain are coordinated to provide this function. Luria therefore proposes that it is important to distinguish between functions that are carried out by special brain areas compared to functional systems that require a complex interaction of brain areas, with each brain area performing a different specialised role.

Luria refers to the coordination and activity of these different brain areas as functional systems. Each cognitive activity such as perception, memory, language and attention requires not one brain area but several, each brain area making an important contribution in its own right but being dependent on the expression of others. These functional systems obviously vary depending on the type of function or faculty being produced. For example, memorising requires not just the hippocampus for storing new memories but also other brain areas for selecting to-be-remembered information, and others that act as a store for the new information. This, then, is some way from the narrow concept of localisation that was introduced by Gall and tentatively revealed by Broca.

Luria's model describes a number of units that interact to provide functional systems. They are described as follows: *the unit for regulating tone and waking and mental states*, which is necessary for the arousal of the brain and which originates in the reticular formation of the brain stem; *the unit for receiving, analysing, and storing information*, which relates to areas within the occipital lobe (vision), the temporal lobe (auditory), and the parietal lobe (somatosensory, i.e. haptic or tactile sensation); finally, *the unit for programming, regulation, and verification of activity*, which Luria associates with the frontal lobe and which allows direction and control of motor movement. It is also clear from his writings that Luria saw the frontal lobes as having a wider role in controlling behaviour, which is in keeping with modern views.

The unit for regulating tone and waking and mental states

The first of these units, *the unit for regulating tone and waking and mental states* (see Figure 1.9), is described as providing the required optimal levels of arousal for the brain (see Figure 9). This unit for regulating tone involves an interaction between the reticular system of the brain stem and the thalamus, which, as indicated above, is a structure important for relaying sensory information. The reticular formation also activates the limbic system, e.g. the amygdala (sometimes referred to as the visceral brain because of its role in emotion), the basal ganglia (with its influence on motor movements), and the cortex (with its role in higher mental functioning). The purpose of this unit is to provide the optimum level of arousal that is suitable for any particular functional requirement. For example, we require a different level of brain arousal when playing chess when compared to the activity of running for a bus. In the next chapter we give some clinical examples of disorders that are associated with a loss of arousal due to damage to this unit.

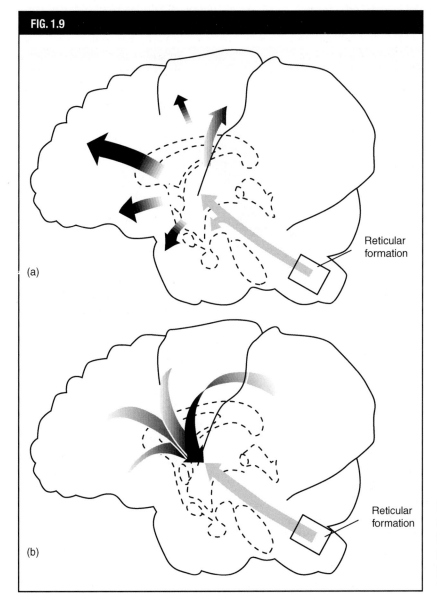

FIG. 1.9

(a)

Reticular formation

(b)

Reticular formation

Luria's model unit for tone, showing an illustration of the effects of (a) ascending and (b) descending tracts (adapted from Luria, 1973).

The unit for receiving, analysing, and storing information

The second unit within Luria's model is *the unit for receiving, analysing, and storing information*. This unit has three zones: the first primary zone includes three primary processing areas for the inputs of basic sensory information. These areas include the striate or calcarine cortex within the occipital lobe for processing visual information, the area of Heschl's gyrus within the temporal lobe for processing auditory information, and the postcentral gyrus within the parietal lobe for the processing of somatosensory (tactile) informa-

tion. Information from these primary zones is followed by two further processing zones. Further analysis takes place in the secondary zone; more often this is referred to as the unimodal association area. This analysis is still modality dependent, e.g. auditory, visual but the perceptual analysis is more complex. The information is then finally processed at the most abstract level in the tertiary zone (polymodal association area) (see Figure 1.10). This final level is *not* modality specific in the sense that it has no particular allegiance to auditory, visual, or somatosensory representation.

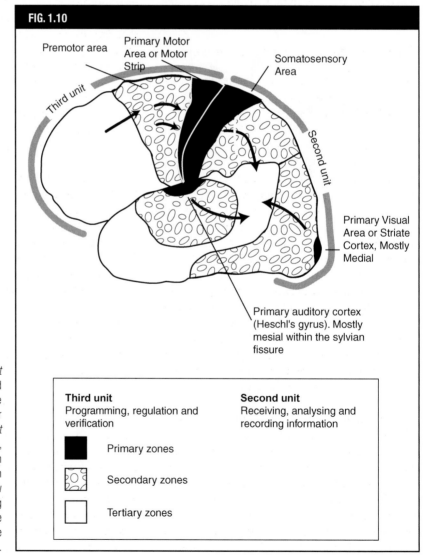

FIG. 1.10

Premotor area

Primary Motor Area or Motor Strip

Somatosensory Area

Third unit

Second unit

Primary Visual Area or Striate Cortex, Mostly Medial

Primary auditory cortex (Heschl's gyrus). Mostly mesial within the sylvian fissure

Third unit Programming, regulation and verification	**Second unit** Receiving, analysing and recording information
■ Primary zones	
▨ Secondary zones	
☐ Tertiary zones	

Diagram of the *second unit* for receiving, analysing, and storing information and the unit for the motor involvement of *the third unit* for the programming, regulation, and verification of activity (adapted from Luria, 1973). Note the flow for the unit receiving information is in the reverse direction compared to the programming of activity.

In summary, this unit describes information being progressively analysed at a more and more advanced level from the registration of basic sensory information, to the secondary zone (unimodal sensory association area) in which the perception of the stimulus for a particular modality (visual, auditory and somatosensory) takes place. From this unimodal area there is a transition to a final tertiary stage in which all the sensory modality inputs are integrated into an abstract amodal code. Luria's tertiary zone is more commonly referred to as a polymodal sensory association area or just the association area. This is an area that recruits information from all the senses at the highest level of analysis.

The unit for the programming, regulation, and verification of activity

The third of Luria's units is *the unit for the programming, regulation and verification of activity*, which is associated with the frontal lobes. The frontal lobes are considered to be important areas for directing and controlling other brain activities. The frontal lobes also control any associated motor behaviour, the movements being prepared in the secondary motor area (usually referred to as the premotor area) and then executed in the primary motor area (the motor strip). Luria sees the *prefrontal cortex* (area anterior to the premotor area in Figure 1.10) as being the tertiary area for the premotor area (secondary zone). From the premotor area where the actions are prepared, the action information is then sent to the primary motor area or motor strip for execution of the final movement. It can be seen that while sensory information is analysed from a primary to a tertiary zone the motor movements are processed in the reverse direction, from tertiary to primary zone.

Luria's stress was on the role of the production of motor movements within the frontal lobes. However, it is clear that he sees this unit as giving direction to all behaviour. In fact, he writes concerning the complex role of the prefrontal lobes as a "*superstructure above all other parts of the cerebral cortex, so that they perform a far more universal function of general regulation of behaviour*" (Luria, 1973, p. 89; Luria's italics).

Later, Luria describes experiments with frontal-lesioned animals which provide evidence that illustrates the tendency for the animal to run automatic routines of behaviour without being able to adapt or control these routines when required. Destruction of the frontal lobes denies the animal an ability to subordinate the animal's behaviour to an internal program. He suggests that the *destruction of the prefrontal cortex leads to a profound disturbance of complex behavioural programs* and to marked *disinhibition of immediate responses to irrelevant stimuli*, thus making the performance of complex behavioural programs impossible (Luria. 1973, p. 91). An illustration of human behaviour losing control due to an inability to resist automatic behaviour comes from a story told to me about a woman who had had a frontal tumour removed and was bathing her baby continually, so much so that the baby's skin had become sore and red. An explanation of this behaviour was that every time she came within sight of the baby's bath in the sink she was triggered by the external stimulus into an automatic routine of washing the baby, being unable to internally control this urge. If the baby's bath had been placed out of sight then the baby may have gone unwashed since again internal control is required to program and plan such behaviour.

The large number of connections between the frontal lobe and practically every other area of the brain suits the teleological role attributed to it (see Figure 1.11 for an example).

Functional systems

Arguments concerning how the brain is organised to produce functions have been largely developed on the assumptions that either the brain is relatively homogeneous and non-specialised or that each brain area has a special role. Luria's model provides a solution that acknowledges specialisation but also draws attention to interdependence between specialised areas. Luria describes three specialised units that are dependent on each other and must act in concert to produce a behaviour. For example, he sees perception as an active process in the way that information is processed and analysed. At the same time this information is fed forward to the prefrontal cortex, which directs

FIG. 1.11

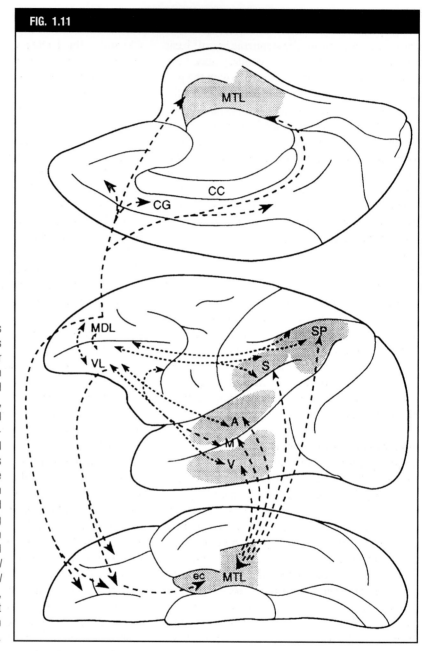

Illustration of the numerous functional connections between frontal and other areas of the monkey brain somatosensory (S), spatial (SP), auditory (A), visual (V), some aspects of Multimodal (M), Ventrolateral (VL), mid-dorsolateral (MDL), Medial temporal lobe (MTL), Corpus Callosum (CC), Cingulate gyrus (CG) (reprinted from Petrides, M., Specialized systems for the processing of mnemonic information within the primate frontal cortex. *Philosophical Transactions of the Royal Society London B, 351,* 1455–1462. Copyright 1996, with permission from the Royal Society).

and controls the selection of particular aspects of the environment for further analysis. At the same time the brain stem is providing the required level of tone or cortical arousal for this activity. The different ways in which these three units cooperate to produce different functions (e.g. speech,

motor activities) are referred to by Luria as different "functional systems" (Luria, 1973).

The three units, one providing arousal, one allowing for the analysis of incoming information, and a third producing and organising behaviour, allow different behaviours to take place. For example, in the case of someone catching a ball in a cricket match, the outfielder, who may have been dreaming after a long period of inactivity, may suddenly hear the ominous whirring sound of a ball travelling at high speed towards him. The auditory unit for processing and analysing information is first activated and allows the interpretation of the whirring sound of the cricket ball and the expectant hush of the other players and spectators. This auditory stimulus alerts the fielder that his services are called upon. The arousal system increases alertness to allow for the emergency situation to be dealt with. The fielder looks up and the unit for analysing information allows the perception of the cricket ball coming towards him. The trajectory of the ball is estimated and the prefrontal cortex coordinates and plans future behaviour. Within this unit for programming, regulation, and verification of behaviour, motor movements are planned and executed that are conducive to catching the ball. The state of arousal is regulated as the fielder steadies himself—he mustn't get too excited. The functional system has in this way contributed to the catching of the ball.

The influence of the cognitive neuropsychology movement

Modern theorising in the area of neuropsychology has been heavily influenced by the cognitive neuropsychology approach to modelling. In the early 1980s a number of cognitive psychologists and psycholinguists became interested in researching brain-damaged patients as a means of supporting and validating theory in areas such as memory and language. It might be difficult to target when the term "cognitive neuropsychology" came into being but the author remembers attending a meeting at the Royal Society in London (UK), which constituted something of a milestone. Among the speakers attending this meeting was a Professor Max Coltheart, who commenced his talk by describing a different approach to researching neuropsychology (Coltheart, 1982). He described the model-building approach. This was an analysis of information processing in which cognitive

functions, e.g. language, could be analysed into component parts. Reading, he said, could be represented by an interaction between the constituent parts of the analysed process. This proposal raised some eyebrows since although there was nothing new about the information-processing analytic approach and indeed there were others at the time that were involved with this approach, the more radical aspect of his proposal was that neuropsychology modelling could be done *without* reference to the underlying neurophysiological mechanism. That is, he argued successfully that behaviour due to brain damage could still be fruitfully analysed without modelling the process in terms of brain mechanisms.

Coltheart went on to propose, based on careful analysis of brain-damaged individuals, that reading disorders could only be fully understood by refined and detailed psycholinguistic analysis. Coltheart postulated that reading included at least two processes. The first was a phonological (sound) representation in which words were read by using certain rules that translate letters into sounds. This allows us to read non-words such as *flerd*. We may have never encountered the non-word *flerd* before but we know from childhood how to pronounce the word by following the rules of pronunciation. There are, however, some irregular words that flout these conventional rules of pronunciation and these irregular words, such as *steak*, just have to be known—we have to learn these words, which have to be stored in some hypothetical lexicon. Thus if we pronounced the word *steak* by the usual rules we would pronounce it to rhyme with *streak* or *leak*. Coltheart reviewed work that showed a possible double dissociation, with some reading-disordered (dyslexic) patients having good performance in experiments requiring knowledge of the irregular words such as *steak* and *pint*, but poor performance with non-words such as *flerd* and *tleck*. A second group of patients were described that had the reverse pattern, with a relatively better performance on reading non-words and poorer performance reading the irregularly pronounced words.

The evidence for Coltheart's theory has been further developed (see Figure 1.12), since this

Illustration of a dual-route model of reading. The orthographic lexicon allows the reading of irregular (and regular) words for a speedy conversion from the physical appearance of the word to its pronunciation. The other route allows a slower process that requires conversion of the letters and letter groups into pronounced sounds according to certain rules.

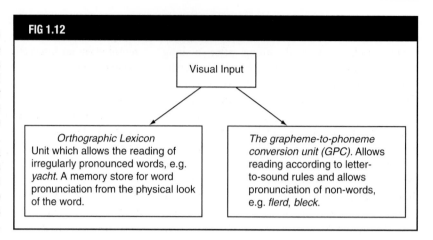

FIG 1.12

Visual Input

Orthographic Lexicon
Unit which allows the reading of irregularly pronounced words, e.g. *yacht*. A memory store for word pronunciation from the physical look of the word.

The grapheme-to-phoneme conversion unit (GPC). Allows reading according to letter-to-sound rules and allows pronunciation of non-words, e.g. *flerd, bleck.*

early work; this and other similar models are discussed in greater depth in Chapter 7).

If Coltheart and colleagues had found a single dissociation, with only cases of patients performing more poorly on non-word reading for example, this would have been less impressive. If this had been the case then there may have been some thoughts that perhaps this was just a very demanding or difficult task. Perhaps the patients performed more poorly on this task merely because they were just more brain damaged. However, he presented evidence that implied a double dissociation.

The term *double dissociation* is used here to denote when two cases or groups have the opposite pattern of impairment. For example, if we have two tasks A and B, one group may be poor at task A, but good at task B, while the other group have the opposite pattern being impaired on task B, but performing normally on task A. When a double dissociation is apparent this result is less likely to be due to the difficulty of the task or a general consequence of more severe brain damage in one of the groups. These results suggest that, for whatever reason, the location of the lesion is an important indicator in influencing the results and suggest a special role of the damaged area in the lost function. If, as was generally the case with Coltheart's patients, the precise area of brain damage was difficult to assess then a double dissociation still increased confidence that different processes were being identified. The useful concept of the double dissociation, and its occa-

sional fallibility, is returned to in future chapters. The analysis of dyslexia is used here to allow the newcomer to neuropsychology an insight into the logic of the process espoused by cognitive neuropsychologists of the time. It was around this same time that the *Journal of Cognitive Neuropsychology* was launched; although it has now broadened its content, in its early days it was mainly devoted to information-processing modelling of the type illustrated above. The influence of the cognitive neuropsychology approach is often referred to in this book in the box and arrow diagrams, which often allow a clearer perspective of the processes involved. Nevertheless, while this analytical approach has proved to be immensely popular, it is increasingly being applied to models that include reference to brain mechanism.

Certain arguments that surrounded this style of research method towards the end of the 1980s provide a challenge to complacency on what was acceptable on research method. The first issue related to the use of single cases versus groups. Normally psychologists prior to the 1980s had studied groups of patients, on the basis that there are certain variations in performance due to the varied experience and backgrounds of the patients and unreliability associated with testing (Caplan, 1988). However, a counter-argument runs that it is not only possible to use single cases to model psychological process but that this is actually desirable (see Caramazza et al. in a special issue of *Cognitive Neuropsychology*, 1988, Volume 5). The advantage of the single-case study is that it allows a detailed analysis of an individual patient profile that is often unique to the individual.

This issue of the use of a single-case study versus groups of subjects is also returned to at various points in this book but a few comments might be made here. First, although these historically early researchers did additionally model brain mechanism, the single-case study has been useful in neuropsychology since the time of Broca and Déjerine. Some of the ground-breaking work of these early researchers has already been mentioned. Sometimes it is necessary to use a rare patient to illustrate a theoretical point. Luria also studied and described the single case to great advantage.

The reasons why the use of groups is preferred by some researchers are the same reasons why group studies are preferred in other areas of psychological research. The individual may be unusual and not representative of other cases; there are also a number of influences on an experiment that may make an individual's response unreliable or invalid.

However, the attraction of using a single case is that the information processing by the patient may be studied in great detail in an attempt to analyse the precise deficit of the patient. This detail is not obscured or swamped by the means of a group of patients—patients who inevitably suffer individually slightly different patterns of deficit. As indicated, the single case is often chosen because it represents a theoretically important distinction. For example, a patient who fails to name an object from its verbal description, but is able to name an object from its visual appearance, might be contrasted with a patient with the reverse deficits to illustrate the existence of two different ways of processing information for naming.

Nevertheless, confidence may be increased if a number of cases have been found that show the same pattern of deficits. For example, as already mentioned, Paul Broca's patient named Tan showed a language disorder following a left frontal stroke in the area that takes his name. Broca was nevertheless restrained in publicising his theoretical ideas comprehensively until he had found at least eight other similar patients. However, it was still the finding of Tan which provided significant information leading to the collection of further cases.

Also, in support of the single case, the rarity of a type of perceptual or language disorder may not mean that the brain of the patient was unusual even prior to brain damage, e.g. developmental disorder causing an unusual representation or organisation of function. The rarity may rather be because the underlying neuropathology is unusual, for example, a tumour in an unusual location (see the rare but crucial cases of agnosia described in Chapter 2). Also in support of the unusual case, there is an experience that when a new neuropsychological disorder is described it is frequently followed in the literature by a series of similar cases. Sometimes the patients are not so rare and the demonstration of the new disorder has taught neuropsychologists to regard existing patients in a new way.

In conclusion, it is a case of "horses for courses", depending on the goal and nature of research a single case or group approach may be appropriate. While the group study has obvious advantages over a single case in that the consistency of a finding may be replicated and fears concerning the unusual representation of a single case may be overcome, the single case study also has obvious advantages that often lead to further group studies. Sometimes a theoretical question can only be investigated on a case-by-case basis. Alternatively the trial of a rehabilitation technique may require application on to number of cases before the validity of the technique is realised.

The second controversy, which was raised within this polemic in the 1980s, relates to the need to model brain mechanisms. Many researchers who saw themselves as cognitive neuropsychologists some 10 years ago would have seen the modelling of brain mechanism in terms of brain structure as being unnecessary, although some might have thought this was desirable. Now it is probably fair to say that most researchers see a clear advantage in attempting to model the brain mechanism at the same time as analysing the process.

The most obvious advantage is that the knowledge base from one area of research, e.g. clinical syndromes, may assist the interpretation of the other information-processing approach.[4] In other words, if the lesioned area is identified then the knowledge of the neurophysiology and past models of various syndromes will help in the interpretation of the results of such modelling described above. Another reason for modelling the brain mechanism is that lesion models or functional neuroimaging (see next section) may help to break down a process into its component parts and reveal the underlying mechanism more elaborately. By using both sources of information there can be a convergence on a solution.

When considering the need to analyse the brain mechanism, group studies may offer information that is denied by the study of the single case. For example, one group approach would to accumulate a number of patients with the same deficit, e.g. comprehension difficulties of a certain kind, and then look at the overlapping scans of the patients to see which area of the brain coincides with the most overlapping lesions (see Kertesz, 1994).

While it is important to describe the lesions associated with a disorder and try to model the brain process underlying the information-processing deficit, there are still difficulties of interpretation that may arise. Apart from the already mentioned problem of patients who show an interesting profile but whose lesions are too diffuse to be analysed, there is also the problem of the selective nature of natural lesions. Natural brain lesions do not, of course, occur randomly. Lesions often follow a pattern of location that is determined by certain neurophysiological constraints such as the positioning of the cerebral arteries. This may have the result that certain quite different disorders may occur consistently together and spuriously look as if they are part of the same syndrome with a common underlying mechanism.[5]

In summary, the cognitive neuropsychological approach of intensive analysis of single cases has

been a productive and useful way of furthering neuropsychology theory. There is also a strong case for group studies, although the research questions may often dictate the approach (Newcombe & Marshall, 1988). While brain process modelling adds a degree of validity to pure cognitive modelling, the analytical approach of cognitive neuropsychology has had and continues to have a very positive influence on modern neuropsychological research.

In this section there has been an attempt to reveal the approaches and epistemology of the original cognitive neuropsychology movement. The purist cognitive neuropsychologist approach promoted some introspection into research methods in the late 1980s. These arguments are now generally muted but the influence of this approach remains and flourishes. Many of the strong champions of this approach are now involved in neuroimaging and other methods of research that focus on brain mechanism and these researchers are to be seen in the forefront of scientific inquiry today.

The functional neuroimaging revolution

As I entered the large and bare laboratory I noted a woman was lying down with her head surrounded by a series of giant steel rings that were wobbling to and fro. The image would not have been out of place in a science fiction film. The patient was completing a task that required her to silently count numbers and while she was doing this her brain was being scanned. She had previously been injected with a small amount of a radioactive isotope, which enabled the movement of blood within her brain to be detected and traced. In this way, as she counted there was a registration of the metabolic reaction within the brain. This was my earliest experience of a positron emission tomography (PET) scan and took place when I visited the University of British Columbia in Canada in the early 1980s.

Functional neuroimaging is a broad term used to describe a method in which the dynamics of brain activation e.g. blood movement, glucose uptake, is scanned in association with performing some psychological task. A brain scan of this type typically takes scans of the brain to provide

---

[4] See a discussion of optic aphasia in Chapter 7.
[5] See discussion on Broca's aphasia in Chapter 7.

a pictorial representation of the metabolic changes during the experimental task. This allows the experimenter to investigate the relationship between brain and behaviour in normal persons or patients with neurological disease. Different methods of functional imaging measure different indices of the brain. For example, when considering PET, the nuclear isotope that is injected and later imaged may have an affinity for highlighting blood flow, while another isotope might be used that has an affinity for glucose uptake (taking far longer).

If blood flow is being imaged then it is understood that blood goes to areas of the brain that require irrigation. Blood carries oxygen and glucose, which are the fuels of the brain's basic unit: the neurone. It is assumed that the brain areas that require increased blood flow are undertaking increased neuronal activity.

Certain assumptions are, of course, made when interpreting the results of neuroimaging studies. For example, there is an assumption that the patients being imaged have a similar motivation to complete the task. A relative deactivation may be associated with poor motivation in some psychiatric groups. However, patient characteristics have not been the main source of concern in this literature.

Even the simplest task requires a number of cognitive processes and some of these are not necessarily of interest to the researcher. For example, if a person is required to press a button upon detecting a target on a screen then there will be brain activations for looking at the stimulus, pressing the button, and many other aspects of cognition. There are so many processes going on even in a simple task that they become impossible to analyse. There may already be a burgeoning literature on the brain response to the perception of visual images and finger motor response during button pressing and the researcher is interested in isolating the attentional response to the target. In order to delineate and isolate the brain changes of interest, the researcher typically runs at least two scans. The first scan looks at the brain activation when the subject presses a button each time they see a stimulus appearing on the screen. The brain images from this scan are then sub-

tracted from a scan in which the task has an additional attentional component. This is referred to as the "subtraction method", in which the brain imaging associated with the control task is deducted from that of the experimental tasks. One can imagine that if you ran a third scan, in which the person was detecting a target at the same time as being subjected to interfering auditory noise, a further subtraction could be carried out in order to identify the structures most associated with the ability to focus attention despite interference.

The subtraction method is still used today although it may make some assumptions about brain function that might be presumptuous. Some functions may be the result of the interaction between brain areas as Luria has suggested; subtracting one of these fails to realise the process. A second possibility not allowed for by this approach is that the new activations assigned to the attentional task in our example are all contributing to attention equally in the same way. It is possible, and even likely, that some structures provide the prerequisite level of arousal or other supporting function rather than the selection of the target per se. For these and other reasons, variations on the subtractive method are often used. One method involves increasing the difficulty of a task. For example, in the task described above in which the subject is required to detect a target from distracting non-targets, scans might be taken for three speeds of presentation. As the presentation speed is increased certain brain structures might be seen to increase activation, while some may show a decrease or levelling out of activation (see Rees, Frith, & Lavie, 1997).

Until the commercial introduction of functional imaging technology neuropsychology research was largely reliant on the lesion method. As indicated, this method typically involves the comparison of two groups of patients; the groups might be distinguished in terms of their lesion location. These groups might be further compared with a control group of subjects without a brain lesion. For example, a group with right parietal lesions might be compared with a group with left parietal lesions. In the end such a study might give information that either the left or right parietal lobe was required to carry out a task, but the results would not tell you whether other structures such as the frontal lobe might also be involved.

The advantage of functional neuroimaging is that the dynamics of a number of brain areas interacting together may be inspected simultaneously. A further advantage is that normal persons can be used. This overcomes the criticism that sometimes brain-damaged patients compensate and complete tasks in a different way from normal persons. Research interest into the adaptation to brain damage is, of course, a bona fide topic (see Chapter 10) and reveals another advantage of functional neuroimaging.

Other advantages emerge when topics such as consciousness or subjective awareness are being investigated. For example, a number of studies, which are discussed in Chapter 8, have found that when we imagine ourselves carrying out a motor activity the brain motor areas activated are very similar to those that are activated when we are actually carrying out the same activity (Jeannerod, 1995). In a similar vein, patients who suffer from the psychiatric disorder of schizophrenia and sometimes complain of hearing voices do actually show an activation in the auditory area of the temporal lobe, which is important for the reception and comprehension of language (e.g. Dierks et al., 1999; Frith, 1999). It is difficult to see how one might research the neuropsychology of such topics, without the functional imaging techniques.

While it must depend on the reason for scanning the brain, fMRI is becoming more popular than PET scan for some purposes. With the fMRI BOLD technique blood oxygen levels are assessed. However, despite similar indices being measured, the fMRI technique and PET are very different technologies. fMRI does not require an injection of a radioactive isotope. This safety difference has favoured the use of fMRI over PET because there are no limitations to the number of fMRI scans that can be taken in a session. fMRI is also favoured because there is better resolution or definition of brain area activation. However, despite the high resolution of the fMRI scan

there is a difficulty in knowing the exact interval in which to scan the behaviour so that the desired activation may be captured. To solve this problem researchers are combining two technologies to allow the actual brain process to be captured. Box 1.1 describes how the electrical readings from the brain are being combined with fMRI to gain the advantages from the two systems.

Despite the clear advantage of fMRI compared to PET there remain some disadvantages. Some areas such as the inferior aspect of the orbital frontal cortex may show artefacts due to increased radiation from the bony surface. An image in the vicinity of sinuses may also cause problems. Also, head movements may cause difficulties and some subjects may be restrained by specially designed masks. During an experiment stimuli are presented via headphones. In the case of visual stimuli the patient who is lying in a confined space may view the experimental material projected on to a mirror. The patient may use a fibre optics response pad because the high degree of magnetisation disallows the usual electrical leads. These conditions inevitably limit the range of experiments that can be carried out.

Also, while functional imaging, using fMRI or PET is becoming more sophisticated, some authors have pointed to disagreement between studies (e.g., see Poeppel, 1996), although such interpretations are not always accepted. Also it should be noted that some structures, such as the hippocampus, tend to show less activation and some of the initial studies into memory failed to show activation in this area despite the undeniable involvement of this structure in the laying down of new memories.

Despite these cautions the functional imaging revolution within neuropsychology is an extremely exciting research innovation and the technology being used in this area is improving rapidly. Already, these methods have allowed enormous insights into the relationship between brain and behaviour and many of these studies have been used and described in this book to support models and argument.

Box 1.1   Measures of the brain's activity over time

The electroencephologram (EEG) is a method of measuring the electrical activity of the brain. Scalp electrodes are used to detect minute variations in electrical activity, which are produced by the many electrical messages of neurones. As might be imagined, while this method is still usefully used to assess such major events as epileptic seizures, the method has some disadvantages since the electrical activity is diffusely represented after having travelled through the cranium. A far more reliable but similar method is to use the method of event-related potential (ERP). With this method the brain's electrical response to an event, such as a single auditory tone, is measured and then repeated again and again. The electrical response is measured for each trial and averaged, giving a more reliable electrical signature. The advantage of the ERP measure is that it can immediately time the event of activation of a particular brain area and is a far more direct measure of neurone response. The functional magnetic resonance imaging (fMRI) scan has the advantage of a greater definition or resolution of the brain area activated than ERP, but the fMRI cannot identify the very rapid progression of brain activation that tracks the progressive analysis of the brain, which takes place within milliseconds.

While PET scans may be taken over time the method requires around a 40-second interval between scans, the scan takes around 30 seconds to complete. Even the fMRI scan may not pick up the very rapid changes that take place in the brain—changes that correspond to electrical changes that take place at intervals as short as 50 ms. For this reason the ERP measure is sometimes used with fMRI (event-related fMRI) in order to inspect the temporal progression of brain activation. In other words, in modern research there is often a convenient marriage between the ERP to indicate the time onset of the scan, and the superior spatial resolution of the fMRI. In this way the brain's response to *specific stages* of a task may be measured.

A GUIDE TO ISSUES COVERED

A solo text allows the privilege of a broad overview across different topic areas, which encourages new theoretical perspectives. While new models are nearly always controversial, the review of an entire area always demands theoretical innovation, especially when theory lags behind evidence. The following is a brief introduction to some of the theoretical issues that are examined in this book.

As indicated, this first chapter is designed to allow for an introduction of some of the terms frequently used in neuropsychology, to give insights into the history of neuropsychology and some initial information on the way neuropsychology is researched. The organisation of this book is such that the early chapters are conceptually simple and perhaps easier to digest than those which follow. They also provide an introduction to issues that are continued throughout this book.

There has already been something of an introduction to Chapter 2. Luria's model is now dated but the idea of basic sensory information being analysed to a progressively greater degree from the primary sensory area (primary zone) through to the polymodal association areas (tertiary zone) is still attractive as a starting point. However, since Luria's work a number of important modifications have been made to this traditional view.

The concept of modulisation has been introduced, which proposes that some areas of the brain appear to perform specialised analysis, e.g. colour, motion. Also, there is the proposal that perception is influenced in the form of a perceptual feedback, in what is referred to as "top-down processing". This view argues that perception uses stored experiences or perceptual memories that contribute to the perceptual process.

In Chapter 3 the important topic of *executive dysfunction* is discussed. Previously, there was a reference to Luria's third unit for the programming, regulation and verification of activity, which is associated with the influence of the frontal lobes. This chapter elaborates on modern formulations within this area. There are many different components in what is referred to broadly as the executive system. Some concern exists within the literature that this is too broad a term. While it is clear that different contributions towards executive function are made by different structures within the frontal lobe, there is still some speculation as to the exact nature of these contributions.

The executive system has a very important place in the discussion of both theoretical and clinical neuropsychology since it influences all the topics under discussion in this book. This important topic has been placed earlier in this book so that the reader is familiar with the basic concepts when they are discussed in more detail in the subsequent chapters. In the final section of this chapter the fractionation of the executive system is given some substance when the different components are referred to with their related neuroanatomical substrates.

In Chapter 4, on *attention disorders*, the theories in this area are discussed alongside the clinical disorder of unilateral neglect. Unilateral neglect is manifested by a failure to take into account and attend to features, usually on the left of a patient, e.g. visual space or one's own body. In this chapter the various components of attention are modelled by the description of four integrated systems. First discussed is the process of *arousal*, which allows the prerequisite alertness. A brief introduction to this system has already been given within Luria's model. The second topic is a relatively new issue, which is discussed as the *perceptual attention system*. This topic leads on from Chapter 2 on disorders of perception and fits with modern theoretical accounts coming from cognitive psychology and cognitive neuroscience (research into cognition using animals and functional neuroimaging). It is proposed that perception is not a passive process and that there are attentional mechanisms within perception that actively seek out certain stimuli at the expense of others. The *orienting system* is next described, which allows a reflexive response to novel information and which is, in turn, combined with a fourth *executive attentional system*, which is controlling the selective attention process. These four systems are then described as being part of an integrated whole to provide a complete model of attention.

In Chapter 5 *memory disorders* are discussed with their associated clinical disorders. At present there is a poverty of cohesive theory which marries the different memory research areas together. For example, the concept of working memory is introduced as a hypothetical memory system which is important for holding information temporarily "online" when some other form of mental operations are taking place. This topic is often researched separately from issues concerning our "knowledge base" of our long-term-memory store. Despite these traditional separations a model is described that shows working memory

to be influenced and interdependent with long-term memory. It is argued within this chapter that the ease with which we learn something is very much dependent on our knowledge base that exists at the time of learning. What we have learned in the long term assists or undermines what we learn in the future and therefore working memory and long-term memory are intimately linked. If this is adopted then a number of advantages follow. For example, it is possible to describe the one control or executive system for both temporary and long-term (stored) memories. Therefore a model is proposed that attempts to explain most memory phenomena within a single parsimonious framework.

Chapter 6 on *asymmetry* could have been omitted from this text and the contents distributed among the various other chapters. Any serious author in this area must feel uneasy in describing the functions of the two hemispheres of the brain as if they functioned separately. This is especially the case when functional neuroimaging studies clearly show the involvement of both hemispheres in the production of most functions. However, experiments that have looked at the performance of patients who have had the two hemispheres of the brain surgically separated are among the most dramatic and interesting within the neuropsychological literature. These studies are also useful to some of the theoretical proposals that are provided at various points within this text. This is a research area which has attracted a great amount of research interest and the asymmetry chapter does serve as an introduction to a chapter on language, being the most asymmetrically organised of cognitive functions.

Chapter 7 on *language disorders* describes work that has come from two different researching approaches. A difference between researchers in this area can be seen when contrasting the extreme interests in clinical syndromes with the psychological process. There are those researchers who propose clinical syndromes that describe a way of categorising patients according to their presenting symptoms. These specialists are interested in the relationship between brain structure and the diagnosis of clinical language disorders. Cognitive neuropsychologists, as mentioned above, have been more interested in analysing the process of language and will more often use the single-case study in trying to dissociate the different types of language disorders. As previously discussed, both these approaches have their advantages and increasingly we are finding researchers who are bridging the gap. Thus although the two parts of this chapter separate out these two approaches to some degree, this chapter aims to find a middle path. The information from the models from one set of research is often used to support or develop the other.

Chapter 8 on *movement disorders* has identified a new model that depicts three separate interacting systems: a *cortical motor system*, which is bound to the relationship between actions and perceptions; a second *basal ganglia system*, which is necessary for automated chains of movements; and a third, *cerebellar system* which is prominent in its contribution to the modification and modulation of movements. There is a focus here on the higher mental control of motor movements rather than the peripheral mechanisms which can be found in other texts.

In Chapter 9 on *emotional and social dysfunction* is certainly a neglected area in some neuropsychology texts. From the clinical perspective, it is one of the commonest and most serious problems suffered by the patient with brain damage. One of the author's research interests has been an attempt to provide modelling of human brain functions in this area, which has in the past received attention from mainly animal researchers. This is certainly one of the most intriguing areas of neuropsychology and the most difficult to research. While an attempt is made here to model the organic or neuroanatomical mechanisms of emotion it is a challenge to dissociate these mechanisms from the environmental and social influences on the patient. For this reason modelling in this area is still very dependent on animal research and is tentative at this stage. The topic of consciousness is a popular topic at the present time and the clinical section within this chapter allows a discussion of some disorders like schizophrenia which are associated with impaired consciousness in the form of hallucinations and delusions. The topic of consciousness

is nevertheless broached in each of the chapters.

Two further chapters on *recovery* and *rehabilitation* bring this text closer to the clinical arena. The area of recovery is proving of increasing interest, especially in the way that research attempts to predict the progress of recovery following brain damage. Discussed here are such issues as the interaction between brain damage and the stage of brain development. Also discussed are the features of the patient that seem to influence their prognosis. Included also is a review of the new work on neural transplantation, which is starting to show some indication of promise.

In the chapter on rehabilitation there is no attempt to discuss all the neuropsychological attempts at rehabilitation. Rather the aim is to illustrate the issues that are important to many areas of rehabilitation using the example of memory remediation. There are a number of ways of researching this area on different levels. The most sophisticated of these is to place research within a context of how a patient's improvement might be predicted by models of their disorder. In other words, if we know the mechanism which is causing the patient's impairment we will be more able to compensate it. Nevertheless there is much value in the many studies that have found improvements to patients despite a lack of knowledge of the neuropsychological mechanism involved. This is true of medical-oriented treatment research as it is of neuropsychological research. Therefore some of this work is also discussed.

There is particular interest in these final chapters in the relationship between what is known about the process of recovery and its implication for rehabilitation. For example, within the clinical arena there appears to be something of a split between rehabilitationists who believe that you should retrain the impaired function, e.g. exercising the paralysed limb, and those who believe that one should work towards compensating for this impairment, e.g. relying more on the unimpaired limb. There is an attempt to answer this conundrum with an inspection of specific areas of rehabilitation that is as old as neuropsychology itself.

In any text on neuropsychology it is inevitable

that the chapter topic suggest unnatural divisions between what, in actuality, are interacting processes. The final Chapter 12 attempts to reflect and identify some of these interactions. Researchers often see themselves as workers within particular areas such as memory or language, but frequently there is some surprise when a researcher is faced with an obvious overlap, as two research areas collide. These discovered commonalities provide a direction towards a more integrated model of neuropsychological process.

This is a time of great change within neuropsychology, which is unsurpassed in the discipline's relatively short scientific history. This book has taken advantage of advances in neuropsychological research but also includes the recent expansion of contributions from cognitive neuroscience and neuroscience. Neuroscience has been traditionally the domain of studies of mechanisms that are at the neuronal level and usually involves non-human subjects. Cognitive Neuroscience has typically used monkeys and other animals to determine the relationship between neurophysiological processes and cognition. However, this area also includes the important functional neuroimaging work with human subjects. These areas of research with the contributions of more mainstream neuropsychology are combined in this book to provide a greater understanding of the relationship between brain and behaviour. This aim to bring together knowledge from these different areas of research lays a foundation towards understanding links between theory and the clinical presentation of the patient in practice. Readers are welcome to contact the author's web page http://www.sites.psych.unimelb.edu.au/andrewes/ with any interesting suggestions that might support this process in future editions.

2

Disorders of perception

INTRODUCTION

Perception includes the analysis of senses such as vision, audition, taste, olfaction (smell) and haptic (perception relating to touch and other somatosensory stimulation). Because of the natural dominance of our visual sensory system, there is much more clinical and research interest in this area. Therefore this chapter deals largely with visual perception and related processes.

As discussed in Chapter 1 our visual processes follow a route that runs from the retina, where visual sensation is first processed, and then to the thalamus, where it is relayed on to the primary visual cortex at the posterior, mainly medial occipital lobe. From this point perceptual processes emerge as the visual information in its unanalysed basic form is subject to further analysis and interpretation. Initially, in this chapter the disorders of sensation are described. These disorders are most commonly associated with a form of disconnection in which the pathway from the retina to the primary visual cortex in the occipital lobe is disrupted.

Following the description of disorders of sensation there is a discussion of the nature of the perceptual analysis that takes place mainly within the occipital lobe. This is described as a complex parallel system that analyses information in a progressively more complex way as the information is passed anteriorly from the primary visual cortex. This is a system that additionally has certain specialised cortical areas that are devoted to the analysis of such percepts as colour and motion.

Although it may be wrong to think of perceptual analysis as a series of stages, it is nevertheless generally assumed that basic analysis of contours takes place early in the primary visual cortex and adjacent areas, while more complex analysis takes place more anteriorly or "downstream". The term "downstream" is used in the context of what is referred to as the *what* pathway, which leads from the primary visual cortex or striate cortex in the occipital lobe to the inferior temporal lobe (see Figure 2.1). This pathway was first identified in monkeys as being important in the process of identification of a visual stimulus (Mishkin, Ungerleider, & Macko, 1983). In short, the "what" pathway is seen as being responsible for the identification of an object.

A second pathway originally referred to by Mishkin and colleagues as the "where" pathway is specialised in locating the position and motion of the object. Milner and Goodale (1995) extended this model, arguing that the "where" pathway was most obviously dedicated to the

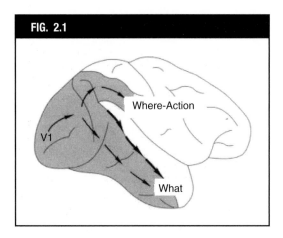

FIG. 2.1

Where-Action

V1

What

The "what" (ventral) and "where-action" (dorsal) pathways.
(adapted from Mishkin, Ungerleider, & Macko, 1983, and
Milner & Goodale, 1995).

preparation of movement, hence the "*where-action*" term used here. There is a description of some of the features of this pathway here, although a more detailed analysis of the role of the "where action" pathway in the preparation of movement is provided in Chapter 8.

These specialised pathways are not merely in one direction. Although it is argued that visually identified objects are analysed in a more and more refined manner with progressive analysis along these pathways, there in now good evidence that constant feedback also exists. This feedback is most likely occurring simultaneously and involves the provision of perceptual information from our experience to help this progressive perceptual process. This might be seen as a process of "shaping" whereby our knowledge of the relationship between the physical contours of an object and its stored information about that object help our perceptual analysis. This process of top-down processing allows this highly complex feat of interpreting the world around us based on the basic two-dimensional visual information that impinges on our retinas. The use of stored perceptual knowledge while at the same time analysing the visual sensation has been referred to for some time by authors (see also Gregory, 1998; Zeki, 1993) but it is relatively

recently that this issue has been given more extensive study.

A strong hypothesis is that the computations that are taking place in the primary visual cortex (striate cortex), which map out our "here and now" visual experience, are at the same time being supplemented by "top-down" information concerning what we already know and what we expect to see. These already stored features are likely to guide our "bottom-up" analysis, which is dedicated to the analysis of the external environment in terms of contour, colour, texture, luminance, and motion. In this manner we do not start afresh each time we perceive; rather we use past stored perceptual experience to metaphorically guide the perceptual analysis of visual information.

Perceptual disorders are discussed initially in this chapter in terms of the clinical syndromes. The distinction between apperceptive and associative agnosia was originally proposed by Lissauer (1890/1988) and has influenced the clinical description and categorisation of perceptual disorders. Disorders of associative agnosia are described in terms of a failure to recognise the meaning of what is perceived. The agnosic patient is able to see the physical form but has no access to the associative meaning of the object that is stored in memory. Apperceptive agnosia, in contrast, is described when the patient has difficulty in constructing the form or structure of the percept in the first place.

The terms apperceptive and associative agnosia are uncomfortably broad in the light of modern research. In the second part of this chapter a more in-depth analysis of the mechanisms of perceptual processes are undertaken. At this point models of object and face recognition are discussed with other features that have drawn research in recent years.

The topical discussion of imagery and perceptual awareness is then developed with a description of patients who clearly have impaired or distorted perception. Finally, there is a broad discussion of how the breakdown of perception in brain-damaged patients may be revealed in a framework that is also useful when describing normal perceptual mechanisms.

VISUAL SENSATION

Visual sensation versus visual perception

Sensation has been described as the product of environmental stimulation prior to its perceptual interpretation (Coren, Ward, & Enns, 1994). The process of visual sensation may be seen as the reception of light (photons) patterns within the retina and the transformation of these patterns into a neural code. The large retinal ganglion cells leading from the retinal area pass this representation onto the primary visual cortex via the lateral geniculate nucleus of the thalamus (one of the nuclei of the thalamus). Any damage or interruption to this pathway in its journey to the primary visual cortex in the occipital lobe invariably leads to what is referred to as a disorder of visual sensation.

Visual perception is said to have occurred if there is evidence that a stimulus has been processed according to its form, colour, motion, or meaning. It is the process by which sensation is analysed for its psychological meaning. Such a definition excludes some visually experienced phenomena that may take place without a stimulus, such as imagery or hallucinations, although it will be argued that the processes, that produce these phenomena overlap or at least depend on processes necessary for perception of the external world.

From a clinical perspective, the distinction between sensation and perception is clearest when viewing the disorder of hemianopia (see Box 2.1). Hemianopia or hemianopsia occurs when a part of the left or right visual field is not available to the patient. This is a disorder of sensation that affects an early stage of visual processing. Another disorder of sensation, which has a similar effect, occurs when cells within the primary visual cortex are damaged. This damage causes what are referred to as scotomas, which occur when patches of cells have died or necrosed within the primary visual cortex. These patches, which fail to receive the inputs of visual sensation, may be due to an infarct following a stroke or when the cells are damaged due to trauma.

The cells within the primary visual cortex have a close relationship with a corresponding area within the retina, so that damage to one specific area within the primary visual cortex affects analysis within a corresponding area within the visual field.

The patient may not normally notice the presence of these scotomas unless they are clinically tested. Perhaps because the eyes are constantly moving and flicking back and forth (saccadic movements) there is sufficient visual information falling on good areas at any one time to compensate for the areas not receiving information. In other words, lack of awareness of impaired sensation (when it occurs) may be due in part to the rapid successive exposure to intact and dead cells. We may not be conscious of the process, in the same way that we are not aware that a movie picture is made up from a series of stills.

Nevertheless, although patients with scotomas and hemianopia do not see the impaired sensation as blacked out patches, objects nevertheless disappear from view if they fall within the area of the scotoma. Patients such as the one described in Box 2.1 do report a dulling of the visual sensation in the area associated with the loss. Also the knowledge that objects actually disappear without awareness has prompted an alternative proposal that this early level of processing is just not available to consciousness (Crick & Koch, 1995). Crick and Koch argue that we are not aware, or conscious, of the products of neuronal activity at the level of the primary visual cortex. They propose that we are only aware of what we process at a higher level of perceptual analysis post areas V1 and V2 (see Figure 2.5) within the association cortex (Behrmann, Moscovitch, & Winocur, 1994; Roland & Gulyas, 1994;). This later analysis has also been associated with imagery.

In following the pathway of visual information from the retina to the primary visual cortex (see Figure 2.2), visual information first strikes the retina in the way that a signal might strike the curved dish of a radar scanner. Information coming in from the left hits the right side of the retina (radar dish). In this way, visual information on the left is received by the right side of each eye and is transferred to the right brain hemisphere.

Box 2.1

Patient CG suffered a haemorrhage in the right occipitoparietal area. At about 11 o'clock at night he had felt a stabbing pain spreading from the right orbit of his eye and posteriorly back over the frontodorsal area of his head. On awaking the next morning he noted that he had difficulty in seeing things in the left half of his vision and was taken to hospital. A week after the event he described his visual impairment.

DA: How has your vision been affected?

CG: Well, it's a funny sensation but my vision seems fuzzy and dim in parts. If I look straight ahead and concentrate on your face then the left lower side of my vision becomes darker or dimmer. But if I look around, which I normally do, this area interferes with the rest of my vision. The area moves around, as I look around. The left lower area is not as dim when I do this, but my whole vision becomes somehow less clear.

DA: To what extent does your problem affect your everyday life?

CG. I thought that I could drive at the start, but when I realised that cars popped up from nowhere on the left side, I realised that I shouldn't be driving. Also, I noticed that when I am cutting things up, while cooking, I cannot see clearly enough. I find I can't read properly either. But I find that I can use a strategy of looking steadily to the left to compensate.

DA: Do you have any other problems?

CG: Well, I have found that I have been a bit weepy and depressed, but I haven't noticed any other difficulties. I can still do most things but it sometimes takes longer because I'm checking back and forth.

CG is suffering from a left lower quadrantanopia. This means that the visual information falling on right upper part of his retina is not being analysed at a cortical level. This is a disorder of sensation (see Figure 2.2).

This means that the bundles of axons, or optic nerve, that project from the right side of the *left eye* has to cross over to the right hemisphere at the optic chiasm (see Figure 2.2). A similar journey is taken by information that hits the left side of each retina from the right visual field, only, in this case the information goes to the left hemisphere. These pathways may be traced out using Figure 2.2

A cardinal rule is therefore that when there is a disorder of visual sensation that affects one side of the visual field it can often be assumed that the damage causing the problem is in the contralateral or opposite brain hemisphere.

As indicated, the main pathway responsible for visual perception travels from the retina to the *lateral geniculate nucleus of the thalami* (LGN) on each side. The synapses at the thalamus have a one-to-one relationship with the cells that map the visual input at the retina. From the LGN the situation becomes more complex since each of the two projections (left and right hemisphere) further subdivide from the thalamus into the *optic radiations* as they head for the primary visual cortex.

It is important at this stage to view a sagittal representation of the primary visual cortex (Figure 2.2). This view of the brain can be realised if the brain is cut down its length along the longitudinal fissure, revealing the mesial aspect (normally hidden inside surface) of the brain. The important landmark sulcus (crease or valley) that is seen here, and is also on the posterior lateral surface of the occipital lobe, is referred to as the calcarine sulcus. Within each hemisphere the optic radiations from the LGN take two pathways as they travel towards the primary visual cortex (striate cortex). The optic radiations, which travel via the parietal lobe, end up above this calcarine sulcus. The second pathway via the temporal lobe involves radiations that terminate below the calcarine sulcus. These last radiations initially sweep forward within the temporal lobe (the Meyer loop), before travelling back below the calcarine sulcus to the inferior aspect of the primary visual cortex (striate cortex). These pathways can be easily remembered by the fact that the parietal lobe is above the temporal lobe (above goes to above, below goes to below the calcarine sulcus). The optic radiations terminate in the primary visual cortex (Brodmann's area 17) in an area referred to as the striate cortex (see Figure 2.3). The primary visual cortex is referred to as "striate", meaning striped, because the cells in this area appear striped when stained. Again, as in the case of the thalamus, there is a mapping of the visual field areas within the primary visual cortex that represents the retina topographically in a one-to-one relationship with the visual field.

Figure 2.2 shows the types of losses of sensation that can occur due to lesions at the various parts of the visual pathway. Broadly, large lesions to the left hemisphere result in difficulties in seeing the right visual field (right homonymous hemianopia); lesions to the right hemisphere may result in a left homonymous hemianopia. Lesions to one of the optic radiations in isolation cause the quadrantanopias (approximately a quarter of

the visual field missing). Lesions to the upper branch of the radiations which travel above cause the lowest quarter of the field to be affected. When patient CG (Box 2.1) described difficulty in seeing the left lower visual field (left lower quadrantanopia) this was suggestive of a either a right parietal lesion or a right occipital lesion above the calcarine fissure. Had he claimed a difficulty in seeing in the left upper visual field (left

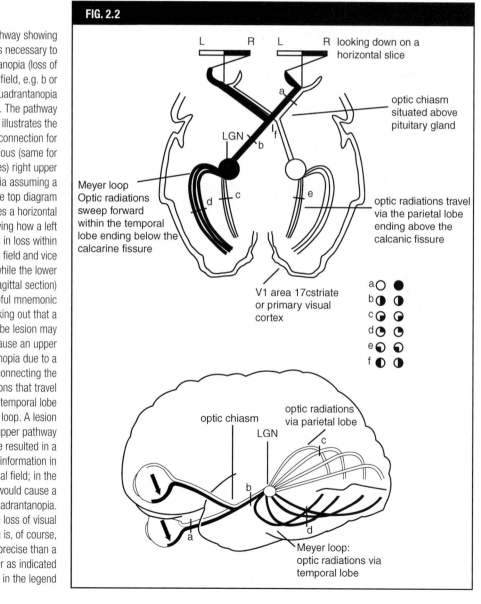

FIG. 2.2

The visual pathway showing the lesion sites necessary to produce hemianopia (loss of half the visual field, e.g. b or (c + d) and quadrantanopia e.g. c, d or, e. The pathway in bold illustrates the necessary disconnection for a homonymous (same for both eyes) right upper quadrantanopia assuming a lesion at d. The top diagram illustrates a horizontal section showing how a left lesion results in loss within the right visual field and vice versa, while the lower diagram (sagittal section) provides a useful mnemonic for working out that a temporal lobe lesion may cause an upper quadrantanopia due to a lesion disconnecting the optic radiations that travel through the temporal lobe via Meyer's loop. A lesion within the upper pathway would have resulted in a loss of visual information in the lower visual field; in the example this would cause a right lower quadrantanopia. The loss of visual information is, of course, usually less precise than a half or quarter as indicated in the legend upper quadrantanopia) then a clinicians thoughts would have turned more towards a right temporal lobe or an inferior occipital lesion. In this way the impairments of the visual field provide clinically useful information for forming hypotheses about a patient.

A pituitary tumour may cause some more unusual sensory disturbances. The pituitary gland is just below the optic chiasm and therefore growth of a tumour can result in a pressure against the mid aspect of the optic chiasm. This may lead to a number of effects including loss of sensation to the nasal aspects of the retina, affecting information on the retina nearest the nose. This results in a loss of some peripheral vision on both sides. Strokes, tumours and traumatic brain injury are the commonest causes of homonymous hemianopia (degradation of much of one half of the visual field). Needless to say hemianopia is a significant handicap especially in the initial stages of adaptation. Part of the problem relates to the subjective nature of this loss of sensation. There is no obvious demarcation from the patient's point of view as to where good sensation ends and poor sensation begins (see Box 2.1). A patient who has a left hemisphere stroke may initially bump into doorways, tables and other obstacles on the right. However, within a few days the patient will often start to adapt to this problem by moving their eyes and head at an angle. In this manner, the reduced visual field is covering a more useful central position.

Sometimes a patient's sensitivity to visual stimuli is tested by a method referred to as perimetry. In this test a spherical frame is placed around the head of the patient. The frame has small lights placed at various points within the patient's visual field. The examiner tests the patient's visual field by switching on lights in various areas of the frame of the cage while the patient looks straight ahead. If a patient fails to detect a light it is assumed that there is a lack of

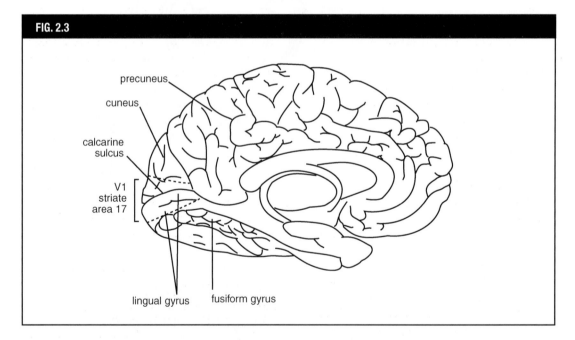

FIG. 2.3

precuneus

cuneus

calcarine sulcus

V1 striate area 17

lingual gyrus   fusiform gyrus

Illustration of the area of destination for the optic radiations. Temporal lobe optic radiations end below the calcarine sulcus and optic radiation travelling through the parietal lobe end up above the calcarine sulcus. Illustrated is the approximate V1 area, which is Brodmann's area 17. This primary visual cortex is sometimes referred to as the striate cortex because when the cortex is cut away revealing a cross-section staining reveals cells that conjugate in clumps presenting a striped appearance. Imaging studies suggest that the fusiform gyrus provides an important pathway for visual information for the "what" pathway.

sensation in that area. Alternatively, with a more rough and ready approach the clinician may sit opposite the patient and will move a finger or other object around the patient's visual field while the patient covers one eye and looks straight ahead at the clinician's nose opposite.

A quick mnemonic for learning the quadrantanopias can be achieved by placing an imaginary cross section of a radar dish in the area of the calcarine sulcus in vertical profile (see Figure 2.2). Damage to the upper part of the radar dish results in occluded vision for information entering from below in the visual field. Using this method it easy to learn that damage to an upper area, e.g. parietal lobe (involving optic radiations that travel above the calcarine sulcus), may cause difficulty in seeing objects below the horizontal view. Using both the retina and calcarine "radar dishes" one may quickly work out that a lesion in the left temporal lobe may cause a right upper quadrantanopia: an impaired ability to see in the right upper quadrant of visual space.

Apart from assessment of the presence or absence of detection of sensory information there are more subtle tests of sensation. Other disorders of sensation may occur due to early lesions within the visual processing stream. The retina projects basic information concerning shape, luminance, form and light frequency to the primary visual cortex.

Tests of sensory discrimination additionally include testing a patient for the presence or absence of light and the discrimination and detection of targets of different sizes and shapes. Also, tests that assess changes in spatial frequency and contrast sensitivity may be carried out (see Figure 2.13a). Patients with difficulties in making these kinds of discrimination may refer to the stimuli as being like a blob (see McCarthy & Warrington, 1990, pp. 23–28) and therefore fail to discriminate at this basic level of sensation discrimination. These disorders of sensation are further discussed under the topic of object recognition.

Before we leave the disorders of sensation it is important to mention the other sensory inputs that have been previously mentioned in Chapter 1. Apart from the paths of visual sensation there are two other pathways that crossover and are also dependent on the thalamus as a relay system. While there are ipsilateral projections the main projections from the cochlea of the inner ear crossover to the medial geniculate body (MG) of the thalamus in the contralateral hemisphere before projecting on to the cortical area called *Heschl's gyrus* (see Figure 2.4). Heschl's gyrus is the primary auditory cortex. From the primary auditory cortex of Heschl's gyrus auditory information is further analysed within Wernicke's area before its final analysis within the association areas. In this way sensation from the left ear is mainly analysed in the contralateral right hemisphere cortex after being relayed via the thalamus. We have already mentioned that the left hemisphere is usually dominant for language. In the chapter on asymmetry we will discuss the right ear advantage for verbal material. Because the right ear projects to the left hemisphere, verbal information presented to the right ear is more efficiently analysed in this medium.

Somatosensory information similarly crosses over at the pyramids within the brain stem. Again this sensory information enters the thalamus before being analysed in the primary somatosensory area. In this way what we feel on the left side of our bodies is mostly analysed in the cortex within the right hemisphere. The primary somatosensory area is organised in a similar manner to the motor cortex (see Chapter 1), with the various parts of the contralateral body being represented so that damage to this area results in a lack of body sensation in the opposite side of the body, left brain damage affecting the perception of right body areas. Figure 2.5 shows a diagram of the thalamus and the various nuclei that are allocated to the different sensory areas.

THE ORGANISATION OF PERCEPTION:HIERARCHICAL AND PARALLEL MODULAR SYSTEMS

Neural pathways within the visual system
In Chapter 1 Luria's model described visual information being analysed progressively from basic percepts to more complex analysis. This

FIG. 2.4

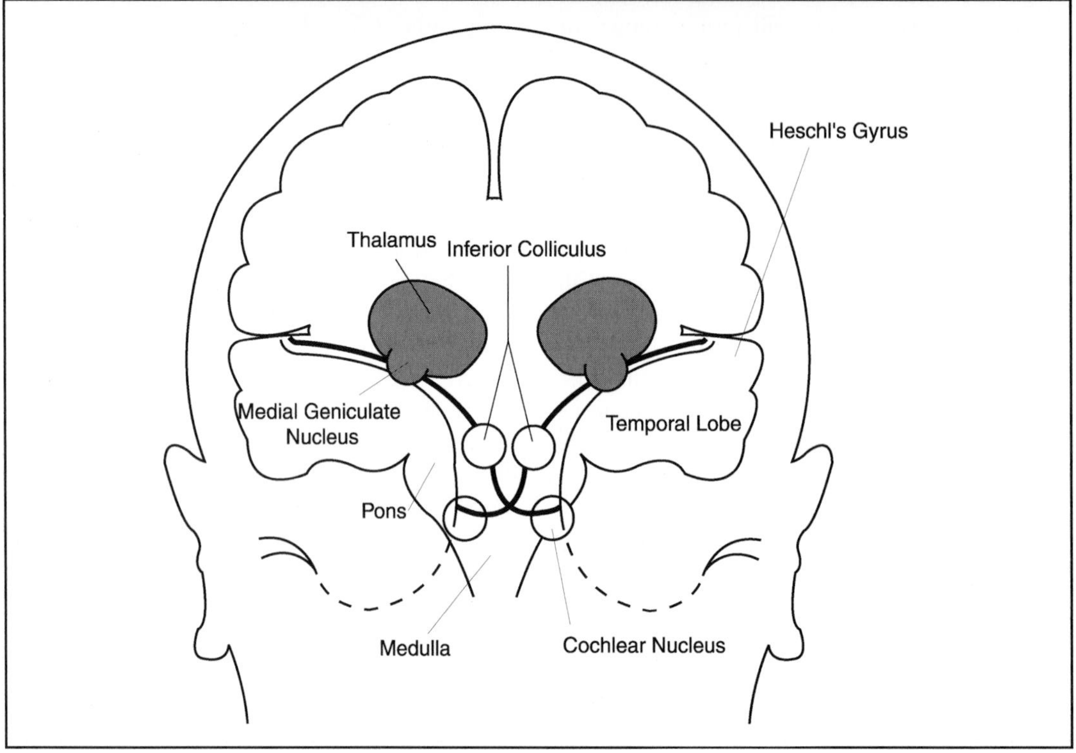

The pathways from the cochlea of the ear travel via the brain stem and the dominant projections, then cross over and travel via the inferior colliculus to the medial geniculate nucleus of the thalamus. From the medial geniculate nucleus there is a projection to Heschl's gyrus on the mesial surface of the superior temporal cortex (within the lateral sulcus or sylvian fissure).

hierarchical analysis describes a process in which more and more information is metaphorically unwrapped from the basic sensory information. This view was heavily influenced by the animal work of co-workers Hubel and Wiesel (1962, 1977), who were awarded a Nobel prize for their work in the 1960s. These researchers placed electrodes in various areas of the occipital cortex of the cat and the monkey to assess cell activity to different types of visual stimuli. This method, which is referred to as single-unit recording, is frequently used today. Typically the animal subject is presented with a stimulus on a screen at the same time the activation of a single brain cell is recorded. If there is increased activation of the cell then it is assumed that the neurone measures some feature of the stimulus. They found indi-

vidual cells in the visual cortex of the occipital lobe that responded selectively to stimuli presented in the visual field. Their progress was slow initially until a serendipitous breakthrough brought about by inadvertently using a cracked slide. The slide projected a light bar of a particular orientation that triggered a cascade of activation from the cells being measured in the cat's brain.

The retina is made up from the light-sensitive but monochrome rods and the cones, which receive colour and definition within the fovea. These retinal cells are connected to bipolar cells, which are in turn connected to large ganglion cells. The axons of these ganglion cells make up what is known as the optic nerve, as discussed earlier. The optic nerve projects to the LGN of

FIG. 2.5

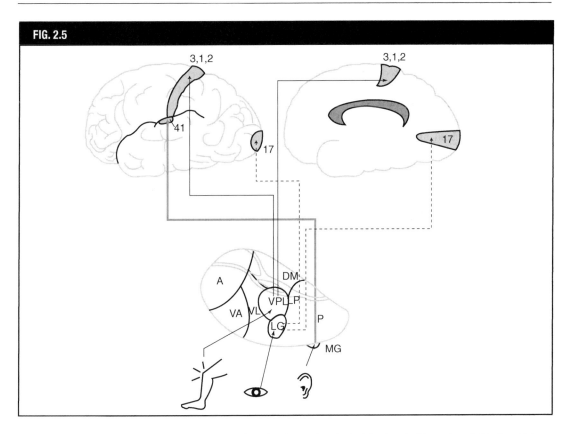

The thalamus acts as a relay station for sensation. It relays visual sensation via the lateral geniculate nucleus (LG) to the striate cortex, auditory information via the medial geniculate body (MG) and then projecting on to Heschl's gyrus. The somatosensory information from the limbs such as touch and where a limb is (proprioceptive) travels via the ventroposterior nucleus (VPL) of the thalamus to the somatosensory area within the cortex within the postcentral gyrus (gyrus posterior to the central sulcus). Other nuclei that are referred to in later chapters include the anterior nucleus (A) and the dorsomedial nucleus (DM) in the context of memory function, the pulvinar (P) in relation to language, the ventral anterior nucleus (VA) and ventral lateral nucleus (VL) in relation to motor movements and projection to these areas from the basal ganglia.

the thalamus. Hubel and Weisel found cells at the LGN were either turned "off" or "on" by a stimulus. Many cells function in this manner, apparently working to produce a visual outline of the object.

Because they found that several cells from the LGN fed into a single cell in the primary visual cortex of area V1, Hubel and Wiesel reasoned that this basic spatial information was being integrated and analysed within the visual cortex. In keeping with this view they found that while cells (simple cells) in the area V1 (striate cortex of the occipital lobe) reacted to bars of light

or darkness, acting as edge detectors, these cells also responded maximally to a particular orientation. Some cells, for example, only fired with a horizontal edge while others responded to slight angle, and so on.

These *simple cells* were also found to be sensitive to location, so that if a particular simple cell were to fire at a maximum rate the stimulus would have to be at a particular angle and a particular location within the visual field. Furthermore, the cells within the primary visual cortex were found to be lined up in such a way that rows of cells responded to a gradually different angle within a

integrated it is a wonder that the product of these two modules arrives at conscious perception at the same time. In fact they do not. Experiments have shown small time differences in our ability to perceive these attributes. While under normal circumstances this difference is not obvious, laboratory experiments show that we see colour before motion by about 60–80 ms (Moutoussis & Zeki, 1997).

Although the primary visual cortex is associated with the analysis of basic form, there is evidence of specialisation within the cell column even at this early stage of processing. The cortex is built up of various cell types within the layers of the cell column (referred to in Chapter 1) and there may be a preponderance of a certain type of cell compared to another, depending on the level of the cell column within the V1 area of the visual cortex. This profile of different cell types at the various levels within the column is referred to as cytoarchitecture. In the primary visual cortex the information from the retina, via the LGN of the thalamus, enters in the fourth of six cell layers at V1 (layer 1 is nearest the surface of the cortex).

Cells within the retina appear to be well adapted for survival. The frog, for example, has retinal cells that are ideal for preying on small moving objects; in fact they ultimately trigger the cells required for predatory behaviour. Other cells, which are specialised for detecting large objects, are directly linked with avoidance behaviours. The eye of the macaque monkey and the human eye have cells that are also specialised with some increased complexity. The neuroscience of the cell types responsible for perception will not be entered into in any detail here, but it is important to make some distinction in terms of the functional importance of two cell types. One type has obvious relevance to the functional role of the "what" pathway while the other has clear associations within the "where-action" pathway. From the lateral geniculate nucleus to the striate cortex there are two streams that are identified by their cell type: the parvocellular and the magnocellular stream (using Zeki' nomenclature). The parvocellular pathway is associated with p or parvo cells which provide the opportunity for detailed information to be provided for the

"what" pathway (Figure 2.7). Such detail includes information about colour, contour, and texture, and the pattern is relatively slow. In contrast the magnocellular pathway is associated with M or magno cells; these larger cells provide for a much faster transference of information and are sensitive to movement. Magno cells lack the ability to transfer detail and are monochrome. The magnocellular pathway dominates the "where-action" pathway.

When showing a movie, which is a series of still pictures shown at speed giving the appearance of movement, the different speeds of these two cell types have to be taken into account. If a black and white film is shown the faster M cells require a higher-speed film so that the motion appears smooth. The magno and parvo streams maintain this separation when they arrive, via the optic radiations, at the striate cortex (V1) and beyond in the various areas of the extrastriate cortex. There is an obvious adaptive advantage for this parallel communication of different forms of information.

Let us trace the pathways of these two streams. The P cells with their slower conduction and more sustained activation, transport information concerning colour and contour from the four Parvocellular divisions in the LGN to V1. The information maintains its functional identity and eventually proceeds to V4, which is specialised for analysing colour and contour as part of the "what' pathway. Part of the magnocellular division (M cells) follows a similar journey to V1 but eventually finds its way dorsally along the "where-action" pathway to area V5, which is important for the analysis of motion. The parvo stream is ideally suited to measuring visual components such as contour and colour, while the other magno stream is important for location and eventually for the integration of visual and body perception towards the preparation for action. There is also a magno stream within the "what pathway" although the functional role is less clear.

Some of these sensitive fast-acting M cells are projected by an alternative route to a structure called the superior colliculus, which is situated on the roof of the brain stem. This alternative

FIG. 2.7

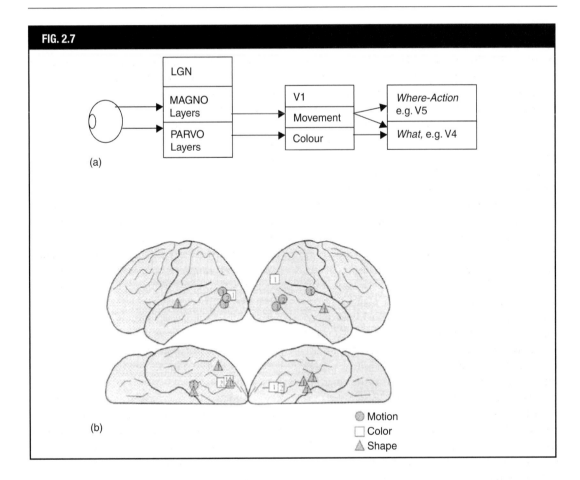

(a) Schematic illustration of the relationship between the parvocellular and magnocellular pathways and the "what" and "where-action" pathways. The pathways are separate and play a specialised role in the analysis of movement and colour. The parvo and magno cell layers within the lateral geniculate nucleus (LGN) of the thalamus project to V1 and then continue along the "where-action" and "what" pathways. (b) Illustration showing areas of activation for PET scan during two types of display. Note that for motion the activation within the extrastriate areas is more dorsal, which is in keeping with the "where-action" pathway. For colour and shape the activations are more inferior, in keeping with the "what" pathway. Note the ventral activations that involve the fusiform gyrus. (reprinted with permission from V.4. Current opinion in Neurobiology, Ungerleider, L.G. & Haxby, J.V. (1994) "What' and 'Where' in the human brain. P160. Copyright, 1994, with permission from Current Biology Ltd).

magnocellular route to the cortex via the pulvinar of the thalamus (not the LGN) bypasses much of the primary visual cortex analysis and is assumed to enter the cortex at a number of points including a point where motion is analysed (V5). This superior colliculus route is seen as having the functional importance of directing attention to novel stimuli and will be discussed in more detail in Chapter 4. For the moment, it is possible to contemplate the evolutionary advantage of this fast-acting magnocellular division, which is both

attention arousing and orients the organism to possible danger or potential prey. There are obvious advantages to an animal that can react fast to information concerning motion within the periphery of visual space. Both the hunter and the hunted need to be prepared and alert for such a contingency.

The identification of the object by the slower parvocellular P cell information acting through the LGN is also obviously important, but the eyes must be directed to the stimulus before this can occur. The animal must start preparations for action prior to the completion of the detailed analysis of the incoming target.

The M cells, when they travel via the LGN and the older and more primitive structure of the superior colliculus, are presumed to act as an early warning system, which acts to select attention towards novel stimuli to allow their eventual identification. As mentioned, within the primary visual cortex this division between magno and parvo cell division is maintained (Wong-Riley, 1979). On arrival at level four of the cell layers, the information from these two cell types goes to other areas e.g. V2. There are also connections within the cell column from level IV to levels II and III. Within levels II and III, two types of cell structure have been recognised through cell-staining techniques. These are referred to as "blobs" dark areas (when stained) which consist of a conjugation, or collection, of cells, and "interblobs", which consist of different types of cells more widely spaced. These blobs (dark) and interblobs (light) have a striped appearance so that VI, the primary visual cortex, is often referred to as the striate cortex (see Zeki, 1993).

When Hubel eventually returned to research this area and reconsidered the V1 area, he was surprised to find that cells within the blobs did not respond to orientation like other cells in the cell column; instead they were wavelength sensitive to colour, with connections to area V4 via V2 (Livingstone & Hubel, 1987). The interblob cells, in contrast, were found to be more sensitive to the analysis of both orientation and movement, having connections with V5 (Zeki, 1993, p. 203). The colour-sensitive P cells predictably have most connections with the blobs, which in turn have connections with V4, which is associated with a module for analysing colour. M cells have predominant connections with the interblobs, which have more connections with the movement module V5. From this perspective specialisation is occurring even at this early stage of analysis within the visual cortex and carries on in the process of module analysis within the "what" and "where-action" streams. Before passing on to these destinations of V4 and V5 pathways extend from V1 to V2 and V3. This kind of branching

out specialisation also occurs at V2. Livingstone and Hubel saw these findings of different layers within cell columns analysing different specialised aspects of the visual sensation as providing good evidence of parallel processing.

Apart from this parallel processing to the different modules, there also appears to be allowance for projections back into V1 from these areas. Originally it was thought that this might be a way in which the different modules might be integrated, but as indicated above the product of these modules remains separate. There is nevertheless opportunity for feedback of information at all levels (Zeki, 1993). At this stage it seems that this may be more related to identification of features for attentional purposes, an issue that is discussed further in Chapter 4. The specialised nature of the perceptual process whereby different attributes such as colour and motion are analysed separately and are finally brought together with their individual contributions towards perception reminds one of the assembly of a car being constructed in a factory. The body of the car is being added to on the assembly line, but at the same time specialised construction of the engine (colour) or electrical components (motion) and body work (form) is going on from simple to more complex levels. These individually assembled units are finally added together to make the final perceptual product. Certain subunits take longer to complete but the differences in times are so small that they are not consciously apparent. The final product relies on the coming together of all these various subprocesses or modules.

Summary

Previously, the notion of a "what" and "where-action" pathways was introduced to describe two streams of processing (see Figure 2.1). In this section two cellular divisions were described that have a functional relationship with these pathways. These divisions have been traced from the LGN to V1 and then to the various parts of the extrastriate cortex. The parvo stream with its specialisation in identifying the colour and contour of objects continues appropriately inferiorly along the "what" pathway, while one magno stream proceeds dorsally along the "where-action" pathway. Perhaps less expected is the finding that a magno stream also exists in the "what" pathway. As indicated, a magno stream has cells with the qualities appropriate to locating and acting upon environmental stimuli and these cells more exclusively dominate the dorsal pathway. Therefore, the parallel processing and specialisation take place at an early stage and are maintained until a late stage of information processing.

Given that the "what" pathway is described within a function of identifying and recognising the percept, it is appropriate that V4 which is involved in colour analysis is located in the fusiform gyrus in a medial and ventral location (see Figures 2.3 and Figure 2.7b). Also, module V5, which appears to be more specialised for the analysis of motion (Plant et al., 1993; Shipp et al., 1994), is located at a more superior location more in keeping with the "where-action" pathway.

Before moving on to discuss some of the human clinical syndromes that are associated with lesions to these respective pathways, it should be noted that the colour module V4 and the motion/location module V5 are not pure: cells that respond to other features are found in these areas. Nevertheless cells within such areas respond more predominantly to such visual stimulations and are more strongly activated in PET scan studies when demands on that function are made. Also, while areas such as V4 are defined as being important for colour it is likely, because of its important position in the pathway, that it has additional perceptual functions related to identification (Shipp et al., 1994, Young, 1991;). For example, the V4 area has also been implicated in the analysis of depth perception (Dobbins, Jeo, Fiser, & Allman, 1998).

In the next section we describe some clinical disorders that describe what happens when the "what" and "where-action" pathways are disrupted.

CLINICAL DISORDERS OF PERCEPTION

Primary perceptual disorders

In the previous sections the pathway from the retina to the visual cortex has been described with the functional influence of parvo and magno cell division on the "what" and "where-action" pathways respectively. Primary perceptual disorders are described here as disorders of perception that are due to the impaired perception of form, colour or motion. Achromatopsia and motion perception represent disorders thay are associated with these two pathways.

Achromatopsia

Patients with this disorder are often found to have lesions in the fusiform gyrus area: area V4 (Zeki, 1993). They sometimes report seeing colours as being washed out or grey. This does not worry someone who is born colour-blind, where this is caused by abnormal sensation at the level of the retina. But if you have acquired this disorder, then eating food that suddenly appears to look like mud can be quite upsetting (Sacks & Wasserman, 1987). Mostly, however, patients may merely lose the depth or strength of colour and sometimes this impairment is isolated to particular colours. Patients with achromatopsia still see motion. Conversely, patients who are unable to see motion may be able to see colour. This double dissociation highlights the modularity of the analysis of these two attributes.

Perception of movement

After damage to the areas described above as V5 patients sometimes complain of poor ability in judging motion. This is a rare disorder but in its most obvious manifestation the patient may complain that life is a series of still photographs. As in the case of a patient reported by Zihl, Von Cramon, and Mai (1983), who saw liquid that was being poured as being frozen, crossing streets was difficult (and clearly dangerous) because she had the impression of being confronted by a car without seeing the movement. Goldstein and Gelb (1918) describe a patient with a bilateral posterior brain injury who reported after observing a rapid arm movement that the hand appeared to be up one moment and down the next without any perception of movement. Sometimes the disorder is milder and may be only contralateral to the brain damage. Plant and colleagues have estimated a location for a sufficient lesion for this disorder is within the lateral gyri of the occipital lobe. They suggest a lesion around 4 cm anterior from the occipital pole is present with their cases and this location is presumed to be within the vicinity of the human location of area V5 (Plant et al., 1993).

The distinction between apperceptive and associative agnosia

The term agnosia comes from the Greek, meaning without knowledge, which accurately describes the predicament of the patient with agnosia. These are patients who can generally be described as having either damage to or a disconnection within the "what" pathway.

Lissauer (1890/1988) originally made the distinction between apperceptive and associative agnosia. Apperceptive agnosias were described as cases in which recognition fails due to an impairment of visual perception despite the absence of any disorder of sensation. These patients do not recognise objects because they do not perceive them normally. In contrast, the patient who has associative agnosia is able to perceive the object normally but fails to recognise the object for what it is. The "normal percept is stripped of meaning" (Teuber, 1968).

As Farah (1990) acknowledges, the terms apperceptive and associative agnosia are often used in two quite different ways. The first relates to Lissauer's original description and describes the relatively rare clinical syndromes. The second sense is much broader and relates to neuropsychological signs. Thus a patient may described as showing some signs or symptoms of apperceptive agnosia without having all the features of the clinical syndrome.

For example, a patient with *signs* of apperceptive agnosia (sometimes referred to as categorisation deficit) may have difficulty in recognising pictures from unusual views (see Fig. 2.17) or an object depicted surrounded by shadows (Warrington & Taylor, 1973). They may have difficulty in recognising embedded figures that are surrounded by confusing and distracting shapes (see Figure 2.8). These patients may have different degrees of impairment. Some with milder problems will recognise objects when shown from a typical viewpoint. If they have signs of apperceptive agnosia in isolation the patient will then recognise the bucket and will know what it is used for once it is placed in a normal orientation. The patient with apperceptive agnosic signs has a conceptual knowledge store intact but there appears some degree of loss of the stored images of common objects in unusual orientations and other depictions with minimal cues. Therefore top-down information about the structural features of objects is impoverished. These patients with apperceptive agnosic signs are often referred to as having apperceptive perceptual disorders but in the few cases that have been reported with the syndrome of apperceptive agnosia the patients are far more impaired.

Apperceptive agnosia

Patients with the syndrome of apperceptive agnosia are more impaired in the basic primary perception of objects (e.g. Shelton, Bowers, Duara & Heilman 1994). They have difficulty in distinguishing between objects. These patients are sometimes described by their relatives as being blind, since they have difficulty in recognising even simple objects and have to rely on certain cues to find their way around. Therefore within the visual modality their perception is so poor that apperceptive agnosia sometimes excludes the testing of associative agnosia. Despite their inability to describe visual stimuli they will show that they are able to identify and name objects presented in other modalities, e.g. auditory, tactile.

Some of the features of sensation are intact in this disorder, for example, their visual acuity. Visual fields can be tested with white objects. Detection of small differences in luminescence, wavelength, and area and small movements are intact, but discrimination of shapes fails. Often these patients compensate for their primary perceptual

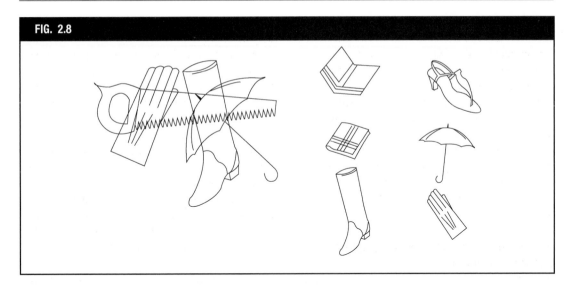

FIG. 2.8

Patients with apperceptive agnosia or categorisation deficit often have difficulty in recognising stimuli that are degraded or interfered with in some way. In this test of overlapping objects the patient with apperceptive agnosia has difficulty in identifying each of the objects. The objects within the overlapping display may be pointed to from the pictures to the right. In this way the test is not confounded in the case of a patient with word finding difficulties. Usually all the objects are from the same category. (adapted from Gainotti, et al., 1989).

difficulties by tracing the item with their fingers, when the subject matter is simple, without irrelevant lines. The diffuse lesions associated with this disorder involve the posterior region and are bilateral. Apperceptive agnosia is often associated with disorders such as carbon monoxide poisoning and mercury poisoning, which affect diffuse cortical areas and cause deterioration of the interconnections between neurones.

Apperceptive agnosia is sometimes confused with "dorsal simultaneous agnosia", which is more properly an attentional disorder (see Chapter 4.) The distinction is clearly made when movement sometimes helps apperceptive agnosics to detect an object from a background, while in the case of dorsal simultaneous agnosia movement makes the analysis of an object more difficult.

In dorsal simultaneous agnosia the subject can use the shape or contour to cue themselves in a top-down manner. For example, knowledge of the colour of an object does to some extent narrow the alternatives in the problem-solving game of identification. For example, something green on the table in the kitchen could be a vegetable of

some kind. Apperceptive agnosics are not helped to the same extent by these cues because their perception may be limited to size, texture, and sometimes colour (see Bauer, 1993; Farah, 1990).

Associative Agnosia

Patients with the associative agnosias are unable to recognise objects or their function. The different types of associative agnosia are described by the sensory modality affected, e.g. *visual* associative agnosia. There is less research in the areas of auditory associative agnosia, e.g. not being able to recognise a dog's bark, or associative olfactory agnosia—an inability to recognise a smell—and therefore we continue to explore the visual examples which are well documented despite their rarity.

Patients with the associative agnosias are able to perceive the physical characteristics of the stimulus. For example, patients with visual associative agnosia are able to copy and match the object they can not recognise and therefore primary perceptual processing appears to be intact.

One of the stronger explanatory theories for

associative agnosia is that the "what" pathway has been disrupted or disconnected. That is, the hypothetical end-point of the "what" pathway, which contains a store of the associative meaning of the percept, is disconnected from the primary perceptual analysis that takes place "upstream". In later chapters on memory and language disorders the association areas will be described as a memory store for knowledge. Using this simplistic description, if this store or stores are destroyed or disconnected from the sensory input then the patient may see without knowing what they are seeing.

As previously discussed, cells have been found within the inferior temporal lobe which only respond to perceptually complete objects or entities. This supports the view that the end-point of recognition of an object is within the temporal lobe. However, as will be discussed in the chapter on language disorders, it is clear that semantic information that allows the analysis of meaning is accessed for visual information as early as Brodmann area 37 (see Figure 1.5). As their disease progresses, patients with Alzheimer's disease lose more neurones from the cortical areas that are associated with the "what" pathway and the storage of semantic information (Giannakopoulos et al., 1999). Due to the loss of neurones in these areas they may start to show an associative agnosia where they fail to recognise and identify objects (Patterson & Hodges, 1995). It is assumed that these patients have agnosia because the memory store is damaged although some disconnection may also be present (Giannakopoulos et al., 1999). Farah (1997) makes the distinction between this type of agnosia due to the destruction of the memory store and perceptual agnosia which is often more easily described by a disconnection from that store (Geschwind, 1965).

As might be predicted, damage to the store of general meaning of concepts that is found in Alzheimer's disease is associated with associative agnosia in more than one sense modality, e.g. visual and auditory, and may be more related to confusions of meaning. In contrast, *perceptual* associative agnosia, which is being discussed here, may be more modality specific and complete. That is, the patient may be able to recognise an object using the tactile sensation when they cannot identify the object by sight. This is because the disconnection only affects a single pathway between the visual sense and the hypothetical knowledge store. This is why the clinical testing of associative agnosia is often performed using different modalities (see Box 2.2). For example, Endo et al. (1992) describe two cases of tactile agnosia where the patients were unable to identify common objects that were placed in the hands. However, the patient was able to name the same objects and categorised their use when the same objects were presented visually.

The left temporal lobes have been found to be particularly important for our memory of the meaning of objects. As we have already discovered in the first chapter, the left hemisphere is dominant for language and it also contains a translation unit that interprets the speech that we hear into meaning. It may be remembered that Carl Wernicke was responsible for drawing scientists' attention to patients who had damage to the area that bears his name. These patients had particular difficulty in understanding speech. The brain is complex but not wasteful: the areas within the vicinity of Wernicke's area which have been described as the association areas within the temporal, parietal, and occipital cortex, have been cited, among other functions, in a broad role as an extended store-house for concepts.

While it has been argued that *visual* associative agnosia must be modelled either by a destruction of this store or by a disconnection, what kind of separation between the visual input and this store is required to cause a disconnection within the "what " pathway ?

A lesion between the primary visual cortex and the association areas is not sufficient on its own because visual information may come across from the right hemisphere via the splenium of the corpus callosum. The corpus callosum, is a wedge of axons that connect one hemisphere with the other and constitutes the largest connection between the two hemispheres. The splenium is the most posterior part of the corpus callosum. It is the splenium that allows visual information to pass from one hemisphere to the other. The lesion therefore has to be a two-way disconnection. It must cut off

---

Box 2.2 Visual associative agnosia: DM (see text for psychometric details)

DA: Do you know what this is here? [Author places a banana in front of DM.]

DM: Yes, I should know what that is.

DA: Without touching it, do you know what it is?

DM: Food.

DA: Would you like to close your eyes and just feel it? Both hands. Feel it all over.

DM: I know as well as I know, you know what day it is, what that is, it is eatable. Lifted off. [Makes a pulling motion at the stalk of the banana as if he is about to peel it.]

DA: Lifted off?

DM: I don't know how you describe that, not to screw it [again makes pulling motion], but to chew it.

DA: Do you want to do what you usually do with it?

DM: Well, yes I will.

DA: Do you want to eat it.

DM: Yes, I would have to strip it away.

DA: Would you like to open your eyes and strip?

DM: Yes.

DA: It is expendable, you don't have to worry about it. Do you know what it is now? You can look at it, if you like. What do you think it is?

DM: Silly isn't it.

DA: You know you have to eat it. Would you like to eat it and then guess what it is?

DM: No, I don't want to eat it.

DA: Oh go on, just have a bite.

DM: I'll just have a little bit [bites banana and chews it for a while]—this is a silly thing. We know all about it, we know the flavour, we know the feel, and you have been deprived of what it is . . . You know that it is good food.

DA: Is it like meat?

DM: No, it is more like . . . you can almost call it vegetable.

DA: Do you think it might be fruit?

DM: Oh yes it has to be fruit.

DA: Is it a grape?

DM: No.

DA: What about an apple?

DM: No.

DA: An orange?

DM: No

DA: Banana?

DM: No. No . . . I can't let him go, here's something quite like, . . . and here I go right back to the stage where I say well if it's not a banana, we wouldn't have this fruit.

DA So you think it's a banana?

DM: Banana is the only one. I know there is worse fruit than that. That is nice fruit, nice flavour. Only trouble is you've lost a banana.

---

the 'what' pathway within the left hemisphere and at the same time block visual information coming across from the right hemisphere via the splenium. The patient who has *visual* associative agnosia may use a number of different sensory systems to bypass the disconnecting visual system. However, humans are remarkably dependent on visual information, as any blindfolded wine-taster will admit; therefore sometimes the alternative sensory system may not dramatically improve recognition of the object (see Figure 2.9).

Because of the rather special requirements of the lesion, visual associative agnosia is relatively rare. Often, as in the case reported in Box 2.2, patients have a stroke involving the occlusion of the *left posterior cerebral artery* (see Figure 2.10). Our patient, DM, was a congenial 59-year-old man who had previously worked as an assessor in the insurance business. The interview was completed 2 weeks after his stroke, when he showed the classical signs of visual associative agnosia. He was unable to recognise even common objects such a bunch of keys and a comb. This was despite a relatively intact level of intellectual functioning as measured on the Wechsler Adult Intelligence scale–Revised. He had an intellectual level within the high average range and his vocabulary and general knowledge were in keeping with this level, as was his digit span. There were no obvious aphasic symptoms, although by virtue of the arterial territory involved with this disorder some of these patients do have auditory comprehension difficulties associated with sensory transcortical aphasia (Kertesz, Sheppard, &

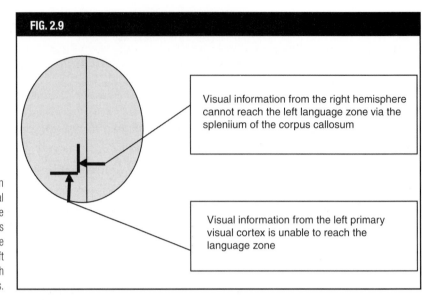

FIG. 2.9

Visual information from the right hemisphere cannot reach the left language zone via the spleniium of the corpus callosum

Visual information from the left primary visual cortex is unable to reach the language zone

Diagram of the lesion required for visual associative agnosia. The visual sensory information is prevented from entering the language area of the left hemisphere from both hemispheres.

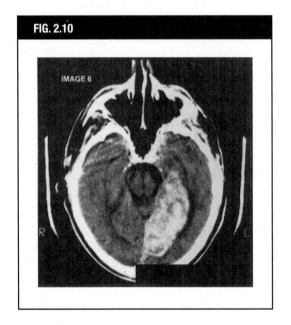

FIG. 2.10

IMAGE 6

A CT scan of the lesion sustained by agnosic patient DM following a stroke involving the left branch of the posterior cerebral artery.

MacKenzie,1982; see Chapter 7 for a description). His constructional skills involving making designs using coloured blocks were remarkably intact. He did show an amnesic performance on a test of learning new information (see a reference to retrosplenium amnesia in Chapter 5). He was able to repeat back a list of words in the normal way but after a delay he failed to recall any items. However, this could not explain his most obvious difficulty in recognising the identity and meaning of objects presented to him visually, even of commonplace articles. This was not just a difficulty in naming the items (anomia): he clearly had no idea what the objects were or what they were used for (visual associative agnosia). DM was not able to recognise any objects represented in picture form on cards and had not been able to recognise most real commonplace objects, with only one exception. The only object that he did recognise (other than the banana eventually) was a pair of glasses. When a pair of glasses was placed in front of him he responded that this is the same as what I was wearing.

The reader of the interview in Box 2.2 will get a feel for this disorder and the extent of his handicap. There are a number of interesting aspects to DM's performance. Firstly, DM uses expressions that are not appropriate for the object. He talks about "lifting", "stripping" and even "screwing" the banana instead of "peeling" it. This illustrates the need to know what an object is prior to using the correct language to describe it.

He also seems to get closer to the identity of the object as more and more information is built up about it. His expression on tasting the banana suggests that his "whole realisation of what it is", is the result of this additional sensory information. However, for our species the visual sense is dominant for identification. Not only are the other senses inferior, they are less practised. Our over-reliance on the visual sense is never more obvious when it becomes impaired. In line with this view is the finding by Ettlinger and Wyke that their agnosic patient's performance was *worse* handling items with eyes open than with eyes closed (Ettlinger & Wyke, 1961). This suggested to the authors that visual information was hindering the process of identification, the patient was inappropriately relying too much on the dominant sensory modality.

Finally DM seems to have only really worked out what the fruit is by a process of deduction, rather than by any instant realisation or perceptual breakthrough. ". . .Where I say well if it's not a banana, we wouldn't have this fruit. . . . Banana is the only one." Sometimes perception may be aided by a logical process, irrespective of the state of the perceptual system.

The drawings of these patients allow another insight into their world. As indicated, these patients are able to copy or match the items that they cannot recognise. DM is able to copy the items that he cannot identify, but it is not an easy task for him. The term that is appropriately used to describe these patients' copying style is "slavish". When DM was copying an item, he was very slow. He appeared to be carefully copying each millimetre of the outline, like a child copying an unfamiliar map (see Figure 2.11). There were no bold strokes that one might expect of a person who was familiar with the object. It was if he was copying the object for the first time. This is a common feature of this disorder and illustrates the importance of using one's experience or top-down processing during normal drawing.

In keeping with this interpretation, DM was asked to draw some objects from memory and was unable to do so. Wapner, Judd and Gardner (1978) report a case that seems to confirm this interpretation of "slavish" copying. Their particular patient could recognise some items and these same items he could copy swiftly and accur-

ately. The patient is reported to have remarked "Can't help but use your natural knowledge in drawing the thing" (top-down assistance). However, for those items he could not recognise his copies were slower and less confident.

In these patients the visual appearance of objects is disconnected from the area of the brain where the meaning of the objects are stored. Other types of visual input are also disconnected in this manner. As we shall learn in Chapter 7 the temporoparietal areas are important for language and therefore the same disconnection that disrupts meaning may also disrupt naming. The patient therefore, also has difficulty in naming (anomia) visually presented objects, although some of these patients may name them when auditory definitions of the objects are given. Such auditory information has a pathway to the hypothetical memory store, which is spared. For similar reasons, patients may often also have a difficulty in reading (alexia). The visual input from the text is not getting through to the brain are that analyses the meaning. However, there are some language-based skills, such as writing, which are achieved without visual input. This results in the strange paradoxical phenomenon of a patient being able to write without being able to read what they have written.

Alexia without agraphia and "letter-by-letter reading"

It is possible to write something in a darkened cellar or in a poorly lit street. While the results might not be tidy, it is possible to write without visual feedback. In the disorder suffered by DM the store for meaning is not disconnected from the brain area responsible for writing. Therefore the strange situation occurs whereby a patient who is asked to write something, such as their name or address, is able to do so. However, if they are then asked to read what they just have written they cannot, because the visual input is disrupted by their lesion. This is referred to as alexia without agraphia;—having a reading disability without the writing disability (see Chapter 7 for a further discussion). Perhaps a more puzzling aspect of some of these patients is that they can often use "letter-by-letter reading". They read out

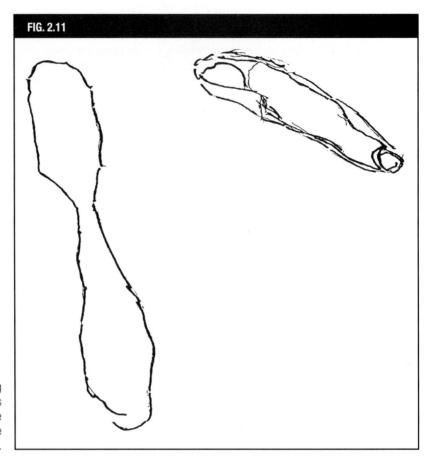

FIG. 2.11

Drawings by DM, illustrating the results of his laborious and slavish copying. On the left is a knife and on the right is a safety pin.

each letter that they see and then deduce the word from the spelling. This is not due to a limited attention span (Shallice, 1988a). The patient's visual processing for letters, for reasons not understood, is still intact.

Colour agnosia

It will be remembered that the "what" pathway was described as proceeding inferiorly via an area referred to as V4. V4 is the site at which much of the colour processing occurs. The analysis of what colours mean or the common associations of colours, e.g. grass is green, blood is red is assumed to take place more anteriorly within this pathway. Therefore a disconnection between the analysis of colours and the meaning of those colours may eventuate in a colour agnosia in which these colour–meaning associations may not occur. The patient perceives the colours and may

match them but cannot retrieve the past associations of these colours, because the same route to the colour meaning is also the route to colour naming. This same left hemisphere is the language hemisphere and therefore the patients are unable to name the colours (colour anomia).

Box 2.3 describes an exchange during the assessment of colour agnosia and anomia in patient DM (transcript from video). The patient was able to match a number of different coloured pens into pairs consisting of red, orange, blue and gold. Therefore at this crude clinical level his sensation for colours was intact. He was also able to talk freely about colours; he says, "I got the impression that they have blues, black, greens, purples, and gold. From then on, they started introducing more extreme colours." and therefore his anomia was not related to a language disorder, i.e. damage to the language area. There was no

---

Box 2.3. Colour anomia and colour agnosia

The patient is presented with coloured pens. There are five colours (red, green, gold, blue, and brown), with two pens of each colour. DM first matches the pens for colour correctly in pairs as evidence that the patient is capable of perceiving the colours at a primary, bottom-up level.

DM: Oh two the same colour. [Starts to match the colours and places similar coloured pens together]
DA: Yes, or so that they are next door to each other.
       [He succeeds in matching the colours up perfectly]
DA: Can you tell me what colour these two here are? How about these?
DM: [A long pause in which DM fails to name colours] Since I grew up they have introduced many more colours. I got the impression that they have blues, black, greens, purples and gold. From then on, they started introducing more extreme colours.
       [He has just failed to name the orange colour and he has now been shown a green pair]
DM: Would it be umm . . . let it go for a second or two and go onto something else and see if we can work it out.
DA: OK, try these last ones. See if you can name the colour of these ones.
DM: Interesting if you would have been here a little earlier. A couple or three days before we would have got better results.
DA: Is that right?
DM: Yes, things are slipping. Oh well.
DA: Maybe if I can tell you some objects, then you can tell me what colour they usually are. For example, a post box. What colour is a post box usually?
DM: What colour would a post box be? Well umm, now this is quite serious.
DA: Or a fire engine?
DM: Umm, I'm sorry about this.
DA: Oh, don't worry. What about the colour of grass?
DM: Grass—green.
DA: Good, and the colour of blood?
DM: Blood . . .
DA: Can you name anything that is the colour of blue, for example? Can you think of anything that is coloured blue around us?
DM: Violets are blue.
DA: Violets—blue?
DM: Are they?
DA: Well no, they are a violet colour, aren't they? It's a little rhyme isn't it?
DM: I think it was, 'roses are red, violets are blue'.
DA: Can you think of anything else that might be coloured blue?
DM: There is another aspect behind this, although what I used to rely on once, it's not as reliable anymore. I'm not getting the talkback that I used to get. Whether that will go on, whether it will improve, I don't know. Things are deteriorating quite a bit.

---

reason to believe that his lack of response was due to an inability to finely discriminate differences between colours and yet he was not even able to guess or say the colour that was most like the one he was seeing.

DM was faced with the unpalatable evidence that he was unable to name colours (colour anomia) or know the colour from meaningful associations of common objects (colour agnosia). The type of excuse he makes for this surprising shortcoming is typical of other accounts in the literature. This may be a genuine attempt at trying to explain the unexplainable. The reader will notice that in Box 2.3, the names of colourful objects are given in the auditory modality. It might be assumed that because the semantic store is seen to be in areas such as the temporal lobe then there would be no disconnection and DM should have no trouble with this task. However, associations for colour

appear to be stored in a more posterior brain area nearer to the V4 area where colour is analysed. Colour agnosia and colour anomia almost always occur together in this syndrome and it is assumed that the meaningful associations of colour are stored in an occipitotemporal lobe site (Goldenberg & Artner, 1991), which is likely to be the damaged site in the case of DM.

Associative and apperceptive face agnosia:prosopagnosia

A broad term for an inability to recognise faces is prosopagnosia. However, there is a distinction within this category between those patients who have a main difficulty in recognising a face (apperceptive face angosia), from those who have an ability to recognise a face but have lost the ability to recognise the identity of familiar faces (associative face agnosia). It can be argued that associative face agnosia, like associative object agnosia, is a type of top-down agnosia—top-down in the sense that the familiarity of faces is something that is learned from experience and is stored in downstream areas over the "what" pathway. For familiarity to be recognised this information must be accessed internally to be matched with the analysed external sensory information.

In one of the earliest case studies of face agnosia Bodamer (Bodamer, 1947; see Ellis, 1996) reports on a patient who described a dog's face as a human face with funny hair. From this, and other examples, it can be assumed that Bodamer's patient was having difficulty perceiving the structural features of the face—a type of apperceptive agnosia.

In terms of the patient with associative face agnosia, the failure to recognise the familiarity of faces may have alarming implications. This may extend to their own family or even their own face as portrayed in the mirror. For these patients the situation might arise in which the patient looks into the mirror and sees the reflection of a stranger. The patient knows that they are the strange looking person since they are the only person in front of the mirror. If the patient speaks they may recognise their own voice, they may even recognise a characteristic gesture in front of the mirror, but the face is completely new to them.

These patients have difficulty in recognising the faces of family and friends or famous personalities. But they may also have difficulty in recognising articles of clothing that they own, their cars, or in one case a farmer failed to recognise some cows that were previously individually known to him (e.g. Bornstein, Sroka, & Munitz, 1969). Nevertheless, faces appear to be special and dissociable from the poor recognition of other articles. Patients may have poor recognition for the familiarity of faces in isolation, while others may have poor recognition of familiarity of articles but be okay with faces.

Many patients with associative face agnosia may also have other associative agnosias, having additional inability to recognise objects (visual associative agnosia); however, alexia (inability to read) appears to be separable. Alexia is more

likely to occur following a left hemisphere lesion while prosopagnosia is more likely to require a bilateral lesion. There are a few cases of patients who suffer from prosopagnosia following right hemisphere lesions in isolation (Damasio, Damasio, & Van Hoesen, 1982; Polster & Rapcsak, 1996; Takahashi et al., 1995). This suggests, with other evidence, that face recognition is more dependent on the right hemisphere. Thus alexia and prosopagnosia appear to be separable and therefore depend to some extent on different brain structures, while object recognition may occur in the presence of either disorder (Farah, 1997). It should be stressed that these patients with *associative* face agnosia are able to recognise faces for what they are; they have, however, failed to gauge the faces' identity or its familiarity. Fortunately, like the other types of agnosias described above, the lesions required for this disorder are rare and usually involve a bilateral inferior occipital lobe area. The critical lesion is below the calcarine sulcus within Brodmann areas 18 and 19 and part of field 37 (see Figure 2.12).

Roesler, Lanquillon, Dippel and Braune (1997) used a computer morphing technique, in which an image gradually changed from one well-known face into another. The faces chosen were well-known personalities and the subjects had to identify the new face as it changed, as soon as possible. Patients with right posterior lesions were later in the recognition of the familiarity of the new face showing mild face agnosic impairment using this method. This interesting study suggests that there may be degrees of prosopagnosia or associative face agnosia. It may not be an all-or-none disorder as is sometimes described.

Patients with *apperceptive face agnosia* have difficulties with recognising a face as a face. Oliver Sacks describes a patient in the popular book *The man who mistook his wife for a hat* as actually attempting to lift his wife's head off to put it on (Sacks, 1986). This is unlike *associative* face agnosia in which patients can discriminate the physical distinction between faces and hats. The previously given example of Bodamer's patient (Bodamer, 1947) who saw a dog's face as being a human face with abundant hair would be seen as showing signs of apperceptive face

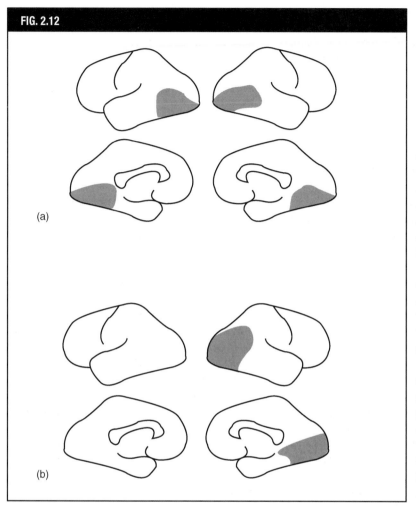

FIG. 2.12

(a)

(b)

Illustration of the lesions commonly found with prosopagnosia (a) associative face agnosia and (b) apperceptive agnosia. (a) Associative agnosia is associated with bilateral damage to the inferior aspect of the occipital lobe. (b) Apperceptive face agnosia is associated with damage to *both* the inferior and the superior aspects in areas 18 and 19, both mesially and laterally with additionally damage to parts of fields 37 and 39. A lesion sufficient to cause this disorder may also take the form of a unilateral lesion in the *right hemisphere* only.

agnosia. Another of Bodamer's patients reported seeing a face as being distorted with one eyebrow and the nose askew and the hair like an ill-fitting cap. Despite this 'metamorphopsia' the patient was able to recognise the identity of patients and therefore in this case at least there was proof of no accompanying associative face agnosia (Bodamer, 1947).

The apperceptive face agnosic may be assessed by being asked to match faces or identify a face when provided with only part of a face. This impairment is not just for faces and may pertain to partial visual information of other visual objects. Patients may also have difficulty in assembling puzzles for similar reasons. It might

be argued that there is no difference between the description of this kind of patient and any other patient with a general primary perceptual disorder. However, Damasio et al. (1982) propose that the inability to recognise the physical features of faces, familiar or otherwise, is sufficiently unusual to warrant the use of the special term 'apperceptive face agnosia'. There are patients who appear to have *specific* difficulties in identifying a face as a face without other difficulties of recognition of objects. Also, while patients with associative face agnosia often have apperceptive impairments they can be shown to be too mild to explain the severity of the associative face agnosia on the basis of the failure of structural analysis of the face. As indicated, even when apperceptive face agnosia is severe the patient may still be able to identify familiar face. There is therefore support for the separation of these two disorders.

OBJECT RECOGNITION

Assessment of perceptual disorder using the single-case approach.

In the previous section on clinical disorders of perception and the description of the classical syndromes some models of the brain mechanisms were described but there was no in-depth discussion of the analysis of the process. A cognitive neuropsychology approach to research using the single-case method has allowed a more in-depth analysis of the underlying mechanism of some of these disorders.

In the first half of this chapter the reader was introduced to the neuroscience of visual information processing with a description of the progressive analysis of visual information within the "what" and "where-action" pathways. There was then a description of clinical disorders, which revealed what happens when this pathway was disrupted. In this last section there is a more theoretical model-building approach that describes the various features of the disorders of perception and what these disorders tell us about the underlying process of visual perception.

New forms of perceptual disorders are constantly being proposed and the view of how we should categorise these disorders is rapidly changing. This approach has resulted in new categories of perceptual disorder although some of these are rather tentative. One of the problems with introducing a new perceptual disorder is the concern that the phenomenon being described is really just a mixture of two already existing disorders. These doubts may be more likely to arise when only one patient with the "new" disorder has been reported.

As argued in Chapter 1, the advantage of the single-case cognitive neuropsychology approach is the greater detail of analysis that goes along

with this approach. For example, in analysing the perceptual performance of such a case, the first stage in the analysis might be to test that the patient has a disorder of sensation. Already discussed is the need to test the elements of acuity, which assesses the patients ability to detect changes in luminance and size) (see Figure 2.13 for an example).

The impairment of acuity must obviously undermine the ability to detect and judge shape, contours, and form, but the relationship in some cases is not as strong as one might predict. There are patients who have moderate to severe problems of acuity, but who are nevertheless able to detect form (e.g., Efron, 1968). There are also patients who have no difficulty with acuity judgements but have a complete failure in detecting form, so there is a case for making the distinction between acuity and shape perception (Warrington & Taylor, 1973). These patients who have adequate *acuity*, but still have difficulty in detecting form, may not be able to match or copy shapes with different contours; this is sometimes referred to as *visual form agnosia*. A further dissociation between acuity and form lies in the neuropathology. Patients with problems of acuity may show this following a unilateral lesion, while poor discrimination of contour in isolation without impaired acuity mainly occurs following a bilateral lesion (Efron, 1968). Both these disorders are associated with posterior occipital lesions.

A further intermediate stage has been realised in which patients may be able match and copy form and contour but they appear to lack the structural templates that allow the shape to be recognised as an object for its physical features. Sometimes these patients may copy and match, but the object can not be identified as in the case of associative agnosia; nevertheless these patients do show some familiarity for the physical characteristics that they are viewing. In one popularly used test the patient is shown some line drawing of animals, e.g. a kangaroo, with similar drawings of chimeras, e.g. kangaroo with emu's head. Similar real and chimeric stimuli using tools have also been designed (see Figure 2.13c). The patient is asked which of the pictures are of real animals or

FIG. 2.13

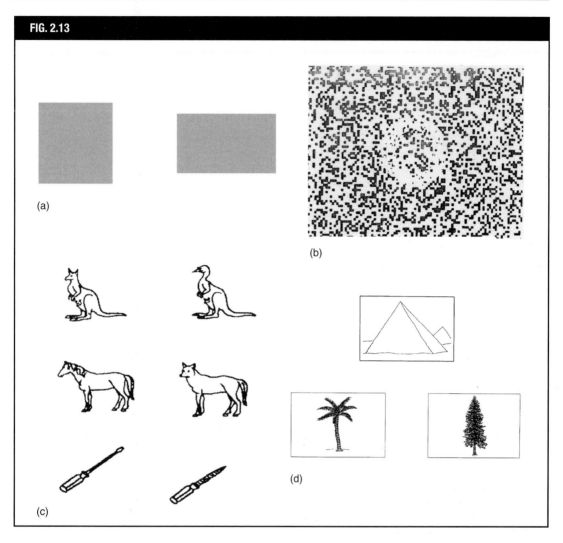

(a)

(b)

(c)

(d)

Illustration of the tests commonly used to analyse the nature of the perceptual disorder: (a) test of acuity; (b) test of appreciation of form or contour (reprinted from Warrington & Taylor, 1973, with permission from Masson, Italy); (c) chimeric stimuli (from Riddoch, & Humphreys, 1987, *Cognitive Neuropsychology*, reprinted by permission of Psychology Press. Ltd, Hove, UK) (d) test of semantic access without the confounding assessment of language output (reprinted from the Pyramid and Palm Trees test by Howard, D. and Patterson, K.E. with permission from the Thames Valley test Company Bury St Edmonds UK).

real objects. If they are able to complete this task successfully then it is assumed that they are able to access the stored structural form of what they are seeing. The patient may not know the meaning of the stimuli, that the stimulus is half kangaroo and emu, but the correct response that it is not a real animal might suggest that there is some physical representation of real animals that is helping this decision. Patients that appear to show this as a separate stage from semantic analysis are capable of performing this task but are unable to match functionally similar objects (semantic analysis) (Chertkow, Bub, & Caplan, 1992; Riddoch & Humphreys, 1987a). The distinction between the top-down semantic and top-down physical representation is therefore being made. There is the implication that just as we have knowledge that helps in the perceptual process we also have memory representations of the physical or structural representations of objects, which allow us to speed up the perceptual recognition process.

The reader will note that the model in Figure 2.14 is referred to as a prototype model. At a later stage within this chapter this model will be further developed. The distinction between structural object identity and semantic identity is attractive and supported by patients with posterior right hemisphere damage who have difficulty in recognising objects in unusual orientations. These patients make mistakes because of the fewer number of physical rather than meaningful features present (see discussion below). Nevertheless, other interpretations are available for the isolated success on the chimeric task. For example, this might represent a deficient refined semantic analysis, such that only broad semantic categories may be judged "real' versus "not-real". Patients with associative agnosia may make broad judgements of this nature in other domains correctly when more specific judgements are not available to them. Therefore, although it is likely that we have physical templates that could be disconnected from specific meaning, more work is required in this area to verify the model.

Tasks that are used to assess perceptual stages in isolation often use a recognition format that does not require a verbal report. If a person fails to respond to a task that requires a verbal response it might be because the patient has a language difficulty. This confusion of what is actually impaired is reduced in the pyramid and palm trees test. In this test the patient has to choose which of the pictured objects goes with a target picture, e.g. a pyramid. Options such as a deciduous tree versus a palm tree allow an assessment of the patient's ability to access the associations of what they are perceiving (see Figure 2.13d) at the semantic knowledge level. Using these types of methods the stage of perceptual breakdown may be analysed.

Integrative agnosia

A number of patients have been described who appear to have lesions that support some degree of both apperceptive and associative agnosia and might be described as intermediate agnosias (Behrmann et al., 1994; Farah, 1990; Humphreys & Riddoch, 1984, 1985; Warrington, 1985). However, Glyn Humphreys and colleagues describe a patient HJA who has been classified as suffering specifically from *integrative agnosia* (Boucart & Humphreys, 1992; Humphreys et al., 1994; Riddoch & Humphreys, 1987a; see also Butter & Trobe, 1994). The patient could match objects and could also draw good renditions of common objects from memory when asked to do so (using the auditory modality). The patient had

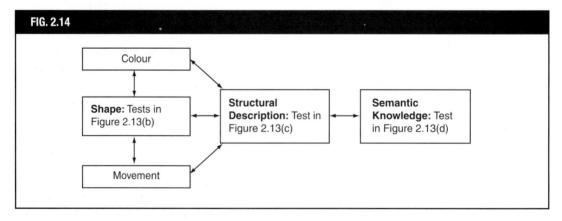

FIG. 2.14

A prototypical model of object recognition with influences from Warrington (1985), Humphreys and Riddoch (1985, 1994), and Farah (1990). The model assumes that processing is to some degree in series but does not discount the possibility of a later stage being completed despite impairment at an earlier stage. There is the capability for top-down processing to facilitate bottom-up processing (see also Humphreys, Riddoch, & Price, 1997).

difficulty in recognising objects presented visually even when he was capable of copying them and therefore could be diagnosed as suffering from visual associative agnosia. However, there were additional deficits in recognising objects, which suggested some difficulty in perceiving the structural or physical components of an object. For example, he was less likely to identify an object if it was in an unusual orientation, the patient also had difficulty in matching or tracing objects that were overlapping (see Figure 2.8). There were additional signs of partially impaired top-down processing. For example, the patient was able to name and recognise some line drawings, but when they contained extra lines that depicted features of the object, these extra lines, which helped normal control persons, hindered this patient. The patient found it easier to identify silhouettes, e.g. objects that are shaded showing just the outline. The patient took longer to analyse any outline especially when grouping or isolation of a figure from a background was required. In short these patients have difficulty "seeing the forest for the trees" when it comes to visual recognition. This patient was, however, able to discriminate real objects from drawn non-objects (see Figure 2.13c), suggesting that the structural representation was intact or that there was some surviving semantic analysis at a basic level. The requisite lesion is assumed to be ventral within the "what" pathway.

In summary, it would appear that the patient with integrative agnosia generally shows the following features:

1. A general inability to recognise objects, despite an ability of the patient to describe or even draw objects from memory.
2. A difficulty in recognition when objects are drawn with more detail or overlapping figures.
3. The patient is generally challenged by any task that requires grouping together of a design towards a whole or a gestalt.
4. The patient has less difficulty in identifying silhouettes or drawings that do not have internal detail even though such detail may normally help controls or other patients.

There is a distinction to be made between patients like HJA with ventral lesions to the "what pathway" and those who have lesions in the "where-action" pathway who suffer from *dorsal simultaneous agnosia*. Both types of patients have difficulty selecting figures from background noise but with the latter patients the problem is more one of attention. That is, they have difficulty in transferring from one local aspect of a figure to another; they have attentional difficulties which are discussed in the next chapter. Both these types of patients may have difficulty with the overlapping figures task for different reasons (Humphreys et al., 1994). However, the integrative agnosic patient will usually take longer to process a visually presented picture irrespective of whether it contains one or many items if there is enough interfering detail in the single object. But a patient with dorsal simultaneous agnosia is only slower if the picture contains more than one item. The dorsal simultaneous agnosic patient will be as quick as controls in processing an image as long as it is a single item (Coslett & Saffran, 1991).

Global versus local processing

One popular hypothesis concerning perceptual processing and differences between the two hemispheres concerns the finding that the left hemisphere appears to be more specialised in the recognition of the prominent *parts* of stimuli, while the right is better at analysing the *holistic* features of visual information. The holistic perception or gestalt relates to the perception of all the features and how they relate to each other. For example, the left hemisphere would, according to this theory, be better able to recognise small parts of a stimulus that do not require an overall integration of those parts. The right hemisphere would in contrast be drawn to analysing the overall picture—how the parts combine to make the whole. From this proposal it should be understood that the hemispheres make different but complementary contributions towards the perceptual recognition process.

Much of the initial work on the local–global distinction tended to employ a paradigm similar to that displayed in Figure 2.15. The test depends

FIG. 2.15

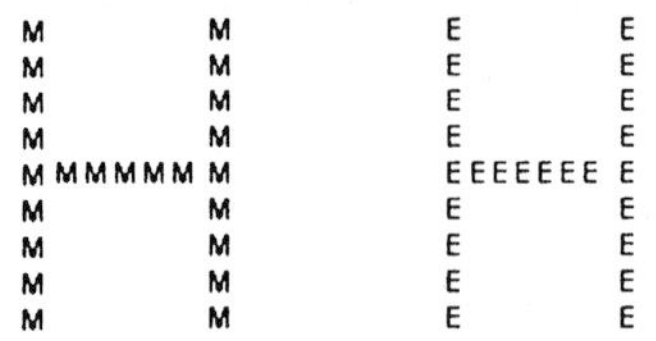

```
M        M            E            E
M        M            E            E
M        M            E            E
M        M            E            E
M MMMMM  M            EEEEEEE  E
M        M            E            E
M        M            E            E
M        M            E            E
M        M            E            E
```

Illustration of global and local stimuli. In deciding whether the two stimuli are the same or different a "same response" would indicate a global level of processing, while a tendency to give a "different response" suggests that a local level is preferred. There are many variations on this theme.

on the relative and absolute size of the local stimuli (small letters) and the global letters (large letters made up from the small letters). With this particular paradigm there is a general tendency for matching decisions of local stimuli to show some interference from global stimuli, but not vice versa. That is, in the above situation there might be a slower judgement of the local stimuli because the correct response to say "different" might be interfered with by the correct response of "same" for the global stimuli.

With similar paradigms *global* judgements are less efficient when patients have a right superior temporal lobe lesion. But if they are required to make a local decision, patients with a left superior temporal lobe lesion show less ability. Also, interference between levels (global versus local) is reduced when one hemisphere is damaged since there is less interference from the type of analysis that normally proceeds from that hemisphere. For example, a patient with a right superior temporal lobe lesion would be less slowed by the interfering global analysis in our example (Doyon & Milner, 1991; Lamb, Robertson, & Knight, 1990). This predilection of the left hemisphere for local analysis and right hemisphere for global analysis is a consistent finding with both normals and split-brain patients (Robertson, Lamb, & Zaidel, 1993). While the contributions are separate, this should not undermine the importance of the integrative approach of the two hemispheres. Nevertheless, there are some percepts that are

more suited to the holistic or global approach. One of these percepts is the human face.

There are additional arguments concerning the global versus local distinction which are related to the perception of certain spatial frequencies. It appears that the right hemisphere is especially advantaged if the global aspects of perception contain high spatial frequencies (Fink, Marshall, Halligan, & Dolan, 1999; For a complete description of this theory see Ivry & Robertson, 1998).

THE SPECIAL CASE OF FACE RECOGNITION

Perception and the recognition of a person's face, name, and identity

There are various ways in which persons may be identified. Their name might be retrieved, or their face may be recognised, or even a person may be identified from biographical details such as a description of who they are or what they have done in the past. Patients have been found who have no difficulty in recognising faces but have difficulty with names, while other patients have been found with the converse problem, being able to recognise a face but having difficulty retrieving the name. These last patients are an exaggeration of the common lament "I never forget a face, but I have trouble with names".[1] The important issue here is that this double dissociation suggests that names and faces are processed separately. If you damage one process you do not necessarily damage another.

But as we have argued, in the case of apperceptive face agnosia, when we are talking about face recognition there must be a process prior to face recognition that analyses the structural or physical aspects of the face. Patients with apperceptive face agnosia have difficulty at this level. Patients with prosopagnosia or associative face agnosia may be able to get though this first stage and recognise what they are seeing as a face but fail in the second stage in recognising its familiarity and identity (see Figure 2.16). Stages that are thought

[1] The issue of the difficulty of remembering names compared to recognising faces is discussed further in the chapter on rehabilitation.

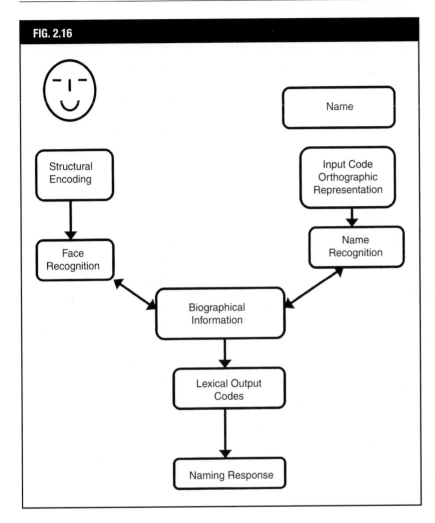

FIG. 2.16

A simplified functional model of face and proper name processing (adapted from Bruce & Young, 1986, and Tempini et al. (1998).

to be associated with normal identification of a face are assumed to be sequential. At the coarsest level of analysis, there are three stages of processing: first, a structural face recognition stage (*Is this a face?*); second, a face recognition stage (*This is a face and it looks familiar or unfamiliar*); a third stage in which the person would be identified for who they are and what they do. That is, the person's biographical information or meaningful information about the identity is required (*I know this person; he is the one who lives in the white house and works for the post office*).

Figure 2.16 shows a box and arrow diagram which reveals the relationship discussed so far that has been derived from the various clinical case studies and studies of normal groups (e.g.

Brennen, Baguley, Bright, & Bruce 1990; Cohen & Faulkner, 1986; Young, Hay, & Ellis, 1985). It should be noted that in this model it is possible to derive someone's name or recognise their face following their identification of what they do and where they come from. An example of this situation might arise when a person sees an actor in a film who is only recognised when the viewer has been told what other films the actor had been in. There are patients who are able to recognise the name, voice, face but still have no ability to retrieve any biographical information. Therefore a special box for biographical or meaningful information about the identity is also required (e.g. Kapur et al., 1995); Kartsounis & Shallice, 1996). Finally there is a further literature and models of the identification of emotion within facial expression, but this is dealt with in the chapter on emotion and social dysfunction.

Neurophysiological evidence for face recognition from animal research

There are now a number of studies that have found cells within the temporal lobe that are specialised for the recognition of faces. These face cells have been investigated by measuring firing rates of individual cells when the animal is presented with faces versus control non-face stimuli or objects. It appears that while cells within the inferior temporal lobe are more important for recognising the identity of a face (a picture of a specific monkey's face), there are cells within the superior temporal lobe (specifically within the superior temporal sulcus) that fire more selectively to certain expressions, movement, and orientation. These findings have been replicated with human subjects (e.g. Puce, Smith & Allison, 2000). There are also a smaller number of cells that seem to respond only to a combination of identity and orientation stimuli (Hasselmo, Rolls, Baylis, & Nalwa 1989; Perrett, Hietanen, Oram, Benson, 1992).

One issue that has been of research interest in recent years is the distinction between *object-centred* and *viewer-centred* perception. Perrett and Oram with colleagues (Oram & Perrett, 1996; Perrett, Oram, Harries et al., 1991) report the existence of some cells that appear to be dependent on the viewpoint of the observer and others that are not.

The majority of cells that have been detected respond to a single orientation of a face. For example these viewer-centred cells may respond maximally to a face at 45% orientation in relations to the viewer. However, there are a few cells in the superior temporal area of the macaque monkey that respond irrespective of the face orientation. These 2–5% of clever cells pick up a face in all the orientations and are referred to as object-centred cells. It might be that these object centred cells might have input from cells that are more restricted in the reception of specific orientations (Ullman, 1998).

The same distribution of cells firing more at certain orientations has been found with stimuli other than faces. However, many questions remain to be answered. For example, it is assumed that cells exist for some of the orientations but not for all orientations. Therefore one theory is that there is some interpolation between viewer-centred angles of orientation. In other words, if there were cells to cope with viewer-centred orientation after the face or object has turned through 40 degrees and 50 degrees then is there some mechanism that predicted the features of the object at 45 degrees. This would be necessary in order to allow the apparently visually smooth turning of the object. Logothetis and Pauls (1995) conducted an experiment to answer this question. Using novel three-dimensional objects that were especially created for the experiment, the primates in this experiment were trained to recognise these originally unfamiliar objects at certain orientations. Cells were then found in the temporal cortex which, after training, showed a significant response to the trained orientations. Despite this apparent specific cell response to the trained orientations they found that the primates still recognised the objects after they were rotated through a further 40 degrees beyond the trained orientation. This suggests some support for the interpolation mechanism described above.

Also, there is an assumption that cell representation for perceived orientation is not linear but categorised. For example, as a face turns away from you there is a sudden loss of identifying features at a certain point that might mark the end and the beginning of a new category of orientation. There may be less need for intense identification of orientation when the facial features are hidden (see Ullman, 1998, for a discussion of these issues).

The distinction in face detection between the inferior and superior temporal lobe in terms of identity recognition and orientation/movement respectively has caused the speculation that these are extensions of the "what" and "where-action" pathways (Oram & Perrett, 1996; Turnbull, Carey, & McCarthy, 1997). Although, there are some areas of overlap, with cells showing a combination of these qualities, this relationship also seems to be supported in terms of the speed of response of cells.

Some differences between face and object recognition

While it may be reasonable to assume that the monkey brain and the human brain have similar functional organisation at the cellular level, there is clearly more hemispheric specialisation within the human brain. Apart from the more obvious left hemisphere dominance for language there is also a distinction in terms of perceptual processing. The human right hemisphere appears to be more proficient at processing facial stimuli when compared to object processing. This is not to suggest a simplistic formula whereby objects are the domain of the left hemisphere and faces of the right hemisphere, but rather to suggest that faces require more right hemisphere involvement in the human brain.

Studies have found a tendency for poor recognition of famous faces to be associated with atrophy in the right temporal lobe in a single case (Patterson & Hodges, 1995). Judgements on faces are certainly usually more accurate and faster when they are presented to the right hemisphere (e.g. Rhodes & Wooding, 1989). Also, as indicated above, a right posterior lesion is sufficient to cause apperceptive face agnosia (Damasio, Tranel, & Damasio, 1990a).

There is also a growing literature showing that the judgement of emotion in faces is better performed by the right hemisphere, although the performance of the left hemisphere is improved when the emotions are given verbal labels (e.g. Stone, Nisenson, Eliassen, & Gazzaniga, 1996). Some studies have investigated patients with substantial damage to the right hemisphere to evaluate the effect of reliance on the left hemisphere. When the difficulty of these patients is analysed further, it appears that patients who have to rely on the left hemisphere have a relatively inefficient strategy of trying to recognise a face by an over-reliance on the recognition of certain facial features—an analysis of the face by its parts, rather than the whole (Polster & Rapcsak, 1996, p. 245; Rapcsak, Polster, Glisky & Comer, 1996; Zaidel, 1990). We are reminded

of the global and local distinction that has been made above.

When thinking about differences between object and face recognition it might be helpful to make the distinction between recognition of features versus global recognition. When talking about visual recognition the right hemisphere appears to be useful at analysing the global aspects of the face while the left seems to contribute by recognising certain features or parts. The term "global" refers to the value of the overall gestalt. The gestalt refers to a visual representation in which the parts of the picture only take their value from their overall interrelationship with one another.

Everyone has two eyes, a mouth, two ears and most us have some hair. The distinction between individuals only becomes really clear when these features are related to each other within their natural position (e.g. Farah, Wilson, Drain, & Tanaka, 1998). In contrast to faces, it is easier to discriminate between objects on the basis of parts or features. The long spout and base of a watering can are quite distinctive. The teeth of a comb could only belong to a comb in the absence of another feature such as a handle.

We have already mentioned the difficulty that patients have in recognising faces when they have right hemisphere damage. What happens when patients have to use their right hemisphere for face processing without the help of the left hemisphere? Moscovitch, Winocur and Behrmann (1997) chose to study a patient with associative object agnosia and dyslexia associated with substantial left hemisphere damage. From this and other studies it is clear that right hemisphere face perception is not analysing eyes or mouths in isolation or even collectively. Given these distinctive aspects of the face placed in a group (not in their correct spatial position) the patient still had difficulty in recognising the identity of the face. It was only when the parts of the face were placed within their spatially correct relationship that the face was most easily recognised—the sum of the parts is not equivalent to the whole.

Moscovitch and colleagues found that their patient had exaggerated difficulty in recognising a face when it was upside down. This well-replicated finding suggests that we have a memory template of an upright face with which new faces are compared. Objects are far less difficult to recognise than faces when they are inverted (Farah et al., 1998). Haxby and colleagues have shown with imaging studies that when faces were inverted an alternative stream of brain activation occurred, suggesting a different process of analysis (Haxby et al., 1999). This suggests that when the template for an upright face no longer becomes useful an alternative strategy has to be used. The template hypothesis is further supported by the finding that different races appear to have different templates. Many people are struck by the difficulty in distinguishing between people when they go overseas for their holiday. The often seemingly racist statement that "they all look alike" is most obviously because there is some variation in memory for face templates between races. If this difficulty in identifying particular individuals from a particular race exists, it is likely to be due to a lack of experience with that race and therefore the confusion is often reciprocated (Rhodes, 1993).

There are an increasing number of imaging studies confirming the separation between the processing of objects and names compared to faces at the initial level of analysis, the activation associated with faces being more bilateral but involving the right hemisphere more. Faces primarily activate the fusiform gyrus bilaterally, and also activate the right areas of the occipital and temporal lobe referred to broadly above as the "what" pathway but also within regions of the middle temporal gyrus (Puce et al.,1996). Both object and faces appear to involve the "what" pathway and structures such as the fusiform gyrus; it is only downstream from this point that differences are most obvious. There is a further anterior middle temporal lobe location that also may be more specialised for faces (Tempini et al., 1998). These locations appear to be further supported also from lesion studies (Damasio, Tranel, & Damasio, 1990a).

Summary

In summary, there is evidence that faces are processed somewhat differently from proper names and other information relating to a person's iden-

tity. The perception of faces deteriorates much more than objects when they are inverted, which suggests that we process the face according to some form of template that is dependent on the correct orientation. For example, if you turn a model train upside down the train is still easily recognisable. If you get a friend to lie on the floor so that you can see their face upside down, you will see how different and strange they look.

The finding of cells in the monkey's cortex of the temporal lobe that specifically respond to faces is now well replicated. Cells in the area of the superior temporal lobe are more sensitive to orientation and faces or bodies moving in a particular direction. These cells are also more sensitive to expression. All these features depend on recognising the spatial constituents of facial features and it is possible that these cells represent the extension of the "where-action" pathway. The inferior aspect of the temporal lobe appears to be more related to identifying the face, which may represent an extension of the "what" pathway.

Apart from the basic problem of face identification there is also the problem of how we recognise a person's face or an object from so many different viewpoints. If one just considers the outline of a face as it changes orientation to the viewer there is a radically different view being presented as the face turns through 90 degrees. It would seem a lot to ask of the perceptual system to recognise all these very different views, as a face rotates away from the viewer. However, this is what the brain actually appears to do. The monkey studies have described a large number of cells that maximally respond to faces at a certain orientation according to the observer (viewer dependent). There are a smaller number of "object or face-centred" cells that have been found to be sensitive to all the different orientations, irrespective of the observer's viewpoint. Given that the outline of a face can vary extensively depending on the angle at which it is seen, these cells must be sensitive to some "faceness" quality that is common to all orientations. Alternatively, and perhaps more likely, these "object-centred" cells have input from all the cells that are individually sensitive to faces in all the different orientations (Ullman, 1998).

Finally, it appears that the right hemisphere has a specific contribution to make towards the perception of faces. The global perception strategy associated with the right hemisphere appears to suit the analysis of the complex features of the face that can only be differentiated by subtle differences in the way the different features are spatially interrelated. As a species we have been (and still are in some parts of the world) very dependent on acknowledging social relationships and emotional facial recognition for survival; our ancestors must have evolved to become very certain on knowing exactly who was dominant and who was "friendly" or "unfriendly". Further examples of this right hemisphere specialty within perception are provided in the next section.

RIGHT HEMISPHERE PERCEPTUAL PROCESSING

The right parietal area and the perception of degraded and unusual viewpoints.

Some disorders of perception are confined to the perception of objects in unusual or degraded presentations. Sometimes referred to as a "categorisation deficit" this type of apperceptive agnosia

is associated with a right inferior posterior parietal lobe lesion (Warrington & Taylor, 1973). This may be evoked in a number of different presentations but was originally found when patients were presented with pictures in an unusual orientation, for example, a bucket is viewed from directly above (see Figure 2.17). Humphreys and Riddoch (1984, 1985) found that varying the number of features (recognisable parts) did not affect these patients' perception to the same extent as changing the contours of the object (see Davidoff & Warrington, 1999, for a confirmation of this view). In other words, for these patients visuospatial aspects or the physical contours were the impediment to recognition, not the availability of meaning.

However, for Humphrey's and Riddoch's associative agnosic patients (with left hemisphere lesion) the reverse was true: the contours were not as important as the amount of meaning cues available. In some sense this is supportive of the structural description stage in the model provided in Figure 2.14. It would appear that the right hemisphere is more dominant for the assessment of structural information, while the left is more important for deciphering the meaning of the structural information.

Consequently, while poor recognition of objects from an unusual viewpoint might best be

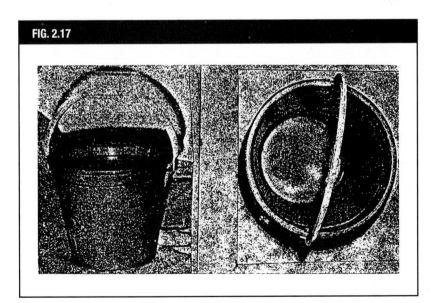

The stimulus on the right is an unusual view of a bucket. Patients with right posterior parietal damage also find photographs of partially shaded and silhouettes of objects difficult to identify. (reprinted from Warrington & Taylor, 1973, with permission from Masson, Italy).

seen as a reduction of the right hemisphere's capacity to analyse detail, the left hemisphere appears to be more specialised in the analysis of the conceptual meaning of the object. A point worth making here is that when objects are in the normal orientation the patient with a right posterior (parietal) lesion is often able to recognise or name the object. Even if the right hemisphere is helping to do this for these patients, it is likely that the left hemisphere is able to do this on its own, possibly by using the familiar contours rather than the details.

Davidoff and Warrington (1999) tested a patient with a substantial right hemisphere lesion. The lesion was sufficiently large to argue that most of this patient's perception was being undertaken by the left hemisphere. Their patient had difficulty in perceiving unusual views, as shown in Figure 2.17. These researchers wanted to find out how the left hemisphere was able to perceive the objects when they were in normal orientation. One theory that is often put forward is that the right hemisphere is capable of holistic perception while the left hemisphere makes an identification through the analysis of typical features of an object. Davidoff and Warrington showed their patient the features in Figure 2.18a and unlike the controls their patient had extreme difficulty in identifying the object by its parts. This rather flies in the face of one version of the global–local view discussed earlier that the left hemisphere is good at analysing the parts or features of a stimulus.

Davidoff and Warrington (1999) then looked at the basis on which objects were named when an object was in a normal orientation. How discriminating was this mechanism? They reasoned that one might still be able to name an object just from its broad outline without perceiving its form or detail with any accuracy. In Figure 2.18b an example of the three choices is given in three conditions. In the first condition the patient was required to recognise the most typical representation of the eagle. The second test required the assessment of shape, and the third required the assessment of colour. The patient performed poorly on these tests compared to controls and therefore it was concluded that while the left hemisphere was able to name objects, given a typical outline, its perceptual abilities were relatively unsophisticated. It was the right hemisphere that analysed such details as provided by shading and subtle perceptual features. Studies of agnosic patients clearly show how important the left hemisphere is for the analysis of meaning, but the right hemisphere has a strength when it comes to analysing the complex shading, details and subtle physical details of visually presented stimuli. When describing the attributes of the left hemisphere abilities in form perception Warrington and Davidoff (1999) describe it as a "bare bones" of perception. The right hemisphere is clearly more useful in its contribution to visuospatial analysis. In Figure 2.23 the model of Figure 2.14 has now been adapted to take into account these relative gifts of the two hemispheres.

This exciting work needs to be extended but there seems to be a convergence of empirical information to support the view that the right hemisphere is a gifted hemisphere when it comes to the structural or physical analysis of an object. This suggests that in the normal brain the two hemispheres work in tandem to perceive an object. The right hemisphere is dominant in the recognition of the structural features, while the left hemisphere supplies the meaning. A further finding of this important study was that this patient was also poor at recognising the orientation of an object. Is this another gift to be attributed to the right hemisphere?

Orientation and the perception of three dimensions

Judgement of orientation

Visual orientation is usually referred to as the ability to judge the angle of objects in space and has been assessed by a number of tasks, including the Benton line orientation (Benton, Varney, & Hamsher, 1978). This test requires the patient to judge the orientation of a line or lines by correctly pointing to the matching line from a number of variously oriented lines in a protractor-like array. When this task is presented in a way that maximises the demands of the orientation judgement by using an optional sample of lines (without the

FIG. 2.18

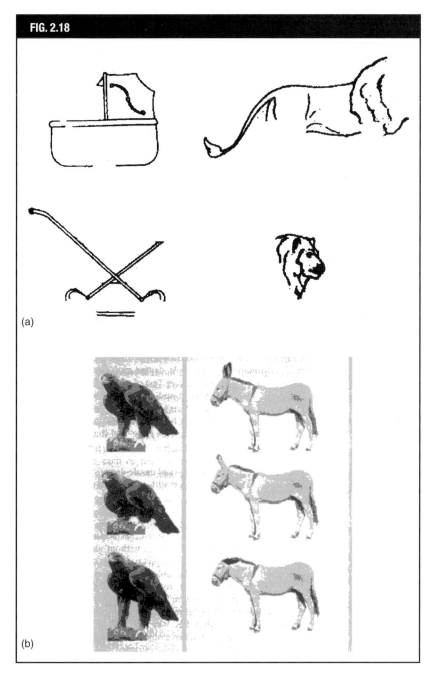

(a)

(b)

Davidoff and Warrington (1999) used features (a) that were shown to the patient and controls one at a time. The right hemisphere-damaged patient had difficulty in identifying an item from the part. In (b), although the patient was able to name objects there was poor judgement of the correct or typical (top) representation (reprinted from Davidoff and Warrington, 1999, with permission from Elsevier Sciences).

protractor array) then the task is sensitive to posterior right hemisphere lesions. The group with left posterior hemisphere lesions performed at the same level as the controls (Mehta & Newcombe, 1996).

There are some individual patients who show extreme difficulty in judging orientation. Turnbull (e.g. Turnbull, Beschin, & Della Sala, 1996) describes a patient (NL) and other patients who tend to rotate their copies of drawings and have poor judgement of orientation. The critical lesion for this disturbance is uncertain but it is quite dramatic, with the patient being somewhat non-plussed by the demand to correctly orient their pictures. If they are given a picture showing a wrong orientation, e.g. a bus upside down, there is a tendency to draw the picture in the right orientation, but this is not inevitable and is despite full knowledge that the aim of the task is to draw the object in the same orientation. There are also similar difficulties in judging the correct orientation from a choice of different orientations. The patient NL is reported to have hanged his pictures at home upside down (presumably these are not all by Jackson Pollack); it is of interest that he shows no obvious constructional distortions in his copies and therefore his impairment is not obviously confounded by other perceptual impairments. Although the two original patients described by Turnbull and his colleagues had a lesion that included the right parietal area and cells have been found in the monkey that respond to rotated motion in the vicinity of V5 (Sakata, Shibutani, Ito & Tsurugai, 1986), there are a variety of lesions associated with this deficit, which include frontal areas. As yet there is no clear indication of the crucial lesions involved with this disorder (see Solms, Turnbull, Kaplan-Solms, & Miller, 1998). Further support for differentiation between the analysis of orientation compared to other perceptions comes from work showing that orientation is processed more slowly than colour and faster than motion (Moutoussis & Zeki, 1997). From this evidence it appears that the mechanism is likely to be separate from other perceptual or constructional impairments. Turnbull, Carey and McCarthy (1997) also argue this point and suggest that the identification within the parietal lobe is within the ventral stream of the "what" pathway within the right hemisphere, while the assessment of orientation is more dorsal, perhaps part of the "where-action" pathway. The orientation module may assist in object recognition within the ventral stream by detecting unusual or rotated orientation of objects.

Topographical orientation
There are some patients who have difficulty in orienting in terms of their spatial location. This might occur when a patient is required to walk from one therapy room to another within a hospital. Semmes attempted to simulate such a difficulty by asking patients to walk along a route described by a map given to the patient (Semmes, Weinstein, Ghent, & Teuber, 1955). The map was a series of lines drawn between a series of circles. Thus the map might describe a pathway going up to the first circle and then to the side for the next circle and so on. On the floor of the room in which the patient was standing was a series of circles in a similar pattern described by the map, and the patient was required to walk along the direction indicated by the primitive map. Patients with parietal damage were worse on this task compared to a control group and another group with lesions in other brain areas. This task was referred to as a test of extrapersonal space. Later Semmes (Semmes, Weinstein Ghent, & Teuber, 1963) was able to show a difference between disorientation on this type of task and that concerning one's own body or personal space. Tests of personal space required subjects to touch their own body in the order indicated on a drawn model. Patients with left frontal lesions had difficulty on this test. Therefore there is a dissociation between extrapersonal and personal space. The frontal patients may do poorly because they have to put themselves into an imaginary situation represented by the model. The task requires the subject to anticipate where to touch if they

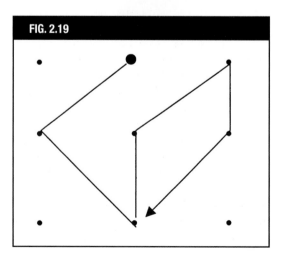

FIG. 2.19

Illustration of the type of maps used by Semmes et al., 1955).

were facing in a particular direction. The knowledge of consequences of action and this form of extrapolation make the task difficult for the frontal lobe patient, whereas the extrapersonal test more obviously requires the judgement of spatial relationships, direction, and orientation. Therefore a parietal lesion might be expected. A recent survey of patients with topographical orientation route-learning difficulties indicates a medial bilateral or right medial parietal/occipital lesion is common with a posterior lesion to the hippocampi (Barrash, Damasio, Adolphs, & Tranel, 2000). It is in this medial parietal area of the precuneus that functional imaging studies show some activation during imagery (Fletcher, Frith, Baker et al., 1995).

Perception of three dimensions

One of the big debates that is a focus of research interest at the present time is how we recognise objects in three dimensions. This seems a rather foolish question until we realise that we retrieve a three-dimensional image from the two-dimensional image that is represented by the light patterns that fall on the retina. These light patterns, if they were just read as they were received, would reveal a flat, shapeless world. Already discussed are the viewer-centred cells that might be in a position to construct three dimensions from a series of orientations. However, it is clear that there are a number of cues that illustrate depth and the three-dimensional nature of the environment.

Our perceptual process interprets the depth perception cues such as perspective, texture, shadows, overlaps, and relative size, giving us an accurate perception of depth. These are learned and must be considered top-down interpretations of the stimulus cues that exist in our environment. There is also the cue of *local* stereopsis, which is cued by ocular convergence. Near images are associated with larger amounts of accommodation because the eyes have to converge on the image more. This cue is used as one of many that allow us to estimate depth, although these are not a property of any one hemisphere.

However, there is one cue that appears to depend more on the right hemisphere, which is

referred to as *global* stereopsis and is tested by looking at stereograms (Julesz, 1971). Global stereopsis appears to depend on a dot-by-dot matching of what is seen in one eye compared to the other. By using special glasses, with one glass green and the other red, steropsis may be created within specially made films that have been shot by two different cameras from a slightly different angle. The colour in one lens blocks out or obscures the angle shot from one of the cameras, so that each eye sees a slightly different film. The objects in the film become so real that the audience may be seen reaching out to grab the passing objects. This mechanism is referred to as binocular disparity and is not dependent on the identification of recognised forms. Stereograms of random dots may appear in three dimensions. The ability to detect depth from stereostopic projections in this manner has been shown to be impaired in patients with right lesions (Carmon & Bechtoldt, 1969); the most sensitive assessment of such a deficit is obtained by using random letter stereoscopic test. More recently, patients following right temporal lobectomy (removal of the anterior portion of the temporal lobe usually to reduce epilepsy) have been found to be more impaired than those following left temporal lobectomy (Ptito, Zatorre, Larson, & Tosoni, 1991). A finding that has been supported by imaging studies is that there is more activation in the right posterior areas when viewing stereograms (Ptito et al., 1993).

Rotation in the 'mind's eye' (image) of three-dimensional images is also seen as more of a right hemisphere skill. Typically, in these kinds of experiments a pair of three-or two-dimensional forms are shown and the subject has to judge whether the two forms match each other. The two forms are in a different orientation, e.g. one of the figures might be turned on its side. Some people appear to make this judgement by rotating one of the forms around in the "mind's eye" until they are both oriented in the same way before making a matching decision. Evidence of greater right hemisphere involvement comes from studies of patients who have right hemisphere lesions (Ratcliff, 1979) and from split-brain studies (see Chapter 6 for methodology) (Corballis &

Sargent, 1989). This is seen as a predominant right hemisphere task rather than the sole domain of the right hemisphere, perhaps because there are a number of different strategies for completing the task.

Constructions and spatial distortions

Constructional apraxia is used by clinicians for convenience rather than as a term with any precise meaning. Constructional difficulties may be due to a large number of different factors some of which some are quite unrelated to apraxia (see Benton & Tranel, 1993, for a discussion). Nevertheless, it is possible that some of these factors may be delineated to reveal a more specific description.

Difficulty in making constructions including drawing, copying designs using coloured blocks, or copying three-dimensional models all require perception, coordinated motor movements and judgement of orientation and spatial relationships, and adequate attention to the task. Constructions are therefore a form of non-verbal final common pathway for many of the higher mental processes described above. Copying a cube is a popular bedside method used by clinicians for assessing constructional impairment. Although they may be unreliable they are sensitive to brain impairment and will prompt further testing. Sometimes when memory for the copy is required later, this exaggerates the impaired performance.

While Alzheimer's disease is commonly associated with memory loss in the laypersons mind, constructional difficulties are also very common (Haut et al., 1994). While the memory loss in this disease is associated with loss of cells from the both hippocampi in the medial temporal lobe, there is also a similar loss of cells within the temporal cortex and the parietal cortex (see Figure 2.20a). This latter cortical atrophy is used to

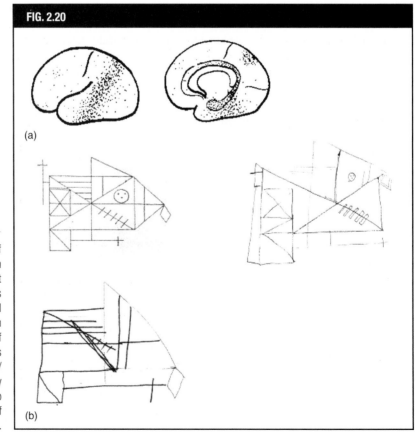

FIG. 2.20

(a)

(b)

(a) Illustration of the areas of cell loss associated with Alzheimer's disease. Most loss in the initial stages is typically from the temporal and parietal cortex. Note in the medial representation of the brain the loss of cells from the hippocampal/ amygdala region. (b) A copy of the Rey figure by a two patients with dementia of the Alzheimer type.

explain the dramatic constructional difficulties that are often associated with this disease (Figure 2,20b). Among the support for this view are studies that have found a relationship between abnormal parietotemporol blood flow using PET scans and constructional difficulties (Gragnaniello, Kessler, Bley, & Mielke, 1998). In stroke patients the parietal lobes and particularly the right parietal lobe are associated with the organisation of spatial relationships. However, the right frontal lobes are also implicated in the flexible and spontaneous production of visuospatial constructions.

The differences in constructional impairments between left and right hemisphere give us an indication of what is going on here. When considering a clinician's view of the incidence of constructional impairments it is likely that there would be a relatively strong view that a right hemisphere lesion is far more likely to result in constructional impairment. According to the reviews of studies (McCarthy & Warrington, 1990) there appears to be a ratio whereby it is roughly twice as common to find constructional difficulties following right hemisphere damage. Also of interest is the proposal that right and left

hemisphere patients make different types of errors and it is likely these two types of constructional impairments have a different mechanism. Patients with right hemisphere damage tend to distort the spatial relationships within the drawing, whereas patients with left hemisphere stroke tend to simplify and leave elements out of the drawing (see Figure 2.21). From the examples below it is evident that some of the constructions of the right hemisphere patients reduce three dimensions to two, which would support the view that the right hemisphere was required for this type of perception. Unfortunately, there is little research that can explain why some left hemisphere patients tend to simplify the diagrams, although the Davidoff and Warrington (1999) study discussed above would suggest that the right hemisphere was adequate at complex visual spatial analysis. Therefore one would expect that patients with left hemisphere lesions would retain the ability to perceive details. It is possible that the global aspects of the object become more salient when the right hemisphere is not supported or balanced by the left hemisphere. The local–global distinction was previously made when referring to the left and right hemisphere

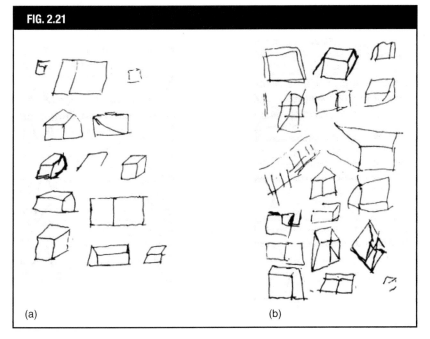

FIG. 2.21

(a)   (b)

Some examples of constructional distortions from patients with (a) right hemisphere damage and (b) left hemisphere damage. The left hemisphere patient's tendency is to simplify the cube, while the right-lesioned patient makes more constructional distortions (reprinted from Piercy, M. Hecaen, H. & De Ajuriaguerro, J. 1960, with permission from Oxford Journals).

meaning of the object when it comes to discrimination between objects. For example, Morris, Abrahams, Baddeley, & Polkey, (1995) required patients following left and right temporal lobectomy to recognise a series of previously presented doors from among other similar doors that had not been previously seen. These doors, which were photographed from houses in Dublin in Ireland by the third author while he was on sabbatical, were individually interesting but because most doors have similar features they were placed in this forced-choice recognition test alongside other doors that were remarkably similar. In some cases they were only distinguishable by the spatial relationship of the features and textures within the doors, e.g. the position of the door-knocker relative to the door-knob. In this study patients with right temporal lobectomy performed more poorly than those with left temporal lobectomy. This is a memory study but a good illustration of the special qualities of processing provided by the right hemisphere.

Summary

It has been argued that that the right hemisphere has certain aptitudes for analysing complex visuospatial visual information. The right hemisphere is able to analyse the subtle spatial and physical cues that allow us to identify objects that are for various reasons hard to identify from physical or structural features. The abilities that allow us to analyse this information require an acknowledgement of the relationships between features in terms of the overall look of an object. The kind of assimilation of the overall relative position of features appears to be largely a right hemisphere achievement. This right hemisphere trick, which we all take for granted, is ideal for detecting small differences in the overall relative position between the features of complex objects and lends itself to the detection of minute differences between faces. It is clear that with the evidence presented above we must update our prototype model in Figure 2.14 and allow for some division of specialisation between the hemispheres. During the remainder of the chapter a model will be developed that takes into account these hemispheric specialisations.

AWARENESS OF A PERCEPTUAL DEFICIT AND IMAGERY

Although the agnosic patient DM is obviously concerned at times that he does not know the identity of the everyday objects presented to him, he is not as devastated as we might be when faced with this kind of lack of knowledge. One might speculate that if a brain-intact person were suddenly transferred to an environment where they were surrounded by incomprehensible objects, then they would be constantly alarmed and worried by this state of affairs. In part, this lack of concern could be explained by the assumption that the objects around the patient are interpreted as being rare and only available to specialised knowledge. In the same way a brain-intact person might wander into an advanced space laboratory and not be alarmed by a lack of knowledge of the strange instruments. However, patients appear to be relatively unaware of their deficit in quite normal surroundings unless they are actually challenged to identify objects.

Patients with associative face agnosia (prosopagnosia) show some evidence of perceptual processing that is not consciously available to them. These patients, who are not aware of the familiarity of faces, nevertheless show signs of differentiating between familiar versus unfamiliar faces in terms of electrodermal responses (measure of sweating rate) (Tranel & Damasio, 1985; see also De Haan, Bauer, & Greve, 1992). Therefore at some level familiarity is being processed. There is of course a problem in knowing what these signs of arousal actually mean: are they just the remnants of processing that is not sufficiently strong to promote conscious recognition? Or are they representative of an emotional processing that is aided by covert perceptual processing? It is possible that this is a minimal activation of the face recognition unit that is not capable of producing conscious recognition rather than "covert recognition" (Breen, Caine, & Coltheart, 2000).

Perhaps the most dramatic illustration of perception without awareness is found in a disorder

2. DISORDERS OF PERCEPTION 79

referred to as "blindsight". These rare patients are not consciously aware of presented stimuli but are able to process the perceptual information at a *basic level*, e.g. geometric forms, movement, and broad changes in light wave frequency. They even make movements (when they are encouraged to do so against their conscious judgement) in the direction of moving objects and they can even manually locate objects in space even though they report being unable to see these objects. They report seeing nothing yet when they are persuaded to make a guess they are able to discriminate between previously presented and novel items, sometimes at levels as high as 80% correct (e.g. Weiskrantz, 1986). However, when they are achieving this high level of accuracy they personally believe that their performance is entirely random (Stoerig & Cowey, 1997).

Cowey and Stoerig (1995) trained monkeys with complete left unilateral occipital removal that included the splenium (part of the corpus callosum that allows the transference of visual information from one hemisphere to another). When these monkeys were trained to respond purely to the *presence* of a stimulus (contralateral to the lesion within the hemianopic field), their performance was not much better than chance, suggesting that they were blind. However, on a task that required the monkeys to make a forced discrimination between stimuli that had been presented in this "blind" visual field, they amazingly performed as well as the controls (again stimuli presented to the contralateral visual field to lesion). The implication is that monkeys, like blindsight patients, were able to make discriminations between stimuli that they did know were present. Although this is a controversial area, the prima facie explanation of this experiment is that the monkeys were motivated to respond to gain nourishment and had learned a successful response. However, this was presumably without awareness of why the response was successful, since they were not able to judge when a stimulus was present or absent.

The lesions of these subjects allows the confirmation that this perceptual process is not within the geniculostriate system (LGN pathway), but is more likely reliant on the alternate visual projection via the superior colliculus and the pulvinar within the thalamus (Cowey, 1994, p. 17). This is a pathway that is more fully described in Chapter 4.

If blindsight occurs when a patient can perceive an object without conscious awareness of that object, quite the reverse situation occurs in the case of Anton's syndrome. Patients with Anton's syndrome are cortically blind, that is, they are unable to see because of the destruction of their visual cortex. However, these patients often deny their blindness even though objective tests show otherwise. This is sometimes referred to as an anosognosia of blindness (other types of anosognosia are referred to in Chapter 4). Goldenberg, Mullbacher, and Nowak, (1995) propose a possible explanation that patients mistake their own imagery for partial sight. If you like, they believe that what they are imagining is what they are seeing. Their patient (HS) was of interest since the lesion was relatively discrete within the visual cortex and included the almost complete bilateral destruction of the primary visual cortex (further atrophy was noted in the right temporo-occipital area). Despite the mountain of evidence that this patient was totally blind, she would describe her sight as only "unreliable". She reported that sometimes things around her would appear very clearly, only to disappear a few minutes later. Sometimes she would reach out for an object, such as a cup, for example, only to find that it was not where she expected it to be (Goldenberg et al., 1995, p. 1374). The authors tested the imagery hypothesis by making the sound related to the object, e.g. rattling keys, scissors opening and shutting, or let her touch the object and then after placing it out of sight would ask the patient whether she saw the object. Without this auditory or tactile stimulus the patient would say that she couldn't see anything, but she would report seeing the object with a stimulus prime. The following dialogue, in which GG is the experimeter and HS is the patient, reveals the test. Although by this time the patient had recovered somewhat, she only had a 5-degree visual window on the right side; apart from this she remained functionally blind.

GG: [moves bunch of small keys, producing sound] *I am holding an object. Do you have any idea what it might be?*

HS: *Could that be a key?*

GG. [silently moves the keys beneath the table. The part of the conversation printed in italics takes place while the keys are hidden from view] *What does it look like?*

HS: *On top there is a big ring, and it has a dark key-bit.*

GG. *Do you see the key well?*

HS: *I am seeing the key* [Goldenberg et al., 1995, p. 1378].

The many similarities between perception and imagery have prompted the proposal that they share the same process and depend on the same neuroanatomic substrates. However, HS had excellent imagery without a primary visual cortex, which suggests that the relationship is not as close as one might expect. A famous English psychologist, Sir Francis Galton who lived at the turn of the nineteenth century, asked his eminent colleagues at the Royal Society whether they could image their breakfast table at their own homes. Some reported very clear images, while a few could not provide any image (Galton, 1883). Individuals vary considerably in their ability to imagine and sometimes studies fail to take this individual difference into account.

Apart from the patient described above with Anton's syndrome and a destruction of area V1, other patients have also been described with destruction at this early stage of bottom-up processing who can pass imagery tests without difficulty. A description of patients with good imagery but with an intermediate agnosia has prompted a number of authors to propose that imagery is dependent on perceptual structures that are higher than feature analysis levels (Crick & Koch, 1995; Roland & Gulyas, 1994). Behrmann et al., (1994) propose that while lower levels may be used to define imagery, this is still a top-down process. They describe a patient with intermediate agnosia whose imagery is satisfactory to the extent that the patient was able to report on images of objects that the patient could not recognise. But there are also patients, who due to their brain damage, have impaired imagery but intact perception, suggesting that for at least some patients top-down perception is not necessarily synonymous with imagery. Farah (1984) reported on 27 patients of whom 8 could be placed within this category. In order to explain this, a mechanism is described that is unique to imagery which drives image generation (Farah, 1984; Kosslyn & Shin, 1994); impaired imaging may occur when perception is spared.

Some recent imaging studies have found that the precuneus is activated reliably during imagery tasks (Fletcher, Frith, Baker et al., 1995). Perhaps because recently researchers have been intrigued by the nature of consciousness a series of functional imaging studies have been conducted into the nature of imagery and this same gyrus in the medial parietal lobe has been found to be activated when subjects image letters (Raij, 1999), are imagining carrying out motor tasks (Ogiso, Kobayashi & Sugishita 2000), imaging navigation along a route (Ghaem et al., 1997) and during the conscious recall of memories (Krause et al., 1999). The precuneus is obviously not the only structure that is activated in these studies and imagery may be a more complex process than it appears. Lesion studies suggest that there are a number of structures that may contribute to imagery for different reasons (Farah, 1988), but it is possible that the precuneus plays an integrative role by allowing the product of perceptual and other processes to come to "mind".

Finally on this topic concerning consciousness, imagery, and perception, has received a great deal of research interest recently, perhaps because it reveals certain counterintuitive findings. It appears that some patients may perceive without realising it, while others think they can perceive when they cannot. While consciousness is clearly closely tied to the associated function it shows that consciousness, like any other function, is the product of brain mechanisms and has for many years been a valid topic for research within neuropsychology.

BOTTOM-UP VERSUS TOP-DOWN DISORDERS AND THE EXECUTIVE INFLUENCE

Bottom-up processing consists of the primary perceptual processes that transform sensation into percepts that have form, colour, movement, and location. It is assumed that the structures that allow such processes are developed early in life. Animal experiments using selective perceptual deprivation suggest there is a critical age in childhood when brain development of the visual cortex occurs to allow these basic primary perceptual analysers to develop. Top-down processing assists in the perceptual process by allowing our learned experience of percepts to narrow the competition between the possible interpretations of the sensory information. It is likely that the updating of what is referred to here as top-down processing is constantly occurring, although there is evidence from persons who have acquired their sight late in life that radical changes in this process may be more difficult as we get older.

Some persons who are born blind and who have gained their sight through surgery for the first time in adulthood obviously lack some of the experience required for efficient top-down processing and some become depressed and somewhat confused by their new perceptual experience. These people nevertheless manage to gain a surprising perceptual knowledge of the world through the tactile, auditory and other senses prior to gaining their sight. Some of their difficulties clearly relate to their lack of experience of objects and are more obviously related to top-down processing.

Gregory (1998, pp. 154–156) describes a patient (SB) who drew a double-decker bus without a front prior to gaining his sight and his drawings remained with this omission a year after he had regained his sight. He also had a clear disadvantage in making perceptual judgements of information not previously experienced. For example, he judged that his feet would just touch the ground if he hung from his window sill, but

the distance was 10 times that distance. Gregory suggests that because of their prior experience in other perceptual domains these people are probably not good illustrations of the way children develop visual perception, but they nevertheless give some indication of the importance of past experience or top-down processing on our perception.

If one were to design a robot to perceive without any prior experience, such a machine would have to use bottom-up processing. This machine would be faced with the gargantuan task of analysing each visual sensation as a fresh experience. It is clear that such a situation in which bottom-up processing is the only method of perceptual analysis does not represent human perceptual processing. We use our past perceptual experience when we perceive objects, which allows the unmanageable to become manageable. The power of this system can be realised when viewing Figure 2.23.

The picture is usually initially perceived as a scene of two figures fighting in a jungle. However, if the viewer is told that the drawing also contains a picture of a boy reading and that the palm tree-like shrubbery in the foreground is the boy's hair, then the alternative interpretation is often seen. Once the boy is identified lying down, every time we look at the picture we see the boy, and the two figures are now seen as symbolising the boy's thoughts as he reads the adventure story. If the reader now looks away from the picture and then looks back, or even if the reader immediately puts the book down and goes on holiday for a week, as soon as the picture is perceived again the boy within the picture is immediately recognised. There is certainly no need to go through the laborious searching process that was originally necessary: so what has changed?

Following the process of problem solving and discovery of the extra dimension within the picture, the brain has changed and accommodated this experience so that perception of that same image may be speeded up when it is next encountered. This top-down processing, which uses past experience to help in the perception of visual sensation, is essential and when it is absent

FIG. 2.23

Illustration of top-down processing. Once the boy is found then future instances of recognition are assisted through our previous experience (with permission from Rauch, 1974).

or damaged then the perceptual process is severely undermined.

There have been a number of experiments that have shown the power of top-down processing in normal subjects without brain damage. For example, Palmer (1975) found that people were more likely to identify ambiguous drawings of objects if they were placed within their normal context, e.g. a breadboard within the context of a kitchen. The context allows the observer to reduce the number of alternatives, thereby allow-ing the top-down process to be of more assistance to the perceptual process.

Using our past experience to help us perceive is not without its drawbacks. When people say "You must be seeing things" they are often referring to a case where top-down processing is probably to blame. The advantage of our perceptual system is also its frailty. This is well illustrated in the research into the unreliability of eye-witness tes-timony and was used to good effect in the stories of some of our great crime writers, such as G.K.

Chesterton and Sir Arthur Conan Doyle. Sometimes what we expect to see interferes with what we are actually seeing.

Returning to the process of neuropsychological modeling of the perceptual process, one should be reminded by the difficulties of perception without top-down processing. A system that analyses patterns of light information to an increasing degree of complexity, from basic line patterns to the final percept, is conceptually a bottom-up process. If bottom-up processing were the only method of perceptual analysis available to us we would be in quite a bit of trouble.

Patients with associative agnosia are a good illustration of a breakdown in top-down processing. There is nothing wrong with these patients' visual analysis of the object, i.e. bottom-up processing is intact. They can match and draw objects. They nevertheless cannot recognise the object and they have no idea what it might be used for or anything else about the object. This lack of top-down knowledge is even apparent when they attempt a drawing of an object (see Figure 2.11). Drawing for these patients taxes the patience of the examiner; it is a long drawn-out process in which the patient makes an uncertain, hesitant copy, as if they are seeing the object for the first time, and in one sense they are.

It is not just the experience of meaning that is fed back to the perceptual process but the physical characteristics of objects and faces that must also be stored and used for future perceptual processing. It has been proposed that the perception of faces is dependent on a stored template of a typical face representation. If the structures that support such a representation are damaged then the patient will inevitably have difficulty in this area. Patients who are unable to recognise familiar faces must have damage to the face representation but also they are impaired in realising the meaning the face potrays. Perhaps this is why a bilateral lesion is often required: both the left hemisphere's ability to find meaning and the right hemisphere's adept handling of the physical features need to be impaired. Even patients who have impaired ability to recognise objects in unusual orientations or have difficulty in recognising the physical features of faces must have impaired top-

down processing; these are aspects we learn to perceive and are dependent on our experience. Damage to this information gives rise to apperceptive agnosic signs.

Apart from the very large amount of analysis required to perceive objects in their typical orientations, each object must be recognised from atypical orientations. While the analysis of unusual views of objects takes longer to recognise, the task would be near to impossible if we did not have some possible templates or neuronal representations of the orientation with which to compare the hypothetical bottom-up image.

The distinction between bottom-up and top-down processing is something of a contrivance that is used here to illustrate the very real and different mechanisms that are in play during the process of perception. The neural mechanisms must perform these processes simultaneously in an integrated manner, each having equal influence except when unusual circumstances exist.

Our modelling so far has been built around cases that have generally shown a certain level of incompetence of perceptual processing when the left hemisphere is to be relied upon in isolation. Also studies have been reviewed that have shown an impaired level of perceptual processing when the right hemisphere has been damaged. Lesion studies and functional imaging studies support a right hemisphere specialisation for face perception. Yet despite these clear demonstrations that the right hemisphere is contributing something special to the perceptual process, we nevertheless see the slavish copying of the associative agnosic when copying everyday objects. The associative agnosic who has a left hemisphere lesion copies objects as if they have never been seen before even in their physical form. How can we reconcile this incompetence in the face of the evidence that the right hemisphere is perceptually sophisticated and contributes to the recognition of objects that would normally be seen as a challenge to our perceptual system?

The evidence of these agnosic patients and the results of studies of patients following a split-brain operation and presentation of object information to the right hemisphere (see Chapter 6) strongly suggests that the two hemispheres work in tandem in the process of perception. The right hemisphere processing can only be fully realised when the left hemisphere is intact to act as a control or command module. As discussed in this chapter the "what" pathway is most obviously revealed in its progressive processing within the left hemisphere. When the left hemisphere is damaged and disconnects the analysis carried out in this hemisphere the patients cease to understand their environment but the physical or structural analysis of the object is also undermined. Therefore the right hemisphere skills may not be fully realised without the identification system of the left hemisphere. This identification automatically and perhaps simultaneously activates the right hemisphere to give a full identification of the physical features of the identified object or face. In most situations the process no doubt takes place in parallel within a network. In cases where the stimulus is degraded, when an object is placed in the shadows, for example, the left hemisphere activates a range of possible alternatives within the right hemisphere, some of which will match better than others with the bottom-up analysis that takes place in the right hemisphere. This trial-and-error matching process, which is organised by the left (identification) hemisphere finally, after some extended processing time, reaches a conclusion. This distribution of duties and skills is not out of keeping with the results of split-brain operations, which are discussed in Chapter 6. Following the separation of hemispheres the right hemisphere still manages to process visual information but this hemisphere's ability is far from exciting on its own and is certainly not consciously realised.

Some experimental evidence for the interplay between bottom-up and top-down processing is now emerging in the literature. As mentioned earlier, even the thalamus has back-projections from areas where it is assumed perceptual analysis is well advanced; the majority of afferent (in) and efferent (out) thalamic connections are with higher cortical areas (Cowey, 1994). There are back-projections at every level of visual perceptual analysis and it is assumed that these allow us to narrow the possibilities and support the more laborious process of bottom-up processing, which would otherwise be starting from scratch for each newly seen object.

The evidence for top-down processing within perception has also been revealed indirectly through animal experiments. For example, the receptive field within V1 cells is small, as described above. However, studies measuring the frequency of individual V1 cells have found that such cells are influenced in their firing by cells that are outside their receptive field. If a figure is shown that depends on its context for its analysis (most of our everyday images depend on contrast between foreground and background) e.g. silhouette, then the individual cells may respond because of the influence from neighbouring cells. In other words a cell may respond to a bar at a 45° angle but whether that bar is seen as part of a protruding bar or a painted bar will depend on the activation of other cells. Information received in one cell is interpreted in terms of the information received by other cells. Studies have found that firing rates are influenced horizontally (other V1 cells) but also in a vertical fashion from V2 and V4 (see Lamme & Spekreijse, 2000, for a review).[2] Therefore, it now transpires that V1 cells, with their reputation as passive contour receptors, are a bit more flexible and there is evidence that they may respond more actively to some forms compared to others—forms that are more in tune with experience and expectations (e.g. Zipser, Lamme, & Schiller, 1996). Studies with humans have assessed the electrical signatures of the brain using event-related potentials (see Chapter 1, Box 1.2) and found that frontal areas modulate and influence the areas within the occipital lobe during a perceptual task (Barcelo, Suwazono, & Knight, 2000). The executive/attentional influence on perception is emerging in the literature, an influence that is discussed further in the next chapter.

Despite the gaps in our knowledge, of all areas in neuropsychology visual perception is arguably the most advanced. The studies of perception, which have realised this modular network system, have set an example for approaches to research in other areas of neuropsychology.

[2] This is one of those papers that, at the time of writing, may be accessed free on the internet via the PubMed site.

3

Executive dysfunction

INTRODUCTION

This chapter acts as an introduction to a theme of executive function that is continued within each of the chapters of this book. Executive influences are present in all the topics of cognitive, emotional, and motor functioning, which perhaps explains why some researchers are questioning whether we can refer to executive functioning as if it were a single entity.

Donald Stuss and the late Frank Benson (Stuss & Benson, 1986), describe the kinds of deficits that may arise when testing a patient with lesions to the prefrontal cortex:

> General deficit in generation or initiation of behaviour; impairment in organisational strategies, monitoring and judgement of responses; a lack of behavioural restraint; deficient hypothesis formation, plan formulation, and shifting established response patterns; and impaired social judgement. (Stuss & Benson, 1984)

In reading this list of potentially highly disabling complaints, one might form the view that such individuals would be measured as having a very low intelligence. However, many of these patients do relatively well on intelligence tests. One possible reason for this is that the typical IQ test involves having well-defined tasks or problems, often requiring the use of well-learned skills, and containing questions that generally lead to a single answer. This finding of preserved performance of patients with manifest prefrontal compromise on measures of intelligence led to some puzzlement in the 1940s and 1950s (Hebb & Penfield, 1940). The question was a reasonable one: What was the role of this large expanse of cortex that was so well developed in the human species? Subsequently, it was realised that novel tasks, requiring flexibility and adaptation, were far more sensitive to damage in this area.

The behavioural problems listed above are not observed in every patient with an anterior lesion. Some patients may have more difficulty with initiation of behaviour, while others may show a lack of behavioural restraint as the main feature (Kertesz, 1994, pp. 568–569). Also, while these problems may be predominantly associated with the frontal lobe and, more specifically, the prefrontal cortex and underlying structures, this is clearly not always the case (Tranel, Anderson, & Benton, 1994). Because the prefrontal cortex has connections to most brain areas, a disconnection from these other brain areas may also result in dysexecutive behaviour. The executive system is, if you like, a series of systems, with each system vulnerable to interference or disruption at various levels. It is assumed that a disconnection between the prefrontal cortex and the specialised centres for various cognitive processes, such as language or memory, will cause dysexecutive signs within that respective process. It should also be noted that this system has some compensatory characteristics, and a ubiquitous finding in the literature is that bilateral lesions are often accompanied by far more serious consequences compared to unilateral lesions.

Because many patients with frontal lesions have either none or only a few of the features described above, and different patients may show different features, one might question whether it is appropriate to use the term "frontal lobe syndrome". The terms "dysexecutive syndrome" (Baddeley & Wilson, 1988) or "adaptive behavioural syndrome" are preferable since they make no assumptions concerning the area of the brain responsible for the dysfunctional behaviour. The term "syndrome" refers to a constellation of signs or symptoms that consistently appear together and describe a common complaint. Therefore it may be useful to use this term in the clinical context in the case of a rare number of patients, but "syndrome" is less useful when more precise communication is necessary (i.e. in a research context or in reference to a clinical neuropsychological assessment). The term "executive dysfunction", the title of this chapter, is often used when no localisation or syndromic implications are being made.

Alexander Luria's "functional systems" model described the executive system as a system that plans, organises, and monitors behaviour and, as illustrated in Chapter 1, the frontal lobe is well placed to carry out this controlling role by virtue of its multitudinous connections with other areas of the brain. However, this description is now seen as an oversimplification. This broad and large brain area, which constitutes one third of the cortex, is made from distinct sub-areas which may be differentiated by cytoarchitecture (the profile of predominant cell type within a column) and functional role. The apparent heterogeneity of symptoms of patients with dysexecutive signs is in line with evidence that there are different

behavioural consequences depending on the location of the lesion within the prefrontal cortex. Towards the end of this chapter a more thorough and detailed description of the associated functional contributions of these areas will be described. Broadly, the structural divisions within the prefrontal cortex (see Figure 3.1) and other areas of the frontal lobe are delineated by both the predominance of certain cell types, connections with other structures and, in some cases, the predominance of particular types of neurotransmitter.

At an introductory level, the frontal lobe is divided into motor-related areas. which include the premotor and primary motor area, the frontal eye fields and Broca's area, and the prefrontal cortex. The prefrontal cortex is the area that is mostly associated with executive functioning. It is generally demarcated according to two features. The first is the less often referred to connections with the medial aspects of the thalamus, and the more commonly recognised is the prevalence of a granular cell within the fourth level of the six levels of cells described by Brodmann and others. At the borders of the prefrontal cortex there is less predominance of the granular cells as they merge with the neighbouring cytoarchitecture. For example, Broca's area is often not included in the prefrontal cortex because the cells in this area start to take on the appearance of the neighbouring motor areas. Similarly, while the orbital frontal cortex is included in the prefrontal cortex, much of the cell structure in this area is not in keeping with the six-level granular characteristics, taking on the features of the neighbouring limbic areas and referred to as the "paralimbic" cortex. The anterior aspect of the cingulate will also be referred to in this chapter in the context of executive dysfunction and while this is not within the prefrontal cortex it clearly has an executive role (Fuster, 1997).

Some familiarisation with these "executive" areas is allowed with a broad description of their functional role. The orbital cortex has important connections with deep areas within the brain that are referred to as the limbic system. A modern description of the limbic system includes such structures as the hypothalamus, septum and

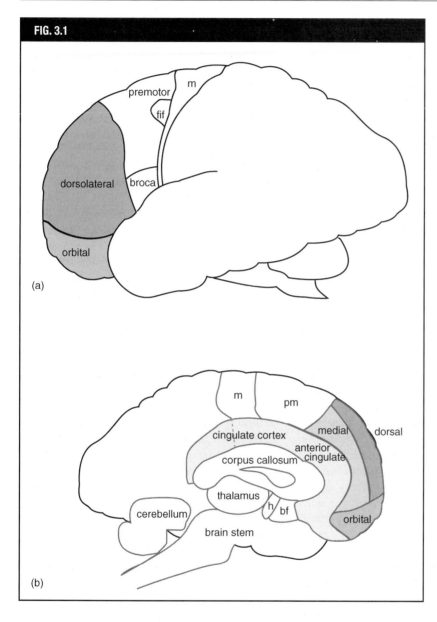

FIG. 3.1

Diagram of the areas of the prefrontal lobe (shaded) ((a) shows the lateral aspect and (b) the medial areas); showing the dorsolateral cortex, orbito-frontal cortex, medial prefrontal cortex, frontal eye fields (fif; newly recognised location), and Broca's area. Also shown are the premotor area (pm) and the primary motor area (m). The anterior cingulate as part of the cingulate is shown. The basal forebrain (bf) is a loose term for an area near the inferior surface of the cortex between the orbital cortex and the hypothalamus (h). Recent research delineating the functional properties of the dorsolateral area into mid and ventro-lateral areas referred to towards the end of this chapter.

amygdala. Animal research shows a close relationship between the limbic system and the production of emotional behaviour. The orbitofrontal cortex is therefore seen to have an important role in regulating and controlling emotions. In keeping with this view patients with orbital frontal lesions sometimes show poorly controlled emotional and socially inappropriate behaviour with poor insight. For example, Welt (1888) gives one of the earliest descriptions of

patients with lesions in this area and describes an overly aggressive patient who was often inappropriately jocular and malicious. There is also evidence that this area has an influence on attention. Patients with damage to this area have a tendency to be easily distracted (Malloy, Bihrle, Duffy, & Cimino, 1993). There are also projections into this area from all the sensory systems and there is firm evidence from animal research that the area has a role in motivation by the association of rewards with behaviour (Rolls, 2000).

The dorsolateral prefrontal cortex (DPFC) has efferent (out) and afferent (in) projections with the tertiary association areas and, to a lesser extent, the secondary areas of the visual, somatosensory, and auditory sensory areas. Accordingly, this area has a specialised role in organising and integrating incoming sensory information. There are also areas that act with these polymodal association areas to keep information in mind, like a buffer store—a place to keep information on a temporary basis while we do something else. The dorsolateral prefrontal cortex also has a key role in the *selection* of information required for attention and has also been found to be important for storing the sequence of events into memory (Milner, Corsi, Leonard, 1991).

The medial area of the frontal lobes, which includes the anterior cingulate gyrus and the supplementary motor area (SMA), is located more posteriorly and is involved in the preparation and direction of learned complex motor movements. The anterior cingulate (AC) has a number of functions, as one might expect given that this is a relatively extensive brain area that has a numerous and diverse connections with other brain areas. More anteriorly there are connections with areas such as the amygdala that are important for the attribution of emotion. When authors refer to the "limbic system" these structures, the amygdala and anterior cingulate are implicated. These areas also have connections with centres associated with attention and the storage of memories such as the thalamus and hippocampus. Additionally, bilateral lesions to the anterior cingulate may result initially in akinesis (patients may be inert, making no spontaneous movement). This region is therefore seen as being important for providing that abstract quality we often refer to as "drive", and patients with bilateral damage in this area may be passive and show little affect or sexual drive. However, parts of the anterior cingulate are also clearly important in tasks that require focused attention.

Other areas exist that are *not* part of the prefrontal cortex but also provide an executive role via their effect on motor movements. These include the frontal eyefields, Broca's area and the premotor area. The frontal eyefields have an important role in the motor movements required of eye movements. Broca's area will be discussed in greater detail later in Chapter 7 but, briefly, this area is associated with the organisation of expression in speech, especially articulation. The premotor area, on the other hand, is associated with the preparation and organisation of motor movements. The executive functioning of this area and motor movements is discussed in more detail in Chapter 8.

It may be easy to realise the functional significance of the four areas of executive functioning that are referred to in this chapter by considering the main neighbouring connections of these areas. The orbitofrontal cortex has many reciprocal connections with limbic system structures such as the amygdala and hypothalamus and therefore the orbital area is associated with emotional control and sensory areas for stimulus–response associations. The dorsolateral area is seen as playing a role in cognition and appropriately has prolific connections with the areas important for analysing incoming sensory information. The medial prefrontal cortex and anterior cingulate areas have connections with the hippocamapal complex and are therefore implicated in playing a role within memory function. These medial frontal areas also have strong thalamic connections which is in keeping with its attributed role within drive and attentional mechanisms.

Later in this chapter the relationship between the various areas of the prefrontal cortex and their associated functions will be discussed further, with some elaboration.

FEATURES OF EXECUTIVE DYSFUNCTION

Control

Inhibition and disinhibition
When we are talking of a person as "losing control" we usually talk of an excess of behaviour. We may talk of someone who is intoxicated as

losing control when they show an exaggerated emotional response with little provocation. A person who shows this kind of behavioural excess is referred to as being "disinhibited". However, there is another sense in which we lose control of our own behaviour, and this is manifested by an inability to initiate behaviour, which is referred to as "inhibition". Strangely, a patient with frontal pathology can, at various times, be both inhibited and disinhibited. Thus, they may have difficulty getting going or initiating a behaviour spontaneously (inhibited), but may also be goaded into some automatic routine of behaviour in a disinhibited manner and then not be able to stop when it is appropriate (disinhibited). An example of this was evident in a recent dementia patient at our centre who, according to MRI brain scan, showed evidence of atrophy in the frontal lobes. On assessment, she lacked any flexibility on a number of tasks and had difficulty in producing a response on others. When asked to produce words beginning with "F" (time allowed, 1 minute) this conservatively dressed older lady produced only three words (inhibited), one of which was a rude four-letter one (disinhibited). She then proceeded to hug and kiss the author fervently when it was time for her to go (disinhibited). Overall, the problem is one of control.

Impulsivity is associated with disinhibition and is strongly but not exclusively related to orbital pathology. This phenomenon may have something in common with distraction in the sense that external stimuli may draw the exclusive attention of the subject. Impulsivity is well illustrated by go–no go tasks (Drewe, 1975). In these tasks, patients are typically asked to make one response to one signal and an absence of response to another signal. For example, the patient is instructed to squeeze or tap the examiner's hand when the examiner says "stop" but must withhold a response to the word "go". There is a tendency in this instance to make the error of squeezing in response to the word "go", when a response should be withheld.

L'hermitte and colleagues (L'hermitte, 1986; L'hermitte, Pillon, & Serdaru, 1986) describe patients with frontal lobe damage who were tested in a somewhat bizarre way. The examiner sat in front of the patient and made various idiosyncratic gestures while largely disregarding the patient. The examiner might scratch their ear or "cock a snook" or fold a sheet of paper. While the control subjects in this experiment remained waiting in their seats doing nothing (other than perhaps wondering about the sanity of the examiner), the patients with frontal lesions (often gross areas of damage, bilateral and inferior aspect) tended to imitate the behaviour. They appeared to be dependent on the external stimuli in some way. If these patients were placed in any situation that was normally associated with a particular activity, e.g. gardening, they would automatically start doing that activity. L'hermitte describes one occasion when a patient was brought to his apartment and was shown around. When the patient was shown the bedroom with the bedspread taken off and the top sheet turned back in the normal way, the patient got undressed to got into bed. L'hermitte describes this behaviour as a dependence on external cues. The patient is set off on an automatic routine of behaviour because of a lack of internal control.

L'hermitte describes behaviour that is disinhibited, but inhibition may also appear as a predominant dysexecutive sign. The patient may sit around looking at television all the time; they may only speak when they are spoken to, showing no initiative in social activities. In tasks testing verbal fluency the patient may reveal a combination of these features. In this task the patient is asked to give a number of exemplars from a category or words beginning with a particular letter within a time limit. As indicated, the patient may give few exemplars showing an inhibition. They may look around the room for items beginning with the letter hoping for an external cue. They may also show disinhibition and break rules and give exemplars not allowed.

Brenda Milner of the Montreal Institute of Neurology was one of the first to note the lack of spontaneous verbal comment in a patient with left lateral prefrontal lesion who otherwise appeared to be intelligent. She then started to use the verbal fluency tasks as a test for these patients. On one occasion she was surprised to see one such patient cover a complete page with words;

however, on closer inspection the patient had written the same phrase over and over again "I can't, I can't, I can't" (Milner, personal communication).

Studies using both PET and MRI show changes in blood flow as the subject completes the verbal fluency task, giving consistent activation in the left prefrontal cortex with some activation in the cingulate (Phelps, Hyder, Blamaire, & Shulman, 1997). However, it is of interest that this activation dissipates as the subject becomes used to the task (Posner & Raichle, 1998). This is perhaps why it may be more diagnostically useful to require the patient to switch from one category to another, i.e. one word from letter to one word of category and so on (Troyer et al., 1998). Patients with left frontal lesions more frequently show verbal fluency problems, while patients with right frontal lesions are more obviously affected by a version of this task that requires the patient to spontaneously generate a number of nonsense shapes, with the restriction that they have three sides (Jones-Gotman & Milner, 1977). Patients with a right frontal lesion may have more difficulty in spontaneously producing a series of meaningful gestures, e.g. the hitchhiking gesture using the thumb (Jason, 1985a).

The important constituents of the tasks described in this section require initiative and controlled selection. In the task of verbal fluency the patient has to initiate a search for specific words. In the go–no go task the patient has to ignore external cues and follow rules that are internalised and are counterintuitive. It should be noted that the verbal fluency task may be failed for reasons other than poor control of response. In Chapter 7 we describe patients who perform poorly on this task because they appear to have damage to a store or lexicon of all words. It should also be noted that the task demands a certain linguistic acumen. For this reason some practitioners make an adjustment in the results of this test for the patients vocabulary or occupational background.

Cognitive flexibility

Cognitive flexibility is a broad term and is allied to the concept of control. Cognitive flexibility is a term that is used to refer to a person's ability to switch from one topic to another. Implicit in this requirement is the demand to curtail or inhibit one behaviour and spontaneously commence another. Tests that measure these characteristics typically set up an automatic expectancy or routine of behaviour in the patient and then require the patient to shift from that expectancy or routine in an independent manner.

The Wisconsin Card Sorting Test (WCST; Grant & Berg, 1948) is perhaps the most famous of the set-shifting tests. This test provides four target cards incorporating different colours, numbers or shapes, which are placed face up in front of the patient (see Figure 3.2). Cards from a pack are placed one at a time underneath one of these four target cards on the basis of a match of either colour, number or shape. Initially, only the clinician knows which of these matching strategies is correct. In the example below, the subject has decided to go for a match according to shape rather than colour or number. The clinician will say "correct" or "incorrect" to the subject's placement, until eventually the subject discovers the correct rule by trial and error. In the easier, perhaps less sensitive, modified version (Nelson, 1976) the patient will be told that the rule has been changed. In the original version pioneered and first used with patients by Brenda Milner, the examiner changes the rule, e.g. from number to colour, without telling the patient. The patient has to work out that this has happened purely by monitoring feedback (i.e. whether their response is designated correct or incorrect by the examiner). Two main measures, the number of categories (rules) achieved and the number of perseverations, are used from this task. At this stage in this chapter it should be noted that even in the most reliable indicator of frontal dysfunction the perseveration measure is somewhat ambiguous.

Perseveration occurs when a behaviour is repeated despite a history of negative feedback. It is therefore in short *a non-adaptive repetition of behaviour*, and although it is often taken as a sign of poor cognitive flexibility this broad description may be misleading. Perseveration occurs in the WCST when the patient doggedly persists with a previously relevant but now irrelevant rule despite

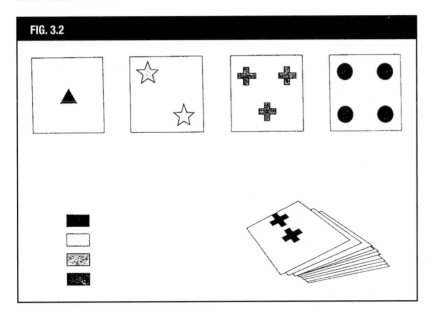

FIG. 3.2

Illustration of the Wisconsin card sorting test indicating the layout of test material as shown to the subject (reprinted From B. Milner, Some effects of frontal lobectomy in man. In J.M. Warren and K. Akert, eds, *The frontal granula cortex and behavior*, copyright 1964, with the permission of The McGraw-Hill Companies).

clear indications that the rule has been changed. Thus, they may continue sorting the pack according to colour, even though the feedback indicates this is no longer the basis on which the cards should be matched.

While the WCST showed much promise originally, recent studies and reviews have questioned whether this is a diagnostically useful task (Bowden, et al., 1998; Hermann, Wyler, & Richey, 1988; Mountain & Snow, 1993), although careful use of the results of this test may be useful (Stuss et al., 2000). The difficulty this task has in the differentiation between patients on the basis of lesion location must be due in part to the multiple-component nature of this task. Even the measure of perseveration is fraught with some ambiguity. Sandson and Albert (1984) and Goldberg (1986) describe the different types of perseveration and describe some of the different mechanisms underlying this behavioural phenomenon. For example, it is conceived of here as a failure to inhibit the old responding, which was previously rewarded. However, perseveration may be caused by a failure to flexibly select new alternatives. There is also the requirement to retain and keep in mind the strategies, the previous response, and its associated feedback. Finally many patients with amnesia without obvious

executive disorder may perseverate merely because they have been unable to remember the history of their responses. Functional imaging studies support the multi-component nature of the task, which finds that the dorsolateral, orbital, parietal, and temporal lobes are all activated during this task (Berman, Ostrem, & Randolph, 1995). Because of its ambiguity this task has been broken down into its components in a computerised version by a Cambridge (UK) group of researchers and this work is reviewed later in this chapter (Robbins, 1998).

The Trail-Making Test B (TMTB) has the advantage as a task measuring flexibility since it is not confounded by memory effects. In this test, the patient has to join numbers and letters alternately e.g. 1-A-2-B-3-C. Our natural inclination is to join B to C is an automatic repertoire of behaviour, which requires some cognitive control to resist. Unlike the WCST, however, which some people without brain damage find too difficult, the TMTB may actually be too easy for some of the more intelligent patients with frontal pathology. Tranel et al. (1994) report the results of seven patients on this task, most of whom did not show signs of impairment on this task. However, all these patients had more than 12 years of education and, although intellectual levels were not given, one suspects they were all above average.

In clinical practice, it is very much a matter of tailoring the task to the capabilities of your patient. Stuss and colleagues report a series of 16 leucotomised schizophrenic patients who showed a deterioration in speed on both TMTA (joining consecutive numbers) and TMTB. The TMTB (requiring the flexible response) was not exaggeratedly worse relative to TMTA when compared to a group of psychiatric and normal controls (Picton, Stuss, & Marshall, 1986). It should also be mentioned that information about the speed taken to complete this task may be less useful clinically than the quality of errors. Individual patients may show a striking perseverative quality in their results that are clearly indicative of a lack of flexibility. This is illustrated in their paper.

The "Stroop task" (Stroop, 1935) is somewhat less ambiguous as a measure of flexibility, which is also associated with frontal dysfunction (Perret, 1974; Golden, 1978b; Vendrell et al., 1995; Andrewes, Alpitsis, & Detering, 2001). This task requires the subject to read a series of words printed in incongruent colours (e.g. the word RED printed in green ink). The subject is required to report *the colour in which the word is printed*. The subject has to inhibit the natural inclination to read the word "red" and instead say "green", the colour of the ink in which "Red" is written. This is sometimes referred to as a "conflict" task since the subject must curb their natural and automatic inclination to read the word. As will be discussed in a later section, practice on these tasks naturally undermine the power of such tasks to assess the prefrontal role.

The author recently developed a test of verbal set-shifting ability called the verbal solutions test (Andrewes, Alpitsis, & Detering, 2001). The test was adapted from Reitan's "word-finding" test (Reitan, 1972a, 1972b). In Reitan's original test, the patient is required to determine the solution to a series of clues. In the current adaptation of this task (see Box 3.1), the subject is first given a hint to prime them towards a convergent solution. However, the clues are ambiguous so that it is possible to proffer two equally correct alternative solutions. In some conditions, the patients

were not provided a hint (neutral) while, in other conditions, the hint was identical to the proffered solution (expected). Further, in the shift-set condition the patients were required to change their mind about the solution and respond yes to a solution that was equally correct but not the same as the hint or prime. Figure 3.3 shows the results using patients who had had brain tumours surgically removed from anterior (frontal) and posterior locations. The anterior lesioned group took longer to respond and made more errors in the set-shifting condition. When compared to controls, patients with Huntington's disease and schizophrenics also have an exaggerated difficulty in the shift-set condition (Hanes, Andrewes, & Pantelis, 1996; Hanes, Andrewes, Pantelis, & Chiu, 1996).

The process of cognitive flexibility that underlies the process of set shifting can possibly be broken down into subcomponents. In the event of shifting from one routine behaviour to another, the patient may theoretically have to undertake two processes. First, the original "expected" behaviour must be *suppressed or inhibited*, then the patient must *initiate* the new response. Burgess and Shallice (1996) used a paradigm to dissociate these two features in a task that required patients to complete sentences (the Hayling Test). In their task, the final word in the sentence was missing and subjects were timed as they completed the sentences (an initiation task). Then subjects were asked to do a similar task, only this time they were required to use a word to complete the sentence that was unrelated to the sentence. In the second task the patient needed to suppress or inhibit their natural inclination to complete the sentence. As predicted, the initiation/completion task was slower in the patients with anterior lesions compared to the posterior lesioned

---

Box 3.1. Example of the shift-set condition

(Hint) Television
(Clues with two solutions)
Most people have one of these things in their house
This thing is a source of entertainment
This thing usually runs on electricity
This thing has different stations to tune into

(Target probe) Could the clues be describing a radio?
NB. Items in brackets were not presented on the screen

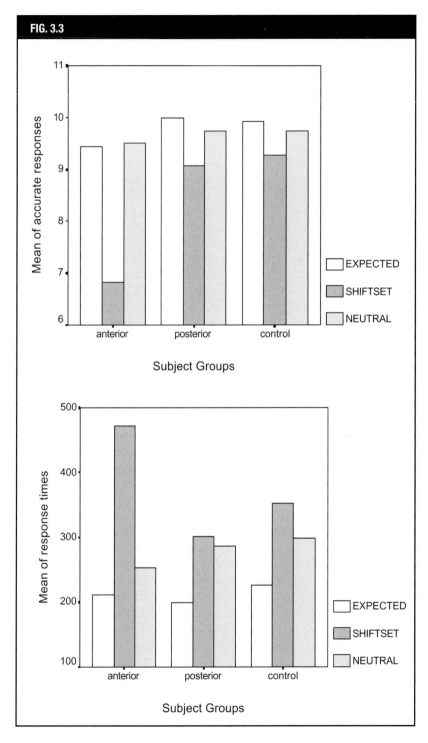

FIG. 3.3

Graph of accuracy and reaction data on the verbal solutions task, showing the significant reduction in accuracy and increased slowing of patients with anterior lesions (anterior of the central sulcus) in the condition where they have to shift their set to an alternative solution. Each group contained 15 subjects matched for age, estimated IQ, vocabulary, memory, immediate memory, and lesion size (Andrewes, Alpitsis, & Detering, in preparation).

patients. The patients not only slowed up in the suppression task but they also tended to make more errors either by going against instructions by completing the sentence or by using a word that was in some way conceptually related to the sentence. Although patients with bilateral frontal lesions in this study did poorly on both tasks, some of the patients with unilateral lesions did more poorly on one task compared to the other. The lack of an association between the performance on these tasks suggested two processes. However, the authors point out that this proposal awaits verification because of other possible interpretations of this finding. Therefore it is possible that a distinction might be made between patients who find initiation more difficult, while others find the inhibition of response more difficult within the process of cognitive flexibility.

Finally, on this topic of cognitive flexibility and control, it should be acknowledged that even without brain damage a person may be poor or good at controlling their own behaviour. It is a commonly held clinical view (but to the author's knowledge, not yet empirically verified) that brain damage to the frontal region may exaggerate the premorbid personality of the patient. For example, if the patient is disinhibited prior to frontal brain damage this aspect of their personality might be exaggerated.

For a similar reason the patient who has difficulties in the area of control should be wary of drugs such as alcohol, which have an effect of reducing control by further depressing cortical function. In summary, one of the primary roles of the executive system is in the stopping, starting, and changing repertoires of behaviour. The issue of control in these patients is further explored below in the section dealing with the effects on social behaviour.

Organisation, synthesis, and judgement

When sensory information is received, there is a tendency to categorise and compare that information in terms of our past experience. This is a critical process, both in terms of our ability to understand and our ability to remember such information. In some patients with frontal dysfunction the ability to appreciate and process material in this manner may be impaired, irrespective of the sensory modality of presentation, e.g. auditory or visual, or whether it is verbal or non-verbal material.

Perception and construction

Studies of patients with problems of a dysexecutive nature often report that the design is seen in terms of its parts rather than as a whole. This tendency is sometimes found in the block design subtest of the Wechsler Adult Intelligence Scale (WAIS-R; Wechsler, 1987), which requires the subject to copy a series of patterns using coloured blocks. Thus, the patient is seen to be constructing a block design in a piece-by-piece matching process and may have little realisation of the relationship of the design to the frame. For example, the patient may attempt to construct the design within a rectangle or other shape when the original is a square. However, the right hemisphere is more homogeneous than the left in its neuroanatomical structure and functional outcome and parietal damage may also cause similar effects.

This effect of piecemeal analysis is also found in a number of other tests such as the Hooper visual organisation test which tests a person's ability to construct puzzles representing objects. Patients with prefrontal lesions may be misled as to the nature of the puzzle by concentrating on the parts rather than the whole. For example, a fish that is made up of a two-part puzzle will be reported as a duck because one of the parts of the puzzle looks like a duck (Lezak, 1995).

This problem of appreciation and synthesis of non-verbal material may also be found in the analysis of verbal material. There is, for example, a tendency for patients to show poor integration on tasks that require an integrated verbal solution. The Reitan Word Finding Test (Reitan, 1972a, 1972b; see Boxes 3.1 and 3.2), referred to in a previous section, requires the patient to find a common solution to a series of clues. The patient understands the nature of the task but generally finds difficulty in finding commonalities towards a converging solution. The result is a separate answer for each clue (see the example below). Failure on this task is not obvious in a number of cases and may only be sensitive to very gross

Box 3.2.   Case: patient HH

Results of the Reitan Word Finding Test (patient's response in italics)

1. Most grobnicks have long tails. *Horse*
2. Grobnicks of a certain breed have short tails. *Cat*
3. Grobnicks can climb trees. *Monkey*
4. Birds are afraid of Grobnicks. *Snakes*
5. Grobnicks are said to have nine lives. *Lizard*

1. Every house has a Grobnick Yard
2. Grobnicks are constructed in different shapes, but the purpose is the same. "House"
3. It would be quite uncomfortable to live in a house that didn't have a Grobnick. "Husband"
4. A leak in a Grobnick is usually detected during a heavy storm. "Drain"
5. Some people are very happy if they have food in their stomachs and a Grobnick over their head. "House"

damage. The patient HH, whose results are presented below, had gross frontal damage from a tumour (meningioma), which may have affected other brain areas through compression (pressing on these areas). There is some support for behaviour like this being due to lesions beyond that of the frontal lobe. Work described below (Humphreys & Forde, 1998; Schwartz, 1995) suggest that such results may be caused by damage of combined frontal areas and brain areas that are responsible for storing schemas. Schemas are scripts that describe commonly experienced situations or actions such as "making a sandwich" or the features that belong to a cat. They can also be knowledge units concerning typical actions or events.

Similarly, the patients used in Reitan's study all had gross cerebral damage. This patient was not amnesic since she obtained a delayed recall of five items on the Auditory Verbal Learning test. She did show a full understanding of the requirements of the task, as demonstrated by getting some items on this task correct. Her response for a number of the items was "house" suggesting some tendency to perseverate.

This difficulty of organisation can be more readily discerned in patients with isolated frontal lesions in the ability of these patients to organise their memory performance (Incisa Della Rochetta & Milner, 1993) (see Figure 3.4). Impaired memory recall is due to a failure to take advantage of the inherent associations between words during retrieval. Patients with left dorsolateral lesions appear to be particularly prone to this type of deficit (Stuss, Alexander et al., 1994). Also, lesions in this prefrontal area interfere with

the patient's ability to remember where, when, and the order of information (e.g. Petrides, Alivisatos, Evans, & Meyer, 1993). See Chapter 5 for a further discussion on these topics.

Judgement

A patient who was assessed by our team recently following a left frontal lobectomy was followed up because of the large number of his rated everyday emotional and social dysfunction. The patient's wife described how exocentric the patient had become but also how he lacked judgement. For example, because he wanted his wife to stay with him at home he had suggested, quite seriously, that 5- and 6-year-old children take themselves to school. A number of case studies have been reported describing patients following bilateral surgical resection who consequently show a lack of judgement. For example, Eslinger and Damasio report on a patient (EVR) who, following his operation, soon established a partnership as an accountant with a man of doubtful reputation and went into a business against sound advice (Eslinger & Damasio, 1985). Part of this appears to be related to inability to judge a sense of proportion at the time a decision is made. Patients with frontal lesions are described by Damasio (1994) who are lured into the unwise betting on cards that, although having a good immediate return, nevertheless have such a penalty in the long term that they are avoided by the more sensible controls subjects (these studies are described in more detail in Chapter 9).

Several tests of judgement have been devised that appear to be related to frontal dysfunction. The cognitive estimations task requires subjects

in this respect. As a final note, it is of interest that in their study it was only a subgroup of frontal patients that showed the difficulties. This indicates the need to study patients with specific lesions to the frontal lobe although the rarity of such patients often precludes the type of research.

In the next chapter we review tasks that have found that divided attention or other tasks where the subject has to resist the effects of distraction activates frontal regions when normal subjects are scanned during functional imaging.

Before leaving this section on attention it is important to briefly discuss the work of Goldman-Rakic (1996) and others who have explored the area of research referred to as working memory. This area is discussed in Chapter 5. As will be argued, the concepts dealt with in this work are closely allied to attention and refer to the ability we have for keeping information "in mind". Monkeys with lesions to an area within the dorsal lateral prefrontal cortex have some difficulty in performing tasks that require this ability even for a matter of seconds. This is a form of internal attention to images and thoughts, which has obvious importance for any task that requires mental manipulation.

Planning, sequencing and monitoring

Problem-solving tasks

In any problem-solving task it is important to plan a sequence of stages leading to a goal (Baddeley & Wilson, 1988). During problem solving it is also obviously important to monitor where you are within the planned series of sequences. Progress must be monitored so that mistakes can be rectified. Milner (1965) used a maze and tested patients with frontal and temporal lobe lesions. Patients with right temporal lobe and right frontal lesions performed more poorly than other groups. Right frontal patients tended to make more errors in terms of rule breaking. Rule breaking involves going against instructions with such procedures as retracing steps and going diagonally instead of vertically or horizontally.

Karnath, Wallesch, and Zimmerman (1991) tested patients on maze learning over a small number of trials and found that patients with

frontomedial lesions did not benefit from experience to the same degree as other patients. They also noted rule breaking. An important aspect of this maze-learning task is that the maze is unseen. That is, the pathway is obscured and only realised through feedback from each response. In the case of the maze used by Milner, which is used frequently by clinical neuropsychologists in Australia, the patient must press buttons by adjacent steps along a pathway within a matrix of 10×10 buttons. A green light signals a correct response; a red light accompanied by a buzzer signals an error. In the Karnath et al. study, the inability to benefit from experience on the second trial was noted on their maze. Clinically, it is most obviously and dramatically noted in a patient on the Milner maze when the patient is able to solve the maze after approximately 10 trials, but who then goes back to make more errors. The patient may wax and wane in this manner, never quite achieving the requisite number of two correct trials without errors. This quality of response is noted by Walsh (1985, p. 153) as *imperfect learning*. Such a sign, when it is marked, does not bode well for the patient's rehabilitation prospects, especially if it is accompanied by a lack of insight into the impaired nature of their own poor performance. In such a case the patient may not make progress in retraining or rehabilitation because they have the dual handicap of being unable to make use of errors to correct performance and also because they fail to consistently compensate for this problem as a result of failure to recognise its existence (see Box 3.3).

Klosowska (1976) presented a task requiring all the elements of planning, sequencing, and monitoring. The goal of the task was to retrieve a cork from an inaccessible and secured narrow container. The goal was achieved by a series of steps that the subjects were required to work out. Initially a water vessel had to be constructed, then the vessel had to be used to gain access to a cork by filling the narrow container with water, thereby allowing it to float to the surface. The 50 patients with unilateral and bilateral frontal lobe damage were far more likely to have difficulty with this task and were often incapable of providing a consistent strategy for solving the task.

> **Box 3.3.** Case illustrating poor planning, sequencing and monitoring
>
> A 50-year-old patient who had suffered a stroke to the right anterior cerebral artery was assessed as having a generally superior premorbid level of intelligence. However, there were signs of poor organisation on a block design test (see above) in which he failed to realise the overall gestalt of the design and had difficulty determining the frame of the construction. On a maze-learning test he reduced his errors to one on the 11th trial then made four errors on the 12th trial. He made zero errors on the 15th trial, then made three errors on the 16th. He made zero errors again on the 18th but returned to making errors and the test was abandoned on the 20th trial when he made three errors. There was extreme difficulty in monitoring and eradicating errors. The requirement for assessment was occasioned because of complaints from his employer, a large scientific organisation. It was reported that he was making a large number of errors in his work. In particular, he no longer seemed to be able to check his experimental data and computer programs and much of his work had to be overseen or corrected by other employees. The man was a pleasant, mild-mannered gentleman who seemed to think he was coping adequately at work.

Tasks such as the Tower of Hanoi, or an important modification of this task called the Tower of London, also embody these qualities of planning and sequencing (Shallice, 1982) (see Figure 5) (see Figure 3.5). These tasks require the patient to work out a spatial solution by shifting beads from one pole to another according to certain rules. The aim of the task is to gain a certain target configuration displayed on a card. The rules require that only one of the three beads can be shifted, one step at a time, from one adjacent pole to the next. The task is made harder because of the limited space on the poles. Patients with frontal lesions have shown a relatively impaired performance on this task (Owen et al., 1991). Also recently, in collaboration with the author, Karl Hanes has extended this task to increase the difficulty with positive results in terms of assessing patients with subcortical disorders such as Parkinson patients and Huntington's disease (Hanes, Andrewes, Smith & Pantelis, 1996). Owen and colleagues also successfully used a computerised version of this task to distinguish between frontal and other patients. Frontal patients took significantly more moves to achieve a correct solution in this study (Owen et al., 1991).

One of the important components within the Tower of London, maze-learning tasks, and other problem-solving tasks is the need to think ahead towards a solution. This may be a major problem in the daily lives of the more grossly affected patient. However all these tasks are constrained to the extent that there are rules regarding how to proceed, and fail to reflect the open-ended nature of everyday tasks.

Everyday planning and goal-oriented behaviour

Not many tasks are open ended to the extent that they reflect the kinds of choice that are available to us in our everyday lives. A task that provides much more challenge to the patient's initiative and ingenuity was designed by Klosowska (1976). This task requires the patient to solve a problem of retrieving a cork from a fixed flask given certain equipment, e.g. cork, burette, flask, metal

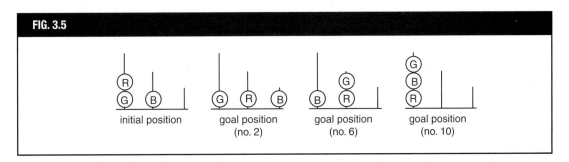

FIG. 3.5

Illustration of three problems of the Tower of London test. The initial position is the same for all three. R stands for red; G, for green; B for blue, (reprinted from T. Shallice, *Philosophical Transactions of the Royal Society of London B, 298, 199–209*, copyright 1982, with permission from the Royal Society).

hook. The subject, after using the hook to open the flask, must then retrieve the cork by pouring a certain amount of water into the flask. This allows the cork to rise to the surface. Patients with frontal versus posterior brain damage were required to give a verbal explanation of how to complete the task. Just over half of the frontal patients, compared to 12% of the posterior patients, had difficulty in giving an explanation. Even without matching of lesion size this suggests some extra difficulty in the frontal group.

This kind of self-goal-directed behaviour is tested in Muriel Lezak's Tinker toy test, in which patients are asked to make models with attachments, e.g. wheels with holes for spokes, that are not unlike "Meccano" or "Lego". Lezak (1995, p. 662) comments on this test: "A number of executive functions appear to contribute to high scoring constructions, including the abilities to formulate a goal and to plan, initiate, and carry out a complex activity to achieve the goal." Patients with difficulty on this task seem to try to gain some inspiration by sorting the pieces into groups according to the shape of the parts provided and have hardly started by the time the 5 minutes is up. The 5-minute time limit was decided upon because of the behaviour of the controls, who had to be curbed from their ambitious and creative activity. With the patients with executive dysfunction, if they do construct something they tend to use a smaller number of pieces and the construction often fails to match the title. Some of the scoring criteria are necessarily subjective but the task appears to be more sensitive than others in predicting re-employment after recovery. Martzke, Swan and Varney (1991) found this task sensitive to impairments in a group of patients, many of whom complained of anosmia (loss of smell often due to olfactory bulb damage) or had orbitofrontal lesions following traumatic brain injury. This test showed impairments when other tests of executive dysfunction showed no impairment. It is important that in this test patients are allowed to construct whatever they wish. This is very much a simulation of many everyday tasks which are also open ended in this way.

For example, preparing a meal may allow a number of alternatives as to how to proceed. The famous neurosurgeon Wilder Penfield, who is mentioned in other chapters for his brain mapping using electrical stimulation at the Montreal Institute of Neurology, gives a poignant yet insightful account of the functioning of his sister after the removal of a frontal lobe tumour:

> One day, about 15 months after the operation, she had planned to get a simple supper for one guest and four members of her own family. She looked forward to it with pleasure and had the whole day for preparation . . . When the appointed hour arrived she was in the kitchen, the food was all there, one or two things were on the stove, but the salad was not ready, the meat had not been started and she was distressed and confused by her long continued effort alone. It seemed that she would never be able to get everything ready at once. With help the task was quickly completed. (Penfield & Evans, 1935)

Luria (1973) proposed that it was the tasks that required several stages which tended to defeat the patient. It is as if the patients had difficulty in distinguishing or keeping track of the various stages. This inability to discriminate between sequences of information is also very much a problem when retrieving information from memory (see Chapter 5). That is, they may adequately recognise a stimulus but not know when or where it was learned. Luria provides questions for his patients such as "There were eighteen books on two shelves, but they were not equally divided: there were twice as many on one shelf as on the other. How many books where there on each shelf?" (Luria 1973, pp. 219–220). His patients with frontal lobe lesions had difficulty in maintaining the original information and consequently misinterpreted the question. However, even when the original question was retained there was no consistent or logical strategy. When solving the problem aloud one patient reported "Of course . . . eighteen books . . . on one shelf and twice as many . . . that means 36 . . . 36 + 18 = 54." Luria proposes that this difficulty may be overcome when the problem is broken down into parts or stages for the patient, in this way providing external support (Luria, 1973, p. 220). Patients have been described who do adequately, and sometimes very well, on structured neuropsychological tests but have great difficulty in their everyday behaviour such as arranging an appointment or making plans for the weekend. The everyday tasks are more open ended and require initiative and the kinds of processes described by Luria (e.g. Shallice & Burgess, 1991a; Goldstein et al., 1993). A patient seen recently by the author showed this difficulty. His wife no longer allowed him to shop following complications associated with an anterior communicating aneurysm. She complained that this ex-school teacher either came back with far less than his shopping list required or far more.

Goldstein et al. (1993) propose that when we use a strategy we must keep it "in mind" like an internal marker. There is the assumption that a person has two states of awareness: one that is focused on doing the task "at hand" and a second that is observing one's own actions and monitoring strategies. It is in this last area that some frontally lesioned patients appear to have difficulty. It is also this last self-awareness area that is essential for observing one's own behaviour and is a prerequisite for appropriate, self-regulated behaviour. Luria describes this process as follows: "Man not only reacts passively to incoming information, but creates *intentions* forms *plans* and *programmes* of his actions, inspects their performance, and *regulates* his behaviour so that it conforms to these plans and programmes; finally he *verifies* his conscious activity, comparing the effects of his actions with the original intentions and correcting any mistakes he has made" (Luria, 1973, pp. 79–80; Luria's italics).

Shallice and Burgess (1991a) also use the internal marker metaphor in their study of three patients who despite scoring well on tests of intellect, memory and traditional tests of frontal dysfunction showed all the hallmarks of poorly planned and poorly organised lifestyle. For example, all three had sustained frontal lobe damage following a road traffic accident. Case 1 is described as having an inability to keep his mind on the task at hand. On one occasion when he was supposed to be in hospital he was discovered on the golf course having originally stepped outside the therapy room to fetch some coffee. The patient was unable to shop because he would go to the shop and buy one thing at a time, returning to the car on each occasion (Shallice & Burgess, 1991, p. 728). A second patient was described as being incapable of completing day-to-day events such as his personal hygiene, cleaning his room or arranging any social event spontaneously. He was well capable of completing these tasks, but even when his wife gave him a specific task to complete he would only carry out parts of it, before reading a newspaper. At work and at home the patient had made poor decisions, showing a lack of judgement. Case 3, like the others, never organised her own leisure time spontaneously and lived a lifestyle that was totally routine, without any attempt at novelty.

Shallice and Burgess (1991a) argued that the problem with neuropsychological tests is that they are not sufficiently open ended and, because of this, they fail to tap the day-to-day challenges in life that require decisions given many options and require the maintenance of a plan towards a goal. Their six-element test required the patients to complete a number of tasks within a time period of 15 minutes. There were three tasks divided into two subtasks (a) and (b), making up the six elements. The only restriction was the subjects were not allowed to do two subtasks consecutively and that they had to attempt all the tasks within the time limit. Typically, the patients would become engrossed or sidetracked by a task and therefore would attempt too few tasks, although on a second testing one subject went to the other extreme and changed tasks 63 times. On two subsidiary tasks the subjects had to judge the time taken over the tasks by looking at a hidden watch from time to time and they would often overrun the time required. These authors also set up a real-life task that involved a shopping expedition. Here again there appears to be failure to keep track of goals and the rules surrounding the task, with shops being visited too often, things not paid for and off-limits shops being visited.

The failures on these tasks are categorised under three headings:

1. *Plan formulation or modification*. The problems here typically seem to be the failure to follow and monitor a plan and the failure to formulate plans. For example, one of the subtasks in the six elements was to dictate how the subject would be going home after the test, and one of the patients wasted time on this task because they could not decide which way to go home.

2. *Marker creation or triggering*. This category appears to be most relevant to what is referred to as prospective memory. Subjects were poor at reminding themselves to do something in the future. This assumes that for us to remind ourselves to do something like pay for something in a shop, we must somehow tag an item as needing payment in the future. This hypothetical tag then triggers this memory after being distracted.

3. *Evaluation and goal articulation*. This appears to refer to a tendency to be poor at monitoring progress within a task. Associated with this is the abandonment of tasks before they are completed; also, carelessness and failure to monitor errors.(Shallice & Burgess, 1991a, p. 728).

Some space was taken to focus on this paper by Shallice and Burgess (1991a) because it highlights the skills that are required in our daily living that we often take for granted—skills that are generally poorly assessed in the clinic. These findings also point to the important teleological role of the frontal structures.

Summary

Efficient problem solving is dependent on planning, sequencing, and monitoring. Tasks that require planning, such as the Tower of London, also require sequencing and monitoring skills and often require other skills such as mental manipulation. Experimental work is required to separate these various sub-components in order to analyse the nature of the executive deficit. As will be argued in Chapter 5, one of the strongest explanations for the frontal patients' difficulty in

remembering the sequence, frequency, or source of memories is that these patients fail to store important contextual cues that allow for this type of information to be recalled. A similar explanation is given here for some of these patients' inconsistent and poor use of strategies. The patient appears to be inconsistently aware of where they are in terms of the overall plan of their actions. It is as if they have lost the bookmarker for their procedures. The studies discussed in this section reveal that in everyday life we have to constantly change our behaviour according to changing circumstances while maintaining a consistent goal. We need to be adaptive.

Personality

Drive

The patient described in Box 3.4 shows many of the features associated with a lack of drive. This was manifested in poor initiative in his business and an inability to carry through a task until its completion. Typically the patient fails to do things on time, knows that something has to be done and even how to do it, but never quite gets round to it. The case in Box 3.4 is at the milder end of the spectrum—patients who have very little residual drive are referred to as adynamic. Adynamic patients may have little spontaneity and require prompting to do even the simplest task. This patient had a right medial frontal lobe lesion following a head injury. Luria (1970) reports on a similar patient with a left medial lesion. Lesions to this area involving the anterior cingulate area have been associated with a lack of drive or adynamia, especially when there is a bilateral lesion, in which case hypokinesia may be evidenced initially.

Impaired social skills

Following severe head injury (traumatic brain injury) patients are often described as behaving in a socially inappropriate way. In the most extreme cases, the patient may make inappropriate sexual advances, masturbate in public, and show aggressive behaviour without much provocation. There are other, milder, instances that may involve inappropriate and hurtful comments—the kind

---

Box 3.4.   Case

A patient with a right frontal haemorrhage on CT scan following a car accident was a freelance welder by trade. Prior to the accident he had a thriving business and would work long hours and employed an assistant. Much of his work was gained by phoning and keeping in touch with prospective businesses. There was little evidence of any deterioration on a wide battery of tests, except for some signs of impairment on a maze-learning test, and he was physically fit. After the accident, he found that he did not work on some days and when he did he could not work long, He was unable to explain why this was the case. He has ceased to phone prospective customers and had to lay off his assistant because of the lack of business. His wife had no complaints about their relationship, although she said that he was no longer much interested in sex.

---

of comments that we may occasionally entertain but would normally keep to ourselves. A story told to me by a colleague illustrates this kind of social inappropriateness. The patient had been recovering from the removal of a frontal lobe tumour. The patient's wife felt that he had been making good progress and since she was something of a social hostess she decided to have the first dinner party since his illness. Her view of his recovery seemed to be confirmed by his "valet-like" politeness during the dinner and as the guests started to leave she was breathing a sigh of relief. However, the patient then proceeded to tell each guest just how interesting or boring they had been during the dinner party. They were also told on this basis whether they would get another invitation to dinner in the future.

Often the patient's relatives do not fully appreciate that such behaviour is largely the consequence of brain damage. When they are counselled and educated on this matter by a clinician, it can do much to relieve the tension and bad feeling within the family (see Chapter 9 for a more comprehensive review of this topic).

Lack of Insight

Awareness of one's own behaviour and the consequences of that behaviour have already been discussed in terms of cognitive skills such as problem solving. This same dysfunction may also influence the interpersonal social skills of a patient and the insight the patient has into their own behaviour.

George Prigatano (1991), who has written a great deal on this issue, makes the comment "assuming the frontal lobes are especially important for the modulation of emotions and the control of behavioural responses appropriate for social adaption, it may be precisely in these

areas that frontal lobe injury affects awareness the most. Furthermore, since the definition of 'one's self' is at least in part obtained by comparing one's characteristics with others, frontal lobe lesions may particularly affect the highest perceptions of one's own self-functioning" (Prigatano, 1991, p. 390). The interesting point therefore made is that lack of awareness is related to the area of deficit and this relationship has already been referred to in other chapters concerning patients with perceptual disorders. Also, Prigatano suggests that we modify our social behaviour by comparisons with others. One might extend this view by suggesting that we also *monitor* our own social behaviour "on-line". We may change what we say in response to the expression or body language of the other person. If you are not able to monitor these signs, sooner or later a "social gaff" will be committed.

A prerequisite for improving or changing behaviour is the acknowledgment that behaviour needs to be altered. If a patient is unaware that they are performing poorly on tasks or in their social relationships, there is little likelihood that they will take advice in a rehabilitation setting (Kinsella, Moran, Ford, & Ponsford, 1988; Prigatano, 1991). For this reason, some effort is made to improve insight and awareness in patients in the rehabilitation setting (Ponsford, Sloan, & Snow, 1995).

Ironically, this lack of insight into one's own problems may be the mechanism for change following some forms of psychosurgery. The early surgical treatments that were used for the treatment of schizophrenia, referred to as prefrontal lobotomy and frontal leucotomy, consisted of radical division of white matter just anterior of the horns of the lateral ventricles. This surgical treatment, therefore, severs many of

---

Box 3.5.   Case: poor insight into inappropriate social behaviour

The patient was assaulted in a car park on leaving a hotel. He received bilateral damage to the dorsolateral aspect of the prefrontal cortex. The patient's wife complained that he no longer went to work as a truck driver and just sat around the house during the day while she went out to work. The wife was exasperated and at her "wits' end" because her husband only carried out tasks when he was directly told. Once she left for work and he was left unsupervised he would do nothing, even when he was left a list of duties. She also complained that he was now short tempered with the children and would lose his temper at the slightest thing. The husband could not understand what all the fuss was about and even when his wife left him with the children some months later he was still convinced that there was nothing especially wrong with his behaviour.

---

the connections with the prefrontal cortex, especially those leading to and from the orbitofrontal cortex. A concise description of the history and evolution of this technique is provided by Walsh (1985, pp. 158–164). There may be some success with this operation with patients who obsessively ruminate to an excessive degree and are not treatable by any other means. However, this success may be due to a reduction in the patient's self-concern (Valenstein, 1990). Put in perhaps a less glamorous light, the patient loses awareness of their difficulties but also they possibly become blunted in other areas of their life, with less favourable ramifications (see Chapter 9 for a discussion).

Also notable is Damasio's finding that patients with prefrontal lesions show far less arousal as compared with controls when faced with pictures containing emotionally laden connotations. This is translated into theory by Damasio (1994), who attributes the lack of reaction and sensitivity (and presumably concern) to an absence of emotional feedback which may guide us to focus on the consequences of situations and actions.

Summary

Patients with anterior lesions may show a wide range of impaired everyday behaviours, but most can be described in terms of three distinguishing types of behaviour that are not necessarily mutually exclusive. These influences on personality are:

1. A lack of drive and difficulty when patients initiate or complete behaviours.
2. Poor social skills, associated with disinhibited behaviour. The patient's behaviour may be embarrassing and inappropriate. These behaviours may occur despite an intact knowledge of appropriate behaviour or social mores (Saver & Damasio, 1991).

3. The patient has a lack of insight. They fail to monitor their own behaviour and the reactions of others. In a social situation this may mean that they obtain degraded feedback from their own behaviour. In the clinical situation this may mean that the patient is a poor judge of their own capabilities and may insist on discharging themselves from hospital or returning to work too early, with sometimes disastrous consequences.

Patients may show fewer of these signs if their lives are relatively protected and structured. For example, a devoted carer may take over the role of the frontal lobes of the patient, organising and initiating behaviours and prompting the patient. In Chapter 9 the effects of frontal pathology on the personality of the patient are further explored.

EXECUTIVE DYSFUNCTION FOLLOWING SUBCORTICAL ATROPHY

It has long been known that patients with a genetic neurological disorder called Huntington's disease (see Chapter 8 for a description) often show the signs of executive dysfunction which may be shown by these patients during the later stages of their disease. The striatum, which includes the caudate nucleus and an adjacent structure beneath it called the putamen, is initially affected in this disease (see diagrams in Chapter 8). The deterioration or atrophy of these structures, especially the putamen, is associated with lack of control over motor movements, which are referred to as choreic. These erratic movements including facial grimacing, a writhing of the trunk, and sudden erratic movement of the arms. As the disease progresses atrophy of mesial–orbital frontal structures also occurs.

The caudate nucleus lies at the apex of the basal ganglia and runs from its anterior aspect (close to the orbitofrontal cortex) posteriorly, providing a connection between the prefrontal cortex and such important structures as the thalamus. From its anterior aspect it rises up dorsally in a curve and receives projections from the adjacent areas within the prefrontal cortex. Therefore from receiving projections from the orbitofrontal cortex ventrally it rises to receive projections from the dorsolateral prefrontal cortex and medial aspects of the frontal lobe. The caudate nucleus therefore acts as an important communication system between the prefrontal cortex with other subcortical structures. The

caudate should be seen as a super-highway from-for information for the five subcortical circuits, of which threeare described here as being are relevant to executive dysfunction. The physiological nature of the circuits were described by Alexander and Crutcher, and their functional and clinical significance have been described by Cummings (Alexander, Crutcher & Delong, 1990; Cummings, 1993; Cummings & Coffey, 2000) (see Table 3.1).

Huntington's disease is a genetic disorder that is associated with atrophy of areas that will undermine both the dorsolateral and the orbital circuits described in Table 3.1. As indicated, the disorganised and disinhibited involuntary choreic movements of Huntington patients are most readily ascribed to atrophy of the putamen, which

TABLE 3.1

The subcortical pathways and circuits that may be undermined in disorders such as Huntington's and Parkinson's disease (see Chapter 6). The functional contributions of the subcortical structures within these three circuits

Subcortical circuit	Circuit connections. The pathway progresses through 1 to 3 or 4 and then returns to 1				Functional significance and clinical syndromes
	1	2	3	4	
Dorsolateral circuit	Convexity of frontal lobe	Dorsolateral head of the caudate nucleus	Globus pallidus and substantia nigra	Medial dorsal thalamic nuclei and ventral anterior	Executive dysfunction
Orbitofrontal circuit	Inferior lateral prefrontal cortex	Inferior caudate nucleus	Pallidum and substantia nigra	Medial portions of the ventral anterior and medial dorsal thalamic nuclei	Emotional and social dysfunction
Anterior cingulate circuit	Cortex of the anterior cingulate gyrus Brodmann's area 24	Ventral or limbic striatum, inc. nucleus accumbens, ventromedial portions of the caudate and putamen	Medial thalamic nuclei		Akinetic mutism (difficulty in spontaneously initiating motor movements), also apathy, lack of drive and focus of attention

Adapted from Alexander, Crutcher, and Delong (1990); Cummings (1993); Cummings and Coffey (200).

is next to and has close interconnections with the caudate. This atrophy is also associated with an imbalance in the neurotransmitter systems described in Chapter 8 and is seen as an important mechanism for the disinhibited movements. The patients may go for many years without obvious mental impairment, while the stage of onset of the personality, motor, or cognitive impairment varies with the individual. Eventually, the same disinhibition shown in their motor movements may also eventually appear in their social behaviour. Some of this disinhibition may appear in the form of irrational temperamental outbursts or inappropriate behaviour. A possible illustration of disinhibition, not necessarily sexual, occurred when one of our patients was arrested for tugging on the pigtails of a little girl while standing in a supermarket queue. Given that this was uncharacteristic behaviour for this person, his diagnosis was used in his defence in the court case.

Apart from such examples of disinhibition there may also be signs of *inhibition* with this disorder, both in terms of slowed thinking (bradyphrenia) and slowed initiation of movements. The cognitive and behavioural manifestations of the disorder are heterogeneous, and as indicated, while signs of depression may in some cases herald the disease, most of the signs of executive system breakdown, when they occur, are evident in the patient towards the more advanced stages of this disorder.

Dysexecutive performance may show on tests such as the verbal fluency tests, WCST, and TMTB, which are described above. These patients may also have difficulties on tasks which require planning, such as maze-learning tasks. Perception remains intact but constructional impairment exists, as indicated by poorly organised copies of complex design (see Figure 3.6). Memory impairment is marked by poor organisation and poor recall rather than recognition (unless the recognition task is made difficult withby the use of a number of distractors) indistractors). In other words, when there are memory retrieval requirements that need the organisation of learned material these patients have difficulties, but in tasks where they merely have to recognise the material in an uncomplicated way they do far better (Brandt et al., 1984).

Around 50% of the progeny of a Huntington's carrier have the disease. Because of this danger of inheritance and because a patient is often in their forties before the clinical signs of the disease are realised, prediction of the disease is important before the decision is made to have a family. Prior to genetic testing neuropsychology provided one means of anticipating this disease. We and others found that presymptomatic patients (patients *without* the clinical signs of motor movements and other clinical signs of Huntington's) sometimes showed subtle signs of poor planning and poor flexibility on neuropsychological testing (e.g. Diamond et al., 1992; Andrewes et al., 1993; Brandt et al., 1984).

Another disorder that is associated with dysexecutive signs, to a lesser extent, is Parkinson's disease. As a group, these patients have difficulty on tasks that involve cognitive flexibility and planning, and as with the Huntington patients these effects are not due to problems of movement that characterise this disorder. There are now extensive studies using the Tower of London with these patients and Owen (1997a) makes the speculative case that the impairment found in these and other patients may be due to subcortical pathology, rather than purely disconnection or frontal cortical atrophy per se.

To follow Owen's argument, it is important to acknowledge that patients with Parkinson's disease and Huntington's disease both suffer from bradyphrenia or slowness of thought process. When patients with Parkinson's disease are compared with patients with frontal lobe lesions, Parkinson patients show more slowed thinking in planning out tasks such as the Tower of London (Owen et al., 1995). Huntington patients also have this exaggerated slowing in planning on both the Tower of London and on a maze task called the Porteus maze. Typically, as the problems become more taxing and demanding so there is an exaggerated increase in the time taken to plan the moves, and since the movement requirements are largely unchanged this increased slowness is unrelated to motor speed requirements of the test

FIG. 3.6

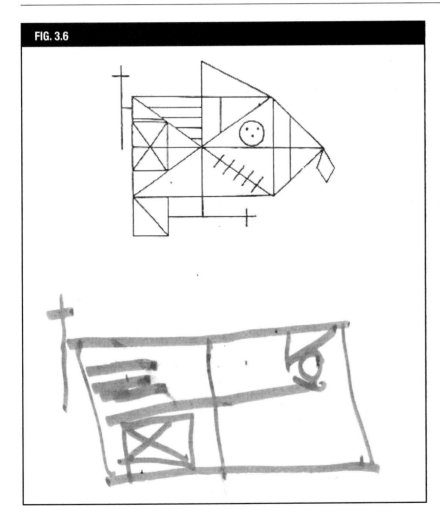

Illustration of a poorly organised copy of a Rey Ostereith figure completed by a patient with Huntington's disease.

(Andrewes et al., 1993; Hanes, Pantelis, Andrewes, & Chiu, 1996).

An interesting question that has been posed by Owen (1997a) is whether this *slowed thinking* is due to a separate mechanism from that supporting the *accuracy* and successful completion of the Tower of London task? Apart from the finding that the slowed thinking does not appear to be linked to frontal cortical lesions, there are two other pieces of information that seem to imply a separation. The first is the finding that the slowness appears at an early stage of the progression of the disease, before there is a significant reduction of task accuracy. The second piece of evidence relates to the treatment of Parkinson's disease with L-dopa. This treatment, which compensates for the loss of the neurotransmitter substance dopamine, acts to ameliorate impaired accuracy on the Tower of London task but fails to improve planning time in the same way (Owen et al., 1995). The implications are, therefore, that the mechanism for bradyphrenia, or slowed thinking, is caused by a separate process compared to other signs of executive dysfunction.

PET scan studies that have evaluated blood flow during Tower of London tasks have implicated both frontal lobe and subcortical structures as contributing of this task. Both of these areas are activated by increased blood flow during a PET scan when subjects are completing the more

scheduling may occur when the sight of a dirty window triggers some automatic schema-driven window-cleaning activity. But contention scheduling may also be triggered by a thought, e.g. "I need to make the children's lunches for school", or the triggering stimulus could be part of another chain of behaviour, e.g. sugar in the cup triggers stirring (Shallice & Burgess, 1991b, p. 126).

What happens when we continue with a routine inappropriately and the SAS fails to cut in and control behaviour away from the automatic routine? Such a situation is referred to as a "capture slip"—we are captured by a routine of behaviour and cannot get away from it. Patients with gross frontal lesions are reputedly particularly prone to making such "capture slips", when either tested in the laboratory (Della Malva, Stuss, D'Alton, & Willmer, 1993) or in everyday life. This is revealed above and in the example given towards the beginning of this chapter when a patient was described as getting into a bed that did not belong to him (L'hermitte, 1986). L'hermitte (1986) describes a series of such capture slips. Patients with gross frontal lobe damage are described as drinking from a cup handed to them even when it is empty. The same patients, when given an orange, peel the orange, even when they are not hungry. Another patient is given a pair of glasses and the patient automatically puts them on despite his already wearing a pair (see discussion on cue utilization behaviour by Stuss, Eskes & Foster, 1994, pp. 152–153). For these patients the SAS is not stepping in to control the automatic behaviour: rather the patient is being controlled externally by perceptual inputs that are triggering the schemas inappropriately. The SAS is "down" and not functioning to intervene when necessary.

Apart from these situations involving a lack of supervisory modulation sufficient to inhibit behaviour, there are various other types of dysexecutive behaviour that Shallice and Burgess (1991b) believe is predicted by their model. For example, sometimes patients with frontal damage are reported as being perseverative in their behaviours: repeating a behaviour over and over again could be seen as being captured by the external environment. The author assessed a patient with bilateral orbitofrontal lesions following a stroke. This patient, having drawn a diagram of two flags crossed from immediate memory, then proceeded to draw the same figure again and again across the page. According to the model the external stimulus of the original request triggered the contention scheduler, which triggered the drawing schema, but after the drawing was completed the contention scheduler was never modified by the supervisory attentional system and therefore the behaviour was repeated. Shallice and Burgess also describe the vulnerability to distraction which they see again as being determined by the tendency for the patient to be dictated to by external stimuli. The patient is described as being without the necessary internal control which would normally be supplied by the SAS.

Persons without brain damage may also fall prey to such automatic behaviour. An example of this might be when a person is driving to the shops at the weekend by the same road he uses to drive to work. A few minutes later he finds himself feeling mildy foolish in the car park at work. The road has triggered the entrenched automatic behaviour. One prediction that can be made from this model is that if the role of the SAS is represented by a prefrontal structure then patients with damage to this area will fail at tasks that require controlled performance away from a natural tendency towards automaticity. For example, there is a well-entrenched and overlearned ability to count in order 1, 2, 3 etc. and therefore the request to produce random numbers is particularly difficult because there is a natural tendency to count in series. We have previously described such tasks as the Trail Making B task in which patients have to join 1 to A, A to 2, 2 to B and so on; this is difficult for some patients with frontal lesions for similar reasons. The patient typically makes the mistake of joining two numbers or two letters consecutively because this is a well-learned response. Humphreys and Forde (1998) similarly found evidence for this attraction towards the automatic response when they asked patients with frontal lesions to undertake novel tasks, e.g. pouring from a cup into a teapot.

This basic SAS model has not been described in any elaborative way here and has since been updated to accommodate more advanced research information relating to attentional processes (Shallice & Burgess, 1998; Stuss, Shallice, Alexander, & Picton, 1995). However, the SAS model is a rather useful framework from which to start our search for a generalist model of executive function.

There are a number of studies that confirm the predictions of the SAS model as a description of executive dysfunction and some of these have already been reviewed in the first half of this chapter. While these authors have moved on from this model, I am sure they will not mind their old model being used as a useful teaching point within this discussion. Although it is well supported in areas that require control and cognitive flexibility, one criticism of this model in its basic form is that the description of dysexecutive behaviour is too simplistic. For example, patients with executive dysfunction do not always make the kind of errors that involve a disinhibited release of automatic behaviour. Schwartz and her colleagues have videotaped patients with traumatic brain injury who showed dysexecutive signs. Although some of these behaviours could be described by the SAS model, e.g. while intending to prepare and pack a sandwich the patient prepared, packed, and then *ate* the sandwich, there were nevertheless other examples that did not fit easily within this framework. For example, these patients were identified as having a tendency towards making disorganised movements. The authors found that patients made a variety of confusions of routine behaviour, while with other tests of everyday activities they found insertions of routines, mixing up routines and omissions. For example, they would sometimes substitute one routine for another, e.g. the patient intended to put the present in the gift-box but ended up putting both the present and the bow in the gift-box. When videotaped in their everyday lives, one patient spooned butter into coffee, and attempted to pour from a closed container. Another patient poured dry cereal into a coffee mug, attempted to shave without plugging in a shaver, and spread shaving cream onto the toothbrush. Of course some of these behaviours may be more easily described as illustrations of

apraxia but the disorganisation that is found in these patients is not atypical of dysexecutive behaviour reported in other studies.

Godbout similarly describes a study in which patients with frontal traumatic brain injury were required to buy the commodities for a three course meal and then cook the meal. "Brownies" were the last item on the menu but the ingredients for this meal had to be put in the oven first, many of the dysexecutive patients with traumatic head injury slipped-up with this kind of planning ahead (Godbout & Fortin, 2000; Godbout & Doyen, 1995). Clearly these examples are not obviously concerned with inhibiting automatic behaviours, which is clearly described by the SAS model, but rather in terms of organising and planning both parts of automatic behaviours and controlled behaviours. There is an apparent difficulty in selecting the correct behaviour, which is presumably associated with poor monitoring of behaviour. Normal people under stress sometimes make these types of errors of poor selection and poor monitoring like these two examples:

When I leave work in the morning, I am in the habit of throwing two dog biscuits to my pet corgi and then putting on my earrings. One morning, I threw the earrings to the dog and found myself trying to attach a dog biscuit to my ear. (Reason, 1992)

At midday we cadets and officers gathered to take "a sight". This required the measurement of the angle between the horizon and the sun. For this navigational routine most of us had second-hand sextants since they were very expensive. However, one of us had a new sextant—a much envied state of the art instrument. This cadet was steadying himself for a measurement, which had to be made at an exact time, being counted down by someone in the chart room. He was concentrating on the task at hand, with the sextant being held steady in one hand and a lighted cigarette in the other. He was adjusting the angle with the hand that also held the cigarette. No one heard the Captain when he came up behind us on the bridge, but his bellow of "No smoking on the bridge!" caused the cadet to instantly throw his new sextant overboard. He was left staring in disbelief at the cigarette he meant to throw. (An incident once described to the author)

These two examples suggest that even persons without brain damage may mix up or misapply automatic behaviours, especially when the situation involves some stress and division of attention. These types of examples also indicate that even when we are carrying out automatic behaviours there is a need for monitoring, even if this need is reduced. This miss-selection or disorganisation of behaviours over time may also occur in the cases when the person is merely engrossed in thought. Most of us have either committed one of these confused activities or know someone who has. Examples have been given of persons who have placed the sugar in the fridge. Quite otherwise normal persons have been unusually in their bedroom looking for something and absent-mindedly started to get undressed for bed.

Schwartz proposes that these examples indicate that even automatic behaviours require some kind of monitoring and scheduling if they are to be run off in the right order in an efficient manner (Schwartz, 1995). Therefore if we are constructing a model of executive function it would seem important to illustrate a variable monitoring process that oversees both the selection of controlled, novel behaviours and also the selection of automatic behaviours that may be triggered by the environment.

In summary, Shallice and Norman's original model provided a useful framework for illustrating how behaviours might be triggered by certain stimuli; also, how these automatic behaviours might be curtailed and replaced by more controlled and supervised processes when the automatic behaviours cease to become adaptive. It has been argued that an extension of this model requires that their be, in addition, a supervision or monitoring of automatic routines. Although such automatic routines may require less monitoring and certainly require less attentional resource (see Chapter 4 for a discussion).

Also, while the model illustrates the situation in which controlled behaviour takes over from automatic behaviour, the model is less clear concerning how behaviours are planned and organised but also, crucially, how the prefrontal cortex acts to select a new behaviour. Unless we are thinking of the prefrontal cortex as a kind of little person in our head we must explain how the prefrontal cortex selects the schema without a map of such schemas; there can be no magic involved here. If we give a selective role to a structure it is important to model how this can occur. A model by Jordan Grafman which is described in the next section focuses on this issue.

Schemas and the frontal lobe?

Schemas represent the knowledge of our world. The schema concept derives from such early theorists as Bartlett (1932) who described among his other work, memory reports of stories that appeared to report gists and themes rather than a verbatim response. These reports also seemed to reflect on the subject's past knowledge and experience as if new information was cast in the framework of old information. The idea of building up a schema or schemas relates to the increase in knowledge of a particular topic, event, or action. The term "frame" or "script" is sometimes used to refer to a similar concept. A schema is a broad term that describes the content of a typical set of ideas or experiences and their logical relationships. This information represents our past knowledge of what is likely to occur given a certain context. For example, the following sentence might violate our schema of going to a restaurant:

Jim went to a restaurant and asked to be seated in the gallery. He was told that there would be a one-half hour wait. Forty minutes later, the applause for his song indicated that he could proceed with the preparation. Twenty guests had ordered his favourite, a cheese souffle. (Bransford, 1979, p. 184)

Having expectations about situations clearly allows us to comprehend and act quickly and anticipate what will happen next. If we go to a children's birthday party then we have a general schema of what this involves: giving of presents, games, tea party with cake. However, we also have quite specific schemas for typical sentence construction, e.g. subject, verb, object. In the SAS model schemas are described as being accessed in an automatic way, often being triggered by external stimuli and resulting in routines of behaviour.

Grafman (1989, 1995) describes a hierarchy of schemas that are stored within the prefrontal cortex. These schemas are referred to as managerial knowledge units. They are represented at nodes, starting at the top at a general and abstract level, with more specific subunits beneath them. At the most abstract level there are broad descriptions that might relate to a wide variety of behaviours; as the elements of the schema become lower in the hierarchy they become more specific. Grafman proposes that these schemas reside in the frontal lobe and without some representation of knowledge at an executive level it would be difficult to see how such information could achieve its role of selecting schemas and their associated routines of behaviour. It would be a bit like wanting to change an article of newly bought clothing without knowing where you bought it.

However, an immediate objection to this proposal might be that although frontal lesions are associated with organisational and retrieval difficulties, damage to this area is not obviously associated with loss of schemas per se knowledge or the knowledge the schemas represent. However, (Grafman, 1989) proposes that there is sufficient redundancy in the system to compensate unless presumably the damage is gross, and then some support for Grafman's theory appears in the literature in the work described by Reitan (1972a, 1972b; see Boxes 3.1 and 3.2), L'hermitte (1983, 1986), and others in this chapter.

This brings us to the advantage of Grafman's model in that it answers a question not satisfied by the SAS model. That is, how can disorganisation of information occur? The poor organisation and selection following damage to the prefrontal cortex may be easily described in terms of the destruction of such schemas that are represented there. The lack of

judgement, which is also described above, may also be described in terms of poor access to relationships within knowledge representations. Poor planning and impaired autobiographical memory may also be represented by the damage to the schematic representation of events, which Grafman refers to as structured event complexes (Grafman, 1989).

Grafman refers to managerial knowledge units as being derived originally from the less abstract schemas, being referred to as structured event complexes. Therefore there is a hierarchy, with the most abstract representations above diverting into more and more specific representations. For example, there may be a managerial unit concerning the general activities regarding a visit to the restaurant, e.g. being shown to the table, choosing something to eat from the menu and receiving the bill or account. But below this more abstract level there are event-related complexes that might relate to what to do when the waiter gives you the wrong change. At the most basic level this schema hierarchy may take on a description of an action such as found in Figure 3.8. However, these may develop and include reference to experiences related to the structured event. The structured event complex (SEC) may comprise representations of stored events that have occurred in the past and will probably occur again in the future.

Grafman (1995) argues that children with their undeveloped prefrontal cortex, may show inconsequential and embarrassing behaviour in certain situations, e.g. restaurants, because they have undeveloped SECs (see Diamond, 1996, for further work in a related area). The emerging functional imaging work in the area of autobiographical memory appears to broadly support Grafman's theory. As will be discussed in Chapter 5 the prefrontal cortex is activated when detailed autobiographical information is being retrieved (Conway et al., 1999) or when there has to be an elaborate search through memory (Henson, Rugg et al., 1999).

The model is useful in describing the breakdown of planning, reasoning, and organisation following prefrontal damage, and some of Grafman's own work reveals some specialisation

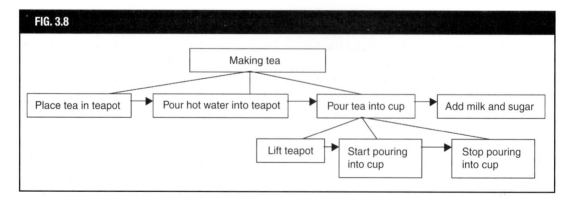

FIG. 3.8

Illustration of the hierarchy of the schema of the type proposed by Graffman (1995) and others. If the patient with frontal damage is asked to undertake the task the patient will have no difficulty in relying on the posterior located schema, but a novel task, e.g. "Pour the cup into the teapot", is made difficult because a schema cannot be relied upon. The patient must start and stop the task and must make a series of selections and transpositions that rely on frontal structures. When the posterior structures containing the schemas are damaged then even commonly learned procedures have to be produced in a controlled manner, relying on frontal structures for selection and organisation. Combined damage to frontal and parietal areas results in disorganised behaviour.

within the prefrontal cortex for certain types of SEC. For example, Sirigu et al. (1998) have found a double dissociation whereby patients with left prefrontal cortex lesions with Broca's aphasia (see Chapter 7) had difficulty in ordering words into grammatical sentences but had no difficulty in ordering a series of actions. In contrast, patients with dorsolateral prefrontal lesions had the reverse problem, having difficulty in ordering actions but no difficulty with the syntax-related tasks.

Partiot et al. (1996) PET scanned normals and revealed a network of activation including the prefrontal cortex and anterior cingulate and areas within the temporal lobe during ordering and predicting membership of scripts such as those shown in Fig 3.8. The right frontal lobe was more activated with temporal sequencing, while the left more activated during the categorisation and membership tasks. The model predicts that an inhibition or disinhibition of response will occur when the representative schema for that response is damaged. Thus disinhibition of a particular SEC may occur if there is less inhibition from competitive schemas within the network. Grafman also proposes that the selection of schemas is in terms of network activation and therefore a switch between schemas is possible, thereby allowing flexibility. There is less development of the mechanisms associated with control in his writings.

Grafman's model allows an insight into a wide variety of executive dysfunction that are somewhat neglected by other models. It is especially strong in allowing a solution to the conundrum concerning how the knowledge stores are selected and searched. However, there is mounting evidence that such knowledge stores are accessed posteriorly within the association areas. In the previous chapter we referred to a disconnection with knowledge centres residing in the temporal lobe, the end of the "what" pathway. In Chapter 5 we discuss the disorder referred to as semantic dementia, which is associated with a loss of knowledge and atrophy of the temporal lobes. Therefore, if the frontal lobes contain schemas of knowledge it is clear that the temporal lobes also contain such knowledge. Also, in seeming contradiction to the view that schemas are located within the prefrontal cortex, patients with frontal lobe lesions may often achieve well on tests of information. We have already mentioned above how these patients may do well on structured neuropsychology tests. As early as 1940 Hebb and Penfield were reporting that IQ (including the test on information knowledge) was not reduced despite gross lesions to the frontal lobes. Lezak (1995, p. 43) reports on a number of interesting cases, one of which includes a description of a professional man who after anoxia associated with an anaesthetic accident retained a high average to superior IQ. The insurance assessor originally saw this as an indicator that the man was intact and required no financial support, until it was realised that the man was both occupationally and socially incompetent. The man was unable to make decisions or organise his recreational pursuits, and he lacked any initiative, being reduced to running errands for his brother's grocery business. The only IQ test which appears to be clearly sensitive in some patients, is Cattell's "culture fair test". This is a problem-solving test that requires the goal to be kept in mind. This test is similar to the Raven Matrices and requires the subject to choose a spatial design that logically fits the one missing from a series. There is a further discussion concerning this test towards the end of this chapter (Duncan, Burgess, & Emslie, 1995).

Studies have already been reviewed above of patients with frontal lesions who show a similar mismatch between their performance on structured tests and their everyday behaviour. These points of evidence seem to counter Grafman's theory that schemas are located within the frontal lobe. Nevertheless, some schematic representation must be accessed in the prefrontal cortex because otherwise the selection of appropriate information would not be possible. As argued above, patients with frontal lesions, while they may be able to respond accurately to well-structured questions, tend to have difficulty in spontaneously organising and selecting such information given internal requirements.

Two possible models present themselves as a solution: either schema knowledge is represented in both the prefrontal cortex and the association cortices (areas of the parietal and temporal lobe) or the prefrontal cortex provides an internal filing system of knowledge representation rather than the knowledge system itself. This latter metaphor is clearly preferred since if there were a duplicate knowledge system then knowledge of the world would still remain when the posterior association areas are destroyed or damaged, because the prefrontal cortex knowledge system would be able to compensate for the loss, but this is clearly not the case. Patients with semantic dementia and Alzheimer's disease with atrophy to the posterior association cortices become agnosic: they cease to recognise the meaning of common objects around them.

If the view of the prefrontal cortex as a filing or directory system is preferred, a library's computer filing system is an appropriate analogy. When we use such a system we are not obviously searching through the books themselves that are located on the shelves: we are merely accessing a directory of where books by a particular author or topic might be found. We are searching representations of where to look for knowledge.

Disorganisation therefore occurs when such a directory system is disrupted or destroyed but the posterior knowledge structure remains to be accessed externally through structured questions from tests or other form. These knowledge systems may be accessed by those close to a patient and therefore in one sense others may act as the patient's frontal lobes, directing their daily lives. In this way they may lead relatively useful lives, as in the case of the man described above by Lezak who lived with his brother. It is a recognised rehabilitation strategy that others can in some circumstances act as the patients frontal lobes.

Earlier in this chapter a study by Schwartz (1995) was described that involved patients with disorganisation of *movements*. She noted that her patients appeared to require both a combined parietal and frontal lesion before a marked disorganisation of movement was noted. The proposal was that the schemas for the behavioural routines (stored posteriorly) and the frontal structures must *both* be undermined for these kinds of confused behaviours to consistently show themselves to a *high degree*. Humphreys and Forde (1998) have also showed that some of their patients had problems with the schema-driven familiar tasks. These authors describe a patient with more isolated left frontal lesions who showed very little impairment unless the condition was made confusing by having a number of distractors, e.g. the provision of both Sellotape and masking tape for making a parcel. The patients with the combined frontal and posterior lesions also showed this vulnerability to interference but exhibited more severe problems in carrying out the tasks. Commonly two types of errors were made: perseveration, in which a stage was unnecessarily repeated; and sequencing errors, getting the stages out of order. Therefore although the number of patients is very small in this study it would appear that combined lesions are required for marked disorganisation of behaviour of this nature (see also Schwartz, 1995). This would support the view that the prefrontal cortex acts in concert with posterior association areas within a network. This view is also held by Grafman (1995). However, when considering the definition of their respective roles it may be useful to see the prefrontal cortex as administering a selective role to a posterior storage system.

In conclusion, many models have neglected to describe the nature of schemas that allows us to act with the benefit of experience. The contribution of Grafman's model has been to propose that the executive system that cannot be seen in isolation from the structure of knowledge. The executive role takes place within this structure. Some parts of this structure are inhibited, while other parts are activated. Many models neglect to discuss the nature of these important schematic representations of knowledge and how it guides behaviour. Modern functional imaging studies appear to support the prefrontal structures in a selection process. The model argued for here declares that one of the roles of the prefrontal cortex is to act as a directory system for knowledge that is located posteriorly. In some ways this is an elaboration of Shallice's SAS: it explains how the system modulates the contention scheduler.

These signposts to the various parts of the knowledge system are referred to here as *directory schemas* . These allow us to access the knowledge schemas that are located within the association areas. Directory schemas allow self-initiated access to knowledge that may be compensated or off set by external commands or stimulation. Directory schemas provide an outline that may even represent the upper layers of the schemas

discussed above. Just as we might wish to access books on crime by a certain author, the directory schema would project to areas that will be fruitfully searched. With less precise information or a broader area of search such a response would obviously take longer.

It is appropriate to talk within this framework of internally and externally driven behaviour (see Petrides, 1998, for a similar view). The latter, externally driven behaviour, would be intact in these patients and would include responses to direct questions and commands from others. It would be predicted that the behaviour of such patients in situations in which external influences stimulate and guide behaviour would be quite normal. Damage to the directory schema system within the prefrontal cortex interferes with the process of self-initiated organisation and self-initiated selection.

An integral part of any internally driven search process is that it is over time. At least two components must be retained over time. The goal or strategy must be maintained, otherwise the patient will see no reason to continue, but information must also be maintained. Models of prefrontal function often include a working memory component that allows this bridging of the temporal gap between search initiation and its final outcome or action.

Working memory

Research by Jacobson (1935) revealed a startling finding that monkeys with bilateral lesions to the prefrontal cortex had the greatest difficulty in holding information over a delay. This finding has been researched extensively in more recent years and various paradigms of measuring delayed response have been used. The classic paradigm involves the placement of food or other reward under one of two wells in front of the monkey. Although there may be no distinguishing feature between the lids of the two wells, the hungry monkey watches intently as the food is placed in the well to the left or right of its cage. A shutter is then brought down to obscure the animal's vision for a brief period, e.g 3–60 seconds. The monkey is then allowed to reach out to one of the two wells in order to retrieve the reward. Monkeys with bilateral lesions to the mid-dorsolateral and mid-ventrolateral prefrontal cortex cannot perform this task accurately—to borrow a phrase, "Out of sight out of mind." However, these findings should be put in perspective. It is not on the first trial that this difficulty is found. When there is no interference of previous trials they can perform this task (Diamond, 1990). There appears to be a dual function of this area, to keep information in mind but also to select out one experience from another in time.

This role of selection over time is also revealed in an experimental task that has been used extensively by Michael Petrides over the years (Petrides, 1991; Petrides & Milner, 1982). The task uses a series of cards each of which contains a number of pictures in different locations. Each card is divided into a grid or lattice, each cell containing a different picture of an object or similar stimulus. In this task the subject is merely required to point at a different picture on each trial. If a patient pointed to a picture on one trial in a certain spatial location then this choice could not be repeated in the next trial. The crucial requirement of these "self-ordering" tasks is to remember what you have previously chosen and on which trial this choice was made, otherwise the same choice will be made twice running. Mid-dorsolaterally lesioned patients or monkeys typically have difficulty in keeping track of this kind of potentially confusing information. In contrast, although they have the greatest difficulty in retaining and using this contextual material, these subjects are able to distinguish information that has been presented from information that has not been presented. Therefore they can decide as well as controls whether a stimulus is familiar and has been previously presented—they just have difficulty in remembering stimulus presentation information; the contextual information of "when", "where" and "which order".

In the light of functional imaging studies with human subjects, lesions in this lateral area of the prefrontal cortex undermine what is referred to as working memory. As we shall discuss in chapter 5 definitions of working memory vary but within these types of paradigms the requirement is often merely to keep more than one piece of information metaphorically "in mind" over trials that are poorly delineated. Some paradigms require an additional alternative task to be conducted, while others involve a series of potentially confusing trials while information is temporally retained. The area involved in the monkey is adjacent to the principal sulcus, which divides the lateral surface of the prefrontal cortex into the dorsal and ventral areas. The principal sulcus is not a feature of the human brain, but studies comparing human and monkey brains have deduced that a similar division may be made within the human brain with the middle and superior frontal gyrus (BA areas 9 and 46) representing the human dorsolateral prefrontal gyrus, while the anterior portion of the inferior frontal gyrus (BA 47, 45) represents the ventrolateral prefrontal cortex (e.g. Pollmann & Von Cramon, 2000, p. 13). A number of functional imaging studies have now been completed that have required human subjects to retain information over brief periods, accompanied by some extra task, and these working memory studies are discussed in more detail in Chapter 5. Suffice it to say that the monkey model has crucial relevance to the modelling of human neuropsychological functioning in this area.

Fuster's long-held theory of prefrontal function seems to support rather than contend with this view of prefrontal function. This theory proposes the prefrontal areas contribute by holding information over a temporal gap until behaviour is required. Cells within the prefrontal cortex have been found that might represent such a process. These cells "reverberate" and maintain activation over time until the required behaviour is enacted. Some of these cells respond to a combination of features or rules rather than a stimulus within a single modality. Thus, for example, some cells respond only to a stimulus that is rewarded or is the correct response, irrespective of its nature, suggesting a higher or more abstract level of processing than the posterior areas to which these cells are networked. Prefrontal cortex cells may also keep firing in anticipation of a response or have a delayed decay (see Fuster, 1997, for a review; Quintana & Fuster, 1999).

While it is well accepted that the prefrontal cortex, especially the mid-dorsolateral and mid-ventrolateral prefrontal areas, act in a role to maintain information "on-line" in the face of interference, other features of this system are more controversial. Some of these will be discussed in Chapter 5, but for the moment it is argued that the prefrontal cortex does not retain information "on-line" through activation of memory or experiences within the prefrontal cortex. It has already been argued that the prefrontal cortex contains directory schemas that activate the posterior knowledge store. The hypothesised role of the prefrontal cortex within working memory is to select out and activate the association areas that represent recent experience. There is an assumption that some modification of this temporary memory is required to tag it with its contextual elements. In this way past events are distinguished from each other, e.g. left versus right food well. The where, when, and order of the memory episode must be encoded and/or retrieved by the prefrontal structures to allow the descrimination between working memories over time.

Allocation of roles within the prefrontal cortex

Jonathan Cohen at Princeton University has been particularly interested in modelling frontal dysfunctioning attributed to schizophrenia (Cohen & Servan-Schreiber, 1992). This group has used tasks such as the Stroop, which is described above. In one elegant experiment Carter and MacDonald and colleagues (Carter et al., 2000; MacDonald, Cohen, Stenger, Carter, 2000) varied the Stroop instructions so that on one trial the subjects were randomly required to report the *colour* of the ink in which the word was written: the colour of the ink might be green when the word reads as RED. (This is a hard task because the colour conflicts with the more natural response to read.) On another trial the subjects were required to read the colour name and ignore the ink colour (easy). The authors conducted event-related fMRI, which allowed a functional image of the subjects both in the instruction period and later in the response period. Functional imaging of the instruction period showed heightened activation of the dorsolateral prefrontal cortex only when the subjects reported the

colour (instructions for the hard task were given). This activation was continued during the hard response only (reporting the colour) but this time the anterior cingulate was also activated. This experiment confirms the involvement of the anterior cingulate in the response to conflict tasks. The random presentation of the high- versus low-conflict task is especially useful since even the Stroop task may be learned and with practice the anterior cingulate is less involved (Gratton, Coles, & Donchin, 1992). One study suggest that it may be the degree of conflict rather than difficulty of the task which involves the anterior cingulate maximally (e.g. Botvinick et al., 1999) and from this and other work the group has proposed that the anterior cingulate is crucial for monitoring and (more recently) controlling conflict.

Their model (Figure 3.9) shows that two control processes are hypothesised. One is most obviously the influence of the instruction set. The prefrontal cortex is therefore seen as having a selective role in activating the appropriate response set (see module representing task demands). From his writings it is clear that Cohen is referring here to the selective process of the dorsolateral cortex. As indicated earlier in the Stroop study, when the instructions announced an attention-demanding process the dorsolateral cortex was activated and this was assumed to be a selective and strategic process that continued throughout the task into the response period. Cohen argues that when tasks require a choice of targets from a large number of distractors the dorsolateral prefrontal cortex is maximally activated to control such a selection. This view has been supported for some time in memory studies. Patients with dorsolateral lesions are well able to judge "familiarity" in recognition tasks, but when the recognition task is made more difficult by increasing the choice of items or making distractors more similar then the subject must retrieve context ("where", "when", and "order" of the stimulus) in order to make a decision. Under these circumstances the recognition task requires a retrieval process similar to that of recall (e.g Leonard, & Milner, 1991a, 1991b). The second monitoring control unit is the anterior cingulate, which according to this model is

FIG. 3.9

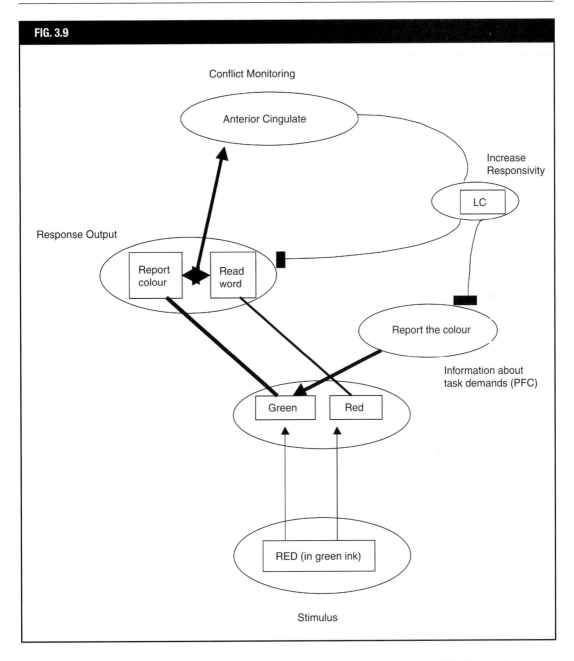

Model of the Stroop task according to Jonathon Cohen and colleagues' model (adapted from Cohen, 2000). See text for a description of this model.

important in monitoring conflict (see Figure 3.9). If more control is required then the anterior cingulate triggers the locus coeruleus, which increases arousal within the system to modulate the requisite arousal for the task.

Some objection may be made concerning a reference to the role of the anterior cingulate purely as a monitoring device. For example, in reviewing the role of the anterior cingulate in the process required of the Stroop and other tasks, Peterson and colleagues describe this as a structure playing a role in the allocation of attentional resources. They further describe its role in the modification of pathway strengths by reducing cross-talk between information processing that underlies a conflicting response (Peterson et al., 1999). Also, studies that are not obviously concerned with monitoring but do require attentional effort in retrieval of specific associations seem to reliably activate this structure, such as selecting words to complete a sentence (Nathaniel, Brown & Ron, 1996). Further support for a non-passive role for the anterior cingulate is reviewed in the next section. In fairness, Cohen's role for the anterior cingulate is not entirely passive (Cohen, 2000). In particular, as indicated, he refers to the modulating role of the anterior cingulate on the noradrenaline neurotransmitter system.

One of the markers for increased arousal associated with the increased presence of noradrenaline within the system is pupil size (Brown et al., 1999; Robertson, Mattingley, Rorden & Driver, 1998). Pupil size turns out to be a relatively sensitive measure of attentional load, that is, the amount of concentration that is being devoted to a task. In terms of Cohen's model the anterior cingulate is seen as driving the locus coeruleus, which in turn modulates the activation at the response output and the information about task demands module (see black rectangles in Figure 3.9). Recently, Coull, Buchel, Friston, & Frith (1999) have lent some support to the view that the frontal cortex does have an influence on the locus coeruleus and the noradrenergic/ norepinephrine system. They reveal a network that includes other structures such as the thalamus and sensory input areas. At present this system appears to have a modulating role that maintains an optimal level of cortical arousal depending on task demands. Therefore if subjects are sleep deprived there is an activation of thalamic regions during a demanding task in what seems to be a bid to compensate for low levels of baseline arousal (Portas et al., 1998). However, there is much to learn about the specific influence of the anterior cingulate within this system.

In summary Cohen's model suggests two control systems. The first control system is related to the selective attention role of the prefrontal cortex (dorsolateral area). This process is involved when instructions (information about task demands) prime a strategic selection. The second control process involves a conflict monitoring role of the anterior cingulate. As demands for focused attention increase, this information is fed back from the anterior cingulate to the locus coeruleus, which in turn increases the level of arousal by increasing levels of noradrenaline.

There are some uncertainties concerning this model, and for the Stroop experiment described above there are alternative interpretations. The prefrontal cortex and anterior cingulate are also modulated additionally by the serotonergic and dopaminergic systems.

Cohen (2000) suggests that the selective strategic skills of the dorsolateral prefrontal cortex and the anterior cingulate may act in concert so that when one is damaged the other will compensate. There appears to be some agreement with other authors when discussing the selective strategic role of the dorsolateral prefrontal cortex. Frith, in reviewing a series of imaging studies, points to the consistent activation of the dorsolateral prefrontal cortex during tasks that require *self-initiated*, *controlled search behaviour*. As soon as a task becomes automatic or easy, this area is less likely to be activated (e.g. Frith, 2000).

Despite the remaining questions concerning the role of the anterior cingulate and the nature of the neurotransmitter modulation, Cohen's specialised connectionist model provides one of the few testable theories in this area. In the remaining part of this chapter there will be an attempt to synthesise what has been learned about executive function and the specific contributions of the frontal lobe structures that serve this function.

Summary of the contribution of models of executive function

In the first part of this section we introduced Norman and Shallice's model, which provides a good introduction to modelling in this area. This model provides a description of how a patient with gross frontal damage may become a slave to external stimuli. From this perspective a perceptual stimulus may initiate a chain of behaviour that the frontal patient finds difficult to control and withdraw from. The explanatory power of such models is limited when describing the mechanism of disorganised behaviour when automatic or controlled behaviours become mixed or are repeated. Such behaviours as planning, organisation, were described in the introductory chapter in the context of Luria's model. These behaviours are worthy of more precise modelling and here Grafman's contribution is useful in proposing that the prefrontal cortex houses schemas that represent our knowledge system and the logical relationships within that system. Disorganisation of behaviour or poor planning occurs when these schema structures are undermined. The weighting of competing activations within the network becomes metaphorically unbalanced.

As a modification of this model, it was suggested that in keeping with some experimental work the frontal lobes may contain maps or directories of our experience (directory schemas), and that knowledge schemas are more likely more posteriorly within the association areas. Therefore combined lesions to both frontal and posterior lesions would have a greater impact on organised behaviour compared to lesions to the anterior area alone. Also, according to this proposal damage to the prefrontal cortex will only affect self-initiated schema activation—schema activation will still take place via the perceptual systems and in this way damage to the directory schemas may be compensated by external cues. Nevertheless, removal of the prefrontal influence in schema activation may result in inappropriate behaviour in which external stimulation triggers maladaptive schema-driven behaviours. In a very real way the patient becomes a slave to the environment.

By assigning a schema selection role to the prefrontal cortex the importance of these prefrontal structures in the temporary maintenance of information becomes clear. Temporary activation of a knowledge schema allows, by whatever mechanism, knowledge to enter awareness. Continued activation allows that knowledge to be maintained by using what is referred to rather broadly as working memory. It is perhaps a sign of species sophistication that abstract goals and strategies may be held in mind while other activities are conducted. In this way experiences may be demarcated in time and critical behaviours may be delayed.

Cohen and colleagues' model was then discussed, which described the role of the dorsolateral prefrontal cortex and the anterior cingulate in selection and monitoring respectively. It was suggested that the literature could be interpreted to provide a more proactive role for the anterior cingulate as a means of allocating attention rather than merely monitoring, although this is still controversial. Also, the possible role of the orbitofrontal cortex was referred to as contributing to the inhibition of a response. These issues are pursued further in the final sections of this chapter.

In the next section there is a more precise delineation of the roles of the various structures that contribute to what is loosely described as the executive system. With this information there is an attempt to provide a minimalist neuropsychological model that describes relationships between frontal structures that represent executive behaviour.

EXECUTIVE DYSFUNCTION AND THE PREFRONTAL CORTEX: THE ORBITAL, DORSOLATERAL, AND MEDIAL SYSTEMS

The difficulty of isolating function within clinical patients with natural lesions

When attempting to assign certain functional roles to brain structure it is important to support the functional imaging studies with lesion studies. The disadvantages of these two methods have been referred to in the introductory chapter. It is probably true that the progress in our knowledge concerning the role of the frontal lobes has been delayed by a dearth of lesion studies, which is in turn due to a scarcity of patients with discrete, clean lesions in this area.

For example, many patients suffering brain

trauma following a car accident suffer frontal contusion and other damage to the poles of the frontal and temporal lobe, but they also suffer shearing of axons in a number of areas including the brain stem. This is the case even with the compulsory wearing of seat-belts and air-bags because of the massive forces of deceleration of the brain upon impact. Shearing of axons within the brain stem and other areas generally reduces functional efficiency of the brain. Brain damage to the orbital lobes and other protruding areas such as the poles of the temporal lobes may also occur. Anosmia (loss of sense of smell) may also accompany such damage because the olfactory bulbs are situated ventrally, just beneath the orbital frontal cortex, and the orbital area also acts (among its other roles) as a type of association area for this sense. Thus loss of sense of smell and disinhibited social behaviour are often associated with ventral damage to the orbital frontal cortex, and this pattern is not uncommonly found by clinicians working with brain trauma patients.

We have already mentioned in Chapter 1 the affect on structures along the midline of the frontal lobe following a stroke involving the anterior cerebral artery. Added to this, one must consider complications following the rupture of an anterior communicating artery aneurysm. This may be followed by many dysexecutive signs, including an impact on organisation and verification of memory (see Chapter 5). However, again because the lesion is frequently diffuse, these patients act as a less than perfect lesion model for the prefrontal cortex and the anterior cingulate.

The dysfunctional social behaviour of patients with *tumours* may also sometimes raise suspicion and prompt assessment. Some of the patients we assess at our clinic have an original referral on the grounds of unusual behaviour, such as the woman who uncharacteristically started to neglect her personal appearance and housework, or the priest who was having difficulty with his teaching and was, according to the nuns, "attending too many masses". Tumour patients may often provide a good source of patients for lesion studies. However, tumours may infiltrate and press on areas remote to the site shown on the scan and

even when they have been removed there is some uncertainty concerning possible regrowth.

As indicated, patients with atrophy of subcortical structures such as those with *Huntington's disease* or *Huntington's chorea* and to a lesser extent Parkinson's disease also show signs of dysexecutive dysfunction in problem-solving tasks (Owen et al., 1992), but this disease is not normally associated with the severity of executive dysfunction described. There are of course a number of differences between individuals and the influence of depleted neurotransmitter systems is not reliably identified.

Finally, there are the patients with dementia. Most commonly, advanced cases of *Alzheimer's disease* often show the disinhibition, associated with loss of cells to the orbital region and other areas of the prefrontal cortex. There is often extreme loss of cells to the area known as the nucleus basalis of Meynert in the basal forebrain, which produces the cholinergic neurotransmitter substances common to this frontal area and which activate structures such as the hippocampus. During the later stages of their disease these patients may show disinhibited behaviour, personal exposure, swearing and aggression, which makes caring for these patients all the more difficult. Although there is increased cell loss from the frontal lobes during this later stage it is not possible to delineate the specific associations between neuropathology and executive dysfunction.

Rarer cases of *frontal lobe dementia*, *Pick's disease*, and *Creutzfeldt–Jakob* disease also show the signs of executive and emotional dysfunction (Neary & Snowden, 1991). These patients may all show the full gamut of disinhibited and inconsequential behaviour that brings the patient to the notice of the clinician. An example is a woman who was eventually diagnosed in our clinic with a frontal lobe dementia who had a benign smile and facile conversation. She came to the notice of her employers at the betting shop where she worked when she gave an undeserving customer $35,000.

Apart from the difficulty in obtaining patients with well-defined natural lesions there is the problem that executive dysfunction may not be limited to patients with frontal lobe pathology. As indicated, the prefrontal cortex functions within a network to other structures. Executive behaviour depends on the efficient interaction with those posterior structures and therefore a pervasive disconnection would theoretically decrease frontal influence sufficient to cause dysexecutive behaviours (e.g. Vilkki, 1992). Large and diffuse posterior lesions may therefore undermine the executive role of frontal structures.

As functional imaging becomes more sophisticated we have come to rely more and more on information in this area. However, caution is required: we must constantly remind ourselves that these studies only represent a secondary measure of brain activation. Blood flow may be moving to an area for various underlying reasons. An avalanche of studies, some of which ascribe "centres" of functional relevance to each new activation, has earned the cynical observation that functional neuroimaging is the phrenology of the twenty-first century. Such a statement is almost always said in jest, but there is always the grain of truth that warns. These problems – and with the aid of other modern imaging techniques – predicate the following sections, which describe studies that have focused on delineating the functional contribution of prefrontal structures and the anterior cingulate towards executive behaviour.

A model of dysexecutive behaviour must, to some extent, attempt to explain the differences between patients with reference to the differences in projections and biochemical influences that exist within the prefrontal cortex (Oscar-Berman, McNamara, & Freedman, 1991). The cortical and subcortical connections and the prevalent neurotransmitter (chemical that allows one neurone to activate another) differentiate areas within the prefrontal cortex (Barbas & Pandya, 1991; Petrides & Pandya, 1994). These are broadly discussed here in terms of the orbitofrontal cortex, the dorsolateral cortex within the prefrontal cortex, and the medial prefrontal cortex including the anterior cingulate.

Orbitofrontal cortex

In general there is support from human and animal research for an orbital role that encourages new associations and inhibits old previously learned associations between reward and behaviour (see Rolls, 2000, for a review). In other words this area is important in allowing us to act flexibly, giving up old ways of responding and taking on new ways. However, in order to complete this important role many others have also drawn attention to its hypothesised ability to take into account emotional reaction to a stimulus. Thus the stress is on defining the nature of the *reward* and behaviour. In many ways this is intuitively reasonable, if we are gaining unpleasant feedback when we make a particular response to a stimulus. For example, if we have been used to doing well on the stock market by investing in a particular share we feel good about it and therefore continue with this behaviour; however, with a downturn in the market this behaviour is less rewarding: we feel bad about the behaviour and cease to invest in the share. It might be predicted that a patient with orbitofrontal damage will not take full advantage of this negative emotional feedback and continue with the old behaviour.

The network of neural projections between the orbitofrontal cortex and other brain areas reveals how this role might be fulfilled. The prefrontal cortex receives projections from the association areas, which allows the area access to analysed sensory information. Although work with non-human animals suggests the strongest role for this area is as an association area for olfactory and gustatory sensory information, one might expect this to be somewhat modified in the human brain. We seem to be more dependent on visual and auditory sensory areas and there are important connections between this frontal area and the end-points of analysis of all these sensory systems. There are further connections between the orbital area and the medial and anterior aspects of the temporal lobe which allows the orbitofrontal cortex influential involvement in the learning of associations.

To allow for the emotional associations described above, there are further important connections between the orbitofrontal cortex between its caudal or more posterior aspect and the limbic system. The limbic system is a general term for a group of structures that are discussed more fully in later chapters. However, the cingulate, hypothalamus, and amygdala are prominently associated with the limbic system and a role in the processing of emotional information. There is therefore a relationship between the orbitofrontal cortex, the sensory areas, the amygdala for emotion, and the medial temporal lobe (including the hippocampus for memory) that allows its role within emotional learning. In short, then, this cortical area is in a well-placed position to register the association between a sensory stimulus and the associated emotional response. The orbitofrontal cortex therefore allows a synthesis between sensory and emotional information so that sensory information may be identified for its motivational characteristics. Neurones have been found in this area that are dedicated to deciding whether the stimulus is rewarding irrespective of its perceptual qualities (Fuster, 1997; Markowitsch, 1988; Rolls, 2000). Also, recent functional neuroimaging work has revealed that certain areas within the orbitofrontal cortex that are activated according to the magnitude of the reward or punishment experienced.

The most obvious indication of the role of the orbitofrontal area comes from patients with brain damage in this area. Most of these unfortunate cases have bilateral damage to this area, which may additionally include some of the medial prefrontal cortex and the anterior cingulate. These patients are described as being disinhibited and terms such as pseudopsychopathic and acquired sociopathy are used to describe persons who appear to be unfeeling in their social behaviour without intention (Blumer & Benson, 1975; Eslinger & Damasio, 1985; Malloy & Richardson, 1994; Malloy, Bihrle, Duffy, & Cimino, 1993; Saver, & Damasio, 1991; Tranel, 1994). This behaviour has been discussed previously, but it is seen here for its mechanism in terms of the orbitofrontal cortex as an agent for behavioural control. The effect of releasing control and, therefore, allowing emotional and socially inappropriate behaviour is seen by some as a failure to register the emotional feedback that is associated with negative behaviour (Damasio, 1994) .

The orbitofrontal area also appears to have an influential role in modulating attention. The influence over the cholinergic neurotransmitter system via the neurones of the nucleus basalis of Meynert in the basal forebrain appears to be important in this respect. This neurotransmitter system is influential in innervating the neocortex, hippocampus, and cingulate (Mesulam, 1988). There is growing support for the role of this neurotransmitter within attention. Lesions in this area could affect a wide variety of behaviours. Most obviously, patients with bilateral lesions in this area may be easily distracted by external cues. They also tend to perseverate (continuing on with a response when it is more appropriate to cease responding), and therefore show a tendency to be captured by a stimulus irrespective of internal goals.

In order to analyse more carefully the mechanisms underlying these general behaviours of disinhibited social behaviour, vulnerability to distraction and the link between stimulus and reward, it is useful to look more closely at the way different areas of the orbitofrontal cortex (OFC) appear to be playing different roles. At this time a functional division may be made between medial aspects, anterior lateral and posterior lateral aspects of the orbitofrontal cortex. For some time animal studies have implicated the orbitofrontal cortex in a role associating reward with the stimulus (see Rolls, 2000, for a review). Functional imaging studies have promoted the view that medial aspects are particularly related to the association of the reward with the stimulus. As indicated, memory for these relationships may be allowed by the connections between the medial orbitofrontal areas and the medial temporal lobe areas, including the hippocampus, which is important for laying down new memories. The medial aspect of the orbitofrontal cortex is seen to be representing the rightness, familiarity, and rewarding aspects to a stimulus (Elliott, Dolan, & Frith, 2000). In humans functional imaging studies suggest that this area is involved in weighing up the correct choice when judgements are required, such as in a situation in which a judgement about several candidate relationships must be made (Elliott, Frith, & Dolan, 1997; Elliott, Rees & Dolan, 1999; Elliott, Sahakian et al., 1997).

In contrast, studies suggest that the anterior–lateral aspects of the orbitofrontal cortex play an inhibiting role. This finding is encouraging because clinical studies of patients, mentioned above, also support an inhibiting role for OFC. Support for an inhibiting role of ventral, inferior prefrontal structures comes also from studies described as "go–no go" tasks, described ealier. These require both flexibility and inhibition of response (Rubia et al., 2000).

The evidence of a role for the orbitofrontal cortex in the inhibition of responses that were previously rewarded is particularly strong. For example, when subjects must learn to respond to stimulus B and not stimulus A, patients with orbital lesions may learn this relationship. However, when the response requirements are reversed so that now stimulus A but not B is rewarded, the patients have significant difficulty in inhibiting the originally learned relationship. Such patients may signify verbally the correct stimulus but then behave again in error (Rolls, 1994). This curious dissociation between "knowing and doing" is reported occasionally during clinical assessment of patients (Teuber, 1964; Walsh, 1991). Dias, Robbins and Roberts (1996) lesioned the orbitofrontal cortex in marmoset monkeys and found significant impairment on a reversal learning task that was not present in the monkeys with lateral frontal lesions (superior to the orbital area). Lesions to the nucleus basalis of Meynert in the basal forebrain, causing a cholinergic depletion in the marmoset, also selectively impairs reversal learning (Roberts, Robbins, Everitt, & Muir, 1992).

The connections from this lateral anterior area of the orbitofrontal cortex with other prefrontal cortical areas, such as the dorsolateral prefrontal cortex (Petrides and Pandya, 1994), would allow the inhibition of other executive behaviour. The more posterior or caudal aspects of the lateral orbital area are more associated with heightened emotional stress response. Given the results of series of MRI with normal patients (Elliott, Dolan, & Frith, 2000) the following scenario reveals the function roles of this complex area.

A gambler wishes to place a bet on a horse. The gambler has previously won money on this particular horse and therefore it is hypothesised that the medial aspects of the orbitofrontal cortex have provided a positive rewarding relationship between this particular horse and the behaviour of betting. The medial aspects of the orbitofrontal cortex are seen as creating reward associations and therefore if the gambler had previously bet on some *other* horses in the race with occasional success then these relationships would be seen to provide some uncertainty. In MRI studies these more medial areas of the orbitofrontal cortex are seen to be activated when such uncertainty exists and a judgement has to be made between alternatives.

To continue with our example, during the pre-race showing of the favoured horse the gambler notes that his horse has a slight limp. The lateral aspects of the orbitofrontal cortex would now be activated in a process that would inhibit the urge to gamble on this horse (inhibition of a previously rewarded response). The gambler decides to "blow caution to the wind" and bet on the horse. During the race, the gambler sees the horse go from first to last position and the caudal or posterior–lateral areas of the orbitofrontal cortex are activated as part of the emotional stress response.

This type of everyday situation has been simulated in gambling experiments with patients by Antonio Damasio's, group (see Bechara, Damasio & Damasio, 2000) and in a series of functional imaging experiments conducted by Elliott and colleagues (e.g. Elliott, Frith, & Dolan, 1997; Elliott, Sahakian, et al., 1997). There is a more substantial review of this work in Chapter 9.

It should be noted that the behaviour of betting on a horse that clearly has a limp can be seen as being "inconsequential"—a type of impulsive behaviour that is not unlike that of patients that have been described as being disinhibited. The same behaviour can also be represented more formally in an experimental situation as an inability to inhibit an old learned rewarding relationship and is similar to the problem of reversal learning in which previously learned behaviour cannot be extinguished or unlearned.

The dorsolateral prefrontal cortex

While there are structural connections between the orbitofrontal cortex and the dorsolateral cortex (Cavada et al., 2000; Petrides & Pandya, 1994), the dorsolateral connections are most obviously with the polymodal association areas (the final area of sensory analysis, which is more sensory neutral in its representation) and other areas involved in the *later* analysis of sensory information. However, the dorsolateral area appears to utilise this information differently when compared to the orbitofrontal cortex: unlike the latter the dorsolateral prefrontal cortex appears to be manipulating and selecting this sensory information. There are also connections with the medial temporal lobe that are assumed to have some association with mnemonic or memory features. The relationship between areas within the dorsolateral cortex and the maintenance of an internal representation of a stimulus (keeping information in mind) has been referred to above and will be returned to in the next two chapters on attention and memory.

This dorsolateral prefrontal area is similarly implicated in selective attention (detecting a target from an array of items). An association is made between selective attention and working memory in Chapter 5. Broadly, attention is required in order to select information that has to be kept "in mind" and the functional imaging studies support the importance of this area in this role.

Supporting evidence for the dorsolateral prefrontal cortex for keeping information "in mind" in working memory additionally comes from the work of Adele Diamond with infants and young children (see Diamond, 1998, for a review). Because the prefrontal cortex is a late-developing area of the brain, infants and young children show performances that sometimes appears not unlike that of adults with lesions to the dorsolateral prefrontal cortex (see Diamond, 1998, for a review). Normal infants (in their first year) have difficulty with keeping information in mind (delayed response tasks), while older children of 3–4 years old may have some difficulty in a children's Stroop task in which the child has to say "night" to a picture of a day scene, e.g. blue sky with sun, and say "day" to a night scene, e.g. black picture with a moon and stars. Also there may be difficulty switching categories, e.g. shape, when previously they had sorted for colour. These skills develop over time in normal infants and young children and it is assumed that this development coincides with prefrontal development, which is more delayed compared to other brain areas (see Chapter 10).

Diamond et al. (1994) and separately Welsh et al. (1990) have studied the development of executive skills in children suffering from a disorder called phenylketonuria (PKU). This is a congenital disorder in which phenylalanine (Phe) is not metabolised and consequently builds up in the system, causing toxic brain effects and retardation in the child. Diet may overcome this problem by reducing Phe but elevated levels may remain and the difficulties in converting the amino acid Phe as a precursor to the amino acid tyrosine also remain. Tyrosine is seen as being important to the development of the dopamine neurotransmitter system, which is influential on prefrontal function. This effect seems to be especially influential in early infancy (Diamond, 1998, p. 149).

Diamond argues that lowered dopamine is likely to be the cause of these *treated* PKU children's poor performance on the "dorsolateral prefrontal-associated tasks". In these children there tends to be a delay in achieving the developmental progress on executive tasks such as the delayed response task. This broad paradigm was described in monkey experiments earlier. In the human infant version the subject has to keep in mind the position of a hidden toy during a brief distraction (Diamond, 1998).

This argument linking developmental problems with the delayed response task and dopamine depletion is more firmly supported than with some of the other children's executive tasks, which are also performed poorly by these children. Diamond's and Welch's work shows a relationship between higher plasma levels of Phe and a decrement in performance on these tasks. As indicated bilateral lesions to the dorsolateral prefrontal cortex in adult monkeys result in impairments in these same working memory-sustained attention tasks and so does dopamine depletion in monkeys following the injection of dopamine atagonists (Sawaguchi & Goldman-Rakic, 1991). Diamond appears to maintain a critical attitude to this theory and she reports that there remains some difficulty in reconciling the inconsistent findings on tasks in this area to a single model (Diamond, 1998).

Given the plethora of imaging studies on the topic of working memory there is no doubt concerning the importance of the dorsolateral prefrontal cortex (DPFC) to tasks that require keeping a series of different items of information in mind over time. More recently researchers have been more interested in differentiating the contributions of different areas within this large area of cortex. This kind of specialisation is discussed in more depth in Chapter 5, but in terms of our goal towards building a model of executive function a few examples will be mentioned at this point. In tasks that require patients to generate words according to a rule, e.g. verbal fluency tasks, the left *ventral* area of the DPFC is consistently activated in functional imaging studies (e.g. Petersen et al., 1988; Raichle et al., 1994) (see Figure 3.10).

In Chapter 5 we discuss the work of D'Esposito and others (D'Esposito, Postle, & Rypma, 2000), who have used event-related functional imaging to find discrete activations within the DPFC that correspond to subtly different roles. The mid-ventrolateral regions were found to be most activated when a stimulus was selected and interfering stimuli was inhibited, while within the mid-dorsolateral region there are areas that are more obviously associated with the manipulation of stimuli that are held "on-line". An example of this last type of processing is the requirement to place a series of random letters in alphabetical order without writing them down.

Functional imaging studies that require subjects to produce and learn a self-initiated series of finger movements find peaks of activation in more dorsal–posterior aspects of this area and both the left and right hemispheres are activated (Frith, 2000). Therefore while there is an overlap of activation, some specialisation appears to exist.

Apart for the need to maintain information "in mind", the feature in common with these tasks is

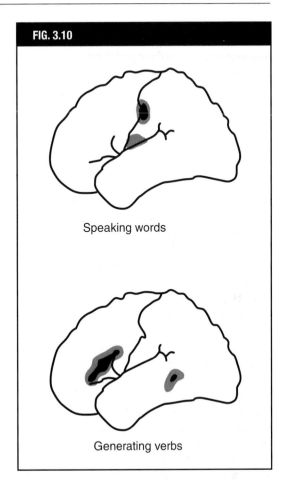

FIG. 3.10

Speaking words

Generating verbs

Illustration of the functional imaging scan (adapted from Posner & Raichle, 1997). In (a) A the subject is reporting a word that appears on the screen in a passive manner. In (b) the subject has to generate a verb associated with the noun presented on the screen (see also Raichle et al., 1994).

that they require self-controlled responses, i.e. not copied or pre-learned, and they also require the selection of a response. However, some tasks have revealed this feature without any obvious working memory component. Raichle required subjects to produce verbs that were associated with nouns presented on a screen, e.g. *pound* for the word *hammer* (Raichle et al., 1994). The left ventral aspect of the DPFC was activated (see Figure 3.10). However, when the subjects were scanned later following practice with the same word associations the DPFC ceased to be activated following the first trial. Similarly, in studies in which subjects have to decide when to make a movement, say with their forefinger, these self-initiated movements are associated with DPFC activation. However, if the subjects merely have to move the same finger every time they hear a tone then the activation in this area is significantly reduced (Jahanshahi, Jenkins, & Brown et al., 1995). Therefore, self-initiated novel decisions to use or select one word or movement compared to another invokes more metabolic processes in the DPFC.

As mentioned, some patients with dorsolateral lesions have problems providing numerous instances given an exemplar, e.g.words beginning a certain letter. They have an impoverished output on these verbal fluency tasks (Jones-Gotman & Milner, 1977). Frith (2000) reviews a number of functional imaging studies using different materials and prefers the description of "sculpting" as a reference to the way a selection of a response is initiated in a controlled manner.

In summary, the DPFC appears to have two broad roles. The first function appears to *contribute* to what we commonly refer to as consciousness. In our daily behaviour we often have to select out an image or stimulus and retain it for inspection or for learning; the DFPC appears to play an important role in this type of working memory. The second role appears to be in a type of *self*-generated selection process—a role that is accentuated when the task is a novel one. In order to make such a selection and search within existing memory banks it is argued that there must exist some form of directory or categorisation of what is available within the memory store. These references are referred to as "directory schemas". It is argued by many authors that for the DFPC to play its organising and selective role on behaviour it must have extensive networks with posterior association areas where sensory and other information is stored. In other words, while the orbitofrontal cortex is broadly seen as contributing to the motivational processes important to the controlling and regulation of behaviour, the DFPC is seen as having a role that is more related to the self-initiated selection and organisation of information.

The medial frontal cortex and the anterior cingulate (AC)

The medial area includes the medial prefrontal cortical area and the anterior cingulate gyrus. At its most anterior and inferior aspect it extends towards the medial aspect of the orbital cortex, while at its most posterior, dorsal aspect, it leads on to motor areas such as the supplementary motor area. The supplementary motor area is associated with the role of flexibility of internally planned motor movements (Roland, Larsen, Lassen, & Skinhoj, et al, 1980). There are also connections with the hippocampus from this medial area. The more posterior areas of the cingulate, 31, 23, 29, and 30, are activated during memory tasks (Fazio et al., 1992). As amnesic patients tend to show decreased activation in the cingulate, basal forebrain, thalamus, and hippocampus this suggests that the anterior cingulate plays a role in a network response within new learning (Grasby et al., 1993).

There are a few recorded cases that have shown akinetic mutism following bilateral lesions to the anterior cingulate. In such cases, the patient is able to track with eye movements, but is largely inert and without speech. Sometimes the supplementary area is also involved. These cases are stroke patients and always include damage to neighbouring areas, although the cingulate (Brodmann's area 24) is most consistently damaged (see Devinsky, Morrell & Vogt, 1995, for a review). When thinking of a mechanism for this disorder it may be wrong to suggest that this is purely an inability to make the required motor response (as is the case with patients with "locked-in syndrome" following brain stem stroke). One female patient who recovered from this akinetic syndrome following bilateral anterior cingulate damage reported that she did not talk because she had nothing to say and that her mind was empty. She could follow conversations but felt no will to reply (Damasio & Van Hoesen, 1983). Although the verbal reports do not necessarily match the mechanism, these kinds of reports seem to support the importance of the anterior cingulate in subserving "drive" or motivation.

While it is still speculative, there is mounting

support for the view that the medial frontal cortex, and in particular the anterior cingulate, is implicated in the behaviour associated with Gilles de la Tourette syndrome (GLTS). These patients have tics and other sudden involuntary movements and may lack internal control in some of their vocalisations. They may swear or suddenly say something rude that one would normally keep to oneself. They also often have marked obsessional symptoms in terms of repeated hand-washing or counting rituals. Support for a connection between the cingulate and GLTS is broadly noted by Devinsky et al. (1995) as follows:

1. Electrical stimulation of the cingulate in monkeys results in the kinds of staccato involuntary sounds that are characteristic of GLTS patients' vocalisations.
2. The anterior cingulate is associated with the initiation of speech.
3. The principal biochemical abnormality is a dopaminergic *hyperactivity* and the cingulate is part of the dopaminergic pathway that comes from the ventral tegmental area.
4. There are similarities in the movements of GLTS and the involuntary human movements following stimulation of the cingulate.
5. There is a reduction of glucose uptake in this area in GLTS subjects.
6. Lesions to the cingulate may result in a decrease in obsessive-compulsive symptoms.

It is possible that GLTS represents an over-stimulation of the initiating qualities of the cingulate. Thus the speculation runs that while lesions to this area reduce spontaneous initiation, the stimulation of this area possibly results in over-initiation of unwanted behaviours that should be contained.

Cingulotomy is a surgical procedure that has been used for various psychiatric disorders with the aim of modifying emotional response. When it is used to reduce pain, patients report that they still feel the pain, but that they seem to worry less about it (Foltz & White, 1962). Chronic pain patients, following a bilateral cingulectomy, may become less concerned about their pain, but they also become less spontaneous and perform less well on tasks such as verbal fluency that require the patient to initiate a number of responses spontaneously.

The cingulate (ventral aspect), which is also seen as part of the limbic system, has projections to the amygdala, which has been described as the central processor of emotion, and the anterior cingulate has an interactive relationship with this structure. The effects of the cingulate on emotion are apparent in epileptic patients. Seizure activity in this area is far more likely to be associated with a report of an emotional response when compared to seizures focused in the temporal lobe (Devinsky, Morrell, & Vogt, 1995).

There is a description in this chapter and in next Chapter 4 of the anterior cingulate being involved in focused attention, in tasks where there is a conflict of responses. PET scan imaging work with such tasks as the Stroop (described above) leads to the belief that the anterior cingulate has a role to play in flexibility and in the spontaneous control of a new response, especially when there are distractions that may encourage an alternative response (Pardo, Pardo, Janer, & Raichle, 1990). There are a large number of tasks that require a spontaneous controlled response which show activation of the anterior cingulate. Also, evoked potential studies that show a representation of the brain's electrical response to stimuli also point to the anterior cingulate as being active at a time just prior to the onset of a controlled response. This evoked response is prior to other motor areas such as the supplementary motor areas that are also often active prior to a response (Devinsky et al., 1995, p. 287).

One of the challenges for modern researchers is to dissociate the role of the DPFC from that of the anterior cingulate in tasks that require self-initiated controlled attention. The difficulty arises because these two structures are often both activated in such tasks. As previously suggested, Cohen and his co-workers have ascribed a monitoring role to anterior cingulate but this description would seem to be too passive a role to fit with some of the lesion studies described above.

Area 32 of the anterior cingulate is activated in the self-generated word and finger movements, described above, and this consistency does suggest that the role is attention related—certainly in the study by Jahanshahi and colleagues described above (Jahanshahi et al., 1995) when comparing the activation of the DPFC with the anterior cingulate. The DPFC appeared to play a more self-initiated selective role since while the dorsolateral area was predominantly activated in this condition, the anterior cingulate was activated more consistently during both the self-selected motor response condition and in a condition that required the subject to monitor a pattern of copied movements. Because the monitoring of copied movements required no self-initiation the anterior cingulate might be seen in a purely attentional role in this task.

However, Petersen and previously Posner have argued that there is increased involvement of the DPFC when the selection or focus on a response is required; there is the proposal that the anterior cingulate is most activated when allocation of attentional resource is required in the face of interference (Posner & Petersen, 1990; Peterson et al., 1999), for example, in the case when a subject is required to be involved in dual tasks (motor movements and verbal generation) rather than single tasks (Fletcher, Frith, Grasby et al., 1995). Therefore in tasks in which the DFPC and the anterior cingulate are both activated it is persuasive that the anterior cingulate is involved in the allocation of resources within a focused attention role. Increased activation of the anterior cingulate occurs when the selection processes of the DPFC require more attentional resource.

The anterior cingulate is especially likely to be involved in controlled responses that require an overcoming of the natural, automatic or reflexive response. The role of this structure in the Stroop task has already been referred to but there is also a role within the control of reflexive eye movements (Paus, 1996). Recent work suggests that the anterior cingulate and the mid cingulate may be divided into a number of different areas playing different roles i.e. different areas for the control of pain compared to attention (Frith & Frith, 1999). Such functional differentiation varies in terms of the exact position between individuals, but func-

tional separation remains constant within an individual (Posner & Rothbart, 1996).

In summary, from these studies the executive role of the anterior cingulate appears to be most obvious in tasks that require some concentration, self-direction, and focus. Tasks that involve the initiation of a response and the direction of attentional *resources* towards a goal of controlled behaviour are seen to tap the function of this structure. Prior to a more definitive functional analysis, it appears also that this structure, which has extensive connections with emotional systems, is also associated with the rather broad and ill-defined concept of "drive".

TOWARDS A MODEL OF EXECUTIVE FUNCTION

It is clear from the functional description of the various areas of the prefrontal cortex and the anterior cingulate that these areas have an adaptive role, especially when novel and controlled behaviours are required. In the first section of this chapter there was a broader description of executive dysfunction under the topics of control, organisation, synthesis and judgement, attention, planning, sequencing and monitoring, and personality. This broad adaptive role might be expected from brain structures that have extensive networked connection with other brain structures and a wide range of influence in the ways in which we adapt to the environment.

In describing a model of the functional influence of the various frontal lobe structures there is obvious uncertainty. However, patterns of functional representation are emerging and these are represented in the minimalist model shown in Figure 3.11. In this model the orbital frontal cortex and the anterior cingulate appear to provide a controlling role. The anterior cingulate is most often associated with initiating behaviours (drive) and the focusing of attention in the presence of distraction. The orbitofrontal cortex is most frequently associated with allowing a motivated association between a sensory signalled reward and a response, but also has areas that appear to

TABLE 3.2

Outline of behavioural and neurophysiological influences of the prefrontal cortex and anterior cingulate

Prefrontal area	Orbital	Dorsolateral	Medial
Neurophysiological influences	1. Projections to the limbic system, e.g. amygdala, hypothalamus, also tertiary areas of the inferior aspect of the temporal lobe 2. Lateral and medial division, with the lateral area having more connections with other prefrontal structures and the medial having more connections with memory-related structures, e.g. hippocampus 3. Influence over cholinergic system in nucleus basalis of Meynert in the basal forebrain 4. Olfactory and gustatory sensory area.	1. Neurones surrounding the principal sulcus work in concert with secondary and tertiary sensory zones within the temporal and parietal lobes 2. Efferents to the premotor area 3. Influence on brain stem monoamine sites, e.g. noradrenaline	1. Cingulate gyrus and SMA have connections to other subcortical motor areas within the basal ganglia 2. Also there are connections with the hippocampus 3. Ventromedial connections with other limbic system areas (amygdala)
Psychological dysfunction	1. Emotional disinhibition 2. Difficulty in maintaining voluntary gaze against distraction Vulnerability to distraction on memory tests 3. Poor discrimination of smell	1. Poor internal representation of sensory information. Poor memory encoding of context, when, where and sequence of to-be-remembered material. Poor selective attention when presented with multiple stimuli 2. Difficulties in sequencing motor movements, especially of the face. 3. Timing and sequencing	1. Cognitive inflexibility, hypokinesis, memory disorders, especially those requiring flexibility. Changing from one set to another 2. Memory impairment 3. Allocating emotional significance 4. Drive 5. Restraining a reflexive or habitually guided visual gaze

be important for controlling and inhibiting that response once it has been created. The position of the orbital prefrontal cortex allows it to direct and combine the sensory information with motivational associations. Such associations are likely to be supplied by the emotional valence created by such structures as the amygdala with which it is connected. The dorsolateral pre-frontal cortex embodies many of the qualities of the other two areas but is more obviously involved with the direction and *autonomous* initiation of search, organisation, and selection

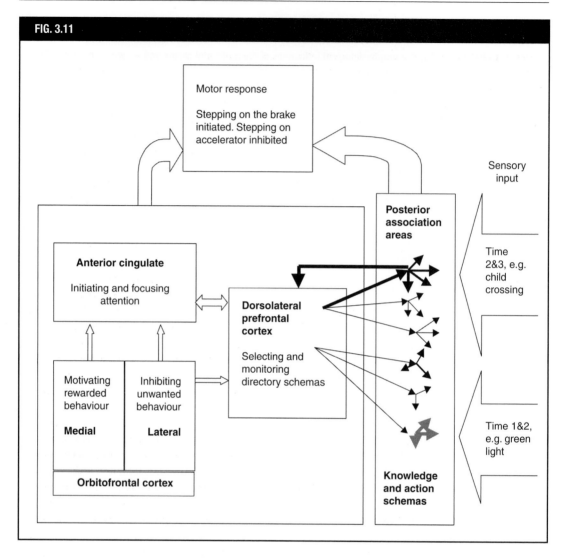

FIG. 3.11

The executive system. A simple framework for describing the influence of the prefrontal cortex in controlling and selecting knowledge units or schemas that initiate routines of behaviours. The anterior cingulate and orbital areas initiate and inhibit schema selection, a selection process that takes place within the dorsolateral prefrontal cortex. The dorsolateral prefrontal cortex both selects and monitors schemas. The novel and non-routine behaviour is produced by serially activating different schemas.

of information that is external (perceptual) or internally represented within working memory.

This model does not illustrate aspects of motor or emotional control, which will be elaborated on in the appropriate chapters. This model has obvious similarities with other models such as the Norman and Shallice, Grafman, and Cohen models described earlier but elaborates on the relationship between function and brain struc-

ture. In this model behaviour is determined by a perceptual trigger or executive control or a combination of these two. The description of the perceptual triggers is no different from that described by Norman and Shallice's contention scheduling at Time 1 for the example in Figure 3.10. The example of the motorist stepping on the accelerator at the green light is described in terms of the green light triggering an action schema that produces the automatic acceleration behaviour. In the case of the unusual behaviour of a child running in front of the car a chain of responses would be occurring. Clearly some emotional associations would be represented by this perceptual stimulus of the child and the orbitofrontal cortex would initiate an inhibition of the action schema normally triggered by the green light. The next stage in the process would be a combined response from the DPFC and the anterior cingulate. The anterior cingulate would allow the allocation of attentional resources to the new novel stimulus. Finally the appropriate "avoiding steering" action schema would be selected via the *directory schemas* within the dorsolateral prefrontal cortex at Time 2. Following this there would be a number of phases involving Time 3, 4 etc. which are not shown in the diagram. These are the controlled adjustments that would be needed during the evasive action. The child might stop running or not be running as fast as the driver thought; an oncoming car may force a decision to swerve in the other direction. With each of these adjustments the activation of the appropriate action schema and the old schema would be inhibited. In this way the author follows Grafman's view that all behaviours involve schema activation. Fast automatic behaviour becomes more resource intensive when there is a constant reselection of different schemas. Novel tasks become resource intensive, and require more attention and "effort" because we cannot rely on one schematic representation; rather we have to select a number of different schemas and parts of schemas in order to complete the required behaviour.

In this example the term action schema is used but it is assumed that there are a number of different types of schemas. This topic is developed more thoroughly in Chapter 5 but it can be seen, for example, that a chess player may select a schema that represents a game strategy of defence that is considered with other strategies prior to any final action being formulated.

A further contribution of this framework is the proposed extended executive responsibility of the prefrontal cortex as a monitoring device. The term monitoring is a rather vague concept: it is

not too different from awareness but assumes some level of checking the external environment, which includes a person's own behaviour. In the examples of "capture slips" cited earlier it is clear that monitoring is more extensive in controlled novel tasks, and when we are extremely aroused or very relaxed "monitoring" sometimes break down and we make mistakes. When discussing the problems that occur when two automatic behaviours are confused, as in the case of some capture slips, Schwartz (1995) argues " . . . if routine action production is as prone to error as this, and it falls to supervisory attention to monitor for errors and correct them before they are overtly expressed, then the supervisory attention system is playing a more active role in routine action production than is generally appreciated"(p. 324). Monitoring is constant, otherwise the executive system would not respond when adaptations are required. Monitoring of automatic behaviour that is represented by a hypothetical single schema, which has been strongly triggered by a perceptual input, taxes prefrontal resources to a lesser degree when compared to the need during novel behaviour, which requires the serial selection of a number of different schemas.

Therefore more changes in the selection of schemas will require more attentional resources. However, there is a second factor that is present in many models and relates to competition between schemas. For example, if the patient is asked to carry out the unfamiliar behaviour of pouring a cup into a teapot, this unfamiliar task may need more monitoring because there is a more entrenched competing schema, which involves pouring the teapot into the cup. Schema strength has a bearing on whether a particular behaviour is activated compared to its competition. If the schema activation required is well learned then it will be triggered more easily by the appropriate perceptual stimulus, but it will also be more likely to interfere with competing behaviours within the same context. Capture slips are more likely to occur when the competing schema is strong or has a high probability of occurring within that same context (Cooper & Shallice, 2000). In Figure 3.11, the perceptual triggering at Time 1 is an entrenched and well-learned response; switching to a less well-learned response would seem to be more challenging according to this model.

Therefore in the model that is developing here attentional resource, referred to generally as monitoring, is required to a greater degree according to three related variables: (a) the number of new schema selections required within a specific time, (b) the strength of the activation of the required schema (the degree to which it has been learned as a response) and (c) the strength of the competing schema(s). Such a relationship is intuitively reasonable but is yet to be empirically tested, although there is a start in this direction by some researchers (e.g. Cooper & Shallice, 2000).

Previously, there has been some discussion concerning the hypothetical "directory schemas" that are represented in Figure 3.11. These are representations within the prefrontal cortex of information that is stored more posteriorly within the association areas. A search within memory for a particular identity, for example, "an object that begins with 'W' and is found on yachts", requires the involvement of directory schemas and a selected self-driven search until we come up with "winch" or "windlass", and no doubt other examples. A judgement concerning "How many camels are there in the Netherlands?" would require a similar use of directory schemas, as would the requirement of organising a set of objects into different self-derived categories. All these tasks require a goal oriented, strategic serial activation of schemas on a trial basis.

There are, needless to say, a number of tricky issues to be resolved and one of these concerns the issue of goals. Goals may be in the form of long-term aims that are responsive to internal states, e.g. satiation, hunger. Alternatively, they may be considered to be responsive to expectations of reward, whether the reward is material or self-esteem related. It is generally assumed that goals are achieved by adopting a strategy or strategies that are maintained over time. Patients with gross frontal damage appear to be unable to maintain behaviour towards achieving a goal. In Chapter 9 is a description of one of the earliest recorded patients to sustain gross frontal damage, called Phineus Gage. Phineus Gage who was the victim of an accident in which a metal bar travelled though his skull when he was acting as a foreman of a gang that was laying track for a railway company. He is described by his treating doctor as "impatient of restraint or advice when it conflicts with his desires, at times pertinaciously obstinate, yet capricious and vacillating, divining many plans for operation, which are no sooner arranged than they are abandoned in turn for others more feasible" (Macmillan, 1986). The same failure to work towards a consistent endpoint may also be seen in the earlier description of Wilder Penfield's sister's difficulty in preparing a meal. Working towards a goal requires all the elements described in this model. The patient must maintain the goal 'in mind' or working memory, appropriate action must be selected over time at appropriate intervals, distractions must be ignored, and previously rewarded behaviour may need to be inhibited. With an internal state such as hunger the subject is constantly prompted by internal physiological states but a more long-term goal without immediate and salient rewarding consequences such as completing a service on a car may be more difficult for the patient. External distractions such as a newspaper lying open on a chair by the car must be ignored. Without focused attention (AC) and self-selection skills (DPFC) and the inhibition of previously rewarded response (orbital) the patient with gross frontal lesions becomes easy prey to such seductive schema-triggering stimuli.

Duncan, Emslie, and Williams (1996) have proposed that goal maintenance has a pervasive impact on the performance of patient with frontal lesions. In Duncan's task a series of pairs of letters and numbers are scrolled on to the screen of a computer vertically. The subject is required to report the letters and not the numbers and it is signalled on the screen whether the subject is to report the letters on the left or the letters on the right. The goal maintenance aspect of this task is challenged because from time to time the subject is asked to switch and report from the other side. Even normal subjects make mistakes on this task and occasionally report from the same side when they have been told to switch, and patients with frontal lesions find this task particularly difficult (Duncan et al., 1996).

Grafman's group (Koechlin et al., 1999) have identified areas of the frontal poles and anterior poles of the temporal lobe that appear to be consistently activated during goal maintenance. Goals may be kept, so to speak, on-line within a type of working memory (see reference to long term working memory in Chapter 5). As this function declines; with old age we may have increased difficulty in maintaining such goals as our working memory declines; such as in the case when we forget why we are visiting the garden shed. As indicated above, we may be distracted from a goal and therefore maintenance of goal-related behaviour may have several underlying causes, which may vary with the individual and the area of prefrontal damage.

Yet despite the importance of this and the other information discussed here there remains the uncomfortable feeling that there is still a need for a "little person in the head" to direct behaviour. When there is a need for a designated controller of behaviour this is always the sign of an incomplete model. Such a need perhaps illustrates that the model is more descriptive than explanatory at this stage. Nevertheless, the need for mannequin or manager that sits in the brain appears to be diminishing and perhaps with it "free will". Neuropsychology, following behaviourism, may turn out to be a second-wave attack on this self-determination notion. The motivational component supplied by the orbitofrontal cortex and which is likely to be given some expression by the anterior cingulate is less well formulated. Our response to the changing environment must inevitably be directed by the nature of brain networks that, in turn, are the consequence of our experience and inherited cognitive efficiency. How much room is there left?

WHY EXECUTIVE FUNCTION?

In closing this chapter it might be of interest to reflect on the nature and purpose of executive functioning and whether we should be using such a term. It might be argued that it is not possible to formulate a generalist model. Stuss et al., (1995)

argue that one of the reasons for a low correlation between different tasks measuring executive functioning is that there are a number of different subtypes of executive functioning and these different types require separate modelling (e.g. Della Sala, Gray, Spinnler, & Trivelli, 1998). For example, in the chapter on memory disorders we discuss the contributions of the prefrontal cortex within what is referred to as working memory. There are also formulations that describe a similar area contributing to the maintaining of information over time or intervals, allowing for the delaying of behaviour (see Fuster, 1995, 1997). Also, there are models for the sequencing and monitoring the context of memory (e.g. Petrides, 1996; See Chapter 5). Frameworks also exist that suggest the way some events or situations are tagged with markers within a kind of somatic memory that can cue emotional associations which are more related to ventromedial areas of the prefrontal cortex (Bechara, Damasio, Damasio, 2000; Damasio, 1994; see Chapter 8). Finally, there are models that relate to disorganised actions (Schwartz et al., 1991). All of these models argue against a unified view of executive function.

As indicated earlier, some researchers have assessed the statistical relationship between the different results of "executive" neuropsychological tests and have come up with the disquieting results that the relationship between these tasks is not much stronger than with "none-executive" tests (Duncan, Johnson, Swales, & Freer, 1997). One of the problems with such studies is that they often fail to measure a wide range of executive dysfunction. There are a limited number of tests that have been normed (standardised on normal persons to allow an indication of abnormal performance) and most of these have been criticised in some way. Another difficulty with such studies is that they sometimes use patients with diffuse brain damage, as in the case of traumatic brain injury. Studies have previously found that the slowness of their information processing is the prominent feature of these patients' performance and this may obscure correlative analysis of more subtle relationships. Support for this view is found when studies of normal subjects do actually find that executive factors that can be identified when the research is carefully carried out (Della Salla et al., 1998; Miyake, Friedman, Emerson et al., 2000).

Finally, when viewing studies that have attempted to find correlations between "executive tests" using patient populations it must be realised that some of these tests may be impaired for more than one reason. For example, verbal fluency may be impaired in patients with left frontal lesions but a failure to access the verbal lexicon may *also* be associated with a difficulty in comprehension associated with aphasia and a posterior lesion on the left side. This last disorder is more obviously a consequence of damage to the lexicon rather than a selection or retrieval difficulty (see Chapter 7). When tasks are used that are ambiguous in this way, intercorrelations between tasks have multiple allegiances and patterns become less clear. When the subject population also has diffuse or different lesions the matrix becomes even more confused, undermining any correlation that might be related to the functional quality of the tests.

One group of researchers has made appeals to normal theories of intelligence based on intercorrelations between intelligence tests, as a means of explaining low undifferentiated correlations between executive and non-executive tests. The suggestion is made that intelligence tests have an underlying executive component, which explains why they are intercorrelated (Duncan et al., 1996). Part of this argument relates to finding that some tests that are good overall estimates of intelligence also test executive function, e.g. problem-solving tasks such as the Raven matrices. This proposal is something of a leap of faith; as argued earlier, non-executive tests may correlate with executive tests within a brain-damaged population for entirely different reasons. The commonality between intelligence test performances in normal subjects may best reveal an inherited cognitive efficiency of the individual rather than any underlying executive component.

The greatest difficulty is that while a reader of this chapter might, hopefully, have a strong feel for what a neuropsychologist means when there is reference to "executive dysfunction" the concept is uncomfortably broad.

The comment has also been made that in order to measure executive dysfunction one must also measure other non-executive functions that are needed to express executive dysfunction. However, this problem is not insurmountable since it is possible to partial out a non-executive component. For example, Bayless, Varney, and Roberts (1989) used a statistical method to co-vary out the constructional requirement of the results on the Tinker Toy test and by doing this found a correlation with the later employment status of the patients in the study. A study by Crepeau, Scherzer, Belleville, and Desmarais (1997) found that tasks such as "complex" photocopying can be broken down into various executive components (see also Goel et al., 1997, and their financial planning task). One of the interesting facets of these studies is the observation of the way different patients in their study failed at the practical task for different reasons. This qualitative information can of course be enormously informative when attempting to analyse the exact nature of dysexecutive behaviour.

Quantification of what we believe to be executive behaviour is sufficiently difficult that sometimes we must turn to other means of measurement. Sometimes we must start by looking at the quality of performance before developing a test that attempts to quantify the quality. In this respect we can learn a great deal from the explorative approach to assessment that was adopted by Alexandra Luria (see Christensen & Caetano, 1996, for a brief description). Anne-Lise Christiansen, who worked with the Lurian approach in Denmark, made a number of visits to Luria's clinic and observed the stimulating interactions between Luria, his patients, and the privileged observers. In such sessions the patient was very much involved with the testing process, which was aimed at exploring the patient's strengths and weaknesses. Also under inspection were the methods that the patients were using to achieve the goals set for them. Modern clinicians often combine a quantitative with a qualitative approach to assessment whereby the patient is not only measured on an objective score, but is observed in their style of performing and is also questioned on the way the results were achieved and the approach to the task. Using this method allowed Luria to formulate his theory about the role of the frontal lobe—a theory of dynamic integration that was formulated long before we could observe such processes using advanced radiological techniques.

At this stage it is clear that what is generally referred to as executive functioning is a product of a fractionated system that is contributed to in different ways by different areas in the prefrontal cortex and the anterior cingulate. It is not too surprising therefore that there are tests which are better at representing some part of this system compared to others. We may wish to abandon this concept eventually, but at present the term remains useful because we know too little about the components of the system (e.g. Robbins, 1998; Shallice & Burgess, 1998).

Finally, one may ask the question why the topic of executive functioning holds so much interest for neuropsychologists. The answer may be that the concept of executive function is very much aligned to our special gifts as humans. When we talk about someone as being clever, it is almost always a comment concerning their creativity and their flexible problem-solving ability. The concept of executive dysfunction has a particular relevance for the human condition. We pride ourselves on our ability to adapt flexibly to the environment. We are even sometimes disappointed when we are deprived of our initiative and our ability to seemingly make our own decisions. Mesulam (1998) comments on the nature of the human species compared to others by reflecting on the way our brain organisation is structured to allow us many more options in determining our response to the environment. Unlike other species, which are restrained to run out stereotyped responses to a particular stimulus, we have many more alternatives depending not only on the present circumstances but also on our estimated future consequences of our actions.

It is perhaps ironic that while intelligence is sometimes referred to as a person's ability to adapt to the environment, this is not what intelligence tests generally measure. We are just starting to measure the real nature of our intellectual strength with neuropsychological tests of executive function. As indicated, such tests require some ingenuity since executive functioning is all about adapting to changing circumstances in an independent and flexible way. As soon as limits are put on behaviour in order to make measurement easier, the more adaptive and creative components are automatically limited. It is a fitting challenge to measure one of the main reasons for our success as a species.

4

Disorders of attention

INTRODUCTION

In the first section of this chapter we briefly attempt to reveal the nature of attention through a description of some of the historical arguments surrounding this process. Defining a concept such as attention is similar challenge to defining such broad topics as intelligence. It is sometimes more helpful to describe the psychological context in which attention has been discussed and researched. In this way the reader will hopefully gain a feeling for the various ways it has been described from a theoretical viewpoint. The neuropsychology of attention is heavily influenced by a long-standing literature of studies carried out on subjects without brain damage. There is a brief review of this literature in the first part of this chapter which sets the stage for the terminology and theoretical discussion that come later in the chapter.

Following this introduction to the area there follows a description of a broad theoretical framework for attention, which allows a build-up of concepts in a hierarchical manner from the basic, primitive components of attention to more advanced cortically controlled components. This is a hierarchical framework from the point of view that each attentional system may in some

circumstances be dependent on a lower level of the hierarchy. All these systems are activated within an integrated circuit or network. The term system is used to denote a description of a group of structures and their biochemical substrates that have an identified functional role. It is understood that these systems may act together in an integrated way towards achieving an attentional goal. They are described in this chapter as the *arousal system* for maintaining cortical tone according to environmental demands; the *orienting system* which is ideally suited for detecting and orienting attention towards novel or unpredictable stimuli; the *perceptual attention system*, which is described as a selective attentional system that allows us to perceive some stimuli while ignoring other stimuli in our environment; and finally the *executive attention system*, which serves to control attention by inhibiting and disinhibiting orienting responses and controlling the perceptual attention system.

Following a discussion of this four-system framework, the fascinating clinical phenomenon of unilateral neglect or hemi-inattention is discussed. Patients with unilateral neglect usually have difficulty in attending to information on the left-hand side following a lesion on the right side, which is often within the inferior parietal cortex near the junction of the occipital and temporal lobes. These patients show features indicating a breakdown of each of the attentional systems. There is a lowered arousal, impaired orienting, and difficulties in areas of vigilance and selective attention associated with the executive attentional system, and finally there are features of these patient's performance which suggest that their attentional impairment influences their perceptual processes.

Also discussed at this point is the related term of anosognosia, which refers to the tendency for patients to be unaware of their own disability, whether it be their own attentional disorder or the left hemiparesis (paralysis of left limbs), which often accompanies this disorder. Also discussed in this section is Balint's syndrome, with the accompanying attentional disorder of dorsolateral simultaneous agnosia. Finally there is a discussion of the more prosaic disorders of attention disorder that handicap all brain-damaged patients and which can be so handicapping in their work and social life.

Unilateral neglect is a reasonably common clinical symptom in the early days following right hemisphere stroke. It is also commonly studied because it is assumed by many to be revealing of the mechanism of attention. For this reason and for the theoretical insights into attention it offers, there is a further discussion of the models that have attempted to describe this facinating disorder.

The discussion of these patients and models describing the mechanisms of neglect lead on to more complex discussions of the relationships between attention and perception and then the relationship between attention and memory.

In the final section of this chapter there is a look at the relationship between the neuropsychology of attention and the terminology. This section is an attempt to focus on the confusion that sometimes exists in the clinical literature, where tests have been adopted without considering the breadth of their cognitive demands.

A BRIEF HISTORICAL BACKGROUND OF THEORY

When researchers talk about attention in the literature, the term "modulation" is frequently used. The term implies that attention influences the efficiency and modifies the performance of other functions. Certainly attention is one of the most variable and pervasive features of cognition and it does appear to be subservient to memory, perception, and language, acting as a go-between to integrate, direct, and influence the involvement of these functions in a flexible manner.

The way attention interacts with other aspects of cognition is evidenced when there is an attempt to define attention. William James, brother of the famous novelist Henry James, wrote one of the most quoted definitions of attention over a hundred years ago. He wrote, "Everyone knows what attention is. It is the taking possession by the mind, in clear and vivid form, of one out of what seem several simultaneously possible objects or trains of thought. Focalisation, concentration of consciousness are of its essence. It implies withdrawal from some things in order to deal effectively with others" (James, 1890, Vol. 1, p. 403).

Donald Broadbent, one of the most influential early experimentalists in this area, was particularly interested in the problem of what happens when this selective attentional system is taxed to its limits. Broadbent was drawn to practical problems relating to attention. For example, he investigated a series of mysterious aeroplane crashes for the RAF and observed the need to redesign an ambiguous altimeter. He was drawn to other practical considerations of how air traffic controllers could concentrate on more than one thing at a time and still make their important life-and-death decisions (Broadbent, 1958; see Baddeley & Weiskrantz, 1993, pp. x–xv, for an interesting history). Much of the cognitive psychology research has been devoted to addressing these issues of divided attention and the *capacity* to attend, and a number of models have been developed to describe this process (e.g. Kahneman, 1973). A classical finding is that when interference is increased above a certain level and or the task requirements are increased then errors start to creep into performance (e.g., Duncan, 1993).

These formulations suggest that our attentional resources are limited in capacity. Anyone who has to both drive at the same time as looking at a map will note this limitation. Research has also addressed the issue of how unfamiliar and inconsistent information requires more attentional capacity, while overlearned and consistent information is processed more automatically and consequently requires less attentional capacity. The concept of *controlled* versus *automatic* attention has been introduced to cover these two types of processing, which are presumed to be on a continuum (e.g. Poltrock, Lansman, & Hunt, 1982; Shiffrin & Schneider, 1977). While there are theoretical arguments, especially about the issue of the relationship between attention and consciousness (e.g. Jacoby, Ste-Marie, & Toth, 1993), from the phenomenological point of view *controlled processes* are generally considered to be serial (looking at one bit of information at a time). They are also slow and are often associated with more conscious awareness. For example, controlled attention may be required in the case when a series of unfamiliar and complex paintings are being viewed for the first time.

Automatic processing, on the other hand, may be illustrated by the situation in which a practised card player surveys their hand rapidly; the information is assumed to be processed in parallel (larger chunks) without much conscious awareness of what is happening. From this perspective, as the activity becomes more familiar it requires less attentional "*effort*" and this concept has also been used in researching the attentional requirements of learning (Hasher & Zacks, 1984). The difficulty with terms such as "capacity" and "effort" is that they need to be measured in some way independently and some believe that methods of measurement are too arbitrary.

Sometimes when we appear to be doing two things at the same time we are actually rapidly going forwards and backwards between two tasks. This may lead to inefficiencies of the type Wiliam James describes: "Where, however, the processes are less automatic, as in the story of Julius Caesar dictating four letters whilst he writes a fifth, there must be rapid oscillation of the mind from one to the next, and no consequent gain in time" (James, 1890, Vol. 1, p. 409). But such a process of dividing our attention may be made more efficient when we are very familiar with one of the tasks.

There are a number of everyday examples in which we find experience and learning may advantage our ability to attend. Therefore, a person may appear to read and type at the same time, or alternatively follow sheet music while playing the piano, dividing their attention between the two tasks with some efficiency. These activities require less attentional resources because they are so well learned. However, even when a competing task is well learned, there is, nevertheless, a tendency to switch attention very rapidly between the two tasks. When the tasks are less familiar, switching attention between tasks must be quicker and take up more time to the extent we might be advised not to follow Julius Caesar's example and instead do one thing at a time.

Awareness has an important relationship with attention, but attention may start prior to conscious awareness (Cohen, Sparling-Cohen, & O'Donnell, 1993). We are often aware of what we are doing when we select a stimulus from among others, but sometimes the process seems automatic and just happens without any conscious control. The term often used for this phenomenon is *preattentive* (Neisser, 1967). An example of the preattentive process occurs when we survey a list of names in a telephone book. Suddenly, the name we are searching for springs out of the page at us. It is as if we have a readiness to perceive a particular pattern and once there is a match that percept is automatically activated. Something similar may occur in what is referred to as the "cocktail party phenomenon". A person is talking to someone at a social gathering when someone mentions their name from across the room in another conversation. The person's attention is suddenly diverted as they become aware that their name is being mentioned. In the experimental situation a little over a third of student subjects will be distracted from their task by their name being presented in the other "unattended" ear (Wood & Cowan, 1995, replication of Moray's original findings).

This phenomenon of being alerted to an "unattended" stimulus posed some questions for the early model makers in the area of attention, for how could a person pick up their name from, say, eight separate conversations without monitoring all these separate conversations simultaneously? Some theoreticians in the 1970s thought that all the conversations in the room were analysed unconsciously for their meaning. For surely we would miss our name if these conversations were not being monitored at this level. This rather unlikely proposal spawned late (semantic/meaning) selection theories of attention (after the physical attributes have been analysed). In support of this view is research that suggests that we are influenced by the meaning of information even when we may not be conscious of that meaning. For example, a typical attention task of the 1970s used a dichotic listening task in which the subject was required to monitor the left ear at the expense of the right ear. If the word *bank* is presented to the left ear then the subject might report the word *bank* as a place where one obtains money. However, if at the same time the word *river* is presented in the other "unattended ear", then the subject is more likely to interpret the ambiguous word *bank* as a bank of a river. This coarse semantic analysis occurs even though the subject is not consciously aware of having heard the word *river* in the "unattended ear" (McKay, 1973).

However, other evidence is suggestive of an earlier stage of filtering. Thus if we are to monitor a message in one ear we may not become aware that the topic of conversation has changed in the other ear, but we are aware if there is a change to a foreign language (Treisman, 1964). In such a situation it is the phonological sounds or the physical structure of the language that has distracted attention, suggesting an early filtering system. This disagreement between models espousing late (semantic/meaning) and early physical selection of features (e.g. phonological/ sound) took place in the 1960s and 1970s and

some light has recently been shed on this argument by work from Lavie (1995).

We have already argued that increased interference may cause on-task errors in this limited capacity system, but what if the task is made easier? Does that leave more capacity to attend to so-called "unattended" information? The answer is probably "yes" and this provides a solution to the disagreement between some of the early studies. Lavie (1995) argues from a series of experiments that there has been a trend for early studies to find early filtering (physical features) of unattended information because these studies generally had a high perceptual load. Later studies tended to have low perceptual load, e.g. detecting a single letter, and tended to espouse a late model of filtering (after meaningful analysis). The argument Lavie supports is that a light perceptual load allows more spare capacity for the more exacting analysis required of the interfering or "unattended" information. This finding has received some neuropsychological support in a study that looked at blood flow in the brain using PET technology (Rees, Frith, & Lavie, 1997). In this study background motion was used as a distraction for a word detection task. In the low-perceptual-load task the subject was required to detect words that were in upper case (physical analysis), while the high-load task required the subject to undertake the more demanding processing task of detecting bisyllabic words. In the higher perceptual load task activations of the area representing the processing of the distracting motion (V5) decreased.

An everyday illustration of Lavie's view would suggest that if, for example, someone is reluctantly listening to an individual at a party and their conversation is predictable and perhaps boring, then as soon as the listener's name is mentioned in another conversation across the room they will be distracted by the event. In contrast, the engrossed listener might miss their name being spoken. However, although this meaningful material might escape the engrossed party-goer's notice, the listener might nevertheless become aware of physical changes (less demanding of physical analysis) in their environment, such as if everyone around them suddenly stopped talking.

The view that we have a certain attentional

capacity and that if it is not being used we have more spare capacity to monitor other "unattended" information around us is attractive, and probably in line with a layperson's understanding. Nevertheless it is also true that in extreme situations distracting interference that is demanding of the subject's attention will undermine the performance on a main task. This situation will also be familiar to us when we are trying to read a book and they are conducting renovations in the next room. In experimental tasks there is an attempt to assess a patient's ability to cope with interference and divided attention in what is referred to as "duel tasks". For example, the subject may be required to track a target while answering questions.

While Lavie's work reveals that we might be more likely to pick up our name at a cocktail party when we are not required to concentrate on our own conversation, this doesn't really answer the question of how we can detect our name from all those other conversations without processing every conversation in the room. One attractive partial solution to this conundrum comes from the researchers Desimone and Duncan (1995). They have proposed that top-down processing, of the type mentioned in Chapter 2, occurs to make us more ready to receive some information at the expense of others. This influences what is attended to in a competitive process. It is understood that cells that represent behaviourally relevant stimuli in our environment are ready to be activated, while at the same time other stimuli which are behaviourally irrelevant may be inhibited. "Behaviourally relevant" refers to stimuli that are important to the person according to past experience. For example, a mother may be alerted by the muted sounds of her baby crying but at the same time be unaware of a loud banging of a gate.

This top-down, competitive process is assumed to work even when we do not set out to search for a particular target. As in the case of the baby crying there must be a process that allows certain percepts to win the competition over others. The process might be described metaphorically as throwing a number of different shapes including stars, circles, and squares on to a board that only

has slots in the shape of circles. All the shapes will slide off the perceptual board except the behaviourally relevant circles, which slot into position. This top-down perceptual readiness to receive some stimuli at the expense of others is not a complete description of the process. We are also predisposed to process objects that are novel, brighter, coloured, and of well-defined shape, and shapes in motion. These shapes are especially likely to be detected if these features are displayed on a background that does not contain other stimuli that have some of these qualities. Even if we ignore the propensity for such features as novelty movement and colour to trigger attentional response, according to this theory features may also be favoured in this competitive parallel perceptual process if there is no competition from similar features.

Later the work by Desimone and co-workers, which has used brain cell recordings during a task requiring attention, is described further. These studies suggest that we can prepare ourselves in advance to perceive a particular target to bias the competitive process towards the stimulus when it arrives on the scene. So we also have some control over this system. We can even train ourselves to look for something in this manner, but it may then be hard to ignore that same information when we decide it is no longer relevant (Shiffrin & Schneider, 1977).

Desimone and Duncan's (1995) competition theory is persuasive since from the evolutionary viewpoint attention and perception must interact in an efficient manner. If there is an acceptance that our ability to process information is limited, then we should be spending that valuable resource on things that matter to us. All other things being equal, it appears that what we perceive most easily is also what we wish to attend to.

While there is clearly an attentional process that allows us to pick out and perceive relevant information from a background, the nature of the background is also important. Work by Watson and Humphreys (1997) illustrates this last point well in their work, showing that that we can instantly detect changes to a background, but the background must be familiar to us. One is reminded of the evolutionary importance of such a skill. A watchful hunter who instantly realises when there is a slight change within a vast visual range of bush is at an obvious advantage. Despite surveying a large expanse of complex scenery, experimental subjects may detect small changes that signal the arrival of a new element with astonishing ease. But the ease with which this is done depends on the *extent that we have had experience with the background scene*. Naturalists may have an advantage in the bush, but city slickers will be more likely to notice small changes to the front of a local store. The top-down information again facilitates our attentional process.

The proposal by Desimone that our attention to a stimulus is a competitive process whereby certain features are selected in a top-down perceptual manner combined with an inhibition of competing or distracting information (Desimone & Duncan, 1995) is reminiscent of previous metaphors of attention as a spotlight (Tsal, 1983). It appears that we can "zoom in" on particular aspects of our environment (Eriksen & Yeh, 1985). Thus small areas of our available visual field may be concentrated upon at the expense of others. Intuitively, we are aware that this is more likely to occur when a task is particularly demanding, or when there is interference that we are trying to "shut out".

The competition theory also predicts that if there is more than one target then the search will be slowed because the targets will compete for the limited capacity. For example, it is slower to search for targets in Figure 4.1(b) when compared to the single target in 4.1(a).

Treisman and Gelade (1980) provide an alternative feature integration theory of attention which also has relevance to the preattentive processes earlier described by Neisser (1967). As discussed earlier, Neisser described preattentive processes as an automatic unconscious type of processing occurring when a feature appears to "pop out" of the page at us. Treisman's theory and her extensions of this theory (e.g. Treisman, 1998) describe this relationship between perception and attention. For example, when we search a white triangle from a background of black squares and black triangles the search speed is very quick. The white triangle appears to "pop

out" at us from the background (see Figure 4.1a). But if there is overlap between all the features of the target and background or distractor stimuli, such as in the case of Figure 4.1b, then this conjunction of features causes a far slower search time that is proportional to the number of distractors. Mathematically reaction-times appear to predict a parallel process in the "pop-out" situation but reaction times are closer to a serial search in the case of the conjuction of features

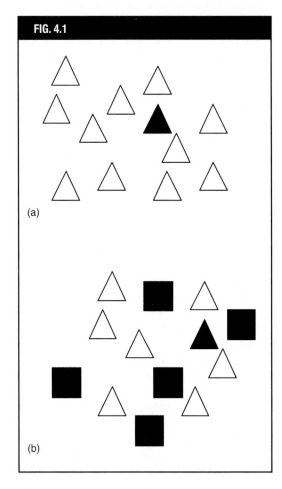

FIG. 4.1

(a)

(b)

(a) A black triangle target leading to "pop-out" parallel processing requiring no integration. (b) Overlap between target and distractors; there are no critical target features that are unique to the target. This conjoint presentation leads to a much slower search, which is assumed to be serial, according to integration theory. Competition theory provides that increased competition between features increases processing time but may remain a parallel process.

(Figure 4.1b). That is, with increasing number of distractors in a conjunction display of the type in Figure 4.1b there is a linear increase of reaction time in trying to find the target. An additive increase in reaction would confirm a serial search; with each extra distractor there will be an incremental increase in reaction time. Whether this is actually obtained is controversial. Duncan (1998) provides evidence that the increases are not additive. Competition theory also predicts a proportionally longer search time for the situation where there is an overlap of features, but this is described more in terms of a parallel search involving excessive competition. As the overlap between the target one is seeking and the competition in the form of distractors is increased, the search is accordingly slowed. Both theories assume a limited-capacity system.

According to Treisman's integration theory the parallel "pop-up" process involves stimuli that are already integrated. However, when a slow serial search is required, there has to be a connecting up between the perceptual features of the target with its location. In our example of Fig. 4.1b the slow serial search occurs because the position of each stimulus and its representative shape and colour must be individually integrated or bound together. In some experimental tasks, when normal subjects are put under duress during a perceptual task (e.g. increasing speed of the task) mistakes are made that show a poor lining up or binding of these features.

Treisman also describes a brain-damaged patient, RM, who is described as having difficulty in judging the location of a target and also had difficulty in gauging the properties of the stimulus when others were present—for example, getting the colour and location of two stimuli mixed up. Therefore the integration theory also has support from a number of sources of evidence (Treisman, 1998).

Desimone and Duncan (1995) are not so persuaded by this parallel versus serial integration description. They argue that the reaction time data for the conjunction tasks do not obviously represent a serial additive search with additional distractors being searched through one at a time. Also, cell representations that underlie percep-

tions may be spatially located with respect to the retina given feed-forward from the V1 area; in other words there is normally no need for spatial integration: it is provided by V1. From the authors' viewpoint it is the increased competition caused by a target and background overlap that slows down a process in the case of Figure 4.1b. They argue that the time differences between Figure 4.1a and Figure 4.1b do not necessarily suggest a distinction between a parallel and serial process: they can both be explained in terms of a parallel process—a process in which search time increases as competition increases. It should be borne in mind that some models may be more useful at describing certain phenomena than others and that both these theories may eventually be found to make a contribution.

At this stage we appear to be some way from describing a comprehensive theory of attention that has general acceptance. Some of the theories will be revisited at a later stage within this chapter. The models of attention that have been developed using normal subjects reveal certain important postulates that have had increasing importance for the neuropsychological literature. This brief overview of findings within attention has been given as a background to a discussion of neuropsychological issues in this area.

Broadly, attention can be described as a limited-capacity process that allows the preferential processing of certain sensory or imaged information at the expense of other available stimuli. By way of a summary the following factors may influence this process:

1. There is an intimate link between our perceptual experience and the ease with which we attend. It is easier to attend to a familiar target stimulus especially if it has a motivational implications. It is also easier to detect the arrival in time of a new stimulus (an arrival of a new object within a scene) when the background is familiar to us. Therefore top-down perceptual processing plays a significant role in our ability to attend.
2. When considering divided attention, our capacity to attend to information or task(s)

appears to be limited. Our capacity to attend may be less challenged and require less conscious control when the perceptual load is light, i.e. a familiar task or small number of targets. When perceptual capacity is metaphorically released due to light perceptual load this allows us to be more capable of monitoring "unattended" information to a greater depth, i.e. more meaningful level rather than purely physical features.

3. Our limited capacity to attend may also be interfered with by a an alternative source. Thus if perceptual load is high and the interfering stimulus is salient then mistakes on the main task will suffer.

4. It appears that we are capable of focusing on or "zooming" in on some features at the expense of others, when the situation demands closer inspection of an object, e.g. a dangerous activity or one requiring great skill or greater attention to detail. This process has been described as a competitive process whereby some perceptually representive brain cells within the cortex may be activated, while others are inhibited. Evidence for such "tuning" is now coming in from animal studies.

5. The attentional preference of processing may be determined by preattentive mechanisms that appear to be perceptually determined, e.g. isolated differences in colour or contour or motion. These stimuli may be detected more rapidly when the background does not contain similar features. These integrated stimuli may also be particular patterns that are seen as holistic because of our experience of the world. This type of stimulus is processed rapidly in parallel; it appears automatic and immediate without any conscious awareness of the process. When we search for stimuli that do not have this distinctive advantage and the features of the target stimulus share all its features with the background, then the process becomes a laborious search that requires either an integration or binding between features such as location, colour and shape

(integration theory). Alternatively, the search is slowed because of greater competition between stimuli (competition theory).

For many years there has been a considerable gap between the cognitive psychology of attention being based on normal subjects and the neuropsychology of attentional disorders. This was partly because investigations into the neuropsychology were driven by the clinical experience of attentional impairment. Cognitive psychological research, in contrast, was centred on testing models of normal attentional processing that were originally often derived from practical everyday problems, e.g.: How do we listen to two messages at once? These differences are now being rationalised, and the two areas of research are moving together. These efforts are in part influenced by applying "normal" theoretical constructs to brain-damaged patients. This has also been accompanied by a renaissance of new techniques for measuring brain activation during experiments that have been developed in the last decade and have allowed closer links between neuropsychological theory and normal models of functioning.

A neuropsychological framework for attention

There are also obvious similarities with the model developed here and those of Posner and Petersen (1990) (see Figure 4.2) and that of Mesulam (1981, 1999) (see Figure 19). The model is made up from different systems, each system with a different functional role. The first arousal system was described in the Chapter 1 as part of Luria's model and this fundamental view has not changed in some of the most recent studies in this area (e.g. Coull, 1998). The patient must have the prequisite cortical tone in order to attend depending on the demands of the environment. While arousal level as supplied by the *arousal system* can be seen as an essential foundation of attention, the orienting reflex can be seen as a further building block for more primitive attentional processes.

The orienting system is associated with a rapid allocation of attention, being a reaction to a startling or novel stimulus. It is assumed that the

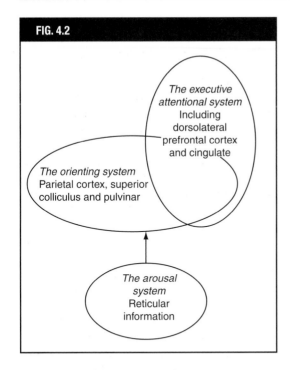

FIG. 4.2

The executive attentional system
Including dorsolateral prefrontal cortex and cingulate

The orienting system
Parietal cortex, superior colliculus and pulvinar

The arousal system
Reticular information

Illustration of the model of Posner and Petersen (adapted from Posner & Petersen, 1990) with some modification of terminology. The executive attention system is illustrated as overlapping with the orienting system but placed predominantly within the right hemisphere.

orienting reflex plays a significant role in survival and this fact alone may explain its presence in so many species. During the orienting reflex attention is rapidly focused on the source of movement or novelty. In its most urgent form it is associated with an additional autonomic, physiological response that prepares the organism for "fight or flight". This might be construed as an emergency response to the presence of a predator or prey. This reflex is discussed in relation to a series of structures centred on the superior colliculus, which is situated on the roof of the brain stem (the tectum). This response is not always adaptive, especially when novel but unimportant stimuli are arriving on the scene frequently. For example, there are occasions in a city when, surrounded by constant novel sounds, we need to inhibit the natural tendency to orient towards the noise. Therefore this system must be add-itionally capable of inhibiting and moderating this reflexive response.

A third system, the *executive attention system*, is a term that is taken from Posner's more recent work (Posner & Rothbart, 1998), which overlaps with the other systems at the parietal area of this attentional system (see Figure 4.2). This system is more obviously involved in the controlled attentional responses. This executive system is described as being important in the detection and selection of targets from a background of dis-tracting features. When our ancestors were hunt-ing on the savannah there would have been the requirement to search for the tell-tale shape of an animal among the grasses. In modern times the pertinent stimuli have become the new occurrence of a "blip" on a radar screen or the change of a traffic light. An important feature of the execu-tive attention system is its involvement in the selection and monitoring of stimuli. In addition to the parietal cortex various structures in the frontal lobe, including the anterior cingulate and the DPFC, have been found to be important when selecting out features from a background. Let us look now at these features in more detail.

The arousal system

General effects of the arousal system on alertness

For attention to occur, a certain level of alertness is required. In Chapter 1 the system for regulating tone was described as a feature of Luria's model and the influence of the reticular formation as an agent for increasing cortical arousal via the thal-amus was also described. More specifically, within the reticular formation are neuronal pro-jections referred to as the ascending reticular activating system (ARAS). This activation was seen as supplying modulated arousal to areas such as the thalamus, cortex, and limbic system (especially the hypothalamus). The ARAS was compared with a descending system that was seen as acting as a feedback system, dampening down the level of arousal within the reticular system of the brain stem (pons and medulla). Arousal is just one of the functions of the structures that make up the reticular formation. The reticular formation is also important for influencing motor and sensory responses. But the main and most important influence on cortical arousal appears to be via the thalamus. The connections within the thalamus are seen to be particularly important and will be discussed in more depth when discussing models of neglect. These connections of the ARAS to the thalamus go to a site within the central area of each thalamus (left and right respectively); this central part of the thalamus is referred to as the intralaminar nuclei. The importance of these thalamic nuclei is demonstrated by the evidence that damage to the intralaminar system results in lowered arousal including lethargy or coma (Castaigne, Buge, Escourolle, & Masson, 1962).

This formation has an unusual neuronal composition, in the form of a network. It has been described as being at the core of the brain stem, like a sausage in a hot dog (Nolte, 1993, p. 167). Bilateral lesions in this area have caused cats to go into a coma and this area was also found to alter EEG rhythmicity (Moruzzi & Magoun, 1949).

Two types of arousal are often referred to when describing the influence of arousal on attention: *tonic arousal*, which refers to diurnal (daily) alterations in arousal, such as the sleep wakefulness cycle; and *phasic arousal*, which is determined by environmental events and is therefore more variable. The reticular formation and the ARAS influence both of these types of arousal.

Tonic arousal has been found to be additionally influenced by the suprachiasmic nucleus (SCN), which is a small structure that is situated above the optic chiasm (see Figure 2.2). A few of the neuronal projections that make up the optic nerve branch off to the SCN to give this structure information concerning the environmental light. The SCN sits in the basal anterior section of the hypothalamus. The SCN has an important role in regulating the circadian rhythm, which describes the fluctuating daily levels of arousal throughout the day, including the sleep–wake cycle. Cohen and Albers (1991) describe a patient with SCN damage. The patient showed huge variability of arousal throughout the day and night with consequent effects on the patient's ability to attend to stimuli. This type of lesion is most frequently

associated with tumours, such as a pituitary or a craniophangioma.

The hypothalamus also has an effect on temporary or autonomic variability in attention. This is an important structure with a number of functions. It plays a pivotal role in integrating emotional and appetitive behaviours (hunger, thirst, and sexual drives) in relation to environmental demands. The hypothalamus is also well placed to control the *fight or flight response*. This refers to the emergency physiological response required to make sudden energetic movements in the face of danger. The dangers that were around when the response was evolving in our ancestors have long gone and have now been replaced by contingencies such as irresponsibly driven fast cars. Anyone who has crossed the road and heard a sudden screech of brakes will attest to the sudden symptoms of increased cardiac output, increased sweating, and sudden alertness that this kind of stimulus causes. These sympathetic autonomic central nervous symptom responses (e.g. see Thompson, 1985, p. 165) are of most interest here in terms of their affect on arousal and, consequently, attention. The physiological response causes a *phasic* or temporary alteration in alertness, which is directly influenced either through hormonal influence via the endocrine system, e.g. adrenal glands, or through the ascending reticular activating system.

The attentional component of the "fight or flight" response is referred to as the "orienting reflex response". This can be associated with a less dramatic response of merely orienting when a novel stimulus is presented. The orienting reflex involves a sudden switching of attention to a stimulus of interest—it is a "what is it" type of response. Some of the attentional components of this response are contained within the sensory attentional system, which is described in the next section.

Because the reticular formation is within the brain stem, damage or insult to the brain stem often causes abnormalities in a patient's state of arousal. Chapter 1 has already referred to the effect of such disorders as subarachnoid haemorrhage and the way that blood haemorrhaging from the circle of Willis may place pressure on the brain stem. Reduced alertness is also associated with vascular disorders (basilar artery) and tumours involving the brain stem. Such patients may fall in and out of sleep. However, loss of consciousness and coma are most frequently associated with traumatic brain injury (TBI). The integrity of the reticular formation may be undermined by a number of different mechanisms associated with TBI, for example excessive intracranial pressure (ICP), which may be caused by oedema (swelling of the cortex). This swelling may in turn cause pressure on the brain stem and undermine the functioning of the reticular formation and sometimes other life-preserving characteristics such as respiration and heart rate. Alternatively, vascular disruption in the area of the brain stem can also result in damage to the reticular system in TBI. In this case, the acceleration of the brain following impact in a motor vehicle accident causes arteries to be wrenched away or dislodged from the brain stem. Also shearing forces may result in the axons of the brain stem, including the reticular system, being severed. These injuries, along with vascular or tumour-related disorders, may be consequently associated with coma or severe states of lethargy.

Sub-systems of arousal contributing to specific functions

Although there is functional imaging evidence to support the role of the reticular formation and some regional areas of the thalamus in extreme de-arousal such as anaesthesia and sleep (Alkire, Haier, & Fallon, 2000), there has been a move away from talking about a brain arousal system as a unitary system (Robbins & Everitt, 1995).

The illustrations in Figure 4.3 depict some of the pathways associated with the different neurotransmitter systems. All these systems area associated with the modulation of brain arousal and attention. While there is still much conjecture concerning their different functional contributions, research at present is very focused on this exciting area at the present time.

The most commonly referred to system is the norepinephrine system or, as it is more commonly referred to in the UK, the noradrenaline system. Since this system projects to wide and disparate cortical areas there is the assumption that it is involved in the general arousal of the cortex and is therefore less specific in its effect compared with other systems. Various studies have confirmed the involvement of this neurotransmitter system in tasks requiring attention. Portas et al. (1998) gave caffeine delivered in cups of coffee to sleep-deprived volunteers and functional imaging revealed increased activation in areas of the thalamus that appeared to be a form of compensatory arousal that was delivered during the attention-demanding task. The source of this system is the locus coeruleus (see Figure 4.3); in the previous chapter Cohen's model (Cohen, 2000) was described in which the anterior cingulate was seen as acting to increase arousal by evoking increased activation within the locus coeruleus. More recently it has been found that drugs that encourage noradrenaline (alpha-2 adrenoceptor agonist) increase connectivity between an attentional network during an attention task. A PET scan study by Coull et al. (1999) has used a statistical method that indicates two directional increases in connectivity. The first appears to be changes centred on the parietal cortex, with increases in connectivity between the locus coeruleus and the parietal cortex and from the parietal cortex and thalamus. The second effect appears also to be drug induced. This involved the effect of the frontal cortex on the connectivity between the locus coeruleus and the parietal cortex. This study is positive support for the influence of the noradrenaline neurotransmitter system on attention as previously proposed by Posner and Petersen (1990).

Other recent studies have been interested in the clinical effects of neurotransmitter systems on brain arousal and task performance. These effects are often most clearly seen in terms of interactions between structures such as the prefrontal cortex, thalamus, and posterior association areas. For some time it has been realised that amphetamines such as methylphenidate (Ritalin) may enhance arousal of the noradrenaline and dopamine systems. This has been found to improve attention and concentration on tasks in normal 10- to 11-year-old boys (e.g., Rapoport et al., 1978) as well as a subgroup of children with

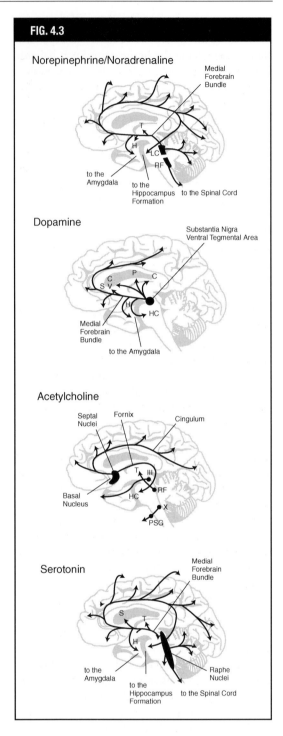

FIG. 4.3

Norepinephrine/Noradrenaline

Medial
Forebrain
Bundle

T
H
LC
RF

to the
Amygdala

to the
Hippocampus
Formation

to the Spinal Cord

Dopamine

Substantia Nigra
Ventral Tegmental Area

C   P   C
S V
H
HC

Medial
Forebrain
Bundle

to the Amygdala

Acetylcholine

Septal
Nuclei   Fornix   Cingulum

T   III
RF
HC
Basal
Nucleus   X
PSG

Serotonin

Medial
Forebrain
Bundle

S
T
H

to the
Amygdala

to the
Hippocampus
Formation

to the Spinal Cord

Raphe
Nuclei

The noradrenaline system is clearly associated with the sleep–wake cycle and innervates the cortex in a non-specific manner. The locus coeruleus (LC), reticular formation (RF) and thalamus (T) are shown. The dopamine system has a clear influence on motor performance, being the transmitter system of the basal ganglia, but this system has also been implicated within sustained alertness, having an influence on frontal regions (Coull, 1998). The hippocampus (HC), septum (S), Cingulate (C), and hypothalamus (H) are shown. The acytycholine (cholinergic) system appears to play a more specific role in selective attention, although there are further implications for a role within memory since it has close connections with the hippocampus (Baxter & Chiba, 1999). Finally, the serotin system is thought to be like nornadrenaline, a general regulator of brain activity wtih its origins in the raphe nuclei (Greek for seam). The raphe nuclei run like a seam within the two halves of the brain stem (adapted from Nolte & Angevine, 1995, with permission from Mosby Yearbook, Inc.).

attention deficit hyperactive disorder (ADHD). Notwithstanding the concerns that are sometimes voiced concerning the indiscriminate use of such treatments (e.g., Safer, 2000), some headway is being made on the specific action of such drugs. Improvements in performance on visuospatial working memory tasks have been associated with functional imaging changes including a reduction in activation within the left DPFC and the posterior parietal cortex in healthy volunteers (Mehta, Owen, Sahakian et al., 2000). Mehta and colleagues required the subjects to play a kind of "Kim's" game on a computer in which red circles were touched consecutively to see whether they covered a blue token. The blue token never appeared under the same red circle twice and therefore the subject had to "keep in mind" their responses for previous trials.

As indicated, methylphenidate may have its effect by modulating either the noradrenaline system or the dopamine system or both to achieve improved performance. There may be different effects of each system on attention, but at present the effect of methylphenidate is most commonly described as having its clinical effect on attention and working memory (tasks requiring the retaining information temporarily in mind) through the enhancement of dopamine levels. In respect of this proposal Diamond (1998) has proposed that children who have failed to satisfactorily develop their frontal dopamine system due to the dietary treatment for phenylketonuria (PKU) show executive dysfunction that overlaps with problems commonly described as working memory or focused attention. This area is discussed more comprehensively in the previous chapter.

Also, investigations that have been more focused on the affects of methylphenidate on ADHD in children and adults also favour the enhancement of the dopamine system as a cause for improved attention. At the present time the dopamine system appears to modulate the frontostriatal system in ADHD patients (Vaidya et al., 1998). According to imaging studies, e.g. single-photon emission computed tomography (SPECT) using an isotope with an affinity for dopamine, the activation of the putamen (part of the basal ganglia within the striatum), a structure associated with motor function (and possibly hyperactivity), is normalised by methylphenidate treatment in ADHD patients (Krause et al., 2000; Teicher et al., 2000).

Finally on the dopamine system, in Chapter 9 the psychiatric disorder of schizophrenia is discussed and one description of this disorder as a depletion of dopamine within a frontostriatal (striatum = putamen plus caudate nucleus) circuit. This frontal de-arousal may be compensated by administration of dopamine agonists. Again there is the association with impaired attention, although schizophrenia is too complex a disorder to attribute cause and effect with any certainty.

The cholinergic (acetycholine) neurotransmitter system, with its source in the basal forebrain (the nucleus basalis of Meynert), consists of two subsystems: the nicotininic, which has a clear influence on attention; and the muscorinic system, which has for some time been seen to have its effect on memory with its projections to the hippocampus. Because a depletion of acetylcholine is associated with atrophy of the nucleus basalis of Meynert within the basal forebrain in Alzheimer's disease there have been attempts at compensating this system through diet and drug treatments aimed at enhancment. There is a large research base that has been devoted to attempts at compensating the depletion of acytylcholine in these patients by increasing the availablity of the neurotransmitter through ingestion (lecithin) or commonly by reducing the breakdown of acetylcholine, i.e. using anticholinesterase drugs. Most of the effects of these studies have been minimal and often ambiguous in their support of treatment. More modern approaches using such drugs as tarcrine (THA) have generally found to have their impact on attention rather than memory (see also Baxter & Chiba, 1999, for support for attention rather than a memory influence for the cholinergic system). These studies produce minimal real life changes although there is considerable risk of side effects (Davies et al., 1990; Levy et al., 2000; Sahakian et al., 1993).

A more prosaic effect of this neurotransmitter is seen in the effects of smoking. The attention of smokers is enhanced by nicotine, which is a nicotinic agonist. However, this stress-reducing support for smokers is of course lost when they attempt to "kick the habit". Hence the common complaint of poor concentration by smokers attempting to withdraw (Kassel, 1997).

Neuropsychological assessment of the effects of poor arousal may be most obvious on tests of vigilance such as a continuous performance task. The continuous performance task was originally developed to investigate the effects of monotonous viewing of radar screens during the Second World War. During these times hours might go by without any sign of the enemy. Nevertheless, detection of the signal when it did eventually arrive was, of course, crucial. These tasks of sustained attention are sometimes referred to as tests of vigilance. They require subjects to detect and respond to infrequently presented targets from a series of distracting stimuli over an extended time period, e.g. responding to the letter "L" from among other continuously presented letters over a period of 20–30 minutes. Typically, performance on this type of continuous performance task is initially satisfactory but quickly falls off as the patient becomes fatigued (Lindsley, 1960). The system that contributes to alertness over time is likely to be a different from that required for an immediate response to cognitive demands and may modulate frontal systems more than parietal areas (Coull, Frackowiak, & Frith, 1998).

A pattern of different subsystems of arousal and their specific contributions to attention are only now emerging, with their contributions to different types of attention from general levels of arousal to working memory. Research in this area is undergoing an understandable resurgence, which is partly due to the use of functional imaging in association with the manipulation of drug levels and task performance. Also driving this research is the ever-present interest in treatment, and even prevention, since many neurological disorders are associated with a depletion of one or more of the neurotransmitter systems discussed.

The orienting system

The orienting system describes a system whereby reflexive and more controlled eye movements are initiated as part of an attentional response.

The sensory attentional system and the orienting reflex

An important distinction has been made in Chapter 2 between the magnocellular (magno) and parvocellular (parvo) streams in the process of visual perception. These systems correspond to two pathways that have specialised roles in transferring coded visual information from the thalamus through to various stages of analysis within the visual cortex. These magno and parvo pathways are recognised as being associated respectively with M and P cells at the level of the thalamus and cortex. As indicated, M cells are generally larger cells that are more sensitive to luminance and movement within the periphery of vision. Both P and M cells find their way to the visual cortex via the lateral geniculate nuclei of the thalamus, which is described in Chapter 2. The M cells in this pathway have a particular role in the analysis of motion within the V5 area and in other ares in the anterior occipital to posterior parietal areas. The M cells, therefore, make an important contribution to the "where-action" pathway. However, there is a *second* "geniculate" pathway for the magno stream which appears to have a particular importance for orienting within attention; this pathway also makes an important contribution to analysing motion and location, especially when the target arrives within the periphery of vision. This pathway projects first to the superior colliculus and then to the pulvinar of the thalamus before projecting mainly to the posterior parietal area, but there are also projections that fan out to points along the V1 to V4 pathway (see Figure 4.4).

La Berge (1995, pp. 143–147) provides a model that describes the complex interaction between the superior colliculus (SC) and other brain areas. Broadly, a functional pattern can be discerned, which describes a number of layers within the SC. The superficial or upper layers of the SC play a role in passing sensory information at high speed to be analysed for location of a target, which is passed on to the cortex. This movement-sensitive mechanism has obvious importance in organisms for detecting sudden movement in the periphery of vision and therefore has obvious pertinence to the survival of many species (see Figure 4.5a).

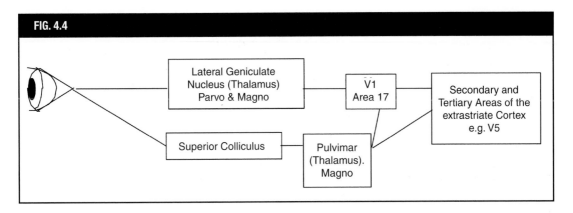

FIG. 4.4

Diagram showing the geniculate pathway via the lateral geniculate nucleus of the thalamus and the collicular pathway travelling via the superior colliculus and the pulvinar of the thalamus.

These superficial layers of the SC have a retinal map and appear to function mainly in a visual receptive mode.

There are also deeper layers of the SC that appear to play a role in both feeding sensory information back to the superficial levels and directing eye movements to the location of the moving object. Therefore the deeper layers are not purely reflexive. Nevertheless, electrical discharge can be measured here *prior* to eye movements and it is likely that these deeper and intermediate areas are instrumental in initiating quick eye movements since there are inputs from other sensory systems (auditory and somatosensory) that give directional cues. These deeper layers of the SC have cells that map visual, auditory, and somatosensory space. The suggestion is that these deeper levels activate the brain stem centres, which in turn activate the muscle movements in the eyes and head turning. However, these deeper layers are themselves potentially triggered by the posterior parietal cortex with further guidance from the frontal eye fields, while the basal ganglia is seen as having an inhibitory or restraining role, although most recently there is some controversy concerning the role of the frontal eye fields. The possibility exists from recent evidence that in humans it acts as a short-term memory system for overt or covert attention (Gaymard, Ploner, Rivaud-Pechoux, & Pierrot-Deseilligny, 1999; Ploner et al., 1999). In other words it acts to keep on-line previous experiences regarding spatial location, but this area needs further research and it is also clear that frontal eye fields have an inhibiting influence on attentional orienting and the SC. This is discussed in greater detail when the executive attention system is discussed later.

Now let us look more at the direction of eye movements and sensory feedback, which appears to be more the domain of the deeper layers of the SC. The deeper layers receive visual sensory feedback from the superior SC and also receive projections from the substantia nigra reticulata of the basal ganglia. As mentioned, the deep and intermediate areas of the SC also receive projections from other sensory areas such as those receiving auditory and somatosensory input. These sensory inputs no doubt enhance the processing of the directional location of an object and may bear on the relationship between direction gaze and the direction of non-visual sensory information discussed below.

Apart from receiving and feeding back from two types of sensory information (auditory and somatosensory), the deeper layers of the SC also play a role in rapid scanning eye movements. When considering the sensory inputs from the auditory and somatosensory areas it is worth taking into account the direction of this influence. Experiments that have assessed the influence of cueing from one modality to another (e.g. auditory information cueing where to look) have suggested that visual orienting can be influenced by auditory cues or somatosensory cues. It appears

FIG. 4.5

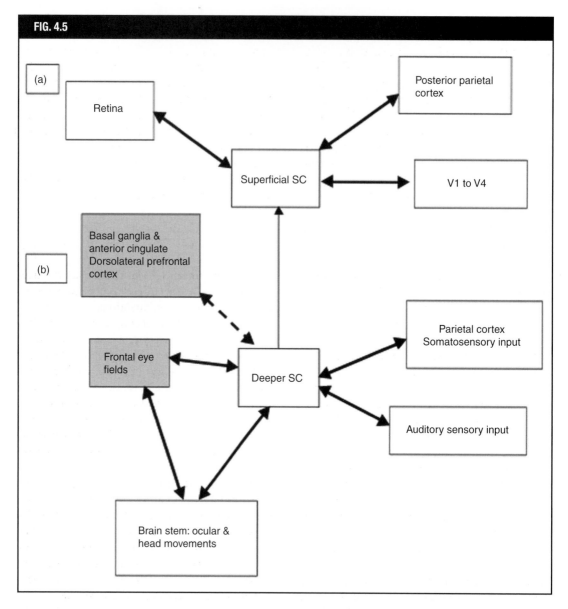

Schematic diagram of SC inputs and outputs. (a) The functional connections of the superficial layers, which act as a fast-tract input from the retina to the "where-action" pathway of the parietal cortex via the pulvinar of the thalamus. A retinal map allows detection of location of any moving object, especially within the periphery of vision. (b) The intermediate and deeper layers within the SC are more concerned with the execution of eye movements via the brain stem. At the deeper levels there are inputs from the auditory and somatosensory areas that help to cue direction. The deeper layers are also controlled by the frontal eye fields (shaded) and the parietal cortex. The basal ganglia and anterior cingulate may have a more indirect influence (dotted line).

that spatial maps of the environment are set up through coordinating sensory inputs. However, in some situations visual cues appear to be dominant; therefore when there is a television picture of someone reading the news the sound will appear to come from that same direction even if this is not the case (see Driver & Spence, 1998). Ventriloquists use this to good effect. Animal experiments investigating cell firing to multisensory stimuli point to the SC as being one of the main coordinating centres for attentional orienting. The recognition of location of objects (spatial mapping) is derived in part from the coordination of sensory inputs and is mediated in part by the SC (e.g. Wallace, Meredith, & Stein, 1998). This activity also takes place in concert with polymodal (representing different senses) areas within the parietal lobe (Andersen, Snyder, Bradley, & Xing, 1997). In short, both the SC and the posterior parietal cortex are assumed to have spatial maps of the environment.

Prior to eye movements, cells fire within the deep SC layers and parts of the basal ganglia and frontal eye fields; the firing of cells in the posterior parietal lobe is less dependent on eye movements by comparison. Because the cells within the basal ganglia are inhibitory it is assumed that they cease to inhibit and release the SC when an eye movement is required, thereby allowing the SC to activate eye movements. La Berge (1995) suggests that, since the frontal eye fields, the posterior parietal cortex, and the basal ganglia influence the same intermediate/deep layers of the SC, it is likely that all these structures combine to activate the SC to direct the oculomotor nuclei in a controlled manner. Ultimately, the eye movement required of an attentional response is initiated by both the deep layers of the SC and the frontal eye fields, which also activate the oculomotor nuclei in the brain stem independently, which in turn act on muscle groups to move the eyes. In animal experiments, on which this model is largely based, this system has an obvious role in fixating and tracking a target (see La Berge, 1995, pp. 150–155).

In summary, the orienting reflex is assumed to be a fast stimulus location detection mechanism, which is assumed to be monochrome (magno

stream). It is a primitive mechanism since it is not well suited to defining the object of attention in an advanced perceptual way. The function of the orienting reflex is to bring the target into the range of the fovea (centre) of the eye to allow analysis of the target. The SC, the frontal eye fields,with the posterior parietal cortex appear to be influential in controlling the reflexive nature of the SC and overruling the system to provide voluntary control for shifts of attention. In the following sections there is a further discussion of the structures and their executive influence.

Habituation

This interaction between the SC and other structures, described above, is only part of the mechanism. The response is more sophisticated since, with a repeated stimulus, there is a reduction in the magnitude of the reflex as the stimulus becomes more familiar. This process of *habituation* may be described in the case when a person is alerted by a strange noise from a nextdoor flat. The same unusual noise is heard at the same time the next evening, with a similar but lesser attentional response. Eventually, the person takes no notice of the noise and is not even aware that it has occurred and is consequently surprised when it is mentioned by a visitor. This is the process of habituation.

To describe this phenomenon in experimental terms there is a reduction of the orienting reflex with repetitions of an initially novel stimulus. As the stimulus becomes more familiar, the orienting reflex is reduced in magnitude and eventually disappears. Generally, the literature reviewed by Cohen et al. (1993, pp. 110–113) provides that the posterior brain structures are not so involved in this process of habituation. Studies with patients with medial frontal lesions to the cingulate (Cohen, McCrae, Phillips, & Wilkinson, 1990), and patients with Wernicke–Korsakoff syndrome (amnesic patients discussed in Chapter 5) and Huntington's disease, implicate anterior structures as being most important. According to Cohen et al. (1993) there is further support for the involvement of the limbic system, especially the amygdala and the hypothalamus. These limbic–hypothalamic–frontal systems activate the

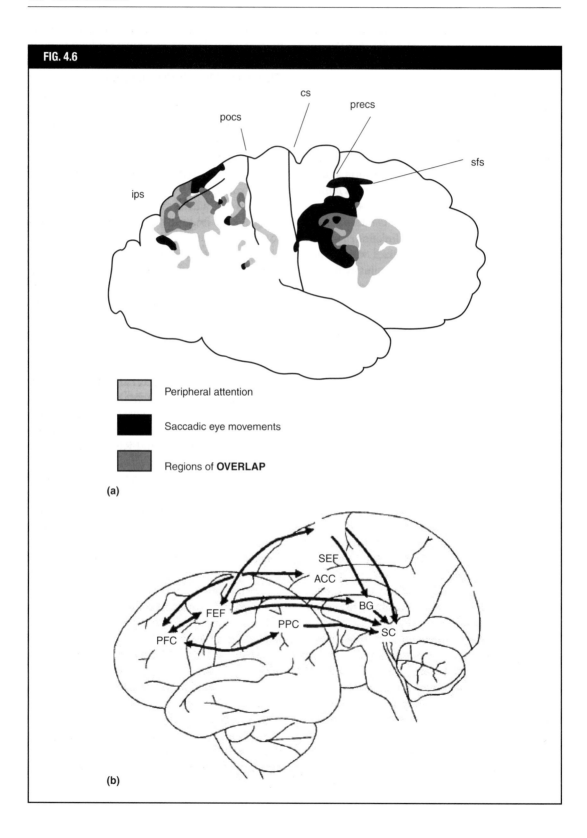

FIG. 4.6

Peripheral attention

Saccadic eye movements

Regions of **OVERLAP**

(a)

(b)

areas are, of course, the frontal eye fields. As indicated, this area, which is activated in Fig 4.6a, is clearly important in guiding and possibly triggering voluntary eye movements and covert (without eye movements) attention.

The second parietal area that seems to play a dominant role in all attentional processes is an area at the junction of the occipital, temporal, and parietal lobes within the inferior parietal cortex. It is this area which when damaged causes an impairment in global processing when the lesion is on the right and an impaired local processing when the lesion is on the left. This phenomenon has been previously discussed in the section on global and local processing in Chapter 2 (see Rafal & Robertson, 1995). Some patients who have damage to this area on the right will go on to show features of unilateral neglect, which is a profound disorder of attention and is discussed in this chapter in some detail. Conceptually, for reasons that will become clear, this area can be seen as involving the orienting, perceptual, and executive attention systems. However, patients with unilateral neglect show abnormal orienting as a classic hallmark of the disorder. Unlike the slowed and inefficient orienting that occurs with damage to the SC the orienting impairment associated with unilateral neglect is very much tied to the nature and competition between stimuli present at the time. It is perhaps not surprising, given the location of this area within the polymodal association area (an area involving an advanced stage of processing of visual, auditory, and somatosensory information), that damage in this area influences the orienting response in relation to the perceptual nature of the input.

The perceptual attention system

In Chapter 2 there was a discussion concerning the various areas of the occipital lobe and the inferior temporal lobe that were important to the identification of an object. A progressive and specialised analysis was described that was seen as following a stream of processing which was referred to as the "what pathway". Apart from this progressive analysis an additional aid to perceptual processing was described in terms of top-down processing. This was described as the influence of past experience in influencing perceptual processing. However, there was little discussion of the mechanism of top-down processing. Is this a passive process in which a template is matched at a late stage of processing or is this a dynamic process whereby there is also the capability to make early stages of processing more sensitive to some features compared to others?

In the review of the literature at the beginning of this chapter there was a discussion of Cherry's cocktail party phenomenon, which describes our tendency in a social situation to become alerted to our own name being mentioned across the room. The question was asked, do we have to unconsciously monitor all the conversations to a "deep level of processing" for meaning before we can recognise our name and bring it to consciousness? It was argued that this is probably not the case and that we can probably be perceptually ready for some stimuli at the expense of others. This view is formulated within Desimone and

(a) Results of a meta-analysis of PET scan data of the activation of areas associated with a task requiring the subject to shift to a target within the periphery of visual space with (saccadic) or without eye movements. There are prominent activations in the superior aspect of the posterior parietal cortex at a point that is seen as being part of the "where-action" pathway. The posterior parietal cortex is involved, especially an area around the intraparietal sulcus (ips) area (see line representing this sulcus). The posterior central sulcus (poc and central sulcus (cs) are also shown. There are also anterior activations corresponding to the precentral gyrus (precs), which is part of the motor strip; these extend anteriorly. There are also activations in the saccadic condition in the frontal eye fields towards the posterior tip of the superior frontal sulcus (sfs); some of the medial activations are not shown (adapted with permission from Corbetta, Shulman, Miezin, & Petersen, 1995). (b) Schematic diagram of the structures believed to be involved with the antisaccade, and a simplified diagram of their connectivity. The prefrontal cortex (PFC), posterior parietal cortex (PPC), the frontal eye-fields (FEF), supplementary eye-field (SEF), superior colliculus (SC), anterior cingulate ACC, and basal ganglia (BG) are shown (reprinted from Everling & Fischer, 1998, with permission from Elsevier Science).

Duncan's (1995) competition theory. Since this account was published there has been much more evidence concerning where this competition takes place. But the first series of experiments, which appear to be the mainstay of competition theory and support the view that there are selective processes of attention within perception, come from Desimone's and colleagues' own work.

The method of research in these studies is cunning in that it matches cell activation with the perception of certain objects and then looks at how this cell activations changes according to attentional demands (Figure 4.7). This seems to be a simple type of experiment but the difficult part would seem to be finding the brain cells in the mentioned area that correspond to the perception of a particular object. To do this the experimenters have to do some detective work: they expose a monkey to a variety of pictures until there is a greater activation of some of the cells that are being measured to a particular picture. They then know in the future that this firing pattern is closely related to the perception of the picture. They then train the monkey to attend to

FIG. 4.7

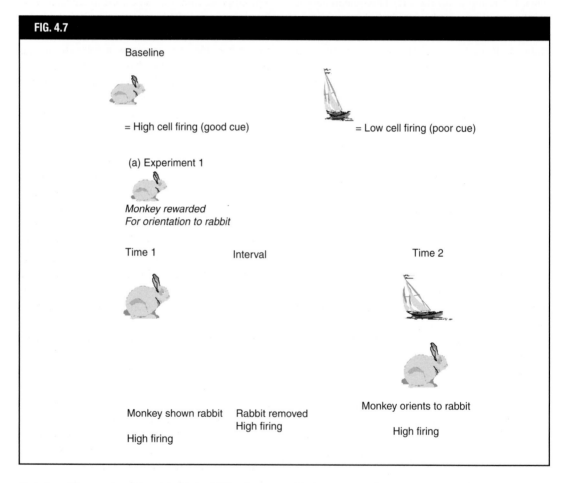

Baseline

= High cell firing (good cue)

= Low cell firing (poor cue)

(a) Experiment 1

Monkey rewarded
For orientation to rabbit

Time 1   Interval   Time 2

Monkey shown rabbit   Rabbit removed   Monkey orients to rabbit
                       High firing
High firing   High firing

Illustration of the experimental work by Chelazzi, Miller, Duncan, and Desimone (1993). Baseline firing patterns are first registered. (a) There is evidence of a maintained high firing during the interval which is accentuated just prior to orientation towards the rabbit. This suggests that a readiness to respond to the rabbit is maintained during the interval. (b) When the poor cue (sailing boat) is presented with the rabbit during the orientation recognition test one might expect a high firing response, given the presence of the rabbit. But the neuronal firing to the rabbit is suppressed, suggesting a selection of the sailing boat at the expense of the rabbit, thereby giving support for a competition theory of attention within perception.

the object so that it is rewarded when the monkey orients to this same object. Having identified the neural signal that is associated with a certain object the experimenter would rightly assume that as soon as the object is presented then the associated cells would fire in an exaggerated way. This occurs but what they also found was that the same pattern of firing existed even before the object they were looking for was presented. It was as if the monkey was thinking or imaging the object in preparation to being shown the stimulus.

Let us describe this important experiment in more detail. Chelazzi, Miller, Duncan, & Desimone (1993) monitored cells within the monkey's inferior temporal lobe and identified two cell types that corresponded to two objects being described respectively as "good cues", which responded maximally, and "poor cues", which responded minimally. In this way the researchers identified a visual stimulus according to a pattern of cell firing compared to a baseline measure. The paradigm used in this experiment involved the presentation of a stimulus (one of the two types of cues) followed by an interval, which was followed by the presentation of two stimuli (one "good" and one "poor") in different peripheral locations, one of these two stimuli (good or poor cue) matching the originally presented cue. The monkey was rewarded with juice if it oriented its eyes in the direction of the stimulus that matched the cue they had been presenting orginally. By using "good" cues (high cell activation) and "poor" cues (low cell activation) the cell activation could be matched to the stimulus.

Two findings were of interest: firstly, there was a prolongation of activation, which matched the original cue type (good or poor) that continued into the interval when no cues or targets were present. It is speculative, but as suggested above, some kind of internal representation of the cue appeared to be maintained, which could be construed as a top-down perceptual process. This view is further supported by the location of these cells within the inferior temporal lobe, an area that is frequently associated with a metaphorical end-point of perception within the "what" pathway.

In the test situation the repeated cue was shown in one location and the non-cue in another. The monkey had been previously trained to look and orient to the cue in order to test the attributes of the neural firing in this task as the monkey oriented towards the target. Chelazzi and colleagues found that just before the monkey oriented towards the stimulus that matched the good cue the firing of the pattern matching the good cue was exaggerated. This suggests a "capture" process, whereby the attention was covertly oriented *prior* to the overt eye movements.

The second finding, which illustrated the competitive nature of the process, showed that when a "poor" cue was originally presented as a future target and the test presentation contained both the "good" cue and the "poor" cue (target), the activation associated with the "good" cue (now a distractor) was *lower* than baseline. In other words, the usual high activation towards "good" cues in this test situation was *suppressed*. This encourages the intuitively appealing view of attention as a spotlight or zoom lens. In this way a stimulus is attended to and focused on at the expense of other competing stimuli (see Desimone & Duncan, 1995, for a review). The finding that the cells representing the target were pre-activated in readiness within the inferior temporal lobe strongly suggested that this was a top-down perceptual process. However, this attentional selection takes place within the perception. Therefor it is referred to here as the perceptual attention system.

There are now studies that have found evidence of this kind of selection in areas other than the inferior temporal lobe. This evidence of selective top-down processing has been found in areas such as V4 and V2 (Reynolds, Chelazzi, & Desimone, 1999) and studies have found the results of this tuning effect as early as V1, although it appears to be reduced at this earlier stage of perceptual processing. Thus in the case of figures that have ambiguous perceptions but the same physical features, such as the faces and the vase figure illustrated towards the end of Chapter 2 around 18% cells are modulated with a change in the perception within the primary visual or striate cortex, while nearly half were involved at a halfway stage around V4 (area MT in the monkey) and all the neurones were involved within the inferior temporal cortex (Leopold & Logothetis, 1996).

When a relevant stimulus is novel, or is familiar but has not seen recently, then there is an accentuated neuronal activity at the level of the visual cortex and to a lesser extent the inferior temporal lobe. As further presentations of the stimuli are provided, the features of the stimulus become familiar and activation becomes more selectively driven at the inferior temporal lobe level (Desimone, Miller, & Chelazzi, 1994). The need to orient to such stimuli is, correspondingly, reduced unless it is actively searched for. This describes a system whereby experience with a perceptual stimulus can increase its tendency to act in a "top-down" fashion. When we have sufficient experience of a stimulus, "top-down" control allows a short-cut in the perceptual process. The increased ease of identification of a percept has the advantage of reducing the need for attentional resources.

This top-down view of the selection of perceptual stimuli is further supported by studies that have assessed the attention to percepts during tasks that illustrate binocular rivalry. Binocular rivalry refers to the situation in which two different images are presented, one to each eye. The reported experience of subjects in this type of experiment is that only one of the two images is seen: either the image presented to the left eye or the one presented to the right. There is no experience of overlapping images or two interfering images, although there may be the experience of alternation, i.e. seeing one image and then the other. Sheinberg and Logothetis (1997) have conducted experiments with monkeys trained to see single images by making a specific response, e.g. pulling a lever. In situations that encourage binocular rivalry, i.e. a different image to each eye, it is possible to see which image the monkey is seeing by its response. By knowing when the monkey was switching from one image to another it was possible to show that implanted electrodes in the anterior temporal lobe were more likely to be activated when compared to striate areas (primary visual area, 17) and early extrastriate areas,

e.g. V4. In other words, it was at the end of the "what" pathway that image switching was most obviously being represented and that perhaps the earlier areas, which had less activation to switching, were involved in the organisation process of perception. This is most obviously a perceptual process, but selective attention can be considered to be involved since monkey (Sheinberg & Logothetis, 1997) and human subjects (Ooi & He, 1999) may apparently select a preferred image during a binocular rivalry task—in the same way that the reader may voluntarily select and concentrate on one of the interpretations of the ambiguous images in Figure 4.8 at the expense of the other. Therefore, this top-down process is very much a perceptual attentional process that is subject to some top-down control.

Electrophysiological studies (Gaetz, Weinberg, Rzempoluck & Jantzen, 1998) have found that the crucial areas of activation during the switching of images, i.e. Necker cube reversal, are generally posterior within the parietal, temporal, and occipital lobes. Functional imaging studies see that the parietal lobe is particularly crucial during the switch (Inui et al., 2000).

In summary, there is a case, given the recent work in this area, for describing a perceptual attentional system that acts to select percepts in a preferential, voluntary manner. Investigations into this network are in their infancy but it is likely that the selection of expected features of our environment allow us to concentrate preferentially on things that matter most to us. This system has obvious advantages but it can also act against us in situations where other intelligent protagonists are attempting to deceive us. The deceptive strategies of the conjurer and pickpocket both know and play upon features of the perceptual attentional system—the tendency to focus on some features of our environment at the expense of others, and to be attracted by movement and salient features within our visual space.

The structures that are functionally important to the perceptual attentional system are not yet fully appreciated, although the anterior temporal lobe and parietal structures clearly play an important role. It is likely that a controlling role exists additionally within the prefrontal

FIG. 4.8

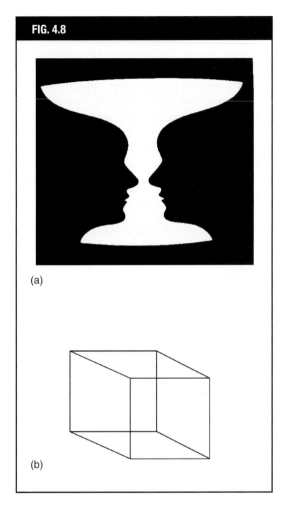

(a)

(b)

(a) An ambiguous figure (reprinted from Hoffman & Richards, 1984, with permission from Elsevier Science). Notice how you can control the perception of either the profile of the vase or the faces using the hypothetical top-down processing. The two percepts are competing and may be selected for attention under voluntary control. (b) The Necker cube (adapted from Cavanagh, 1987, with permission from Academic Press), allows two perspectives by turning the image inside out. Studies show the frequency of reversals by requesting subjects to indicate by lever or button as a reversal is made.

cortex. Lesion studies have found that frontal lesions are associated with reduced frequency of Necker reversals (Teuber & Mishkin, 1954) although a brain-damaged control was not used for this study. However, this and other data have

been recently discussed favouring of a right frontal influence on such tasks (see Sengpiel, 2000). Therefore a broad model sees a final executive attention system that influences all the other systems referred to so far. The nature of the perceptual attention system will be elaborated on towards the end of this chapter when the quality of perceptual deficits is described in relation to disorders of attention.

The executive attention system and its influence on the orienting and perceptual attention and arousal systems

The executive attention system and the orienting system

The previous chapter illustrated the important influence of the executive system in the control, organisation, and monitoring of behaviour. This description included a reference to the executive influences on attention. We now elaborate on this influence by looking at the processes underlying controlled search and monitoring within attention.

First, it is appropriate to refer back to the section on the orienting system. The archetypal task for demonstrating orienting requires the subject to orient to a flash of light or other signal in the periphery. Eye movements are tracked and a button is pressed when the target is located. Antisaccades occur when the subject is required to orient away from the target and this controlled response, which requires the containment of a reflexive response in the other direction, is assumed to involve some executive control.

Recent support for this view comes from a method referred to as transcranial magnetic stimulation (TMS) (Muri, Rivaud, Gaymard et al., 1999). TMS may be used with human subjects and acts to very temporarily disable certain specific brain areas through magnetic radiation. When TMS is applied to the prefrontal cortex area many more express saccades occur to the contralateral side; also antisaccades are slower. These results suggest that the dorsolateral area within the prefrontal cortex has a special inhibiting or controlling role on reflexive orienting. Such movements may be voluntarily controlled by the frontal eye fields and a modern location for this area can be seen in the activation that occurs at the junction of the precentral gyrus and the superior frontal sulcus, as shown in Figure 4.6 (Pollmann & von Cramon, 2000). There is some activation of this area even in an orientation response.

Henik, Rafal, & Rhodes, 1994; Rafal and Robertson (1995) compared patients with DPFC lesions with patients with DPFC lesions plus lesions to the frontal eye fields. When the frontal eye fields were additionally lesioned there were two effects. First there was a quickening of reflex orienting to the contralateral field, which is explained as a disinhibition of the SC on the same *ipsilesional* side. In other words, the frontal eye field is seen as having a controlling influence on reflexive responding; when this is removed then the reflexive orienting becomes unfettered and hyperreflexive. If the frontal eye field is important for controlled orienting then one would expect a voluntary shift of gaze to the contralateral field to be slower, and this was also found in the study. In this way contralateral externally triggered (reflexive) orienting is faster but contralateral voluntary orienting (controlled) is slower. However, there is a further effect of slowing reflexive orienting on the ipsilesional side to a point where it is no faster than a voluntary shift. This might be difficult to interpret without considering a system that is balanced at the cortical level. The left frontal eye field has inhibiting forces that are normally balanced by the right frontal eye field. If you remove the left frontal eye field then the inhibiting power of the right becomes too powerful and overly inhibits the reflexive orienting to the ipsilesional side. This idea of lateral balance between orienting systems is not a new one and has been supported by animal studies showing that slow orienting due to a cortical lesion has actually been improved by a second contralateral lesion within the orienting system (Kinsbourne, 1993).

Studies such as those by Henik and colleagues are somewhat complex and must be confirmed in their interpretation; however, at present the frontal eye field is seen to have a role in voluntary shifts of attention and the control of reflexive

orienting when this is appropriate. This role for the frontal eye field has been confirmed in monkey work that has recorded cell activation during voluntary attention shift (Schall, Hanes, Thompson, & King, 1995). The reader will be aware that several structures have been accredited with such a role and one of the research aims at the present time is to define a network of structures that include the frontal eye field, parietal cortex, DPFC, and anterior cingulate with reference to the individual contribution of these structures (see Posner, 1995, for a discussion).

Selective attention and divided attention: roles for the DPFC and the Anterior Cingulate

The DPFC has been associated with a prominent executive role on the orienting system as described earlier but the DPFC has also been described as playing an important role in tasks that require selective attention. Richer et al., (1993) found that patients with frontal lesions made significantly more errors as the number of items to be searched increased. Studies using a variety of techniques suggest complex tasks of selective attention that require a target search show additional involvement in attention of the DPFC within a network with the parietal cortex and other structures (Knight, Grabowecky, & Scabini, 1995). These dorsolateral frontal areas appear to be involved in keeping track of the search process (Petrides, 1996) and also appear to play an integrative role by allowing attentional and perceptual processes to work in concert (Barcelo et al., 2000).

In support of this integrating role of the prefrontal cortex, patients with frontal lobe lesions often have difficulty in tasks that require a spatial search of stimuli for particular features. Part of this problem appears to be strategic. As discussed in the previous chapter, Luria (1973) described a number of such patients, who show a disorganised search for features in pictures when their eye movements are monitored, and this kind of finding has been well replicated using other paradigms. Teuber (1964), for example, describes an experiment in which patients with frontal lesions found difficulty in matching a centrally placed target shape with a shape on the periphery from among other distracting shapes. Typically the search was poorly organised, lacking any efficient strategy (see also Knight et al., 1995). Therefore there is evidence from a number of areas that the executive attention system modulates what has been described here as the perceptual attention system.

With the previous description of the role of the anterior cingulate within habituation, there is a further role for this structure within tasks requiring focused attention. There are a number of paradigms that test this kind of attention. In the previous chapter there was a description of the Stroop test (Stroop, 1935), which provides a good example. In this test the word "BLUE" would be written in red ink, for example. The patient is required to report the colour of the ink, *red*, and not name the word. This is a difficult task because the subject has to restrain themselves from the automatic tendency to read the word and focus on the requirements of reporting the colour. Functional imaging studies have consistently found the right anterior cingulate to be activated in such tasks (e.g; Pardo et al., 1990). With practice subjects come to learn the task and the task becomes more automatic, with the anterior cingulate and other structures becoming less activated as this occurs (Raichle et al., 1994). Given the network of connections between the parietal cortex, anterior cingulate and DPFC one might speculate that the anterior cingulate acts as a kind of intermediary between the DPFC and the parietal cortex. The parietal cortex processes the spatial location of the stimulus and the DPFC provides the initiating semantic selection requirements, while the anterior cingulate allows an integration between the two areas (see also Posner, 1995, p. 620). However, the anterior cingulate is likely to have more than a mere translation or integration role given its specific activation in tasks that require concentration and effort or when tasks are novel and demanding. In Chapter 3 it was argued that activation of the anterior cingulate occurs when the strategic selection processes of the DPFC require more attentional resources. Therefore the integrating role of the anterior cingulate must be seen in a role that

brings attentional resources to focus on the spatial location taking into account the information provided by the DPFC.

Finally, before leaving this section on selective attention some mention should be made of the overlap between this topic and the selection of past memories for awareness. In the section on the perceptual attentional system the influence of the DPFC on the top-down selection of visual attributes was described. Such a system assumes that a perceptual memory store is accessed to guide selective processes during a search of visual space. Some part of this selective process may be present when we select information from memory without reference to external stimuli. When we keep information "in mind" it is assumed that specific information is attended to externally and then maintained in some internal form. When a selective element is involved to the extent that more than one element must be maintained, then this involves a representation within "working memory". Both working memory and spatial attention involve the activation of the DPFC in concert with other structures already mentioned and, although the areas of activation are not identical, functional imaging studies do indicate some overlap when similar materials are being assessed (LaBar, Gitelman, Parrish, & Mesulam, 1999).

The involvement of attention within a temporary memory or buffer system is dealt with more comprehensively towards the end of this chapter and in the next chapter. At this point it is sufficient to mention that the influence of the executive attention system may be described in the control, selection, and focus on external and internally represented stimuli.

Sustained attention and alertness: the role of the executive attentional system in vigilance

In the introduction to this chapter there was mention of the importance of a type of attention that in everyday terms referred to "keeping watch" or monitoring over extended periods of time. This could be seen as a crucial skill towards survival for a number of species and is quite different from the kind of concentration that is required when carrying out immediate tasks. This monitoring role, which is described here as the alert system, was originally described by Posner and Petersen (1990). These authors referred to a sustained visual attention system, which maintains attentional alertness and is based within the right parietal and right frontal areas. *Sustained* visual attention is required by the vigilance tasks that have been previously mentioned. These 20–30-minute tasks typically require the subject to detect target letters appearing in a particular order, and false positive errors and "hits" provide a ratio that can be represented in a measure of signal detection sometimes referred to as "d" prime.

While there appears to be some agreement in the way vigilance and the hypothetical alerting process can be measured, there is still some discussion concerning the arousal mechanism, which maintains a readiness to respond despite lengthy periods without much need for response. Posner and Petersen (1990) reviewed animal work suggesting that this alertness involves a right hemisphere-biased noradrenaline system (e.g. Robinson, 985). There is some support for the influence of this neurotransmitter on attention as described earlier. There is an increased connectivity between a network of structures that include the parietal cortex, the thalamus, the frontal cortex, and locus coeruleus (Coull et al., 1999).

A study using PET scan seems to support part of Posner and Petersen's proposal. Coull et al. (1998) used a task that required subjects to detect a letter of a certain colour from among other letters of different colours; some features of the distractors were overlapping or conjoint with the target, i.e. same letter, different colour. These letters were presented one at a time in a serial fashion and the subjects were brain scanned at different intervals longitudinally (at three points during the 18-minute sustained attention task). When the brain activations on this task were compared with the activations on a control task, which merely required the subject to detect the presence of a stimulus without any discrimination required, there was a clear difference over time. The *right-sided* prefrontal (dorsolateral and ventrolateral) and parietal activations were maintained over time. However, these activations quickly died

away on the control task. This and other studies suggest that over time the thalamic arousal is reduced during such tasks and such de-arousal is associated with slowing in reaction time. Coull (1998) proposes that because in their own study the activation of the parietal and frontal areas was maintained despite a reduction in thalamic arousal there may be two arousal systems involved, one arousal system for subcortical structures contributing to attention and another supplying arousal to prefrontal cortical areas. These two systems are yet to be clearly identified. The cholinergic system and the noradrenaline systems are obvious candidates for the thalamic arousal. But the suggestion at this time is that the second system which serves the prefrontal cortex is a dopamine neurotransmitter system (see Figure 4.3). Such a system would be in a position to modulate arousal within frontal structures that have been found important to sustained attention over extended periods.

Robertson et al. (1995) have also been influenced by the Posner and Petersen model. They reasoned that if the orienting system and the alert/sustained attention system overlapped (see Figure 4.2), then training in one should benefit the other. These authors trained patients with unilateral neglect, who showed difficulty in orienting to and attending to the left. This disorder is discussed in the next section, but the point to be made here is that training on the sustained attention task *also* appeared to improve performance on these patients' ability to orient their attention to one side. General improvements to attention have also been achieved by methods aimed at increasing the arousal of the patient during the task, which is also in keeping with the interaction between systems (Robertson et al., 1995).

Interactions between the four systems

In summary, four systems have been described: the arousal system, the orienting system, the perceptual attention system, and the executive attention system. Arousal levels affect the other systems, providing the prerequisite cortical tone for attention. However, while originally a single system was envisaged by early theorists (see Chapter

1), it is becoming clear that there are several arousal systems that appear to have specialist roles. In this model the parietal cortex acts in a pivotal role in the spatial allocation of attention for both the orienting and the executive attention systems. It is assumed that the network of systems is integrated but finally orchestrated by the executive attention system.

The nature of this controlling executive role is poorly understood as yet and the strength of this influence may depend on the nature of the task. The overlap between systems and the overall influence of the executive attention system may be revealed in some of the earlier discussion that described the inhibiting role of the frontal eye field over reflexive orienting, also the apparent influence of the frontal eye field within voluntary shifts of attention. The influence in controlling the orienting system was also described in some studies that had temporary disablement of the DPFC. The DPFC has also been described as contributing towards the completion of tasks involving selective attention, in particular when organised strategies of search are required.

Seemingly, separate influences of the executive attention system come from work that has investigated Posner and Petersen's alerting system. Here again we are reminded of interactions between different systems, in particular the arousal that maintains alertness over long and boring periods of monitoring which is typically required in the continuous performance task that assesses vigilance.

Illustrations of the diagrammatic relationship between the four systems are given in Figure 4.9. The model assumes that there is a controlling and inhibiting influence on the other three systems by the executive attention system. This influence would extend to the arousal system which itself is depicted here as having a broad influence in maintaining optimal arousal in all the systems. Developments of this simple model would see the fractionation of these arousal components and the evolution of various subsystems that highlight the separate executive roles that are emerging at the present time. Further development of this model would no doubt also point to the lateralised nature of attention, as described in the depic-

tion of Posner and Petersen's original model in Figure 4.2. More activation on the right is frequently noted in functional imaging studies that have studied orientation and shifts of attention (Corbetta & Shulman, 1998). Already mentioned is the apparent lateralisation of attention to the right side in studies of continuous performance tasks and alertness. However, other tasks measuring selective attention are not necessarily so dependent on right hemisphere processing (Passingham, 1998).

One of the main supports for the view of a right hemisphere dominance for attention is found in studies of the clinical disorder of unilateral neglect. Given that this disorder typifies a clinical representation of attention breakdown in orientation the right parietal cortex is often seen at the hub of the attentional system.

A CLINICAL DESCRIPTION OF ATTENTION DISORDERS

Clinical signs of unilateral neglect

Unilateral neglect is the syndrome that typifies a clinical disorder of attention. A broad description of this disorder from the clinical perspective may help to place some of the experimental literature in perspective.

Unilateral neglect is a disorder of attention and should not be confused with the sensory loss of hemianopia, which was described in Chapter 2. Patients with unilateral neglect have impaired attention to the side contralateral to their lesion (see Box 4.1.) Because this disorder is usually associated with a right-sided lesion in the inferior parietal lobe, the left side is usually neglected or ignored. Visual neglect from clinical assessment (e.g. copying Rey Figure, see Figure 4.10) is relatively frequent in acute stroke patients, often involving the middle cerebral artery. Although in the first 3 days after stroke neglect can occur following lesions on either side, 3 months later the vast majority of cases with neglect have a right hemisphere lesion. Around 33% of stroke patients at this time show a left-sided neglect associated with right hemisphere damage (Stone,

Wilson, Wroot, et al., 1991). When looking at its clinical manifestation, chronic neglect tends to be predominantly a right hemisphere, left attentional neglect phenomenon.

The effects of neglect may be dramatic. Patients will only draw the right half of a picture, or comb the right side of their hair or eat from the right side of their plate (McFie, 1975). For this reason allowances have to be made when arranging the patient's belongings around their bedside and the patient should be communicated with from the appropriate side, usually the patient's right side. If a patient is asked to attend to a previously ignored object, they will often acknowledge the presence of the object in a rather nonchalant or diffident way. Therefore, although the stimulus is available to the patient's perception, they have merely failed to attend to the stimulus (see Box 4.1).

Neglect is a complex disorder with many variants. Patients may manifest their neglect in the visual, auditory, or somesthetic (haptic) modalities and also in terms of movement (kinetic). Neglect can be isolated to one or a combination of these modalities and there are experimentally derived subtypes within these broad categories. Sometimes a stimulus is acknowledged on the neglected side and the patient may mistakenly report its presence as if it appeared on the non-neglected side. Thus, for example, a patient may be given an auditory stimulation on the their left neglected side and claim that the sound came from the right. Or, in the case of kinetic (hypokinesia) neglect, the patient may be asked to raise their left hand and, if they respond at all, they may raise their right hand. However, if then their left hand is held or stimulated in some way, this extra focusing cue may be enough for the patient to respond with the correct hand. Similarly, in the case of visual neglect, extra visual cues may attract the patient's attention towards the neglected side so they may notice something they had not attended to before.

One of the striking features of neglect is an apparent lack of awareness of the continuation of a visually presented object into the left field. In Figure 4.10 there is a copy of the Rey figure by a 61-year-old female patient with left-sided visual neglect. She had suffered right frontoparietal damage following complications associated with the clipping of a right middle cerebral artery aneurysm. When drawing she reached the left side of her copy, went over a few lines on that side as if she was finishing off, then went back to the right side of the drawing to tidy up and before finishing. When asked if she was finished, she said she had completed the copy.

Any picture that is being copied may have what are considered global aspects (perception of the overall) and having meaningful subparts or objects within the global aspects. For example, a seascape that includes ships, a lighthouse, and a horizon are the global aspects but the ships and lighthouse are local objects. Patients with neglect will often ignore the whole left half of the picture; this is referred to as viewer-centred neglect. However, some patients neglect the left side of parts of objects within the global picture, which is referred to as object-centred neglect (see Figure 4.11 and the copy of the house and the tree). It is tempting to interpret this as a case of the patient focusing in or "zooming in" on the object, because it is more difficult to complete and is a complete entity. This extra concentration would result in the patient being only aware of the object, which is then neglected on the left. However, this interpretation is undermined by the finding that some patients have object-centred neglect without viewer-centred neglect (Driver & Halligan, 1991).

Other frame of reference distinctions have been made such as in terms of head position or body position (extracorporeal space) (Kooistra & Heilman, 1989). Patients may have neglect according to any or a combination of these directional planes and may show different orientations of neglect at different times or with different materials (this issue is returned to later in this chapter).

The attentional nature of neglect is sometimes revealed in the patient's memory and imagery for objects. The famous experiment by Bisiach and Luzzatti (1978) illustrates this process well. These researchers required visual neglect patients to describe a well-known square in Milan, Italy, from their memory using imagery. These authors found the patients failed to describe the left side

FIG. 4.11

Copy of house and field by a patient with visual unilateral neglect. Note the object-centered neglect for half of the tree to the right centre of the picture and the environment-centred neglect for the left half of the drawing and the pine tree on the left.

of the square. However, when the patients were requested to describe the image of the same scene, but from the opposite direction, they managed to report on the previously neglected side of the square, which was now imaged on the right. The patients were now unable to describe details of the previously reported side, which was now in their imagination on the left. See Box 4.2 concerning a patient who was tested by the author in this manner.

There are now commercially available tests that can identify the variety of everyday manifestations of neglect and other attention disorders (e.g., Robertson, Ward, Ridgeway, & Nimmo-Smith, 1996). There are also a number of other neuropsychological tests that have been traditionally popular with clinicians and these will be referred to during the course of this chapter. However, the nature of this clinical disorder may

be initially assessed using a less reliable bedside approach. These tests can be revealing for initial management purposes and prior to a more in-depth assessment of the disorder.

Prior to testing, some attempt should be made to verify whether the patient has some sensory or perceptual problems that might confound the assessment. In the case of testing visual neglect, the clinician may ask the patient to focus on the clinician's nose and then to detect one of the clinician's fingers moving from outstretched hands, one at a time. This test is also used to test hemianopia, which should make the clinician cautious in their interpretation. Some patients with severe neglect may look at the fingers of the tester (on their right) as soon as they start moving, despite repeated instructions to stay focused on the tester's nose. The patient may also be asked to draw common stimuli from a copy and from memory.

Alternatively, the patient might be asked to cancel out stimuli, e.g. a series of lines that cover a page. Patients typically cancel the lines in the left visual field. Perhaps the most popular test of visual neglect is to ask the patient to bisect a series of lines down the middle. The patient who attends to the right side of each line tends to bisect towards the right. Some clinicians feel that this test is just a bit too popular and some patients have so much practice at bisecting lines that they become quite good at it, using pencils as measurers and probably other little strategies to compensate.

The patient may then be asked to carry out an action with the neglected body side, e.g. "Lift your left hand." A rough and ready clinical test for auditory neglect requires the clinician to stand behind the patient making a sound, e.g. rubbing the fingers, in one ear and then the other. The somesthetic modality is similarly tested by touching either side of the body, e.g. face or legs, with the patient's eyes closed. There is sometimes a greater evidence of neglect in more distal body parts, e.g. arms rather than shoulders.

All these signs must be interpreted with the possibility that the body parts may have lost sensation for other reasons (anaesthesia).

Extinction to stimuli may also be tested. Extinction occurs when the patient is required to detect two stimuli, one on each side, with the patient typically reporting one stimulus on the non-neglected side. For example, the patient might be touched bilaterally on both cheeks or both knees when eyes are closed. Some caution must be used in the interpretation of this feature, since "extinction to double simultaneous stimulation" may be present in normals and there is some argument that it may be a separate but related disorder of neglect (Heilman, Watson, & Valenstein, 1993; Vallar, 1993).

Whether extinction can be considered a separate disorder from other forms of neglect is discussed below. However, this sign is often the last to disappear after many other signs of neglect have remitted (Weinstein, 1994). Therefore it is often seen as a sign of neglect that has recovered and that bilateral stimulation is a particularly demanding task which manages to evoke the remnant of this disorder.

Some problems may arise in testing visual

Box 4.2.   Neglect within imagery

The following is a transcription taken from a video of a patient with neglect. The patient is a 24-year-old young man who was recovering from surgical treatment for a ruptured right middle cerebral artery aneurysm. The patient claimed he had no difficulty in seeing or being aware of the left side and then proceeded to show severe left-sided neglect on a number of clinical tests. The patient was asked to describe his home from memory, while looking at the house from the front. The house was the usual Australian suburban bungalow with a front aspect, which included a central door and two windows on either side. He first spends some time describing his bedroom, which he describes as being straight ahead, but later it becomes apparent that this is the "rightmost" room in the front of the house. When probed about the other rooms in the house, he describes his brother's room, which is behind his own bedroom, again on the right of the house. When the patient's attention is drawn to the front of the house again, the author declares that there must be a door. He then describes a door. A picture is then drawn of the front of the house as he has described it so far and this is presented to the patient. Eventually the patient locates where the front door is on the picture. We pick the dialogue up at this point.

GD: No, inside the wall past my room (referring to his brother's room) and then the door is there. [Quickly and rather reluctantly points to the position of the front door at a position he is imagining it, which appears to be central]
DA: OK, fine. Now what about the other side of the house as you are looking at it. What's over on the other side? Do you know what's there?
G.D: Nothing.
DA: Nothing?
GD: Straight over the back? [The patient still wants to go anywhere but to his left]
        At this point the author draws the patient's house as it is described so far.
DA: I mean as you're looking facing the front of the house. You have two windows. Are there any other windows there in the front? [The author points to the area on the left of the drawing]
GD: [Nods his head] There's mine, it's there (points to the right), and then the front window there. [Quickly and briefly points to the left of the front door]
DA: Front window, what's in the front window?
GD: Nothing.
DA: There must be some room behind it.
GD: Lounge room.

neglect, when it is confounded by a sensory or perceptual impairment. The patient should always be asked if they have noted any sensory impairments. If they are deaf in one ear, for example, they will usually own up to this (Vallar, 1993, p. 40). Some patients also have anaesthesia, which includes a loss of sensitivity in the neglected limb.

Observation of the patient will often be useful in determining whether neglect is present. Patients who have hemianopia alone may soon compensate for their disorder by moving their head at an angle in order to prevent bumping into objects on the left. Another distinction may be made when patients with neglect are asked to read a sign such as "Outpatients". These patients tend to read the most meaningful component on the right, i.e. the word "patients". Although the experimental results reviewed below suggest that sometimes these patients will guess the first part of the word, they nevertheless report a whole word. A patient with hemianopia and no neglect, in contrast, when asked to look straight ahead to read such a sign, just as they see it, will sometimes report seeing a proportion of the word rather than a meaningful whole. However, when both neglect and hemianopia exist together, which is not uncommon, detection of hemianopia may not be clear cut (Vallar, 1993).

While the most frequently experienced lesion associated with neglect involves the junction of the temporal, parietal, and occipital lobe at the inferior parietal lobule (see Figure 12), there are other lesioned areas associated with neglect: for example, the reticular formation, the anterior cingulate gyrus, and the basal ganglia (Vallar, 1993). Occasionally neglect will be found following lesions to the frontal lobe. An example of this was noted in the case of a patient whom the author assessed with a right frontal lobe tumour. She had first come to clinical notice following an incident when she was driving along the road and scraped along a row of parked cars on her left-hand side. Other lesion locations, such as the thalamus, are also discussed below. Many of the functional imaging studies have failed to find activation during attentional orienting in the typical left inferior parietal lobule.

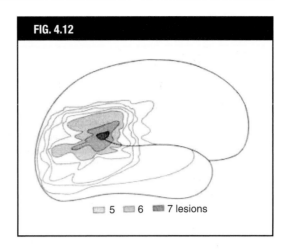

FIG. 4.12

5 ☐ 6 ☐ 7 lesions

A composite contour map of seven patients with severe neglect (reprinted from Vallar & Perani, 1986, with permission from Elsevier Science).

Clinical signs of anosognosia

Patients who have neglect often have far less insight into their disorder when compared to patients who suffer only hemianopia. Often, some of the more severely affected patients will not even admit that they have a problem at all. Even when these patients" attention is drawn to their neglect and they are shown that they have missed out half of the drawing, they often respond "oh yes" or "mm". They tend not to say in an alarmed manner, "How could I have missed that?"

In its severest form it can be a complete denial of the existence of neglect. This lack of insight, or anosognosia, presents a challenge for those involved in the rehabilitation of such patients. Some authors report that, in terms of rehabilitation, changes in behaviour are only noted when there are changes in awareness (Antonucci et. al., 1995). If one is not aware of a deficit, compensation obviously becomes problematic. "Why should I try and compensate for a problem I don't have?" It is sometimes reported that patients will parrot verbally the instructions of their occupational therapist: "I must look to the left," and then do nothing of the kind.

Anosognosia (*a* meaning without; *noso*, disease; *gnosia*, knowledge) is a general term used to refer to the ignoring of an illness. The term was originally coined to refer to a loss of or

---

Box 4.3. Mild signs of anosognosia

The following dialogue is taken from a video of a 48-year-old nursing sister who suffered from complications associated with a right middle cerebral artery stroke. She has a left hemiplegia and is in a wheelchair. This patient is somewhat recovered and is now showing more insight, although she still shows marked signs of neglect on copying tasks. The dialogue below illustrates some of the difficulties and frustrations these patients endure; also, the personification of her paralysed limb, which is seen as a mild sign of anosognosia for hemiplegia. For the purposes of the instructive nature of the video the patient is led to talk about an area that had been noted by other staff, i.e. that had been shown spontaneously by the patient previously. The patient is likely to have additional problems with the perception of spatial relationships.

VW: I still realise that I'm missing a lot on the left, on my lunch tray, when I'm looking for something on the left hand side and there are things that I just can't . . . I spend so much time looking for things. You feel as if you have run a mile, a couple of miles.
DA: There is a tendency for you to speak to your hand too?
VW: I keep telling it, talk to me, work. There are a couple of times when it works, then it doesn't do it the next day, and I am not very impressed with it.
DA: So it has a personality of its own?
VW: It sure has . . . a terrible one.
DA: Right, okay , now the good news for you is that you have improved a lot, haven't you?
VW: Yes.
DA: I mean before you wouldn't even admit to being unaware of the left-hand side, but now are you realising that you have to compensate?
VW: Um, I keep imagining a little green man on my shoulder, to tap you all the time, to remind you. Cos although you are conscious of these things, but you're still not doing it all the time . . . doing it properly. It's the slowness of picking things up that frustrates me. Like yesterday trying to work out the dates, and I had the diary with me, and I couldn't work it out.

---

recognition of hemiplegia, which is also sometimes associated with neglect. The term has now broadened in its connotation. Therefore it now covers not only the lack of awareness associated with neglect, but also any number of disorders of awareness such as Anton's syndrome (the ignoring of blindness, see Chapter 2) or even the ignoring of memory disorders, as is found with Wernicke–Korsakoff syndrome (see Chapter 5). Anosognosia for hemiplegia may appear without neglect and therefore is seen as a separate but strongly associated disorder.

Sometimes neglect can be misdiagnosed as a psychiatric case, suffering from hysterical or somatic conversion, or even as malingering. This is especially the case when the presentation is not associated with common neuropathological signs that accompany a right-sided cortical lesion. Recently we had the experience of such a patient with a colloidal cyst of the third ventricle, which produced pressure in the area of the posterior right thalamus. This particular patient also had a tendency to ignore his own body parts (anosognosia) on the left-hand side, which was also associated with hemianaesthesia (a loss of sensation).

Anosognosia for hemiplegia occurs when the patient fails to acknowledge their disability associated with hemiparesis; patients may not acknowledge their disability and even claim that they have moved their limb in response to the examiner's command despite the limb being stationary. Anecdotally, the most extreme cases are described when a patient believes that an arm or other body part belongs to another person.

Sacks (1985, p. 53) reports on a patient who attracted the attention of staff when he fell out of bed. He had woken up to feel a strange leg beside him; thereupon he threw his own leg out of bed. He was surprised when he was forced to follow the leg on to the floor. The patient reported that as soon as he landed on the floor his leg suddenly became his own.

There is now a developing literature on the influence of physical stimulation in reducing neglect and perhaps the stimulation of hitting the floor may have reduced the anosognosia in this case. Clinically the disorder is normally less dramatic. A patient who shows little concern for their left limb may be suffering from a milder form of anosognosia for hemiplegia. More often the anosognosia for hemiplegia is seen in terms of nonchalance concerning their paralysed limb. It may be revealing when a patient is seen lying with the paralysed limb in an awkward position. Alternatively, they may refer to the paralysed limb in the third person as if it was a separate entity (see Box 4.3; see Weinstein, 1994, for further examples).

In this initial section there has been a description of the salient clinical features of unilateral neglect; a more in-depth experimental review of this disorder takes place in the next section. However, a broad picture of common presentations is useful, as is the realisation of how a patient's life is commonly handicapped by this disorder. If these patients are viewed in an occupational therapy setting of a mock kitchen, for example, one becomes aware of how even routine tasks become a challenge. Important features of recipes on the left-hand side are missed out. The patient cannot find certain ingredients that are placed on the left-hand side, flour is knocked over and ovens are left open—it is a frustrating process for both patient and therapist.

Dorsal simultaneous agnosia and Balint's syndrome

Dorsal simultaneous agnosia is a relatively rare disorder of attention and the term agnosia is arguably misused. Patients with this disorder typically have a small focus of attention such that they can only look at a small portion of their visual field at any one time. If you place two pencils in front of the patient, they will often report seeing only one, and will have to be directed to view the other. Readers of the literature can be forgiven for conceptualising dorsal simultaneous agnosia as a case of bilateral neglect and they often have a bilateral parietal lesion that accounts for their disorder. But there are additional difficulties to the attentional problems suffered by these patients; in particular, problems of locating objects and consistently maintaining an object's identity from other objects. There are difficulties of integrating features. For example, in the case of the overlapping figures task described in Chapter 4 there is a difficulty in seeing more that one figure.

The term simultaneous agnosia was originally coined by Luria and is seen as the attentional feature of Balint's syndrome (translation: Harvey &

Milner, 1995). Balint reported his case at the turn of the nineteenth century and he related the following signs in his patient:

1. A limited field of attention and a difficulty in concentrating on a particular object (simultaneous agnosia). Balint describes how he was able to sit down beside his patient's left side quite unnoticed (the sound of passing carriages cloaked any alerting sound); however, any visual movement to his right was immediately noticed. Balint's patient was able to read short words but only when instructed and by a process of scanning backward to each letter. Spontaneously he was only able to read right most single letters, although he was limited to a right angle from the midline of around 40 degrees. When his attention was drawn to preceding letters he was surprised that they existed and was able to read these, but could not attend to more than one letter at a time. More importantly, Balint showed that it was not the size of the object that mattered (this was also the case with RM, described earlier). If one large drawing was chalked on a board he saw this, but when two objects were drawn taking up the same area he still saw only one. Even when two objects were superimposed, he saw only one. The patient nevertheless showed no signs of sensory impairment or agnosia. He was able to recognise all the objects he detected.

2. Optic ataxia, an inability to reach for objects. Balint noticed that his patient could touch his own body parts when requested, but as soon as Balint requested an action that was within vision his arm movement went off to the right. Thus, when carving some meat, his right hand containing the knife was feeling round the right side of the plate. Interestingly, when drawing a house he appeared to be only able to focus on one part of the drawing at a time, so that his organisation was poor, drawing the windows outside the house.

3. The patient also showed what Balint described as a "paralysis of gaze", which

has also been referred to as "sticky fix-ations" when referring to disordered sac-cadic eye movements. This involves an impairment in the patient's voluntary eye movements and has been found on its own in patients with lesions to the superior col-liculus (Harvey & Milner, 1995). The patient showed no signs of apraxia (disorder of controlled functional movements) or agraphia (inability to write) that were not related to his very narrow attention span, poor location when reaching and a paralysis of gaze.

Like Balint's syndrome, patients suffering from simultaneous agnosia in isolation are seen to bump into things and are often seen groping their way around furniture like a blind person when navigating their way through a room. Coslett and Saffran (1991, p. 1523) describe it as being "char-acterised by the inability to interpret complex visual arrays, despite preserved recognition of single objects." That this is an attentional limita-tion rather than a limitation of visual field is illus-trated by experiments by Luria (Luria, Pravdina-Vinarskaya, & Yarbuss, 1963) and others that indicate that the *number of objects* is more important than the breadth of the visual field. However, as in the case of RM these patients' perception of location is also often impaired. Coslet and Saffran's patient, for example, had to use particular landmarks to find her way around the house. Their patient also reported that when watching TV characters in a play would strangely appear to be having heated arguments on their own, as if it was with themselves. In a fight sequence a character would suddenly be sent reel-ing across the room for some unknown reason. This disorder is generally seen as a disconnection or destruction of the dorsal "where-action" pathway, while the inferior "what" pathway remains, to allow the patients to identify objects accurately.

In some ways, Balint's syndrome represents the breakdown of many of the attentional features described in this chapter. The paralysis of gaze would certainly suggest some undermining of the system represented within the orientation system.

The failure to locate and select objects for percep-tion in a controlled manner suggests many of the features of the executive and perceptual attention systems.

General disorders of attention

The clinical neuropsychology of attention is the-oretically still "finding its feet". When a neu-ropsychologist reports that a patient has difficul-ties of attention it is clearly not very meaningful without some qualification. Given the intangible nature of attention it is perhaps not surprising that we still often refer to global descriptions such as "slowed information processing", "impaired attentional scanning", and "difficulties in tasks measuring concentration".

Given the large number of brain structures that are involved in attentional processes it is also per-haps not surprising that, with few exceptions, there is often little specific connection between attentional function and localisation. Tests of unilateral neglect are perhaps the most developed assessments, but these specialised assessments ignore the host of patients who have less dramatic but, nevertheless, functionally handicapping attentional deficits.

One of the commonest sequelae of TBI con-cerns problems of concentration and attention but despite a large literature on the subject this research has arguably provided more questions than answers. There is a general tendency for patients with moderate to severe head injury to be down on all the attention tasks administered (e.g., Ponsford & Kinsella, 1992). Also, many of the differences between TBI patients and controls are accounted for in terms of "speed of information processing". That is, when the differences in speed of information processing between the TBI and the control group are statistically taken out, group differences often disappear (Spikman, Van Zomeran, & Deelman, 1996). These findings are little less surprising when the level of atten-tion testing is considered. Tests of attention, which are popular within clinical and experi-mental testing, are generally at a relatively high level of the hierarchy given the model in Figure 4.9. Often the test which is seen to be *just* measur-ing speed of information processing is challenging quite a sophisticated set of cognitive skills that involves most of the attentional systems described above. Therefore if one subtracts a control task that requires a selective search and orientation then it is possible that one is removing an assessment of the efficiency of many of the structures that are being assessed by the main experimental task. This is what Spikman et al. (1996) refer to as "throwing the baby out with the bath water."

However, even allowing for the problem of removing the contribution of tasks to a higher level of functioning than is assumed, there are still areas of doubt. Spikman et al. (1996) found no significant difference between groups when tasks requiring no obvious flexibility were removed from these that required no flexibility, e.g. Stroop task, despite using a large sample of 60 patients.

There may be further problems when assessing the contribution of different systems of attention when the patients suffer from a deficit that affects all attentional processes equally. A consistent neuropathology associated with TBI is the severing or shearing of axons within the brain stem. The effects of damage to the brain stem on arousal in terms of coma have already been discussed. But axonal shearing may have a longer-term effect on arousal and consequently all facets of attention. If one then subtracts or partials out the effect of de-arousal on "speed of information processing" then the same effects on other attentional tasks may also be removed.

It may not be an exaggeration to propose that most popular clinical tasks designed to assess attention are testing all the systems of attention that have been discussed here. These tasks are also often chosen for research purposes given their sensitivity. There is now a literature that is particularly interested in the topic of mild head injury. Part of this interest is based on scepticism concerning long-standing complaints by patients following head trauma associated with only a brief period of unconsciousness. Such complaints are referred to collectively as the post-concussional syndrome. They include dizziness, headache, fatigue, blurred vision, sensitivity to noise and light, insomnia, difficulty in concentrating, irritability, memory difficulties, and anxiety (Dikman, Temkin & Armsden, 1989). Sometimes these symptoms may actually increase with time, especially if there is litigation concerning claims that are outstanding (Rutherford, 1989). This is a complex and controversial issue and it is certain some patients genuinely report these symptoms and some, for whatever reason, do not recover when litigation has been settled. The personality of the patient, their social situation, and their grievances appear to interact with difficulties in recovery (see Chapter 9). Also, there are consistent reports of attentional deficits and these post-concussional symptoms following mild head injury in patients following a brief period of consciousness after sports injuries involving no element of litigation or compensation.

Many clinical tasks, are designed to be sensitive to subtle attentional deficits that are sometimes associated mild head injury, appear to be aimed at challenging the patient's attentional capacity. These tasks clearly involve the highest level of the attentional hierarchy and the activation of a large number of brain areas. Gronwall and Wrightson (1974) studied a group of mild head injury (MHI) patients.[1] These patients had mostly received their concussion following New Zealand-based rugby injuries and therefore compensation was not a confounding issue. They used Gronwall's Paced Auditory Serial Addition Task (PASAT), which requires the subject to add the last two spoken numbers in the following fashion. The clinician's voice is typically taped to present numbers at a specified rate as follows:

Clinician: 2
Clinician: 4
Patient: 6 (2 + 4)
Clinician: 3
Patient: 7 (4 + 3)
Clinican: 2
Patient: 5 (3 + 2)
etc

It should be noted that as the patient adds 4 to 3

[1] Various definitions of MHI exist. Often a period of less than 20–30 minutes loss of consciousness or a length of post-traumatic amnesia (coma + disorientation) of less than 1 hour is used. There is normally no indication of clinical neurological involvement after this period.

in this example to produce the sum 7, they must at the same time keep "in mind" that 3 was the last number. This task could be construed as one of divided attention but is probably more properly referred to as testing working memory. The attention to something retained "in mind" is maintained while the patient attends to the process of mental arithmetic. The task has three speeds and can be somewhat harassing to the patient if they fail to keep up with the process. Despite the task's sensitiveness those patients with MHI were generally free of measurable impairment as a group by the second assessment at a little over 1 month following injury.

There was a tendency for those showing impairment after MHI to be also complaining of post-concussion symptoms. Most of those MHI patients who had difficulty in returning to work also showed impairment on the PASAT. More modern studies have also found memory impairment (e.g. learning lists of words) for a similar length of time. But attention difficulties remain predominant in the case of MHI (see also Gentilini, Nichelli, & Schoenhuber, 1989). Also, a history of a previous similar accident appears to exaggerate impairment (Gronwall & Wrightson, 1975), as is sometimes found when less successful boxers are assessed. Individuals may show more prolonged effects especially when they have evidence of damage on CT scan (Barth, et al., 1989), although recently SPECT scan has been found to be far more sensitive to MHI than structural scans. A number of recent studies that have shown abnormalities in MHI patients using SPECT scans; these abnormalities are not evidenced using more commonly used structural scanning methods such as CT and MRI scans (e.g., Kant, Smith-Seemiller, Isaac, & Duffy, 1997). Some of these studies have found relatively long-term evidence, e.g. 1 year post injury, in as many as 50% of patients who suffer persistent post-concussional symptoms. Therefore while scepticism as to the organic nature of these complaints is no doubt warranted in some cases, these studies certainly suggest that long-term complaints may have an organic basis. However, to get these research findings into perspective according to the New Zealand research only 5%

of all MHI patients complain of persistent symptoms after 1 year (Gronwall & Wrightson, 1998).

Another task that is likely to be sensitive to MHI is the telephone task from the Test of Everyday Attention (Robertson et al., 1996; see also Gronwall, personal communication). Again this is a form of divided attention task in which material must be kept in mind. These tasks have a common ingredient according to the model above: that they are at the top of the proposed hierarchy. They involve the activation of sensory, parietal, and frontal areas and the tasks are determined by an enforced rate of speed.

Tasks that are also found to be challenging and sensitive to attentional disorder include two tests from the series of Wechsler Adult Intelligence tests (WAIS-R, WAIS-III). The digit symbol subtest is seen to be one of the most sensitive tests to a very broad range of patients with brain impairment (Lezak, 1995). The task requires the conversion of a series of numbers into a code at speed. The task is a good general measure of deterioration because it measures attention speed, an orienting response, a search for the appropriate code, and a motor response. A similar measure, the symbol digit modalities test (Smith, 1973), which is without the motor response, is also sensitive to attentional deficit. Another measure from this WAIS battery commonly associated with attention is the digit-span. This task requires the subject to repeat back a list of digits of increasing length. The subject has to repeat the digits in the same order that they are given. As an indication that this test is on the border between attention and memory, the task is sometimes referred to variously as a test of attention span, short-term memory, or immediate memory. The subject is required to keep the digits "in mind" before they are repeated back. Unless the patient has a language disorder this part of the test is not sensitive to deterioration. However, the next part of this test, which requires the patient to repeat the digits back in the reverse order, is more challenging and more likely to be sensitive to patients who are showing deterioration on other tasks. Again this last task requires the patient to keep the number in mind while mentally manipulating the reverse order.

Therefore there is an executive component. These two tasks are described in the next chapter when discussing memory tasks and towards the end of the chapter in terms of the overlap between memory and attention.

Modern clinical neuropsychological endeavours are often not aimed at localisation issues. These are generally taken care of by the increased technological expertise that is associated with brain imaging. There is arguably a greater need to look at the patient's capacity to attend in trying to predict their everyday competence.

With reference to this need to link everyday requirements of attention and measures of attention Alderman (1996) provides an example of how this issue might be approached. He reported on patients with severe TBI and executive dysfunction. The patients were divided into two groups according to how they responded to therapy. He found those who had not responded to therapy (mainly behaviour modification) experienced extreme difficulty in a test which divided attention task. Alderman used a divided attention task in which a tracking task was completed with various secondary tasks, e.g. repeating back a series of digits. The worst performance on the tracking task occurred when the subject was involved in conversation with the experiment. As Alderman points out, this is a reasonable simulation of the patients everyday exposure to competing stimuli and perhaps the reason for their failure to take note of attempts to reduce negative and increase positive behaviours. Given the complexity of the attentional system we are probably a long way from developing a set of diagnostic tests of attention that cover a broad spectrum of attentional disorders. Therefore the kind of ecological validity in clinical testing which looks at the impact of the disorder on the patient's daily life is one of the more useful research approaches at the present time.

One way of assessing a patient's attention is by finding out the situations that are most often associated with inattention. For example, Ponsford and Kinsella (1991) surveyed therapists regarding the attentional difficulties of TBI patients. Most commonly the therapists reported "slowness in performing mental tasks", difficulties in "being able to pay attention to more than one thing at a time", "making mistakes because he or she wasn't paying attention properly", "missing important detail", and "having difficulty on concentrating". The partners of patients with brain damage notice other day-to day difficulties. Figure 4.13 illustrates of our own work (Andrewes et al., 1998) on patients following brain surgery using the Everyday Functioning Questionnaire (EFQ), which includes a section on concentration. On questionnaires that were filled in by partners and patients independently, the partner's questionnaire tended to be more discriminating. The rating of each question within the questionnaire was on a visual analogue scale and involved marking on a 10 cm line a point between "no problem" at one end and "big problem" at the other end. The EFQ questionnaire showed brain surgery patients rating towards the "big problem" end of the scale in over 20% of the cases. Their rating was far in excess of the control group attending the same neurosurgical outpatient clinic who had had surgery to areas not including the brain. More positively, we found that the concentration scale showed the strongest recovery when looking at time since surgery (Andrewes et al., 1998).

These complaints of not being able to concentrate in the presence of distraction may be of such gravity that these patients avoid social situations altogether. It is a clinical observation that these kinds of complaints are also prevalent among patients who have suffered from TBI.

A proposal that seems to be gaining some support is that tasks of attention which are subjectively seen as requiring a high attentional capacity, such as divided attention tasks, also according to functional imaging e.g. PET and fMRI, involve the prefrontal cortex to a greater extent (Coull, 1998). Many tests of attention used by clinical neuropsychologists involve assessment at this level of the proposed hierarchy and probably owe there popularity to their ability to pick up modest levels of attention deficit. Perhaps because of the large number of brain structures involved, the tests are not usually seen as supplying information that is useful for localisation. Consequently

FIG. 4.13

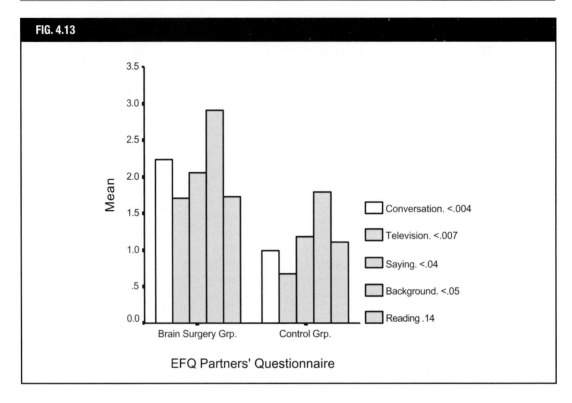

Graph illustrating means for the items of the concentration scale of the EFQ, using the report of partners of patients following brain surgery. The rating was on a 10cm visual analogue scale, the label "no problem" at one end and "big problem" at the other. All questions were preceded by the statement "Does the patient have difficulty in concentrating?" The individual questions' means and p-values are "When following a conversation?" (conversation, 20% rated over 5), "On a television programme?" (televison, 13% over 5), "On what people say?" (people saying, 15% over 5), "When there is a lot of background noise" (background, 24% over 5), and "When reading a book or newspaper" (reading, 17% over 5). The sample included postoperative brain surgery patients ($n = 140$) and controls ($n = 42$) with extracerebral lesions who were attending the same neurosurgical outpatient department (see Andrewes, Hordern, & Kaye, 1998).

many of these tests are also diagnostically non-specific. For example, the digit symbol subtest of the WAIS-R, in which the patient has to decode a series of numbers into symbols at speed, requires the subject to shift attention scan and search for the appropriate symbol. The symbol, which is unfamiliar, must be copied and the performance is speeded by learning some of the code trans-formations or keeping them in mind to speed up the process, which is completed within a time limit. The task is more sensitive to deterioration compared to all the other subtests in the WAIS-R regardless of where the lesion is located Lezak (1995, p. 378).

However, the point to be made here is that most clinical measures of attention tend to be of this broad nature and there is at present very little scientific guidance as to the terminology and tasks that might indicate a more informed approach. Towards the end of this chapter the subject is revisited in an attempt to describe a cor-respondence between process and task.

MODELS OF NEGLECT

Neuropsychological models of neglect
The finding that a right-sided lesion is more likely to show obvious neglect suggests that the right

hemisphere has a dominant role in attention and this is now well accepted. This explanation proposes that the right hemisphere contains attention control for both the left and right side, while the left side controls the attention for only the right hemi-space (Heilman et al., 1993; Mesulam, 1981, 1999). In the case of a lesion to the left hemisphere, there is a backup system, because the right hemisphere caters for both sides. If there is a lesion to the right side, then the right hemi-space is catered for by the intact left hemisphere, but there is no back up system for the left hemi-space (see Figure 4.14).

This state of affairs, in which the right hemisphere is seen as dominant for attention catering for both sides, has been supported by the results of imaging studies. Corbetta and colleagues found that a shift in attention to the left and right was associated with right parietal activation while the left hemisphere only showed increased blood flow with a shift to the right (Corbetta, Miezin, Shulman, & Petersen, 1993).

However, despite the ability of the right hemisphere to cope with both sides, damage to the left hemisphere's attentional centres may still be detected. In this case, a milder form of neglect may be revealed by using a more demanding test (see Figure 4.15) (Ogden, 1985). The less frequently experienced right neglect is not only milder but also recovers more quickly.

Evidence for the dominance of the right hemisphere for attention is also present in the finding that patients with right-sided damage may also show some mild signs of impairment in right visual space, despite the left hemisphere backup system. Weintraub and Mesulam (1987) found that in a cancellation test, in which subjects were required to cross off multiple short lines on a page, patients with right hemisphere stroke were slower than patients with left hemisphere stroke on this task, even on cancellation of material in the right visual field. This suggests that the intact right hemisphere is more important for attention to the right side when compared to the left hemisphere (Robertson, 1993). In other words, the right hemisphere not only takes care of both sides, but it is also the main resource for attention on those two sides. In further support of this

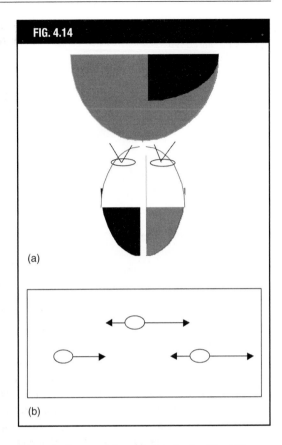

FIG. 4.14

(a)

(b)

Schematic diagram of the control of attention. The right attentional system is dominant and controls attention bilaterally. A lesion in the left hemisphere is compensated by the right. There is no compensation for the contralateral area if there is damage to the right attentional systems. A more representational diagram (b) is shown (adapted from Mesulam, 1999), indicating that neglect affects orientation rather than visual space per se. The longer arrows signify a stronger tendency to orient to the left. Right and left orientation are normally relatively equal, with the right hemisphere being responsible for orientation to both sides, while the left hemisphere is involved in orientation to the right.

view, Robertson et al. (1994) found that 17 out of 90 cases with *right* hemisphere damage and left neglect also had some right-sided neglect. This view of the right hemisphere as the attention hemisphere is adopted most prominently in a model by Posner and Peterson (1990; see also Posner, 1995).

Kinsbourne's (1993) model of neglect is

FIG. 4.15

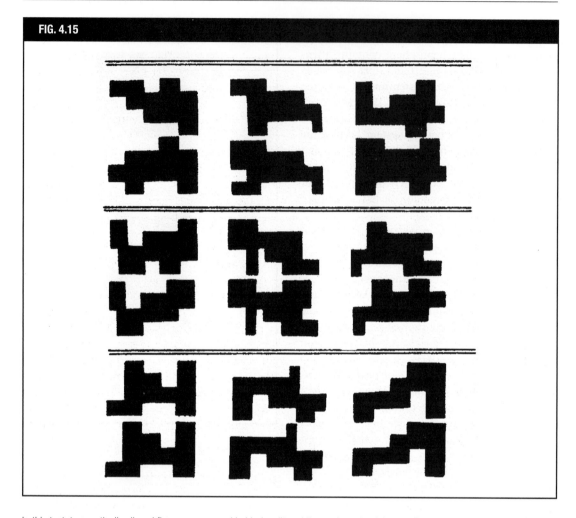

In this test, two vertically aligned figures are passed behind a slit and thus only parts of the two figures are shown at any one time. The subject has to judge whether the two figures positioned in line above each other are the same. Sometimes the figures are the same, but for others a difference can only be detected on the left side, while with other figures the differences can only be detected on the right side of the figures. Patients with the more typical neglect for the left side have difficulty in making the judgement when the difference between the two figures is on the left side, but the less typical patients with left hemisphere lesions also made errors for differences that appeared on the right side (reprinted from Ogden, 1985, with permission from Elsevier Science).

slightly different in interpretation, since he prefers to describe neglect in terms of orientation rather than processing of areas or sides. To put this another way, he argues that describing neglect should be in terms of a left orienting (right hemisphere) and a right orienting (left hemisphere) system. The systems balance each other until one of the hemispheres is damaged. Therefore, the damage to the right hemisphere results in the left

hemisphere's right orienting system taking control and becoming dominant, and consequently the patient tends to orient their attention to the right like a magnet. Indeed, more severe damage to the right system results in even more severe orientation to the right, in the case of left neglect (Vallar, 1993).

Additional support for Kinsbourne's view comes from literature on the preference of eye movements. Persons with and without brain damage will often direct their gaze to the side to which they are attending, even when they are attending to auditory stimuli (Gopher, 1973) or tactile stimuli (Honore, 1982). There is a tendency for the majority of neglect patients to show disordered eye movements, with an incidence that ranges from 64% to 82% (Albert, 1973; Hecaen, 1962). Neglect patients even have reduced eye movements to the left during sleep within rapid eye movement (Dorrichi, Guariglia, Paolucci, & Pizzamiglio, 1990). Perhaps most important, in terms of supporting Kinsbourne's model, is the finding that tracking a target towards the neglected side is impaired even within the non-neglected side. Tracking towards the non-neglected side is relatively normal when tracking a target into non-neglected space (e.g. Farne, Ponti, & Ladavas, 1998). Also, when these patients are left to search for a non-existent letter within a sphere that surrounds them, their eye and head movements suggest a failure to explore the neglected side. In other words, it is not so much that they cannot attend to the left side as a failure to orient to that left side. It is a failure to orient both overtly (eye movements) and covertly (without eye movements) (Karnath, Niemeier, & Dichgans, 1998). This supports the orientation hypothesis along with other findings from the same group who showed that the subject's viewing of space on the neglected side was not compressed as has been thought. Karnath and Ferber (1999) showed that when neglect patients sat in the dark they were able to correctly space out a series of 10 LED lights distributed in the horizontal plane when they were required to space two at a time. In the experiment two green lights were shown in the required position and during the spacing exercise these were then turned off. Without external distractions to pull the focus of attention to the right, the patients spaced the led lights correctly even on the neglected side. Therefore no compression of the space was found to the left.

Evidence for the magnet metaphor also comes from the cancellation task. In this task the patient is typically asked to cancel out all the objects, lines, or letters on a sheet of paper. Typically the patient starts on the far right side and then cancels a few further items towards the left before completing the task. The patient therefore fails to cancel the majority of items to the left of the rightmost border of the paper. In a cunning experiment, Mark and colleagues decided to get patients with neglect to erase the detected items instead of cancelling them. This had the effect of improving performance dramatically. Using the magnet metaphor the right border was changing as they erased the items on the right, allowing them more and more access to the leftmost items (Mark, Kooistra, & Heilman, 1988).

Also in keeping with the orienting view is the finding that when patients are lured or cued to look towards the left side this reduces neglect; this method is commonly used in rehabilitative techniques with these patients. For example, neglect of memories may be ameliorated by directing the imaged gaze towards the neglected area; this is similar to the process the author was using in Box 4.2 (Meadore, Loring, Bowers, & Heilman, 1989). Also, patients are generally assisted by cueing with many kinds of stimulation towards the neglected side, e.g. ice in the left ear, mild electrical stimulation (TENS machine) of left body parts (Coppa, Sterzi, Vallar, & Bisiach, 1987; Farne et al., 1998).

Kinsbourne's theory is also useful since, as opposed to one side of visual space being neglected (with a cut-off at the centre), a gradation of neglect is predicted. The attentional gradient may be illustrated by the example in which there are two items within the right "non-neglected side". In this situation the patient orients towards the rightmost of these two items and may ignore the leftmost item even though they are both in the non-neglected side according to other tasks. An example of this can be seen in the task shown in Figure 4.16, where the patient is attending to the right digit of two-digit numbers. If the patient had been consistent in the neglect of a certain side of space then she would have realised that at least some of the traced numbers were part of a larger number. The metaphor of a magnet or gravitational pull is often used to describe this type of imbalance of orientation.

Further evidence of this magnetic attraction

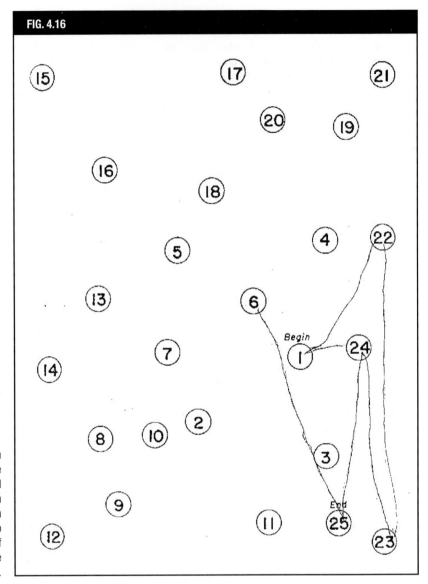

FIG. 4.16

The Trail Making Test, Form A. Test showing the tendency for the unilateral neglect patient to focus on the right side of each number in an attempt to follow the instructions of linking consecutive numbers.

may be illustrated when these patients have difficulty in reorienting to the neglected side when they are originally given an invalid cue to the right (Posner, Walker, Friedrich, & Rafal, 1984). In this popularly used paradigm the subject faces a screen and fixates the eyes on a central point. A large proportion of the time a cue appears, e.g. a pointer, just prior to the onset of a target, e.g. a light. The target may be to the left or right of the screen, depending on which side the cue is pointing. As one might predict, a warning where the light is about to arrive significantly helps normal and neglect patients. However, when on some trials the light appears on the opposite side to the one indicated by the cue both groups have difficulty, but the neglect patients have exaggerated difficulty in disengaging from the cued side when the target appears on the neglected side of the screen. In this paradigm the presentation of the stimulus is very quick and so there is no time in which to make eye movements. The process is therefore referred to as requiring *covert attention*.

In their studies Posner and colleagues found that neglect patients were well able to direct their attention towards the neglected field when they were cued in that direction, but when they were falsely cued to the right they had the greatest difficulty in returning to the left towards the target. The limitation of referring to unilateral neglect purely as a disorder of disengagement becomes clear when these patients are observed in their clinical situation. If the patient sitting facing the examiner is asked to concentrate on the examiner's nose and the examiner raises a single presentation of the right hand (the patient's neglected left side) then the patient will orient towards the movement and the hand and acknowledge its existence (something like orienting to a cue in Posner's experiment). However, if two hands containing objects and both objects are raised simultaneously (test of extinction), the patient will report only on the object in the examiner's left hand (to the patient's right). In other words it is when there is competition between stimuli that the stimulus which is rightmost is attended to; there is therefore an *engagement* problem, which is equivalent to the disengagement problem described by Posner.

This engagement difficulty is described in Box 4.1, when the the patient is asked if the examiner's hands are in his pockets. The question is asked of two competing stimuli and the patient orients to the author's left hand on the patient's right to verify the answer the question. As indicated, in situations were there are two competing stimuli the patient will orient to the rightmost stimulus. This problem of engagement in the face of competitive stimuli has been observed experimentally (e.g., Karnath et al., 1998) and the way that orienting is apparently controlled by the quantity and quality of the information suggests that the magnet metaphor is the most useful. There is an attraction and once it is attracted there is a difficulty in pulling away.

However, there are findings that do not fit so easily with Kinsbourne's model. As indicated, one study found right hemisphere-damaged patients to show unexpected attentional impairment on the wrong ipsilesional side (Robertson et al., 1994). Additionally, other studies have found

that some left neglect patients (usually more severely affected) show an additional small neglect on the right side, a kind of bilateral neglect (Small, Cowey, & Ellis, 1994). It is possible that the orientation problems are bilateral in this case so the magnet has moved more to the centre, but this evidence does suggest that a problem with spatial mapping may also be involved.

These findings do not dispute that the right hemisphere is the dominant hemisphere for attention, which corresponds to the view taken by Posner and Petersen (1990). This model of attention, which posits a right dominance of attention, is further supported by studies that have found patients with left hemisphere strokes attending more efficiently when compared to those with right hemisphere strokes even when the right hemisphere patients do not have neglect. Such right hemisphere-damaged patients may be slower in reaction time tests (e.g., Howes & Boller, 1975). Such impaired attentional performance is not obviously dependent on the mechanism responsible for orientation and may involve frontal structures as well as parietal structures (Rueckert & Grafman, 1998; Wilkins, Shallice, & McCarthy, 1987). Tests that show these kinds of attentional deficits require patients to monitor information presented in a serial format over an extended period. These tests of sustained attention, which require long-term vigilance, may have some overlap with the orientation system (see Figure 4.2).

Robertson (1993) describes a process of rehabilitation for patients that appears to support the intimate relationship between the parietal and executive systems within the Posner and Petersen model. The relevant feature of this model proposes that poor vigilance is due to poor arousal within the right hemisphere (Heilman et al., 1993, takes a similar view). Robertson and colleagues increased *subjective* arousal by requiring their neglect patients to tell themselves to "attend!" and rap on a desk at the same time. These instructions were trained first to be performed overtly and then covertly, with consequent improvements in performance (Robertson et al., 1995). Whether the patients managed to increase their neurophysiological arousal or whether they were just improving their cueing strategies is not clear. But in keeping with the overlap posited by Posner, the improvements in sustained attention appeared to have some positive effects on the unilateral neglect of these patients (parietal orienting system).

In summary, there appear to be at least two mechanisms that are revealed by ongoing work. One of these mechanisms has been described by Kinsbourne (e.g., Kinsbourne, 1993), who proposes a left and right *orientation* mechanism that is controlled by the contralateral hemisphere. This is attractive, since these patients often appear to be "magnetised" towards the right rather than having a strict spatial division. However, this theory is less strong in explaining the greater preponderance and severity of neglect following right parietal lesions. This finding would suggest that the right hemisphere is dominant for processes of attention. In fact patients with right-sided lesions, whether they have difficulty in orienting or not, show impaired attention on tasks compared to patients with left lesions, suggesting that the right hemisphere, especially the parietal and frontal cortex, is dominant for attention. This last information rests more easily with Posner and Petersen's model (Posner & Petersen, 1990).

A lateralised arousal system is an important component of this model, and some models that describe the neural mechanisms underlying the clinical presentations of attentional disorder see a reduced arousal within a network as an important mechanism contributing to unilateral neglect.

Neurophysiologically based models of neglect

Arousal models

A model by Heilman et al. (1993) posits a neural circuit that is responsible for attention. Their proposal is that neglect is caused by a de-arousal of this system through a disconnection that may occur at a number of points. This model allows for the finding that the thalamus is an important relay for the sensory modalities.

The role of the thalamus in perception as a sensory relay has already been referred to in previous chapters. The lateral geniculate nucleus of the thalamus is important for the transmission of visual information, the medial geniculate nucleus (MGN) of the thalamus for auditory information and the ventral, posterolateral nucleus for somatosensory information (see Figure 2.5). While the pulvinar of the thalamus is clearly important for orientation (see discussion of the orienting system above), Heilman and colleagues are more interested in another aspect of the thalamus that is responsible mainly for arousal and is referred to as the intralaminar nucleus. Work by Singer and others (Singer, 1977; Yingling & Skinner, 1975) has provided that the sensory relay areas within the thalamus may be individually or collectively suppressed by the nucleus reticularis (NR). This may be the system that is influential for enhancing attention to some areas of our environment at the expense of others (La Berge, 1995). By inhibiting or suppressing these areas of the thalamus, the NR allows dominance of one sensory system over the other, in the manner, for example, that a person who is blindfolded may suddenly become acutely aware of the smells and sounds which surround them. Even the slightest noise is boosted for a more in-depth analysis.

The NR, in turn, is controlled and activated by the ARAS, which as indicated above is a general term for an arousing influence that supplies tone or arousal to this and many other areas of the brain. Heilman and colleagues are uncertain which neurotransmitter system is implicated but believe the cholinergic system is the most likely to be involved.

These authors describe a chain reaction in which the ARAS stimulates the NR, then the NR *disinhibits* the respective sensory areas of the thalamus, thereby enhancing sensory transmission (see Figure 4.17). In this way the NR acts as an inhibitor until it is activated.

Heilman et al. (1993) propose that neglect may be caused by damage to the mechanism that arouses and activates the NR. Damage to the reticular system would reduce the effect of the ARAS on the NR. Reduced activation of the NR would have the consequence of the NR inhibiting the thalamus, which in turn would reduce the relaying of sensory information. This view is supported by studies that have created unilateral

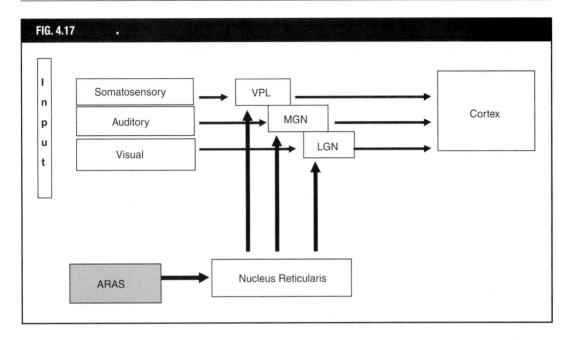

FIG. 4.17

Diagram illustrating the way the arousal supplied by the ascending reticular activating system (ARAS) is modified by the nucleus reticularis (NR). The NR selectively inhibits arousal of the various sensory relays within the thalamus. These sensory relays correspond to the ventralis posterolateralis (VPL) for somatosensory input, the medial geniculate nucleus (MGN) for auditory sensory input, and the lateral geniculate nucleus (LGN) for visual input (adapted from Heilman, Watson, & Valenstein, 1993).

neglect following unilateral lesions to the reticular formation within the brain stem (Reeves & Hagamen, 1971). Alternatively, damage to the unimodal association areas within the cortex may mean that the novelty of a stimulus is not evaluated. Because this information is not fed back to the thalamus (see Figure 4.18) via the NR, the NR is again not sufficiently activated to disinhibit the thalamus. However this time the neglect is confined to one modality, e.g. visual (Heilman et al., 1993, p. 296). From this one model one might expect that thalamic lesions may sometimes result in neglect and this is indeed the case. It is argued therefore that neglect might be caused by damage or disconnection of one of these circuits and this will in turn cause a de-arousal sufficient to cause neglect.

One of the difficulties in describing the neuroanatomical model of neglect from animal research is that the location of lesions necessary for neglect in the monkey are different from those in humans (Heilman et al., 1993). Despite this

uncertainty, cases of neglect have been studied in humans, which allow some clarification of comparable cortical pathways that are functionally equivalent for the purpose of providing a model of neglect. Heilman, Watson, and Valenstein's neuroanatomical model of neglect has been influential and includes the thalamic mechanism (in Figure 4.17) that is incorporated in the diagram of a simplified adaptation of their model in Figure 4.18. Broadly, Heilman, Watson, and Valenstein's model (Heilman et al., 1993, p. 294) proposes that there is a circuit linking key structures that have been associated with neglect in lesion studies. Each of these structures is independently aroused by the ARAS from the mesencephalic area of the reticular system, as described earlier.

Although unilateral neglect is caused by de-arousal of an attentional system made up from structures that are connected into a complex circuit, the different structures have different functional roles that contribute to attention. The

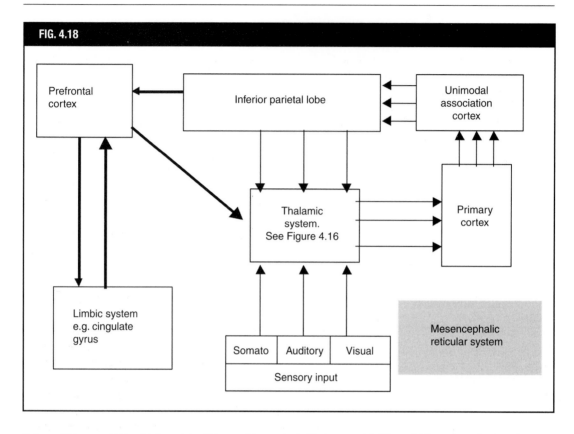

FIG. 4.18

Heilman, Watson, and Valenstein's model, which associates neglect with de-arousal. In this model the various structures have different roles. The cingulate supplies a motivational component; the inferior parietal cortex provides a spatial map of the environment play. The unimodal association areas detect novelty and top-down selection of important stimuli, which are also fed back to the thalamic arousal system illustrated in Figure 4.17. Neglect may only affect one sensory system since there are unimodal connections within a circuit that leads to and from the thalamus; thus de-arousal within one sensory modality may occur (adapted from Heilman & Valenstein, 1993).

inferior parietal lobe has cells that fire just prior to a response, are location sensitive and are therefore seen as important for directing attention (Goldberg & Robinson, 1977; Mountcastle, Andersen, & Motter, 1981). These parietal cells are sensitive to both rewarding and aversive stimuli and therefore probably do not determine the state of motivation but rather select attention for "important" stimuli that have the potential to be critical to survival (Heilman et al., 1993).

The prefrontal cortex may be important for coordinating the stream of processing responsible for identifying a stimulus and the location of the object, and help in the prediction of where a stimulus might be likely to arrive. The DPFC is also seen as being particularly important for detecting novelty and responds irrespective of the modality of the input. Studies that have measured an evoked potential (electrical brain response to an unexpected auditory stimulus measured on the scalp) find this response diminished when there is damage, especially on the right (see review by Knight et al., 1995). Knight and colleagues also provide similar evidence for the importance of the prefrontal cortex for sustaining, selecting, and anticipation of a stimulus (see also Richer et al., 1993). The association areas influence the inferior parietal lobe via the prefrontal cortex (Heilman et al., 1993).

The cingulate and other structures of the limbic system, e.g. amygdala, have been associated with a motivational role (Mesulam, 1985) and lesions within the medial frontal lobe result in reduced concern in patients who have had this surgical treatment for chronic pain that may have an attentional component (Cohen et al., 1993).

Lesions to the basal ganglia have also been associated with visual neglect, often in a mild form. Areas within the basal ganglia that may be important are the right putamen and caudate nucleus (Damasio, Damasio, & Chui, 1980; Ferro, Kertesz, & Black, 1987). Patients with lesions to the basal ganglia and the prefrontal cortex also show difficulty in switching and selecting attention unless there are salient cues (Bradshaw et al., 1992; Georgiou et al., 1996).

The theory of Heilman and colleagues that these circuits are linked and the de-arousal of the brain structures within these circuits result in the neglect syndrome is attractive, especially when considering brain stem pathology. Neglect following brain stem lesions, however, does not appear to be common. Their de-arousal model is also supported by studies that have used self-alerting techniques (Robertson et al., 1995), although the dependence on arousal as a major mechanism for neglect seems to underplay the variation in presentations of neglect.

Mesulam's model

Mesulam's (1985, 1999) model in Figure 4.19 predicts the broad symptoms of neglect according to a network of structures similar to those proposed by Heilman and colleagues. Further, these structures contribute different functional roles within this attentional network. The frontal eye fields assist in the overt and covert directional shift in attention, while the parietal cortex contributes to the sensory/perceptual aspects of neglect. The cingulate subserves motivational aspects of neglect as in the case of Heilman's model. The role of the collicular system has already been described in the section on the orienting system.

Although these arousal models specify differential roles for structures within a circuit, this is not obviously found in studies. For example, a large study of 120 patients with a variety of

neglect measures failed to find a relationship between the pattern of neglect and Mesulam's neuroanatomical subtypes (McGlinchey-Berroth et al., 1996). Mesulam recognises that the same symptoms may result from lesions to these different structures because they make up a network. Also a network, being made up of a multitude of connections, has sufficient redundancy that a lesion might have to be extensive if a disconnection was to occur. The attentional network has certain areas of convergence which are more vulnerable to disruption and one of these areas is in the inferior parietal, where spatial coordinates of visual space are seen to be connected with the various sensory systems in this association area (Mesulam, 1998).

One of the few differences within this "network" has been found recently and reported by Mattingley Mattingley et al. (1998). They found differences between patients with neglect following parietal versus frontal lesions, with the former patients showing more motor-related neglect. These patients were equated on cancellation tests but in a reaching task that varied the initial position of the reaching hand they identified a motor component that was more obviously impaired in the parietal patients. They varied the motor contribution by placing the starting position of the hand in various starting locations (in and out of located space). Motor neglect was reduced when the patient reached towards a green light and the hand was initially placed within the neglected field. This result would be expected given the location of the parietal lesion topographically near to what is referred to here as the "where-action pathway" (see a more elaborate description of this system in Chapter 8). However, this is not in keeping with the predictions of Mesulam's (1999) model, which sees the more anterior lesions being associated with more motor neglect.

Monkey studies that have investigated shifts of attention show that frontal eye field activation precedes the shift and that the role is to direct eye movements or covert attention in the general direction rather than to the exact location (Mesulam, 1999). Lesions in the monkey equivalent area cause severe contralateral neglect and the animal fails to retrieve motivational relevant

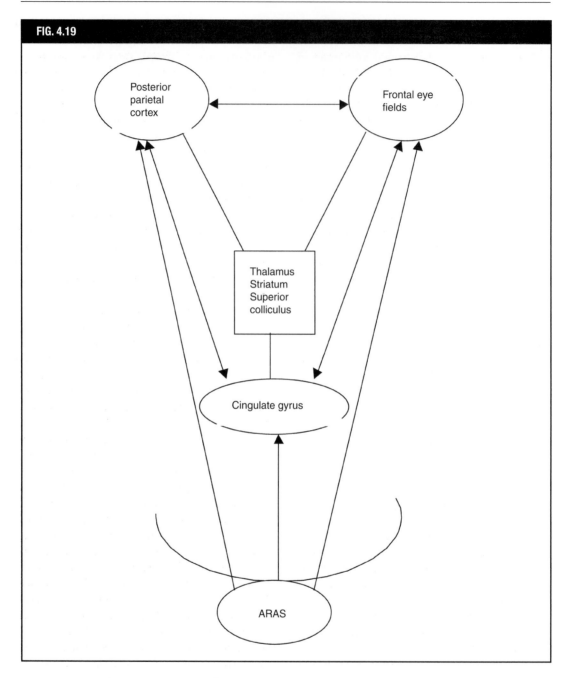

FIG. 4.19

Adaptation illustrating Mesulam's model of attention (adapted from Mesulam, 1999). Each structure has a different role in contributing to the attentional process. The ascending reticular activation system (ARAS) supplies the requisite arousal for the system. A motivational role is attributed to the cingulate , while the parietal cortex provides a sensory spatial map of the environment. The frontal eye fields provide a motor component allowing orientation with the central features of an arousal system (reprinted from M.M. Mesulam, *Philosophical Transactions of the Royal Society of London B*, 29, 1325–1346, copyright 1999, with permission from the Royal Society.)

stimuli from that sector (e.g., Keating & Gooley, 1988; Kennard, 1939). A recent monkey lesion study showed that combined lesions to both the cortical association areas (superior temporal) and the frontal eye field caused a neglect that was not obvious when the frontal eye field was lesioned on its own (Scalaidhe, Rodman, Albright, & Gross, 1997).

This finding predicts that some kind of occulomotor neglect might be associated with lesions in the frontal eye field and suggests that this type of neglect may be related to oculomotor orienting required by shifts of attention (see Figure 4.6). It is probably helpful to specify which motoric system one is referring to when describing motor neglect. A further difficulty, as Mesulam acknowledges, is the rarity of neglect following lesions to the cingulate. Further evidence may prove to support Mesulam's model but some uncertainty underlies all attempts to model this enigmatic condition at present. What is becoming clear is, and is well illustrated in both Heilman and colleagues' and Mesulam's models, is that the effects of lesions on neglect may be exaggerated when more than one of these structures is lesioned. This is certainly in keeping with a network of structures working in concert to produce a function.

Variations in the presentation of unilateral neglect and theoretical implications

Numerous case studies have been published revealing the large number of variations in the presentation of neglect. Moreover, it is possible to show differential grouping of performance on neglect tasks using statistical techniques. For example, Kinsella et al. (1993) identified two main factors in their principal components analysis study of 40 unilateral right hemisphere stroke patients. The first factor included results on tests of scanning stimuli in space, such as cancellation and line bisection, while the second factor loaded most heavily on internal imagery representation measures, such as a blindfold tactile maze, spontaneous drawings, landscape, and scenery. However, more commonly reported is a dissociation between poor correlation between line cancellation and line bisection (Binder et al., 1992; Hal-

ligan & Marshall, 1995). Halligan and Marshall (1998) illustrate the distinction between line bisection and cancellation and the dependency on internal computations of the former when describing two patients with bidirectional neglect (one patient had a left stroke and the other a right stroke). Both patients showed line bisection and cancellation but in opposite fields (e.g. showing neglect for line bisection in the left field while showing neglect for the right field in the cancellation task). However, the fields were opposite for the two patients.

Costello and Warrington (1987) report on a patient who showed a marked right-sided neglect when copying, drawing, and doing line bisection tasks. However, this patient's neglect for reading words was on the left side. A more commonly found discrepancy is between visual neglect and unilateral hypokinesia. With unilateral hypokinesia, the patient is reluctant to carry out requested or modelled motor activities within their left hemi-space. Of course, when a patient completes a test for neglect, such as drawing and line bisection, the motor and perceptual components are confounded. However, various experiments have been able to discover that these two types of neglect are separable and respectively occur to various degrees in different patients. Bisiach, Germiniani, Berti, and Risconi (1990) used a system of pulleys that allowed the patients to manipulate a pointer. Pulling in one direction allowed the pointer to move in the opposite direction so that, in one condition, the patient would move their arm into the left side while, perceptually, the pointer moved to the right. In other words they were able to test neglected motor movements while providing a visual image that was not testing their visual neglect. Similarly, Coslett and Saffran, (1991) videorecorded the patients" hand movements during a line bisection task, their actual movements being out of sight. By moving the VDU into the left versus right hemisphere they were able to show dissociations between these two forms of neglect.

Most commonly in the clinic, visual unilateral neglect is assumed to be to the left side but often little notice is taken to determine the frame of reference: for example, whether it is to the left of the midline of the patient's visual space, as they are facing (viewer centred) or whether it is to left side of the environment (environment centred) irrespective of their view at the time. Studies have manipulated the frame of reference by requiring the patient to alter the directional alignment of their head, either off to the left or right, to see if the neglect for parts of the scene alters. Such studies generally find that both the environment and the view influence neglect and when the scene and environment are in line there appears to be something of a combined effect (e.g., Calvanio, Petrone, & Levine, 1987; Ladavas, 1987).

Object-centred neglect, discussed further in the next section (see Figure 4.11), is not always present in patients with neglect and there is evidence that some patients may have object-centred neglect without viewer-centred neglect and visa versa (Chatterjee, 1994). As discussed previously, object-centred neglect appears to be related to the perception of the object and may occur with relative independence compared to viewer-centred neglect, e.g. towards the right or middle of a viewed scene.

Distinctions have also been made between patients who have neglect in personal space (body areas), peripersonal space (within reaching distance), and extrapersonal space (within walking distance, using laser light for the bisection) (Bisiach, Vallar, Perani, Papagno, & Berti, 1986; Calvanio et al., 1987; Halligan & Marshall, 1991).

In terms of testing in the clinic it is commonly found that a patient who has recovered from most signs of measured neglect nevertheless retains some signs of hemi-inattention on an extinction test when stimuli are applied bilaterally in a simultaneous manner, e.g. the clinician asks the patient to close their eyes while they touch both knees or cheeks at the same time. The patient in such a case may report only the right-sided stimulus, whatever the modality of presentation. Some caution may be required in considering this as purely a remnant of neglect that has been elicited by a more difficult or demanding test. Sometimes this response may be found in patients following lesions not normally associated with neglect, albeit in a milder form (reported by Duncan, 1998).

The inability to read words correctly because the "leftmost" letters are ignored is referred to as unilateral dyslexia (Kinsbourne & Warrington, 1962). As indicated when describing the clinical manifestation of this disorder, often a word will be read in terms of the most "rightward" meaningful letters, e.g. *patients* from "outpatients". When words are rotated through 180 degrees, it is the final letters that are misread, which are now to the left (Ellis, Young, & Flude, 1987), e.g. *out* from "outpatients". There will also be occasions when a word is partially identified and, instead of scanning back, the patient appears to guess at the word. Accordingly, the more ambiguous a word is, the more likely these patients are to make an error, especially when the ambiguity is only resolved by knowledge of the "leftmost" letters of the word. If there is a random string of letters then, paradoxically, the left-most letter may be reported but other "left-sided" letters ignored, as if there is some checking procedure to make sure the word does not make sense (Riddoch, Humphreys, Cleton, & Fery, 1990).

Hemianopia may interact with neglect to alter the type of error. Thus, a central presentation (both disorders) may produce an omission of the initial letters, e.g. CAT to AT and CHAIR to HAIR, while a rightward presentation (not affecting left hemianopia but neglect still omits the left side) of a word results in a substitution, e.g. BAT to EAT, BELIEF to RELIEF (Young, Newcombe, & Ellis, 1991). Patients have been reported who have a left lesion and difficulty in reading the rightward ends of words, and patients have also been reported who have shown little reading neglect but have been found to have neglect in spelling "out loud" and writing (Caramazza & Hillis, 1991; see Ellis, Young, & Flude, 1993, for a further discussion).

These cases are theoretically interesting and indicate that neglect is a fractionated disorder. However, one should sometimes be reminded of the bigger picture; when an unselected group of neglect patients is considered, these double dissociations between types of neglect task performance do not represent the average presentation of this disorder. McGlinchey-Berroth and colleagues found three factors, including a number of search and other tasks in the first factor, line bisection in the second factor, and reading in the third factor, when a principal components analysis was conducted on the results of 120 patients. However, the authors remark that "impairments in these three factors were commonly associated" (McGlinchey-Berroth et al., 1996, p. 449). Reading was found to be least common. They argue, with Halligan and Marshall (1995), that line bisection is more often dissociated from other tasks because it requires a computation of an imaginary midpoint, while reading may be compensated by internal semantic cues.

In summary it is not impossible, but unlikely, that these different presentations of neglect are contributed to solely by a single mechanism (such as arousal) within a common circuit unless the modularisation continues throughout the circuit. For example, if arousal is the product of the brain stem and thalamic components then these should affect all types of neglect equally unless the brain stem and the thalamus are similarly divided into modules. This possibility should not be discounted out of hand but the single mechanism seems less strong in the presence of such variation (see Humphreys & Riddoch, 1994, for further arguments for variable mechanism explanations).

Also, the preponderance of cases associated with the inferior parietal lobe in humans (Vallar, 1993) suggests that there is some crucial mechanism within this area and that this contribution should be outlined with respect to other structures. In the study by McGlinchey-Berroth et al., (1996) some of the sample of 83 patients had lesions in more than one of the chosen general areas. However, as an indication of the commonest areas involved around, 51% had lesions in a lateral temporal/parietal area, around 43% had lesions in the capsular–striatal area and 28% had lesions within the dorsolateral frontal area. Experiments using monkeys have found that the neglect caused by right parietal lesions may take longer to recover from when compared to neglect caused by frontal dorsolateral lesions (Crowne & Mah, 1998). For those seeking a unitary explanation of neglect or a model that fails to acknowledge such structures this data might be explained in terms of some brain areas being more vulner-

able to natural lesions due to the distribution of cerebral arteries or bottlenecks in neural projections. Nevertheless, models proposing differential contributions from different brain areas remain attractive given the description of the variation in presentation described above.

Rizzolatti and Berti (1993) propose that the viewer-centred attentional space is represented, in the same way that perceptual processes are mapped out. If there are numerous fields of brain cells each catering for different types of spatial representation, e.g. personal, extrapersonal space, then some of the complexities could be resolved. A modular approach is also favoured by the same group (Berti, Ladavas, & Corte, 1996) when theorising about anosognosia. As discussed earlier, they found many dissociations when assessing the lack of awareness to various different neglect signs. It may be helpful in the clinical arena to assume that there are different modules with different neuroanatomical locations. Often in the case of major stroke, damage will affect all the closely situated modules, but this is not invariably the case and an appropriately directed rehabilitation programme must obviously be based on comprehensive assessment. However, this compartmentalisation of different types of neglect does not undermine models that take a broader view of a single network of structures contributing to the attentional process. It is possible that neglect requires a prerequisite lesion to a network and that the nature of neglect is only determined at one point within that network, such as the parietal cortex—in other words a disconnection between different structures of the type described described by Mesulam or Heilman and colleagues with a specific lesion in one of the structures, which determines its presentation.

In summary, the arousal theory from Heilman et al. (1993) has been a long-standing and influential model and is one of the few models that gives a comprehensive account of the neuroanatomical and biochemical underpinning of attentional processes. Details of this model have not been thoroughly explored here and the reader should be referred to the original writings of these authors. Also, these authors report on the functional relevance of the network of structures it describes. The model explains neglect in terms of an arousal mechanism. There is support for the de-arousal hypothesis from experimental work and also from rehabilitative techniques. Some approaches to rehabilitation have aimed to increase arousal and alertness in order to reduce neglect (e.g. Robertson, Mattingley, Rorden, & Driver, 1998).

However, models may be more or less helpful when describing different levels of function. Other models that argue for modules serving particular roles within attention are also favoured because they explain the individual variation in the manifestation of neglect according to lesion site. The literature on the relationship between the location of the lesion and features of neglect suggests that some brain areas are more crucial than others within a right hemisphere-dominant network or circuit of structures (e.g., Posner & Petersen, 1990). There also appears to be an increasing acceptance that neglect is a disorder of orientation, implicating an imbalance in the orienting system as described earlier in this chapter. Posner and Petersen's model appears to be satisfying many of these features at one level. Future models will additionally have to include an explanation for the variety of presentations of this intriguing disorder.

Models of anosognosia

In a previous section on models of neglect some comment was made about studies that had stimulated neglect patients by either cueing the patients to attend to the left or through increasing arousal. One of the difficulties in transferring such measures to rehabilitation is the problem of insight or awareness of the neglect: the problem of anosognosia. Anosognosia presents in two common forms: first, in terms of a failure to acknowledge the patients neglect; and second, in terms of a failure to acknowledge that a limb(s) contralateral to the lesion is paralysed.

The least plausible explanation for anosognosia is the denial theory. This proposes that the patient fails to acknowledge their disorder by way of some kind of "defence mechanism"—a defence against the overwhelming anxiety concerning their loss of function. The most obvious argument against this view is the localised nature of the disorder. A patient is unlikely to deny a disorder that is commonly associated with particular lesion sites but not with others that are equally handicapping. Also, there is a tendency to recover within the acute stage following brain damage, whereas (hysterical) conversion disorders associated with psychological denial do not follow a recovery curve—quite the reverse, they tend to manifest chronically. Finally, anosognosia appears to be quite specific: a patient may have anosognosia for an upper limb but not the lower limb, or the patient may ignore one particular neglect feature, i.e. neglect for drawing, but then acknowledge neglect in another area (Berti et al., 1996). If this were a denial reaction then one would have thought it would be less specific and attached to complaints that were most severe, but this is not the case (see Heilman, Barrett & Adair, 1998, for further arguments).

One argument for psychological denial comes from the belief that anosognosia is associated with a right hemisphere lesion only because patients with left hemisphere lesions commonly have aphasia and therefore cannot communicate their denial. However, even if this were taken seriously, studies using the Wada test (see chapter on memory disorders for a description), in which one hemisphere is anaesthetised, seem to go against the denial interpretation. Although there is some discrepancy between studies, they generally show that there is an awareness of contralateral limb paralysis when the left hemisphere is anaesthetised but that this is less likely when the right hemisphere is paralysed (see Heilman et al., 1998, for a review of these studies).

Various other theories have been considered and found wanting. For example, anosognosia for hemiplegia cannot be consistently blamed on inattention to that limb associated with unilateral neglect, as anosognosia for limb hemiplegia is not always related to the severity of neglect or even the existence of neglect. Some patients have severe unilateral neglect and no anosognosia for hemiplegia, while other patients have been reported with anosognosia but are without neglect. Berti et al. (1996) come to the conclusion that, like unilateral neglect, anosognosia is modularised. Their view is based on the testing of 34 neglect patients, around a quarter of whom showed some form of anosognosia. The two types of anosognosia tested in this study were related to either an inability to point to their left paralysed limb, using their right hand (personal neglect or asomatognosia), or an inability to recognise the impairment of the left limb (anosognosia for hemiplegia). The more severely affected patients with the latter complaint claimed to have been able to move their paralysed arm to touch the experimenter's hand, when in reality they had done no such thing. One patient claimed to have touched the experimenter's hand with the neglected limb even when the limb was placed in the patient's non-neglected right visual field. In this study 47% of those with drawing neglect failed to acknowledge this impairment, although this was not always associated with the severity of neglect. Other examples of the specific nature of this disorder appear in this study. Some patients had anosognosia for their reading neglect but not for neglect indicated by their drawing from memory. One patient had anosognosia for the upper limb but not in the lower limb, while another patient had the reverse condition. The findings of Berti et al. (1996) encourage the view that anosognosia can be considered a separate disorder and which can present in a specific form.

Nevertheless, there are two other theories that are worth considering and which do not necessarily discount Berti and colleagues' modular approach. The first concerns a theory by Geschwind that depicts anosognosia as a form of disconnection syndrome. That is, there is a disconnection between the two hemispheres so that the left language hemisphere cannot report on the knowledge held about the limb in the right hemisphere. Left limbs are largely controlled by the right hemisphere so only the right hemisphere would know that the left limb is paralysed. If the left speech hemisphere is unaware of this information because it is only available to the right hemisphere, then the self-report may indicate that there was nothing wrong with the left arm. Certainly, the experiments discussed in Chapter 6 would support such an interpretation. However, when considering this interpretation it must be realised that these patients' visual input should transfer the information to each hemisphere and patients should still be able to mime or indicate in some non-verbal way the nature of the affliction, but this does not occur. Also, such patients tend to choose bimanual tasks over unimanual tasks, indicating that they do not even have tacit knowledge of their hemiparesis (Ramachandran, 1995).

Finally, a theory has been developed by Heilman et al. (1998) suggesting that anosognosia for hemiplegia is explainable in terms of a failure within an intention to make a movement. They refer to patients with phantom limb who, despite amputation of the limb, feel as if they are nevertheless making a movement with their non-existent limb. The feeling of making a movement may therefore be registered early in the process, before movements are made. It is of interest that patients with anosognosia report making a movement, even when there is no initiating attempt to make the movement according to registered proximal muscle movements (pectoralis majores), also suggesting that the illusion is based on false information prior to this stage. These same muscle movements were measured in other patients with hemiparesis who did not show anosognosia (Gold, Adair, Jacobs, & Heilman, 1994). The intentional deficit theory (Heilman et al., 1998) proposes that the intention is present but because there is no feed-forward to move the limb and no feedback to indicate that the limb has not moved, the patient does not acknowledge the problem. A prediction runs from this, that providing feedback by some external means will overcome the lack of internal feed-forward and feedback. There are mixed results when testing this prediction. Using visual and somatosensory feedback Adair et al. (1997) conducted an experiment that involved asking 15 patients with anosognosia to squeeze the experimenter's hand both in and out of view. Only 4 of the 15 discovered their weakness using this method and only one achieved this improvement when the limb was in view. At this stage, the intentional feedback proposal remains of interest but requires further assessment before it can be seen as having broad implications for this disorder.

In summary, there appears to be a consensus that a denial mechanism is the least likely explanation for anosognosia. Anosognosia is a relatively common, but by no means necessary, accompaniment of unilateral neglect and like neglect is also more often found following a right lesion. Nevertheless, neglect is not a strong contender as a broad explanation for this disorder. Other theories that model difficulties in terms of feedforward and feedback are emerging, but at this time it is most useful to conceive of anosognosia as being a multifaceted disorder that may have a number of manifestations and is not uniform in the area it affects. The proposal that we may have a representative map of body area and that our awareness of those areas may be undermined by cells representing those areas is gaining some ascendancy. Findings that patients may have a specific loss of limb awareness encourages such views. Within a single patient there is sometimes awareness for one type of neglect but not for others and therefore again the models that provide a modular explanation are provided some support.

RELATIONSHIPS BETWEEN ATTENTION AND PERCEPTION WITHIN ATTENTIONAL DISORDERS

Implicit perception within attentional disorders

There is evidence from a number of different areas that an implicit or non-conscious perception is sometimes maintained for the left side in subjects who have unilateral neglect. It appears that some patients are able to process information in a preattentive manner on the left neglected side without being consciously aware of the material. Marshall and Halligan (1988) described a patient who was shown two houses, one above the other. Both left sides of the two houses were on the neglected side of the patient and on this side one of the houses was depicted as being on fire. The patient reporting to the experimenter that there was no difference between the houses, when asked to report which house she would prefer to live in

would always choose the one that was not on fire. This experiment does not always work with patients but the phenomenon clearly exists. A more traditional experimental demonstration of implicit perception has been achieved in a priming paradigm. This paradigm is illustrated by a situation in which a person is first presented the word (the prime), which helps the speed of recognition of a second word. For example, the prime *nurse* has the effect of quickening the recognition of the semantically related word *doctor*. McGlinchey-Berroth et al. (1993) showed that unlike a patient with hemianopia their neglect patients benefited from a prime presented in the left neglected side, which positively influenced the processing of material in the right, non-neglected side.

Therefore, patients with neglect do perceive and analyse the meaning of material in the neglected side, up to a certain level. This semantic analysis is no doubt at a rudimentary or course level since patients often guess and make mistakes about the identity of an object or word when identifying material that is on the left side. Berti et al. (1992) investigated patients following temporal lobectomy who showed extinction with certain speeds of bilateral presentation of stimuli. In other words these patients who did not show neglect had difficulty in identifying the object contralateral to the lesion when two objects were presented at the same time on both sides (see earlier discussion of extinction). These patients were able to make categorical judgements on objects presented in the contralateral field to their parietal lesion (same–different judgements), but while being able to name the object in the ipsilateral they could not do this for the contralateral field.

Also, awareness of information is proportional to the amount of information presented. If, for example, the patient is asked to search for a target among a number of distractors, e.g. searching for a "T" amongst other letters, the subject will search through more letters towards the left given a large display that is extended into the neglected visual field when compared to a small one that is just present on the non-neglected side. There appears to be an implicit assessment of the overall size of the display that includes the neglected side for this to occur (Grabowecky, Robertson, & Treisman, 1993).

The important issue here is that these studies all provide evidence that the neglect patients may be unaware of the presence of a stimulus but nevertheless process the "unattended" information at some preattentive level.

If a part of an object is presented in a patient's neglected field the patient will sometimes voluntarily seek out its identity by scanning to the left. But this is a "grudging process" that is only given when the identity of the object is uncertain according to its rightmost features. An illustration of this comes from a study by Humphreys and Riddoch (1992), who presented two types of drawings of objects to a subject with neglect: one type of drawing with the identifying feature to the left and the other type with the identifying feature to the right. They found that the patient only drew the left neglected part of the object when it had some crucial identifying aspect, e.g. the spout of a watering can when it was pointing to the left. Even then there was a tendency to misplace this aspect towards the right, so that the spout of the watering can was superimposed on the drawing of the right side of the can (see Figure 4.20). When the object was identifiable by its rightward features then only the right half was drawn. It would appear that orientation was only pursued until the object was perceptually identified.

Sometimes it appears that perception will actually drive or override attention in a more direct way. Some patients who show extinction (unable to detect the left object when two are shown in the left and right visual fields) but without the full-blown syndrome of neglect may be more likely to acknowledge a stimulus to the left if it is part of a perceptual whole, even when it is only an illusion. For example, certain illusions are based on our readiness to perceive shapes according to our common perceptual experience. For example, in Figure 4.21 illusions (a) and (b) are both seen by patients with an extinction paradigm (bilateral presentation), but the left side of (c) and (d) are not (Mattingley, Davis, & Driver, 1997). It is of interest that when viewing (b) one patient described seeing the rod shoot through the block

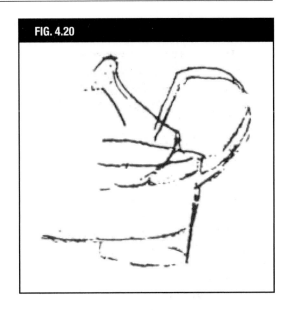

FIG. 4.20

When the part of the stimulus that is crucial to identifying the object is on the left then often this left part is drawn by the patient and not ignored. However, it is drawn towards the right (reprinted from Humphreys & Riddoch, 1993, with permission from Lawrence Erlbaum Associates Ltd).

from right to left (Mattingley et al., 1997, p. 672).

Viewer-centred and object-centred neglect: a case of perceptual versus spatially influenced neglect?

The topic of object-centred and viewer-centred neglect has been referred to and the coexistence of these two types of neglect appearing in the one patient was mentioned earlier (see Figure 4.11). In this illustration, the failure to complete the left side of the house in a part of the copied picture is an example of object-centred neglect, while the loss of the pine tree to the left is viewer-centred neglect. The critical difference between these two types is that in the former there is neglect for part of a holistic percept. Patients may be found with object-centred and not viewer-centred neglect, whereas still others may be found to have viewer-centred but not object-centred neglect (Chatterjee, 1994; Humphreys & Heinke, 1998).

Object-centred neglect appears to disregard the holistic nature of objects. For example, in the experiment by Humphreys and Heinke (1998)

FIG. 4.21

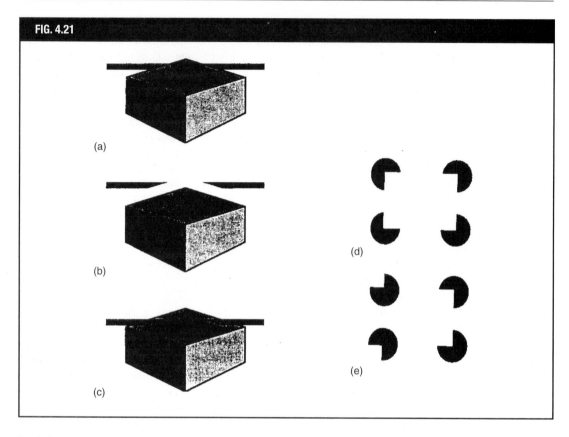

For designs (a) and (c) there was no extinction. The patient with extinction (not neglect) when viewing (a) said she saw the bar shooting behind the box from right to left, suggesting that perceptual processes and depth perception overruled attentional difficulties. The patient was more likely to just see the right part of the stick when viewing (b). When viewing the pacman in (d) the patient saw all the pacman and the illusion of the square, while only the right pacman tended to be seen with (e). (reprinted with permission from Mattingley, Davis, & Driver, 1997, *Science, 275,* 671–672. Copyright 1997 American Association for the Advancement of Science).

object-centred neglect patients were unable to judge whether the two halves of a chimeric face were of the same sex. In a chimeric presentation one half from one face is joined to the other half of another face. In this experiment the face was placed within a central presentation. Some of these patients were, nevertheless, able to make the same judgement of two whole faces placed either side of the patient while facing ahead. Patients were also found with the opposite problem.

It would appear that object-centred neglect is more perceptually than direction based. By way of supporting this view are studies that have found that half of an individual object may be neglected even when placed to the right of the viewer. Also, object-centred neglect may occur to the left side of an object even when it is rotated so that left ends up as right. For example, imagine if in Figure 4.11 the picture to be copied contained a house blown over on its side, rotated through 90 degrees so that it rested on its right side. In such a case, if our patient had copied the house in this orientation than according to the results of some studies (e.g. Behrmann & Moscovitch, 1994) the same portion of the house would have been neglected, but of course now the neglected portion would be uppermost compared to the overall scene.

While it can be argued that there is a dissociation between object-centred and viewer-centred neglect, it is possible that certain conditions may predispose a person with viewer-centred neglect to show object-centred neglect. The first condition appears to be the need to identify the object as a separate object with an identity of its own. The second condition possibly relates to the ease of perception or the ease of construction. This view has not been verified but it is interesting that some patients who have more subtle versions of the disorder may show object-centred neglect for a word when it is rotated but show no such neglect when the word is normally oriented (Behrmann & Moscovitch, 1994). It could be argued that when difficulty is increased or the patient has additional constructional difficulties attention becomes more focused and the object actually becomes viewer-centred. This speculation is not disregarding the likelihood that some patients are more prone to object-centred neglect because of the nature of their lesion.

The literature discussed above suggests that perceptual wholes, e.g. perceptual groupings and some illusions, may be attended to in the normally neglected field or extinguished field. This seems to be in contradiction to the phenomenon of object-centred neglect. It is possible that there is additional interference with the perceptual system in this last group of patients.

In the next section the discussion turns to the topic of dorsal simultaneous agnosia. It is of interest that some patients with simultaneous agnosia, who appear to have the most limited attention span of all patients, are still, unlike the patient with object-centred neglect, able to attend to a single object irrespective of its size.

Dorsal simultaneous agnosia and perceptual integration

At the beginning of this chapter, the integration theory of Treisman and Gelade (1980) was discussed as a model describing the integration between attention and perception. Among the predictions of this model is that stimuli selected on a top-down or bottom-up basis as separate from the background do not require such integration. These are the stimuli that are said to "pop up" from the background. They are perceived without conscious effort and are assumed to be processed

in parallel. This type of perception is contrasted with a search for a target whose features overlap (conjoint) with the background stimuli. In such a case the integration theory predicts that attention is required to couple the features of a stimulus with its location in space, and is associated with an effortful conscious serial search.

Friedman-Hill, Robertson, and Treisman (1995) described a patient, RM, with simultaneous agnosia who had difficulty with such integration. In a search task he had no difficulty in detecting a letter according to a distinct colour, e.g. detecting a red X from among blue X's. He also had no difficulty in detecting the X from a background of O's even when they were the same colour. Therefore in the "pop-up" parallel processing type of task he was successful. But when the distracters or background stimuli were a mixture of red O's and blue X's he performed poorly, taking as long as 5 seconds to complete the search and making errors a quarter of the time. RM complained "When I first look at it, it looks blue and it changes real quick to red. I see both colours coming together . . . Sometimes one letter is going into the other one. I get double identity. It coincides" (Friedman-Hill et al., 1995, p. 1301). To try and compensate for this he at one time designed a type of telescope from a piece of paper. This paper cylinder confined his vision to a smaller area to avoid the discomforting difficulties that occurred when he had to search the environment for objects that were not perceptually discrete compared to the background. Therefore it is not merely a massive bilateral neglect: the patient also had difficulties in screening out distracting features and maintaining a constant integration of features within a single object.

When dorsal simultaneous agnosia as a feature of Balint's syndrome was discussed earlier in the chapter there was a description of how only one object or entity was seen at a time. This was irrespective of size; thus if two tiny letters were presented only one letter was reported at a time, and if a very large letter was drawn on a board the patient was still able to read the letter.

The top-down perceptual influence on attention is well illustrated in studies using two figures superimposed or presented in the same space. For example, if a cross is placed to fill a circle, the patient will see the cross or the circle but not both, even though they form one design. Similarly if two triangles are placed on top of each other to make a star, the patient will see one triangle at a time (see also Luria, 1973). A number of more recent studies have confirmed this type of effect. For example, if a display contains circles some of which are red and some green then errors are often made when the subject is asked to state whether or not there are two colours present. This is because of seeming concentration on one circle, and the metaphor of the magnet is again appropriate. However, if two circles of different colours are joined by a black line then two colours are reported, presumably because the dumbbell entity is seen as a gestalt—a single percept.

Summary of issues relating to the relationship between attention and perception

In the earlier discussion of a neuropsychological framework for attention there was a description of a selective and competitive activation of some perceptually oriented cell groups at the expense of others in a perceptual attention system. Our attentional capacity is limited and so there seems to be a constant competitive process whereby some stimuli within our environment receive special consideration while others are suppressed. The research by Desimone and colleagues argues that during an anticipated search for a particular target we start the competitive perceptual process even before the target arrives on the scene. When it does arrive and it is not surrounded by distracting stimuli then the process of attention must be speeded up because this preattentive process is one of matching external states with internal ones. Metaphorically it is as if we look for a match to a template. When this kind of processing takes place there is a clear "what" pathway activation but little involvement of the more attention-related "where action" pathway as represented by areas within the parietal cortex.

Thus the perceptual attentional system remains intact in patients with lesions isolated to the parietal cortex. Therefore it would seem that while the allocation of attentional resources denies these perceptual/attentional resources expression they may nevertheless interact and bias attention. Thus when only half of a complete object is seen then the intact perceptual attention system somehow communicates this and attentional scanning is controlled by intact areas, that allowing identification of the object.

Desimone and Duncan's (1995) competition theory accounts for the preference for the perception of the whole object. However, integration theory provides a better explanation for RM's confusion (Freidman-Hill et al., 1995). In some ways Treisman's integration and Duncan and Desimone's competition theory are dealing with different aspects of the same process. The integration theory may be seen to be dealing more specifically with the process of binding features of stimuli to location and seems to refer to a dysfunctional perceptual attention system, while competition theory may refer more to the limited-capacity attention feature of this system.

ATTENTION AND WORKING MEMORY

The work of Michael Petrides of the Montreal Neurological Institute has been influential in studies concerning the monitoring and ordering of remembered information and information that has to be kept metaphorically "in mind" (see Petrides, 1998, for a review). In these borderlands of attention that overlap with memory research there is a common executive influence within attention and memory that organises, selects, and monitors stimuli for the purposes of maintaining storage into or retrieval from memory. This attention for "memories" or "thoughts" is also a focus of the work of Goldman Rakic (e.g., Golman-Rakic, 1995). This work and that of Petrides is discussed under the topic of working memory in Chapter 5. A discussion of this and other similar work is further developed in future chapters. Attention to what is kept in mind is referred to as working memory. The information may have been given to the person from an external source or retrieved from a person's past memory. There may be a number of reasons why someone might have to keep information in mind in a temporary fashion. There may be the requirement to temporarily hold the information prior to its manipulation, as in the case of mental arithmetic. Or the information may only have to be retained briefly prior to it being written down, as in the case of a person looking for a pen in order to write down a telephone number. Many tests of attention include such requirements of keeping information "on-line".

Work by Goldman-Rakic in her laboratory at Yale provides evidence that centres which have been described so far have interconnections via networks, as illustrated in Chapter 5 (Goldman-Rakic, 1995). She proposes that, in a situation in which an animal is maintaining attention on an internal representation of an object, all the structures within the network are activated simultaneously. This, however, does not deny the functional specialisation of the different areas but, rather, illustrates the integrated nature of the cerebral response (Goldman-Rakie, 1995, p. 59). These neural circuits also illustrate how the different circuits (e.g. SC circuit) described above are likely to link up with the other circuits described to influence attention behaviour.

Patients with lesions in the DPFC have difficulty in monitoring and keeping a record of the order and location of past stimuli. Patients with bilateral parietal lesions also have difficulty in monitoring, but the deficit is rather one of taking in more than one object at a time, whereas the dorsolateral prefrontal patients are poorly organised and fail to metaphorically tag episodes or events for contextual information that might distinguish one event from another (e.g. Milner, Corsi, & Leonard, 1991).

It is clear that some tests of attention will overlap with working memory tasks. Engle describes a list of working memory tasks compared to short-term-memory tasks (Engle, Tuholski, Laughlin, & Conway, 1999). Broadly, the working memory tasks have some executive content that requires prefrontal structures and are often identical to tasks that are described as taxing attention (Engle, Tuholski et al., 1999). Subjects who have an excellent working memory also do very well on

traditional tasks of attention (Engle, Keane, & Tuholski, 1999). Perhaps the most disparate working memory and attention tasks are keeping information "in mind" compared to "shifting attention" to a cue task, yet even with these tasks there is considerable overlap in the brain areas that are activated (LaBar et al., 1999). In Chapter 5 a case is made that the process of working memory and attention are in fact overlapping.

RELATIONSHIP BETWEEN TERMS OF ATTENTION AND PROCESS

Terminology in the study of attention

In the experimental and clinical literature there have been a number of attempts to define terms such as the following:

1. *Information processing speed.* This is a vague term, which may mean a general slowing on, for example, straightforward reaction time to targets that are presented in a serial fashion without distraction. Sometimes there may be the requirement to join a series of numbers in the right order.
2. *Selective attention.* E.g., a task that requires the selection of a target from background stimuli.
3. *Spatial attention task.* E.g., the subject is required to shift attention to a new location.
4. *Focussed attention.* E.g., the subject may have to select a particular stimulus (target) from a background of other stimuli that have overlapping or partially overlapping features calling for a controlled search (generally not "pop-out").
5. *Divided attention.* E.g., the subject has to monitor and perform two separate tasks that are competing, as in the case of a dual task.
6. *Sustained attention or vigilance.* E.g., lengthy (20 minutes plus), usually serial presentation of stimuli from which the subject must detect the occasional target from among a series of distractors, e.g. letter "L" from other letters.

Sometimes there is a need to be reminded that these commonly used terms are a typology of tasks and not verified, isolated cognitive processes as some authors might imply. One way of increasing confidence that there exists a separate process of selective attention compared to, say, divided attention might come from what is referred to as a *double dissociation*. This is found when one group of patients with lesion A is found to be significantly impaired on a focused attention task, for example, but not on the divided attention task, while another group with lesion B has the opposite pattern. Such a result would encourage the view that selective and divided attention were served by two different brain mechanisms. Unfortunately, this kind of evidence is lacking, and given the evidence reviewed above, such a distinction is unlikely to be found. This does not of course mean that these terms are not useful and do not have clinical relevance in that one task may be taxing one brain mechanism more than another. Nevertheless, it may be time to reorient our perspectives on performance in tasks and their relationship to brain processes.

The business of estimating the involvement of brain areas according to task type and functional imaging results is obviously not straightforward. For example, while some imaging studies have found differences between focused and selective attention, many have failed to find differences between such supposedly distinct tasks. For example, auditory tasks of focused attention (monitoring and making decisions in one ear while ignoring stimuli in the other ear) do not seem to activate different areas from divided attention task (duel tasks attending to both ears at the same time) (Benedict et al., 1998). Divided attention tasks may show similar areas of activation to sustained activation tasks (Johannsen et al., 1997).

While there are differences between these different tasks in terms of the extent of activation in different areas, in terms of the broad areas the differences are not as obvious as one might expect. Sometimes two seemingly quite different tasks are only differentiated by the degree of activation within a particular area (Carter, Mintun, & Cohen, 1995). Therefore it might be time to

abandon this typology of tasks for a more research-based differentiation. A start is made towards this goal in the list of tasks below.

Non-conjunctive feature detection

At the lowest level of attentional demand a task requiring the detection of a feature from a background appears to challenge areas within the striate, extrastriate cortex and the inferior temporal lobe. This task, which involves a "pop-out" search (See Figure 4.1a) appears to predominantly involve the "what" pathway. The striate, extrastriate cortex, and the inferior temporal lobe are most frequently activated in the PET and fMRI studies (Corbetta & Shulman, 1998). Activation of the parietal cortex is less likely. In some sense this might be seen as a straightforward test of perception but, as argued above, there are attentional features to such a task.

Conjunction feature detection

In this task, which requires a search because of the overlap between target and background stimuli (see Figure 4.1b), there is superior parietal activation. If there are a small number of distractors then the activations associated with a shift of attention would be minimised. When compared with feature detection tasks involving searching for a colour against a different background or motion against a different background there was little parietal activation compared with a search where there was conjuction between target and distractors involving both these qualities (Corbetta, Shulman, Miezin, & Petersen, 1995). Studies that temporarily incapacitate brain areas using transmagnetic stimulation also show that the parietal cortex is important for conjunction tasks but not for feature detection tasks (Ashbridge, Walsh, & Cowey, 1997) .

Shift of attention

There is a simple task that involves no instructions to the subject, and the subject has to passively sit there until a light is suddenly presented on a screen at different locations. This reflex response is associated with parietal cortex activation without obvious frontal involvement (Yantes & Jonides, 1990; Corbetta & Shulman,

1998). However, as soon as the subject has responded intentionally to detect a target and there is some controlled aspect to the task then frontal structures are involved even when a motor response is subtracted. Typically with these tasks the subject has to press a button as soon as they detect a stimulus. In some studies such as spatial attention tasks there is a cue that is helpful for most trials in directing attention. However, on some occasions the cue is contradicted and the target is presented on the opposite side. In such tasks there are two main areas that are activated in excess of control conditions in fMRI and PET studies. There are some differences between the very many studies that have looked at these shifting attention paradigms, but a meta-analysis by Corbetta and Shulman (1998) revealed a parietal–frontal network that is relatively consistent (see also Figure 4.6). There is usually activation of the superior and more inferior parietal areas. These include the postcentral gyrus and the intraparietal sulcus. The second area involves the precentral gyrus and the supplementary eye fields (superior aspect of the central sulcus on the mesial aspect of longitudinal fissure) (see Chapter 8 for a discussion on these motor areas). Finally there is an area at the posterior tip of the superior frontal sulcus at the junction with the precentral gyrus which is thought to correspond to the frontal eye field activation in controlling eye movements (see Figure 4.6). There are other brain areas that are not always prominent in imaging studies but which are clearly important from animal research. The SC, basal ganglia and cingulate are clearly implicated in such tasks.

Monitoring/selection tasks

This refers to tasks in which there is the necessity to keep information in mind or monitor progress during a search, for example in a task requiring a search for a target through a large display. In such a task there is a conjunction between the features of the target and distractors such that there is a competitive overlap. If there is a search for more than one target then the identities of such stimuli would also have to be kept in mind. An auditory version of such a task would require the subject to repeat back a series of digits in the reverse order. In such a situation the subject must remember the digits forward and then mentally reverse them. Such tasks involve extra bilateral activation of areas within the dorsolateral prefrontal cortex. In the case of a visual search task then ,of course, the areas required of shifting attention would additionally be involved.

Divided attention tasks

If the task becomes even harder and various distracting sounds are presented to the subject then the visual sensory input will be activated and the auditory sensory input would, in theory, have to be suppressed by the thalamic system (La Berge, 1995). The anterior cingulate will also act to inhibit any orienting reflex to distracting stimuli (Corbetta et al., 1991). La Berge (1995) argues that the thalamus (possibly the pulvinar) has a role in accentuating stimulus identification from a background, something like turning up the gain. The outline of the stimulus is amplified, while the cells activated by the surround are inhibited. A role for the nucleus reticularis in suppressing one modality to allow another to be disinhibited was described earlier. Frith and Friston (1996) found that the mid thalamus was activated when the auditory modality was attended to at the expense of the visual modality but not vice versa, which is not confidently explained but does show a filtering role for the thalamus.

This attentional system is made up from a number of components that are more or less activated depending on task demands. Table 4.1 allows a tentative start to defining task requirements based on embryonic functional imaging research. While the arousal system is necessary for all tasks and many of the components will be required at the same time, it is of course possible to design a task that minimises or maximises the use of one particular component. Recent work shows that it is simplistic to think of functional activation in a linear manner. Some structures appear to supply a prerequisite role, while others play a role that increases with the demands of a task. A further perspective is to look at the connectivity between structures that may have particular relevance to the topic of attention, which appears to depend on relationships between

TABLE 4.1

A broad guide to brain areas that are more activated depending on the task requirement

Name of component	Function	Structures involved
Arousal	Cortical arousal	Reticular formation, intralaminar nucleus of the thalamus. Medical geniculate nucleus. Global features, cortical and subcortical
Feature detection (no overlap between target and distractor)	Focus on important perceptual features at the expense of others. Driven by top-down perceptual processes and motivational factors	Predominantly the striate, extrastriate cortex and inferior temporal lobe and inferior temporal lobe
Conjunction task (overlap between target and distractor)	Selection of target from overlapping distractors	Striate, extrastriate cortex and inferior temporal lobe, and parietal and frontal activation
Attentional shift	Orient towards a target from overlapping distractors	Structurtes described as being part of the orienting system. Superior colliculus, parietal cortex, frontal motor area controlling eye movements
Monitoring/selection	Resistance to distraction and controlled search. Keeping information in mind	Parietal cortex, cingulate and dorsolateral prefrontal cortex
Modality focus	Selection of one modality at the expense of another during distraction	Additional thalamus activation, especially when visual modality ignored for auditory modality

structures described as relying on neuronal networks.

Due to a number of factors subcortical structures are often not clearly revealed in these imaging studies. However, from research results derived from animal studies involving tasks that require shifts of attention the collicular system is clearly involved (see earlier, under "Orienting reflex"). This system is used even when the state is a preparatory one, prior to a shift, or even when eye movements are suppressed in some way in the presence of an orienting eliciting stimulus.

OVERVIEW

In the first part of this chapter we described a framework that served a purpose in clarifying one

of the most complex and pervasive areas in neuropsychology. When talking of attention one invariably talks about limitations of the organism in its ability to process information. Attention can be described as a limited-capacity process that allows the preferential processing of certain sensory or imaged information at the expense of other stimuli.

In the variety of literature reviewed so far a model of attention is emerging that allows for some elaboration on existing models. Various systems have been identified that contribute to attention. The *arousal system* will influence both the quality of attention and our capacity to attend. In turn, this level of arousal will affect our ability to respond quickly and reflexively to important stimuli that might signal danger or novelty. Thus an arousal system was described which in turn affects the efficiency of other systems. The acknowledged complexity of this system has increased in the last two decades to describe different arousal subsystems that are dependent on different neurotransmitter networks whose specialised functions are only now being defined.

The *orienting system* was also described as a feature of this model, which has a role in initiating and controlling shifts of attention that are rapid and reflexive. As discussed, there are obvious "natural selection" reasons for this phylogenetically archaic system. The accent is on speedy orientation to bring peripheral targets within the receptive area of the fovea for closer inspection and analysis. Such an automatic response needs to be controlled on occasions, either in the presence of a large amount of superfluous distraction or in the case when concentration on a single demanding task is imperative. Novel stimuli are particularly likely to cause distraction but as the stimuli become more familiar then orientation becomes less likely within a process of habituation. This suggests that there is some preliminary analysis that verifies whether the peripheral stimulus is familiar or not. This suggests some triggering process by some cortical areas such as the parietal cortex.

The *perceptual attention system* provides a conceptual interface between perception and attention. The major role of this system is to allow the organism to attend to relevant features of our environment. This process, which is sometimes referred to as tuning, appears to potentially influence relatively early stages of perceptual processing in a top-down manner that allows our experience and expectations to support a perceptual process that would otherwise be laborious and non-adaptive. Patients who have difficulty in orienting to the left following parietal lesions still retain this ability to focus on or seek out perceptually whole objects, thereby showing that a part of this system remains functionally intact. As argued above, pop-out feature detection does not require the integrity of the parietal cortex—it is only when there is a competition between features that the parietal cortex is involved.

The *executive attention system* drives and directs the attentional process when there are distracting, confusing, or competing elements within the sensory system. The importance of the association area within the right parietal cortex within this system is clear. There is some agreement that the area within the inferior parietal cortex, which is often damaged in cases of neglect, is important for integrating all the perceptual features into a visuospatial map of our environment. This area interacts with the prefrontal cortex such as the dorsolateral prefrontal cortex and also the anterior cingulate and the basal ganglia, to provide a control system for attention. This system may have its own arousal system, which is important for sustained alertness (Posner, 1995; Posner & Petersen, 1990).

An argument was made that the frontal structures within this system controlled reflexive orienting. It is likely that this controlling influence is late to develop in children. Posner and Rothbart (1998) describe how young children who are upset by something are very easily distracted by the mother to another stimulus, so that tears can be turned to laughter quite quickly. As discussed in Chapter 10 the frontal cortex develops far more slowly than other brain areas. Therefore the orienting system may be more dominant in the early years of childhood and more conducive to external control without the internal control supplied by frontal structures.

One disorder that appears to exemplify a breakdown within the executive attention system and the network between the prefrontal cortex and the parietal areas is that of unilateral neglect. This dramatic and relatively common clinical disorder in the early days following right hemisphere stroke is yet to be theoretically described in a comprehensive manner. Any theory must account for the following features:

1. This is a disorder of orientation in which the patient is attracted to one side, usually the right, as if attracted by a magnet.
2. The expression of the disorder is determined by the nature of the available stimuli. In other words it not merely an orientation deficit but dependent on whether there are *competing* percepts. Thus the environment is ignored according to units of perception.
3. Neglect is predominantly a right hemisphere disorder.

4. It often involves a lesion to the inferior right parietal lobule.

5. There are other brain areas which when lesioned are associated with neglect, albeit less frequently.

6. It is associated with overt and covert orientation difficulties.

7. It is a fractionated disorder, suggesting that there are different types of neglect both in terms of sensory modality, e.g. auditory neglect, and also in terms of frame of reference, e.g. object centred, viewer centred.

There are theories of neglect which explain some of these features better than others, but none, at the present time, manage to explain all of these features in a comprehensive and persuasive manner. It may be helpful to see neglect as breakdown in the hub of the attentional system. It is, if you like, at the centre of a network, the go-between for the perceptual system, the orienting system, and the arousal system, and therefore features of impairment in all these systems are associated with unilateral neglect.

Despite some consensus of what is important to study within attention there is still some obvious uncertainty as to how to proceed with measuring attention. For example, how should we measure the limited capacity of attention? Although this chapter has frequently referred to the topic of attentional capacity, an agreed independent measure of this concept has yet to be devised. It might be predicted that tasks that challenge the attentional system at the highest level and involve all the systems described so far would therefore challenge the capacity of the system. Alternatively, a measure of frontal activation may reveal a measure (see Passingham, 1998). In keeping with this last view is the finding that tests of divided attention, which subjects often describe as being subjectively stressful, are associated with more intense and widespread brain activation, especially involving the anterior cingulate and DPFC (Corbetta et al., 1991). It appears, however, that the activation of areas according to cerebral blood flow are not always related to attentional load in a straightforward manner. Some structures are activated in a linear way with increased attentional load, while other areas appear to reach a threshold and plateau while other areas decrease in activation. Rees et al. (1997) found that when this auditory stimulus became the priority task then activation of the auditory sensory area increased. However, the area did not then increase in activation in a linear fashion with increased demands as the task was speeded up and made more difficult. In fact, *deactivation* of the inferior temporal lobe did correlate with demand for reasons which are at present unclear (see also Carter et al., 1995). Therefore cerebral blood flow, which is in itself a secondary measure of neuronal activation, does not as yet supply the answer to this problem of attentional capacity.

Attention is the most perplexing and enigmatic area of research at the present time. It has been described as modulating all the other areas of cognition and the way the topic of attention merges with other topics is a point of interest in the next chapter on memory disorders and is discussed in the final chapter of this book.. However, despite this overlap with other topics, attention remains a topic in its own right that influences all other functions but retains its own identity.

5

Memory disorders

INTRODUCTION

Memory is a complex function and although many models exist few are devoted to a comprehensive description of memory from a neuropsychological/functional perspective. Therefore to enhance the reader's understanding of this topic the first part of this chapter is devoted to describing a model of memory that attempts an up-to-date, but parsimonious, representation of the research findings. In order to achieve this end the initial approach is to describe the bare bones of a theory and to elaborate on this later in the chapter.

The second part of this chapter introduces more specialised topics. Some of these issues are under discussion within the literature at the present time and an attempt has been made to impart some of the flavour of these discussions and the way the process of scientific discovery emerges, in some cases, within a relatively brief period of time.

In the third part of this chapter is a discussion of the different types of amnesia and their various presentations. Clinically amnesia is the most dramatic representation of a memory disorder. Amnesia constitutes a profoundly impaired ability to learn new information, which severely handicaps the patient's everyday life. Patients with amnesia often have to be supervised and cared for in some way. They will leave things on a stove, leave a fire on, fail to pay bills and have difficulty in remembering whether they have been shopping or even whether they have had a particular meal.

While there is no agreed upon objective criteria for amnesia, generally such patients recall nothing or a negligible amount of information after a delay filled with interference. Amnesia may be *anterograde*, which is an inability to remember events and other information since an illness, or *retrograde*, in which memories stored prior to the illness or accident are not retrieved, recalled, or recognised (Figure 5.1). The topic of retrograde amnesia is discussed next and how the mechanism for this type of amnesia is mostly but not completely separate from that of anterograde amnesia. In the final part of this chapter there is a return to the model discussed in first part. This final summary takes into account the new information described since this section.

Some of the complexity of memory is due to the influence of so many other areas of cognition. It can be seen as the hub of a wheel that is surrounded by the spokes representing all the other cognitive functions. Sometimes, for this reason, memory is referred to as "the final common pathway". Memory impairment may be the result

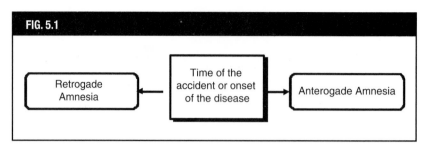

Retrograde amnesia relates to an inability to remember events prior to the illness or accident, while anterograde amnesia is the inability to learn information after the accident.

of attentional, perceptual, motor, or executive dysfunction. Other functional impairments may therefore impinge on our ability to store or retrieve memories. Perhaps, because of the inter-dependence with other areas and because memory is so important to our efficient functioning in our everyday lives we notice when it deteriorates, and memory impairment is one of the most commonly reported disorders. This is true of both normal persons and those who are suffering brain damage (Andrewes et al., 1998; Kapur & Pearson, 1983).

TOWARDS A NEUROPSYCHOLOGICAL MODEL OF MEMORY

An overview

There has been a long-standing interaction between the models of memory provided by cognitive psychologists and the clinical findings of neuropsychologists. There is a symbiosis in which one often feeds upon the work of the other and many theoreticians who have been cognitive psychologists have become neuropsychologists partly in a bid to provide substantial support for their modelling.

Some clinical confusion occurs because of the use of popular terms such as short-term memory. Often one hears a clinician say "The patient has a problem with their short-term memory," meaning that the patient has difficulty in remembering new information in any permanent way. This is a misuse of the scientific term, which refers to a brief memory store lasting a matter of seconds. Luckily, this term has been largely superseded by the term *working memory* (WM), a modern substitute

for the short-term memory concept. It is still a brief memory store with a decay rate of a few seconds but the concept has been extended. Working memory allows us to manipulate information in mind during, and prior to, the process of storing information into memory. Working memory is not used just for learning: it may be used for keeping information on-line while doing other everyday tasks such as learning to read or even retrieval of permanent memories. It is closely allied to attention and may be seen as a temporary "buffer" store for information while other mental manipulations are taking place.

Information that is learned is stored in what is referred to as the long-term memory store (LTMS). However, for this to happen the material has to be stored into memory by what is referred to here as the consolidation system. The consolidation system, which includes such structures as the hippocampus (see Figure 1.3), is often not mentioned in cognitive psychology models. Perhaps this is because these models were originally developed on subjects who had nothing wrong with the process of memory storage. However, the need for positing such a system is clear since there are some patients who have an intact working memory but an inability to consolidate memories into a form that is more permanent. In other words, these patients are able to manipulate information and keep this information in mind for brief periods (working memory). They also have the ability to retrieve information from the LTMS (for information learned prior to the brain damage). But they are unable to store new permanent memories into the LTMS since the onset of their brain damage because in these cases the consolidation system is damaged. For new

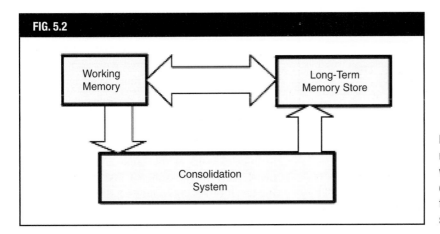

FIG. 5.2

Working Memory

Long-Term Memory Store

Consolidation System

Illustration of the relationship between working memory, the consolidation system and the long-term memory store.

long-term memories to be created an intact consolidation system is required (Figure 5.2).

In summary, WM is described as a process for keeping information "in mind" while other mental activities take place. WM may be seen as a "holding bay" or "buffer store", while relationships are found within the LTMS which would allow a more permanent storage. WM in this instance therefore develops and holds these new associations while the process of consolidation takes place.

The role of the consolidation system is to strengthen these new activations of WM that take place in the LTMS in such a way that the old information and the new information are linked together to become permanent features of the LTMS. In the next section the features of WM, the consolidation system, and the LTMS are identified. However, because these concepts are rapidly developing at the present time it is important to indicate some of the history and arguments associated with these three concepts.

Working memory

Some historical influences in the development of a working memory model from the cognitive psychology perspective
In the 1970s Graham Hitch teamed with Alan Baddeley to produce a model of WM. The concept evolved from short-term memory (STM) (See Box 5.1 for a brief description), from a perceived need to define a temporary memory system that catered for everyday needs. Previously, STM was described by Atkinson and Shiffrin (1968) as a temporary memory store for material, prior to being stored more permanently. The function of this hypothetical buffer memory store was to allow the vivid holding in mind of a limited amount of information, while that information was processed and analysed further.

The model below gives a simplified version of Atkinson and Shiffrin's 1968 model. In this model, rehearsal of information within STM allowed for this information to be refreshed and maintained in STM. This rehearsal prevented decay and forgetting. The frequently used example of this is the situation when we might rehearse a phone number until we find a pen to write it down. The rehearsal process was also seen, at the time, as the major way of increasing the permanence of the memory, allowing the information to be transferred to long-term memory. The greater the amount of rehearsal the more likely the material, e.g. the phone number, would be transferred to the LTMS. This would in turn free up space within this limited-capacity STM, allowing more information to be rehearsed and so on (see Box 5.1 for a further discussion, and Figure 5.3).

The conceptual development of working memory has two research origins. One of these areas has been made famous by researchers such as Patricia Goldman-Rakic and colleagues. This work was most interested in mapping the relationship between brain areas and pathways

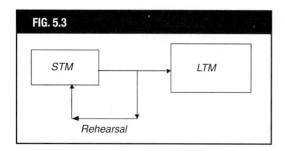

FIG. 5.3

STM — LTM

Rehearsal

Illustration of Atkinson and Shiffrin's (1968) control processes involved in transferral from STM to LTM. In this model information within the limited-capacity STM is refreshed through rehearsal. With increased rehearsal the information will enter LTM, thereby freeing up space within STM. If rehearsal is prevented then information decays from the STM buffer over a matter of seconds (adapted from Atkinson & Shriffin, 1968).

associated with working memory (Goldman-Rakic, 1987, 1995). This work is referred to later in the chapter when discussing the neuroanatomical correlates of WM. A second, conceptually separate approach was developed through work with humans and was developed by Alan Baddeley and Graham Hitch (Baddeley & Hitch, 1974). These last researchers were not originally concerned with brain relationships and neuroanatomical considerations but were searching for a practical purpose for the older concept of STM. These two approaches to WM may be seen as separate, using quite different methods of testing, although recently some links between these two approaches have been appearing in the literature. At this point we are most concerned with the original human literature spearheaded by the Baddeley and Hitch model.

When they originally developed their WM model Alan Baddeley and Graham Hitch (Baddeley, 1986; Baddeley & Hitch, 1974) had the very practical opinion that STM must be useful for something more than just remembering telephone numbers and word lists. They reasoned that STM might be used as a temporary store while conducting mental activities such as mental arithmetic or verbal reasoning tasks. They argued that if such tasks relied on the same STM then mental arithmetic performance should be undermined by

filling STM to capacity with a series of digits (see digit-span in Box 5.1). In this way the subject would have to carry out two tasks at the same time to see if they interfered with each other; if they did, then the subject must be using the same resource. For example, the subjects might have to remember a list of six digits as a priority task (STM nearly full to capacity, see Box 5.1), but subjects would also have to carry out the other arithmetic tasks at the same time. If the arithmetic performance suffered and deteriorated as the result of having to retain a digit-span, then it could be assumed that STM capacity was also being used during the mental arithmetic task. It could therefore be deduced that STM was being used as part of a kind of "working memory".

Initially, little effect was found in such experiments. The findings suggested to Baddeley (1986) that somehow the STM used by the mental arithmetic, for example, was in some way flexible and that mental arithmetic could rely on an alternative encoding. In other words, the phonological STM that digit-span relied on could be by passed by using another type of STM—one that perhaps might rely more on imagery, for example. The visuospatial sketchpad was proposed as a separate STM store for the visuospatial modality (see illustration of WM model below). The updated WM included different types of STM, the phonological store and the visuospatial sketchpad, which were now referred to as slave systems (See Figure 5.4).

A *central executive* was also proposed to deploy these slave systems. In this way the central executive allowed one slave system to be used over another depending on the demands made on the individual. In some ways the central executive now takes over those roles originally referred to by Atkinson and Shiffrin (1968) as control processes.

The most researched slave system, the phonological store, is specialised to process the sounds of words. The phonological store is a temporary memory store that has many of the features of the older STM (see Box 5.1), although the limited capacity is now attributed to the central executive (Gathercole & Baddeley, 1993). The phonological store is associated with an articulatory loop,

Box 5.1. Features of the modal model of short-term memory

This model of memory was referred to as modal because it conformed to the ideas of many theorists of the time. Models of the STM and LTM dichotomy, such as the Atkinson and Shiffrin model (1968), were supported by some of the following research findings:

1. The store decayed rapidly. If rehearsal was prevented then the store would decay or be interfered with over a number of seconds, e.g. 18 seconds, for less meaningful material (Brown, 1958; Peterson & Peterson, 1959). In the figure below subjects were shown three letters (no vowels) and they had to repeat back the letters after a period of distraction in which they would count backwards from a number. The time of the distraction (counting backwards) was varied and it was found that the longer the period of repeating backwards the less likely the letters were remembered.

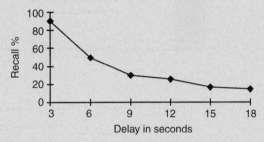

2. The measure that is taken as the neuropsychological gold standard for the capacity of STM is the digit-span test. This test requires a person to repeat a series of numbers in the right order. The random numbers chosen are read by the examiner at the rate of one number per second. Most people can repeat back seven digits and only start making mistakes when faced with an eight-digit number, but there is a large amount of individual variation to some extent related to intelligence. Therefore an impaired STM in certain brain-damaged patients is sometimes taken as a low digit-span relative to the subject's level of intelligence, i.e. 2 or 3. There are reasons to believe that digit-span overestimates the STM capacity and this issue is discussed below.
3. Another measure of STM that is commonly used comes from the finding that when a subject is asked to immediately recall a list of words they tend to have a strategy of repeating back the last words in the list first. This is as if they wish to offload the last items quickly before they are lost and are still "in mind". This "recency effect" is associated with STM storage. In keeping with expectations, these words decay rapidly compared to others in a list of words if the subject is *unexpectedly* distracted. *All* measures of STM are surrounded by controversy and arguments about what is being measured; however, within the limitations and artifical constraints of these experiments, these results have been well replicated.
4. Because of the vulnerability of STM to phonological interference it is assumed that phonological encoding (the sound of the word) is the main form of encoding for this store.

which takes over from Atkinson and Shiffrin's rehearsal mechanism (see Figure 5.3). The articulatory loop may refresh the phonological store in the same way that rehearsal refreshes STM in the older model. The original model proposes that rehearsal may be subvocal (rehearsing under-the-breath or silent) or vocal (aloud). Apart from the previous STM experiments confirming the phonological characteristics of the phonological store a series of further experiments have also found that immediate recall of the digit-span is heavily influenced by the time it takes to say the numbers in the span. If the articulatory rehearsal mechanism was not refreshed within around 2 seconds then the contents of the phonological store would decay (Baddeley, 1986).

Because the store proposed is time limited

rather than chunk or item limited it matters a lot how quickly you can articulate the words to refresh them. One might make a comparison with a short conveyor belt that allows boxes to drop off the end (forgotten) if they are not brought back to the beginning by hand (recycled by the articulatory loop).

As discussed, the digit-span test is seen as the main assessment of phonological store and requires the subject to immediately repeat back a series of numbers in the right order. If the numbers 5–6–9, for example, are spoken in English, the words for these numerals are relatively short when compared to the same numerals spoken in other languages such as Welsh, for example. Persons, who for these and other reasons, take longer to say the numerals have shorter digit-spans (Ellis

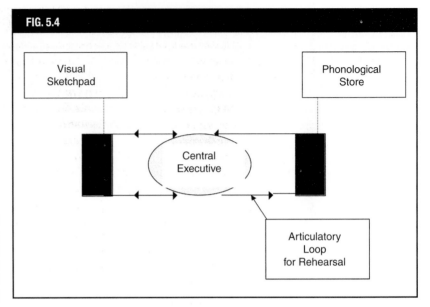

FIG. 5.4

Illustration of Baddeley and Hitch's model of working memory (adapted from Baddeley, 1986, by permission of Oxford University Press.)

& Hennelly, 1980). Theoretically this is explained according to the nature of the phonological store. Because the store is based on the sound of the words and has the attribute of rapidly decaying, the quicker the words are pronounced the greater the number can be retained prior to their inevitable decay. To return to the conveyor belt analogy, the longer the boxes (longer-sounding words), the fewer can be placed on the conveyor belt at any one time. This limitation according to the spoken length of a word is referred to as the *word length effect*. If a list or string of words has to be immediately repeated back in the same order then the repeated span performance will improve with short words compared to longer multisyllable words (Baddeley, Thomson, & Buchanan, 1975). Therefore it appears that whether the meaning or semantics of the words is influential or not in such experiments, the time it takes to say the words—the phonological characteristics of the words—is certainly significant. Also, the *word length effect* occurs when the words are presented in an auditory or visual presentation, which suggests that in the case of visually presented words some conversion to a phonological code might take place.

Further results supporting the predominance of the phonological code are provided by experiments which find that subjects are more easily distracted by verbal material that is phonologically similar to the to-be-repeated material when compared to a distraction that is semantically (meaningfully) similar to that material (Salamé & Baddeley, 1982).

In summary, the working memory model describes a phonological store that has taken over many of the features of the old STM system. The store has the characteristics of being vulnerable to decay and interference and quickly fades away in around 2 seconds unless it is refreshed by rehearsal through the articulatory loop.

The visuospatial sketchpad, the non-verbal equivalent of the phonological store, has been less vigorously researched. Experiments often use a tracking task in which the subject had to manually follow a target to test this type of memory (e.g. Baddeley, Grant, Wright, & Thomson, 1975). Simultaneously, in such experiments, the subjects were required to retain the visuospatial location of items (numbers) within a 4   4 spatial matrix (spatial equivalent to digit-span) (Brooks, 1967). Extensive interference was found between the two tasks, resulting in increased errors on the tracking task. This suggested that the tracking task was competing for the same spatial processing resources required of the non-verbal/spatial equivalent of the digit-span task. Baddeley and Lieberman (1980) confirmed the features of the visuospatial sketchpad as a store that was spatial rather than merely visual in nature and also a store that was involved with imagery tasks.

Although new models are appearing in the literature at the present time (see Miyake & Shah, 1999), Baddeley and Hitch's WM model has been the most influential in thinking about the nature of brief, non-permanent memory. Also, the distinction between the phonological store with its articulatory loop (subvocal rehearsal) and the visual sketchpad is supported by a number of studies (e.g., Shah & Miyake, 1996). The independent existence of the phonological store compared to the visual sketchpad is also supported by neuropsychological case studies showing that patients may have problems with either store, quite independently (Vallar & Papagno, 1995a; see discussion below).

However, despite this support, many studies with non-brain-damaged subjects have failed to find the expected interference effects with everyday tasks, suggesting that the model may have limited application. The phonological store is a strongly implicated resource in a relatively small number of everyday tasks. Interesting studies have been completed suggesting that we might use different stores depending on the stage of our development. For example, when remembering the presentation of a series of pictures, young children of 5 years are more likely to rely on imagery and presumably the visuospatial sketchpad. But as they get older they appear to rely on a more verbally based encoding or translate into verbal encoding more easily (Hitch, Halliday, Schaafstal, & Schraagen,1988). A relationship has been found between a children's capacity to learn to read and the working memory phonological store capacity as measured by the digit-span test (Gathercole, 1994; Gathercole & Baddeley, 1993) but this relationship is less obvious in adult reading (see Just & Carpenter, 1992). Further influence of phonological WM appears to be present during retrieval from long-term-memory (Baddeley, 1997).

In conclusion, this WM model has confirmed Baddeley and Hitch's view that the old STM can be used for purposes other than just storing new memories. Therefore the idea of a buffer store that is *mainly* important for holding new information prior to storage into LTM is challenged; nevertheless, some researchers believe that it is time for this model to be extended (see Baddeley, 2000). This point will be returned to at a later point within this section.

Some historical influences in the development of a working memory model from the neuropsychological perspective

Warrington and Shallice (1969) described a patient, KF, who had a severely impaired STM (digit-span of one), but strangely he had an ability to transfer items into LTMS (as evidenced in learning on a paired-associate task). This was a dramatic finding at the time because it was assumed that the patient, with his profoundly impaired digit-span, had a severely impaired phonologically based STM store. If Fig. 5.3 is surveyed it is clear that in a traditional model transfer into LTMS is dependent on the integrity of STM. If KF had a severely reduced STM then how could he learn new information, since the model described in Fig. 5.3 allows for no alternative entry into LTMS. The dual-entry system of the WM model, however, proposed that an intact visuospatial sketchpad might compensate for a deficient phonological store. By the use of imagery some verbal material could be converted to visuospatial encoding. This is the view that has been argued for other patients with impaired phonological stores (see Vallar & Papagno, 1995a).

Vallar and Papagno (see Vallar & Papagno, 1995a, for a review) report on a patient, PV, with an impaired phonological store. On a number of measures, PV is clearly able to place information into LTMS, presumably by using coding that is alternative to phonological encoding. Sometimes, however, the to-be-learned information apparently defied any attempts to use an alternative code. For example, when PV tried to learn new Russian words, which presumably required her to remember the pronunciation of words, she had great difficulty (Vallar & Papagno, 1995b).

Apart from these specific instances the evidence

of flexibility in encoding appears to be endemic. It is likely that some patients who are particularly impaired in their phonological store may learn to use an alternative encoding even when completing such gold-standard phonological store tasks as the digit-span (see Howard, 1995; Martin & Breedin, 1992). Sometimes experimenters, who assess the phonological store, give the patient pronounceable non-words to repeat back, e.g. flard, chrine, rather than the digit-span. Because we have no knowledge of such words they have no meaning or, at least, less meaning than digits. Non-words are therefore assumed to be reliant purely on a phonological encoding. Howard's patient (1995) could only repeat back a *single* nonsense syllable, e.g. "tord". Nevertheless, despite this resoundingly impaired ability to keep phonological material in mind, this patient was able to repeat back three digits which seemed to be in excess of expectations given the performance on the nonsense words. The authors concluded from their research that the patient was using a visual encoding, imagery, or semantic store to retain the digits.

Other illustrations of such flexibility come from Butterworth, Campbell, and Howard (1986), who describe a successful student who had little difficulty with reading or auditory comprehension despite her digit-span of four.

Other slave systems?

The research strength supporting the phonological store and the visuospatial sketch-pad within working memory is undeniable and in the case of the phonological store impressive, but there are now an increasing number of models that allow for semantic (meaningful, conceptual) encoding within brief memory. By semantic the author is referring to association with concepts other than those related to the phonological or purely visual information. Some of these models suggest a conceptual short-term memory (CSTM) that in some way activates LTMS very briefly. The CSTM can be distinguished from the phonological store because of its speed of access. Potter (1993) argues for this store and describes experiments that show that we can extract semantic information at very high speeds and can also

learn this information at relative high speeds compared to phonological information. She proposes that when we learn in our everyday life we rarely resort to rehearsal for new learning, as some traditional models would suggest. Potter suggests that learning is often effortless and fast. Hopefully, for example, the reader is using this type of memory storage facility.

Also, the point is sometimes made that while the phonological code appears to be most important in some WM tasks, this is the case only when certain conditions exist. For example, when there is a limited set of items, e.g. digits and these are used repetitively over trials, so the potential for interference exists, a resort to a phonological code appears to be more likely; also, when an articulated response is required, rather than pointing or choosing as in a recognition task. When serial recall is required this may also alter the apparent characteristics of the WM towards a time-based phonological encoding (see Cowan, 1995, pp. 77–93). But even here one should not disregard the semantic influence in learning. For example, Hulme, Maughan, and Brown (1991) found that memory-span for pronounceable Italian words is increased when the English-speaking subjects are taught the meanings of those words. The capacity of STM or the slave systems of WM may be dependent on the experience of the learner in the area tested. That is, it depends on the contents and structure of their LTMS, whether it be phonological or semantic. This has been noted on word list learning and phrase learning for some time (Glanzer & Razel, 1974; Shulman, 1971). There are STM studies that indicate strongly the use of a store other than a phonological store. Simon (1974) reports his own ability to immediately recall a series of well-known phrases such as "All's fair in love and war" and "To be or not to be, that is the question" and found that he could remember three or at most four of these sayings. If these were retained within a phonological store then it would have to be far in excess of seven items.

Miller (1956, 1994) proposed that we are able to retain seven "chunks" of information. To take a well-used example, it might present a challenge to repeat back the letters CI-ATI-AFB-IGI-FD-

AIB-M. But if the same letters are placed in the format CIA-TIA-FBI-GI-FDA-IBM they might be repeated back more easily, especially if you live in the USA. Seventeen letters have been reduced to seven chunks. Glanzer and Razel (1974), using a different method of calculation, found a reduced capacity but still based on chunks. For example, they found that well-known phrases such "A stitch in time . . . " took up equivalent space when compared to a single word in a list of unrelated words.

It is now realised that Miller was probably in error in terms of the actual number of chunks. Our working memory for meaningful material may vary depending on our expertise in an area. For example, doctors, chess players and other professionals all appear to have prodigious ability to remember relevant material very quickly after a brief presentation. Experimenters have been attracted to use concise, unambiguous materials such as lists of words and numbers, but these studies have misrepresented our capacity to remember in many everyday situations (Jenkins, 1974; Kintsch, 1998). Also, when considering unrelated information, if persons are asked to repeat back information, e.g. digits, without warning (no time for rehearsal) then around four chunks is more accurate (see Cowan, in press). In other words when digit-span is being measured then there may be the influence of both chunking and phonological rehearsal. Thus in a "running span" in which a large series of digits is presented, e.g. 45, and the subject is unexpectedly asked to recall the last digits heard, they will recall the last 4.2 digits on average (Pollack, Johnson, & Knaff, 1959).

Models that seem to need some integration with Hitch and Baddeley's model see the need for a temporary semantic store for functional reasons. Schneider and Detweiler (1988), and more recently Ericsson and Kintsch (1995) and others (Gobet, 1998; Vicente & Wang, 1998), have argued for a temporary memory for semantic information which takes into account a person's knowledge and experience. Ericsson and Kintsch provide the example of being interrupted during reading and how we have no difficulty in reporting back the themes of what we have just read (Ericsson & Kintsch, 1995). Some working memory models might propose that such interference would cause a complete loss of the theme of the book, but this does not happen. Therefore the decay or interference curve referred to in Box 5.1 is not relevant here. Ericsson and Kintsch argue for a long-term working memory (LTWM), which has a decay period that is between STM and the decay of permanently stored long-term memories. They also illustrate how a person's expertise in a particular area may extend their LTWM (Ericsson & Kintsch, 1995). A number of studies these authors review provide evidence that comprehension is not unduly interfered with by the articulatory loop or interfering phonological material. For example, people may even read aloud without impairing their comprehension and a person's individual reading proficiency is not related to their STM as measured by digit-span. Adult reading proficiency is related to the ability to retrieve facts and associations from the text (Ericsson & Kintch, 1995; Just & Carpenter, 1992, see discussion of Cowan, 1995, pp. 90–92).

From the work reviewed so far, it is clear that storage of semantic information may be extremely rapid, especially when it is congruent with the individual's experience. If a person is very familiar with the material, it is as if we have a ready-made template or structure in our memory store that we merely have to modify (Gobet, 1998). This encourages the view that semantic or meaningful WM is a temporary activation of the LTMS that holds that experience. It is possible that these brief and longer WMs are on a continuum and dependent on the content of the task and the task requirement.

The idea of STM as a temporary activation of the LTMS is not a new idea (e.g. Melton, 1963; Waugh & Norman, 1965). More recently, this view has been modelled and researched by a number of authors (e.g. Anderson, 1983; Cantor & Engle, 1993; Cowan, 1988, 1995; Schneider & Detweiler, 1988; Shiffrin & Schneider, 1977).

However, while this view is intuitively reasonable, the nature of the activation process is still being researched from the psychological perspective in normal subjects (Anderson, 1983; Anderson, Bothell, Lebiere, & Matessa, 1998; Conway

& Engle, 1994; Kimberg, D'Esposito, & Farah, 1997). Some of these models tend to place the capacity limitation in terms of the extent of activation within the hypothetical LTMS. For example, Anderson's ACT theory (Anderson, 1983) proposed that memory retrieval is slowed when there are a larger number of associations to the to-be-remembered item (e.g. Andrewes & Maude, 1990). From another perspective activation is referred to from the perspective of the neurophysiological level. Later there is a discussion of how patterns of cells or cell assemblies are stimulated to represent memories—an issue that is broached in the next section on consolidation.

Neuropsychological studies of patients who have a semantic WM impairment are few in number. However, Martin and Romani (1995) described a patient whom they propose has a limited semantic WM. This case, Alan, was able to learn material for permanent storage in the LTMS given certain conditions, but performed poorly on tasks that required the retention of one chunk of semantic information (using Miller's terminology). In one of the experiments they describe, Martin and Romani gave the patient two types of sentences to process. These researchers asked Alan and the control subjects to simply indicate whether a series of sentences were sensible. Sometimes we can tell whether a sentence is sensible just by reading the first few words. Other sentences require reading from beginning to end before a judgement can be made. Alan had difficulty in judging sentences that required the retention of the meaning of a number of chunks compared to a few.

In a task that required the subject to judge whether a sentence made sense, Alan was able to judge a sentence, in which the verb came early, e.g. *The children played in the water that was blue, cold and dry until they got tired.* Note the sentence is building a familiar picture according to our experience of children and water. However, he had great difficulty when, in another condition, the verb came late and the sense or theme of the sentence was delayed, e.g. *Jeeps, men, and women were walking the streets.* In this last sentence it is difficult to integrate the meaning of the sentence until quite late in the sentence. Jeeps, men, and

women do not give a hint as to what is to come so we must keep the meaning of these individual words "in mind" until there is a knowledge of what is being referred to. Because their analysis discounted an impaired phonological store explanation they preferred the view that Alan's poor performance was due to a reduced semantic span.

Alan could learn information and place the information into long-term memory when it was in structured sentences but not when it was in unrelated words. The implication is that the capacity of the semantic slave system was therefore challenged when the material is less familiar and more difficult to integrate into the ready-made structures within the LTMS. According to the view followed here the single unrelated words are still activated within the LTMS but until some form of associations are found they require continued activation, which is a limited-capacity system.

In the next section the question is asked: What is the nature of this limited capacity? And how can we be limited within one modality, eg. phonological, visuospatial, semantic, but not in another?

A limited-capacity system

There are several theories concerning where the limitations of capacity exist within models of WM. For example, Gathercole and Baddeley (1995) propose that the central executive is limited in capacity. Baddeley has referred to Shallice's model as a provisional model of the central executive. In this model the SAS is the component that allocates attentional capacity. While there therefore appears to be an assumed close relationship between attention and WM few theoreticians have attempted to describe this relationship. Cowan's model of WM is one of the few models that relates attention to WM unambiguously (Cowan, 1988, 1995). He proposes that attention and WM are intimately linked. His model sees attentional capacity as influencing and defining STM e.g. phonological store, visual sketchpad, capacity. What is attended to both externally and internally involves an activation of the LTMS (see Figure 5.5).

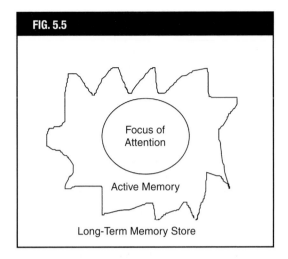

FIG. 5.5

Focus of Attention

Active Memory

Long-Term Memory Store

Illustration of working memory module activation of LTMS (adapted from Cowan, 1988, 1993).

Using this model it can be seen that we may be consciously aware of information and attend to information held within the stores of our WM. However, when our attention is distracted elsewhere, the activation of the LTMS will decay or be interfered with. As indicated, the decay is not immediate: there is a delay of some seconds, during which an area of the LTMS will be activated that is in excess of the focus of attention. An analogy can be made with a blowtorch: when the blowtorch of attention is fired at the coals (LTMS), they glow and continue to glow as long as they receive attention. When the torch is directed at another area of the fire, the coals that are left still glow for a while. In the same way the activated LTMS remains activated for a moment after attention has been directed elsewhere, but will then decay unless refreshed by further attention, e.g. rehearsal. It can be seen that a reduced ability to focus attention on the area activated within the LTMS reduces the capacity of that store. Functional imaging studies are just starting to evaluate the relationship between attention and WM. For example, Jiang et al. (2000) in a task that required subjects to recognise familiar targets from among equally familiar distractors, the extrastriate areas of activation reduced over trials, which they took as a reduced need to analyse the perceptually familiar material. But

activation was maintained for targets in the frontal areas associated with WM which they took as an indication for the need to maintain target identification within WM during the attention task.

It is likely that the measure of capacity is dependent on the type of slave system or store, with phonological and spatial encoding being more time based, while semantic encoding is chunk based, e.g. ˜4 chunks (Cowan, in press). Whether or not the central executive is divided into areas of specialisation for phonological, spatial, and semantic is controversial at the present time. It appears from functional imaging studies that the specialisation of type of information is not as obvious within the frontal cortex when compared to the posterior association areas (Owen, 2000) and that within the DPFC, at least, there is a more sure division between the functional role within WM e.g. maintenance versus manipulation (D'Esposito et al., 2000). These functional roles will be discussed towards the end of this chapter.

The model in Figure 5.6 illustrates the revised model as described so far. The important feature of this model is that it allows for information to be encoded for meaning in a temporary form. The characteristics of this semantic store may be somewhat different from the other two stores (see Ericsson & Kintsch, 1995, for their concept of LTWM). One of the predictions made by this model is that there may be some differences between cultures in their ability to encode information and keep it in mind depending on the experience and knowledge characteristics of that culture. Some Australian aboriginals, in particular, developed non-verbal memories for visuospatial displays, such as memory for rocks or objects (Drinkwater, 1976). Given that these temporary stores are dependent on the activation of our previous experience as represented by our LTMS our ability to learn will depend on the ease with which we can overcome the limited-capacity temporary buffer system. This will, according to theory, depend on the ease with which the material is assimilated into our LTMS (see Curran, 1980, for a discussion on the influence of cross-culteral experience on cognition). For example, a person

FIG. 5.6

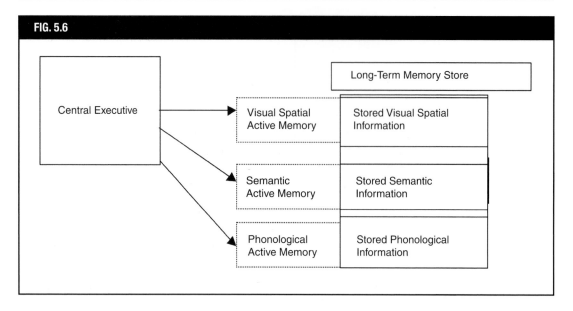

The active memory model. Phonological, visuospatial (Sketch-pad), and semantic active memories are described as a temporary activation of the long-term memory store. The central executive acts to deploy resources to allow efficient use of the limited capacity available. For example, more resources may be given to one area of active memory versus another, or divide resources to more than one area, depending on the nature of the material to be learned or processed.

who is brought up as an English speaker will have fewer problems in learning Spanish words compared to Chinese because the phonological sounds of English and Spanish are more similar compared to English and Chinese. This relationship between experience and ease of assimilation within the LTMS is well supported from various studies. For example, while most memory performances of university lecturers/professors deteriorate normally with old age their memory for prose is maintained at a level equivalent to much younger persons (Shimamura et al., 1995). Pools players who gamble on results of football matches are able to learn fictitious football results with greater ease than non-pools players, even when the names of the teams are supplied (Morris, Tweedy & Gruneberg, 1985). Expert gymnasts are able to repeat a longer series series of routines with greater facility than non-experts (Tenenbaum, Tehan, Stewart, & Christensen, 1999). There is therefore a prediction that there is a relationship between the immediate span of a particular material and the ease with which we learn that material. This was discussed previously in terms of the greater span of chess moves found in expert chess players.

We have conducted a recent study with subjects using a variation of our problem-solving paradigm (see Figure 5.7). This study shows a relationship between knowledge of a set a clues and the working memory semantic span of this material. With random clues there is clear difficulty in finding compatible shematic relationship within the LTMS; accordingly fewer clues are repeated back and kept on-line. It should be noted that BR (see Box 7.7 for a dscription of this patient) a patient who has a severely impaired phonological store capacity but is still able to repeat back a series of clues without difficulty. Therefore the encoding requirement for this task is clearly not phonological.

There are some remaining complexities and difficulties to be resolved in our prototype model, and these will be revisited and clarified towards the end of this chapter. For the present we can summarise that a model has been described that allows some modular activation of the LTMS. The approach at this stage contains many of the

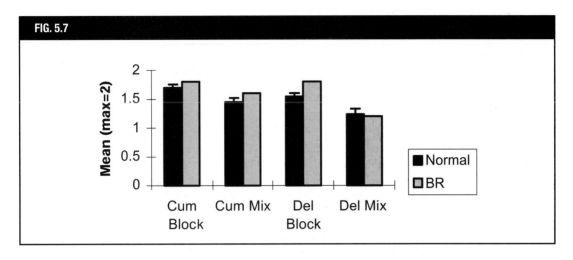

FIG. 5.7

Twenty-five subjects without cerebral impairment were presented two sets of five clues in series, each set leading to a single solution. The clues were either presented cumulatively (CM) or in a delayed (DI) presentation in which each clue was removed after it was presented. Subjects were presented clues within three formats or conditions as follows: In a blocked (Blk) order with the presentation of the first set of five then the second five; in a mixed condition (Mx) in which the 10 clues were presented in a random order; the final condition involved the presentation of random clues (Rnd) from different clue sets; these last clues were independently rated as not converging on any solution. After clue presentation subjects were asked to repeat back the clues and provide two solutions; the order of this requirement was randomised. Subjects report fewer clues and solutions in the delayed (working memory) condition ($p \leq .001$, $p \leq .001$). Fewer solutions and clues were repeated back following the random clue presentation when compared to the other two conditions ($p < .01$). Fewer solutions were obtained in the mixed condition compared to the blocked condition ($p < .01$). Fewer clues were repeated in the delayed mixed compared to the delayed cumulative condition ($p < .01$)

features of models provided by Cowan (1988) and Schneider and Detweiler (1988), but the formulation is relatively rudimentary. The semantic active slave system or module has different characteristics compared to the phonological module. For example, it has been argued above that while the phonological store is time based and decays after around 2 seconds unless refreshed, our ability to retain semantic material is more reliant on the size of the information chunks. Whether this is related to the familiarity of the material used has yet to be assessed; for example, it might be found that phonological units may be similarly chunked. The nature and size of those chunks are dependent on our ability to perceive relationships or meaning within the information.

Much of the research that has investigated encoding appears to have searched for a single code to fit a theory. However, such research may almost always be reinterpreted in terms of finding a dominant encoding of many encodings. Indeed,

when research has been more interested in assessing the breadth of encoding of memories it is clear that more than one type of encoding has been used in any situation (e.g., Hulme et al., 1991, 1999; Rubin & Wallace, 1989; Shulman, 1971).

The intuitive view is that everything we learn has some semantic encoding by virtue that it would be without meaning otherwise. Some temporary activations may be dominantly phonological or visuospatial merely because the meaning in the material is still being processed. The huge history of cognitive psychology experiments that have used word lists, consonants, and numbers in an endeavour to keep their experimental presentations tight and controlled have tended to exaggerate the use of encodings that would generally be seen as inefficient in everyday remembering—encodings that rely on sound and shape in the absence of integrated meaning (Neisser, 1997).

The consolidation system

The term *consolidation* is used to describe a neuropsychological mechanism that allows memories to be stored more permanently. This is a broad definition and the term has been used in a variety of contexts to describe the strengthening of memories over brief periods, to periods as long as several years. It is assumed at present that any type of storage resulting in greater permanence of memories involves the structures described in this section.

The neuropsychological perspective allows us to discuss the brain structures, such as the hippocampus, parts of the thalamus and possibly the mammillary bodies, in terms of the engine room of the consolidation process. This view is based on patients who have become amnesic due to damage to these structures. The model proposed here is that these structures act to "stamp in" the activations within the LTMS so that they become more permanent features of this store. How this occurs at the cellular level is as yet not clear, but this issue is discussed in the final part of this section.

The hippocampus

It could be argued that the most famous case in the history of neuropsychology is the amnesic patient HM. He was operated on by a neurosurgeon, William Scoville, for his epileptic seizures in the mid-1950s and was subsequently researched by Dr Brenda Milner, a neuropsychologist at the Montreal Institute of Neurology in Canada. HM became amnesic following surgery to both temporal lobes. This unusual surgical procedure is said to have been prompted by the logic that if seizures that start in one temporal lobe can be cured by the removal of the temporal lobe in that hemisphere, then removal or resections of both sides might reduce seizures that affected both brain hemispheres. His surgery included a resection of the hippocampus and adjacent cortical structures such as the parahippocampal gyrus. These medial structures (towards the middle of the brain) of the temporal lobe are diagrammed in Figure 5.8, with the other consolidation structures to be discussed. These structures include the hippocampus which were

later found to be crucial to the strengthening or consolidation of memories.

Unilateral anterior temporal lobectomy has been used for many years as a treatment for temporal lobe epilepsy when it is resistant to drug therapy (refractory epilepsy). Typically, the *en bloc* resection removes the anterior 4–6 cm from the pole of the temporal lobe, although sometimes the cortex is preserved and the hippocampus and/or the amygdala is removed in isolation. Unless there is an undetected lesion in the contralateral hemisphere, patients suffer *far* less memory impairment following a unilateral lesion, when compared to a bilateral lesion. This suggests there is normally some substantial compensation by the remaining temporal lobe and hippocampus.

There is now well-replicated evidence that there is more verbal memory impairment following left temporal lobectomy (often the side that supports language). There is also evidence that there is *some* form of non-verbal memory impairment, such as maze-learning, following right temporal lobectomy (e.g. Milner, 1965; Powell, Polkey & McMillan, 1985). Recent functional imaging using fMRI showed among the areas activated predominant *right* hippocampus activation over all the subjects (Gron et al., 2000). However, differences were found between males and females: females showed more right prefrontal activation than males, while the males showed extra reliance on the hippocampus on the left side. These results are interpreted by the authors as supporting the research (Sandstrom, Kaufman, & Huettal, 1998) arguing that females rely on memory for landmarks (requiring WM to keep these in mind), whereas males rely on landmarks and a geometric sense of where things are (mediated more by the hippocampus). This highlights the specialties of the two hemispheres.

As can be seen, these medial structures interface with the mesial (inside) surface of the temporal lobe. The degree of pre-surgical hippocampal cell loss prior to surgery in the epileptic patient can be gauged by assessing the surgical specimens of the removed hippocampus following temporal lobectomy. As an estimation of the degree of atrophy present prior to the operation the post-surgical hippocampus specimen may be histologically examined for cell loss. Using this method some proof has been found of the direct relationship between the amount of hippocampal cell loss within these specimens, reflecting the amount of hippocampus that was healthy prior to surgery and pre-surgery memory impairment. This cell loss is not so strongly related to language impairment and therefore the memory loss is unlikely to be due to this factor (e.g. Matkovic et al., 1995; Sass et al., 1992).

Other supportive evidence that the hippocampus is the important structure for new learning and the consolidation of memory comes from other measurements prior to surgery in temporal lobe epilepsy patients. When the volume of each of the hippocampi is measured using MRI scans (like X-rays of the brain but more sensitive to the presence of fluid content), the volume of the left hippocampus is significantly correlated with verbal memory. Also, some studies have found that the right hippocampus is significantly correlated with some visuo-spatial memory which test memory for location (e.g. Kilpatrick, Cook, Murrie, & Andrewes, 1997; Trenerry et al., 1993). The patient, whose MRI scan and EEG are illustrated in Figures 5.9(a) and 5.9(b), had a delayed verbal memory well within the normal range. However, on a test of maze learning she went for 23 trials and still failed to reach criterion, which was well below the expected level of performance for someone of her intelligence.

Patients may suffer a greater degree of memory deterioration following a temporal lobectomy when the temporal lobe epilepsy is at a late age of onset, as compared to early-age onset (in childhood) (Andrewes, Dinjin et al., 2000). This advantage for patients with "early-onset" temporal lobe epilepsy is theoretically explained by the better early reorganisation of language and memory skills, either to the contralateral hemisphere or sometimes within the same hemisphere in the case of language (Rasmussen & Milner, 1977). This is allowed for by the greater plasticity or malleability of the developing brain of the child (Hiscock & Kinsbourne, 1995) (see Chapter 10 for a further discussion).

Both hippocampi following early-onset temporal lobe epilepsy tend to be volumetrically small, but they are generally smaller on the side of the focus of the seizure (Cook et al., 1992). Patients with early-onset temporal lobe seizures in childhood have often had febrile seizures in infancy although the cause of hippocampal sclerosis is uncertain. It should be pointed out that the relationship in the other direction does not hold; that is, the majority of babies who have febrile seizures do not go on to have any obvious problems.

The temporal lobe epilepsy of these patients is often associated with hippocampal sclerosis (atrophy). There will be a return to the subject of the hippocampus and its relationship to memory storage later, but for the moment it is sufficient to know that, although one hippocampus may compensate for the other, when both the left and right are undermined the consequence is amnesia, as was the case with patient HM. In the introduction to this chapter two patients were described who had amnesia. The second patient, TJ, suffered from a disease called herpes simplex encephalitis: she had bilateral atrophy of the temporal lobes, which included the hippocampi. The first patient, EM, with his history of alcoholism, also suffered from amnesia but he would have had atrophy in quite different brain areas, including parts of the thalamus (dorsomedial nucleus and/or anterior thalamus) and the mammillary bodies (see Fig 5.8).

The issue of the differential role of structures associated with the consolidation system is returned to in a later section.

How does the consolidation system create permanent memories?

These consolidation structures are not the final storage place of memories but rather the structure involved in storing or "stamping in" the memory to a more permanent form. We shall explore these areas in detail when the LTMS is discussed in the next section. However, it is obvious that there are areas within the cortex that are acted on by the consolidation structures. These areas of the cortex that provide the store for long-term memories are assumed to be changed, and the change must be relatively permanent. This

FIG. 5.8

H   = Hippocampus
F   = Fornix
E   = Entorhinal Cortex
T   = Thalamus
AT   = Anterior Thalamic Nucleus
M   = Mammillary Body
CING = Cingulate
CC   = Corpus Callosum
AM   = Amygdala
OF   = Orbitofrontal Cortex
S   = Septum
SU   = Subiculum
D   = Dentate Gyrus

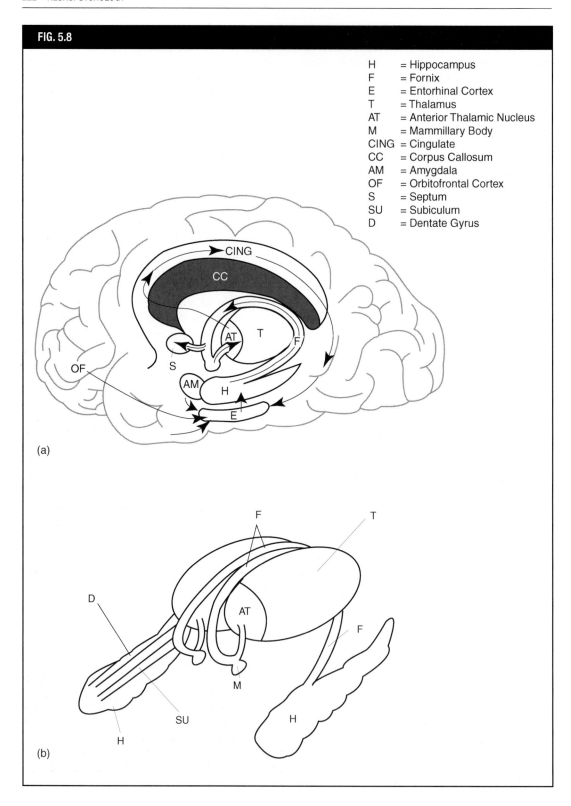

must be so because if our brains are given electric shocks or we become temporarily unconscious we sometimes lose a few of these memories but most of them survive. Therefore they are unlikely to be purely reliant on chemical changes—they are too robust. The most obvious candidate for the process of storing permanent memories within the cortex are changes in the way brain cells are linked up and activate each other. The exact mechanism by which these memory structures store new memories is still uncertain. However, the "cell assembly" theory provides a derivation of many of the modern models of consolidation at the brain cell level.

A famous Canadian psychologist, Donald Hebb, developed this influential model of how memories are formed at the neuronal or brain cell level in 1949. He proposed that long-term memories were represented in the cortex as "cell assemblies". A cell assembly is the name given to a hypothetical group of brain cells that represent a memory. This group of cells habitually fire in a particular pattern. Hebb proposed that repetitive firing of brain cells in a consistent pattern resulted in structural changes between the cells. This allowed the pattern to fire with greater facility and eventually in a permanent circuit.

Using non-human animal models, electrical stimulation can cause extensive "reverberation" of neuronal circuits for a lengthy period after stimulation. According to this model, two hypothetical cell assemblies, each representing a word, could be combined through repetitive stimulation into a larger cell assembly in a task that required the learning of a paired associate (two words learned together). Peter Milner (1989, p. 26) suggests that memories may be more or less permanent depending on the amount of firing within a pattern. These stimulations are assumed to be provided by the hippocampus and are referred to as *tetanic stimulation*. With sufficient strength such stimulation may develop *long-term potentiation*, which is the term used to describe a cell assembly or group of neurones that now respond with greater facility after repetitive stimulation in the experimental situation. This view fits well with the model of WM proposed because it assumes that memories may be more or less permanent depending on the degree of stimulation and the extent that the structures are already present. For example, expert chess players are able to remember the positions in up to five chess boards after a brief presentation (see Gobet, 1998, for a review). But this seemingly miraculous performance is only achieved if the chess positions represent real games, rather than random placement of pieces. In terms of the cell assembly model this is explained because the cell assemblies are pre-existing and require little modification.

The long-term memory store

The LTMS is a depository for memories. LTMS is a broad, encompassing term that has been fractionated so that there are subtypes of memory stores, each with their own research literature. For example, memory for knowledge is referred to as *semantic memory* and encompasses knowledge about objects, e.g. what a toothbrush is and what its uses are and also knowledge concerning facts, e.g. who won a particular race in the last Olympics. Also, within this hypothetical LTMS are stored *autobiographical memories*, which include the detailed memories of our per-

(a) Illustration of the structures that make up the consolidation system. There are pathways from a number of cortical areas to the entorhinal cortex, which provides a major input to the hippocampus. These include the amygdala and the orbitofrontal cortex, which together are seen to supply an emotional and motivational context to memory. Other areas including the parahippocampal cortex are thought to supply an input from the association areas. The pathway from the entorhinal cortex within the medial cortical area of the temporal lobe through the hippocampus is dominantly one way. From the hippocampus there is a projection to the septum and mammillary bodies via the fornix. From the mammillary body there is a projection to the anterior thalamus, from which there are projections to the cingulate. From a pathway within the cingulate there is an eventual return to the entorhinal cortex. Broadly therefore there is a relatively complex circuit, which is yet to be understood, but clearly has a role in the consolidation of memories. (b) Bilateral three-dimensional model of the crucial structures shown in (a).

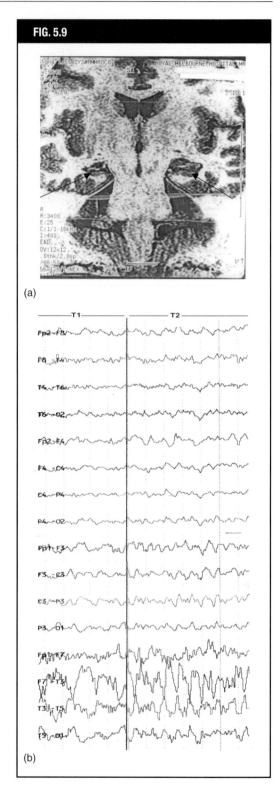

FIG. 5.9

(a)

(b)

(a) MRI of a patient with diagnosed right temporal lobe epilepsy. The scan, which is a coronal section with the brain sliced from top to bottom (see Appendix 1), shows mesial sclerosis in the right hippocampal formation as indicated by a smaller volume of the hippocampus (right is on the left side of scan).The area below on the right and left which looks like antlers is the white matter (axons) within the temporal lobe). (b) EEG of a patient with left temporal lobe epilepsy (see towards the bottom of output). At time 1 (T1) nearer the onset of seizure activity there is a developing reverse phase shift (peaks of the wave form are negative when the surrounding waves are positive) and the higher amplitudes are developing at T3 (the midtemporal lobe region). At Time 2 (T2) the seizure activity has developed further with rhythmical activity at around 7 HZ becoming salient.

sonal history. Also referred to is our memory for events (*episodic memory*) with their context, e.g. that the man who served me in a shop on Thursday was wearing a turban. Knowledge about the meaning and sounds of words is referred to as *the lexicon or lexical memory*. Other subtypes have been referred to and some of these terms appear to be slightly overlapping. The LTMS is therefore a store of all our more durable memories.

Within the clinical situation a patient's semantic memory is tested by their knowledge on a subtest of information from an intelligence assessment scale such as the WAIS or a test of naming objects such as the Boston Naming Task. These would constitute measures of semantic memory. Patients who do poorly on these types of tests tend to have lesions or atrophy to the cortex of the temporal lobe. These patients who have semantic dementia and those with Alzheimer's disease are discussed in detail later. In these extreme disorders they lose not only their knowledge about facts but also about the objects around them. They suffer from agnosia. However, unlike the agnosia described in the chapter on perceptual disorders this is not a disconnection between the visual input and the LTMS for concepts; rather it is a destruction of the LTMS itself.

Alternatively, the patient in the clinic may be asked to recall past events in their life (autobiographical memory). This may be done formally, in a test of remote memories that occurred prior to the accident or prior to the onset of the disease. In other words this would be a test of the patient's retrograde amnesia, although such a test may include other information such as memory of information that has been learned at a particular time prior to the onset of the disease.

A more in-depth discussion of *semantic memory*, the hypothetical knowledge base, and *retrograde amnesia* is continued in the advanced topics section below. For the sake of clarity we will complete this discussion of a preliminary model of memory with a section on how WM the consolidation system and the LTMS interact to produce permanent memories. This is necessarily a purely psychological perspective, which hopefully will assist the reader in understanding the functional role of these three units.

The interaction between working memory, the consolidation system, and the long-term memory store

In the 1970s Craik and Lockhart provided a new way of looking at memory, referred to as "the levels of processing framework" (Craik & Lockhart, 1972). This framework is no longer fashionable for reasons to be outlined, but is relevant to points being made here. The broad underpinning of this framework was the view that how one processed information determined how permanently it was remembered. Broadly, the framework proposed that deeper levels of encoding resulted in more permanent memories. The following examples show the nature of the incidental learning paradigms that were used to test the predictions of this framework. To prevent subjects from using other encodings of their own, the ultimate requirement to remember the words in italics below was a secret. By keeping this learning *incidental* it was hoped that the subject would not use their own extra strategies of encoding that might spoil the test of the encodings embedded within the task requirements. The words in italics would be the words to be remembered in a later surprise learning test:

> Does this word contain a capital letter? *toWn*. (Shallow level.)
> Does this word rhyme with bight? *spite*. (Intermediate level.)
> Does this word belong to the category of living things? *robot*. (Deep level.)

The "deeper" level of processing generally resulted in more permanent remembering as predicted, but researchers lost interest in this approach because of a number of criticisms concerning its validity. Among the criticisms of this framework were that certain types of distinct shallow encoding of words such as *zebra* or *xylophone* may actually result in a more enduring memory than some supposed semantic "deep" encoding. Also, in some experiments it was argued that "shallow" processing may be less well remembered because it drew attention away from semantic attributes, rather than the use of the type of encoding, e.g. orthographic (look of the word) versus phonological (sound of the word), per se. Also, the frameworks assumption, that phonetic processing necessarily preceded semantic processing, although intuitively appealing, was not always supported (Baddeley, 1978; Nelson, Walling, & McEnvoy, 1979). However, the levels of processing framework provided the valuable lesson that the focus should be more on how we process information (elaborative rehearsal, associations with other meaningful material), rather than merely how often information was repetitively rehearsed (maintenance rehearsal). A very large number of studies provided that elaborative encoding, which aimed to find multiple meaningful connections between the item and what is already known, was beneficial to new learning. This was especially the case if these associations encouraged encoding that was *distinct* from the associations used for other to-be-remembered items.

The valuable lesson from this research is that memory is aided by elaborate yet distinct encodings of memory. Also, these experiments provided that the more attention and *effort* a person put into these elaborate encodings, the more likely the item will be learned (see Bransford, 1979). These lessons are as relevant and important in today's research as they were then, especially in the area of the management of memory disorders.

From the neuropsychological perspective, areas within the prefrontal cortex would be seen as playing a key role in the working memory role towards strategic remembering. In a study using PET scan and the levels of processing framework, Kapur et al., (1994) compared a condition in which the subjects were either required to decide whether words were living or non-living (deep level) or whether the word contained the letter "a" (shallow level). The eventual surprise recognition test showed 75% of words recognised in the deep condition versus 57% in the shallow condition, as expected. However, the encoding process associated with the deep-level encoding involved a far greater activation of prefrontal areas—areas that overlapped with WM tasks. Similar results have been obtained using fMRI (see Buckner & Koutstaal, 1998, for a review of this area). The implication is that the prefrontal areas, which hold information in mind, are also those areas that seek out relationships within the LTMS.

In terms of the present discussion this research highlighted the need to find relationships between what you have already learned and what you wish to learn. From the cognitive perspective it can be seen as part of a strategy of using past knowledge to store new knowledge in a way that allows associations to be made during storage of the memory. It can also be seen as a way of setting up a retrieval structure through those same associations.

It has been proposed that the contents of slave systems within WM involve activations of the LTMS. However, the role for the central executive is assumed to be important in the strategic searching for further associations that will allow the contents of the slave systems to be assimilated within the LTMS with increased ease.

There is a relationship between the size of information chunks rehearsed within WM and the ease with which we learn information. Also mentioned is the tendency for experts in their field such as Grand Master chess players to have a prodigious memory for particular types of materials with which they work (see Ericsson & Kintsch, 1995). There is an obvious relationship between experience and the nature and structure of the LTMS that represents our stored memories. The LTMS is determined by what we do and experience. The levels of processing framework literature allows the realisation of what we must do to capitalise on that experience. Piaget, a famous expert on children's cognitive development, also theorised about how children developed their thinking by using the term *assimilation*. This described the process of adapting external stimuli to one's own mental structures (Piaget, 1970).

Most types of mnemonics or strategies of remembering are based on this premise that we must not only find associations with what we already know but we must also remember the associations we have used for the original storage of memories so that we can use them later for retrieval. To use the library analogy we need to place the book in a filing system that exists within the library but we also need to keep a record of where that book is kept within the filing system.

From the cognitive perspective a description has now been given of how we can maximise the consolidation process by using strategies. These strategies are given priority or selected by the central executive within the WM. The strategies themselves may be held in a WM but since these are also activations of the LTMS (see Cowan, 1995, for arguments supporting this view) they may take more or less resources depending on how well learned they are. The process of searching for new associations takes up some of the limited capacity. When these new associations have been found they are then metaphorically stamped into LTMS by the consolidation system.

It is possible that this ability to capitalise on the memory structure that exists prior to surgery may assist patients to learn even when they are amnesic (Andrewes & Gielewski, 1999). A patient whom I assessed some years ago illustrates this point. The patient had originally been diagnosed as amnesic. This diagnosis at first seemed to be supported by the memory tests administered. This patient had a history of chronic alcoholism and a diagnosis of Wernicke–Korsakoff syndrome; he presumably had severe atrophy of part of his consolidation system, namely his thalami and mammillary bodies. His very poor memory on all delayed tests of memory seemed to confirm this diagnosis. There was some surprise though when he did rather better on an experimental word list that contained food names. He was told of this considerable improvement and he responded that prior to entering hospital he had been a waiter for many years. Therefore, despite his handicap, he still found it easier to learn a list of food names. He had retained the strategies and the structure of his LTMS, which was rich in food-related associations, to compensate for his damaged consolidation system. The ability to take advantage of the structure of the LTMS may not be a significant advantage to some amnesic patients. However, if the other aspects of the system are intact, as is apparent in some imaging studies (Buckner & Koutstaal, 1998), then residual consolidation structures may be useful in encouraging new learning of information that is congruent to the patient's experience.

Summary and comment

So far a broad model has been developed to allow an initial framework for the remainder of this chapter. Any memory model is controversial but the one chosen here fits well with the neuropsychological perspective and the author's interest in the management and rehabilitation of memory disorders. In this model the relationship between learning and the LTMS is paramount. The hypothetical cell assemblies need little modification by the consolidation system if the LTMS contains information that has some overlap with what is to be learned. Students who know something about a lecture prior to their attendance are always at an advantage not only because they have less to learn but also because they have metaphorically ready-made coat hangers on which they can place the clothing of their new knowledge. This is an associative node model of long-term memory which has been in the literature for many years but has been relatively ignored.

WM is limited in capacity but as yet there is no agreement by authors as to where those limitations reside. The capacity appears to vary with the area of the LTMS being activated, with the phonological store being apparently time limited, but semantic information is more limited to the number of chunks of information (see Cowan, in press, for a further comprehensive discussion). Capacity limitations may affect both the limitations of attention within the system and also the nature of the LTMS structure, e.g. phonological, semantic. It is possible that limitations of capacity may be at more than one level, depending on the location of the lesion. Patients with WM limitations within one modality, e.g. phonological or visuospatial, suggest that for these patients capacity may be limited at the store level. The issue whether the central executive itself may be divided into different modalities is more controversial and is discussed in the final section of this chapter.

The consolidation system is seen as necessary for the permanent storing of information. It should be noted, however, that the storage process does not finish with the initial exercise of learning. Every time we recollect a fact or event through retrieval, the memory is strengthened or further consolidated by the consolidation system. Consolidation is a process used in the context of new learning but is one that can occur over a number of years. It is likely, as Moscovitch, Goshen-Gottstein, and Vriezen (1993) argue, that the hippocampal system may be automatically triggered and so we sometimes remember information that we did not intend to remember at the time. To some extent this may depend on the amount of attention that is paid to an event or subject matter and may be influenced by our level of arousal.

Also discussed was the relationship between WM and attention (Cowan, 1988, 1995). It was proposed that what we select for attention also overlaps with the content of the slave systems, e.g. phonological store. WM, however, also involves activations within the LTMS, which is slightly beyond our focus of attention since preceding areas of attention focus may retain activation for a period before decaying or being interfered with.

The central executive within the WM model was a psychological concept and was not originally given a neuroanatomical association (Baddeley, 1986). Nevertheless, the central executive has been associated with Shallice's SAS model, discussed in a previous chapter, and is strongly associated with the prefrontally based network. Work with PET scan and MRI has confirmed that WM tasks involve the activation of the prefrontal cortex (Cohen, Perlstein et al., 1997; D'Esposito, Postle & Rypma, 2000). Certainly, the teleological role assigned to the central executive, as a flexible, strategic and directive mechanism, reflects what is sometimes missing in patients with damage in this area (Shallice & Burgess, 1996). Also, studies of primates and monkeys' ability to hold information "in mind" or attend to stimuli that are absent over short durations have implicated the DPFC as part of a network of connections with other brain areas (e.g., Goldman-Rakic, 1996). This has prompted models that posit the central executive as being resident in the prefrontal cortex and the phonological slave systems as being part of the posterior language zone (see Gupta & MacWhinney, 1997). This last issue and the wider influence of the central executive within memory are discussed further in later sections of this chapter.

NEUROPSYCHOLOGICAL ISSUES AND MEMORY DISORDERS

Explicit versus implicit memory: memory without consolidation

Some excitement has been produced by the finding that amnesic patients are capable of learning in certain conditions using what is referred to as implicit memory. Implicit memory requires no conscious recall of the event of learning and is usually applied to learning materials that in some way were previously associated. For example, if *bread* and *jam* are presented to an amnesic patient, the patient will later respond with the word *jam* when given the stem *bread*. You might argue that this is purely by chance, but if the patient were just guessing then they might have easily responded with the word *butter*, which is also strongly associated with *bread*. However, this implicit learning is more likely to occur if the patient is asked to give the first word that comes into their head. If the same amnesic patient is asked what word they learned which was paired with bread they will say "I don't remember doing any such learning task" and in their confusion may even produce the wrong item. Therefore in implicit memory there is no memory for the event of learning. This last aspect is one of the main features distinguishing implicit from explicit memory. Some authors have used the terms nondeclarative and declarative memory to describe implicit and explicit memory, respectively, because with explicit memory the subject is able to declare conscious knowledge that they have had to remember the information.

Sergei Korsakoff (cited by Schacter, 1987), a Russian physician who wrote the seminal paper on what was to become the amnesic condition called Wernicke–Korsakoff syndrome, gives an illustration of implicit memory in a description of one of his patients. This amnesic patient had previously been given an electric shock but had no memory at all for this incident. However, on a later occasion the patient passed the nondescript apparatus responsible for the shock and Dr Korsakoff was surprised when the patient remarked that he was probably going to be administered an electric shock. This information was volunteered by the patient without conscious recall of the event of previously being shocked and is an incident of implicit remembering. Dan Schacter of Harvard University is one of the leading researchers who has helped to define this concept. He proposes that "Implicit memory is revealed when previous experiences facilitate performance on a task that does not require conscious or intentional recollection of previous experiences" (Schacter, 1987, p. 501).

Elizabeth Warrington and Larry Weiskrantz (Warrington & Weiskrantz, 1968) provided some of the earliest modern experimental work on amnesia and implicit memory. These studies provided evidence that amnesic patients were able to learn the identity of deteriorated pictures and words in which parts of the image were missing (see Figure 5.10). The subjects were required to say what the picture represented; if they failed they were given a less degraded version, and so on, until they guessed the object. On subsequent trials, both normal and amnesic subjects were able to identify an object at an earlier or worse state of degradation, showing that some learning must have taken place. Over trials, both normals and amnesic patients showed that they could learn to recognise the most degraded version.

Another task used by Warrington and Weiskrantz was a stem completion task. These experiments are sometimes referred to as *priming* since they lead the subject to respond in a particular way through experience. For example, if an amnesic patient is presented with the word "STRING" as a prime and later is asked to complete the stem "STRI . . . " they will complete the word as "STRING", even though there are many other common words with the same stem, some of which may be equally or even more common.

These first experiments with amnesic patients were given theoretical substance years later (e.g. Graf & Mandler, 1984; Graf & Schacter, 1984; Schacter, 1987). In these studies the full import-

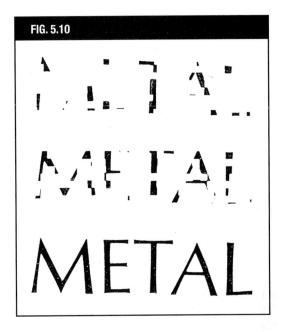

FIG. 5.10

With these degraded stimuli following Gollin (1960), Warrington and Weiscrantz (1968) showed that eventually their amnesic patients were able to learn to recognise and identity the most degraded word following a number of presentations. Such patients would usually have little memory of the learning trials despite a learning performance that approached that of the controls (reprinted by permission from *Nature*, Warrington & Weiskrantz, 1968, copyright 1968 Macmillan Magazines Ltd).

ance of the instructions were realised. The instructions were found to be crucial to the success of implicit remembering. Implicit memory was most likely to be optimal when the learning was incidental and the task was not seen as a memory task by the patients. Use of the patient's conscious or explicit memory often interfered with the process. To avoid the use of explicit or intentional memory the task was not presented to the subject as a memory task. Subjects were therefore merely asked to complete the question or other task to ensure that attention was drawn to the stimulus (see Schacter, 1987, 1995, for a brief review of this subject).

As indicated above, except when the learned material is built up over a series of trials, tasks that illustrate implicit memory in amnesic subjects typically use material that is well known or familiar to the subject, prior to the onset of amnesia. The evidence that amnesic patients have relatively intact implicit memory has prompted some theorists to propose that implicit memory is the activation of pre-existing memory representations within the hypothetical LTMS (Graf & Mandler, 1984). Even when apparently unfamiliar material has been used, the activation hypothesis is still attractive. For example, McAndrews, Glisky, and Schacter (1987) used a paradigm in which the subjects were given a solution to the meaning of a series of sentences that were difficult to comprehend. For example, when the sentence *The haystack was important because the cloth ripped* was provided with the solution *parachute*, the amnesic subjects gave the same solution when they were later presented with the same sentence. Therefore even when material is unfamiliar it has a familiar knowledge basis or schema that has been learned previously. When elaborative sentences are used that are anomalous and make no sense according to our past experience (e.g. "The dusky *cow* multiplied the *employer*"), implicit memory effects are not found (Schacter & Graf, 1986).

As suggested, implicit memory is typically tested in a partially cued, e.g. stem, degraded, or recognition presentation, e.g. the original and other words are presented for acceptance or rejection. This might also be taken to favour an activation view. According to the activation hypothesis, implicit memory would require access and activation of the LTMS, independent or without support of the consolidation system.

However, it would appear that this view is more acceptable for perceptual rather than semantic or meaningful encodings. As indicated, one of the features that often distinguishes implicit from explicit memory (any conscious recall of information) is that explicit memory is more likely to be improved by semantic encoding. For example, explicit memory is improved by a condition in which the meaningful content of words is analysed, e.g. *Is this word a living thing?*, compared to analysis that promotes less associations, e.g. *Does this word have a letter n?* This is the paradigm that underpins the levels of processing perspective on memory, referred to in a previous section (Craik

& Lockhart, 1972). Implicit memory, in contrast, is not affected by such manipulation in tasks where words have to be identified after priming (Jacoby & Dallas, 1981). Also, when considering priming, e.g. presenting a word prior to its stem on testing, implicit memory deteriorates when the modality of presentation, e.g. auditory or visual, varies between presentation and testing (Schacter & Church, 1992). The view that this activation is perceptual in nature is supported by PET scans showing occipital activations during implicit memory tasks (see Schacter, 1997, for a review). This contrasts with retrieval from explicit memory, when a subject has intended to learn something. When the process of retrieval is considered in explicit remembering there is more prefrontal involvement (e.g. Tulving, Kapur, & Craik, 1994).

A topic of recent interest to researchers using functional imaging techniques is whether the two hemispheres have different roles during retrieval. At this stage it appears that if one considers verbal information the activation of the left versus right hemisphere tends to depend on the type of retrieval task used. In tasks of free recall in which the *generation* of a response is required then it would appear that the left dorsolateral and ventrolateral prefrontal cortex is activated more within a network that includes temporoparietal areas and the hippocampal complex. We are reminded of the prefrontal activation associated with verbal fluency test, described in Chapter 3. Therefore the left prefrontal cortex, especially the dorsolateral are appears to importance when the memory task requires the elaboration of encoding involving a search of semantic memory. However, a similar area in the right prefrontal cortex is activated in recognition tests, especially when recognition of the context is required, e.g. recognition whether the word was spoken in a male or female voice. Here the accent is more on the retrieval of episodic information. These kinds of results have been modelled within what Cabeza and colleagues refer to as the generate–recognise asymmetry model or GRAM (Cabeza et al., in press). Further analysis has been conducted looking at the apparent specialisation of ventrolateral (VPFC) versus dorsolateral (DPFC) and anterior prefrontal cortex (APFC; Brodmans area 10).

These results are emerging at the present time but a series of studies by the group at the Institute of Cognitive Neuroscience at University College London (Wellcome Department of Cognitive Neurology) have identified the VPFC as important in specifying retrieval cues. When tasks become more uncertain and complex and *monitoring* of response is required the DPFC is more likely to show additional activation (to avoid the repetition of a response). The APFC appears more likely to be activated when the source context is retrieved (whether an item was new or old-previously presented) (e.g., Henson, Rugg et al., 1999; Henson, Shallice, & Dolan, 1999).

Implicit memory has been shown to have a variable duration of around a few hours, but this may vary depending on the kinds of information described. In an experiment by McAndrews, and Milner (1991) (see description above) the duration for implicit memory may actually be around a week. Therefore the type of material and task is important, just as it is for explicit memory. However, the duration of implicit memory appears to be independent of explicit memory for the same material. Also, implicit memory is less influenced by interference when compared to explicit memory (Moscovitch et al., 1993; Schacter, 1995). It would appear that these two types of memory differ enough in performance to suggest that these two memory types are served by brain structures that are not completely shared.

The implicit–explicit memory distinction is supported first and foremost by the finding that amnesic patients, who have profound difficulties in remembering that requires conscious recollection, are nevertheless capable of implicit remembering. Moscovitch proposes (Moscovitch et al., 1993, pp. 643–644) that the consolidation system structures, especially the hippocampal formation, are important for explicit memory and the consciousness or awareness of memories, although this does not explain why those amnesic patients without hippocampal lesions are also not capable of storing conscious memories. It is possible, however, that the thalamic amnesias are due to the effect they have on the functioning of the hippocampus.

As indicated, implicit memory appears to survive in patients who are amnesic, although it is true that implicit memory performance is slightly lower for these patients when compared to normals. However, normal groups are probably advantaged by using some explicit memory during an implicit memory task (Jacoby, Toth, & Yonelinas, 1993; Mayes, Van Eijk, & Isaac, 1995). Thus normal subjects may consciously remember being previously presented with a word, even if there was no requirement to learn the word at the time, and for this reason adjustments to their scores have to be made or special paradigms developed for overcoming this problem (Mayes et al., 1995).

Just as explicit memory has modal features, as discussed in terms of the model above, e.g. phonological, visuospatial, so, predictably, there is evidence of modules in the case of implicit memory. Left cortical damage is associated with impaired verbal implicit memory, while right cortical damage is associated with impaired non-verbal implicit memory (Schacter & Church, 1992).

Other dissociations may be found between types of implicit memory, especially when considering memory for procedures dependent on motor movements. Amnesic patients sometimes show an intact ability to learn simple practised motor movements over a series of trials. The amnesic patient HM was able to learn to draw a star when drawing from a reflection in a mirror. With experience HM was able to learn these procedures at rates not too dissimilar to normal persons, yet would not remember doing the task previously (Milner, 1970). Gardener (1974) describes a Wernicke–Korsakoff patient who learned a new piano piece but failed to remember learning the piece. When asked by a health worker to play the piece the patient protested that he could not play the piece. The patient was enormously surprised when he found that he could play it. This implicit motor learning, which does not require conscious recollection, is also referred to as *procedural memory*. Patients with motor disorders such as Parkinson's or Huntington's disease, who have lesions in the basal ganglia, are more often impaired in learning these motor movement-related tasks. However, they are not so impaired on verbal implicit tasks. This contrasts with Alzheimer patients, who have bilateral cortical atrophy to the temporal and parietal lobe. These patients have the opposite pattern of impairment: they have impaired verbal implicit memory but relatively intact memory for procedures (e.g. Butters, Heindel, & Salmon, 1990). Therefore there is a possible double dissociation, with the basal ganglia being important for implicit motor learning (procedural memory) and the cortex being more crucial for verbal and pictorial visuospatial implicit learning. However, further work is required in this area to confirm this dissociation.

Prospective memory

Memory-impaired brain-damaged patients frequently complain of an inability to remember to do things in the future (Kapur & Pearson, 1983). This type of self-reminding has been referred to as remembering to remember (Harris, 1980). Most definitions of prospective memory include the feature of requiring the subject to remember a specific task or action at some time in the future (e.g. Sohlberg, White, Evans, & Mateer, 1992, p. 129). This is distinct from retrospective memory, in which a person is reminded of the event of learning through supplied cues such as a recognition choice or a specific request for recall. Nevertheless, in some experimental work, recognition cues are used as a means of testing prospective memory (e.g. Maylor, 1993). When the cues are not specifically identified at the time of presentation as recognition cues, the subject must remind themselves that the recognition cue has previously been identified as a reminder. Therefore the critical feature of prospective memory is the remembering of *intentions* to carry out a task or action in the future (see Kvavilashvili & Ellis, 1996, for further discussion).

Einstein and McDaniel (1990) considered two types of prospective remembering tasks:

1. Time based, in which the person has to remind themselves to undertake the activity at a particular time (e.g., Wilkins & Baddeley, 1978).
2. Event based, in which an event is the triggering cue for the activity, e.g., "I must remember to hang out the clothes to dry in the event that I cease to hear the noise of the washing machine."

West and Craik (1999) proposed that time-based prospective remembering is more vulnerable to forgetting given its greater reliance on self-reminding. This contrasts with event-based prospective remembering, where the event acts as a cue for self-reminding.

Of course it is not always certain that event-based prospective memory is not just another form of retrospective memory. For example, when we recall something in a cued recall test is it so different from the situation in which we are cued at some time in the future?

Certainly, because the subject has to distinguish between bona fide cues or events and this occurs over time, this type of remembering requires some controlled monitoring and therefore patients with frontal lesions might be expected to have difficulty in this area (Glisky, 1996). One might predict that patients with frontal lobe lesions may have more difficulty with time-based prospective memory since this requires more spontaneity and more self-initiated monitoring. McDaniel et al., (1999) looked at event-based prospective memory and varied the saliency of the event on the basis that a less salient event would require more executive monitoring. It was found that persons who did more poorly on frontal tests did more poorly on this task irrespective of the condition. This area of memory research is in its infancy but one suspects that the practical implications of work in this area will make it popular in the future.

Semantic memory within the long-term memory store

Autobiographical memory is a form of LTMS and this will be discussed further under the topic of retrograde amnesia. Rather than cover all the different types of LTMS, the focus here will be on semantic memory. This is justified on the grounds there has been most focused neuropsychological research in this area and that at this stage there appear to be some similarities when describing the different types. For example, patients who are poor at remembering one type of LTMS are usually poor at remembering another type (Squire, 1992).

The term *semantic memory* was introduced by Endel Tulving as a memory store for facts and knowledge e.g. the name of the Prime Minister of Australia, or how many legs an emu has. It is the part of the LTMS that represents the knowledge of objects, facts, and concepts and their interrelationships (Tulving, 1972, 1983).

Semantic memory may have a representation in a number of brain areas although to date most research has focused on the temporal lobe cortex. The most common clinical example of impaired semantic memory is the patient with Alzheimer's disease. Such patients often initially have most cell loss within the temporal and parietal lobes. However, these patients have a number of other confounding difficulties, the most obvious of which is a deterioration of the consolidation system, with the cell loss from the hippocampi. A rarer group of patients, favoured for research for their purer loss of semantic memory, are referred to as suffering from *semantic dementia*.

Semantic dementia

The term *semantic dementia* has been proposed to describe a patient who fails at tests of semantic memory but who is without other confounding impairments (Hodges, Patterson, Oxbury, & Funnell, 1992; Snowden, Goulding, & Neary, 1989).[1]

In one of their papers, Hodges and colleagues (Hodges et al., 1992) describe a semantic dementia patient, PP, a 69 year old English women with a two year history of memory loss for peoples" names, places, and impaired comprehension for terms. At the onset she had difficulty in recognising familiar persons by sight (prosopagnosia), voice or description. The authors describe how, when she was asked "Have you ever been to America," she replied "what's America?" When asked what was her favourite food she responded "food, food, I wish I knew what that was." (Hodges, Patterson, & Tyler, 1994, p. 508). She is reported as remembering day-to-day activities and appointments, suggesting that her new learning (consolidation system) was intact. However, as Patterson and Hodges (1995) point out, some new learning must be undermined when it involves learning information or words that are no longer present in semantic memory. One suspects the problem may be similar to that of trying to remember a word in another language without knowing its meaning.

On a task that required PP to recognise famous faces, her performance was described as very poor. On one occasion this British patient was asked which one of the faces was the Queen. The patient responded eventually, "I've heard of the Queen, but I wish I knew what it was." (Hodges et al., 1994, p. 509). Interestingly, although PP's comprehension of sentences was profoundly impaired to the point that she had difficulty in understanding instructions, she maintained an awareness and knowledge of syntax.

The association area within the anterolateral temporal lobe is favoured as an area important to semantic memory since there are now a number of semantic dementia patients who are described as having atrophy in this particular area (Patterson & Hodges, 1995, p. 123). These patients have a deterioration in their naming ability and their production of words from a category; they are similar to Alzheimer patients in this respect. Patients who suffer from semantic dementia often illustrate their loss of the meaning of objects by placing articles in their houses in unusual positions: a kitchen utensil might be placed on the coffee table. They may also draw objects within pictures in such a way that it is obvious that they haven't the slightest idea how the object is used.

Testing in the laboratory may misrepresent their abilities in the home since they are more likely to recognise an object if it is familiar and in familiar surroundings. For example, a patient might recognise their own kettle within the con-

---

[1] The disorder of semantic dementia is succinctly described by Hodges, Patterson, and Tyler (1994): (1) the selective impairment of semantic memory causing severe anomia, impaired single word comprehension (both spoken and written), reduced exemplars on category fluency tests and an impoverished fund of general knowledge; (2) relative sparing of other components of language output, notably syntax phonology; (3) normal perceptual skills and non-verbal problem-solving abilities; (4) relatively preserved autobiographical and day-to-day (episodic) memory; (5) a reading disorder with the pattern of surface dyslexia. (Hodges et al., 1994, p. 507).

text of their own kitchen, but not when it is placed in another room (Snowden, Griffiths, & Neary, 1994). This is of course true of other patients such as Alzheimer patients and therefore any change from their own surroundings to a nursing home may initially result in increased confusion.

The progressive breakdown of semantic memory may offer some clues as to the nature of storage within LTMS. Patients often misname a less frequently experienced item by the name of a more common item. Patients, when faced with a picture of a camel, for example, may refer to the camel as a horse. A picture of a church may be referred to as a house. In more advanced cases, the patients may call everything that is deemed to be living as a common animal such as a dog. The ability to discriminate is eroded, often to the most commonly experienced exemplar. This type of deterioration is a hallmark of semantic memory deterioration and might suggest that storage within semantic memory occurs in terms of a hierarchy or a tree-like structure. For example, with animals as the trunk of a metaphorical tree, the concept branches divide off into domestic animals versus wild animals, then the twigs of the branches divide further into the types of animals within that category. The dementia causes the twigs to be eaten away, followed by the branches etc. (Hodges et al., 1994). This hierachical view of semantic memory was favoured by early models based on normal subjects (e.g., Collins & Quillian, 1969) and McCarthy and Warrington also note that the superordinate level is less vulnerable (1990, p. 135). Patterson and Hodges (1995) provide a perceptual explanation for this effect. They favour the view that when we look at a picture of an animal it has only a few features that distinguish it from other animals, but many features that distinguish it as an animal as opposed to some non-living thing. For example, many animals have four legs, whiskers, fur and a tail. You only have to pick up on one of these features to realise that it is an animal. However, specific features distinguishing the type of animal are not as common. For example, you only have to lose out on a very few features to start interpreting a picture of a wolf as a dog. However, there is also an effect whereby more commonly experienced items are more likely to be retained compared to less commonly experienced items, perhaps because their representation within the LTMS is frequently rehearsed and consolidated (Snowden et al., 1994). However, two points should be made first. When we refer to experience we are referring to day-to-day autobiographical experience. These patients are able to talk about day-to-day events since their hippocampus is able to store and retrieve this information in a semi-permanent manner. However, because this is now adding to past stores of information the information they have on these commonly experienced items is very idiosyncratic and based on their own use rather than any common definition. For example, a water jug might be described as a receptacle for flowers (Snowden, Griffiths, & Neary, 1999).

An alzheimer patient seen by the author was happy to call a guinea-pig a cat because according to these laws the guinea-pig was a less commonly experienced animal on a day-to-day basis but its appearance in a picture also had many features in common with a cat.

Can semantic memory be divided into subtypes associated with different brain areas?

One of the controversies within this literature concerns whether semantic memory can be further divided into subtypes. Patients have been found who appear to have some differential impairment of performance, suggesting different types of semantic memory. Beauvois (1982) decribes a patient who was anomic (naming difficulty) only for visually presented objects. To take a more common example a number of patients are found who have more difficulty in gauging the meaning of abstract words, e.g. emotion, compared to more concrete words, e.g. pig. But other patients have been found who have the reverse difficulty: these patients have difficulty in recognising concrete words, e.g. yacht, with better recognition for abstract words, e.g. emotion. Warrington (1975) and Warrington and Shallice (1984) describe such patients and the differences are quite marked, with around 90–93% of abstract words being comprehended, and only

50–63% of concrete words obtaining a satisfactory definition.

However, even within the category of concrete words, further differences have been found, in particular, the finding that some patients have a selective impairment in comprehending words or pictures that represent "living things" compared to "non-living things" (inanimate objects). This has been found in subjects from different countries and therefore is not obviously an artefact of language (e.g., Gainotti & Silveri, 1996; McCarthy & Warrington, 1988; Sartori & Job, 1988). Some patients have also been found who have the reverse pattern, with poorer comprehension of "non-living things" compared to "living things" (Warrington & McCarthy, 1983, 1987). There is evidence also of patients having difficulty with words representing indoor objects (plate) compared to outdoor objects (bus) (Warrington & McCarthy, 1987). When one patient(s) has an intact function "a", for example the ability to name "living things" but has impaired function "b", naming "non-living things", while another patient(s) has a reverse pattern with function "a" being impaired and "b" intact, then this is referred to as a "double dissociation". It is often assumed that a "double-dissociation" signals that the two functions, i.e. naming of "living" and "non-living things", must be served by different brain areas.

With a bewildering number of semantic memory subtype dissociations one might be tempted to become a little cynical, especially when some of the bizarre subtypes are reported by a double dissociation based on two single patients. Let us inspect the mechanism of the double dissociation in one of the commonplace examples. If, to take a hypothetical example, a double dissociation exists between the recognition of food words and words for tools, case 1 would have to show impairment in comprehending food but not tools, while case 2 would require the reverse impairment with tools but not food. If only one patient or group showed a single dissociation, one could argue that food and tools were served by the same store and that one category was just harder than the other and there was just a gradation, so a double dissociation is more impressive. However, we have

already noted that comprehension within semantic dementia is influenced by a person's individual experience. If case 1 (in the hypothetical example above) has been a cook (good at food names), while case 2 has worked in a garage (experienced with tool names) then the double dissociation suddenly looks less exciting (see Miller, 1993, for an elaboration of such arguments).

However, despite such dangers many of these dissociations are based on a number of replications. For example, the double dissociations between the naming of living things and non-living things is well replicated and cannot be regarded to be due to any mistake of method or spurious interpretation. There are, however, a number of different explanations for this difference. The first is that the usual balance of worst performance on living things is due to a word frequency effect. A long-standing finding is that words occurring more frequently in literature are more likely to be remembered and recognised (word frequency effect). Other artefactual features that also affect performance include the visual complexity of the object and subjective familiarity of the item (Stewart, Parkin, & Hunkin, 1992). When these variables have been controlled for, the effect disappears with some individual patients (Funnell & Sheridan, 1992; Stewart et al., 1992). But this is not the case when the differential between these two categories (living and non-living things) is large (Gainotti & Silveri, 1996; Sartori, Miozzo, & Job, 1993).

The double dissociation found between patients who have ability to remember living but not non-living things and vice versa is now generally accepted and has survived attempts to discredit it. But what does it mean? Do these different types of information or categories have separate representations within the cortex and, if so, how does the brain make this distinction at the neuronal level?

The first evidence, not sitting easily with the category view, was the finding that impaired ability to name and comprehend pictures of *living things* was often accompanied by poor naming and comprehension for items of *food*. An explanation for this was supplied by reframing the division by classifying living things plus food as belonging to a superordinate category of items categorised by their looks (sensory), compared to those items that are more readily recognised by their function, e.g. inanimate tools (Warrington & Shallice, 1984). A number of authors warmed to this view and varied the visual distinctiveness of food and animal items to test the basis for this sensory/functional view point (Gaffan and Heywood, 1993; Gainotti and Silveri, 1996; Laiacona, Barbarotto, & Capitani, 1993).

At present a consensus is forming that categories or classes of objects are differentiated in terms of brain location in accordance with their perceptual and analytical requirements (see McCarthy & Warrington, 1990). According to PET scan studies of normal subjects, and lesion studies which have investigated object naming, different brain areas are involved in the naming of tools, animals, and familiar faces, for example. These differences may be based on the analysis typically required of the category (Martin, Wiggs, Ungerleider, & Haxby, 1996). Brain locations deemed to be important for the storage of tools are found to be close to the same areas that are important for action words in the temporal lobe. Activations in these radiological studies have also been found in areas within the premotor area, which is close to the area associated with the imagery for motor movements. These coincidences have been interpreted by Martin and colleagues as being associated with the related conceptual knowledge of tools as manipulated objects. Animals, in contrast, are found to be located in different areas including the medial and inferior temporal lobes, with more posterior involvement than some other attributes, which is interpreted as being related to the requirement for visual analysis as necessary physical differentiations between animals (Damasio et al., 1996). Familiar faces require different areas again, which include the left and right temporal pole. This may reflect the fine-grained perceptual requirements and the semantic context associated, for example, with person's occupation (Damasio et al., 1996; Burton et al., 1991). This location is also close to the amygdala and its important role of processing emotional faces (see a discussion of this topic in Chapter 9).

In summary, the LTMS is described as being functionally heterogeneous. It appears that information is stored in the vicinity to areas of the cortex that are near to the functions that are most relevant to their recognition or use. Objects that are most frequently seen are stored in the vicinity of perceptual processes, while information about items that are handled are stored near to areas that are associated with motor movements and manipulation. It might be predicted that damage to the brain may follow specific deficits in semantic memory, but also that some patients may show a deficit that is specific to the modality of presentation. For example, Sheridan and Humphreys describe a case that was unable to recognise an item when it was presented visually, but could recognise the same item when described verbally (Sheridan & Humphreys, 1993).

The research undertaken in the area of semantic memory has been discussed in greater detail because it represents an excellent example of how neuropsychological research develops: being driven by opinion evolving through systematic research. When discussing the basis of semantic memory and its tendency to be separated into different modules or categories according to the required perceptual analysis, one is brought home to the overlap between memory and perception. In some sense semantic memory could be construed as the source of top-down perception feeding the "what" pathway (see Gaffan, 1996). There are also links with language since naming impairment (anomia) may be classified as part of a language disorder that has one of its causes associated with a damaged semantic memory. If you like, semantic memory is the common ground where memory meets perception and language.

The executive Influence on memory

Patients with lesions to the prefrontal cortex may have difficulty in organising information during both storage and the retrieval of memory. For example, when tested with word list learning over trials such patients may recall words in an inconsistent order (Incisa Della Rochetta & Milner, 1993; Stuss, Alexander et al., 1994). This may mean that the patient fails to increase their recall over trials in the same way that non-brain-damaged subjects are able to since they fail to build on past associations. They appear to use inconsistent strategies of organisation (Stuss, Alexander et al., 1994). *Unless* there are many distracting items to choose from, recognition is far easier for such patients since there is no need for this organising retrieval process (Janowsky, Shimamura, & Kritchevsky, 1989).

Prisko (1963) originally found that while patients with frontal lesions had no difficulty in remembering stimuli (e.g. words) on a test of recognition, they did have difficulty in knowing which of two previously presented items had been presented first. These patients had difficulty keeping track of the order in which items had been presented. Similarly, patients with prefrontal lesions also have problems on tasks that require them to recall which item has been presented last or more recently (e.g. Milner & Petrides, 1984). Patients with left dorsolateral prefrontal lesions have particular difficulty making these kinds of judgements (Milner, Corsi, & Leonard, 1991). Milner and colleagues have found a relationship in which a left-sided lesion is associated with more difficulty with verbal material, whereas a right-sided lesion is more associated with impairment of visuospatial material, e.g. designs.

Similarly, patients with prefrontal lesions also have difficulty in remembering where they originally learned a fact (source memory; Janowsky, Shimamura, & Squire, 1989). This type of finding has been illustrated in various studies, using different paradigms. The explanation favoured by many researchers is that the patient fails to monitor and learn the context of the items to be remembered. The context relates to the environmental features associated with the presentation of the information: for example, that a particular word was presented before another within a certain list at a certain time and was presented by a certain examiner at a time that the patient's stomach was rumbling—these are all contextual features that might help us distinguish when and where something was learned.

Some patients with prefrontal lesions appear to have difficulty storing contextual features of an event so that they are left with having to judge

material as either familiar (deemed recent) or non-familiar (deemed non-recent). If non-recent items are repeated (increasing familiarity), then patients can be tricked into believing the item is recent, when it is not. Normal subjects are less easily fooled because they can remember the event of learning and its context (Huppert & Piercy, 1976).

Petrides (1996) reviews work arguing that the ventrolateral areas of the dorsofrontal cortex are important for strategic remembering and that when this area is damaged the patient may still learn prose or paired associates and other information that requires little use of strategy. However, as soon as active encoding and retrieval of certain features are required these patients will have difficulty.

One way of overcoming the difficulty of storing these contextual features might be to require these patients to use a strategy that makes them pay more attention to the context. McAndrews and Milner (1991) increased the saliency of contextual cues by requiring patients to manipulate and use the to-be-remembered items, e.g. turn the to-be-remembered egg-timer. With these kinds of manipulations, the frontal patients" performance was markedly improved up to the level of patients with posterior lesions. The impairment of contextual memory has also been put forward as an explanation for some types of amnesia (see below).

Failure to monitor context is also found in maze-learning tests. Patients with anterior lesions may fail to learn from their mistakes (Karnath et al., 1991). Corkin (1965) (unseen tactile maze) and Milner (1965) (visual maze) have both provided maze tasks that have been found to be sensitive to right frontal lobe damage.

Remembering a series of movements demonstrated by the examiner is more obviously impaired in patients with left parietal lesions and some of these patients would no doubt be showing clinical signs of apraxia (see Chapter 8). Patients with right frontal lesions also have some difficulty in remembering a series of *examiner-defined* hand movements when they are unseen. This impairment associated with right frontal lesions is most obviously due to the poor internal maintenance of movements (WM). This is not obviously due to long-term memory storage per se since, unlike temporal lobe-lesioned patients, delayed recall makes little difference to performance of the right frontally lesioned patients (Leonard & Milner, 1991a, 1991b). In both these tasks it is as if the patient is unable to distinguish one past trial from another.

The ability to reproduce a series of facial movements is most impaired in patients with prefrontal lesions and this is seen to be mainly due to dorsolateral lesions (Kolb & Milner, 1981b).

Many patients with prefrontal lesions do not have executive memory disorders. However, when Milner and colleagues surveyed the scans of those patients who had difficulty in remembering the order of items, they found an area within the dorsolateral cortex of the prefrontal cortex around the principal sulcus that was most commonly lesioned (Milner et al., 1991). This area is similar to the area Goldman-Rakic found that interfered with a monkey's ability to register information in memory over brief periods.

While patients with prefrontal lesions, especially in the dorsolateral regions, have some difficulty in organising and retrieving information that may help them remember the order and "recency" of memorised information, they nevertheless often have a reasonable level of memory function in terms of the quantity of what they recall. Thus, such a patient may, when clinically assessed, achieve a score that is in keeping with normal subjects of the same age and sex. It is only when the qualitative features of recall are viewed that the nature of their impairment is fully realised. Such features as poor organisation, inconsistency of recall, and a tendency not to keep track of what they have already recalled are hallmarks of dysexecutive remembering (Wheeler, Stuss, & Tulving, 1997).

Remembering that is less influenced by these factors such as two-choice recognition and cued recall. Difficulties on recognition tests have been noted but this is more obviously the case when a large number of foils or distractors are introduced (forced-choice recognition with words similar to the those in the list). In such a presentation there is a tendency to make false-positive choices (Wheeler, Stuss, & Tulving, 1995). Some of these features are not exclusive to these patients, but, with other clinical evidence, they are part of a dysexecutive pattern. Finally, it must be considered that these qualities are an *influence* on memory performance. If the consolidation system and its associated structures are intact and the executive requirements of the task are minimised by using a highly structured task of learning paired associates, then the problems noted above will also be minimised. This kind of information is important to clinicians who are assessing the nature and profile in a patient who is suspected to have problems of organisation within memory.

Because these influences may, to some extent, be compensated by an intact consolidation system, the dysexecutive influence may become more obvious in patients with damage to the consolidation system. This issue is dealt with in the next part of this chapter.

AMNESIA

Introduction

As the cases in Box 5.2 illustrate, amnesia can come in many forms depending on the areas of the brain that are damaged. Ideally, a model of the memory process must be able to describe these amnesic syndromes and be able to predict the pattern of memory deficit from the lesion site(s). This chapter is concerned with such models and a description of the various clinical syndromes that support them. Given the differences in the profiles of the two cases, it is clear that different types of amnesias potentially provide useful information concerning the mechanisms of memory.

There has already been some discussion of the classic case of amnesia of HM and the bilateral excisions to his hippocampi which caused his dense amnesia. In this section, we start by discussing amnesia due to another cause. These Wernicke–Korsakoff syndrome patients, who were referred to at one time as typifying the amnesic syndrome, have damage to the diencephalic structures, which include the thalamus. These patients will first be discussed and the very interesting quality of their amnesia, which is suggestive of frontal lobe dysfunction or disconnection. This will be followed by a more in-depth discussion concerning the mechanisms of other amnesias.

There has over the years been something of a conflict between the animal literature on amnesia and the human literature. Recently a new model of the extended hippocampal system has been proposed that attempts to bring these two literatures together. So far the human literature fails to support the theory but the discussion of this model does allow the descriptions of the puzzling connections that are between structures within the consolidation system.

Finally, there will be a discussion of "forgetting curves" and amnesia. The question is asked, even though amnesics and severely memory-impaired patients may show some evidence of retention given certain materials with certain presentations, do they show the same kinds of memory forgetting compared to other persons?

Executive influence on amnesia and the Wernicke–Korsakoff syndrome?

Global amnesia is usually associated with profound loss of memory for all the modalities, for example, verbal material (list learning and prose), visual memory (nonsense figures), and visuospatial (maze learning). The patient typically shows virtually no new learning over the long term. Therefore in a test of memory that includes a period of interference between presentation and recall, there is virtually no memory after guessing has been accounted for. However, immediate memory (repeating back a series of digits) or WM is often intact. Apart from this anterograde amnesia, there is further difficulty in remembering events prior to the onset of disease or injury. This retrograde amnesia is often, but not always, temporally graded (see below). Temporally graded retrograde amnesia shows itself as a most obvious difficulty in remembering events just prior to the onset of the disease with less difficulty in remembering more remote events, e.g. schooling, early job description, although the

pattern is dependent on the type of memory being tested. Therefore there will be a different gradient when assessing detailed autobiographical material when compared to factual knowledge, for example. These features of amnesia may even occur with a background of intact intellectual function as examined using tests of intelligence such as the WAIS-R (see Squire and Zola, 1997, for a discussion). However, this description of pure amnesia may be influenced by damage to areas outside of the *consolidation system*. In such a situation the amnesia takes on extra symptoms and the memory loss has a certain pattern or profile. These deviations are determined by, and specific to, the nature of the type of brain damage, disorder and disease process.

In earlier writings, the amnesic syndrome was typified by one type of patient with the disorder called Wernicke–Korsakoff syndrome. With this disorder there is a progression of the disease from a sudden onset of confusion and sleepiness, sometimes accompanied by delusions and confabulation (producing stories about their circumstance that are inaccurate or not anchored in time). This is referred to as the Wernicke's encephalopathy stage. In the second stage, the patient becomes more stable and less confused and Wernicke's encephalopathy gives way to a profound and chronic amnesia, which is the Korsakoff part of the Wernicke–Korsakoff syndrome. Originally diagnosed by a Russian physician, Sergei Korsakoff, these patients most often have a history of chronic alcoholism, although some of Korsakoff's original patients had different aetiologies (Victor, Adams, & Collins, 1971; Victor & Yakovlev, 1955). This disorder is relatively rare and seen to be due to thiamine (vitamin B_1) deficiency. Although thiamine is undeniably implicated from research with non-human animal models, it is so much more commonly associated with alcoholism in humans that it is tempting to consider an interaction between alcohol and thiamine deficiency. Also, while some malnourished, thiamine-deficient prisoners of the Second World War are recorded with amnesic symptoms, they typically recovered relatively quickly after vitamin treatment (Spillane, 1947).

Traditionally, Wernicke–Korsakoff syndrome

Box 5.2.   Cases of amnesia

Case EM

The patient is a 50-year-old man with a past history of chronic alcoholism. He is looking agitated and anxious when he comes into the office and, before there is a chance of introducing myself, he goes into a long story concerning how he came into hospital. He hurriedly recounts a strange tale that he is the victim of clinical error. He reports that he came to the hospital to visit his brother. He tells how the ward sister mistook him for his brother during the visit and mistakenly kept him in hospital, while his sick brother was sent home. This far-fetched story is related with such complete conviction, it is tempting to check the notes just in case something of this nature has actually happened.

Other than this strange story, the patient seems to be quite normal at first during the interview. But something is clearly wrong, for when describing his present favourite TV show he describes characters in a long-running series who have been written out of the script or died some 10 years ago. When asked who is the Prime Minister he responds, identifying someone who was in power some 10 years previously. The patient was assessed and found to be suffering from a profound amnesia. He was diagnosed as having Wernicke–Korsakoff syndrome. Despite his profound inability to remember, he genuinely does not believe that he has a memory problem. He fails to recognise me when I see him again later that afternoon. The story concerning the brother is found to be a fabrication or, in clinical parlance, a "confabulation".

Case TJ

A 30-year-old woman, has been diagnosed as having had a viral infection of the brain, referred to as herpes simplex encephalitis. She had been found unconscious in her flat by neighbours 2 months previously. Like the Korsakoff patient, she is also an amnesic. She is unsure of the reason for her assessment, even though she has been informed of this a few minutes previously and she asks me for other information which she has been told repeatedly. However, unlike the 50-year-old Wernicke–Korsakoff patient, she realises she has a profound and debilitating memory impairment and carries round a tape recorder in an vain attempt to compensate for her amnesia. Sadly, every time she plays the recording it means little to her since she does not remember the context of the conversations. For her, it is as if she has turned on the radio halfway through an unfamiliar programme.

---

has been referred to as the "the amnesic syndrome" as it was once seen as a pure example of amnesia without confounding impairments. The patients show some intellectual deterioration but strikingly mild when compared to a catastrophic loss of memory. But the term "amnesic syndrome" is used less often now since it is realised that Wernicke–Korsakoff syndrome has special qualitative features setting it apart from other amnesias. In other words, it is less of a pure standard than was originally assumed. It is now realised that each type of amnesia has its own neuropsychological profile dependent on the pattern of brain damage or neuropathology caused by the disease.

Early studies of Wernicke–Korsakoff syndrome come to some agreement that lesions to the thalamus (medial thalamic lesions such as the dorsomedial nucleus, magnocellular division) and to lesser extent the mammillary bodies are associated with amnesic consequences (Adams, Collins, & Victor, 1962; Warrington & Weiskrantz, 1978). Other areas of damage in these patients include the anterior cerebellum and the brain stem and are more associated with ataxia (wide-based gait) and nystagmus (jerky eye movements when tracking a moving finger). However, while these findings remain supported, there is more recent evidence that there are other common lesions in these patients that may contribute to the special flavour of this amnesia. In particular, a CT scan study by Shimamura, Jernigan, and Squire (1988) noted some evidence of dorsolateral prefrontal cortical atrophy inferred from sulci widening. These signs of pathology were found to correlate with tests of executive dysfunction. Perhaps even more interesting, from the point of view of the present discussion, is an MRI scan study by Butters (1984), which found the involvement of the basal areas of the frontal lobe and some orbital prefrontal cortical areas. These last lesions are not unlike those presented by the anterior communicating artery aneurysm—a patient group whose amnesia (when it is present) is also associated with confabulation. The lesions to the midline of the thalamus have recently been verified and the mammillary body atrophy seems to be a less reliable accompaniment of the disease (Visser et al., 1999). There is a difficulty in isolating the crucial lesion in a brain that has many areas of damage due to chronic alcohol abuse. Recently, in a study involving a cell count measure of atrophy, Harding, Halliday, Caine, and Kril (2000) confirmed that the mamillary bodies were not critical in Wernicke–Korsakoff syndrome by comparison with chronic alcoholics without amnesia. Their findings support the anterior thalamus as being the crucial lesion that separated the amnesic from the non-amnesic alcoholics. This finding, while needing replication, is perhaps more in keeping with expectations since, as described below, the anterior thalamus is more directly part of a consolidation circuit that includes the hippocampus.

As illustrated in the anecdotal case study in the introduction to this chapter (see Box 5.2), there is a tendency, under certain conditions, for these patients to confabulate. The patient described in the introduction recounts a mythical mistake in which he was retained in hospital while his sick brother was sent home. This is an example of confabulation. The patient clearly believes what he is saying so there is no obvious attempt at deception. While it is possible that there is a continuum, Kopelman (1987) distinguishes between spontaneous and provoked confabulation. Most commonly, the Wernicke–Korsakoff syndrome patient will be provoked into confabulation if they are asked about some topic of memory, for example when they are asked about a story that has just been presented. Spontaneous confabulations are rarer, and tend to be more bizarre. Broadly they can be described as the ingenuous fabrication of past memories.

Some confabulations are a rationalisation for a patient's resent circumstances, as in the case of the patient who had been 10 years in an institution and told the author that he was in hospital because he had been bitten by a dog. In this case there was no knowledge of how long the patient had been in hospital and he thought the prime minister of England was a politician who had left office some 15 years previously. However, as Talland (1965) points out, many confabulations are actually vaguely true memories that have been misplaced in time. This was true of one of the first patients witnessed by the author, who believed that he was a cook on a sheep station, which had been true some 20 years previously. The inability to judge and select past memories according to their temporal context is a particular problem for these patients.

Confabulation is also associated with frontal damage in an amnesia that is sometimes associated with anterior communicating aneurysm. Fischer, Alexander, D'Esposito, and Otto (1995) reported a series of anterior communicating artery aneurysm patients (see Chapter 1 for a description), and compared two groups: one being made up of "spontaneous" and the other "provoked" confabulators. This study confirmed a previous single-case study by Kapur and Coughlan (1980) that confabulation is correlated with measures of executive functioning, e.g. flexibility and planning. As these measures improve the confabulation remits. The degree of confabulation has also been related to the degree of damage to, or disconnection from, prefrontal areas (Fischer, Alexander, D'Eposito & Otto, 1995). A pattern emerges whereby amnesia, in addition to prefrontal lesions, may be the necessary conditions for the occurrence of this confabulation and lack of insight, and this may also be true of Wernicke–Korsakoff patients. It is possible that patients with Wernicke–Korsakoff syndrome, anterior communicating artery aneurysm, or basal forebrain lesions who have amnesia may have a type of frontal type amnesia that is caused by damage or disconnection between memory circuits and frontal mechanisms. This hypothesis has been entertained but requires confirmation.

Modern surgery techniques often mean that the repair of an aneurysm within the circle of Willis system leaves the patient with relatively little impairment (Andrewes et al., 1998). However, complications, which may include the rupture of the aneurysm or vasospasm (related to the constriction of the artery) of the anterior cerebral arteries at the time of surgery or prior to surgery, may result in severe neuropsychological impairments (Stenhouse, Knight, Longmore & Bishara, 1991). As indicated some of these patients confabulate, as in Wernicke–Korsakoff syndrome, especially in the acute stages (Alexander & Freedman, 1984). These patients may show a dense anterograde amnesia and some amnesia for more recent past events prior to the complication (see comments below concerning retrograde amnesia). Also, like Wernicke–Korsakoff patients, they may have little insight into their amnesia and other limitations. It is of interest that medial orbital areas which may be damaged when the circulation to the anterior cerebral arteries is undermined, have predominant connections to the medial anterior aspects of the thalamus, which is the area associated with damage in Wernicke–Korsakoff patients.

Patients have been noted to have amnesia following damage to the basal forebrain on its own, so this is sometimes seen as one of the sources of amnesia in these cases (Alexander & Freedman, 1984; Damasio et al., 1985). Case studies have attempted to be more specific about the area sufficient to cause damage and Morris, Bowers, Chatterjee, and Heilman (1992) argue for an area referred to as the "diagonal band of Broca", which is responsible for cholinergic innervation of the hippocampus. However, as the authors point out, the finding needs some replication and the problem is that within the basal forebrain area there are a number of possible candidates that might equally be influencing memory.

Theoretical Interpretations concerning the amnesia of Wernicke–Korsakoff syndrome

We have already discussed how patients with lesions to the dorsolateral prefrontal cortex have difficulty in judging and recalling how recently they have seen learned information and how they find difficulty in remembering where they have seen something and in what order they have seen remembered items. Also a theory has been referred to that describes these amnesias as a failure to remember the context of a remembered event. This has also been a prominent theory for the amnesic patients with Wernicke–Korsakoff syndrome (Winocur, 1982; Winocur & Kinsbourne, 1978; Huppert & Piercy, 1976). As discussed, context refers to features that are present at the time and place of the learning experience. The theory proposes that we must attach, or tag, the to-be-learned information with contextual features present at the time of learning. In this way, when we racall or recognise the material later we are able to realise when and where we have learned the information. However, this theory of Wernicke–Korsakoff syndrome has its detractors.

Andrew Mayes and Peter Meudell, at Manchester University proposed an alternative theory

for Wernicke–Korsakoff syndrome amnesia. They proposed the quality of performance of these patients was just a reflection of the quality of a weak memory—a quality that you find in normal subjects if you delay their retrieval time sufficiently. To put this another way, they set out to demonstrate the weak memory hypothesis by trying to simulate amnesia in normal subjects. They found that under these conditions the normal subjects would have similar difficulties in judging the recency or frequency of presentation of an item in memory (see Mayes, Meudell, & Som, 1981; Meudell & Mayes, 1981).

Nevertheless, in any experiment it could be argued that it is too difficult to simulate the level of memory impairment found in amnesic patients. When this difficulty of balancing the strength of the memory trace is achieved by comparing patients with different forms of amnesia, Wernicke–Korsakoff patients appear to show an exaggerated difficulty in judging recency and temporal order when compared with herpes simplex encephalitis patients, who have medial temporal lobe damage (e.g., Hunkin & Parkin, 1993; Parkin, Leng, & Hunkin, 1990).

To place these findings in some perspective, it is well established that patients *without* amnesia, but with mid-dorsolateral frontal lesions, have difficulty in remembering the order, recency, and source of their memory (where and when they learned an item), as is argued above. From the experimental standpoint, the issue whether the Wernicke–Korsakoff syndrome represents a case of frontal amnesia is yet to be confirmed but there is perhaps more evidence to support this than there is to negate this view. Some patients with anterior communicating artery aneurysm appear to be similar in this respect and these two types of amnesic patient groups appear to be different from others who have damage to the hippocampus without other damage.

Despite the controversial aspects of the theory, it appears that, for whatever reason, Wernicke–Korsakoff patients and some patients with frontal lesions have particular difficulty in judging the validity of their memories. This view is not disputed by the finding that these patients (assuming care has been taken over the diagnosis) have no insight whatsoever into their amnesia. In the author's study 12 Wernicke–Korsakoff patients (Andrewes, 1984) rated their own memory on a visual analogue scale (a simple 10 cm line) in comparison to the general public. All these amnesic patients, except for one, rated their memory as average and put a mark in the middle of the line. Only one patient rated himself as being marginally below average and when asked about this he said, "Well, I'm getting on in years, I doubt my memory is as good as those younger than me." This lack of insight is not necessarily shared by other patients—patients who may be equally amnesic.

These Wernicke–Korsakoff patients have difficulty in judging their own memory and fail to judge how recently they learned an item, but they also have difficulty in judging the accuracy of their own memories. They may be encouraged into making false-positive responses by their being misled as to the contents of the list that they have just had to remember. For example, if you ask these patients if they remember any names of toys in the list, they will give a string of toy names even when there were none in the original list (Andrewes, 1984). These patients' intellectual capacity is largely intact and they fully understand the requirements of the task.

It is of interest that patients with gross frontal lobe damage perform similarly in this respect. Schacter and colleagues describe a patient following a right frontal stroke who also performed in this manner by the gross false recognition of items that were not in the previously presented list. This tendency was overcome when the patient was guided by the categories of words contained in the learning list (Curran et al., 1997). The mechanism for this high preponderance of false positives during retrieval is uncertain. However, it appears that patients with frontal lesions tend to be lax in their criterion. Rapsack and colleagues requested their frontally lesioned patients to be more strict in their criterion for the recognition of a series of faces, with a resulting significant reduction in false-positive errors (Rapcsak et al., 1999).

There is now a large literature on the topic of false recognition in memory and typically, in the study of normal subjects, words from the to-be-learned list, e.g. *door, glass, pane*, and *frame*, are accompanied during a recognition test by words that are semantically related, e.g. *window*. Given the appropriate conditions subjects will confidently recognize the word *window* as being previously presented when this is not the case. They will even do this when they have been forewarned of this manipulation (Roediger & McDermott, 1999).

Several studies have shown that we tend to show more evidence of false recognition as we get older (e.g. Koutstaal, Schacter, Galluccio, & Stofer, 1999). The mechanism for this trend may be due to the general decline in brain cells in the frontal lobe and the reduced reliance on the frontal lobes in the retrieval of the source of memories. When we find that a memory item is familiar it may be for various reasons—the item may merely be associated with the one we have had to learn. In order to check whether this "uncertain" item was learned we must retrieve the context of learning. We must remember the event of being shown the item for learning (source memory) in order to check the validity of the word so that we can determine whether it is "familiar" for the right reasons. Elderly people and patients with frontal lobe damage are less able to check up on "uncertain" memories in this manner. They may have a tendency not to remember the details and rely on a kind of gist recall (rough indication of the meaning rather than specific attributes). An alternative theory is that frontal lobe patients do not monitor or check their memory output sufficiently (see Melo, Winocur, & Moscovitch, 1999, for additional explanations). A tendency to make false positives could be due to a combination of these mechanisms since frontal pathology may be associated with both a failure in recalling the source of a memory and also difficulty in monitoring output.

There is an important link between frontal damage, false recognition, and a memory aberration that has already been referred to as a confabulation. Confabulations in Wernicke–Korsakoff syndrome and anterior communicating artery aneurysm patients may be associated with a mixing up of temporal context, like excessive false recognition, this is in keeping with a failure of "source" memory. It should be noted that patients with medial temporal lobe-associated memory impairment make false-positive errors but this is exaggerated when frontal pathology additionally exists (Melo et al., 1999). However, some "bizarre", "fantastic", and delusional confabulations may be due to additional or different dysfunction that is yet to be clearly outlined (Kopelman, 1999).

Functional neuroimaging studies of subjects undergoing memory tasks are starting to show consistent results, indicating specialisation of the prefrontal cortex for verifying retrieval of memories. This issue is discussed later in this chapter (e.g., Fletcher, Frith, Grasby, et al., 1995). Studies using event-related fMRI (Schacter et al., 1997) and ERP (Fabiani, Stadler, & Wessels, in press) have confirmed frontal involvement during false recognition in studies with normals using the type of paradigm described above.

In terms of its clinical expression, in its most moderate form it may merely involve the excessive false recognition of items in a recognition test (Delbecq-Dérousiné, Beauvois, & Shallice, 1990; Curran et al., 1997). In its most florid form this retrieval uncertainty may translate into confabulation. This lack of certainty regarding judgements of the patient's own memory may also contribute to these frontal amnesic patients' lack of insight into their own memory impairment, although this is yet to be verified.

Patients *without* frontal amnesia, like the herpes simplex encephalitis amnesic patient without dysexecutive features on testing (see Box 5.2), have far more insight into their amnesia (see also Andrewes & Gielewski, 1999).

Summary of some executive influences on memory

Patients who have memory impairment and prefrontal lesions may have difficulty in encoding and retrieving memory for the context of the event. These patients also have difficulty in retrieving the order of items learned, when or how recently items were learned and the context or place of learning (source memory). Also, these patients may inconsistently recall items and show poor organisation of what they have learned. Such patients may have less trouble in recognising material because they do not have to organise and actively retrieve during a simple recognition task. However, if the recognition task is sufficiently difficult, with a number of distracters, their performance will fall off because of the increased need to use a retrieval process.

Theories that have tried to explain the underlying mechanism of Wernicke–Korsakoff amnesia have proposed that these patients have a difficulty in encoding the context of their memories. That is, when it comes to retrieving their memories they have little idea of where or when they learned the information. This, with their lack of insight into their own memory impairment and their tendency to make excessive false-positive responses and sometimes show confabulation, are some of the reasons that these patients perform as though they have frontal damage. There is an emerging link between frontal pathology, the propensity to make excessive false recognitions, confabulation, and difficulty in retrieving or checking the context of memory.

Finally, it should be noted that some authors are weary of using the term "frontal amnesia". This term seems to imply that the frontal damage causes the amnesia; this may be the case with a select few patients with basal forebrain lesions, but generally frontal lesions merely influence the quality of the amnesia or memory impairment. Frontal lesions give a profile to an amnesia that is caused originally by damage to the consolidation system.

Other amnesic syndromes

HM had bilateral damage to the hippocampal formation and the adjacent medial cortical structure and was densely amnesic. In many ways this case may be seen to be the archetypal amnesia associated with relatively selective damage to the consolidation system, without damage to other functional areas. Some accounts reporting the HM experience of his amnesia describe this as waking from a dream. It is difficult to imagine the type of isolation that might be felt when there is no memory of what has previously happened to you. Since that time research has shown that small discrete lesions to the hippocampi in area CA1 lead to a less dense amnesia when compared to lesions that include a larger area of the hippocampal formation (e.g. hippocampus plus the entorhinal cortex). Lesions such as those suffered by HM, which include the hippocampal formation plus the perirhinal and parahippocampal cortices, result in the densest amnesia. Severe memory impairment may occur following bilateral damage to the entorhinal, perientorhinal, and parahippocampal cortices in isolation (Squire & Zola, 1997). The mechanism appears to relate to the relationship between unimodal and multimodal association areas within the temporal, parietal, and frontal lobes. Both the perientorhinal (with afferents mainly from the visuo-auditory association areas) and parrahippocampal (afferents mainly from the parietal lobe association areas) have inputs into the entorhinal cortex, which in turn has afferents from the hippocampus (see Figure 5.11). Therefore at least one influence of damage to these areas on the

FIG. 5.11

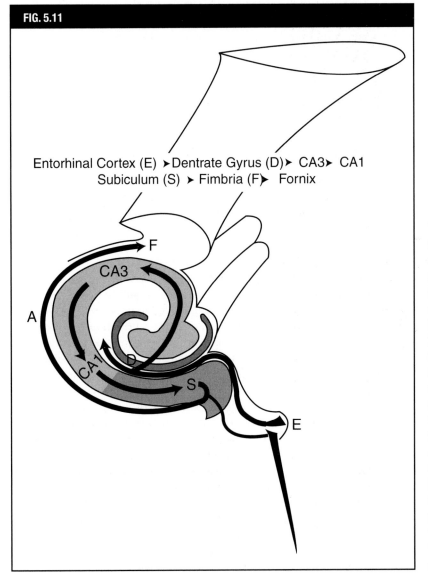

Entorhinal Cortex (E) ►Dentrate Gyrus (D)► CA3► CA1 Subiculum (S) ► Fimbria (F► Fornix

The hippocampal formation. This schematic diagram illustrates the circuit within the hippocampus a structure which is also shown in Figure 5.7. The direction of flow is mainly one-way with Inputs from cell layers I and II of the entorhinal cortex travel via the dentate gyrus, CA3 and CA1 to the subiculum, then to the fimbria via the Alveus (A). The fimbria develops into the fornix. However, as can be seen, there are lesser projections which return to the lower cell layer of 5, the entorhinal cortex, providing a circuit.

hippocampus appears to be disconnective (Squire & Zola, 1997).

The CA1 cells of the hippocampus may be especially vulnerable, since there is most cell loss in this area in patients with temporal lobe epilepsy and also in patients who have suffered anoxia in adulthood (Parkin & Leng, 1993). A bilateral lesion in the cell area CA1 of the hippocampus has eventuated in amnesia in animal models (Parkin & Leng, 1993, p. 83) and a similar relationship has been found with individual patients who have suffered from anoxia. Anoxia due to attempted suicide (e.g. strangulation, carbon monoxide poisoning), cardiac arrest, and other causes may result in ischaemia within the hippocampal areas, which are especially vulnerable (Medalia, Merriam, & Ehrenreich, 1991). Even bilateral lesions confined to area CA1, alone, have been found to be sufficient to result in amnesia (Zola-Morgan, Squire, & Amaral, 1986). The circuit described below within the hippocampus is one-way and therefore a disconnection may cause dysfunction in the whole circuit.

Amnesia may also occur following damage to the thalamus in isolation. While Wernicke–Korsakoff patients would be classed as a thalamic amnesia, some space has been devoted above to the argument that frontal lesions resulting in a disconnection between the consolidation system and frontal structures may have a marked influence on the presentation of this type of amnesia. Other cases of thalamic amnesia do not present with these dysexecutive features. Because discrete thalamic damage, like hippocampal damage, in isolation is rare, patients are referred to by their initials. Patient NA is one patient who has been extensively studied. As a radio operator in Guam, NA was spending some recreational time making a model aeroplane. A colleague, pointing a miniature fencing foil from behind, disturbed him. NA spun round unexpectedly on his revolving chair and the point of the foil entered his brain through his nose. He became amnesic from that time onwards, being unable to remember anything new in any permanent way. Later following a CT brain scan he was found to have damage to the left thalamus (Cohen & Squire, 1981), although some controversy surrounds the precise nature of this lesion[2]. Another patient, BY (Winocur et al., 1984), who had a bilateral thalamic infarct, has also been reported to have amnesia. The critical lesions for these patients have been assumed include the dorsomedial nucleus of the thalamus (as is the case with Wernicke–Korsakoff syndrome). However, Kapur et al. (1996) describe a case with anterior thalamic lesions. As indicated earlier it is of interest that the nuclei in the anterior thalamus have more direct connections with the hippocampi.

The patient HM had widespread bilateral damage to the medial temporal lobe. Some patients who have had unilateral temporal lobectomy become amnesic following their surgical procedure. However, when this occurs it is assumed that the contralateral, unoperated hippocampus has a silent or unrecognised lesion. In other words the patient has been unwittingly been given a bilateral lesion. This does not happen often but when it does, and the brain has been available at post-mortem, this situation of a bilateral lesion has been confirmed.

In order to avoid this amnesic consequence, and at the same time indicate the location of language (left, right hemisphere or bilateral), patients are given a Wada test (intracarotid sodium amytal procedure) prior to surgery (Jones-Gotman, Rouleau, & Snyder, 1997). Dr Wada initially researched this method on monkeys and it was eventually adopted as a presurgical technique to pre-empt post-surgical amnesia. During this rather dramatic procedure one brain hemisphere (same side as surgery but sometimes the other side as well, separately) is anaesthetised, in an attempt to simulate the effects of the removal of a temporal lobe. A patient who is found to be amnesic under these conditions signals that there might be a lesion in the other hippocampus, the one that is not to be removed. In this procedure the catheter from which the anaesthetising agent issues is presented usually to the internal carotid artery in the brain. The procedure uses a plastic catheter, which is inserted into the femoral artery below the groin

[2] It is now believed that additional medial temporal lobe areas were also damaged (Squire et al., 1989).

and is persuaded upwards by the radiologist using a radiological technique, which provides an outline of the arteries (arteriogram) to trace the position of the catheter. The anaesthetic agent is then presented to the arteries in one hemisphere (e.g. middle cerebral artery). Ideally, the posterior cerebral artery should be the direct target since this artery sweeps forward and irrigates the hippocampus more directly; however this is less commonly done because this more precise location of the catheter is associated with greater risk to the patient. The neuropsychologist has around $1\frac{1}{2}$–2 minutes in which to test the patient. The patient may be drowsy and is likely to be aphasic when the left hemisphere is anaesthetised. Therefore the patient may have to point in a recognition format in order to show any memory. Needless to say, the procedure lacks reliability and patients who fail on one occasion may pass on another. Nevertheless, it is the only safeguard against amnesia that is available at the present time and the correct use of memory items, e.g. objects, may show very useful results and increase the accuracy of postoperative prediction (see Dade & Jones-Gotman, 1997, and other papers in this special issue). This test is discussed further in Chapter 6.

Research with monkeys has confirmed the human experience that bilateral lesions to memory structures may cause more severe memory impairment (Mishkin, 1982). Squire (1992) reviews more recent work with monkeys showing that the more extensive the lesion to the hippocampal formation the greater the degree of anterograde amnesia. Research by Zola-Morgan and Squire and colleagues illustrates that damage to the parahippocampal gyrus, which allows the hippocampus communication with unimodal (primary and secondary sensory areas) and polymodal areas of the cortex (tertiary association areas), results in more severe anterograde amnesia (Squire, 1992). It is of interest to note that HM had a similar area excised, that is, the hippocampal complex including the amygdala and adjacent parahippocampal areas.

Of recent interest is a type of amnesia referred to as retrosplenial amnesia. For some time it has been known that bilateral occlusion of the posterior cerebral artery results in amnesia and this

has been researched in monkeys (Bachevalier & Mishkin, 1989). This amnesia is assumed to be due to a lack of irrigation of the hippocampi on both sides. However, some agnosic patients (see DM in Chapter 2) have amnesia after a unilateral lesion on the left (Carlesimo, Casadio, Sabbadini, & Caltagirone, 1998). There have even been some reports of amnesia following a right posterior cerebral arter infarct (Yasuda et al., 1997). The location for the critical lesion in these cases may be a retrosplenial one (posterior to the splenium of the corpus callosum. The reason for this is poorly understood but is is thought to be due to a disconnection between the semantic system and the hipocamppi. It is of interest that these cases often additionally have associative agnosia (Carlesmo et al., 1998) and may be on a circuit that is activated with prefrontal areas during the acquisition of memory (Shallice et al., 1994). This is an area of current research interest.

While the hippocampal and parahippocampal areas are clearly important to memory, the amygdala seems to be less important. Studies reported by Squire (1992) indicate that additional bilateral damage to the amygdala did not induce more severe amnesia.

The amygdala has, been found to have a rather specialised role in the remembering of emotional faces (Markowitsch et al., 1994; Young et al., 1995). This structure also has a more general role in the processing of emotional information and emotional response (see Chapter 9 for a further discussion).

Even quite discrete lesions within the area of the hippocampus may be sufficient to cause amnesia. As indicated earlier, bilateral lesion in the cell area CA1 of the hippocampus has eventuated in amnesia in animal models and individual patients who have suffered from anoxia (Parkin & Leng, 1993, p. 83; Zola-Morgan et al., 1986). Anoxia due to attempted suicide (e.g. strangulation, carbon monoxide poisoning), cardiac arrest, and other causes may result in ischaemia within the more vulnerable hippocampal area (Medalia et al., 1991) (See Box 5.3).

Finally, the importance of the mammillary bodies and the fornices should not be ignored;

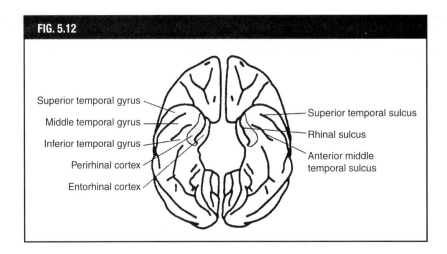

FIG. 5.12

Superior temporal gyrus
Middle temporal gyrus
Inferior temporal gyrus
Perirhinal cortex
Entorhinal cortex

Superior temporal sulcus
Rhinal sulcus
Anterior middle temporal sulcus

Position of the perirhinal and the entorhinal cortex. The polymodal association areas responsible for analysing objects (end-point of the "what" pathway) feed into the perirhinal cortex and then to the entorhinal cortex and the hypocampus. It is therefore an object recognition input rather than a spatial information process. Spatial attributes are believed to have a greater input via the parahippocampal gyrus (Reprinted from Buckley and Gaffan, 1968, with permission from *Neuropsychologia*). See Figure 5.8 for the relationship of the this area to the extended hippocampal complex.

implicated in these spatial memory tasks, which are seen to involve recall, and Aggleton and Saunders describe these as the extended hippocampal complex. The subiculum of the hippocampus projects to the anterior thalamic nuclei and the hippocampus also projects to the mammillary bodies via the fornix (see Table 5.1). Severe memory impairment in humans following bilateral lesions to the anterior thalamus and fornix (Gaffan, 1994; Gaffan et al., 1991) has been reported, although this is relatively rare. The animal literature suggests that when more than one lesion exists within this extended system there is an incremental affect on the animal's memory.

Aggleton and Saunders (1997) argue from a retrospective analysis that this division in animal research can be made also in human research. However, the human literature is not so supportive of their theory. A study by Miller, Lai, and Munoz (1998) has failed to endorse the Aggleton and Saunders proposal. This study of temporal lobectomy patients found little difference on two-choice recognition between patients with additional lesions to the entorhinal cortex compared to those without such a lesion. Also, Manns and Squire (1999) have found impaired performance

on two clinical tests of recognition memory (doors and people test) in patients with isolated hippocampal damage. However it is of interest that children who have severe hippocampal damage early in life have relatively intact recognition on these tests (Vargha-Khadem, Gadian, et al., 1997). In fact, the few cases of early-onset hippocampal damage suggest that these patients have developed a great deal of scholastic knowledge despite an amnesic level of performance on recall tests of new learning. Therefore even if Aggleton and Saunders' theory fails to apply obviously to the human amnesia literature the adaptive process shown by young amnesic patients may support a version of their theory in which familiarity recognition may be taken over by extra-hippocampal structures.

Forgetting and amnesia
There is a distinction between difficulty in learning (storing) something and the forgetting rate once something has been learned. For example, in experiments testing forgetting, without manipulating interference, the typical forgetting curve is evidenced. First found by Hermann Ebbinghaus (1885), one of the founders of a modern experi-

TABLE 5.1	
A broad description of the two systems within the consolidation system	
Structures supporting familiarity recognition	Perirhinal and Entorhinal cortex and medial thalamus
Structures supporting retrieval of context within recognition and recall	Hippocampal complex, fornix, mammillary body and anterior thalamus (extended hippocampal system)
See Aggleton and Saunders (1997) for a more detailed description of the connections).	

mental approach in memory, this curve describes most forgetting taking place over the first hour and levelling out at 8 hours. Ebbinghaus used the rather artificial material of word syllables. More ecologically valid material with more personal relevance, such as the memory for classmates in high school, may have a more gradual forgetting curve (Bahrick, Bahrick, & Wittilinger, 1975). Forgetting rates may also be increased in the presence of interference and may merely decay over time without interference (see Baddeley, 1997, for a discussion). Interference is increased by making the interference material more similar to the to-be-remembered material.

The difficulty of comparing forgetting rates in patients with different severity of memory disorders lies in the initial need to increase the various groups' memory to an equivalent level. This is necessary since a higher level of initial learning may give one group an advantage over the other; it cannot be assumed that a low level of memory has a similar forgetting curve to high levels of memory. One method of gaining this equivalence is to present the material longer to the more memory-impaired group, e.g. 25 seconds compared to 1 second. This works to differentially increase initial levels of learning for the memory-impaired group. There are other difficulties, for example in knowing when to start the interval of retention—before or after the presentation. This makes findings in this area difficult to appraise. Huppert and Piercy (1979) provided the most careful pioneering work in this area, with the surprising evidence that amnesic Wernicke–Korsakoff patients had a remarkably similar for-

getting rate when compared to controls. These researchers and others have argued that temporal lobe-based memory impairment is associated with a faster forgetting rate, but this has not been found in most recent studies (e.g., Kopelman & Stanhope, 1997) (see Figure 5.13). Perhaps the main certainty is that when forgetting is tested by recognition, e.g. two-choice, then memory decay curves are remarkably similar for Wenicke–Korsakoff and amnesic patients with temporal lobe lesions and controls when the periods tested vary from delays of 1 minute to 20 minutes (Kopelman & Stanhope, 1997). However, when recall is required and the material has to be retrieved, then the memory-impaired and amnesic patients appear disadvantaged when compared to controls. Nevertheless, the exaggerated forgetting in the case of recall is subtle when compared to the impaired acquisition of information (Kopelman & Stanhope, 1997).

Of course, the retrieval mechanisms required of recall may depend on structures other than just the consolidation system and when patients with often diffuse lesions are tested there is some uncertainty in estimating the cause of these differences.

Summary

Much of this section is summarised within Box 5.3 on page 248, which sets out the various types of lesions and neurological disorders associated with amnesia. Amnesia may be associated with *isolated* thalamic lesions although this is relatively rare and therefore the role of the thalamus within the consolidation system is still poorly

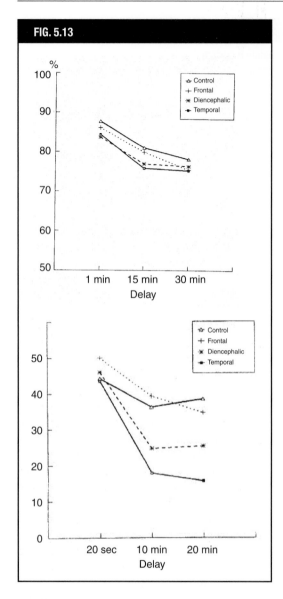

FIG. 5.13

Forgetting curves for patient groups when recognition and recall are required. The forgetting rates only differed from controls in the recall condition (reprinted from Kopelman & Stanhope, 1998, with permission from Elsevier Science).

executive influence such that the amnesia may show a lack of judgement either from a high rate of false positives, e.g. check that an item has been recognised when it was not presented or as manifested in a lack of insight into their own amnesia. These "frontal amnesia" patients show poor organisation and consistency between learning trials. They have difficulty in judging the context of the information when they do show some learning. They are able to show some learning of information when they make simple familiarity judgements, e.g. two-choice recognition, but have great difficulty in judging when, where, or how recently they have seen the item. This finding has led to a theory that attributes their amnesic condition to a failure to retrieve the context of learning.

The animal research referred to above suggests further reasons for caution. Aggleton and Saunders provide a theory, which is as yet not supported by the human literature. Their suggestion is that lesions to different areas of the thalamus might alter the nature of the amnesia. The mammillary bodies and the anterior thalamus have direct connections to the hippocampus via the fornices and it has been suggested that these structures together may represent an extended hippocampal system. However, there are more substantial connections between the medial thalamus and the rhinal cortex (the area of the cortex that receives projections from the hippocampus) which might have special relevance to the judgement of familiarity. The connections between these areas are more complex than suggested above and many connections are overlapping (see Aggleton & Saunders, 1997).

The hippocampal complex contributes to consolidation in an additive way to memory impairment. The greater the number of damaged structures within the extended hippocampal structures, the greater the amnesia. These structures may be differentially involved in amnesia but these roles have not, as yet, been clearly identified in humans.

Forgetting is technically described as the loss of memory over time. Amnesic patients have the greatest difficulty in storing new memories but have less problem retaining that information once it has been stored. Nevertheless, while forgetting

understood. There are some amnestic syndromes that show an amnesia which is likely to be influenced by frontal dysfunction through direct damage or from a hypothesised disconnection between the consolidation system and the frontal structures. Such patients show an undermined as tested by two-choice recognition appears to be normal, the forgetting rate is worse for some amnesic patients when recall is required. To some extent these variable results might be predicted. Recall and other forms of memory retrieval demand additional skills compared to memory alone. For example, the impaired organisational skills of the frontal patients might be expected to undermine recall more than recognition. The interaction of frontal dysfunction and the consolidation system are further discussed in the next section when retrieval and forgetting of longer-term, remote memories are discussed.

THEORETICAL PERSPECTIVES ON RETROGRADE AMNESIA

The unreliability of past memories

The amnesic patients referred to so far have all had ongoing difficulties storing new memories into the LTMS. They cannot learn new information after the illness or injury and therefore have anterograde amnesia. Retrograde amnesia is an inability to recall memories stored prior to the illness or accident.

Measurement of retrograde amnesia is not an easy process. We are reminded of some of our past memories through discussions with friends or because something in the media has cued the memory. However, every time we recall these old memories we may subtly change them for various reasons relating to our feelings or experience at the time of recollection. A substantial amount of research looking at the unreliability of witness testimony would support this view (Belli & Loftus, 1996; Loftus, Miller, & Burns, 1978).

In the case of memories recalled in adulthood which have been stored in childhood the intervening growth of neurones within the brain and their interconnections will have significantly changed. This is one theory for the cause of lost early memories, e.g. before 3–5 years of age, a phenomenon referred to as "infantile amnesia" (Baddeley, 1997, p. 220). From the psychological perspective we can never recreate our perspective at the time we first stored the memory. Our under-standing of events when we are young, "when Christmas trees were tall", is different from our adult understanding. Therefore old memories are often gradually distorted or updated over the years to fit with the adult memory structure and perspective. The effect is similar to the game of "Chinese whispers", which involves passing a whispered message form one person to another. The kinds of results are illustrated in the story of the general who told his adjutant on the battlefield to pass on the urgent message "Send reinforcements, we are going to advance." After the message was passed on several times a bemused commander eventually received the message "Send three and four pence, we are going to a dance."

While longitudinal studies on the accuracy of memory recall are scarce, there is evidence to support the unreliability of past memories. Ulric Neisser, a noted cognitive psychologist, has researched the deceptive nature of past memories, even when they can be extraordinarily vivid (Neisser, 1982; Neisser & Harsch, 1992). Neisser's first hint that these types of memories may not be reliable came when investigating one of his own memories. He had a clear memory of an incident in his childhood when he was watching a baseball game on television. The programme was interrupted by a newsflash that the Japanese had bombed Pearl Harbour. He then remembered going upstairs and telling his parents. He remembered all this clearly as if it was a direct recording of the event. This kind of vivid memory is referred to as a "flash-bulb" memory (not to be confused with a photographic memory). However, later he realised that the memory must have been at least partly false since there were no baseball games on television at that time of the year on television. This kind of realisation prompted him to conduct a study in which subjects were asked what they were doing just at the time they heard of the Challenger space shuttle disaster (Neisser & Harsch, 1992). As a result of the publicity preceding the NASA launch there were many reasons to think that the disaster would result in similar "flash-bulb memories" to those associated with the assassination of John F. Kennedy. Subjects were asked what they were doing at the time they heard the news. They were asked first just after the event and then later at a follow-up, 3 years later. At 3 years after the event most had distorted versions of their activities of the time. A quarter had quite different versions of the original event and many of these were convinced of the validity of their false memories. Some of these false memories were quite dramatic, e.g. running through a dormitory screaming out the news, and they were often astonished when they viewed the true version of their activities in their own handwriting.

How these changes occur is not certain but an interference theory would suggest that each time we recall a remote memory it is changed subtly to fit with our present knowledge system and our expectations. However, the extent to which this occurs may depend on other factors such as the initial motivation to recall accurately and the personal significance of a memory. The accuracy of a memory may increase if we wish to retell the story about that memory a number of times just after the event. Under these conditions we may then retain reasonable accuracy, as did the Californian earthquake subjects in a similar experiment a year and a half after the event (Neisser et al., 1996). There was no relationship between the level of subjective arousal and accuracy of later recall in this study, suggesting that this was not the factor that was influential in this study. Neisser speculates that because persons involved in this earthquake commonly regaled friends with their version of what they were doing at the time, these memories were rehearsed frequently just after the event and were consequently less vulnerable to interference.

Sometimes changes in brain structure in adulthood, such as traumatic brain injury, may interfere further with the accuracy of recalled memories from our past. Even when the patient has recovered from a period of retrograde amnesia, they may misplace memories in time (Whitty & Zangwill, 1977). Again we have cause to ponder the reliability of remote memory recall in the case when an important traumatically brain-injured witness is called to give evidence on events that occurred just prior to a particular fateful accident.

Unless we have access a number of significant persons who have shared the patient's past life events, autobiographical remote memories may be difficult to verify. There are no guarantees that the personal memories are accurate, or indeed that they occurred. This inability to check many of our memories led to criticisms of some interesting experiments by Wilder Penfield at the Montreal Institute of Neurology. Penfield mapped the cortex to identify the function of areas of the brain prior to brain surgery. Such mapping was achieved by giving a mild electrical stimulation within the exposed brain while the patient was conscious. The brain itself is insensitive to pain, so the patients were able to freely report any experiences they might have had at the time of stimulation. Patients sometimes had what he referred to as "flashbacks". For example, he reports that when he stimulated one patient in the exposed hippocampus, the female patient MM declared, "A familiar memory—the place where I hang my coat up—where I go to work" (Penfield & Roberts, 1959, p. 47). Most of these flashbacks were of inconsequential events and reported as if the person were actually re-experiencing the situation. Many of the areas that elicited these reports were within the temporal lobe, which is not out of keeping with modern theory implicating this area as a storage place for memories, but these accounts could have been explained as visual or auditory hallucinations—although, in the above case, Penfield was persuaded that this report was a bona fide memory and refers to the work of his colleague, Brenda Milner, showing the relationship between the hippocampi and the storage of memory (at that time the case of HM).

It is of interest that on one occasion when Penfield stimulated areas around the junction of the *right* occipital and temporal lobes, the patient responded by reporting a sudden feeling of familiarity that she had been through the operation before. This was, of course, not the case and Penfield interprets this experience as a feeling of *déjà vu*, which is now known as a cardinal sign of *right* temporal lobe epilepsy. Unfortunately, the origins and the nature of many of these fascinating reports are uncertain but the work is a tribute to the early pioneering skills of this great neurosurgeon.

While assessment of the reliability of auto-biographical events provides a challenge, the use of public events, which can be verified by past news reports, also has problems. Items within such a test must be of equivalent difficulty. Also some events cannot be used because they are frequently rehearsed as part of our history or in quiz games. Despite these and many other difficulties, questionnaires have been developed to show clear evidence that when brain damage has occurred there is often a temporal gradient of recall whereby older memories are relatively better preserved. That is, people remember information around the time of their childhood with greater ease when compared to the years just prior to the disease or accident. This retrograde amnesia curve is referred to as the temporal gradient.

The nature of retrograde amnesia and the influence of the hippocampus

Many amnesic patients have both anterograde and retrograde amnesia, but the anterograde amnesia is often most salient and the retrograde amnesia harder to detect. The most common clinical co-occurrence of anterograde and retrograde amnesia is in the case of TBI (see Box 5.4). In such cases, where retrograde amnesia exists, it will typically shrink after a period of recovery so that the only memory loss is for events just prior to the accident. Sometimes the period of retrograde amnesia is longer but unless they are suffering dementia patients are invariably able to remember who they are, where they went to school and other broad information about themselves that has been consistent throughout there lives, e.g. birth date. The soap opera character who has difficulty remembering his or her own past and identity, and yet is able to remember a social engagement and chat intelligently over a candle-lit dinner, does not exist in reality.

While anterograde amnesia is frequently accompanied by retrograde amnesia, it is extremely rare to find retrograde amnesia without some kind of anterograde memory. When this does occur to any degree, the clinician is often reasonably suspicious. The complaint may sometimes be a cover for some criminal or other unpalatable behaviour. The author came across this with a young man who claimed amnesia for the event of stealing a car and another who had assaulted his father-in-law during this period; both were found to be malingering on tests.

This association whereby retrograde amnesia is in some way dependent on the presence of anterograde amnesia may provide a valuable clue to the mechanism of some types of retrograde amnesia. Squire (Squire 1992; Squire & Zola, 1997) proposes a theory that explains this relationship and the finding that more recent remote memories are more vulnerable within retrograde amnesia. His view is that retrograde (before the event) memories, which are more recent, are less consolidated and therefore more vulnerable to destruction than more remote memories, which are well rehearsed and consolidated. Further, he proposes that the more recent memories are more reliant on the hippocampal structures for retrieval. Squire notes that, within certain limits, there appears to be a relationship between the severity of anterograde amnesia and the severity of retrograde amnesia for the *more recent* retrograde memories (Squire, 1992, p. 217). In other words the ability to consolidate new memories (hippocampus) is related to the retrieval of recent retrograde memories, which also depends on the hippocampus and the evidence for retrograde amnesia. Retrograde remote memories may be only partially interfered with by minor hippocampal damage. Thus a patient with isolated damage within area CA1 of the hippocampus tends to have very little, if any, retrograde amnesia, while more extensive damage to the hippocampus and the related adjacent cortical structures would be associated with greater retrograde amnesia (Zola-Morgan et al., 1986).

In support of this view, Zola-Morgan and Squire (1990) conducted an experiment in which monkeys learned a discrimination task to a high-accuracy criterion, on different stimuli, at different intervals prior to surgery. Different intervals of 2–16 weeks prior to surgery were chosen so that the effect of extended consolidation (16 weeks interval) was compared to 2 weeks interval (very little time for consolidation of memory). It was found that the control monkeys were best at recognising the stimuli learned most recently, in

---

> **Box 5.4.   Post-traumatic amnesia and retrograde amnesia following traumatic brain injury**
>
> The presence of anterograde amnesia and retrograde amnesia is sometimes associated with head injury or TBI. Many cases of TBI show evidence of anterograde amnesia. This term covers and includes the period just following the accident when the patient is in a disoriented state. The period of disorientation within anterograde amnesia is referred to as Post-traumatic amnesia (PTA). When a patient is reliably out of PTA it is apparent that there is a loss of memory for events during periods of PTA. When the patient is reliably out of PTA (the patient may slip in and out towards the end), retrograde amnesia may be tested.
>
> The patient may initially have difficulty recalling their activities on the days preceding the accident; memories may be patchy, with "islands" of intact memory. The islands may not recover in strict chronological sequence (Whitty & Zangwill, 1977). The period of retrograde amnesia may, however, shrink so that eventually the patient may only have difficulty remembering the events in the final few seconds or minutes leading up to the accident. However, there are many individual differences in this process (Schacter & Crovitz, 1977) and with more exacting testing, using a questionnaire, there may be more remote memory impairment than is suggested by informal history taking. The period of PTA is taken as the period of coma plus the period of disorientation.

the manner of the typical forgetting curve. However, the monkeys with bilateral lesions to the hippocampal and parahippocampal areas showed the inverse relationship, with the material that was learned at the greater interval (prior to testing) being better remembered. In other words, the results are in keeping with the view that lesions to the hippocampal complex interfere with the consolidation process, thereby explaining the finding that the most recent retrograde memories are more vulnerable (See also Yoneda, Mori, Yamashita, & Yamadori, 1994).

For humans this period of extended consolidation in which the memories are vulnerable to disturbance are seen, according to this theory, to last as long as 3 years after storage. Although this is somewhat controversial HM, with his destruction of the hippocampus, had a retrograde amnesia of 3 years initially (Milner, 1970). Patients who undergo bilateral electroconvulsive therapy (ECT) also show memory retrograde memory impairment, which is assumed to be related to disturbance of hippocampal functioning. Thus retrograde amnesia has a temporal gradient that may[3] show a gradual reduction of retrograde amnesia. This is assumed not to be measurable prior to the 3-year period (Squire, Slater, & Chace, 1975). Peter Milner's (1989) adaptation of Hebb's model, described earlier, fits well with this view. Milner sees the soft synapses being set up within the limbic system and the hippocampus,

while the hard synapses are created within the cortical areas. He also proposes that if there is damage or other insult to the areas within the cortex, the memories represented by those synapses will be lost.

Let us make two predictions from Squire's theory. First, patients with bilateral damage to the hippocampus will have a limited retrograde amnesia for information that is not completely consolidated. There seems to be some support for this, as discussed above. Second, the theory predicts that if there is additional cortical damage in the cortical areas where memories are stored there will be additional retrograde amnesia. Certainly in disorders such as *some* herpes simplex encephalitis patients (Cermak & O'Connor, 1983) and Alzheimer's dementia (Beatty, Salmon, Butters, et al., 1988) there is a more complete retrograde amnesia, although some early, perhaps more redundant memories, are preserved. This is in keeping with the Squire–Milner view since in this situation recent retrograde memories are associated with damage to the hippocampal complex—associated with "soft" synapses—and more remote retrograde memories are associated with more extensive cortical structures and "hard" synapses.

So far the proposal has been made that the consolidation system also acts as a structure involved in the retrieval of recent retrograde memories, hence the association: severe anterograde loss of recent retrograde memories. One can predict that if the usually more vulnerable hippocampi are preserved but large cortical areas are damaged then more remote retrograde mem-

---

[3] The severity of anterograde and retrograde amnesia following ECT has been found to be related to many factors, such as the size of the voltage used and the placement of the electrodes (bilateral > unilateral left > unilateral right).

ories may be impaired but the patient would have preserved memory both following the injury (no anterograde amnesia) and preserved recent retrograde memories. A few such cases have started to emerge that might fit this description (Kapur et al., 1992; Markowitsch et al., 1993; Calabrese et al., 1996).

However, there are some results that are less easy to explain with the Squire theory. For example, there are some patients who appear to have a flat retrograde amnesia curve. That is, they appear to remember events or information equally poorly whether it occurred early or late during their lives. Huntington patients show a flatter retrograde amnesia compared to Alzheimer patients (Beatty et al., 1998). Therefore, the influences contributing to retrograde amnesia are clearly more complex and perhaps the more anterior damage of the Huntington patients involves a retrieval mechanism that applies to both recent and remote memories. There is also an emerging literature that has found a dissociation between autobiographical memory (memory for personal life events) and memories that are more easily attributable to semantic memory. In a PET scan study by Conway et al. (1999) the subjects were given a word such as *cinema* from which they were required to recall a personal event that came to mind. They give the following example of a response:

When did I go to the cinema a lot? When I was a student. I lived in a student hall near Russell Square and we used to go to the art cinema there and I remember sitting in the dark in big red seats watching *The Spirit of the Beehive*.

Subtracting control tasks, which included a pre-learned paired-associate task that gave the patients a stem, the authors found two interesting findings. The first was the left frontal activation, which might be expected given the generative nature of this task (see GRAM discussed earlier). They also found that both recent and remote autobiographical memories retrieved involved activation of the hippocampi. There are now reported cases encouraging the view that auto-biographical memories may be dissociated from semantic memories. For example, Hunkin et al. (1995) report a patient who had impaired auto-biographical memory but was able to recall personal and public information. This does not discount Squire's proposal for the retrieval of semantic memories; for example, HM was able to name objects and had satisfactory information and vocabulary scores according to the Wechsler Intelligence Scale. Therefore retrieval of some remotely learned information is not dependent on the hippocampus. However, it is likely that Moscovitch and Nadel's (1998) multi-trace theory, which proposes a greater hippocampal dependence on retrieval, is relevant to the retrieval of detailed autobiographical material given the results to date. It should be noted that when recollecting a personal event from one's past life there is often a problem-solving component and possibly a search through various schemas representing such events (see Grafman's schema theory in Chapter 3). It might be predicted that a selective search process is not used merely for auto-biographical memories but also for any past memories that require details from the past. It would be predicted that the hippocampus and the prefrontal cortex must work in concert to produce this detailed information. When such structures are not intact then the detail may be lost and perhaps only the "gist" of what has happened remains. Do those patients who were previously described as making false-positive recognition mistakes have a similar problem? No doubt this relationship will be researched in the future.

Patterns of retrograde amnesia following thalamic damage and other disorders

Finally, these theories concerning the retrieval of remote and retrograde memories make a prediction that amnesics with *isolated* thalamic damage will show no appreciable retrograde amnesia. Patient NA (Cohen & Squire, 1981), who had damage to the left thalamus following an accident when a fencing foil accident entered his nostril,[4]

---

[4] Although it is now believed that additional medial temporal lobe areas were also damaged (Squire et al., 1989). As indicated above, a minority of cases with isolated thalamic damage have been shown to have no measurable retrograde amnesia.

and patient BY (Winocur et al., 1984), who had a bilateral infarct, were reported to have little and no retrograde amnesia respectively. There is also a case reported by Kapur et al. (1996) who presented with anterior thalamic lesions (rather than dorsomedial) and, as these authors suggest, a more extensive type of disconnection from connecting systems (including the hippocampus) might be required to produce retrograde amnesia. Clinically, however, the more common experience is that amnesia associated with thalamic lesions is also often accompanied by retrograde amnesia (Hodges & McCarthy, 1995) and some of these vascular and tumour-related cases show a temporal gradient, that is, recent retrograde memories were more affected than more remote earlier memories. These patients have relatively intact hippocampi so neither these theories can readily explain the failure to retrieve recent retrograde memories unless one assumes that the hippocampus and other structures are de-aroused due to thalamic damage.

At one time a possible explanation for the thalamic Wernicke–Korsakoff temporally graded retrograde amnesia was seen as being due to poor storage of memories. Since most Wernicke–Korsakoff patients have a history of chronic alcoholism, constant inebriation may have interfered with the storage of memories even before the onset/diagnosis of disease. However, as a "strong" hypothesis, this explanation has become less popular.

The first evidence against the poor storage theory involves the case of university professor PZ (Butters, 1984) who wrote his autobiography just prior to the onset of the symptoms of the alcoholic Wernicke–Korsakoff syndrome. His autobiography showed no obvious evidence of temporally graded retrograde amnesia just before the onset of the disease, and therefore the storage of memories up until onset appeared to be relatively intact. This evidence does not support the poor storage theory.

The second piece of evidence concerns the phenomenon of transient global amnesia (TGA). At present the cause of TGA is controversial (Goldenberg, 1995; Kritchevsky, Zouzounis, & Squire, 1997; the associated problems are transitory global anterograde amnesia, lasting minutes to a few hours). This is well illustrated with the case of a man who came to my notice through a neighbour. The man's wife had been severely berating him for felling a tree in his garden that his wife wanted to preserve. This is not such an uncommon story but for the fact that the husband denied having any memory of committing the deed. On the face of it, it appeared the man was making some kind of excuse; however, there were other recent events he could not remember and the man was considerably depressed by his apparent brief loss of memory. After a few hours his new learning appeared to recover. Interestingly, TGA is also associated with a temporally graded retrograde amnesia during the period of amnesia (Hodges & McCarthy, 1995). Again, a poor storage explanation is not useful because of the sudden onset of this disorder. This evidence seems to go against a theory suggesting origional poor storage as an explanation.

Finally, while the storage hypothesis is untenable because of its sudden onset and disappearance, it is also too long in the case of Wernicke–Korsakoff syndrome (sometimes two decades). This not easily explained by hippocampal dysfunction, according to Squire's proposal (Parkin, 1996, p. 214). Measuring retrograde amnesia is a difficult process for a number of methodological reasons, but the temporal gradient for Korsakoff patients does appear to go back at least 15 years, and in some studies longer. Korsakoff patients do have a multiplicity of lesions including frontal involvement (Shimamura, Jernigan, & Squire, 1988), which may allow a third mechanism for retrograde amnesia: the poor selection and discrimination of memories from a dysexecutive influence.

Some support for this dysexecutive view of temporally graded retrograded amnesia in Wernicke–Korsakoff syndrome comes from a study by Verfaellie, Reiss, and Roth (1995). They looked at levels of knowledge of vocabulary (measure of semantic memory) in Korsakoff and other amnesic patients. Although Korsakoff patients do not have semantic dementia and have equivalent WAIS-R vocabulary scores when compared to controls, Verfaellie and colleagues found that Korsakoff patients had poorer knowledge for particular words that were introduced into the English language more recently, prior to the onset of their disease, e.g. Velcro. Further, they found a temporal gradient, just like the temporal gradient for recall of the past events. Interestingly, they found a relationship between retrograde amnesia on their task and measures of executive function (WCST, Verbal Fluency Test, and Trails B; see Chapter 3). They found less evidence for a temporal gradient in a recognition test when compared to a recall test, which supported the view that retrograde amnesia with a temporal gradient was due to retrieval difficulty, also encouraging the dysexecutive nature of these patients' retrograde amnesia.

Summary

The retrieval of remote memories is clearly fraught with problems of reliability and its measurement provides a challenge. There are two emerging theories that attempt to explain retrograde amnesia. Retrograde amnesia is often present with a temporal gradient; that is, more remote past memories are better preserved. Damage to the hippocampal formation (hippocampus plus entorhinal cortex) and their projections (within the perirhinal and parahippocampal cortex) may be associated with relatively smaller periods of retrograde amnesia (up to 3 years). These structures are therefore seen to be important for retrieving memories in addition to storing them (Squire, 1992). Patients with lesions in these areas may have difficulty in recalling their most recent memories because they are dependent on the hippocampal complex for their retrieval, as the memories are still in the process of being consolidated. A hypothetical process, transforming memories from soft synapse cell assemblies within the hippocampus to hard synapses and independent representation within the cortex, describes this consolidation process.

A second theory (Moscovitch & Nadel, 1998) appears to be more relevant to detailed autobiographical memories. In this case detailed event-specific knowledge (ESK) (see Conway et al., 1999, for a description of a model) may require the hippocampus for retrieval and the frontal structures. The multi-trace model proposes that older ESK may be more difficult to recall because there are fewer surviving traces. Therefore a search process is necessary.

There is a third and last theory to explain the 15-year-old temporal gradient found in thalamic amnesias such as Wernicke–Korsakoff syndrome. In the case of patients with thalamic/diencephalic lesions, such as is found with Wernicke–Korsakoff patients, the problem may be aggravated due to poor retrieval associated with frontal dysfunction or a disconnection from frontal structures. It is possible that old memories are more resistant to forgetting, because older memories are more consolidated due to extra-rehearsal (Pitres, 1895) and they may need less organisation on retrieval. Such rehearsal may make these memories easier to retrieve because they are sourced by a relatively stronger memory trace, such strength being related to redundant storage within metaphorically "hard" synapses. Relationships found between tests of executive functioning and retrograde amnesia in these patients lend support to the prefrontal retrograde amnesia connection in Wernicke–Korsakoff patients. PET scan work (see Conway et al., 1999, for a brief review) suggests that an activation of the left dorsolateral and ventrolateral areas are important for the generative strategy involved in "dredging up" an ESK of an autobiographical memory.

A NEUROPSYCHOLOGICAL MODEL OF MEMORY

While at one time there were a considerable number of general models of memory that took into account memory functioning in its entirety, at the present time there is a tendency for modern theorists to provide more specialised models, e.g. models of WM, autobiographical memory. Because of this lack of direction at the present time a model is provided here as a means of making overall sense of the neuropsychological literature in this area. This will allow the student a base from which more complex formulations might be added.

The model illustrated below has attempted to recreate a dynamic picture of memory. The three functional units—the previously proposed WM consolidation system, and LTMS—are included in this model, although the executive system that was originally applied to the WM system now takes on a broader role with its extra involvement with the consolidation system. These units are referred to as functional because although they have associated neuroanatomical structures they are primarily identified here by their roles in encoding, storing, and retrieval of memories. Support for the model is supplied largely from arguments and description of studies supplied earlier. However, some new information is supplied below giving a neuroanatomical context for the revised model.

Working memory revisited

Earlier in this chapter there was the proposal of a model of WM that contained elements from different models of WM. Firstly, the views proposal by Cowan, Engle, Anderson, and others that WM was an activation of the LTMS was adopted. The nature of that activation was described as a focus of attention plus a fast-decaying component of any previously activated area. These combined activations will be referred to here as active memory. This is equivalent in its role to the old term of short-term memory, but this term gives a better representation of the theoretical formulation adopted here. Thus we may attend to the memory of an incident and bring it to consciousness within active memory; however, after attention has been focused away the remaining trace will decay, but it will be more or less enduring depending on the extent that it is assimilated into the LTMS. As indicated previously, Ericsson and Kintsch (1995) made the observation that we clearly remember the content of the book as we are reading it, even though as we are reading past information is being replaced by new information. If someone distracts us we are still able to "pick up the thread" and recall the semantic theme of what we have recently read. Given the discussion within the chapter on executive dys-

function the analogy of the directory schema is clearly important here. Certain areas of the association areas are activated by frontal structures that allow the new information (what we are reading) to be assimilated within themes that we already have stored in the LTMS.

It is assumed that in the same way we may attend to an external stimulus and with the mechanism of top-down processing (see Chapter 2) our LTMS will be activated and the percept will remain active as an image when we look away. The image is retained within consciousness in our active memory. With the need to work and manipulate the information within the active memory there is the need for an executive system (central executive) and with this additional component the new model of WM is complete. Creating a new memory is not of course merely a matter of activation. Depending on the novelty of the information the material may need rearrangement—modification of the existing store so that the new information is assimilated.

The analogy of a blowtorch was used for the interface between the LTMS and attentional processes. Active memory is seen as a combination of what is being attended to plus the remnant of previous activations. When the attentional blowtorch moves on, there remains a delay before the previous activated or remnant area dissipates; this may be a very brief period of decay in the case where unusual or meaningless information is presented but may be far longer if the information is thematically familiar. During the interval and before the information dissipates entirely it may be reactivated (strategically rehearsed, repeated, or imaged) and returned to consciousness.

The focus of attention, as it moves over the LTMS is directed by the central executive, or the executive system, as it has been broadly described in Chapter 3. Phonological, semantic, visuospatial, and other aspects of the LTMS may be accessed. It is likely that under normal circumstances the consolidation is also activated to a low degree. There is an assumption by some authors that conscious recollection requires activation of the hippocampus (Moscovitch, Goshen-Gottstein, & Vriezen, 1993). It is uncertain what is exactly meant by this, but within the model proposed here these patients show awareness of active memory as revealed by their self-report in STM experiments. Therefore, while there may be impaired consciousness of the *event* of learning after damage to the consolidation system, most authors would agree that this could be explained by the view that the consolidation of the event had not occurred in the first place. There also may be difficulty in consciously recalling events in detail even prior to the time of damage but this may be quite specific and not general to all memories (Milner, 1970). Therefore it may be argued that consciousness for memories may be augmented by the hippocampus.

Animal-based models of working memory

There are various definitions of WM which at one time was a source of irritation. Some animal cognitive neuroscience researchers seem to refer to WM as keeping something in mind, whereas researchers with human subjects seemed to require an extra dimension of a subsidiary or additional task while keeping information in mind. Researchers in functional imaging research have often used a "two-back" or "three-back" task, which shows a series of three items that are required to be maintained in memory. The subject is then asked to recognise or remember the "last but one item" (item before the last presented item) or the "last but two item". It should be noted that if the subject was asked to recall the last item then no executive requirement would exist and WM would not be tested. Cowan (1995, p. 100) describes WM as follows: "there is no reason to doubt that WM is based on that activated information along with central executive processes." Baddeley (1992) describes WM as "a brain system that provides temporary storage and manipulation of information necessary for such complex tasks as language comprehension, learning and reasoning." D'Esposito, Postle, and Rypma (2000), a functional imaging researcher, describes WM as "the short-term retention of information that is no longer accessible in the environment, and the manipulation of this information." Therefore there is some consensus that WM requires the short-term retention or temporary activation of an internal representa-

tion with some requirement of executive processes. This executive component may involve the manipulation of the information being maintained or some other potentially conflicting subsidiary task. These broad definitions cover a huge area of our everyday cognition, whether we are retrieving a memory, or involved with mental arithmetic or other problem-solving exercise. Sometimes we may be speaking while thinking of what we are going to say next; such a process would also require WM.

The design of WM tasks may depend on the context of the task to provide the WM component. Some tasks don't appear to be testing WM when the behaviour of a single trial is analysed, i.e. asking for a report or response to a presentation after a short unfilled delay. However, such tasks must be seen in the context of a series of trials that are very similar. It is almost certain that when this occurs the subject is not only responding to the active representation of what has just been presented, but is also inhibiting previous activations and responses to previous trials. In other words the executive component is required to dissociate and differentiate previous trials from the present trial. This is no doubt the case in the delayed response task used by such researchers as Patricia Goldman-Rakic.

The work of Goldman-Rakic (Goldman-Rakic, 1987; Goldman-Rakic & Friedman, 1991) and others has been influential in providing a model of prefrontal lobe function as it applies to area 46, the area surrounding the principal sulcus in the monkey. Goldman-Rakic and others at Yale University have worked with a paradigm that is quite simple in its conception. The paradigm, which supports the animal model, is described as follows:

A monkey sits in a cage and looks out on two dishes, one to the left and one to the right. The experimenter then places a piece of food in one of the two dishes under a cover in full view of the monkey. Then a shutter is brought down for a few seconds to obscure the view of the two feeding areas. When the two dishes with their covers are revealed again, the hungry monkey has a seemingly simple task of remembering which stimulus dish contains the food.

However, the monkey with a bilateral lesion in the area of the principal sulcus area (the mid-dorsolateral prefrontal cortex) just chooses the first dish that draws its attention. As Goldman-Rakic puts it, "Out of sight out of mind." There is nothing wrong with the choice when the food dishes remain in view or even on the first trial of this paradigm (no WM requirement; just reporting form active memory). Also, if the food dishes are clearly marked, e.g. with a star, the monkey is able to learn over trials that the food always turns up under that star, irrespective of the side of the star, and associative memory is therefore intact. The monkey with the mid-dorsolateral lesion only has difficulty when the internal representation of the stimulus has to be relied upon and the location of the food is changed over trials. This paradigm has been successfully used with human populations and patients with frontal dysfunction are especially challenged by variants of this task (Oscar-Berman et al., 1991).

Goldman-Rakic (1996) and colleagues have been able to map areas within the dorsolateral prefrontal cortex that relate to abilities on this delayed-response paradigm. By measuring the responses from individual neurones during this task and manipulating either the spatial constraints or the spatial and visual identification of the target, she has shown that:

1. Areas within the mid-dorsolateral cortex (areas 46 and 8) are specialised for keeping on-line the spatial attributes of the target (position of the target with respect to other stimuli). This area in the dorsolateral cortex has neural projections to the inferior posterior parietal lobe which as discussed in the previous chapter, has important mapping representations for spatial location.

2. Areas within the inferior convexity, the more ventral areas of the lateral prefrontal cortex (areas 12/45), are more obviously related to identification of the attributes of the target. If the original place of the food can be identified by a pattern or colour then

monkeys with lesions in this area have more difficulty. There is some continuity with what we have learned about the "what" pathway in previous chapters and this model. It is hypothesised that the end-point of the "what" pathway within the inferior temporal cortex links up with this more inferior area of the prefrontal cortex with a continued functional role to identify the target.

3. Areas within the prefrontal cortex area are divided according to the characteristics of the stimuli in the environment as described in paragraphs 1 and 2, but this information is directed to multiple brain areas specialised in sensory processing, memory processing, and motor movement processing. In other words, each specialised module has its own network of connections with other posterior areas representing memory (medial temporal lobe) spatial location (parietal cortex), and in terms of the author's own model of LTMS (various cortical areas within the association cortex such as the temporal lobe and parietal cortex) (see Figure 1.11 for a distribution of some of these connections). The important implication is that the prefrontal cortex, according to this model, is divided into modules according the attributes of the perceived object. The dorsal (upper) areas are used for spatial attributes, while the more ventral (lower) areas are important for identification of the object.

Contributions of functional imaging studies to modelling working memory

Most of these conclusions have been found to be true also of functional imaging studies with human subjects (Courtney, Petit, Haxby, & Ungerleider, 1998), with some modification and elaboration. These researchers support the view that the "what" and "where-action" pathways continue their specific analysis on to the prefrontal cortex in different contributions to WM. When human subjects are required to orient towards a stimulus or spatial location then the parietal–dorsolateral pathway (see Figure 5.14) is activated. According to Petrides and Pandya

FIG. 5.14

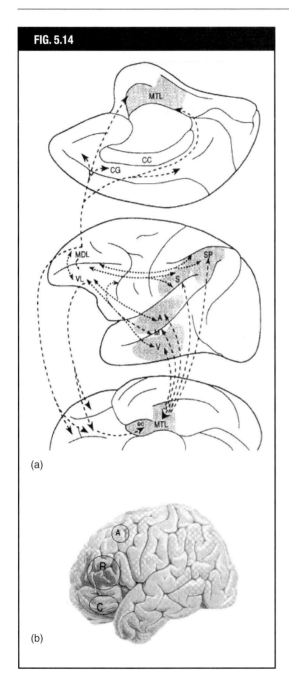

(a)

(b)

(a) Schematic diagram representing features of the Petrides model (reprinted from Petrides, M., Specialized systems for the processing of mnemonic information within the primate frontal cortex. *Philosophical Transactions of the Royal Society London B, 351,* 1455–1462. Copyright 1996, with permission from the Royal Society). The model proposes that information is received and selected at the mid-ventrolateral area (VL) in the monkey brain and is then transferred to the mid-dorsolateral area (MDL) for more abstract or higher-level processing. It can be seen that there is a circuit that includes the medial temporal lobe (MTL; memory) and the cortex of the temporal lobe, which has associations with the LTMS and the parietal cortex, which is important for defining a map of spatial location (inferior parietal cortex and motor movements, e.g. eye movements in the superior posterior parietal cortex. There are some differences in the location of the areas identified in 13(a) and those of the human brain 13(b).

When looking at 13(b) It is worth referring to Figure 1.5(a). It is now becoming clear that the functionally equivalent area of the monkey brain area 46 MDL actually includes some of area 9 in the human brain (see area B in part b). Also shown is the equivalent mid-ventrolateral area C. When considering connections with the inferior parietal cortex and the influence of this area in determining spatial location within WM, this area is evidently more posterior and superior in area 8, being on an apparent continuation with the frontal eye fields (see area A) (Petrides and Pandya, 1999; Pollmann & von Cramon, 2000).

(1999) and also work by Pollmann and von Cramon (2000), using event-related fMRI, the activation for locative WM may relate to an area described in Fig. 5.14 as area "A". This area overlaps with the activation involved in the orientation of eye movements in attention shift experiments.

Michael Petrides from Montreal Neurological Institute (e.g. Petrides, 1996) argues from research studies that the association of dorsolateral pathways with spatial information and ventrolateral pathways with objects is not consistent but rather depends on the amount of processing required of

match. Rypma and D'Esposito (1999) found that in the first encoding stage when the letters were extended there was more activation of the mid-dorsolateral area. During the delay period when the series of consonants were being maintained there was an activation of the left posterior areas, as found previously, the load of maintaining information in mind involved the association area. An additional analysis of individuals showed that the encoding overload that caused the mid-dorsolateral area was most likely related to the individual's WM capacity. Correlations between the reaction time of an individual and the extent of activation within the mid-dorsolateral area had a relatively high and significant correlation of $r = .76$ with their retrieval rate: the time taken to scan through the digits and recognise a match.

Finally, using the same paradigm they manipulated proactive interference by varying the relationship between two consecutive trials. For example, for trial 1 a series of letters would be presented, which included the letter "z" for example. After a delay the probe letter "z" was presented and the subject would judge whether it matched one of the letters in the sample. Then a second trial was given and this time the series did not contain the letter "z", but the probe letter "z" was shown again. With the letter "z" shown in the previous trial the subject would presumably restrain or inhibit the tendency to make a match. During these more confusing and interfering trials the mid-ventrolateral area was activated, suggesting a selective mechanism within this area (D'Esposito et al., 2000). An illustrated summary of these results is presented in Figure 5.15b. Petrides' adapted model is presented in Figure 5.14a. It may be seen that at the present time there is a converging view of prefrontal function within working memory—a view that started with the earlier macaque monkey work of Goldman-Rakic and has been elaborated on by Petrides' lesion work with monkey and human subjects. The present-day functional neuroimaging work tends to support the Petrides proposal but indicates that each position is to some extent complementary.

The role of the central executive

Most models provide that WM has a role in both manipulating temporary memory and also in retrieving and storing permanent memories. This has important consequences for how we view past findings in the literature. For example, some space in this chapter has been devoted to discussing the influence of frontal structures on memory. These influences are the same influences that may direct short-term remembering and activate the LTMS according to this model. It is implied by this model of LTMS activation that retrieval of consolidated memories takes place by the activation of these memories within the LTMS. The view that WM is involved with any information that reaches a level of conscious awareness, including the retrieval of long-term memories, is held by many researchers (Salamé & Baddeley, 1982). There has been a discussion about patients with lesions to the left dorsolateral prefrontal structures, who are more likely to show difficulty in monitoring and remembering the order of previously learned verbal information. Also, a similar problem with visuospatial remembering may occur following lesions to the same area in the right prefrontal lobe.

The executive influence is clearly overlapping with the previously described attentional executive system but there are also roles that are specific to memory such as control of the consolidation system. However, as indicated, it should be noted that WM and the retaining of information on-line are not seen as being dependent on the consolidation system. If, as is the case with amnesia, the consolidation system is destroyed, the model still allows for WM to function independently of this system (see Figure 5.16). The argument for executive control of the consolidation system comes from studies describing the executive influence on memory, discussed earlier in this chapter. Also, there is an extensive literature showing that performance following strategic and intentional learning is superior compared to incidental learning. Some of these intentional learning strategies may be relatively automatic and not reach consciousness within WM; it is nevertheless assumed that the medial temporal lobe is influenced by executive control during these states, and there are certain reciprocal pathways between the prefrontal cortex and the medial temporal lobe that would allow such influence (see Figure 5.14).

The executive system is seen to be important in the guiding of LTMS search and selection as part of the WM process. However, it is argued by some that WM is either not or only minimally required in many instances of learning (Moscovitch,

1994a; Potter, 1993). Often learning appears to be instantaneous, without any need for manipulation of material or obvious recoding of material. In such cases the executive system is still seen to be important in the attention process that is required to select one area of the LTMS as opposed to another. However, less attentional resource would be required and presumably less involvement of the consolidation system since the

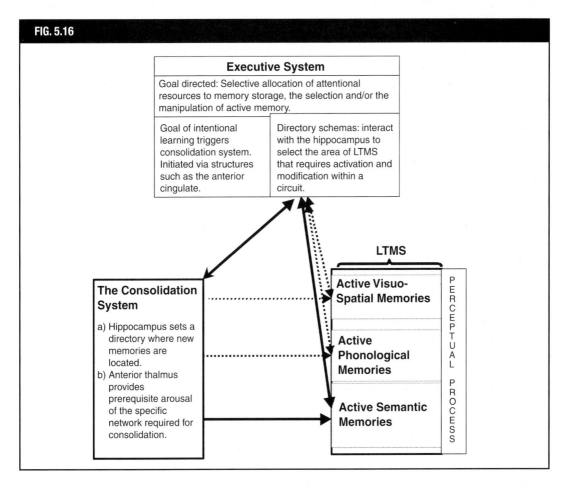

The active model of memory. The process of working memory is the activation of the LTMS under the control of the executive system. This is a limited-capacity system that allows a variable allocation of attentional resource to any of the areas depending on the goals of the organism. Global capacity limitations may reduce the allocation of resources to the consolidation system, active memory and its manipulation of other functions such as language or perception. Each of the units, e.g. consolidation system, LTMS, may be damaged to reduce attentional capacity within a more specific area within the system. In the example, the heavier lines to the semantic active memory illustrate an example when this activation is selected over the other two modalities. Task requirements dictate the degree to which any one modality is activated. Working memory is the combined involvement of the executive system and the various active LTM memory modules. It should be noted that working memory is not reliant on the consolidation system for its function.

structure representing the memory store would require less modification.

Finally, some comment should be made concerning the capacity of this system. There is a limited capacity of attention that has to be shared with perceptual processes and any other information processing (see Figure 5.16) at the executive level. Recent research suggests that these are separate but related processes (Haxby, Petit, Ungerleider, & Courtney, 2000; Morris, Paxinos, & Petrides, 2000). When people are so deep in thought that they look "straight through you" one might speculate that most of their capacity is being concentrated on internal WM rather than the perceptual analysis involving the external environment. At other times resources may be entirely allocated to the external environment, as in the case of soldering a circuit board or scoring a football goal.

It is assumed that attentional capacity within WM may be influenced at the global level by damage to the executive system. Limitations may be less specific and more related to poor selection processes and difficulties with dual tasking. Alternatively, attentional capacity may be limited at a local level when damage to a particular area of the LTMS may result in a limited-capacity active memory of that area. Such isolated active memory impairment might reduce the capacity of phonological active memory, for example. Already described are patients such as PV (see the description of our BR in Chapter 7). In this way a patient may have a limited-capacity phonological active memory but an intact visuospatial active memory. Therefore many of the findings that have previously been used to support more traditional models would be seen to give equal support an active memory model.

A similar model of capacity limitations confined to specific WM slave system(s) is discussed by Riddoch and Humphreys (1995). There are a number of studies that have confirmed this view of separate temporary store systems with normal subjects, some of which have been discussed above; these studies apply equally to the active memory model. What remains to be confirmed is that patients with dysexecutive signs affecting working memory have a general capacity limita-

tion on WM task performance. This certainly would be predicted given the results in this area so far (e.g., Alderman, 1996; Moscovitch, 1994a).

The consolidation system

The consolidation system strengthens new memories with a circuit that is described in Figure 5.14 for the monkey. Something similar is confirmed within the human brain in functional imaging studies. Some confirmation that the structures describe function in a network is evident from PET scan studies (e.g., Tulving et al., Craik, 1994), although hippocampal activation is sometimes difficult to detect. Amnesic patients have been PET scanned when attempting new learning. These scans have then been compared with those of normal subjects completing the same learning task. The amnesic patients show abnormal deactivation of frontal areas, the thalamus and hippocampus, thereby encouraging the view of memory as a network response involving specific integrated circuits (Fazio et al., 1992).

There is also the theory discussed in a previous section that the consolidation system is influential in retrieving memories under certain circumstances. It has been argued that the retrieval of recently stored information is more dependent on the hippocampi, but that this structure may also be required to retrieve the details of personal or autobiographical memories over a far longer period.

While the consolidation system may have its full effect in intentional learning under executive control, the consolidation system may also act automatically to store information that we were not intending to learn (Moscovitch, 1994a, 1994b). It is a well-replicated finding that intention to learn has an effect to improve memory over and above incidental learning, but there is also some control over what we intend to forget (Bjork, 1972). The active model of memory in Figure 5.16 allows that some aspects of WM may be intact while the consolidation system is no longer functional. As indicated, patients such as HM and Wernicke–Korsakoff patients may keep information on-line and maintain it briefly without being capable of consolidating memories, although it should be said that Wernicke–

Korsakoff patients do not have efficient temporary memories when the task challenges executive skills. These patients are, for example, vulnerable to proactive interference in tasks measuring temporary retention of material (see Butters & Cermak, 1977). Therefore, given the arguments concerning the dysexecutive memory performance of these patients one might predict impairment on WM tasks as a consequence of executive dysfunction. However, on tasks that are without an executive component such as forward digit-span these patients are not significantly impaired compared to controls (Butters & Cermak, 1977).

This activation of the LTMS without a consolidation system would allow for implicit remembering on the grounds that activation on its own strengthens existing memory structure. Remembering novel relationships would not be possible without the consolidation system, since this would require rearrangement and modification of the existing structure of the LTMS. However, lesser incremental modifications of existing structure may be possible and perceptual activations would make such activations stronger and more likely in the future. Therefore implicit memory may be described in this context by this model.

A reported case of a boy with amnesia following cardiac arrest is of interest in this respect. The associated anoxia caused significant damage to the hippocampal system when the boy was only 8 years old. Yet despite his amnesia he has been able to keep up with his peers at school in many areas, which would be assumed to be reliant on an intact consolidation system. His knowledge of such skills as mathematics is relatively intact. Therefore it is possible that the power of incremental learning of an implicit nature without a consolidation system may be underestimated (Broman, Rose, Hotson, & Casey, 1997; see also Vargha-Khadem, Gadian et al., 1997).

Long-term memory store
Many researchers have become interested in the interaction between WM and existing LTMS (see discussion in the first part of this chapter). Bad-

deley proposes that "Returning to the role of LTM in WM: one way of conceptualizing a hypothetical general retrieval system might be through the concept of the central executive. Such a system should be able to encode and retrieve information both from the slave systems and from temporary activated components of long-term memory" (Baddeley, 1996, p. 23). Therefore, although long-term storage of memories is dependent on the integrity of structures such as the hippocampus, memories may be made more permanent through strategies that take into account the nature of the existing LTMS. Elaborative rehearsal strategies, which seek out relationships between what is to be learned and what has already been stored in memory, are designed to take advantage of existing LTMS knowledge structures. Elaborative rehearsal and retrieval search may be two examples of how WM interacts with the LTMS (see the discussion on the levels of processing literature above).

The LTMS is described as a heterogeneous entity made up of various specialised stores or modules. This LTMS structure may be important to perception as well as new learning. A congruence between the sensory input and the contents of the LTMS would allow top-down processing and increased ease of perception and, if the material is required to be learned, increased ease of accommodation within the LTMS. Unusual novel material requires more bottom-up processing and more attentional resources, and will take longer to assimilate within the LTMS. WM has more involvement in the latter process since the information must be held on-line while relationships between the sensory input and the contents of the LTMS are sorted, manipulated, and selected.

Dynamic integration of the executive system, consolidation system and active memory within the the long-term memory store
The active memory model assumes that the central executive allows the priorities of learning to be achieved, by the selection, integration, and discrimination of memories within the LTMS. These "control processes" of memory must be directed in a flexible way by the central executive

in accordance with the nature of the to-be-learned or retrieved information, the goals, and context of the learning situation. Without the hypothetical central executive the learning process lacks direction and organisation. However, the goal of learning is just one of the many demands made on this system which may be used for problem solving and other tasks that require mental manipulation. It is also assumed by some authors (e.g. Shallice & Burgess, 1998) that the same executive processes that are used when there is a maintenance of information may also be deployed when there is no requirement of keeping information in mind. That is, for example, when problems are written down and diagrammed.

Without experience of what is being attended to, the objects around us would have no meaning, they gain meaning from top-down perceptual processing, which originates in the LTMS. It is likely that this process is separate but related to the WM process in that it is also dependent on dorsolateral frontal integrity.

This temporary activation of the LTMS does not necessarily lead to more permanent storage unless the consolidation system is also involved. The consolidation system "stamps" and consolidates the new information into the LTMS, and within this model may also be controlled in this process by the prefrontal cortex. More specifically, the basal forebrain may also provide neurotransmitter control of hippocampus activation. The cholinergic system, which has its source within the basal forebrain, influences attentional processes and probably plays an important role in enhancing and focusing on the information to be remembered (Baxter & Chiba, 1999; Coull et al., 1999). The model provides that some mechanism must coordinate the selection of the area of activation within the LTMS and at the same time influence the consolidation system to activate that same area(s) in order to modify it. Figure 5.14 which shows the neuronal networks of the monkey brain, show how these activations are achieved within a network. However, it remains likely, given this circuit, that LTMS may be activated without the involvement of the part of the circuit that involves the medial temporal lobe. Therefore these two, normally coordinated, activations must be separate since patients who have severe damage to the consolidation system are still able to focus attention on, and retrieve information from, the LTMS (stored prior to the onset of the disease).

The model presented here is influenced by other modular models of memory (Cowan, 1995; Moscovitch & Umilta, 1990; Schneider, 1993). The contribution here is an attempt to place the literature on WM and consolidation on a basis that is both simplified and integrated, which is in accordance with up-to-date knowledge of neuropsychology. This minimalist model will hopefully give the reader a starting point towards understanding this complex and controversial area.

6

Disorders of cerebral asymmetry

INTRODUCTION

Pure disorders of asymmetry are rarely found in clinical practice. They are most commonly found in stroke patients (Bogen, 1993), but even in these patients it may not be recognised because of the predominance of symptoms such as aphasia which appear concurrently. Nevertheless, the theoretical importance of this area outweighs practical considerations of this sort.

Prior to discussing a range of findings that relate to the asymmetry of the hemispheres it should be noted that there is a certain glamour associated with some of the findings in this area. The consequence of this is that some of the research findings are often quoted out of context in the popular literature. This has resulted in an inevitable oversimplification of the laterality of different functions between the two brain hemispheres. Persons who are researching and reviewing this area often make the point that many of the findings of laterali-sation often act to draw attention away from the more important need to realise that all func-tions depend on an integration of analysis pro-vided by both hemispheres (e.g. Levy, 1985). As Beaumont (1997) argues, there is room for scepticism when some of the methods used in laterality research are scrutinised. Beaumont proposes that "Where the influence of hemi-spheric specialization remains, the lateral asym-metries are small in magnitude and subject to considerable individual variability." (Beaumont, 1997 p. 111).

There is an enduring puzzle concerning the adaptive significance of there being two brain hemispheres rather than one. Solutions to this puzzle are usually sought in terms of natural selection and some authorities have suggested that an animal with two brain hemispheres may be more likely to survive and consequently pass on its genes if one hemisphere is damaged. This argument is less impressive if one considers that for two hemispheres, or even three, to be chosen over one, the change must be generally adaptive for the species. Therefore if severe damage to one side of the brain was a common occurrence and cause of death then one might concede that two hemispheres might be eventually be favoured over one. This would indeed be a violent world and for similar reasons you might expect us to have two hearts.

The difficulty in finding a reason for two hemispheres may be because it is based on some biological imperative unrelated to the environment. Bilateral organs are more common than single organs and perhaps this has its origin in cell mitosis and perhaps selective mechanisms for the instance of a single organ must be sort. Apart from these speculations, an equally puzzling and related finding is that most of the senses and movement are projected contralaterally to the opposite hemisphere. Only the olfactory bulbs, which are situated in the philogenically older parts of the brain, project mainly to the ipsilateral hemisphere. With the contralateral control of movements and contralateral sense reception there is a more obvious adaptive purpose since a fast reflexive motor response may be made by the same brain hemisphere that receives the relevant sensory information (Coghill, 1964). The left hemisphere, which controls the right arm, also receives the visual information from the right side. Without decussation (crossing over) and two eyes this would not occur, although this, of course, is hardly an argument for two hemispheres.

The contralateral control over ipsilateral control of movement for *simple* unimanual response is well documented from a number of sources (see Hartlage & Gage, 1997, for a review). There is also evidence according to cerebral blood flow using PET scan (e.g. Kawashima, Yamada, & Kinomura, 1993) that the left hemisphere is activated for right hand movements but that both ipsilateral and contralateral hemispheres are more likely to be involved in left hand responses especially when a series of movements is required. This would suggest that the left hemisphere is more often involved and somehow more important than the right for complex movements (this issue is further discussed in Chapter 8).

In confirmation of this apparent left hemisphere dominance, a little over 90% of us are right-handed for most manipulative tasks. Since our right hand is largely controlled by the left brain hemisphere, this suggests that there are left hemisphere structures that are important for complicated and dexterous acts. The left hemisphere is also dominant for language. This is known from studies of language disorders following strokes, the temporary effects of ECT (Pratt & Warrington, 1972), and also from work with a previously discussed clinical technique called the Wada test, which looks at the behavioural result of anaesthetising much of one hemisphere.

The Wada technique was named after its inventor and involves anaesthetising one brain hemisphere to simulate the effects of surgery. As discussed in Chapter 5 this method is often used with epilepsy patients prior to temporal lobectomy. Sometimes there is a concern that the contralateral hippocampus is not supporting memory functioning and that a loss of a temporal lobe on one side will result in a bilateral loss of function, resulting in an amnesia similar to that suffered by HM (see Chapter 5). The procedure is also used as a means of assessing the laterality or side of language. The surgeon will often be more sparing of areas within the temporal lobe if they realise that it is the language hemisphere. Usually, the complete loss of speech (aphasic arrest) is striking when the left hemisphere is anaesthetised; the patient is often only able to point when this occurs during testing.

Evidence from the different sources referred to above combine to reveal that nearly all of us (95–98%) who are right-handed have language housed in the left brain hemisphere. Therefore, the vast majority of people are both right-handed and have language in the left hemisphere of the brain. This preference for one limb over another throughout a species is rare. There are reports of dextrality (preference for the right) and sinistrality (preference for the left) in some species of monkey for particular tasks but the evidence is not strong. Typically an individual monkey has a paw preference but this is different from one individual to another. There is, however, some evidence of laterality in some species of birds. Nottebohm and colleagues (Nottebohm, 1979) have established that some species of songbirds, e.g. oscine passerine, are more likely to have their vocalisation interrupted with a left brain lesion. Also, some species of parrots have a preferred

TABLE 6.1

Speech lateralisation as related to handedness using epilepsy patients

Handedness	Number of cases	Left hemisphere	Right hemisphere	Bilateral
Right	140	96%	0%	4%
Left	122	70%	15%	15%

Reprinted from Rassmusen and Milner (1977), with permission from the New York Academy of Sciences.

"footedness" for certain tasks (Bradshaw, 1989). Nevertheless, despite these tendencies found in other species, a pervasive and consistent laterality of function appears to be peculiar to the human species.

There is also a tendency for arithmetic and gesture (communicative movements) conventions, such as American sign language, to be controlled from this same valuable left hemisphere. This has earned the left hemisphere a reputation of being analytical and Corballis has suggested that language, gesture and manual dexterity all have this analytical feature in common. All these functions are capable of being reducible to units that can be rearranged in a countless number of creative ways. Corballis argues that this ability is a distinctively human attribute that explains our exceptional ability to adapt, manipulate and, in some situations, control our environment (Corballis, 1991).

Even in the small percentage (i.e. approximately 10%, smaller in some Asian societies; Hartlage & Gage, 1997) of us who are left- or mixed-handed, there is a greater tendency to have speech in the left hemisphere (around 70–80%) (McKeever, Seitz, Krutsch, & Van Eys, 1995; Rasmussen & Milner, 1977). Interestingly, the remaining third of these minority left-handers (20–30%) have unusual lateralisation of function, with around half having right hemisphere language dominance while half appear to have language in both hemispheres. Some caution must be raised concerning the exact nature of these figures, which are based on an epileptic population and are, therefore, associated with pathology. However, other studies with ECT patients do lend support to this general pattern (Pratt & Warrington, 1972).

Dextrality is found in infants who might have little opportunity to learn this behaviour. The percentage of 1- to 7-day old infants who "step out" with their right foot when placed in an upright position is 88%, and this is similar to the incidence of right-handedness in the population (Melekian, 1981). Despite cultural diversity, right handedness has been shown to be prevalent in all human societies and this feature has considerable historical consistency over many thousands of years. For example, there are many biblical references to the predominance of right-handedness. As a consequence, some form of genetic theory for handedness is required to account for this evidence.

One of the most persuasive models for handedness and hemispheric allocation of language is Marion Annett's genetic theory (Annett, 1985). Broadly, this and other popular competing theories propose that most of us inherit a genetic predisposition for handedness and speech in the left brain hemisphere, while a minority with no such predisposition will have these functions randomly distributed. The theory posits that most right-handedness is due to inherited right shift allele (RS +). However, some will inherit two RS − alleles, which promotes no genotypic bias to left or right handedness. The model predicts a greater correspondence between right-handedness and localisation of language in the left hemisphere since, barring some interfering pathology, most right-handers will have one or two RS + alleles and will be predetermined to have both right-handedness and left localisation of language.

Box 6.1. Handedness questionnaires

There are a number of measurements for handedness and laterality (see Dean & Reynolds, 1997, for a review). Apart from the usual issues of reliability, a variety of issues should be considered when making a choice of measures:

1. Most measures may be criticised on the grounds that each reported task, e.g. "Which hand do you use when drinking?", should be measured on a continuum, i.e. sliding scale such as a visual analogue or Likert scale.
2. Some measures, measure left/rightness according to subscales revealed through factor analysis. One should be aware that there may be a discordance between such tasks which, for example, use a particular eye compared to one which purely involves the hand.
3. Questionnaires should demonstrate some concurrent validity in thata self-report in the questionnaire should have a relationship with actual performance.

From the theoretical perspective some caution is also required in assuming there is a *direct* relationship between handedness and the laterality of language even in normal populations (Beaumont, 1997). This is especially the case when dealing with a brain-damaged population. There is some evidence that a hemispheric shift in language from the left to right, when injury is at a young age, requires more severe damage compared to a shift in handedness (e.g. Zurif & Bryden, 1969).

However, in the minority of cases people will have inherited the more unusual combination of two RS – alleles, in which case handedness and side of language may be either left or right and the necessary correspondence between language and handedness disappears. Although there are competing models of handedness, such genetic models do seem to allow a best fit to the data, when certain societal influences on handedness and the effects of brain damage are allowed for. Because of the degree of uncertainty in lateralising with left-handers, sometimes a handedness questionnaire (e.g. Oldfield, 1971) is required when lateralisation of function is important for clinical purposes. There has been some recent discussion concerning the approach to testing handedness, which is not as straightforward as it may seem (See Box 6.1).

While the left brain hemisphere has obvious skills for language, the right hemisphere also has areas of specialisation as well, although they may be less pronounced. For example, tasks that require the understanding of spatial relationships and physical orientation of objects around us are more associated with the right hemisphere. These and other non-verbal skills and behaviour with a right hemisphere advantage will be discussed in greater length later in the chapter and are discussed in Chapter 9.

In keeping with this cerebral asymmetry of function is an asymmetry of brain anatomy. It is important to note that there are large differences in the relative size of various brain structures between individuals. Despite these individual differences consistent hemispheric differences have been found between the brain structures, even at the cell level, between the two hemispheres. Also, some of the earliest findings have been well replicated and provide the most obvious relevance to functional lateralisation. In particular, Geschwind and Levitsky (1968) found that the left hemisphere has an enlarged area called the planum temporale, which is situated on the mesial surface of the temporal lobe. When following this area around, within the sylvian fissure we come to an enlarged superior aspect of the temporal lobe. This area is important for language and is also larger on the left (Wada, Clarke, & Hamm, 1975). The right hemisphere has a smaller planum temporale but there is a doubling in size of Heschl's gyrus (see Figure 6.1). The left and right Heschl's gyri, serving as the primary auditory sensory areas, have a similar role in processing auditory stimuli at a basic acoustic level (see illustration in Chapter 1). Other findings include different sizes and shapes of the two hemispheres and different inclinations of the slope and size of the sylvian fissures (see below).

Although it might be too speculative to attribute any specific functional meaning to these differences, there is clear anatomical support for cerebral asymmetry of function. Differences in the size of the planum temporale appear to have a better relationship to handedness compared to language but many factors may conspire to bias this relationship depending on the population of investigation (Beaton, 1997). The most enduring description of this area is with Heschl's gyrus as

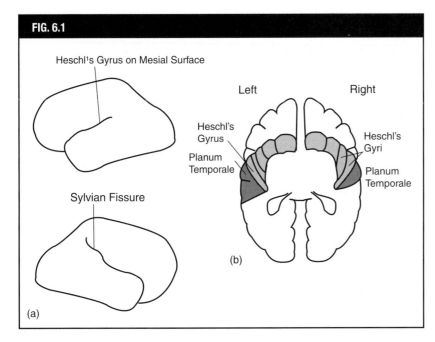

FIG. 6.1

Heschl's Gyrus on Mesial Surface

Left

Right

Heschl's Gyrus

Planum Temporale

Heschl's Gyri

Planum Temporale

Sylvian Fissure

(b)

(a)

(a) shows the slope of the sylvian fissure with a longer and steeper slope in the right hemisphere. (b) The planum temporale is on the shows the planum temporale is on the mesial superior surface of the temporal lobe (see also Figure 7.9). This diagram reveals the superior aspect of the temporal lobes after the dorsal aspect of the brain has been cut away. Note the smaller planum temporale and larger Heschl's gyrus in the right hemisphere.

an area for the input and analysis of phonological aspects of the basic acoustic information that is imported from the auditory system—in other words, converting sound frequencies into sounds that represent word forms.

One method that has contributed more than any other to our knowledge of asymmetry of function is the "split-brain operation". Although a controversial area, much has been learned concerning the respective functional contribution of the two brain hemispheres from studies of patients who have had their brain hemispheres separated at the cortical level.

THE SPLIT-BRAIN OPERATION

The left-sided localisation for language is clearly and most dramatically demonstrated following a split-brain operation or commissurotomy. This operation involves the sectioning or removal of the commissures (see Figure 6.2), thereby denying communication between the two hemispheres at a cortical level, other than via the optic chiasm. The optic chiasm, which allows visual informa-

tion from the retina to cross over from one retina to the contralateral hemisphere, is not sectioned in this procedure in human research and therefore a special divided visual field presentation is required when demonstrating the isolated function of a hemisphere (see Figure 6.3). The commissures are seen to be a later evolutionary development in the placental mammals. Also, the ontological development of the corpus callosum in the fourth gestational month in the human species might suggest some particular purpose or functional significance of these large interhemispheric connections. Levy (1985) suggests that the commissures exist to play a role in the development of hemispheric organisation and allow attentional control and regulation of the hemispheres. It appears that some specialisations, such as handedness, develop and become more defined with the increasing age of the child. Even a small degree of functional specialisation of the hemispheres would seem to require some cooperation and integration. Therefore there may be some credence to the view that the commissures have evolved with the increasing need for cross-talk between the hemispheres. It seems reasonable to argue that such specialisation might be made

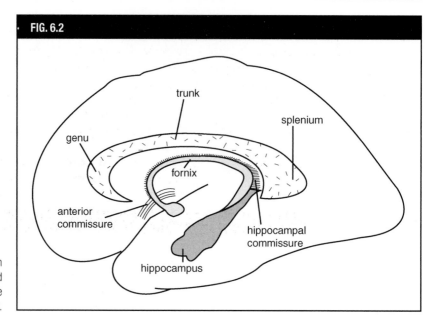

FIG. 6.2

Cross-section of the main commissures, which would be revealed if the brain were cut in half longitudinally.

more swiftly with interhemispheric transfer and that this specialisation may have had some adaptive significance for our tool-making ancestors (Corballis, 1991).

These commissures consists of bundles of nerve fibres, which are made up of millions of axons, referred to as white matter because of the white appearance of the myelin sheath along the stalk or length of each neurone. The function of these nerve fibres is to pass information from one brain hemisphere to another. When these are severed they disconnect one hemisphere from the other at the cortex, with the effect that these hemispheres are cortically quite separate and independent from each other, just as one might disconnect so many telephone lines.

The corpus callosum, the largest of the commissures, was a subject of mystery for some years. As early as the 1930s split-brain operations began to be conducted, in which the commissures were severed for epileptic seizures that were *secondarily generalised*. These were seizures that started in one hemisphere (partial) and spread to the other hemisphere (became generalised). At this time few could see any obvious ill effects following this operation. Sperry (1964) cites a nerve physiologist from Yale University in the 1940s who wryly suggested the role of the corpus callosum seemed to be to aid in the transmission of epileptic seizures from one to the other side of the body. It was not until the 1960s that interesting reports started to emerge, illustrating the behavioural significance of the split-brain operation (commissurotomy).

Some of the effects of severing the various sections of the corpus callosum can be anticipated by looking at the position of the lesion with respect to the functional significance of the adjacent cortical area. Connections between the different hemisphere regions are, for the most part, homotopic (same area) and at the same cytoarchitectonic cortical level (Brodahl, 1981 p. 804; Innocenti, Aggoun-Zouaoui, & Lehmann, 1995).

The callosal fibres have been traced with most accuracy in the monkey, where they proliferate in the mid-posterior frontal region and in the association areas of the parietal lobe. They appear to be absent in the primary motor areas representing distal parts of limbs and also in the primary visual area. From this evidence it appears that when interhemispheric transfer takes place it is more like to be after some preliminary hemispheric analysis prior to the final execution of the movement, perhaps during a preparation phase.

Motor movements are communicated via other areas such as the premotor area, especially the initiation of a movement, which no doubt supports bimanual coordination (see Geffen, Jones, & Geffen, 1994, for a review).

However, there is also clearly transformation of sensory information between the two hemispheres. The trunk of the corpus callosum has also been found to be important in transferring haptic information concerning the form of objects and other somatosensory information from one hemisphere to another (Bentin, Sakar, & Moscovitch, 1984; Geffen, Nilsson, & Quinn, 1985). For example, when touched on a particular finger on the right hand, blindfolded patients with this mid-callosal area sectioned would have difficulty in wiggling the same finger of the left hand. Perhaps the most important area of the corpus callosum in terms of the surgical procedure for epilepsy and the experimental findings, is the splenium. The splenium is at the slightly bulbous posterior end and, as one might predict given its position relative to the occipital lobe, it is important for transferring visual information (Greenblatt, Saunders, Culver, & Bogdanowicz, 1980). Because the splenium of the corpus callosum plays such a vital role it is often spared in the modern surgical procedures.

Finally, other commissures other than the corpus callosum play important roles. The anterior commissure provides interhemispheric connections between the olfactory bulbs, which is important for our sense of smell. The anterior commissure also provides interhemispheric communication between the amygdalae, important for emotional processing, the piriform cortex, the entorrhinal area, and aspects of the temporal cortex. The hippocampal commissure connects the hippocampal formation, supporting important integrating processes relating to memory.

Most of the neuropsychological findings that are reported here relate to commissurotomy, which involves the severing of all commissures with the exception, in some cases, of the anterior commissures. This dramatic disconnection involving the severing of vast nerve bundles might be expected to result in equally dramatic behavioural deterioration, but as indicated the signs after the

initial recovery of the patient are often subtle and may only be identified following careful and, in some cases, ingenious testing. The more common modern neurosurgical treatment is a partial callosotomy; this involves severing the anterior two-thirds of the corpus callosum and avoids many of the psychological consequences of a commissurotomy (Blume, 1984; Gordon, Bogen, & Sperry, 1971).

THE SPLIT-BRAIN DISCONNECTION SYNDROMES

A disconnection is said to occur when the neuronal projections that normally connect the two brain areas are severed. This may result in a constellation of neuropsychological signs, which consistently appear in the company of each other and therefore earns the title of a syndrome. The disconnection syndrome associated with split-brain surgery is of particular interest since it provides information concerning the asymmetry of brain function.

SPECIALISED CONTRIBUTIONS OF THE TWO HEMISPHERES

Left hemisphere specialisation

One of the clearest demonstrations of the left hemisphere's specialisation is provided by this surgical treatment. In various ways this split-brain operation allows the isolation of a sensory input to one brain hemisphere. In the case of olfaction, our sense of smell is regulated by the phylogenetically older projections of the olfactory bulbs. As indicated, this is unlike other sensory systems since they are ipsilateral (going to the same side). Therefore, something that is smelt with the right nostril is isolated to the right hemisphere in the split-brain patient. When the patient is presented the smell of mint to the right nostril, which is connected to the right hemisphere only, the patient is unable to name the smell. But when

FIG. 6.3

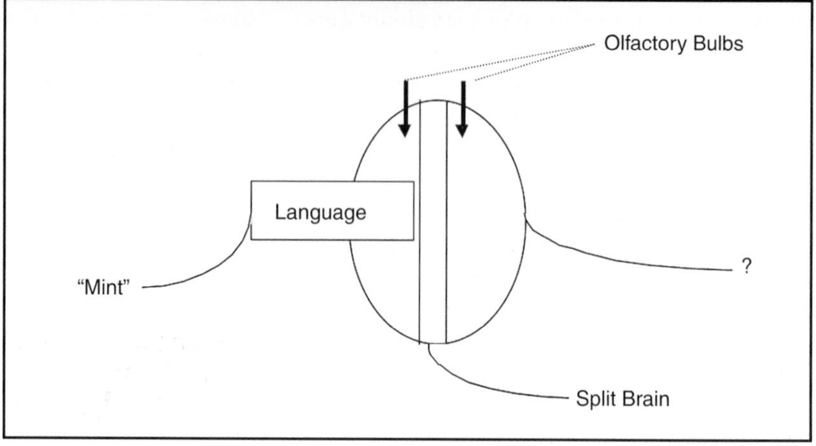

When the smell of mint is presented to the right nostril, with the left nostril blocked, this information cannot be passed over to the left hemisphere to be named in the split-brain patient. The patient may match two smells but cannot name the smell.

the smell is presented to the left nostril, which is connected to the left language hemisphere, the patient can easily name the smell "mint". Although the split-brain subject is unable to name the smell, they are still able to differentiate the mint smell from other smells and easily match with a similar one, smelt by the same nostril (Gazzaniga, 1967). It is merely the linguistic expression of the smell that is unavailable.

Disconnection between the two hemispheres may occur through naturally occurring lesions such as those due to stroke and tumours. Liepmann was one of the earliest writers to observe such patients and at the same time formulate an influential theory in this area (Liepmann & Maas, 1907). He observed that if a patient showed a left-handed agraphia (inability to write), the patient was also unable to carry out verbal orders using the left hand. For this last phenomenon he introduced the term apraxia. This ideomotor apraxia is not due to any weakness, paralysis, or loss of dexterity of the left hand, but rather because it is attached directly to a right hemisphere that is disconnected from the language hemisphere. The right hemisphere is not supported by the normal writing or full verbal comprehension prerequisite to the understanding of written sentences. The connections between the hemispheres and the neuronal projections to the upper limbs decussate (cross over) below the commissures at the level of

the brain stem. As a result, commissurotomy does not interfere with these connections required of the execution of limb movement. A request to use the right arm in some way is executed without difficulty by the left hemisphere, which understands the instruction (see Figure 6.3). However, the right hemisphere, which projects to the left arm does not understand this request and the command to move the left arm is not carried out (Gazzaniga, 1967; Geschwind, Kaplan, & Levy, 1962).

A disconnection syndrome can also be demonstrated using visually presented material. However, in this case the separation of the visual input to one hemisphere versus another is not straightforward. Information going to each retina is shared between the two hemispheres. The right side of each retina goes to the right hemisphere while the left side of each retina goes to the left hemisphere. As can be seen from Figure 6.4, the nasal (nearest the nose) projections from each eye cross over at the optic chiasm. In order to test the respective function of each hemisphere in "split-brain" patients an experimental procedure was designed to separate the visual information received by the left compared to the right sides of the two retinas. This was achieved, in the case of testing the right hemisphere, by getting the patient to look straight ahead at a dot on the screen, while information was then flashed briefly from the left, which hit the right side of the curved surface of both retinas and was thereby transferred to the right hemisphere in isolation. With the commissures severed the information is confined to that hemisphere and cannot be transferred across to the other hemisphere (see Figure 6.4).

Gazzaniga and Sperry (1967) found that when objects or names were flashed to commissurotomy patients so that they went solely to the right hemisphere, the patients could not name the item. They were unable to transfer this information to the left (language) hemisphere because of their commissurotomy. In this situation the patient commonly said that they had not seen anything other than perhaps a flash of light. This result might suggest that simple objects (e.g. spoon, orange) presented to the right hemisphere were never processed. However, in one experiment it was clearly shown that the patient was able to pick out the originally presented object from under a screen, even though they claimed not to have seen it. The object was picked out using the left hand (connected to the right hemisphere) and therefore, although the subject was

not conscious of seeing the item, it was, nevertheless, processed and, indeed, remembered (see Figure 6.5).

The question often posed by students is: How could the right hemisphere understand the instructions sufficiently to reach out with the left hand?, for the left hand is connected to that right hemisphere without language. The answer must be "With great difficulty" in some cases because of this type of ideomotor apraxia, which has already been discussed. However, according to some reports, these patients typically become very clever at overcoming this problem through a process of visual cueing. The left hemisphere understands the question and moves the right hand in some way to communicate what is required of the left hand. Alternatively, the experimenter might have to coax or lead the right hand into the required action.

A second question that perhaps more obviously springs to mind is if the patient is not aware of seeing anything except for a flash of light then it might be difficult to persuade the patient that reaching for the item is a worthwhile exercise. The following reported dialogue illustrates this

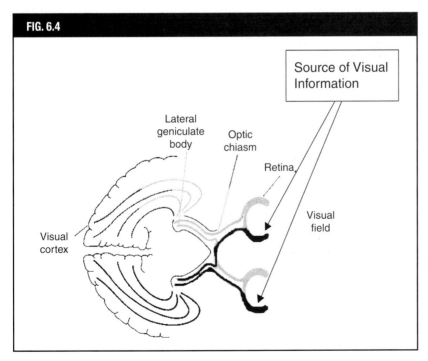

FIG. 6.4

Source of Visual Information

Lateral geniculate body

Optic chiasm

Retina

Visual field

Visual cortex

The visual pathways allow the presentation of visual information to be isolated to one hemisphere in the split brain patient.

such as counting to ten and expletives may be produced in patients who have no other means of expression. This evidence illustrates that the split-brain patient is not always an adequate model for isolated hemisphere functioning, if only because the patient still retains the other hemisphere and there is not the same imperative to use the right hemisphere for expression. Certainly, as will be discussed in future chapters, imaging techniques have shown some bilateral posterior activation during comprehension tasks but more unilateral left posterior and anterior activation when the task requires the expression of language. This area of discussion is returned to when discussing interhemispheric transfer and the recovery of language in the split-brain patient.

Auditory sensory inputs are similar to visual inputs in that they are also contralateral; however, there are also ipsilateral projections. Nevertheless, the main source of auditory information goes to the contralateral hemisphere. Thus the main projections from the left ear go to the right hemisphere and those of the right ear go to the left hemisphere. The difficulty of the right hemisphere with language can be demonstrated when earphones are used to isolate the presentation of stimuli. In an experiment where information is presented in a 'dichotic' fashion, different verbal information is presented to each ear. The patient tends to make better judgements on verbal information presented in the latter because the right ear has its main connections with the left brain hemisphere, especially when there is competition. It appears that the demands of a conflicting input (dichotic presentation) overcomes any compensation that might be allowed by relying on the lesser ipsilateral connections. Relationships have been found this right ear advantage and other measures of laterality (Bryden, 1988).

In summary, studies that image the brain during various tasks suggest that both hemispheres are involved in the completion of a wide variety of behaviours. Even when one hemisphere appears to be more activated than the other there is inevitably a contralateral activation suggesting contributions being made towards the completion of the task being carried out. Nevertheless, there is a case to be made that while the two hemi-spheres act in concert the contributions of the two hemispheres are often quite different. The clearest difference that is not shared is the general specialisation of the left hemisphere for the *expression* of language. The left hemisphere may have special structural advantages that suit it to the analysis and production of speech. That same left hemisphere also often appears to be dominant for the manipulation of movements—a dominance that is commonly expressed in terms of right-handedness. The left hemisphere is also associated with awareness of symbols such as language and objects. However, as argued, some analysis of the meaning or semantic qualities of symbols also appears to take place in this right hemisphere. There is evidence from studies of patients with gross damage to the left hemisphere and split-brain patients that they may act on a certain level of semantic analysis. Split-brain patients may pick out objects using the left hand by drawing or picking out objects that have been processed by the right hemisphere. However, the comprehension of the right hemisphere for language appears to be far less developed than the left. There is some evidence of comprehension of simple words without any syntactic or phonetic capability (Zaidel, 1978).

Right hemisphere specialisation

The left hemisphere is often referred to as the dominant hemisphere, although some have objected to this designation (Bogen, 1997; Sperry, 1984b). It is probably true that the right hemisphere advantages are not matched in terms of degree with the left hemisphere advantages in terms of the modern everyday requirements. However, the known number of areas of right hemisphere advantage is expanding and its importance is gradually being appreciated (Van Lancker, 1997).

The right hemisphere appears to be superior to the left in some aspects of face perception (Levy, Trevarthen, & Sperry, 1972). Levy and colleagues presented chimeric faces, composed of two different half faces, to commissurotomy patients. In this way the different face halves were presented to different brain hemispheres. Later the subjects tended to recognise the whole face belonging to the half previously presented to the right hemisphere. In other words, in a later recognition task of whole faces, each half face being reunited with its other half, patients tended to choose the face that included the half previously presented to the right hemisphere, and the faces that included the half that was originally presented to the left hemisphere were more likely to be ignored. Also, the right hemisphere has an advantage over the left in detecting and interpreting emotional expression (Gazzaniga et al., 1975). These findings have been generally supported by other studies with stroke patients with some modification (see Chapters 7 and 9).

Other advantages for the right hemisphere appear to be in the remembering of random tones, melody and music, although with musicians and those who are used to analysing music for its composition the left hemisphere may have more influence (e.g., Plenger et al., 1996).

More interest has been focused on the right hemisphere's advantage over the left on tasks requiring spatial analysis and construction. For example, studies with split-brain patients have found the left hand (right hemisphere) to be better at discriminating non-verbal shapes by touch (Gazzaniga, 1987a). The constructional advantage of the right hemisphere is also shown in a study by Bogen and Gazzaniga (1966).While the left hand (right hemisphere) of the patients in this study was untidier it was capable, unlike the right hand, of drawing cubes and other objects in three dimensions. There is an interesting film in which Dr Gazzaniga presents a split-brain patient constructing a puzzle. The patient's two hands appear to be arguing with each other. The left hand, which is attached to the right hemisphere, is better at the task, but the right hand, connected to the left hemisphere, comes in and messes things up. At one stage the right hand takes hold of the left hand as if it was an interfering stranger and draws it away (see Gazzaniga, 1985).

It is important to note, however, that the two hemispheres may solve the same problem in quite different ways. Therefore when integrated the left hemisphere may make a valuable contribution. In one experiment reported by Levy (1974) the results showed that there was a different type of contribution from the right hemisphere compared to the left on a constructional task. Her results suggested that, given the problem of copying a design using blocks, the left hemisphere tends to analyse the detail of the puzzle, fitting each block in a piecemeal fashion to make a whole. In contrast, the right hemisphere takes a more holistic approach based on the resemblance of the pattern of the blocks to the overall pattern of the design (see also see De Renzi's similar arguments concerning the contributions of both hemispheres to construction; De Renzi, 1982).

This distinction between holistic/right and analytic/left is taken up by a number of authors, although there is some difficulty in operationalising this distinction (Bradshaw & Nettleton, 1983, p. 185). The global (right) and local (left) distinction has also been discussed in Chapter 2. Hellige and Sergent (1986) argue that such broad labels as holistic/analytic or global/local for right versus left hemisphere processing, respectively, are inappropriate since processing is qualitatively variable depending on task demands. For example, they cite their own work and that of Levy showing that an advantage may be given to one hemisphere over the other by varying the nature of the stimuli and increasing one or other processing requirements. To take an example where the holistic–local distinction may be swapped because of the task, these authors found that presentations of consonant–vowel–consonant such as "TAM" were processed holistically as units by the left hemisphere but as individual letters by the right hemisphere. In terms of their own research on an STM task they found that the left hemisphere had an advantage when the memory load was increased. However, if the memory load is reduced and the perceptual information degraded the right hemisphere presentation becomes advantaged. The relationship is therefore not quite as straightforward as sometimes suggested.

While Gazzaniga appears to be in sympathy with this global-right/local-left distinction, he makes the point from his experiments that the left and right hemisphere are equally good at perceiving and *matching* visuospatial material. It is only when the patient has *to use their hands* in the pursuit of construction or drawing that the differences emerge (Gazzaniga, 1985). It would be interesting to know the extent this was linked to the "where-action" pathway. The reader may have become aware in Chapter 2 of apparent ubiquitous links between the "where-action" and right hemisphere function and comparable links between the "what" pathway and left hemisphere function, although it may be too early to formulate a theoretical relationship. This issue of the dissociation of action-related judgements and perceptual judgements is further pursued in Chapter 8.

The appreciation of music and discrimination of tones have also been found to be more dominant in the right hemisphere, with the temporal lobe being especially implicated (Milner, 1962). Also, it is possible that females are more lateralised than males in the detection of melody (Boucher & Bryden, 1997). As indicated, professional musicians appear to be dependent on the left hemisphere compared to non-musicians. It is assumed that the left hemisphere comes into play when analysis of composition is required, in contrast to the more holistic enjoyment of music by the non-musician (Bever & Chiarello, 1974). One should be reminded, however, that musicians generally have a greater representation of music according to an fMRI study and this may be dependent on the number of years they have practised (Pantev, Oostenveld, Engelien et al., 1998).

Before leaving this section dealing with the specialisation of the brain hemispheres according to split-brain research, some reservations should be voiced concerning the generalisation of these findings to the normal brain. Beaumont (1997) and others have questioned research into cerebral lateralisation on a number of grounds. One criticism concerns the relevance of split-brain research. It is noted that researchers might be advised to be wary of whole-heartedly accepting the results from the divided brain research as being revealing of the function of the normal undivided brain. Obviously, the interaction of the whole brain is not capable of representation or expression in a split-brain patient other than at a subcortical level. Therefore when we look at these results we are only learning part of the story.

Also, the whole is not always equivalent to the sum of its parts. For example, the possibility exists that one hemisphere may need the other to express its analysis, or a particular task can only be solved by the collaboration of both hemispheres. If we are to take this argument even further then an extreme view might be that the split brain is forced into aberrant or unusual modes of processing that are not conducted in the normal brain.

As mentioned in the introduction of this chapter, modern radiological studies using PET and fMRI clearly show a significant amount of involvement of both hemispheres in most tasks and it is highly likely that the two hemispheres are working to complement each other. Such interactions are not available for observation in the split-brain patient, so only part of the story concerning hemispheric involvement is being revealed in these patients. However, the stronger argument that what is left is distorted or biased and misleading is less credible. Many of the findings with split-brain patients have also been found or replicated using natural lesion studies, studies of patients following radical surgical procedures such as hemispherectomy (one half of the brain removed), and normal groups when special experimental techniques have been used. This is not to say split-brain patients do not perform differently from normal subjects with disadvantages and perhaps even some advantages in artificial experimental situations (Gazzaniga, 1987b); rather it is to support a view concerning the relative usefulness of investigating hemispheric specialisation in these patients.

A second reservation relates to the experimental methodology used in laterality research. The task constraints of testing hemispheric processing include presenting information towards the periphery of visual space in rather unusual conditions that might favour one side of presentation over another depending on the nature of the stimulus. Most of the concerns in this area have either been countered or have modified testing procedures (see Beaumont, 1997). Nevertheless, for these types of methodological reasons and the difficulties in assuming normal brain representation, it is clearly proper to retain some caution when surveying the split-brain research.

Finally, the full split-brain operation of commissurotomy is rarely done these days. This is a difficult operation partly because of the large network of veins that overlies the corpus callosum. When it is done it is usually a callosotomy rather than a commissurectomy. This procedure involves the resection of the anterior parts of the corpus callosum, allowing visual information to be transferred over at the splenium. This operation is still carried out in some circumstances to stop seizure activity from travelling from one hemisphere to the other—in other words, to prevent a generalised seizure and its associated loss of consciousness. However, because of the rarity of this full split-brain operation these subjects are seldom encoutered and many studies are presented with small numbers of subjects. It is not uncommon to find a study with around three subjects or even one subject. Therefore, sometimes conclusions have been drawn from patients who either have unusual organisation of function, have a confounding disorder, or less complete sectioning of the brain than was originally understood—although, the "rogue" cases are often identified in retrospect when results have failed replication.

However, while keeping in mind these reservations it is probably fair to say that most neuropsychologists view split-brain research as providing significant insights into the respective contributions of the two hemsiphieres.

ALIEN HAND AND CONSCIOUS AWARENESS

Cases of one hand acting independently of the other are sometimes reported, in which the hand (or foot) appears to act independently as if without the knowledge of the patient. This is usually the left hand (right hemisphere) in a right-handed person (Bogen, 1985). This phenomenon, referred to as the "alien" or "anarchic" hand, is reported with such examples as one hand undoing a shirt while the other hand goes along afterwards doing up the same garment; or in the case of the super-

market where one hand takes down an item, which the other hand then immediately places back on the shelf. This last behaviour is of course sometimes found in normal shopping behaviour, although when the left hand appears to move of its own volition something more than the power of advertising is at work.

Patients reported by Bogen (1985) used to talk about their wayward hand in the third person in much the same way as a neglect patient sometimes talks about their left arm (see anosognosia in chapter 4). One patient reported by Bogen (1993, p. 361) who had a wayward left leg complained for several years of "an inability to get his left foot to go in the same direction as the rest of him." It appears, then, that there is a greater likelihood of poor awareness of those functions that are governed by the right hemisphere, which can lead to its apparent independence. Many patients do not show this "alien" or "anarchic" hand. When it does persist it is sometimes associated with mesial frontal damage and therefore the original cause may interact with a tendency to be disinhibited in one's actions (Bogen, 1993; Della Sala, Marchetti & Spinnler, 1991; Feinberg, Schindler, Flanagan, & Haber, 1992). With a number of these originally reported patients, resection was associated with a "neighbourhood lesion". That is, there is some pathology, such as a tumour, which has prompted the surgery in the first place and, therefore, it is possible that some of the rarer symptoms of commissurotomy may not be due to bisection of the hemispheres alone.

However, the phenomenon of the "alien" hand and the lack of conscious awareness of images presented to the right hemisphere correspond well with the idea that conscious awareness or monitoring of cognition is largely a left hemisphere process. This, of course, does not discount that the right hemisphere is not the most important hemisphere for attention as is argued in Chapter 4 but rather argues that awareness of movements and other attentional processes are likely to require the involvement of the left hemisphere.

THE CLINICAL PRESENTATION OF DISCONNECTION SYNDROME

Introduction

The presence of disconnection signs in patients who have suffered a stroke or tumour is probably more common than is generally realised. Some stroke patients may initially show some signs of disconnection because of the interruption of the passage of information from one hemisphere to another. Some of these naturally occurring lesions are associated with "neighbourhood signs". Therefore, as indicated, it may not always be correct to attribute these signs to disconnection per se, but rather to the damage of adjacent brain structures. For example, anterior callosal lesions may be associated with patients who show indifference or apathy to events around them. This might be found in the case of a "butterfly" glioma in the genu (anterior aspect of the corpus callosum), the wings of this malignant tumour symmetrically spreading and infiltrating both frontal lobes. This inability to speak and make spontaneous movements is likely to be related to bilateral damage to the cingulate gyrus in the medial frontal cortex. Bogen cites a translation of a study proposeing that tumours involving the splenium were likely to produce memory dysfunction (Escourolle, Haw, Gray, & Henin, 1975). However, Geffen, Walsh, Simpson, and Jeeves (1980) argue that this, again, is not due to the disconnection per se but is rather a neighbourhood sign and possibly represents an influence of arterial supply on the hippocampus. It will be remembered that the posterior cerebral artery sweeps forward to irrigate the hippocampi.

In physiotherapy there is an obvious interest in the coordination between the contralateral limbs. Tasks that require coordination of both hands such as doing up a parcel with string may be revealing. Also, a clinician may be referred a patient who has been misdiagnosed with a psychiatric dissociative disorder because of symptoms of "alien" hand. Therefore some assessment of callosal disconnection is an advantage, even when there is no access to sophisticated experi-

mental equipment (the reader is referred to Bogen, 1993, for a more in-depth discussion of these issues). The following tests may consolidate the understanding of asymmetry of function and the features of this syndrome.

Unilateral left-handed anomia

This is relatively easy to test. The patient fails when asked to feel and name an unseen common object with their left hand (right hemisphere). Testing of both hands is obviously important to reduce the likelihood of confounding causes of this impairment. *Asteriognosis* is the name used to describe an inability to recognise objects by touch. This may be contributed by a somatosensory area lesion in the postcentral gyrus (see diagram in Chapter 1) or a more posterior lesion that may affect spatial analysis of the object. However, right hemisphere lesions may affect patients bimanually, whereas a left hemisphere lesion is more likely to affect patients unilaterally on the contralateral side (right hand) (Semmes, 1965). Therefore, a unimanual left-handed asteriognosis is more likely to be evidence of disconnection. Further corroborative evidence may be obtained if the patient is then asked to retrieve the same object from beneath a screen (rather than an unreliable blindfold) with the same hand. This ability to match provides evidence of intact sensory system, thereby encouraging a disconnection interpretation.

Pseudo double hemianopia

This may occur if there is a natural lesion that includes the splenium (see Figure 6.2). The transference of visual information from one hemisphere to another will be impeded. Information that is briefly presented in the left visual space will be transferred to the right hemisphere, and can therefore be pointed to with the left hand but not the right (the left hemisphere has no knowledge of this stimulus). Therefore if the patient is asked to sit on their left hand so that they can only point with their right (left hemisphere) and are asked to keep silent and fixate their gaze straight ahead, they will fail to point at something presented in left visual space (this will become clear to the reader if the situation is diagrammed). Of course, a patient who has hemianopia or attentional neglect may also fail at this task. However, an additional failure to point at a stimulus in the right visual field (left hemisphere) when pointing with the left hand (right hemisphere) is taken as a more confident sign of disconnection (in this case there is the additional problem of the right hemisphere understanding the instruction). Typically, with a test of this nature the examiner asks the patient to focus on their nose while they wiggle one of their fingers in the periphery of vision. This is obviously a rough and ready approach to testing and the examiner should be aware of various hints and tricks a patient can get up to, to communicate the occurrence of stimuli to the other hemisphere. It is also important to have all the combinations of visual field presentations and hand pointing to reduce the possibility of confounding disorders.

Hemialexia (left side)

Many clinicians do not have a tachistoscope or other experimental device for separating the visual fields but it may still be possible to show an inability to read words presented in the left visual field while having no difficulty in reading words in the right visual field. However, further support for a disconnection interpretation would be to find that the patient is successfully able to retrieve the same presented article in the left visual field from under an obscuring screen using the left hand. This may be a less reliable indicator if there is a left hemianopia since this is commonly associated with a right posterior stroke and the patient is unable to use their left hand because of left hemiparesis. However, with such cases the patient without disconnection may still be able to write what they have been presented in their left visual field, with their right hand without dysgraphia.

Unimanual pseudo apraxia and agraphia

The right hemisphere does not understand instructions that which might involve the left hand that is directed by it in the split-brain patient. Unilateral ideomotor apraxia, when it is associated with the split-brain patient, is a little different from other types of ideomotor apraxia (see Chapter 8). This type of ideomotor apraxia is perhaps more appropriately named a disconnec-

tion apraxia since the request to move the left hand is understood by the left hemisphere, but the latter has no way of passing this message on to the right hemisphere, which is supposed to execute the movement. This is not a kinetic dyspraxia where there is a physical weakness due to hemiparesis or other physical incapacity. In order to dismiss the possibility of confounding motor disorders, Bogen (1993) suggests the patient be allowed to carry out the activity naturally, e.g. opening the door with the left hand, in order to make sure the person is capable of making the necessary controlled motor movements. Alternatively, the patient is asked to carry out the request using both hands, if the action is easy to imitate. Unilateral pseudo agraphia (left hand) is simply tested by requesting the patient to write something with their left hand. Again the disorder is not attributable to physical weakness or other disability that undermines the capability to make the requisite motor movements.

RECOVERY FROM SPLIT-BRAIN SURGERY

As discussed, following commissurotomy there is sometimes an initial period of akinetic mutism, which passes, to reveal the usual signs of disconnection. Some signs are more resistant to recovery compared to others; according to Bogen, the signs of unimanual apraxia (failure of motor response of the left limb to command) and unimanual dysgraphia (inability to write with the left hand) are more likely to recover, especially in younger persons. Unilateral left-handed anomia (naming items held unseen in the left hand) and hemialexia (reading in left visual space) are more resistant to recovery (Bogen, 1993, p. 344).

Some of this recovery is due to the patient becoming clever at using strategies that allow external communication to each hemisphere, i.e. in reporting proceedings of a task verbally. Other recovery may be due to the strengthening of ipsilateral projections (Gazzaniga, 1987a). However, these explanations do not totally satisfy some researchers in this area.

A clue as to how this recovery may take place is present in a condition referred to as agenesis of the corpus callosum. In this condition a person is born without a corpus callosum; there is generally little evidence of impairment and, therefore, it is understood that some compensation must have taken place. These patients do show some signs of a lack of bilateral coordination on motor tasks but they are usually only revealed on specially designed tests: for example, in the case where a subject has to move a cross-sight along a diagonal line by moving a right-hand wheel, which moves the sights vertically, while the other wheel moves the sights horizontally (Jeeves, Silver, & Jacobson, 1988). As is the case with some split-brain patients, these patients typically still have an anterior commissure and this is generally larger than normal (Bogen, 1993). Also, these persons have a larger bundle of nerve fibres that runs longitudinally where the corpus callosum would have been. Therefore it is possible that some compensation takes place by running information longitudinally to the anterior commissure.

Gazzaniga argues against the agenesis explanation as an explanation for recovery in split-brain patients. He has found no differences between patients with commissurotomy and the proportions of their anterior commissure and those with just a complete callosotomy (the corpus callosum is sectioned without other commissures). He is therefore not impressed by the anterior commissure compensation theory (Gazzaniga, 1987a). The explanation for recovery is yet to be satisfactorily explained, although some subcortical connections clearly allow for intercommunications between the hemispheres of a limited nature. The importance of these connections is given further discussion in the following section.

THE NATURE OF INTERHEMISPHERIC INTEGRATION

It is perhaps unnecessary to propose that the split-brain case provides some difficulties when making assertions concerning integrated brain functioning. The split-brain experiments provide a picture that may lead to a view that there are two brains. This is true in the sense that they appear to be able to function independently when they are separated. Indeed, studies with monkeys have shown that by isolating the experience of the hemispheres one hemisphere can learn information that the other hemisphere does not know (Gazzaniga, 1967). However, there is more obviously one brain when the activation of the whole brain is studied during a task using functional imaging or when assessing brain electrical activity. Even for strongly lateralised behaviours such as speech, the right hemisphere provides motor mechanisms for speech and the appropriate prosodic tonal qualities of the voice that are essential for the non-verbal communicative aspects of speech. These split-brain experiments tell us little, as yet, about this processes of integration.

However, while the process by which the two hemispheres collaborate remains a matter of speculation more is known concerning the extent and nature of subcortical transfer. The brain areas below the cortex, such as the brain stem, thalamus, and the colliculi, remain intact during commissurotomy. In Chapter 4 the superior colliculus was referred to with the pulvinar of the thalamus and parietal cortex as being important for orienting during attention, especially when there is movement in the periphery of vision. Therefore some interhemispheric transfer of attentional information is possible. For example, reaction time to a target presented in a position within the visual field of one hemisphere may be reduced by providing a directional cue or arrow in the visual field of the other hemisphere. In this way, despite cortical disconnection, one hemisphere helps the other to direct attention to a particular location within the visual field, e.g. to the left (Holtzman, 1984).

Also, there is transference of emotional tone from one hemisphere to the other. It is assumed that this would be because the two hemispheres are joined at the hypothalamus. Some researchers have found that a connotative influence presented in one hemisphere may bias selection of information presented in the other hemisphere (e.g., Lambert, 1991). However, although controversial, the evidence is generally against the transference of perceptual information following commissurotomy (Gazzaniga, 1987a). Gazzaniga argues that there is actually less interhemisphere communication than has been previously suggested; his studies show that there is some interhemispheric transmission of basic information, e.g. detection of the presence of a stimulus in the other visual field, but not a discrimination between verbal stimuli (see also Corballis & Trudel, 1993). Corballis (1993) suggests that sometimes transference of perceptual information may be found due to poor method. For example, when a split-brain subject is asked whether two stimuli projected to different hemispheres are the same or different, a correct response may be due to chance when a recognition paradigm is used with a limited number of choices. The patient may often raise the accuracy of their judgement by guessing which of the options is most likely.

Although Gazzaniga et al. (1979) have noted the recovery of some right hemisphere language in a split-brain patient after 2 years, this may be the exception rather than the rule. Bogen argues that the recovery or development of language in the split-brain right hemisphere is actually less than is sometimes reported of patients following gross left hemisphere damage (Bogen, 1993). When the left hemisphere is removed in adulthood there is some recovery of *limited* verbal output (Burklund & Smith, 1977; Code, 1997). Bogen proposes that when the hemisphere is disconnected but remains intact, the lesser verbal abilities of the right hemisphere may initially be absent or suppressed by the present left hemisphere that is still intact. If the mechanism for an absence of language in the right hemisphere is suppression then there must be some means of communicating that suppression. Some authors have postulated that some subcortical communication within the brain stem may be responsible for transmitting that inhibition (Johnson, 1984).

To extend Bogen's line of thinking on suppression, it is a possibility that attentional processes may be responsible for the lack of right hemisphere language development. The control of attentional resources (how much one can attend to at the same time) is shared between the hemispheres. If one hemisphere is given a task, the capacity of the other half brain is, accordingly, reduced (Gazzaniga, 1987b). Therefore unlike the case of the patient with gross left hemisphere damage there will be deactivation of the right hemisphere during language tasks because attentional resources are allocated to the intact left hemisphere. In contrast, in the case of patients with gross damage to the left hemisphere, the right hemisphere would enjoy all the attentional resources required to improve speech capacity. This speculation is in line with PET studies showing increased right hemisphere activation in response to language tasks following left hemisphere stroke (e.g. Cappa et al., 1997), although it must be mentioned that even here such recovery tends to be related more to comprehension than to expression (Gainotti, 1993b).

The above example, in which the patient's hands appeared to argue over the best way of approaching a constructional solution, raises the important question as to how these two hemispheres integrate their respective skills towards a solution in the intact brain. In the case of constructional skills, that presumably requires the sophisticated integration of the skills of both hemispheres; the commissures must be useful not only for feedback but also for allowing executive direction. The skills and frailties of either hemisphere must be encouraged and discouraged respectively.

Comment is often made concerning the amazing adaption of the spilt-brain patient following surgery. These patients may go about their daily business without obvious handicap. But is this adaptation more apparent than real? Are situations involving less routine tasks where the patient is disadvantaged? In some experiments the split-brain patient may actually be at an advantage because there is less interference between different images projected to the two visual fields (Gazzaniga, 1987b). However, this advantage is only achieved in a contrived experimental situation. Other evidence would suggest that the split-brain patient is more disadvantaged. The split-brain patient may show a general lack of processing efficiency on tasks requiring concentration over a period of time (10–30 minutes).

Dimond (1976) was interested in comments made by Sperry (1974) implying that split-brain patients were generally poorer at performing some tasks than one would expect. "One gets a general impression from working with these [split-brain] patients over long periods that their overall mental potential is affected by the commissurotomy. Perseverance in tasks that are mentally taxing remains low in most of the patients as does also the ability to grasp broad, long-term or distant implications of a situation" (see also Zaidel & Sperry, 1974). Dimond gave these remarks some empirical substance by showing that split-brain subjects had far more difficulty in attending to material in their environment when given a vigilance task lasting 30 minutes when compared to the partial split-brain subjects. The partial split-brain patients were assumed to have interhemispheric transference of visually presented information. In this task subjects were required to press a button to detect stimuli in the

left or right visual field. Their results are reproduced in Figure 6.6.

The cause of this deterioration is described in terms of a lack of responding given a left hemisphere response, with the right hemisphere associated with over-responding, thereby causing false positives. The poor detection by the left hemisphere may be explained in terms of the right hemisphere dominance for attention, but the reason for the increased false positives of the right hemisphere is less obvious. The results do suggest that the corpus callosum, especially the splenium, is important in allowing for the switching of attentional resources from one hemisphere to another. In conclusion, tasks that require either the combined skills of both hemispheres or the integration of attentional resources over time, illustrate the importance of interhemispheric communication. The two halves may perform independently but they have some disadvantages when they are in isolation. Of course, in such a study it is difficult to get two groups of such rare patients that are equivalent, but the results are sufficiently dramatic to illustrate a point. Split brains act more like two halves than two brains.

The commissures are clearly more important than was realised in the 1930s, or indeed in the 1950s when a famous neurophysiologist, Karl Lashley, shared his puzzlement with others at the time by jokingly suggesting that the commissures were perhaps useful for preventing the two hemispheres from sagging. However, while much has been learned since this time and the case of the split-brain patient has been useful in illustrating the specialty skills of the hemispheres, this research method has not been equally successful in answering the important question of how these two hemispheres cooperate and maximise these skills. This is one of the intriguing question, that remain to be answered.

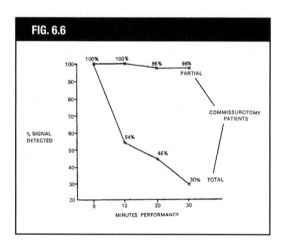

FIG. 6.6

A graph illustrating the results of Dimond, showing reduced vigilance in split-brain subjects (reprinted from Dimond, 1976, with permission from Oxford Journals).

certain roles in the production and comprehesion of language.

The older structural models of language disorders provide a way of describing and modellir common presentations of language dysfunctio This approach to modelling is referred to as tl *syndrome approach* because originally patien were classified according to a collection of cor monly occurring aphasic signs. Some aphasias a named after the researchers who were influenti in bringing the types of language disorders people's attention. For example, Broca's aphas is broadly described as a disorder of speech pr duction, while Wernicke's aphasia is a disorder speech comprehension. However, not only ha the descriptions of these syndromes been que tioned but research has also challenged tl precise brain areas likely to produce these sy dromes. Indeed, some researchers are of the opi ion that it is just too hard to model language this manner. This discussion of the vario clinical types of aphasia is therefore necessari critical. Nevertheless, a revision of the older pe spectives is timely and this section is complete with a proposal for a new model of languaj disorders.

Some of the most exciting new work in the are of language is from the cognitive neur psychological perspective, which attempts analyse the stages necessary for a breakdown language. The latter half of this chapter is mo devoted to this work concerning acquired difficu ties, in carrying out arithmetical calculatio (acalculia), writing difficulties (dysgraphias) ar reading difficulties (dyslexias).

FIG. 7.1

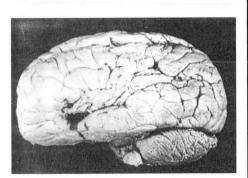

(a)

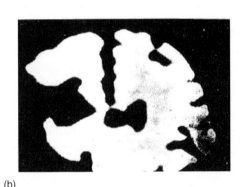

(b)

a) The brain of Paul Broca's patient, Tan (Monsieur Leborgne), was rediscovered in a museum and was then subjected to CT can. (b) Note the gross subcortical extent of the lesion in the coronal section (reprinted from Signoret et al., 1984, with permission from Harcourt Publishers).

HISTORICAL NOTES

In 1861 Paul Broca, a French surgeon, describe the post-mortem findings on two patients wh had suffered severely impaired language functio ing before their deaths. The first of these tw cases, a patient known as Tan, was to becon most famous. Tan was named after one of the fe utterances he would say. This restriction w evident from reports from the nuns who we

nation been available at the time of these early arguments, whether Marie would have a more elevated place in aphasiology history.

Lecours and colleagues describe a transcript of these earnest arguments at consecutive meetings of the Société de Neurologie de Paris in 1908. At this time Déjerine (responsible for the disconnection theory of agnosia) and his wife Madame Déjerine (a respected anatomist of the time) were the main antagonists to Marie. Dejerine argued that Broca's aphasia was separate from Wernicke's aphasia, because the anterior broca aphasia is largely a disorder of speech production and comprehension difficulties are mild. Marie countered that comprehension difficulties were only mild because the lesioned area is further away from the main language centre of Wernicke (Lecours et al., 1992). As indicated, Marie's proposal was that anterior or Broca's aphasia was not a proper aphasia, but a motor disorder. He was referring to the disorders of articulation found in these patients that are associated with the poor coordination of the motor movements required of speech. This view of Broca's aphasia is not completely accepted by modern theorists. As we shall argue, there are clear symptoms of aphasia that are associated with an anterior Broca's type aphasia. But, as will be argued in this chapter, in another sense Marie was accurate when describing the effect of the lesion if it were isolated to Broca's area. Marie's contribution is also important because he drew attention to the importance of subcortical lesions in aphasia.

It is possible that, in part, the controversies supplied by Marie and others led to a more ready acceptance of a purely psychological description of aphasia, championed by such authors as Head (1926). Head described the different aphasias irrespective of their neuroanatomical correlates, describing verbal, semantic, nominal, and syntactic aphasias. Correlative neuroanatomical descriptions became less popular, in the same way that many cognitive neuropsychological descriptions of language disorders have sometimes seen this aspect as being of lesser importance or irrelevant to their particular theoretical goals.

The influence of Head and others was followed by new holistic descriptions of brain organisation. These proposals, in contrast to the localisationist approach, were largely against the idea of different brain areas playing different roles. According to this scheme it was not where the lesion occurred but how much brain was damaged which mattered most. The holistic perspective of brain organisation, while ultimately found lacking in support, may have maintained the momentum of the purely psychological approach (Geschwind, 1965, p. 240). We now know that relatively discrete lesions in particular areas may cause considerably more aphasic symptoms than larger lesions elsewhere in the brain. This is true

even within the areas that have been identified as being important for language (Naeser, 1994).

The influence started to swing the other way with the publications of Norman Geschwind in the 1960s. Geschwind's influence stemmed not only from his own work but also from his charismatic influence on his many bright and energetic followers at the Veterans Administration Hospital in Boston. Geschwind drew attention to the original theory provided by the early localisationists such as Wernicke and Lichtheim with a modified model of his own. The model described the language areas of Broca and Wernicke and other areas; each area was described as playing a particular role. Geschwind made predictions concerning aphasic symptoms if these different areas were damaged or disconnected from each other. However, some influential thinkers were not in agreement with Geschwind's early proposals. Initially, Luria was clearly not in sympathy with Geschwind's views (Luria & Hutton, 1977), although later he was to formulate a correlative neuroanatomical model, which he admitted was similar to Geschwind's (Luria, 1980).

Some of the complexities and uncertainties that have caused such historical controversy are due to the multiple higher cortical influences on the language process. The influences of memory, perception, and executive disorders on language allow the many presentations of language disorder. Also, as indicated below, there is considerable variability in the representation of language between individuals, which has also undermined attempts at modelling. This has made analysis and agreement between researchers unlikely. The same variety of language disorders has led to the proliferation of a bewildering number of terms, many of which describe overlapping concepts.

Nevertheless, with some modification, the original views of two language systems, one anterior system for expression and production of speech, and a second posterior system for comprehension with its important connections to the auditory and visual sensory areas, remained popular although somewhat modified. These and other broad differences have led over the years to certain aphasic syndromes being proposed and developed that are based on the original work of the first localisationists. For example, *Broca's aphasia* is a disorder typified by impairment in the production and expression of speech. This is associated with lesions in the area originally described that was apparently affected in his patient "Tan". *Wernicke's aphasia* is the name given to patients who have a dominant difficulty in comprehending language and is similarly associated with the area originally described by Carl Wernicke. Both these syndromes are associated with particular patterns of symptoms that include an inability to repeat back sentences. *Conduction aphasia* is revealed when an inability to repeat back is the main symptom. There are also syndromes that are referred to collectively as transcortical aphasias, which are not associated with poor repeating back (repetition). Although it is generally realised that the traditional syndromes such as Broca's aphasia describe symptoms that are due to different mechanisms, many researchers remain interested in working within this framework. This provides a focus of interest for many researchers who are most interested in understanding how the brain is organised in its production and comprehension of language.

In the early 1980s a new movement of cognitive neuropsychology, spearheaded by a journal of the same name, provided an alternative approach to research that depended on deducing levels of analysis of language mainly using case studies (previously referred to in the introduction). These researchers, who often came from cognitive psychology (study of memory, perception, and attention in normal subjects) and from a psycholinguistic tradition, had already been preceded by others with a similar background, but now the approach to research was clearly identified and intensified. Many researchers in this group soon became assertive in proposing that the single-case methodology was *more* warranted compared to group studies because of the individual variation between patients. There was concern that by using groups the analysis of crucial differences between patients was blurred. Nevertheless, this view was not by any means accepted in many quarters. Others claimed that group studies were still useful for all the reasons that psychologists had usually studied groups rather than rely on one potentially unreliable case. The cognitive neuropsychology approach was often less concerned about the neuroanatomical basis of language disorders. They reasonably proposed that a phenomenon could be analysed at various levels and that one of their main aims was to describe normal language processes without reference to neuroanatomy. In the next section some of the flavour of this approach to their research is introduced. It is of interest that this journal of cognitive neuropsychology has since changed in its content and is more observant of cognitive–structural relationships. However, the original introduction of this journal and its consequent impact on scientific thinking in this area was of immense historical significance and much of the work discussed in the second half of this chapter are the products of its influence.

SOME INTRODUCTORY CONCEPTS: THE EXAMPLE OF ANOMIA

Anomia, briefly, is an inability to name when confronted with a stimulus. The naming difficulty occurs in all modalities of presentation, e.g. visual, auditory, and tactile, and it is a pervasive problem among aphasics. Anomia occurs in most types of aphasia and often the only sign left after a patient largely recovers from aphasia is some residual signs of anomia. Anomia cannot be assumed to exist if the patient is denied access to the sensory input prerequisite to naming. For example, a patient with a visual impairment such as hemianopia is not necessarily seen as suffering anomia if they fail to name an article presented in the area of their impaired visual field.

As more and more interesting cases of patients with anomia are described, models of anomia have become increasingly complex. Some look like a map of the underground to the initiate. However, these "boxes and arrows" models of the type illustrated in Figure 7.2 become easy to understand if they are built up from the basics. The first issue, which is clearest, is the distinction between naming and knowledge of the name's meaning. A common situation in both aphasic

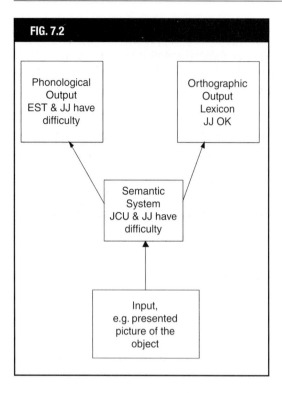

FIG. 7.2

Phonological Output
EST & JJ have difficulty

Orthographic Output Lexicon
JJ OK

Semantic System
JCU & JJ have difficulty

Input, e.g. presented picture of the object

A hypothetical output system for naming. Separate systems are assumed due to a dissociation of impairments. Expression of naming may be in speech and the dependence on the selection of the phonological attributes of the word or, alternatively, the orthographic features—the physical, visual appearance—of the name. The model assumes that the meaning (semantic features) of the name must be selected prior to its output. This example is used to provide a model of the logic of cognitive neuropsychology. More elaborate and sophisticated models exist illustrating the input and output model of naming (e.g. Caramazza, 1988).

and normal speech occurs when we know quite a bit about an object, but the name eludes us. We might say "You know that thing you navigate with . . . it's used on ships to measure the angle between the horizon and the sun or stars. It begins with 's' and it's on the tip of my tongue . . . Oh yes, it's a sextant!" This "tip of the tongue phenomenon" has been investigated in subjects with and without aphasia and it does help a subject if the first letter of the name is provided (Brown & McNeill, 1966). This encourages the view that we have a store or lexicon from which we retrieve the name, in the same way a library

book might be more easily found if we know where it is stored. While giving a first letter of an object is often helpful, giving more information about the object is not so helpful in name retrieval, which suggests a separation between the semantic (meaning) store and the name *lexicon.*

While an inability to name an object, despite access to knowledge of the object's use and function, is a relatively common occurrence with aphasic patients, patients with the reverse problem are far rarer. However, the existence of such patients who are able to name without knowledge encourages the view that separate naming and semantic analysis systems do exist. Howard and Orchard-Lisle (1984) describe a patient referred to as JCU who was able to give the name when cued with a letter but the response sometimes resulted in an error, but the error was such that a word from a similar category was produced, e.g. a tiger would be called a lion. The authors concluded that the patient had a naming difficulty because of imprecise semantic analysis. More commonly, other patients such as EST (Kay & Ellis, 1987) were able to give precise information about the objects that they could not name. The patient was unable to access to a lexicon of the phonological representations of the semantic information. The hypothetical store containing the sound of the words representing the object was impaired or disconnected in some way. So far it seems reasonable to propose two stages of analysis: one analysing the meaning (semantic analysis) of the to-be-named item and a second analysing the phonological constituents of the word describing the item.

Of course, when we name an object the name can be spoken or written. Hillis and Caramazza (1991a) describe a patient, JJ, with damage to the left temporal lobe area and the basal ganglia following a stroke. JJ was unable to give the meaning of 32% of the words (irregular words) that he could read. He could write the name of items presented to him and also spell these words correctly. This case offers the view that the patient had specific access to the form of the words that he read. Irregular words such as *mint, yacht, chaos,* and *steak* are not pronounced by using the sound or

Box 7.1. Ojemann, Ojemann, Lettich, & Berger (1989) electrical mapping study

Of their 117 patients epileptic patients around 33% failed to show an anterior speech zone. Interestingly, more females than males gave evidence of an anterior speech zone. Males with low verbal levels of intelligence tended not to show an anterior inferior speech area. Also, the areas found to be responsive to speech arrest during naming were not confined to the traditional areas described by Broca and Wernicke. As indicated, the anterior inferior areas were particularly variable. No relationship was found between the area of cortex apparently taken up by language and intelligence, although there was a trend with lower IQ being associated with a smaller area.

There was no obvious support for reorganisation of language in this study, with the areas of patients with perinatal lesions not differing from those with lesions in adulthood.

Electrical mapping of the cortex is a process that is presumed to inhibit or inactivate groups of neurones. The method may therefore be assumed to be relatively crude. Without detracting from the usefulness of these and other studies, no differential arrest of categorical words, e.g. living versus non-living things, has been found. Therefore the subtle effects that might be expected from lesion studies are not always revealed by this method. It should also be kept in mind that these are patients who had electrical mapping prior to surgery. Generalisation to normal groups cannot be assumed.

These reservations aside, the findings of Ojemann's group, while drawing attention to the large number of individual differences, replicate findings of the earlier findings of Penfield and colleagues. Stimulation studies are especially useful in pointing out the areas that are important for articulation — the areas that play a role in the production of the motor components of speech.

phonological rules, but must be learned and recognised for their form. An orthographic lexicon is required that stores all these unusually pronounced words. With this introduction it may be possible to see how the cognitive neuropsychologist might set about model making. We have not cited enough evidence yet, but we are beginning to model the existence of different stores and output systems on the basis of logical deduction.

At this point some verification of the terms used so far is necessary. While the *phonological* structure (how a word is analysed for its sound or pronunciation) may be important for spelling regular words, writing requires knowledge of the visual form of the word, which is referred to as orthography. For example, the word *sale* has a different *orthography* from the word *sail* because the words *look* physically different, but phonologically they are identical given most accents. We can often work out the orthography of a word from its sound, but irregular words need to be remembered if they are to be spelled correctly. They require a memory store or *lexicon* like a dictionary. It is assumed that the semantic system, which stores the meaning or attributions of the word, accesses the orthographic lexicon and the phonological analyser in parallel. The logic for this view comes from the finding that a patient may have difficulty with the orthographic lexicon but not with the phonological analysis system, while other patients may have the opposite difficulty. If one followed the other there would be

interference such that an earlier stage would interfere with a later stage — the information would get "cut off at the pass". This does not always happen so the parallel model in Figure 7.2 is assumed.

A number of patients have now been described who have superior writing naming abilities when compared to spoken naming (e.g. L'hermitte & Derouesne, 1974). Other patients may have the opposite difficulty, with writing being far worse than spoken naming (Caramazza & Hillis, 1990). These patients often show clear knowledge of the meaning of the words, so the difficulty does appear to be at these two output stages. Caramazza & Hillis (1990) describe patients whose spoken word naming was far worse then their naming when writing, which also supports the independence of these two systems (see Figure 7.2). This introduction into the cognitive neuropsychology approach to modelling illustrates the way single cases that are rare, and therefore could never be studied on a group basis, help define and model the language process.

The cognitive neuropsychology approach will be covered in more depth towards the end of this chapter. The next section of this chapter will, however, be more concerned with models of language that have been developed using a different but equally valid approach often looking for similarities between patients. This syndrome approach attempts to group patients according to their symptoms.

THE LANGUAGE AREA

In Chapter 6, attention was paid to the left brain hemisphere's specialised role in language. Although the significance of the neuroanatomical differences between the structure of the two hemispheres is yet to be fully understood, some of the more obvious contrasts take place in the vicinity of what is described as the language area. For example, there are differences between the hemispheres in Broca's area. More cortex is hidden within the sulci on the left in this area and this area is larger, with denser dendritic growth, compared to the equivalent right area (Falzi, Peronne, & Vignolo, 1982; Scheibel et al., 1985).

A variety of procedures have identified what is broadly described as the left perisylvian area as a language area. Most notably, the use of electrical stimulation of the brain has been used to map out the functional importance of this area. Patients who have been candidates for the surgical treatment of epilepsy are often used on the basis that electrical stimulation may evoke and thereby localise a seizure focus. A second use of such a technique is to map out the area used for language so that this can be avoided during surgery. The brain is largely insensitive to pain and a local anaesthetic was originally sufficient to allow the brain area to be exposed.

Electrical mapping of the cortex is a process that is presumed to inhibit or inactivate groups of neurones. The method may therefore be assumed to be relatively crude. Without detracting from the usefulness of these and other studies, no differential arrest of categorical words, e.g. living versus non-living things, has been found. Also, the stimulation method is used with patients who often have lesions that may result in some anomalies in the distribution of language.

Stimulation within the perisylvian area, including Wernicke's and Broca's areas, often results in the patient responding with an arrest of speech, if the patient is talking. Wilder Penfield of the Montreal Institute of Neurology used this method to define the areas described in Figure 7.3. These same areas run the risk of long-term aphasia when they are excised (Rasmussen & Milner, 1976).

While these areas are still seen to be important, more recent work by Ojemann, Ojemann, Lettich, & Berger (1989) had placed these early findings in perspective. Of prime importance is the need to realise that these averaged findings are poorly representative of the variability found among individuals (see Box 7.1 for a discussion of some of their results). If the areas that are most frequently associated with naming failure are inspected (Figure 7.3b) then certain patterns reveal themselves. However, account must be taken of how the failure to name a picture or make a naming error during electrical stimulation may be due to a number of different reasons. Ojemann supports the findings of Penfield in targeting certain motor areas for spoken language, such as the supplementary motor areas (see also the areas that parallel the motor strip). These areas are far more forgiving when lesioned and result in articulation disorder for around 1 week, often followed by a complete recovery (Ojemann, 1994). The posterior language zone is more obviously related to aphasic symptoms. He reports that a lesion within 2 cm of a speech area may result in mild aphasic symptoms evident on tests a month later. Also, on this evidence excision of the superior gyri of the left temporal lobe is not advised irrespective of individual differences found between patients.

Work with stroke patients who have aphasic symptoms has also been useful in isolating this language area, which can be seen as extending beyond the traditional language areas described by Broca and Wernicke, and is again predictably subject to some marked individual differences (Kertesz, 1993b; Rasmussen & Milner, 1976).

A MODEL OF LANGUAGE DISORDERS

Lichtheim (1885) published a monograph in *Brain* that provided a model of aphasia with a number of supporting case studies. This work was important because it allowed certain predictions if the connections between specialised brain areas

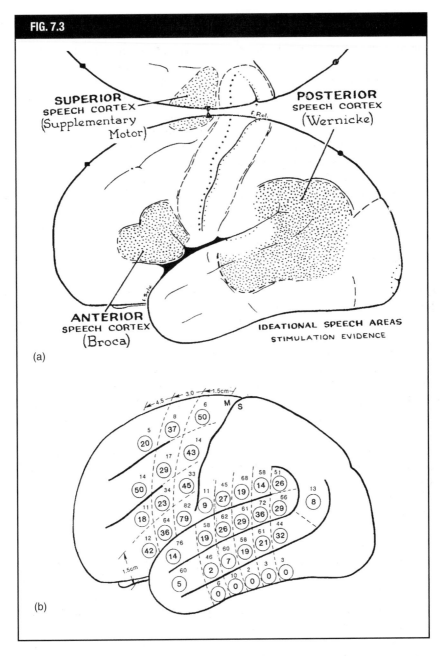

FIG. 7.3

(a) Illustration of the perisylvian speech areas, following the electrical mapping work of Penfield and Roberts (reprinted from Penfield and Roberts, 1959, with permission form Princeton University Press). Negative motor areas may be associated with sudden meaningless articulations involving motor movements such as tongue movements. Language areas are associated with a cessation of speech following electrical stimulation of the cortex. The anterior and posterior speech areas correspond remarkably well with the surgeon's areas based on interference following cortical excision, except the posterior speech area tends to extend ventrally. This work somewhat overlooks the range of individual differences encapsulated by the later work of Ojemann. (b) Results of Ojemann's electrical mapping study. The numbers in the circles indicate the number of patients who consistently failed in naming during stimulation in that area (reprinted from Ojemann, Ojemann, Lettich, & Berger, 1989, with permission from the *Journal of Neurosurgery*).

were severed. The work of Lichtheim and Wernicke provides the basis of theory underlying what is sometimes referred to as the syndrome approach. Lichtheim retained the work of Broca, designating the anterior area of Broca as a centre for expression and production of language, while Wernicke's area was designated an area of comprehension. Lichtheim's contribution was to provide a model that described some of the aphasias as a disconnection between these main centres and provided case studies to support his theory. Much later the 1960s saw a revival of the popularity of this approach (Geschwind, 1965, 1970). Geschwind clarified and linked Lichtheim's model with the visual input system, describing the processing of visual information from the visual cortex to the angular gyrus prior to the analysis for meaning in Wernicke's area (See Figure 7.4). This model, which is sometimes referred to as the Wernicke–Geschwind model of language, could equally be called the Wernicke–Lichtheim–Geschwind model. This model is presented first in order to allow the reader a background towards more modern formulations.

The model proposes that connections between specialised centres allow the progression from sensory input to speech output. The model in Figure 7.4 contains two areas of sensory input, the visual area for reading and the auditory area for analysing auditory input. The basic sensory inputs are analysed at Heschl's gyrus for auditory input and the striate cortex for visual information. In this model the angular gyrus, as part of the association area, is seen as an area for translating from one sensory modality to another: from the visual modality to the auditory and vice versa. The transformation of the basic auditory information at Heschl's gyrus into the phonological representation of words and then to their meaning is assumed to take place in Wernicke's area. For the meaning of visual information, e.g. reading material to be realised, there must be an initial translation of the visual input in the visual cortex. This visual information is then sent to the angular gyrus in order that it may be translated into an auditory modality for meaning. The translation in this polymodal association area of the angular gyrus is therefore necessary before it may finally be translated for meaning in Wernicke's area. Finally, for the production of speech, Geschwind (1970) proposes that the meaning of what is to be said must be transferred

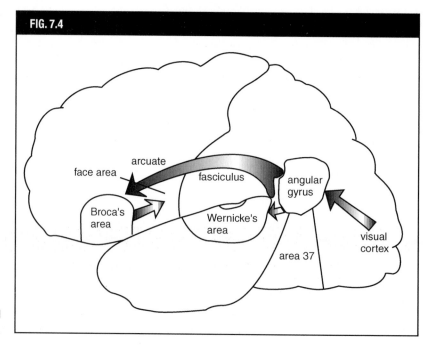

FIG. 7.4

The Wernicke–Geschwind model.

from Wernicke's area to Broca's area via a group of axons called the arcuate fasciculus. Within Broca's area the sentence to be spoken is planned and organised before it is sent on to the "face area" within the motor strip. The face area is then responsible for activating and executing the appropriate motor movements for the articulation of speech, which has been pre-programmed within Broca's area.

As indicated, the phonological conversion of the spoken word into auditory meaning takes place in Wernicke's area. This same area is also important for deducing meaning during the reading process. The word, when it is read, must be transferred from the primary visual cortex to the secondary and tertiary areas before it arrives within the association area, at the angular gyrus. The transformation from visual to auditory modality is necessary for access to Wernicke's area and the translation of the orthographic (physical visual form) representation of the script into its meaning.

Reading aloud requires an additional stage, requiring the transferral of auditory information (acoustic/phonetic/semantic) into a speech form. The acoustic/phonological information must be sent first to the area of Broca. As indicated, in this model this is achieved by transferring information via the supramarginal gyrus along the long axons, referred to as the arcuate fasciculus. When the information arrives at Broca's area, it is assembled into the required sequential order for spoken language before being sent posteriorly to the "face area" for the execution of the tongue, lips, and other muscle movements required for speech. In other words, Broca's area plans and orders the information for spontaneous speech. Table 7.1 illustrates the variety of stages involved in various language functions.

The Wernicke–Geschwind model is a useful model to start theoretical thinking about language disorders, although the discussion concerning some of the modern views of language disorders demands some considerable refinement of this model.

While there are a number of reputable alternative classification systems, in clinical practice the Boston system and the one proposed by Luria have been especially influential. The Boston-based work has been led by Norman Geschwind, Frank Benson, Harold Goodglass, Edith Kaplan, and numerous colleagues. Another approach with a strong therapeutic influence is provided by Luria (see Kagan & Saling, 1988, for an introduction). There are many similarities between the classifications of the two groups. The Boston approach will be the main instructional framework used here.

The Boston approach divides the perisylvian aphasias into *Broca's aphasia*, which is marked predominantly by difficulties in expression or production of language with some specific difficulties in comprehension of syntax, and *Wernicke's aphasia*, which is predominantly a disorder of comprehension. The third type is referred to as *conduction aphasia*, an aphasia in which repetition is the main impairment. Finally, *global aphasia* is associated with features of both Broca's and Wernicke's aphasia.

A number of studies of stroke patients appear to support the essential prediction that Broca's aphasia is more often associated with an anterior stroke, while posterior stroke is more often associated with Wernicke's aphasia (Basso, Lecours, Moraschini & Vanier, 1985; Naeser & Hayward, 1979). As will be argued, even studies that have been critical of the usefulness of this syndrome approach may still be reinterpreted as

TABLE 7.1		
Serial involvement of areas according to the Wernicke–Geschwind model		
Reading	Visual cortex → angular gyrus → Wernicke's	
Repetition	Heschl's gyrus → Wernicke's area → ararcuate fasciculus → Broca's → face area	
Reading aloud	Visual cortex → angular gyrus → Wernicke's → arcuate fasciculus → Broca's area → face area	

supporting this very general view (Willmes & Poeck, 1993).

THE PERISYLVIAN APHASIAS

As the name suggests, these aphasias are associated with lesions around the sylvian fissure, broadly within the language area described in Figure 7.3. The work of Kertesz and others has indicated that the areas that produce perisylvian aphasias extend well beyond the sylvian fissure and well beyond the areas originally described by Broca and Wernicke (Kertesz, 1979).

Within the Boston classification of language disorders, a further broad division can be made between those disorders that are related to poor repetition and those where repetition is intact. Poor repetition of words, numbers, and sentences is associated with perisylvian lesions and disorders such as *Broca's, Wernicke's and conduction aphasia*. This group of aphasias is distinct from the group of *transcortical aphasias* which are associated with extra-perisylvian damage and which are found to have an intact repetition.

Broca's aphasia

Main features
As indicated above, the Wernicke–Geschwind model sees the area of Broca as a centre that is important for language production. Alternative terms that are sometimes used to refer to symptoms similar to Broca's aphasia are non-fluent or expressive aphasia. Patients diagnosed with this syndrome often have lesions that are in excess of broca's area (see Figure 7.5). These patients have difficulty planning and organising their speech and this is well illustrated in the extract in Box 7.2 where a patient attempts a description of the Cinderella story. The slashes between the words indicate pauses and illustrate the "effortful" nature of articulation. This articulatory difficulty with speech is sometimes accompanied by grimaces or contorted facial expressions, as if the words are an effort to get out.

With this type of aphasia there is a noted hesitation in the initiation of an articulation (Alexander & Benson, 1991) and in planning, sequencing, and executing the articulation. The articulation problems are related to the motor control of speech and are sometimes referred to as verbal apraxia. Verbal apraxia may disappear when the patient is asked to repeat back stereotyped phrases that are well learned, such as the alphabet. The distinction between verbal apraxias and dysarthria is important. Dysarthria is a motor impairment that distorts all speech sounds relatively indiscriminately and often (not always) relates to subcortical damage, e.g. basal ganglia involvement. Verbal apraxia affects particular words, especially if they are difficult to pronounce, e.g. tongue-twisters, or are less familiar to the patient. Associated with a verbal apraxia, is a buccofacial apraxia which is seen as being more associated with damage to the face area within the motor strip. This relates to the execution of motor movements associated with the execution of speech and is tested by requesting the patient to make movements like blowing out a match or moving their tongue from one side of their mouth to another. It should be noted that because this aphasic syndrome is associated with lesions to the anterior branch of the middle cerebral artery the motor areas are likely to be affected. For example, Broca's aphasia is often accompanied by paralysis of the right upper limb.

Much of the speech in the transcript contained in Box 7.2 is agrammatic as well as being poorly planned and organised; that is, it lacks the joining or function words. As one would predict, many of these difficulties are not merely confined to speech but often also appear in the patient's written language and reading. The patient may have paraphasias, in which case the wrong word is used, e.g. table for bed (verbal/semantic paraphasias); or a word sounding like the word is used, e.g. school instead of stool (literal/phonological paraphasias). These paraphasias are looked at in more detail when discussing Wernicke's aphasia.

Naming impairment (anomia) can occur with all types of perisylvian aphasias and is always poor in Broca's aphasia. However, confrontation naming tends to demonstrate a better vocabulary than would be expected, given the paucity of

FIG. 7.5

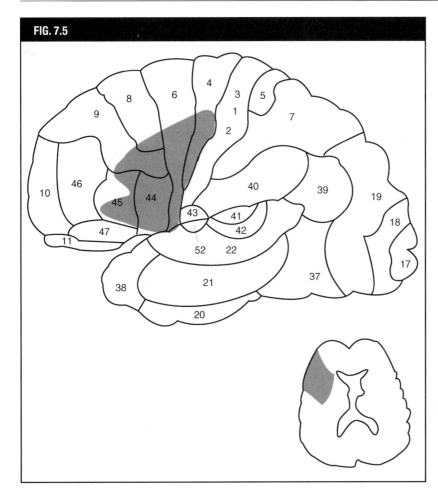

Some of the the lesion sites in patients with Broca's aphasia (adapted from Damasio, 1991). Broca's area 45 is involved but also 44 and some of the premotor area. The oblique slice of the brain gives an example of the subcortical damage.

Box 7.2.   Illustration of speech of a Broca's aphasia patient

Cinderella's story

"a mother/ . . . three kids/ . . . bad mother/one kid beautiful/ . . . rich/Italian/ . . . mother/ . . . stepmother/ . . . talk about Cinderella/Cinderella/clean my house/ . . . you Cinderella/close the door/ . . . Cinderella like jail/ . . . mother . . . three kids/ . . . I love mother/ . . . Cinderella walk ball/ . . . people ball/ . . . rich rich people/ . . . man and Cinderella dance dance dance party/ . . . one/ . . . dance dance dance/ . . . dance every time/ . . . ball beautiful people/ . . . people watched Cinderella/ . . . Cinderella . . . beautiful clothes . . . and garments/ . . . twelve o'clock night/Cinderella/oh no/oh no/ I'm sorry/I'm sorry people/I love you baby/ . . . walk walk/tumble/ . . . one shoe bye-bye/ . . . Cinderella . . . pumpkin cab/ . . . oh shoe/oh please/oh well/walk pumpkin car/."

Excerpt from Saffran, Berndt, and Schwartz (1989)

---

words used in spontaneous speech (Benson & Ardila, 1996). Therefore the spontaneous use of words is more obviously impaired when compared to the cued situation. Also, better results are obtained when naming the actual object compared to an outline of the object on a card (Goodglass & Kaplan, 1983).

Agrammatism

Agrammatism is an obvious feature in the "Cinderella" transcript (Box 7.2); nouns, verbs, and adjectives that have a high meaning content are provided at the expense of the correct tenses of verbs and conjunctions, which give sentences their syntactical meaning. This is sometimes referred to as telegraphic speech, because it is reminiscent of the telegrams sent by impoverished persons. The telegrams were costed according to the number of words used, and were accordingly often abbreviated without the use of syntax, e.g. "Send . . . money . . . clothes . . . have . . . holes".

Over recent years the analysis of agrammatism has been a popular focus of research. It is evident that not only do patients have difficulty in producing sentences that have syntactical flow, but some patients also have difficulty understanding sentences due to poor appreciation of these same grammatical constructs (e.g. Berndt & Caramazza, 1980a, 1980b; Goodglass, 1993). This is shown clearly in some patients using reversible sentences. A reversible sentence is one that is pivoted on a verb, so that when the noun phrases either side of the verb are swapped the sentence still makes sense. For example, *John loved Mary* is reversible since *Mary loved John* also makes sense. There is a tendency for patients showing agrammatism to switch the nouns in such sentences, thus revealing a difficulty in using syntax to determine the subject/object relationships. Patients with Broca's aphasia may have more difficulty extracting the meaning of such reversible sentences (Schwartz, Saffran, & Marin, 1980b).

Patients are often able to read even complex sentences when they are non-reversible. For example, the sentence "The bike which the girl is riding is blue" may cause fewer problems than anticipated. If the sentence is broken down into meaning units then the result, "bike/girl/riding/blue" is less dependent on the grammatical comprehension, for the bike, not the girl, is most likely to be blue (Schwartz, Fink, & Saffran, 1995). If an understanding of the syntax is necessary for sentence comprehension then the agrammatic Broca's aphasia patient may have some difficulty. This is especially true of passive sentences in which the patient is fooled by the order. For example, in the reversible sentence, *The boy was hit by the ball*, the patient not comprehending the passive syntax may assume the more usual subject acts on object construction, allowing the interpretation of *The boy hit the ball*.

The mechanism for this difficulty is uncertain.

Contrary to expectations, Schwartz, Saffran, and Marin, (1980b) have shown that agrammatic patients are actually able to judge whether sentences are syntactically correct, even though they may have difficulty in extracting the meaning and are unable to construct such sentences themselves. This has prompted Berndt and Caramazza (1981) to propose that agrammatism might be due to a lack of attentional resource. They argued that the syntax judgement task may require less attention since patients carrying out this task were not overloaded or additionally hampered by the analysis of the meaning (semantics) of such syntax. They called this the trade-off hypothesis. There is some evidence that these patients have extra difficulty with long sentences (Kolk & Weuts, 1996). Although these authors take this into consideration, there is a universal tendency for impairments due to brain damage to be accentuated under conditions that require increased attentional resources.

There is also support for a second, "mapping hypothesis", which proposes that the problem is one of converting the syntax into meaning (Berndt & Caramazza, 1981). In other words, these patients' agrammatism is explained in terms of a difficulty in using the words that surround the nouns and verbs such as prepositions, and the different endings of verbs, e.g. kick*ed* versus kick*s*, and the other grammatical features that modify the meaning of a sentence. These patients often have an inability to retrieve words that are of syntactical relevance. Therefore there is the difficulty in recruiting syntactical information from a hypothetical syntax lexicon (Caramazza, Berndt, Basili, & Koller, 1981; Goodglass, 1983). The mapping hypothesis is supported at the expense of the trade-off hypothesis by the finding that even small sentences with very simple syntactical elements cause difficulty for these patients.

For practical purposes, the important lesson is that these patients have difficulty on tasks that require the *active* retrieval and production of syntactical-related procedures. If one assesses the *comprehension* of these patients on such material, using aphasic controls without agrammatism, there may, however, be little difference in terms of comprehension ability between Broca patients and other patient groups (Caplan, Baker, & Dehaut, 1985; Goodglass et al., 1979). Therefore while comprehension of syntax is undeniably a problem with Broca's aphasia, a sense of proportion allows that it is the grammatical expression that is the relatively outstanding impairment. These patients with anterior lesions have less difficulty when less spontaneity is required, as in the case of recognition of correct versus incorrect sentences.

Just as the patient with anterior lesions with memory impairment may have less difficulty recognising memorised material and more difficulty actively retrieving information, so the anterior-lesioned patients with agrammatism will also have more difficulty in spontaneously producing grammatical constructions. In some ways this may be seen as a dysexecutive language disorder. Certainly there is evidence that poor organisation of the sentence is sometimes a problem for some patients with agrammatism (Saffran, Schwartz, & Marin, 1980b).

For this reason, the patient, during a clinical examination, will often be asked to undertake tasks that require spontaneous sentence constructions. For example, the patient might be asked to describe the weather on the day of the assessment, or their previous work. These requests reveal the features of agrammatism in speech and writing.

A comment on Broca's aphasia and the broad nomenclature of agrammatism

Many criticisms have been made concerning the conceptual integrity of Broca's syndrome, but two appear to be most important: the first concerns the lesion location of Broca's aphasia, while the second relates to the individual variability of the type of agrammatism expressed.

Some mention has already been made regarding the criticism that Broca's aphasia appears to be a collection of signs that are more related to the pathway of the cerebral arteries associated with stroke than to any unified functional explanation for the collection of deficits (Poeck, 1983b). This criticism has been given some teeth from a study by Mohr et al. (1978), who showed that cases with lesions isolated to Broca's area often showed an isolated verbal apraxia, but not necessarily the other features that are also described as part of Broca's aphasic syndrome. The lesion site traditionally associated with this syndrome therefore appears to be misleading. The presence of other Broca signs was often associated with lesions widely in excess of the Broca's area. Of these patients, who had smaller lesions that were more defined, most had lesions within the frontal region. Vanier and Caplan (1985) describe lesion data for 20 patients with the agrammatic form of Broca's aphasia. Some of these patients had extensive lesions involving most of the tributaries of the middle cerebral artery, which made interpretation difficult. Of those with small lesions, four were frontal (most overlapped Broca's area, with one on the right side in an area equivalent to Broca's, and three were subcortical lesions in which areas of the arcuate fasciculus, the insula, and the corona radiata were involved. The neurosurgeons Wilder Penfield and Lamar Roberts (1959, p. 203), when discussing their lesion studies, suggest that surgical removal of Broca's area (usually associated with brain tumour) frequently results in a recovery of language within a brief recovery period. They were of the opinion that a subcortical lesion is required for more permanent aphasic symptoms (Penfield and Roberts, 1959, p. 203). They go on to say "On the contrary, in the posterior speech area any large destruction that involves cortex and the underlying projection areas of the thalamus would certainly produce the gravest aphasia.".

Past studies using PET and MRI have tended to be difficult to interpret. Tasks were often passive, because patients had to be completely still during scanning. However, more recently devices including masks and body moulds have reduced the motor movement and allowed subjects a less passive role. Studies that include constructing and speaking sentences show activation that is very much more frontal than passive listening (Xiong et al., 1998). Also, if one thinks of difficulty in initiating a sentence spontaneously as a key difficulty with Broca's, it is important to note the activation studies that show anterior activation in studies requiring selection or generation of verbal output (see Figure 3.10).

A study by Metter and colleagues (reviewed in Metter & Hanson, 1994) looked at the uptake of glucose in the brain using PET. This method allows the inspection of hypometabolism due to the influence of brain damage; these areas of hypometabolism (measured relative to the contralateral hemisphere) may then be compared to CT scans of the damage due to stroke (area of infarction). These studies are interesting since they estimate that the effects of brain damage are far greater than expected. The direction of effects is not merely an expansion of area of damage but affects some brain areas more than others — areas that are presumed to have a functional relationship with the damaged area. These researchers confirm that patients showing the signs of Broca's aphasia inevitably have subcortical damage, e.g. anterior internal capsule, lenticular nuclei. They also support the view that Broca's aphasia is not necessarily related to damage to Broca's area per se. If one considers Marie's (1906) study described earlier in the brief historical review, it is interesting that in addition there is found hypometabolism involving posterior language areas in the parietal and temporal lobes. The area of metabolism was far more asymmetrical in Broca's compared to conduction and Wernicke's aphasic patients. That is, the left hemisphere appeared to be involved in relative isolation. This pattern has been confirmed in studies using PET in quite a different way, which have looked at the change in blood flow in normal persons during expressive speech (see Poeppel, 1996; Xiong et al., 1998). We will return to the possibility of posterior language production centres later in this chapter.

In summary, the localisation of Broca's aphasia is very variable from one individual to another and fails to show a clear and consistent relationship with the area originally described by Broca, although frontal areas are mostly associated with this aphasic syndrome. Nevertheless, recent functional imaging studies reveal that Broca's and left prefrontal areas with their adjacent subcortical areas play an important role in the spontaneous expression of speech. This and the surrounding areas are well placed to play out the usual executive role in initiating and organising speech pro-duction, which is eventually executed in the lowest, ventral area of the motor strip. This area is involved in the motor movements required of speech (see Figure 7.3b; Ojemann found the area just anterior to this motor area, the most consistently involved in the interference of naming).

A second modification of the concept of Broca's aphasia and agrammatism comes from a series of findings from a linguistic perspective. It is argued that the term is too broad since it may take so many different forms. Differences between patients have been found who have a different degree of agrammatism within speech production versus comprehension (Kolk, Van Grunsvan, & Keyser, 1985; Schwartz et al., 1980a). These results suggest the system for the *production* of syntactical language is separate from the system required for *comprehension of syntax*.

However, even within the production of syntax there may be even further differentiation. Analysis of individual patients suggests that different mechanisms underlie difficulties with syntax. For example, patients have been found who omit function words and inflections but who show little difficulty with word order (Tissot, Mounin, & L'hermitte, 1973). Conversely, patients have also been found who have difficulty with word order, but have far fewer problems in using function words and inflection words in their speech (Saffran, Schwartz, & Marin, 1980a).

In formulating a model that describes the disruption of syntax it is important to start with the notion that content and function words may be processed differently. Content words are subject to a familiarity effect: the more familiar or frequently used content words such as *husband* or *nurse* are responded to far more quickly than words such as *kidney* or *broker.*

Function words that includes conjunctions, e.g. *and, because*, prepositions, e.g. *to, by, in*, and other words that are crucial for grammatical constructions such as *what, where, who* may appear to be more intact in some patients compared to others, but when during testing the content and function words are matched for familiarity, i.e. the extent they appear in the literature, then differences sometimes disappear (Ellis & Young, 1996, p. 125). Nevertheless, it is possible that our knowledge for content and the use of function words are stored in different brain areas. Manning and Warrington (1996) have described a patient who had good ability to retrieve the meaning of content words such as verbs, but poor ability in retrieving knowledge concerning verbal syntax.

A model by Garrett (1976) proposes that in order to produce utterances we first formulate the meaning of what we have to say. This intended meaning automatically activates the appropriate function words required of the sentence. A plan of the functional relationship is then formulated as a series of slots, e.g. subject object verb. Then the nature of the syntax is formulated in terms of a framework which includes a verb and its tense e.g. past or present. In the next stage the verbs and content words are adapted according to whether they are referring to the singular or plural. The phonological representations of the content words are then accessed from a lexicon using the semantic representation. In the next level these content words are placed within the syntactic framework. This is followed by the phonological specification of the function words and other grammatical elements. Within this framework elements that make up a sentence are first planned in terms of a framework and last of all assembled into the final product. This adapted and shortened version of Garrett's model is summarised below. The levels are as follows:

1. Conceptual formulation of the sentence.
2. Framework of functional relationships within the required sentence, e.g. subject, verb, object.
3. Framework of the syntax including the tense of the verb and the position of a word and whether it is singular or plural.
4. Access and preparation of the phonological representation of content words retrieved from a store or lexicon, which allows access to the sounds of words given their meaning.
5. Access and preparation of the phonological representation of the syntactual elements represented in the framework previously designed in level 3.

One of the assumptions of this model is that errors may occur within a level but not between levels. As Garrett suggests, content words are often exchanged with each other in error and syntactual features are often exchanged but there is little evidence of content interfering with syntax. An example of the content words being exchanged while syntax remains unchanged came most notably from a Dr Spooner, who was a don at Oxford University. A relative of the author, who was one of his students recalled on one occasion when meaning to say "The cat dropped on its paws", he said instead "The cat popped on its draws". These spoonerisms are more likely to occur given certain conditions. For example, with words from the same syntactic class as in *dropped* and *popped* exchanges can occur over greater distances, while other content exchanges require closer positions within a sentence, as in the case of saying "key cars" instead of "car keys". Harley reports that from a corpus of several thousand speech errors there was not one instance of a content word being exchanged with a function word (Harley, 1995). While, function and content words are not interchanged sometimes there is interaction between sound and meaning. In the above example *paws* and *draws* are real words that have meaning, but they also sound the same. As Harley points out, the serial nature of Garrett's model cannot be completely accepted since many errors combine semantic and phonological features simultaneously. When a person makes an exchange it is more likely with a real word, not just a word sounding like the original. Therefore there appears to be an interaction between what a person means to say (level 1) and the phonological representation of what he means to say (level 4).

Nevertheless there appears to be a good argument for the separation of the content words from syntactical elements of the type that change tense, for example. The sentence *She slants her writing* becomes *She writes her slanting* and not *She writing her slants* (Butterworth, 1979; Garrett, 1982). Even more convincing is the finding that in studies aimed at disrupting reading through electrical stimulation of the brain, areas have been found that do not disrupt the fluency of reading but produce errors in verb errors, verb endings, pronouns, prepositions, and conjunctions

(Ojemann, 1994, p. 49). Friederici (1995) argues from work looking at electrical patterns associated with tasks that this syntactical analysis occurs within the left anterior brain areas.

Somewhat supportive of a late phonological access to syntactical elements (i.e. within spoken language the syntax is added after words have been decided upon) is the finding that patients who produce neologisms (substituting non-words for words) use the grammar that is appropriate to the neologism rather than the real word. For example, the neologism *dislap* which displaces *declare* becomes *dislapt* and not *dislaped* to suit *declared*. In other words, the neologism is first decided upon with the other content words and then later the syntax and grammatical elements are added based on those content words and modifying them if necessary. Pronunciation of the suffixes, such as *ed* for the past tense, is therefore produced at a relatively late stage after the neologism and other content words have been chosen (Garrett, 1980).

Garrett' framework allows some description of the different forms of agrammatism. As indicated, some patients may have difficulty in retrieving function words, which may represent a breakdown of level 5. Alternatively, a patient may not be able to organise or access their sentences for expression, which might be seen as a failure to access a framework for syntax at level 3. Or they may have difficulty in organising or accessing the order of the content words, which could be illustrative of a failure to comprehend reversible sentences, as described above. Needless to say, such speculations make a number of assumptions: least of all is the assumption that the model applies to both comprehension and expression equally. However, such models may eventually be useful for classifying patients who may require different therapeutic interventions depending on the type of agrammatic disorder.

Typology of severity within Broca's aphasia
Some authors suggest a division, often used by clinicians, between a "little Broca's" or "aphasia-type 1" and "large Broca's" or "aphasia type 2". They are distinguished largely in terms of the associated pathology (Benson, 1996): type 1 little

Broca's aphasia is confined to the cortex, or immediate subcortical structures, while type 2 Broca's aphasia is more extensive, involving the opercula, precentral gyrus, anterior insula and periventricular white matter and/or the posterior inferior deep white matter. Broadly, the more severe type 2 is associated with much more white matter disconnection from frontal lobe areas. Type 2 or big Broca's aphasia is described by Alexander, Benson, and Stuss (1989) as involving many more motor signs, e.g. right hemiplegia, pronounced articulation problems and dysarthria. Hesitancy in verbal initiation and output, restricted grammar, and poor word finding are also more severe. A number of studies have now found that more extensive white matter lesions are associated with this type and it is also accompanied by a slower recovery (e.g. Kertesz, 1993b).

Although Broca's aphasia is seen as having a better recovery profile when compared to Wernicke's, some patients with type 2 have a poor prognosis. Naeser et al. (1989) looked at the recovery of patients with Broca's aphasia and found that those with additional lesions in an area referred to as the medial subcallosal fasciculus (MScF) tended to have a poor recovery. The MScF is a relatively small band of white matter beneath the corpus callosum (subcallosal) and acts to connect the SMA and other areas of the anterior cingulate (area 24) with the caudate and eventually the putamen. It is not essential for the reader to know the exact nature of these connections. However, in Chapter 8 the caudate and putamen will be introduced as structures that make up part of the basal ganglia; the putamen is especially important for motor movements. The SMA and other areas of the cingulate have been described in relation to the initiation of behaviour in Chapter 3. So here we have a system that from its affects on language impairs articulation, especially the internally driven initiation of the articulatory components of speech. Patients with these lesions and Broca's aphasia, whose comprehension is relatively intact, may show little recovery of spontaneous speech. Of interest here is Broca's original patient Tan (Monsieur Leborgne), who many years later was found to have a lesion in this very area (see Figure 7.1). Tan also failed to improve his spontaneous speech up until his death.

Normally small Broca's aphasia has a far better prognosis. The following is a description of a patient with a small Broca's aphasia who initially had no evidence of a lesion on CT scan taken several months after noted deterioration, but had signs of paralysis with lower right face droop, accompanied by sudden aphasic symptoms. HH is a 64-year-old retired foreman of a company making aircraft parts. Six months previously he and his wife noted some signs of difficulty when speaking with friends. There were also signs of right hand weakness. He complained that sometimes he had difficulty in producing the right words. He said, "Sometimes it comes out strange" (see Box 7.3).

HH showed some difficulty in placing his tongue to alternate sides of his mouth, suggesting a mild *buccofacial apraxia*. When tested he had some difficulty in repeating words such as "caterpillar" and "baseball bat", showing some signs of articulatory difficulty. His comprehension was intact but when he was asked to write a description of his job as foreman some of the sentences were not grammatically correct. He had a reduced digit-span of only three items forward.

There has been particular interest over recent years in a progressive dementing disorder referred to as primary progressive aphasia (PPA). A wide variety of presentations have been reported, the most frequent of which starts with signs of Broca's aphasia (Mesulam & Weintraub, 1992). These patients show many of the features of Broca's aphasia initially, but may become mute and deterioration in areas of memory heralds a dementia which is typically associated with dysexecutive signs and is then sometimes referred to as a type of frontal lobe dementia (see Box 7.8). This type of PPA is associated with signs of anterior atrophy. A second variety, which is more likely to involve the temporal lobe, is referred to in the section describing transcortical sensory aphasias (Kertesz, Davidson, & McCabe, 1998).

Wernicke's aphasia

The main features

Overlapping with the conditions referred to as receptive aphasia or sensory aphasia, Wernicke's aphasia, unlike Broca's aphasia, is characterised by fluent speech. Sometimes the speech has an excessive flow as if there is nothing to stop it — a feature that is referred to as a "press of speech". Contrasting with Broca's there is an excess of grammatical words but a paucity of meaning. These patients often provide evidence of circumlocutions, which usually involve describing the word rather than naming it. For example, "the farm animal that needs to be milked" as a circumlocution for "cow". Because of their fluidity of speech, the Wernicke's patient will often compensate for their word-finding difficulties by using these circumlocutions.

The comprehension of Wernicke patients may be tested by visual confrontation naming: requesting the names of *objects* or *body parts* will often show their comprehension difficulties. A difficulty arises sometimes when the examiner is not sure whether a failure of response is due to other factors. If the patient shows the ability to imitate the actions of the examiner then some of these doubts concerning sensory perception may be reduced.

For example, while the patient may be able to *imitate* the movements of the tongue, which indicates they do not have buccofacial apraxia, they may have difficulty understanding the request for the same movement. Sometimes the patient is able to understand some instructions but not

---

Box 7.3. The initial speech assessment of a patient with a small Broca's aphasia.

HH: Sometimes I say "yes" . . . [halts in mid sentence] when I mean "no". I realise immediately afterwards that I have said the wrong thing and . . . correct myself.

DA: Does this happen often?

HH: . . . [Appears to be thinking about what to say and lunges forward as if forcing out the word] "No" (we both saw the humour in the situation, but he refrains from elaborating).

DA: How does this affect your everyday life?

HH: It's problem when . . . converse with the mates.

Box 7.4. A comparison of Wernicke's and Broca's aphasic description of the cookie theft story shown in Figure 7.6. The Wernicke's speech is fluent and sometimes quite rapid. In contrast, the Broca's patient's speech is hesitant and full of pauses

Wernicke's *patient description, from Goodglass (1983)*:

"Well this . . . mother is away here working her work out o' here to get her better, but when she's looking, the two boys looking in the other part. One their small tile into her time here. She's working another time because she is getting, too."

Broca's patient description from Helm-Estabrooks et al., (1981, p. 425):

"Well . . . see . . . girl eating no . . . cookie . . . no . . . ah . . . school no . . . stool . . . ah . . . tip over . . . and ah . . . cookie jar . . . ah . . . lid . . . no . . . see . . . water all over . . . spilled over . . . yuck . . . Mother . . . daydreaming."

others. These patients may, for example, be able to carry out whole-body commands such as stand up or take a bow.

Wernicke aphasic patients may have difficulty with syntax, but it is different in quality from that seen with Broca's aphasia. The Wernicke's patient has difficulties that are referred to as paragrammatic: they are less significant and more related to construction than the poor retrieval of syntax-related words. The two descriptions of the famous cookie theft picture (see Figure 7.6 and Box 7.4) gives an indication of these qualitative differences.

Repetition of a sentence provided by the examiner is generally poor with Wernicke's and the patient's speech is often paraphasic. There are both *phonemic paraphasias*, in which the patient may use the wrong phone and change the sound of a word, e.g. *trar* for *tar*. There are some *semantic paraphasias* when the patient may give a word that means something similar to the required word. For example, the patient may substitute a word for another word, such as "dog" instead of "cat". In some aphasic examinations, comprehension is tested by asking the patients to respond "yes" or "no" to reduce the confounding difficulties of expression that may exist. However, as was the case with a patient interviewed at our hospital (see Box 7.5), with some Wernicke's patients the difficulty

FIG. 7.6

Cookie theft picture from the Boston aphasia exam (reprinted from Goodglass & Kaplan, *The assessment of apashia and related disorders*, 2nd edition, copyright 1980, with permission from Lippincott Williams & Wilkins).

Box 7.5.   Illustrating the comprehension difficulties of the Wernicke's patient (transcript from video)

SP: Could you tell me where you are?
Frank: . . . Yes, er, I just don't feel too good.
SP: Are you in hospital at the present time?
Frank: . . . That is really one thing, really I feel bad you know. Mm . . . I'm not really feeling too good.
SP: What's wrong with you, Frank?
Frank: Well I don't know, to be honest you just er, there will be a few days I feel shy. Saturday was bad, I get bad, Sunday and today.
SP: Where do you live?
Frank: . . . I don't know to be honest, we've got a lot of things my dad.
SP: Do you live in East Keilor?
Frank: . . . Sorry? Yeh well fair outside things, you can't do warn. I can talk but I can't show up myself. I can't put the voice. It would be one thing if I could talk. But I can't talk so people can see it.
SP: Are you married, Frank?
Frank: . . . I was news to due to be.

---

in comprehension does not require such careful testing.

Unlike the Broca's patient, who has frequent hesitation during a sentence, the Wernicke's aphasic patient may show some brief hesitation just prior to answering the sentence, possibly because the patient is checking the meaning of the question (Butterworth, 1979). Although the grammar is fluent, the words that give the sentence the depth of meaning are somewhat absent. This is sometimes referred to as "empty speech". The patient often will not ask for the question to be repeated and therefore the ability to monitor their own understanding is impaired. When the patient answers a question that has not been asked, the answer is often appropriate to a question that might be asked under the circumstances. There are a number of verbal or semantic paraphasias. When the patient "Frank" (see Box 7.5) says he cannot "talk" or that people cannot "see" his speech we know the intended meaning. We also understand the difficulties he is having in trying to communicate and the isolation that he must be feeling. The area of damage associated with Wernicke's aphasia is far larger than originally described by Wernicke (see, Figure 7.7), although stimulation studies described earlier suggest that the extent of the area is perhaps exaggerated by individual variation and the posterior superior temporal gyrus is still seen as being more crucial.

In the dialogue of the Wernicke's patient in Box 7.5 there are a number of paraphasias. There are *verbal paraphasias* or *semantic paraphasias* such as the substitution of the word "see" for "hear". The words are from a related meaning but the precise meaning is wrong. There are also literal or phonemic paraphasias, which are phonologically based and sound like the original phrase: "I was news to due to be" instead of "I used to be." Sometimes the patient will use *neologisms*, which are new words created by the patient, without meaning. In its most extreme form, the same neologism may appear frequently and is referred to as *jargon*. At one time the term *jargon aphasia* was used to denote a separate aphasia but the patient is now more likely to be classified as a Wernicke's aphasia patient with jargon (Benson & Ardila, 1996).

The use of jargon by these patients is made more unusual by evidence that these patients are apparently oblivious to their errors. One of the first patients I interviewed as a student had jargon aphasia and not having been told what to expect, it was difficult, initially, for me to believe the validity of what I was hearing. However, the seriousness of the patient's face revealed the lack of insight into the extraordinary things he was saying. The excerpt in Box 7.6 is a transcript from an assessment by a speech pathologist at our hospital.

It is of interest that although this patient uses more neologisms and frequently uses the neologism "prentice" as a substitute, the patient is more able to comprehend the question when compared to the other Wernicke's patient reported in Box 7.5. Many of the reported patients who extensively use jargon also have poor comprehension (e.g. Hough, 1993). But the finding that severe comprehension impairment does not

attributes. The jargon aphasic patient always appears to know what they are saying; that is, they appear to have satisfactory intentions. For example, often their speech makes sense if neologisms are substituted for real words.

It is clear from the dialogue of the patient Tom above that the concept of May is understood; however, when corrected, he responds almost indignantly, "That's correct, Naym prentice." Therefore the patient understands the word, but still proceeds with the faulty phonological output. If one accepts that this patient and others are aware of the meaning of the word they are trying to produce then a faulty semantic analysis is a less likely explanation. Also, the finding that comprehension difficulties and jargon are rather poorly related would suggest that there is, in some way, a faulty communication between the semantic analysis and the phonetic production.

Paraphasic errors of the type shown by Tom are commonly found with this disorder (Butterworth, 1985): for example, when he substitutes *May* for *Naym*. These and other speech errors would suggest there is a predominant breakdown in the phonetic production at the output stage. If the phonological analysis breakdown were at the input stage then this would presumably interfere with comprehension. In the case of pure word deafness — a disorder in which the patient is unable to hear the phonological form of the words — the reverse is true. That is, the phonological input is impaired but the word-deaf patient may be able to produce faultless speech output. Pure word deafness is associated with bilateral lesions to the area referred to in Figure 7.9 as the posterior temporal plane.

While, as indicated, the patient with jargon may present in different ways, the finding that in some patients comprehension is relatively preserved also supports previous arguments that phonological output analysis may take place independently of semantic analysis. This model for jargon aphasia and the above discussion encourages the view that there are two phonological systems: one for input and one for speech output — this has also been argued by other authors (e.g. Monsell, 1987; Nickels, Howard, &

Best, 1997; Shallice, 1988a). Thus in the case of jargon aphasia it would appear that input necessary for comprehension including the phonological and semantic analysis may be relatively unimpaired compared to a phonological output system that includes neologisms.

But if the patient's comprehension is relatively preserved, this still leaves unresolved the question why these patients are not aware of their own mistakes. Kertesz (1981, p. 110) describes a relatively complex model showing a parallel phonological and semantic analysis. Kertesz describes jargon aphasia as being due to the auditory monitor unit becoming disconnected from both the phonological and semantic processor. Some confirmation for this model, or versions of this model, comes from recent animal work describing two routes to the anterior speech area. The first runs dorsally and is broadly described within the Wernicke–Geschwind model. This dorsal route is described by Hickok (2000) as allowing conscious introspection of verbal phonological output. If there is destruction of this area then a second ventral route will be utilised but there is no conscious monitoring of this route. The argument for this last route comes from monkey experiments that have revealed these separate dorsal and ventral pathways from the auditory cortex to an area homologous to the anterior speech areas in humans (Romanski, Bates, & Goldman-Rakic, 1999). Hickok's proposal relates to an explanation of conduction aphasia and will be discussed in the next section. However, if there is a search for an explanation for jargon aphasia it could be related to the destruction of this proposed "conscious introspective" dorsal pathway, which includes the supramarginal gyrus (see Hickok, 2000. p. 99, note 4). Therefore if there is sufficient damage to this pathway and adjacent areas responsible for phonological production there will result paraphasias and neologisms combined with a destruction of conscious introspection of phonological segments within speech. However, the unconscious ventral pathway is still intact for some degree of comprehension. Damage to areas responsible for semantic analysis will degrade the output further, giving rein to the full spectrum of jargon aphasias.

Conduction aphasia

Both Broca's and Wernicke's aphasia are associated with impaired repetition. When this is the predominant sign and comprehension and expression are relatively intact, the disorder is described as a *conduction aphasia*. It has been questioned whether this type of aphasia deserves a separate entity. This challenge comes from those who believed it to be a recovered form of Wernicke's aphasia. However, many patients who conform to this disorder (Benson & Ardila, 1996; Goodglass & Kaplan, 1983; Tonkonogy, 1986) do not have a history of Wernicke's recovery (Damasio & Damasio, 1980).

Many of the patients who were described in Chapter 5 as having an isolated working memory disorder with a poor digit-span (repeating back a list of digits in the right order) but adequate storage into the LTMS have recovered from a condition originally diagnosed as conduction aphasia. It is now realised, however, that there is more than one mechanism for conduction aphasia, of which impaired working memory must be considered as one of the explanations.

Conduction aphasia has been seen as supporting the Wernicke–Geschwind model since there is a putative disconnection between the area of reception and the motor area of expression (see Figure 7.8a). According to the Wernicke–Geschwind model, words of the examiner would be registered and analysed in Wernicke's area and then this information would be sent to Broca's area for repetition via the nerve fibres of the arcuate fasciculus. As indicated, these nerve fibres run longitudinally and connect Wernicke's with Broca's area. The finding that damage to an area within the supramarginal gyrus and the insula is often associated with conduction aphasia appears

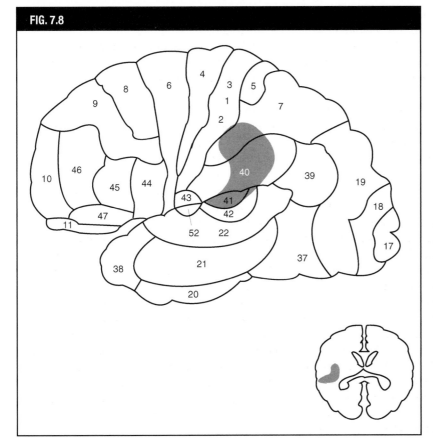

FIG. 7.8

A composite lesion of six patients with conduction aphasia. The lateral view and oblique slices are shown, lowest top left. The insula is often involved, which is shown on the oblique slices, the superior regions of the supra marginal gyrus and the primary auditory area (adapted from Damasio, & Damasio, 1989, and Damasio, 1981).

Box 7.7.   Conduction aphasia

BR awoke one morning and noticed the clock radio sounded "tinny". He said he felt a little strange and noted that he had difficulty reading a Qantas frequent flyer advertisement. His wife found his speech largely unintelligible and he was taken to hospital for tests. He was described broadly in his notes as having both an expressive and receptive aphasia. There were no signs of weakness in any of his limbs and this was taken as a possible indication that he was suffering from a more posterior-based language disorder. His CT scan revealed a left parietal infarct. BR was seen by the author 9 months after his stroke. At this time, BR was able to pass all the comprehension section of the Boston Aphasia Examination. There appeared to be some difficulty understanding the content of the longest story, although this was likely to be due to the misunderstanding of the crucial word "lion" in this sentence. When this word was clarified the passage was repeated and his comprehension was perfect. This misperception of words was not obviously a difficulty with comprehension, but rather related to the patient's complaint of not being able to hear the word distinctly. Although BR's comprehension of sentences was intact, he found comprehension of complex material such as mental arithmetic questions impossible, but when he was allowed to read the questions, he was able to perform closer to his expected level The patient's age-scaled scores on WAIS-R were: Information, 12 ; Digit-span, 3 ; Similarities, 8; Vocabulary, 12; Arithmetic (BR reads questions), 8; Picture completion, 9; Block design, 13; Digit symbol, 7.

On a task that required him to name a series of pictures he was largely satisfactory, although his pronunciation of some items revealed literal/phonemic paraphasias. These errors also appeared on a test of general knowledge (Information). For example, when naming an Eagle he said "Egel". When he was asked what was the Koran, he responded, "It was the book of Mahobin" instead of Mohammed. For Einstein he said "Eisten"; for "energy" he said "enedy". There was also an occasion when he was able to correct himself. When asked who wrote Hamlet he responded "Bill Wickman", then corrected himself and said "No, Bill Shakeman" and then said "Shakespurce" and then finally said "No, Bill Shakespeare". BR's writing was largely intact, but again there were the occasional mistakes that were reminiscent of his difficulties with speech. When required to write about his previous job, he substituted words that were not appropriate. For example, the word *write* was substituted for the word *read* and instead of *today* he wrote *to date*. As implied previously, his silent reading appeared to be without fault but his reading aloud showed the same difficulties as his speech and writing. As might be expected with this syndrome, repetition was extremely difficult for this patient. He was able to repeat back three digits forward (although only two consistently) in order and two digits backwards. When given the numbers 6439 he repeated back 4669, and 7286 was repeated back as 2782. With longer numbers he just repeated back the first three numbers and then gave up.

---

to support this disconnection theory. These areas are close to the arcuate fasciculus and therefore a disconnection of this communicating circuit could conceivably stop information travelling from the posterior to the anterior language zone.

The case in Box 7.7 is a description of a patient seen by the author who displays many of the features of conduction aphasia. Most obviously his severely impaired repetition performance is the cardinal sign. There are literal or phonemic paraphasias but when these occur there is often either uncertainty concerning the mispronunciation or an attempt to correct himself. Therefore, unlike the jargon aphasia patient, this patient and other conduction aphasic patients may correct their errors of expression. These repeated self-corrections, which improve over a series of pronunciations, are referred to as *"conduit d'approche"*. Therefore according to the the theoretical formulation proposed above the damage would not be sufficient to destroy the conscious output of this system.

Simmons (1990) argues that conduction aphasic patients make mainly phonemic paraphasias rather than semantic paraphasias. However, the indication that some patients with more posterior lesions are reported as showing evidence of semantic paraphasias has resulted in this researcher proposing a continuum with more posterior conduction aphasia, showing more Wernicke's features, while the more anterior lesions show more articulatory difficulties and Broca's features (Simmons, 1990, p. 56).

A comment on conduction aphasia

The phonemic paraphasias, the difficulties with repetition and the ability to self-correct on occasions are typical of a conduction aphasia (Goodglass & Kaplan, 1983), but are these symptoms expected from a disconnection as the Wernicke–Geschwind model proposes? The fluent speech, with an ability to monitor one's own speech, suggests that expression and reception of language are to some degree intact with the connections between these areas. If, however, the centre for meaning and semantic interpretation (Wernicke's area) is disconnected from the centre of expression (Broca's area) then there should be more than just repetition failure. Theoretically a complete disconnection between these two centres should result in the patient not being able to say anything intelligible or meaningful. Even a partial disconnection should result in a predominance of semantic paraphasias or speech that is empty of meaning in repetition, but this is not the case.

At least two types of conduction aphasia have been identified: one type that is associated with lesions to the posterior supratemporal plane within the auditory cortex, and a second that is more obviously a problem of working or short-term-memory, associated with lesions to the supramarginal gyrus and the underlying arcuate fasciculus.

In terms of the first type, the phonemic paraphasias, which are often reported with conduction aphasia, are perhaps more readily explained as damage or disturbed connections to a phonological based lexicon or store that is important for the output and production of language. This is certainly the view of Hickok (Hickok, 2000; Hickok & Poeppel, 2000). Hickok proposes that these patients' phonemic errors are particularly important and are most likely due to damage to a phonological output system. (see Figure 7.9 illustrating the posterior supratemporal plane area, which includes the Heschl's gyrus and the planum temporale).

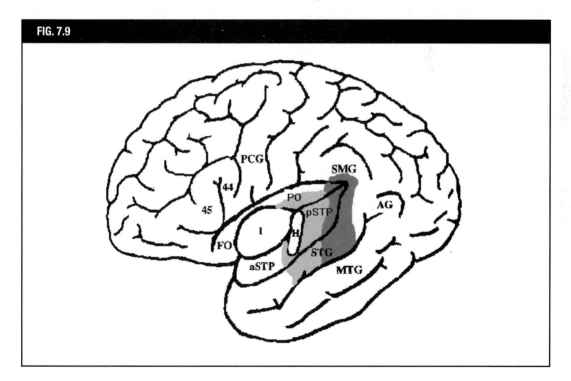

FIG. 7.9

Showing the language areas with the areas inside the Sylvian fissure, with the Sylvian fossa exposed (heavy line). The combined areas of Heschl's gyrus (primary auditory area and the planum temporale are referred to by Hickok as the posterior temporal plane. Areas shown include the anterior and posterior supratemporal plane (aSTP, pSTP); the planum temporale is subsumed by the area pSTP. The functional areas according to the cytoarchitecture are roughly as follows. Heschl's gyrus (H) (white) is the primary auditory cortex. The light-grey area represents a unimodal auditory area and the dark-grey area a transitional field between the unimodal sensory cortex and multimodal integration (association) area. Also shown are the insula (I), parietal operculum (PO), frontal operculum (FO), supramarginal gyrus (SMG), angular gyrus (AG), superior temporal gyrus (STG), middle temporal gyrus (MTG), precentral gyrus (PCG), and Brodman's areas 44 and 45. The authors propose that this *bilaterally* is an area important for sound-based speech which interacts with the frontal motor area to produce speech. However, they also propose that there is a separate interaction between this area and the comprehension area which is more posterior, around the junction of the occipital temporal and parietal lobes (adapted from Hickok & Poeppel, 2000, with permission from Elsevier Science).

Hickok's argument for the existence of this phonologically based speech production unit comes from three main planks of evidence:

1. Electrical stimulation of the posterior supratemporal gyrus (pSTP) produces speech errors that are characterised within repetition of words and symbols (Penfield & Roberts, 1959).
2. Functional imaging results implicate the activation of the pSTP during speech production (Hickok et al., 1999; Levelt et al., 1998).
3. He believes the intact comprehension in these patients relates to comprehension abilities of the right hemisphere (bilateral lesions to the pSTP are associated with pure word deafness and this disorder is also associated with phonological paraphasias) (Buchman et al., 1986).

This arguement is not entirely convincing in that one would expect that reliance on the right hemisphere for comprehension would result in more comprehension difficulties than is often found with these patients. While it is well established that at least one type of conduction aphasia is due to impaired phonological reproduction, the location of the lesion remains controversial. These cases are perhaps more in keeping with a partial disconnection from Broca's area or damage to the phonological output system. It would be predicted that these patients have most difficulty in repeating back words that are longer and less frequent (Shallice & Warrington, 1977).

Hickok (e.g., Hickok, 1999) and other authors have suggested that conduction aphasia can be explained also by a second type that is more obviously a disorder of short-term or active memory. This group of conduction aphasic patients have difficulty in repetition that is largely unrelated to reproduction or comprehension. These patients have a similar size of repetition span irrespective of whether words or numbers are repeated back (e.g., Caramazza, Basili et al., 1981; Shallice & Warrington, 1977).

Damasio and Damasio (1980) provide evidence of relatively discrete white matter damage (lateral to the insula) in five of six conduction cases, with damage to the putamen in one case. The projections from this vicinity of the insula lead to the thalamus and may then progress to Broca's area or join a motor circuit that includes the putamen (see Figure 7.8b). As indicated some of these cases also include lesions to the arcuate fasciculus — the longitudinal axons that connect the anterior and posterior language areas as described in Geschwind–Wernicke's model — keeping alive the original explanation of a disconnection between reception and expression (e.g. Ardila, Rosselli, & Pinzon, 1989; Damasio & Damasio, 1980; Murdoch, 1988). However, it is perhaps just as likely, given the symptoms of these patients, that disconnections from a phonemic lexicon occur due to disconnection of projections to the thalamus (see Figure 7.8b), when the insula, SMG locations are considered (see Figures 7.9 and 7.13). The insula has attracted increased interest in recent years and is one of the areas that is activated during working memory experiments (e.g. D'Esposito, Postle, & Rypma, 2000) and therefore again we have the implication for an active memory explanation.

Global aphasia

Occlusion of the main stem of the left middle cerebral artery results in impeded flow in both the anterior and posterior branches of this artery. The result may be a large infarct involving most of the language area which may, during the early stages, cause a complete loss of speech. The patient may be mute, combined with a loss of comprehension. This is obviously a traumatic consequence to the patient, who occasionally respond in an extreme emotional reaction, i.e. a catastrophic reaction (Goldstein, 1948).

There may be recovery of language expression and comprehension over time and some patients can recover to reveal an aphasia that is mostly reminiscent of Broca's aphasia; comprehension recovers but speech production difficulties may remain (e.g., Kertesz, 1993b; Willmes & Poeck, 1993). Caplan and Hildebrandt (1986) are unable to explain this pattern of recovery from global to Broca's aphasia. One possible solution concerns the more redundant brain representation of comprehension. PET scan results of language in non-brain-damaged populations tend to support the view that passive comprehension activates both hemispheres in the temporoparietal language areas (Poeppel, 1996). In contrast, expression seems to be a more unilateral anterior phenomenon (Xiong et al., 1998) and therefore does not have a back-up right hemisphere system. In support of this view is work looking at occipital asymmetries and the degree of left language dominance (Kertesz & Naeser, 1994). Kertesz and Naeser report studies that show a relatively high negative correlation between recovery following gobal aphasia and occipital asymmetry as measured on CT scan. The larger the asymmetry, with the left occipital lobe being wider and longer, the less the recovery. This relationship held for comprehension but not for production of speech. In other words there is support for the view that higher asymmetry of language in the individual is associated with poorer recovery of comprehension.

It is possible that such an asymmetry factor is responsible for a number of global aphasics not recovering to any extent. However, the mechanisms surrounding recovery in these patients is uncertain and some who recover do not transform into Broca's type aphasia. The position of the lesion may, to some extent, determine the progression of recovery. For example, Naeser (1994) reports (using CT scan 3 months post recovery) that the degree of destruction of Wernicke's area correlates with the likely recovery of comprehension.

Continuing with Naeser's research, but on the issue of the importance of lesion location in global aphasia, she has also shown that apart from the massive cortical infarcts found with this language disorder, relatively discrete lesions may cause global aphasia. This occurs when there is a lesion to a subcortical area called the temporal isthmus. The temporal isthmus is an area containing the auditory connections between the medial geniculate thalamus and Heschl's gyrus. The reader will recall that the auditory system within the ear, including the cochlea and basilar membrane, transfers auditory input to the thalamus before this information is transferred (via the temporal isthmus) to Heschl's gyrus for analysis

in the cortex. When the lesion includes the temporal isthmus but does *not* include Wernicke's area then some recovery of comprehension is more likely (Naeser, 1994, p. 257).

THE TRANSCORTICAL APHASIAS

As indicated, these extrasylvian aphasias, originally described by Wernicke in 1981, are distinguished from the perisylvian syndromes by the patient's ability to repeat back.

According to Lichtheim's model a disconnection between Wernicke's and Broca's areas resulted in an inability to repeat back (input could not travel to output); damage to Broca's (output damaged) or Wernicke's area (input damaged) results in similar problems. Lichtheim's original problem was to account for an aphasic performance that was associated with poor comprehension but at the same time did not show repetition problems (see Figure 7.11). To cope with this another conceptual system was proposed that could be damaged. In this way, if the Wernicke's to Broca's pathway was undamaged, repetition could occur but comprehension was undermined. A lesion to this conceptual system would result in transcortical sensory aphasia. For a similar reason a lesion between Broca's area and the concept area would result in many of the Broca signs but, at the same time, repeating back would be intact. This last lesion would result in transcortical motor aphasia.

The naturally occurring lesion, which is often, but not always, associated with these types of aphasias, is referred to as a watershed infarction. As can be seen from Figure 7.10, the deprivation of arterial blood supply to the extremities of the arterial tributaries causes a necrosis or death of brain cells in the shaded area. This *infarction* (death of brain cells) is caused by *ischaemia*, which is a deprivation of oxygen and nutrients such as glucose. These watershed infarctions are seen to be due directly to atherosclerosis (thickening of the artery walls). Alternatively they may be caused by micro-emboli, minute particles that are flicked off, from plaques (solid dead matter,

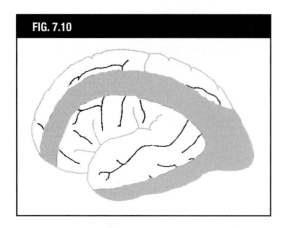

FIG. 7.10

Illustration of the watershed zone, the area incorporating the final narrow tributaries of the major arteries which are consequently prone to the watershed infarction.

cholesterol) on the wall of the artery and travel up the carotid arteries with the blood flow to the brain. These emboli eventually lodge in the artery as it narrows. This problem is obviously more likely to occur when the constriction is at the narrower, more terminal stages of the arteries. Therefore it is at the borders between the ends of the tributaries of the major arteries that the watershed infarction occurs.

Where the infarction occurs in the watershed zone will dictate whether there are aphasic signs and the nature of the transcortical aphasia. When it is in the anterior region, especially near the motor area, the symptoms are more likely to affect the motor aspects of aphasia and some of these symptoms are similar to Broca's aphasia. These anterior transcortical aphasias are referred to as *transcortical motor aphasias.*

When the damage is in the posterior area, and symptoms are more likely to be receptive and there are difficulties with comprehension, the connection with Wernicke's aphasia is inevitable. These posterior transcortical aphasias are the *transcortical sensory aphasias.* In this way the nomenclature gives a lead to the symptoms expected.

The transcortical aphasias may be further differentiated according to a more precise localisation and its associated symptoms. It is an over-simplification to propose that transcortical motor aphasia (TMA) is a Broca's aphasia but with repetition intact or that transcortical sensory aphasia (TSA) is a Wernicke's aphasia with repetition intact. However, to the initiate this is a useful guide. There are many differences other than intact repetition.

Transcortical motor aphasia and poor initiation of speech

Within the TMA group two types may be discerned (Benson & Ardila, 1996). TMA is associated with poor spontaneity and initiation of speech and this may show itself in other areas of the patient's behaviour.

Type I TMA is associated with a prefrontal lesion, superior to Broca's area or within the lateral aspect of dorsolateral area of the prefrontal cortex. TMA type I cases may show more difficulty in the comprehension of complex sentences, which is more associated with superior, dorsolateral lesions. Patients with type I TMA often have special difficulty in following commands. Luria (1973) referred to this type of aphasia as dynamic aphasia. This appears to have a dysexecutive nature since comprehension is often good. Luria (1966) describes this as a dissociation between language and overt behaviour and may be explained by the patient in terms of a situation where the command sounds as if it is addressed to somebody else (Benson & Ardila, 1996 p. 150). There may a difficulty on tasks that require sponteneity. For example, on tasks were the subject has to produce as many exemplars of a category as possible (e.g. animals) they may show an impoverishment of response with a dysexecutive flavour. There may, for example, be perseveration in naming or, in category tasks, a failure to keep to a category and the naming of parts instead of the whole and other dysexecutive problems.

However, while failing in their spontaneous speech these patients may repeat back, sometimes to an excessive degree, echoing repeatedly what the examiner has just said. This apparently blind repeating of the experimenter is referred to as echolalia and has caught the interest of many of the earlier researchers (Lichtheim, 1885; Wernicke, 1881). Echolalia and the lack of hemiparesis in some cases have led to a misdiagnosis of an acute psychiatric condition (Benson & Ardila, 1996). This is a relatively rarely reported disorder but when it is reported there are frontal lesions that involve relatively deep and medial areas (Hadano, Nakamura, & Hamanaka, 1998).

Type II TMA is associated with lesions in the anterior cingulate and the left side of the supplementary motor area (see Figure 7.2). In Chapter 3 there is a description of the inertia sometimes suffered by patients in the early stages of recovery from bilateral cingulate lesions. In such cases there may initially be a lack of movement (akinesia) and mutism (no speech). Later, as the patient recovers, it may be realised that the patient has a lack of affect, slow motor response, poor memory, and a lack of insight when the lesions are anterior and inferior within the cingulate (Damasio & Van Hoesen, 1983). As discussed in Chapter 3, these anterior–inferior cingulate lesions are associated with reduced motivation and drive.

The SMA, which is associated with the preparation of automatic movement routines, has extensive connections with the basal ganglia and is associated with the preparation of a movement routine. Some of the features of poor initiation of speech and movement are found in Parkinson's and Huntington's disease, where patients have damage to these circuits, which are intimately related to the SMA (see Chapter 8). Following lesions to the SMA, the patient often recovers quickly from mutism, suggesting to some that the main impediment is purely motor in origin rather than a "true" aphasia. With this syndrome, writing is especially undermined. However, the aphasic symptoms, (of the type normally associated with perisylvian lesions) are largely resolved after 6 weeks, leaving slowed writing and speech (Masdeau et al., 1978). Recovery may even be after a few days following a small left supplementary motor area lesion (Damasio & Van Hoesen, 1983). With type II TMA there may be accompanying paresis of the lower extremities, by virtue of the position of the lesion and its relationship to the primary motor strip (see Chapter 8). Although tumour or trauma may be implicated, occlusion of the left anterior cerebral artery is frequently associated with this disorder.

In such cases the paresis of the lower extremities, but *preservation* of motor movements of the upper limbs and face, are useful diagnostic indicators (Benson & Ardila, 1996).

Both type I and II TMA are, like Broca's aphasic patients, assisted in their speech initiation by cueing. Thus completion of a sentence is easier for these patients when compared to structuring and initiating their own sentence. The recovery of TMA type I may be more protracted, when compared to type II, and also less amenable to treatment (Gonzalez Rothi, 1990).

While both type I and type II TMA are associated with poor initiation of speech, there are differences between the two types. Type I patients may go through elaborate motor movements to try and initiate speech and sometimes the patient may repeat the instructions of the examiner in an echolalic manner. For both types of TMA writing may be a particular problem, especially in Type I. In contrast, silent reading and comprehension may be relatively intact, and therefore there may be dysgraphia without alexia (Rubens, 1975). Dysgraphia without alexia is the reverse situation of the posterior disconnection syndrome, which is described below in a discussion of alexia. This pattern of impairments is in keeping with the Wernicke–Geschwind model, which describes anterior mechanisms for writing and posterior mechanisms for reading.

In summary, it would appear that type II TMA, with its involvement of the SMA or the anterior cingulate, is more associated with motor initiation symptoms and drive. With type II, recovery of motor symptoms coincides with the recovery of aphasic signs (Freedman, Alexander, & Naeser, 1984). This contrasts with the more dorsolaterally located type I TMA, which has more dysexecutive signs including poor category fluency, with some perseveration in naming tasks, echolalia of an instruction, poor initiation of a spontaneous response but better cued response (Benson & Ardila, 1996).

Transcortical Sensory Aphasia and Poor Comprehension.

In contrast to TMA, patients with *transcortical sensory aphasia* (TSA) have fluent expression.

But, like TMA, TSA is associated with intact repetition. Rapcsak and Rubens (1994) describe TSA as follows: "linguistically, the hallmark of TSA is the dissociation between impaired semantic processing and relatively preserved syntactic/phonological competence" (p. 311). With TSA intact repetition is taken to extremes on occasion; these patients may repeat back anything that the clinician or researcher provides for the patient, even if it is nonsense, with the proviso that it conforms with the structure or syntax of the patient's natural language. In a milder form, the patient may start to answer the question and then incorporate what the examiner has just said within their own speech, which is generally not very meaningful. Therefore the patient will repeat but have poor comprehension of what they or the examiner are saying.

Again, as with TMA the two types are identified by lesion location: type I TSA is associated with damage to areas inferior to the angular gyrus and temporal lobe and is more associated with signs of a disconnection between the visual and auditory sensory modality. This aphasia has been referred to as amnestic aphasia (Luria, 1976) and is associated with extreme difficulty in naming pictures and objects. It also has many of the semantic paraphasic features of Wernicke's aphasia. Kertesz et al. (1982) report a group of these patients that show a number of interesting features. The first is that although they are able to repeat back they failed to comprehend (see also Schacter, McGlynn, Milberg, & Church, 1993). The articulation of patients was intact and their speech was fluent but empty of meaning, and included many semantic paraphasias and jargon. A proportion of the patients had tactile agnosia (astereognosia, identifying objects by touch) and many had visual object agnosia (see Chapter 2). The lesions for these patients were generally not overlapping with Wernicke's area. They were more posterior and tended to be more inferior to the angular gyrus.

Type II TSA is sometimes referred to as semantic aphasia (e.g. Luria, 1966, 1976) or semantic anomia. There are word-finding difficulties and empty speech, using a low number of content words with circumlocutions. Luria made a par-

ticular study of these patients and noted how they have difficulty in comprehending complex sentence construction, especially where the relationships between clauses is important, or some linguistic manipulation is required, such as in the case of double negatives and possessives. Type II is associated more with superior angular gyrus and posterior parietal damage. Type II is often accompanied by the signs of Gerstmann's syndrome, although the status of the syndrome is controversial (Gerstmann, 1930; 1957).[1]

Finally on the topic of transcortical aphasias there is a group of patients with features of both TMA and TSA who are referred to as mixed transcortical aphasias. This type of aphasia is probably due to widespread, diffuse lesions that affect both the areas responsible for TMA and TSA individually. Patients with widespread watershed infarction are sometimes found with this disorder (see Figure 7.10).

Comment on the Transcortical Aphasias

Geschwind proposed that a disconnection between Wernicke's area and the association cortex was required for a comprehension deficit without repetition (Geschwind, 1965, p. 286).

The disconnection interpretation proposed by the Wernicke–Geschwind model might be difficult to sustain on the grounds that there are auditory comprehension difficulties in isolation (see also Berndt, Basili, & Caramazza, 1987; Schacter et al., 1993). Some of these patients are actually able to repeat back without understanding the meaning of what they are saying — this is not in keeping with a disconnection with an intact Wernicke's auditory input/phonological/semantic analysis area (Caplan & Hildebrant, 1988, p. 298). If there is a disconnection, how does the

---

[1] Gertsmann's syndrome includes the neuropsychology signs of poor right/left discrimination of body parts, acalculia, agraphia and finger agnosia, e.g. difficulty in detecting the number of fingers between two fingers with eyes closed. Poeck and Orgass (1975) and others have questioned its status as a syndrome since the individual signs, individually, occur more frequently in isolation than collectively. However, clinicians often find this grouping of symptoms diagnostically useful. Kertesz (1994, p. 6) defends the use of this and other syndromes by arguing that the main advantage of the syndrome is that they are more likely to be located to a localisable lesion, whereas single symptoms are usually not.

phonological information for repetition get past such a disconnection when the auditory semantic information does not?

TSA is often associated with agnosia and tactile agnosia. Even if the lesion location is ignored, the multimodal nature of these semantically related complaints suggests an area is damaged that has a direct responsibility for semantic analysis.

It is also difficult to rationalise how the TSA patients have speech that is empty of meaning and anomia, given that according to the Wernicke–Geschwind model Wernicke's area would remain intact (Kertesz et al., 1982). These arguments discourage a disconnection explanation, but the location removed from Wernicke's area encourages the view of a separate or extended semantic system.

Generally, the symptoms of TSA suggest that a centre for semantic analysis has been undermined or at least a centre that recruits semantic information from other areas. The areas commonly associated with TSA have been viewed broadly as an association area. They are downstream from a number of sensory areas and therefore well positioned to serve such a role. Rapcsak and Rubens (1994) discuss Lichtheim's (1885) attempt to overcome this dilemma of a comprehension impairment without impaired repetition. Lichtheim gave more substance to Carl Wernicke's formulation and proposed a separate concept centre (see Figure 7.11).

The same criticisms that are levelled at Wernicke–Geschwind model may also be levelled at Lichtheim's model. Lichtheim did not propose a location for the concept area, but rather saw it as being spread and distributed among a number of areas. Although the model takes care of comprehension difficulties with impaired repetition (a lesion to the auditory image in Wernicke's area) and comprehension difficulties without impaired repetition (lesion disconnecting auditory image from concept area), there is still some unease concerning the usefulness of this model. First, TMA is largely a disorder of articulation with dysexecutive features that relate to difficulties in initiation and possibly the planning of speech. Comprehension difficulties are not described as a key feature of this disorder and therefore a disconnection

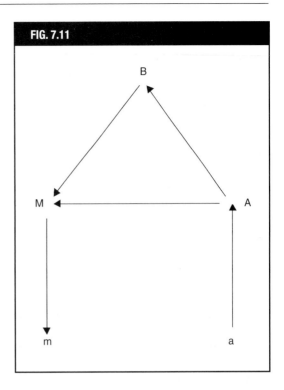

FIG. 7.11

A simplified Lichtheim's model of aphasia. A disconnection between a (Wernicke's area, auditory images) and B (the concept area) results in TSA. A disconnection between B (concept area) and m (Broca's area, centre for motor images) results in TMA according to this model (Lichtheim, 1885).

with a concept centre would not seem to be a useful way of describing TMA.

In terms of TSA there is more interest in Lichtheim's model. With the loss of access to the concept centre with its consequent reduction of comprehension, however, the word images are still analysed within Wernicke's and this information may be sent forward to Broca's to allow repetition. But a transferral of meaning from B to M should allow naming and yet this is often impaired in TSA cases. Similar criticisms of the Wernicke–Geschwind model can therefore also be made of Lichtheim's model.

A more useful model proposes that TSA results from a lesion to a part of the semantic system that is separate from the semantic system for auditory phonological analysis (Alexander, Hiltbrunner, & Fischer, 1989; Berndt et al., 1987; Rothi, 1990). A situation that could be seen as

brain cells (grey matter) residing beneath the cortex. Such aphasia, if it were identified, should have qualitative features that were *consistently* found following a lesion in that structure, thereby indicating that the structure played a distinctive role in the process of language. This does not include those previously discussed aphasias that are associated with syndromes such as Broca's aphasia where the symptoms may be contributed to by subcortical disconnections of white matter. This rather pedantic formulation is necessary because there is some argument that damage to subcortical structures such as the thalamus is associated with aphasia not because it is a centre for processing language, but rather because it is just a relay station that allows connection to other areas. Such explanations are often sought in terms of a disconnection between language centres. A further alternative explanation that is sometimes aired concerns the effect of lesions on the metabolism of adjacent areas. Thus if the quality of aphasia is similar in typology to that expected following a lesion to an adjacent cortical area then the suspicion is that the cortical area is actually responsible for the aphasic symptoms and not the subcortical area.

A good place to start this discussion is with the early work described by Penfield and Roberts (1959). These researchers have been already mentioned in their work mapping out the anterior and posterior language areas using stimulation techniques. These neurosurgeons also describe some surgical work that has particular repercussions for the Wernicke–Geschwind model. As part of the procedure for the surgical removal of tumours Penfield and Roberts (1959) report disconnecting and lesioning of areas surrounding the language areas with either temporary or no effect on language. Needless to say, this is not supportive of the Wernicke–Geschwind disconnection model. According to this model disconnection would result in aphasias such as conduction aphasia. While they do not discount intercortical connections between these areas, they do provide an argument that all language areas are interconnected by the thalamus. A description of some of these connections is given in Figure 7.13. In the examples, it can be seen that there are extensive

two-way (efferent and afferent) projections between parts of the posterior language zone and the nuclei of the thalamus such as the pulvinar (see Figure 7.13). There are similar connections between the SMA and the thalamus. It will be recalled that stimulation of the left SMA causes speech arrest, which is most obviously related to the motor aspects of speech. Lesions in this area cause a transcortical motor aphasia that tends to recover relatively quickly if the lesion is discrete (Penfield & Roberts, 1959). This and subsequent work suggests strongly that even if information is transferred in the manner that the Wernicke–Geschwind model indicates, there are alternative pathways that are just as important.

If the evidence supports certain areas of the thalamus as being possible junctions for areas that are important to language processing, then the next consideration is the role that the thalamus has to play in this process. First, as indicated, lesions in subcortical areas, whether within subcortical nuclei or white matter, do have a pronounced effect on adjacent cortical areas. Radiological measures such as PET, SPECT and fMRI are capable of representing the functional activation of the brain and these radiological methods have found that there are signs of abnormal effects on the brain which are in excess of the damage revealed by such measures as MRI and CT.

For example, Pappata et al. (1987) found that four patients with deeply located brain lesions showed a significant metabolic reduction for both oxygen uptake and glucose uptake in the overlaying cerebral cortex using PET, but these abnormalities were not detected on MRI. These and other studies have suggested that the damage to subcortical nuclei may cause language impairment because of the inevitable hypometabolism and oedema, which reduces the efficiency of cortically based language areas.

Studies using PET technology may use a variety of methodologies depending on the goals of research. A particularly useful method of studying the effect of brain damage on surrounding structures is the use of an isotope that has an affinity for glucose. This method takes around 40 minutes to activate areas that are using up the glucose and therefore is not much use for studying

FIG. 7.13

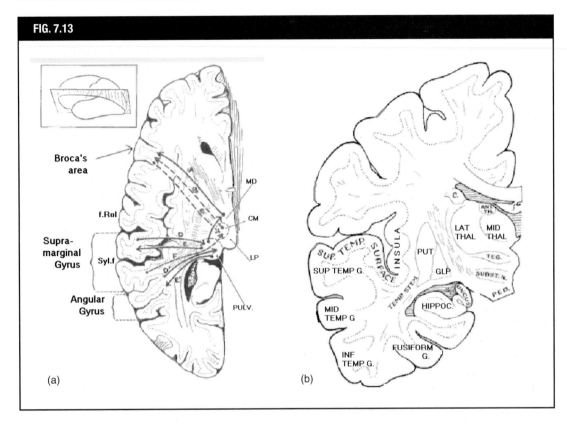

(a) Illustration showing connections between the thalamus and the language areas (Penfield, W. & Roberts, L., *Speech and brain mechanisms*. Copyright © 1959. Reprinted by permission of Princeton University Press). Various areas of the thalamus are indicated: medial dorsal nucleus (MD), centrum medianum (CM), lateral posterior nucleus (LP), pulvinar (PULV). (b) Coronal slice, showing the relative position of the subcortical structures to the perisylvian language area: putamen (PUT), globus pallidus (GLP), thalamus (THAL) (adapted from Penfield, 1956).

functions in real time. However, the method is very useful for looking at the effect of lesions on brain metabolism. Metter and Hanson (1994) describe a series of studies that investigated patients 3 months post stroke and found reduced glucose uptake in areas remote from those found to be damaged, according to MRI and CT scans. The most reduced activity in these remote areas were cortical areas that were connected with the damaged subcortical regions. When Metter and Hanson (1994) investigated some *control cases* who had *right* lesions, they serendipitously failed to find these remote effects. Therefore they suggest that perhaps it is only structures that are *functionally* related which are undermined.

Metter and Hanson (1994) further found that

lesions to the thalamus, for example, may produce Wernicke's or Broca's type symptoms depending on the area lesioned. Broca's symptoms are more likely to occur if an area of the thalamus is damaged that has predominantly anterior cortical projections. The picture is more confused with posterior connections (perhaps because speech production mechanisms also exist posteriorly) but the lesson remains. Remote effects need to be considered and the aphasic symptoms need not be due to a subcortical lesion so much as an interference with connections to cortical regions. This kind of work does not, of course, rule out a subcortical contribution to language processing, but rather argues for caution when attributing cause and effect.

In searching for an aphasia that can be directly accounted for by a subcortical lesion, two methods have been proposed to overcome the remote effects interpretation. The first is to conduct measures of hypometabolism (PET scan) to rule out cortical interference. If aphasic symptoms remain without remote effects on the cortex then this is stronger support for a subcortical language centre. The second is to correlate the size of the subcortical area of damage with aphasic symptoms. If more damage to the subcortical structure is associated with more language impairment, then this would be useful support against an alternative cortical cause for aphasia. Michael Alexander and colleagues have used both these methods (D'Esposito & Alexander, 1995). They found that many of the aphasic symptoms disappear during the acute recovery phase in patients with supposed subcortical aphasia, leaving mainly motor symptoms. These motor symptoms are described as a dysexecutive articulation disorder which is not readily measurable on standard aphasic batteries.

Nadeau and Crosson (1997) appear to support this view for *most* subcortical aphasias. They believe that the symptoms following a particular subcortical lesion are too heterogeneous to be ascribed to the structure that is meant to cause them and that the hypometabolism and interference effects on cortical areas are most likely the cause of these effects. However, this area of discussion is still ongoing and there remains more solid evidence for aphasia associated with thalamic lesions.

Looking at a comprehensive review of studies, however, Nadeau and Crosson (1997) believe evidence for language disorders following thalamic damage remain relatively firm. The description of aphasia following lesions to thalamic areas include:

1. Anomia in spontaneous language.
2. Poor performance on verbal fluency tasks (e.g. providing words starting with a letter within a time limit).
3. Problems with naming to confrontation.
4. Minimally impaired comprehension and repetition (Crosson, 1992, p. 90).

Cambier, Elghozi, and Graveleau (1982) additionally describe reduced vocal volume (hypophonia), aspontaneity in oral expression, pauses in oral expression, and word-finding deficit (with frequent perseveration).

Murdoch (1990) and others argue that thalamic aphasia has features that are too specific to be blamed on neighbourhood lesions. It is also of interest that PET scans of normal subjects who are involved in language tasks do show activation in the thalamic area (e.g. Ingvar, 1983). Also, as described above, there is a consistent finding of reduced metabolism in this area in patients with aphasia (Metter, 1995).

The analysis of the area of the thalamus involved and the mechanism for the aphasic symptoms is not entirely clear. Thalamic aphasia is generally not found following modern stereotactic surgical procedures for Parkinson's disease. This rules out the involvement of certain ventrolateral nuclei with links to the putamen. There is more support for the involvement of the pulvinar. The pulvinar is one of the few areas of the thalamus that consistently results in anomia during stimulation studies (Ojemann, 1977). However, some reservations concerning the role of the pulvinar must be entertained on the grounds that stimulation may affect connecting areas, e.g. posterior language zone (Ojemann, 1977). Also, surgical lesions in this area have been less likely to result in aphasia; however, Crosson (1992) explains this in terms of the rather specific area of the pulvinar that is devoted to speech (superior anterior). In support of the case for the pulvinar, Crosson and colleagues have investigated a case of left pulvinar haemorrhage (Crosson et al., 1986). This patient presented with semantic difficulties in reading and writing. The patient tended to rely on phonetic encoding when reading, for example. See description of surface dyslexic below.

In their most recent formulation on the cause of thalamic aphasia, Nadeau and Crosson (1997) favour a de-arousal interpretation of thalamic aphasia. They build an argument for a breakdown of circuit that links the reticular formation, the thalamus and the frontal lobe in a system that is assumed to be important to the role of attention and arousal within language. Because this is a system that affects language processes, rather than a structure responsible directly for language, one might expect the features of quicker recovery that are found with thalamic aphasia. It is of interest that a number of patients who have been reported by Cappa and colleagues, Cappa, Papagno, Vallar, and Vignolo (1986) as having left thalamic haemorrhage are only temporally aphasic for about a month after stroke onset, which is perhaps more in keeping with this explained role for the thalamus.

In summary, a number of subcortical nuclei within the basal ganglia and thalamus have been cited as being the direct cause of aphasia. That is, these structures play a role in the processing of language. The present view provides that these structures often affect language largely because they are functionally connected to areas that are responsible for language. The strongest role for the involvement in language is given to the thalamus, especially the nuclei referred to as the pulvinar. The thalamic role may be described as being part of a circuit that boosts the focus or selectivity of a function when it is required. The thalamus is therefore more than just a link between language centres. The thalamus is more likely to act as a metaphorical amplifier that relays and accentuates resources delivered to one function over another, according to the behavioural requirements of the organism (see Chapter 4 for further discussion). There is also likely to be a second but related role for the thalamus with other subcortical structures in relation to the mechanism that underlies articulation.

The nuclei within the thalamus may also allow some structures within the basal ganglia, premotor area and supplementary motor area a balanced motoric expression of language. This is certainly the view of Crosson (1992), in the formulation of his model of subcortical influences in language.

Crosson (1992) provides a model that describes a loop or circuit involving the structures of the basal ganglia, the ventral anterior nucleus of the thalamus, and the language zones of the anterior and posterior cortex. The basal ganglia includes a number of structures that appear to allow for the timing of internally driven motor movements. However, at present theorising in this area is inevitably speculative. Crosson proposes a circuit that involves connections between the posterior language cortex and the head of the caudate nucleus, the globus pallidus, the ventral anterior thalamus, and the anterior language cortex. This cortico-pallido-thalamo-cortical loop (CPTC) is assumed to play the role of releasing the speech-associated movements prerequisite to a section of speech. In other words, when preparing narrative speech the motor movements for such speech require appropriate timing.

The topic of subcortical aphasia is an important reminder of the role of subcortical connections in linking different cortical areas and subcortical areas that make a contribution to language. The thalamus appears to be at the centre of a system providing interconnection between the language areas and areas that are important for planning, i.e. anterior cortical areas and those important for producing articulation (the SMA–basal ganglia circuit). Needless to say, any model of language must take these contributions into account.

LANGUAGE AND THE RIGHT HEMISPHERE

The right hemisphere contributes prosody to speech. Prosody refers to the variations in tone and pitch that add to the meaning of what we say. A discussion of this issue also takes place in Chapter 9, where there is a broader discussion of emotion and how this affects communication and the perception of emotion in both verbal and non-verbal domains.

Imagine the situation at mealtime when a child says "Pass the potatoes" rather rudely. The mother corrects the child—"*Please* pass the potatoes"—upon which the child responds in an aggrieved tone "I asked first." The mother's attempt to instil some manners into the child has misfired because the child has not received the meaning of the elements of prosody. The mother has put stress on the word *please* in order to draw attention to the significance of that word but there was also a disapproving tone, which was missed by the child. Here tone, stress on a word which includes accentuating the first phoneme of *please* with an increased volume of speech on that word are all aspects of prosody, which are so important in communication.

Patients with right hemisphere damage may be aprosodic and when this is present it may be quite startling. A young man who came onto our ward following a head injury had this problem and he spoke in a monotone, like a robot or one of those computer messages that is made from splicing together pieces of digital speech. There was no rise and fall or inflection of speech whatsoever. Some patients with left hemisphere damage may also be aprosodic but this tends to be more due to difficulties in articulation. If the process of speaking is so difficult and effortful, as in the case of Broca's-type aphasia, then prosody of speech is also affected. If the articulation demands are made easier then the prosody returns but this is not the case for a right hemisphere-damaged aprosodic patient and is less obviously impaired in those left hemisphere-damaged patients who are often quite fluent irrespective of the demands made on articulation (Ross, Thompson, & Yenkosky, 1997).

Some patients have a problem with comprehending prosody (Blonder, Bowers, & Heilman, 1991; Bowers et al., 1987). The only way these patients know someone is saying something happy or sad is by the context. If someone talks about mistakenly running over their favourite cat, they assume that the message is sad not from the tone of voice but rather from the subject matter. If the emotional valence of the sentence is ambiguous then the message may be misconstrued, such as in the case of a friend happily saying that they had at last broken up with their boyfriend. In order to test the emotional perception of speech, experiments sometimes have neutral sentences such as "The boy played football" read in a sad or a happy tone of voice. In this situation these patients have difficulty in detecting the tone of the sentence because they have to make the decision purely on the grounds of prosody.

One theory, which has had mixed support, is

whether patients with anterior right hemisphere damage are more likely to show difficulties in the production of prosody in speech while posterior lesioned patients have difficulty with comprehension of prosody. This proposal by Ross provides a prosodic analogue for Broca's and Wernicke's aphasia (Ross, 1981). Although intuitively attractive, this hypothesis has tended not to be supported consistently. It is true that expressive and perceptive/receptive emotional impairment is not highly correlated and the lack of a relationship suggests they are managed by separate structures. But Borod et al. (1996) found that instead of Ross's anterior–posterior relationship, perceptual impairments related to neocortical lesions, while expressive communicative disorders tended to be subcortical. Cancelliere and Kertesz (1990), however, found cortical and subcortical lesions (basal ganglia) were associated with both expressive and receptive emotional prosodic impairments. Many studies using PET technology indicate some homotypic activation within the right hemisphere during comprehension and expression respectively, but there is no obvious indication that this is related to prosody in such a way to support Ross's theory.

The right hemisphere does appear to have some limited speech expression, so that when patients have major destruction to the left hemisphere they may still be capable of swearing and using other emotionally charged words; also singing and some stereotyped phrases appear to be produced by the right hemisphere (Code, 1997). Code makes the interesting point that popular songs often include a stereotyped phrase and that this might be related to the reception of music being a more right hemisphere process in non-musicians (Bever & Chiarello, 1974). A speech therapy called melodic intonation therapy encourages aphasic patients to sing sentences they are unable to say, thereby making use of the right hemisphere's musical function in this area.

The comprehension capabilities of the right hemisphere have already been discussed in Chapter 6. Some frequently used, concrete words are understood by the right hemisphere, even if the patient is unaware that they have been shown the word. The right hemisphere appears to have an additional gift of being able to comprehend the overall context or theme that is present in a sentence. Sometimes an overall knowledge of what is being referred to helps our comprehension. If you hear a snatch of a conversation while on a bus or on a train it can sometimes be quite intriguing. Immediately, you start making inferences about what is being said. Persons with right hemisphere damage tend not to be good at making such thematic inferences. For example, Beeman (1993) presented a series of statements to right hemisphere-damaged patients in the form of a story and then tested the patients and an elderly control group for the recognition of events and facts that could be inferred compared to those that were stated explicitly. For example, halfway through one of the stories there is the statement: *Then he went to the bathroom and discovered that he had left the bathtub water running.* Later in the story there is the statement: *The mess in the bathroom took a long time to mop up.* Later the subjects were asked whether the bathtub had overflowed or whether another scenario had occurred, and fewer of the right hemisphere patients correctly chose the inferred statement concerning overflowing. This was not related to memory since they had no difficulty with choosing a statement that represented information that was explicitly stated. Most obviously, this kind of difficulty is related to maintaining the context or underlying theme of what is being said. For example, in another study patients were given sentences that would normally have a certain meaning but because of the context had a different meaning. For example, in the case of someone saying "Can you open the door?" this is often taken to mean "will you open the door for me?" (Brownell, Michel, Powlenson, & Gardener, 1983), not "Are you capable of opening the door?" But within the context of the question being addressed to someone in a wheelchair, the right hemisphere-damaged were still tempted towards the more usual interpretation.

This failure to infer from context was also found by Brownell, Potter, Bihrle, and Gardener (1986), who also looked at right hemisphere-damaged patients' ability to make correct inferences. They presented sentences that would

normally lead to an obvious assumption about a person but then alter that assumption with a further statement. For example, *Sally approached the movie star with pen and paper in hand. She was writing an article about famous people's views on nuclear power.* Despite the evidence that Sally was unlikely to be an autograph hunter the first sentence still resulted in many right hemisphere-damaged patients choosing a statement suggesting that she was. In this last study there would appear to be an additional rigidity of thought in which the literal interpretation is always maintained. Therefore not only is there a failure to make inferences, but there is also a tendency to choose the most literal interpretation and not alter it. This may be due to a tendency for the left hemisphere to be more convergent in its approach to semantics. Studies that have presented single words to the left versus right visual field have found that subjects respond more quickly to familiar or high-frequency words while the right hemisphere presentation responded equally quickly to high- and low-frequency words. For Beeman (1993) this suggests that the left hemisphere may be more convergent and literal in its interpretation, while the right hemisphere might be more responsive to alternative interpretations.

A number of studies have suggested that right hemisphere-damaged patients may have a reduced sense of humour. For example, Brownell et al. (1983) provided the sentences leading up to a joke and asked the subjects to choose the punch-line. For example, the neighbourhood borrower approached Mr Smith on Sunday afternoon and inquired, "say, Smith, are you using your lawn mower this afternoon?" "Yes, I am", Smith replied wearily. The patient then had an option of various punch-lines. The right hemisphere-damaged subjects were as likely to choose such statements as "The grass is always greener on the other side" as the correct punch-line: "Fine, then you won't be needing your golf clubs. I'll just borrow them." Surprise is one of the elements of humorous constructions but this did not seem to be the element lacking since the right hemisphere-damaged patients chose surprise endings just as often as the control group.

As one might predict from these studies right

hemisphere-damaged patients also have difficulty in interpreting conversational requests when they are indirect (Stemmer, Giroux, & Joanette, 1994) and when choosing formal versus informal terms, according to status and familiarity. These patients may make errors of etiquette, for example calling an unknown bank manager *Hank* instead of *Mr Jarvis* (Brownell et al., 1997). These problems can have clear consequences for social interaction for some patients. Many patients with right hemisphere damage do not have these problems to any obvious degree but occasionally one comes across a patient who clearly has difficulty in making inferences and following a theme within a conversation. The same patients may also have difficulty in picking up non-verbal cues. For example, they may be oblivious to non-verbal cues indicating that someone wants to take a turn in the conversation or wishes to curtail a conversation.

TOWARDS A NEW MODEL OF LANGUAGE DISORDERS

Is it possible to model relationships between language functions and brain areas?

In one of the earlier sections of this chapter there was some discussion about individual differences and the anterior representation of language according to stimulation studies. These studies have questioned the anterior representation of language for many, although the involvement of Broca's area in articulation and in the spontaneous production of speech is still supported by studies using technology such as PET and fMRI. Nevertheless, the argument could be made that the localisation of different types of aphasia is too uncertain to be of any use and we should concentrate on analysing the types of impairments from the psychological viewpoint alone, without reference to brain structure. In this chapter we have argued how in many cases the use of such terms as Broca's aphasia or agrammatism is too broad to be helpful in describing any one individual patient. However, given these reservations, is it still possible to predict the lesioned area

according to the diagnosed traditional syndromes given the theory?

Studies that have looked at the fit between classical syndromes and localisation have generally supported the Boston Diagnostic Classification System, which divides aphasia into the syndromes discussed. This classification system has a leaning towards favouring the Wernicke–Geschwind model, since it was originally proposed by researchers who were greatly influenced by Norman Geschwind. Indeed this classification has received some support. A fit was found for 17 of the 19 patients assessed by Naeser and Hayward (1978), although two patients with small lesions in Broca's area, failed to show impaired repetition.

Basso et al. (1985) studied 207 aphasic patients (removing those without radiology and those with purely sub-cortical lesions), acknowledging that they did not use a battery of tests that would lead to an objective classification score. They comment on the two main difficulties with the syndome approach, the first being that only around a third of patients fit cleanly into one of the classified syndromes as they are described psychologically, e.g. Broca's, conduction, and Wernicke's. The second issue concerned the difficulty in matching the aphasic features of the syndrome to the supposed associated lesion area. Part of the difficulty related to the uncertainty of measuring the area of damage from the CT scans used by these authors. Thirteen per cent of the patients had "exceptional findings"; 9.7% of these had global aphasia with (according to scan reports) no lesion in Wernicke's area. The authors do not see this finding as a huge threat to the integrity of the model. Nevertheless, seven patients with anterior lesions had Wernicke's aphasia and six with posterior lesions had non-fluent (Broca's) aphasia. The authors conclude that the syndrome model turns out to be roughly valid for most of the cases and propose that these principles should be "adhered to as a basis of standard teaching" (Basso et al., 1985, p. 226). This study and a long-running series reported by Kertesz (1979) appear to statistically support the continued use of the syndrome.

Willmes and Poeck (1993) are less impressed by

the syndrome approach and criticise the interpretation of Basso and colleagues. In their study they used the Aachen Aphasia Test with 221 patients. If the cortical lesions are considered, there appears to be a trend of anterior lesions being associated with Broca's aphasia and posterior lesions being associated with Wernicke's aphasia (Willmes and Poeck, 1993; see table on p. 1533). However, in terms of syndrome/localisation prediction, these results are spoiled largely by the poorly predictive classification of "amnestic aphasia" patients. This classification, where the predominant feature is an inability to name, is not universally accepted as a separate type of aphasia. Naming impairment is associated with lesions throughout the language areas and many aphasic patients will recover to have a residual impairment in naming. In the case of mild aphasia, naming may be the only difficulty. The difficulty using naming impairment as a type of aphasia comes mainly from the number of different mechanisms that may cause this problem. Nevertheless, the Willmes and Poeck study is certainly more thorough than most and takes into account the stage of recovery, which may alter the presentation of the language disorder.

Apart from the very considerable differences between studies in terms of the type of measurements used in measuring aphasia and the issues of stage of recovery of the patient, some of these studies are keen to point out the limitations of the technology used, e.g. CT scans. However, studies that use PET technology in order to look at the relationship between aphasia and hypometabolism have their own problems of interpretation, which may also be difficult to resolve. For example, is a 50% reduction in metabolism in an undamaged area equivalent to the effect of a 50% reduction in a damaged area (Metter & Hanson, 1994, p. 128)? Metter and Hanson (1994), in looking at the relationship between hypometabolism using PET and ratings on the Western Aphasia Battery, found the "frontal regions are most markedly depressed for Broca's aphasia" (p. 130). However, this was most closely related to the degree of subcortical damage, especially hypometabolism of the head of the caudate and thalamus. They talk of a frontal–subcortical system.

The other more definite finding was the relationship between poor comprehension and hypometabolism in the temporoparietal cortex, which has been found in a number of studies. Looking at all their aphasic patients it is perhaps instructive that posterior areas, which are seen to be theoretically important to the language process, are particularly implicated following posterior damage to the language area. Of these, 97% of hypometabolic abnormalities were found in the angular gyrus, 89% in the supramarginal gyrus and 87% in the lateral and transverse superior temporal gyrus.

In summary, the above brief review may take an optimistic or pessimistic interpretation. On the one hand it is certainly time to move on from the old descriptions of syndromes; nevertheless, the syndrome classification has been sufficiently successful to motivate interest in further defining the relationship between structure and function. Syndromes are being replaced by sub-syndromes and in some areas the gap appears to be narrowing between the sub-syndromes and the formulations of those researchers who are primarily interested in testing single cases and are generally more interested in isolating the nature of the impairment more thoroughly.

Should we use the term syndrome?

There has been a large amount of discussion in the literature concerning the use of terms such as Broca's aphasia to describe a syndrome. A syndrome is a collection of symptoms that commonly appear together in a consistent manner. It is sometimes assumed that they appear together more than they appear apart (Poeck & Orgass, 1975) and, mostly in medicine, it is assumed that there is a common underlying mechanism to the symptoms that make up a syndrome. The arguments for and against the use of this term will not be reviewed here (see Caplan, 1988; Caramazza and McCloskey, 1988; Coltheart, 1980, p. 23; Kertesz, 1994; Shallice, 1988a pp. 33–34). However, protagonists who argue against the syndrome approach often base their opinion on the belief that language disorders are too complex and vary too much between individuals. To try and categorise language disorders in this way would inevitably be misleading. Those researchers or clinicians who refer to syndromes are referred to as syndromists and the tone is usually unfavourable. It is widely implied that such researchers have no understanding of the complexity underlying the terms that they use. But do these syndromists actually exist, or are they something of "a straw man"? It is difficult to find modern researchers who believe in syndromes in the simplistic way that is often described. Most researchers who are primarily interested in researching the relationship between brain organisation and language do so with a healthy scepticism concerning the state of knowledge in this area. One should be reminded that there are also problems in studying a single symptom while ignoring collections of symptoms on the assumption that a single symptom represents a single mechanism. Some single mechanisms may only be represented adequately by a collection of symptoms. The arguments against using the syndrome description were, nevertheless, important to avoid complacency and a simplistic, prejudicial approach towards research in this area (see Kertesz, 1994a, for a further discussion).

Revisions to the Wernicke–Geschwind model

In this first section many inadequacies of the Wernicke–Geschwind model have been revealed but some consistencies remain. The radiological findings from PET and fMRI have not removed the mystery of the mechanism underlying language disorders. Some reviews of the literature in this area are somewhat cynical and point to the inconsistencies of results between different studies (Chertkow, & Murtha, 1997; Poeppel, 1996). This is certainly a difficult methodological area to work in. It is also hampered by brief presentations in the cases of PET and limitations placed on paradigms to reduce movements of the subject. Paradigms may be limited by the need for subjects to keep totally still and for this reason masks and body moulds have been designed so that the patient is able to talk during the procedure (Muller et al., 1998). Generally, these studies reveal that more left anterior areas are involved during the production of speech. Simple passive listening tasks often cause activation in

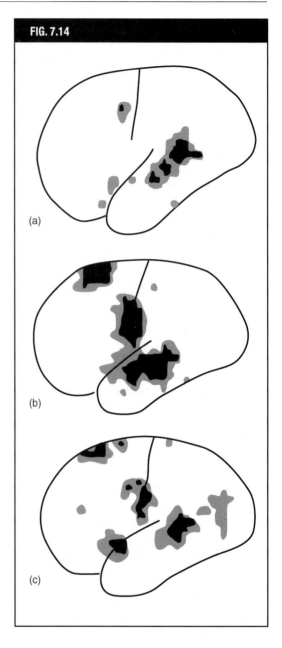

FIG. 7.14

(a)

(b)

(c)

Illustration of a scan measuring cerebral blood flow (adapted from Lassen, Ingvar, & Skinhoj, 1978). (a) Silent listening with the predominant activation of Wernicke's area. (b) Speaking aloud with the activation of Wernicke's area for the reception of speech, precentral area and Broca's for the expression of speech, the mouth area and the supplementary motor area for the motor movements. (c) Reading allowed with more activation of the occipital lobe for visual processing and the frontal eye fields for eye movements.

the posterior language zone, e.g. the superior gyrus of the temporal lobe, this activation being bilateral (sometimes more left than right). However, when decisions have to be made on phonological material the supramaginal gyrus and Broca's area are more likely to be activated even without the requirement of speech output. Areas in the primary motor strip around the "face area" and the areas of the supplementary motor area are activated when the motor movements are isolated, i.e. silent tongue and lip movements. Also, the anterior cingulate is activated when the verbal task demands attention (Petersen et al., 1988). Tasks that require complex sentence construction during speech or lexical association include activation of inferior anterior areas, including areas anterior to Broca's area (Xiong et al., 1998). These findings are generally in support of an anterior speech production system and a posterior speech comprehension system, but with more overlap between the two systems than the Wernicke–Geschwind model would allow (Chertkow & Murtha, 1997; Poeppel, 1996).

Perhaps the least controversial component of the language model (see Figure 7.15) is the allocation of Broca's area as a centre important for the motor movements required of articulation. Both lesion and PET studies have now identified Broca's area as an area important for articulation. As previously discussed, the work of Mohr (1976), and others since, indicate that when lesions are isolated to Broca's area the impairment tends to be confined to a speech apraxia following the initial recovery period. The effortful speech and the hesitations are there but the aphasic symptoms such as agrammatism and paraphasias are either absent or mild, and when they are present they recover quickly. An analysis of the nature of these articulation impairments suggests that it is the timing of phonetics which affects the prosodic content (the appropriate timing and rise and fall of the voice) (Blumstein, 1995, p. 924). But there is an argument discussed above that the impairments of prosody are secondary to articulatory problems and the right hemisphere is more directly committed to prosody.

Following on to the next stage, PET scan work also supports the primary motor area (e.g. face

area), the supplementary motor area and the basal ganglia as structures that are important for the execution of movements required of speech (e.g. Petersen et al., 1988). This argument is also made when discussing subcortical aphasia. The involvement of these motor areas in speech is further discussed in Chapter 8.

The second area that is often more confidently proposed is the location devoted to auditory input. Heschl's gyrus has been identified as the area important for the analysis of the acoustic stimulus. Also, while Wernicke's area is no doubt important for semantic analysis of the acoustic profile of the word, the area for semantic analysis is probably more widespread. Certainly, the superior gyrus of the temporal lobe is activated during passive listening in PET studies and, while there is often more activation on the left, there is also activation at a similar area on the right (Demonet et al., 1992; Petersen et al., 1988; Zattorre, Evans, Meyer, & Gjedde, 1992).

The structural correlates between auditory input and speech output are less clear. As indicated, when the subject is required to make decisions on phonological information, more left-sided anterior areas are activated. For example, when Demonet et al. (1992) requested subjects to detect the occurrence of the sound of "b" followed by the sound of "d" in a word, the supramarginal gyrus and Broca's area were activated. These and other findings in this area suggest to some authors such as Gupta and MacWhinney (1997) that although the input and output stages of phonological analysis take place interactively in both posterior and anterior speech zones, the output phonological analysis takes place more anteriorly. A number of authors argue that rather than just one phonological system, there are separate systems for input and output phonological analysis (Monsell, 1987; Nickels et al., 1997; Shallice, 1988a) although the brain structures associated with such a distinction are uncertain. Hickok (2000) proposes that a phonological output system exists posteriorly in the posterior supratemporal plane, which is situated next to Heschl's gyrus within the sylvian fissure. Hickok proposes that damage to this area is associated with one type of conduction aphasia.

aphasia, while the Wernicke's route with its conscious monitoring of output is impaired.

5. The Wernicke–Geschwind model proposed that pathways between language areas were via projections that were direct; these travelled beneath the grey matter but were not subcortical in the sense of travelling via subcortical structures. Nerve fibres such as the arcuate fasciculus are still seen as being important, but it is argued here and elsewhere that projections to structures such as the thalamus should also be considered as projections between language areas or modules (see Figure 7.13).

6. The right hemisphere clearly plays a role in providing prosody for speech and is influential in the production and reception of prosody. A further role is likely in terms of the comprehension of themes or the coherence of narrative. This role is still being defined but it appears that any communication has a context that includes knowledge concerning social mores within communica-

tion and inferences concerning predictions given certain scenarios. The right hemisphere plays a role in language that is less tied to the structure of language but more related to what is referred to as coarse semantic coding of language: the meaning of language within a social and emotional.

In the introduction to this chapter there was a discussion of the early history of research and language modelling that was provided by the early localisationists. One hundred and thirty years later we have improved our knowledge, but in some measure this has made us less certain. However, further technical improvements in brain scanning are likely to increase our theoretical sophistication in this area in the not too distant future.

In the remainder of this chapter there will be more concentration on specialty topics such as dyslexia and agraphia within a modelling approach chosen by those researchers who broadly describe themselves as cognitive neuropsychologists.

PART 2: A COGNITIVE NEUROPSYCHOLOGICAL PERSPECTIVE

ANOMIA ACCORDING TO SENSORY MODALITY

In the first part of this chapter there was an introduction to the topic of the case study approach to the analysis of anomia. In this last part of this chapter we continue with the topic of anomia within a single modality, e.g. visual, auditory.

Difficulties in naming in one particular modality of sensory input are rare, but when found are of considerable theoretical importance. When anomia is isolated to visual presentations it is referred to as *optic aphasia*, when confined to the auditory modality it is referred to as *auditory aphasia*, while *tactile aphasia* is the name used to

describe a difficulty in naming by the touch of an object. The use of these terms is accepted when the patient shows some knowledge of the object, otherwise without knowledge the patient would be seen as suffering from agnosia.

While theoretically optic aphasia and visual associative agnosia are distinguished by whether the patient has knowledge of the meaning of the to-be-named object, optic aphasic patients do have impaired semantic processing. Knowledge of the object within patients diagnosed with optic aphasia is far from perfect and we shall eventually argue that these two diagnostic categories of optic aphasia and visual associative agnosia are actually closely related. The issues surrounding the arguments on the nature of anomia are revealing of the thought processes that eventually create useful modelling within neuropsychology, even if the eventual answer to the conundrum of optic aphasia looks suspiciously like the resurrection of theory that was originally formulated at the turn of the century.

The research in this area has developed a number of new ways of testing anomia but some traditional methods are still used. The object naming task, as part of the Boston Aphasia Examination, is often used for testing naming and requires the patient to name a series of pictures. The Peabody test involves the reverse requirement but without a speech requirement: the subject is required to pick out the picture that is the best representation of a word in print. Less frequently, a clinician may give a definition and ask the patient to name the object described (auditory modality), or name an object from feel while their vision is obscured in some way (tactile modality). The distinction between anomia and agnosia is important and patients may often know what an object is used for and where it is usually found without being able to name the item. These patients have anomia but not agnosia. Patients with optic, auditory, or tactile aphasia who have naming difficulties only within a specific modality but remain able to recognise an object's conceptual identity are very rare and it will eventually be considered, as others have done, whether we should be using these terms.

An assumption in these naming exercises is that the object is sensed correctly. Often the patient is required to show that they are able to match the object from a choice of objects. Modern experimental work has developed a whole new set of tests that has helped to define the nature of the anomia in a more comprehensive manner (e.g. Warrington, 1975; Riddoch & Humphreys, 1987b; Coslett and Saffran, 1991). One of these, the test of composite parts, requires the judgement of whether a pictorially presented object is real or not real. Some of the "not real" pictures contain drawings that are a composite, containing features of different animals, e.g. a kangaroo with a chicken's head, see Figure 2.13. Such a judgement can sometimes be made even when the patient is unable to identify or recognise a kangaroo or chicken on its own. This has suggested to some authors (Riddoch & Humphreys, 1987a)

that we can match objects with our memory for their physical structures without recourse to meaning. In other words, we might be able say a picture of a chicken is real without being able to identify it because we are able to match it with a stored template of the physical features of a chicken. Other tests require a purely semantic judgement, as in the case of the "pyramid and palm trees test", in which the patient is required to match objects for their conceptual similarity. The palm tree is matched with the pyramid rather than the deciduous tree (note: no naming is required). These tests are therefore designed to analyse the area of breakdown without providing a confounding explanation (see examples of these tests in Chapter 2, Figure 2.13).

While the presence of optic, auditory, or tactile aphasia is important support for a modality-specific naming impairment, the case of optic aphasia has been most frequently studied. Patients with optic aphasia are significantly better at naming objects when they can feel the object or when the object is defined verbally, compared to a visual presentation. The disorder is often associated with a left occipital lesion (involving the left posterior cerebral artery). These patients may have a right hemianopia and often have difficulty naming colours (colour anomia) and also an inability to read (alexia). The syndrome clearly has many features in common with visual associative agnosia, which is discussed in Chapter 2. Like the agnosic patient, the patient will often not be able to give the meaning of the object verbally, but the same patient will, strangely, be able to show knowledge of the meaning by miming the object's use through gesture. If the same object is presented in another modality through verbal definition or tactile presentation, the naming of the object is clearly facilitated. Optic aphasia is, as the name suggests, a naming difficulty with visually presented material.

The finding that anomia and agnosia may be specific to a modality has prompted the multi-modular model, which is illustrated in Figure 7.16. Note there remains a central semantic system: when this store is damaged then the patient would have agnosia for all modalities. Damage to the naming output would result in difficulty in naming in all the modalities. Damage to the visual semantic analysis would result in visual associative agnosia, for example. The case of optic aphasia is difficult to model. The patient is not able to name, but semantic analysis is getting through to allow miming. A disconnection is required to stop naming within one modality and yet the semantic analysis must be getting through in some measure for the patient to show some knowledge of the object to-be-named.

The structural analysis stages illustrated within the model are supported by work with a patient called JB (Riddoch & Humphreys, 1987a). JB had the features required of optic aphasia. JB was able to name objects described by definition in the auditory presentation with equal facility when compared to controls. However, when the researchers used a set of pictures for visual naming (the items were selected because they could also be mimed) JB had great difficulty in naming the objects. JB could, however, make gestures that indicated knowledge of some of the objects he could not name. JB was only able to name 20 out of 44 objects presented visually compared to 44/44 for definitions presented in the auditory modality. Of the 24 objects presented visually which drew an *incorrect* naming response, 11 objects were given correct gestures (45.8%). Also a correct gesture sometimes accompanied a naming error when the error was not even semantically close to the name (Riddoch & Humphreys, 1987, p. 138). Nevertheless, Riddoch and Humphreys were not happy that miming was a convincing test of semantic knowledge. They proposed that the use might be correctly mimed not because of knowledge of the article, but rather because of structural or physical analysis of the pictured object. For example, in the case of a corkscrew the spiralling grooves might limit the way the item might be used, e.g. screwing motion. In this way the meaning of the grooves would be the only thing that would need to be analysed.

Apparently in support of this view the authors found that JB did well on the test that presented composite parts (see Chapter 2, Figure 2.13). They proposed that the structural knowledge of the item was intact. For example, when JB was presented with a composite that was half screw-driver and half chisel (not a real object), JB could check this against a stored *physical* image of a screwdriver in order make the decision that the object was not real. Their model contained a multi-modular structural analysis system, which is included within Figure 7.16. However, their position saw no necessity for a multi-modular semantic system (Riddoch, Humphreys, Coltheart, & Funnell, 1988).

Shallice (1988b) disagreed with Riddoch and colleagues' physical cue type interpretation. He argued for the multi-modular semantic analysis system against the view that the semantic information of these patients was in some way degraded when miming. Shallice refers to cases where the dissociation is much more pronounced than in the case of JB. Among other cases, he refers to the optic aphasic patient of Gil et al. (1985), who could mime 100% of the items.

Shallice (1988b) proposes a multiple semantic system dominated by two lines of evidence. The first is *modality-specific priming*: the finding that some patients' naming is more helped by giving a cue or prime in one modality rather than another. For example, a patient "A" might name a "pyramid" when provided with a definition preceded by an auditory prime of the word *pharaoh* rather than a picture prime of a *pharaoh*, while a patient "B" might be more helped by the picture than the auditory presentation (e.g. Warrington & Shallice, 1979). The second line of evidence is that of *modality-specific aspects of semantic memory disorders*. Warrington (1975) described two patients with opposite impairments: one patient, EM, was most successful when given a picture description, while the other patient, AB, was most successful when given an auditory description. This suggested to the author that EM had more damage to her auditory semantic system, whereas AB had relatively more damage to a visual semantic system. These lines of evidence and their interpretation have been criticised by (Riddoch et al., 1988). However, both these models fail to show how semantic analysis reaches the miming stage when it fails to reach the naming stage, whether it is following modality-specific semantic analysis or following structural analysis. This conundrum is illustrated in Figure 7.16.

FIG. 7.16

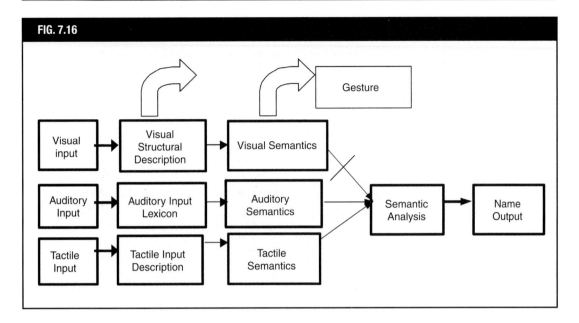

A simplified multiple modality model. There must be a disconnection between semantic analysis to stop naming within the visual domain in isolation. The dilemma for modelling optic aphasia is to allow the semantic information access to miming.

A step towards finding the answer comes from the case study of the optic aphasic, MP (Coslett & Saffran, 1991). MP was reported as a dramatic illustration of optic aphasia: the patient was unable to name any objects visually, compared to 92% in the tactile modality. Further, this study provides evidence for a possible structural explanation for optic aphasia. This patient showed intact semantic knowledge in the visual modality by matching objects from the same category. Strangely, MP claimed not to have seen some stimuli he was capable of matching. A number of features of this patient reminded the authors of the responses of the right hemisphere in the split-brain research. The reader will remember the following features discussed in Chapter 6 given presentation of visual stimuli to the right hemisphere:

1. A lack of awareness of the visual stimuli input.
2. An inability to express in language what has been seen.
3. An ability to comprehend high-imagery common nouns.
4. A failure to process syntax in terms of suf-

fixes, e.g. a failure to recognise that *tigered* is incorrect.

There were also within-category, word–picture matching errors suggesting a course semantic analysis which is reminiscent of the right hemisphere language capabilities already mentioned above. Interestingly, this type of performance is also shown by patients suffering from deep dyslexia[2].

In this way Coslett and Saffran (1991) build up an argument for optic aphasia that was first introduced by Freund a century ago (see De Bleser, 1990, for a description). Freund worked in Carl Wernicke's clinic and was therefore working with models of language disorders similar to the one revived by Geschwind. Freund proposed that damage to the left occipital region and the splenium (the posterior end of the corpus callosum, which is important for transferring visual information) means that the objects cannot be named.

[2] Deep dyslexia, which is discussed later in the chapter, is a disorder whereby the patient makes semantic errors in reading, i.e. reading *time* for the word *clock*. It is mentioned here because one of the theories for this disorder is that reading takes place via a right hemisphere route.

Box 7.8. Too many terms?

The most common type of primary progressive aphasia (PPA) is a deteriorating disorder that presents with dysfluent speech and a Broca's type aphasia. Kertesz reports on a patient with a second, less common type of PPA who could be referred to as having transcortical sensory aphasia (Kertesz et al., 1998). This type of PPA has a profound anomia that is related to a loss of recognised meaning of an object. For example, Kertesz reports a question to their patient:

Q. What is a tool used to drive a nail into a piece of wood?
A. What is a tool? (Kertesz et al., 1998, p. 391).

Naming went from 52/60 high frequency to 25/60 low frequency to zero within the 6 years of deterioration in a disorder that is often marked initially by no impairment of recent memory. Kertesz and colleagues use the term *semantic aphasia* and *semantic dementia* interchangeably as a means of describing this patient. They note that Head (1926) first used the term semantic aphasia when describing what had previously been termed by Wernicke as transcortical aphasia. It could be argued that this type of PPA is *not* a transcortical aphasia since other than the naming impairment, which is associated with a degeneration of semantic analysis, aphasic symptoms are not predominant. This and other patients have been found to be able to name colours (colour anomia seems to be more influenced when lesions are more posterior). Patients are typically able to categorise visual objects and therefore they would be seen as having optic aphasia rather than agnosia (see description of optic aphasia below). In many ways semantic dementia is a preferable term in describing a patient that progressively deteriorates in their ability to analyse semantically without the additional cognitive and personality deterioration that is typically found in Alzheimer's disease (see Chapter 5 for further discussion of this disorder). This and other cases have shown atrophy in the left temporal cortex but often not in the hippocampi, hence the *relatively* intact recent memory. The neuropathology of these patients is often suggestive of Pick's disease. This clearly is one area where the nomenclature needs some clarification since we have a patient with a variant of primary progressive aphasia who could also be described as suffering from transcortical sensory aphasia, semantic aphasia, semantic dementia, and optic aphasia, and who may be suffering from a type of dementia called Pick's disease. While there will be many disagreements with these somewhat facetious proposals, it is inevitable that as knowledge expands within an area diagnoses and labels will metaphorically bump into each other.

In order to access the centre for verbal meaning the visual information must therefore be analysed within the right hemisphere. The result would be an inability to name with a *partial* visual associative agnosia. The assumption is that the right hemisphere contains its own non-verbal semantic system that contains some semantic referents for objects, hence the partial agnosia. Partial agnosia, a partial loss of knowledge of visually presented objects, is a feature common to most optic aphasia cases. In terms of a simplified model of the type espoused by Coslett and Saffran (1991), a combination of both structural and semantic representations are allowed for analysis (see Figure 7.17). A disconnection between these two systems allows patients the ability to match and draw objects without being able to express knowledge of their full meaning. A disconnection between the two hemispheres and a large lesion within the left occipital region may give rise to an optic aphasia because of the reliance on the right hemisphere. Some semantic information can nevertheless be analysed by the right hemisphere which can be expressed through miming. The object is not named because visual access to the left language hemisphere is denied.

If the poor semantic analysis is due to the rather course semantic encoding of the right hemisphere then this should show up on a task that demands a fine degree of semantic analysis. In keeping with this is evidence from semantic matching tasks that if semantic distracters are used (distracters may be items that are close to the meaning of the two to-be-matched items) then patients with optic aphasia do more poorly (Hillis & Caramazza, 1995). The assumption is that a well-defined semantic analysis requires access to the left hemisphere.

Since this disconnection explanation is identical to that of visual associative agnosia and these optic aphasia patients appear to have some limited semantic access, the question remains why some patients have the capacity to undertake more semantic analysis than others. Could there be a continuum between optic aphasia and agnosia? Should the term optic aphasia be dropped and designated as mild visual associative agnosia? De Renzi and Saetti (1997) argue that the variation in semantic access is dependent on the extent to which the individual has the propensity to analyse objects for semantics in the right hemisphere. If an individual has such a right hemisphere capability prior to the stroke then a left hemisphere stroke (left posterior cerebral

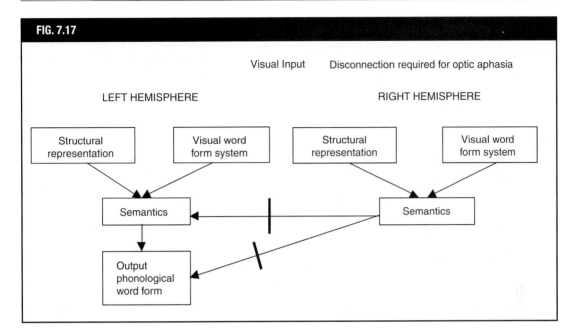

FIG. 7.17

A box-and-arrow diagram of a simplified model of the callosal disconnection required for optic aphasia following Coslett and Saffran (1992).

artery) will result in a mild agnosia (and a diagnosis of optic aphasia). However, if the individual has less of this semantic analysing ability in the right hemisphere prior to stroke then the individual will show little knowledge or recognition of the object and be diagnosed with a visual associative agnosia. One is reminded of the same individual differences that predict the degree of recovery from global aphasia which Kertesz and Naeser (1994) researched and associated with occipital lobe asymmetry.

The final issue, yet to be addressed, is how the patient is sometimes able to show knowledge of an object through mime. None of the models described indicate how the semantic analysis that takes place in the right hemisphere is represented by gesturing. Some readers of Chapters 2 and 4 may have already guessed the best candidate for an answer to this question. In those chapters the distinction between the "what" and "where-action" pathways is described and the evidence for the "where-action" pathway. While the "what" pathway is involved in object identification and runs ventrally from the visual cortex to

the temporal lobe, the pathway that analyses the location of the object and is important for visually guided manipulation runs dorsally from the visual cortex and relies on occipito-parieto-frontal structures (see Chapter 8). It is possible that mime is the non-verbal representation of the object using the coarse right hemisphere semantic analysis and the "where-action" pathway for expression. Feirreira et al. (1997) argue this position, although a preserved "where-action" dorsal stream explanation may not suit all of the patients described above. The patient of Coslett and Saffran (1992), for example, did not have this ability to illustrate semantic analysis through gesture, although the patient did have some semantic recognition skills as described. The differences between these patients may be due to the variation in lesion site and premorbid individual differences in the localisation of language.

Feirreira et al. (1997) have taken the issue of miming using right hemisphere semantic analysis further by arguing from PET studies for the support of a separate semantic system for perceptual/motor analysis (e.g. Martin, Wiggs, Ungerleider,

FIG. 7.18

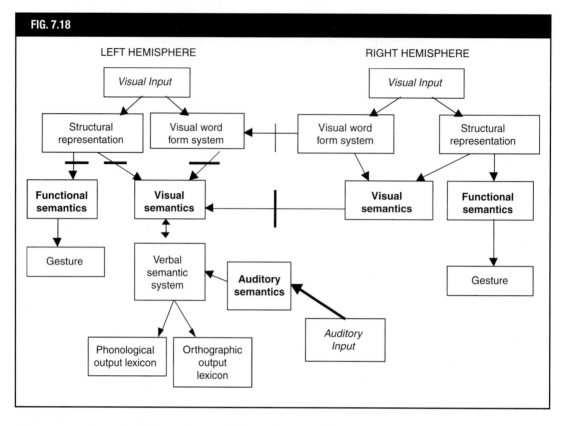

A box-and-arrow diagram illustrating a reliance on right hemisphere analysis for object and word naming as found in optic aphasia and visual associative agnosia. Note the disconnections within the left hemisphere which cut visual analysis off from the semantic system. See Chapter 2 for a more neuroanatomical description.

& Haxby, 1996). The diagram in Figure 7.18 retains features of the models of Riddoch and Humphreys (1987a), Shallice (1988b), and Coslett and Saffran (1992).

In summary, the most acceptable explanation of optic aphasia is that individual patients may use the right hemisphere to provide functional information necessary for accurate gesture. It is possible also that some of the visual associative agnosic patients who have been previously reported would also be found to be capable of miming or broad recognition of verbal conceptual information, if they had been tested in this area. If the degree of semantic impairment is merely due to an individual's premorbid right hemisphere capacity for semantic analysis and the espoused mechanism for optic aphasia is identical to that of agnosia, then it would seem that the term optic aphasia is defunct and that we should really be talking about mild agnosia versus severe agnosia. In keeping with this view, Benke (1988) reports on a visual associative agnosic who during the process of recovery became able to mime and therefore recovered from being an agnosic and became a patient with optic aphasia.

No doubt many will feel they need to know more about the neuropsychological mechanism that underpins the relationship between visual information processing and mime before they are willing to relinquish the term of optic aphasia. On the other hand, perhaps we should be using fewer terms and aiming for parsimony until a more complex situation is supported—a kind of innocent until proved guilty plea for parsimony (see Box 7.8 for a further whimsical note on the plethora of labels).

The case of optic aphasia is a good example of how the analytical skills of cognitive neuropsychology may be combined with the disconnection models originally supplied by the syndrome-localisationist school.

ACALCULIA

Acalculia is a broad term for a disturbance in the ability to calculate. This disorder may be due to a wide variety of impairments in the perception, comprehension, and manipulation of numbers. A person's ability to calculate may be affected by the various aphasias discussed above. A patient who has difficulty in initiating speech because of a transcortical motor aphasia, for example, will also have difficulty in initiating the production of numbers in speech. Similarly, the patient with Wernicke's aphasia who has difficulty in comprehending words may also have equal difficulty in comprehending the symbolic value of numbers. Just as these patients may make paraphasic errors with words, so they will also repeat back different numbers, leave out numbers and place them in the wrong order. Therefore the disorder of acalculia may often reflect the associated language disorder. However, this type of acalculia is reasonably seen as being secondary by some authors (McCarthy & Warrington, 1990). By the same reasoning, *spatial acalculia*, when the patient has difficulty spatially setting out written calculations, along with other similar visuospatial difficulties is also seen as secondary (Hecaen & Albert, 1978). With spatial acalculia, which is often associated with right hemisphere damage, the patient may set out columns so that they are out of line. The same patient may succeed when given a mental calculation. Patients who have neglect may fail to attend to the left-hand side of written numbers when carrying out a calculation. All the above calculation difficulties are generally not seen as "primary". That is, the problems of calculation are seen as a by-product or secondary to a more fundamental mechanism of impairment.

Frontal acalculia

In some ways frontal acalculia may be considered secondary if only because the kinds of errors these patients make also appear in their other behaviours for similar reasons. Patients with damage in the prefrontal cortex may have difficulty in serial operations. This may occur when solving problems that require a patient to keep one step of the calculation in mind while conducting a second or third operation (Luria, 1966; Rosselli & Ardila, 1989). Luria (1966) describes a patient who had a large tumour removed from the posterior left frontal region. Luria gave the patient a series of problems that required the patient to work through several stages of a problem prior to gaining a solution. For example: *Some farmers had 12 hectares of land. From each hectare they took 5 cwt of grain; they sold one-third to the state. How much was left for them?* Another question was used by Luria: *On two shelves there were 18 books, but there were two books fewer on one shelf than on the other. How many books were there on each shelf?* Luria reports the patient's tendency was to fail to plan an approach to the question. The patient immediately entered into the calculations without deliberation and without a plan, and was also easily distracted by irrelevant associations.

Once the patient was told how to solve the problem, the patient would then proceed to solve similar questions accurately without difficulty. However, when the nature of the problem was changed and required a different strategy, the patient would continue to use the old, now inappropriate strategy. Luria reports also that there was a sense from the dialogue of the patient that some information was not being kept on-line, which could be explained in terms of a breakdown of working memory (Luria, 1966, pp. 449–459). Sometimes there is perseveration of a response, so that a number is added to the solution again and again.

Computational impairments in acalculia

When computational impairments are disproportionate to other deficits they are seen as "primary" and this is often referred to as *anarithmetia* (Hecaen, Angelergues, & Houiller,

1961). This type of impairment may be present to a greater degree following lesions in the angular gyrus. Luria (1966) made the observation that disorders of calculation associated with left parietal damage may also be related to disordered grammatical structure. The description of transcortical sensory aphasia may include a difficulty in transposing sentences which, because of their structure, require some mental manipulation, for example, the double negative or the passive sentence. Anarithmetia also involves this type of syntactical computational disorder with numbers such as in a situation when the order of the numbers is confused. Therefore there appears to be a common reason for the appearance of grammatical difficulties and acalculia in some patients who suffer sensory transcortical aphasia.

With anarithmetia there is a particular difficulty in transcoding, that is, in completing successive operations required in solving mathematical problems (Rosselli & Ardila, 1989). It may be more than a coincidence that damage to the angular gyrus is also associated with the signs of impaired left–right orientation and *finger agnosia*—disorders that also require some mental manipulation of learned structures. These disorders sometimes appear together in what is sometimes referred to as Gerstmann's syndrome, being associated with a left parietal lesion. The word *digit* comes from the Latin *digitus*, which also means finger. Counting on one's fingers has an ancient history which goes back to at least 2000 BC and is likely to account for the decimal system (see Butterworth, 1999, for an informative account). It is therefore appropriate (but not necessarily significant) that finger agnosia (a failure in identifying fingers when touched with eyes closed) often accompanies acalculia of the anarithmetia type following lesions within the left parietal area.

There may be good evolutionary reasons why these two facilities are housed close together. It seems that while adults generally use various automatic and well-learned strategies to complete mathematical problems, children often start to learn to count using fingers. Children who have finger agnosia often, but not always, have impaired mathematical ability, although statements concerning cause and effect are of course difficult (Suresh & Sebastian, 2000).

However, while dense acalculias, which are sometimes so severe that the patient has difficulty in manipulating numbers in excess of four, are commonly associated with a left parietal lesion, there is now evidence that the right hemisphere is also involved in mathematical reasoning. Therefore in comparing patients on a graded difficulty arithmetic test (involving subtraction and addition) patients with left hemisphere lesions are most impaired; patients perform equally badly compared to controls on an arithmetical reasoning test (e.g. subject required to select a number that fits a series 2, 4, 6 _?) (Langdon & Warrington, 1997). These authors speculate that the right hemisphere is superior to the left in a task requiring the estimation of the magnitude of a number. Thus in the arithmetical reasoning test the right hemisphere may have an advantage in judging some spatial representation of the series progression, a rough appreciation of the relative intervals between numbers. The left hemisphere conducts the verbal commutation to test out the hypothesis provided by the right.

The determination that acalculia may be a primary disorder is quite simply deduced by discounting alternative reasons for acalculia. For example, patients may be aphasic assuming that the specific left parietal lobe area is spared (Rossor, Warrington, & Cipolotti, 1995), or amnesic (e.g., Delazer & Girelli, 2000) or have severely impaired short-term memory (Butterworth, Cipolotti, & Warrington, 1996) and still perform adequately at arithmetic. There are also patients who know all the mathematical rules and strategies required to solve mathematical problems but are nevertheless unable to undergo the procedure required of calculation (Warrington, 1982). There are other patients who have these cognitive areas intact (e.g. Cipolotti, Butterworth, & Denes, 1991) and yet have acalculia. Therefore acalculia may be considered a primary disorder in some patients.

Interactions between experience and patterns of impaired calculation

Sometimes a patient may retain the rules of complex calculations but be excessively slow at performing these calculations. Children take longer to make additions of two digits compared to a single digit. This difference is often minimal in adulthood since there is a certain amount of automaticity; the need for metaphorical finger counting is reduced. Some brain-damaged patients may retain the rules of calculations, e.g. percentages, proportions, but lose the automaticity, which varies premorbidly according to the occupation and experience of the patient (Warrington, 1982). On this topic it is a pity that some papers on acalculia often neglect to note the past occupational experience of the patient. Intuitively one might expect to find differences in some self-reports of strategies used in approaching mathematical problems that might also be revealing.

A feature found in several case studies (McCloskey & Caramazza, 1987; McCloskey, Sokol, & Goodman, 1986) is the tendency to show errors only within certain number categories, e.g. tens. For example, two numbers ending in 0 might be interchanged so that 20 might be misread as 30. The teens 13–19 are also interchanged, but substitutions between these boundaries are far less likely. For example, 18 would be less likely to be read as 28 (going between teens to twenties), but 18 could be read as 19. This suggests that a number production system is categorised in some way (McCloskey & Caramazza, 1987).

Some patients have been found to have difficulty judging which of two numbers are larger. This may be because the patient has difficulty processing the order of the numbers or because the symbolic magnitude is not realised (Delazer & Butterworth, 1997; McCloskey and Caramazza, 1987).

All these impairments—automaticity, categorisation of numbers, and judgement of numbers—suggest that there is a semantic system for numbers that allows the subject to know what numbers mean.

A model of acalculia is provided by McCloskey and Caramazza (1987), who in their subsequent publications describe comprehension inputs and production outputs within a central semantic system. These inputs and outputs vary according to whether the numbers are represented verbally or in arabic numerical form (see Figure 7.19). The model proposes that the semantic representation specifies the basic quantities of the number and computes the answer to the problem. The comprehension (input) and production (output) are further specified into *phonological encoding* for the auditory reception of numbers and their expression. The *graphemic* form allows reading input and written output. Syntactic processing errors in the case of arabic numerals occur when the number order is disturbed. This model is supported by a series of dissociations. For example, Macaruso, McCloskey, and Aliminosa (1993) report on a patient, RH, who when given a verbal form of number made an error in transcoding the number either into the arabic or verbal form, e.g. seventy-four → 84, forty-nine → four-eight. He was much more successful, however, when transcoding an arabic form into an arabic or verbal form, e.g. 84 to eighty-four. Cipolotti, Warrington, and Butterworth (1995) describe the opposite problem in a patient who could manipulate and transcode numbers when they were presented verbally but had difficulty with arabic numerals.

Some patients appear to have an acalculia that is confined to a particular modality. Not contained in the Macaruso model is a reference to the relationship between acalculia and working memory in which auditorily presented material is particularly impaired (Logie, Gilhooly, & Wynn, 1994). Cases have been reported that are similar to the conduction aphasic patient BR described earlier. It is understood that in such cases the patient is unable to retain numbers in a phonological store, as part of a working memory impairment. From this view comes the prediction that the patient would be able to perform calculations when the material is presented in another modality. When the author was testing this patient there was the expectation of a difference between modality of presentation, but the difference was far more dramatic than expected. BR's performance was so dismal under auditory

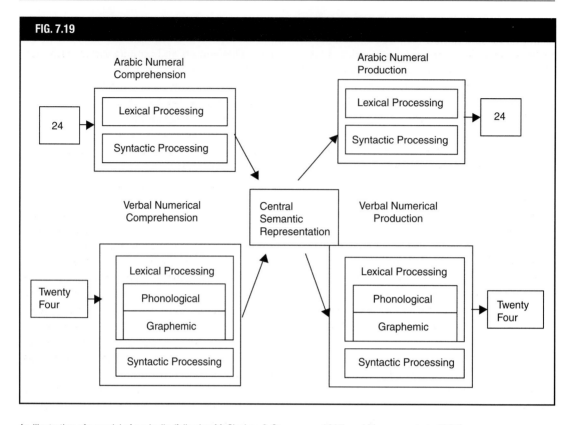

FIG. 7.19

Arabic Numeral Comprehension

Lexical Processing

Syntactic Processing

24

Arabic Numeral Production

Lexical Processing

Syntactic Processing

24

Verbal Numerical Comprehension

Lexical Processing

Phonological

Graphemic

Syntactic Processing

Twenty Four

Central Semantic Representation

Verbal Numerical Production

Lexical Processing

Phonological

Graphemic

Syntactic Processing

Twenty Four

An illustration of a model of acalculia (following McCloskey & Caramazza, 1987, and Macaruso et al., 1993).

presentation (mental arithmetic) that he gave up on the simplest items, e.g. "What is four plus five dollars?" He was not even game to attempt an answer to the question, "If you buy 6 dollars worth of petrol and pay for it with a 10-dollar note, how much change should you get back?" When allowed to read the question that was placed in front of him during problem solving BR was able to supply an adroit correct answer to such questions as "A coat that normally sells for $60 is reduced by 15% in a sale. What is the price of the coat during the sale?" In other words, when auditory working memory was not required during the arithmetical performance he showed an ability that was in keeping with his pre-stroke administrative work role.

Since BR had significant problems on a number of working memory tasks that tested the capacity of a phonological store, it is of interest that in this patient mental arithmetic ability appeared to be dependent on this same store. The patient PV, who is discussed by Vallar and Papagno (1995a, p. 143), is similar in this respect. She showed an inability to perform auditory working memory tests, had a left perisylvian lesion and had particular difficulty in working out change in shops.

In seeming contradiction to this theoretical interpretation are the results of a patient, MRF, who was studied by Butterworth, Cipolotti, and Warrington (1996). Despite a forward digit span of only three, MRF was well able to perform mental arithmetic with an auditory presentation. One possible explanation for MRH's ability in this area comes from a structural model of working memory provided by Gupta and MacWhinney (1997). They propose that impaired repetition, as measured by digit-span, may be undermined for different reasons depending on the area of the lesion. In the case of some perisylvian conduction aphasic patients, it is assumed that the capacity of the phonological store within working memory is reduced (as would be the case with BR and PV). If the lesion is more anterior, however, the articulatory loop is more likely to be affected. The slower speed of articulation has the effect of reducing digit-span. As indicated in Chapter 5, digit-span is correlated with speed of articulation even to the extent that nationalities that have longer names for numbers have reduced average digit-span when compared to nations that have shorter number names, e.g. Welsh compared to English children.

Butterworth and colleagues describe their patient as suffering from "dysfluent aphasia" (Broca's type?) and therefore according to the Gupta and MacWhinney model there might be an articulatory slowness that was interfering with the patient's digit-span—a slowness might not interfere with covert mathematical abilities when out-loud or subvocal calculation was not required.

In summary, acalculia is a broad term that needs to be further defined prior to planning any form of remedial intervention. The reasons for acalculia may be related to a dysfunction in one particular modality (visual versus auditory), number ordering (syntax), numeral representation (verbal versus arabic), impaired working memory function such as impaired articulation or impaired phonological store capacity, and finally executive dysfunction (frontal acalculia). Most of these acalculias are accompanied by similar errors in aphasic symptoms and therefore may be just one manifestation of a language disorder.

Acalculia may occur, as indicated above, without aphasia or working memory impairment as a primary acalculia being associated with a lesion in the vicinity of the angular gyrus (Cipolotti et al., 1991; Takayama, Sugishita, Akiguchi, & Kimura, 1994). These rarely reported patients who have acalculia in isolation or have a disproportionate difficulty with numbers have been referred to as suffering anarithmetia. These patients have mainly computational difficulties in which symbolic errors (knowing the relative magnitude of numbers) may be present. There may also be difficulty in transcoding or completing a series of stages within a math-

ematical problem. A syntactical computational disorder with numbers, such as in a situation when the order of the numbers is confused, may also be present. At present the cognitive neuropsychological analysis of acalculia presents one of the most fruitful approaches to analysing this interesting disorder.

THE AGRAPHIAS

Agraphia is an acquired inability to write, while dysgraphia refers to an impaired ability to write. This disorder has already been mentioned as a component in the various aphasic syndromes. For example, patients with a dysfluent, Broca's type aphasia may sometimes have the same agrammatic speech in their writing with the loss of "joining words" and/or poor syntax, for example, as they do in their speech. The paraphasias, which are present in an aphasic patient's speech, may also occur in their writing.

How common is "pure agraphia" without aphasic symptoms? Basso, Taborelli, and Vignolo (1978) found only 2 out of 500 with left hemisphere damage who were found to have agraphia without aphasia. Most reported cases of agraphia in isolation appear to involve damage to the left angular gyrus or just posterior to this structure (see Figure 7.20). Often this is described with acalculia and other features of what is referred to as Gerstmann's syndrome. In such cases there is distortion of letter forms and reduplications of strokes, and there may be a choice of letters not appearing in the alphabet. Semantic errors are less likely. However, localisation of any of the different types of agraphia is fraught with uncertainty (Roeltgen, 1994).

Another rare form of agraphia involves a type of apraxia. Apractic agraphia is more obviously a difficulty of the fine motor coordination required of writing and most often involves the left superior parietal lobule (Alexander, Fischer, & Friedman, 1992). In this type of apraxia the patient may resort to using "block" letters. Such cases are assumed to be due to a loss of the memories dedicated to writing movements. The

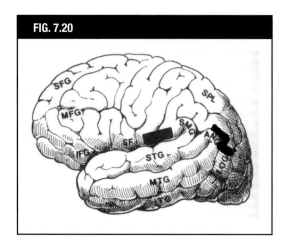

FIG. 7.20

Illustration of the brain areas that when lesioned may be associated with dysgraphia. The lesion area posterior to the angular gyrus (ANG) is associated with lexical agraphia and the area anterior to the supramarginal gyrus is associated with phonological agraphia. The middle (MFG) and superior frontal gyrus (SFG) are shown with the middle (MTG) and superior temporal gyrus (STG) (reprinted from Roeltgen & Heilman, 1984, with permission from Oxford University Press).

patient is likely to be able to spell orally. Finally, isolated agraphia has been noted following frontal lesions, in particular, lesions to the area of the precentral gyrus or motor strip (Rapcsak, Arthur, & Rubens, 1988). A pattern of posterior speech zones interacting with anterior motor areas is attractive but the lack of consistent evidence makes modelling in this area hazardous.

The distinction between writing and spelling is sometimes made. Two forms of agraphia, surface dysgraphia and phonological dysgraphia, have been distinguished according to certain patterns of spelling errors. Surface or orthographic agraphia is marked by the patient's tendency to make errors suggesting that there is an over-application of phonological rules (grapheme-to-phoneme conversion, GPC) when spelling. English language has a large number of words with orthography that has little relation to pronunciation. Irregular words such as *steak* in the context of *I ate the steak* provide a challenge for the surface agraphic patient. When asked to write the word they might assume the more usual rules of pronunciation that follow words such as *make*,

bake, or *wake* and therefore write the word *stake*. A patient with surface agraphia when asked to write the word *sugar* may well spell the word *shugger*, according to the sound of the word. The GPC is intact but the lexicon or memory store containing all those irregular words that we must learn to pronounce is not functioning. Baxter and Warrington (1987) describe a patient, KT, who spelt *knock* as *noc* and *build* as *bild*. Sometimes the more common irregular words are spared.

A second spelling disorder of phonological agraphia is rarely discovered because it often only becomes obvious when the subject is asked to spell non-words. This patient has a vocabulary-based or lexicon-based spelling but is unable to spell according to the sound of the word, which, as indicated, is the only way the surface agraphic is able to spell. These patients might be able to spell *encyclopaedia* but be unable to spell the simple non-word *frid*. In such patients it is clear they have a vocabulary store or lexicon of the words but they are unable to sound out the words to help their spelling of words not previously encountered. They do not have a GPC. Shallice (1981) describes such a patient who had difficulty in spelling syllabic sounds. In order to compensate, the patient tried to find a related meaning to the sound in order to spell it. The occasional lack of success with this strategy was revealing of the patient's reliance on a lexicon. For example, when asked to spell the sound *na* he responded *gn* (from the word *gnat*). This same patient could spell such words as *genealogy*. As indicated there is a great deal of uncertainty in terms of the localisation of agraphias but there is some support for a location for phonological agraphia that appears to overlap with the area sometimes attributed to conduction aphasia. The area that appears to be most over-lapped in the scans of these patients appears to be within the anterior area of the supramarginal gyrus and the insula (see Figures 7.9 and 7.13 for an illustration of this area). The reader will note that this is not out of keeping with the model provided earlier in which the phonological analysis is associated with this particular area.

These two types of agraphia provide evidence for a lexicon (like a dictionary) for words according to the look of the word (orthography), which is damaged in the case of surface dysgraphia, and a system that converts phonological attributes into graphemes (non-word spelling), which is damaged in the case of phonological dysgraphia.

A third disorder of deep dysgraphia presents in terms of an inability to write the correct meaning of a word. For example, Bub and Kertesz (1982) describe a patient, JC, who made semantic substitutions, e.g. *time → clock, chair → table*. Other patients have been reported with even more specific semantic difficulties for function words and less common abstract words (Baxter & Warrington, 1985). Figure 7.21 illustrates the components required to satisfy the disorders of surface, phonological, and deep dysgraphia.

ALEXIA AND AGRAPHIA

This topic gives an ideal opportunity to contrast the syndrome approach with that of the cognitive neuropsychology approach.

Alexia with agraphia

Alexia is a term used to describe patients who are unable to read, while dyslexia is strictly used to denote an impaired reading ability. The most common form of reading disorder is associated with the posterior syndromes such as Wernicke's aphasia and transcortical sensory aphasia. This is sometimes referred to as parietal–temporal alexia. Déjerine reported one of the earliest cases in 1891. He described a patient with a lesion to the angular gyrus. This patient's aphasic condition recovered, leaving alexia with agraphia (inability to read or write). Patients with this disorder typically have a difficulty in reading *letters* and words and therefore this is different from occipital alexia, in which the patient often has alexia without agraphia, and is able to read letters only (see Table 7.2 below).

Because both reading and writing are impaired in alexia with agraphia, this encourages the view that a central mechanism for language has been interfered with. When alexia is accompanied by agraphia other signs of aphasia usually accompany these impairments, especially problems in the comprehension and expression of spoken language, poor repetition, and anomia (Benson & Ardila, 1996). In contrast, occipital alexia is not associated with these other language disorders but is a frequent accompaniment of visual associative agnosia.

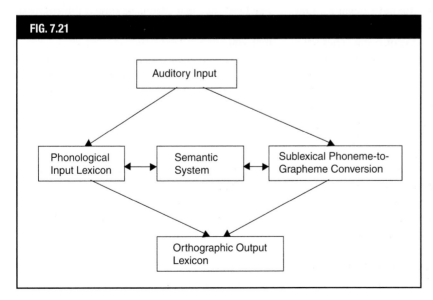

FIG. 7.21

Auditory Input

Phonological Input Lexicon

Semantic System

Sublexical Phoneme-to-Grapheme Conversion

Orthographic Output Lexicon

A breakdown in the dual-route model at the phonological input route will cause surface dysgraphia and a reliance on spelling words according to sound, while a breakdown in the sublexicon will cause phonological dysgraphia and an inability to spell non-words. A breakdown at the semantic level would cause deep dysgraphia.

TABLE 7.2		
Alexia clinical subtypes		
Alexia with agraphia	Alexia without agraphia	Frontal alexia
Parietal–temporal	Occipital	Frontal
poor comprehension for words and letters	Letter-by-letter naming intact	Poor comprehension for words and letters
No or little comprehension	Good comprehension of spelled words	Better comprehension of nouns and adjectives compared to syntax
Accompanied by agraphia	Mild or no agraphia	Dysgraphia similar in quality to alexia
Surface alexia	Pure alexia	Often part of Broca's aphasia

Alexia without agraphia (occipital alexia)

This disorder acts to confirm the visual input disconnection. One of the strongest explanations for *alexia without agraphia* is a disconnection between the visual input and the centre required for language analysis. A disconnection explanation is strong because it is associated with a double disconnection that disallows visual information from entering the left hemisphere for analysis. The lesion that cuts off visual information must first deny entering from the left visual cortex and at the same time deny entry of visual information across the corpus callosum (at the splenium) from the right hemisphere. These patients, who often have additionally visual associative agnosia, or so-called optic aphasia and colour anomia often also have alexia without agraphia. The dual requirements of the lesion contribute to the rarity of the disorder. These two disconnections usually follow stroke involving the left posterior cerebral artery (see Chapter 2).

This complex disconnection was originally described by Dejerine in 1892, and was described and elaborated on again by Geschwind in the 1960s (Geschwind, 1962, 1965). The patient has the ability to write, since the lesion does not damage the angular gyrus and other more anterior language areas which serve writing are intact. Meaning and orthographic form of what is to be written can therefore be formulated and sent to the premotor area in preparation for the execution of the writing movements in the appropriate motor areas for hand and upper limb movements necessary for writing. The patient cannot read what he had written because the visual information is cut off from the language-processing areas (the patient DM described in Chapter 2 had this difficulty). These patients are therefore in the strange situation of not being able to read their own writing. Writing with this disconnection might be roughly likened to a normal person writing with the lights out: the patient is able to write but unable to monitor his or her own writing. While their spontaneous writing is often with ease, when the patient is asked to copy a sentence their copies are reminiscent of a child in kindergarten who has not experienced the word before. The style of copying is "slavish" and because these patients may also have agnosia and therefore have no knowledge of what they are copying, like DM, they may also have similar difficulties in copying objects and other visually presented material.

On occasions the lesion required for the left hemisphere disconnection of the incoming visual information may be more anterior than the more common posterior cerebral artery left occipital lobe stroke. But in such cases the areas in the vicinity of the angular gyrus are assumed to be disconnected (Greenblatt, 1977). However, there appears to be growing evidence that area 37 may be equally if not more important as an association area important to reading and naming in both normal persons and the congenitally blind Braille reading (Buechel, Price, Frackowick & Friston, 1998). This is seen as a convergence zone for a number of modalities and is implicated in patients with anomia as well.

Alexia without agraphia is sometimes associated with a phenomenon referred to as letter-by-letter reading. This occurs when a patient reads out each letter separately and then deciphers the spelling presumably through the auditory route. How these patients are able to do this is still something of a mystery. If they can read letters, why not words? Letter-by-letter reading is a slow process that may reveal that these patients are utilising some kind of reduced capacity to attend, since the letters to be read are sometimes missed, irrespective of whether the patient is requested to read the end letters first or last. Also as the letters are read there is a tendency for the patient to slow down (Berndt & Mitchum, 1995).

Frontal dyslexia

The features of frontal dyslexia are similar to the quality of dysfluent speech and it often accompanies Broca's aphasia. When this becomes a prominent feature there is a difficulty in reading and writing and the patient may find it so difficult that it becomes an aversive process. As indicated above, the patient may have a preserved ability to read words that have a high meaningful content but have difficulty in reading words and suffixes etc. that modify the words in the sentence according to syntactical rules.

The cognitive neuropsychologist's approach to studying alexia is described in the next and final section.

THE ACQUIRED DYSLEXIAS

Dyslexia is often used to describe a children's difficulty in reading and much of the terminology used in this developmental dyslexia is shared with the adult acquired disorder discussed here (Coltheart & Rastle, 1994).

The dyslexias are divided into those that are *peripheral*, which is a dysfunction of the early stages of reading in the visual perceptual analysis system, and the *central dyslexias*, which are assumed to occur at a later stage. The earlier-staged peripheral dyslexias include *letter-by-letter reading*, discussed above in connection with

occipital dyslexia, *attentional dyslexia*, which may occur with Balint's syndrome, and finally *neglect dyslexia*. These last two have been previously referred to in Chapter 4. The terminology for dyslexias is controversial and there is some disagreement as to whether all the peripheral dyslexias, such as attentional dyslexia, should be classified as such (Warrington, Cipolotti, & McNeil, 1993). The prefix *dys* in dyslexia reveals that the discussion of central dyslexias is more concerned with an impairment, rather than an inability to read. It is true though that in contrast to the central dyslexias, the peripheral dyslexias often constitute an inability to read, at least by normal routes. While controversy within some of the peripheral dyslexias is in terms of the stage of processing, controversy exists within the central dyslexias more in terms of the identity of these dyslexias and the best ways to model them.

The central dyslexias

Surface dyslexia

Research into the central dyslexias is precise in defining the psychological components by studying patients who make specific error types. Just as paraphasias give a clue to the nature of the underlying mechanisms of spoken language, errors in reading or paralexias provide evidence of mechanisms underlying dyslexia. For example, some patients who suffer from *surface dyslexia* are similar to surface dysgraphic patients in making errors in reading or spelling, relying on the way the word sounds, according to the normal rules of GPC. The surface dyslexic may have the greatest difficult in reading words that do not obey such rules. According to Figure 7.21 there is a breakdown in the route that allows the use of the orthographic lexicon. The orthographic lexicon is a store containing all words according to their appearance.

The terminology used for dyslexia is very similar to that used for dysgraphia above. The surface dyslexic patient will read the word *pint* with the more regular pronunciation of *mint*. The same patient may read the word *have* with the more regular pronunciation sound of the word *save*. *Pint*, *have*, *colonel*, *yacht*, and *ache* are all examples of exception or irregular words. Patients who are bilingual may have more problems in reading aloud in languages like English and French, which have many of these exception words when compared to languages that have few irregular pronunciations, such as Russian or Spanish (Luria, 1960, p. 334; Masterson, Coltheart, & Meara, 1985). Because the surface dysgraphic patient is relying on the GPC unit the patient is confused in terms of the way the word sounds. A patient may say *"nice"* when reading the word *niece* or say *"decease"* when reading *disease* (Marshall & Newcombe, 1973). The errors are according to the sounds of the pronunciation of words rather than their appearance. Sometimes a word is misread through the regularisation of an irregular word, e.g. the word *gauge* might be read as *gorge*; then the semantic interpretation is according to the pronounced response and in this case it might be understood as a dip or valley (Coltheart, 1981). This would suggest that the semantic lexicon has been accessed after or at the same time as the phonological analysis.

The more frequently used irregular words (in terms of everyday use) are found to be less difficult and therefore one cannot make a clear dichotomous distinction between regular and irregular words when analysing the difficulties of these patients. Because they can use rules of pronunciation, many surface dyslexics will be able to read non-words like *flart* or *trard*. With these patients it is clear that the GPC system is intact, but another recognition component or lexicon that allows us to read irregular words like *yacht* is impaired. On the small and rather confusing number of cases available, surface dyslexia is most frequently found in patients with a lesion of the left temporal lobe in the posterior middle and superior gyri (Patterson, Coltheart, & Marshall, 1985).

The cases are often not as clear cut as presented here; nevertheless, *reliance* on the route that converts letters into their sounds according to the regular rules of GPC is the primary sign of this disorder. Most patients with surface dyslexia will also have surface dysgraphia. In other words, they tend to spell words phonetically and may not be able to write words that have an irregular pronunciation. However, this is not always the case and one patient has been reported who has surface dyslexia but with the signs of phonological dysgraphia—the reverse pattern of impairment (Beauvois & Derouesne, 1979).

Phonological dyslexia

It is easiest to remember the distinction between surface and phonological dyslexia by noting that with *phonological dyslexia* the hypothetical *phonological* conversion unit (grapheme-to-morpheme conversion unit) is impaired. Unlike surface dyslexics, these patients have been found to have difficulty converting graphemes to phonemes, especially when confronted with non-words. These patients with phonological dyslexia have the contrasting problem and cannot read non-words like *trard*. Nevertheless, the evidence that they can often read most other words suggests that the orthographic lexicon can often be relied upon in adult reading. In other words, we often read by the look of the word rather than the sound when we become efficient readers.

Therefore while phonological dyslexic patients have no difficulty with irregular words like *yacht* and *ache*, they may also read some common regular words because these words are recognised without recourse to the sound of the word using GPC. Again, it is rare that this dyslexia appears in a pure form, but because these purer cases exist this encourages the "two-route models" that make the distinction between an orthographic and phonological analysis.

Phonological dyslexics make particular errors that illustrate the breakdown of the phonological system or what is referred to as the grapheme-to-phoneme conversion unit. These paralexic errors may show an ignoring of the sound of the word and a preference to take account of the visual representation of letters. For example, the patient may read the word *dame* as *made* or *deal* as *lead*.

The reader will have noted the similarities between the models for the quality of spelling errors in dyslexia and dysgraphia in Figure 7.21. The overwhelming majority of reported patients with surface dyslexia also have surface dysgraphia and, as indicated, without specialised tests a good way to show their strategy of reading is sometimes through their spelling. This high correlation between the two disorders suggests that the orthographic lexicon for reading input is the same lexicon that is used for writing output. In other words, a single orthographic lexicon could serve for both reading and writing.

The reverse pattern, however, is not so common. A number of patients who have surface dysgraphia do not additionally have surface dyslexia. However, some argue that writing is more demanding, and therefore a patient with a mild impairment will still show the dysgraphia but fail to show the easier reading task impairment diagnostic of dyslexia. There are ever-present cues and contexts in reading, e.g. the word after the target word, which are not present in writing.

However, against the single orthographic lexicon for both reading and writing is the finding that patients who are trained to reduce their surface dysgraphia do not necessarily also improve their surface dyslexia. In the reverse direction, training surface dyslexic patients on reading does not help their spelling (see Weekes & Coltheart, 1996, for a discussion). Also, as Coltheart (1996) points out, reading generally involves posteriorly

related brain processes and a case of surface dysgraphia has been reported following frontal damage (Rapcsak et al., 1988). It is possible there is a dependence on the same lexicon normally and so with damage to the lexicon both reading and writing are affected. But after brain damage a new organisation is set up that is dependent on the modality of training; this would be in keeping with reorganisation theories of recovery discussed previously.

To return to the issue of a model for acquired dyslexia, although the dual route is preferable to a single-route model there are a few difficulties with the model proposed in Figure 7.22, especially in terms of modelling phonological dyslexia. The first issue concerns the pseudohomophone effect. Pseudohomophones are non-words that when spoken sound like real words. For example, the typed word *brane* is a non-word, but when it is spoken out loud it is indistinguishable from the real word *brain*. Normal subjects and patients are faster at naming pseudohomophones than other non-words and patients with phonological dyslexia are more likely to be able to name a non-word if it is a pseudohomophone. This is difficult for the model since in our example the word *brain*

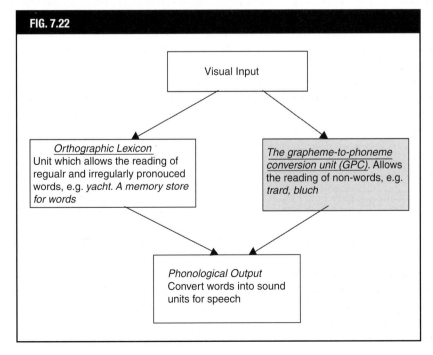

FIG. 7.22

Visual Input

Orthographic Lexicon
Unit which allows the reading of regualr and irregularly pronouced words, e.g. *yacht. A memory store for words*

The grapheme-to-phoneme conversion unit (GPC). Allows the reading of non-words, e.g. *trard, bluch*

Phonological Output
Convert words into sound units for speech

A disruption of the route involving the orthographic lexicon would be associated with surface dyslexia and a reliance on the regular letter-to-sound rules (GPC). A disruption in the grapheme-to-phoneme route results in phonological dyslexia, in which the patient is unable to read non-words.

would be stored in the orthographic lexicon (the way the word looks), while the non-word is read with the aid of the GPC. There are no direct interconnections between the GPC and the orthographic lexicon that allow the benefit derived from naming a pseudohomophone.

One of the classical French-based experiments on phonological dyslexia (Derouesne & Beauvois, 1985) found that their patient, LB, read the non-word *Kok* as *Coq* (with instructions that encouraged seeking real words). This advantage of patients and normal subjects being helped by pseudohomophones in non-word reading is well replicated. The problem with the model in Figure 7.22 is that the GPC, which reads the non-word *brane*, does not simultaneously have access to real words such as *brain* in the orthographic lexicon. *Brain* and other real words are contained in the orthography lexicon and they must be additionally processed through the phonological output before the congruity of the sound between *brane* and *brain* is appreciated. A non-word has to travel down the GPC and it cannot be sounded out until it has passed the GPC so how can phonological dyslexic patients who have damage to the GPC make use of the sound of the word in order to extract the real word that sounds similar.

One way of dealing with this difficulty is to allow a phonological output to have feedback to the GPC. If some information gained access to the GPC and passed through to the phonological output, the phonological output could in turn access the orthographic lexicon to access the real word *brain* that sounds the same as the non-word. One model, referred to as "the dual route cascade model" provided by Max Coltheart and colleagues seems to cope better with the pseudo-homophone conundrum (Coltheart, Curtis, Atkins, & Haller, 1993; Coltheart & Rastle, 1994) (see Figure 7.23).

In this computer-based model GPC unit is capable of reading non-words by access to about 240 rules of pronunciation. There are no whole non-words, just phonemes and their spelling patterns, e.g. IGH → sol/ai/. The dual route cascade model is a computer-based model with a GPC unit that is capable of reading non-words by access to about 240 rules of pronunciation. GPC is a slower serial reading process, which is in accordance with intuitive descriptions of non-word reading. For example, when giving a reading test, subjects who have never previously encountered the word often pronounce the word *somnambulist* correctly. But the pronunciation is slow, and there is an obvious strategy of splitting up words into units, according to an understanding of the rules of pronunciation: "som-nam-bu-list". The GPC is being used.

One of the predictions of the model concerns

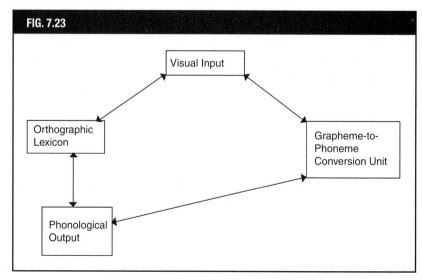

FIG. 7.23

Dual-route cascade model (adapted from Coltheart & Rastle, 1994).

this cascade feature. The model runs on the assumption that during the reading process the visual input is analysed by both routes, cascading down the two routes simultaneously. When there is some conflict at the phonological output stage between the results of the two routes then more cascading of analysis takes place back down the routes, feeding the information back from each side, allowing an interaction between the two analyses.

The word *has* appears very commonly in the literature and is referred to as a "high-frequency word". On the grounds that we are faster at reading words that we have experienced most often it is not surprising to find that high-frequency words are expedited through the orthographic lexicon. The high-frequency word reaches the output before the GPC has completed its analysis —the race is over without any need for interaction. High-frequency words result in quick and accurate recognition; this was found also to be true even for high-frequency irregular words, e.g. steak. However, a different prediction is given for low-frequency irregular words. In such a case the orthographic lexicon may be slow to recognise such a word as *banal* or *simile* and the GPC may win the race, giving the wrong pronunciation. If each route comes up with a different answer then further checking back within the orthographic lexicon may further delay a response. This intuitive description of the model, which is simulated using mathematical equations, predicts these and other phenomena (e.g. Coltheart & Rastle, 1994). This model is particularly attractive when describing the better pseudohomophone reading by phonological dyslexics since if phonological output is activated back to the orthographic lexicon a real word that matches the sound of the non-word may be found.

Deep dyslexia

The third type of dyslexia, deep dyslexia, is denoted by a tendency to read a word for another word with a similar connotation. For example, these patients may read *fly* for *air*, *sick* for *ill*, *tree* for *bush*, and *liar* for *bad*. Note that these errors are made when the patient is given a list of words to read and are not necessarily due to guessing

given the context of the sentence. When the stimulus and response are analysed, they do not follow a pattern of being orthographically or phonologically similar to each other. The patient has nevertheless made a form of semantic analysis but it is not well defined. The necessary lesions for these types of dyslexias are uncertain. One theory provides that the lack of semantic definition is due to a right hemisphere analysis of the type described above for optic aphasia. The right hemisphere is therefore seen as providing a less precise, coarser definition of the word (Coltheart, 1980).

The first point of interest is that deep dyslexia has much in common with phonological dyslexia. Both disorders are associated with poor non-word reading, but even more interesting is the evidence that when patients recover from deep dyslexia they often become phonological dyslexics (Friedman, 1996; Glosser & Friedman, 1996). The association between deep dyslexia and difficulty with non-word reading provides a problem for "box and arrow" models since two units require lesioning both a semantic lexicon (for impaired meaning) and a GPC unit (poor non-word reading). An alternative way of describing this disorder is in terms of an overlapping diagram (see Figures 7.12 and 7.15). This allows the patient to recover from a combined disorder to a single disorder in much the same way that Wernicke's aphasia may recover to conduction aphasia as the area of the brain affected is reduced.

Recently, Farah, Stowe, and Levinson (1996) have shown a further possible link between phonological dyslexia and deep dyslexia by showing that under certain demanding conditions phonological patients also show the semantic difficulties found in deep dyslexics. They describe a model which, like that of Plaut, McClelland, Seidenberg, and Patterson (1996) (see Figure 7.24), appears to cope with deep and phonological dyslexia as a continuum by accentuating the interaction between orthography, phonology, and semantics.

This model has its original foundation on the parallel distributed processing model provided by McClelland and Rumelhart (1986). The brain and its neuronal pathways are seen as distributed

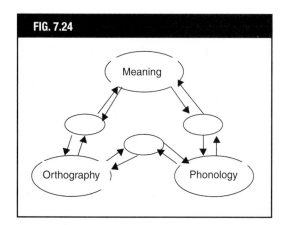

FIG. 7.24

A model of the interaction between the three systems following Plaut, McClelland, Seidenberg, & Patterson, 1996).

networks and hence deviate from the traditional modular approach. In the modular approach information is analysed for a particular attribute, i.e. phonology, and then passed on to the next module for further analysis. The connectionist approach, which is espoused by the parallel distributed processing-based models, allows continuous analysis within all the levels (modules) at the same time. Analysis is built up from partial to whole by a matching process occurring within all the levels, e.g. orthography, phonology, and semantic, at the same time. In the process of reading, the model assumes that the visual stimuli of a letter are detected and matched with stored representations in an orthography unit. The features of the letter and the position of that letter are matched with stored words in the lexicon. For example, if the word *truck* is the stimulus then initially all the words starting with *t* will be activated. The words with an initial letter other than *t* will be inhibited. This process is also undertaken for the second letter and so on. All the words in the store will have various degrees of activation. Groups of letters will be analysed for phonology and meaning at the same time for all the words containing the same letters. For example, if the words *tru* had been identified the meaning of the word *truck* would be activated, but also the meaning of the musical instrument *trumpet*. When the system steadies the word *truck*, its phonological attributes and its meaning will enjoy the most

activation. The computer achieves this through mathematical formulae and continuously monitors the matches and mismatches between the target word and activations within its levels and also with bottom-up activation and top-down feedback. The system is totally interactive and these interactions are represented in the "hidden levels" (represented above as empty ellipses between the three systems). This broad intuitive description does not do justice to modern versions of the parallel distributed processing model and the original model did not have semantic attributes. However, readers wishing for a more comprehensive description of the rationale of the parallel distributed processing model are referred first to Coltheart (1996) and also to Harley (1995) before attempting more advanced descriptions.

These connectionist models may be artificially lesioned by interfering with the matching process and supplying random weights to the activations favouring one attribute over another; this dampens down and impedes the matching process.

In terms of a model by Plaut et al. (1996), understanding normal, non-words are not present in the lexicons and so they are read by analogy. For example, if most words that contain the letters *ake* are pronounced as in the word *take*, then the non-word *nake* will be pronounced in a similar fashion. The continuous interaction between phonology and semantics, for example, supports the view that as we learn the pronunciation of words we also learn and associate these sounds with meanings. Just as important within this model is the implication that when some meaning is lost or damaged the whole unit performs less efficiently. This is because there is also less support for the analysis within the other levels in this interactive system. One of the predictions is that if some lost words are relearned then there may be a carry-on effect that might help to regain other non-treated but related words. There is mixed support for this in the literature (see further discussion below).

In the case of deep dyslexia, difficulty with semantics will also result in a follow-on deterioration in non-word reading because of the close interactions between the phonological and semantic systems (see Patterson, Suzuki, & Wydell, 1996).

Interactions between semantics and orthography may also account for the surface dyslexia that may appear in the presence of additional semantic impairments in the case of some dementia groups. For example, surface dyslexia (reliance on the GPC, damage to the orthographic lexicon) has also been associated with semantic errors, most notably with Alzheimer's disease (Hodges et al., 1992; Funnell, 1996). Also the dementing disorders that affect language, referred to as primary progressive aphasia (Parkin, 1993; Watt, Jokel, & Behrmann, 1997), have similarly been found to have semantic difficulties and surface dyslexia in some cases. The Plaut model would seem to deal better with these less "pure" cases of surface dyslexia where the patients also have some difficulty reading non-words. These cases have most difficulty reading irregular words but also have a lesser difficulty reading non-words. These type 2 surface dyslexics may fit a more interactive model, while the purer cases may be more easily predicted by the dual route cascade model (Coltheart, 1996). This is a rapidly advancing area at the present time, but these two examples from the many models that have been advanced will hopefully give the reader some introduction to these two contrasting approaches to modelling.

One of the areas that continues to be of interest concerns the recovery of language and rehabilitation. Some patients have shown unexplained improvements in non-treated words during rehabilitation—improvements that cannot be readily explained by spontaneous recovery. Connectionist models would seem to provide a ready explanation for these effects since new learning should provide some reduction of uncertainty for other words through inhibition. However, the improvements have not always been in the direction predicted by connectionist modelling (Coltheart, 1996). Also, some studies have found generalisation in the form of improvements in non-treated words whereas other studies have not. Plaut (1996) argues that this variety of results might be expected in a model whose outcome depends on which systems are involved, e.g.

orthography or phonology, and whether a system is damaged or disconnected. For example, in the above model a disconnection between phonology and meaning in one direction may have a different effect on reading when compared to a disconnection in the reverse direction.

The use of connectionist models to model language disorders is not without controversy. Farah (1995) provides an excellent target paper that describes solutions to a number of neuropsychological impairments using parallel distributed processing-based computer modelling. In the same journal are a very large number of comments on the advantages and disadvantages of this method of modelling and the underlying assumptions. One point that is often made is that because the model involves distributed networks it does not necessarily mean that the model concerned is not modular, i.e. making assumptions that certain localised brain areas are specialised to carry out certain functions. Both the above models are, of course, modular in the sense that they assume specialised local analysis.

The two respected models described above are quite different and it is unlikely that they are both correct. It might be obvious, but worth noting, that it is possible to make an accurate prediction concerning a behavioural outcome without simulating the way the brain achieves this end. The same goal may be achieved by quite different routes. This criticism can, of course, be made of any type of modelling. However, by adding constants and various other additions to a model, it can be made to fit the data. A model gains a more confident following when it is based on empirical data and there is a demonstration that a large number of different predictions are satisfied.

Finally on the topic of epistemology there are a number of possible frameworks that have not been discussed and the choice of models must to some extent be restrained by the assumptions concerning how the human nervous system is capable of performing (see Kohonen, 1990).

FINAL COMMENT

In the first part of this chapter there was an attempt to inspect the nature of the different syndromes that have been typically described within aphasiology. These syndromes when dissected become more complex than they first appeared. Agrammatism, for example, was fractionated into several types that had various explanations. Past views of the analysis of auditory meaning and the semantics of reading had to be questioned and the comprehension of language was seen as being determined by a much more extensive and complex neurofunctional area than had previously been acknowledged in theory. Despite a general dissatisfaction of aphasiologists with past general models of langauge mechanism the focus has been to model parts of the process rather than a synthesis of all the information in this area. For this reason a new model of language function was proposed; although it should be noted that not much of the model is original, the contribution here is to integrate the various theoretical contributions of authorities in this area.

The second part of the chapter was more focused on the cognitive neuropsychological contributions. Here there appeared to be reverse flow of analysis; while the discussion of the various syndromes went from simple to complex, cognitive neuropsychological analysis often appeared to be going from complex to simple as neurological concepts were introduced. For example, when discussing optic aphasia initially there was a minute dissection of the structural and semantic analysis processing implied by this disorder. However, once the functional/neuroanatomical features of the left and right hemisphere were combined with this analysis, the model became simpler and was clarified. In this endeavour combining the analytical approach of neuropsychology with clinical knowledge of syndromes seemed to be an advantage.

Many researchers are, of course, hybrids. They are interested in syndromes and the dissection of the psychological components of a disorder. They can see the advantages and disadvantages of both approaches. The classical cognitive neuropsychological approach is to investigate, usually rare, single cases in a manner that dissects the exact nature of the language impairment. There is less interest in neuropathology and the matching of brain areas with impairments—models may be entirely psychological without reference to brain structure. However, more and more functional neuroimaging is being involved to give a neuroanatomical dimension. In contrast, the classical syndromist approach is traditionally more focused on consistencies between patients and often uses groups of patients, but here again there is a change to a more analytical approach as the two sides move together.

In this chapter research has been described that is based on at least two methodological approaches to group research. One approach is to research a group in which all subjects have the same pattern of symptoms, e.g. a certain type of agrammatism, and assess the common area of lesion location, sometimes overlapping the brain scans. The second approach that is sometimes used involves the other side of this coin, which is to investigate the symptoms of all the patients who have a lesion within a particular brain area. Sometimes the area is identified by the first method and then discrepancies are noted from a non-selective sample of patients with lesions within the identified area.

The introduction of the cognitive neuropsychology approach to research in this area has highlighted some of the problems and frailties of the group approach. With good reason, cognitive neuropsychologists have been concerned with the possibility of disguising the *real* nature of the disorder, which might be obscured by grouping patients with subtly different complaints. A consistent message from this camp is that the variations between patients are more important than the consistencies. There is also the fear that trusting in the existence of a syndrome may lead to prejudicial false assumptions concerning the true nature of the disorder and pre-empt further investigation and proper scrutiny of the validity of the syndrome. There is the warning of the inherent danger of oversimplifying the issue and grouping together symptoms that may have quite different underlying mechanisms. For example, the finding of co-occurrence of symptoms may alternatively be a "red herring": two symptoms might be caused by a different mechanism only appearing together because they are both dependent on brain areas that are coincidentally close and which are irrigated by the same cerebral artery. Something of this nature has obviously occurred in the case of the original description of Broca's aphasia.

With this kind of methodological introspection comes the realisation that some of the terms used by cognitive neuropsychologists such as "phonological dyslexia" and "deep dyslexia" may be seen as syndromes themselves. The assumption that they are distinct identities might discourage research towards a phenomenon that might actually represent some kind of continuum. This has led to the suggestion that we should not be using these global descriptions. For example, instead of referring to phonological dyslexia perhaps we should instead be talking in terms of the actual manifested behaviour such as impaired non-word reading.

Nevertheless, consistent patterns of symptoms have, and always will be, useful when seeking out the relationships between brain and behaviour. As has been found in medicine, sometimes two symptoms turn out to be from one cause. Alternatively, a consistent pattern may lead towards identifying an important underlying neuropsychological mechanism or a relationship between two mechanisms. Therefore the lesson is that synthesis is as important as fractionation in aphasiology. This is as true of the area of language as it is in other areas of neuropsychology.

8

Movement disorders

INTRODUCTION

Movement disorders are described in this chapter
in terms of three motor systems. Each motor system is identified on the basis of a separate and
identifiable functional role. It is nevertheless true
that they are interdependent in terms of both
their sensory excitation and their expression.

In this chapter there is a discussion of three
systems in terms of their contribution to the
preparation, modulation, and execution of
movements. The three systems, which are diagrammed in Figure 8.1, will be described and it is
hoped that this will be referred to throughout the
chapter as they are individually described. Figure
8.1 does not illustrate the important connections
between the systems and the brain stem and
spinal cord, which are obviously required for the
execution of movements. Some of these pathways
are illustrated in Figure 8.5. These connections
will be described as the systems themselves are
discussed.

This chapter broadly follows a format of
describing these three systems. First are the areas
of the cortex that related to action in response
to external sensory cues. This *cortical motor system* includes the *premotor area*, the *primary motor
area* within the frontal lobe, *and the somatosen-*

sory areas within the parietal cortex. The premotor area is important for the preparation of
movement and receives sensory information from
the parietal cortex and other areas. The parietal
cortex is especially important for movements that
are guided by sensory information for motor
action since it is here that a spatial map is
attached to body parts so that a person has knowledge of where their limbs are at any point in time.
The primary motor area (M1) or motor strip is
described as having a more direct role in the execution of movement. A second system, the *basal
ganglia system*, is then described, which is based
on the *basal ganglion* and its links with the cortical system. The basal ganglion has cortical
expression via such structures such as the *supplementary motor area*. As can be seen from Figure 8.8, the basal ganglion is not just one structure but a collection of different structures, which
reside deep within the brain. A complex array of
feedback loops joining these nuclei is believed to
have a special influence on the programming of
movements. While the exact role is unknown,
there is implied involvement in initiating movement and the smooth programming of a sequence
of movements. This is not to disallow the influence of the basal ganglia in other types of movements but rather indicates an influence that is
more obvious. The third system is the *cerebellar*

FIG. 8.1

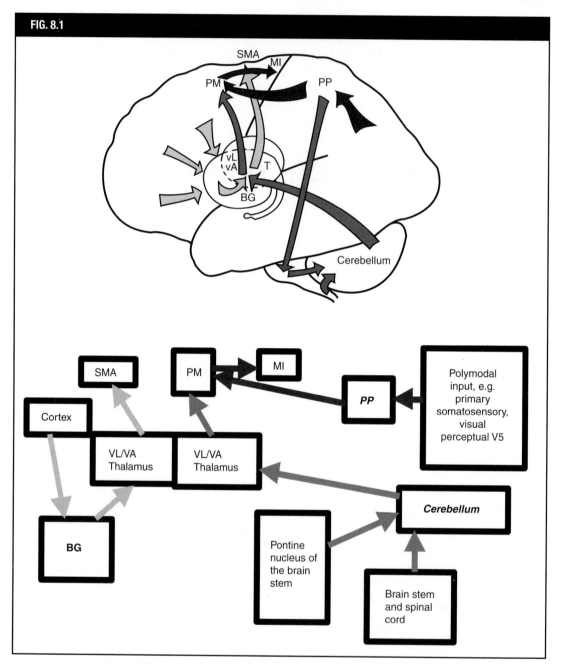

Schematic diagram of the three motor systems with their main pathways. The thalamus is situated behind the basal ganglia (BG). *The cortical motor system* includes a circuit joining the posterior parietal cortex (PP) to the premotor area (PM) and then on to the primary motor area or motor strip (M1). *The basal ganglia system* has inputs from various cortical areas. There are complex loops between the structures that make up the basal ganglia before it outputs to the ventrolateral (VL) and ventroanterior (VA) nuclei of the thalamus. From the thalamus there are projections to the supplementary motor area (SMA). *The cerebellar motor system* includes main pathways from the posterior parietal cortex (PP). This visual/body information is complemented by proprioceptive information from the brain stem and spinal cord. The cerebellum outputs to the premotor area via the VL and VA of the thalamus. Many pathways are not shown but the functional logic of the main circuits is preserved.

motor system, which appears to have a more moderating role on movement. By moderating it is meant that it may be most important for correcting and adjusting movements that require coordination of a number of muscle groups and may also be important for posture. These modifications to movements are seen to be learned and stored in the cerebellum. These three systems are described in terms of the disorders that are likely to occur when there is damage to one of these

In the first section, some introductory concepts are described. The relationship between areas within the primary motor and sensory areas and their influence on the execution and sensation of different body areas are discussed. This relationship has already been referred to in Chapter 1 and describes the behavioural results of electrical stimulation on the primary motor cortex and the sensory cortex respectively. Second, the connections between the cortex, brain stem, and spinal cord are described and the connections with the various subcortical structures. Still within the section on the cortical system there is a discussion of the interaction between movement and perception. This work is the product of relatively recent research and involves what has been previously described as the "where-action" pathway. Areas within the posterior parietal cortex are described that have been found to be as important as some premotor areas in the preparation for movement. In this section our amazing ability to integrate what we see with what we do is discussed. The relationship between our body parts and our external environment is described as being manufactured by a network of connections between the parietal cortex and some areas of the frontal cortex such as the premotor area. By integrating different sensory systems within a spatial map of where our limbs and other body parts are in space, perception can be translated into action. The last area of discussion within this first section relates to theories and descriptions of apraxia, the disorder of skilled movements.

In the second section the basal ganglia system is described as a motor system that has its expression within the cortex but appears to make a special contribution to the balanced production of motor routines. Parkinson's disease and Hunting-

ton's disease are both disease processes that ultimately are associated with atrophy and disorder to the nuclei and their interconnections that make up the basal ganglia. The basal ganglion is made up of a highly complex interaction of structures that are looped together and finally output through the thalamus and cortical areas such as the supplementary motor area. There are some difficulties with present models in explaining improvements following the surgical treatment of Parkinson's disease. Improvements in movement have been found following surgical destruction of certain areas within the basal ganglia but sometimes these improvements are not easy to explain. Parkinson's disease remains the disorder which has provided us with the most information concerning the functional importance of the basal ganglia.

Finally there is a section describing the influence of the cerebellum on motor movements. Sometimes described as the "little brain" it is attached to the brain stem and is situated under the shelf provided by the occipital lobe. Movements that require balance and coordination are often undermined by damage to this area, which has connections to the other motor areas described.

THE PRIMARY MOTOR AND SENSORY AREAS

The functional relationship between the primary motor and sensory areas

While Paul Broca is sometimes seen as the father of the experimental study of localisation, not far behind his example is the animal work of Gustav Fritsch and Eduard Hitzig in 1870 (see Pauly, 1983). Fritsch and Hitzig electrically stimulated the frontal cortex of dogs and showed the limb movements on the opposite side of the body. They found that stimulation within a particular area of the motor cortex elicited a contralateral movement from a specific limb, and if a lesion was made in that same area then the dog became clumsy with that same limb.

Box 8.1. A description of the Jacksonian march

The patient was referred to the author's research when he was a student. The patient was living in the community and after the doorbell was rung a man in his early forties appeared at the door. He initially made his greetings quite normally from the door of his flat when his speech suddenly became slurred and distorted and his face started to contort. Next his hand and arm started to tremble and shake and he started a strange movement reminiscent of waving goodbye. The involuntary movement then subsided. For someone who had not witnessed an epileptic seizure, it was something of a shock to see uncontrolled activity of this nature. What I had witnessed was living proof that the primary motor area represents different areas of the anatomy. The seizure activity spread through the motor strip travelling from the face area up though to the area responsible for the upper limbs. The man had suffered a focal seizure referred to as the Jacksonian seizure, the travel of the seizure activity over the primary motor area being referred to as a Jacksonian march.

Not long after Fritsch and Hitzig's work was published Vladimir Betz discovered the large pyramidal cells within what was later referred to as layer V of the cell column. Specific stimulation of these cells produced movement in the same motor area that Fritsch and Hitzig found to be motor responsive. It was now generally recognised that a cortical area had been found that was specialised for movement.

The type of epileptic seizure described in Box 8.1 is named after Hughlings Jackson, a famous nineteenth-century neurologist. Jackson had a particular interest in epilepsy, which may in part have come from his unwillingly witnessing of his own wife's motor seizures. He believed, some time before the use of the EEG, that brain function could be understood through epilepsy (Lassek, 1970). The Jacksonian seizure is a simple motor seizure that starts in one area of the motor cortex and travels along adjacent cells involving the body areas sequentially. Sometimes, as Jackson reports, the seizure activity follows the path of the motor strip in the reverse direction: the seizure starts in the foot (mesial dorsal area) and eventually passes down the arm (ventrally) (Lassek, 1970).

It is rare to observe a direct relationship between neuroanatomy and function, but the motor and sensory cortices illustrate this relationship clearly. Electrical stimulation of the primary motor area results in a movement in the body part represented in that area (Penfield & Roberts, 1959) (see Figure 8.3).

The greater the dexterity and the finer the manipulation required, the greater the cortical area devoted to that body area. In this way an extensive area is devoted to the hand and fingers within the motor strip, while a disproportionate area of the primary somatosensory area, within the postcentral gyrus, is devoted to the lips, face, and hands.

As can be seen in Figure 8.2, the precentral gyrus and the postcentral gyrus lie either side of the central sulcus and represent the primary motor and sensory area respectively. The *primary motor area* or *motor strip* follows the precentral gyrus down from its dorsal aspect and disappears into the central sulcus being represented mesially. The postcentral gyrus on the posterior side of the central sulcus is dedicated to the *primary sensory area*. The primary sensory area is visible for its length along the postcentral gyrus and represents body parts that are similar to the motor area on the other side of the central sulcus.

The supplementary and premotor areas are activated earlier than the motor strip and the main role of these areas is seen as being more preparatory in nature, with the main efferents providing an output to the primary motor cortex. However, *some* cells within these areas also have a direct role in the execution of movement. As can be seen from Figure 8.2 a significant proportion of efferents find their way down to the pons within the brain stem and then to the cerebellum. In other words the relationship between the area and function is not clear cut and some axons leading from these preparatory motor areas also lead directly to the brain stem as part of the corticospinal tract, without being directed through the primary motor cortex first. However, the role of the motor strip is more obviously directly related to the execution of movement. Some of the giant pyramidal cells discovered by Betz have the longest axons—some travel all the way down the spinal cord—and the *direct* control of *fine motor* movements is more exclusively the domain of the primary motor area. Less often recognised, and researched more recently, are the preparatory

FIG. 8.2

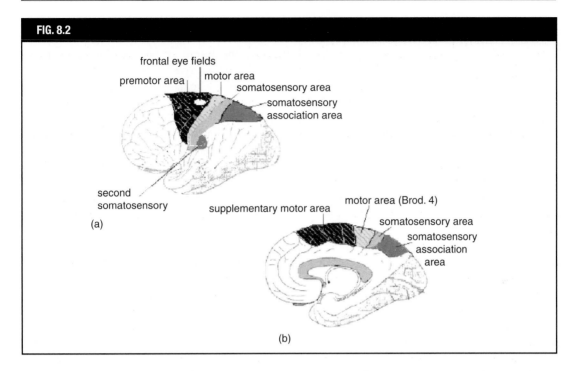

frontal eye fields
premotor area   motor area
somatosensory area
somatosensory
association area

second
somatosensory
(a)

supplementary motor area

motor area (Brod. 4)
somatosensory area
somatosensory
association
area

(b)

Illustration of the primary motor, premotor, and somatosensory areas with other sensory and association areas form the lateral (a) and the medial (b) perspectives. Figure 1.6 shows the artery distribution to these areas. Figure 1.10 also shows the direction of the flow of projections from the premotor to the motor area; also, the flow from the somatosensory area to the somatosensory association areas. There are some projections from the primary somatosensory areas to the second somatosensory areas; also projections from the somatosensory areas anterior to the premotor area.

motor areas within the parietal cortex (see Figure 8.2). These last areas are at one of the end-points of the "where-action" pathway, which was first discussed in Chapter 2 but is more fully described in this chapter.

Paralysis of limbs is a clinical sign that is diagnostically helpful since from this one may deduce the area of brain damage and with some experience this obvious behavioural information may give the clinician an indication as to the cognitive deficits that might be expected given the assumed location (see Figure 8.4). Following a stroke involving the anterior cerebral artery, paralysis of the legs is more likely, while strokes involving the middle cerebral artery are more likely to involve upper limbs. Strokes involving the *internal capsule* may also be followed by paralysis since this is the area that tracks the motor axons leading from the cortex to the brain stem. *Paralysis* is a term used to describe when there is a total loss of controlled movement; often the loss is less severe and is referred to as *paresis*. A stroke patient is referred to as having a hemiparesis when one half of their body is disabled, often because of an infarction of areas of the motor cortex that are important to movement. This type of motor disorder is referred to as *pyramidal* because, as already mentioned, the motor cortex has large pyramidal cells that transmit messages to the brain stem and then on to the spinal cord to eventually elicit muscle movements.

Of course not all paresis is the result of damage to these areas. Later we will discuss damage to *extrapyramidal* areas such as the basal ganglia that may result in paresis but also in other movement disorders.

As indicated, some of these long axons from the Betz cells proceeding from the motor strip

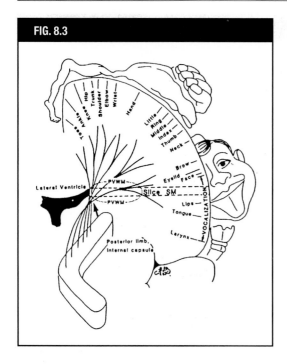

FIG. 8.3

Illustration of the relative size of the various attributes of the primary motor areas according to the area of the brain devoted to the various motor areas. Also shown are the descending pyramidal tract the extension of which is seen in Figure 8.4(b). The pyramidal tract pathways are located in the posterior limb of the internal capsule. There is a similar distribution for the primary sensory somatosensory area (see Figure 8.4(b) (reprinted from Naeser et al., 1989, with permission from Oxford University Press).

terminate in the brain stem while others go all the way down the spinal cord. But before they reach the spinal cord *most* of these axons cross over to the other side of the body at an area within the brain stem referred to as the pyramids.

Because of this *decussation* or switching over of the corticospinal tract to the contralateral side prior to activation of the limbs, a *right* hemisphere stroke results in a *left* hemiparesis and a left hemisphere stroke results in a right hemiparesis. Typically, the stroke patient has contralateral flaccid limbs just following the stroke, but as some recovery takes place some rigidity or spasticity sets in. Further recovery may be accompanied by some recovery of proximal control (nearest the body) returning first. Hands may recover some

movement but fingers tend to function as a unit rather than individually. Although not clearly shown the output of the cerebellum also crosses over before it arrives at the thalamus.

A patient who has made some recovery following anterior cerebral artery stroke may be identified by the way they move their leg. The patient moves the limb by the action of the upper, proximal part of the limb, with the distal parts of the limb being dragged and propelled forward by the swinging of the more mobile upper limb.

Finally on the issue of the primary motor and sensory areas, it appears that recent research is starting to show a less straightforward view of these areas. There is, for example, some overlap between the area (cells) responsible for the activation of the thumb, index finger, ring finger, and wrist representations. Also, there may be more than one representation associated with a particular body part. More interesting from the point of view of recovery is the finding that some movement areas may increase in size with learning, an issue that is discussed in Chapter 10 (Roland & Zilles, 1996).

Connections Between the Cortex, Brain Stem, and Spinal Cord

The primary motor and primary sensory cortex can be seen as one of the last stages of brain activation prior to activation within the spinal cord. As indicated, some of the neurones in this area go directly to the motor neurones within the spinal cord in order to activate the limbs. Alternatively some go to the thalamus, basal ganglia, or brain stem. These fibres are funnelled down within the *internal capsule* in what is referred to as the *corticospinal tract*. As described, the corticospinal tract decussates and switches over to the contralateral side of the brain stem at the pyramids within the medulla.

This same tract also carries somatosensory information from the primary sensory area and other areas within the parietal lobe (Brodmann areas 5 and 7). Eventually, this information descends to the spinal cord and then returns in a feedback loop. Two types of sensory information are returned to the three motor areas. Somatosensory information includes tactile information and

FIG. 8.4

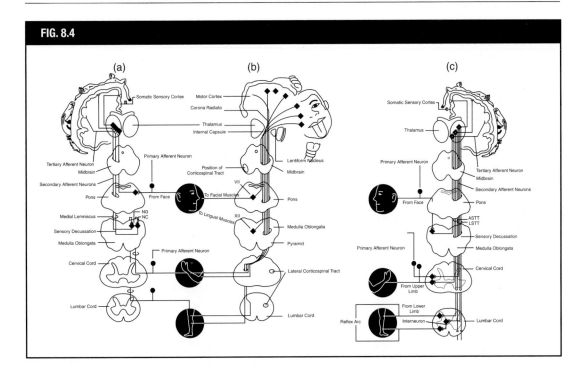

A simplified illustration of the connections between the cortex, brain stem, and spinal cord. The *two ascending pathways* include (a) the spinothalamic tract, which transports information concerning pain, temperature and some information concerning touch and pressure, and (c) the medial lemniscus pathway (within the posterior column), which takes tactile and proprioceptive information from the joints that allows feedback concerning the position of the limbs. Many of these pathways to the somatosensory areas decussate (cross over) where the peripheral projections leave the spinal cord. Some of the ascending pathways with proprioceptive information reach the cerebellum via the spinal cord and the spinocerebellar tract as indicated in Figure 8.1. (b) The descending pathway of the corticospinal tract proceeds from areas such as the pyramidal neurones, e.g. Betz cells from the primary motor areas within the precentral gyrus and other motor neurones. The corticospinal tract travels via the internal capsule and then decussates within the pyramids of the brain stem. Often they terminate on the interneurone within the spinal cord at the level of the appropriate limb, which is activated by the connected motor neurones.

also propioceptive information gives information on the relative positions of the limb. This is returned via the thalamus to the primary sensory area.

Of course, not all motor neurones are designed to activate limbs. Other areas such as our face for expression and our tongues for vocal expression must be activated. Neurones that are devoted more to the area of the face, for example, descend from the face areas within the motor and sensory cortex in a similar manner alongside the corticospinal tract in what is referred to as the *corticobulbar tract* (bulbar is a term used broadly to refer to the *bulbous* brain stem or medulla). These

last axons terminate in various areas of the brain stem and, among other functions, help to innervate the appropriate cranial nerves with other descending fibres from the frontal, parietal cortical areas. For example, fibres from the face area in the motor cortex innervate the eighth cranial nerve with the eventual contralateral innervation of the lower facial muscles. But the same system results in bilateral innervation of upper facial muscles (see Nolte, 1993, p. 198, for a detailed treatment of this and other related issues). Another important pathway involves two adjoining tracts: a *corticorubral tract*, which carries information from the premotor area to the nucleus ruber (red nucleus), and a second tract from the red nucleus called the *rubrospinal tract* that crosses over in the ventral tegmentum of the midbrain and then descends to the spinal cord. The red nucleus also receives information from the cerebellum (see later section on the cerebellum). The vestibular nucleus also receives input from the cerebellum at the start of another descending tract. These last tracts are important in maintaining muscle tone (see Figure 8.4).

The reader is referred to texts such as those by Noback, Strominger, and Demarest (1991). Nolte and Angevine (1995) provide some excellent illustrations of the various motor pathways with the associated neurotransmitter systems.

THE CORTICAL MOTOR SYSTEM

The premotor area and the preparation for movement towards external stimuli

From animal studies and studies with humans using radiological techniques such as PET and fMRI, the premotor area has been divided into two main areas: the premotor dorsal area (PMD) and the premotor ventral area (PMV) (Wise, Boussaoud, Johnson, & Caminiti, 1997). Essentially, it may be difficult to talk about the function of these areas without reference to the nature of the task. In some simple, well-learned tasks, the premotor area and the primary motor area (M1) are activated simultaneously, with few obvious differences in function. However, in more complex novel tasks a hierarchical relationship is revealed. The premotor area is often activated prior to M1, but sometimes simultaneously with the activation of M1 (Roland & Zilles, 1996) (see Figure 8.6).

A distinction can be made between the roles of these subdivisions of the premotor area (see Figure 8.5). Area PMD is more related to changes in target location and visual gaze, while PMV is more related to the integration of oral, facial movements, e.g. coordination of movements during eating. PMV is sensitive to movements around the face. The critical feature of the premotor areas is the feedback this area gains from

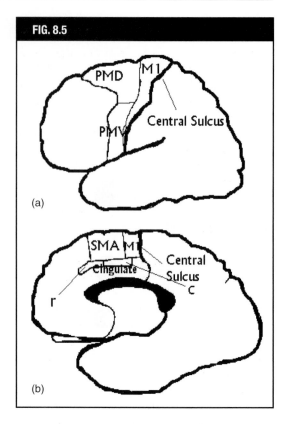

FIG. 8.5

(a)

(b)

(a) The premotor dorsal area (PMD) and the ventral premotor area (PMV). The visible aspect of the primary motor area (M1) is shown; the inferior aspect is within the central sulcus. (b) The supplementary area and the cingulate motor area, within the cingulate, rostral (r) and caudal (c) areas, are outlined (adapted from Roland & Zilles, 1996).

the visual and somatosensory areas. Both PMD and PMV receive visual sensory projections, which is in line with a role in motor movements using visual feedback (see Figure 8.1).

There are also projections from somatosensory association areas. As briefly referred to above, there are three ways that information may guide the position of the limbs: *exteroceptive* cues, which relate to the tactile sensitivity to external stimuli—we know we have reached an object because we can feel it; second, *visual* cues—we know that our limb is going in the direction of the salt cellar, because we can see it; finally, *proprioceptive* cues relate to the internal feedback we may gain from the position of our joints and the relative weight of an arm when it is outstretched. It is the proprioceptive cues and exteroceptive cues that are seen to be received from the somatosensory area and which allow us to reach for something we have dropped in a darkened car, for example. The premotor area appears to be well connected to make use of exteroceptive, visual, and proprioceptive cues and is more likely to be active during movements, especially when visually guided movement changes are required (Mushiake, Inase, & Tanji, 1991). Other motor areas such as the basal ganglia, the Supplementary Motor Area (SMA), and the cingulate area shown in Figure 8.6 are more consistently first activated prior to movements and have a clear role in the orchestration of movements. The premotor area is seen as especially important when movements are being directed and changed by sensory feedback such as in a reaching movement.

There is a simultaneous activation of the premotor area with connected somatosensory–parietal association (see links in Figure 8.1), especially the posterior parietal cortex, prior to movement. Therefore there may be some predictions being made concerning the proprioceptive feedback pending the movement. Kalaska and Crammond (1995) propose that these somatosen-sory areas, which are at the end-point of what we refer to as the end of the "where-action" pathway, may hold a model or image of the body position for the forthcoming movement. This feed-forward may also be the cause of what is referred to as "phantom limb". In this situation the patient feels the position of their arm as if it was there, despite amputation. If the experience of a phantom limb is due to its maintained cortical representation, it would be predicted that later this feeling is reduced. This is because monkey work has shown that representation of a body part eventually disappears (see discussion of this research in Chapter 10). The creation of conscious awareness of limb parts is clearly related to the somatosensory representation in the cortex since feelings of the amputated limb may occur following stimulation of a body part situated adjacent and close to the amputated body part. The seemingly weird situation may arise whereby a touch on the cheek of the amputee may result in the subjective impression that his or her limb has been touched.

In Chapter 10 the work on cortical reorganisation following limb and digital amputation is discussed further. However, for the moment it should be noted that monkeys who had had a

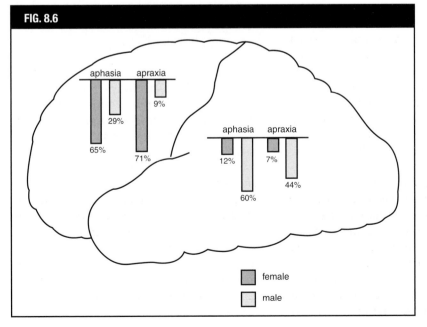

FIG. 8.6

Illustration of associations between aphasia and apraxia. Differences between females and males are evident, which may be due to differences in organisation (adapted from Kimura, 1992). A percentage of those patients have a lesion in the anterior or posterior lesion respectively, e.g. of those female patients who have an anterior lesion 65% show aphasia.

digit removed lost the cortical representation of that digit which became occupied instead by neighbouring digits. Something similar takes place in the case of limb amputation to the extent that it appears that the area originally responsible for the sensation of the limb is now invaded by sensation for parts of the face. The argument runs that stimulation of the face now, by default, activates the remnants of the amputated limb representation. In this way conscious awareness may be described at a purely central brain area and must be a "top-down" process. The patient is still aware of the limb despite visual evidence to the contrary because the limb still has brain representation. This may wear off in time with some patients but frequent phantom limb experience may itself be a process that maintains its representation given what we know about the relationship between practice, training, and cortical representation.

This phenomenon is revealing of the nature of the consciousness that relates to action. In some sense, if a tool is used frequently the tool becomes a part of the hand. We know without thinking exactly where the paintbrush is without thinking about it; we become instantly aware if the paintbrush travels over an area that has a different texture of canvas even if our eyes are shut. We have no neural connections to the object we are holding, whether it is a tissue or a steering wheel, but we are not aware of this peripheral neural discontinuation.

Experiments with monkeys have shown that repeated manipulation of a tool results in a representation of that tool within the cortex. Therefore brain representation does not require peripheral neural representation for it to claim conscious awareness. The "bottom-up" stimulation may create a cortical representation that will encourage a corresponding form of conscious awareness. Something of this process is used with the treatment of phantom limb pain.

Patients with phantom limb may experience a huge amount of pain on occasions, as if their fingers are gripping very tightly through the palm of their hand. Ramachandran (1998) describes a therapeutic method that has been found to ameliorate these terrible sensations in these patients. If

the patient's right arm, for example, has been amputated the patient, who is sitting at a table, has their left arm reflected in a mirror in such a way that the patient sees two arms, one each side. The patient is then requested to release the grip maintained by both hands (the left and imaginary reflected hand). This method apparently reduces the pain sensation and the awareness of the phantom limb pain in some but not all patients.

The power of the visual signal on movement and sensation is revealed in this disorder of phantom limb. There are areas specialised for visual and non-visual sensory inputs within the somatosensory area. When the non-visual somatosensory afferents to the premotor area are disconnected (deafferentation), the subject is still able to reach for an object using purely visual cues, although when visual cues are reduced there is a deterioration in performance (Aglioti, Beltramello, Bonazzi, & Corbetta, 1996; Gordon & Soechting, 1995).

Finally, as one might predict, when movements are relatively novel the premotor area and M1 are activated during the movement, but when the movement is learned the premotor area is more likely to be involved prior to the movement and not continued through the movement. In the novel situation the controlled movement of the limb with sensory feedback would be most important until the movement becomes routine (Jackson & Husain, 1996).

The integration of perception with movement: the "where-action" pathway

Until recently the preparation for movement has been seen as mainly involving frontal areas such as the premotor area and the SMA, which is discussed later in this chapter. However, work predominantly using monkeys has now shown that posterior parietal areas are also involved in the preparation for movement and that these areas are closely interconnected with the motor areas of the frontal lobe. Figure 8.1 shows some of the areas that have been found to be involved in this network. This work may ultimately prove to be important in explaining the distribution of such attentional disorders as unilateral neglect since it would appear that one of the functional roles of these areas is to map out three-dimensional space in terms of the positions of the limbs and other body parts and the direction of gaze.

Perhaps the best way of discussing this particular issue is to describe what happens when we make the simple movement of reaching out to pick up a glass of water from the table. First there must be some perceptual processing that identifies the glass of water. Such processes were discussed in Chapter 2 and they involve what has been described as a stream of information processing referred to as the "what" pathway. After identifying the glass there must then be two further stages. One stage requires the locating of the position of the glass with reference to sensory information. The glass does not contain fizzy water (no auditory input) and therefore there must be a reliance on visual input for determining its location. However, it is not enough to locate the glass according to the visual input: the position of the glass with reference to the arm's position during the action must also be accounted for. If during reaching there was a dependence on visual feedback a number of things would go wrong. There would have to be a concentration on the position of the limb as well as the target and constant corrections would have to be made as our hands approached the glass. The movement would not be smooth and if someone turned out the lights the movement would have to be terminated. Therefore we must have a plan or image of where the limb is and its relationship to the glass. It is of interest that when PET scans are taken of persons imaging a motor movement the brain areas that are activated are very similar to those areas when the person is conducting the actual movement (Jeannerod, 1995). This research would of course be good news to sports psychologists. However, it is uncertain how helpful imaging would be in refining a motor skill since when we make movements we are not very good in consciously being aware of what is going on. For example, Fourneret and Jeannerod (1998) biased the feedback of the position of an object using a video of the subject's arm movements. Subjects made corrections over trials allowing for the bias but were not very good at reporting afterwards what kind of corrections they had made. Therefore while a tennis player may realise their error when making a double fault they may make a further double fault because they do not have a good conscious grasp on the motor movements they are making. When reporters ask soccer players about the experience concerning the amazing goal they scored, the response is typically mundane: "I just hit it and it was in the back of the net."

Nevertheless, sensory feedback is of course required from the limb itself even if we are not aware of this with any precision. The evidence suggests that when making a movement we unconsciously monitor where our hand is through proprioceptive cues. Sensors trigger these somatosensory cues, which are assumed to be located, among other areas, at the position of our joints. If we misjudge the distance between ourselves and the glass of water or we decide to reach for the salt instead we need to feed back any visual information. This information is presumed to be integrated within the posterior parietal cortex in the form of a map of visual space containing the location of where our limbs and head are in relation to the glass.

Patients with bilateral lesions to this area of the posterior parietal cortex often miss the glass altogether, reaching out to the side and then having to feel their way to one side until their hand bumps into the glass (see a description of Balint's syndrome in Chapter 2).

Cells within the posterior parietal area of the monkey's brain appear to function in response to the changing position of objects in space. These cells are responsive to a moving object, not just in terms of direction but also in terms of the depth of placement. These cells have been found to be dependent on the visually positioned location of the object irrespective of the position of the hand or limb movement. Other cells have been found to depend on the position of the limb rather than the position of the target to which the limb is moving. Still other cells appear to combine this information. Cells have been found in areas within the parietal cortex that fire maximally to both visual and proprioceptive cues in such a manner that it is clear that space with respect to a certain body part is being mapped (Colby, Duhamel, & Goldberg, 1996). Therefore, one of the roles of this area of the parietal cortex appears to be in assessing both visual information and somatosensory information. In some ways these two sensory inputs are being combined and integrated.

However, there are also cells within this posterior parietal area that, like the premotor cortex, appear to be devoted to the preparation of movement. There are cells within areas that are most active just prior to intended movements. Also, these cells are still activated when preparing for movement even when darkness is imposed on the monkey when the visual information is removed (Ferraina et al., 1997). Therefore, as indicated, while visual cues may be needed when assessing the position of the object, the plan can be carried out irrespective of the availability of visual cues during the performance of the act. Some areas are still activated in this area even if the movement is voluntarily restrained as in a go–no-go task (see Chapter 3 for a description). Other cells within the primary motor area (M1) are, however, only activated when a movement actually takes place. Therefore, as indicated, there is a distinction between areas that are important for the preparation for movement and those responsible for the execution of movement.

From this evidence it is clear that the integration of sensory information takes place mainly within the posterior brain areas within the parietal cortex, but that the preparation for movement towards external stimuli takes place in both in the posterior (parietal) and anterior brain areas (e.g. premotor areas) in concert.

A second level of separation concerns the body part that the action refers to. Thus cells within the area in the monkey referred to as the lateral intraparietal area (LIP) have been found to be selectively responsive to the position of the object in relation to the eyes, while other areas are responsive to position in relation to other body parts (Andersen, Snyder, Bradley, & Xing, 1997). Other areas have been found to be selective for the position of the arms. But some other areas—premotor and posterior parietal areas—appear to combine information on the direction of gaze with the direction of limb movements (Battaglia-Meyer et al., 1998; Boussard, Jouffrais, & Brem-

mer, 1998). Therefore there appears to be a hierarchy in which different sensory inputs are amalgamated to form an integrated motor response. Importantly, there is the clear message that movement is represented in terms of body part-centred coordinates (Graziano & Gross, 1998). There is supportive evidence for this role within human imaging studies. Clower and colleagues used subjects who wore prisms, which misaligned their visual input with their actual hand position (Clower et al., 1996). While it is known from lesion studies that the cerebellum is important in such adaptation (see discussion below), in this PET study the contralateral parietal area was also found to be activated. These posterior parietal areas were once thought of as being solely concerned with the location of an object within personal space. But these recent findings clearly confirm the role of these posterior parietal areas in the preparation of movements through the integration of the spatial coordinates of body parts from somatosensory information with that of visuoperceptual information. Therefore the term "where-action" pathway appears to be appropriate.

Given the results showing specific areas being responsible for different body parts prior to integration it is not surprising to find that some patients have attentional disorders that are also specific to a particular body part (see Chapter 4).

Finally, some comment should be made with regard to the apparently parallel way some posterior parietal and frontal premotor areas work together. There are many posterior areas that are activated simultaneously with frontal areas. This suggests that the network described by Graziano and Gross (1998) involves extensive connections between these anterior and posterior areas.

In summary, two lessons may be learned from this distribution of networked cell areas with their various specialties. The first concerns the dissociation between the visuospatial representation of an object and the representation of the limb in space with reference to that object. It is therefore possible to accurately estimate the distance of the object and its size but then not be able to reach for it because the information for position of the limb in space is missing. Such a patient with this problem was described in Chapter 2. Jeannerod and colleagues describe a patient, AT, with a lesion to the "where-action" pathway, in the occipitoparietal dorsal area (Jeannerod, Arbib, Rizzolatti, & Sakata, 1995). This patient was unable to pick up or make accurate preparatory grasping movements when reaching towards the object. Kleist (1923) originally commented on this dissociation between perception and action when discussing constructional dyspraxia. He described patients with constructional disabilities as often having a difficulty in transforming an adequate visual perception into appropriate action. In this way praxis is separated from perceptual processes.

The second lesson concerns the importance of some posterior parietal areas in the preparation for action in response to external stimuli. In general there is now considerable evidence for confirmation that the posterior parietal cortex is a centre that prepares for action rather than just an area that is influential in integrating visual information with information concerning the position of the limb. Also, the functional nature of these areas suggests that if they were disconnected or damaged this might be expected to result in poorly directed movements. Patients originally described by Holmes who had missile wounds in these areas were clearly disadvantaged in this respect (Holmes, 1918).

APRAXIA AND THE MOTOR ENGRAM

The possibility that movements and gestures are similar to language, with their own memory store or engram and side of dominance, has been considered since Liepmann proposed his theory of *apraxia* at the beginning of the twentieth century (Liepmann, 1900).

Apraxia is an acquired disorder of movement affecting gestures and controlled movements in the absence of paresis (paralysis of limbs) or other muscular disorder that may prevent basic motor movements. Apraxia is also separate from disorders of comprehension and perceptual disorders that may interfere with the knowledge of what is required in gesturing during a command to mime a gesture.

Gestures may be referred to according to three main forms. First, there are transitive movements that involve objects, such as combing the hair or brushing the teeth. Second, there are intransitive gestures that do not involve objects, and which usually involve interpersonal communication such as saluting or waving goodbye. Third, there are intransitive, non-representational movements that are meaningless hand gestures. Transitive gestures are more likely to elicit apraxia, and increasing the complexity of movements by increasing the number of gestures in the sequence also increases severity of the apraxic response (Kimura & Archibald, 1974).

Different forms of apraxia

Four forms of apraxia are commonly tested within the clinical setting. First, *ideomotor apraxia* is illustrated by an inability to use gestures (make the actions of someone knocking in a nail) using the upper limbs. Second, *buccofacial apraxia* involves difficulty in making movements with the lips (blowing out a candle) and tongue (move the tongue to the side of your mouth) on command. Third, *verbal apraxia* or *motor aphasia* is further discussed in Chapter 7. Lastly, the definition of *ideational apraxia* is most controversial and some authors have suggested that it is just a

---

Box 8.2. Observations of a patient with ideomotor apraxia

The patient, a man in his thirties, has some aphasic signs of anomia (naming) following a left hemisphere stroke. Observation of this patient shows that he has difficulty when instructed to mime a common task, such as using a hammer to drive in nails. He has this difficulty when using either hand and also fails even when asked to imitate these commonly recognised actions. When asked to mime the action of combing his hair he reaches up his right hand and with his right hand flat, presumably to represent the comb, his hand goes round in a rather erratic and irregular circular motion. The motion is sufficiently recognisable to suggest to the examiner that the patient knows what action he is trying to perform, but the action is really nothing like that of someone combing their hair.

severe ideomotor apraxia. Traditionally, ideational apraxia has been seen as an inability to form sequences of actions. It is not as common as ideomotor apraxia, and Poeck suggests that it is only seen in about 4% of aphasic patients (Poeck, 1985). These patients are able to perform single actions, but have difficulty in stringing the acts together; they are often able to imitate gestures, but have more difficulty under instruction (pantomime). The disorder is obvious in the patient's everyday life, since it affects such tasks as "preparing a meal" or "making tea". When making tea one of our patients placed the tealeaves into the cup, followed by the water, and then she poured the water and the tea leaves from the cup to the teapot.

Aphasia and apraxia

When the non-dominant hand movements are compared with dominant hand movements (usually right) then PET scan results tend to show contralateral activation in the case of the dominant hand, but with non-dominant movements there are also ipsilateral areas of activation (e.g. Kawashima et al., 1993). This left laterality is also maintained in motor learning exercises, e.g. pursuit rotor, in human subjects (Grafton et al., 1992). This suggests a specialised functional role in the left hemisphere for complex movements.

Apraxia has traditionally been seen as a disorder involving the left hemisphere, which especially involves the parietal lobe. The resultant effect is usually on the gesture of both the left and right limbs (Kimura & Archibald, 1974; Kolb & Milner, 1981b). Alternative areas that may be involved include the prefrontal cortex and the supramarginal gyrus (Liepmann, 1913). A close relationship has been found between aphasia and apraxia, whereby aphasic patients often additionally show signs of apraxia. However, the relationship varies according to whether you are male or female (Kimura, 1992; Kimura and Watson, 1989). The association between the two disorders is shown in Figure 8.6, with females being more prone to show aphasia and apraxia (hand movements) with anterior lesions, while males are more likely to show aphasia and apraxia (hand movements) with posterior lesions. Kimura argues that

because females have a more anteriorly organised language and apraxic system they may be more likely to escape these deficits following left hemisphere stroke, merely because stroke involving posterior regions is more common.

There have been a number of attempts to explain this relationship between apraxia and aphasia in the left hemisphere. Kimura proposed that language evolved from gesture in our hominid ancestors (Kimura, 1979). Some have argued that these patients have difficulty in expressing or understanding symbols in any modality (Duffy & Duffy, 1990). This relationship between apraxia and aphasia might alternatively suggest that the area subserving language is merely close to that subserving learned movements. Finally, it has also been proposed that the link between apraxia and aphasia is explainable in terms of patients not comprehending instructions.

This last proposal seems to be the most unlikely as a general explanation of apraxia. If apraxia were due to a misunderstanding of instructions then it would always be accompanied by a disorder of comprehension, which is not the case. There are a number of reported cases of apraxia that are not aphasic (Liepmann, 1913). Also poor correlations have been found between apraxia and aphasia, with the exception of global aphasia (Kertesz & Hooper, 1982), and a closer relationship between aphasia and buccofacial apraxia, the latter relationship probably being due to geographical vicinity of the face area to the language zone (Kimura & Watson, 1989). Although the disorder of global aphasia is most associated with apraxia it is associated with imitation as much as pantomime. If it were due to poor comprehension then a closer relationship should have been found with pantomime, especially with those global aphasics who have severe auditory and comprehension difficulties, but again this is not the case (Lehmkuhl, Poeck, & Willmes, 1983). The finding of a higher correlation with a disorder such as global aphasia may relate purely to the fact that a larger brain area is damaged and therefore more likely to include the area contributing to the apraxia. Therefore this isolated correlation is most in keeping with the explanation that it is an overlapping of neighbouring disorders.

Heilman and Rothi (1993) argue from a similar point of view and show that the *severity* of symbolic impairment in apraxia is not related to the severity of the symbolic deficit in aphasia. Therefore the first proposal that they are both closely situated neuroanatomically is the most persuasive explanation for the coincidence of these two disorders. Nevertheless, the neuroanatomical locations for aphasia and apraxia are not too dissimilar and an interesting evolutionary link has been made between the use of communication using gesture and the development of language, which may have been a development peculiar to *Homo sapiens*. Corballis (1999) extends the arguments made by Kimura (1979) in suggesting that gestures preceded language as a means of communication, and sign language is learned very readily by our relatives the chimpanzees.

Another link between gestures and communication might be seen to be deriving from the work of Rizzolatti and colleagues (Rizzolatti, Fadiga, Gallese, & Fogassi, 1996). These researchers found neurones in the anterior premotor area (F5, rostral area of the ventral premotor area) that fire selectively during movements and also when the monkey *observes* other monkeys or experimenters making movements. From functional imaging studies these "mirror" neurones appear to be present in Broca's area (also possibly in the parietal area) in humans. This has led to a thesis that this area of the monkey may also be tuned to symbolic signing and possibly provides a precursor for language in humans (Rizzolatti & Arbib, 1998). Humans have a remarkable facility for using sign language. Nevertheless, sign language cannot always be seen as an inferior means of communication. Some tribes of Australian Aborigines and North American Indians may use sign language with a high degree of sophistication. Certainly, silent communication of an iconic nature, which may be quicker than spoken communication, has a distinct advantage when hunting or during a military sortie.

A neuroanatomical analysis of apraxia

As indicated, apraxia is noted to be most frequent and most severe in patients with lesions to the left hemisphere (Jason, 1985b). When the number of movements in a sequence are increased, the effects are exaggerated (Harrington & Haaland, 1991, 1992). Also, for left hemisphere patients (but not patients with right hemisphere lesions), patients' hand movements become more poorly controlled or distorted, with an increase in sequence (Roy & Square, 1985). Marteniuk et al. (1987) required normal subjects to perform a two-movement task. In both conditions the first movement was identical. For the second movement, the patient was either required to place the object precisely, or was merely required to throw the object into a box. The first movement was significantly faster when it was followed by a less complex movement. The studies of Jason have verified the relationship of this planning movement with left hemisphere involvement. Therefore, within sequencing there is a planning component which when added to the memory component may exaggerate laterality effects, with the more severe impairment being more likely to be lateralised to the left (Jason, 1985a, 1985b).

There is a tendency for a patient to present with more than one apraxia: for example, a concordance of limb, oral, and verbal apraxias in 73% of left hemisphere-damaged patients (Roy & Square, 1996). As previously suggested, there is a tendency for limb apraxias to be located posteriorly with severe deficits in the temporal and parietal lobe. However, there is a tendency for oral (buccofacial) apraxias to be more likely to be localised anteriorly (Kimura, 1982; Kolb & Milner, 1981b). Given the tendency for a high concordance in the appearance and severity of different apraxias Kimura (1982) proposed that the apraxias may be controlled by a single underlying motor system. There is now sufficient evidence to allow that memory for movement and the complexity of movement involves the left hemisphere more than the right. But are there particular areas that are more likely to contain the memories of the images of movement pattern?

Lesions to such areas as the SMA may result in apraxia but are not reliably associated with apraxia. Arguments for the left supramarginal gyrus as an engram or memory store for complex movements are based on the evidence that apraxia is frequently associated with lesions around this area. However, as Roy and Square (1985) argue, this could equally reflect a disconnection between sensory and motor areas. The disconnection theories of apraxia, involving the corpus callosum, are discussed in Chapter 6. Disconnection provides a good explanation of some unilateral left-handed apraxias on the grounds that verbal instructions do not reach the motor area of the right hemisphere (affecting the contralateral left upper limb), but such disconnections do not explain the more common bilateral apraxia (Roy & Square, 1985).

The disconnection theory could be placed in terms of the memory for movements, a kind of movement engram, being disconnected from the contralateral or ipsilateral systems for preparing and executing motor movements. This would require a callosal disconnection and a disconnection between the engram and the anterior motor system. This would seem a rather demanding dual lesion, which would perhaps make apraxia rather more rare than it is.

These callosal disconnection theories are perhaps better at explaining unilateral apraxia and illustrate the importance of testing with both hands and imitation, because if the verbal instructions are not getting across the patient should still be able to imitate since this would not require the engram. Where the disconnection occurs may determine the modality that is disconnected. For example, apart from the patients who fail only because of misunderstanding an instruction, there are some patients who fail with tactile stimuli, some with visual cues, e.g. imitation only (De Renzi, Faglioni, & Sorgato, 1982; Heilman, 1975; Ochipa, Gonzalez Rothi, & Heilman, 1992).

A broader neuroanatomical model is provided by Heilman and Rothi (1993). This model predicts that there is an engram situated within the vicinity of the supramarginal gyrus and angular gyrus in the parietal lobe. This memory system for a series of movements has some obvious advantages. For example, repeating a learned gesture makes it quicker and easier to perform. Also it allows greater ease of learning new actions by allowing us to transfer parts of these programmes to other similar programmes. For example, learning to play tennis would help us to learn other

related bat and ball sports. Heilman and Rothi suggest that these motor memories be called *praxicons*. When these are destroyed then the patient would not only be unable to perform the motor movement on request, but they would also be unable to imitate or *recognise* the correct movement from other movements. These patients should also have difficulty in learning new motor skills.

Heilman and Rothi do not favour the premotor area as a preparation for complex movement. Rather, they would see the SMA as being more important, taking into account electrical stimulation work and PET scan data, and also the finding that a premotor area lesion rarely coincides with ideomotor apraxia. This might appear to fly in the face of the above discussion concerning reaching to external objects. However, it must be borne in mind that we are referring to *internally driven movements*. There may be no external objects to be grasped in testing for apraxia; the patient has to rely on movement knowledge concerning typical actions.

Watson, Fleet, Gonzalez-Rothi, and Heilman, (1986) reported patients with lesions to the medial frontal lobe, including the SMA, which have been followed by bilateral ideomotor apraxia. Lesions to the basal ganglia and thalamus may also be associated with ideomotor apraxia (Basso, Luzzatti, & Spinnler, 1980). Therefore the basal ganglia, thalamic, SMA circuit or motor loop, described later on in this chapter, may also be involved in the planning and preparation of complex learned movements that may be executed in the primary motor cortex and some caudal (posterior) aspects of the premotor area.

Ideational apraxia, which is associated with poor sequencing of movements, has been attributed to lesions within the frontal lobe (Kolb & Milner, 1981b; see a discussion of this issue in Chapter 3). However, De Renzi (1985) reviews the evidence to support this view from a wide range of findings and comes to the general conclusion that, irrespective of the type of test, left parietal lesions cause most severe impairment while frontal lesions, irrespective of side, cause lesser problems. De Renzi points out that some studies have found a poor relationship between difficulties in *manipulating objects* and those who have difficulties in *miming gestures from memory* irrespective of whether sequences or single movements are involved. There is some logic to the view that poor sequencing of movements as an isolated impairment may require a lesion in both the frontal and parietal lobe. This would be argued on the grounds that the frontal lobes are important in organising the order of movements when they are not reliant on a routine or schema supplied by the parietal cortex. Isolated poor sequencing of movements due to selective frontal lesions would then only occur when the gestures required are meaningless and therefore the intact parietal cortex is of no use in supplying the routine. The literature appears to support this view in terms of this last proposal (Jason, 1985a).

In summary, despite the popular inclusion of the premotor area in models of apraxia, the involvement of this area in engram- or memory-driven actions would not necessarily implicate this area when testing involves mimed movements that are internally driven. What we now know about the premotor area is its importance for the manipulation of external stimuli. It is of interest that ideomotor apraxia is rarely reported following lesions to premotor areas (Faglioni & Basso, 1985, p. 14). The view that there is an engram which often shows a left parietotemporal dominance is supported from a number of studies (see Roy & Square, 1994, for a review). There may also be a more anterior representation in some individuals, in the same way that some individuals have a more anterior representation of language (see Chapter 7). Sequencing of movements is more obviously impaired following frontal lesions when meaningless gestures are required. Meaningless gestures are not capable of being run off by a schema resident within the motor engram. Some patients may suffer from a disorganisation of recognised movements but the necessary lesion is uncertain. As discussed in Chapter 3 and argued by Schwartz (1995), such a disorder may require both a parietal lesion (to negate a reliance on motor engram), making motor movements planned rather than driven by a schema, and a second frontal lesion to interfere with the ability to sequence and organise.

The mechanism for apraxia is still something of a mystery, but we will return to the issue of a model of apraxia after reviewing the research on other motor systems such as the basal ganglia.

A functional analysis of apraxia and assessment

A frequent functional differentiation is made between *production* and *conceptual* errors. Production errors relate to the spatiotemporal accuracy of the movement. For example, one of our patients with ideomotor apraxia when asked to comb his hair made a strange oblique motion some way above and to the side of his head with the flat of his hand. The motion was just recognisable as an attempt to mime combing of the hair. It was assumed from these rather strange motions that the patient knew the concepts associated with hair combing, but there was a breakdown in the production of the movements required for the combing action.

In contrast to the ideomotor apraxias with their production difficulties are the patients who do not get to the production stage because they may not know what a comb is for, or they make no connection between combs and combing. Heilman and Gonzalez Rothi (1993) describe *conceptual apraxia* as an inability to recognise the way a tool is associated with an object and the implications of the use and mechanism of the tool, e.g. a heavy object is required for driving in a nail. These conceptual features would be associated with semantic memory rather than memory for motor routines. Rather than ideomotor apraxia the term conceptual apraxia has been coined, and patients with semantic dementia or Alzheimer's disease are likely to have difficulty with the conceptualising the use associated with the object (Ochipa et al., 1992). It is probable that ideational apraxia, which is described above as a poor sequencing of movements, may also, in some patients, be related to a poor knowledge of the objects rather than a knowledge of the procedural steps of the movement or difficulty in sequencing.

There are two main ways of testing apraxia, either by instruction requiring a pantomime of the movement or by the request to imitate.

However, additional tests may be used if there is a suspicion that poor comprehension of instructions, or poor perception during imitation, is interfering with performance. With a test of pantomime the clinician asks the patient to carry out the gesture. For example, "I would like you to make the movements as if you were hammering a nail" (transitive gesture—use of an object) or "I would like you to give me a military salute" (intransitive gesture). In the case of imitation the patient merely has to imitate the commonly recognised gesture.

Typically patients with ideomotor apraxia are often able to approximate the gesture and they sometimes use "body parts as objects". For example, the extended finger may be used to represent a toothbrush. Alternatively, as was the case in the above example, the extended hand might be used to signify a comb.

However, other qualitative errors may be revealed in the case of ideational apraxia when the sequence of a series of acts, such as placing a letter in an envelope, sealing the envelope and placing a stamp on the letter, is performed in the wrong order, i.e. the envelope may be sealed before the letter is placed in the envelope. Alternatively, a patient may repeat or perseverate a particular action or omit an action. These last errors may occur even when the gesture is in error and even when the patient may recognise the correct gesture (Poeck, 1985, p. 101). Patients with apraxia also appear to be clumsy, ungainly and poorly controlled in their movements (Gonzalez Rothi & Heilman, 1985).

Advice concerning testing varies and it may be true that it is more useful to analyse the nature of the breakdown of gesture rather than use a diagnostic label, some of which may be less helpful. It is important to differentiate the patient who has poor conceptual knowledge of gestures from those who merely have difficulty in carrying out gestures. For example, a patient with Alzheimer's disease may not perform a gesture because the knowledge stores relating to the recognition of that gesture are destroyed. Such a patient should be distinguished who only has the engram or memory store for the movements impaired but nevertheless has knowledge about the gesture

(recognition of a gesture by others but without the ability to express the gesture).

It is also important to compare gestures to instruction with imitated gestures since failure with instruction may be due to comprehension of language. It is also important to test each upper limb separately for, as discussed, an isolated problem with a left limb occurring only with instruction might signal a disconnection of language or the motor engram from the right hemisphere or damage to contralateral areas responsible for the execution of movement. Finally, it may be useful to test meaningless sequences of movements versus meaningful sequences of manipulated objects to test frontal contributions to praxis.

THE BASAL GANGLIA SYSTEM

Introduction

Diseases such as Huntington's and Parkinson's disease are associated with structural and biochemical lesions to aspects of the basal ganglia. The basal ganglia is a broad name for a number of different structures (see Figure 8.7). The individual functional significance of these structures is still a subject of controversy and this is in part because the connections between these structures is very complex. It is probably fair to say that if the basal ganglia were on the outside of the brain we would know a great deal more about them than we do. However, these collections of nuclei and their interconnections are situated deep in the brain subcortically. Disorders affecting the basal ganglia are often referred to as extrapyramidal, with the implication that they are not related to the agranular motor cortex (primary motor area). However, it is now known that the basal ganglia are part of a complex loop that depends eventually on the pyramidal motor cortex for its expression. The term extrapyramidal may remain a useful clinical term, however, since there is a special aetiology and pattern of movement disorder that reflects a breakdown of the basal ganglia system.

Nevertheless, apart from the direct connections

FIG. 8.7

Basal ganglia	Corpus striatum	Striatum	Lenticular nucleus
Caudate nucleus Putamen Globus pallidus Subthalmic nucleus Substantia nigra	Caudate nucleus Putamen Globus pallidus	Caudate nucleus Putamen	Putamen Globus pallidus

Some commonly used terms that are used when discussing the basal ganglia (adapted from Nolte, 1993).

with the brain stem, the basal ganglia are seen more as a modulator of pyramidally executed motor movements. The modulation is seen as being most important in the planning and driving of routines of complex motor movements (with less reliance on external sensory feedback). Appropriately, the main cortical output of this subcortical loop is the SMA, which influences the primary motor area.

In recent years the roles of the basal ganglia have been extended. However, the motor aspect of the basal ganglia, which is of interest here, has its input *from a number of cortical areas*. The first structure that receives the input from the cortex is the phylogenetically youngest group of structures within the basal ganglia, called the *striatum*. The striatum includes two structures: the *putamen* and the *caudate nucleus*. At one time the striatum was thought to be one structure; certainly its ontogeny (development following birth) gives the impression of being one structure in its development. But the putamen and the caudate are structurally and histologically distinct, and play different functional roles (Nolte, 1993). The putamen has more implications for movement, while the caudate acts more as a "super-highway" for nerve fibres travelling to and from the prefrontal cortex and other brain areas.

The striatum is situated within the deep area of the brain with its head, the putamen, placed just above the orbital frontal cortex. Its tail, the caudate nucleus, sweeps round in an arc, situated on the wall of the lateral ventricles (see Figure 8.8 and Appendix).

The putamen, having taken information from the cortex, projects this to other structures that are phylogenically older. The putamen first projects to the *external globus pallidus* (see Figure 8.8) and then onto the *internal globus pallidus*. There is more than one connection between the external globus pallidus (GPe) and the internal globus pallidus (GPi). One of these connections is with the *substantia nigra, pars reticulata* (SNr), both directly and also via another important motor structure, the *subthalamic nucleus* (STN). The substantia nigra has assumed special influence within this system as an area of pathology within Parkinson's disease. The substantia nigra (named for the dark-coloured cells) is the source of the dopamine transmitter that has a key influence on the efficient function of the basal ganglia.

There is also a direct route to the GPi from the putamen (see Figure 8.8). Most of the output projections of the putamen are inhibitory and GABAergic. However, the output efferents of the STN are excitatory (glutamatergic). There are other important structures that will be referred to in the context of Parkinson's disease.

The supplementary motor area and the cingulate motor area

The basal ganglia is not the sole activator of the supplementary area. The topic of the SMA and the cingulate motor area (CMA) could also be discussed as part of the cortical system. While there are some variations in the roles of these areas that may depend on the activity required, the special feature of these motor areas is their role in the preparation of movements of all kinds. However, it is well suited to the assumed role of the basal ganglia in their function within the timing and preparation of complex routines of

Structures of the basal ganglia and their interconnecting pathways (a) give an indication of the position of the striatum (putamen plus the caudate nucleus) deep within the brain beneath the cortex. The arrows indicate the various cortical pathways, the "what" and "where-action" pathways, and entry from the medial temporal lobe. Also indicated are the projections from the orbital and dorsolateral cortex to the caudate. (b) Structures hidden behind the striatum to which the putamen projects. The coronal slice, taken at around the position indicated on (b), is shown in diagram (c). Diagram (c) shows some of the efferents and afferents with the cortical areas. Note how there is a loop going from the cortical areas that feeds into the caudate and from the striatum (caudate plus putamen) to the globus pallidus and then to the thalamus and back to the cortex within the motor area (especially the supplementary motor area). See Appendix 4 for the relationship with the middle cerebral artery.

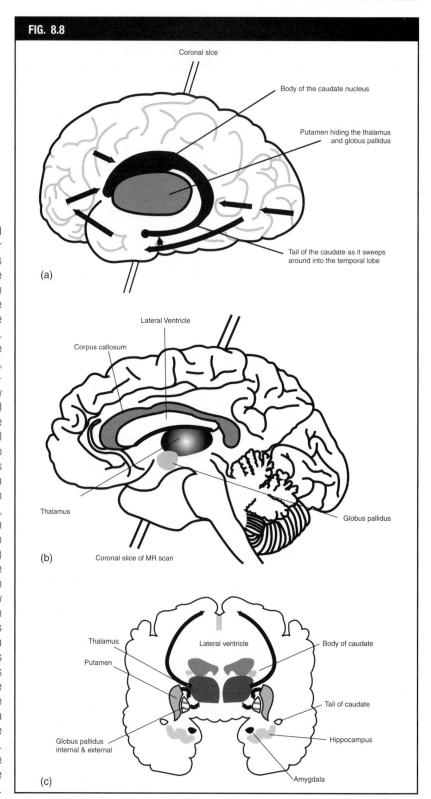

FIG. 8.8

(a)

Coronal slce

Body of the caudate nucleus

Putamen hiding the thalamus and globus pallidus

Tail of the caudate as it sweeps around into the temporal lobe

(b)

Lateral Ventricle

Corpus callosum

Thalamus

Coronal slice of MR scan

Globus pallidus

(c)

Thalamus

Putamen

Globus pallidus internal & external

Lateral ventricle

Body of caudate

Tail of caudate

Hippocampus

Amygdala

behaviour. The SMA lies within the medial region on the mesial aspect of the longitudinal fissure just anterior to the precentral gyrus (see Figure 8.6b). The SMA receives afferents from the prefrontal cortex and acts as the cortical representative of a subcortical loop, which includes the basal ganglia and ventral lateral nuclei of the thalamus. This last system is described in the next section. Less is known concerning the more recently identified CMA (Wise, Boussaoud, Johnson, & Caminiti, 1997). Even the boundaries of these areas are changing with increased knowledge of the surrounding cell types. Just anterior to the SMA and the M1 there is the development of the identity of the CMA; see Figure 8.5b; Roland & Zilles (1996). Unilateral movements generally activate M1 unilaterally in the contralateral hemisphere; however, unilateral movements tend to influence the SMA more bilaterally. Certainly when there is damage to the SMA then the more obvious impairment is on tasks that require bilateral coordination, e.g. tying up shoelaces (Cunnington, Bradshaw, & Iansek, 1996).

Some aspects of movements seem to separate the function of the SMA from the premotor area. There is the tendency for the SMA to be more frequently involved with the preparation of complex movement routines that are more internally driven (Passingham, 1996). The SMA seems to be less directly involved in the process of ongoing sensory feedback. Also, unlike the premotor area, the SMA is less involved once the motor movement has been initiated. Both the SMA and premotor area are important for sequences of movement, but the SMA appears to be especially important. Finally, the SMA and the CMA seem to be important in inhibiting movements that would normally occur routinely, for example the no-go response in the go–no-go task (see Chapter 3) Dettmers et al., 1996; Vidal, Bonnet, & Macar, 1995).

At one time the SMA was seen to be involved in the preparation of limb and body movements, but now it has been well demonstrated that this area is also important for planning fine motor movements involving the dexterous use of digits. Even when only one digit is moved in a simple movement the SMA may be involved (Ikeda et al., 1995). Also, there is a frequent association with speech. Electrical stimulation studies have found that stimulation of the SMA may result in sudden noises from the conscious patient. There is a rapid movement of the tongue (Luders et al., 1988). Also PET scan results often show an activation of the SMA during spontaneous speech (Larsen, Skinhoj, & Lassen, 1978). This and other information has given this structure the reputation as an essential feature for programming the muscle activity necessary for speech (see Crosson, 1992, for a review).

However, the exact contribution of the SMA to the programming of complex routines of movements is not completely clear. There are some studies, for example, which point to quite a specific role in the timing of movements (see Cunnington et al., 1996).

Finally, when discussing these structures it is likely that the SMA and the CMA will be divided further in the future since the areas that are more anterior serve a more preparatory role when compared to areas within these structures, which are posterior and nearest to the precentral gyrus (Dettmers et al., 1995). It is likely that the designated pre-supplementary area may have a more executive role than the SMA, e.g. changing and inhibiting motor plans (Dettmers et al., 1995; Jackson & Husain, 1996).

Huntington's disease

George Huntington's father was a general practitioner, practising in New England at the end of the nineteenth century, and as a child he used to go with his father on his medical rounds. It was on these visits to his father's patients that he first saw patients with this disorder. As he watched from the window of his father's carriage, he was impressed and fascinated by their strange writhing involuntary movements and later made the disorder the subject of his MD thesis in 1872 when he himself was completing his medical qualifications.

This introduction to the disease may not have occurred at this time had Huntington been situated elsewhere, for this genetic disease is distributed to areas that illustrate the geographical movements of the original carriers. In New

England, where Huntington first encountered patients, the original carriers had reportedly been one of the first Pilgrim Father settlers. There are other geographical pockets of the disorder, which also illustrate the spread of the disorder according to a genetic influence. For example, in Australia, one of the early settlers to the state of Tasmania had Huntington's disease and some of the descendants have made their way across the sea to the nearby state of Victoria, and consequently Victoria has many sufferers.

One geographical location that has proved to be a focus of Huntington's disease research is a seaport in Venezuela. The disease was carried there by a sailor and because this was a small, relatively isolated community, it is of special interest to researchers. There occurs here the relatively rare occurrence in which two carriers have married. Combined genetic inheritance is associated with a greater genetic abnormality, which may result in a more severe Huntington's disease with an earlier onset and more rigidity (Kremer, Weber, & Hayden, 1992). All the carriers in the world may be eventually traced back in their family tree to persons coming from the village of Bures in seventeenth-century Suffolk, England.

Huntington's disease or Huntington's chorea is a genetic disorder that is autosomal dominant with full penetration. Therefore the gene always expresses itself in the disease and if one parent has the disorder then, on average, half of the offspring will also inherit the disorder. Since the disorder often does not show obvious symptoms until the patient is in their forties, a patient would often already have made a decision to have a family prior to knowing whether they were a carrier of the gene. This difficulty is somewhat eased by genetic testing, since a genetic *marker* for the disorder has been found on the short arm of chromosome 4. However, the severe repercussions of having this disease means that some persons do not wish to know, and some may even take the test and then at the last moment decline to know the results. Needless to say, such an issue requires considerable sensitivity in supporting the patient during this process.

The progression of the disease is varied, but is associated most obviously with chorea (from the Greek word for dance) and other motor symptoms. However, emotional problems such as major depression may precede these symptoms (Beighton and Hayden, 1981; see Chapter 9) and psychometrically measurable cognitive deterioration may also precede motor symptoms (Diamond et al., 1992; Lyle & Gottesman, 1977). Therefore there is some variability in the initial symptoms at onset and any of these three areas of personality, cognitive, or motor dysfunction may appear first (Bennett & Curiel, 1989).

Huntington's disease is often described as an excess of movement, while Parkinson's disease is associated with a poverty of movement. This is an oversimplification since there is some common ground. For example, Huntington's patients will, like Parkinson patients, be slow at initiating movements. This may be demonstrated in a simple clinical test. If the examiner asks the patient to clap on the examiner's hand at a signal, the delay is often clearly visible.

With progression of this disease there is atrophy of the striatum, initially most notably in the putamen and the caudate (Sax et al., 1983). With such an area of destruction, involving so many connections between the prefrontal cortex and other cortical areas, the damage to the caudate is associated with a number of dysexecutive signs. Eventually, with the spreading of the effects of the disease within the brain, a progressive deterioration of personality and intellect leads to dementia and death after 15–20 years. However, it must be noted that the length and severity of progression of the disease are quite varied, so that patients may go for some time without showing these cognitive signs in their daily lives.

Figure 8.9 illustrates the affect of atrophy at point "a" on the inhibitory GABAergic projections in Huntington's disease. This leads to an imbalance with the inhibitory dopamine input from the substantia nigra. This type of dopaminergic neurone (DA2) has an additional inhibitory effect on the GABA projections with the result that not only are the projections weaker due to the disease, but the effect of DA2 is to accentuate this deficit. The GPe is less inhibited, which leads to a chain reaction of inhibitory and excitatory imbalances culminating in reduced inhibition of

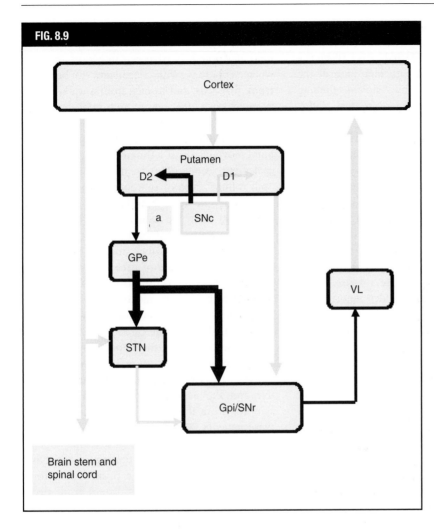

FIG. 8.9

Model of the neuroanatomical disruption due to Huntington's disease. Dark lines indicate inhibitory neuronal projections; light lines are excitatory. Broad lines are abnormally accentuated in their effect; narrow lines indicate reduced effect. See text for description (adapted from Wichman & DeLong, 1996).

the nucleus within the *ventrolateral nucleus of the thalamus*. This reduced inhibition consequently results in overactivation of the excitatory effects of the thalamic nuclei on the SMA. The relationship between the ventrolateral nucleus of the thalamus and the SMA has been verified in Parkinson patients using PET scan (Davis et al., 1997).

In this way the model predicts an overactivation of the motor cortex, thus producing excessive poorly controlled movements (Wichman & DeLong, 1996). There are two attractive features when assessing the above model as a description of Huntingdon's disease. The first is that injection of a dopamine antagonist may reduce motor symptoms temporarily (Marsden, 1987). This, according to the model, would redress the

imbalance of GABA to some degree, and allow an increased inhibition of the GPe towards normal inhibitory levels. The second plausible effect of this model concerns the virtual biochemical disablement of the excitatory effect of the STN on the GPi/SNr. This is in keeping with the findings of Huntington-like symptoms following a lesion to the STN (ballism, referred to below).

Although the putamen is initially involved within the basal ganglia motor circuit, it is assumed that this is not associated with the *advanced* motor signs that are the hallmarks of this disorder (Albin, Young, & Penney, 1989). Damage to the projections between the putamen and the subthalamic nucleus is seen to be more crucial in this respect. Isolated lesions to the STN are associated with many of the Huntington's disease motor signs, whereas lesions to the putamen are not. A disorder referred to as ballism is a rare syndrome associated with infarction of the STN. It is characterised by "violent, flinging motions of the extremities" (Albin et al., 1989, p. 367).

Huntington's disease commences with clumsiness and falls. The uncontrolled movements that follow during the progression of the disease are *choreic*: they may take the form of sudden erratic movements, e.g. sudden throwing out of the arm. There are also typically a number of tics, facial grimaces, forced staring, jerks of the head or arm. In severe cases, there may be bouts of *ballism*. These involuntary movements are collectively referred to as *dyskinesias*. There are also effects on the vocal emissions: sudden snorts and exclamations, and poor control of voice volume. The voice may become dysarthric (consistently distorted) and eventually unintelligible.

Sometimes the patient may appear to adjust an involuntary action for a more natural looking one. The patient is unaware of the extent and nature of their own movements. Patients are often surprised at the extent of their motor dysfunction when viewing a video of themselves. This inability to see themselves as others see them is not related to tested measures of executive dysfunction as one might expect. Snowden suggests that this is probably due to poor physiological feedback rather than "denial of illness" or lack of insight (Snowden, Crauford, & Neary, 1995, and personal communication).

Parkinson's disease

James Parkinson was a physician working in the East End of London, England, when he first noticed patients suffering from "paralysis agitans" shuffling along the streets. In 1817 he described the disorder in the following terms: "Involuntary tremulous motion with lessened muscular power, in parts not in action and even when supported, with a tendency to bend the trunk forwards, and to pass from a walking to a running pace, the senses and intellects being uninjured." Parkinson here describes the "resting tremor" that is most obvious in the fingers of the hand moving against a thumb at approximately 7 cycles per second. This tremor is the repetitive "pill rolling" type of movement, which initially affects one side more than the other. The tremor disappears when the hand is used. The lack of balance is represented by the leaning forward, which Parkinson describes, and the "festination of gait" or quickening of pace may result in the patient falling over as the movements fail to keep up with the forward momentum.

Symptoms of Parkinson's disease usually start to appear after the age of 50 years and affects around 1 in 1000 of the population. The incidence rises in the later years. Hughlings Jackson describes two types of motor difficulties: the positive and the negative symptoms. The positive symptoms are the tremor and rigidity found in these patients. Marsden (1987) argued that it is not profitable to investigate these in the hope of revealing the normal functioning of the basal ganglia. This is because the positive symptoms are an abnormal response of distant brain mechanisms released by the basal ganglia damage. "It is the negative symptoms, functions that are lost, that provide the crucial clues" (Marsden, 1987, p. 283). The negative symptoms, *akinesia* (inability to move), the *hypokinesias* (reduction of spontaneous movement), and *bradykinesias* (slowness in making an ongoing movement) are the focus of interest when attempting to unravel the mysteries of the basal ganglia. It is of interest that these movement difficulties have generally been found

---

Box 8.3. Observations of a patient with Parkinson's disease

The elderly man was shuffling very slowly towards the edge of the platform, using a walking stick for support. He waited patiently for his train, which duly arrived. The doors slid open and several passengers passed by the man and boarded the train. But the man failed to move despite there being the same destination for all trains. After a few moments the doors of the train slid closed. Just as the train started to move off, the man, who was obviously very angry at his own immobility, cried out, and coming to life made a sudden movement; bringing up his walking stick, he struck the train as it moved off. The man was observed later to have both the tremor and the mask-like face that may accompany the disease.

to be independent of the clinical signs of tremor and rigidity (positive signs). Therefore, the patient may have a worse tremor on one side, but show equal bradykinesia (negative sign) with either side (Castiello, Bennett, & Scarpa, 1994; Marsden, 1982).

The akinesia is made more frustrating because of its unpredictability. The frustration arises because the patient knows what they want to do but their limbs will not obey. With luck the height of the leg movement will merely be reduced but sometimes the patient is entirely frozen, and unable to move. This is illustrated by the description of the patient at the beginning of this section.

The rigidity found in these patients may be revealed if the limb or flexible joint of the patient is moved; there may be resistance followed by movement sometimes referred to as cogwheeling. Akinesia (inability to move) may be a separate mechanism to bradykinesia (slowness of ongoing movement). Clinically and experimentally they may not correlate and akinesia may respond to treatment when bradykinesia may not.

The model of Wichman and DeLong (see Figure 8.10) is able to describe Parkinson's disease as being due to a suppression of the motor cortex through the inhibiting influence of the thalamus.

It should be noted that while with Huntington's disease there is an excess of activation from the thalamus to the cortical motor area, the opposite is true in the mechanism for Parkinson's disease. This situation stems originally from the depletion of neurones within the dark pigmented

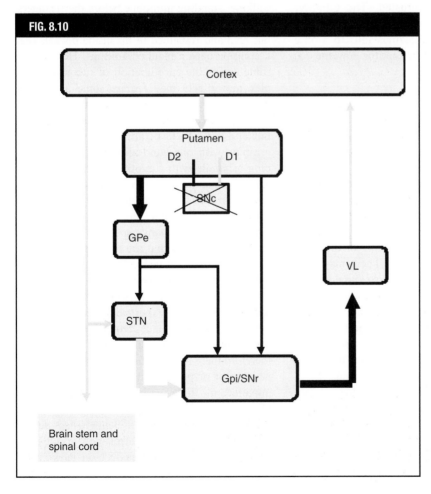

FIG. 8.10

A model of the neuroanatomical disruption due to Parkinson's disease. Dark lines indicate inhibitory neuronal projections; lighter lines are excitatory. Broad lines are abnormally accentuated in their effect; narrow lines indicate reduced effect. See text for a description (adapted from Wichman & DeLong, 1996).

cells in the substantia nigra, pars compacta (SNc).

The roles of the two dopamine receptors DA2 and DA1 are inhibitory and facilitatory respectively. When you take away these influences, then the D1 neurones cease to facilitate the direct inhibiting GABA projections to the GPi/SNr (the right-most route from the putamen in the diagram). The opposite effect occurs on the depletion of the D2ergic neurones (to the left of the diagram). Without the inhibiting effect of D2ergic neurones the inhibiting GABA projections to the GPe are unchecked and thereby reduce the inhibiting effect of the GPe on both the STN and GPi/SNr. Because the STN is not inhibited in its excitatory role it increases the activation of Gpi/SNr. The net result is two inputs that no longer inhibit the GPi/SNr and another input whose excitatory input is accentuated. The GPi/SNr thus exerts an unrestrained inhibitory effect on the thalamus, and the thalamus fails to arouse and initiate the SMA when a motor movement is required.

Movement difficulties with Parkinson's disease

Various features of Parkinson's disease seen in the daily lives of patients provide clues to the nature of their movement disorder. As part of the bradykinesia or slowing of movement there is a tendency to slow down towards the end of a movement. The amplitude of the response becomes less and less. The patient may show signs of micrographia, with small writing or drawings becoming smaller and smaller. There may be a tendency to reach out for an article and not quite achieve the range, thereby necessitating a further second movement in order to reach the goal (Marsden, 1987). However, this may not be due to insufficient force but rather the poor preparation for movement. Parkinson patients may use excessive force on some tasks, and an analysis of handwriting in these subjects would suggest that the problem may be overcome if smaller chunks of movement are required (Phillips, Bradshaw, Iansek, & Chiu, 1993).

There are certain conditions that predispose Parkinson's disease patients to movement difficulties and these are not obviously related to their rigidity. In particular, patients are more likely to show difficulties in conditions involving simultaneous tasks involving both upper limbs. Schwab, Chafetz, and Walker (1954) found that when a Parkinson's disease patient was required to squeeze a bulb with one hand and draw a triangle with the other, their performance broke down and became exaggeratedly slow, with some patients resorting to doing one task, then the other, in a sequential manner. Schwab and colleagues describe everyday situations in which the patient may find it difficult to undertake two movements together; they recount a story told by a patient: "when walking across a hotel lobby room in front of the usual number of strangers to pay his bill, he reached into his inside pocket with his left hand to get his wallet. At once he stopped walking, standing immobile before the strangers. Becoming aware of this, he then resumed walking but his hand remained in his inside pocket, suggesting perhaps a planned holdup." However, to some extent the coordination of two such complex motor acts may require some aspects of planning and executive control that may not be present when carrying out simple tasks. When the bilateral tasks are less complex, e.g. reaching and grasping with one hand and reaching and gripping a handle with the other hand, then differences from controls are not so obvious (Castiello & Bennett, 1997). The precise difficulty with simultaneous movements has yet to be clearly defined. There are many aspects of the naturally described situation that are not present in either of the experimental tasks. The man in the hotel lobby is carrying out two complex motor tasks but they are normally routines not under conscious control. The experimental task described by Schwab and colleagues requires two tasks that are complex but not well-learned routines and therefore there is the coincidental requirement of new motor or procedural learning, which is also impaired in these patients (see discussion in Chapter 5). Finally, the experimental task described by Castiello and Bennett uses simple tasks under conscious control with visual feedback, which has the least effect on Parkinson's disease patients.

Another situation that brings out the movement difficulties of these patients is the sequential task involving "perturbations" or changes in movements. In these tasks the patient starts to reach for a lighted globe and the target is suddenly changed—an alternative globe suddenly lights and becomes the target. The subject has already started to reach for one globe and therefore has to adjust movements after being committed to the first movement. Under these conditions Parkinson's disease patients perform relatively well if the size of the target is maintained. But if the change in direction or distance *also* requires a change of grasp type from a whole hand grasp (large globe) to a precision finger grip (very small target) then the Parkinson's disease patient is far slower at changing the hand manipulation as the hand moves through the air (Castiello, Bennett, & Scarpa, 1994). There is a difficulty in another study when releasing the original grip (Castiello, Bennett, & Stelmach, 1993a).

Other studies similarly show that when there is a change in the motor programmes these patients are slowed to in an exaggerated manner. For example, in a paradigm requiring the subject to flex the arm by pushing a lever and also in some conditions to squeeze the lever at the same time, the time taken for Parkinson's disease patients to do both in sequence is far in excess of either of these movements in isolation when compared to controls (Benecke et al., 1987). This has also been found to be the case for Huntington's disease patients (Thompson et al., 1988) and those with a stroke involving the right SMA. In terms of the above discussion on the right SMA lesion it is of interest that this result pertained to both limbs bilaterally (Dick et al., 1986).

Brotchie and colleagues have shown that a proportion of neurones in the anterior globus pallidus discharge in a phasic manner at the end of a wrist movement (Brotchie, Iansek, & Horne, 1991a, 1991b). As explained above, the globus pallidus is seen as influencing the inhibitory effect of the thalamus on the SMA. Therefore it is in the starting and termination of independent movements that there appears to be a significant difficulty with these patients.

The finding that visual and other sensory cues

are particularly helpful to these patients has encouraged the view that the basal ganglia are functionally helpful for the preparation of complex motor movements that are "*internally driven*". As argued above, the premotor area is seen as being more important for controlled movements to external stimuli and this area is more preserved in Parkinson's disease patients.

There is some evidence that visual cues help both Parkinson's disease and Huntington's disease patients. Sometimes, patients may report that visual sensory information may help to overcome akinesia. For example, in their daily life a patient may search for some visual cue, such as the change in the look of the pavement, which may help them initiate movement. Patients have been known to throw a piece of paper in front of them to keep them moving. Perhaps this allows other motor mechanisms such as the premotor area with its visual feedback to take over in a controlled non-routine way. The way visual feedback may assist movements is well illustrated in studies by Bradshaw and colleagues. In an experiment in which Parkinson's disease patients had to press buttons towards a goal, it was found that when the next button press required was cued by lighting up the button, patients were more assisted than controls if the cue was given in sufficient time to guide performance (Georgiou et al., 1994), both for the initiation of response and movement time. Similar results have been obtained with Huntington's disease patients (Bradshaw et al., 1992). The view that the visual aspect of the stimulus may be important is supported by the finding that other prior non-visual (e.g. verbal warning) preparatory cues are less helpful with these patients (Stelmach, Worringham, & Strand, 1986).

Treatment and therapy for Parkinson's disease

The traditional treatment for Parkinson's disease is to increase the amount of dopamine, which has been depleted by the destruction of the substantia nigra. The therapy relieves some of the clinical symptoms of tremor and akinesia but is less successful in reducing bradykinesia. This might be of concern if bradykinesia is seen as being due to the mechanism described in the model above. Nevertheless, in keeping with Wichman and DeLong's model, when the patient has been administered L-dopa for some time, increasingly higher doses are required to maintain freedom from akinesia and tremors; overdoses may occur, resulting in dyskinesias, e.g. sudden saluting movements. This would be more in keeping with the kind of imbalance associated with Huntington's disease and Wichman and DeLong's model.

Wichman and DeLong (1996) admit that there are some problems in reconciling their model with the finding that the surgical destruction of the ventrolateral area of the thalamus or the GPi results in the relief of symptoms. Pallidotomy is not a new treatment for Parkinson's disease, but technical advances and increased knowledge concerning the correct location of the lesion have meant that stereotactic ablation of the GPi has resulted in favourable results (e.g. Baron et al., 1996). Disruption of the globus pallidus by electrical stimulation (electrodes inserted in the GPi allowing patient control) acting as a temporary ablation may be seen as an even more favourable effect without the problems of recovery following brain lesions (Davis et al., 1997).

But as Wichman and DeLong admit, these results are less favourable for their model. Without any inhibition of the thalamus then the thalamus should have an overactive effect on the SMA and cause dyskinesias as in the Huntington's disease model above. Destruction of the thalamic nuclei might be expected to cause no arousal of the SMA resulting in akinesia. The authors propose that these surgical treatments might reduce the variations in activation or unbalanced noise from the basal ganglia. In partial support of this view it has been found that when the GPi receives electrical stimulation causing its disruption (equivalent to temporary ablation) the cerebral blood flow in the SMA increases to normal level in Parkinson patients (Davis et al., 1997). There remains an unease that if movements return to near normal (even bradykinesias are reduced in the Davis et al., 1997, study), when this circuit is virtually disconnected, how does this conform with the basal ganglia as a

structure with a supposed major contribution to movement (Wichman & DeLong, 1996)?

Finally, it should be noted that both Huntington's disease and Parkinson's disease show bradykinesia. Bradykinesias may therefore require a separate model to allow for this co-occurrence. The basal ganglia are obviously important in the progression of both these diseases but the mechanism still holds some mysteries.

THE CEREBELLUM SYSTEM

Introduction

Luigi Luciani was one of the first great contributors to research in this area and published a monograph on the cerebellum in 1891 (see description and comments in Manni & Petrosini, 1997). His early research with dogs and primates found that hemicerebellectomised animals tend to lose the ability to stand on the same or ipsilateral side of the operation. After a few weeks, muscle tone would return, but movements were awkward and the animal would walk with exaggerated steps, the gait being clumsy and hesitant. There was also some abnormality of the eye movements or nystagmus. The dogs' movements were described as losing their normal measure and harmony.

Later Gordon Holmes (cited by Manni & Petrosini, 1997) was to describe patients with gunshot wounds to the cerebellum in a manner similar to that used by Luciani, as follows (comments in italics):

1. Postural disturbances.
2. A tendency to fall on both sides when standing with feet close together.
3. A drunken sailor's gait, with a wide stance and unsteady balance.
4. An intentional tremor, most noticeable when the patient is at the end of the movement, when most concentration is required (see Figure 8.11).

Human research into the movement disorders and the cerebellum are rather sparse. This is

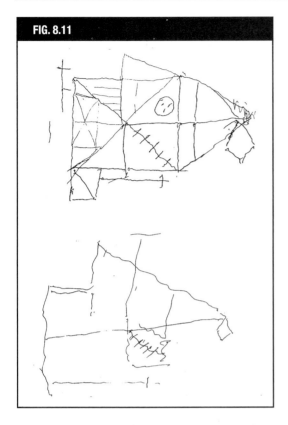

FIG. 8.11

The performance of a patient with cerebellar atrophy—a copy of the Rey Ostereith complex figure and a delayed recall. Note the worse tremor occurs during the possibly more demanding memory task. Unlike Parkinson's disease, which is associated with a resting tremor, patients with cerebellar atrophy have an intentional tremor, which is apparent when they make a movement.

largely because the commoner involvement in natural lesions involves widespread atrophy that often involves additional brain areas. Other subjects with brain surgery following malignant tumour removal are not so common and also have confounding problems in terms of treatment and again other areas are sometimes involved. However, the area has become the focus of some recent research and there has been a return to the use of animal models.

It is easy to see why this structure of the cerebellum attracts interest. Cerebellum means "little brain", although its size is deceptive. It is even more deeply folded than the cortex and if it were flattened out it would cover an area over half that of the cerebral cortex. This densely packed structure contains a large number of granule cells, e.g stellate cells. It actually contains more cells than the cortex (Glickstein, 1998, p. 262). The cell structures within the cerebellum are particularly interesting, with input or afferent neurones, referred to as mossy fibre cells. There are also climbing cells that have dendrites which entwine round the strange-looking Purkinje cell that acts to output signals (see Nolte, 1993, pp. 337–359). The structure of the cerebellum is illustrated in Figure 8.12.

The connections of the cerebellum suggests a modifier of motor responses rather than an executor. The input is from the motor and somatosensory cortex, while the output is to the thalamus before returning to the cortex. The largest afferent input travels from the sensory and motor cortex via a nucleus within the pons in the brain stem (the pontine nucleus). There is a lesser input from the spinal cord and brain stem (via the inferior peduncle). Finally there is an efferent output (via the superior peduncle) to the ventrolateral and ventroanterior nucleus of the thalamus, from which point there is a return to the motor and premotor cortex (see Figure 8.1).

As indicated, the major input to the cerebellum is from the pons, which conveys information from the posterior parietal cortex and motor areas. This information has been found to be related to visual stimuli in terms of direction and velocity rather than shape (Quinn, Didier, Baker, & Peterson, 1998). This is a hyper-fast magno pathway and therefore it is assumed that the cerebellum is important for modifying movements that are dependent on visual sensory information in which movement parameters are important.

Contribution of the cerebellum to movement

These everyday behavioural signs have been analysed to reveal three areas that appear to be mainly found following damage or atrophy to the cerebellum. The first, posture, has been described above, the second is the coordination of movements and the third is the learning of certain movements.

which is contralateral but similar in pattern to that found following lesions to the cerebral cortex. It appears that the cerebellum really is a little brain. It is interesting that Luciani, all those years ago, referred to the possibility of the cerebellum contributing to what we would call today cognitive processes, something that we are only now confirming.

GENERAL SUMMARY

The motor system is made up from the basal ganglia, cortical motor and somatosensory areas, the cerebellum, and some specialised motor areas within the brain stem. When looking at these motor areas one can see a blueprint for survival. It is important to make complex, accurate movements quickly. Our ancestors would have starved had they not had the facility to throw a weapon with precision. A simple throwing motion requires the interplay of many muscle groups, which must be timed perfectly. While the functional contribution of the basal ganglia is still a source of controversy, there is growing evidence that it is involved with the initiation and run of an automatic series of movements that have their expression within structures such as the SMA and other cortical motor areas. With the multitude of afferents from the frontal cortical areas to the basal ganglia it is no surprise that the disorders associated with pathology of the basal ganglia are disorders of motor control.

The cerebellum, in contrast, is more obviously related to the modification of these automatic movements after they have started. This is clearly not always the case but when the target of the action has suddenly moved mid-flight corrections must be made very quickly. For example, given the speed of a bowler in a game of cricket or baseball, certain predictions concerning the nature of the type of ball being delivered must be made. The ball is often travelling too fast to see and preparations for a batting stroke must therefore be made in advance. The bowler or deliverer's hold of the ball is such important

information for the receiver that there will often be elaborate attempts to mislead by sleight of hand or blatant covering of the bowling hand until the last moment. The batter or receiver will have prepared the kind of stroke they are going to play even before the ball leaves the bowler's hand—there is often just not the perceptual speed to do otherwise (McLeod & Jenkins, 1991). According to the proposals made here the automatic run of programmed movements, and their timing, are the contribution of the basal ganglia system. However, in our example, the bowler will, at the last minute, change the pace of the ball or place a disguised spin on the ball. The batter will then consequently make some rapid adjustments to the stroke to make allowance for the change in velocity and direction. These rapid adjustments are contributed in part by the cerebellum.

The final contribution concerns the control of novel movements. Sometimes we have to make visually guided movements that are unplanned and unusual, such as removing a splinter from a finger. Such movements are more obviously contributed to by the cortical motor system and involve the pre-somatosensory and premotor area with expression in the motor strip.

This functional broad overview is given to clarify functional differences between three systems and does not, of course, describe the many additional features or the overlap in contributions of these areas. For example, in the description of the cerebellum as a modifier of complex runs of movement we are at the risk of overlooking the important role this structure has in making any movement that requires constant adjustment for balance. Even simple movements require corrective motion and modification in order to retain equilibrium. This broad description also undermines the integration between the systems. When imaging studies are being undertaken then the movements are often limited to finger movements because of the importance of keeping the subject's head still, so there are few studies that look at the integration of these systems that must take place.

Also, it is wrong to overlook the interdependence of the systems on each other. For example, the premotor area and SMA provide an output for motor behaviour that is programmed and adjusted in the other two systems. Also, there has been a discussion in this chapter of the importance of the posterior parietal cortex and its role in setting up an internal map of the spatial relationships between externally targeted objects and various body parts. This process must be seen as an essential prerequisite to any directive movement since even if one is responding to a target from memory this map must be metaphorically referred to. Thus although lesions to the cerebellum and the basal ganglia may cause significant and dramatic movement disorders, the most significant effect on movement is from bilateral lesions to the posterior parietal cortex, as illustrated in such disorders as Balint's syndrome and its variants, which were described by Holmes (1918).

9

Emotional disorders

INTRODUCTION

What is emotion?

Emotions are normally a response to environmental events and are goal directed. An emotional response is seen as being contingent upon
some form of appraisal of the environment and is
influenced by an internal goal; it is often associated with intense feelings. These feelings are
accompanied by expressions of positive or negative affect (see Lazarus, 1991). *Affect* is a term
used to describe both these reported internal feelings combined with the external manifestations
that are associated with specific feelings, e.g.
laughter, fearful appearance, envious looks. *Mood*
describes an enduring emotional state that is part
of the temporary disposition of an individual.
These are descriptive definitions and it should be
noted that there are patients who have the
external affect without the associated feelings.
These disorders of pathological crying and laughter, which are discussed later in the chapter, illustrate that it may be possible to distinguish
between *internal affect*, the subjective feelings
reported, versus the *external affect*, relating to the
outward, behavioural expression of the emotional state. Also, while emotions are usually
goal-directed and a reaction to environmental

events, they may also be spontaneously evoked
during electrical brain stimulation either through
artificial means or during an epileptic seizure.
Therefore a distinction between *reactive*
(neurophysiologically stimulated affect) and
spontaneous affect may also be made.

Human emotions may be studied by using a
number of techniques. Unlike other species, the
report of emotional behaviour according to the
subject or an observer of the subject through a
questionnaire may be used. Also, behavioural
measures such as a rated observation of categorised facial expressions may be used. Alternatively,
measures of psychophysiological changes in
arousal, such as heart rate or electrical brain
activity (using EEG), allow the monitoring of
arousal levels during the presentation of an
emotionally arousing stimulus. However, all of
these measures are to some extent uncertain.
Behavioural and psychophysiological measures
are ambiguous since they may be associated with
more than one state of arousal. Also, subjective
reports are sometimes unreliable, especially in the
clinical arena when patients may wish for more or
less sympathy. Also, some observers may not be
impartial. These problems of measurement contribute to the challenges in researching the nature
and mechanisms underlying emotional behaviour.

Difficulties in defining and researching

emotions are also met when surveying the non-human research on which much of our neuro-anatomical understanding of emotion is based. Non-human studies of emotion have tended to focus on emotions such as fear, if only because they are more clearly identified by behavioural responses, e.g. freezing behaviour. Variations between species in both the relative size of brain structures and differences in the adaptive significance of emotional behaviours place limitations on generalisation of these findings to the neuro-psychology of human emotion. Nevertheless these studies of other species are nevertheless, essential, since human research enjoys far less opportunity for controlled and systematic lesion studies.

While it may be argued that research into humans allows closer contact with the area of interest, conceptually this area has its own prob-lems. Although research into emotional and social difficulties following brain damage is a worthy topic of research, if only because it is so commonly reported, there remain difficulties in determining the extent of environmental influ-ences from organic influences (Andrewes, Hor-dern, & Kaye, 1998). These two factors cannot be separated but it is possible to reveal the relative importance of their contribution. Some of the earliest studies of emotion in animals and man have shown how this is possible. These early stud-ies clearly illustrate that emotional dysfunction is contributed to by a neurobiological factor.

The emergence of the emotional brain

In his classic work *The expression of the emotions in man and animals* Charles Darwin in 1872 (republished 1967) asserts that emotions are inherited as a behavioural pattern of each species and have particular survival value. For example, for humans and other primates the expression of surprise or fear is accompanied by the raising of the eyebrows and eye widening, which may help to increase visual acuity. In rage, species often bare their teeth, which may help in the prepar-ation for biting. The human species has a wide variation in expressed emotion that has obvious value in communication in social situations. We cry, blush and laugh for reasons that have signifi-cance for the way we interact and manipulate one another in social situations. There is evidence of culturally based learning of emotional expres-sion, which is discussed below. Nevertheless, the view that these emotions have a biological foun-dation and by implication some evolutionary sig-nificance is encouraged by the finding that certain emotions such as anger, fear, disgust, surprise and happiness are recognised by subjects, irrespective of the culture in which they live (Ekman & Friesen, 1971). Also congenitally deaf and blind children may express these emotions appropriately, even when there is no obvious way they could have learned these responses (Goodenough, 1932).

It appears that we are predisposed to produce and recognise well-defined emotional subtypes. This allows the idea that certain brain areas and/or biochemical brain systems are devoted to these processes. A broad description of such areas may be gleaned from models devoted to phylogenic evolution. From the macro-evolutionary perspec-tive, where the progression from reptiles to mammals is considered, emotions may be seen as developing further sophistication and complexity as evolution progresses. MacLean (1993) argues for a broad model describing the phylogenic evo-lution of brain structure from the reptilian brain to the modern neomammalian brain. This model depicts the modern human brain as possessing some of the characteristics of pre-species devel-opment. In other words the model (see Figure 9.1) proposes that the effect of evolution on the brain is one of modification rather than replace-ment; the new model is a combination of the old model with additions that modify the old parts. MacLean accounts for the association of emo-tional expression with certain deep areas of the brain that were developed at an earlier stage; this area was referred to by MacLean as the limbic system. This, with other theories, provides that the human brain has evolutionarily older areas relating to the reptilian brain that have been fur-ther developed in the paleomammalian era, with the final stage of development taking place in the neomammalian stage. The reptilian brain function is predicted from the behaviour of modern-day lizards, which, for example, includes

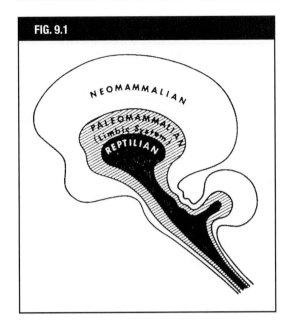

FIG. 9.1

MacLean's (1993) model, illustrating a symbolic evolution of the three main neural assemblies leading to the forebrain of advanced mammals. The progression is from the reptilian brain to that of early mammals and finally to late mammals (reprinted from MacLean, 1993, with permission from Guilford Press).

preparation and establishment of a home site, defence of territory and other basic activities. Further development of this brain blueprint allows for behaviours not evidenced in reptiles; these include nurturing and child-caring attributes, vocal signalling and play, with its associated emotional development The model allows that there is an intermediate development of the brain structures associated with the development of emotional behaviour within the paleomammalian stage that is modulated and controlled eventually by the later development of the neocortex in the final neomammilian stage of evolutionary development.

MacLean's proposal of cortical control of a more primitive emotional system reflects some of the earliest experimental work contributing to a neuropsychological understanding of emotion. Early studies in the 1920s by such researchers as Cannon and Bard (Cannon, 1927) provided evidence that cats deprived of their neocortex would make sudden and inappropriate displays of rage, illustrating the importance of neocortical control and guidance. Walter Cannon used these results as part of a refutation of the James–Lange theory of emotion (see Box 9.1).

These studies by Cannon preceded those of Hess, who demonstrated that brain areas such as the hypothalamus could be electrically stimulated by the use of electrodes, producing similar results to decortication. On stimulation Hess's cats would spit and hiss in response to any immediately available stimuli, although an actual attack was often restrained. In addition to these demonstrations of behaviours, referred to as "sham rage", more recent studies have found that a number of brain sites may produce aggression, but more sites have been found to inhibit aggression during electrical stimulation (Slegal & Edinger, 1983). Some structures, like the basomedial amygdala, lateral prefrontal cortex and septal area, may inhibit aggression within a circuit that is modulated by neurotransmitter systems such as dopamine (Shalkh, Lu, MacGregor, & Siegal, 1991).

The behavioural response is also dependent on environmental demands. From this perspective an emotional circuit may be serving behaviours of different types, e.g. fear, aggression, depending on the area of stimulation and the environmental stimuli, e.g. threat, food (Valenstein, Cox, & Kakolewski, 1970). The structure or combination of structures that are eventually activated depends on the environmental requirements placed on the organism.

Glickman and Schiff (1967) proposed that there were two main sites of stimulation: those which elicited an approach response and those which elicited withdrawal. These responses were manifested in terms of species-typical response, so that an approach behaviour for carnivores may be seen as an attack, whereas a "fear" response in the same animal would be seen as a withdrawal response. However, a herbivore, such as a mouse, may have a different repertoire of approach–avoidance responses. Other difficulties relating to the interpretation of these studies concern the effect of electrical stimulation. At one level it might be interpreted as stimulation but more

---

Box 9.1.

The James–Lange theory of emotion proposed that emotions were the product of self-observed physical or bodily reactions to a stimulus. For example, we may note that we are trembling and accordingly become afraid. This model would seem to be rather counterintuitive since, as critiques pointed out at the time, sometimes emotional feelings precede physical response and some observable bodily changes are not specific to a particular emotion. We may tremble with rage as well as fear or even when we are just plain cold.

Studies by Walter Cannon (1927) and colleagues at the time disputed the James–Lange theory, with the observation that after transections of the cervical spinal cord people still experienced emotions. However, there is some support for a version of this theory, since our feelings may be influenced by cognitive interpretations of our physical or bodily response, especially when we are persuaded towards a particular interpretation of physical responses that are ambiguous and difficult to explain. For example, the Singer–Schachter attribution theory of emotion was derived from an experiment which found that subjects may be led towards reporting particular emotional feelings that are being demonstrated by a confederate of the experimenter. However, this is dependent on the subject experiencing arousal that is not easily explained by other causes. In this case the subject had been given adrenaline, but was misled into believing that it was a vitamin injection (Schachter & Singer, 1962). While there is psychological evidence and some neurological support for a weak form of the James–Lange feedback theory, Cannon seems to be generally correct in his criticism.

Walter Cannon's and his colleagues' found that emotions could be evoked even after the removal of the neocortex, demonstrated the origin of emotions in terms of brain mechanisms. However, modern formulations of emotions allow that an emotional response follows on from cognitive appraisal (e.g. Lazarus, 1966). For example, a stimulus is analysed and perceived as a threat and an emotional response eventuates to cope with that threat. Both cognitive appraisal and the emotional response are controlled by brain mechanisms that are important to our survival.

---

obviously the effects are a long way from this Frankenstein image and more likely result in temporarily ablating the area of electrical stimulation.

While interpretation of the early decortication and the stimulation studies may be controversial in their modern interpretation, they provided evidence of structures beneath the cortex that are specialised in the production of emotions. MacLean's evolutionary model provides a model whereby higher cortical areas are seen as controlling these more "primitive" emotional centres—a model that has many implications both for neuropsychology and psychotherapy. The model suggests that when cortical control is reduced, emotional responses will be less restrained and less appropriately displayed. In the clinical neurological setting reduced control may be associated with brain injury to the cortex, which may be further aggravated by drug effects. For this reason patients with brain damage often have an exaggerated response to the cortical depressant effects of alcohol, for example. Accordingly many patients following traumatic brain injury may be warned by their clinicians about the need for redefining their level of alcohol intake.

The limbic system and emotion circuits

While some early stimulation studies may have favoured a broad division of circuits that were either approach or withdrawal oriented and some of the later studies stressed an interaction between environment and brain, cases of epileptic patients suggest that this description is not inevitable. Studies of humans who suffer particular epileptic syndromes such as temporal lobe epilepsy suggest modules exist that produce *specific* evoked emotions which are not necessarily dependent on interaction with environmental demands. Epileptic seizures may be associated with isolated behaviours associated with emotions such as laughter, intense feelings of pleasure, fear, or aggression. These responses may be isolated to a single emotion that is highly consistent and invariable in a particular patient. On occasions such patients may report the feelings associated with that emotion in the early "aura" stages just prior to a seizure. Also, some drugs have been found to have highly specific effects on emotions. For example, the drug cholecystokinin (CCK) has produced reliable fear responses that are similar to panic attacks (Bradwejn, 1993; Harro, Vasar, & Bradwejn, 1993). These attacks have also been related to limbic system activation according to radiological studies. More specifically, this neuropeptide (hormone) is secreted and possibly mediated by the amygdala. These studies do not deny the importance of interaction with the environment, but there is nevertheless the implied support for specific *emotional modules* that may refer to a particular emotion functioning within an emotional system.

MacLean originally described the limbic system as a series of communicating subcortical nuclei (see MacLean, 1993). Based on the writings of Papez (1937), MacLean included in this circuit the hypothalamus, anterior thalamus, cingulate gyrus and hippocampus. MacLean added to this "Papez circuit" several additional structures, including the amygdala, septal nuclei, orbitofrontal cortex and portions of the basal ganglia. However, LeDoux and others (LeDoux, 1993; Rolls, 1994) argue that this limbic system, although influential, has become superseded. A more modern view according to LeDoux allows that while the hippocampus may be important in the retrieval of emotionally related experience (Gray, 1995), in the human, it is more obviously associated with memory (see Chapter 5) rather than emotion per se. LeDoux cites the amygdala as being most consistently associated with emotion and describes a model in which the amygdala is a central processor of emotion. The other structures referred to within MacLean's limbic system also play important roles but they are seen by LeDoux as supporting roles.

THE EMOTIONAL SYSTEM

The amygdala: the central processor of the emotional system

The early studies
The amygdala is named after the Greek word for almond, which could be said to approximate its shape. It is justified in its position as the centre for emotional analysis by a large body of animal research (e.g. LeDoux, 1993, 1995). The amygdala lies within the medial aspect of the temporal lobe and is recognised for its role in analysing the emotional significance of information. Its amorphus structure has sparked a recent controversy as to whether it is a single structure rather than many structures, and some of the different roles of these structures will be identified.

One of the early studies, which highlighted the amygdala's role in social and emotional behaviour, was conducted by Heinrich Kluver and Paul Bucy (Kluver & Bucy, 1939). These researchers operated on wild monkeys and found that when these animals were given bilateral lesions to the anterior/inferior temporal lobe, which included the amygdala, there resulted some remarkable changes in behaviour. In the laboratory, these monkeys lost much of their aggression and also their fear of humans. Immediately after surgery they became docile, without much facial expression. There were also some features that further suggested some difficulty in recognition of the social significance of features around them. The monkeys became indiscriminate in their sexual habits and tended to mount males or females, or even inanimate objects. There were also signs of visual agnosia: there was increased exploration of objects with the mouth and eating of materials not previously ingested. The few human cases of similar gross bilateral destruction of the temporal lobes have performed in a similar manner (Marlowe, Mancall, & Thomas, 1975, pp. 55–75). Therefore it is thought that the full syndrome is realised with a bilateral, anterior and inferior lesion. With today's evidence of cases of semantic dementia (see Chapter 5 it is likely that the temporal lobe cortical lesions are, at least to some degree, to blame for this apparent agnosia for objects and lack of appreciation of social mores seen in monkeys and human subjects. Later, when more controlled experiments were performed, discrete bilateral lesions to the amygdala were found to be essential for the passive–tame emotional changes in this syndrome (Weiskrantz, 1956).

Kling, Lancaster, and Benitone (1970) went to Zambia and studied the effect of bilateral amygdalectomy on monkeys that were later released back into their troupe post surgery. Much of the oral exploration and other agnosic signs were less prominent, which might be expected since the temporal lobe cortex was not severely lesioned. The poor social skills evident in Kluver and Bucy animals remained. They observed a failure to pick up on social cues important to the social hierarchy and interpersonal relationships between monkeys, which meant that they were quickly socially isolated and were dead within several weeks. In contrast, monkey's with *dorsolateral frontal lesions*, although handicapped, survived, retaining their social bonds. It is understood that a major contributor to the social failure of the amygdalectomised monkeys relates to their *lack of response* to socially significant cues (Kling & Brothers, 1992).

Perceptual processing of emotionally and socially relevant facial stimuli

Emotional response in our daily lives is almost always preceded by some form of appraisal and this has been a crucial component of emotional frameworks since the early work of Arnold Lazarus in the 1960s. Lazarus showed films of emotionally arousing incidents such as the events leading up to a sawmill accident. He found that according to psychophysiological arousal (sweating as measured by galvanic skill response) it was the *anticipation* of the gruesome event, rather than viewing the accident itself, that caused most arousal in the subjects. Of course, the producers of Hollywood horror movies use this mechanism in order to build up suspense to an unbearable degree. It is therefore what we think and believe which alters emotion. For example, a person might be standing on a bus when he or she feels something prodding them from behind. We instantly become angry when we see that a rude man is doing this with a walking stick. However, anger turns to sympathy when we realise the man is blind. The event has not changed, it is only our appraisal of the situation that has altered our emotional reaction.

How we appraise events is therefore a very important predictor of how we react to them (see Figure 9.2). While modern issues have replaced the discussion of this early perspective (e.g. Lazarus, 1991), this simple model remains the basis of many cognitive behavioural psychotherapies that try to change the way we interpret arousing events in our lives in order to reduce depression or anxiety.

The amygdala is just one unit within a system which is dedicated to appraising emotion stimuli. While the work with non-human subjects illustrates the significance of the amygdala in processing emotional information, isolated bilateral damage to these structures is rare in humans. There are, however, a few studies that have similarly shown that damage to the amygdala may impair the judgement of socially significant facially significant facial expression. Young and colleagues report a single case study of a woman, DR, who had bilateral partial amygdalotomy who was poor at recognising and matching faces with emotional expression and had difficulty in recognising social facial signals (Young et al., 1995). This kind of result has been replicated by other studies (Adolphs, Tranel, Damasio, & Damasio, 1995). Also, PET studies of normal subjects have confirmed this involvement of the amygdala in emotional perception. Using PET, Morris et al. (1996) found the left amygdala showed more activation when pictures of fearful faces were shown, whereas the right was more sensitive to happy faces, the happiest face evoking the least activation. There are a number of other studies of normal subjects that have noted the

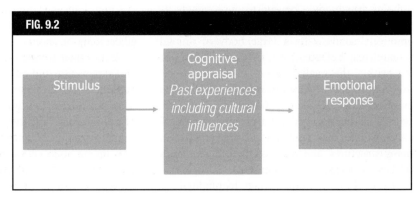

FIG. 9.2

Basic model, illustrating the interdependence between cognitive appraisal and emotional response.

Stimulus → Cognitive appraisal *Past experiences including cultural influences* → Emotional response

activation of the amygdala during PET scans when subjects are confronted with negative faces, e.g. mutilated faces. Later, when conditioned emotional response is discussed, it is argued that the right amygdala may be more specialised for processing the unconscious emotional processing (Morris, Ohman, & Dolan, 1999).

A question that remains of interest is whether our appraisal of emotion can influence our personality. Tranel and Hyman (1990) provide one of the first reported case studies of isolated bilateral destruction of the amygdala where personality of the patient is briefly discussed. The unusual lesions were associated with Urbach–Wiethe, a rare genetic disease. The patient came to the clinic with a "history of personal and social inadequacy" (Damasio, 1994). In terms of the patient's personality the report mainly discusses the nature of the patient's interactions during testing. These were described as inappropriately familiar: the patient was coquettish and was prone to make sexual innuendoes. More recently, Adolphs, Tranel, and Damasio (1998) report a further study that used this patient again. The study examined an unusual topic. The question was asked, could this patient (SM), and two other patients also with isolated bilateral amygdala damage, judge the approachability and trustworthiness of persons given photographs of the faces compared to verbal descriptions? The patients responded normally to the verbal descriptions of characteristics associated with untrustworthiness, but were significantly impaired compared to controls on judging the photographs.

Generally, the patients made the mistake of missing the negative characteristics of these faces, rating them far more positively. It is of interest that patient SM, who is referred to above in the Tranel and Hyman (1990) study, spontaneously commented that in real life she would not know how to judge if a person were trustworthy. This was apparently consistent with her tendency to engage in unsuitable relationships (Adolphs et al., 1998, p. 417). This group has completed a further recent study to confirm that these patients are able to judge faces for positive affect but not for negative affect, e.g. hostile, aggressive. This and

other studies suggest that the amygdala may be particularly important for registering fear or fear-related emotions (Adolphs et al., 1999). This is not related to the perception of the physical features of the faces but seems to be related to the visual features of emotion since they adequately detect prosody in speech. It is of interest that Geschwind, when commenting on the Kluver and Bucy experiments, notes that although tame to visual stimuli, they would become excited and angry when their chains were pulled, as if access to aggression within another sensory modality was still intact (Geschwind, 1965).

In conclusion, the amygdala is important for evaluating facial cues that have negative social significance. Indeed animal research has found groups of cells within the amygdala that are sensitive to specific facial features (Leonard, Rolls, Wilson, & Baylis, 1985). However, the role of the amygdala is extended beyond this area.

Personality, mood and the amygdala

So far a reasonable argument has been made for the amygdala in the perceptual processing of emotion of faces. This in itself could be seen as an explanation for some of the personality changes seen in the monkey experiments. Is there evidence to support changes in emotional expression that are not obviously related to perceptual analysis?

The clearest support for the amygdala as an agent of personality comes from animal research showing that a lesion to the *central* amygdala results in tameness and that a chemical stimulation of the same area results in behavioural signs of fear and aggression (Davis, 1992). Some suggestion that this type of result may also apply to humans comes from the literature on psychosurgery, which has been devoted to reducing unwanted aggression in patients and in some cases prisoners. Powell (1979) reviews a series of psychosurgery studies that have reportedly shown a reduction of behavioural disorder and aggression in patients who have undergone amygdalectomy or amygdalotomy (see also Ramamurthi, 1988). For the most part these studies suggest that these patients become more calm, obedient, and controllable. Unlike the effects of frontal lobotomy and leucotomy these patients are not reported to show a lack of interest or disinhibited social difficulties described below. However, salutary points are noted by Powell (1979); the patients that were chosen for surgery in many of these studies were largely mentally subnormal and secondly there are problems with design and outcome measures used in this area. These studies are described as crude and inadequate without long-term follow-up. Also, because of the poverty of measures used, other possible negative effects of amygdalectomy (resection including disconnection), such as increased anxiety and depression, are generally not assessed (Powell, 1979, pp. 4–55). Finally, there is uncertainty concerning the mechanism of the increased calmness of the patient. If it is a placidity born of a failure to evaluate social cues then although these patients might be more easy to manage this might be at a general cost to the quality of their other social interactions. It should also be mentioned that the earliest experiments of Kluver, Bucy, Kling, and colleagues found a reduction but not a complete absence of emotional expression in their monkeys. Thus in the face of an extreme social reaction by another, such as rage, the monkey would retreat or defend itself. The threshold for such reaction was therefore raised rather than removed. A recent study of the effect of stereotactic amygdalotomy (isolated destruction) as a means of reducing aggression found a reduction but not an elimination of aggressive response. These authors also consider the possibility that this might merely be due to a reduced capability in the subject's ability to process facial cues that are likely to elicit emotional response (Lee et al., 1998).

Support for the amygdala as a possible generator of emotional expression comes from studies of patients with temporal lobe epilepsy. In the case of temporal lobe epilepsy seizures involve a number of structures within the limbic system. Also, it might be difficult to determine whether such endogenous electrical stimulation acts to ablate or stimulate. However, if we are to accept that bilateral removal of the amygdalae causes placidity and a lack of fear, then stimulation might have the opposite effect, as in the case of the animal experiment reported above. There is some evidence to suggest that epilepsy patients report feeling fear and apprehension when the amygdala is stimulated (Vaernet & Marsden, 1970). Also, fear is the most commonly reported emotion with temporal lobe epilepsy, and the amygdala is often implicated in the diagnosis of such cases (Strauss, Risser, & Jones, 1982).

Models of the amygdala as a central processor of emotion

When natural selection was modelling the nature of our abilities, the fear response would have been a frequent, not to say useful response. Today, we have plenty of depression and anxiety, but not much old-fashioned fear. However, we seem to make up for this unnatural scarcity through our nightmares and by our predilection for horror movies. Therefore although fear-provoking non-human experiments may seem to be less meaningful for the modem urban dweller, fear may remain a useful focus of research into the neuropsychology of emotion in human and non-human subjects.

In keeping with this view Joseph LeDoux (1995, 2000) has produced a detailed model of the neural mechanisms of the fear response. This has led to the isolation of the amygdala structures as being the most significant in the application of emotional significance to a stimulus. LeDoux provides evidence from his own laboratory and the research of others, describing the amygdala as being responsible for the processing and production of the fear response, including the triggering of increase in autonomic activity that allows the adaptive expression of "freezing", "flight", or "fight" responses.

The amygdala is divided into a series of nuclei, each area with its specific role, in much the same way as the thalamus is divided into specialised areas. LeDoux's model proposes that the lateral amygdala receives and integrates the sensory information provided by the cortex and thalamus and other brain areas. This information is then converted into action by projecting this information onto the central amygdala, which initiates the emotional response (LeDoux, 1995; LeDoux & Muller, 1997).

When considering the *direct* sensory/perceptual

inputs, the amygdala does not differentiate between the modality of the input. According to LeDoux's model (LeDoux, 1995) the lateral amygdala receives three main sources of input: (1) from the medial nucleus of the thalamus; (2) from the inferior colliculus; and (3) from the polymodal association cortex. The model allows inputs from the thalamus and inferior colliculus and the later stages of perceptual analysis. These projections would allow on-line orientation towards the feared stimuli. The afferents (inputs) into the amygdala from the association areas (also olfactory) allow fully analysed information from all the sensory modalities. According to animal research the first two inputs (thalamus and inferior colliculus) described above are essential for conditioning to occur, while the third is important for discrimination between conditioned and non-conditioned stimuli. All three inputs allow for the appropriate external stimuli to be registered; the central amygdala in some way labels these identified stimuli with the fear emotion and initiates certain physiological mechanisms that give rise to the fear behaviour. It is when the central amygdala is lesioned that the tameness of the animal becomes apparent. The animal becomes easier to handle and their blood levels of stress hormones are lower (Davis, 1992).

Finally, something should be said about how projections from nuclei in the amygdalae are seen to activate a second unit, which provides the emotional response. This consists of the hypothalamus, which influences much of the biochemical processes associated with an emotional reaction. To achieve this the hypothalamus has connections with the pituitary gland, which produces hormones necessary for initiating the autonomic activity associated with the autonomic response (e.g. fight, flight, preparation). These hormones in turn activate the adrenal glands (in the medulla of the brain stem), which release catecholamines, such as adrenaline and noradrenaline which stimulate physiological reactions. The exact nature of this autonomic response is beyond the scope of this text, but such reactions as pupil dilation, sweating, increased heart rate, blood pressure, and breathing rate are some examples of such a fight or flight response which

is originally initiated by the central amygdala. Also, pathways within the brain stem execute other emotionally associated behavioural responses, e.g. laughter, crying. In this system the amygdala is seen as a modulator of the emotional response (LeDoux, 1993).

The animal research on the function of the amygdala reflects, in an interesting way, on psychiatric manifestations related to anxiety. For example, there are high concentrations of opiate/benzodiazepine receptors within the amygdaloid complex and it is likely that anti-anxiety medication such as benzodiazepines have their effect on the basolateral amygdala, which projects to the central amygdala (Sanders & Shekhar, 1995), although there are other areas which are also affected by benzodiazepines.

A structure that has received less recent research focus is the septum. The septum receives projections from the orbitofrontal cortex and connects with the thalamus (Gloor, 1986) and may act to inhibit the amygdala. As indicated above, lesions to the amygdala may increase placidity in an animal; however, septal lesions may increase rage. Carlson (1977) reports the lowering of rage threshold in animals with septal lesions and describes an incident he witnessed as an undergraduate, when a "septal" rat chased two laboratory technicians around the animal room (Carlson, 1977, p. 451). The inhibitory role of the septum may be revealed in the hyperemotional state of the animal when this structure is lesioned. The response varies with the species; a mouse, for example, with the same lesion will show excessive fear and escape (Carlson, 1977). Studies since this time have generally interpreted the aggression following septal lesions as being related to a defence response that is most obviously due to increased anxiety. This response may be manipulated in rats by the injection of nicotinic agonists and antagonists in a structure that is responsive to cholinergic influence (e.g. Ouagazzal, Kenny, & File, 1999).

LeDoux's model illustrates the amygdala's capacity to influence an emotional response (see Figure 9.3). Later in this chapter two other important influences on the amygdala will be discussed from a broad perspective. The first relates to the many projections between the amygdala

FIG. 9.3

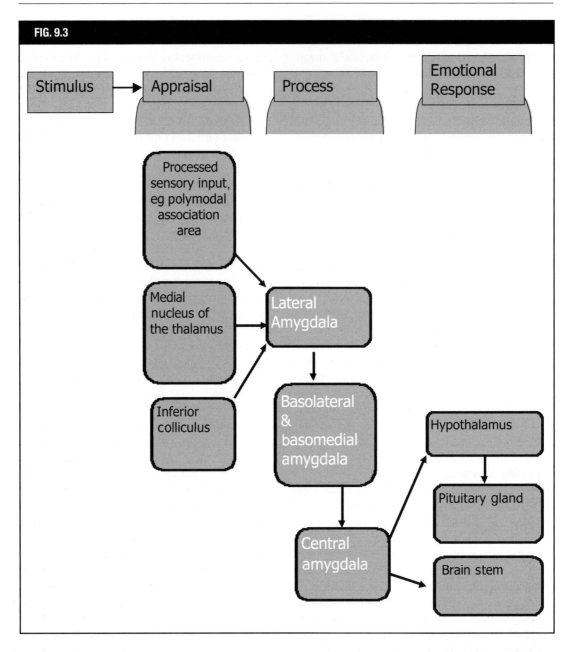

Sensory inputs and outputs of the nuclei of the amygdala (adapted from LeDoux, 1995). In terms of the original model it is possible to see the structures to the left as appraising the stimulus—an orientation response to a possibly threatening stimulus involving the inferior colliculus with its connections to the superior colliculus. The polysensory areas will then be able to complete the perceptual analysis required to appraise the stimulus. This appraisal is followed by the amygdala producing the emotional response and the activation of an emotional response through the triggering of an autonomic response via the hypothalamus. The various parts of the diagram are placed within the framework of Figure 9.2.

and the hippocampus which allow an emotional context to be attached to a memory. The second relates to the apparent influence of the orbito-frontal cortex on the amygdala in controlling emotional behaviour and the association of rewards with particular behaviours.

Finally, it is important to see the amygdala as the hub of an integrated system. An indication that it plays a central role is supported by its apparent influence on a number of different emotional behaviours, e.g. emotional face, emotional associations of conditioning, and contextual memory; this central role is also confirmed by the effect of disconnection of other related structures from the amygdala; also, the similarity of these disconnection behaviours to those following bilateral lesions to closely related structures such as the anterior temporal cortex and the dorsomedial nuclei of the thalamus (Horel, Keating, & Misantone 1975; Muller, Baumgartner, Rohrenbach, & Regard, 1999).

In summary, the amygdala is described as a central processor of emotionally relevant stimuli. There is input to the amygdala from both attentional (thalamus) and perceptual identification (anterior, inferior temporal lobe), which may allow for the identification of conditioned and other learned emotional response (through close connections with the hippocampus and orbitofrontal cortex). Also, it is hypothesised that input from past memory stores (temporal lobe) will influence the judgement of the appropriateness of the emotional response. The output structures of the amygdala are hypothesised to activate the various autonomic and behavioural manifestations of the emotional response (see Figure 9.3).

It should be said that the generalised emotional processing role proposed by LeDoux and others is based on non-human animal studies and is yet to be confirmed in humans. From the human evidence the small but persistent evidence paints a picture of a more restricted role. According to this literature, the amygdala is specialised in the learning and evaluation of the associated social and emotional connotations of visually presented faces although such a limitation is probably largely limited by the type of experiment that is commonly conducted.

Nevertheless the amygdala is well placed to influence the production of emotional behaviour via other structures such as the hypothalamus and the brain stem. Some of the author's own work, which is reviewed in this chapter, does implicate the amygdala and its associated structures as being important in the production and modulation of emotional *behaviour*. This has been shown in studies using patients with unilateral temporal lobectomy, which includes the removal of the amygdala on one side; some of the author's own work in this area will be discussed when reviewing the clinical effect of lesions. It is also clear from the early experiments by Kluver and Bucy, Kling and colleagues, and some rather unreliable psychosurgery data that bilateral amygdalectomy or amygdalotomy does not remove emotional expression entirely, but it may reduce or neutralise an emotional response. Research with humans in this area is still at an embryonic stage.

The perception and communication of emotion

The perception and appraisal of emotion
In our initial simple model of emotional appraisal (Figure 9.2) there is the assumption that emotional stimulus is cognitively appraised. The emotional stimulus within the environment must first be perceived and analysed. The happy facial features of a person or the sad expression of the voice are initially analysed by their perceptual features. We have already discussed the role of the amygdala in the perception of emotional and socially relevant features of faces. However, there is a large literature which implicates other cortical and subcortical structures, which are predominantly in the right hemisphere and which also appear to process such information. At this stage it is important to make the distinction between the intellectual appraisal of emotion, e.g. recognition that a face is angry without any emotional reaction to the face, and the emotional appraisal of emotional stimuli, e.g. fearful appraisal of an angry face. It is possible that the amygdala is involved with both of these types of processing, while the literature looking at the intellectual

analysis of emotional labelling may be dependent on more cortically based analysis (Borod, Haywood, & Koff, 1997; Heilman & Gilmore, 1998). It is assumed that the polymodal association areas play some significant part in this role. The apparent specialisation of the right hemisphere in the perception and communication of emotional significance is one of the more thoroughly investigated issues in the neuropsychological emotional literature.

A large amount of research has been devoted to the analysis of emotional faces as the material of investigation. A comprehensive study by Bowers, Bauer, Coslett, and Heilman (1985) looked at seven tasks using this material. The left- and right-hemisphere stroke patients in this study were equated for visuospatial ability on other tasks, and an impairment in the performance of the right-hemisphere lesioned group on three of the tasks was found, which appeared to be measuring the categorising of facial emotional emotions. Other studies have confirmed these findings (e.g. Blonder et al., 1991; Borod, Koff, Perlman-Lorch, & Nicholas, 1986; Cicone, Wagner, & Gardener, 1980). There are also the findings with split-brain patients referred to in Chapter 6, which suggest that the right hemisphere is capable of emotional analysis without verbal mediation.

The specialisation of the intact right hemisphere is illustrated in a number of studies with normals, which have found that the left visual tachistoscopic presentation of emotional faces (to the right hemisphere) is responded to at a faster rate and more accurately when compared to a right visual field presentation (e.g. Suberi & McKeever, 1977). A study by Benowitz et al. (1983) found that a split-brain subject was able to identify filmed facial expressions when they were projected to the right hemisphere but had difficulty when they were presented to the left. However, Stone and colleagues found little right hemisphere advantage in a task that required matching photographs of emotional faces. This was especially the case when the subject was given a strategy of labelling the emotions during the left hemisphere presentations (Stone, Nisenson, Eliassen, & Gazzaniga, 1996). Therefore there may

be some compensation by the left hemisphere's ability to decode classic emotional expressions into verbal labels.

There is also evidence that patients with right hemisphere damage judge emotional expressions to be less intense (e.g. Christman & Hackworth, 1993). Thus if patients are shown a face that registers an emotion and unbeknown to the subject it is made up of two mirror images, the right hemisphere-damaged patients will tend to rate the left half (going to the right side of the right retina and onto the same-sided hemisphere) as being less emotional.

There may also be a lateralisation of the amygdala with the right amygdala more sensitive to the unconscious rapid emotional response associated with classical conditioning. In a paradigm in which a negative, e.g. mutilated, face is shown briefly followed by a neutral mask, the subject will report that they have seen nothing. However, they will often show a skin conductance (arousal) response that indicates some form of subliminal perception has taken place. Also during such presentations the right amygdala is often more activated than the left (Morris, Ohman, & Dolan, 1998). These last findings are in keeping with a model by LeDoux and Muller (1997) proposing that the analysis of threatening information may be processed at high speed prior to conscious awareness. This more direct route, in which the sensory information via the thalamus (pulvinar in the case of visual and the medial thalamus in the case of the auditory stimulus) directly activates the amygdala, is fast but lacks full definitive cognitive appraisal. In contrast, with the second slower, more indirect route, the amygdala is activated only after perceptual cortical analysis has taken place within the "what" pathway. This model appeals to the need for a fast input when a stimulus may be briefly appraised as being dangerous. Natural selection has provided us with a mechanism that allows us to react immediately in the situation where if you know what it is, it's too late. The right amygdala may be more reactive to such unconscious assessment of fear-related stimuli, (Morris, Ohman, & Dolan, 1998). Also, the evidence from patients with "blindsight" and imaging studies implicates this more *direct* route

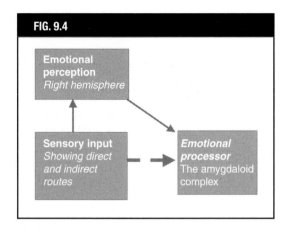

FIG. 9.4

Emotional
perception
Right hemisphere

Sensory input
*Showing direct
and indirect
routes*

*Emotional
processor*
The amygdaloid
complex

A rudimentary model illustrating two inputs one direct route (dotted arrow) and one indirect route via a right hemisphere based cortical system. The direct route possibly involves an input via the inferior colliculus and/or the thalamic connections (see Figure 9.3). This fast access route without detailed analysis, which may have survival implications when a threatening stimulus must be processed. The second, more indirect, route allows more detailed conscious appraisal of the stimulus but has the disadvantage of slower processing time. The right hemisphere analysis of emotion (emotional perception) illustrates a strength within that domain rather than the sole region of analysis.

from the retina, to the superior colliculus to the pulvinar of the thalamus (see Chapter 4 for a description of this high-speed orienting system) (Morris et al., 1999) (see Figure 9.4).

Emotional messages within speech

As previously indicated (see the topic of prosody in Chapter 7), the emotional inflection of speech is obviously a vital aspect of communication. Patients with right hemisphere stroke have been found to have relative difficulty in perceiving the emotional tone in speech (e.g. Bowers et al., 1987). Blonder et al. (1991) found that the right hemisphere patients were impaired compared to the left hemisphere group in their ability to accurately discriminate and match the emotional tone. In this study neutral sentences, e.g. "The boy played football", were read with different emotional tones, e.g. sad, happy. In addition to the emotional tone or prosody of the voice there is also a meaningful content of speech, which may

signify the emotional content. The subjects of Blonder et al.'s (1991) study were also given sentences that conveyed emotion in the verbal content without the intonation, e.g. "Tears fell from her eyes"; the sentences were produced by a computer with a clear but neutral tone. Such sentences are slightly ambiguous since we may cry when we are laughing very hard. The right hemisphere damaged group were also impaired on this task. However, on a task that gave extra information regarding a situation, e.g. "You were delighted by the bonus", the right hemisphere damaged group showed no disadvantage. In the latter task the emotional content could be more likely inferred from the common situation involving the bonus and this extra information presumably allowed the right hemisphere damaged patients to compensate from knowledge stored in the opposite left hemisphere. But this result is rather open to interpretation. The description of the right hemisphere as being important for the comprehension of emotional communication must be tempered by the finding that apart from the cortical lesions many of these patients have subcortical lesions, especially within the basal ganglia area (e.g. Starkstein et al., 1994).

Apart from the apparent specialisation of the right hemisphere for the reception of emotional verbal communication, the right hemisphere may also be important in the expression of emotion within language. There is evidence that patients with right hemisphere damage communicate their emotions less efficiently (Borod et al., 1996). When asked to produce a story of a personal experience relating to each of seven negative or positive emotional categories, patients with right hemisphere stroke were rated as using less emotional content when compared to left hemisphere stroke patients. It is interesting that patients with aphasia associated with a left hemisphere lesion will improve in their speech if they use words with emotional significance (Bloom, Borod, Obler, & Gerstman, 1992), while right hemisphere-damaged patients tend to avoid the use of these words (Bloom, Borod, Obler, & Koff, 1990).

Apart from the emotional content or tone of speech the right hemisphere is also important for the facial expression of emotion. The lower left facial movements, which are controlled by the right hemisphere, are reportedly more expressive than other areas of the face (see Asthana & Mandal, 1997, for a thorough treatment of this issue). People recorded on video in a restaurant were seen to be more expressive on their left side, which is innervated by the right brain hemisphere (Moscovitch & Olds, 1982; see Borod et al., 1997, for a review). Other work makes an important distinction in terms of posed versus spontaneous facial expression, with only the latter being impaired in right brain-damaged patients (see Borod, 1992, for a review). A further differentiation may be made between cortical and subcortical influences on the expression of facial emotions. Damasio (1994, pp. 141–143) argues from work by Guillaume-Benjamin Duchenne in the mid-nineteenth century that for a smile to be natural looking there must be a contraction of two muscles of the zygomatic major, which allows the ends of the mouth to turn upwards, and the orbicularis muscle, which affects the musculature around the eyes. Duchenne argued that only the above-mentioned mouth muscles could produce a smile in a voluntary manner and these movements produced the "smiles of politeness". He proposed that for smiling the orbicularis (around the eyes) could only be moved in an involuntary manner making the genuine-looking smile difficult to manufacture. Damasio (1994) proposes that the orbicularis is controlled subcortically in the region of the cingulate, while the smiling mouth is more controlled by cortical mechanisms (e.g. motor strip). According to Damasio's clinical experience, the stroke patient with particular damage to the cortex may not be able to smile on command but be able to smile spontaneously when told a joke. In contrast, the patient with an appropriate subcortical lesion may only be able to produce a "pyramidal smile" (of politeness) on command, but fail to smile spontaneously. This is an interesting proposal and may explain why it is so difficult to produce a genuine-looking smile for a photograph; the muscles around the eyes will only complete the genuine smile response when they are activated spontaneously without control (subcortically). Modern air hostesses and stewards in the better airlines often manage to smile

frequently under conditions of great duress and these smiles are often difficult to distinguish from the genuine article. However, one suspects some considerable training is at work here.

At one time the lack of emotionality found in the Parkinson's disease patients was assumed to be exclusively due to their motor symptoms. For example, their mask-like facial appearance and the sometimes monotone voice were seen to be purely difficulties of executing the required facial movements. But studies of these patients have found both expressive and perceptive disorders additional to any motor influence. In the study by Blonder, Gur, & Gur (1989) no lateralisation effects were found between those patients with more right-sided signs of Parkinson's disease and those with left hemiparkinsonism. While this may be equivocal evidence one would certainly expect worse expression on the facial side more affected by motor symptoms if the impairment was motor based. The amygdala has reciprocal projections to the basal ganglia and therefore there is opportunity for the basal ganglia influence on facial expression and reception of emotion. In keeping with this view Cancelliere and Kertesz (1990) found that in addition to cortical lesions subcortical lesions (basal ganglia) were also associated with both expressive and receptive emotional prosodic impairments.

The work of Kolb and Milner (1981a) draws attention to the effect of frontal lesions on emotional perception and expression. They found that frontal lesions produced a lessening of emotional expression. Furthermore, work by Hornak, Rolls, and Wade (1996) found that patients with ventral frontal lesions were impaired in their ability to perceive emotional expressions and situations and it was these patients who tended to show the behavioural and socially embarrassing behaviour.

While right hemisphere-damaged patients may show more impairment in the perception and expression of emotions in situations of communication, compared with left hemisphere-damaged patients, some left hemisphere-damaged patients may also show these problems (Cancelliere & Kertesz, 1990). Most of the studies described above have used stroke patients who inevitably have both cortical and subcortical damage, and therefore do not help a great deal in specifying the underlying mechanism for these impairments. In some ways the findings appear to be not unlike those of unilateral neglect in that problems of emotional communication are associated with a variety of lesions within a hypothesised emotional system or network, although differences in the quality and/or the severity of the impairment may yet be found when comparing patients with different lesions.

This brief selective review has concentrated on positive results, which in the main have been replicated, but there are many disagreements and controversies within this area. This may be partly due to differences in methods of testing emotional judgement; whether, for example, posed or spontaneous material is being used, or the type of medium being used for presentation video or photos, or split visual field.

Some authors have sought to explain why the right hemisphere is dominant for the perception and expression of emotion as a means of communication. One argument runs that the right hemisphere is more differentiated and less compartmentalised when compared to the left. Thus it has been argued that left hemisphere lesions produce more discrete functional impairments when compared to focal lesions in the right hemisphere (Semmes, 1968). From a neurophysiological standpoint there are more neuronal interconnections within the right hemisphere compared to the left and more connections with paralimbic structures (Liotti & Tucker, 1995). Liotti and Tucker suggest that the less differentiated structure of the right hemisphere suits the analysis of complex material that requires analysis of internal relational structure rather than a recognition of parts (Burton, 1994). Thus the analysis of a smiling face is dependent on the relative position of the lips, the muscle movements around the eyes and no doubt a number of other cues that may be less consciously processed. All these different signals must come together at exactly the right time with the correct intensity of each component. This process of analysis during social communication is therefore complex and may lend itself to more holistic or gestalt processing. This complexity that defies the analysis of parts may be a special skill that suits the right hemisphere's analysis of non-verbal material such as face perception and the processing of subtle contextual elements within object identification (see also Chapter 2).

Finally, when considering the perception of emotions it must be conceded that a number of structures have been found to be involved. In this and previous sections we have described the amygdala, the right cortical influence and the apparent involvement of the basal ganglia, also discussed in the contribution of the orbitofrontal cortex, and this last influence will be discussed more comprehensively in the next section. While these structures may contribute to the process in subtly different ways it is probably important to think of a network response in which a series of structures contribute towards the final response.

The executive influence on emotion and the frontal lobes

A discourse on the influence of the frontal lobes on personality must first begin with a historical visit to the psychosurgery procedure of frontal lobotomy or leucotomy, which was most popular from the late 1930s through to the late 1950s. The term lobotomy refers to the more radical surgery involving the removal of the frontal lobes (almost vertical incision just anterior to the tip of the lateral ventricles). Leucotomy is often seen as a less severe surgery, which involves the severance of white matter, causing an often more discrete disconnection between the prefrontal cortex and other brain areas. The use of these terms has not been exact and has varied depending on the country, with lobotomy being the more popular term in North America and leucotomy being favoured in the United Kingdom (Walsh, 1987). Whatever the term used, early psychosurgical treatments of this nature included substantial resection of areas within the frontal lobe.

During the period in which the treatment was in its heyday, a very large number of operations were carried out by medical practitioners, often without any neurosurgical background, using relatively crude equipment. Jasper (1995) describes a typical operation in which the patient

---

Box 9.2. Signs of pseudo-depression

A 28-year-old male, GT, was the pillion passenger on a motor cycle. The driver of the bike decided that he would just make it under the descending boom at a railway crossing without warning his passenger. The bar hit GT, throwing him off the bike, rendering him unconscious. He was in a coma for 3 weeks and there was evidence of a haematoma (collection of blood) in the left frontal region on CT scan, which was evacuated, and there was also evidence of contusion to the frontal lobe. Prior to the accident the patient had worked satisfactorily for many years as a groundsman for the local council. Following the accident the patient eventually returned to work, but he was unable to maintain his employment. According to his notes, his foreman could not leave him unsupervised. The foreman would no sooner be out of sight than he would stop work. His wife reported that at home he had little conversation and would sit around doing nothing for most of the day. Prior to the accident he was known as a sociable person, "the life and soul of the party", but now people had stopped coming round because he was such poor company. He no longer made conversation and would only respond when directly asked a question. According to his wife, they had had no sexual relations since his accident and this was as much due to his lack of interest as it was to hers. She felt that he was a totally changed man and that up to that point (it was now 2 years since the accident) she had stayed with him out of duty, but she was not sure how long she could keep this up (she left him soon after). On interview GT clearly did not have insight into the extent to which his relationship was threatened or the way that he was reportedly behaving.

Box 9.3. Signs of pseudo-psychopathy

The author assessed a 23-year-old young man 3 years after a severe head injury who had lost his sense of smell as a result of his head-on collision. This is sometimes an indication of orbital damage, given the location of the olfactory bulbs. His level of intelligence was within the high average range and there were no dysexecutive signs on such tests as the controlled word association test, a maze-learning test (Milner pathway, Austin electronic maze) or Trails B. However, his history, radiological findings, and personality were clearly related to a history of severe head injury with over a month of post-traumatic amnesia. While he was popular prior to the accident he now had no friends. His parents confirmed suspicions that part of his problem was that he had no judgement when it was appropriate to relinquish an argument and that he would lose his temper far too easily. He had no girlfriend at the time of assessment but had become quickly engaged to a girl who he said "turned out to be a simpleton." He said bitterly that these were the only kinds of persons that could be bothered with him. During the interview he would fly into an angry tirade when touchy issues were discussed. When asked about his plans for the future he responded that he did not have a future any more, all he had was the present. He made it clear that any provident behaviour such as applying for a job was beyond him.

---

and dominergic with their origin in various brain stem nuclei. It is of interest that Drevets et al. (1997) have found significant reductions in volume of activation within this area, especially on the left side in patients with familial depression and bipolar affective disorder (manic depression). The implications are to confirm this area as major area for the regulation of emotion in both brain-damaged and psychiatric patients. In Box 9.2 there are some illustrative features of pseudo-depression from a case study.

This case illustrates the lack of drive and adynamia (inertia and lack of spontaneity) associated with the pseudo-depression type. Stuss, Gow, and Hetherington (1992) propose that pseudo-depression occurs most often in the context of lesions to the convexity of the dorsolateral cortex of the prefrontal lobe. Patients who alternate between pseudo-depression and pseudo-psychopathy may have lesions in both the ventral and the dorsal areas, but as Stuss and colleagues (1992, p. 354) suggest, this model must remain to be confirmed. Often patients may show features

of both personality types and there is sometimes no good relationship between the patients' measured cognitive deterioration and the personality of these patients (see Box 9.3). Saver and Damasio (1991) report the case of a patient whose only manifestation of impairment was severely disrupted social behaviour. Therefore, in this patient, also, performance on neuropsychological tests did not predict everyday behaviour. Interestingly, they found that with this and other patients there was an obvious rift between knowledge of required behaviour and the actual behaviour of the patient. Saver and Damasio found that this patient's knowledge of appropriate responses to social dilemmas and knowledge of social conduct was intact. There was a conflict, therefore, between knowledge and practice. Hornak et al. (1996) seem to support this view of knowledge not being congruent with behaviour, with a report that their ventral frontal patients when reminded of their behaviour looked back on their social gaffs with some distress. Hornak and colleagues propose that part of the problem, at least, was a deficit in the expression and/or perception of emotional behaviour. That is, their own emotional responses and the emotional responses of others were being poorly monitored at the time of the inappropriate behaviour.

A possible further cause of inappropriate social behaviour is an inability to register in advance the consequence of such behaviour. Bechara, Damasio, Damasio, and Anderson (1994) report a gambling game that was presented to both patients with frontal lesions and a control group. The subject was presented with four packs of cards referred to as A, B, C, and D. After each card was turned over the subject was given a pay-back of pretend money. Turning over cards in A or B pack resulted in better pay-back than C or D. However, on infrequent occasions turning over a card would receive a penalty. In this experimental game, the penalty was so large for cards from pack A and B that the best strategy was to stick with the lower pay-back packs of C and D. Typically, the control group would go from picking cards from A and B initially and then by the end of the session be using only packs C and D. The ventromedial frontal patients, in contrast, were more likely to be maintaining their choice for A and B, despite becoming bankrupt on a number of occasions. One frontal patient who was investigated further could remember many of his decisions and realised his error in retrospect, but at a later point repeated his earlier mistaken strategy in an identical way. Damasio and colleagues have extended the study by using skin conductance to measure emotional arousal physiologically. Both normals and frontals showed the same level of physiological response to the punishing and rewarding consequences of their pack choice (positive and negative) in this gambling game. However, differences arose as the game progressed: the normal group and the brain-damaged controls, but not the frontal patients, showed an increased tendency to sweat as they considered turning over a card from the potentially "bad" A or B packs. Not only did the frontals not show emotional signs of arousal in anticipation of a poor decision, but also they tended not to report a "hunch" that there might be something not quite right or dangerous about the bad A and B packs. Normals tended to go through a "hunch" stage in which there was some "gut feeling" that the A and B packs had problems, through to a "conceptual" stage when they were consciously aware that the A and B packs were poor packs to choose. In the conceptual stage they consciously realised that despite the big pay-backs these were ultimately wiped out by occasional big penalties. Despite not going through the "hunch" stage a proportion of ventromedial patients still reached the "conceptual" stage, although many of these still made the error of choosing the wrong packs. There was therefore the strange rift between knowledge and action which is occasionally reported with these patients (for a review see Bechara et al., 2000).

These gambling and other experiments suggest some important information concerning these patients that may bear on emotional and social dysfunction (see Damasio, 1994, for a more in-depth argument towards this view). If these patients are unable to anticipate the consequences of their problem-solving behaviour, they may have similar difficulties in anticipating the consequences of their social behaviour. They can judge the past, but have difficulty in anticipating the future and judging future consequences. This is perhaps what the young head-injured man meant when he said that he had no future, only a present (see Box 9.3). Therefore when neuropsychological testing fails to predict a dysfunctional personality it may, at least in some cases, be because we are using the wrong tests.

The exact neuroanatomical mechanism for the influence of the prefrontal cortex on emotional and social dysfunction is as yet uncertain, but there are now an increasing number of these cases with bilateral lesions to the ventral/orbital area (Damasio, 1997). Damasio (1994) introduced a *somatic marker theory*, which may provide an explanation, at one level, why their frontal patients failed to report the "hunch stage" and failed to respond in an emotional manner on psychophysiological measures. This theory is discussed in the next section when we review processes of emotional conditioning.

Summary

Patients with lesions to certain areas of the frontal lobe may be seen to have poor emotional control and social dysfunction. They may be disinterested and apathetic, but they may also be outspoken, bombastic, and tactless. These personality subtypes were referred to by Blumer and Benson (1975) as pseudo-depressive and pseudo-psychopathic respectively. One could argue that the inspiration for the very large number of frontal lobotomies given to psychiatric patients in the 1950s and 1960s was the reduction of agitation towards a type of pseudo-depressive state—a similiar state that was noticed originally in research with some individual chimpanzees. However, the other less palatable results of such surgery appeared to have been ignored at this stage because of the frantic treatment needs of the time. The moral difficulties involved in these surgical procedures are well illustrated in such films as *One flew Over the Cuckoo's Nest*, in which the surgical procedures were used not so much for the patient's benefit but rather as a means of controlling the patient for management purposes.

These features of pseudo-depression and pseudo-psychopathy may not be mutually exclusive and so some patients may be reclusive and apathetic for some time but then later, with the right cues or with recovery, become more extrovert and antisocial. There may be a common mechanism for these difficulties, which are modified by the extent to which the drive or spontaneity of the patient is undermined. In recent years the mechanism for these socially dysfunctional behaviours has been given special attention. It is perhaps helpful in determining the cause of this emotional disorder that at least some of these patients have an intact knowledge base of how to behave given certain situations. Also, some patients may look back on their behaviour with distress. There will be others, however, who look back without any insight into their past behaviour. In looking for a cause of antisocial behaviour it is clear that some patients have difficulty in anticipating the consequences of their behaviour at the time the behaviour occurs. There may be a number of reasons why these patients may on occasion make poor social decisions. One

possible explanation which is receiving support at the present time is the somatic marker theory, which proposes that these patients fail to create an emotional "early warning system" that may guide our behaviour when the consequences are not consciously recognised.

Finally, in terms of the progression and extension of our broad model of emotional systems, we are at the stage of being able to acknowledge the controlling influence of ventral frontal structures. While it is likely that there are other frontal influences, it is clear from case studies reviewed above that the ventromedial area must have some contribution to emotional control and allowing socially appropriate behaviour (see Figure 5).

Learning new emotional associations and acquired emotional information

New emotional associations

The updating of perceptions and their emotional connotations requires the learning of new associations. Since the work of Mishkin and colleagues revealed the role of the amygdala in the association of conditioned response with reward and punishment (e.g. Jones & Mishkin, 1972) an effort has been made to define the exact nature of the amygdala's role in memory. A distinction has been made between the remembering of the emotional connotations associated with a discrete stimulus and its context and emotional conditioning in which there is a sympathetic (autonomic) response that may generalise to conditions similar to the original stimulus. It is important, for example, for us to remember the context in which a bear was originally experienced, e.g. a particular cave; such declarative memories would involve the hippocampus. However, it is also important for the emotional response to be attached to that same memory (hippocampus in association with the amygdala). It is also important to have a conditioned response to the same cave. This may involve a quick and sudden emotional response to the cave (or caves like the original one) even prior to any conscious acknowledgement that this is the cave where I was originally attacked by a bear (e.g. Phillips & LeDoux, 1992). This suggests that

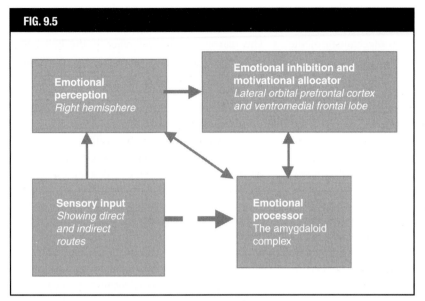

FIG. 9.5

Emotional perception
Right hemisphere

Emotional inhibition and motivational allocator
Lateral orbital prefrontal cortex and ventromedial frontal lobe

Sensory input
Showing direct and indirect routes

Emotional processor
The amygdaloid complex

An extension of the model provided in Figure 9.4. The control of emotional response is no doubt a complex mechanism that may depend on many factors yet to be defined. In a social situation they may be impulsive and disinhibited which may be related to a failure to anticipate consequences of behaviour, or may have difficulty in monitoring their own behaviour and that of others.

the amygdala may work in tandem with the hippocampus to produce an emotional memory. The amygdala is important for the classical conditioning of an emotional response to a stimulus, but the hippocampus gives the response a useful context. This has been preliminarily confirmed in a human study by a double dissociation between patients with isolated amygdalectomy versus a patient with hippocampal removal (Bechara et al., 1995). A patient with selective bilateral damage to the amygdala did not acquire conditioned autonomic responses to visual or auditory stimuli but did acquire the declarative facts about which visual or auditory stimuli were paired with the unconditioned stimulus. In contrast, a patient with selective bilateral damage to the hippocampus failed to acquire the facts, but did acquire the conditioning (see also Markowitsch et al., 1994) (see Figure 9.6).

To describe the amygdala system and the conditioned response without reference to the orbitofrontal cortex is to neglect the form the association or integration between the autonomic response and the stimulus takes. Rolls (2000) refers to the importance of cells within the orbitofrontal cortex that respond to reward or punishment. Therefore cells are found in this area that

respond to a stimulus only as long as a response to that stimulus is rewarded. Other cells appear to be sensitive to punishment. The orbitofrontal cortex also has areas that represent senses of smell, taste, and vision. Therefore the orbitofrontal cortex may influence the organism's response to reward and punishment in a sustained way that is referred to in the learning theory literature as operant conditioning. This provides an alternative explanation of poor responses to gambling contingencies as described in the Bechara experiments described earlier. Rolls found that patients with ventral prefrontal lesions (lesions overlapping with the orbital but not the dorsolateral cortex) performed very much like monkeys with lesions in the same areas on a task in which a stimulus was associated with a reward on some trials and then punishment on others. Patients tended to respond to the originally positively rewarded stimulus even when it became a punishing stimulus. There was therefore impaired reversal and extinction after orbitofrontal lesions. The patients' performance was correlated with their documented disinhibited and socially inappropriate behaviour in their everyday life (Rolls, Hornak, Wade, & McGrath, 1994). These results have particular relevance to a theory that attempts to explain the socially incompetent behaviour of some patients with orbitofrontal lesions.

The exact neuroanatomical mechanism of the prefrontal cortex on emotional and social dysfunction is as yet uncertain, but there are now an increasing number of such cases involving bilateral lesions to the ventral/orbital area (Damasio, 1997).

Somatic marker theory

Earlier there was a discussion of how patients with ventromedial lesions had difficulty in choosing the right pack in a gambling game experiment. The patient's behaviour was explained in terms of poor emotional feedback at the stage in the game when the patient was not fully aware of the rationale for the correct decision. During this stage normal subjects were able to use a "hunch" mechanism that appeared to be related to some kind of emotional feedback that the patients lacked. This response is clearly related to their ventral lesion but given the research described above by Rolls there is probably an involvement in the way that conditioning is linked to emotional response, a type of classical conditioning that involves an interaction between the orbitofrontal cortex, the amygdala, and the hippocampus (see Figure 9.6) and possibly the somatosensory area. This proposal is described by Damasio (1994) as the somatic marker theory.

The somatic marker theory proposes that there is an emotional response warning against behaviour that has a negative consequence, and this emotional response may precede conscious acknowledgement of why the response is a bad one. When considering the patients' behaviour in the gambling game, they initially behave normally. When they receive a penalty they immediately switch to another pack just like the normal subjects, but it is as if they cannot resist returning to the packs that provide the high rewards. It must be considered that these patients appear to act not unlike children who find it hard to resist a cookie or biscuit even when they know the theft will result in punishment.

It is understood that the negative emotional response is attached or tagged to the "wrong"

behaviour. The reader might be surprised that the word "somatic" is used in the title of this theory. The reason for this reference is the belief that when we anticipate another person's feelings in response to our behaviour, we do this by simulating those feelings in ourselves. Thus Adolphs et al. (2000) researched patients with a variety of lesions and found that patients with lesions to the right somatosensory cortex within the parietal cortex have most difficulty in recognising emotions from pictures of faces. These authors' interpretation is that when we recognise an emotion we actually simulate that emotion. The somatic marker may be created within the ventromedial cortex (areas including the medial areas of the orbital and the ventral area of the medial prefrontal cortex and anterior cingulate) and learned through an interaction between the amygdala and hippocampus. However, the feelings themselves are seen as being directly represented within the somatosensory cortices.

Their somatic marker theory proposes that we may refrain from saying something that is hurtful or lacking in tact or making a wrong decision because we have a quick emotional information system that informs us to hold back. This may be close to what we refer to as intuition. However, can all the socially inappropriate behaviour be blamed on such a mechanism? And can this explain what Bechara et al. (2000) refer to as cognitive impulsiveness? The theory is based on a relatively select amount of data using indirect measures of arousal such as skin conductance and therefore there is room for the development of this and other theories.

Finally, it is worth speculating on the relationship between some anxiety disorders and the influence of prefrontal structures and the orbitofrontal and anterior cingulate on the amygdala. LeDoux and Muller (1997) propose that excessive anxiety may cause amnesia for a traumatic event in childhood. Thus while emotional associations may improve memory for an event, an excess of arousal may incapacitate memory function. The conditioned emotional response would nevertheless be registered by the amygdala through the direct route referred to above. According to this theory the unconscious registering of an emotional association would not be available for later conscious recovery since it was not stored in the first place. But the emotional reactivity to the stimulus might remain. However, there is no obvious reason why such conditioning should not be extinguished over time. Thus, for example, if there is an unfortunate incident in which a child is frightened by a frog, subsequent innocuous experiences with frogs should reduce and eventually extinguish the conditioned fear, but for some reason this does not occur in these individuals.

It is possible that this extinction process may not occur at this young age because the brain is not sufficiently developed. Phobias mainly have their onset prior to puberty. The common onset of a long-term phobic reaction to a stimulus may be related to ontological development of brain structures, since the frontal structures are the last to fully develop and there may be insufficient control on the conditioned response such that the arousing stimulus fails to extinguish or habituate. It will be remembered that in the studies by Cohen and colleagues patients following cingulotomy failed to habituate in a normal manner (see Chapter 4), although it is clear that therapy that encourages the extinction process is often helpful with these patients (Cohen et al., 1990).

It is possible that some individuals have a predisposition towards maintaining a post-traumatic stress condition for possibly related reasons. Rauch et al. (2000) reported an fMRI study of patients who had post-traumatic stress disorder in which there was a heightened reaction to stimuli associated with a traumatic event. Such patients often have an excessive autonomic arousal when faced with stimuli associated with the original traumatic event. In Rauch et al.'s study, treatment-resistant patients where exposed to emotionally arousing material. These patients showed an excessive activation of the amygdala with an *underactivation* of the anterior cingulate when compared to normals.

An acquired store of emotional and social knowledge

So far there has been a discussion of the perception and expression of emotional communication at a relatively crude level, as if they exist in isolation of cultural expectations. We must know when it is appropriate to laugh or cry, and when it is acceptable to be facetious. It is assumed that these social rules are stored in much the same way as other knowledge. Some of this knowledge is handed down to us through the culture in which we develop. For example, Briggs (1970) suggests that certain tribes of Eskimo are not only less likely to express anger but they are also less likely to feel this emotion. Also, Tahitians have few words for longing, loneliness, or sadness possibly because these states are less often recognised (Levy, 1984). Needless to say, we are never free from the emotional and social influences of our past and those who have had an unusual upbringing will readily concede to this view.

It is likely that the Kluver–Bucy syndrome includes a destruction or disconnection from the store containing this social experience and knowledge. Apart from a timid and placid emotional presentation attributed to the destruction of the amygdala, these patients and Kluver and Bucy's monkeys with bilateral anterior inferior temporal lobe lesions also show an agnosic response towards stimuli, such as eating items that would not normally be eaten. They also behave in a socially inappropriate manner, with changes in sexual orientation. One explanation is that the social behaviour is undermined by a lack of information about appropriate behaviour. Therefore cases of visual agnosia in these monkeys may be associated with an additional removal of the memory store for rules concerning social interaction—a memory store that may well be housed within the temporal cortex.

Earlier in this section the patients of the Damasio group were described with their ventromedial lesions. These patients had clearly acquired and retained knowledge concerning social behaviour. Therefore the ventromedial aspects of the frontal lobes are clearly less likely to be a depository of such information. However, patients who have sustained damage in this area

---

Box 9.4. A case of Pathological Laughter

JM has a high average intellectual level with some slight deterioration noted on the block design. His performance on tasks assessing executive dysfunction are unremarkable, e.g. verbal fluency, maze learning and Trails B. CT scan shows a deep right hemisphere lesion of uncertain origin. His main presenting problem is an irrepressible tendency to laugh. At times a mildly funny comment, at other times events quite unrelated to humour, such as the unusual movement of someone's arm, will set him off. He says that he feels embarrassed when his family visits him in hospital. He may laugh at something that is not funny, and then his family around the bedside start to laugh, because they see the humour of the situation and this depresses him. During this interview (transcripted from a VCR tape) the patient, JM, has an expression on his face that suggested that he was continuously trying to suppress his laughter.

Interviewer: Do you have any difficulty controlling your laughter?
JM: Sometimes I do. [Snorts with laughter, but tries to control himself.]
Interviewer: What sort of things make it worse?
JM: Things that are different—once I get used to them [looks as if he is trying not to laugh] I try not to laugh . . . [laughs, then brings himself under control].
Interviewer: I gather you work at St Christopher's Hospital. What job do you do?
JM: Bacteriologist. [Two bursts of laughter.]
Interviewer: How do you become a bacteriologist?
JM: [Laughs, for about 5 seconds.] You go to the university and do a BSc then you do a course at the Institute of Technology.
Interviewer: When you laugh is it because you feel happy inside?
JM: Sometimes it is, sometimes it just comes out.
Interviewer: Do you sometimes feel sad inside when you laugh?
JM: Sometimes, but very rarely.

---

within the basal temporal lobe region, the bursts of laughter caused by this stimulation were more "strident" and "brisk" than was normally the case. Patients also reported a change in their perception during this stimulation. One patient reported a funny feeling, a feeling of happiness and dizziness, while the other patient reported that the meanings of things changed in a funny way and "things sounded really funny" (Arroyo et al., 1993, p. 762).

Most commonly gelastic seizures are abnormality associated with the hypothalamus, temporal lobe, and cingulate gyrus (Arroyo et al., 1993). Arroyo and colleagues argue that while the anterior cingulate is particularly important in the initiation of the motor components of emotions, including the accompanying vocalisations, the basal temporal lobe areas are more likely to be involved in the internal affect from the self-report of the few studies that are available. While pathological laughter and crying are referred to in the literature, there is as yet a poor definition of this disorder and how it varies from other disorders of disinhibited emotion. Also, because such disorders are relatively rare they have yet to be studied scientifically in any quantity and therefore theoretical discussion of this area remains tentative. However, at this point there appears to be a mechanism for the external affect of patients that

appears to be dissociable from internal affect and pathological emotions are not obviously related to the poor control shown by patients with frontal dysfunction. In Figure 9.7 the unit for the emotional response is supplied to cope with this dissociation. If one assumes that the amygdala is the central processor of emotion then a disconnection between the amygdala and the brain stem may result in a pathological emotional response without the proper emotional association. Loss of control of such an emotional response would require a second lesion disconnecting the orbitofrontal area from the amygdala. The model is now complete.

Summary

Despite the uncertainty and confusion in this area, a beginning has been made in modelling units of an emotional system. The system is made up of functional modules associated with certain roles. It would appear that the amygdala acts as an emotional processor, initiating the physiological arousal and external affect associated with an emotional response. The amygdala has features that allow the subject to make decisions concerning facial qualities such as "trustworthiness". There is also evidence that a bilateral lesion may affect personality but there are a small number of human cases and the evidence for this is

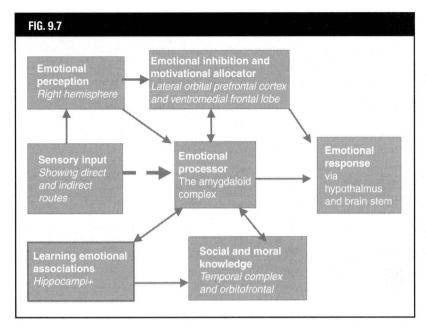

FIG. 9.7

Emotional perception
Right hemisphere

Emotional inhibition and motivational allocator
Lateral orbital prefrontal cortex and ventromedial frontal lobe

Sensory input
Showing direct and indirect routes

Emotional processor
The amygdaloid complex

Emotional response
via hypothalmus and brain stem

Learning emotional associations
Hippocampi+

Social and moral knowledge
Temporal complex and orbitofrontal

The complete emotional system with the added module for production and execution of the emotion. The cases of pathological emotions indicate a separate need for this module.

strongest in the animal literature and it is uncertain how much of this is due to a disconnection from sensory inputs to an emotional system. The central amygdala, with its connection with the hypothalamus, has been especially identified with this role. The amygdala appears to have two methods of receiving external sensory information. The first pathway is via a "quick and dirty process" probably involving a similar system that is referred to in Chapter 4 as the collicular pathway within the orienting system. In this way the organism may receive non-specific warning of a stimulus that suddenly arrives on the scene—a stimulus that may herald danger and require an autonomic response involving the physiological responses associated with "fight" or "flight" response. The second is more indirect and involves the "what pathway" and such areas as the orbitofrontal cortex.

One of the roles of the orbitofrontal cortex appears to be its ability to identify a stimulus according to its motivating characteristics. It could be seen as a structure that is important for linking sensory information with the emotional connotations according to its rewarding or punishing properties. In this way not only is emotional response to stimuli flattened but also

decisions made according to conditioned emotional response are also undermined. The information from such a process may indicate to an adolescent whether it is good to ask to borrow the car when their parent has returned after a harrowing day at the office. Experimentally it has been shown to affect emotionally based "hunch" decisions on a simulated gambling task.

The final two units are the unit for the storage of information concerning social knowledge, incorporating the multiplicity of influences on a person's moral and social development, and a second unit that is involved in the execution of external affect, the outward manifestations of an emotional response.

It is possible that well-designed functional imaging studies will allow the next development of modelling in this area. But these studies will need human and animal lesion studies for guiding task design and interpretation. Apart from the limitations already mentioned, functional imaging tasks are also necessarily somewhat artificial. It may be possible to present positive or negative imagery or visual information that has emotional connotations, but it might not be easy to re-create the emotional reaction and stress associated with everyday events. For example, it might be difficult to create the emotional reaction to a heated family argument or the extreme embarrassment and disappointment associated with being unable to remember one's phone number. In the next section there is a look at some of the questionnaire work that has attempted to access everyday emotional and social reactions of patients.

FURTHER ASPECTS OF EMOTIONAL AND SOCIAL DYSFUNCTION FROM THE CLINICAL PERSPECTIVE

Issues concerning the measurement of emotional and social dysfunction following brain damage

Emotional disturbance and social dysfunction following brain damage are common complaints. We have already described some of these problems, especially with reference to damage to areas within the temporal and frontal lobes. The extent of the problem is well illustrated from our own surveys of postoperative brain surgery patients. We originally surveyed 90 patients following brain surgery using a questionnaire filled in by the partner of the patient (Andrewes et al., 1998). We found that on average emotional and social dysfunction was the greatest complaint when compared to a variety of other cognitive complaints such as memory and concentration. Our various control groups including a group who had had neurosurgery to extracerebral areas, and another group with terminal cancer also rated this as their greatest problem. However, the brain surgery patients were significantly worse and as an indication of the margin in our original study we found that 37% of the brain surgery patient's scores were greater than 95% of the control group (see our preliminary study: Andrewes et al., 1998).

Despite these results suggesting that brain damage may affect emotionally related behaviour in a direct fashion, there remains some uncertainty concerning the cause of this behaviour, which provides such stress in the homes of these patients. Such emotional or social dysfunction could be caused by many factors:

- The direct result of structural damage undermining the integrity of a neurobiologically based emotional system, which may interact with the patient's premorbid personality.
- A reaction to the patient's own failures in areas where he or she used to succeed. Patients often report anger and frustration when confronted with the evidence that they cannot complete a task that they have previously completed with ease (Reitan & Wolfson, 1997).
- Disconfirmation of the patient's expected recovery; a loss of relationships and support. Patients may initially be surrounded by "well-wishers", but when the "dust settles" and friends realise that the patient's problems may be long term even those who are nearest to the patient may feel that they can no longer cope (Bond, 1984).
- Environmental factors such as financial problems associated with the illness and a forced change in lifestyle.

Frequently these factors interact. For example, the patient may be constantly fatigued (organic factor). This may reduce the patient's ability to cope with the frustration of not being able to complete a task (reaction to his own deteriorated abilities); the consequent outburst may upset the partner of the patient and undermine the relationship, so the partner becomes cold and removed (reduced social support); the patient feels deserted and becomes more depressed and angry, which further alienates friends, and so on. These kinds of chain reaction do occur and are commonly reported. Some families are stronger or have the resources to cope more proficiently. The following retrospective report from a clinical psychologist following traumatic brain injury illustrates such positive coping. "I was also subject to fits of rage and had a hair-trigger temper that could be ignited instantly by the smallest incident. This all became so difficult for my family (themselves under great stress) that my wife finally insisted that we see the psychiatrist who had worked with me while I was in the hospital" (Linge, 1990).

During different stages of recovery different mechanisms may exist because of an interaction of the emotional response with the cognitive recovery of the patient. For example, during the initial stages of recovery organic factors may predominate. Take the example of the retrospective report of this patient who suffered a stroke. This early report is not too dissimilar to the early problems described above associated with head injury. "I recalled very real anger at the least, or no, provocation when I first came home, little furies that seem now to have been unprovoked" (LaBaw, 1968).

However, while early emotional reactions often appear to be related to a lack of control, later emotional and social dysfunction may paradoxically be associated with a patient's improvement. The patient in the earlier stages often lacks insight into their own impairments and predicament in life. The patient may be contained and in some cases treated like a difficult child (Oddy, Coughlan, Tyerman, & Jenkins, 1985). However, improvement of the patient's mental function is often associated with increased insight and consequent depression. There are now a number of studies providing evidence that with recovery from brain damage the patient becomes more aware of their deficits and may take stock more realistically of their future prospects. This may lead to depression and anxiety and consequently instead of the patient becoming easier to handle they become more difficult. They go from being a passive invalid to being more proactive, and interpersonal difficulties are noted that were not apparent previously (Fleming & Strong, 1995; Malia, Powell, & Torode, 1995). To the carer who is expecting a progressive recovery of the type associated with a physical injury this is a confusing and dispiriting period.

Further, emotional reaction may occur when a patient returns to work or becomes sufficiently improved to undertake a new activity. A patient recently assessed by the author described the panic he had felt during the first week after suffering a visual field defect. Apart from the realisation that he was not seeing things normally, he complained of a sensation of being bombarded with visual information with which he could not cope. This was sufficient to cause him some considerable anxiety. The personal nature of these reports from those with expertise in the area brings home the human side of neuropsychology, which is too often neglected (see Narinder Kapur's book of a collection of these accounts; Kapur, 1997).

In our research, rather than rely on tests developed to assess psychiatric disorders we have attempted to create a test of emotional dysfunction that is more relevant to the problems suffered by patients with brain damage. We have used factor analysis, which statistically sorts the answers to questions into categories or scales so that questions that are responded to in a similar way are grouped together. Taking a rather strange analogy, factor analysis is a bit like having a very large box filled with a number of different types of birds, all flapping about in panic-stricken confusion. You let them all go and they settle on the land nearby in their various groupings, different flocks of birds all roosting with their same kind. Factor analysis does a similar magic with items of questionnaires in such a way that if, for example, a large number of persons rate, say, five questions in much the same way, these five questions will be grouped together to make the same scale. In our study (Andrewes, Kaye, Aitken et al., submitted) we used the reports of both patients and partners (someone who was close to the patient and knew them well). We collected patients from the neurosurgery outpatients of our hospital (the Royal Melbourne Hospital) and from another Melbourne hospital (St Vincent's Hospital) over a 4-year period to collect one of the largest samples of such patients. We used patients following brain surgery for the various complaints indicated in Table 9.1. See Box 9.5 for a description of the scales with examples of their associated items.

As indicated, emotional upset may be caused by a number of factors other than brain damage and therefore we have been careful to use controls who have also had neurosurgery to extracerebral areas. These control patients had a variety of neurological disorders, including carpal tunnel syndrome, spinal operations and other painful complaints, some of which would have been

TABLE 9.1

A description of the diagnostic groupings of the self-rating (*n* = 225) and partner-rated patients (*n* = 211). There was a lower number of partners due to some failure of partners to supply ratings of the patient

Surgical treatment				
Self-rating			Partner-rating	
Diagnosis	%		Diagnosis	%
Brain tumour	53.8		Brain tumour	50.7
AVM	3.6		AVM	3.3
TL epilepsy	23.6		TL epilepsy	22.7
VP shunt	2.2		VP shunt	2.4
Aneurysm	12.0		Aneurysm	15.6
Cyst	2.2		Cyst	2.4
Other	2.6		Other	2.8

Box 9.5

The Emotional and Social Dysfunction Questionnaire (ESDQ) was developed using factor analytic techniques with patients following brain surgery. Two versions of the questionnaire were devised: a self-rated version and a version that allowed a partner's perspective of the patient. Below are some of the items within the scales. Cronbach alpha of scale is shown in brackets.

Partner's ESDQ: 1. Anger (.94) e.g. Is he/she short tempered (short fused)? 2. Helplessness (.92) e.g. Does he/she feel without hope? 3. Indifference (.91) e.g. Does he/she appear to be indifferent to things that would normally cause him or her concern? 4. Emotional Dyscontrol (.88) e.g. Does he/she cry one moment and laugh the next? 5. Inappropriate (.80) e.g. Does he/she sometimes talk about sex too much? 6. Fatigue (.78) e.g. Does he/she need more sleep during the day? 7. Maladaptive (.91) Does he/she behave in a way that is too silly and childlish? 8. Insight (.80) e.g. Do others sometimes say that he or she has difficulties with personal relationships that the patient does not see him or herself?

Self-Rating ESDQ: 1 Anger (.93) e.g. Are you short tempered (short fused)? 2. Emotional Dyscontrol (.93) e.g. Do you sometimes cry or laugh for no apparent reason? 3. Helplessness (.92) e.g. Do you have panic attacks? Inertia (.81) e.g. Do others sometimes remark that you never start or complete things? Fatigue (.79) Do you need more sleep during the day? Indifference (.90) e. g. Do you feel uninterested in things going on around you? Inappropriate (.83) e.g. Do you find that sometimes you talk about sex too much? Euporia (.86) e.g. Are you sometimes unconcerned about your well-being?

associated with treatment dissatisfaction. We have also included in our controls terminally ill cancer patients in the same proportion as the patients in our sample to the brain surgery group who had had malignant brain tumours removed. Despite the use of this rigorous control group, when rated by their partners the brain surgery patients still showed significantly more emotional and behavioural problems on each of the scales. However, the patient's questionnaire appeared to be not as reliable and failed to show differences with the control group to the same degree (see Figure 9.8 and Box 9.1 for examples of items).

THEORIES OF LATERALISED EMOTIONAL EXPRESSION WITHIN THE CLINICAL CONTEXT

Davidson (1993) and colleagues (Davidson, 1993; Davidson & Irwin, 1999) propose that the anterior regions and the amygdala of the left hemisphere supports positive emotions and approach behaviours, while the right hemisphere supports negative emotions and withdrawal behaviour. This is argued for general cognitive-based behaviours but especially for particular emotions. Davidson

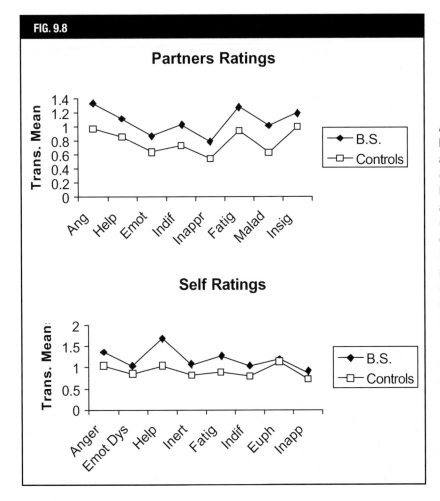

FIG. 9.8

A comparison between the brain surgery ($n = 211$) and the control group ($n = 46$) on the Partner's ESDQ. A discriminant analysis found separation (Wilks' $L = .903, \chi = 21.1$, d.f. $= 8, p \leq .005$). On an individual scale basis all scales showed a significant separation of $<.005$. An overall separation (Wilks' $L = .904, \chi = 26.2$, d.f. $= 8, p \leq .001$) was found on the self-rating version and although a number of scales were significant or approached significance at the $\leq .05$ level only the Fatigue and Helplessness scales were $p \leq .01$.

argues that the left frontal area subserves positive emotions while the right hemisphere subserves negative emotions. Hence this is sometimes referred to as a valence hypothesis.

Davidson's own research is perhaps the most persuasive support for his theory. Davidson et al. (1990) presented positive and negative film clips to non-brain-damaged subjects. Brain activation using EEG was used as a measure of the laterality of response to a negative versus a positive film clip. Measures were taken during the period that their faces were either happy or disgusted respectively. They found, as predicted, that increased right-sided brain activity (disappearance of alpha waves) during facial activity was associated with disgust. Also, the asymmetry was only evident in the anterior areas, as predicted. There was no dif-

ference between the hemispheres in the amount of cortical activation in the periods without facial affect and therefore the authors argue that the difference was related to the emotional response.

A further study followed up individual differences found in the initial studies. It was found that subjects reporting highest on measured depression or rating negative disposition had less left frontal activation (Henriques & Davidson, 1991; Schaffer, Davidson, & Saron, 1983). In this way increased activation in the left frontal hemisphere is associated with a positive response, but if a person has a predisposition to being depressed then there is generally less activation in that same hemisphere at baseline. Results of studies using young children were in a similar direction; in this study the *reduced* activation (increased alpha) found in the left frontal EEG was associated with inhibited behaviour, such as "clingy" behaviour and a fear of strangers. *Increased* left activation of the left frontal area was associated with an extreme group of *dis*inhibited children. It should be noted that in this last study the main variation of EEG asymmetry was found in the left hemisphere rather than a reciprocal relationship with the right (Davidson et al., 1994).

If the left frontal hemisphere is associated with positive emotions and this area is destroyed then there is nothing to counterbalance or inhibit the role of the depressive influence of the right frontal areas and therefore a patient with a left frontal lesion should generally be more depressed. One way of settling this issue would be to assess patients' emotional style when one brain hemisphere is anaesthetised. This occurs in the Wada technique, which is referred to in Chapter 5. Considering the limitations of using this paradigm there has been surprising agreement. Five studies have shown a higher incidence of depressed mood with ablation of the left hemisphere (Ahern et al., 1994; Christianson et al., 1993; Lee et al., 1990; Rossi & Rosadini, 1967), while one study (Lee et al., 1990) has additionally found elation of mood and laughter more associated with a right hemisphere procedure. A further study found no relationship in terms of facial expressions (Kolb & Milner, 1981a).

Further support for the valence theory comes from left hemisphere stroke studies. Gasparrini, Satz, Heilman, and Coolidge (1978) found patients with a left hemisphere lesion rated themselves higher on the depression scale of the MMPI when compared to right hemisphere patients on this measure of psychiatric personality. But more persuasive clinical evidence for the left versus right distinction comes from the work of Robinson, Kubos et al. (1984). They found a relationship in a small and select population of stroke patients for left anterior lesions to be associated with depression. Of course, this might be explained by the tendencies for patients with aphasia (left hemisphere) to react negatively to their loss of speech (Gainotti, 1993a). Goldstein (1948) described the "catastrophic reaction" of

the patient as an intense emotional reaction to the realisation of the aphasic consequences of their stroke. But while this influence and the influence of other handicaps cannot be discounted, Robinson, Kubos et al. (1984) were able to show that depression was not related to aphasia severity. They found, with a small number of subjects, that left anterior stroke patients and to a lesser degree right posterior lesions were associated with more depression. Sinyor et al. (1986) also found that depression did not relate to functional impairment. They found, however, that a relationship existed with distance from *both* the left and right frontal poles. There was also a relationship with right posterior lesions as found by Robinson's group.

These studies mentioned so far are based on hospital samples that may be selective in other ways, such as the exclusion of aphasic patients with comprehension difficulties. Ideally, a non-selective sample of stroke patients should find similar patterns. House et al. (1990) followed up 73 consecutive stroke patients who had received CT scan. Around half were seen within 6 months of stroke and the others within 12 months, at which time comprehensive testing and interviewing of each patient were carried out. These authors found no relationship between the left or right location of lesion. CT scan found a weak relationship between the location of lesion and the frontal poles. Sharpe et al. (1990) followed up 60 stroke patients and similarly found no significant relationship, although this was over 3 years post stroke. Two more recent studies are more supportive not only of more depression but also more anxiety following left hemisphere stroke (Astrom, 1996; Castillo, Starkstein, Federoff et al., 1993).

Although the stroke literature tends to be supportive of the valence hypothesis as it applies to the left hemisphere. In some ways stroke patients may not be the best sample to assess this theory. The negative results may be indicative of the tendency for both left- and right-sided stroke patients to be handicapped and older. Also, pathology such as atherosclerosis affects a number of areas and even when a stroke is in one hemisphere impairments associated with pathology in the other hemisphere cannot always be ruled out.

Valence theorists often cite a paper by Starkstein, Boston, and Robinson (1988) as partial support for the predictions following right hemisphere damage (Davidson, 1993). The existence of mania or elation following right anterior damage would support a release or disinhibition of the positive emotional disposition of the left. However, Starkstein and colleagues support a case for a more complex model of emotional function that includes subcortical mechanisms. Although most of their patients with mania had right-sided anterior lesions, nearly half had right subcortical lesions involving the thalamus, hypothalamus, and periventricular areas. Also, they pointed to the rarity of these cases even to the point of speculating on a possible genetic predisposition. Many of these mania patients also suffered bouts of depression and as the authors suggest some would have gone on to receive a diagnosis of bipolar affective disorder (manic-depressive disorder). Starkstein and Robinson (1991) report how the valence hypothesis was tested in one manic patient with right hemisphere lesion. They argued that if the mania were the result of the left hemisphere release of positive mood, then anesthetising the left hemisphere in a Wada procedure with this patient should at least balance the situation and restore the right (negative) influence. However, the patient remained as manic as ever during this procedure.

While Gainotti (1989) proposed that there is more elation and euphoria in right hemisphere-damaged patients, the thorough study by House et al. (1990) described earlier failed to find this relationship. Gainotti referred to the indifference of right hemisphere patients, especially those with right posterior lesions who showed signs of neglect and anosognosia. He proposed that this indifference to their condition caused an unrealistic appraisal of their situation, resulting in a more positive outlook. Some of these patients also suffer from anosognosia, which is an indifference to impairments, especially those impairments represented on the contralateral side (see Chapter 4). However, the disorders associated with anosognosia are often associated with right *posterior*

damage, although in many cases the disorder may remit relatively quickly after stroke, e.g. within the first few weeks of recovery. These cases may not, therefore, be sufficient to support Davidson's broad-based theory of anterior laterality and emotional dysfunction.

In an interesting paper Ross and Rush (1981) describe four patients with right hemisphere stroke who deny depression that clearly exists when carers' and relatives' reports are taken into account. Some of these patients had pathological laughter and crying (excessive and often unwarranted) and often reported feeling no emotion during these bouts. However, antidepressants reduced the signs of depression such as irritability, withdrawal and lack of appetite that were reported by partners. In other words, some right hemisphere patients may not be in touch with their own emotions and close second-hand analysis of behaviour by a partner may be required to diagnose some of these patients. Starkstein et al. (1991) have further confirmed evidence of this group of patients with right hemisphere lesions who are depressed yet deny their depression. These and other papers suggest that brain-damaged patients' self-report measures of emotion should be accompanied by partner reports.

In conclusion, the evidence in support of the valence hypothesis from stroke studies is not straightforward. Nevertheless, the issues of research are clearly complex in terms of the selection of patients and method of assessment when denial of symptoms and a lack of insight are present. However, there are indications that increased anxiety and other types of exaggerated emotional response may also be a feature of left hemisphere stroke. For example, House, Dennis, Molyneaux et al. (1989) report a study of stroke patients in which they surveyed the incidence of emotionalism in stroke patients. They describe emotionalism as "the habit of weakly . . . yielding to emotion." They found a clinical level of emotionalism, as measured by the Beck Depression Inventory and psychiatric assessment, at a higher incidence in left hemisphere lesioned patients (57%), compared to patients with lesions in other areas (19%), right hemisphere stroke counterparts, although this difference appeared to change over time with recovery. Sometimes the drop-out rate of patients threaten longitudinal work, although methods can be argued to rectify this situation (Cicchetti & Nelson, 1994). Nelson and colleagues used a questionnaire from their studies that allowed dimensions of Indifference, Depression, Mania, and Pragnosia (defect of emotional communication) using an absent/present checklist. Finally, Starkstein and colleagues rated 53 stroke patients following CT scan and found a greater preponderance of anxiety plus depression in left hemisphere lesion subjects, although patients with depression alone tended to have basal ganglia lesions (Starkstein et al., 1990).

Our group has also completed a study with patients following brain surgery and we confirm similar findings independently using the questionnaires that have already been described. In Figures 9.9 and 9.10 are the results of a comparison between patients following left and right lesions, which suggest differences between the groups according to gender. The left hemisphere-lesioned females act in accordance with Davidson's theory by showing negative responses such as anger and depression in the form of feelings of helplessness and "giving up". However, the right hemisphere males were generally rated as having more dysfunction following a right lesion. The males provide more support for the observations of Gainotti (1989, 1993a) indicating that these subjects tend to lack socially appropriate behaviour, in this case showing more inappropriate behaviour and maladaptive behaviour. The

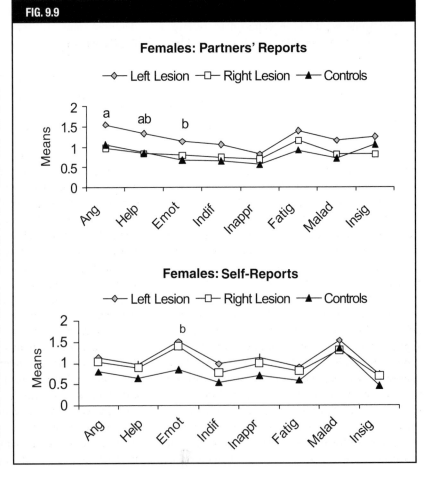

ESDQ Partner Rating and Self-Rating Laterality Profile for Females showing transformed means. Subjects compared included the left lesion group (*n* = 29; 11 frontal, 5 temporal tumour removal, 13 temporal lobectomy epilepsy), the right lesion group (*n* = 29; 9 frontal, 6 temporal tumour removal and 14 temporal lobectomy epilepsy) and 20 controls. The groups were of equivalent age, level of education and time since surgery. A level of <.01 was accepted (Bonferonni correction); "a" denotes a significant difference between the left and the right lesion group and "b" denotes a significant difference between a lesion group and controls.

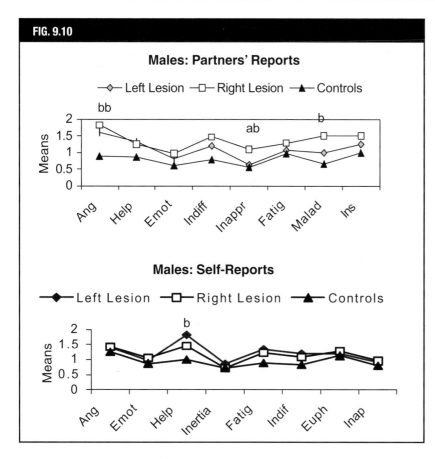

FIG. 9.10

Males: Partners' Reports

—◇— Left Lesion —□— Right Lesion —▲— Controls

Means: 2, 1.5, 1, 0.5, 0

Ang Help Emot Indiff Inappr Fatig Malad Ins

Males: Self-Reports

—◆— Left Lesion —□— Right Lesion —▲— Controls

Means: 2, 1.5, 1, 0.5, 0

Ang Emot Help Inertia Fatig Indif Euph Inap

ESDQ (Partner Rating) Laterality Profile for Males. Subjects in left group (n = 19; 4 frontal and 6 temporal tumour removal and 9 temporal lobectomy). The right group (n = 17; 4 frontal and 5 temporal tumour removal and 8 temporal lobectomy). The groups were equivalent in terms of their age, level of education, and time since surgery. Overall the right-lesioned group were rated worse than the left ($F = 2.29$, $p < .05$). A level of $<.01$ was accepted (Bonferonni correction); "a" denotes a significant difference between the left and the right lesion group and "b" denotes a significant difference between a lesion group and controls.

anger ratings are not obviously different between the two lesioned groups of males although they are clearly worse compared to controls. Interestingly, the left males rate themselves as significantly worse compared to controls and again one is reminded of possible cultural differences in the expression and possibly the partners have not picked up subtle differences that might be more clearly expressed in females.

Of course, with results such as these that provide a different profile for males and females it might be tempting to look for alternative explanations. One might suggest, for example, that these interesting results are merely due to the assessing partners being mainly of the opposite sex. However, these lateralisation effects exist despite comparisons with controls who are similarly assessed by partners of the opposite sex. It is possible that even though these men are Australian they may

be more prone to reveal their lower threshold for asocial behaviour in talking in an inappropriate fashion than women with the same damage, and with the right questions a more subtle form of asocial behaviour might reveal itself in females. However, the differences between male and female left lesions is not so easy to explain completely along these lines.

The view of a flip-flop emotional system that is balanced in such a way that the left hemisphere is damaged releasing the right hemisphere and vice versa is not convincingly supported by the literature. Already mentioned is the study by Starkstein and Robinson (1991), who found no balancing effect on emotions of a manic patient during a left hemisphere Wada procedure. Also, while there is relatively consistent support for negative emotions following left lesions, the evidence following damage to the right is far

commonly verbal and auditory (David & Cutting, 1994). In the case of auditory hallucinations the patient may believe, for example, that they hear voices, believing them to be coming from some external source or from inside their head. They are often linked to a delusion; for example, in the case of an auditory hallucination, the voices are seen to be due to some form of possession or that the message has in some way been transmitted to the patient. The voices that the patients hear often have a different accent from the patient's own voice. It may be a foreign voice or have an accent suggesting a different geographical location or socio-economic background to the patient. While some of these hallucinations are seen as pleasant, the content of the voices is often derogatory, vulgar, or abusive (Nayani and David, 1996).

The higher risk of a suicide attempt, as a direct response to hallucination, bears witness to the suffering they may cause and the experience that they are often out of the patient's control (Falloon & Talbot, 1981). Nayani and David (1996) report that all their 100 subjects heard voices rather than experiencing thoughts and the majority (73%) heard them in a conversational tone, while 14% described whispers and 13% shouting. Therefore according to self-report these experiences, in most cases, can be clearly distinguished from thoughts or "thinking out loud". They are often reported to be real, which is diagnostically important, although there may be some realisation of their hallucinogenic quality in the more chronic stages of the disorder (Frith, 1992).

The identification of a hallucination and its distinction from a delusion is not always straightforward. Sometimes the patient's persecutory ideation may be confused with a hallucination. For example, if the patient says "They are shouting my name in the streets" this may mean that the patient thinks or believes this to be the case (delusion) without actually hearing the shouting (hallucination). There is also the problem when recording a hallucination because of the incoherence of speech that is sometimes present.

For these and other reasons, hallucinations within schizophrenia provide a special challenge for theoreticians partly because there appears to be many aspects or components of this disorder that require explanation. This review focusses on two components which are seen to underlie hallucinations. The first is the mechanism for *false perception*, hearing and seeing things which are not there. This *false perception* aspect is not uncommon in a number of patient populations and is experienced sometimes, albeit infrequently, by "normal" persons. The second component is a *false attribution*. This relates to the patient's belief in the voices and the failure to realise the likelihood that they are imaginary.

There are various competing theories that attempt to explain schizophrenic hallucinations, and given the apparent heterogeneity of neuro-pathology found in these patients (Arnold, 1999) it is possible that differences in mechanism exist between patients. Certainly when surveyed there is variation in the reported nature of the hallucination (Nayani & David, 1996). However, there are consistencies that demand explanation even if any modelling must be tentative at this stage.

False perception and subvocal speech

Many authors have favoured the explanation that verbal auditory hallucinations are misattributed inner speech (e.g. David, 1999). The argument follows the view that the patient hears their own subvocal voice and takes it for a voice of another identity. Three studies have found a direct relationship between subvocal speech and hallucinations each with a single patient. The scarcity of these results may be related to the difficulty in getting patients to cooperate. Only one out of ten of McGuigan's (1966) patients complied in a study which found that measured oral muscle movements just preceded reports of hearing voices. Green and Preston (1981) amplified a patient's subvocal speech by use of a throat microphone. Not only did the subvocal speech correspond to reported hallucinations but they were in a different voice to the patient's normal voice. Gould (1949) describes a patient who heard voices most of the time and noticed that the patient made noises from her nose and mouth. When these noises were amplified, whispers could be heard which the patient sometimes responded to in her normal voice. For example:

Patient whispers: "She knows she is the most wicked thing in the whole wide world. The only voice I hear is hers. She knows everything. She knows all about aviation."

Patient in normal voice: "I heard them say I have a knowledge of aviation."

There is conflicting evidence on the issue whether occupying the vocal musculature reduces hallucinations. Green and Kinsbourne (1990) found reduction in reported hallucinations by getting the patients to hum but the relationship to the frequency of hallucinations remains uncertain. However, competitive distraction of this kind generally helps to reduce hallucinations in the short term (Shergill, Murray, & McGuire, 1998). The nature of this subvocal speech may not be entirely synonymous with what Baddeley refers to as phonological or articulatory loop since it seems to be able to coexist with short-term memory tasks (David & Lucas, 1993). On the other hand, a patient who suffered a hallucination of her thoughts being echoed and broadcast showed that her condition did interfere with short-term memory performance (David, 1994).

While the source of the hallucinations appears to be subvocal speech in some patients, it is uncertain whether this is generally the case or even whether the voices continue when subvocal speech is in some way blocked. To place this issue in perspective it is of interest that most of the schizophrenic patients surveyed by Nayani and David (1996) heard more than one voice; 57% had experienced, in addition to the reported voice or voices, sounds of crowds of persons talking or mumbling together. These kinds of hallucinations are more difficult to explain by the subvocal theory.

Functional imaging evidence supplies some support for the subvocal model, finding that brain areas activated during a hallucination are the same cortical areas that are also involved in subvocal speech in normal persons. Secondary auditory areas, speech-related premotor areas and part of Broca's area have been found to be activated (McGuire et al., 1993). David et al. (1996) compared a single subject over a number of sessions. On some of these sessions the patient was hallucinating almost continuously, while on other sessions the hallucinations had ceased as a response to medication. On each of these sessions the subject was subjected to tapes of spoken words or in another condition visual stimuli. Using fMRI David and colleagues found activation of the auditory association area during a hallucination, which was attenuated or reduced when it coincided with listening to a hallucination. There was no activation in the primary auditory association area. In contrast to this finding, a recent fMRI study (Dierks et al., 1999) showed additional activation during hallucinations of the primary auditory sensory area within Wernicke's area and Heschl's gyrus. Frith in an editorial reflects on the importance of these findings since this study delivers neurometabolic evidence that this subvocal speech may be perceived as external speech through the activation of this sensory reception area. There is now mounting evidence that top-down perceptual activation may influence the neuronal activation even within the primary visual cortex and therefore activation at primary sensory reception areas may be due to the influence of initial activation at a higher level. The indication that the primary auditory sensory area is activated does not necessarily argue for the hallucination as a kind of irritation of the sensory apparatus. Such random excitations are not in keeping with the consistent and often stereotyped prose that is frequently reported. The neuropsychological evidence would suggest that in many cases the hallucination has been processed comprehensively at a conceptual level.

False perception and a top-down tyranny?

While the subvocal production of auditory hallucinations may have some sway as a hypothesis, this proposal would suggest that the patient has some control over their hallucinations. If this were the case one might expect that they would be less objectionable and less likely to be the consequence of frequent suicide. Also, while there is a good argument that *some* patients may mouth their hallucination subvocally it would appear that the more important issue is the out-of-control aspect which often dominates a hallucination. Some evidence for this comes from studies which seem to suggest that schizophrenic patients may be dominated by their "top-down" processing at the expense of their "bottom-up" perceptions. The influence of our expectations (top-down) is clearly important to the normal perceptual process but there is a balance to the extent that what we actually see (bottom-up) drives and dominates the perceptual process. With schizophrenic hallucinations it would appear that often the bottom-up processing is overridden, and the top-down processing dominates. For example, Bentall and Slade (1985) presented patients a series of single words, half of which were the word "*who*" within a background noise; other presentations were just the background noise without any word. In this study the patients who suffered hallucinations were more likely to hear the word "*who*" when just the background noise was presented. This result could also be interpreted as a general tendency towards misperception but then the patients might be expected to have heard an equal amount of just noise in some of the noise conditions. Also, Done and Frith (reported in Frith, 1992) presented nonwords in the form of randomly paired phonemes on a computer and there was no greater preponderance for the patients to perceive these as words more than controls. It appears that the mechanism is more likely to be related to the internal expectancies of the patient. It is as if a top-down process has taken over in these patients' perception. In another study showing this evidence, Haddock, Bentall, and Slade (1995) gave hallucinators and controls the suggestion that when they heard the word *tress* repeated over and over they might hear other new words. Both groups heard extra words such as *stress* and *dress*, but the hallucinators imagined that they heard many more words, including such words as *caressed* and *christ*.

David (1999) in reviewing this specific area describes these hallucinations as having a "precise content which is often highly personalised to the voice hearer." He describes the complex relationships that develop between the patient and the voices and the way the patient describes the voices as being more powerful than the patient (David, 1999, p. 96). Therefore the content of such hal-

lucinations appears to be part of stored scenario that is well developed. In terms of cognitive theory these scenarios can be seen as schemas that are well represented in the patient's knowledge structure and are constantly activated, apparently without the patient's control. It is as if these patients are constantly ready to tune in to the contents of their delusion. Schneider (1976) reveals this feature in a study where schizophrenic patients were requested to attend to one ear of the stereo headphones while to-be-ignored distracting material was presented in the other ear. Schneider provided a pseudo-hallucination in the "unattended ear". The patients were more distracted by the pseudo-hallucination compared to controls (Schneider, 1976). In summary, it appears that while the evidence for the self-production of schizophrenic hallucinations is strong, and while they may be manifested in terms of subvocal speech, it is likely that a hallucination is originally the product of a delusional schema which is prone to involuntary activation (Nayani & David, 1996).

A neuropsychological explanation has been sought for this apparent top-down tyranny in the form of a laterality hypothesis. This proposes that in these patients the right hemisphere is relatively more dominant compared to the left hemisphere and the hallucination is the result of undue influence from a normally quiescent right hemisphere. This theory points to findings with split-brain patients in which the patients may manifest independent goals of the two hemispheres, as in the case of the anarchic hand (Bogan, 1993). Normally when verbal material is presented simultaneously to both ears there is a right ear advantage in detection that is attributed to the left hemisphere verbal dominance. The left hemisphere (right ear) advantage for verbal recognition has found to be less obvious in patients with hallucinations (Bruder, Rabinowicz, & Towey, 1995). There is also evidence that when listening to external speech there is less activation in the left language areas and more activation in the right temporal lobe in these patients compared to control subjects. There also appears to be a relative smaller volume of these critical left temporal lobe brain regions in schizophrenics who suffer such hallucinations, providing possible evidence of greater neuropathology in the left compared to right temporal lobe (Levitan, Ward, & Catts, 1999). The evidence that patients sometimes hear short expletives might also encourage the view that hallucinations are the consequence of interfering right hemisphere speech, given the nature of this type of speech (Code, 1997). However, such hallucinatory experiences are less common than propositional speech which reduces the validity of any strong right hemisphere hypothesis of this nature. While the isolated right hemisphere speech capabilities have not been experimentally assessed to the author's knowledge, the production of propositional language is not seen as being within the capability of the right hemisphere according to the split-brain research (Gazzaniga, 1993). A relatively less efficient and smaller left hemisphere may nevertheless support the likelihood of greater neuropathology in the left hemisphere in schizophrenic patients rather than any greater language dominance of the right.

A better direction in searching for the generator of hallucinogenic material comes from its nature. If these false perception experiences are elicited from the patient's own memory system then there is the expectancy for additional areas of activation to the cortical areas discussed so far. For example, because memories are involved and many hallucinations have an extreme emotional content one might expect that the hippocampus and the amygdala might be involved in this process, the hippocampus being involved in the retrieval of recent episodic (conscious recollection) and the amygdala as a source of emotional evaluation. Epstein and colleagues have found this to be the case (Epstein, Stern, & Silbersweig, 1999). These researchers used a technique whereby the patient is required to press a button when they experience a hallucination; in this way the brain activation, according to PET scan, may be matched with the hallucination. They confirmed that within a context of decreased prefrontal deactivation within the cingulate area there was a concomitant increase in activation within areas including ventral striatal areas, the amygdala and the hippocampus within the medial temporal lobe, areas have

been described as part of an emotional circuit by Gray (1999).

Further evidence for the support for medial temporal lobe involvement comes from two other areas of research. First, the hippocampus and adjacent areas of the entorhinal cortex have been targeted as areas that often show abnormalities associated with schizophrenia (e.g. Van Hoesen, Augustinack, & Redman, 1999). Also, in line with the involvement of the temporal lobe, there are a few patients with temporal lobe epilepsy who also suffer from verbal auditory hallucinations. In contrast to schizophrenic patients, these temporal lobe epilepsy patients often described the hallucinations in retrospect as being unreal (Stevens, 1999). Early physicians observed a relationship between the low cortical arousal of schizophrenics and the low incidence of epilepsy in these patients. This link was combined with the finding that hallucinations only occurred in epileptic patients when the incidence of their seizures was reduced and their EEG nearly normalised. This apparent incompatibility between seizures and hallucinations led to electroconvulsant therapy (ECT) being used to reduce schizophrenic symptoms, which is maintained as a course of treatment by some clinicians even today (Bogerts, 1997). Therefore there is a link between the structures important for memory retrieval and emotion which may be seen as a mechanism for a top-down tyranny.

A top-down tyranny of a similar kind may occur when we dream. The observation of similarities between dreaming and hallucinations is attractive. Functional imaging of REM sleep and hallucinations have not been compared directly but there are differences when schizophrenic patients are imaged who have been known to hallucinate (Hobson, Stickgold, & Pace-Schott, 1998). Nevertheless, there is a similar accentuated activation between the two conditions in the amygdala and hippocampus and ventral aspects of striatal structures (including the nucleus of accumbens) coincident with a relative hyperactivity of the cholinergic system in REM sleep. Also both conditions are associated with de-arousal of the dorsolateral prefrontal cortex. However, the cingulate appears to be aroused during REM and possibly de-aroused during hallucinations (Epstein, Stern, & Silbersweig, 1999). With REM there is a neurotransmitter control of these changes with a shutting down of the noradrenaline neurotransmitter system, which is responsible for cortical tone. This change acts to *prevent* any kind of sensory input. When normal persons are REM sleep deprived they may start to hallucinate during waking, which is also associated with a rebound of excessive REM when they have uninterrupted sleep. The link between dreaming and sleep-related hallucinations and schizophrenia is yet to be confirmed but comparisons are intuitively reasonable and the focus of research interest at the present time.

In summary, the functional imaging research appears to confirm the view that there is a top-down mechanism since the structures that appear to be frequently activated are also responsible for retrieving memories and are associated with emotional content. The top-down tyranny hypothesis is highly speculative at the present time and even more uncertain but just as intriguing is the attributive nature of hallucinations. It is perhaps difficult for us to imagine a hallucination but one expects that rationality might prevail and the hallucination might be disbelieved or at least questioned, for such an experience could be easily discounted by a logical thought process. For example, why does the patient assume that there is a third person involved with the hallucination when sensory evidence would suggest otherwise. What is the mechanism for this kind of false attribution?

False attribution and disinhibition theory

One explanation for false attribution is that the reality of the internal experience is accentuated by an information-processing block of some kind—a kind of sensory information block that is apparently neurochemically set up in dreaming and is the kind of explanation proposed by a disinhibition theory (Schultz & Melzack, 1991). This follows the finding of an association of visual hallucination in patients with some kind of sensory impedance, such as in the case of a scotoma or a severing of the optic nerve. In these and other similar cases the blockage in input is seen to *dis-*

inhibit internal top-down images. For example, patients with Anton's syndrome following destruction of the visual cortex often believe they see objects that are not there (Goldenberg, Mullbacher, & Nowak, 1995). McGhie and Chapman (1961) described the self-reported information-processing experiences of schizophrenic patients in terms such as "Things are coming in too fast. I lose my grip of it and I get lost. I am attending to everything at once and as a result I do not attend to anything" and "My thoughts get all jumbled up. I start thinking or talking about something but I never get there." Also, from a standardised questionnaire Freedman and Chapman (1971) gained similar self-reports of poor attention and also thought blocking, which disrupted speech and impaired perception of speech. The most common reports were of poor focused attention. About half of the schizophrenic patients reported that they were unable to ignore irrelevant stimuli.

These reported difficulties of poor executive attention, organisation, and monitoring are reminiscent of the cognitive dysfunction that is often associated with frontal lobe dysfunction. In keeping with this neuropsychological association is the finding that apart from the temporal lobe structural abnormalities there are also those relating to the prefrontal cortex and frontostriatal areas (Arnold, 1999).

It is now well accepted that schizophrenia is a neurodevelopmental disorder (Parnas, 1999), being commonly clinically diagnosed in the late teens or early twenties. The final diagnosis is preceded by a pre-schizophrenic stage when the symptoms become consolidated and a prodromal stage in which the symptoms are more sporadically manifested for about 4 years prior to diagnosis. Symptoms of poor motor coordination, emotionality, and learning difficulties may, however, occur much earlier. A retrospective survey (Walker, Diforio, & Baum, 1999) has found that symptoms of these kinds started to occur in some cases as early as 4 years old. It is not known why the disorder manifests itself in the late teens, but it is of interest that the frontal lobes are the last areas to reach maturity through the process of neural pruning. Also, there is support for cytoarchitecture abnormalities in cortical areas and reputably within the dorsolateral prefrontal cortex and the cingulate, but also in the temporal lobe (see Arnold, 1999, p. 42, for a review).

There is now a large literature on the proposed similarities between the performance of patients with schizophrenia and patients with frontal lesions (e.g. Goldberg, Hyde, Kleinman, & Weinberger, 1993) and more recently comparisons have been made with patients suffering degeneration in frontal–striatal regions (e.g. Robbins, 1990; Hanes, Andrewes, Pantelis, & Chiu, 1996). Many of these comparisons have found some differences between other patient groups, although some may be quite subtle (e.g. Hanes, Pantelis, Andrewes, & Chiu, 1996). Scores on the clinical tests of executive abilities tend to be more correlated with negative signs (reduced spontaneity etc.) rather than positive signs and comment has been made about the heterogeneity of the neuropsychological profile of these patients. However, Poole, Ober, Shenaut, and Vinogradov (1999) have recently found that a go–no-go test of the type eliciting disinhibited behaviours was correlated with the incidence of hallucinations. It is possible that there may be some link between the process of the self monitoring which is important within executive tasks and false attribution.

A further link between frontal dysfunction and hallucinations has been found when considering the aberrant frontal neurotransmitter function in schizophrenia. Schizophrenia has been treated traditionally by drugs that reduce the influence of the neurotransmitter dopamine. Certain types of dopamine have an inhibiting effect on arousal within the frontal lobes, especially within the striatal areas, e.g. basal ganglia. A simple explanation is therefore that some of the symptoms of schizophrenia may be reduced by increasing frontal arousal. How this occurs remains controversial but even if the mechanism is not as direct as is sometimes assumed there is converging evidence that the dopamine hypothesis is useful in explaining some of the symptoms of schizophrenia.

Recently, it has been shown that a normal level of dopamine within the frontal cortex is essential to other brain areas as well—brain areas that are also implicated in the mechanism of hallucin-

ations. An interesting interaction between the temporary reduction of dopamine and the normalisation of the functional arousal within the schizophrenic brain has recently been found using PET functional imaging techniques. Chris Frith and colleagues have been researching schizophrenic patients using a verbal fluency task in which patients were required to provide exemplars of category or words beginning with a certain letter (see review of this work by Dolan et al., 1999). When schizophrenic patients without drug therapy were compared with controls, marked differences were found most obviously in the areas of the anterior cingulate and superior temporal lobe. The cingulate was underactive and the temporal lobe activations were excessive compared to controls. However, when a dopamine challenging drug, apomorphine, was administered to the patients their scans became more like that of the controls, with increased activation of the cingulate and reduced activation of the temporal lobe areas (Fletcher et al., 1996).

This exciting work suggests there is a neurochemically modulated balance between brain structures of the anterior cingulate and the temporal lobe. Is it possible that the overarousal of the medial temporal areas and de-aroused cingulate found during hallucinations (Epstein et al., 1999) is somehow altered to reduce hallucinations? There is no answer to this question at present because the neurochemical relationship between these two areas is yet to be defined with any certainty (see Gray, 1999, for a discussion). However, the link between false attribution and the anterior cingulate is encouraged further by neuroimaging work with autistic children, which finds an association between anterior cingulate activation and "theory of mind tasks". It appears that a sense of self and a theory of what others are thinking is determined by adequate functioning of this structure and this may well have an influence on misdirected attribution during hallucinations (Frith & Frith, 1999). There are only a few reported cases of isolated bilateral anterior cingulate damage. But such patients do have a self-report that is reminiscent of a loss self-determination. An interesting interchange between doctor and patient is recorded in a case study of a 35-year-old woman who had suffered an embolic infarct in the left cingulate and supplementary motor area, reported by Damasio and Van Hoesen (1983). The patient suffered akinetic mutism during the first month and was non-reponsive to her doctor's questioning, but showing no signs of frustration with her predicament. After some substantial recovery she was asked why she did not respond to questions and she responded that "she did not talk because she had nothing to say." Her mind was "empty". "Nothing mattered". She said that she could follow the doctor's conversation but felt no will to reply to the questions. This kind of reaction is reported following cingulotomy as a psychosurgical treatment for chronic pain. In this case the patient still feels the pain but somehow fails to care anymore (Foltz & White, 1962).

These same feelings of passivity, of being controlled and a lack of intention or will are also reported as features of schizophrenia (Frith, 1992). Frith and Done (1989) see a failure to monitor the patient's own intentions as a key feature of schizophrenic behaviour and this has particular relevance to the false attribution of hallucinations. There is also evidence that these patients have difficulty in monitoring their own thoughts and this could be a clue to their misattribution of their own internal productions as coming from other persons. Schizophrenic patients may have difficulty in distinguishing between statements that have been thought or imaged by the patient, compared to statements that have been stated aloud or imagined to have been said by others. Furthermore, they have a bias in assuming the source was external (Keefe, Arnold, Bayen, & Harvey, 1999). This cannot be attributed to poor memory on its own and is not unlike a dysfunctional "source memory" (Janowsky, Shimamura, & Squire, 1989), which has been seen to be related to frontal dysfunction (Rugg, Fletcher, Chua, & Dolan, 1999). Broadly, there is therefore a difficulty in allocating a context of the original conditions that existed when something was originally learned, e.g. whether the word was said in a male or female voice. This difficulty in monitoring the source, i.e. internal versus external, and a tendency to misattribute

the source externally is, of course, very like some patients' tendency to attribute their subvocal speech to external voices. Most studies have found this type of source misattribution to be more obvious in patients with a history of delusions and hallucinations (e.g. Bentall, Baker, & Havers, 1991).

Frith and Done (1989) required patients to predict the consequence of their own actions without visual feedback. In a computer-driven tracking task patients were exaggeratedly undermined in their performance compared to a condition when they could not rely on visual feedback of their intended actions (Frith & Done, 1989). Therefore the false attribution of hallucinations may well have its origins in an inability to monitor the products of their own mentation and their own paranoid ideas become externalised because of a failure to realise that they are a product of the patient's own top-down processing, whether this be manifested in subvocal speech or perceptions that are dominated by their own top-down processing.

Summary

To conclude, there are various loose ends that need to be tied before a credible model of hallucinations within schizophrenia can be proposed. Nevertheless there are some interesting leads in this detective story that appear to favour certain assumptions, represented in condensed form in Figure 9.11.

The first is that the language areas are activated during auditory hallucinations. At present there are unfortunately very few studies that have attempted to isolate hallucinations and compare these with controls. Some of these have used patients who are apparently continuously hallucinating, while other studies have asked the patient to press a button when they experience a hallucination. Either of these two methods are hampered by the imaging method used. A combination of event-related potential and fMRI may eventually prove to provide the answer, although the difficulty is in coinciding the timing of the scan with the hallucination in such psychiatric patients. At present there appears to be solid evidence that the auditory association

FIG. 9.11

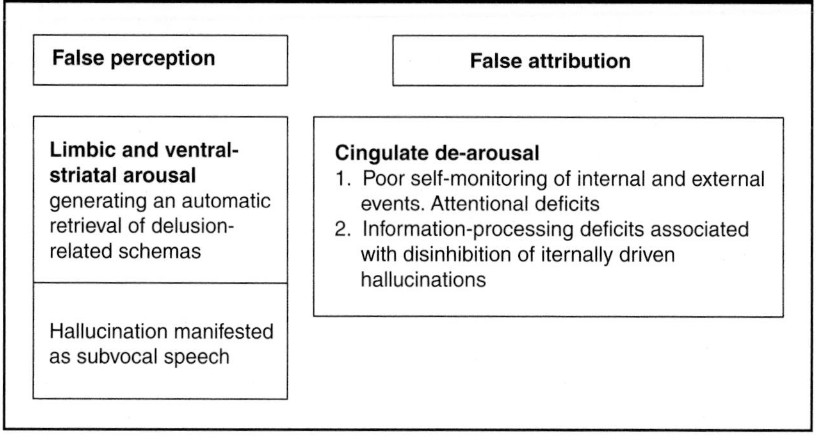

False perception		False attribution

Limbic and ventral-striatal arousal generating an automatic retrieval of delusion-related schemas	**Cingulate de-arousal** 1. Poor self-monitoring of internal and external events. Attentional deficits 2. Information-processing deficits associated with disinhibition of iternally driven hallucinations
Hallucination manifested as subvocal speech	

A schematic illustration of the factors that influence hallucination production in schizophrenic patients.

area is activated during auditory hallucinations but other areas of activation need to be confirmed by replication. At this point it appears that some patients produce their own hallucination. This is likely to be a top-down process in the sense that the hallucinations are tied to delusions and possibly additionally to subvocal speech.

The second assumption concerns the mounting evidence that the source or engine for hallucinations resides within a limbic ventral–striatal circuit. Imaging work seems to favour this view. Hallucinations are clearly not random irritations of a sensory system. They are personalised, culture-oriented productions that are highly related to the patient's own emotional themes of delusion. If this area is the source of hallucinations then certain predictions may be made. First, it appears that this area is overaroused in schizophrenic patients and that the hippocampus is implicated. Patients often complain of hallucinations many times a day and sometimes continuously. The hippocampus is important for the retrieval of recent memories but is also a consolidator of memories and therefore it is possible that each hallucination is in some way consolidating itself, reinforcing the likelihood of its returning. This might suggest that cognitive behavioural treatments should seek to reduce the incidence of hallucinations but also perhaps attempt to change their nature

and make them more benign (Shergill et al., 1998).

A final assumption is that the de-arousal of the frontal systems is in some way relevant to the verisimilitude of the hallucination. A tentative argument has been made that an imbalance in the activation between frontal cingulate structure and medial temporal lobe assists the hallucinatory process and enhances its sense of reality. Here most clearly the dopamine-based frontal lobe, which includes the cingulate, seems to be most crucial, although de-arousal of the dorsolateral prefrontal cortex has also been noted. Certainly, there seems to be some kind of an imbalance between these frontal systems and the ventral–limbic circuit, which may be normalised by reducing the presence of inhibiting dopamine. The question whether the cingulate plays an important role in the false-attribution of the hallucination remains unanswered. However, reviewed here are certain aspects of poor discrimination and impaired information processing which may encourage this view of the process of the hallucination. The first relates to inhibition and the finding that schizophrenia patients suffer numerous difficulties of attention, and problem-solving that may reduce the quality of information processing. This would, according to theory, act to encourage the event of a hallucination. The second relates to the difficulties in self-monitoring these patients have when trying to make judgements on experiences that might be internal or external. Figure 9.6 shows a description of how these processes may interact. This is a preliminary model that has no explanatory power at present. We are left with many important questions. There is still very little information on why these experiences are so often negative and often paranoid in their content. Also, because schizophrenic patients suffer so many cognitive deficits it is all too easy to ascribe a functional association to an phenomenon such as a hallucination. There remains a need to further isolate the crucial cognitive dysfunction that encourages the hallucinatory experience.

Capgras syndrome

Capgras is a strange disorder in which the patient believes their family are imposters. These patients may return home to their family after some form of traumatic brain injury to find that they have been replaced by look-alikes. Originally described by two French psychiatrists, Capgras and Reboul-Lachaux, in 1923 it was for many years seen as a psychiatric disorder and given a Freudian explanation. However, there are many features that indicate its organic nature which are described below. One of these is the finding that it can be modality specific; thus Ramachandran (1998) describes a patient who overcomes his syndrome and believes in the identity of his parents when he is on the telephone. However, the sound of their voices is not sufficient to dissuade him from his belief that they are not his true parents when he is with them. The disorder cannot be explained as an associative face agnosia, for some patients are capable of recognising familiar famous faces and of course they see their family as looking just like their real family. Nor can it be explained in terms of an apperceptive face agnosia since they are capable of matching faces accurately.

Ramachandran found that when presented with family photos a Capgras patient failed to show the usual emotional sweating response as measured by skin conductance or galvanic skin response. Ramachandran proposes that there is a disconnection between the recognition of a person's face and the emotional associations with that face which is mediated by the amygdala within the temporal lobe. Other disconnection explanations have been proposed (Bauer, 1986; Ellis & Young, 1990) but these have lost favour since they depend on a dorsal pathway being capable of some form of face identity recognition. A dorsal pathway is extremely unlikely given our modern knowledge of the neuroanatomical correlates of face recognition (Breen et al., 2000) (see also *Cognitive Neuropsychology*, special issue, Volume 17, 2000).

A more plausible model involves a single ventral pathway, which is important for face recognition. From this pathway the affective association is accessed within the inferior medial temporal lobe at the amygdala. In the case of Ramachandran's patient he proposes that his patient has a disconnection at this point, but a different pathway leading to the amygdala from the auditory system is intact. This explains the patient's ability to recognise the valid representation of his parents when he is talking to them on the phone. A similar theory is proposed by Breen et al. (2000; see Figure 9.12).

The question remains, if a person returns from hospital and finds that he no longer feels any emotional attachment to his family and is emotionally indifferent to their facial features, would this be sufficient for them to declare that they must be imposters? Even if the person now had different emotional reactions that contrasted dramatically with the old emotional response they remembered, one might suspect that the patient would blame his misperception on the brain trauma or some other factor before deciding that these people who looked just like his family were imposters. One has to remember that these patients are emphatic and argue against the logic supplied by both clinicians and family.

Alexander, Stuss, and Benson (1979) describe a 44-year-old man who suffered head injury. The patient had experienced auditory hallucinations and delusions associated with stress but had never acted on them. Some $2\frac{1}{2}$ years following the accident he informed Alexander that he had two families. The old family was seen to be younger

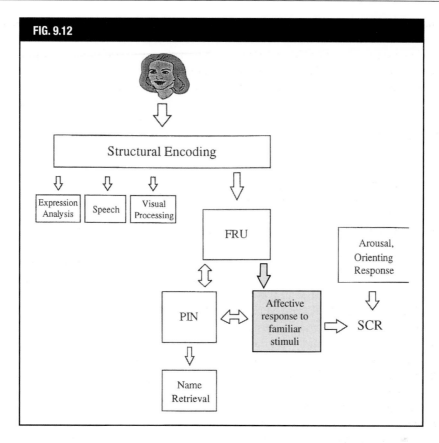

FIG. 9.12

The patient with Capgras fails to show an emotional arousal response to family photographs because of a disruption from the emotional associations mediated by such structures as the amygdala. From structural encoding the face recognition unit (FRU) signals the familiarity of the face. The personal identity nodes (PIN) supply semantic and biographical information about the person. Because of the disconnection with the emotional processor the usual emotional response to family members is not present in the skin conductance response (SCR). This model is an adaptation of one by Bruce and Young (1986) (from Breen et al., 2000, reprinted by permission of Psychology Press Ltd, Hove, UK).

and he claimed he had not seen his original family since around a month after the accident and had been taken home by a new wife to a new family, although they looked the same. From an interview they quote:

E: Isn't that [two families] unusual?
S: It was unbelievable!
E: How do you account for it?
S: I don't know. I try to understand it myself, and it was virtually impossible.
E: What if I told you I don't believe it?
S: That's perfectly understandable. In fact,

when I tell the story, I feel I am concocting a story . . . It's not quite right. Something is wrong.

The question whether the emotional disconnection is sufficient to explain the dogged determination to continue with a belief that is clearly preposterous is something that will no doubt be subject to further research in the future. Further disconnections between the face recognition unit and the personal identity nodes are not considered on the grounds that such patients may identify famous faces, but perhaps more sensitive assessment of the personal identity node is required. Also, many of these patients have a history of psychosis and there is a quality in these reports that the patient has suffered some form of hallucinatory condition in the past. This is a rare disorder and when it occurs it is often associated with a dementing process, so it remains a difficult topic to research.

Other psychiatric disorders

There is evidence of organically related depression in patients who suffer from basal ganglia related disorders such as Parkinson's disease and Huntington's chorea. This depression is not necessarily a response to the debilitating nature of their disease. Major depression not infrequently pre-dates the onset of clinical symptoms in the case of Huntington's disease (another basal ganglia motor disorder) (Peyser & Folstein, 1990) and the motor symptoms and stress due to the disability of Parkinson's disease correlate poorly with depression in Parkinson's disease (Robins, 1976). There seems to be a general acknowledgement that depression in these disorders may be due to organic, possibly biochemical abnormalities associated with these diseases. It is of interest that there is a tendency for more depression to be associated with anterior subcortical lesions, e.g. head of the caudate (Starkstein, Robinson, & Price, 1987), especially when the lesion is on the left side (Starkstein, Robinson et al., 1988a).

There is some support for this organic interpretation from functional imaging studies. Thus whether over- or underactivation is noted there is often abnormal metabolism in a subgenual (inferior to the genu, which is the anterior aspect of the corpus callosum) orbital area (Drevets & Raichle, 1995). There is also some involvement of the anterior cingulate. Most of this abnormal activity is in what is referred to as the paralimbic regions, being inferior and medial (Mayberg, 1997). This inferior frontal area is associated with abnormal activation in other disorders.

Patients with obsessive-compulsive disorder (OCD) suffer obsessions that often take the form of repetitive ruminations concerning the dangers of such issues as germ contamination and additionally have compulsions, with difficulty in refraining from certain behaviours, e.g. continuous hand-washing. These patients appear to have abnormalities in the orbital area that may be structural and not just biochemical (Szeszko et al., 1999). Abnormalities in this area might be expected given what we know about the orbito-frontal cortex and the attribution of an inhibiting role for this structure. The patient with OCD may be classified with more than an hour of repetitive compulsive behaviour which is often accompanied by significant subjective distress.

From these characteristics one may predict that these patients will show dysexecutive signs on neuropsychological tests and while results are variable this does seem to be the case when these patients are compared to a control group of patients who are normal or have panic disorder. However, these differences on such tasks as attention shifting when compared to normal controls and panic disorder do not show when the OCD patients are compared to those with depression (Purcell, Maruff, Kyrios, & Pantelis, 1998). Of course, many of these patients with OCD also suffer some depression but given the association of depression with abnormal metabolism in an inferior frontal area this may mean that both these groups of patients have dysexecutive signs. The OCD patients nevertheless do show slower motor initiation and impaired spatial working memory when compared to depressed patients.

GENERAL SUMMARY

Throughout this chapter there has been a conscious attempt to return to the theme that emotions are related to interactions between certain brain structures and environmental demands on the organism. Even the early research involving the stimulation and excitation of certain brain structures showed an awareness of the importance of this interaction. Certainly, the work by Kluver and Bucy was mostly interesting because of the way these animals interacted socially with the other members of their group—something that might have been missed with a pure laboratory study. This is an area that demands a number of research strategies and some allowance for confounding influences when brain–behaviour relationships are sought.

Following a review of some background history of research in this area, a neuropsychological model of emotional behaviour was developed based on human and other animal research. The small number of studies with humans confirms other animal studies that indicate the important role of the amygdala as a central processor of emotion. Most obviously roles for the amygdala have been found in conditioning and also in the perception of emotion. However, there are expectations that the amygdala and other related structures may also influence personality and other facets of emotional behaviour. There is some progress towards this goal in the clinical research reviewed in the second half of the chapter, although this work has yet to isolate and identify specific roles of brain structures that play a role in emotional behaviour.

When looking at the review of more recent findings in this chapter, certain patterns of research begin to emerge. Patients with right hemisphere lesions, especially stroke patients, are generally more likely to be impaired in their perception and expression of emotion within verbal and non-verbal communication. However, when the everyday behavioural expression of emotional and social behaviour is considered then it could be argued that the left hemisphere has a more controlling role, with more dysfunction in patients following left hemisphere lesions. Differences between the sexes were reported that showed qualitative differences, with right lesioned males reporting more inappropriate behaviours while left lesioned females report more anger and helplessness. More subtle differences in emotional dysfunction have also been referred to, such as groups of patients including those with posterior right hemisphere lesions who may ignore their own handicaps and emotional behaviour.

These general patterns overlook equally important influences on both communication and expression of emotion, some of which are not so readily lateralised. Patients with subcortical lesions are also found to have emotional problems and disorders of emotional communication, especially those with thalamic and basal ganglia lesions. Changes following frontal lobe damage and patient groups such as those with Parkinson's or Huntington's disease were also discussed which appear to have their own emotional/social profile. A variety of mechanisms have been put forward; for example, reduced cortical control, which was initially referred to in the early stages of this chapter when referring to MacLean's evolutionary model. In this model the phylogenetically primitive limbic system is directed and controlled by the evolutionarily more recent neocortex. In the early stages of brain injury disinhibition is sometimes posited as an explanation for a lack of emotional control. In particular, the orbital area of the prefrontal lobe is seen as having an inhibiting role on limbic structures such as the amygdala.

In line with the control of emotional and social behaviour was a discussion of work with patients who had ventral and ventro-orbital lesions. The question here was why these patients commit embarrassing behaviours when they know the etiquette surrounding these behaviours. Poor judgement in other areas such as on gambling tasks appears to be revealing difficulties in emotional conditioning which helps to give instant feedback on the advisability of launching into a particular behaviour. Further animal work was discussed suggesting that emotional learning, as described by classical conditioning, is dependent on a combination of structures that include the amygdala, the hippocampus and the orbitofrontal cortex. The orbital area appears to play a role in integrating the emotional response with the stimulus in a bid to identify and distinguish between rewarding and punishing events. Further problems within social interaction may also occur because the patient fails to pick up on the feelings of others. This may be part of a specific perceptual problem and here again the amygdala appears to be implicated among other predominantly right hemisphere structures.

While the model developed in this chapter referred to the role of the amygdala as a central processor and the frontal areas as a means of controlling and integrating emotional behaviour, less certainty was placed on a store for social knowledge. It was proposed that a knowledge system that was developed and influenced by our experience and cultural values existed to guide our behaviour. Such information is imparted to us by parental and societal influence but is dependent on an intact emotional system for its development. The temporal cortices were a possible area that might be implicated in this storage system given the importance of these cortices for other areas of memory. Also, the apparent lack of social knowledge in Kluver–Bucy syndrome might also implicate this area. However, further research is required to deduce the nature of this store of knowledge concerning social mores and cultural values.

Finally, a case was made for a module that was important for the execution of external affect. Several sources of evidence were presented to support a possible dissociation between the expression of emotion compared to the feelings that are associated with the expression—a dissociation between internal and external affect. Disorders which exhibit a compulsion to show crying or laughter in excess of the experienced emotion and certain seizure types suggest that a case can be made for a separate unit devoted to the mechanical production of the outward appearances of emotion.

The attention within this chapter then turned to clinical issues. Initially there was a discussion of the growing literature that was emerging to show neuropsychological mechanisms for disorders that at one time were seen as purely functional. Neuropsychiatry is a growing science that lends itself to neuropsychological analysis. The most intriguing puzzle at present is the mechanism for the hallucinations of schizophrenic patients and why they appear so real to the patients. Functional imaging has offered an opportunity to make some gains in knowledge within this territory. It is likely that some real

headway in understanding this phenomenon will be made using this research technique.

Obsessive compulsive disorder has also received recent research attention and a picture is unfolding here of a condition that may have some dysexecutive signs which could explain the repetitive behaviour of these patients. Like schizophrenia studies, studies of depressed patients have increased in association with the functional imaging techniques. These studies are now investigating the changes of brain metabolism following successful treatment. It is likely that future studies will investigate why some patients fail to respond to certain treatments using these techniques.

Despite the attempts here to theorise about the neuropsychological components of emotional behaviour one is reminded that theories that attempt to explain mechanisms of personality dysfunction are based on a relatively small number of case studies. It would not be too surprising to find that the emotional and social dysfunction found in patients with frontal lobe damage, for example, are due to more than one mechanism. For example, the ventromedial-damaged patients reported by Damasio have damage to structures that are differentiated at a physiological level. Orbital areas have different projections from the medial areas with which they connect. Given what we know about the attention control and initiating roles of medial frontal areas, e.g. anterior cingulate, and the stimulus–reward integration and inhibition characteristics of the orbital areas, it is possible that such patients suffer a damaging combination of deficits. That is both a failure to focus away from distracting and motivating stimuli (anterior cingulate), difficulties in controlling response, with a failure to make on-line distinctions between behaviour that has negative or positive consequences (orbital prefrontal cortex). Damage to either structure in isolation might be coped with, but a vulnerability to distraction, impulsivity plus an inability to make immediate on-line decisions without some deliberation is a close description of Phineus Gage and likely to lead to maladaptive social behaviour.

It is highly likely that eventually subtypes of emotional dysfunction due to brain dysfunction will be identified and this will allow tailored therapeutic management of emotional disorders. In this way patients may be treated on a prescriptive basis for what is arguably the most destructive handicap faced by both patients and those who try to support them.

10

Recovery from brain damage

INTRODUCTION

Knowledge of the recovery process is essential to any student of the health sciences; any clinician who deals with brain-damaged patients and their families will eventually be asked about the prognosis of the patient. How long will the patient take to recover? Will the patient be left with lasting handicap? Will they be able to return to work? These are just some of the questions put by anxious family members. Responses at this time should be cautious and some clinicians refrain from even using the word "recovery" (Lezak, 1995). Patients whose cases were originally considered hopeless and yet who go on and manage some intellectual achievement, such as passing a degree, regularly contribute to media stories entitled "My doctor said I would never recover."

Patients often misunderstand and misinterpret advice for a number of reasons. Sometimes this is due to the effect of anxiety on information processing and memory; however, there are other times when the clinician is misled into generalising too freely from the evidence of the classical recovery curve in Figure 10.1.

Curves such as this one tend to provide for most of the recovery taking place in the first 3 months, with the rate of recovery levelling off at the 9-month mark and reaching an asymptote after an interval of about 1 year. While many individuals do show this kind of recovery pattern, there are a number of positive and negative factors that can undermine and distort the normal progression of recovery from brain damage. The factors that may affect the recovery process are the main topic of discussion of the current chapter.

In the first half of this chapter there is a focus on *the mechanisms of recovery*. These mechanisms are described in terms of the chronological process of recovery. The acute phase immediately following brain damage, which may include trauma, surgery, disease, or other brain insult, is followed by a description of the more advanced stages of recovery. The initial stage of recovery can be seen as a process of "damage control" as the brain undergoes an *acute neurophysiological response* to brain insult. The next stage, termed the *adaptation phase*, can metaphorically be seen as the "healing stage". In the adaptation phase the phenomena of plasticity, diaschisis, and local reorganisation are discussed. These are all ways in which the brain reacts and adapts to neuronal damage in a positive way. Among the discussions which take place within this section is the effect of age on recovery. While it has long been seen as an advantage to have a lesion at an early age, this is not always the case. Here there is particular reference

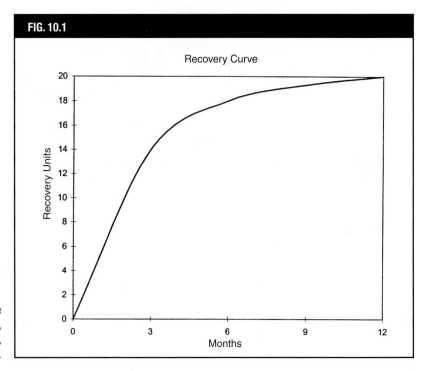

FIG. 10.1

Recovery Curve

The classical recovery curve (see Newcombe, Marshall, Caravick, & Hiorns, 1975, for examples).

to the disadvantage when damage is in the very early stage at a particular time when the foundations of the brain structure are in the process of development.

Descriptions of these neurophysiological processes of adaptation are followed by a discussion of psychological compensation in the form of *functional adaptation*. An example of a functional adaptation might be the use of a fist-like grip for lifting a cup when the brain areas representing the more orthodox thumb and index pincer-grip are damaged. There is also reference here to the influence of functional adaptation on our brain structure. Thus in the case of the fist-like grip, with repetitive use this type of compensatory grip will become natural and automatic as it gains a more dominant brain representation. These changes are illustrative of what is referred to broadly as brain *plasticity*. But these brain changes and associated changes in strategy are also dependent on the extent of *redundancy*; that is, the extent to which the remaining undamaged brain areas are able to take on the functional adaptation. If the damaged area includes the complete area devoted to motor function and there is further damage to

surrounding areas then there might be little redundancy of function; there would be no surviving brain tissue that could be adapted to hand movements. Some parts of the brain are very specialised in their function and have very little redundancy even when damage is discrete and to a small area.

The second half of this chapter is more clinically oriented. First, the *characteristics of the patient* that influence the rate of recovery are described. This includes such factors as severity of injury, age, and personality of the patient. This is followed by a discussion of the *general characteristics of recovery*, such as the emotional states associated with recovery, the way cognitive function recovers and psychosocial outcome. In the final section the *factors that encourage recovery* are described. These include factors that are relevant to those dealt with in Chapter 11 and include environmental stimulation and recognised specialised hospital treatments. The issue of transplantation of neural tissue is also discussed. Finally, a broad model for the recovery process is provided that describes the multifactorial influences on recovery.

MECHANISMS OF RECOVERY

The acute neurophysiological response

Oedema and neural shock

The early stages of recovery depend on the type of brain insult sustained by the patient. For example, there may be different effects associated with hypoxia compared to haemorrhage, which may have different consequences again compared to that of traumatic brain injury (TBI).

Oedema (brain swelling) is a frequent consequence of traumatic brain damage (TBI) during this stage of recovery. Oedema is one of the agents that, through its action, applies compression to the brain stem and which then leads to coma (see Chapter 1). Oedema is also commonly associated with other lesions such as stroke, and brain tumours such as meningiomas which press on brain structures. It may be initially visible on radiological scans in the areas surrounding those that are more permanently damaged. Oedema is associated with ruptured tissue and the collection of fluid around the brain cells. This, in turn, may cause further oedema through pressure and obstruction of major cerebral veins, thereby causing a build-up of cerebral blood volume (hyperaemia). Oedema is, on occasions, responsible for increased intracranial pressure (ICP). This would have to be monitored in cases when the brain stem with its life-preserving functions, e.g. respiration, is threatened by this increase in pressure.

Following, for example, a road traffic accident a person may go into coma for a number of reasons. Some of these are described in Chapter 1 and relate to pressure on the brain stem following haemorrhaging, e.g. subarachnoid hemorrhage or cortical oedema pressing on the brain stem. Despite the lack of arousal associated with coma some activity may take place. Some patients may even be induced to move the position of their limbs, which might be used for the practical purpose of reducing the occurrence of limb contracture, the limb rigidity caused by lack of movement during coma (Shiel et al., 1993). In this study the level of coma (e.g. Glasgow Coma Scale, (Teasdale & Jennett, 1976)) was not related to the ability of the patient to carry out simple movements such as removing a cloth from the face, it should not therefore be assumed that this is a totally passive state. While there is a remarkable variation in the presentation during coma, the potentially active nature of this state is well illustrated in this second-hand report following a severe head injury: "My wife was with me almost round the clock for the first two weeks and for several hours per day thereafter until I was discharged. She tells me that even when I was unconscious my body was constantly in motion, tugging at the traction, trying to move my limbs immobilised by casts, testing out my limits of movement. On some level, it would seem that my body was fighting on its own even when my brain was unable to function" (Linge, 1990).

Other effects of cerebral insult include a temporary imbalance of biochemical substances, referred to as neural shock (Luria, 1973). This disturbance of neurotransmitter substances may be ameliorated over the few days following trauma. These and other acute effects may, depending on the severity, be reduced over the days and weeks following the event and lead to a recovery of cognitive functions that were being suppressed by these mechanisms. This type of recovery is sometimes referred to as "artefact recovery", because in one sense it is not recovery at all since the functions were merely in suspension and were not actually lost in the first place. Therefore, some of the early rapid recovery that is seen in the early stages (e.g. first few weeks) is due to a resolution of the acute negative neurophysiological consequences of brain insult and may not be indicative of more permanent damage.

Diaschisis

Another example of artefact recovery is present in the phenomenon of diaschisis. Von Monakow used this term in 1914 to describe the observation that function may return suddenly following injury. Finger and Stein (1982) refer to the case of a sailor who was admitted to a North American hospital. After a period of being mute (without speech), the patient started speaking with little fault in a southern drawl to a nonplussed and

Studies that have investigated redundancy in animal subjects initially map out the functional representation of the cortex in the area of interest. This may be done by placing electrodes in brain areas and gauging the electrical response when a behaviour is carried out. Alternatively, the brain may be given electrical stimulation in various areas and the behavioural response is assessed (see Chapter 7 for this kind of experiment with human epileptic subjects). Often the motor cortex is chosen for its well-defined response of movement corresponding to different body areas. In this way a number of experiments have shown that a group of cortical neurones may maximally fire in response to a particular action of an animal, e.g. wrist movement of the monkey. Typically, when mapping out the cortical area, there are some neurones that respond to a lesser extent in the periphery of these cell groups. The second stage of such an experiment would be to excise those maximally responsive cells and allow recovery to take place. The responsiveness of the area is later measured again after some recovery to find that those cells that were originally responding infrequently during pre-lesion mapping are now firing maximally and have therefore taken over the role of the damaged neurones (see Figure 10.2). In other words, plasticity has occurred because there is some redundancy for this function. This result is often explained by arguing that in the animal without a lesion the firing of the main group normally inhibits these neurones on the periphery. Thus when the main group is destroyed, the remaining neurones are freer to respond (Wall, 1980; see Bach-Y-Rita, 1990, for a discussion).

Redundancy is sometimes supported in another sense. In this case the redundancy relates to alternative routes to achieve the same function. For example, a model of language includes cortical and subcortical routes (see Chapter 7). Sometimes language impairment is only temporary, as in the case of a thalamic lesion. This may be explained in terms of an alternative substitute route becoming more dominant (see Papanicolaou, Moore, & Deutsch, 1989, for this line of argument; see Poeck, 1990, for arguments against).

One of the important therapeutic issues for discussion is whether the plasticity associated with training depends on the degree of redundancy of a function. That is, can one predict that in the case where a scan shows little hope of redundancy should the clinician then decide on a rehabilitation programme that concentrates on alternative ways of completing the behavioural goal? Such a question is crucial since the decision will accelerate or retard the recovery of a patient.

Plasticity during brain development

The relationship between brain development in infancy and recovery from brain damage is sufficiently complex to warrant a complete description of this process. Early brain development prior to birth mainly involves two processes: first, neurogenesis, a process in which new brain cells are formed and multiply through mitosis; and, second, the process of cell migration, in which these new brain cells are by degrees positioned to form more mature brain structures such as the cortex.

At present, most of what we know about brain injury during brain development is extrapolated from non-human studies. Nevertheless some tentative statements may be made concerning the human case. Depending on the area of the brain being considered, neurogenesis and cell migration are near to completion some days after birth (see Figure 10.3a) (Kolb, 1995). Injury during this time does not bode well for the infant's eventual recovery.

If these early processes of development are interfered with then there are two negative implications. The first relates to a reduced number of brain cells. The second implication relates to the repercussion of injury on eventual brain development. Insult to the brain during cell migration may affect brain development to the extent that the patient's brain structure may be more broadly affected and may even cause distortions in brain development (Kolb, 1995).

The third overlapping process (see Figure 10.3b) of differentiation and neuronal maturation involves axonal and dendritic development and extensive synaptogenisis (increased interconnec-

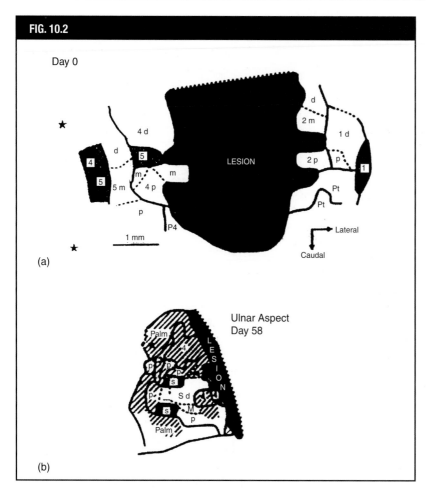

FIG. 10.2

Day 0

(a)

Ulnar Aspect
Day 58

(b)

Mapping of the brain area representing motor areas (a) before and (b) after recovery. The shaded area has been reorganised to include areas such as 3, which were originally damaged (reprinted from Jenkins, Merzenich, & Recanzone, 1990, with permission from Elsevier Science).

tions between neurones). This will also be undermined by lesions during the cell migration since synaptogenesis depends on the earlier stage for its successful completion. All these factors may contribute to the thinning of the cortex in adulthood.

According to animal experiments, bilateral frontal brain lesions during the early stage of brain development leads to reduced synaptogenesis and cortical thinning, both in the area of the lesion and other areas within the same hemisphere. There is the implication from these experiments with rats that injury in frontal areas has more far-reaching effects on brain function when compared to lesions in other areas (see Kolb & Whishaw, 1989, pp. 257–267). The cause

of this reduced tree-like branching out of dendrites (arborisation) is likely to reflect a reduced stimulation from the damaged area (neurones projecting *into* healthy tissue) (Kolb & Whishaw, 1989). This mechanism may also be responsible for the accompanying reduced size of subcortical nuclei that project into those areas. For example, lesions to frontal cortical regions may influence the synaptogenisis that takes place in the caudate nucleus and thalamus.

In contrast, posterior lesions are more likely to be associated with sensory and motor symptoms and are associated with reduction in the size and projections of the thalamus and other structures connected with these cortical areas (Kolb & Whishaw, 1989). Therefore the effect of injury on

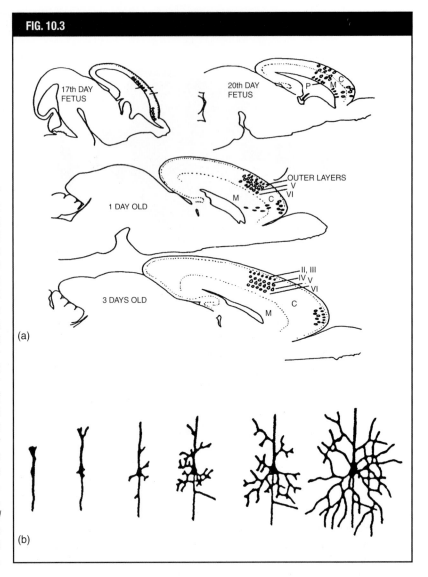

FIG. 10.3

(a) The various stages of brain development associated with microgenesis and cell proliferation. The cells are assembled on the surface of the neural groove, which later become the lateral ventricle; as the brain develops, these cell layers develop outwards so that these initial layers later make up the uppermost superficial cell layers at 17 months. (b) The process of synaptogenesis. Axons and dendrites lengthen to allow increased contact with other neurones. Synapses are attached to spines on the surface of the dendrites. (Reprinted from Kolb, B. (1995). *Brain plasticity and behaviour*. New Jersey, with permission from Lawrence Erlbaum Associates).

brain development is dependent not only on the area damaged, but also the areas with which the area is networked. The function of the brain area may be a guide as to the other areas that will be affected. When considering the executive responsibility that has been attributed to the prefrontal cortex there is no surprise that damage to this area is likely to implicate many other brain areas.

Banich, Levine, Kim, and Huttenlocher (1990) report on the longitudinal intellectual scores of a group of children with congenital injuries show-ing evidence that these children "grow into deficits" (see Figure 10.4). That is, as they become older they become progressively more disadvantaged. This must in part be because of their inability to learn and organise efficiently. These difficulties mean that the child has a disadvantage that is cumulative in its effect and would cause the child to fall further and further behind in their studies. Also, as the requirements of schoolwork become more complex and demanding the children's poverty of intellectual resources will also become more obvious.

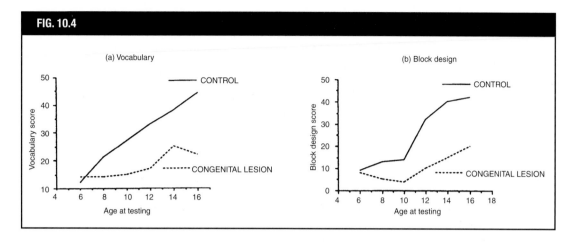

FIG. 10.4

(a) Vocabulary

(b) Block design

"Growing into deficits" (reprinted from Branich et al., 1990), with permission from Elsevier Science).

The next stage of brain development goes from one of the worst times to have an injury to one of the best times. Broadly, in early childhood the number of synapses, or connections between neurones, builds up to a level far in excess of what is eventually required in adulthood. Therefore there is a rapid increase in synaptogenesis which, with the lengthening of the axon, myelinisation (development of fatty insulating tissue surrounding the axon) and increased dendrite formation, causes a fourfold increase in brain size during the first 3–4 years of life. This massive increase in synapses is then followed by a reduction or *pruning* in the number of synapses, which eventually levels out to adult levels. This process of synaptic pruning levels out to adult levels at around 7 years in the visual cortex in humans, but may continue up to 16 years in the far more delayed process within the frontal cortex (Huttenlocher, 1990).

Given the results of investigating non-human recovery, it appears that if injury occurs during or just after this maximal period of synaptogenesis, before synapses have been reduced to adult levels, then the outcome is the most favourable (Kolb, 1995). This finding is intuitively appealing since the pruning of excessive synaptic connections may be seen as a process by which environmental conditions may mould the brain by retaining environmentally useful connections and patterns at the expense of less useful configurations. This

is a highly adaptive mechanism since if there is a lesion the synaptic pruning will take this limitation metaphorically into account as the brain adapts flexibly according to its structural resources (see Huttenlocher, 1990, for a reference to these theories). Kolb (1995, p. 75) proposes that there are reservations regarding the generalisation of rodent research in this area to humans because of the non-equivalence of the times in the developmental stages. However, he suggests: "Indeed, it might be reasonable to expect that there would be more plasticity during the period of overproduction of synapses, as the larger number of synapses might lead to an enhanced capacity to adjust to injury."

The ratio between the excess of synaptic connections and the final adult level varies with the complexity of the species. For example, the level of excessive synaptic connections in the human and monkey is far in excess of the cat. Therefore, the advantages of this relatively late postnatal adaptation are not available to all species to the same extent and might be expected to favour the human brain. Also, as mentioned, there may be further delays in some brain areas compared to others. As might be expected, the areas with the attributed complex integrating functions such as the frontal cortex are the last to develop. Synaptic decline in the frontal cortex does not even start or at least is not noticeable until around 7 years of age (Huttenlocher, 1990). Thus one may speculate that the frontal cortex may have a different window in terms the optimal period for injury. In other words, while early lesions in the frontal area may have a poor prognosis lesions later on in childhood may be more forgiving because of an extended period of synaptogenesis. An open mind is required on these issues.

Further compensatory responses to injury in childhood

While there has been a discussion of cortical thinning in response to the earliest lesions when the brain cell structure is still developing, quite a different story presents itself following hemidecortication. Animal studies suggest that the remaining hemisphere does not require the stimulation of the lost hemisphere but actually increases its size as if responding to a greater involvement and stimulation having to act in isolation. The development of the surviving hemisphere has been associated with increased length of dendrites and dendritic spines, which is associated with increased synaptogenesis and increased recovery of function.

As suggested, there is the assumption that brain development is undermined by a lack of stimulation. However, when the cortex of one hemisphere is damaged early enough there is no abnormal lack of stimulation from one hemisphere to another because the corpus callosum does not fully develop until a relatively late stage. This thickening of the healthy hemisphere is therefore most dramatic with early hemidecortication.

During this critical early stage removal of the cortex from one hemisphere of the rat has the effect of greater arborisation and synaptogenesis within the remaining hemicortex and its subcortical areas (thalamus) (Kolb, Gibb, & van der Kooy, 1992; Kolb & Whishaw, 1989). This same thickening does not appear to occur to the same extent when hemidecortication is in adulthood, presumably because by this time the corpus callosum is fully developed and degeneration occurs across from one hemisphere to the other.

Thickening of the healthy hemisphere of the infant following hemidecortication is due in part to the setting up of new ipsilateral connections in the intact hemisphere. This remarkable physio-

logical adaptation of the hemidecorticated infant has been found to result in a significant sparing of cognitive function when later measured in adulthood. However, bilateral lesions during the critical developmental period are associated with very poor outcome. Bilateral lesions are associated with cortical thinning rather than cortical thickening.

In summary, plasticity appears to interact with the time and stage of brain development. It may be difficult to generalise from rat studies to the human, but recovery in the rat is poorest when the processes of neurogenesis and cell migration are still occurring. This appears to be prior to around 5 days of postnatal development, but may extend to a later time interval, especially when the frontal cortex is considered. The equivalent period in the human is uncertain but probably within the first months postnatally. Lesions during this critical period causes cortical thinning which when measured later in adulthood is represented by stunted neuronal formation and a reduced number of synapses. Bilateral and incomplete unilateral lesions result in a worse prognosis and this is likely to cause thinning, but also aberrant interfering with new connections between neurones. The best outcome, arguably better than lesions in adulthood, occurs when the number of synaptic connections is maximised. This stage is followed by synaptic pruning, which is assumed to allow some adaptation to brain damage.

Cortical thickening of the undamaged hemisphere takes place as a response to early complete hemidecortication. This is most dramatically supported by relatively good recovery of these subjects, even when the operation takes place close to and within the early critical developmental period.

Sex differences and mechanisms of plasticity

Kolb and Stewart (1991) found that male rats had a thicker right cortex when compared to the left, which was not evident in female rats. However, they have also found serendipitously that if the mother of a male pup is subjected to stress during pregnancy, then this greater thickness of the right cortex fails to occur (Stewart & Kolby, 1988).

Male rats generally have more cortical neurones compared to females (Reid & Juraska, 1992), although females appear to compensate with greater synaptic density, as represented by a greater quantity of dendritic material. However, the differentiation is more complex since when some specific areas of the frontal cortex are surveyed in females they are found to have a thicker cortex, with more brain cells. Male and female rat brains are different and these differences appear to be driven by hormonal differences that are present at birth.

Human males and females have a slight mean advantage over each other depending on the skill tested. Differences have also been found in non-human animals. On an alternation task requiring a flexible shifting of a learned response, Clark and Goldman-Rakic (1989) found male monkeys were superior compared to females. A suggestion that the females were possibly using a different brain area for this task when compared to the male monkeys came from the finding that lesions to the orbital cortex severely impaired the males' performance but not the females'. The performance of female monkeys was, however, improved to the level of the males if they were treated pre- and postnatally with testosterone. However, the treated females then became as vulnerable to orbital lesions as the males on this task. In other words, hormones appear to influence skills and the area of the brain used by those skills, and consequently the effect on recovery following damage to a particular brain area differ. Similar differences have been found in rat studies, with differential impairment being measured following frontal lesions depending on the task (Kolb & Cioe, 1996).

Some of these differences may also contribute to differences in plasticity between the sexes. Measures of synaptic recovery (dendritic spines) were blocked in males following gonadectomy, while there was less arborisation in the case of females following perinatal exposure to testosterone (Kolb & Stewart, 1995).

Finally, enriched environments have differential effects on synaptogenesis in male and female rat development, with males showing more dendritic development within the visual cortex and females showing more development within the hippocampus (Juraska, 1986). Therefore one might predict that the rehabilitation experience might affect males and females differentially and that hormone levels may play a role in recovery of the patient, but it is too early to speculate how this might happen. In summary, there appears to be hormonal effects on the development of brain structures, the functional brain relationship and the mechanisms of recovery.

In one study reported by Kimura (1992) reasoning ability was found to be related to hormonal levels in humans; however, little is known concerning the recovery rate in humans. McGlone (1980) provides evidence that aphasia following stroke is significantly more common in males compared to females. This may not be due to a more bilateral representation of language in the female brain, but rather to more diffuse representation of language within the left hemisphere in the female. There is evidence of more anterior representation of language in females (Ojemann et al., 1989) and this more diffuse representation of language may possibly render females less vulnerable to language disorder following stroke.

The reorganisation of language and plasticity

Children have greater recovery of language when compared to adults following damage in the dominant hemisphere. Part of this better age-related prognosis for language is due to the apparent ease with which children may reorganise language either within the same hemisphere or in some cases to the opposite hemisphere. One might expect such reorganisation to be most successful during the period of maximum synaptic contact, just prior to or at the start of pruning, perhaps before 5 years old. Woods and Teuber (1978) studied children and found that all those who had aphasia prior to 8 years recovered speech, although the recovery time was very variable, from 1 month to 2 years. In terms of the left hemisphere dominance of speech being present early, it is of interest that of the 34 children with left hemisphere lesion, 25 had an initial aphasia,

explanation for recovery, especially in adulthood. Modern studies of motor recovery often use video recording or high-speed film to capture the different ways the lesioned animal achieves its goal. Often the animal eventually achieves a similar speed and accuracy of performance but a new set of movements or skills is used which is only apparent when the animal is viewed in slow motion.

Nevertheless, there is evidence of neurophysiological recovery of the damaged area which may eventually reinstate some of the original behavious in non-human research. The process, however, may take some months (Jenkins et al., 1990). We still know very little about the ongoing long-term rate of neurophysiological processes of recovery. There are numerous case studies of lengthy recoveries in the literature. For example, Geschwind (1985) describes a number of such patients, including one patient who was severely aphasic in the first year and was still showing evidence of aphasia after 6 years, but whose aphasia had substantially cleared after 18 years.

There is now increasing evidence that adult monkeys and rats show reorganisation of function following excision of a cortical area and that this is related to the redundancy of the system and the post-lesion behaviour and environmental conditions. If the lesion is too extensive or the undamaged area is too distant from the position of the original representative cortical area then reorganisation is less likely to take place. However, reorganisation between neighbouring motor areas has been found and when this neighbouring area is no longer being used then such reorganisation is encouraged. For example, Jenkins removed the third digit in a monkey and then after some months the cortical area was reassessed; it was found that the area representing this digit had disappeared and had been replaced by extended representation of the neighbouring digits (Jenkins et al., 1990).

Nudo, Milliken, Jenkins, and Merzenich (1996) provide evidence that there is no clear division between functional adaptation and mechanisms of plasticity by finding that whether the monkey is lesioned or not training a muscle group will increase its representation at the expense of other representations. These results have been found with other species and one study found suggestions from a scanning procedure that changes occur in Braille readers. These subjects, who had used extensive Braille reading since childhood, showed a much larger brain area in the right hemisphere which controlled the use of the left hand (Pascual-Leone et al., 1993).

Also, if a monkey is lesioned in a representative area of a particular movement and that movement is not carried out in post-lesion training then the area is less likely to show recovery through the usual reorganisation mechanism. In other words, reorganisation associated with redundancy may be encouraged through training or alternatively retarded by a lack of training or restraining (Nudo & Milliken, 1996). The motto "use it or lose it" appears to be true of motor behaviours and although this view has only been recently supported scientifically, physiotherapists have assumed this to be the case for some time. The big question for rehabilitationists is whether they wish to try and reinstate the original behaviour or a functional adaptation. In making this decision there must be consideration of the severity of the lesion: is there undamaged tissue sufficient to allow redundancy? If this is judged not to be the case then functional adaptation or achieving the goal by different means must be considered. Whether reinstitution of the original behaviour or a different way of achieving the same goal in the form of a functional adaptation is being sort, the literature promotes the view that the patient must be active and stimulated during their recovery. However, not all programmes take this into account. Stein and Glasier (1992) point out that during rehabilitation the normal cortical reorganisation that occurs in the natural setting could be interfered with by confining a patient to training procedures that may not be relevant to everyday functioning. They also quote figures revealing that some 65% of nursing home patients in the state of California are either physically or chemically restrained, proposing that this "may actually produce or exacerbate some of the behavioral impairments that the therapist is seeking to avoid" (Stein & Glasier, 1992, p. 15).

The new research, which throws light on the

relationship between training and plasticity, encourages some deliberation when designing a rehabilitation programme to suit a patient. Should we train for functional adaptation or the regaining of the lost behaviour? Should we now be taking into account the potential redundancy and the severity of the lesion when making these decisions?

Summary

Unless brain damage is severe there is often a rapid recovery in the first few months after brain insult. A proportion of this recovery can be attributed to artefact recovery—recovery of function that has been suspended due to the negative physical interfering effects of brain trauma. The regaining of this function, when such factors as neural shock and oedema have subsided, is taken over by a greater prominence of what is referred to here as the adaptation phase. Local reorganisation during the adaptation phase includes such neuronal processes as sprouting and regeneration. When the developing brain is considered there will also be synaptogenesis and consequent cortical thickening in undamaged areas. The plasticity that takes place during this time is likely to correspond closely to the behavioural experience of the animal. The adaptation phase constitutes a dynamic interaction between the nature of the injury and the functional response to environmental demands.

There is generally evidence of greater plasticity in children compared to adults. At one time it was thought that this was inevitably the case and was referred to as the Kennard principle. However, recently a more complex picture has emerged whereby lesions in childhood result in more adaptation, except when the lesion occurs in infancy during the time the brain cells are increasing (neurogenesis) and taking up their position as the brain structure is formed (cell migration). Lesions during this time (approximately within the first year and congenitally) can disrupt brain development and cause disadvantages both in school and later in life. If you have to have a brain injury then a far better time to have it is when a third stage of synaptogenesis is reaching a point where there is an excess of synapses, around the time when a reduction is occurring (synaptic pruning). As a general rule, function following childhood lesions and adult lesions is qualitatively different. Adult injury may result in more severe isolated deficits when compared to the more broad intellectual impairments suffered by children. This appears to be due to the tendency for the brain areas to become more specialised and show less plasticity as we get older.

Plasticity during brain development includes a compensatory thickening of the cortex in the undamaged hemisphere. This is most obvious in the case of hemidecortication. There are a number of factors that may hasten or retard plasticity, including the interaction with hormones that are likely to differentially influence the nature of the recovery process in males versus females. Other trophic factors not discussed here also play a role. Such factors include the biochemical support provided by glia such as astrocytes—the cells that normally play a supportive role in the healthy functioning of neurones.

The extent of the reorganisation of language to the contralateral hemisphere following early injury is uncertain. Cases of hemidecortication teach us that this may be complete but other cases of childhood injury and epilepsy suggest that such reorganisation may be as much within the left hemisphere as in the contralateral hemisphere.

When viewing the factors that encourage plasticity in the brain, some areas may be more forgiving than others. Some areas of the brain allow for significant redundancy while others, such as the hippocampus and the visual pathways, are highly specific in their function and allow very little. Evidence was reviewed that suggested that, within limitations, recovery in adulthood may be associated with undamaged cortical areas taking on the functional representation of neighbouring damaged areas. This is the restitution of the original function.

An alternative and perhaps more realistic goal in many cases is the attempt to bypass the damaged ability and train the patient to achieve the same goal by using an alternative behaviour. This is the functional adaptation approach. However, both adaptation and restitution or reorganisation are similar in one way. Both are associated with changing brain structure, which is driven by the activities and training of the lesioned animal. Thus even functional adaptation is associated with a changing functional representation of the brain. The evidence that training will enhance cortical representation and unused functions will be less represented promotes the view that the therapy process within rehabilitation must be carefully chosen. Functional adaptation may ultimately result in ungainly and less efficient behaviours but damage may sometimes allow little scope for redundancy. As a description of the underlying mechanism of both these approaches to rehabilitation, plasticity is the neurophysiological adaptation of brain structure to damage as a consequence of an interaction between the redundancy of the area lesioned and the post-lesion experience. It is influenced by a number of factors, including the stage of brain development, hormonal influences, and premorbid experience.

This accent on the experience of the individual stresses the practical implication that ecologically valid training is essential so that neurophysiological structure is in tune with the demands made on the patient once they leave hospital. In the remainder of this chapter we look at recovery on another level that is closer to everyday clinical experience.

FEATURES THAT INFLUENCE THE RECOVERY PROCESS: A CLINICAL PERSPECTIVE

Characteristics of the individual

Severity of brain damage
The overriding factor affecting recovery is the severity of brain damage. This can be judged by the size of the lesion or, in the case of traumatic brain injury (TBI), by the length of coma or post-traumatic amnesia (PTA), or by the initial severity of the functional deficit. These indicators all have their various disadvantages. While the size of the lesion has been found to be a consistent indicator of functional recovery in children

(Aram & Eisele, 1992), Irle (1987) argues more generally from the literature that smaller lesions may in fact under some circumstances be more of a disadvantage. This is especially the case when surviving neurones are inhibitory and when neuronal regeneration results in connections that are maladaptive. Also, although PTA may have a better relationship with prognosis than coma alone, this is still an unreliable predictor and often not reliably measured (Lezak, 1995, p. 174). In the case of recovery from aphasia the initial severity of aphasic disturbance is also taken as a good indicator of final outcome (Kertesz, 1993b). However, even here there are some provisos depending on the structures being undermined (Naeser, 1994).

Age
Leaving aside comparisons with children, which have already been discussed, age within adulthood does not seem to be as strong a factor as one might presume. When looking at age effects in adulthood some studies fail to find an age effect (Keenan & Brassel, 1974), with correlations tending to be rather weak. However, relationships with age do exist when the measures are broad, such as the incidence of morbidity, mortality and returning home after stroke. One of the difficulties in making comparisons between age groups is the marked difference in age associated with different types of disorders. Thus, while young patients tend to be suffering from TBI, older patients tend to suffer more from strokes and so comparisons are difficult to make. Recently, Katz and Alexander (1994) found an age relationship in patients with TBI. They found patients over the age of 40 years had significantly longer PTA and had a worse functional outcome.

There is possibly a relationship between the effects of brain insult and the later acceleration of deterioration in old age. There is some evidence that head injury when it occurs at a young age may exacerbate cognitive decline when the same person reaches old age (Corkin, 1989). Further support for the accelerated intellectual decline of older persons with a history of brain lesions is a study of a group of patients who received a frontal lobotomy (Hamlin, 1970). A year after their surgery their level of intellectual function appeared recovered and was near to their pre-surgical levels. However, when they were assessed around 10 years later they were found to have deteriorated more compared to their peers. Although there is some uncertainty in this area (Kolb, 1995) brain cells tend not to renew in the same way that cells in the peripheral nervous system do. Therefore loss of cells due to ageing must accumulate with cell loss sustained due to other causes, e.g. head injury. While some sustain cell loss and apparently compensate through increased arborisation or complex dendritic growth of the neurones, no doubt there is a point or threshold of cell density below which the first signs of dementia appear. Certainly, the higher incidence of a history of brain injury in patients with Alzheimer's disease seems to support this view. However, one must be wary of research that is based on correlations, since such persons may be more prone to accidents for some third common reason.

Personality and intelligence

Depression and passivity are often associated with poor recovery (Robinson & Benson, 1981). It is seen as important to intervene with drug therapy when stroke is associated with depression for this reason.

Whether or not intelligence can influence recovery can be answered in two ways. Most obviously, highly intelligent persons may recover faster because they are more ingenious in their ability to adapt to the environment with their new handicap. In the same vein, persons of low intelligence may deteriorate to a similar degree as someone with a high intelligence with an identical lesion and deteriorate to a level where they may require support for activities of daily living. For example, if a person goes from an IQ of 90 to one of 70 this is more problematic for their everyday functioning than if a person goes from 120 to 100 (average) IQ. This is not to suggest that these two changes can be equated in terms of being due to equally severe brain damage. Nevertheless, the point is worth making that some persons have less to lose before they get into trouble with handling money or driving a car, for example. Therefore

the question of intelligence cannot be dissociated from the issue of how the intelligence interacts with environmental demands and the degree of "handicap".

An attempt to answer this question in a more scientific manner may be undermined by the limitations of the measures used. For example, the popular Wechsler Adult Intelligence Scale–Revised (WAIS-R) may not be as discriminating between patients at the top end or at the bottom end of the scale and other tests may also have varying degrees of reliability at different levels (Chapman & Chapman, 1973). In other words, a drop-off of IQ for a patient at the high end may not be equivalent to a similar drop-off at the lower end of the scale in terms of the patient's everyday adaptability. Recovery on the same or different scales in patients who are originally matched on degree of deterioration involves the same problems.

In terms of stroke patients, studies that have been less interested in these extremes have generally found that such factors as health, educational level, and employment have little effect on recovery when compared to factors such as aphasic symptoms, e.g. comprehension and fluency (Keenan & Brassel, 1974). Therefore, if a person has a particular functional difficulty, like memory impairment, this may to some extent outweigh socio-economic factors. However, socio-economic status of a patient and the degree of family support are also critical and may influence the rate of recovery in patients who have suffered TBI (Sbordone, 1987) or stroke (Kelly-Hayes & Paige, 1995).

The motivation and attitude of the patient often impress the rehabilitationist as an important factor. However, this important factor, which may be a feature of the patient's personality prior to brain insult, has generally been difficult to assess and may be confounded by a number of other issues.

Characteristics of the disorder

Stroke

Stroke is a term that is often preferred to cerebrovascular accident (CVA). Stroke is a good description of the sudden nature and impact of the event and some clinicians object to use of the word "accident" since the term draws attention away from preventive medicine and the factors that often herald and predict the onset of stroke. Recovery from stroke is often described in terms of two stages. The first stage involves an extensive biochemical and vascular recovery and the reduction of oedema—in fact many of the processes described above as part of the acute phase of recovery. There are a number of pharmacological interventions that may be used to stabilise and compensate the biochemical imbalances caused by the stroke (see Kertesz, 1993b, p. 648). This first stage in the hours and days after stroke is accompanied by a substantial amount of recovery of function. The second stage of recovery, which is associated with improvement of the patient over the months and years after stroke, is associated more with the other recovery mechanisms described above as functional adaptation.

Because stroke patients are generally an older population of patients they are more likely to remain dependent on a carer when compared to other diseases. If they survive, about a third will require assistance with activities of daily living (ADL) and a fifth will require assistance with ambulating after 1 year, with motor recovery plateauing at around 3 months (Kelly-Hayes et al., 1988; Pak & Dombovy, 1994). Around half of these patients have dysphagia (related to a difficulty in swallowing) and half of these dysphagia patients may show signs of difficulty with aspiration (drawing of breath). This is especially the case when there is brain stem or bilateral involvement, a good proportion of these patients only showing signs of such difficulty during a measurement technique referred to as videofluoroscopic evaluation (e.g., Gordon, Hewer, & Wade, 1987).

After the initial recovery phase in which cognitive recovery is most noticeable, the picture remains more static for about 5 years, and in older patients there is an increased functional deterioration and institutionalisation (Pak & Dombovy, 1994). Although there is an even greater proportion of patients who *claim* aphasic symptoms from self-report, a smaller number

(around a quarter) of these patients are diagnosed aphasic in the acute stage, which is reduced to around 12% at 6 months. Hemianopia is found in about a sixth of patients in the acute phase and around half of the survivors have some residual hemiparesis after 6 months. These deficits are understandably accompanied by primary and secondary depression in many cases (see Chapter 9 for a discussion). Within the stroke group there are variations according to aetiology (Kelly-Hayes et al., 1988). For example, haemorrhagic strokes initially have a greater risk of mortality, with the death of around a half of all patients, compared to less than a quarter of infarct patients. However, the survivors of haemorrhagic stroke tend to have a better prognosis.

Traumatic brain injury (TBI)

There is a similar variation in recovery from TBI. The variety of lesions sustained following TBI are associated with a corresponding variation in recovery profiles. A patient with severe TBI will go through a period of coma and PTA (period of coma plus a phase of disorientation and confusion). The period of confusion is usually proportionally four times longer than the period of coma. PTA is often found to be a better indicator of prognosis when compared to coma, especially with milder head injury. However, relationships between PTA and prognosis remain moderate (about a third of the variance; Brooks, 1984) and may be more useful with axonal injuries (diffuse shearing of axons, especially in the brain stem) when compared to focal lesions (Katz & Alexander, 1994).

Nevertheless, although indicators such as coma may be inadequate predictors of cognitive function after recovery, lengthy coma duration and their neurophysiological correlates are obviously an important consideration where the survival and recovery of the patient are concerned. As already described, the associated pathology of coma may include swelling of the cortical areas (oedema) which may press on those brain stem areas that are important for such functions as respiration and arousal. For this reason, intracranial pressure is often monitored. The recovery curve will vary depending on the severity of head injury in such a way that the more severely head-injured person may experience a lesser recovery and have a prolonged recovery period lasting for some years (see Figure 10.5). It should also be noted that the slope of recovery for more severe TBI is more gradual. Such curves have obvious implications for the time of introducing rehabilitation, the type of rehabilitation used, and the expectancies in terms of rate of improvement.

Differential neuropsychological recovery and measurement issues

Features of neuropsychological recovery vary significantly with the disorder and location of the damage. The preceding chapters have covered these issues and drawn attention to the way the distribution of the cerebral vascular system may dictate the nature of the cognitive deterioration. For example, language impairment often follows left middle cerebral artery stroke. The nature of head injury following a motor vehicle accident also gives rise to common patterns of cognitive deficit.

Commonalities exist, however, with the patient in the initial phases of recovery invariably having difficulty concentrating, being easy to fatigue and being irritable in terms of their mood. Memory as the final common pathway is, of course, affected by these factors and often structures such as the hippocampus or thalamus are damaged, giving rise to primary memory disorder (one due to direct damage to the structures responsible for memory).

The measurement of cognitive recovery is fraught with methodological problems and varies according to the type of cognitive process being assessed. This is well illustrated in a study looking at recovery of IQ by Brooks et al. (1984). In this study, although the mean results of the individuals looks like the recovery curve in Figure 10.1, a plot of the individual results shows that the mean is not at all a good representative of how the individuals perform. The performance of the individuals is extremely variable. Some of these differences are due to the type of measurement. For example, IQ scores are designed to be

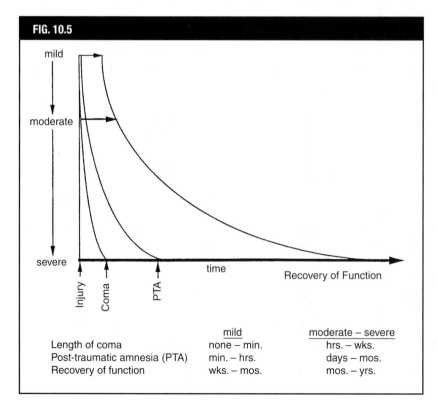

FIG. 10.5

	mild	moderate – severe
Length of coma	none – min.	hrs. – wks.
Post-traumatic amnesia (PTA)	min. – hrs.	days – mos.
Recovery of function	wks. – mos.	mos. – yrs.

Course of recovery from diffuse axonal injury following TBI of different severities. Note that with severe TBI the patient's recovery is more gradual and over a longer period (reprinted with permission from Katz, D.I., Neuropathology and neurobehavioral recovery from closed head injury, *Journal of Head Trauma and Rehabilitation, 7,* 1–15, © Aspen Publishers, Inc.).

highly reliable but are not the measure of choice if subtle changes in cognitive efficiency are required. Indeed, some subtests of IQ measures are excellent indicators of how the patient was prior to the accident (referred to as Hold tests). In contrast, measures of aphasia may be more sensitive but may be prone to ceiling effects, so that a recovery curve asymptotes or ceilings too early, partly because the test is too easy at the upper end of the scale. In such a case the patient may improve further but because the test is too easy the improvement is not measurable.

These points concerning measurements aside, the view of recovery as represented in Figure 10.1 is often upheld although it is generally elongated, with a more gradual slope and a later asymptote in the case of more severe brain insult. Nevertheless, there are still some important points to be made about individual differences of the type that

can be seen in Figure 10.6. For example, Sbordone (1987) argues that the recovery from TBI at 9 months and a year may be made lower because of emotional problems such as depression that often accompany this stage of recovery. He also points out that some recovery curves are based on selective samples and that intervals of measurement may distort the curve. He, like many recent authors, points to evidence of longer-term recovery in some cases (see also Lezak, 1995).

Finally, on the subject of cognitive recovery, there is evidence for different rates of recovery of different functions, which is likely to depend on the potential for redundancy of the structure representing the function. A study by Teuber (1975) clearly illustrates the variability of recovery depending on the cognitive process being measured. He showed that some visual problems such as scotomas (visual blind spots) might be rela-

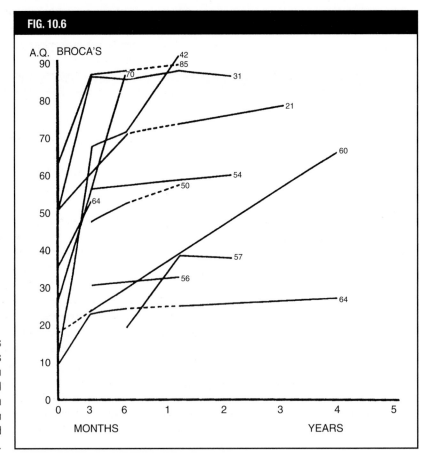

FIG. 10.6

Recovery from Broca's aphasia. Interrupted lines indicate duration of speech therapy. A.Q. = overall score (reprinted from Kertesz, 1985, with permission from Oxford University Press).

tively permanent, whereas language and constructional disorders invariably show obvious improvements. Functions such as constructional disorders may depend on a number of different structurally independent brain areas for their expression. Such functions may be more conducive to strategic compensation or functional adaptation whereby the functional goal is achieved by different means.

Recovery from amnesia is less likely because of the specialised nature of the structures that represent memory, e.g. the hippocampus. Patient HM, mentioned in the chapter on Memory, has not recovered from his amnesia over many years (Milner, 1966). However, when *one* anterior temporal lobe with the hippocampus is removed, there is substantial recovery of memory by 1-year follow-up. Patients following left temporal lobectomy complain of more memory impairment compared to those following right temporal lobectomy and there is great variation between individuals. Ojemann and Dodrill (1985) found that patients following left anterior temporal lobectomy have a 22% decline in memory at 1 month and 11% decline 1 year postoperatively. Generally, memory impairment following right temporal lobectomy is both less noticeable to the patient and less obvious on objective measures of memory when compared with left temporal lobectomy.

Assuming the hippocampi are intact then memory impairment may be dependent on the integrity of a number of other functions and memory often appears to take longer to recover. One study has shown extended recovery for these patients, taking place over several years (Blakemore & Falconer, 1967), although this last result may have been influenced by selective drop-out of patients at follow-up. Wade, Wood, and Langton Hewer (1988) followed up stroke patients regularly and found a more prolonged recovery curve for memory when compared to unilateral neglect. Neglect, a disorder of attention, appears in a great number of right hemisphere stroke patients (also to a lesser degree following left hemisphere stroke); however, many recover in 2 weeks (Wade et al., 1988) (see Figure 10.7). It is possible that neglect is more influenced by the acute recovery

processes when compared to some other functions, although this finding may be due to issues of measurement. Robertson (1999) suggests that recovery is rapid for deficits that are subserved by a number of circuits. According to this principle there is limited scope for recovery from hemianopia since the paths from the retina to the primary visual cortex are relatively discrete. On the other hand, the complex system that supports language allows for more redundancy.

Measures across functions may not be of comparable difficulty. There are also recovery profiles within the domain of a particular function: different language disorders may have different recovery profiles, e.g. Wernicke's versus Broca's having a different pattern (Kertesz, 1993b). In terms of recovery outcome transcortical aphasias have an excellent recovery prognosis, while global aphasia, which usually involves an occlusion of a large part of the middle cerebral artery, has a poor and slower recovery (Kertesz, 1993b). Some of these results may reveal nothing more than a well-demonstrated negative association of recovery with the size of lesion and differential measures of the different types of aphasia.

However, as discussed under the section relating to global aphasia in Chapter 8, it is important to know where the lesion is before the functional recovery is predicted. The nature of the aphasia may change during recovery. Severe global aphasias may recover to reveal a type 2 "large" Broca's aphasia. Type 1 "small" Broca's and conduction aphasia may recover and leave a mild anomia. Some of the agrammatism of Broca's may recover, while the articulation difficulties may remain, illustrating the different mechanisms underlying the features of a syndrome. The comprehension of Wernicke's aphasias may be more likely to recover than some aspects of Broca's, perhaps because comprehension may be compensated to some degree by right hemisphere structures. The more specialised role of Broca's area may be less easily compensated by other brain areas (Benson & Ardila, 1996, pp. 345–347). These aphasias do tend to follow the classic recovery pattern of most recovery in the first 3–6 months, but global aphasia, with its associated large area of infarction, may show most recovery

FIG. 10.7

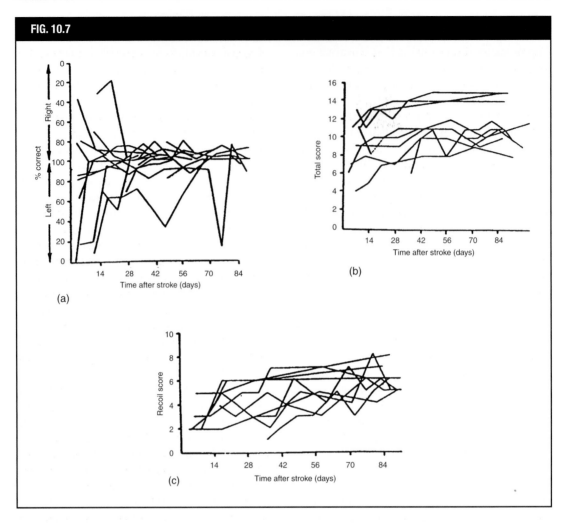

Recovery curves for (a) 15 patients with neglect showing percentage correct on worst side, (b) 10 patients on digit span, repeating back digits, forwards plus backwards (reprinted from Wade et al., 1988, *Journal of Neurology, Neurosurgery and Psychiatry, 51*, 10–13, with permission from the BMJ Publishing Group). (c) Words correctly recalllled from a list of 10 words (reprinted from Blakemore & Falconer, 1967, *Journal of Neurology, Neurosurgery and Psychiatry, 30*, 364–367, with permission from the BMJ Publishing Group).

between 6 months and a year (see Kertesz, 1993b, for a more in-depth review of this topic).

As mentioned earlier, most profiles of recovery will depend on the means of measurement. However, even when some consistency and reliability of a measure are assumed the mean recovery curve may be very misleading when the individual results are considered.

Recovery and psychosocial issues

Emotional and social dysfunction following brain damage is often an underrated problem in the literature. Surveys of patients following brain damage find that social and emotional dysfunction is rated as the biggest problem compared to a range of other cognitive deficits such as concentration, memory, and organisation (Andrewes et al., 1998;

Irle, Peper, Wowra, & Kunze, 1994; McKinlay et al., 1981). Depression and other signs of emotionality are very common in stroke patients (House et al., 1989; Robinson, Starr, & Price, 1984), patients with TBI (e.g., Kinsella, Moran, Ford, & Ponsford, 1988), and following brain surgery (Andrewes et al., 1998).

Other signs of emotional dysfunction apart from depression include emotional lability (emotional response is variable and poorly controlled) and often there is irritability and fatigue. Sometimes there is hostility and aggression, which are often associated with frustration at not being able to perform on tasks that were previously easy. A poignant paper by Frederick Linge, a clinical psychologist who suffered a head injury, describes these kinds of experiences (Linge, 1980).

There are also problems of poor social skills, which provide particular difficulties when it comes to social interaction (Godfrey, Knight, & Marsh, 1989). Partners may complain of poor social skills with often inappropriate and hurtful childishness, which may continue over many years post brain injury in some cases (e.g. after 7 years; Oddy et al., 1985). In terms of TBI, during the initial period after the accident the patient is an invalid and head injuries are often accompanied by physical injuries that can be easily understood and identified by carers as limiting factors associated with a "sick" person. However, after 9 months to a year the patient may have largely recovered from physical injuries and is more active and less subdued. The patient is now becoming more insightful into their problems and limitations and is consequently becoming depressed with their situation (Malia, Powell, & Torode, 1995; Sbordone, 1987). With recovery, the patient, depending on the location and severity of their injury, is now showing many of the emotional and other trying symptoms described above. Counter to expectations, from the carer's perspective the patient appears to be getting worse, not better. Disillusioned expectations may affect the patient as well. Sbordone makes a comment that many patients are told that they will continue to recover for 1 or 2 years (Sbordone, 1987). When they reach the end of this period and reflect on their situation, they become depressed, thinking there is no further recovery in sight, even though many go on to make further improvements. Education and counselling during these times of recovery are obviously essential.

These difficulties have enormous repercussions for the patient's relations. As Sbordone points out, "when someone in the family becomes brain-injured, it is the family that must bear this burden. Families are frequently devastated by the enormous financial, emotional and psychological burdens which are placed upon them" (Sbordone, 1987, p. 32). Sbordone goes on to describe the brave face and denial tactics of family members, who put on a "command performance" despite the horrendous guilt and stress they are undergoing. Unless the family is treated as well as the patient, the patient will eventually lose crucial and necessary support. It is an unfortunate statistic that many patients become separated and end up living in isolation following their accident (Florian, 1991).

Return to work must depend on many factors, including the level of unemployment and the employment requirements of the country concerned. For the severely head-injured, the outcome is often poorer compared to the rest of the population. For those with severe head injury less than a third of these patients return to pre-accident employment levels and many are unemployed (Brooks, McKinlay & Symington, 1987; Oddy et al., 1985). However, the issue of the type of brain damage and its severity is important. For example, Lezak (1995), when reviewing the literature on post-war penetrating missile wounds, finds a more optimistic outcome, with 75% being re-employed for a longer time of follow-up in European societies. Clearly the cause of brain damage and the economic climate of a country must be considered when judging these studies.

Psychosocial recovery depends on a number of features but is influenced markedly by the extent to which executive functions are impaired. Vilkki and colleagues found that tests such as intelligence tests were not useful in predicting work status and social activity. The tests that were most useful were tests of dysexecutive functioning or "cognitive flexibility" (Vilkki et al., 1994).

FACTORS THAT ENCOURAGE RECOVERY

The time of treatment

Factors that affect treatment in the acute phase of recovery are different from those when the initial recovery form physical trauma has taken place. Recently there have been a number of advances in the treatment of patients just after they have had their stroke or head injury. Previously, artefact theory was referred to as a way of looking at recovery in these early stages, a regaining of functions not originally lost. However, how much may be regained at this stage may depend on how the patient is treated during this time.

Following the Falklands War some soldiers who had sustained extensive wounds and loss of limbs made a remarkable recovery when left on the battlefield overnight in sub-zero temperatures. This and other experiences have promoted a new way of looking at the recovery process. Although more recently this area has been a popular research topic there has been some knowledge on the beneficial affects of cooling on coma or stroke victims during the very early phase of recovery (e.g. Vacanti & Ames, 1984). This perhaps ameliorates some of the more toxic recovery processes and oedema. However, later after the acute recovery phase stimulating drugs that increase the level of arousal may be used in combination with increased patient stimulation to hasten the process of recovery and diaschisis (Feeney, 1997). Further studies are needed before the nature of these early findings can be confirmed.

Another possible advance concerns the use of streptokinase within the first 3 hours after stroke. Streptokinase is used as a kind of anticoagulant agent in order to reduce ischaemia. At present, this treatment is still under review and the treatment may increase haemorrhage and mortality unless the nature of the stroke is correctly identified using CT scan (Osborn, LaMonte, & Gaasch, 1999).

When considering recovery after this acute stage, animal experiments generally allow that early treatment is better than late treatment (Black, Markowitz, & Cianci, 1975). Although it is ethically difficult to allow for the effects of spontaneous remission when assessing this factor of recovery, Cope and Hall (1982) give some evidence in favour of early treatment with human subjects. As indicated, patients may benefit from rehabilitation some years after brain insult when they were previously not capable of taking advantage of a programme at an earlier time. In the next chapter, it is argued that intervention is important at all stages of recovery just so long as it takes into account the limitations and requirements of the patient at each stage of their recovery.

As early as 1917, Elizabeth Dunn reported the first successful case of transplanting cortical tissue in the mouse. She documented a successful graft in 2 out of 50 cases using neonatal donors and adult hosts. However, interest in this type of work was sporadic until the 1960s, when unequivocal evidence of neuronal regrowth was starting to be demonstrated (Dunn, 1971).

Environmental enrichment

Kolb (1995) recounts an anecdote concerning Donald Hebb, the famous Canadian psychologist who in the 1950s conducted an experiment in which he left one group of rats in a bare laboratory cage while he took another group home to let them loose in his house. He must have had a very understanding wife since it was much later that he collected his home-based rats, who no doubt had a very stimulating time in the interim. He took these home-experienced rats back to his laboratory, where they were tested on their ability in solving a maze. They performed significantly better than their old companions who had been stuck in their cage during this time.

In a review of the effects of an enriched environment Will and Kelche (1992) conclude that this type of extra stimulation also improves the performance of animals following brain lesions. Typically, in these studies brain-lesioned rats are compared with sham-lesioned rats (extracerebral lesion). They are pre-tested and each group is then further divided and placed in either an enriched cage with interesting objects, tunnels etc. or a standard bare cage. When tested later on a task, such as a maze, the rats with the enriched environmental experience tend to improve compared to those from the unstimulating environment. Also, interestingly, these lesioned rats appear to benefit more from this experience when compared to rats without lesions, suggesting some interaction between the recovery process and the environmental stimulation (Kolb & Elliott, 1987).

The neurophysiological correlates of environmental enrichment are increased dendritic growth and synaptogenesis and increased vascularisation (Kolb, 1995, p. 27; Rosenzweig, 1984). The animal findings with enriched environments are more consistently found in young (5-10 days old) compared to older rats or very young rats (1 day old). In the case of very young rats the advantages are offset by interference with the process of synaptogenesis as described earlier. These experiments have also found more effects if rats are kept in groups rather than in isolation: social interaction is, of course, stimulation in itself (Will & Kelche, 1992).

The implications are clear—it is important to have some kind of stimulation during recovery. Some homes may offer more stimulation than some hospitals and, therefore in some circumstances the patient may be better off as an outpatient. Some expensive private hospitals keep patients in isolated private rooms that may not be conducive to recovery.

Nevertheless, there is a good case for supporting the use of a specialised rehabilitation unit according to studies reviewed by Pak and Dombovy (1994). A carefully designed Norwegian study (Indredavik et al., 1991) is especially encouraging, with figures after 3 months showing only 15% remaining on the stroke unit compared with 39% on the medical wards. A higher proportion of the stroke unit patients were independent in ADL. In patients whose age was less than 75 years or who had mild to moderate deficits, the process of rehabilitation was accelerated and for the rest they were more likely to be returned home with some measured advantage of having experienced a stroke unit.

In summary, there is sufficient evidence that some stroke rehabilitation units will reduce time in hospital and reduce institutionalisation. But as Pak and Dombovy point out, the important ingredients are yet to be identified. However, it is clear that good results can be achieved if "acute treatment is standardised, systematic, and closely linked to early mobilization, intensive rehabilitation and family education" (Pak & Dumbovy, 1994, p. 468).

Neural repair and transplantation within rehabilitation

There is an exciting new area encouraging the prospect that the advances of some neurological diseases may be halted and even remediated by the transplantation of neural tissue. This is seen by many as the next stage of advancement in the field of rehabilitation. It has already been argued that there is some impediment to the process of reorganisation and regeneration within the brain. However, the application of techniques whereby this might be changed is starting to show some benefits in human clinical trials.

While cell division and regeneration of the neurone occur in the peripheral nervous system (outside of the brain and spinal cord), the renewal of lost neurones through cell division does not so easily occur in the adult mammal and regeneration of the neurones is generally inhibited within the central nervous system. This is not a property of the central nervous system neurone, but rather the environment in which it is placed. If such a neurone is placed artificially within a peripheral nervous system laboratory-created environment then many of the regeneration properties of the peripheral nervous system may be demonstrated (Barker & Dunnett, 1999). Within the central nervous system there are two main types of cell: the neurones and the glial cells. Glial cells provide a supportive role to the neurones when there is brain damage but they are also thought to inhibit the regrowth of damaged neurones.

The story of neural transplant is largely one of overcoming these inhibitory factors. This section reviews some of the findings in this area that have been used for the treatment of Parkinson's disease. This disorder of movement is described in more detail in Chapter 8 but briefly the disease is associated with the atrophy of cells in the substantia nigra that produce dopamine. The consequent depletion of this neurotransmitter within the basal ganglia affects and disables the patient's ability to make movements. The features of the targeted cell loss in a specific crucial area make this disease a natural vehicle for testing the efficacy of neural transplant treatment.

Of those grafting methods that have made it from the animal literature to the stage of human clinical trials, two types of grafts have been tried sufficiently to allow some evaluation. The first are grafts from the adrenal medulla. There are two adrenal medullae, which are located on each side, just above the kidneys. These structures are chosen because they release dopamine and adrenaline. The clear advantage is that by using the patient's own neural tissue it is possible to overcome rejection of the transplant due to suppression of the immune system.

Adrenal medulla grafts do survive transplantation but may have a limited longevity. The grafts have been found to promote neuronal sprouting even when the graft itself has degenerated. This result and the bilateral improvement from unilateral grafts suggest to some that the improvement is caused by elicitation of neurotrophic substances (substances that encourage neural regeneration), e.g. nerve growth factor, in the host (Stein & Glasier, 1992).

Generally, in human clinical trials adequate improvements at the 6-month period were generally dissipated or dissipating at 18 months (Goetz et al., 1989). Given that there are two invasive operations—one for harvesting the adrenal gland and the other for making the graft—it is perhaps not surprising that there are side effects along with the recorded improvements. Side effects are going to be high anyway in frail and elderly patients with such invasive treatments. Some studies have found that the majority of subjects experience "prolonged alteration of mental state", psychiatric reaction, and neuropathology such as haemorrhage and infarction, as a consequence of this type of surgery (Quinn, 1990). The exact mechanism or mechanisms that are

successful within this procedure are not certain and given there is only evidence for modest temporary improvements at present the treatment effects must be balanced with the rather serious side effects. For this reason it is generally thought that the animal research should continue without further human trials for the time being (Barker & Dunnett, 1999, p. 110).

More success has been noted with the transplant of fetal tissue. The grafts required have strict criteria: they must be from a fetus of a certain age, e.g. around 1–2 months of gestation; the neuronal tissue to be taken from the donor must be matched with the area of the graft site in the host (homotopic); there must also be a number of additional factors in place before success is maximised. For example, the cavity for the graft must have vascular irrigation, there must be some means of reducing an immune suppression response and neurotrophic factors which encourage neuronal growth must also be in place. It is also an advantage if the host is younger rather than older. Under these and other restricted conditions the probability of success of recovery of *some of the symptoms* is likely and there are reports that anti-parkinsonian drug treatments are consequentially more effective, although the length of the success of this treatment is still uncertain (e.g., Freeman et al., 1995).

Assessments of the efficacy of this treatment are important before anything can be said about the outcome. Barker and Dunnett (1999) complain that all too frequently surgery is conducted without serious assessment of outcome. Apart from the before-and-after neurological assessment of movement one would hope that neuropsychological and some form of psychiatric assessment would also be conducted. Because the effects of neurosurgical treatment are inevitably confounded with the pre and post-surgery drug treatment, the exaggerated advantage on the affects of this therapy should also be reported. An assessment during maximum drug effect must be compared with minimal drug influence. Therefore an assessment during the "on" period (just after drug administration) must be compared with an assessment of the "off" period (on waking with less drug advantage) both before and after grafting. Also, a before-and-after MRI and PET scan would also be seen as advantageous (see Barker & Dunnett, 1999, p. 155). The former would be able to identify whether or not the graft had degenerated and the PET scan, using an isotope with an affinity for dopamine, would be used to assess the dopamine compensatory effects of the graft.

Finally, it must be realised that encouraging neuronal growth and the production of dopamine in an area does not necessarily replace skills previously lost due to the disease process. The phrase used for this psychological process of recovery is *learning to use the transplant*. In an experiment by Brasted et al. (1998) it was shown that performance in grafted rats only improved more than in rats with a lesion without grafting when they were additionally given training. There has already been some discussion in this chapter on the importance of stimulation and enriched environments on recovery. This also applies to patients following neural grafts. According to arguments provided in this chapter the patient

should receive extensive physical and psychological rehabilitation for the full benefits of the graft to be realised. The ethical issues surrounding this type of research mean that alternative sources of donor tissue are being sought.

At present it seems unlikely that transplants are going to be useful with Alzheimer's disease but the prospects for Huntington's disease seem better at this stage given the animal literature (see Barker & Dunnett, 1999).

A multifactorial influence on recovery outcome

One of the messages from the earliest part of this chapter is the understanding that the brain, whether damaged or otherwise, is not a static entity. Experience constantly changes brain structure and therefore the quality of experience following brain damage is clearly a key issue. Decisions on the nature of training must be guided by a number of factors. The patient's everyday requirements, the limitations imposed by the extent or severity of brain damage, the time

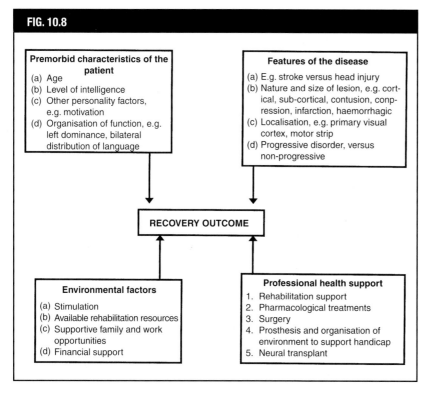

FIG. 10.8

Premorbid characteristics of the patient
(a) Age
(b) Level of intelligence
(c) Other personality factors, e.g. motivation
(d) Organisation of function, e.g. left dominance, bilateral distribution of language

Features of the disease
(a) E.g. stroke versus head injury
(b) Nature and size of lesion, e.g. cortical, sub-cortical, contusion, conpression, infarction, haemorrhagic
(c) Localisation, e.g. primary visual cortex, motor strip
(d) Progressive disorder, versus non-progressive

RECOVERY OUTCOME

Environmental factors
(a) Stimulation
(b) Available rehabilitation resources
(c) Supportive family and work opportunities
(d) Financial support

Professional health support
1. Rehabilitation support
2. Pharmacological treatments
3. Surgery
4. Prosthesis and organisation of environment to support handicap
5. Neural transplant

Factors influencing recovery from brain damage.

dysexecutive syndrome are used as examples of major limitations to rehabilitation. Using these examples, rehabilitation is seen as a process that is determined by, firstly, understanding the limitations, setting reasonable goals, and then designing a programme that effectively compensates for the patient's limitations.

While broad ranges of disorders are referred to, these various issues are mainly discussed with reference to the remediation of memory disorders. This example is provided to illustrate certain areas of controversy and principles of remediation—principles that are also applicable to other areas of rehabilitation.

THE RELATIONSHIP BETWEEN THEORIES OF RECOVERY AND REHABILITATION

In discussing the relationship between recovery and rehabilitation it is important to identify the meaning of the rather broad term referred to as function. The term is identified in Chapter 1, which talks of certain brain areas being associated with different behavioural roles, in the same way that the kidneys or the liver serve different roles. A *function* is therefore a behavioural role that is specified and linked to a particular brain area. In the context of rehabilitation it is rare that functions are well specified and therefore the term *behaviour* is preferred as a broad term for any identified activity, e.g. lifting a cup to drink, remembering information. However, in the theoretical approach to linking recovery with rehabilitation, functions, which are represented by hypothetical brain areas, may be referred to in order to illustrate the relationship between theoretical concepts of recovery and approaches to rehabilitation.

It has been popular to describe the remediation of brain-damaged patients according to three alternative approaches (Glisky, 1995; Wilson, 1989; Zangwill, 1947). Each of these has their own underlying theoretical assumptions as follows:

1. *Retraining of impaired function.* Rehabilitation is initiated with the goal of reallocation of the lost function within the brain or the amelioration of damaged tissue through the mechanisms of reorganisation described in the previous chapter. Consequently, it might be assumed that if a person is trained on any memory task, the hippocampus will be positively reorganised and memory will be improved generally. This is sometimes referred to as the "mental muscle" approach. The metaphor provides that exercise will cause improvement in any task that uses that particular part of the brain. In the previous chapter animal experiments were described which showed how training could, within certain limits, influence brain structure. Thus the brain representation of a function might be increased or enhanced at the expense of another, assuming that there was sufficient redundancy.

2. *Functional adaption.* Sometimes known as behavioural substitution in this case rehabilitation is achieved by using alternative functions to achieve the same behavioural goal. The assumption is that damaged brain structures can be "side-stepped" by substituting behaviours that are already supported by preserved brain structures. Thus the patient who is no longer able to judge distances is trained to rely more on the sense of touch when picking up an object (Golden, 1978a, 1978b).

3. *Compensation.* With compensation rehabilitation is achieved by increasing the efficiency of the remaining damaged function. This might be described in the case where a patient is taught to use a diary (external aid) to reduce the frequency of missing appointments. This is similar to functional adaptation but there is a reliance on artificial means or strategies to boost the performance of the damaged function. An alternative function is not specifically relied upon; rather the accent is on behaviours that will support what is remaining of the damaged function. In the case of compensation a number of different methods may be used depending on the demands of the

situation. There is not the concentration on a single alternative way of carrying out the behaviour.

In the example of a patient having a paralysed left leg following a right hemisphere stroke, a method of *compensation* would be to use a special caliper to make that left leg function more efficiently. In contrast, *functional adaptation* may also be encouraged, with a greater reliance on the right leg to support weight. The patient may also be given physiotherapy, exercising that left leg with the aim of improving brain plasticity and the brain representation of left leg movements. This last approach would be one of *retraining*. Of course the therapist may have little control over some of these forces of recovery. For example, the therapist may constantly remind the patient not to use functional adaptation but this may still inevitably occur because the patient may do some things quite automatically. Nevertheless, research should eventually show us the approach that we should be using and stressing without patients.

The first of these three approaches (retraining) makes the assumption that training in itself may encourage the neurophysiological recovery process. As indicated, this process includes concepts such as the reorganisation of an impaired function to undamaged areas (plasticity), and local neurophysiological mechanisms of neuronal repair and compensation, such as collateral sprouting and denervation supersensitivity, discussed in the preceding chapter. The last two approaches do not deny these processes of recovery, but they make no reliance on them. However, as previously argued, reliance on another behaviour (the greater use of the right leg in our example) will inevitably detract from the use of the original behaviour (the use of the left leg). Consequently the brain representation of the left leg may be undermined. Alternatively, a prothesis such as a caliper may also reduce the use of the impaired ability. Therefore even when functional adaptation and compensation are used the implications for brain organisation and representation may also have to be considered. In the previous chapter the animal literature suggests that

recovery training of one function at the expense of another will inevitably result in plastic brain changes even in healthy brain tissue.

It could be argued that, if the patient were taught a strategy encouraging the use of alternative *preserved* cognitive resources (functional adaption), or strategies aimed at increasing efficiency of remaining damaged function (compensation), then the process of recovery would be expedited. However, this may not always be the strategy that is ultimately best for the patient. There are instances when "direct training" may be stressed over these alternative approaches. For example, when the damaged brain areas are adjacent to spared brain areas that have a similar function then, according to animal research, there would be potential for a mechanism whereby redundancy would allow reorganisation of function to spared brain areas. In this case retraining might be favoured. The recent literature on recovery provides that if a motor function is not used then the brain representation of that function will be reduced rather than extended. This reduction of representation of the damaged function is associated with an increase in representation of the substituted spared function. Thus if a patient has paresis of one arm then naturally they will use the other arm to complete tasks that were previously the domain of the paralysed arm (functional adaptation). Theoretically this would result in greater representation of the good arm at the expense of the arm with paresis. This might not be positive for the patient if the new strategy results in an inefficient or ungainly way of completing a task. Such a functional adaptation approach might place limitations on the patient's potential for recovery. For example, a patient may come to rely too heavily on the good right arm to lift them from a wheelchair. However, if the patient is forced to use retraining, which involves the use of the impaired arm in combination with the good arm, the movement may eventually be more successfully carried out and cause less embarrassment because the movement looks more natural. In recovery terms, at the neural level this last strategy would encourage representation of the previously damaged function to be located within the undamaged motor strip and somatosensory area.

It should be noted, however, that there might be limitations to the retraining approach when dealing with some elderly stroke victims. The animal literature involves adult animals but rarely do you note the specific use of aged animals being used, which would more realistically simulate the stroke situation. As indicated, recovery is influenced by many factors; if a patient is statistically likely to have a second stroke within a year is it fair to commit them to a long-term retraining programme when a programme focused on functional adaptation may give more immediate benefits to the patient? As research is extended we will start to get some answers to these important questions.

While, under some circumstances, emphasis may be given to the retraining approach with motor functions, the reliance on this as a main approach is less certain when considering cognitive functions such as language, memory, and attention. Retraining is undeniably beneficial in these areas but the results of training appear to be quite specific. Often it is found that there is little carry-over from one task to another. If the patient is exercised on a single task, say remembering a list of words, the patient is likely to improve only on the task being trained. There is not a general improvement in memory. Not only is there likely to be no generalisation from one task to another but there tends to be no carry-over from training on one type of material to another, e.g. numbers to letters within the same task. This has been found to be true for normal subjects, the elderly, memory-impaired patients, and amnesic patients alike (Berg, Koning-Haanstra, & Deelman, 1991; Chace & Ericsson, 1981; Dolan & Norton, 1977; Glisky, Schacter, & Tulving, 1986; Godfrey & Knight, 1985; Goldstein & Malec, 1989). The area of attention is more controversial, with some studies showing generalisation to other laboratory-based tasks (e.g. Gray, Robertson, Pentland, & Anderson, 1992) while others show no generalisation either to laboratory or everyday tasks (Ponsford & Kinsella, 1980; Wood & Fussey, 1987; see Ponsford, 1990, for a review).

It is quite possible that the retraining approach on some cognitive processes may show a tendency towards greater generalisation than others, just as different cognitions may recover at different rates (Teuber, 1975). However, this is yet to be convincingly demonstrated. Given the inconsistent evidence available, generalisation within a function such as language or memory should not be assumed. For this reason, if retraining (repetitive training on a single task) is pursued, it would be advisable to train the patient on tasks that have a direct relevance to the patient's everyday life, e.g. learning information. This message is particularly germane when considering the use of a number of computer programs that are commercially designed specifically for retraining brain-injured patients. Many of these programs provide exercises, which, although entertaining, are not necessarily relevant to the patient's adaptation to life circumstances (see Glisky, 1995, for a balanced discussion of the benefits and concerns regarding computerised memory training). A point should be made here that the "direct training" method should be distinguished from the arguably more profitable method of training a patient in strategies that can be applied flexibly, or the method of building up skills in an incremental fashion. This approach is more in keeping with the compensation approach described above. These approaches are discussed further below.

Finally, on the subject of the relationship between recovery and rehabilitation, there is a growing realisation that, although there is some evidence that early intervention is preferable to late intervention (see previous chapter), the recovery process tends to be more prolonged in the case of severe injury. There is a new understanding that a later intervention may be useful when a more severely impaired patient has sufficiently recovered to benefit from an intervention (Sbordone, 1987). Patients are generally prepared for different types of rehabilitation at different stages of their recovery and some patients may be given fruitful remediation some 3 or 5 years after their brain insult—rehabilitation that they were not previously able to benefit from.

THE APPLICATION OF TECHNIQUES

General applications

Ecological validity

The research literature for both memory-impaired aged and younger brain-impaired subjects is replete with experiments on list learning. These are useful studies, especially when determining the comparative benefits of different mnemonics. Wilson (1987), for example, found that a mnemonic referred to as the aeroplane story detail (see Addendum 1) gave the best results when compared with other popularly learned mnemonics. Also, it may be useful to test the patient's ability to use imagery or some other method, irrespective of the material used. Further, when lists are learned by these techniques patients in memory groups may gain some confidence and some feeling of pride in their achievements (Pattern, 1972). However, the number of studies using lists as material probably outweighs the practical benefit of using such material. Certainly lists must be remembered when going shopping and for remembering to do things in the future, but lists can also be written down. A survey by Harris (1980) showed that around 50% of housewives use lists. Therefore while remembering a list is definitely useful, the everyday application of such learning material must also be considered. It could be argued that training in remembering how to use lists or when to check lists, or even training in remembering where to check lists (Andrewes & Pannella, in preparation), is a more useful pursuit for the rehabilitationist.

"Ecological validity" is a popular phrase among those who are interested in applied research. The message from those who espouse ecological validity is that if theory is to be generalisable to the real world, then that research should use materials and situations that are based in the real world (see Neisser, 1978, for an elegant argument towards this view). However, while such research is important, basic research using word lists may also be essential in illustrating principles of learning.

Examples of useful basic research.

There is now an extensive literature on implicit memory that has been originally prompted by work with amnesic patients (see Chapter 5 for a discussion). Briefly, some amnesics can learn certain material, especially if it relates closely to information they have learned prior to the onset of their amnesia. The only practical drawback is that they do not remember the event or even the context of learning. This is unfortunate since, sometimes when we recollect information, we can discount some potential false memories by recalling the situation when the information was originally learned. For example, in the case where a person is trying to remember when they deposited something at the dry cleaners, they might say to themselves, "Well it might have been Thursday, when I usually put my dry cleaning in. Oh no. It was last Friday because I remember talking to the dry cleaning man after work and saying that it was good that it was the end of the week." Amnesics do not have these explicit memories available to them. In having only implicit memory available, they can only say both Thursday and Friday seem familiar or likely days and then perhaps remember the wrong day. The amnesic patient is therefore more vulnerable to memories of competing strength or familiarity. Baddeley and Wilson (1994) found just this when they compared learning words in a condition where error making was allowed during learning compared to a condition when error making was avoided. The amnesics were far more affected by error making when compared to non-amnesic groups. If they recalled the wrong word, then they were much more likely to repeat it again as a response. The response in error increased the strength of the item, causing it to become more familiar. The patients had no explicit memory of making a mistake and therefore could not use this memory to disregard a response that nevertheless had some feeling of familiarity. The lesson is an obvious one—if you are teaching memory-impaired patients, especially if they are amnesic, it is advisable to reduce the likelihood that an error will be made during learning.

One method that capitalises on the errorless learning principle is called the "vanishing" cues technique, in which the subject only has to learn small pieces of information at a time. For example, Glisky et al. (1986) managed to teach amnesic subjects to learn to use computers. Also, names of persons have been learned using this technique. Typically, this method uses the whole name with just the end letter missing; following a series of correct trials a second letter is removed and so on.

A second principle, which also could contribute to an errorless learning approach, is that of the expanded rehearsal technique (Landauer & Bjork, 1978). This technique works on the principle that the length of time between presentation and a request for recall is gradually increased. Schacter, Rich, and Stampp (1985) used this technique to teach memory-impaired patients to link personality characteristics to a series of different faces. The importance of gradually expanding the interval between presentation and recall is that, on each occasion, recall requires some retrieval effort. Theoretically, by doing this, the patient is setting up retrieval cues in the process of learning to recall from long-term memory. With the concept of errorless learning this is a useful principle based on basic research that has numerous applications.

A common rehabilitation technique is to reduce the challenge to the patient's information-processing limitations by presenting information incrementally, learning parts or chunks of information and then adding these components at a later stage. For example, in a study by von Cramon and Mathes-von Cramon (1990) patients with many signs of dysexecutive syndrome were found to be significantly improved on a number of measures when they were given a staged programme which was focused on learning to solve problems. The patients were taught over four modules, each module concentrating on a different part of the problem-solving process according to a taxonomy of problem-solving behaviours; while the results are not without some ambiguity of interpretation, they suggest that some generalised improvement occurred on other untrained problem-solving tasks. In other words skills had been learned that could be transferred to other areas.

An investigation of the effects of prospective memory training by Sohlberg et al. (1992) used a similar building-up-skills and lengthening the interval prior to remembering, thereby combining the expanded rehearsal and dividing the task up into small units.

The point being made in this section is that basic research, sometimes using normal subjects, may outline principles of learning or problem-solving that are usefully adopted by rehabilitationists. Such principles, which will be referred to frequently during this chapter, are invaluable since they can be represented using a wide variety of contexts and materials.

Specific applications

In the early 1980s Barbara Wilson's work using internal strategies to achieve goals within the institution was an inspiration to clinicians. The work of Wilson and others led to the introduction of books devoted to the area of memory rehabilitation (Wilson, 1987; Wilson & Moffat, 1992). This work was largely hospital based and aimed at such practical goals as learning the names of staff. Much of this early work, which was improvised and mnemonic based, had an impact on the methods of memory rehabilitation and should be seen as important reading for those attempting to work in this area.

Wilson is keen to adopt an individual approach and would be the first to note that a technique needs to be tailored to the patient (Wilson, 1992b). The accent here will therefore be to focus on some of the problems associated with the implementation of these techniques and the useful alternative approaches.

Learning names to faces

Both normal persons and memory-impaired patients find it difficult to remember names of people (Kapur & Pearson, 1983). This is a problem at one level because there is no obvious association between our names and how we look or behave. This was not, of course, always the case for our forebears who were often called after their trade, e.g. Smith, Tailor, Baker. One way of getting around this conundrum is to make an association between name and face by using visual imagery (see Addendum 1). This method has been used successfully with patients in an institutional setting, where there is support and supervision for the patient. For example, Wilson (1987, p. 113) describes a study in which a severely head-injured 21-year-old man was found to learn staff members' names significantly faster when rehearsal was used without imagery.

In a study by Lewinsohn, Danaher, and Kikel (1997) with patients who had mostly suffered from stroke, imagery was provided for these patients across a three-stage learning programme. Although there were trends towards significant gains when patients were tested immediately and at 30 minutes compared to controls, this apparent advantage disappeared when the patients were tested a week later. Perhaps the main difference between this study and others is the perceived usefulness of the training. Thus, if the patient wants to learn the names of staff members they will be motivated to learn them and will rehearse them whenever they meet the staff member. However, if the names are artificially derived and do not belong to anyone the patient knows, then they will not be inclined to remember this meaningless material or the practising of a technique.

One of the difficulties in applying this technique is that not every person, impaired or otherwise, can form images or use these images to associate them with a name. This strategic process is probably especially difficult for some brain-impaired patients (Crovitz, Harvey, & Horn, 1979; Richardson & Barry, 1985; Wilson, 1987) and is often beyond the capabilities of Alzheimer patients, for example (Backman, Josephsson, Herlitz, & Stigsdotter, 1991). Glasgow, Zeiss, Barrera, and Lewinsohn (1977) showed how they adapted the face–name technique to overcome this problem. They describe the case of a 23-year-old head-injured college student with a left frontal oedema, right hemiparesis, and dysphasia. The patient had some difficulty in using imagery and so a less complex imagery training technique was devised. The patient found that, by writing the names on the back of an index card and then imaging the face while rehearsing the name at three scheduled times a day, the patient learned 30 names and naming errors went from four at base-line to one per day. This patient was using this technique as an outpatient and therefore, in this case, the patient was able to initiate the method independently. Wilson (1987, pp. 110–113) describes using a similar method, in which photographs were used when the patient could not remember the image of the face. This method was used successfully with a severely memory-impaired patient with a malignant tumour; the patient was able to learn 10 staff members in a cumulative fashion, only adding a name when the preceding one had been learned. When the patient went away for 6 weeks, upon returning he was able to recall eight of the names, relearning the last two without any difficulty.

The previously mentioned vanishing cues technique, in which the letters of the names are slowly removed over trials to provide a diminishing partial cue, has been successfully used even with amnesic patients. In some studies the last letter is removed first before testing, followed by the next letter and so on (Jaffe & Katz, 1975). With other versions of this method, the patient is required to guess in the hardest condition with very few letters; the letters are then increased until a correct answer is given, and the patient then starts again until the name is guessed in the hardest condition (Thoene & Glisky, 1995). The method in which the patient does not have to guess too much may be preferable (to promote errorless learning). This technique lends itself to computer presentation and has also been found to be useful in teaching amnesic subjects computer skills (e.g., Glisky et al., 1986).

Thoene and Glisky (1995) compared three methods of learning the names to faces and professions of persons (with imaginary names supplied, e.g. Carol Oliphant). Three methods were compared: the method of vanishing cues, a simplified visual imagery mnemonic, and a video presentation with additional background information (e.g. where they came from and where they went to university). The mnemonic method was found to be superior. An error analysis suggested that names were learned in the vanishing cues condition but not always associated with the face. The mnemonic was therefore superior in its facilitation of the association. An interesting finding was that the video condition provided better recall of the person's profession. As the authors point out, it is possible that, in this case, an enriched schema of the person's identity made available more retrieval cues for the person's profession. Whether or not the same results could have been obtained with natural names, the lesson is a good one. As Thoene and Glisky (1995) point out, these amnesic patients are capable of making *new* semantic associations and are therefore not necessarily dependent on implicit memory, at least as it would normally be construed (see also Kovner, Mattis, & Pass, 1985).

Most recently, Downes et al. (1997) have shown that the imagery technique, which aims at providing an image that connects a face with a name in a meaningful manner, may be enhanced if the patient was exposed to the face before having to associate it with the name and was required to make a series of personality judgements about the face, e.g. friendliness, honesty, dominance. This strategy nearly doubled recall compared to imagery alone.

When considering the use of the face–name imagery mnemonics for less severely memory-impaired patients, the question of independence has to be considered. Such patients may, for example, want to use the mnemonic technique independently and spontaneously in their daily lives. The studies reviewed above suggest that there might be some difficulty in (a) transferring this skill to the real world, and (b) dealing with the cognitively demanding process of using this technique.

In a recent study of our own (Andrewes, Kinsella, Murphy, & Alderton, 1996), we aimed to teach elderly persons living in the community a range of efficient memory strategies for dealing with their reported memory difficulties. A new approach was taken whereby the patients were given a number of techniques that they could use either in combination or on their own. For example, for learning names to faces, they were given the visual imagery technique (see Addendum 1). But they were also instructed that they could make a rhyme with a meaningful association and they were advised to repeat back the name after an introduction as much as possible

during a conversation. In order to increase generalisation, the experimental group was given a training handbook, which contained a description of the techniques with a series of practice exercises. The appendix contained a series of photographs, most of which were of the same generation as the subjects and some merely had Christian names to increase the ecological validity. While some countries may be more formal it is common in Australia for persons to meet informally and just exchange Christian names. The control group was given a placebo treatment involving a pamphlet that described a series of mnemonics for learning lists. There was a significant increase on the more objective laboratory tasks, which tested the subjects' ability to remember names to faces both before and one month after the intervention. There was also a significant benefit for the experimental group in the patients' everyday lives according to a memory diary they kept from day to day. The diary, which was filled in for 3 weeks after the intervention, recorded the proportion of times they remembered— compared to forgot—a checklist of situations. At the follow-up, 4 months after the intervention, the experimental group were still showing the benefits of training according to a questionnaire surveying the use of the techniques (see Table 11.1). The survey indicates that, while some patients had a preference for some strategies rather than others, with only few exceptions most of the strategies were used to some extent. Some of these were clearly already used given the pre-intervention assessment. This kind of field research is aimed at determining the benefits of certain approaches towards rehabilitation, rather than the benefits of one particular method versus another. The provision of a smorgasbord of techniques allows the subject to choose the technique that suits their own situation. The extension of training into the patient's daily life allows the skills to generalise to the everyday situation. Finally, the use of a handbook means that memory-impaired patients do not have to memorise the techniques on a single occasion of training. We have initial results that this kind of approach is also useful with clinically diagnosed memory impaired-patients.

TABLE 11.1

Percentage of subjects reporting using a specific memory strategy for each of the handbrook areas at follow-up (strategy use questionnaire) for the memory-handbook group (*n* = 17) and the control group (*n* = 17)

Technique according to area	Memory handbook	Controls
Remembering a person's name		
Repeating back	76.5%	58.8%
Rhyming	47.1%	5.9%
Meaning	76.5%	52.9%
Imagery	47.1%	23.5%
Rehearse	2.4%	76.5%
Remembering to do something in the future		
Internal cueing	41.2%	23.5%
External cueing	100%	100%
Peg word system	0%	0%
Diary/alarm method	41.2%	23.5%
Remembering where you put something		
Set place	100%	100%
Imagery	23.5%	0%
Retrace steps	100%	58.8%
Remembering information		
First letter	5.9%	29.4%
Link mnemonic	0%	0%
PQRST	35%	23.5%
Remembering how to get somewhere		
Write a map	76.5%	82.4%
Landmarks	88.2%	70.6%
Look behind	353.3%	58.8%
Remembering numbers		
Split into two	52.9%	76.5%
Give them meaning	17.6%	35.3%

Remembering to do something in the future (prospective memory)

This is another commonly reported memory problem (Kapur & Pearson, 1983). Although it is unlikely that prospective memory will eventually be classified as a distinct memory system, there are *certain* features of this type of memory that set it apart from retrospective memory. Prospective memory refers to the self-reminding required to remember an action or event at some point in the future. Harris (1980) refers to prospective memory as remembering to remember. However, most definitions include the feature of having to remember a specific task or event at some time in the future (e.g. Sohlberg et al., 1992, p. 129). Einstein and McDaniel (1990) considered two types of prospective remembering tasks: (1) *time based*, in which the person has to remind themselves to undertake the activity at a particular time, e.g. a dentist appointment; and (2) *event based*, in which an event is the triggering cue for the activity, e.g. "I must hang out the clothes to dry in the event that I cease to hear the noise of the washing machine." Patients with executive dysfunction may have particular problems with prospective remembering because they appear to have an inability to tag information for future remembering.

External aids are seen to be one of the most useful means of reminding for prospective memory. These are most naturally used memory joggers. They are more popularly used in everyday remembering than internal aids (mnemonics) both for normal (Itons-Peterson & Fournier, 1986) elderly (Cavanaugh, Grady, & Perlmutter, 1983) and memory-impaired patients (Wilson, 1992a). Learning and remembering a mnemonic has a memory requirement on its own and a mnemonic takes effort to apply, while an external aid merely requires a habit or routine. The following are some examples of the external aids that might be used to compensate impaired prospective memory: leaving something by the door so that it is not forgotten at the time of leaving the house; leaving messages or notes in a prominent place that you know will be observed during the domestic routine, e.g. bathroom mirror; and leaving an empty carton or tin as a reminder that the item needs replacing.

In a 3-year follow-up of patients leaving hospital, Wilson (1992a) found that the use of memory strategies had increased. Some of the most commonly used items as prospective memory supports were notebooks/notes, wall calendars/wall charts, lists, alarm clocks, asking others to remind them, using a watch with a date, appointments diary, writing on the hand and using a dictaphone or tape recorder.

Some studies have attempted to increase a patient's ability to use a notebook. For example, Sohlberg et al. (1992) describe a single case study in which the patient had suffered from a subarachnoid haemorrhage, resulting in severe impairment of memory and other areas of cognition. The patient showed poor insight and some impulsivity. The programme consisted of gradually extending the length of time between the request and the time the task (checking a notebook) was required to be executed. If two consecutive mistakes were made, then a cueing was instigated with reminders every 15 seconds. The training was interspersed with naturalistic tasks to assess generalisation. The study was persuasive, showing improvement on the training and the naturalistic tasks.

One of the most successful accounts of the use

of external aids is described by Wilson and Hughes (1997). The subject, JC, was a university student when he became amnesic following the clipping of an aneurysm involving the posterior cerebral artery. The patient was given information about the use of mnemonics, reminders, and diary keeping but over the years following his release from hospital he built up an elaborate and complex reminding system which allowed him to live independently, run a small business from home, and enjoy a social life. The sophistication of the system increased by degrees, from a system that used an hourly alarm allowing him to look at his diary so that he could keep track of the past events, to a more complex and highly organised filofax-driven system that allowed him to keep appointments in the future. Among the measures used was a colour-coded note system for different topics, e.g. eating out. The use of a dictaphone allowed him to back up and elaborate on notes taken during the day and was reviewed at set times such as in the evening. Various stick-on notes were used and reminders were kept in areas that were related to the topic, e.g. shopping lists placed in the kitchen. This is a rather remarkable adaptation to amnesia, which the authors believe was due to some extent to age and intelligence.

Prosthetic devices have also been used to advantage. There are a number of organisers on the market, although many are complicated to use (Kapur, 1995). They have the advantage of giving a specific message when it is required and also have a sound or alarm that draws the person's attention to the reminder. Small computers with screens that can be written on and provide a printed message at a prearranged time can therefore be used to good effect. However, often patients forget where they have put them and most have too many functions and are complicated to use. The simplest method is the diary-alarm method (Kurlychek, 1983), in which the patient is trained to check their diary at intervals according to a regular chime or alarm provided by a wristwatch. One of the most sophisticated methods reported is the use of a pager that is sent radio-controlled messages originating from a central computer which supplies a preprogrammed diary of events (Hersh & Treadgold, 1992, cited in Wilson, 1995).

Remembering something in the past (retrospective memory)

Here again external aids have been found to be useful. For example, in the follow-up of patients described above (Wilson, 1995), the strategy of leaving often mislaid articles, e.g. keys, glasses, in a special and consistently labelled place was often used by patients.

Remembering information

Learning of information is a practical requirement that is likely to be of interest to a variety of patients who wish to return to the workplace or their studies. However, the techniques available appear to have limited application for brain-damaged patients. Aeschelman and Snoy (1982) used visual imagery for learning prose and found some gains, but the patient was still only able to recall 30% of the material and the significance of this improvement in real terms is difficult to assess.

Glasgow et al. (1977) managed to teach a modified version of the PQRST technique (see a description in Addendum 1) to a 22-year-old female graduate who had suffered a car accident, which involved a coma of 5 days duration. The injury had been followed by aphasic symptoms and some right-sided paresis. She had largely recovered from these symptoms at the time of the study. However, although she was doing well at university, she was considering leaving because of her memory problems. The programme was reported to be effective and increased the self-confidence of the student to the extent that she took on more subjects at university. However, this case may have been successful because the patient's impairment was only mild. In collaboration with the author, Matotek (1987) has also researched this technique using four single cases. All cases were around 6 months into their recovery, except for one (case 4), who was 2 years following TBI. All patients had indications in their WAIS-R scores of "average" or above, premorbid intellect level: case 1 was a 35-year-old male, a computer consultant, who had received a

right temporal lobectomy following an encephalitis that was assumed to be herpes simplex. He had largely recovered memory but still showed slow information processing and was the slowest of all the cases in using the technique. Case 2 was a 21-year-old female secretary who had been involved in a motor vehicle accident, with 1 week of coma and 17 days PTA. CT showed a cerebral oedema. She had mild signs of memory impairment and was described by therapists as having fluctuating insight and lacking in self-confidence at times. Case 3 involved a 20-year-old clerk who also had a motor vehicle accident, with 7 days of coma and PTA of uncertain length. Originally CT showed contusion of the right and left frontal lobes. This patient had severe memory impairment and was unable to learn the Austin maze. Case 4 was a 25-year-old male who, prior to his head injury, left university to sell encyclopaedias. CT revealed a right frontal haematoma and the patient had been unconscious for 3 weeks. The length of PTA was not reported. He had discharged himself from rehabilitation hospital and was reported to have been uncooperative, verbally aggressive and showed lack of insight, with largely intact memory and some dysexecutive signs on tasks such as the Austin maze, verbal fluency and L'hermitte board. Training took place over 16–18 sessions, with half of the sessions being conducted at baseline. The exposure time to the material was kept constant throughout baseline and treatment, although it varied somewhat between individuals.

The results showed that only cases 1 and 2 showed statistical improvement. These patients did not require more than three sessions of supervised learning on the technique. Case 3, on the other hand, who had moderate to severe learning memory disorder, was still learning the technique on the eighth session and was not making any obvious progress. In contrast, case 4 learned the technique in three sessions but then refused to use it, saying he was "too lazy". Only cases 1 and 4 could describe the PQRST process in its entirety on immediate follow-up. At follow-up (5–7 months) after patients had been discharged, only cases 1 and 2 were using an approximation of the original method that was certainly more sophisticated than the pre-intervention techniques used. Case 1 used a simplified PQRST, which included extracting the main ideas during the first reading of the prose passage, and re-reading the passage to integrate detail into the remarks already constructed. Case 2 used an even more simplified technique of "chunking" information when reading magazines and articles and managed to learn to associate the main points in the passage to the details. At 6-month follow-up, case 3 could remember the sessions but nothing about the PQRST technique. This patient was totally reliant on his diary, which he used constantly to support his severe memory problem. Case 4 was never induced to use the technique during the session, let alone at follow-up, and this was despite his university training. From these and other studies (e.g. Crosson & Buenning, 1984) it would seem that mnemonic techniques are only successfully taken on in an independent fashion, by mildly impaired and motivated patients.

This does not, of course, disallow that more impaired patients might be helped with simplified techniques if they were trained over a longer period. Case 4 had all the behavioural signs and neuropsychological results of a dysexecutive syndrome. Despite being able to learn the technique quickly and having a high premorbid level of intelligence, this patient showed little spontaneous inclination towards the use of the technique. This was despite initially expressing an interest in the project and coming to each session.

The last description of the difficulties of providing useful memory management techniques through the use of mnemonics brings home the need to realise the limitations of patients.

THE LIMITATIONS OF THE PATIENT

The limitations of the patient must, of course, be assessed by methods that are appropriate to the goals of the assessment. Diller (1992) has noted the shortfall of neuropsychological tests in predicting the everyday functioning of the patient.

However, while ecologically valid tests are important, especially when measuring recovery of a patient or the response to treatment, diagnostic tests are also useful.

Amnesia

Patients with amnesia are understandably difficult to rehabilitate and train (e.g. Benedict, Brandt, & Bergey, 1993), especially when amnesia is associated with other forms of cognitive impairment, which is often the case with disorders such as Alzheimer's disease.

However, some diseases, such as herpes simplex encephalitis, may present in a variety of degrees of deterioration from isolated memory impairment to a case where there is aphasia and total dependence for ADL. When memory is affected in relative isolation and insight is intact, these patients may be able to undergo some form of rehabilitation, as the following case study illustrates.

Case report: JR

JR, a 25-year-old female patient, was admitted to hospital suffering from headache and nausea upon her admission. She was found to have poor recall for the previous week and earlier she had had a grand mal fit. After being given acyclovir, penicillin, and Dilantin (phenytoin) she improved over the next few days but then deteriorated over the following 5 days and became amnesic. A diagnosis of herpes simplex encephalitis was made. During the first year of recovery a diagnosis of amnesia was confirmed by neuropsychological assessment. At this time JR was both apathetic and subdued, which alarmed her mother since this was quite unlike her bouncy and outgoing premorbid personality.

Her measured IQ, in the "Average" to "High Average" range was also not in keeping with her academic history of gaining a distinction in law at a premier university. In the second year following her illness, she became depressed and had suicidal ideation as her insight increased and she started to realise the full portent of what she had lost. Her mother said that at this time things were hard to cope with since JR would prolong any feelings of anger or sadness she had without remembering why she was feeling the emotion. She would repeatedly ask her mother why she felt the emotion, and having been told why she would then renew the negative emotion in an endless circular fashion. Her MRI scan results indicated evidence of damage to both left and right hippocampi and amygdala, being more severe on the left than the right.

The author assessed JR 3 years after her illness (see Box 11.1) and, by this time, many of the

Box 11.1

Psychometric scores for JR

Test	Age/scale scores	Other tests	
Information	12	COWAT	F = 19/4*, A = 17/3*, S = 20/4*
Digit-span	14	Trail making	A = 30 s, B = 44 s
Vocabulary	17	Logical memory	2% imm. = 9.5, 1% delay = 0
Arithmetic	11		
Comprehension	18	* Number of repeats.	
Similarities	16		
Picture completion	11		
Block design	13		
Digit symbol	16		
Est. full-scale IQ	132 Superior		

Milner Maze-Learning Trials

Auditory verbal learning test

Trial	1	2	3	4	5	INT	Del Rec	RECOG
1994	7/+3	7/+1	6	8	9	7/+1	1/+2	10/+5
1996	7/+2	7/+1	7	9	9/+1	7/+2	0/+1	9/+3
Expected Mean (Sd)	7.7 (1.9)	10.5 (2.0)	12.2 (2.4)	12.0 (1.6)	12.9 (1.5)	7.9 (2.0)	11.6 (1.2)	14.2 (0.8)

problems described above had ameliorated. Her emotional responses were no longer perseverated although she remained despondent at times about her position in life. She had regained much of her previous personality but, as her mother pointed out, her amnesia meant that she was limited in social interaction since she could only respond to the "here and now". There were no obvious signs of frontal dysfunction in her test results and she was well capable of winning speech-making competitions. In fact, at her toastmasters club she was able to prepare and read a well-structured 3-minute speech. Box 11.1 provides a brief review of her neuropsychological test results (see Andrewes & Gielewski, 1999, for a more comprehensive account). She clearly remained amnesic both in terms of her memory for word lists (delayed recall on AVLT, Geffen et al., 1990), recall of prose on the Wechsler memory scale Delayed Logical Memory test (Wechsler, 1987), and maze learning. Repetitions in her verbal fluency test (Benton & Hamsher, 1976) were another indication of her amnesia.

However, there did appear to be an improvement in the sense that her intellectual level had improved since her first assessment to a "very superior" level. Her "vocabulary" and "information" WAIS-R subtests (Wechsler, 1981) and verbal fluency score all suggested semantic memory was largely preserved. Another important preserved resource was her remote memory (see Andrewes & Gielewski, 1999), which also seemed to have recovered to an adequate level. Given these pluses, the author suggested to the mother that she might be able to carry out a filing job at her old law firm. There were, however, a number of difficulties; for example, she still had relatively frequent minor seizures around once a week. This was explained to the law firm and, while we waited on a decision, a number of interventions were carried out with JR. She had already attended a number of sessions at a government-run institution. During this time she had been trained to keep a diary. She had also been taught how to keep track of her place in a job by checking off after completing each stage (Burke, Zencius, Wesolowski, & Doubleday, 1991). These two interventions were to prove the most valuable

preparation when she finally went to work some months later.

The first task set by the author was to learn the names of the photographs of the staff she was to work with. After an unsuccessful attempt to teach JR a visual imagery mnemonic, JR's mother's help was enlisted. Her mother was told that it was important to learn the name of one face at a time and that learning should be errorless. By this time preliminary arrangements were made for JR to work in the library and photographs of the library staff were taken so that JR could be familiar with key personnel before she started work. The vanishing cue technique was used, in which the full name was first rehearsed with the photo of the person for three trials. Following three trials the name of the person was supplied with the final letter of the last name missing. Eventually the initials of the name were sufficient to trigger the name, and eventually no cues were required other than the photograph.

JR's first job was updating law files. The job was divided into four stages that involved taking out the first alteration in the file, finding the insertion point in the file, unclipping the file, and then removing the outdated section and replacing it with the updated section—a simple enough procedure if one can remember whether the document in your hand is the one that has just been replaced or the one to be replaced. Above her desk was a set of numbered instructions that she checked off at each stage in the process. Also above her desk was a photograph of the woman who was in charge of the library, with her name below (this was only replaced with another staff member when she was confident of the name without reference to the photograph). She also had a map to show her the way to the toilet. For the first 3 months, she attended the library twice a week for half a day. She was taken by taxi to and from work. She was accompanied at work on each occasion by a speech pathologist, although, in the last month, the speech pathologist was present only once a week. The author was keen to point out that only one job was to be learned at a time and, given the experience reported in other case studies, the progress was likely to be tortuously slow and hopes should not be raised too high. However, progress was far quicker than expected. JR managed to learn the task without prompting from the therapist in three sessions. She was going to the toilet with her map and without being accompanied by the therapist after a single month. She started to learn a new job of checking in books using a computer, which provided more challenges, but within 8 months she was able to undertake three jobs in the library. She is still reminded of her former life by the books she now puts back in the shelves. Full accounts of the training procedures have been published (Andrewes & Gielewski, 1999). Broadly the process was achieved by reducing each job to a series of routines that could be learned like a habit. It would be tempting to say she was using implicit memory because, of course, she had no memory of the learning experience. However, this might be to underestimate her achievements given the rather limited scope with which implicit memory is researched. My colleague Elizabeth Gielewski has since tried something similar with another amnesic patient without the same success, and perhaps one cannot ignore the important rehabilitation setting which was so similar to her original workplace and her high degree of intelligence in making an important contribution towards her successful outcome.

One should also not discount the importance of her relatively intact executive skills—skills that allowed her to take the initiative and try out new solutions to problems. In the next section there is a discussion of patients who lack such skills, and who provide some of the biggest challenges to the rehabilitationist.

Dysexecutive behaviour and rehabilitation

The case of TW (see Box 11.2) reveals a number of features of dysexecutive syndrome that undermine attempts at rehabilitation. Firstly, there was a certain lack of insight into his condition. The patient had a vague awareness that he was unable to do the timetables anymore, but the patient's wife had a far better realisation of what was going wrong with his behaviour. She reported what appeared to be a lack of motivation and difficulty in making even simple everyday decisions. The second feature was the patient's inability to function without supervision and the necessary cueing of his responses, as if he had lost his will to function independently. His level of intelligence was adequate but these tests were convergent and progressed towards a single solution. They did not test his ability to take the initiative and try different strategies to achieve a goal. The patient performed relatively well in structured situations; it was only when initiative, spontaneity, and creativity were at a premium that the importance of the intact executive system was realised.

This lack of awareness or lack of insight is seen as being a cardinal sign of dysexecutive syndrome (Stuss, 1991). A failure to acknowledge or moni-

---

Box 11.2. Case report: TW

The patient, TW, was a schoolteacher in his fifties. He had suffered a right frontoparietal stroke that involved the anterior branch of the middle cerebral artery. His wife reported that he had briefly returned to teaching but had not coped at all well. When the patient was personally asked about his performance he was a bit vague. However, he suggested that, prior to the stroke, the principal always asked him to construct the school time-table. He said that he was seen as especially skilled in this area and gained some enjoyment from the task. However, since the stroke, he was not capable of doing this task and was not sure why this was the case.

His performance on intelligence tests was within the "high average" range and was generally unremarkable, with the exception of some difficulty on the block design subtest, a test of construction that requires the subject to copy designs using a set of coloured blocks. On a number of tests that have been associated with frontal dysfunction his performance (e.g. verbal fluency, colour form sort and Trails B) he was within the expected range. However, on a test requiring him to learn an electronic maze he showed severe difficulty. He frequently broke the rules of the task and was poor at monitoring his errors. Although he made good progress at first, he never achieved two errorless trials, At one point, after 21 trials he managed to complete the maze without error, but then on the next trial made four errors, and so on.

I was impressed by the man's keenness to be involved in rehabilitation and his generally intact and high level of intelligence, and it was recommended that he go to a special rehabilitation centre. However, on following him up 3 months later I was informed that he had been taken off the programme because of his lack of initiative. He was assigned to a workshop and would readily understand how to do the tasks and would start the task off when supervised. But, a few minutes later he would be standing by his bench not being able to continue with his work unless he was prompted or cued.

tor one's own deficiencies is a common clinical problem. It has been frequently found in patients with severe TBI, and is particularly predominant in some of the dementias such as Alzheimer's and Huntington's chorea and patients following brain surgery (McGlynn & Kazniak, 1991). For example, Oddy et al. (1985) asked the patients and their families to describe their behaviour. Of these severely head-injured patients only 53% self-reported residual memory problems whereas 79% of the patients' families had noted the patients' memory impairment. Forty per cent of the families also reported childish behaviour in the patient, which the patients never acknowledged. Objective evidence of this lack of self-awareness comes from a number of studies showing that, when reports are compared with objective testing, the relatives' or partner's reports are far more accurate and reliable compared with the patient's self-report (Andrewes et al., 1998; Sunderland, Harris, & Gleave, 1984). This schism between the patient's judgement and reality causes a huge hurdle for rehabilitation. Obviously, if the patients are not aware of their own behaviour, then there will be little motivation to overcome that deficiency. The lack of awareness of one's own behaviour also means that mistakes will not be monitored and the patient is robbed of any means of learning new behaviours.

These kinds of results have led some clinicians to have a negative and fatalistic attitude towards patients with dysexecutive neuropsychological signs. However, there are many ways that these patients' lives may be improved if allowance is made for their impairment. Even in cases that seem to be hopeless the therapist may be of assistance.

Compensating executive dysfunction

The model of the executive system has already been described in Chapter 3. In the case of ED (see Box 11.3) there was a breakdown in the initiating of behaviour, suggesting that her ability to control her own behaviour had accordingly declined. Two options would increase the likelihood of triggering the hypothetical "washing-up schema". The first might be the encouragement of the self-initiation through instruction. This sometimes works with such patients; however, the patient was too impaired for this to work. The initiation of the schema was in this case encouraged by starting the patient off on the schema-driven behaviour. In the same way in this model as in previous schema-driven behaviour the initiation of a routine will trigger the rest of that routine. A further encouragement to the desired behaviour was theoretically achieved by exposing the patient to environmental stimuli that might also trigger such a schema. In this case the patient was taken to the sink, which with its utensils and washing-up liquid provided an environmental cue that would help to trigger the "washing-up schema". The simple model of the therapist, or in the last case the husband, standing in for the

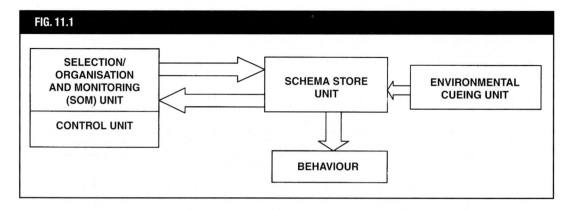

The executive system: a simplified model that illustrates the essential features for the rehabilitation perspective (see Chapter 3 for a full description of this system).

missing functional component within the executive system works in a number of commonly used situations within rehabilitation. According to this model the patient will sit around without any spontaneity. But when a plate of food is placed in front of them, they will be triggered into a routine of eating until the stimulus is removed. The person is literally under the control of the environment as it impinges on them (L'hermitte, 1983). Any external cues such as instructions, lists, or other prompts may be helpful.

Often therapies are aimed at compensating both the control unit and the selection, organisation, and monitoring (SOM) unit, but some therapies clearly favour one over the other. Finset and Andresen (1990) used a "process diary", which clearly had positive results on the patient's SOM behaviour. The diary functioned to selectively increase attention to their surroundings, their own behaviour, and their therapeutic goals. The use of this diary also had the effect of organising and structuring their daily lives. The process diary was a file that allowed for the insertion of various work sheets or forms that were provided by the therapist. The patient and the therapist filled in these forms during their daily sessions (see Finset & Andresen, 1990, for details and case examples). Initially, the process diary has a very simple purpose of defining the treatment goals of the diary itself—the reason why they should find the diary useful. The diary subsequently contains details of orientation: when the patient came into hospital, why they are in hospital etc. As therapy progresses the process diary expands to contain

clearly divided sections such as *planning* (listing future activities), *memory* (listing memory strategies), *diary* (an actual diary, filled in on a daily basis), *self-evaluation* (strong and weak points noted), *special assignments* (e.g. reporting back in the next session on the TV news seen between sessions), *feedback on behaviour* (given a particular target behaviour such as rudeness to staff; negative feedback is given on one page with goals achieved on the other).

One of the assignments was aimed at compensating control unit problems and was referred to as *training initiative* (passive patients were given assignments to increase their involvement with activities or persons on the ward). The authors present evidence that this method helped severely impaired patients who showed many dysexecutive, signs e.g. impulsivity and disinhibition. Patients who were previously adynamic (lacking in spontaneity) became far more goal oriented and showed more initiative on ADL tasks.

The process diary has two main benefits. Firstly, it provides structure for the patient which the patient is unable to provide for themselves. In terms of the executive model it provides the organisation that the SOM unit was not able to provide. Secondly, it also compensates for impaired memory. The patient has continuous access to the process diary and this allows the patient to rehearse the information and refer to it. The process diary provided an external cue for activities that could not be initiated by the control unit. Finally, the diary became a routine itself and

---

Box 11.3. Compensating the control unit: case report—ED

The patient ED was suffering a frontal lobe dementia following two separate instances of coma associated with lithium toxicity. The 55-year-old female patient had became comatose on two occasions following two general anaesthetic operations undertaken at two small private hospitals.

The patient was severely impaired on all tests of flexibility and to a lesser extent on tests of memory. There were signs on an MRI scan of frontal atrophy. The husband complained that the patient was no longer active around the house, despite her tremendous energy and industry prior to the deterioration. He was sure that the patient was still able to do housework and he said that his wife wanted to help around the house with such duties as sweeping and washing-up but, for some reason, never got around to it. Information was provided to the husband in a way that would allow him to apply his therapeutic information in a flexible and appropriate manner. His wife's problem was described to him as a poorly functioning starter motor in a car. This function of the frontal lobes was sensitively explained to the husband with the use of a model brain. It was suggested to him that, on the next occasion when she wanted to do housework, he should gently start her off on the routine. On the next appointment the husband was full of enthusiasm. He had found, for example, that in the case of washing-up, if his wife was guided gently into starting on the washing-up she would happily go on to complete the process. Although the patient deteriorated beyond being able to do these tasks after a further 6 months, this simple measure provided some lifting of spirits initially in a depressing situation.

> **Box 11.4.** Compensation of the SOM unit to distract attention away from external cues: case report—JL
>
> A similar technique, which the author has found useful with two patients, is referred to as the ZYX method, in which the patient is distracted by saying the alphabet backwards to themselves. This method was used in the case of a right frontoparietal stroke patient who complained that in the earlier stages of his recovery he tended to cry for very little reason, but now he tended to laugh too much and, once he started laughing, could not stop. Usually (unlike the pathological laughter patient described in Chapter 9), the laughter was appropriate, e.g. when someone made a joke. It was just that he found it hard to stop once he started. John said that once he started others around him would start laughing, which made it even harder for him to stop. He said that, apart from the embarrassment, it would physically hurt his sides. He was instructed to say the alphabet backwards on any occasion that he felt laughter coming on. In a later assessment he reported that it worked very well indeed until he learned how to say the alphabet backwards with ease, whereupon he had to switch to counting backwards in threes. In this case attention is distracted from triggering environmental cue by using a strategy that reorients the SOM unit.
>
> This method also worked well for a patient who found that, following the removal of a right frontal benign tumour, she was moved to tears with very little encouragement. This caused her some embarrassment in public places such as restaurants. Both these patients had only mild signs of neuropsychological impairment on tests, and therefore it is possible that there was sufficient executive capacity to allow them to strategically assist the modulation of their attentional focus.

therefore theoretically the habit of filling in the diary formed a hypothetical diary filling-in schema which was cued by the various environmental stimuli that were always present when the diary was completed.

In the more intact patient, *the patient* themselves may change the environmental cues and thereby curtail the triggering of an unwanted behaviour. While there may be no research to support these methods, they are sometimes used by clinicians known to the author. Patients with poor emotional control that may or may not be due to frontal damage may be given strategies which increase the ease with which they can avoid the external stimuli that trigger the emotional behaviour. Typically patients, and more often their partners, complain that the patient is easily moved to anger with little provocation. They are described as having a "short fuse" and their emotional response is quite out of keeping with the minor event causing the loss of temper. Advice that is often used with varying success is for the patient to leave the situation as soon as they feel they are losing their temper. In terms of the executive system framework, the success of this method would lie in changing the environmental cues. The patient, because of their impairment, is unable to change the direction of their own selective attention unit in a controlled manner. The patient is, however, able to change the environment by going outside and away from the triggering event. The example of a child calming down when they go to their room might be an everyday example of this occurring. Of course,

this method assumes that the patient has a sufficiently intact control unit to break the chain of behaviour and this cannot always be assumed. Nevertheless, patients with disinhibited behaviour of this kind do find these types of techniques useful.

What is going on when these techniques are found to be successful with what appears to be an impossible situation? Two main themes seem to be running through these cases in that two forms of treatment strategies are working. The first, referred to at the beginning of this section, proposes that in some cases it is appropriate to act as the patient's frontal lobes and guide them and prompt them. This is an especially appropriate strategy when the patient has a close relationship with a carer.

The second strategy is somewhat different. Here an automatic routine is set up to compensate for a behaviour that is more usually internally selected using the hypothetical SOM unit. The process involves training an automatic link between the external cue and a behaviour. The diary cues a routine and then cues within the diary cue further routines. These trained habits reduce the need for the SOM and control unit. A further example of this process is that of a young medical practitioner with executive dysfunction following TBI who showed an inability to monitor his errors and check his own work spontaneously. He was trained to check his work (von Cramon & Matthes-von Cramon, 1994) in a process in a training programme that required him to check each time, irrespective of whether he thought it was necessary. In this way the environmental cue of work completion automatically cued a checking process without the need for initiative or controlled directory selection of routines. The goals were achieved without the SOM and control units by forming a habit or schema that was cued by the environment.

Awareness of environmental cues and the influence of the SOM on schema selection

According to our model, a behavioural routine is selected either by the environmental cues or by more internally modulated selection processes involving the control and SOM unit. We have already described cases in which the control and SOM unit may be compensated; however, sometimes it is sufficient to enhance the saliency of environmental cues, making them more powerful.

Sometimes the signals from internal states that modify goals such as thirst and hunger are not available and therefore the appropriate schema is not triggered, placing the patient at risk. A good example of this occurring is the case of a woman whose hypothalamus was removed during the excision of a tumour (Johnston, Burgess, McMillan, & Greenwood, 1994). This woman of "low average" intelligence did not have any indication of when she was thirsty and consequently became seriously dehydrated. A token economy programme was successfully implemented which required her to drink a certain amount of water from a measuring flask at certain times during the day. She was rewarded by exchanging the tokens for rewards to be purchased at the hospital canteen; the tokens were eventually faded when the behavioural routine was learned.

A more complex case is described by Burgess and Alderman (1990) of a patient who had no awareness of the volume of his voice. His speaking voice was "excessively loud". He was described as having marked intellectual deterioration with language and memory deficits and "exhibiting a frontal lobe syndrome". The volume of the patient's voice was measured using a meter and the patient was successfully encouraged to read single words at the level marked on the meter. This was done by giving the patient encouragement to read at the marked level and

fining the patient (response cost) if the patient read too loudly. The patient was also given the inducement that he could leave the session if he reached a prearranged target performance. There was little generalisation between the reading of words and the reading of phrases and the difficulty of the material had to be moderated, but eventually the patient showed mastery with the phrases and an ability to moderate his own voice volume using the meter. Unfortunately this achievement did not generalise to his speech outside the sessions. But the evidence that he did have the potential to independently moderate his own speech volume prompted the use of a microphone headset so that he could monitor his volume throughout the day. The authors describe this as a failure of controlling voice volume according to social context (e.g. speak quietly in a chapel, but loudly at a football match). The patient was described as losing his monitoring capacity. The programme allowed him to compensate for a breakdown of this monitoring process.

Modification of behavioural routines

Some approaches to therapy can be conceived as setting up new schemas by encouraging certain behaviours given a set of conditions. Severely brain-damaged patients may show gross signs of impaired higher cortical functioning to the extent that behavioural modification techniques are one of the few ways of helping the patient towards acceptable social behaviour. Such patients may not only show dysexecutive signs but also severe memory impairment and low levels of intellectual function. Sometimes the patient will show a routine of behaviour that is inappropriate but is nevertheless unwittingly rewarded. Often the patient is attempting to draw attention to themselves in an understaffed environment in which the patient probably feels alone and neglected. Because the patient does not have the intellectual resources to attract attention by positive means, various disruptive behaviours may be enacted such as pulling or grabbing at nurses as they pass, abusive language, incoherent shouting, or screaming.

Often the patient places themselves unwittingly

information may be best delivered after patients have left hospital.

Further, questions remain of the cognitive neuropsychological approach, which analyses the *process* that is impaired prior to its compensation (Berndt & Mitchum, 1995). These efforts are not always successful for reasons that are poorly understood, but ultimately this is a research path that is likely to bear fruit in future years.

The area of neuropsychological rehabilitation research is a fascinating area that shows tensions in how to proceed with research and practice. Some propose a holistic approach to therapy (Ben-Yishay, 1996), while others see a strict analytic approach in which the cause of impaired performance is analysed and consequently compensated (Robertson, 1999; Robertson & Murre, 1999). In some ways both approaches may make sense, given different goals. Thus when applying rehabilitation at the "coalface" account has to be taken of the individual's limitations, personality needs and requirements, and their family milieu and other support systems. However, there remains the requirement for studies that clearly analyse performance breakdown and then attempt to compensate the process that is impaired irrespective of the patient's characteristics. Such approaches attempt to outline principles that guide rehabilitation approaches.

This chapter has argued broadly that it is no longer useful to merely refer to techniques as if they may be usefully applied to all patients with a particular disorder. Rehabilitationists must take into account three key factors: needs, limitations, and feasibility. In terms of *needs* the patient has to ask whether the skills taught will enhance the patient's everyday coping. The *limitations* of a patient will limit what can be done and one should not ignore the possibility that a severely impaired patient will need a different approach to rehabilitation depending on their stage of recovery. Sometimes skills may be taught at one stage of recovery because they will be useful at a later stage. For example, an amnesic patient may be taught to check off items completed to provide a base training for later interventions. The *limitations* of the patient have been discussed in this chapter in terms of the areas that require compensation, and such information can only be gained by a comprehensive assessment of the patient's strengths and weaknesses. Finally, a programme will not be *feasible* unless the patient is motivated and there is the requisite support from both clinical resources and significant others. In practice and rehabilitation research this chapter has broadly argued the need for tailoring the rehabilitation to the patient.

ADDENDUM 1

Internal strategies

Most mnemonics (pronounced *nemonics*) are designed to:

1. Increase the organisation of material according to one's previous experience. The previous experience may be in terms of a familiar room in the case of the method of loci or familiar rhyme as in the case of the peg word system. These familiar memories are sometimes referred to as schemas.

2. Provide cues at the time of storing the memory that encode the memory in such a way that it can be easily retrieved. For example, often an association is made between the well-learned schema and the to-be-remembered information. The schema is easy to retrieve from memory and therefore acts as a useful cue for the to-be-remembered information. While the supervised use of these techniques is useful they tend not to be used independently by clients once they have returned home.

Aeroplane story

Crovitz (1979) reports the use of this technique for remembering a list of words. Words are linked by a story involving passengers in an aeroplane, e.g. The *Giraffe* is eating a *sausage* and handing the next passenger a *gun*. The words in italics are in the list. Other variations on this theme exist (e.g. Kovner et al., 1985).

Names to faces using visual imagery

A commonly referred to mnemonic for learning names to faces (McCarty, 1980), this mnemonic requires the subject to find an association between the person's name and some distinctive aspect of their face (e.g. Mr Miller with his ears out like a windmill). If a distinctive feature of the face is within the imagery so much the better. Try and use features that are not likely to change.

Rhyming associative method of learning names to faces

A man's name, Graham, may be remembered because the person has a grey beard ("grey-ham"). Sometimes the association may be quite weakly related to the person but nevertheless effective. For example, a woman with the name of Gail might be remembered by imagining her long hair blowing in a gale of wind. A woman's name Lois might be remembered because she is short ("low-es") and stout. Ambiguity of a word should be avoided. Wilson (1987) describes how a patient was taught the name of a nurse called Anita by the action of the nurse shaking her hair (making it "neat-a"). The patient then proceeded to call anyone who adjusted their hair "Anita".

PQRST method

Another commonly used method in the rehabilitation literature is the PQRST method (Robinson, 1970). This is a study method that has been used to help patients remember information from texts and is of obvious advantage to a student. The technique requires the patient to first preview (P) the material, skimming through, picking out key words and surveying diagrams and pictures in order to obtain a good idea of what the chapter or article is about. From this perusal, the patient is then able to write down a list of questions (Q) that they hope to be answered by the material. The person then reads (R) the material, actively answering the questions as they go. Additional questions with the answers are added if necessary. The next stage requires the patient to rehearse or state (S) the questions and answers. Finally, the questions are written down without the answers and the patient tests (T) themselves.

External memory aids

External strategies are more likely to be used independently and spontaneously. For example, they may consist of placing items that are frequently mislaid, e.g. glasses, keys, in a consistent and special place. Alternatively, they may consist of environmental adaptations. These may take the form of painting the toilet doors red so that they can be easily recognised—a measure that is reported to markedly reduce the incidence of incontinence in a geriatric ward (Harris, 1980)—or of using an electronic organiser that draws attention to an appointment by giving off an alarm.

Memory groups

These are groups that are run for a number of memory-impaired patients. The accent is on patients having fun with various memory games and exercises. Patients discuss their problems and sometimes increase their awareness of their own problems and how to solve them from others.

ADDENDUM 2

Some behaviour modification terms

The term *behaviour modification* causes some unwarranted ethical concerns. If one were to be more realistic the term behavioural influence is perhaps more realistic. Nevertheless the same question should be asked of a behaviour modification programme and any other type of treatment: "Will it benefit the patient?"

Target behaviours are those that are identified for reduction or increase. Communication of these behaviours by precise definitions is necessary to avoid inconsistent response by staff. *Rewards,* e.g. ice cream, become *reinforcers* when they motivate and change behaviour. Other than asking a patient what they like, the patient's behaviour may be observed to assess their favourite activity. Using the *Premack principle* it is understood that a patient's most frequent behaviour is often the most potent reinforcer. Often the aim is to reduce unwanted behaviour but at the same time increase appropriate behaviour. If the unwanted behaviour is reduced on its own then there is a danger of the patient replacing the gap in behaviour with another equally unwanted behaviour.

Increasing behaviours

Positive reinforcement. Rewards increase behaviour, e.g. one hour's TV for making a bed.

Negative reinforcement. Behaviour is increased in order to avoid an aversive event, e.g. returning a library book to avoid a fine. This is termed *avoidance* if a stimulus indicates the threat of an aversive event.

Differential reinforcement of other behaviours (DRO). Reinforcing alternative, competing behaviours to the behaviour targeted for reduction, e.g. public masturbation is reduced by positively reinforcing appropriate activities requiring use of the hands.

Intermittent reinforcement schedule. When a reward for behaviour is delivered inconsistently for a behaviour, e.g. attention to disruptive behaviour on some occasions but not on others, then this intermittent reinforcement can build up the expectancy that reward will eventually come through perseverance. In much the same way a gambler bets once more just in case of a win. This schedule is therefore resistant to extinction and may be a common cause of the programme's failure.

Token economy. Sometimes severely impaired patients on a ward are motivated to perform domestic duties and keep up with their personal hygiene by reward using tokens, which can be exchanged at the hospital shop. There is an obvious advantage in the patients exchanging tokens for goods they want rather than working for a reward that is assumed to be reinforcing. Nurses are encouraged to use social praise when they give the tokens and eventually the tokens are faded, leaving just the praise—the patients continuing making beds and helping out reward nurses' behaviour.

Reducing behaviours

Positive punishment. Introducing negative consequences to reduce behaviour, e.g. subjecting a patient to an unpleasant smell (Wood, 1987). These methods are less often used because of the negative association with the carers and there are a number of ethical considerations.

Negative punishment. Withdrawing positive consequences to reduce behaviour, e.g. withdrawing ice cream if the patient is aggressive.

Extinction. Ignoring target behaviour, sometimes referred to as "time-out on the spot" (TOOTS), e.g. the patient's swearing is ignored. Time-out in an isolated room is less often used because of its negative connotations being a type of positive punishment.

Response cost. Inappropriate behaviour receives negative punishment within a token economy. When the undesirable behaviour occurs a token is removed from the number of tokens that are initially given to the patient at the beginning of the day.

12

Integration between neuropsychological functions

Neuropsychology texts may be seen to have evolved through three generations. The first generation of texts discusses the relationship between brain behaviour in terms of brain areas; in such a book chapter titles refer to the various lobes of the brain. It is only relatively recently that methodologies within neuropsychological research have allowed a more complex perspective. These technological advances in research methodology encourage a perspective that sees interactions between brain areas—interactions that are more easily allowed within the context of function rather than one specific brain area. This is the approach of this text, which may be seen as a second-generation approach to the description of neuropsychology.

However, even here there are disadvantages: terms such as perception, attention, and memory have been derived from thoughts and philosophies at a time lacking the benefit of modern neuropsychological research. There must there-fore be some uneasiness in accepting these divisions without question. It has suited psychologists to write about such topics as perception or language as different and separate topics, partly because connections between such topics were not foreseen or obvious. We sometimes need to be reminded that we have created these terms, and that the supposed divisions between one function and the next is sometimes blurred and less precise than is sometimes presumed.

A third generation of texts must point to the way these functions overlap. Some kind of a start towards this goal is attempted here and readers will have noted within these chapters how at least one topic overlaps and dovetails with another. In this final chapter these connections are highlighted as a contribution towards a more integrated approach to neuropsychology. Finally in this chapter is a discussion of the topic of consciousness. This has perhaps been a neglected topic in modern psychology up until some 10 years ago. The study of conscious awareness of our external environment, and our internal environment in terms of imagery and thought, is one of the final frontiers of neuropsychological investigation. Consciousness not only involves an integration of the processing within different functions but it appears to have a key role in allowing us to direct and control these functions. This illusive topic is still at the stage of being defined but it is important to tentatively discuss some of the initial findings in this area prior to a more thorough understanding in the future.

This chapter refrains from introducing new information, being more reflective in its tone. Figure 12.1 shows a model that reflects the arguments produced here towards synthesis and integration.

LINKS WITHIN THE LONG-TERM MEMORY STORE (LTMS): THE INFLUENCE OF PAST EXPERIENCE ON MEMORY, ATTENTION, PERCEPTION, AND LANGUAGE

As a hypothetical store for our past memories the long-term memory store (LTMS) acts to provide a top-down processing base for the learning of new memories. But the store also provides a basis on which we seek out new information about our perceptual world and allows us to communicate information through language. These functions involve quite different types of stored information. For example, it is argued in Chapter 2 that when perceiving a face there is some kind of stored representation of a typical or prototype face with which the face is matched. When listening to language it is also assumed that a lexicon of stored words is being accessed; these words are also a part of this hypothetical LTMS. The stored information, which is helpful to top-down processes within perception, may not overlap with those of the language information, although for some features of information they may share semantic information. For example, there may be connections between a stored template for what might be seen as a typical Japanese face and the word "Japanese", as being associated with Japan in this way connections are assumed to exist between modalities.

Even when skilled motor movements are considered these are presumed to be stored movement routines which when damaged cause ideomotor apraxia. The stored arrangement of movements for, say, "hammering in a nail" may be linked within the LTMS to information regarding carpentry, words for the tools used and the visual information that defines these tools. In Chapter 5 there was discussion of evidence for a model of semantic memory which described the location of information for inanimate objects, e.g. tools, being stored in the vicinity of a lexicon of actions of the type that might be required in the use of such objects.

Thus while studies are keen to show divisions within the LTMS even within types of memory, e.g. living and non-living things, it may be useful

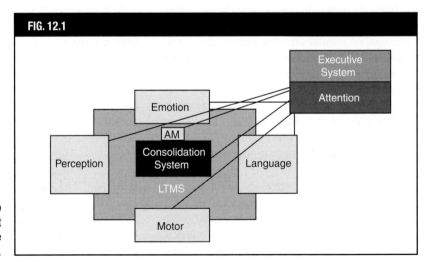

FIG. 12.1

A model of the relationship between the different systems including active memory (AM).

to see a common function of the LTMS as a source of top-down processing, a provision of an experience base that allows behaviour and information processing in a general sense. We are good at finding statistical divisions within science but poorer at showing integration.

The consolidation system described in Chapter 5 must be capable of storing information in such a way that this type of integration between the different functions is realised. The current view is that a pattern of motor movements is learned with more reliance on such areas as the basal ganglia. This procedural memory is implicit and is not dependent on explicit recollection of the event of learning.

ATTENTION WITHIN PERCEPTION

The top-down processing referred to in Chapter 2 is a means of describing a process whereby past experience may assist in speeding up the perceptual process. Until recent years little was known concerning the dynamics of this system. A match with templates could be one explanation of how this occurs. When we are shown a "mask" we process the outline and then compare these rudimentary features with likely objects and items that we have stored in our perceptual memory. If a match occurs between the facial features of the mask with the stored knowledge of a face then a process of recognition is unconsciously instituted. These templates or knowledge systems are presumed to be situated within the end-point of what has been referred to as the "what" pathway in such areas as the inferior temporal lobe. However, recent evidence shows that this is not merely a perceptual process. We may select out certain features in our visual environment at the expense of other features. As discussed, this top-down influence is more obviously influential at "late" stages of perception in V4 and the inferior temporal lobe, although research with monkeys has suggested that the competitive influence of attention on perception may be even earlier at V1.

From these studies of single-cell recordings it is clear that some kind of feedback from top-down processing has some influence even at early stages of perceptual processing. Therefore certainly according to our definition of attention there are attentional processes that appear to interact with perception. Perception itself appears to be a competitive process. Any description of a perceptual process must take into account the attentional process that guides it. A person may not perceive something because they are attending to another feature within their environment.

In the work of Chelazzi, Miller, Duncan, and Desimone (1993), their monkeys appeared to have a perceptual readiness for some objects compared to others. This selectivity may have more influence when there is a demand to process two or more competing percepts. But the point remains that there is a significant overlap between processes of attention and perception when one percept is being selected at the expense of another, although the overlap is not complete.

However, the model is clearly incomplete. Most obviously the information that guides this attentional system is dependent itself on the knowledge basis on which the perceptual system is functioning. In order to search for a face at the expense of other stimuli there must be a memory store of what a face looks like: a long-term memory store representation guides the search mechanism. There may even be a conscious awareness of the face within our working memory system as the search takes place—a process that is guided by motivational constraints and directed by a central executive. These motivational constraints are themselves determined by sensory receptors that motivate us to hunger, thirst, or social requirements present or future. In this last formulation we are going beyond the previous discussions in a bid to present an overall illustration of the integration in a macro model of the type referred to in the introduction of this book.

EXECUTIVE INFLUENCES ON ATTENTION, PERCEPTION, MEMORY, AND LANGUAGE

In the initial stages of this book there was a description of the executive system and towards the end of this chapter there was a comment that some theorists were unhappy with the idea of a single executive system. At one level this view has been confirmed since in each of the chapters on attention, perception, memory, and language there has been a description of executive influences. Virtually all of these have been described in terms of frontal dysfunction, although clearly at this point there is an imprecise relationship between the prefrontal cortex and the attributed role. There are now several publications that have pointed to the isolated dysexecutive signs within a particular domain of functioning. For example, patients with executive dysfunction in the area of syntax organisation but not in the organisation of actions, and there are many other similar dissociations. The breakdown of executive function may be very discrete, suggesting some form of modularisation. This does not, however, deny some form of integration of these modules in the same way that perception or memory is an integrated system. It is a personal view that the fashion to fractionate rather than integrate is influenced by two factors. The first is straightforward and relates to the nature of statistical analysis, which may only detect differences with any surety; the second related factor is that journals are accordingly driven to accept papers that show statistical differences. If we had a method of showing equivalence with the same confidence our approach to modelling would be quite different. It is reasonable to argue that the brain is actually a very integrated system. In fact when looked at from a structural point of view there are planes within the brain that have similar roles, e.g. the gyri of the temporal lobe, the "what" pathway. Whatever the process of evolution in the adaptation of the brain to the environment it is unlikely to promote an uneconomic approach to function; therefore it is perhaps overdue that we look for synthesis rather than compartmentalisation.

The similarities between the attention and the executive system have been noted by a number of authors. For example, Norman and Shallice's supervisory attention system is referred to by some authors as a central executive and has been described here as part of the executive system. The executive attention system arguably coordinates the various executive modules by limiting activation of one module at a time. However, we are a long way from learning how this system is controlled or how goals are realised.

Some theorists have suggested that consciousness plays an integrating role. This is a fashionable area of research but it is likely that there is more than one type of conscious activity. For example, visual imagery is likely to be a different form from internal body awareness since they may be impaired in a separate manner. Traditionally, psychologists have been naturally suspicious that what we are conscious or aware of is actually a representation of the underlying processing. This scepticism is well founded: apart from the cases of Anton's syndrome, blindsight, anosognosia, and confabulation, in which conscious representation is in error, there are also cases of normal persons in which reports of conscious activity have been misleading (Nisbett & Wilson, 1977). It is clear that the concept of "active memory" as described in Chapter 5 has a close relationship with conscious awareness.

In the last decade within neuropsychology it has been popular to modularise. This trend to compartmentalise and fractionate behaviour–brain relationships has clearly advanced our knowledge of brain mechanism and reveals a fundamental truth that the brain has neurones that are specialised at performing certain analyses and are capable of passing on this information to build up knowledge of the world. Our ability to recognise the global integrating features are less advanced, but with the advent of advances in functional imaging techniques this challenge is starting to be met.

Appendix

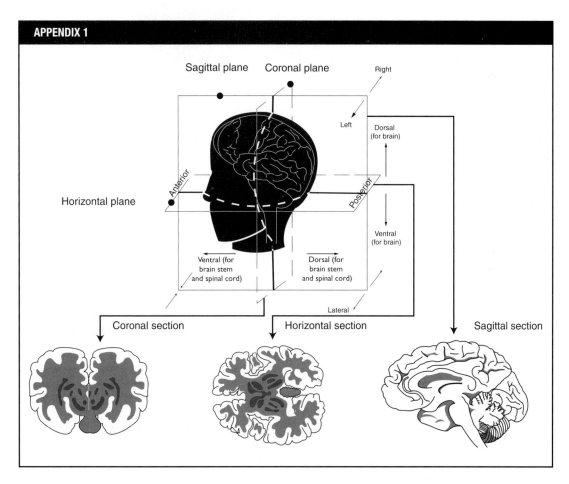

An illustration of the terminology used to describe the various relative locations of the brain. The various sections are often referred to in imaging work using MRI and CT scans. It should be noted that because the brain stem is placed in a position at an angle with the brain compared to other species dorsal and ventral relate to different spatial locations depending on whether the cerebrum or the brain stem is referred to. Terms that get over this problem are rostral (beak, anterior aspect) and caudal (tail, towards the end of the brain stem towards the spinal column), which are terms that apply to the central nervous system with more unity.

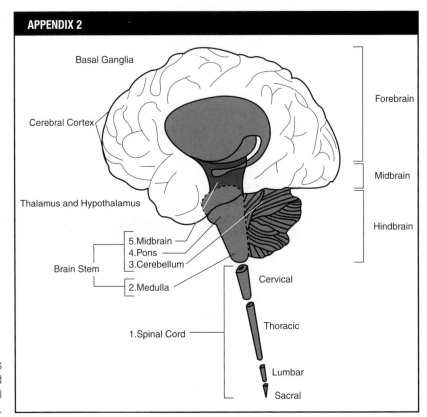

APPENDIX 2

Basal Ganglia

Cerebral Cortex

Thalamus and Hypothalamus

Brain Stem
- 5. Midbrain
- 4. Pons
- 3. Cerebellum
- 2. Medulla

1. Spinal Cord

Forebrain

Midbrain

Hindbrain

Cervical

Thoracic

Lumbar

Sacral

An illustration of the terms used to describe areas and levels within the central nervous system.

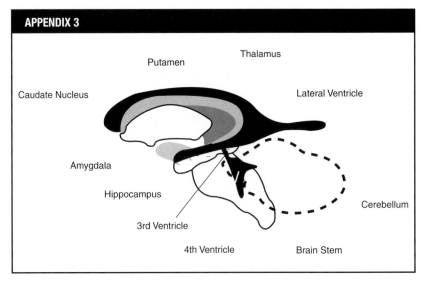

APPENDIX 3

Putamen

Thalamus

Caudate Nucleus

Lateral Ventricle

Amygdala

Hippocampus

3rd Ventricle

4th Ventricle

Cerebellum

Brain Stem

The brain contains a number of spaces or ventricles that allow for the circulation of cerebrospinal fluid. Sometimes tumours may block communication between ventricles, especially at the narrowing of the ventricles. This is associated with increased brain pressure and a widening of the ventricles, which is associated with obstructive (tension) hydrocephalus, sometimes referred to as non-communicating hydrocephalus.

APPENDIX 4

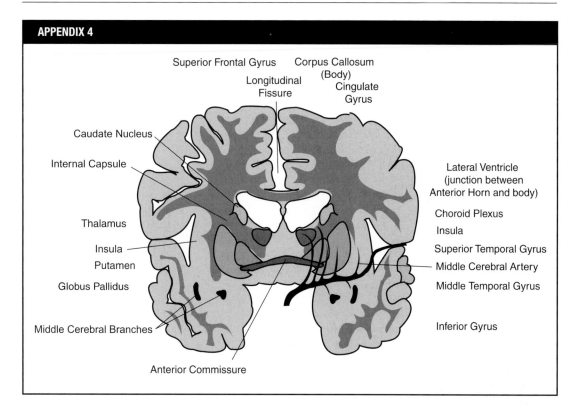

Superior Frontal Gyrus
Corpus Callosum (Body)
Longitudinal Fissure
Cingulate Gyrus
Caudate Nucleus
Internal Capsule
Thalamus
Insula
Putamen
Globus Pallidus
Middle Cerebral Branches
Anterior Commissure
Lateral Ventricle (junction between Anterior Horn and body)
Choroid Plexus
Insula
Superior Temporal Gyrus
Middle Cerebral Artery
Middle Temporal Gyrus
Inferior Gyrus

A coronal slice of the brain indicating the subcortical structures. Included is the pathway of the middle cerebral artery and the tributaries that infiltrate the motor areas of the basal ganglia and the internal capsule. Sometimes small lacunar infarcts occur in this area. These strokes are associated with other motor problems and sometimes hemiparesis of the contralateral side. The posterior limb of the internal capsule contains corticospinal motor fibres on their way from the cortex to the brain stem (see Chapter 8).

References

Adair, J.C., Schwartz, R.L., Na, D.L., Fennell, E., Gilmore, R., & Heilman, K.M. (1997). Anosognosia: Examining the disconnection hypothesis. *Journal of Neurology, Neurosurgery and Psychiatry, 63*, 798–800.

Adams, R.D., Collins, G.H., & Victor, M. (1962). Troubles de la memoire et de l'apprentissage chez l'homme: Leurs relations avec des lesions des lobes temporaux et du diencéphale. In *Physiologie de l'Hippocampe* (pp. 273–296). Paris: Centre National de la Récherche Scientifique.

Adolphs, R., & Tranel, D. (1999). Intact recognition of emotional prosody following amygdala damage. *Neuropsychologia, 37*, 1285–1292.

Adolphs, R., Damasio, H., Tranel, D., Cooper, G., & Damasio, A.R. (2000). A role for somatosensory cortices in the visual recognition of emotion as revealed by three-dimensional lesion mapping. *Journal of Neuroscience, 20*, 2683–2690.

Adolphs, R., Damasio, H., Tranel, D., & Damasio, A.R. (1996). Cortical systems for the recognition of emotion in facial expressions. *Journal of Neuroscience, 16*, 678–687.

Adolphs, R., Tranel, D., & Damasio, A.R. (1998). The human amygdala in social judgement. *Nature, 393*, 470–474.

Adolphs, R., Tranel, D., Damasio, H., & Damasio, A.R. (1995). Fear and the human amygdala. *Journal of Neuroscience, 15*, 5879–5891.

Adolphs, R., Tranel, D., Hamann, S., Young, A.W., Calder, A.J., Phelps, E.A., Anderson, A., Lee, G.P., & Damasio, A.R. (1999). Recognition of facial emotion in nine individuals with bilateral amygdala damage. *Neuropsychologia, 37*, 1111–1117.

Aeschelman, S.R., & Snoy, M.T. (1982). Enhancing the recall of prose in a brain-injured client with mnemonic instruction. *Human Learning, 1*, 165–170.

Aggleton, J.P. & Saunders, R.C. (1997). Anatomical basis of anterograde amnesia. *Memory, 5*, 49–71.

Aglioti, S., Beltramello, A., Bonazzi, A., & Corbetta, M. (1996). Thumb pointing in humans after damage to somatic sensory cortex. *Experimental Brain Research, 102*, 92–100.

Aguirre, G.K., & D'Esposito, M. (1999). Topographical disorientation: A synthesis and taxonomy. *Brain, 122*(9): 1613–1628.

Ahern, G.L., Herring, A.M., Tackenberg, J.N., Schwartz, G.E., Seeger, J.F., Labiner, D.M., Weinand, M.E., & Oommen, K.J. (1994). Affective self-report during the intracarotid sodium amobarbital test. *Clinical and Experimental Neuropsychology, 16*, 372–376

Albert, M.L. (1973). A simple test of visual neglect. *Neurology, 23*, 658–664.

Albin, R.L., Young, A.B., & Penney, J.B. (1989). The functional anatomy of basal ganglia disorders. *Trends in Neuroscience, 12*, 366–375.

Alderman, N. (1996). Central executive deficit and response to operant conditioning methods. *Neuropsychological Rehabilitation, 6*, 161–186.

Alderman, N., & Burgess, P.W. (1990). Integrating cognition and behaviour: A pragmatic approach to brain injury and rehabilitation. In R. Ll. Wood & I. Fussey (Eds.), *Cognitive rehabilitation in perspective.* (pp. 204–209). London: Taylor & Francis.

Alexander, G.E., Crutcher, M.D., & Delong, M.R. (1990). Basal-ganglia and thalamocortical circuits: Parallel substrates for motor, occulomotor, "prefrontal" and "limbic" functions. *Progress in Brain Research*, *85*, 119.

Alexander, G.E., DeLong, M.R., & Crutcher, M.D. (1992). Do cortical and basal ganglionic motor areas use "motor programs" to control movement? *Behavioral and Brain Sciences*, *15*, 656–665.

Alexander, M.P., Baker, E., Naeser, M.A., Kaplan, E., & Palumbo, C. (1992). Neuropsychological and neuroanatomical dimensions of ideomotor apraxia. *Brain*, *115*, 87–107.

Alexander, M.P., & Benson, D.F. (1991). The aphasias and related disturbances. In R.J. Joynt (Ed.), *Clinical Neurology* (Vol. 1, Ch. 10). Philadelphia: Lippincott.

Alexander, M.P., Benson, D.F., & Stuss, D.T. (1989). Frontal lobes and language. *Brain and Language*, *37*, 656–691.

Alexander, M.P., Fischer, R.S., & Friedman, R. (1992). Lesion localization in apractic agraphia. *Archives of Neurology*, *49*, 246–251.

Alexander, M.P., & Freedman, M. (1984). Amnesia after anterior communicating artery aneurysm rupture. *Neurology*, *34*, 752–759.

Alexander, M.P., Hiltbrunner, B., & Fischer, R.S. (1989). Disturbed anatomy of transcortical sensory aphasia. *Archives of Neurology*, *46*, 885–892.

Alexander, M.P., Naeser, N.A., & Palumbo, C.L. (1987). Correlations of subcortical CT lesion sites and aphasia profiles. *Brain*, *110*, 961–991.

Alexander, M.P., Stuss, D.T., & Benson, D.F. (1979). Capgras syndrome: A reduplicative phenomenon. *Neurology*, *29*, 334–339.

Alkire, M.T., Haier, R.J., & Fallon, J.H. (2000). Toward a unified theory of narcosis: Brain imaging evidence for a thalamocortical switch as the neurophysiologic basis of anesthetic-induced unconsciousness. *Conscious Cognition*, *9*(3): 370–386.

Andersen, G., Ingemann-Nielsen, N.M., Vestergaard, K., & Riis, J.O. (1994). Pathoanatomic correlation between poststroke pathological crying and damage to brain areas involved in serotonergic neurotransmission. *Stroke*, *25*, 1050–1052.

Andersen, G., Vestergaard, K., & Riis, J.O. (1993). Citalopram for post-stroke pathological crying. *Lancet*, *342*, 837–839.

Andersen, R.A., Snyder, L.H., Bradley, D.C., & Xing, J. (1997). Multimodal representation of space in the posterior parietal cortex and its use in planning movements. *Annual Review of Neuroscience, 20*, 303–330.

Anderson, J.M., Gilmore, R., Roper, S., Crosson, B., et al. (1999). Conduction aphasia and the arcuate fasciculus: A reexamination of the Wernicke–Geschwind model. *Brain and Language*, *70*, 1–12.

Anderson, J.R. (1983). *The architecture of cognition*. Cambridge, MA: Harvard University Press.

Anderson, J.R., Bothell, D., Lebiere, C., & Matessa, M. (1998). An integrated theory of list memory. *Journal of Memory and Language*, *38*, 341–380

Anderson, S.W., Bechara, A., Damasio, H., Tranel, D., & Damasio, A.R. (1999) Impairment of social and moral behavior related to early damage in human prefrontal cortex. *Nature Neuroscience*, *2*(11). 1032–1037.

Andrewes, D.G. (1984). *The analysis and compensation of rehearsal as a learning strategy in Korsakoff psychosis patients*. Unpublished PhD thesis, London University.

Andrewes, D.G. (1989). The behaviour modification of disruptive behaviour in the brain-damaged patient. *Journal of Behavior Therapy and Experimental Psychiatry*, *20*, 261–264.

Andrewes, D.G., Aitken, S., Parr, C., Mitchell, P., & Kaye, A. (2001). The development of a scale for measuring emotional and social dysfunction following brain surgery. Manuscript in preparation.

Andrewes, D.G., Alpitsis, R., & Detering, P. (2001). Cognitive inflexibility in patients with frontal lobe lesions. Manuscript in preparation.

Andrewes, D.G., Dinjin, P., Layton, T., Puce, A., Kilpatrick, C., & Bladin, P. (2001) Effects of unilateral temporal lobectomy on verbal and visuospatial recognition memory: The role of laterality and age of onset. Manuscript in preparation.

Andrewes, D.G., Gibbs, A., Chiu, E., Dennis, C., Bradshaw, J.L., & Bradshaw, J.A. (1993). Presymptomatic and advanced neuropsychological signs of Huntington's disease. In J. Hendy, D. Caine, A. Pfaff & E. Hannan (Eds.), *The life cycle: Development, maturation, senescence*. Proceedings of the 16th Annual Brain Impairment conference, Sydney, November 1992. Bowen Hills, Queensland: Australian Academic Press.

Andrewes, D.G., & Gielewski, E. (1999). The work rehabilitation of a herpes simplex encephalitis patient with anterograde amnesia. *Neuropsychological Rehabilitation*, *9*, 70–99.

Andrewes, D.G., Hordern, C., & Kaye, A. (1998). The Everyday Functioning Questionnaire: A new measure of cognitive and emotional status for neurosurgical outpatients. *Neuropsychological Rehabilitation*, *8*, 377–391.

Andrewes, D.G., Kaye, A., Aitken, S., Parr, C., Bates, L., & Murphy, M. (Submitted). The ESDR: a new method of assessing emotional and social dysfunction in patients following brain surgery.

Andrewes, D.G., Kinsella, G., Murphy, M., & Alderton, K. (1996). Using a memory-handbook to improve everyday memory in community dwelling older adults with memory complaints. *Experimental Ageing and Research, 22,* 305–322.

Andrewes, D.G., & Maude, D. (1990). A computerised clinical test of forgetting based on the ACT model of memory retrieval. *International Journal of Man–Machine Studies, 32,* 233–244.

Andrewes, D.G., & Pannella, G. (2001). The remediation of prospective memory. Manuscript in preparation. *Neuropsychological Rehabilitation.*

Annett, M. (1985). Left, right, hand and brain: The right shift theory. London: Lawrence Erlbaum Associates Ltd.

Antonucci, G., Guariglia, C., Judica, A., Magnotti, L., Paolucci, S., Pizzamiglio, L., & Zoccolotti, P. (1995). Effectiveness of neglect rehabilitation in a randomized group study. *Journal of Clinical and Experimental Neuropsychology, 17,* 383–389.

Aram, D.M., & Eisele, J.A. (1992). Plasticity and recovery of higher cognitive functions following early brain injury. In I. Rapin & S.J. Segalowitz (Eds.), *Handbook of neuropsychology: Vol. 6. Child neuropsychology* (pp. 73–92). New York: Elsevier Science.

Ardila, A., Rosselli, M., & Pinzon, O. (1989). Alexia and agraphia in Spanish speakers: CAT correlations and inter-linguistic analysis. In A. Ardila, & F. Ostrosky (Eds.), *Brain organisation of language and cognitive processes* (pp. 204–206) New York. Plenum Press.

Arguin, M., & Bub, D. (1993). Modulation of the directional attention deficit in visual neglect by hemispatial factors. *Brain and Cognition, 22,* 148–160.

Army Individual Test Battery (1944). *Manual of directions and scoring.* Washington, DC: War Department, Adjutants General Office.

Arnold, S.E. (1999). Cognition and neurpathology in schizophrenia. *Acta Psychiatrica Scandinavica, 99* (suppl. 395), 41–50.

Arroyo, S., Lesser, R.P., Gordon, B., Uematsu, S., Hart, J., Schwerdt, P., Andreasson, K., & Fisher, R.S. (1993). Mirth, laughter and gelastic seizures. *Brain, 116*(4), 757–780.

Ashbridge, E., Walsh, V., & Cowey, A. (1997). Temporal aspects of visual search studies by transcranial magnetic stimulation. *Neuropsychologia, 35,* 1121–1131.

Asthana, H.S., & Mandal, M.K. (1997). Hemiregional variations in facial expression of emotions. *British Journal of Psychology, 88* (3): 519–525.

Astrom, M. (1996). Generalised anxiety disorder in stroke patients. *Stroke, 27,* 270–275.

Atkinson, R.C., & Shiffrin, R.M. (1968). Human memory: A proposed system and its control processes. *Psychology of Learning and Motivation, 2,* 89–195.

Atkinson, R.C., & Shiffrin, R.M. (1977). Human memory: A proposed system and its control processes. In G. Bower (Ed.), *Human memory: Basic processes* (pp. 110–113). New York: Academic Press.

Bachevalier, J., & Mishkin, M. (1989). Mnemonic and neuropathological effects of occluding the posterior cerebral artery in *Macaca mulatta. Neuropsychologia, 27*(1), 83–105.

Bach-Y-Rita, P. (1990). Brain plasticity as a basis for recovery of functions in humans. *Neuropsychologia, 28,* 547–554.

Backman, L., Josephsson, S., Herlitz, A., & Stigsdotter, A. (1991). The generalizability of training gains in dementia: Effects of an imagery-based mnemonic on face–name retention duration. *Psychology and Aging, 6,* 489–492.

Baddeley, A.D. (1966). Short-term memory for word sequences as a function of accoustic, semantic and formal similarity. *Quarterly Journal of Experimental Psychology, 18,* 362–365.

Baddeley, A.D. (1978). The trouble with levels: A re-examination of Craik and Lockhart's framework for memory research. *Psychological Review, 85,* 1–8.

Baddeley, A.D. (1986). *Working memory.* Oxford: Oxford University Press.

Baddeley, A.D. (1992). Working memory. *Science, 255,* 556–559.

Baddeley, A.D. (1996). Exploring the central executive. *Quarterly Journal of Experimental Psychology, 49A,* 5–29.

Baddeley, A.D. (1997). *Human memory: Theory and practice.* Hove, UK: Psychology Press.

Baddeley, A.D. (1998). Recent developments in working-memory. *Current Opinion in Neurobiology, 8,* 234–238.

Baddeley, A. (2000). The episodic buffer: A new component of working memory? *Trends in Cognitive Science, 4,* 417–423.

Baddeley, A.D., & Della Sala, S. (1996) Working memory and executive control. *Philosophical Transactions of the Royal Society London B Series, 351,* 1397–1404.

Baddeley, A.D., Della Sala, S., Papagno, C., & Spinnler, H. (1997). Dual task performance in dysexecutive and non-dysexecutive patients with frontal lobe lesions. *Neuropsychology*, *11*, 187–194.

Baddeley, A.D., Grant, S., Wright, E., & Thomson, N. (1975). Imagery and visual working memory. In P.M.A. Rabbitt & S. Dornic (Eds.), *Attention and performance* (Vol. 5, pp. 205–217). London: Academic Press.

Baddeley, A.D., & Hitch, G.J. (1974). Working memory. In G.A. Bower (Ed.), *The psychology of learning and motivation* (Vol. 8, pp. 47–90). New York: Academic Press.

Baddeley, A.D., & Hitch, G. (1977). Recency re-examined. In S. Dornic (Ed.), *Attention and performance* (Vol. 6, pp. 647–667). Hillsdale, NJ: Lawrence Erlbaum Associates Inc.

Baddeley, A.D., & Hitch, G. (1993). The recency effect: Implicit learning with explicit retrieval? *Memory and Cognition*, *24*, 146–155.

Baddeley, A.D., & Lieberman, K. (1980). Spatial working memory. In R. Nickerson (Ed.), *Attention and performance* (Vol. 8, pp. 521–539). Hillsdale, NJ: Lawrence Erlbaum Associates Inc.

Baddeley, A.D., Thomson, N., & Buchanan, M. (1975). Word length and the structure of short-term memory. *Journal of Verbal Learning and Verbal Behavior*, *14*, 575–589.

Baddeley, A.D., & Warrington, E.K. (1970). Amnesia and the distinction between long- and short-term memory. *Journal of Verbal Behaviour and Verbal Learning*, *9*, 176–189.

Baddeley, A.D., & Weiskrantz, L. (Eds.) (1993). *Attention: Selection, awareness, and control: A tribute to Donald Broadbent*. New York: Clarendon Press.

Baddeley, A.D., & Wilson, B. (1988). Frontal amnesia and the dysexecutive syndrome. *Brain and Cognition*, *7*, 212–230.

Baddeley A., & Wilson, B.A. (1994). When implicit learning fails: Amnesia and the problem of error elimination. *Neuropsychologia*, *32*, 53–68.

Badecker, W., & Caramazza, A. (1985). On considerations of method and theory governing the use of clinical categories in neurolinguistics and cognitive neuropsychology: The case against agrammatism. *Cognition*, *20*, 97–125.

Bahrick, H.P., Bahrick, P.O., & Wittilinger, R.P. (1975). Fifty years of memory for names of faces: A cross-sectional approach. *Journal of Experimental Psychology: General*, *104*, 54–75.

Baizer, J.S., Kralj-Hans, I., & Glickstein, M. (1999). Cerebellar lesions and prism adaption in macaque monkeys. *Journal of Neurophysiology*, *81*, 1960–1965.

Banich, M.T., Levine, S.C., Kim, H., & Huttenlocher, P. (1990). The effect of developmental factors on IQ in hemiplegic children. *Neuropsychologia*, *28*, 35–47.

Barbas, H., & Pandya, D.N. (1991). Patterns of connections of the prefrontal cortex in the rhesus monkey associated with cortical architecture. In H.S. Levin, H.M. Eisenberg, & A.L. Benton (Eds.), *Frontal lobe function and dysfunction.* (Ch. 2, pp. 35–58). Oxford: Oxford University Press.

Barcelo, F., Suwazono, S., Knight, R.T. (2000). Prefrontal modulation of visual processing in humans. *Nature Neuroscience*, *3*, 399–403.

Barker, A., & Dunnett, S.B. (1999). *Neural repair, transplantation and rehabilitation*. Hove, UK: Psychology Press.

Baron, M.S., Vitek, J.L., Bakay, R.A.E., Green, J., Kaneoke, Y., Hashimoto, T., Turner, R.S., Woodard, J.L., Cole, S.A., McDonald, W.M., & DeLong, M.R. (1996). Treatment of advanced Parkinson's disease by posterior Gpi pallidotomy: 1-year results of a pilot study. *Annals of Neurology*, *40*, 355–366.

Barrash, J., Damasio, H., Adolphs, R., Tranel, D. (2000). The neuroanatomical correlates of route learning impairment. *Neuropsychologia*, *38*, 820–836.

Barth, J.T., Alves, W.M., Ryan, T.V., Macciocci, R.W., Rimel, J., Nelson, J., & Nelson, W. (1989). Mild head injury in sports: Neuropsychological sequelae and recovery of function. In H. Levin, H.W. Eisenberg, & A.L. Benton (Eds.), *Mild head injury* (pp. 257–275). Oxford: Oxford University Press.

Bartlett, F.C. (1932). Remembering: A study in experimental and social psychology. London: Cambridge University Press.

Basso, A., Gardelli, M., Grassi, M.P., & Mariotti, M. (1989). The role of the right hemisphere in recovery from aphasia: Two case studies. *Cortex*, *25* (4), 555–566.

Basso, A., Lecours, A.R., Moraschini, S., & Vanier, M. (1985). Anatomical correlations of the aphasias as defined through computerised tomography: Exceptions. *Brain and Language*, *26*, 201–229.

Basso, A., Luzzatti, C., & Spinnler, H. (1980). Is ideomotor apraxia the outcome of damage to well defined regions of the left hemisphere? Neuropsychological study of CT correlation. *Journal of Neurology, Neurosurgery and Psychiatry*, *43*, 118–126.

Basso, A., Taborelli, A., & Vignolo, L.A. (1978). Dissociated disorders of speaking and writing in aphasia. *Journal of Neurology, Neurosurgery and Psychiatry*, *41*, 556–563.

Bastian, A.J., Mink, J.W., Kaufman, B.A., & Thach, W.T. (1998). Posterior vermal split syndrome. *Annals of Neurology*, *44*, 601–610.

Battaglia-Meyer, A., Ferraina, S., Marconi, B. et al. (1998). Early motor influences on visuomotor transformations for reaching: A positive image of optic ataxia. *Experimental Brain Research*, *123*, 172–189.

Bauer, R. (1986). The cognitive psychophysiology of prosopagnosia, In H. Ellis, M. Jeeves, F. Newcombe, & A. Young (Eds.), Aspects of face processing (pp. 253–267). Dordrecht: Martinus Nijhoff.

Bauer, R.M. (1993). Agnosia. In K.M. Heilman & E. Valenstein (Eds.), *Clinical Neuropsychology* (3rd ed., pp.215–263). Oxford: Oxford University Press.

Baxter, M.G., & Chiba, A.A. (1999). Cognitive functions of the basal forebrain. *Current Opinion in Neurobiology*, *9*, 178–183.

Baxter, D.M., & Warrington, E.K. (1985). Category specific phonological dysgraphia. *Neuropsychologia*, *23*, 653–666.

Baxter, D.M., & Warrington, E.K. (1987). Transcoding sound to spelling: single or multiple sound unit correspondence? *Cortex*, *23*, 11–28.

Bayless, J.D., Varney, N.R., & Roberts, R.J. (1989). Tinker toy test performance and vocational outcome in patients with closed head injuries. *Journal of Clinical and Experimental Neuropsychology*, *11*, 913–917.

Beaton, A.A. (1997). The relation of the planum temporale asymmetry and morphology of the corpus callosum to handedness, gender, and dyslexia: A review of the evidence. *Brain and language*, *60*, 255–322.

Beatty, W.W., Salmon, D.P., Butters, N., Heindel, W.C., et al. (1988). Retrograde amnesia in patients with Alzheimer's disease or Huntington's disease. *Neurobiology of Aging*, *9*, 181–186.

Beaumont, J.G. (1997). Future directions in laterality. *Neuropsychology Review*, *7*, 107–126.

Beaumont, J.G., & Davidoff, J.B. (1992). Assessment of visuo-perceptual dysfunction. In J.R. Crawford, D.M. Parker, & W.W. McKinlay (Eds.), *Handbook of Neuropsychological Assessment* (pp. 115–140). Hove, UK: Lawrence Erlbaum Associates Ltd.

Beauvois, M.F. (1982). Optic aphasia: A process of interaction between vision and language. *Philosophical Transactions of the Royal Society of London, Series B*, *298*, 35–47.

Beauvois, M.F., Saillant, B., Meninger, B.V., & L'her-mitte, F. (1978). Bilateral tactile aphasia, a tacto-verbal dysfunction. *Brain*, *101*, 381–401.

Bechara, A., Damasio, A.R., & Damasio, H. (2000). Emotion, decision making and the orbitofrontal cortex. *Cerebral Cortex*, *10*, 295–300.

Bechara, A., Damasio, A.R., Damasio, H., & Anderson, S. (1994). Insensitivity to future consequences following damage to human prefrontal cortex. *Cognition*, *50*, 7–12.

Bechara, A., Tranel, D., Damasio, H., Adolphs, R., Rockland, C., & Damasio, A.R. (1995). Double dissociation of conditioning and declarative knowledge relative to the amygdala and hippocampus in humans. *Science*, *25* (269), 1115–1118.

Beeman, M. (1993). Semantic processing in the right hemisphere may contribute to drawing inferences during comprehension. *Brain and Language*, *44*, 80–120.

Beeman, M., & Chiarello, C. (Eds.). (1998). *Right hemisphere language comprehension: Perspectives from cognitive neuroscience.* Hillsdale, NJ: Lawrence Erlbaum Associates Inc.

Behrmann, M., & McLeod, J. (1995). Rehabilitation for pure alexia: Efficacy of therapy and implications for models of normal word recognition. In R.S. Berndt & C.C. Mitchum (Eds.), *Cognitive neuropsychological approaches to the treatment of language disorders* (pp. 149–180). Hove, UK: Lawrence Erlbaum Associates Ltd.

Behrmann, M., & Moscovitch, M. (1994). Object centered neglect in patients with unilateral neglect: Effects of left–right coordinates of objects. *Journal of Cognitive Neuroscience*, *6*, 1–16.

Behrmann, M., Moscovitch, M., & Winocur, G. (1994). Intact visual imagery and impaired visual perception in a patient with visual agnosia. *Journal of Experimental Psychology: Human Perception and Performance*, *20*, 1068–1087.

Beighton, P., & Hayden, M.R. (1981). Huntington's chorea. *South African Medical Journal*, *59*, 250.

Belli, R.F., & Loftus, E.F. (1996). The pliability of autobiographical memory: Misinformation and the false memory problem. In D.C. Rubin (Ed.), *Remembering the past: Studies in autobiographical memory* (pp. 157–179). New York: Cambridge University Press.

Benecke, R., Rothwell, J.C., Dick, J.P.R., Day, B.L., & Marsden, C.D. (1987). Simple and complex movements on and off treatment in patients with Parkinson's disease. *Journal of Neurology, Neurosurgery and Psychiatry*, *50*, 296–303.

Benedict, R.H.B. (1989). The effectiveness of cognitive remediation strategies for victims of traumatic head-injury: A review of the literature. *Clinical Psychology Review, 9*, 605–626.

Benedict, R.H.B., Brandt, J., & Bergey, G. (1993). An attempt at memory retraining in severe amnesia: an experimental single-case study. *Neuropsychological Rehabilitation, 3*, 39–51.

Benedict, R.H., Lockwood, A.H., Shucard, J.L., Shucard, D.W., Wack, D., & Murphy, B.W. (1998). Functional neuroimaging of attention in the auditory modality. *Neuroreport, 5*, 121–126.

Benke, T. (1988). Visual agnosia and amnesia from a left unilateral lesion. *European Neurology, 28*, 236–239.

Bennett, T.L., & Curiel, M.P. (1989). Early neuropsychological presentation of Huntington's disease with and without choreoathertoid movements. *International Journal of Clinical Neuropsychology, 11*, 91–95.

Benowitz, L., Bear, D., Mesulam, M., Rosenthal, R., Zaidel, E., & Sperry, W. (1983). Non-verbal sensitivity following lateralized cerebral injury. *Cortex, 19*, 5–12.

Benson, D.F. (1996). My day with Luria. *Journal of Geriatric Psychiatry and Neurology, 9*, 120–122.

Benson, D.F., & Ardila, A. (1995). Conduction aphasia. In H.S. Kirshner (Ed.), *Handbook of speech and language disorders*. New York: Marcel Dekker.

Benson, D.F., & Ardila, A. (1996). *Aphasia: A clinical perspective*. Oxford: Oxford University Press.

Bentall, R.P., Baker, G.A., & Havers, S. (1991). Reality monitoring and psychotic hallucinations. *British Journal of Clinical Psychology, 30*, 213–222.

Bentall, R.P., & Slade, P.D. (1985). Reality testing and auditory hallucinations: A signal detection analysis. *British Journal Clinical Psychology, 24* (3), 159–169.

Bentin, S., Sakar, A., & Moscovitch, M. (1984). Intermanual information transfer in patients with lesions in the trunk of the corpus callosum. *Neuropsychologia, 22*, 601–611.

Benton, A.L., & Hamsher, K. de S. (1976). *Multilingual aphasia examination*. Iowa City: University of Iowa.

Benton, A., & Tranel, D. (1993). Visuoperceptual, visuospatial, and visuoconstructive Disorders. In K.M. Heilman & E. Valenstein (Eds.), *Clinical neuropsychology* (3rd ed., Ch. 8, pp. 165–213). Oxford: Oxford University Press.

Benton, A.L., Varney, N.R., & Hamsher, K. de S. (1978). Visuospatial judgement: A clinical test. *Archives of Neurology, 35*, 364–367.

Benton, S.L., Glover, J.A., & Monkowski, P.G. (1983). Employing review procedures in elaboration of prose schemata. *Psychological Reports, 52*, 167–170.

Ben-Yishay, Y. (1996). Reflections on the evolution of the therapeutic milieu concept. *Neuropsychological Rehabilitation, 6*, 327–343.

Ben-Yishay, Y., Piasetsky, E.B., & Rattok, J.A. (1987). A systematic method for ameliorating disorders in basic attention. In M. Meier, A.L. Benton, & L. Diller (Eds.), *Neuropsychological rehabilitation* (pp. 165–181). New York: Churchill Livingstone.

Berg, I.J., Koning-Haanstra, M., & Deelman, B.G. (1991). Long-term effects of memory rehabilitation: A controlled study. *Neuropsychological rehabilitation, 1*, 97–111.

Berman, K.F., Ostrem, J.L., Randolph, C. et al. (1995). Physiological activation of a cortical network during performance of the Wisconsin Card Sorting Tests: A positron emission tomography study. *Neuropsychologia, 33*, 1027–1046.

Berndt, R.S., & Caramazza, A.A. (1980a). A redefinition of the syndrome of broca's aphasia. *Applied Psycholinguistics, 1*, 225–278.

Berndt, R.S., & Caramazza, A.A. (1980b). Semantic operations deficits in sentence comprehension. *Psychological Research, 41* (2–3), 169–177.

Berndt, R.S., & Caramazza, A.A. (1981). Syntactic aspects of aphasia. In M.T. Sarno (Ed.), *Acquired aphasia* (pp. 157–181). New York: Academic Press.

Berndt, R.S., Basili, A., & Caramazza, A. (1987). Dissociation of functions in a case of transcortical sensory aphasia. *Cognitive Neuropsychology, 4*, 79–101.

Berndt, R.S., & Mitchum, C.C. (Eds.). (1995). *Cognitive neuropsychological approaches to the treatment of language disorders*. Hove, UK: Lawrence Erlbaum Associates Ltd.

Berti, A., Allport, A., Driver, J., Dienes, Z, Oxbury, J., & Oxbury, S. (1992). Levels of processing for visual stimuli in an "extinguished" field. *Neuropsychologia, 30*, 403–415.

Berti, A., Ladavas, E., & Corte, M.D. (1996). Anosognosia for hemiplegia, neglect, dyslexia, and drawing neglect: Clinical findings and theoretical considerations. *Journal of the International Neuropsychological Society, 2*, 426–440.

Bever, T.G., & Chiarello, R.J. (1974). Cerebral dominance in musicians and nonmusicians. *Science, 185*, 537–539.

Binder, J.R., Marshall, R., Lazar, R.M., Benjamin, J., & Mohr, J.P. (1992). Distinct syndromes of hemineglect. *Archives of Neurology, 49*, 1187–1194.

Bird, M., & Luscz, M. (1991). Encoding specificity, depth of processing and cued recall in Alzheimer's disease. *Journal of Clinical and Experimental Neuropsychology*, *13* 508–520.

Bisiach, E., Germiniani, G., Berti, A., & Risconi, M.L. (1990). Perceptual and premotor factors of unilateral neglect. *Neurology*, *40*, 1278–1281.

Bisiach, E., & Luzzatti, C. (1978). Unilateral neglect of representational space. *Cortex*, *14*, 129–133.

Bisiach, E., Vallar, G., Perani, D., Papagno, C., & Berti, A. (1986). Unawareness of disease following lesions of the right hemisphere: Anosagnosia for hemiplegia and anosagnosia for hemianopia. *Neuropsychologia*, *24*, 471–482.

Bjork, R.A. (1972). Short term storage: *The order output of a central output of a central processor* (Vol. 1). Hillsdale, NJ: Lawrence Erlbaum Associates Inc.

Black, P., Markowitz, R.S., & Cianci, S. (1975). Recovery of motor function after lesions in the motor cortex of the monkey. In *Ciba Function Symposium No. 34: Outcome of severe damage to the central nervous system* (pp. 65–84). Amsterdam: Elsevier.

Black, S.E., & Behrmann, M. (1994). Localization in alexia. In A. Kertesz (Ed.), *Localization and neuroimaging in neuropsychology* (Ch. 11, pp. 331–376). San Diego: Academic Press.

Blair, R.J., Morris, J.S., Frith, C.D., Perrett, D.I., & Dolan, R.J. (1999). Dissociable neural responses to facial expressions of sadness and anger. *Brain*, *122* (5), 883–893.

Blakemore, C.B., & Falconer, M.A. (1967). Long-term effects of anterior temporal lobectomy on certain cognitive functions. *Journal of Neurology, Neurosurgery and Psychiatry*, *30*, 364–367.

Blakemore, S.J., Rees, G., & Frith, C.D. (1998). How do we predict the consequences of our actions? A functional imaging study. *Neuropsychologia*, *36*, 521–529.

Blinkov, S.M., & Glesner, J.I. (1968). *The human brain in figures and tables*. New York: Basic Books.

Blonder, L.X., Bowers, D., & Heilman, K.M. (1991). The role of the right hemisphere in emotional communication, *Brain*, *114*, 1115–1127.

Blonder, L.X., Gur, R.E., & Gur, R.C. (1989). The effects of right and left hemiparkinsonism on prosody. *Brain and Language*, *36*, 193–207.

Bloom, R.L., Borod, J.C., Obler, L.K., & Gerstman, L.J. (1992). Impact of emotional content on discourse production in patients with unilateral brain damage. *Brain and Language*, *42*, 153–164.

Bloom, R.L., Borod, J.C., Obler, L.K., & Koff, E. (1990). A preliminary characterization of lexical emotional expression in right and left brain-damaged patients. *International Journal of Neuroscience*, *55*, 71–80.

Blume, W.T. (1984). Corpus section for seizure control: Rationale and review of experimental and clinical data. *Cleveland Clinic*, *51*, 319–332.

Blumer, D., & Benson, D.F. (1975). Personality changes with frontal and temporal lobe lesions. In D.F. Benson & D. Blumer (Eds.), *Psychiatric aspects of neurologic disease* (pp. 151–170). New York: Grune & Stratton.

Blumstein, S.E. (1995). The neurobiology of the sound of language. In M.S. Gazzaniga (Ed.), *The Cognitive Neurosciences* (Ch. 59, pp. 915–930). Cambridge, MA: Bradford Books.

Boarman, D., Lesser, R.P., & Gordon, B. (1995). Auditory speech processing in the left-temporal lobe: An electrical interference study. *Brain and Language*, *51*, 269–290.

Bodamer, J. (1947). Die Prosopanosie. *Archiv für Psychiatrie und Nervenkrankheiten*, *179*, 6–54.

Bogen, J.E. (1985). The callosal syndromes. In K.M. Heilman & E. Valenstein (Eds.), *Clinical neuropsychology* (2nd ed., pp. 295–338). New York: Oxford University Press.

Bogen, J.E. (1993). The callosal syndromes. In K.M. Heilman & E. Valenstein (Eds.), *Clinical neuropsychology* (3rd ed., pp. 337–407). New York: Oxford University Press.

Bogen, J.E. (1997). Does cognition in the disconnected right hemisphere require right hemisphere possession of language? *Brain and Language*, *57*, 12–21.

Bogen, J.E., & Gazzaniga, M.S. (1966). Cerebral commissurotomy in man: Minor hemisphere dominance for certain visuospatial functions. *Journal of Neurosurgery*, *23*, 394–399.

Bogerts, B. (1997). The temporolimbic system theory of positive schizophrenic symptoms. *Schizophrenia Bulletin*, *23*, 423–435.

Bond, M. (1984). The psychiatry of closed head injury. In N. Brooks (Ed.), *Closed head injury: Psychological, social, and family consequences* (pp. 148–178). New York: Oxford University Press.

Bondarko, V.M., & Yakovlev, V.V. (1993). Recognition of rotated visual objects. *Sensory Systems*, *7*, 102–108.

Boring, E.G. (1929). *A history of experimental psychology*. New York: Appleton Century Crofts.

Bornstein, B., Sroka, H.A., & Munitz, H. (1969). Prosopagnosia with animal face agnosia. *Cortex*, *5*, 164–169.

Borod, J.C. (1992). Interhemispheric and intrahemispheric control of emotion: A focus on unilateral

& Ellis, A.W. (1991). Understanding covert recognition. *Cognition 39* (2): 129–166.

Burton, M. (1994). Learning new faces in an interactive activation and competition model. *Visual Cognition, 1,* 313–348.

Butter, C.M., & Trobe, J.D. (1994). Integrative agnosia following progressive multifocal leukoencephalopathy. *Cortex, 30,* 145–158.

Butters, N. (1984). Alcoholic Korsakoff's syndrome: An update. *Seminars in Neurology, 4,* 226–244.

Butters, N. (1987). *Procedural learning in dementia: A double dissociation between Huntington disease and patients on verbal priming and motor learning,* Paper presented at the meeting of the International Neuropsychological Society, San Francisco.

Butters, N., & Cermak, L. (1977). *Alcoholic Korsakoff's syndrome.* New York: Academic Press.

Butters, N., Heindel, W.C., & Salmon, D.P. (1990). Dissociation of implicit memory in dementia: Neurological implications. *Bulletin of the Psychonomic Society, 28,* 359–366.

Butterworth, B. (1979). Hesitation and the production of verbal paraphasias and neologisms in jargon aphasia. Brain and Language, *8,* 133–161.

Butterworth, B. (1985). Jargon aphasia: Processes and strategies. In S. Newman, & R. Epstein (Eds.) *Dysphasia* (pp. 61–97). Edinburgh: Churchill Livingstone.

Butterworth, B. (1999). *The mathematical brain.* London: Macmillan.

Butterworth, B., Campbell, R., & Howard, D. (1986). The uses of short-term memory: A case study. *Quarterly Journal of Experimental Psychology, 38A,* 705–738.

Butterworth, B., Cipolotti, L., & Warrington, E.K. (1996). Short-term memory impairment and arithmetical ability. *Quarterly Journal of Experimental Psychology, 49,* 251–262.

Byng, S. (1988). Sentence processing deficits: Theory and therapy. *Cognitive Neuropsychology, 5,* 629–676.

Byng, S., Nickels, L., & Black, M. (1994). Replicating therapy for mapping deficits in agrammatism: Remapping the deficit? *Aphasiology, 8,* 315–342.

Cabeza, R., Anderson, N.D., Kester, J., Lennartsson, E.R., & McIntosh, A.R, (in press). Involvement of prefrontal regions on episodic retrieval: Evidence for a generate–recognize asymmetry model. *Brain and Cognition.*

Calabrese, P., Markowitsch, H.J., Durwen, H.F., Widlitzek, H., Haupts, M., Holinka, B. & Gehlen, W. (1996). Right temporofrontal cortex as critical locus for the recovery of old episodic memories. *Journal of Neurology, Neurosurgery & Psychiatry, 61,* 304–310.

Calvanio, R., Petrone, P.N., & Levine, D.N. (1987). Left visual neglect is both viewer centred and body centred. *Neurology, 37,* 1179–1183.

Cambier, H., Elghozi, D., & Graveleau, P. (1982). *Neuropsychologie des lesions du thalamus: Rapport de neurologie.* In Congres de psychiatrie et de Neurologie de langue francaise, Paris.

Cancelliere, A.E.B., & Kertesz, A. (1990). Lesion localization in acquired deficits of emotional expression and comprehension. *Brain and Cognition, 13,* 133–147.

Cannon, W.B. (1927). The James–Lange theory of emotions: A critical examination of an alternative theory. *American Journal of Psychology, 39,* 106–124.

Cantor, J., & Engle, R.W. (1993). Working memory capacity as long term memory activation: An individual differences approach. *Journal of Experimental Psychology, Learning Memory and Cognition, 19,* 1101–1114.

Caplan, D. (1987). *Neurolinguistics and linguistic aphasiology.* Cambridge, UK: Cambridge University Press.

Caplan, D. (1988). On the role of group studies in neuropsychological and pathopsychological research. *Cognitive Neuropsychology, 5,* 535–548.

Caplan, D., Baker, C., & Dehaut, F. (1985). Syntactic determinants of sentence comprehension in aphasia. *Cognition, 21,* 117–134.

Caplan, D., & Hildebrandt, N. (1986). Language deficits and the theory of syntax: A reply to Grodzinsky. *Brain Language, 27,* 168–177.

Caplan, D., & Hildebrandt, N. (1988) *Disorders of syntactic comprehension.* Cambridge, Mass.: MIT Press.

Cappa, S.F., Papagno, C., Vallar, G., & Vignolo, L.A. (1986). Aphasia does not always follow left thalamic hemorrhage: A study of five negative cases. *Cortex, 22,* 639–647.

Cappa, S.F., Perani, D., Grassi, F., Bressi, S., Alberoni, M., Franceschi, M., Bettinardi, V., Todde, S., & Fazio, F. (1997). A PET follow-up study of recovery after stroke in acute aphasics. *Brain and Language, 56,* 55–67.

Cappa, S.F., & Vallar, G. (1992). The role of left and right hemispheres in recovery from aphasia. *Aphasiology, 6,* 359–372.

Caramazza, A. (1983). The selective impairment of phonological processing: A case study. *Brain and Language, 18,* 128–174.

Caramazza, A. (1988). Some aspects of language processing revealed through the analysis of acquired aphasia: The lexical system. *Annual Review of Neuroscience, 11*, 395–421.

Caramazza, A., Basili, A.G., Koller, J.J., & Berndt, R.S. (1981). An investigation of repetition and language processing in a case of conduction aphasia. *Brain and Language, 14*, 235–271.

Caramazza, A., Berndt, R.S., Basili, A.G., & Koller, J.J. (1981). Syntactic processing deficits in aphasia. *Cortex, 17*, 333–348.

Caramazza, A., & Hillis, A.E. (1990). Where do semantic errors come from? *Cortex, 26*, 95–122.

Caramazza, A., & Hillis, A.E. (1991). Levels of representation, co-ordinate frames, and unilateral neglect. *Cognitive Neuropsychology, 7*, 391–445.

Caramazza, A., McCloskey, M. (1988). The case for single-patient studies. *Cognitive Neuropsychology, 5*, 517–527.

Carlesimo, G.A., Casadio, P., Sabbadini, M., & Caltagirone, C. (1998). Associative visual agnosia resulting from a disconnection between intact visual memory and semantic systems. *Cortex, 34*, 563–576.

Carlson, N.R. (1977). *Physiology of behaviour.* Boston, MA: Allyn & Bacon.

Carmon, A., & Bechtoldt, H.P. (1969). Dominance of the right cerebral hemisphere for stereopsis. *Neuropsychologia, 7*, 29–39.

Carter, C.S., Macdonald, A.M., Botvinick, M., Ross, L.L., Stenger, V.A., Noll, D., & Cohen, J.D. (2000). Passing executive processes: Strategic vs. evaluative functions of the anterior cingulate cortex. *Proceedings of the National Academy of Science USA, 97*, 1944–1948.

Carter, C.S., Mintun, M., & Cohen, J.D. (1995). Interference and facilitation effects during selective attention: An H215O PET study of Stroop task performance. *Neuroimage, 2*, 264–272.

Carter, C.S., Perlstein, W., Ganguli, R., Brar, J., Mintun, M., & Cohen, J.D. (1998). Functional hypofrontality and working memory dysfunction in schizophrenia. *American Journal of Psychiatry, 155*, 1285–1287.

Cascino, G.D., Jack, C.R., Parisi, J.E., et al. (1991). Magnetic resonance imaging-based volume studies in temporal lobe epilepsy: Pathological correlations. *Annals of Neurology, 30*, 31–36.

Castaigne, P., Buge, A., Escourolle, R., & Masson, M. (1962). Ranollissement pedonculaire median, tegmento-thalamique avec opthalmolpegie et hypersomnie. *Review Neuologique, 106*, 357–367.

Castiello, U., & Bennett, K.M.B. (1997). The bilateral reach-to-grasp movement of Parkinson's disease subjects. *Brain, 120*, 593–604.

Castiello, U., Bennett, K.M.B., & Scarpa, M. (1994). The reach to grasp movement of Parkinson's disease subjects. In K.M.B. Bennett and U. Castiello (Eds.), *Insights into the reach to grasp movement* (pp. 215–237). Amsterdam: Elsevier Science.

Castiello, U., Bennett, K.M.B., & Stelmach, G.E. (1993a). Reach to grasp movement of blind subjects. *Experimental Brain Research, 94*, 163–178.

Castiello, U., Bennett, K.M., & Stelmach, G.E. (1993b). The bilateral reach to grasp movement. *Behavioural Brain Research, 56*, 43–57.

Castiello, U., Scarpa, M., & Bennett, K. (1995). A brain-damaged patient with an unusual perceptuomotor deficit. *Nature, 374*, 805–808.

Castillo, C.S., Starkstein, S.E. Federoff, J.P., Price, T.R., & Robinson, R.G. (1993). Generalised anxiety disorder after stroke. *Journal of Nervous and Mental Disease, 181*, 100–106.

Cavada, C., Company, T., Tejedor, J., Cruz-Rizzolo, R.J., & Reinoso-Suarez, F. (2000). The anatomical connections of the macaque monkey orbitofrontal cortex: A review. *Cerebral Cortex, 10*, 220–242.

Cavanaugh, J.C., Grady, J.G., & Perlmutter, M. (1983). Forgetting and the use of memory aids in 20 to 70 year olds' everyday life. *International Journal of Aging and Human Development, 17*, 113–122.

Cavanagh, P. (1988) Pathways in early vision. In Z. Pylyshyn (ed.), *Computational processes in early vision* (pp. 239–261) Norwood, NJ: Ablex.

Cermak, L.S., & O'Connor, M. (1983). The anterograde and retrograde retrieval ability of a patient with amnesia due to encephalitis. *Neuropsychologia, 21*, 213–234.

Cermak, L.S., Reale, L., & De Luca, D. (1977). Korsakoff patients' non-verbal and verbal memory: Effects of interference and the mediation on rate of information loss. *Neuropsychologia, 15*, 303–310.

Chace, W.G., & Ericsson, K.A. (1981). Skilled memory. In J.R. Anderson (Ed.), *Cognitive skills and their acquisition* (pp. 141–190). Hillsdale, NJ: Lawrence Erlbaum Associates Inc.

Chafetz, M.D., Friedman, A.L., Kevorkian, C.G., & Levy, J.K. (1996). The cerebellum and cognitive function: Implications for rehabilitation. *Archives of Physiological Medicine and Rehabilitation, 77*, 1303–1308.

Chapman, L.J., & Chapman, J.P. (1973). Problems in the measurement of cognitive deficit. *Psychological Bulletin, 79*, 180–185.

Chatterjee, A. (1994). Picturing unilateral spatial

neglect: Viewer versus object centred reference frames. *Journal of Neurology, Neurosurgery and Psychiatry*, *57*, 1236–1240.

Chelazzi, L., Miller, E.K., Duncan, J., & Desimone, R. (1993). A neural base for visual search in inferior temporal cortex. *Nature*, *363*, 345–347.

Chertkow, H., Bub, D., & Caplan, D. (1992). Constraining theories of semantic memory processing: Evidence from dementia. *Cognitive Neuropsychology*, *9*, 327–365.

Chertkow, H., & Murtha, S. (1997). PET activation and language. *Clinical Neuroscience*, *4*, 78–86.

Christensen, A.-L., & Caetano, C. (1996). Alexandr Romanovitch Luria (1902–1977): Contributions to neuropsychological rehabilitation. *Neuropsychological Rehabilitation*, *6*, 279–303.

Christianson, S.A., Saisa, J., Garvill, J., & Silfvenius, H. (1993). Hemisphere inactivation and mood-state changes. *Brain and Cognition*, *23*, 127–144.

Christman, S.D., & Hackworth, M.D. (1993). Equivalent perceptual asymmetries for free viewing of positive and negative emotional expressions in chimeric faces. *Neuropsychologia*, *31*, 621–624.

Cicchetti, D., & Nelson, L. (1994). Re-examining threats to the reliability and validity of putative brain–behaviour relationships: New guidelines for assessing the effect of patients lost to follow-up. *Journal of Clinical and Experimental Neuropsychology*, *16*, 339–343.

Cicone, M., Wapner, W., & Gardener, H. (1980). Sensitivity to emotional expressions and situation in organic patients. *Cortex*, *16*, 145–158.

Cipolotti, L., Butterworth, B., & Denes, G.A. (1991). Specific deficit for numbers in a case of dense acalculia. *Brain*, *114*, 2619–2637.

Cipolotti, L., & Warrington, E.K. (1995). Semantic memories and reading abilities: A case report. *Journal of the International Neuropsychological Society*, *1*, 104–110.

Cipolotti, L., Warrington, E.K., & Butterworth, B. (1995). Selective impairment in manipulating arabic numerals. *Cortex*, *31*, 73–86.

Clark, A.S., & Goldman-Rakic, P.S. (1989). Gonadal hormones influence the emergence of cortical functioning in non-human primates. *Behavioural Neuroscience*, *103*, 1287–1295.

Clower, D.M., Hoffman, J.M., Votaw, J.R., Faber, T.L., Woods, R.P., & Alexander, G.E. (1996). Role of the posterior parietal cortex in the recalibration of visually guided reaching. *Nature*, *383*, 618–621.

Cockburn, J. (1996). Assessment and treatment of prospective memory deficits. In M. Brandimonte, G.O.

Einstein, & M.A. McDaniel (Eds.), *Prospective memory: Theory and applications* (Ch. 17, pp. 327–351). Hillsdale, NJ: Lawrence Erlbaum Associates Inc.

Code, C. (1997). Can the right hemisphere speak? *Brain and Language*, *57*, 38–39.

Coghill, G.E. (1964). *Anatomy and the problem of behaviour*. New York: Hafner.

Cohen, G., & Faulkner, D. (1986). Memory for proper names: Age differences in retrieval. *British Journal of Developmental Psychology*, *4*, 187–197.

Cohen, J.D. (2000). Anterior cingulate and prefrontal cortex: Who's in control? *Nature and Neuroscience*, *3*, 421–423.

Cohen, J.D., Perlstein, W.M., Braver, T.S., Nystrom, L.E. Noll, D.C., Jonides, J., & Smith, E.E. (1997). Temporal dynamics of brain activation during a working memory task. *Nature*, *386*, 604–608.

Cohen, J.D., & Servan-Schreiber, D. (1992). Context, cortex, and dopamine: A connectionist approach to behavior and biology in schizophrenia. *Psychological Review*, *99*, 45–77.

Cohen, N.J., & Squire, L.R. (1981). Retrograde amnesia and remote memory impairment. *Neuropsychologia*, *19*, 337–356.

Cohen, R.A., & Albers, H.E. (1991). Disruption of the human circadian and cognitive regulation following a discrete hypothalamic lesion: A case study. *Neurology*, *41*, 726–729.

Cohen, R.A., McCrae, V., Phillips, J.E., & Wilkinson, H. (1990). Neurobehavioural consequences of bilateral medial cingulotomy. *Neurology*, *40*, 198.

Cohen, R.A., Sparling-Cohen, Y., & O'Donnell, B.F. (1993). *The neuropsychology of attention*. New York: Plenum Press.

Colby, C.L., Duhamel, J.R., & Goldberg, M.E. (1996). Visual, presaccadic and cognitive activation of single neurons in monkey's lateral intraparietal area. *Journal of Neurophysiology*, *76*, 2841–2852.

Collins, A.M., & Quillian, M.R. (1969). Retrieval time from semantic memory. *Journal of Verbal Learning and Verbal Behaviour*, *8*, 240–247.

Coltheart, M. (1980). Deep dyslexia: A review of the syndrome. In M. Coltheart, K.E. Patterson, & J.C. Marshall (Eds.) (pp. 12–16) *Deep dyslexia*. London: Routledge.

Coltheart, M. (1981). Disorders of reading and their implications for models of normal reading. *Visible Language*, *15*, 245–286.

Coltheart, M. (1982). The psycholinguistic analysis of acquired dyslexias: Some illustrations. *Philosophical Transactions of the Royal Society London, Series B*, *298*, 151–164.

Coltheart, M. (1985). Cognitive neuropsychology and the study of reading. In M.I. Posner & O.S.M. Marin (Eds.), *Attention and performance* (pp. 3–37). Hillsdale, NJ: Lawrence Erlbaum Associates Inc.

Coltheart, M. (1996). Phonological dyslexia: Past and future issues. *Cognitive Neuropsychology, 13,* 749–762.

Coltheart, M., Curtis, B., Atkins, P., & Haller, M. (1993). Models of reading aloud: Dual-route and parallel distributed processing approaches. *Psychological Review, 100,* 589–608.

Coltheart, M. & Rastle, K. (1994). Serial processing in reading aloud: Evidence for dual-route models of reading. *Journal of Experimental Psychology: Human Perception and Performance, 20,* 1197–1211.

Conrad, R. (1964). Acoustic confusions in immediate memory. *British Journal of Psychology, 55,* 75–84.

Conway, A.R., & Engle, R.W. (1994). Working memory and retrieval: A resource-dependent inhibition model. *Journal of Experimental Psychology, General, 123,* 354–373.

Conway, M.A., Turk, D.J., Miller, S.L., Logan, J., Nebes, R.D., Meltzer, C.C., & Becker, J.T. (1999). A positron emission tomography (PET) study of autobiographical memory retrieval. *Memory, 7,* 679–702.

Cook, M.J. (1994). Mesial temporal sclerosis and volumetric investigations. *Acta Neurologica Scandinavica, 152,* 109–114.

Cook, M.J., Fish, D.R., Shorvon, S.D., Straughan, K., & Stevens, J.M. (1992). Hippocampal volumetric and morphometric studies in frontal and temporal lobe epilepsy. *Brain, 115,* 1001–1015.

Cooper, R. & Shallice, T. (2000). Contention scheduling and the control of routine activities. *Cognitive Neuropsychology, 17,* 297–338.

Cope, D.N., & Hall, K. (1982). Head injury rehabilitation: Benefit of early intervention. *Archives of Physical Medicine and Rehabilitation, 63,* 433–437.

Coppa, S., Sterzi, R., Vallar, G., & Bisiach, E. (1987). Remission of hemineglect during vestibular stimulation. *Neuropsychologia, 25,* 775–782.

Corballis, M.C. (1991). *The lopsided ape.* New York: Oxford University Press.

Corballis, M.C. (1993). Split decisions: Problems in the interpretation of results from commissurotomized subjects. *Behavioural Brain Research, 64,* 163–172.

Corballis, M. (1999). The gestural origins of language. *American Scientist, 87,* 138–145.

Corballis, M.C., & Sargent, J. (1989). Mental rotation in a commissurotomized patient. *Neuropsychologia, 26,* 13–26.

Corballis, M.C., & Trudel, C.I. (1993). Role of the forebrain commissures in interhemispheric integration. *Neuropsychology, 7,* 306–324.

Corbetta, M., Miezin, F.M., Dobmeyer, S., Shulman, G.L., & Petersen, S.E. (1991). Selective and divided attention during visual discriminations of shape, color, and speed: Functional anatomy by positron emission tomography. *Journal of Neuroscience, 11,* 2383–2402.

Corbetta M. (1998). Frontoparietal cortical networks for directing attention and the eye to visual locations: identical, independent, or overlapping neural systems? Proceedings of the National Academy of Science USA., 95, 831–8.

Corbetta, M., Miezin, F.M., Shulman, G.L., & Petersen, S.E. (1993). A PET study of visuospatial attention. *Journal of Neuroscience, 13,* 1202–1226.

Corbetta, M., & Shulman, G.L. (1998). Human cortical mechanisms of visual attention during orienting and search. *Philosophical Transactions of the Royal Society, 353,* 1353–1362.

Corbetta, M., Shulman, G.L., Miezin, F.M., & Petersen, S.E. (1995). Superior parietal cortex activation during spatial attention shifts and visual feature conjunction. *Science, 270,* 802–805.

Coren, S., Ward, L.M., & Enns, J.T. (1994) *Sensation and perception.* Orlando, FL: Harcourt Brace (4th ed.).

Corkin, S. (1965). Tactually-guided maze learning in man: Effects of unilateral cortical excisions and bilateral hippocampal lesions. *Neuropsychologia, 3,* 339–351.

Corkin, S. (1989). Penetrating head injury in young adulthood exacerbates cognitive decline in later years. *Journal of Neuroscience, 9,* 3876–3883.

Corwin, J., & Bylsma, F.W. (1993). Translations of excerpts from Andre Rey's Psychological examination of traumatic encephalopathy and P.A. Osterreith's. The complex Figure copy test. *Clinical Neuropsychologist, 7,* 3–15.

Coslett, H.B., Bowers, D., Fitzpatrick, E., Haws, B., & Heilman, K.M. (1990). Directional hypokinesia and hemispatial inattention in neglect. *Brain, 113,* 475–486.

Coslett, H.B., Bowers, D., & Heilman, K.M. (1987). Reduction in cerebral activation after right hemisphere stroke. *Neurology, 37,* 957–962.

Coslett, H.B., & Saffran, E.M. (1991). Simultanagnosia. To see but not two see. *Brain, 114*(4), 1523–1545.

Coslett, H.B., & Saffran, E.M. (1992). Optic aphasia and the right hemisphere: A replication and extension. *Brain and Language, 43,* 148–161.

Costello, A.D., & Warrington, E.K. (1987). The dissociation of visuospatial neglect and neglect dyslexia. *Journal of Neurology, Neurosurgery and Psychiatry, 50*, 1110–1116.

Coull, J.T. (1998). Neural correlates of attention and arousal: Insights from electrophysiology, functional neuroimaging and psychopharmacology. *Progress in Neurobiology, 55*, 343–361.

Coull, J.T., Buchel, C., Friston, K.J., & Frith, C.D. (1999). Noradrenergically mediated plasticity in a human attentional neuronal network. *Neuroimage, 10*, 705–715.

Coull, J.T., Frackowiak, R.S., & Frith, C.D. (1998). Monitoring for target objects: Activation of right frontal and parietal cortices with increasing time on task. *Neuropsychologia, 36*, 1325–1334.

Courtney, S.M., Petit, L., Haxby, J.V., & Ungerleider, L.G. (1998). The role of prefrontal cortex in working memory: Examining the contents of consciousness. *Philosophical Transactions of the Royal Society London, Series B, 353* (1377), 1819–1828.

Courtney, S.M., Ungerleider, L.G., Kreil, K., & Haxby, J.V. (1996). Object and spatial visual working memory activate separate neural systems in the human cortex. *Cerebral Cortex, 6*, 39–49.

Courtney, S.M., Ungerleider, L.G., Keil, K., & Haxby, J.V. (1997). Transient and sustained activity in a distributed neural system for human working memory. *Nature, 386* (6625), 608–611.

Cowan, N. (1988). Evolving conceptions of memory storage, selective attention, and their mutual constraints within the human information. *Psychological Bulletin, 194*, 163–191.

Cowan, N. (1993). Activation, attention, and short-term memory, *Memory and Cognition, 21*, 162–167.

Cowan, N. (1995). *Attention and memory: An integrated framework*. Oxford psychological series, 26. New York: Oxford University Press.

Cowan, N. (1999). An embedded processes model of working memory. In A. Miyake & P. Shah (Eds.), *Models of working memory: mechanisms of active maintenance and executive control* (Ch. 3, pp. 62–102). Cambridge, UK: Cambridge University Press.

Cowan, N. (in press). The magical number 4 in short-term memory: A reconsideration of mental storage capacity. *Behavioral and Brain Sciences, 24* (1).

Cowan, N., Winkler, I., Teder, W., & Naeaetaenen, R. (1993). Memory prerequisites of mismatch negativity in the auditory event potential (ERP). *Journal of Experimental Psychology: Learning Memory and Cognition, 19*, 909–921.

Cowan, N., Wood, N.L., & Borne, D.N. (1994). Reconfirmation of the short-term storage concept. *Psychological Science, 5*, 103–106.

Cowey, A. (1994). Cortical visual areas and the neurobiology of higher visual processes. In M.J. Farah & G. Ratcliff (Eds.), *The neuropsychology of high-level vision: Collected tutorial essays* (pp. 3–31). Hove, UK: Lawrence Erlbaum Associates Ltd.

Cowey, A., & Stoerig, P. (1995). Blindsight in monkeys. *Nature, 373*, 247–249.

Craik, F.I.M., & Lockhart, R.S. (1972). Levels of processing: A framework for memory research. *Journal of Verbal Learning and Verbal Behaviour, 11*, 671–684.

Crawford, M.P., Fulton, J.F., Jacobson, C.F., & Wolf, J.B. (1948). *Research in nervous and mental diseases: Vol. 27. The frontal lobe* (pp. 3–58). Baltimore: Williams & Wilkins.

Crepeau, F., Scherzer, B.P., Belleville, S., & Desmarais, G. (1997). A qualitative analysis of central executive disorders in a real-life work situation. *Neuropsychological Rehabilitation, 7*, 147–165.

Crick, F., & Koch, C. (1995). Are we aware of neural activity in the primary visual cortex? *Nature, 375*, 121–122.

Crosson, B. (1992). *Subcortical functions in language and memory*. London: Guilford Press.

Crosson, B., & Buenning, W. (1984). An individualized memory retraining program after closed-head injury: A single case study. *Journal of Clinical and Experimental Psychology, 6*, 287–301.

Crosson, B., Parker, J.C., Warren, R.L., Kepes, J.J., Kim, A.K., & Tulley, R.C. (1986). A case of thalamic aphasia with post-mortem validation. *Brain and Language, 29*, 301–314.

Crovitz, H. (1979). Memory retraining in brain-damaged patients: The airplane list. *Cortex, 15*, 225–234.

Crovitz, H.F., Harvey, M.T., & Horn, R.W. (1979). Problems in the acquisition of imagery mnemonics: Three brain-damaged cases. *Cortex, 15*, 225–234.

Crow, T.J. (1980). Positive and negative schizophrenic symptoms and the role of dopamine: II. *British Journal of Psychiatry, 137*, 383–386.

Crowder, R.G. (1993). Short-term memory: Where do we stand? *Memory and Cognition, 21*, 142–145.

Crowne, D.P., & Mah, L.W. (1998). A comparison of hemispatial neglect from posterior parietal and periarcuate lesions in the monkey. *Psychobiology, 26*, 103–108.

Cummings, J.L. (1993). Frontal sub-cortical circuits and human behaviour. *Archives of Neurology, 50*, 873–880.

Cummings, J.L., & Coffey, L.E. (2000). Geriatric neuropsychiatry. In J.L. Cummings & L.E. Coffey (Eds.), *Textbook of geriatric neuropsychiatry* (2nd ed., Ch. 1, pp. 3–16). New York: American Psychiatric Press.

Cunnington, R., Bradshaw, J.L., & Iansek, R. (1996). The role of the supplementary motor area in the control of voluntary movement. *Human Movement Science, 15*, 627–647.

Curran, T., Schacter, D.L., Norman, K.A., & Galluccio, L. (1997). False recognition after a right frontal lobe infarction: Memory for general and specific information. *Neuropsychologia, 35* (7), 1035–1049.

Curran, V. (1980). Cross-cultural perspectives on cognition. In G. Claxton (Ed.), Cognitive psychology: New directions (pp. 300–335). London: Routledge.

Dade, L.A., & Jones-Gotman, M. (1997). Sodium amobarbital memory test: What do they predict? *Brain and Cognition, 33*, 189–209.

Damasio A.R. (1989). Time-locked multiregional retroactivation: A systems-level proposal for the neural substrates of recall and recognition. *Cognition, 33*, 25–62.

Damasio, A.R. (1991). Neuroanatomical correlates of aphasias. In M.T Sarno (Ed.), *Acquired aphasia* (2nd ed., pp. 45–70). New York: Academic Press.

Damasio, A.R. (1994). Descartes error: Emotion, reason and the human brain. New York: Grosset, Putnam.

Damasio, A.R. (1997). Towards a neuropathology of emotion and mood. *Nature, 386*, 769–770.

Damasio, A.R. (1998). Investigating the biology of consciousness. *Philosophical Transactions of the Royal Society, 353*, 1879–1882.

Damasio, A.R., & Anderson, S.W. (1993). The frontal lobes. In K.M. Heilman & K.M. Valenstein (Eds.), *Clinical neuropsychology* (3rd ed., pp. 409–448). Oxford: Oxford University Press.

Damasio, A.R., Damasio, H., & Chui H.C. (1980). Neglect showing damage to frontal lobe and basal ganglia. *Neuropsychologia, 18*, 123–132.

Damasio, A.R., Damasio, H., & Van Hoesen, G.W. (1982). Prosopagnosia: Anatomic basis and behavioural mechanisms. *Neurology (NY), 32*, 331–341.

Damasio, A.R., Graf-Radford, N.R., Eslinger, P.J., Damasio, H., & Kassell, N. (1985). Amnesia following basal forebrain lesions. *Archives of Neurology, 42*, 263–271.

Damasio, A.R., Tranel, D., & Damasio, H. (1990a). Face agnosia and the neural substrates of memory. *Annual Review of Neuroscience, 13*, 89–109.

Damasio, A.R., Tranel, D., & Damasio, H. (1990b). Individuals with sociopathic behaviour caused by frontal damage fail to respond autonomically to social stimuli. *Behaviour, Brain Research, 41*, 81–94.

Damasio, A.R., & Van Hoesen, G.W. (1983). Focal lesions of the limbic frontal lobe. In K.M. Heilman & P. Satz (Eds.), *Neuropsychology of human emotion* (pp. 85–110). New York: Guilford Press.

Damasio, H. (1981). Cerebral localization of the aphasias. In M.T. Sarno (Ed.), *Acquired aphasia* (pp. 27–50). New York: Academic Press.

Damasio, H., & Damasio, A. (1980). The anatomical basis of conduction aphasia. *Brain, 103*, 337–350.

Damasio, H., & Damasio, A.R. (1989). *Lesion analysis in neuropsychology*. New York: Oxford University Press.

Damasio, H., Grabowski, T.J., Tranel, D., Hitchwa, R.D., & Damasio, A.R. (1996). A neural basis for lexical retrieval. *Nature, 380*, 499–505.

Daneman, M., & Carpenter, P.A. (1980). Individual differences in working memory and reading. *Journal of Verbal Learning and Verbal Behaviour, 19*, 450–466.

Darwin, C. (1967). *The expression of the emotions in man and animals*. Chicago: University of Chicago Press (originally published in 1872).

David, A.S. (1994). Thought echo reflects the activity of the phonological loop. *British Journal of Clinical Psychology, 33*, 81–83.

David, A.S. (1999). Auditory hallucinations: Phenomenology, neuropsychology and neuroimaging update. *Acta Psychiatrica Scandinavica, 99* (Suppl. 395), 95–104.

David, A.S., & Cutting, J.D. (1994). *The neuropsychology of schizophrenia*. Hove, UK: Lawrence Erlbaum Associates Ltd.

David, A.S., & Lucas, P. (1993). Auditory-verbal hallucinations and the phonological loop. *British Journal of Clinical Psychology, 32*, 431–441.

David, A.S., Woodruff, P.W., Howard, R., Mellers, J.D., Brammer, M., Bullmore, E., Wright, I., Andrew, C., & Williams, S.C. (1996). Auditory hallucinations inhibit exogenous activation of auditory association cortex. *Neuroreport, 22* (7), 932–936.

Davidoff, J., & Warrington, E.K. (1999). The bare bones of object recognition: Implications from a case of object recognition impairment. *Neuropsychologia, 37*, 279–292.

Davidson, R.J. (1993). The neuropsychology of emotion and affective style. In M. Lewis & J.M. Haviland (Eds.), *Handbook of emotions* (pp. 143–154). London: Guilford Press.

Davidson, R.J., Eckman, P., Saron, C.D., Senulis, J.A.,

& Friesen, W.V. (1990). Approach/withdrawal and cerebral asymmetry: Emotional expression and brain physiology. I. *Journal of Personality and Social Psychology, 58*, 330–341.

Davidson, R.J., Finman, R., Rickman, M.D., Straus, A., & Kagan, J. (1994). Childhood temperament and frontal lobe activity: Patterns of asymmetry differentiate between wary and outgoing children: Brain asymmetry predicts affective response to films. *Journal of Sensory Systems, 7*, 102–108.

Davidson, R.J., & Irwin, W. (1999). The functional neuroanatomy of emotion and affective style. *Trends in Cognitive Science, 3*, 11–21.

Davies, B., Andrewes, D.G., Stargatt, R., Ames, D., Tuckwell, V., & Davis, S. (1989). Tacrine in Alzheimer's disease. *Lancet*, 15 July, 163–164.

Davies, B., Andrewes, D.G., Stargatt, R., Ames, D., Tuckwell, V., & Davis, S. (1990). Tetrohydroaminoacridine in Alzheimer's disease. *International Journal of Geriatric Psychiatry, 5*, 317–321.

Davis, K.D., Taub, E., Houle, S., Lang, A.E., Dostrovsky, J.O., Tasker, R.R., & Lozano, A.M. (1997). Globus pallidus stimulation activates the cortical motor system during alleviation of parkinsonian symptoms. *Nature and Medicine, 3*, 671–674.

Davis, M. (1992). The role of the amygdala in fear potentiated startle: Implications for animal models of anxiety. *Trends in Pharmacological Sciences, 13*, 35–41.

Dean, R.S., & Reynolds, C.R. (1997). Cognitive processing and self-report of lateral preference. *Neuropsychology Review, 7*, 127–142.

De Bleser, R. (1990). Modality specific dissociations. In H. Goodglass & A. Wingfield (Eds.), *Anomia: Neuroanatomical and cognitive correlates* (Ch. 4, pp. 94–117). London: Academic Press.

De Haan, E.H.F., Bauer, R.M., & Greve, K.W. (1992). Autonomic and behavioural evidence of covert recognition in prosopagnosia. *Cortex, 28*, 77–95.

Dejerine, J. (1891). Sur un case de cécité verbale avec agraphie, suivi d'autopsie. *Compte rendu des Seances de la Société de Biologie, 3*, 197–201.

Dejerine, J. (1892). Contribution a l'étude anatomopathologique et clinique des différentes variétés de cécité verbale. *Memoires-Societe Biologie, 4*, 61–90.

Delazer, M., & Girelli, L. (2000). Priming arithmetic reasoning in an amnesic patient. *Brain and Cognition, 43*, 138–143.

Delazer, M., & Butterworth, B. (1997). A dissociation of the number meanings. *Cognitive Neuropsychology, 14*, 613–636.

Delbecq-Dérousiné, J., Beauvois, M.F., & Shallice, T.

(1990). Preserved recall versus impaired recognition. *Brain, 113*, 1045–1074.

Della Malva, C.L., Stuss, D.T., D'Alton, J., & Willmer, J. (1993). Capture errors and sequencing after frontal brain lesions. *Neuropsychologia, 31*, 363–372.

Della Sala, S., Gray, C., Spinnler, H., & Trivelli, C. (1998). Frontal lobe functioning in man: The riddle revisted. *Archives of Clinical Neuropsychology, 13*, 663–683.

Della Sala, S., Marchetti, C., & Spinnler, H. (1991). Right sided anarchic (alien) hand: A longitudinal study. *Neuropsychologia, 29*, 1113–1127.

Delporte, H. (1995). Art and the early hominids. In J.P. Cahneux & J. Chavaillon (Eds.), *Origins of the human brain*. Oxford: Clarendon Press.

Demonet, J.F. Chollet, F., Ramasay, S., Cardebat, D., et al. (1992). The anatomy and phonological and semantic processing in normal subjects. *Brain, 115*, 1753–1768.

Denes, G., & Semenza, C. (1975). Auditory modality-specific anomia: Evidence of a case of pure word deafness. *Cortex, 11*, 401–411.

De Partz, M.P. (1995). Deficit of the graphemic buffer: Effects of a written lexical segmentation strategy. In R.S. Berndt & C.C. Mitchum (Eds.), *Cognitive neuropsychological approaches to the treatment of language disorders* (pp. 129–147). Hove, UK: Lawrence Erlbaum Associates Ltd.

De Renzi, E. (1982). *Disorders of space exploration and cognition*. New York: Wiley.

De Renzi, E. (1985). Methods of limb apraxia examination and their bearing on the interpretation of the disorder. In E.A. Roy (Ed.), *Advances in psychology: Vol. 23. Neuropsychological studies of apraxia and related disorders* (pp. 45–62). Amsterdam: North-Holland.

De Renzi, E., Faglioni, P., & Previdi, P. (1977). Spatial memory and hemispheric locus of lesion. *Cortex, 13*, 424–433.

De Renzi, E., Faglioni, P., & Sorgato, P. (1982). Modality specific and supramodal mechanisms of apraxia. *Brain, 105*, 301–312.

De Renzi, E., & Saetti, M.C. (1997). Associative agnosia and optic aphasia: Qualitative or quantitative difference? *Cortex, 33*, 115–130.

Derouesne, J., & Beauvois, M.F. (1979). Phonological processing in reading: Data from alexia. *Journal of Neurology, Neurosurgery and Psychiatry, 42*, 1125–1132.

Derouesne, J., & Beauvois, M.F. (1985). The "phonemic" stage in the non-lexical reading reading process: Evidence fron a case of phonological alexia. In K.E. Patterson, J.C. Marshall, & M. Colt-heart (Eds.), *Surface dyslexia* (pp. 399–458). Hillsdale, NJ: Lawrence Erlbaum Associates Inc.

De Schutter, E., & Maex, R. (1996). The cerebellum: Cortical processing and theory. *Current Opinion in Neurobiology, 6*, 759–764.

Desimone, R. (1998). Visual attention mediated by biased competition in extrastriate visual cortex. *Philosophical Transactions of the Royal Society London, Series B, 353*. 1245–1255.

Desimone, R., Albright, T.D., Gross, C.G., & Bruce, C.J. (1984). Stimulus selective properties of inferior temporal neurons in the macaque. *Journal of Neuroscience, 4*, 2051–2062.

Desimone, R., & Duncan, J. (1995). Neural mechanisms of selective visual attention. *Annual Review of Neuroscience, 18*, 193–222.

Desimone, R., Miller, E.K., & Chelazzi, L. (1994). Interaction of neural systems for attention and memory. In C. Koch & J. David (Eds.), *Large-scale theories of neuronal function* (pp. 75–91). Cambridge, MA: MIT Press.

D'Esposito, M., & Alexander, M.P. (1995). Subcortical aphasia: Distinct profiles following left putaminal hemorrhage. *Neurology, 45*, 38–41.

D'Esposito, M., Ballard, D., Zarahn, E., & Aguirre, G.K. (2000). The role of prefrontal cortex in sensory memory and motor preparation: An event-related fMRI study. *Neuroimage, 11*, 400–408.

D'Esposito, M., Postle, B.R., Ballard, D., & Lease, J. (1999). Maintenance versus manipulation of information held in working memory: An event-related fMRI study. *Brain and Cognition, 41*, 66–86.

D'Esposito, M., Postle, B.R., & Rypma, B. (2000). Prefrontal cortical contributions to working memory: Evidence from event-related fMRI studies. *Experimental Brain Research, 133*, 3–11.

Dettmers, C., Fink, G.R., Lemon, R.N., Stephan, K.M., Passingham, R.E., Silbersweig, D., Holmes, A., Ridding, M.C., Brooks, D.G., & Frackowiak, R.S. (1996). Relation between cerebral activity and force in the motor areas of the human brain. *Journal of Neurophysiology, 74*, 802–815.

Devinsky, O., Morrell, M.J., & Vogt, B.A. (1995). Contributions of anterior cingulate cortex to behaviour. *Brain, 118*, 279–306.

Diamond, A. (1990). The development and neural bases of memory functions as indexed by the AB and delayed response tasks in human infants and monkeys. *Annals of the New York Academy of Sciences, 608*, 266–309.

Diamond, A. (1998). Prefrontal dysfunction in childhood disorders. In A.C. Roberts, T.W. Robbins, & L. Weiskrantz (Eds.), *The prefrontal cortex and cognitive functions* (Ch. 11, pp. 144–150). New York: Oxford University Press.

Diamond, A., Ciaramitaro, V., Donner, E., Djali, S., & Robinson, M.B. (1994). An animal model of early-treated PKU. *Journal of Neuroscience, 14* (5), 3072–3082.

Diamond, R., White, R.F., Myers, R.H., Richard, H., Mastromauro, C., et al. (1992). Evidence of presymptomatic cognitive decline in Huntington's disease. *Journal of Clinical and Experimental Neuropsychology, 14*, 961–975.

Dias, R., Robbins, T.W., & Roberts, A.C. (1996) Dissociation in prefrontal cortex of attentional and affective shifts. *Nature, 380*, 69–72.

Dick, J.P.R., Benecke, R., Rothwell, J.C., Day, B.L., & Marsden, C.D. (1986). Simple and complex movements in a patient with infarction in the right supplementary motor area. *Movement Disorders, 1*, 255–266.

Dierks, T., Linden, D.E., Jandl, M., Formisano, E., Goebel, R., Lanfermann, H., & Singer, W. (1999). Activation of Heschl's gyrus during auditory hallucinations. *Neuron, 22*, 615–621.

Dikman, S.S., Temkin, N., & Armsden, G. (1989). Neuropsychological recovery: Relationship to psychosocial functioning and postconcussional complaints. In H.S. Levin, H.M. Eisenberg, & A.L. Benton (Eds.), *Mild head injury* (Ch. 15, pp. 229–245). New York: Oxford University Press.

Diller, L. (1992). Neuropsychological rehabilitation. In F.D. Rose & D.A. Johnson (Eds.), *Recovery from brain damage* (pp. 105–114). New York: Plenum Press.

Dimond, S.J. (1976). Depletion of attentional capacity after total commissurotomy in man. *Brain, 99*, 347–356.

Dobbins, A.C., Jeo, R.M., Fiser, J., & Allman, J.M. (1998). Distance modulation of neural activity in the visual cortex. *Science, 281*, 552–555.

Dodgson, M.C.H. (1962). *The growing brain: An essay in developmental neurology*. Bristol: Wright.

Dolan, M.P., & Norton, J.C. (1977). A programmed training technique that uses reinforcement to facilitate acquisition and retention in brain damaged patients. *Journal of Clinical Psychology, 33*, 495–501.

Dolan, R.J., Bench C.J., Liddle, P.F., Friston, K.J., Frith, C.D., Grasby, P.M., & Frackowiak, R.S. (1993). Dorsolateral prefrontal cortex dysfunction in the major psychoses: Symptom or disease specificity? *Journal of Neurology, Neurosurgery and Psychiatry*, *56*, 1290–1294.

Dolan, R.J., Fletcher, P.C., McKenna, P., Friston, K.J., & Frith, C. (1999). Abnormal integration related to cognition in schizophrenia. *Acta Psychiatrica Scandinavica Supplement*, *395*, 58–67.

Doody, R.S. (1993). A reappraisal of localisation theory with reference to aphasia. Part 2: Language theories from outside neurology. *Brain and Language*, *44*, 327–348.

Dorrichi, F., Guariglia, C., Paolucci, S., & Pizzamiglio, L. (1990). Severe reduction of leftwards REMs in patients with unilateral hemiinattention. In J. Horne (Ed.), *Sleep 90*. Bochum, Germany: Pontenagel Press.

Downes, J.J., Kalla, T., Davies, A.D.M., Flynn, A. et al. (1997). The pre-exposure technique: A novel method for enhancing the effects of imagery in face–name association learning. *Neuropsychological Rehabilitation*, *7*, 195–214.

Doyon, J., & Milner, B. (1991). Right temporal-lobe contribution to global visual processing. *Neuropsychologia*, *29*, 343–360.

Drevets, W.C., Price, J.L., Simpson Jr, J.R., Todd, R.D., Reich, T., Vanniere, M., & Raichle, M.E. (1997). Subgenual prefrontal cortex abnormalities in mood disorders. *Nature*, *386*, 824–827.

Drevets, W.C., & Raichle, M.E. (1995). Positron emission tomographic imaging studies of human emotional disorders. In M. Gazanigga (Ed.), *The cognitive neurosciences* (pp. 1153–1164). Cambridge, MA: MIT Press.

Drewe, E.A. (1975). Go–no go learning after frontal lesions in man. *Cortex*, *11*, 8–16.

Drinkwater, B.A. (1976). Visual memory skills of medium contact Aboriginal children. *Australian Journal of Psychology*, *28*, 37–43.

Driver, J., & Halligan, P.W. (1991). Can visual neglect operate in object centred coordinates? An affirmative single-case study. *Cognitive Neuropsychology*, *8*, 475–496.

Driver J., & Spence C. (1998). Cross-modal links in spatial attention. *Philosophical Transactions of the Royal Society London, Series B*, *353*, 1319–1331.

Duffy, R.J., & Duffy, J.R. (1990). The relationship between pantomime expression and recognition in aphasia: The search for causes. In G.E. Hammond (Ed.), *Cerebral control of speech and limb movements* (pp. 417–499). Amsterdam: Elsevier.

Duncan, J. (1993). Similarity between concurrent visual discriminations: Dimensions and objects. *Perception and Psychophysics*, *54* (4), 425–430.

Duncan, J. (1998). Converging levels of analysis in cognitive neuroscience of visual attention. *Philosophical Transactions of the Royal Society London, Series B*, *353*, 1307–1317.

Duncan, J., Burgess, P., Emslie, H. (1995). Fluid intelligence after frontal lobe lesions. *Neuropsychologia*, *33*, 261–268.

Duncan, J., Emslie, H., & Williams, P. (1996). Intelligence and the frontal lobe: The organisation of goal-directed behaviour. *Cognitive Psychology*, *30*, 257–303.

Duncan, J., Johnson, R., Swales, M., & Freer, C. (1997). Frontal lobe deficits after head injury: Unity and diversity of function. *Cognitive Neuropsychology*, *14*, 713–741.

Duncan, J., & Owen, A.M. (2000). Common regions of the human frontal lobe recruited by diverse cognitive demands. *Trends in Neuroscience*, *23*, 475–83.

Dunn, E.H. (1917). Primary and secondary findings in a series of attempts to transplant the cerebral cortex in the albino rat. *Journal of Comparative Neurology*, *27*, 656–682.

Ebbinghaus, H. (1885). *Uber das Gedachttnis*. Leipzig: Dunker. (Translation by H. Ruyer and C.E. Bussenius (1913). *Memory*. New York Teachers College, Columbia University.)

Eccles, J.C. (1989). *Evolution of the brain: creation of the self*. London: Routledge.

Efron, R. (1968). What is perception? *Boston Studies in Philosophies of Science*, *4*, 137–173.

Einstein, G.O., & McDaniel, M.A. (1990). Normal aging and prospective memory. *Journal of Experimental Psychology: Learning, Memory and Cognition*, *1*, 717–726.

Ekman, P., & Friesen, W.V. (1971) Constants across culture in the face and emotion. *Journal of Personality and Social Psychology*, *17*, 124–129.

Elliott, R., Dolan, R.J., & Frith, C.D. (2000). Dissociable functions in the medial and lateral orbitofrontal cortex: Evidence from human neuroimaging studies. *Cerebral Cortex*, *10*, 308–317.

Elliott, R., Frith, C.D., & Dolan, R.J. (1997). Differential neural response to positive and negative feedback in planning and guessing tasks. *Neuropsychologia*, *35*, 1395–1404.

Elliott, R., Rees, G., & Dolan, R.J. (1999). Ventromedial prefrontal cortex mediates guessing. *Neuropsychologia*, *37*, 403–411.

Elliott, R., Sahakian, B.J., Michael, A., Paykel, E.S., & Dolan, R.J. (1997). Neural response to feedback on planning and guessing tasks in patients with unipolar depression. *Psychological Medicine*, *28*, 559–571.

Ellis, A.W., & Young, A.W. (1996). *Human cognitive neuropsychology: A text book of readings*. Hove, UK: Psychology Press.

Ellis, A.W., Young, A.W., & Flude, B.M. (1987). "Afferent dysgraphia" in a patient and in normal subjects. *Cognitive Neuropsychology*, *4*, 465–468.

Ellis, A.W., Young, A.W., & Flude, B.M. (1993), Neglect and visual language. In I.H. Robertson & J.C. Marshall (Eds.), *Unilateral neglect: Clinical and experimental studies* (pp. 233–255). Hove, UK: Lawrence Erlbaum Associates Ltd.

Ellis, H.D. (1996). Bodamer on prosopagnosia, In C. Code, C.W. Wallwesch, Y. Joanette, & A.R. Lecours (Eds.), *Classic cases in neuropsychology* (Ch. 6, pp. 69–74). Hove, UK: Psychology Press.

Ellis, H.D., & Young, A. (1990). Accounting for delusions of misidentification. *British Journal of Psychiatry*, *157*, 239–248.

Ellis, N.C., & Hennelly, R.A. (1980). A bilingual word-length effect: Implications for intelligence testing and the relative ease of mental calculation in Welsh and English. *British Journal of Psychology*, *71*, 43–52.

Endo, K., Miyasaka, M., Makishita, H., Yanagisawa, N., & Sugishita, M. (1992). Tactile agnosia and tactile aphasia: Symptomological and anatomical differences. *Cortex*, *28*, 445–469.

Engle, R.W., Keane, M.J., & Tuholski, S.W. (1999). Individual differences in working memory capacity and what they tell us about controlled attention, general fluid intelligence, functions of prefrontal cortex. In A. Miyake & P. Shah (Eds.), *Models of working memory: Mechanisms of active maintenance and executive control* (Ch. 4, pp. 102–135). Cambridge, UK: Cambridge University Press.

Engle, R.W., Tuholski, S.W., Laughlin, J. E., & Conway, A.R.A. (1999). Working memory, short-term memory, and general fluid intelligence: A latent-variable approach. *Journal of Experimental Psychology, General*, *128*, 309–331.

Epstein, J., Stern, E., & Silbersweig, D. (1999). Mesolimbic activity associated with psychosis. *Annals of the New York Academy of Sciences*, *877*, 562–574.

Ericsson, K.A., & Kintsch, W. (1995). Long-term working memory. *Psychological Review*, *102*, 211–245.

Eriksen, C.W., & Yeh, Y. (1985). Allocation of attention in the visual field. *Journal of Experimental Psychology: Human Perception and Performance*, *11*, 583–597.

Escourolle, R., Haw, J.J., Gray, F., & Henin, D. (1975). Aspects neuropathologiques des lesions du corps calleaux. In F. Michel & B. Schott (Eds.), *Les syndromes des disconnexion calleuse chez l'homme*. Lyon: Hôpital Neurologique.

Eslinger, P.J., & Damasio, A.R. (1985). Severe disturbance of higher cognition following bilateral frontal lobe ablation. *Neurology*, *35*, 1731–1741.

Eslinger, P.J., & Grattan, L.M. (1993). Frontal lobe and frontal–striatal substrates for different forms of human cognitive flexibility. *Neuropsychologia*, *31*, 17–28.

Ettlinger, G., & Wyke, M. (1961). Defects in identifying objects visually in a patient with cerebrovascular disease. *Journal of Neurology, Neurosurgery and Psychiatry*, *24*, 254–259.

Everling, S., & Fischer, B. (1998). The anti-saccade: A review of basic research and clinical studies. *Neuropsychologia*, *36*, 885–899.

Fabiani, M., Stadler, M.A., & Wessels, P.M. (2000). True but not false memories produce a sensory signature in human lateralized brain potentials. *Journal of Cognitive Neuroscience*, *12*, 941–949.

Faglioni, P. & Basso, A. (1985). Historical perspectives on apraxia. In E.A. Roy (Ed.), *Advances in Psychology: Vol. 23. Neuropsychological studies of apraxia and related disorders* (pp. 3–34;). Amsterdam: North-Holland.

Falloon, I.R.H., & Talbot, R.E. (1981). Persistent hallucinations: Coping mechanisms and implications for management. *Psychological Medicine*, *11*, 329–339.

Falzi, G., Perrone, P., & Vignolo, L.A. (1982). Right left asymmetry in anterior speech region. *Archives of Neurology*, *39*, 239–240.

Farah, M.J. (1984). The neurological basis of mental imagery: A componential analysis. *Cognition*, *18*, 245–272.

Farah, M.J. (1988). Is visual imagery really visual? Overlooked evidence from neuropsychology. *Psychological Review*, *95*, 307–317.

Farah, M.J. (1990). Visual agnosia: Disorders of object vision and what they tell us about normal vision. Cambridge, MA: MIT Press.

Farah, M.J. (1994). Neuropsychological inference within an interactive brain: A critique of locality assumption. *Behavioural and Brain Sciences*, *17*, 43–104.

Farah, M.J. (1995). Current issues in the neuropsychology of image generation. *Neuropsychologia*, *33*, 1455–1471.

Farah, M.J. (1997). Distinguishing perceptual and semantic impairments affecting visual object recognition. *Visual Cognition*, *4*, 199–206.

Farah, M.J., Stowe, R.M., & Levinson, K.L. (1996).

Gardener, H. (1974). *The shattered mind*. New York: Random House; London: Vintage Books.

Gardiner, J.M., Craik, F.I.M., & Birtwisle, J. (1972). Retrieval cues and release from proactive inhibition. *Journal of Verbal Learning and Verbal Behaviour, 11,* 778–783.

Garrett, M.F. (1976). Syntactic processes in sentence production. In R.J. Wales & E.C.T. Walker (Eds.), *New approaches to language mechanisms* (pp. 231–225). Amersterdam: North-Holland.

Garrett, M.F. (1980). The limits of accommodation. In V. Fromkin (Ed.), Errors in linguistic performance, slips of the tongue, ear, pen and hand (pp. 263–271). New York: Academic Press.

Garrett, M.F. (1982). Production of speech: Observations from normal to pathological language use. In A.W. Ellis (Ed.), *Normality and pathology in cognitive functions* (pp. 19–76). London: Academic Press.

Gasparrini, W.G., Satz, P., Heilman, K.M., & Coolidge, F.L. (1978). Hemispheric asymmetries of affective processing as determined by the Minnesota multiphasic personality inventory. *Journal of Neurology, Neurosurgery and Psychiatry, 41,* 470–473.

Gathercole, S.E. (1994). Neuropsychology and working memory: A review. *Neuropsychology, 8,* 494–505.

Gathercole, S.E., & Baddeley, A.D. (1993). *Working memory and language*. Hove, UK: Lawrence Erlbaum Associates Ltd.

Gaymard, B., Ploner, C.J., Rivaud-Pechoux, S., & Pierrot-Deseilligny, C. (1999). The frontal eye field is involved in spatial short-term memory but not in reflexive saccade inhibition. *Experimental Brain Research, 129* (2), 288–301.

Gazzaniga, M.S. (1967). The split brain in man. *Scientific American, 217,* 24–29.

Gazzaniga, M.S. (1983). Right hemisphere language following bisection: A 20 year perspective. *American Psychologist, 38,* 525–537.

Gazzaniga, M.S. (1985). *The social brain*. New York: Basic Books.

Gazzaniga, M.S. (1987a). Cognitive and neurologic aspects of hemispheric disconnection in the human brain. In P.J. Magistretti (Ed.), *Discussions in neurosciences* (Vol 4). Geneva: FESN.

Gazzaniga, M.S. (1987b). Perceptual and attentional processes following callosal section in humans. *Neuropsychologia, 25,* 119–133.

Gazzaniga, M.S., Risse, G.L., Springer, S.P., Clarke, A.B., & Wilson, D.M. (1975). Psychologic and neurologic consequences of partial and complete cerebral commissurotomy. *Neurology, 25,* 10–15.

Gazzaniga, M.S., & Sperry, R.W. (1967). Language

after section of the cerebral commissures. *Brain, 90,* 131–138.

Gazzaniga, M.S., Volpe, B.T., Smylie, C.S., Wilson, D.H., & Le Doux, J.E. (1979). Plasticity in speech organization following commissurotomy. *Brain, 102,* 805–815.

Geffen, G.M., Jones, D.L., & Geffen, L.B. (1994). Interhemispheric control of manual motor activity. *Behaviour Brain Research, 64,* 131–140.

Geffen, G., Moar, K.J., O'Hanlon, A.C., Clark, C.R., & Geffen, L.B. (1990). Test–retest reliability of a new form of the Auditory Verbal Learning Test. *Clinical Neuropsychologist, 2,* 251–259.

Geffen, G., Nilsson, J., & Quinn, K. (1985). The effect of lesions of the corpus callosum on finger localization. *Neuropsychologia, 23,* 497–514.

Geffen, G., Walsh, A., Simpson, D., & Jeeves, M. (1980). Comparison of the effects of transcortical tumours. *Brain, 103,* 773–788.

Gentilini, M., Nichelli, P., & Schoenhuber, R. (1989). Assessment of attention in mild head injury. In H.S. Levin, H.M. Eisenberg, & A.L. Benton (Eds.), *Mild head injury*. New York: Oxford University Press.

Georgiou, N., Bradshaw, J.L., Iansek, R., Philips, J.G., & Mattingly, J.B. (1994). Reduction in external cues and movement sequencing in Parkinson's disease. *Journal of Neurology, Neurosurgery and Psychiatry, 57,* 368–370.

Georgiou, N., Bradshaw, J.L., Phillips, J.G., Chiu, E. (1996). The effect of Huntington's disease and Gilles de la Tourette's syndrome on the ability to hold and shift attention. *Neuropsychologia, 34,* 843–851.

Gerloff, C., Altenmuller, E., & Dichgans, J. (1996). Disintegration and reorganization of cortical motor processing in two patients with cerebellar stroke. *Electroencephalography and Clinical Neurophysiology, 98,* 59–68.

Gerstadt, C.L., Hong, Y.J., & Diamond, A. (1994). The relationship between cognition and action: Performance of children 3½–7 years old on the Stroop-like day–night test. *Cognition, 53,* 129–153.

Gerstmann, J. (1930). Zur Symptomatologie der Hirnlaesionen im Ubergangsgebiet der unteren Parietalund mittelerem Occipitalwindung. *Nervenarzt, 3,* 691–695.

Gerstmann, J. (1957). Some notes on the Gerstmann syndrome. *Neurology, 7,* 866–869.

Geschwind, N. (1962). The anatomy of acquired disorders of reading. In J. Money (Ed.), *Reading disability: Progress and research needs in dyslexia.*

Baltimore: Johns Hopkins University Press. pp. 115–119.

Geschwind, N. (1965). Disconnection syndromes in animals and man. *Brain, 88,* 237–294.

Geschwind, N. (1970). The organisation of language and the brain. *Science, 170,* 940–944.

Geschwind, N. (1985). Mechanisms of change after brain lesions. *Annals of New York Academy of Science, 457,* 1–11.

Geschwind, N., Kaplan, E., & Levy, J. (1962). A human deconnection syndrome. *Neurology, 12,* 675–685.

Geschwind, N., & Levitsky, W. (1968). Human brain: Left–right asymmetries in speech region. *Science, 161,* 186–187.

Geyer, S., Ledberg, A., Schleicher, A., Kinomura, S., Schormann, T., Burgel, U., Klingberg, T., Larsson, J., Zilles, K., & Roland, P.E. (1996). Two different areas within the primary motor cortex of man. *Nature, 382,* 805–807.

Ghaem, O., Mellet, E., Crivello, F., Tzourio, N., Mazoyer, B., Berthoz, A., & Denis, M. (1997). Mental navigation along memorized routes activates the hippocampus, precuneus, and insula. *Neuroreport, 8,* 739–744.

Giannakopoulos, P., Gold, G., Duc, M., Michel, J.P., Hof, P.R., & Bouras, C. (1999). Neuroanatomic correlates of visual agnosia in Alzheimer's disease: a clinicopathologic study. *Neurology, 52,* 71–77.

Gil, R., Pluncheon, C., Toullat, G., Michenau, D., Rogez, R., & Levevre, J.P. (1985). Disconexion visuo-verbale (aphasie optic) pour les objets, les images, les couleurs et les visages avec alexie "abstractive". *Neuropsychologia, 23,* 333–349.

Glanzer, M., & Cunitz, A.R. (1966). Two storage mechanisms in free recall. *Journal of Verbal Learning and Verbal Behaviour, 5,* 351–360.

Glanzer, M., & Razel, M. (1974). The size of the unit in short term storage. *Journal of Verbal Learning and Verbal Behaviour, 13,* 114–131.

Glasgow, R.E., Zeiss, R.A., Barrera M., Jr & Lewinsohn, P.M. (1977). Case studies on remediating memory deficits in brain-damaged individuals. *Journal of Clinical Psychology, 33,* 1049–1054.

Glickman, S.E., & Schiff, B.B. (1967). A biological theory of reinforcement. *Psychology Review, 74,* 81–109.

Glickstein, M. (1998). Cerebellum and the sensory guidance of movement. In G.R. Block & J.A. Goode (Eds.), *Novartis symposium foundation: Vol. 218. Sensory guidance of movements* (pp. 252–271). Chichester, UK: Wiley.

Glisky, E.L. (1995). Computers in memory rehabilitation. In A.D. Baddeley, B.A. Wilson, & F.N. Watts (Eds.), *Handbook of memory disorder* (pp. 557–575). Chichester, UK: Wiley.

Glisky, E.L. (1996). Propsective memory and the frontal lobes. In M. Brandimonte, G.O. Einstein, & M.A. McDaniel (Eds.), *Prospective memory: Theory and applications* (Ch. 13, pp. 249–266). Hillsdale, NJ: Lawrence Erlbaum Associates Inc.

Glisky, E.L., Schacter, D.L., & Tulving, E. (1986). Learning and retention of vocabulary words in amnesic patients: Method of vanishing cues. *Journal of Clinical and Experimental Neuropsychology, 8,* 292–312.

Gloor, P. (1986). Role of the human limbic system in perception, memory and affect: Lessons for temporal lobe epilepsy. In B.K. Doane, & K.E. Livingstone (Eds.), *The limbic system: Functional organization and clinical disorders.* New York: Raven Press.

Glosser, G., & Friedman, R.B. (1996). The continuum of deep/phonological alexia. *Cortex, 26,* 343–359.

Gobet, F. (1998). Expert memory: A comparison of four theories. *Cognition, 66,* 115–152.

Godbout, L., & Doyen, J. (1995). Mental representation of knowledge following frontal-lobe or postrolandic lesions. *Neuropsychologia, 33,* 1671–1696.

Godbout, L., & Fortin, N. (2000). *The scripting of activities of daily living in traumatic brain-injured patients: Shallice's model revisited.* In Abstracts, Cognitive Neuroscience Society annual meeting (p. 110). Dartmouth, Hanover, USA.

Godfrey, H.P.D., & Knight, R.G. (1985). Cognitive rehabilitation of memory functioning in amnesiac alcoholics. *Journal of Consulting and Clinical Psychology, 53,* 555–557.

Godfrey, H.P.D., Knight, R.G., & Marsh, N.V. (1989). Social interaction and speed of information processing following very severe head injury. *Psychological Medicine, 19,* 175–183.

Goel, V., Grafman, J., Tajik, J., Gana, S., & Danto, D. (1997). A study of the performance of patients with frontal lobe lesions in a financial planning task. *Brain, 120* (10), 1805–1822.

Goetz, C.G., Olanow, C.W., Koller, W.C. et al. (1989). Multicentre study of autologous adrenal medullary transplantation to the corpus striatum in patients with advanced Parkinson's disease. *New England Journal of Medicine, 320,* 337–341.

Gold, M., Adair, J.C., Jacobs, D.H., & Heilman, K.M. (1994). Anosognosia for hemiplegia: An electrophysiologic investigation of the feed-forward hypothesis. *Neurology, 44,* 1804–1808.

Goldberg, E. (1986). Varieties of perseveration: A

comparison of two taxonomies. *Journal of Clinical and Experimental Neuropsychology, 8,* 710–726.

Goldberg, E., & Bilder Jr, R.M. (1987). The frontal lobes and hierarchical organization of cognitive control. In E. Perecman (Ed.), *The frontal lobes revisited* (pp. 159–184). New York: Erlbaum.

Goldberg, E., Podell, K., & Lovell, M. (1994). Lateralization of frontal lobe functions and cognitive novelty. *Journal of Neuropsychiatry, 6,* 371–378.

Goldberg, M.E., & Robinson, D.L. (1977). Visual responses of neurons in monkey inferior parietal lobule: The physiologic substrate of attention and neglect. *Neurology, 27,* 350.

Goldberg, T., Hyde, T.M., Kleinman, J.E., & Weinberger, D.R. (1993). Course of schizophrenia: Neuropsychological evidence for a static encephalopathy. *Schizophrenia Bulletin, 19,* 797–804.

Golden, C.J. (1978a). *Diagnosis and rehabilitation in clinical neuropsychology.* Springfield, IL: Charles C. Thomas.

Golden, C.J. (1978b). The Stroop Color and Word Test: A manual for clinical and experimental uses. Chicago: Stoelting.

Goldenberg, G. (1995). Transient global amnesia. In A.D. Baddeley, B.A. Wilson, & F.N. Watts. (Eds.), *Handbook of memory disorders* (pp. 109–134). Chichester, UK: Wiley.

Goldenberg, G., & Artner, C. (1991). Visual imagery and knowledge about the visual appearance of objects in patients with posterior cerebral artery lesions. *Brain and Cognition, 15,* 160–186.

Goldenberg, G., Mullbacher, W., & Nowak, A. (1995). Imagery without perception: A case study of anosognosia for cortical blindness. *Neuropsychologia, 33,* 1373–1382.

Goldman-Rakic, P.S. (1987). Circuitry of the prefrontal cortex and the regulation of behavior by the representation of knowledge. In F. Plum & V. Mountcastle (Eds.), *Handbook of physiology* (Vol. 5, pp. 373–417). Bethesda, MD: American Physiological Society.

Goldman-Rakic, P.S. (1993). Specification of higher cortical functions. *Journal of Head Trauma Rehabilitation, 8,* 13–23.

Goldman-Rakic, P.S. (1995). Anatomical and functional circuits in the prefrontal cortex of nonhuman primates. In H.H. Jasper, S. Riggio, & P.S. Goldman-Rakic (Eds.), *Epilepsy and the functional anatomy of the frontal lobe. Advances in Neurology,* Vol. 97 (pp. 51–65). New York: Raven Press.

Goldman-Rakic, P.S. (1996). The prefrontal landscape: Implications of the functional architecture for understanding human mentation and the central executive. *Philosophical Transactions of the Royal Society, 351,* 1445–1453.

Goldman-Rakic, P.S., & Friedman, H.R. (1991). The circuitry of working memory revealed by anatomy and metabolic imaging. In H.S. Levin, H.M. Eisenberg, & A.L. Benton (Eds.), *Frontal lobe function and dysfunction* (pp. 72–91). Oxford: University Press.

Goldstein, G., & Malec, E.A (1989). Memory training for severely amnesic patients. *Neuropsychology, 3,* 9–16.

Goldstein, K. (1942). *After effects of brain injuries in war.* New York: Grune & Stratton.

Goldstein, K. (1948). *Language and language disturbances.* New York: Grune & Stratton.

Goldstein, K., & Gelb. A. (1918). Psychologische Analysen Hirnpathologischer Falle auf Grund von Untersuchungen Hirnvertiletzer. *Zeitschrift für die Gesamte Neurologie Psychiatrie, 41,* 1–142.

Goldstein, K., & Scheerer, M. (1941). Abstract and concrete behaviour: An experimental study with special tests. *Psychological Monographs, 53* (2, whole no. 239).

Goldstein, L.H., Bernard, S., Fenwick, P.B.C., Burgess, P.W., & McNeil, J. (1993). Unilateral frontal lobectomy can produce strategy application disorder. *Journal of Neurology, Neurosurgery and Psychiatry, 56,* 274–276.

Gollin, E.S. (1960). Developmental studies of visual recognition of incomplete objects. *Perceptual and Motor Skills, 11,* 289–298.

Gonzalez-Rothi, L.J.G., & Heilman, K. (1985). Apraxia. In K. Heilman & E. Valenstein (Eds.), *Clinical neuropsychology* (pp. 131–150). New York: Oxford University Press.

Gonzalez-Rothi, L.J.G. (1990). Transcortical aphasia. In L.L. La Pointe (Ed.), *Aphasia and related neurogenic language disorders* (pp. 78–95). New York: Thieme.

Gonzalez-Rothi, L.J.G., Raymer, A.M., Maher, L., Greenwald, M., & Morris, M. (1991). Assessment of naming failures in neurological naming disorders. *Clinics in Communication Disorders, 1,* 7–20.

Goodale, M.A., & Milner, A.D. (1992). Separate visual pathways for perception and action. *Trends in Neuroscience, 15,* 20–25.

Goodenough, F.L. (1932). Expression of the emotions in a blind–deaf child. *Journal of Abnormal and Social Psychology, 27,* 323–333.

Goodglass, H. (1983). Linguistic aspects of aphasia. *Trends in Neuroscience,* June, 241–243.

Goodglass, H. (1993). *Understanding aphasia.* San Diego: Academic Press.

Goodglass, H., Blumenstein, S., Statlender, S., Gleason, J.B., & Hyde, M.R. (1979). The effect of syntactic encoding on sentence comprehension in aphasia. *Brain and Language*, 7, 201–209.

Goodglass, H., & Kaplan, E. (1983). *The assessment of aphasia and related disorders* (2nd ed.). Philadelphia: Lea & Febiger.

Gopher, D. (1973). Eye movement patterns in selective listening tasks of focussed attention. *Perceptual Psychophysics*, 14, 259–264.

Gordon, A.M., & Soechting, J.F. (1995). Use of tactile afferent information in sequential finger movements. *Experimental Brain Research*, 107, 281–292.

Gordon, C., Hewer, R., & Wade, D. (1987). Dysphagia in acute stroke. *British Medical Journal*, 295, 411–414.

Gordon, H.W., Bogen, J.E., & Sperry, R.W. (1971). Absence of disconnecting syndrome in two patients with partial section of the neocommissures. *Brain*, 94, 327–336.

Gould, L. N. (1949). Auditory hallucinations and subvocal speech; objective study in a case of schizophrenia. *Journal of Nervous and Mental Disease*, 109, 418–427.

Grabowecky, M., Robertson, L.C., & Treisman, A. (1993). Preattentive processes guide visual search: Evidence from patients with unilateral visual neglect. *Journal of Cognitive Neuroscience*, 5, 288–302.

Graf, P., & Mandler, G. (1984). Activation makes words more accessible, but not necessarily more retrievable. *Journal of Verbal Learning and Verbal Behaviour*, 23, 553–568.

Graf, P., Mandler, G., & Hayden, P. (1982). Simulating amnesic symptoms in normal subjects. *Science*, 218, 1243–1244.

Graf, P., & Schacter, D.L. (1984). Implicit and explicit memory for new associations in normal and amnesic subjects. *Journal of Experimental Psychology: Learning Memory, and Cognition*, 11, 501–518.

Grafman, J. (1989). Plans, actions and mental sets: Managerial knowledge units in the frontal lobes. In E. Perceman (Ed.), *Integrating theory and practice in clinical neuropsychology* (Ch. 4, pp. 93–138). Hillsdale, NJ: Lawrence Erlbaum Associates Inc.

Grafman, J. (1995). Models of prefrontal cortical function. *Annals of the New York Academy of Science*, 769, 337–368.

Grafton, S.T., Mazziotti, J.C., Presty, S., Friston, K.J., Frackowiak, R.S., & Phelps, M.E. (1992). Functional anatomy of human procedural learning determined with cerebral blood flow and PET. *Journal of Neuroscience*, 12, 2542–2548.

Gragnaniello, D., Kessler, J., Bley, M., & Mielke, R. (1998). Copying and free drawing by patients with Alzheimer's disease of different dementia stages, *Nervenartz*, 69, 991–998.

Grant, D.A., & Berg, E.A. (1948). A behavioural analysis of degree of reinforcement and ease of shifting to new responses in a Weigl-type card-sorting problem. *Journal of Experimental Psychology*, 38, 404–411.

Grasby, P.M., Frith, C.D., Friston, K.J., Bench, C., Frackowiak, R.S.J., & Dolan, R.J. (1993). Functional mapping of brain areas implicated in auditory–verbal memory function. *Brain*, 116, 513–525.

Gratton, G., Coles, M.G., & Donchin, E. (1992). Optimizing the use of information: Strategic control of activation of response probability effects on stimulus evaluation and response processes. *Journal of Experimental Psychology*, 4, 480–506.

Gray, J.A. (1995). A model of the limbic system and the basal ganglia: Applications to anxiety and schizophrenia. In M.S. Gazzaniga (Ed.), *The cognitive neurosciences* (pp. 1165–1181). Cambridge, MA: MIT Press.

Gray, J.M., & Robertson, I. (1989). Remediation of attentional difficulties following brain injury: Three experimental case studies. *Brain Injury*, 3, 163–170.

Gray, J.M., Robertson, I., Pentland, B., & Anderson, S. (1992). Microcomputer-based attentional retraining after brain damage: A randomised group controlled trial. *Neuropsychological Rehabilitation*, 2, 97–115.

Gray, T. S. (1999). Functional and anatomical relationships among the amygdala, basal forebrain, ventral striatum, and cortex. *Annals of the New York Academy of Sciences*, 877, 439–444.

Graziano, M.S.A., & Gross, C.G. (1998). Spatial maps for the control of movement. *Current Opinion in Neurobiology*, 8, 195–201.

Grech, P.L. (1993). *Complex figure copying in Huntington's disease: Visuo-perceptual, spatial and constructional underpinnings of performance.* Unpublished honours thesis, University of Melbourne.

Green, E., & Howes, D.H. (1977). The nature of conduction aphasia: A study of of anatomic and clinical features and of underlying mechanisms. In H. Whitiker & H.A. Whitiker (Eds.), *Studies in neurolinguistics* (Vol. 3, pp. 123–156). New York: Academic Press.

Green, M.F., & Kinsbourne, M. (1990). Subvocal activity and auditory hallucinations: Clues for behavioral treatments? *Schizophrenia Bulletin*, 16, 617–625.

Green, P., & Preston, M. (1981). Reinforcement of vocal correlates of auditory hallucinations by auditory feedback: A case study. *British Journal of Psychiatry, 139*, 204–208.

Greenblatt, S.H. (1977). Neurosurgery and the anatomy of reading: A practical review. *Neurosurgery, 1*, 6–15.

Greenblatt, S.H., Saunders, R.L., Culver, C.M., & Bogdanowicz, W. (1980). Normal inter-hemispheric visual transfer with incomplete section of the splenium. *Archives of Neurology, 37*, 567–571.

Greenwald, M.L., Raymer, A.M., Richardson, M.E., & Rothi, L.J.G. (1995). Contrasting treatments for severe impairments of picture naming. In R.S. Berndt & C.C. Mitchum (Eds.), *Cognitive neuropsychological approaches to the treatment of language disorders* (pp. 17–49). Hove, UK: Lawrence Erlbaum Associates, Ltd.

Gregory, R.L. (1998). Eye and brain: The psychology of seeing (5th ed.). Oxford: Oxford University Press.

Gron, G., Wunderlich, A.P., Spitzer, M., Tomczak, R., & Riepe, M.W. (2000). Brain activation during human navigation: gender-different neural networks as substrates of performance. *Nature Neuroscience, 3*, 404–408.

Gronwall, D. (1989). Cumulative and persisting effects of concussion on attention and cognition. In H.S. Levin, H.M. Eisenberg, & A.L. Benton (Eds.), *Mild head injury*. New York: Oxford University Press.

Gronwall, D.R., & Wrightson, P. (1974). Memory and information processing capacity after closed head injury. *Lancet, ii*, 605–609.

Gronwall, D.R., & Wrightson, P. (1975). Cumulative effects on concussion. *Lancet, ii*, 995–997.

Gronwall, D.R., & Wrightson, P. (1998). Mild head injury in New Zealand: Incidence of injury and persisting symptoms. *New Zealand Medical Journal, 111*, 99–101.

Gupta, P., & MacWhinney, B. (1997). Vocabulary acquisition and verbal short-term memory: Computational and neural bases. *Brain and Language, 59*, 267–333.

Guttman, M. (1992). Dopamine receptors in Parkinson's disease. *Neurologic Clinics, 10*, 377–386.

Hachinski, V., and Norris, J.W. (1985). *The acute stroke*. Philadelphia: F.A. Davis.

Hadano, K., Nakamura, H., & Hamanaka, T. (1998). Effortful echolalia. *Cortex, 34*, 67–82.

Haddock, G., Bentall, R.P., & Slade, P.D. (1995). Auditory hallucinations and the transformation effect: The role of suggestions. *Personality and Individual Differences, 19*, 301–306.

Halligan, M.W., & Marshall, J.C. (1991). Left neglect for near but not far space in man. *Nature, 350*, 498–500.

Halligan, M.W., & Marshall, J.C. (1995). Within- and between-task dissociations in visuo-spatial neglect: A case study. *Cortex, 31*, 367–376.

Halligan, P.W., & Marshall, J.C. (1998). Neglect of awareness. *Conscious Cognition, 7*, 356–380.

Halstead, W.C. (1947). *Brain and intelligence*. University of Chicago Press: Chicago.

Hamlin, R.M. (1970). Intellectual function 14 years after frontal lobe surgery, *Cortex, 6*, 299–307.

Hanes, K.R., & Andrewes, D.G. (1995). Cognitive flexibility and complex integration in Parkinson's disease, Huntington's disease and Schizophrenia. *Journal of the International Neuropsychological Society, 1*, 545–553.

Hanes, K., Andrewes, D.G., & Pantelis, C. (1996). Brief assessment of executive control dysfunction: Discriminant validity and homogeneity of planning, set shift and fluency measures. *Archives of Clinical Neuropsychology, 11* (3), 185–191.

Hanes, K.R, Andrewes, D.G, Pantelis, C., & Chiu, E. (1996). Subcortical dysfunction in schizophrenia: A comparison with Parkinson's disease and Huntington's disease. *Schizophrenia Research, 19*, 121–128.

Hanes K.R., Andrewes, D.G., Smith, D., & Pantelis, C. (1996). A brief assessment of executive dysfunction: Homogeneity and discriminant validity of planning, set-shift and fluency measures. *Archives of Clinical Neuropsychology, 30*, 185–193.

Hanes, K.R., Pantelis, C., Andrewes, D.G., & Chiu, E. (1996). Brief Report: Bradyphrenia in Parkinson's Disease, Huntington's Disease and Schizophrenia. *Cognitive Neuropsychiatry, 1*, 165–170.

Hanley, J.R., Young, A.W., & Pearson, N.A. (1991). Impairment of the visuo-spatial sketch pad. *Quarterly Journal of Experimental Psychology, 43A* (1), 101–125.

Hanlon, R.E., & Edmondson, J.A. (1996). Disconnected phonology: A linguistic analysis of phonemic jargon aphasia. *Brain and Language, 55*, 199–212.

Harding, A., Halliday, G., Caine, D., & Kril, J. (2000). Degeneration of anterior thalamic nuclei differentiates alcoholics with amnesia. *Brain, 123* (1), 141–54.

Hare, M.E. (1905) Cited in *Oxford dictionary of quotations* (3rd ed., 1981, p. 242). Oxford: University Press.

Harley, T.A. (1995). *The psychology of language: From data to theory*. Hove, UK: Lawrence Erlbaum Associates Ltd.

Harrington, D.L., & Haaland, K.Y. (1991). Hemispheric specialization for movement sequencing: Abnormalities in levels of programming. *Neuropsychologia, 29*, 147–163.

Harrington, D.L., & Haaland, K.Y. (1992). Motor sequencing with left hemisphere damage. *Brain, 115*, 857–874.

Harris, J.E. (1980). Memory aids people use: Two interview studies. *Memory and Cognition, 8*, 31–38.

Harro, J., Vasar, E., & Bradwejn, J. (1993). CCK in animal and human research on anxiety. *Trends in Pharmacology Science, 14*, 244–249.

Hart, R.P., Wade, J.B., Calabrese, V.P., & Colander, C.C. (1998). Vigilance performance in Parkinson's disease and depression. *Journal of Clinical and Experimental Psychology, 20*, 111–117.

Hartlage, L.C., & Gage, R. (1997). Unimanual performance as a measure of laterality. *Neuropsychology Review, 7*, 143–156.

Harvey, M., & Milner, A.D. (1995). Balint's patient. *Cognitive Neuropsychology, 12*, 261–264.

Hasher, L., & Zacks, R.T. (1979). Automatic and effortful processing in memory. *Journal of Experimental Psychology: General, 108*, 356–388.

Hasher, L., & Zacks, R.T. (1984). Automatic processing of fundamental information: The case of frequency of occurrence. *American Psychologist, 39*, 1372–1388.

Hasselmo, M.E., & McClelland, J.L. (1999). Neural models of memory. *Current Opinion in Neurobiology, 9*, 184–188.

Hasselmo, M.E., Rolls, E.T., Baylis, G.C., & Nalwa, V. (1989). Object-centered encoding by face-selective neurons in the cortex in the superior temporal sulcus of the monkey. *Experimental Brain Research, 75*, 417–429.

Hausen, H.S., Lachmann, E.A., & Nagler, W. (1997). Cerebral diaschisis following cerebellar hemorrhage. *Archives of Physiological Medical Rehabilitation, 78*, 546–559.

Haut, M.W., Weber, A.M., Wilhelm, K.L., Keefover, R.W., et al, (1994). The visual reproduction subtest as a measure of visual perception and constructional functioning in dementia of Alzheimer's type. *Clinical Neuropsychologist, 8*, 187–192.

Haxby, J.V., Petit, L., Ungerleider, L.G., & Courtney, S.M. (2000). Distinguishing the functional roles of multiple regions in distributed neural systems for visual working memory. *Neuroimage, 11* (5), 380–391.

Haxby, J.V., Ungerleider, L.G., Clark, V.P., Schouten, J.L., Hoffman, E.A., & Martin, A. (1999). The effect of face inversion on activity in human neural systems for face and object perception. *Neuron, 22*, 189–199.

Head, H. (1926). *Aphasia and kindred disorders of speech*. London: Cambridge University Press.

Hebb, D. (1945). Man's frontal lobes: A critical review. *Archives of Neurology and Psychiatry, 54*, 10–24.

Hebb, D.O. (1949). *Organization of behaviour*. New York: Wiley.

Hebb, D.O., & Penfield, W. (1940). Human behaviour after extensive bilateral removals of the frontal lobes. *Archives of Neurology and Psychiatry, 44*, 421–438.

Hecaen, H. (1962). Clinical symptomology in right and left hemisphere lesions. In V.B. Mountcastle (Ed.), *Interhemispheric relation and cerebral dominance* (pp. 215–243). Baltimore: Johns Hopkins University Press.

Hecaen, H. (1976). Acquired aphasia in children and the ontogenesis of hemispheric functional specialisation. *Brain and Language, 3*, 114–134.

Hecaen, H. (1983). Acquired aphasia in children: Revisited. *Neuropsychologia, 21*, 581–587.

Hecaen, H., & Albert, M.L. (1978). *Human neuropsychology*. New York: Wiley.

Hecaen, H., Angelergues, T., & Houiller, S. (1961). Les variétés cliniques des acalculies au cours des lesions retrorolandiques. *Revue Neurologique, 105*, 85–103.

Heide, W., Blankenburg, M., Zimmermann, E., & Kompf, D. (1995). Cortical control of double-step saccades: Implications for spatial orientation. *Annals of Neurology, 38*, 739–748.

Heilman, K.M. (1975). Defective motor learning in ideomotor apraxia. *Neurology, 25*, 1018–1020.

Heilman K.M., Barrett A.M., & Adair J.C. (1998). Possible mechanisms of anosognosia: a defect in self-awareness. *Philosophical Transactions of the Royal Society of London B, 353*, 1903–1909.

Heilman, K.M., & Gilmore, R.L. (1998). Cortical influences in emotion. *Journal of Clinical Neurophysiology, 15*, 409–423.

Heilman, K.M., & Rothi, L.J. (1993). Apraxia, in K.M. Heilman & E. Valenstein (Eds.), *Clinical Neuropsychology* (Ch. 7, pp. 141–164). Oxford: Oxford University Press.

Heilman, K.M., Gonzalez-Rothi, L.J., & Valenstein, E. (1982). Two forms of ideomotor apraxia. *Neurology, 32*, 342–346.

Heilman, K.M., Watson, R.T., & Valenstein, E. (1993). Neglect and related disorders. In K.M. Heilman & E. Valenstein (Eds.), *Clinical neuropsychology* (3rd ed.). Oxford: Oxford University Press.

Hellige, J.B., & Sergent, J. (1986). Role of task factors in visual field asymmetries. *Brain and Cognition, 5,* 200–222.

Helm-Estabrooks, N., Fitzpatrick, P.M., & Barresi, B. (1981). Response of an agrammatic patient to a syntax stimulation program for aphasia. *Journal of Hearing and Speech Disorders, 46,* 422–427.

Henik, A., Rafal, R., & Rhodes, D. (1994). Endogenously generated and visually guided saccades after lesions of the human frontal eye fields. *Journal of Cognitive Neuroscience, 6,* 400–411.

Henriques, J.B., & Davidson, R.J. (1991). Left frontal hypoactivation in depression. *Journal of Abnormal Psychology, 100,* 535–545.

Henson, R.N.A, Rugg, M.D., Shallice, T., Josephs, O., & Dolan, R.J. (1999). Recollection and familiarity in recognition memory: An event related fMRI study. *Journal of Neuroscience, 19,* 3962–3972.

Henson, R.N.A, Shallice, T., & Dolan, R.J. (1999). Right prefrontal cortex and episodic memory retrieval: A functional MRI test of the monitoring hypothesis. *Brain, 122,* 1367–1381.

Hermann, B.P., Seidenberg, M., Haltiner, A., & Wyler, A.R. (1995). Relationship of age of onset, chronological age and adequacy of preoperative performance to verbal memory change after anterior temporal lobectomy. *Epilepsia, 36,* 137–145.

Hermann, B.P., Wyler, A.R., & Richey, E.T. (1988). Wisconsin card sorting test performance in patients with complex partial seizures of temporal-lobe origin. *Journal of Clinical and Experimental Neuropsychology, 10,* 467–476.

Hickok, G. (2000). Speech perception, conduction aphasia, and the functional neuroanatomy of language. In Y. Grodzinsky et al. (Eds.), Language and the brain (Ch. 4, pp. 87–104). New York: Academic Press.

Hickok, G., Erhard, P., Kassubek, J., Helms-Tillery, A.K., Naeve-Velgarth, S. et al. (1999). Auditory cortex participants in speech production. *Cognitive Neuroscience Society Abstracts,* Vol. 97, San Francisco.

Hickok, G., & Poeppel, D. (2000). Towards a functional neuroanatomy of speech perception. *Trends in Cognitive Sciences, 4,* 131–138.

Hillis, A.E., & Caramazza, A. (1991a). Mechanisms for accessing lexical representations for output: Evidence for a case of category specific semantic deficit. *Brain and Cognition, 40,* 106–144.

Hillis, A.E., & Caramazza. A. (1991b). The effects of attentional deficits on reading and spelling. In A. Caramazza (Ed.), *Cognitive neuropsychology and neurolinguistics: Advances in models of language processing and impairments* (pp. 211–275). Hillsdale, NJ: Lawrence Erlbaum Associates Inc.

Hillis, A.E., & Caramazza, A. (1995). Cognitive and neural mechanisms underlying visual and semantic processing: Implications from optic aphasia. *Journal of Cognitive Neuroscience, 7,* 457–478.

Hiscock, M., & Kinsbourne, M. (1995). Phylogeny and ontogeny of cerebral lateralization. In R.J. Davidson & K. Hudgahl (Eds.), *Brain asymmetry* (pp. 535–578). Cambridge, MA: Bradford Books.

Hitch, G.J., Halliday, M.S., Schaafstal, A.M., & Schraagen, J.M.C. (1988). Visual working memory in young children. *Memory and Cognition, 16,* 120–132.

Hobson, J.A., Stickgold, R., & Pace-Schott, E.F. (1998). The neuropsychology of REM sleep dreaming. *Neuroreport, 16* (9), R1–14.

Hodges, J.R., & McCarthy, J.A. (1995). Loss of remote memory: A cognitive neuropsychological perspective. *Current Opinion in Neurobiology, 5,* 178–183.

Hodges, J.R., Patterson, K., Oxbury, S., & Funnell, E. (1992). Semantic dementia. *Brain, 115,* 1783–1806.

Hodges, J.R., Patterson, K., & Tyler, L.K. (1994). Loss of semantic memory: Implications for the modularity of mind. *Cognitive Neuropsychology, 11,* 505–542.

Hoffman, D.D., & Richards, W.A. (1984). Parts of recognition. *Cognition, 18,* 65–96.

Hoffman, R.E., & McGlashan, T.H. (1997). "Voices" in schizophrenia: Synaptic elimination, neurodevelopment, and the mechanism of hallucinated "voices" in schizophrenia. *American Journal of Psychiatry, 154,* 1683–1689.

Holmes, G. (1918). Disturbances of visual orientation. *British Journal of Ophthalmology, 2,* 449–468.

Holtzman, J.D. (1984). Interactions between cortical and sub-cortical visual areas: Evidence from human commissurotomy patients. *Visual Research, 24,* 801–813.

Honore, J. (1982). Posture oculaire et attention sélective à des stimuli cutanés. *Neuropsychologia, 20,* 727–730.

Hopfinger, J.B., Buonocore, M.H., & Mangun, G.R. (2000). The neural mechanisms of top-down attentional control. *Nature and Neuroscience, 3,* 284–292.

Horel, J.A., Keating, E.G., & Misantone, L.J. (1975). Partial Kluver–Bucy syndrome produced by destroying temporal neocortex or amygdala. *Brain Research, 94* (2), 347–359

Hornak, J., Rolls, E.T., & Wade, D. (1996). Face and voice expression identification in patients with emotional and behavioural changes following ventral frontal lobe damage. *Neuropsychologia, 34,* 247–261.

Horrenstein, S., Chung, G., & Brenner, S. (1978). Aphasia in two verified cases of left thalamic hemorrhage. *Annals of Neurology, 4,* 177.

Hough, M.S. (1993). Treatment of Wernicke's aphasia with jargon: A case study. *Journal of Communicative Disorders, 26,* 101–111.

House, A., Dennis, M., Molyneux, A., Warlow, C. & Hawton, K. (1989). Emotionalism after stroke. *Nature, 298,* 991–994.

House, A., Dennis, M., Warlow, C., Hawton, K., & Molyneux, A. (1990). Mood disorders after stroke and their relation to lesion location. *Brain, 113,* 1113–1129.

Howard, D. (1995). Short-term recall without short-term memory. In R. Campbell & M.A. Conway (Eds.), *Broken memories: Case studies in memory impairment* (Ch. 20, pp. 285–301). Oxford: Blackwell.

Howard, D., & Orchard-Lisle, V. (1984). On the origin of semantic errors in naming: Evidence from the case of a global aphasic. *Cognitive Neuropsychology, 1,* 163–190.

Howard, R.J., ffytche, D.H., Barnes J., McKeefry D., Ha, Y., Woodruff, P.W., Bullmore, E.T., Simmons, A., Williams, S.C., David, A.S., & Brammer, M. (1998). The functional anatomy of imagining and perceiving colour. *Neuroreport, 20* (9), 1019–1023.

Howes, D., & Boller, F. (1975). Simple reaction time: Evidence for focal impairment from lesions of the right hemisphere. *Brain, 98,* 317–332.

Howes, D., & Geschwind, N. (1964). Quantitative studies of aphasic language. *Research Publication Associate with Nervous Mental Disease, 42,* 229–244.

Howseman, A.M., & Bowtell, R.W. (1999). Functional magnetic imaging techniques and contrast mechanisms. *Philosophical Transactions of the Royal Society, 354,* 1179–1194.

Hubel, D.H., & Wiesel, T.N. (1962). Receptive fields, binocular interaction and functional architecture in the cat's visual cortex. *Journal of Physiology, 160,* 106–154.

Hubel, D.H., & Wiesel, T.N. (1977). The Ferrier lecture: Functional architecture of macaque monkey visual cortex. *Proceedings of the Royal Society of London, Series B 198,* 1–59.

Hulme, C., Maughan, S., & Brown, G.D.A. (1991). Memory for familiar and unfamiliar words: Evidence for a long-term memory contribution to short-term-memory span. *Journal of Memory and Language, 30,* 685–701.

Hulme, C., Newton, P., Cowan, N., Stuart, G., & Brown, G. (1999). Think before you speak: Pauses, memory search, and trace re-integration processes in verbal memory span. *Journal of Experimental Psychology, Learning, Memory and Cognition, 25,* 447–463.

Humphreys, G.W. (1998). Neural representation of objects in space: A dual coding account. *Philosophical Transactions of the Royal Society London, Series B, 353,* 1341–1351.

Humphreys, G.W., & Forde, E.M.E. (1998). Disordered action schema and action disorganisation syndrome. *Cognitive Neuropsychology, 15,* 771–811.

Humphreys, G.W., & Heinke, D. (1998). Spatial representation and selection in the brain: Neuropsychological and computational constraints. *Visual Cognition, 5,* 9–47.

Humphreys, G.W., & Riddoch, M.J. (1984). Routes to object constancy: Implications from neurological impairments of object constancy. *Quarterly Journal of Experimental Psychology, 36a,* 385–415.

Humphreys, G.W., & Riddoch, M.J. (1985). Author's correction to "Routes to object constancy". *Quarterly Journal of Experimental Psychology, 37a,* 493–495.

Humphreys, G.W., & Riddoch, M.J. (1992). Interactions between object- and space-vision revealed through neuropsychology. In D.E. Meyer & S. Kornblum (Eds.), *Attention and performance XIV.* Hillsdale, NJ: Lawrence Erlbaum Associates Inc.

Humphreys, G.W., & Riddoch, M.J. (1993). Interactive attentional systems and unilateral visual neglect. In I.H. Robertson & J.C. Marshall (Eds.), *Unilateral neglect: Clinical and experimental studies* (pp. 139–167). Hove, UK: Lawrence Erlbaum Associates Ltd.

Humphreys, G.W., & Riddoch, M.J. (1994). From phenomena to models. *Neuropsychological Rehabilitation, 4,* 141–142.

Humphreys, G.W., Riddoch, M., Donnelly, N., Freeman, T., Boucart, M., & Muller, H.M. (1994). Intermediate visual processing and visual agnosia. In M.J. Farah & G. Ratcliff (Eds.), *The neuropsychology of high-level vision: Collected tutorial essays* (pp. 63–103). Hove, UK: Lawrence Erlbaum Associates, Ltd.

Hunkin, N.M., & Parkin, A.J. (1993). Recency judgements in Wernicke–Korsakoff and post-encephalitic amnesia: Influences of proactive interference and retention interval. *Cortex, 29,* 485–500.

Hunkin, N.M., Parkin, A.J., Bradley, V.A., Burrows, E.H., et al. (1995). Focal retrograde amnesia following closed head injury: A case study and theoretical account. *Neuropsychologia, 33,* 509–523.

Hunt, M. (1982). *The universe within: A new science explores the human mind*. New York: Touchstone.

Hunton, D.L., Cornetta, M., Shulman, G.L., Miezin, F.M., & Petersen, S.E. (1995). Common areas of parietal activation for shifts of spatial attention and tasks involving the conjunction of visual features. *Society Neuroscience Abstracts, 21*, 937.

Huppert, F.A., & Piercy, M. (1976). Recognition memory in amnesic patients: Effect of temporal context and familiarity of material. *Cortex, 12*, 8.

Huppert, F.A., & Piercy, M. (1979). Normal and abnormal forgetting in organic amnesia: Effect of locus of lesion. *Cortex, 15*, 385–390.

Huttenlocher, P.R. (1990). Morphometric study of the human cerebral cortex development. *Neuropsychologia, 28*, 517–527.

Ikeda, A., Luders, H.O., Shibasaki, H., Collura, T.F., Burgess, R.C., Morris, H.H. & Hamano, T. (1995). Movement related potentials associated with bilateral simultaneous and unilateral movements recorded from the human supplementary motor area. *Electroencephalography and Clinical Neurophysiology, 95*, 323–334.

Incisa Della Rochetta, A., & Milner, B. (1993). Strategic search and retrieval inhibition: The role of the frontal lobes. *Neuropsychologia, 31*, 503–525.

Indredavik, B., Bakke, F., Sohlberg, R. et al. (1991). Benefit of a stroke unit: A randomized controlled trial. *Stroke, 22*, 1026–1031.

Ingvar, D.H. (1983). Serial aspects of language and speech related to prefrontal cortical activity: A selective review. *Human Neurobiology, 2*, 177–189.

Innocenti, G.M., Aggoun-Zouaoui, D., & Lehmann, P. (1995). Cellular aspects of callosal connections and their development. *Neuropsychologia, 33*, 961–987.

Institute for Personality and Ability Testing (1973). *Measuring intelligence with culture fair tests*. Champaign, IL: Institute for Personality and Ability Testing.

Inui, T., Tanaka, S., Okada, T., Nishizawa, S., Katayama, M., & Konishi, J. (2000). Neural substrates for depth perception of the Necker cube: A functional magnetic resonance imaging study in human subjects. *Neuroscience Letter, 282*, 145–148.

Irle, E. (1987). Lesion size and recovery of function: Some new perspectives. *Brain Research Reviews, 12*, 307–320.

Irle, E., Peper, M., Wowra, B., & Kunze, S. (1994). Mood changes after surgery for tumors of the cerebral cortex. *Archives of Neurology, 51*, 164–174.

Itons-Peterson, M.J., & Fournier, J. (1986). External and internal memory aids: When and how often do we use them? *Journal of Experimental Psychology, 115*, 267–280.

Ivry, R.B., & Robertson, L.C. (1998). *The two sides of perception*. Cambridge, MA: MIT Press.

Jackson, S.R., & Husain, M. (1996). Visuomotor functions of the lateral pre-motor cortex. *Cortex, 6*, 788–810.

Jacobson, C.F. (1935). Function of the frontal association areas in primates. *Archives of Neurology and Psychiatry, 33*, 549–569.

Jacoby, L.L., & Dallas, M. (1981). On the relationship between autobiographical memory and perceptual learning. *Journal of Experimental Psychology: General, 110*, 306–340.

Jacoby, L.L., Ste-Marie, D., & Toth, J.P. (1993). Redefining automaticity: Unconscious influences, awareness, and control. In A.D. Baddeley & L. Weiskrantz (Eds.), *Attention: Selection, awareness, and control: A tribute to Donald Broadbent* (pp. 261–282). New York: Clarendon Press.

Jacoby, L.L., Toth, J.P., & Yonelinas, A.P. (1993). Separating conscious and unconscious influences of memory: Measuring recollection. *Journal of Experimental Psychology: General, 122*, 139–154.

Jaffe, P.G., & Katz, A.N. (1975). Attenuating anterograde amnesia in Korsakoff's psychosis. *Journal of Abnormal Psychology, 84*, 559–562.

Jahanshahi, M., & Frith, C.D. (1998). Willed action and its impairments. *Cognitive Neuropsychology, 15*, 483–533.

Jahanshahi, M., Jenkins, I.H., Brown, R.G., Marsden, C.D., Passingham, R.E., & Brooks, D.J. (1995). Self-initiated versus externally triggered movements. I. An investigation using measurment of regional cerebral blood flow with PET and movement-related potentials in normal and Parkinson's disease subjects. *Brain, 118*, 913–933.

James, W. (1890). *The principles of psychology*. New York: Holt, Rinehart & Winston.

Janowsky, J.S., Shimamura, A.P., & Kritchevsky, M. (1989). Cognitive impairments following frontal damage and its relevance to human amnesia. *Behavioral Neuroscience, 103*, 548–560.

Janowsky, J.S., Shimamura, A.P., & Squire, L.R. (1989). Source memory impairment in patients with frontal lobe lesions. *Neuropsychologia, 27*, 1043–1056.

Jason, G.W. (1985a). Gesture fluency after focal cortical lesions. *Neuropsychologia, 23*, 463–481.

Jason, G.W. (1985b). Manual sequence learning after focal cortical lesions. *Neuropsychologia, 23*, 483–496.

Jasper, H.H. (1995). A historical perspective: The rise and fall of prefrontal lobotomy. In H.H. Jasper, S.

Reggio, & P.S. Goldman-Rakic (Eds.), *Epilepsy and the functional anatomy of the frontal lobe. Advances in Neurology*, vol. 97 (pp. 97–114). New York: Raven Press.

Jeannerod, M. (1995). Mental imagery in the motor context. *Neuropsychologia, 33,* 1419–1432.

Jeannerod, M., Arbib, M.A., Rizzolatti, G., & Sakata, H. (1995). Grasping objects: The cortical mechanisms of visuomotor transformation. *Trends in Neuroscience, 18,* 314–320.

Jeeves, M.A., Silver, P.H., & Jacobson, I. (1988). Bimanual co-ordination in callosal agenesis and partial commissurotomy. *Neuropsychologia, 26,* 833–850.

Jenkins, J.J. (1974). Remember that old theory of memory? Well, forget it. *American Psychologist, 29* (11), 785–795.

Jenkins, W.M., Merzenich, M.M., & Recanzone, G. (1990). Neocortical representation dynamics in adult primates: Implications for neuropsychology. *Neuropsychologia, 28,* 573–584.

Jetter, W., Poser, U., Freeman Jr, R.B., & Markowitsch, H.J. (1986). A verbal long term memory deficit in frontal lobe damaged patients. *Cortex, 22,* 229–242.

Jiang, Y., Haxby, J.V., Martin, A., Ungerleider, L.G., & Parasuraman, R. (2000). Complementary neural mechanisms for tracking items in human working memory. *Science, 287* (5453), 643–646.

Johannsen, P., Jakobsen, J., Bruhn, P., Hansen, S.B., Gee, A., Stodkilde-Jorgensen, H., & Gjedde, A. (1997). Cortical sites of sustained and divided attention in normal elderly humans. *Neuroimage, 6,* 145–155.

Johnson, L.E. (1984). Bilateral visual cross-integration by human forebrain commissurotomy subjects. *Neuropsychologia, 22,* 167–175.

Johnston, S., Burgess, J., McMillan, T., & Greenwood, R. (1994). Management of adipsia by a behavioural modification technique. *Journal of Neurology, Neurosurgery and Psychiatry, 54,* 272–274.

Jones, B., & Mishkin, M. (1972). Limbic lesions and the problem of stimulus-reinforcement associations. *Experimental Neurology, 36,* 362–377.

Jones-Gotman, M., & Milner, B. (1977). Design fluency: The invention of nonsense drawings after focal cortical lesions. *Neuropsychologia, 15,* 653–674.

Jones-Gotman, M., Rouleau, I., & Snyder, P.J. (1997). Introduction: Clinical and research contributions of the intracarotid amobarbital procedure to neuropsychology. *Brain and Cognition, 33,* 1–6.

Joschko, M. (1986). Clinical and neuropsychological

outcome following psychosurgery. In I. Grant & K. Adams (Eds.), *Neuropsychological assessment of neuropsychiatric disorders.* New York: Oxford University Press.

Julesz, B. (1971). Foundations of cyclopean perception. Chicago: University of Chicago Press.

Juraska, J.M. (1986). Sex differences in developmental plasticity of behavior and the brain. In W.T. Greenough & J.M. Juraska (Eds.), *Developmental neuropsychobiology* (pp. 409–422). Orlando, FL: Academic Press.

Just, M.A., & Carpenter, P.A. (1992). A capacity theory of comprehension: Individual differences in working memory. *Psychological Review, 99,* 122–149.

Kagan, A., & Saling, M.M. (1988). *An introduction to Luria's Aphasiology.* Baltimore, MD: Paul H. Brookes.

Kahneman, D. (1973). *Attention and effort.* Englewood Cliffs, NJ: Prentice-Hall.

Kalaska, J.F., & Crammond, D.J. (1995). Deciding not to GO: Neuronal correlates of response selection in a GO/NOGO task in primate premotor and parietal cortex. *Cerebral Cortex, 5,* 410–428.

Kant, R., Smith-Seemiller, L., Isaac, G., & Duffy, J. (1997). Tc-HMPAO SPECT in persistent post-concussion syndrome after mild head injury: Comparison with MRI/CT. *Brain Injury, 11,* 115–124.

Kapur, N. (1995). Memory aids in the rehabilitation of memory-disordered patients. In A.D. Baddeley, B.A. Wilson, & F.N. Watts (Eds.), *Handbook of memory disorder* (pp. 533–557). Chichester, UK: Wiley.

Kapur, N. (1997). *Injured brains of medical minds.* Oxford: Oxford University Press.

Kapur, N., & Coughlan, A.C. (1980). Confabulation and frontal lobe dysfunction. *Journal of Neurology, Neurosurgery and Psychiatry, 43,* 461–463.

Kapur, N., Ellison, D., Smith, M.P., McLellan, D.L., & Burrows, E.H. (1992). Focal retrograde amnesia following bilateral temporal lobe pathology: A neuropsychological and magnetic resonance study. *Brain, 1,* 73–85.

Kapur, N., Friston, K.J., Young, A., Frith, C.D., & Frackowiak, R.S. (1995). Activation of human hippocampal formation during memory for faces: A PET study. *Cortex, 31,* 99–108.

Kapur, N., & Pearson, D. (1983). Memory symptoms and memory performances of neurological patients. *British Journal of Psychology, 74,* 409–415.

Kapur, N., Thompson, C., Cook, P., Lang, D., & Brice, J. (1996). Anterograde but not retrograde memory loss following combined mammillary body and medial thalamic lesions. *Neuropsychologia, 34*, 2–8.

Kapur, S., Craik, F.I., Tulving, E., Wilson, A.A., Houle, S., & Brown, G.M. (1994). Neuroanatomical correlates of encoding in episodic memory: Levels of processing effect. *Proceedings of the National Academy of Sciences USA, 91*, 2008–2011.

Karbe, H., Kessler, J., Herholz, K., Fink, G.R., & Heiss, W.D. (1995). Long-term prognosis of post-stroke aphasia studied with positron emission tomography. *Archives of Neurology, 52*, 186–190.

Karnath, H.O., & Ferber, S. (1999). Is space representation distorted in neglect? *Neuropsychologia, 37*, 7–15.

Karnath, H.O., Niemeier, M., & Dichgans, J. (1998). Space exploration in neglect. *Brain, 121* (12), 2357–2367.

Karnath, H.O., Wallesch, C.W., & Zimmerman, P. (1991). Mental planning and anticipatory processes with acute chronic frontal lobe lesions: A comparison of maze performance in routine and non-routine situations. *Neuropsychologia, 29*, 271–290.

Kartsounis, L.D., & Shallice, T. (1996). Modality specific semantic knowledge loss for unique items. *Cortex, 32*, 109–119.

Kassel, J.D. (1997). Smoking and attention: A review and reformulation of the stimulus-filter hypothesis. *Clinical Psychology Review, 17*, 451–478.

Katon, W., & Roy-Byrne, P.P. (1991). Mixed anxiety and depression. *Journal of Abnormal Psychology, 100*, 337–345.

Katz, D.I. (1992). Neuropathology and neurobehavioral recovery from closed head injury. *Journal of Head Trauma and Rehabilitation, 7*, 1–15.

Katz, D.I., & Alexander, M.P. (1994). Traumatic brain injury: Predicting the course of recovery and outcome of patients admitted to rehabilitation. *Archives of Neurology, 51*, 661–670.

Kawashima, R.K., Yamada, S., & Kinomura, T. et al. (1993). Regional blood flow changes of cortical motor areas and prefrontal areas in humans related to ipsilateral and contralateral hand movement. *Brain Research, 623*, 33–40.

Kay, J., & Ellis, A.W. (1987). A cognitive neuropsychological case study of anomia: Implications for psychological models of word retrieval. *Brain, 110*, 613–629.

Keating, E.G., & Gooley, S.G. (1988). Saccadic disorders caused by cooling the superior colliculus or the frontal eye field, or from combined lesions of both structures. *Brain Research, 438*, 247–255.

Keefe, R.S.E., Arnold, M.C., Bayen, U.J., & Harvey, P.D. (1999). Source monitoring deficits in patients with schizophrenia: A multinomial modelling. *Psychological Medicine, 29* (4), 903–914.

Keenan, S.S., & Brassel, E.G. (1974). A study of the factors related to prognosis for individual aphasic patients. *Journal of Speech and Hearing Disorders, 39*, 257–269.

Kelly-Hayes, M., & Paige, C. (1995). Assessment and psychologic factors in stroke rehabilitation. *Neurology, 45*, (2, Suppl. 1), S29–S32.

Kelly-Hayes, M., Wolf, P.A., Kannel, W.B., Sytowski, P.D., D'Agostino, R.B., & Gresham, G.E. (1988). Factors influencing survival and need for institutionalization following stroke: The Framlingham study. *Archives of Physiological Medicine and Rehabilitation, 69*, 415–418.

Kendrick, K.M., & Baldwin, B.A. (1987). Cells in temporal cortex of conscious sheep can respond preferentially to the sight of faces. *Science, 236*, 448–450.

Kennard, M.A. (1939). Alterations in response to visual stimuli following lesions to the frontal lobe in monkeys. *Archives of Neurology and Psychiatry, 41*, 1153–1165.

Kensinger, E.A., & Schacter, D.L. (1999). When true memories suppress false memories: Effects of ageing. *Cognitive Neuropsychology, 16* (3–5), 399–415.

Keppel, G., & Underwood, B.J. (1962). Proactive inhibition in short-term retention of single items. *Journal of Verbal Learning and Verbal Behaviour, 1*, 153–161.

Kertesz, A. (1979). *Aphasia and associated disorders*. New York: Grune & Stratton.

Kertesz, A. (1981). The anatomy of jargon. In J.W. Brown (Ed.), *Jargonaphasia* (pp. 63–112). New York: Academic Press.

Kertesz, A. (1985). Recovery and treatment. In K. Heilman & E. Valenstein (Eds.), *Clinical neuropsychology* (2nd ed., pp. 481–500). Oxford: Oxford University Press.

Kertesz, A. (1993a). Clinical forms of aphasia. *Acta Neurochirurgica Supplement* (Wien), *56*, 52–58.

Kertesz, A. (1993b). Recovery and treatment. In K.M. Heilman & E. Valenstein (Eds.), *Clinical neuropsychology* (3rd ed., Ch. 17, pp. 647–674). Oxford: Oxford University Press.

Kertesz, A. (1994). Localization and function. In A. Kertesz (Ed.), *Localization and neuroimaging in neuropsychology* (Ch. 1, pp. 1–33). San Diego: Academic Press.

Kertesz, A., Davidson, W., & McCabe, P. (1998). Primary progressive semantic aphasia: A case study. *Journal of the International Neuropsychological Society, 4*, 388–398.

Kertesz, A., & Hooper, P. (1982). Praxis and language: The extent and variety of apraxia in aphasia. *Neuropsychologia, 20*, 275–286.

Kertesz, A., & Naeser, M.A. (1994). Anatomical asymmetries and cerebral lateralization. In A. Kertescz (Ed.), *Localization and neuroimaging in neuropsychology* (Ch. 8, pp. 213–239). San Diego: Academic Press.

Kertesz, A., Sheppard, A., & MacKenzie, R. (1982). Localisation in transcortical sensory aphasia. *Archives of Neurology, 39*, 475–458.

Kilpatrick, C., Cook, M., Murrie, V., & Andrewes, D.G. (1997). Degree of left hippocampal atrophy correlates with severity of neuropsychological deficits. *Seizure, 6*, 213–218.

Kim, J.J., & Thompson, R.F. (1997). Cerebellar circuits and synaptic mechanisms involved in classical eyeblink conditioning. *Trends in Neurosciences, 20*, 177–181.

Kimberg, D.Y., D'Esposito, M., & Farah, M.J. (1997). Cognitive functions in the prefrontal cortex: Working memory and executive control. *Current Directions in Psychological Science, 6*. 185–192.

Kimura, D. (1979). Neuromotor mechanisms in the evolution of human communication. In H.D. Steklis & M.J. Raleigh (Eds.), *Neurobiology of social communication in primates* (pp. 197–219). New York: Academic Press.

Kimura, D. (1980). Neuromotor mechanisms in the evolution of human communication. In H.D. Steklis & M.J. Raleigh, (Eds.), *Neurobiology of social communication in primates: An evolutionary perspective*. New York: Academic Press.

Kimura, D. (1982). Left-hemisphere control of oral and brachial movements and their relationship to communication. *Philosophical Transactions of the Royal Society of London, Series B, 298*, 135–149.

Kimura, D. (1992). Sex differences in the brain. *Scientific American, 267*, 118–125.

Kimura, D., & Archibald, Y. (1974). Motor functions of the left hemisphere. *Brain, 97*, 337–350.

Kimura, D., & Watson, N. (1989). The relation between oral movement control and speech. *Brain and Language, 37*, 565–590.

Kinsbourne, M. (1971). The minor cerebral injury as a source of aphasic speech. *Archives of Neurology, 25*, 302–306.

Kinsbourne, M. (1981). Cognitive deficit and the unity of brain organisation: Goldstein's perspective updated. *Journal of Communication Disorders, 14*, 181–194.

Kinsbourne, M. (1993). Orientational bias model of unilateral neglect: Evidence from attentional gradients within hemispace. In I.H. Robertson & J.C. Marshall (Eds.), *Unilateral neglect: Clinical and experimental studies* (pp. 63–86). Hove, UK: Lawrence Erlbaum Associates, Ltd.

Kinsbourne, M., & Warrington, E.K. (1962). A variety of reading disability associated with right hemisphere lesions. *Journal of Neurology, Neurosurgery and Psychiatry, 25*, 339–344.

Kinsella, G., Moran, C., Ford, B., & Ponsford, J. (1988). Emotional disorder and its assessment within the severe head injured population. *Psychological Medicine, 18*, 57–63.

Kinsella, G., Olver, J., Ng, K., Packer, S., & Stark, K. (1993). Analysis of the syndrome of unilateral neglect. *Cortex, 29*, 135–140.

Kintsch, W. (1998). *Comprehension: A paradigm for cognition*. Cambridge, UK: Cambridge University Press.

Klein, R., & Harper, J. (1956). The problem of agnosia in the light of pure word deafness. *Journal of Mental Science, 102*, 112–120.

Kleist, K. (1923). Kriegsverletzungen des Gehirns in ihrer Bedeutung für die Hirnlokalisation und hirnpathologie, In O. von Schjernimg (Ed.), *Handbuch der arztlichen Erfahrung im Weltkriege, 1914/1918* (Vol. 4). Leipzig: Barth.

Kling, A., & Brothers, L.A. (1992), *The amygdala: Neurobiological aspects of emotion, memory, and mental dysfunction*. New York: Wiley–Liss.

Kling, A., Lancaster, J., & Benitone, J. (1970). Amygdalectomy in the free-ranging vervet (*Cercopithecus aethiops*). *Journal of Psychiatric Research, 7*, 191–199.

Klosowska, D. (1976). Relation between ability to program actions and location of brain damage. *Polish Psychological Bulletin, 7*, 245–255.

Kluver, H., & Bucy, P.C. (1937). "Psychic Blindness" and other symptoms following temporal lobectomy. *American Journal of Physiology, 119*, 352–353.

Kluver, H., & Bucy, P.C. (1939). Preliminary analysis of the temporal lobes in monkeys. *Archives of Neurology and Psychiatry, 42*. 979–1000.

Knight, R.T., Grabowecky, M.P., & Scabini, O. (1995). Role of human prefrontal cortex in attention control. *Advances in Neurology, 66*, 21–34.

Knoll, N.E.A., & Tu, S.F. (1988). The bizarre mnemonic. *Psychological Research, 50*, 28–37.

Knowlton, B.J., & Fanselow, M.S. (1998). The hippocampus, consolidation and on-line memory. *Current Opinion in Neurobiology, 8*, 293–296.

Koechlin, E., Basso, G., Pietrini, P., Panzer, S., Grafman, J. (1999). The role of the anterior prefrontal cortex in human cognition. *Nature, 399* (6732), 148–151.

Kohonen, T. (1990). Notes on neural computing and associative memory. In J.L. McGaugh, N.M. Weinberger, & G. Lynch (Eds.), *Brain organisation and memory: Cells, systems, and circuits* (pp. 323–337). New York/Oxford: Oxford University Press.

Kolb, B. (1990). Recovery from occipital stroke: A self-report and an enquiry into the visual processes. *Canadian Journal of Psychology, 44*, 130–147.

Kolb, B. (1995). *Brain plasticity and behaviour*. Hillsdale, NJ: Lawrence Erlbaum Associates Inc.

Kolb, B., & Cioe, J. (1996). Sex related differences in function following prefrontal lobe lesions in rats. *Behavioral Neuroscience, 110*, 1271–1281.

Kolb, B., & Elliott, W. (1987). Recovery from early cortical damage in rats: Effects of experience on anatomy and behaviour following frontal lesions at one or five days of age. *Behavioural Brain Research, 26*, 47–56.

Kolb, B., Gibb, R., & van der Kooy, D. (1992). Cortical and striatal structure and connectivity are altered by neonatal hemidecortication in rats. *Journal of Comparative Neurology, 322*, 311–324.

Kolb, B., & Milner, B. (1981a). Observations on spontaneous facial expressions after focal cerebral excisions and after intracarotid injection of sodium amytal. *Neuropsychologia, 19*, 505–514.

Kolb, B., & Milner, B. (1981b). Performance of complex arm and facial movements after focal brain lesions. *Neuropsychologia, 19*, 491–503.

Kolb, B., & Stewart, J. (1991). Sex related differences in dendritic branching of cells in the prefrontal cortex in rats. *Journal of Neuroendocrinology, 3*, 95–99.

Kolb, B., & Stewart, J. (1995). Changes in neonatal gonadal hormonal environment prevent behavioral sparing and cortical morphogenisis after early frontal lesions in male and female rats. *Behavioral Neuroscience, 109*, 285–294.

Kolb, B., & Whishaw, I.Q. (1989). Plasticity in the neocortex: Mechanisms underlying recovery from early brain damage. *Progress in Neurobiology, 32*. 235–276.

Kolk, H., Van Grunsvan, M.J.F., & Keyser, A. (1985). On parallelism between production and comprehension in agrammatism. In M.L. Kean (Ed.), *Agrammatism*. Orlando, FL: Academic Press.

Kolk, H., & Weuts, M. (1996). Judgements of semantic anomaly in agrammatic patients: Argument movement, syntactic complexity, and the use of heuristics. *Brain and Language, 54*, 86–135.

Kooistra, C.A., & Heilman, K.M. (1989). Hemispheral visual inattention masquerading as hemianopia. *Neurology, 39*, 1125–1127.

Kopelman, M.D. (1985). Rates of forgetting in Alzheimer-type dementias and Korsakoff's syndrome. *Neuropsychologia, 23*, 623–638.

Kopelman, M.D. (1987). Two types of confabulation. *Journal of Neurology, Neurosurgery and Psychiatry, 50*, 1482–1487.

Kopelman, M.D. (1999). Varieties of false-memory. *Cognitive Neuropsychology, 16*, 197–214.

Kopelman, M.D., Guinan, E.M., & Lewis, P.D.R. (1995). Delusional memory and frontal lobe dysfunction. In R. Campbell & M.A. Conway (Eds.), *Broken memories: Case studies in memory impairment* (Ch.11, pp. 137–153). Oxford: Blackwell.

Kopelman, M.D., & Stanhope, N. (1997). Rates of forgetting in organic amnesia following temporal lobe, diencephalic, or frontal lobe lesions. *Neuropsychology, 11*, 343–356.

Kopelman, M.D., & Stanhope, N. (1998). Recall and recognition memory in patients with focal frontal, temporal lobe and diencephalic lesions. *Neuropsychologia, 36*, 785–796.

Koski, L., & Paus, T. (2000). Functional connectivity of the anterior cingulate cortex within the human frontal lobe: A brain-mapping meta-analysis. *Experimental Brain Research, 133*, 55–65.

Kosslyn, S.M., & Shin, L.M. (1994). Visual mental images in the brain: Current issues. In M.J. Farah & G. Ratcliff (Eds.), *The neuropsychology of high-level vision: Collected tutorial essays* (pp. 269–299). Hove, UK: Lawrence Erlbaum Associates Ltd.

Koutstaal, W., Schacter, D.L., Galluccio, L., & Stofer, K.A. (1999). Reducing gist-based false recognition in older adults: Encoding and retrieval manipulations. *Psychology and Aging, 14*, 220–237.

Kovner, R., Mattis, S., & Pass, R. (1985). Some amnesic patients can freely recall large amounts of information in new contexts. *Journal of Clinical and Experimental Neuropsychology, 7*, 395–411.

Krause, B.J., Schmidt, D., Mottaghy, F.M., Taylor, J., Halsband, U., Herzog, H., Tellmann, L., & Muller-Gartner, H.W. (1999). Episodic retrieval activates the precuneus irrespective of the imagery content of word pair associates: A PET study. *Brain, 122* (2), 255–263.

Krause, K.H., Dresel, S.H., Krause, J., Kung, H.F., & Tatsch, K. (2000). Increased striatal dopamine transporter in adult patients with attention deficit hyperactivity disorder: Effects of methylphenidate as measured by single photon emission computed tomography. *Neuroscience Letters, 12* (285), 107–110.

Kremer, B., Weber, B., & Hayden, M.R. (1992). New insights into the clinical features, pathogenesis and molecular genetics of Huntington disease. *Brain Pathology, 2*, 321–335.

Kritchevsky, M., Zouzounis, J., & Squire, L.R. (1997). Transient global amnesia and functional retrograde amnesia: Contrasting examples of episodic memory loss. *Philosophical Transactions of the Royal Society London, Series B, 352*, 1747–1754.

Kurlychek, R.T. (1983). Use of a digital alarm chronograph as a memory aid in early dementia. *Clinical Gerontologist, 1*, 93–94.

Kvavilashvili, L., & Ellis, J. (1996) Varieties of intention: Some distinctions and classifications. In M. Brandimonte, G.O. Einstein, & M. A. McDaniel (Eds.), *Prospective memory: Theory and applications.* Hillsdale, NJ: Lawrence Erlbaum Associates Inc.

LaBar, K.S., Gitelman, D.R., Parrish, T.B., & Mesulam, M. (1999). Neuroanatomic overlap of working memory and spatial attention networks: A functional MRI comparison within subjects. *Neuroimage, 10*, 695–704.

LaBaw, W.L. (1968). Thirty-three months of recovery from trauma, a subjective report: Closed brain injury. *Medical Times, 96*, 821–829.

La Berge, D. (1995). *Attentional processing.* Cambridge, MA: Harvard University Press.

Ladavas, E. (1987). Is the hemispatial deficit produced by right parietal damage associated with retinal or gravitational coordinates? *Brain, 110*, 167–180.

Laiacona, M., Barbarotto, R., & Capitani E. (1993). Perceptual and associative knowledge in category specific impairment of semantic memory: A study of two cases. *Cortex, 29*, 727–740.

Lamb, M.R., Robertson, L.C., & Knight, R.T. (1990). Component mechanisms underlying the processing of hierarchically organised patterns: Inferences from patients with unilateral cortical lesions. *Journal of Experimental Psychology: Learning, Memory and Cognition, 16*, 471–483.

Lambert, A.J. (1991). Interhemispheric interaction in the split-brain. *Neuropsychologia, 29*, 941–948.

Lamme, V.A., & Spekreijse, H. (2000). Modulations of primary visual cortex activity representing attentive and conscious scene perception. *Frontiers in Bioscience. 5*, D232–243.

Landauer, T.K., & Bjork, R.A. (1978). Optimal rehearsal patterns and name learning. In M.M. Gruneberg, P.E. Morris & R.N. Sykes (Eds.), *Prac-tical aspects of memory* (pp. 625–633). London: Academic Press.

Lane, R.D., Reiman, E.M., Ahern, G.L., Schwartz, G.E., & Davidson, R.J. (1997). Neuroanatomical correlates of happiness, sadness, and disgust. *American Journal of Psychiatry, 154* (7), 926–931.

Langdon, D.W., & Warrington, E.K. (1997). The abstraction of numerical relations: A role for the right hemisphere in arithmetic? *Journal of the International Neuropsychological Society, 3*, 260–268.

Lange, C.G., & James, W. (1922). *The emotions.* Baltimore: Williams & Wilkins.

Larsen, B., Skinhoj, E., & Lassen, N.A. (1978). Variations in regional cortical blood flow in the right and left hemispheres. *Brain, 101.* 193–209.

Lassek, A.M. (1970). *The unique legacy of Doctor Hughlings Jackson.* Springfield, IL: Charles C. Thomas.

Lassen, N.A., Ingvar, D.H., & Skinhoj, E. (1978). Brain function and blood flow. *Scientific American. 239*, 62–71.

Lavie, N. (1995). Perceptual load as a necessary condition for selective attention. *Journal of Experimental Psychology: Human Perception and Performance. 21*, 451–468.

Lazarus, A.A. (1966). Behaviour rehearsal vs. nondirective therapy vs. advice in effecting behaviour change. *Behaviour Research and Therapy. 4*, 209–212.

Lazarus, R.S. (1991). Progress on a cognitive-motivational relational theory of emotion. *American Psychologist, 46*, 819–834.

Leckman, J.F., Pauls, D.L., Peterson, B.S., Riddle, M.A., Anderson, G.M., & Cohen, D.J. (1992). Pathogenesis of Tourette syndrome: Clues from the clinical phenotype and natural history. *Advances in Neurology, 58*, 15–24.

Lecours, A.R., Chain, F., Poncet, M., Nespoulos, J.-L., & Joanette, Y. (1992). Paris 1908: The hot summer of aphasiology or a season in the life of a chair. *Brain and Language, 42*, 105–152.

Lecours, A.R., Osborn, E., Travis, L., Rouillon, F., & Lavallee-Huyn, G. (1981). Jargons. In J.W. Brown (Ed.), *Jargonaphasia* (pp. 39–61). New York: Academic Press

LeDoux, G., & Pitts, C. (1995). A case study evaluation of the effects of different techniques for the treatment of anomia. In R.S. Berndt & C.C. Mitchum (Eds.), *Cognitive neuropsychological approaches to the treatment of language disorders* (pp. 51–65). Hove, UK: Lawrence Erlbaum Associates Ltd.

LeDoux, J.E. (1993). Emotional networks in the brain. In M. Lewis, & J.M. Haviland, (Eds.), *Handbook of emotions* (pp. 109–119). New York: Guilford Press.

LeDoux, J.E. (1995). In search of an emotional system in the brain leaping from fear to emotion and consciousness. In M.S. Gazzaniga (Ed.), *The cognitive neurosciences* (pp. 1049–1063). Cambridge, MA: MIT Press.

LeDoux, J.E. (2000). Cognitive-emotional interactions: Listen to the brain. In R.D. Lane & L. Nadel (Eds). *Cognitive neuroscience of emotion: Series in affective science* (pp. 129–155). New York: Oxford University Press.

LeDoux, J.E., & Muller, J. (1997). Emotional memory and psychopathology. *Philosophical Transactions of the Royal Society London, Series B, 29* (352), 1719–1726

Lee, G.P., Bechara, A., Adolphs, R., Arena, J., Meador, K.J., Loring, D.W., & Smith, J.R. (1998). Clinical and physiological effects of stereotaxic bilateral amygdalotomy for intractable aggression. *Journal of Neuropsychiatry and Clinical Neuroscience, 10*, 413–420.

Lee, G.P., Loring, D.W., Meader, K.J., & Brooks, B.B. (1990). Hemispheric specialization for emotional expression: A reexamination of results from intracarotid administration of sodium amobarbital. *Brain and Cognition, 12*, 267–280.

Lehmkuhl, G., Poeck, K., & Willmes, K. (1983). Ideomotor apraxia and aphasia: An examination of types and manifestations of apraxia syndromes. *Neuropsychologia, 21*, 199–212.

Leng, N.R.C., & Parkin, A.J. (1989). Aetiological variation in the amnesic syndrome: Comparisons using the Brown–Peterson task. *Cortex, 25*, 251–259.

Lenneberg, E.H. (1967). *Biological foundations of language*. New York: Wiley.

Leonard, C.M., Rolls, E.T., Wilson, F.A.W., & Baylis, G.C. (1985). Neurons in the amygdala of the monkey with responses to selective for faces. *Behavioural Brain Research, 15*, 159–176.

Leonard, G., & Milner, B. (1991a). Contribution of the right frontal lobe to the encoding and recall of kinaesthetic distance of information. *Neuropsychologia, 29*, 47–58.

Leonard, G., & Milner, B. (1991b). Recall of the end-position of examiner-defined arm movements by patients with frontal- or temporal-lobe lesions. *Neuropsychologia, 29*, 629–640.

Leopold, D.A., & Logothetis, N.K. (1996). Activity changes and early visual cortex reflect monkey's percepts during binocular rivalry. *Nature, 379*, 549.

Lesser, R., & Algar, L. (1995). Towards combining the cognitive neuropsychological and the pragmatic in aphasia therapy. In R.S. Berndt & C.C. Mitchum

(Eds.), *Cognitive neuropsychological approaches to the treatment of language disorders* (pp. 67–92). Hove, UK: Lawrence Erlbaum Associates Ltd.

Levelt, W.J.M., Praamstra, P., Meyer, A.S., Helenius, P., & Salmelin, R. (1998). An MEG study of picture naming. *Journal of Cognitive Neuroscience, 10*, 553–567.

Levin, H.S., Mattis, S. Ruff, R.M., Eisenberg, H.M., Marshall, L.F., et al. (1987). Neurobehavioural outcome following major head injury: A three centre study. *Journal of Neurosurgery, 62*, 96–100.

Levine, B., Robertson, I.H., Clare, L., Carter, G., Hong, J., Wilson, B.A., Duncan, J., & Stuss, D.T. (2000). An experimental–clinical validation of goal management training. *Journal of the International Neuropsychological Society, 6*, 299–312.

Levitan, C., Ward, P.B., & Catts, S.V. (1999). Superior temporal gyral volumes and laterality correlates of auditory hallucinations in schizophrenia. *Biological Psychiatry, 46*, 955–962.

Levy, J. (1974). Cerebral asymmetries as manifested in split-brain man. In M. Kinsbourne & W.L. Smith (Eds.), *Hemispheric disconnection and cerebral function*. Springfield, IL: Charles C. Thomas.

Levy, J. (1985). Interhemispheric collaboration: Single-mindedness in the asymmetric brain. In C.T. Best (Ed.), *Hemispheric function and collaboration in the child* (pp. 11–31). New York: Academic Press.

Levy, J.A., Parasuraman, R., Greenwood, P.M., Dukoff, R., & Sunderland, T. (2000). Acetylcholine affects the spatial scale of attention: Evidence from Alzheimer's disease. *Neuropsychology, 14*, 288–298.

Levy, J., Trevarthen, C., & Sperry, R.W. (1972). Perception of bilateral chimeric figures following hemispheric disconnection. *Brain, 95*, 61–78.

Levy, R.I. (1984). Emotion, knowing and culture. In R.A. Shweder & R. A. LeVine (Eds.), *Culture theory: Essays on mind, self, and emotion* (pp. 214–237). Cambridge, UK: Cambridge University Press.

Lewin, R. (1993). *The origin of modern humans*. New York: W.H. Freeman.

Lewinsohn, P.M., Danaher, B.G., & Kikel, S. (1977). Visual imagery as a mnemonic for brain-injured persons. *Journal of Consulting and Clinical Psychology, 45*, 717–723.

Lezak, M. (1995). *Neuropsychological assessment* (3rd ed.). Oxford: Oxford University Press.

L'hermitte, F. (1983). "Utilization behaviour" and its relation to lesions of the frontal lobes. *Brain, 106* (2), 237–255.

L'hermitte, F. (1986). Human anatomy and the frontal lobes. Part II: Patient behaviour in complex and social situations: The "environmental dependency syndrome". *Annals of Neurology, 19*, 335–343.

L'hermitte, F., & Derouesne, J. (1974). Paraphasies et jargonaphasies dans le language oral avec conservation de langage écrit: Génese des neologismes. *Review Neurolique* (Paris), *130*. 21–38.

L'hermitte, F., Pillon, B., & Serdaru, M. (1986). Human anatomy and the frontal lobes. Part I: Imitation and utilization behaviour: A neuropsychological study of 75 patients. *Annals of Neurology, 19*, 326–334.

Lichtheim, L. (1885). On aphasia. *Brain, 7*, 433–484.

Liepmann, H. (1900). Das Krankheitschild der Apraxie (motorischen Asymbolie). *Monatsschrift für Psychiatrie und Neurologie, 8*, 15–44, 102–132, 182–197.

Liepmann, H.K. (1913). *Motor aphasia, anarthria, and apraxia*. In Transactions of the 17th international congress of medicine, Section XI, Part II, pp. 97–106.

Liepmann, H., & Maas, O. (1907). Fall von linksseitiger Agraphie und Apraxie bei rechts-seitiger Lahmung. *Journal of Psychology and Neurology, 10*, 214–227.

Lindsay, P.H., & Norman, D.A. (1976). *Human information processing* (2nd ed.). New York: Academic Press.

Lindsley, D.B. (1960). Attention, consciousness, sleep and wakefulness. In J. Field, H.W. Magoun, & V.E. Hall (Eds.), *Handbook of physiology* (Vol. 3, pp. 1553–1593). Washington, DC: American Physiological Society.

Linge, F.R. (1980). What does it feel like to be brain damaged? *Canada's Mental Health, 28*, 4–7.

Linge, F.R. (1990). Faith, hope and love: Nontraditional therapy in recovery from serious head injury, a personal account. *Canadian Journal of Psychology, 44*, 116–129

Liotti, M., & Tucker, D.M. (1995). Emotion in asymmetric corticolimbic networks. In R.J. Davidson & K. Hugdahl (Eds.), *Brain asymmetry* (pp. 389–424). Cambridge, MA: MIT Press.

Lissauer, H. (1890/1988). A case of visual agnosia with a contribution to theory. *Cognitive Neuropsychology, 5*, 157–192.

Livingstone, M.S., & Hubel, D.H. (1987). Connections between layer 4B of area 17 and the thick cytochrome oxidase stripes of area 18 in the squirrel monkey. *Journal of Neuroscience, 7*, 3371–3377.

Llinas, R., Ribary, U., Contreras, D., & Pedroarena, C. (1998). The neuronal basis for consciousness. *Philosophical Transactions of the Royal Society London, Series B, 353*, 1841–1849.

Loftus, E.F., Miller, D.G., & Burns, H.J. (1978). Semantic integration of verbal information into a visual memory. *Journal of Experimental Psychology: Human Learning, 4*, 19–31.

Logie, R.H., Cubelli, R., Della Sala, S., Alberoni, M., & Nichelli, P. (1988). Anarthria and verbal short-term memory. In J. Crawford & D. Parker (Eds.), *Developments in clinical and experimental neuropsychology* (pp. 203–211). New York: Plenum Press.

Logie, R.H., Gilhooly, K.J., & Wynn V. (1994). Counting on working memory in arithmetic problem solving. *Memory and Cognition, 22*, 395–410.

Logothetis, N.K., & Pauls J. (1995). Psychophysical and physiological evidence for viewer-centered object representations in the primate. *Cerebral Cortex, 5*, 270–288.

Luders, H., Lesser, R.P., Dinner, D.S., Hahn, J.F., Morris, S.H. et al. (1988). Localization of cortical function: New information from extraoperative monitoring of the patients with epilepsy. *Epilepsia, 29* (Suppl. 2): S56-S65.

Luders, H. Lesser, R.P., Hahn, J. et al. (1991). Basal temporal language area. *Brain, 114*, 743–754.

Ludlow, C.L., Rosenberg, J., Fair, C., Buck, D., Schesselman, S., & Salazar, A. (1986). Brain lesions associated with nonfluent aphasia fifteen years following penetrating head injury. *Brain, 109* (1): 55–80.

Luria, A.R. (1960). Differences between disturbances in speech and writing in Russian and in French. *International Journal of Slavic Linguistics and Poetics, 3*, 13–22.

Luria, A.R. (1966). *Human brain and psychological processes*. New York: Harper & Row.

Luria A.R. (1970). The functional organization of the brain. *Scientific American, 222*, 66–72.

Luria, A.R. (1973). *The working brain*. Harmondsworth, UK: Penguin.

Luria, A.R. (1976). *Fundamentals of neurolinguistics*. New York: Basic Books.

Luria, A.R. (1980). Neuropsychology in the local diagnosis of brain damage. *International Journal of Clinical Neuropsychology, 2*, 1–7.

Luria, A.R., & Hutton, J.T. (1977). A modern assessment of the basic forms of aphasia. *Brain and Language, 4*, 129–151.

Luria, A.R., Pravdina-Vinarskaya, E.N., & Yarbuss, A.L. (1963). Disorders of ocular movement in a case of simultanagnosia. *Brain, 86*, 219–228.

Lyle, O.E., & Gottesman, I.I. (1977). Premorbid psychometric indicators of the new gene for Huntington's disease. *Journal of Consulting and Clinical Psychology, 45*, 1011–1022.

Lynch, J.C., & McLaren, J.W. (1989). Deficits of visual attention and saccadic eye movements after lesions of the parietooccipital cortex in monkeys. *Journal of Neurophysiology, 61*, 4–90.

Macaruso, P., McCloskey, M., & Aliminosa, D. (1993) The functional architecture of the cognitive numerical-processing: Evidence from a patient with multiple impairments. *Cognitive Neuropsychology, 10*, 341–376.

MacDonald, A.W., Cohn, J.D., Stenger, V.A., & Carter, C.S. (2000). Dissociating the role of the dorsolateral prefrontal and anterior cingulate cortex in cognitive control. *Science, 9* (288), 1835–1838.

MacLean, P.D. (1993). Cerebral evolution of emotion. In M. Lewis & J. Haviland (Eds.), *Handbook of emotions*. New Brunswick, NJ: Guilford Press.

Macmillan, M.B. (1986). *A wonderful journey through skull and brains: The travels of Mr Gage's tamping iron*. New York: Academic Press.

Maher, L.M., Gonzalez-Rothi, L.J., & Heilman, K.M. (1994). Lack of error awareness in an aphasic patient with relatively preserved auditory comprehension. *Brain and Language, 46*, 402–418.

Mai, N., Bolsinger, P., Avarello, M., Diener, H.C., & Dichgans, J. (1988). Control of isometric finger force in patients with cerebellar disease. *Brain, 111*, 973–998.

Malia, K., Powell, G., & Torode, S. (1995). Coping and psycho-social function after brain injury. *Brain Injury, 9*, 607–618.

Malloy, P., Bihrle, A., Duffy, J., & Cimino, C. (1993). The orbito medial frontal syndrome. *Archives of Clinical Neuropsychology, 8*, 185–201.

Malloy, P.F., & Richardson, E.D. (1994). Assessment of frontal lobe functions. *Journal of Neuropsychiatry, 6*, 399–409.

Mandler, G. (1980). Recognising: The judgement of previous occurrence. *Psychological Review, 87*, 252–271.

Manni, E., & Petrosini, L. (1997). Luciani's work on the cerebellum a century later. *Trends in Neurosciences, 20*, 112–116.

Manning, L., & Warrington, E.K. (1996). Two routes to naming: A case study. *Neuropsychologia, 34*, 809–817.

Manns, J.R., & Squire, L.R. (1999). Impaired recognition memory on doors and people test associated with damage limited to the hippocampal region. *Hippocampus, 9*, 495–499.

Marie, P. (1906). Revision de l'aphasie de 1861 à 1866; Essai de critique historique sur la génese de la doctrine de Broca. *Semaine Médicale 26*, 241–247.

Mark, V.W., Kooistra, C.A., & Heilman, K.M. (1988). Hemispatial neglect affected by non-neglected stimuli. *Neurology, 38*, 1207–1211.

Markowitsch, H.J. (1988). Anatomical and functional organization of the primate prefrontal cortical system. In H.D. Steklis & J. Erwin (Eds.), *Comparative primate biology: Vol 4. Neurosciences* (pp. 99–153). New York: Alan R. Liss.

Markowitsch, H.J., Calabrese, P., Haupts, M., Durwen, H.F., Liess, J., & Gehlen, W. (1993). Searching for the anatomical basis of retrograde amnesia. *Journal of Clinical and Experimental Neuropsychology, 15*, 947–967.

Markowitsch, H.J., Calabrese, P., Wurker, M., Durwen, H.F., Kessler, J., Babinsky, R., Brechtelsbauer, D., Heuser, L., & Gehlen, W. (1994). The amygdala's contribution to memory: A study on two patients with Urbach–Wiethe disease. *Neuroreport, 5*, 1349–1352.

Markowitsch, H.J., & Kessler, J. (2000). Massive impairment in executive functions with partial preservation of other cognitive functionas: The case of a young patient with severe degeneration of the prefrontal cortex. *Experimental Brain Research, 133*, 94–102.

Marlowe, W.B., Mancall, E.L., & Thomas, J.J. (1975). Complete Kluver–Bucy syndrome in man. *Cortex, 11*, 53–59.

Marsden, C.D. (1982). The mysterious motor function of the basal ganglia: The Robert Wartenberg Lecture. *Neurology, 32*, 514–539.

Marsden, C.D. (1987). What do the basal ganglia tell premotor cortical areas? In *Motor areas of the cerebral cortex: Ciba Foundation Symposium* (Vol. 132, pp. 282–300). Chichester: Wiley.

Marsden, C.D. (1994). Parkinson's disease. *Journal of Neurology, Neurosurgery and Psychiatry, 57*, 672–681.

Marshall, J.C., & Halligan, P.W. (1988). Blindsight and insight in visual spatial neglect. *Nature, 336*, 766–767.

Marshall, J.C., & Halligan, P.W. (1995). Seeing the forest for the trees? *Nature, 373*, 521–523.

Marshall, J.C., & Newcombe, F. (1973). Patterns of paralexia: A psycholinguistic approach. *Journal of Psycholinguistic Research, 2*, 175–199.

Marteniuk, R.G., MacKenzie, C.L., Jeannerod, M., Athenes, S., & Dugas, C. (1987). Constraints on human arm movement trajectories. *Canadian Journal of Psychology, 41*, 365–378.

Martin, A., Wiggs, C.L., Ungerleider, L.G., & Haxby, J.V. (1996). Neural correlates of category-specific knowledge. *Nature, 479*, 649–652.

Martin, N., & Saffran, E.M. (1990). Repetition and verbal STM in transcortical sensory aphasia: A case study. *Brain and Language*, *39*, 254–288.

Martin, R.C. (1993). Short-term memory and sentence processing: Evidence from neuropsychology. *Memory and Cognition, 21*, 176–183.

Martin, R.C., & Breedin, S.D. (1992). Dissociation between speech perception and phonological short-term memory deficits. *Cognitive Neuropsychology*, *9*, 509–534.

Martin, R.C., & Romani, C. (1994). Verbal working memory and sentence comprehension: A multiple-components view. *Neuropsychology*, *8*, 506–523.

Martin, R.C., & Romani, C. (1995). Remembering stories but not words, in R. Campbell & M.A. Conway (Eds.), *Broken memories: Case studies in memory impairment* (Ch. 19, pp. 267–284). Oxford: Blackwell.

Martin, T.A., Keating, J.G., Goodkin, H.P., Batian, A.J., & Thach, W.T. (1996a). Throwing while looking through prisms. I. Focal olivocerebellar lesions impair adaption. *Brain, 119*, 1183–1198.

Martin, T.A., Keating, J.G., Goodkin, H.P., Batian, A.J., & Thach, W.T. (1996b). Throwing while looking through prisms. II. Specificity and storage of multiple gaze-throwing calibrations, *Brain, 119*, 1199–1211.

Martzke, J.S., Swan, C.S., & Varney, N.R. (1991). Postraumatic anosmia and orbital frontal damage: Neuropsychological and neuropsychiatric correlates. *Neuropsychology*, *5*, 213–225.

Masdeau, J.C., Schoene, W.C., & Funkenstein, H. (1978). Aphasia following infarction of the left supplementary area: A clinicopathologic study. *Neurology*, *28*, 1220–1223.

Masterton, J., Coltheart, M., & Meara, P. (1985). Surface dyslexia in a language without irregularly spelled words. In K.E. Patterson, J.C. Marshall, & M. Coltheart (Eds.), *Surface dyslexia* (pp. 215–223). Hillsdale, NJ: Lawrence Erlbaum Associates Inc.

Matkovic, Z., Oxbury, S.M., Hiorns, R.W., et al. (1995). Hippocampal neuronal density correlates with preoperative non-verbal memory in patients with temporal lobe epilepsy. *Epilepsia, 36*, S93.

Matotek, K.M. (1987). *Remediation of memory for prose in memory impaired individuals: Evaluation of the Porst technique.* Unpublished Msc Thesis, University of Melbourne.

Mattingley, J.B., Bradshaw, J.L., Bradshaw, J.A., & Nettleton, N.C. (1994). Recovery from directional hypokinesia and bradykinesia in unilateral neglect. *Journal of Clinical and Experimental Neuropsychology, 16*, 861–876.

Mattingley, J.B., Davis, G., & Driver, J. (1997). Preattentive filling-in of visual surfaces in parietal extinction. *Science, 275*, 671–672.

Mattingley, J.B., Husain, M., Rorden, C., Kennard, C., & Driver, J. (1998). Motor role of human inferior parietal lobe revealed in unilateral neglect patients. *Nature, 12*, 392.

Mayberg, H.S. (1997). Limbic–cortical dysregulation: A proposed model of depression. *Journal of Clinical Neuroscience, 9*, 471–481.

Mayes, A.R., Meudell, P., & Som, S. (1981). Further similarities between amnesia and normal attenuated memory: Effects with paired associate learning and contextual shifts. *Neuropsychologia, 19*, 655–664.

Mayes, A.R., Van Eijk, R., & Isaac, C.L. (1995). Assessment of familiarity and recollection in the false fame paradigm using a modified process dissociation procedure. *Journal of the International Neuropsychological Society, 1*, 469–483.

Maylor, E.A. (1993). Aging and forgetting in prospective and retrospective memory tasks. *Psychology and Aging, 8* (3), 420–428.

McAndrews, M.P., Glisky, E.L., & Schacter, D.L. (1987). When priming persists: Long lasting implicit memory for a single episode in amnesic patients. *Neuropsychologia, 25*, 497–506.

McAndrews, M.P., & Milner, B. (1991). The frontal cortex and memory for temporal order. *Neuropsychologia, 29*, 849–859.

McCarthy, R.A., & Warrington, E.K. (1987). The double-dissociation of short-term memory. *Brain, 110*, 1545–1563.

McCarthy, R.A., & Warrington, E.K. (1988). Evidence for modality-specific meaning systems in the brain. *Nature, 334*, 428–429.

McCarthy, R.A., & Warrington, E.K. (1990). *Cognitive neuropsychology: A clinical introduction.* San Diego: Academic Press.

McCarty, D.L. (1980). Investigation of a visual imagery mnemonic device for acquiring face–name associations. *Journal of Experimental Psychology: Human Learning and Memory, 6*, 145–155.

McClelland, J.L., & Rumelhart, D.E. (1986). *Parallel distributed processing: Explorations in the microstructure of cognition* (Vol. 2). Cambridge, MA: MIT Press.

McCloskey, M., & Caramazza, A. (1987). Cognitive mechanisms in normal and impaired number processing. In G. Deloche & X. Seron (Eds.), *Mathematical disabilities: A cognitive neuropsychological perspective* (pp. 201–220). Hillsdale, NJ: Lawrence Erlbaum Associates Inc.

McCloskey, M., Sokol, S.M., & Goodman, R.A. (1986). Cognitive processes in verbal number processing: Inference from the performance of brain-damaged subjects. *Journal of Experimental Psychology, 115*, 313– 330.

McDaniel, M.A., Glisky, E.L., Rubin, S.R., Guynn, M.J., & Routhieaux, B.C. (1999). Prospective memory: A neuropsychological study. *Neuropsychology, 13* (1), 103–110.

McFie, J. (1975) *Assessment of organic intellectual impairments.* New York, Academic Press.

McFie, J., Piercy, M., & Zangwill, O. (1950). Visual spatial agnosia associated with lesions of the right hemisphere. *Brain, 73*, 167–190.

McGhie, A., & Chapman, L.J. (1961). Disorders of attention and perception in early schizophrenia. *British Journal of Medical Psychology, 34*, 105–116.

McGlinchey-Berroth, R., Bullis, D.P., Milberg, W.P., Verfaellie, M., Alexander, M., & D'Esposito, M. (1996). Assessment of neglect reveals dissociable behavioral but not neuroanatomical subtypes. *Journal of the International Neuropsychological Society, 2*, 441–451.

McGlinchey-Berroth, R., Milberg, W.P., Verfaellie, M. et al. (1993). Semantic processing in the neglected visual field: Evidence from a lexical decision task. *Cognitive Neuropsychology, 10*, 79–108.

McGlone, J. (1980). Sex differences in human brain asymmetry: A critical survey. *Behavioral and Brain Sciences. 3*, 215–263.

McGlynn, S.M., & Kazniak, A.W. (1991). Unawareness of deficits in dementia and schizophrenia. In G.P. Prigatano & D.L. Schacter (Eds.), *Awareness of deficit after brain injury* (pp. 84–110). Oxford: Oxford University Press.

McGuigan, F.J. (1966). Covert oral behaviour and auditory hallucinations. *Psychophysiology, 3*, 73–80.

McGuire, P.K., Shah, G.M.S., Murray, R.M. et al. (1993). Increased blood flow in Broca's area during auditory hallucinations. *Lancet, 342*, 703–706.

McGuire, P.K., Silbersweig, D.A., & Murray, R.M. (1996). The functional neuroanatomy of verbal self monitoring and auditory imagery. *Psychological Medicine, 26*, 29–38.

McKay, D.G. (1973). Aspects of theory and comprehension, memory and attention. *Quarterly Journal of Experimental Psychology, 25*, 22–40.

McKeever, W.F., Seitz, K.S., Krutsch, A.J., & Van Eys, P.L. (1995). On language laterality in normal dextrals and sinistrals: Results from the bilateral object naming latency task. *Neuropsychologia, 33*, 1627–1635.

McKinlay, W.W., Brooks, D.N., Bond, M.R., Martinage, D.P., & Marshall, M.M. (1981). The short term outcome of severe blunt head injury as reported by relatives of the injured persons. *Journal of Neurology, Neurosurgery and Psychiatry, 44*, 527–533.

McLeod, P., & Jenkins, S. (1991). Timing accuracy and decision-time in high-speed ball games. *International Journal of Sport Psychology, 22*, 279–295.

McMillan, T.M., Robertson, I.H., & Wilson, B.A. (1999) Neurogenesis after brain injury: Implications for neurorehabilitation. *Neuropsychological Rehabilitation, 9*, 129–133.

Meadore, K.G., Loring, D.W., Bowers, D., & Heilman, K.M. (1989). Hemisphere asymmetry for eye gaze mechanisms. *Brain, 112*, 103–111.

Medalia, A.A., Merriam, A.E., & Ehrenreich, J.H. (1991). The neuropsychological sequelae of attempted hanging. *Journal of Neurology, Neurosurgery and Psychiatry, 54*, 546–548.

Mehta, M.A., Owen, A.M., Sahakian, B.J., Mavaddat, N., Pickard, J.D., & Robbins, T.W. (2000). Methylphenidate enhances working memory by modulating discrete frontal and parietal lobe regions in the human brain. *J Neuroscience, 20*, RC65.

Mehta, Z., & Newcombe, F. (1996). Dissociate contributions of the two cerebral hemispheres to judgements of line orientations. *Cortex, 32*, 335–339.

Melekian, B. (1981). Lateralization in the human newborn at birth: Asymmetry of the stepping reflex. *Neuropsychologia, 19*, 707–711.

Melo, B., Winocur, G., & Moscovitch, M. (1999). False-recall and false recognition: An examination of the effects of selective and combined lesions to the medial temporal lobe/diencephalon and frontal lobe structures. *Cognitive Neuropsychology, 16*, 343–359.

Melton, A.W. (1963). Implications of short-term memory for a general theory of memory. *Journal of verbal learning and verbal behaviour, 2*, 1–21.

Mesulam, M.M. (1981). A cortical network for directed attention and unilateral neglect. *Annals of Neurology, 10*, 309–325.

Mesulam, M.M. (1985). Attention, confusional states and neglect. In M.-M. Mesulam (Ed.), *Principles of behavioural neurology* (pp. 125–168). Philadelphia: F.A. Davis.

Mesulam, M.M. (1988). Central cholinergic pathways: Neuroanatomy and some behavioural implications. In M. Avoli, T.A. Reader, R.W. Dykes, & P. Gloor (Eds.), *Neurotransmitters and cortical function: From molecules to mind* (pp. 237–260). New York: Plenum.

Mesulam, M.M. (1998). From sensation to cognition. *Brain, 121*, 1013–1052.

Mesulam, M.M. (1999). Spatial attention and neglect: Parietal, frontal and cingulate contributions to the mental representation and attentional targeting of salient extrapersonal events. *Philosophical Transactions of the Royal Society London, Series B, 29* (354), 1325–1346.

Mesulam, M.M., & Weintraub, S. (1992). Primary progressive aphasia: Sharpening the focus on a clinical syndrome. In F. Boller, F. Forette, Z. Zhachturian, M. Poncet, & Y. Christen (Eds.), *Heterogeneity of Alzheimer's disease* (pp. 43–66). Berlin: Springer.

Metter, E.J. (1995). PET in aphasia and language. In H.S. Kirshner (Ed.), *Handbook of neurological speech and language disorders* (pp. 187–212). New York: Marcel Dekker.

Metter, E.J., & Hanson, W.R. (1994). Use of positron emission tomography to study aphasia. In A. Kertesz (Ed.), *Localization and neuroimaging in neuropsychology.* (Ch. 5, pp. 123–147). San Diego: Academic Press.

Meudell, P., & Mayes, A.R. (1981). Normal and abnormal forgetting: Some comments on the human amnesic syndrome. In L.A. Ellis (Ed.), *Normality and pathology in cognitive function.* Academic Press: London.

Miall, R.C. (1998). The cerebellum, predictive control and motor coordination. In G.R. Block & J.A. Goode (Eds.), *Sensory guidance of movements: Novartis symposium foundation* (Vol. 218, pp. 272–290). Chichester, UK: Wiley.

Miceli, G., Mazzucchi, A., Menn, L., & Goodglass, H. (1983). Contrasting cases of Italian agrammatic aphasia without comprehension disorder. *Brain and Language, 18*, 65–97.

Miller, E. (1984). *Recovery and management of neuropsychological impairments.* Chichester, UK: Wiley.

Miller, E. (1993). Dissociating single cases in neuropsychology. *British Journal of Clinical Psychology, 32*, 155–167.

Miller, G.A. (1956). The magical number seven, plus or minus two: Some limits on our capacity for processing information. *Psychological Review, 63*, 81–97.

Miller, G.A. (1994). The magical number seven, plus or minus two: Some limits on our capacity for processing information. *Psychological Review, 101*, 343–352.

Miller, G.A., & Buckhout, R. (1973). *Psychology, the science of mental life.* New York: Harper & Row.

Miller, L.A., Lai, R., & Munoz, D.G. (1998). Contributions of the entorhinal cortex, amygdala and hippocampus to human memory. *Neuropsychologia, 36*, 1247–1256.

Milner, B. (1977). Wilder Penfield: His legacy to neurology. Memory mechanisms. *Canadian Medical Association Journal, 116*, 1374–1376.

Milner, A.D., & Goodale, M.A. (1995). *The visual brain in action.* Oxford: Oxford University Press.

Milner, B. (1962). Laterality effects in audition. In V.B. Mountcastle (Ed.), *Interhemispheric relations and cerebral dominance.* Baltimore: Johns Hopkins University Press.

Milner, B. (1964). Some effects of frontal lobectomy in man. In J.M. Warren & K. Akert (Eds.), *The frontal granular cortex and behaviour* (Ch. 15). New York: McGraw-Hill.

Milner, B. (1965). Visual guided maze learning in man: Effects of bilateral hippocampal, bilateral frontal and unilateral cerebral lesions. *Neuropsychologia, 3*, 317–338.

Milner, B. (1966). Amnesia following operation on the temporal lobes. In C.W.M. Whitty & O.L. Zangwill (Eds.), *Amnesia* (1st ed.). London: Butterworths.

Milner, B. (1970). Memory and the medial temporal lobe regions of the brain. In K.H. Pribram & D. E. Broadbent (Eds.), *Biology of memory.* New York: Academic Press.

Milner, B. (1975). Psychological effects of focal epilepsy and its neurosurgical management. *Advances in Neurology, 8*, 299–321.

Milner, B., Corsi, P., & Leonard, G. (1991). Frontal lobe contribution to recency judgements. *Neuropsychologia, 29*, 601–618.

Milner, B., & Petrides, M. (1984). Behavioural effects of frontal lobe lesions in man. *Trends in Neurosciences, 7*, 403–407.

Milner, P. (1989). A cell assembly theory of hippocampal amnesia. *Neuropsychologia, 27*, 23–30.

Mimura, M., Albert, M.L., & McNamura, P. (1995). Towards a pharacotherapy for aphasia. In H.S. Kirshner (Ed.), *Handbook of neurological speech and language disorders* (pp. 465–482). New York: Marcel Dekker.

Mishkin, M. (1982). A memory system in the monkey. *Philosophical Transactions of the Royal Society London, Series B, 298*, 85–95.

Mishkin, M., Ungerleider, L.G., & Macko, K.O. (1983). Object vision and spatial vision: Two cortical pathways. *Trends in Neurosciences, 6*, 414.

Mitchum, C.C., & Berndt, R.S. (1995). The cognitive neuropsychological approach to treatment of language disorders. In R.S. Berndt & C.C. Mitchum (Eds.), *Cognitive neuropsychological approaches to the treatment of language disorders* (pp. 1–6). Hove, UK: Lawrence Erlbaum Associates Ltd.

Miyake, A., Friedman, N.P., Emerson, M.J., Witzki,

A.H., Howerter, A., & Wager, T.D. (2000). The unity and diversity of executive functions and their contributions to complex "frontal lobe" tasks: a latent variable analysis. *Cognitive Psychology, 41*, 49–100.

Miyake, A. & Shah, P. (Eds.) (1999). *Models of working memory: Mechanisms of active maintenance and executive control.* New York: Cambridge University Press.

Mohr, J.P. (1976). An unusual case of dyslexia with dysgraphia. *Brain and Language, 3*, 324–334.

Mohr, J.P., Pessin, M.S., Finkelstein, S., Funkenstein, H.H., Duncan, G.W., & Davis, K.R. (1978). Broca aphasia: Pathologic and clinical. *Neurology, 28*, 311–324.

Monsell, S. (1987). On the relationship between the lexical input and the lexical output pathways for speech. In A. Allport, D.G. McKay, & W. Prinz, (Eds.), *Language perception and production: Relationships between listening, speaking and reading and writing* (pp. 273–311). London: Academic Press.

Morris, J.S, Frith, C.D., Perrett, D.I., Rowland, D., et al. (1996). A differential neural response in the human amygdala to fearful and happy facial expressions. *Nature, 383*, 812–815.

Morris, J.S., Ohman, A., & Dolan, R.J. (1998). Conscious and unconscious emotional learning in the human amygdala. *Nature, 393*, 467–470.

Morris, J.S., Ohman, A., & Dolan, R.J. (1999). A subcortical pathway to the right amygdala mediating "unseen" fear. *Proceedings of the National Academy of Sciences USA, 16* (96), 1680–1685.

Morris, M.K., Bowers, D., Chatterjee, A., & Heilman, K.M. (1992). Amnesia following a discrete basal forebrain lesion. *Brain, 115*, 1827–1847.

Morris, P.E., Tweedy, M., & Gruneberg, M.M. (1985). Interest, knowledge and the memorizing of soccer scores. *British Journal of Psychology, 76*, 415–425.

Morris, R.G., Downes, J.J., Shahakian, B.J., Evenden, J.L., Heald, A. & Robbins, T.W. (1988). Planning and spatial working memory in Parkinson's disease. *Journal of Neurology, Neurosurgery and Psychiatry, 51*, 757–766.

Morris, R.G., Abrahams, S., Baddeley, A.D., & Polkey, C.E. (1995). Doors and people: Visual and verbal memory after unilateral temporal lobectomy. *Neuropsychology, 9*, 464–469.

Morris, R., Paxinos, G., & Petrides, M. (2000). Architectonic analysis of the human retrosplenial cortex. *Journal of Comparative Neurology, 421*, 14–28.

Morris, R.G., Polkey, C.E., & Cox, T. (1998). Independent recovery of memory and language

function during intercarotid sodium amytal test. *Journal of Clinical and Experimental Neuropsychology, 20*, 433–444.

Morrison, J.H., & Foote, S.L. (1986). Noradrenergic and serotenergic enervation of cortical, thalamic and tectal visual structures in Old and New World monkeys. *Journal of Comparative Neurology, 243*, 117–28.

Morton, J. (1980). The logogen model and orthographic structure. In U. Frith (Ed.), *Cognitive approaches in spelling.* London: Academic Press.

Moruzzi, G., & Magoun, H.W. (1949). Brain stem and reticular formation and activation of the EEG. *Electroencephalography and Clinical Neurophysiology, 1*, 455–473.

Moscovitch, M. (1982). Multiple dissociations in amnesia. In F.K.M. Craik & S. Trehub (Eds.), *Aging and cognitive processes* (pp. 55–78). New York: Plenum Press.

Moscovitch, M. (1994a). Cognitive resources and dual-task interference effects at retrieval in normal people: The role of the frontal lobes and medial temporal cortex. *Neuropsychology, 8*, 524–534.

Moscovitch, M. (1994b) Memory and working with memory: Evaluation of a component process model and comparisons with other models. In D.L. Schacter & E. Tulving (Eds.), *Memory systems* (Ch. 9, pp. 269–310). Cambridge, MA: MIT Press.

Moscovitch, M. (1995). Recovered consciousness: A hypothesis concerning modularity and episodic memory. *Journal of Clinical and Experimental Neuropsychology, 17*, 276–290.

Moscovitch, M., Goshen-Gottstein, Y., & Vriezen, E. (1993). Memory without conscious recollection: A tutorial review from a neuropsychological perspective. In C. Umilta & M. Moscovitch (Eds.), *Attention and performance* (Vol. 15). Cambridge, MA: Bradford Books.

Moscovitch, M., & Nadel, L. (1998). Consolidation and the hippocampal complex revisited: In defence of the multi-choice model. *Current opinion in Neurobiology, 8*, 297–300.

Moskovitch, M., & Olds, J. (1982). Asymmetries in spontaneous facial expressions and their possible relation to hemisheric specialisation. *Neuropsychologia, 20*, 71–81.

Moscovitch, M., & Umilta, C. (1990). Modularity and neuropsychology: Implications for the organization of attention and memory in normal and brain damaged people. In M.E. Schwartz (Ed.) *Modular processes in dementia* (pp. 1–59). Cambridge, MA: MIT Press.

Moscovitch, M., Winocur, G., & Behrmann, M. (1997). What is special about face recognition? Nineteen experiments on a person with visual object agnosia and dyslexia but normal face recognition. *Journal of Cognitive Neuroscience, 9,* 555–604.

Moscovitch, M., Winocur, G., & McLachlan, D. (1986). Memory as assessed by recognition and reading time in normal and memory impaired people with Alzheimer's disease and other neurological disorders. *Journal of Experimental Psychology: General, 115,* 331–347.

Mountain, M.A., & Snow, W.G. (1993). Wisconsin Card Sorting Test as a measure of frontal pathology: A review. *Clinical Neuropsychologist, 7,* 1108–1118.

Mountcastle, V.B., Andersen, R.A., & Motter, B.C. (1981). The influence of attentive fixation upon the excitability of the light sensitive neurons of the posterior parietal cortex. *Journal of Neuroscience, 1,* 1218–1245.

Moutoussis, K., & Zeki, S. (1997). Functional segregation and temporal hierachy of the visual perceptive sytem. *Proceedings of the Royal Society London, Series B, 264,* 1407–1414.

Muller, A., Baumgartner, R.W., Rohrenbach, C., & Regard, M. (1999). Persistent Kluver–Bucy syndrome after bilateral thalamic infarction. *Neuropsychiatry, Neuropsychology, Behaviour and Neurology, 12,* 136–139.

Muller, R.A., Rothermel, R.D., Behen, M.E., Muzik, O., Mangner, T.J., Chakraborty, P.K., & Chugani, H.T. (1998). Brain organization of language after early unilateral lesion: A PET study. *Brain and Language, 62,* 422–451.

Mumby, D.G., Pinel, J.P.J., & Dastur, F.N. (1993). Mediodorsal thalamic lesions and object recognition in rats. *Psychobiology, 21,* 27–36.

Murdoch, B.E. (1988). Computerized tomography scanning: Its contribution to the neuroanatomical basis of aphasia. *Aphasiology, 2,* 437–462.

Murdoch, B.E. (1990). *Acquired speech and language disorders: A neuroanatomical and functional neurological approach.* London: Chapman & Hall.

Muri, R.M., Rivaud, S., Gaymard, B., Ploner, C.J., Vermersch, A.I., Hess, C.W., & Pierrot-Deseilligny, C. (1999). Role of the prefrontal cortex in the control of express saccades. A transcranial magnetic stimulation study. *Neuropsychologia, 37,* 199–206.

Murray, E.A., & Mishkin, M. (1998). Object recognition and location memory in monkeys with excitotoxic lesions of the amygdala and hippocampus. *Journal of Neuroscience, 18,* 6568–6582.

Musen, G., & Squire, L.R. (1993). On the implicit learning of novel associations by amnesic patients and normal subjects. *Neuropsychology, 7,* 119–135.

Mushiake, H., Inase, M., & Tanji, J. (1991). Neuronal activity in the primate premotor, supplementary motor and precentral motor during visually guided and internally determined sequential movements. *Journal of Neurophysiology, 66,* 705–718.

Nadeau S.E., & Crosson, B. (1997) Subcortical aphasia. *Brain and Language, 58,* 355–402.

Naeser, M.A. (1994). Neuroimaging and recovery of auditory comprehension and spontaneous speech in aphasia with some implications for treatment in severe aphasia. In A. Kertesz (Ed.), *Localization and neuroimaging in neuropsychology* (pp. 245–291). San Diego: Academic Press.

Naeser, M.A., & Hayward, R.W. (1978). Lesion localization in aphasia with cranial computed tomography and the Boston diagnostic aphasic examination. *Neurology, 28,* 545–551.

Naeser, M.A., & Hayward, R.W. (1979). The resolving stroke and aphasia: A case study with computerized tomography. *Archives of Neurology, 36* (4), 233–235.

Naeser, M.A., Palumbo, C.L., Helm-Estabrooks, N., Stiassny-Eder, D., & Albert, M.L. (1989). Severe nonfluency in aphasia: Role of the medial subcallosal fasciculus and other white matter pathways in recovery of spontaneous speech. *Brain, 112,* 1–38.

Nakamura, K., Kawashima, R., Ito, K., Sugiuro, M., Kato, T., et al. (1999). Activation of the right inferior temporal lobe cortex during assessment of facial emotion. *Journal of Neurophysiology, 82,* 1610–1614.

Nathaniel, J.D.A., Brown, R., & Ron, M.A. (1996). Memory impairment in schizophrenia: Its relationship to executive function. *Schizophrenia Research, 21,* 85–96.

Naveh-Benjamin, M., & Ayres, T.J. (1986). Digit-span, reading rate and linguistic relativity. *Quarterly Journal of Experimental Psychology, 38,* 739–751.

Nayani, T., & David, A.S. (1996). The auditory hallucination: A phenomenological survey. *Psychological Medicine, 26,* 177–189.

Neary, D., & Snowden, J.S. (1991). Dementia of the frontal lobe type, In H.S. Levin, H.M. Eisenberg, & A.L. Benton (Eds.), *Frontal lobe function and dysfunction* (pp. 304–317). Oxford University Press.

Neisser, U. (1967). *Cognitive neuropsychology.* New York: Appleton-Century-Crofts.

Neisser, U. (1978). Memory: What are the important questions? In M.M. Gruneberg, P.E. Morris, & R.N. Sykes (Eds.), Practical aspects of memory (opening address) (pp. 3–24). London: Academic Press.

Neisser, U. (1982). Snapshots or benchmarks. In U. Neisser (Ed.), *Memory observed: Remembering in natural contexts*, (pp. 43–48). New York: Freeman.

Neisser, U. (1997). The ecological study of memory. *Philosophical Transactions of the Royal Society London, Series B, 352*, 1747–1754.

Neisser, U., & Harsch, N. (1992). Phantom flashbulbs: False recollections of hearing news about Challenger. In E. Weinograd & U. Neisser (Eds.), *Affect and accuracy in recall: Studies of flashbulb memories* (pp. 9–31). Cambridge, UK: Cambridge University Press.

Neisser, U., Weinograd, E., Bergman, E.T., & Schreiber, C.A. et al. (1996). Remembering the earthquake: Direct experience vs hearing the news. *Memory, 4*, 337–357.

Nelson, D.L., Walling, J.R., & McEnvoy, C.L. (1979). Doubts about depth. *Journal of Experimental Psychology: Human Learning and Memory, 15*, 24–44.

Nelson, H.E. (1976). A modified card sorting task sensitive to frontal lobe defects. *Cortex, 12*, 313–324.

Nelson, H.E., & O'Connell, A. (1978). Dementia: The estimation of pre-morbid intelligence levels using the new adult reading test. *Cortex, 14*, 234–244.

Nelson, L.D., Cicchetti, D., Satz, P., Sowa, M., & Mitrushina, M. (1994). Emotional sequelae of stroke: A longitudinal perspective. *Journal of Clinical and Experimental Neuropsychology, 16*, 796–806.

Nelson, L.D., Cicchetti, D., Satz, P., Stern, S., Sowa, M., Cohen, S., Mitrushina, M., & Van Gorp, W. (1993). Emotional sequelae of stroke. *Neuropsychology, 7* (4), 553–560.

Newcombe, F., & Marshall, J.C. (1988). Idealisation meets psychometrics: The case for the right groups and the right individuals. *Cognitive Neuropsychology, 5*, 549–564.

Newcombe, F., Marshall, J.C., Caravick, P.J., & Hiorns, R.W. (1975). Recovery curves in acquired dyslexia. *Journal of Neuroscience, 24*, 127–133.

Nickels, L., Howard, D., & Best, W. (1997). Fractionating the articulatory loop: Dissociations and associations in phonological recoding in aphasia. *Brain and Language, 56*, 161–182.

Nisbett, R.E., & Wilson, T.D. (1977). Telling more than we can know: Verbal reports on mental processes. *Psychological Review, 84*, 231–259.

Noback, C.R., Strominger, N.L., & Demarest, R.J. (1991). *The human nervous system* (4th ed.). Philadelphia: Lea & Febiger.

Nofzinger, E.A., Mintun, M.A., Wiseman, M., Kupfer, D.J., & Moore, R.Y. (1997). Forebrain activation in REM sleep: An FDG PET study. *Brain Research, 770*, 192–201.

Nolte, J. (1991). *Principles of neurobiology* (int. ed.). St Louis, MO: Mosby Yearbooks Inc.

Nolte, J. (1993). The human brain: An introduction to its functional anatomy (3rd ed.). St Louis, MO: Mosby Yearbooks Inc.

Nolte, J., & Angevine Jr, J.B. (1995). The human brain: In photographs and diagrams. St Louis, MO: Mosby Yearbooks Inc.

Norman, D.A., & Shallice, T. (1986). Attention to action: Willed and automatic control of behaviour. In R.J. Davidson, G.E. Schwartz, & D. Shapiro (Eds.), *Consciousness and self regulation* (Vol. 4). New York: Plenum Press.

Nottebohm, F. (1979). Origins and mechanisms in the establishment of cerebral dominance. In M.S. Gazzaniga (Ed.), *Handbook of behavioural neurobiology: Vol 2, Neuropsychology* (pp. 295–344). New York: Plenum.

Nudo, R.J., & Milliken, G.W. (1996). Reorganisation of movement representations in primary motor cortex following focal ischemic infarcts in adult squirrel monkeys. *Journal of Neurophysiology, 75*, 2144–2149.

Nudo, R.J., Milliken, G.W., Jenkins W.M., & Merzenich, M.M. (1996). Use-dependent alterations of movement representations in primary motor cortex of adult squirrel monkeys. *Journal of Neuroscience, 16*, 785–807.

Ochipa, C., Rothi, L.J., & Heilman, K.M. (1992). Conceptual apraxia in Alzheimer's disease. *Brain, 115*, 1061–1071.

Oddy, M., Coughlan, T., Tyerman, A., & Jenkins, D. (1985). Social adjustment after closed head injury: A further follow-up seven years after injury. *Journal of Neurology, Neurosurgery and Psychiatry, 48*, 564–568.

Ogden, J. (1985). Contralesional neglect of constructed images in right and left brain damaged patients. *Neuropsychologia, 23*, 273–277.

Ogden, J. (1988). Language and memory functions after long recovery periods in left hemispherectomized subjects. *Neuropsychologia, 26*, 645–659.

Ogiso, T., Kobayashi, K., Sugishita, M. (2000). The precuneus in motor imagery: A magnetoencephalographic study. *Neuroreport, 11*, 1345–1349.

Ojemann, G.A. (1975). Language and the thalamus: Object naming and recall during and after thalamic stimulation. *Brain and Language, 2*, 101–120.

Ojemann, G.A. (1977). Asymmetric function of the thalamus in man. *Annals of the New York academy of Sciences, 299*, 380–396.

Ojemann, G.A. (1994). Cortical stimulation and recording in language. In A. Kertescz (Ed.), *Localization and neuroimaging in neuropsychology* (Ch. 2, 35–53). San Diego: Academic Press.

Ojemann, G.A., & Dodrill, C.B. (1985). Verbal memory deficits after left temporal lobectomy: Mechanism and intraoperative prediction. *Journal of Neurosurgery, 62*, 101–107.

Ojemann, G.A., Ojemann, J.G., Lettich, E., & Berger, M. (1989). Cortical language localisation in left, dominant hemisphere. *Journal of Neurosurgery, 71*, 316–326.

Oldfield, R.C. (1971). The assessment and analysis of handedness: The Edinburgh Inventory. *Neuropsychologia, 9*, 97–114.

Ooi, T.L., & He, Z.J. (1999). Binocular rivalry and visual awareness: The role of attention. *Perception. 28*, 551–574.

Oram, M.W., & Perrett, T. (1996). Integration of form and motion in the anterior superior temporal polysensory area (STPa) of the macaque monkey. *Journal of Neurophysiology, 76*, 109–129.

Orban, G.A., Dupont P., Vogels, R., Bormans, G., & Mortelmans, L. (1997). Human brain activity related to orientation discrimination tasks. *European Journal of Neuroscience, 9*, 246–259.

Osborn, T.M., LaMonte, M.P., & Gaasch, W.R. (1999). Intravenous thrombolytic therapy for stroke: A review of recent studies and controversies. *Annals of Emergency Medicine, 34*, 244–255.

Oscar-Berman, M., Mcnamara, P., & Freedman, M. (1991). In H.S. Levin, H.M. Eisenberg, & A.L. Benton (Eds.), *Frontal lobe function and dysfunction* (pp. 230–255). Oxford: Oxford University Press.

Ouagazzal, A.M., Kenny, P.J., & File, S.E. (1999). Stimulation of nicotinic receptors in the lateral septal nucleus increases anxiety. *European Journal of Neuroscience, 11*, 3957–3962.

Owen, A.M. (1997a). Cognitive planning in humans: Neuropsychological, neuroanatomical and neuropharmacological perspectives. *Progress in Neurobiology, 53*, 431–450.

Owen, A.M. (1997b). The functional organization of working memory processes within human lateral frontal cortex: the contribution of functional neuroimaging. *European Journal of Neuroscience, 9*, 1329–1339.

Owen, A.M. (2000). The role of the lateral frontal cortex in mnemonic processing: The contribution of functional neuroimaging. *Experimental Brain Research, 133*, 33–43.

Owen, A.M., Doyon, J.M., Petrides, M., & Evans, A.C. (1996). Planning and spatial working memory examined with positron emission tomography (PET). *European Journal of Neuroscience, 8*, 353–364.

Owen, A.M., James, M., Leigh, P.N., Summers, B.A., Marsden, C.D., Quinn, N.P., Lange, K.W., & Robbins, T.W. (1992). Fronto-striatal cognitive deficits at different stages of Parkinson's disease. *Brain, 115*, 1727–1751.

Owen, A.M., Roberts, A.C., Polkey, S.E., Sahakian, B.J., & Robbins, T.W. (1991). Extra-dimensional versus intra-dimensional set shifting performance following frontal lobe excisions, temporal lobe excisions or amygdalo-hippocampectomy in man. *Neuropsychologia, 29*, 993–1006.

Owen, A.M., Roberts, A.C., Polkey, C.E., Sahakian, B.J., & Robbins, T.W. (1993). Contrasting mechanisms of impaired attentional shift performance in patients with frontal lobe excision or Parkinson's disease. *Brain, 116*, 1159–79.

Owen, A.M., Sahakian, B.J., Hodges, J.R., Summers, B.A., Polkey, C.E., & Robbins, T.W. (1995). Dopamine dependent fronto-striatal planning deficits in early Parkinson's disease. *Neuropsychology, 9*, 126–140.

Owen, A.M., Stern, C.E., Look, R.B., Tracey, I., Rosen, B.R., & Petrides, M. (1998). Functional organization of spatial and nonspatial working memory processing within the human lateral frontal cortex. *Proceedings of the National Academy of Sciences USA, 95*, 7721–7726.

Pak, R., & Dombovy, M.I. (1994). Stroke. In D. Good & J. Couch Jr (Eds.), *Handbook of neurorehabilitation*. New York: Marcel Dekker.

Palacios, J.M., Niehoff, D.L., & Kuhar, M.J. (1981). [3H] Spiperone binding sites in brain: Autoradiographic localization of multiple receptors. *Brain, 213*, 277–289.

Palmer, S.E. (1975). Visual perception and world knowledge. In D.A. Norman, D.E. Rumelhart, & the LNR Research Group (Eds.), *Explorations in cognition*. San Francisco: Freeman.

Pandya, D.N., & Yeterian, E.H. (1996). Comparison of prefrontal architecture and connections. *Philosophical Transactions of the Royal Society London, Series B, 351* (1346), 1423–1432.

Pantev, C., Oostenveld, R., Engelien, A., Ross, B., Roberts, L.E., & Hoke, B. (1998). Increased auditory cortical representation in musicians. *Nature, 392*, 811–814.

Papagno, C., & Baddeley, A. (1997). Confabulation in a dysexecutive patient: Implication for models of retrieval. *Cortex, 33*, 743–752.

Papanicolaou, A.C., Moore, B.D., & Deutsch, G. (1989). Reorganization of cerebral function following lesions in the left hemisphere. In P. Bach-Y-Rita (Ed.), *Traumatic brain injury* (pp. 105–119). New York: Demos.

Papez, J.W. (1937). A proposed mechanism of emotion. *Archives of Neurology and Psychiatry, 38*, 725.

Pappata, S., Tran Dinh, S., Baron, J.C., Cambon, H., & Syrota, A. (1987). Remote metabolic effects of cerebrovascular lesions: Magnetic resonance and positron tomography imaging. *Neuroradiology, 29* (1), 1–6.

Pardo, J.V., Pardo, P.J., Janer, K.W., & Raichle, M.E. (1990). The anterior cingulate cortex mediates processing selection in the Stroop attentional conflict paradigm. *Proceedings of the National Academy of Sciences USA, 87*, 256–259.

Parkin, A.J. (1993). Progressive aphasia without dementia: A clinical and cognitive neurological analysis. *Brain and Language, 44*, 201–220.

Parkin, A.J. (1996). *Explorations in cognitive neuropsychology* (pp. 188–219). Oxford: Blackwell.

Parkin, A.J., & Leng, N.R.C. (1993). *Neuropsychology of the amnesic syndrome.* Hove, UK: Lawrence Erlbaum Associates Ltd.

Parkin, A.J., Leng, N.R.C., & Hunkin, N.M. (1990). Differential sensitivity to contextual information in diencephalic and temporal lobe amnesia. *Cortex, 26*, 373–380.

Parkin, A.J., & Walter, B. (1991). Short term memory, ageing, and frontal lobe dysfunction. *Psychobiology, 19*, 175–179.

Parnas, J. (1999). From predisposition to psychosis: Progression of symptoms in schizophrenia. *Acta Psychiatrica Scandinavica, 99* (Suppl. 395), 20–29.

Partiot, A., Grafman, J., Sadato, N., Flitman, S., & Wild, K. (1996). Brain activation during script event processing. *Neuroreport, 29* (7), 761–766.

Pascual-Leone, A., Cammarota, A., Wassermann, E.M., Brasil-Neto, J.P., Cohen, L.G., & Hallett, M. (1993). Modulation of motor cortical outputs to the reading hand of Braille readers. *Annals of Neurology, 34*, 33–37.

Passingham, R.E. (1996). Functional specialization of the supplementary motor area in monkeys and humans. *Advances in Neurology, 70*, 105.

Passingham, R.E. (1998). Attention to action. In A.C. Roberts, T.W. Robbins, & L. Weiskrantz (Eds.), *The prefrontal cortex and cognitive functions* (Ch. 10, pp. 131–143). New York: Oxford University Press.

Pattern, B.M. (1972). The ancient art of memory: Usefulness in treatment. *Archives of Neurology, 26*, 25–30.

Patterson, D.E., & Morton, J. (1985). From orthography to phonology: An attempt at an old interpretation. In K.E. Patterson, M. Coltheart, & J. Marshall (Eds.), *Surface dyslexia* (pp. 91–118). Hove, UK: Lawrence Erlbaum Associates Ltd.

Patterson, K.E., Coltheart, M., & Marshall, J. (1985). *Surface dyslexia* (pp. 335–359). Hove, UK: Lawrence Erlbaum Associates Ltd.

Patterson, K., & Hodges, J.R. (1995). Disorders in semantic memory. In A.D. Baddeley, B.A. Wilson, & F.N. Watts (Eds.). *Handbook of memory disorders* (pp. 167–186). Oxford: Oxford University Press.

Patterson, K., & Shewell, C. (1987). Speak and spell: Dissociations and word-class effects. In M. Coltheart, G. Sartori, & R. Job (Eds.), *The cognitive neuropsychology of language* (pp. 273–294.). Hove, UK: Lawrence Erlbaum Associates Ltd.

Patterson, K., Suzuki, T., & Wydell, T. (1996). Interpreting a case of Japanese phonological alexia: The key is in phonology. *Cognitive Neuropsychology, 13*, 803–822.

Pauly, P.J. (1983). The political structure of the brain: Cerebral localization in Bismarckian Germany. *International Journal of Neuroscience, 21* (1–2), 145–149.

Paus, T. (1996). Location and function of the human frontal eye-field: A selective review. *Neuropsychologia, 34*, 475–483.

Paus, T., Kalina, M., Patockova, L., Angerova, Y., et al. (1991). Medial versus lateral frontal lobe lesions and differential impairment of central gaze fixation in man. *Brain, 114* (5), 2051–2067.

Penfield, W. (1956). Functional localisation in temporal and deep sylvian areas. *Nervous & Mental Diseases, 36*, 210–226.

Penfield, W., & Evans, J. (1935). The frontal lobe in man: A clinical study of maximal removals. *Brain, 58*, 115–133.

Penfield, W., & Roberts, L. (1959). *Speech and brain mechanisms.* Princeton, NJ: Princeton University Press.

Penney, C.S. (1975). Modality effects in short-term verbal memory. *Psychological Bulletin, 82*, 68–84.

Perrani, D., Bressi, S., & Cappa, S.F. (1993). Evidence of multiple memory systems in the human brain: A [18F] FDG PET metabolic study. *Brain, 116*, 903–919.

Perret, E. (1974). The left frontal lobe of man and the suppression of habitual responses. *Neuropsychologia, 12*, 323–330.

Perrett, D.I., Mistlin, A.J., & Chitty, A.J. (1987). Visual cells responsive to faces. *Trends in Neurosciences, 10*, 358–364.

Perrett, D.I., Hietanen, J.K., Oram, M.W., & Benson, P.J. (1995). Organizations and functions of cells responsive to faces in the temporal cortex. Philosophical Transactions of the Royal Society London B, *335* (1273), 23–30.

Perrett, D.I., Oram, M.W., Harries, M.H., Bevan, R., Hietanen, J.K., Benson P.J., & Thomas, S. (1991). Viewer-centred and object-centred coding of heads in the macaque temporal cortex. *Experimental Brain Research, 86*, 159–73.

Perrett, D.I., Oram, M.W., Hietanen, J.K., & Benson, P.J. (1995). Issues of representation in object vision. In M.J. Farah, & G. Ratcliff (Eds.), *The neuropsychology of high-level vision: Collected tutorial essays* (pp. 33–63). Hove UK: Lawrence Erlbaum Associates Ltd.

Petersdorf, R.G. (1983). *Harrison's principles of internal medicine* (10th ed.). New York: McGraw-Hill.

Petersen, S.E., Fox, P.T., Posner, M.I., Mintun, M., & Raichle, M.E. (1988). Positron emission tomographic studies of the cortical anatomy of single word processing. *Nature* (London), *331*, 585–589.

Peterson, B.S., Skudlarski, P., Gatenby, J.C., Zhang, H., Anderson, A.W., & Gore, J.C. (1999). An fMRI study of Stroop word–color interference: Evidence for cingulate subregions subserving multiple distributed attentional systems. *Biolical Psychiatry, 45*, 1237–1258

Peterson, L.R., & Peterson, M.J. (1959). Short-term retention of individual items. *Journal of Experimental Psychology, 58*, 193–198.

Petrides M. (1991). Function specialization within the dorsolateral frontal cortex for serial order memory. *Proceedings of the Royal Society London B, 246* (1317), 299–306.

Petrides, M. (1996). Specialised systems for the processing of mnemonic information within the primate frontal cortex, *Philosophical Transactions of the Royal Society London Series B, 351*, 1455–1462.

Petrides, M. (1998). Specialized systems for the processing of mnemonic information within the primate frontal cortex. In A.C. Roberts, T.W. Robbins, & L. Weiskrantz (Eds.), *The prefrontal cortex: Executive and cognitive functions.* (pp. 103–116). New York: Oxford University Press.

Petrides, M., Alivisatos, B., Evans, A.C., & Meyer, E. (1993). Dissociation of human mid-dorsolateral from posterior dorsolateral frontal cortex in memory processing. *Proceedings of the National Academy of Sciences, 90*, 873–877.

Petrides, M., & Milner, B. (1982). Deficits on subject-ordered tasks after frontal- and temporal-lobe lesions in man. *Neuropsychologia, 20*, 249–262.

Petrides, M., & Pandya, D.N. (1994). Comparative architectonic analysis of the human and macaque frontal cortex. In F. Boller, & J. Grafman (Eds.), *Handbook of neuropsychology* (Vol. 9 pp. 17–58). New York: Elsevier Science.

Petrides, M., & Pandya, D.N. (1999). Dorsolateral prefrontal cortex: Comparative cytoarchitectonic analysis in the human and the macaque brain and corticocortical connection patterns. *European Journal of Neuroscience, 11*, 1011–1036.

Peyser, C.E., & Folstein, S.E. (1990), Huntington's disease as a model for mood disorders. *Molecular and Chemical Neuropathology, 12*, 99–119.

Phelps, E.A, Hyder, F., Blamaire, A.M., & Shulman, R.G. (1997). FMRI of the prefrontal cortex during overt verbal fluency. *Neuroreport, 8*, 561–565.

Phillips, J.G., Bradshaw, J.L., Iansek, R., & Chiu, E. (1993). Motor functions of the basal ganglia. *Psychological Research, 55*, 175–181.

Phillips, R.G., & LeDoux, J.E. (1992). Differential contribution of amygdala and hippocampus to cued and contextual fear conditioning. *Behavioural Neuroscience, 106*, 274–285.

Piaget, J. (1970). Extracts from Piaget's theory. In P.H. Mussen (Ed.), *Manual of child psychology,* Vol. 1 (pp. 703–732). New York: Wiley

Picton, T.W., Stuss, D.T., & Marshall, J.C. (1986). Attention and the brain. In S.L. Friedman, K.A. Kilvington, & R.W. Peterson (Eds.), *The brain, cognition and education* (pp. 19–79). New York: Academic Press.

Piercy, M., Hecaen, H., & Ajuriaguerra, de J. (1960). Constructional apraxia associated with unilateral cerebral lesion: Left and right sided cases compared. *Brain, 83*, 225–242.

Pierrot-Deseilligny, C., Gaymard, B., Muri, R., & Rivaud, J. (1997). Cerebral ocular motor signs. *Journal of Neurology, 244*, 65–70.

Pitres, A. (1895). Etude sur l'aphasie chez les polyglottes. *Revue Medicine, 15*, 873–899.

Plant, G.T., Laxer, K.D., Barbaro, N.M., Schiffman, J.S., & Nakayama, K. (1993). Impaired visual motion perception in the contralateral hemifield following unilateral posterior cerebral lesions in humans. *Brain, 116*, 1303–1335.

Plaut, D.C. (1996). Relearning after damage in

connectionist networks: Toward a theory of rehabilitation. *Brain and Language, 52*, 25–82.

Plaut, D.C., McClelland, J.L., Seidenberg, M.S., & Patterson, K.E. (1996). Understanding normal and impaired word reading: Computational principles in quasi regular domains. *Psychological Review, 103*, 56–115.

Plenger, P.M., Breier, J.W., Wheless, J.W., Ridley, T.D. et al. (1996). Lateralisation of memory for music: Evidence from intracarotid sodium amobarbitol procedure. *Neuropsychologia, 34*, 1015–1018.

Ploner, C.J., Rivaud-Pechoux, S., Gaymard, B.M., Agid, Y., & Pierrot-Deseilligny, C. (1999). Errors of memory-guided saccades in humans with lesions of the frontal eye field and the dorsolateral prefrontal cortex. *Journal of Neurophysiology, 82*, 1086–1090.

Plum, F., Schiff, N., Ribary, U., & Llinas, R. (1998). Coordinated expression in chronically unconscious persons. *Philosophical Transactions of the Royal Society London, Series B, 353*, 1929–1933.

Poeck, K. (1983a). Ideational apraxia. *Journal of Neurology, 230*, 1–5.

Poeck, K. (1983b). What do we mean by "aphasic syndromes?" A neurologist's view. *Brain and Language, 20*, 79–89.

Poeck, K. (1985). Clues to the nature of disruptions to limb praxis. In E.A. Roy (Ed.), *Neurological studies of apraxia and related disorders* (pp. 99–109). North-Holland: Elsevier.

Poeck, K. (1990). Some considerations on language and the brain. In J.C. Eccles & O. Creutzfeldt (Eds.), *Experimental brain research series 21: The principles of design and operation of the brain*. Heidelberg: Springer.

Poeck, K., & Orgass, B. (1975). Gerstmann syndrome without aphasia: Comments on the paper by Strub and Geschwind. *Cortex, 11*, 291–295.

Poeppel, D. (1996). A critical review of PET studies of phonological processing. *Brain and Language, 55*, 317–351.

Pollack, I., Johnson, I.B., & Knaff, P.R. (1959). Running memory span. *Journal of Experimental Psychology, 57*, 137–146.

Pollmann, S., & Von Cramon, D.Y. (2000). Object working memory and visuospatial processing: Functional neuroanatomy analyzed by event-related fMRI. *Experimental Brain Research, 133*, 12–23.

Polster, M.R., & Rapcsak, S.Z. (1996). Representations in learning new faces: Evidence from prosopagnosia. *Journal of the International Neuropsychological Society, 2*, 240–248.

Poltrock, S.E., Lansman, M., & Hunt, E. (1982). Automatic and controlled attention processes in auditory target detection. *Journal of Experimental Psychology: Human Perception and Performance, 8*, 37–45.

Ponsford, J.L. (1990). Editorial. Psychological sequelae of closed head injury: Time to redress the imbalance. *Brain Injury, 4*, 111–114.

Ponsford, J.L., & Kinsella, G. (1980). Evaluation of a remedial programme for attentional deficits. *Journal of Clinical and Experimental Neuropsychology, 10*, 693–708.

Ponsford, J.L., & Kinsella, G. (1991). The use of a rating scale of attentional behaviour. *Neuropsychological Rehabilitation, 1*, 241–257.

Ponsford, J., & Kinsella, G. (1992). Attentional deficits following closed-head injury. *Journal of Clinical and Experimental Neuropsychology, 14*, 822–838.

Ponsford, J.L., Sloan, S., & Snow, P. (1995). *Traumatic Brain Injury: Rehabilitation for everyday and adaptive living*. Hove, UK: Lawrence Erlbaum Associates Ltd.

Poole, J.H., Ober, B.A., Shenaut, G.K., & Vinogradov, S. (1999). Independent frontal-system deficits in schizophrenia: Cognitive, clinical and adaptive implications. *Psychiatry Research, 85*, 161–176.

Portas, C.M., Rees, G., Howseman, A.M., Josephs, O., Turner, R., & Frith, C.D. (1998). A specific role for the thalamus in mediating the interaction of attention and arousal in humans. *Journal of Neuroscience 18*, 8979–8989.

Posner, M.I. (1995). Attention in cognitive neuroscience: An overview. In M.S. Gazzaniga (Ed.), *The Cognitive Neurosciences* (pp. 615–624). Cambridge, MA: Bradford Books.

Posner, M.I., & Petersen S.E. (1990). The attentional system of the human brain. *Annual Review of Neuroscience, 13*, 25–42.

Posner, M.I., Petersen, S.E., Fox, P.T., & Raichle, M.E. (1988). Localization of cognitive operations in the human brain. *Science, 240*, 1627–1631.

Posner, M.I., Rafal, R.D., Choate, L.S., & Vaughan, J. (1985). Inhibition of return: Neural basis and function. *Cognitive Neuropsychology, 2*, 211–228.

Posner, M.I., & Raichle, M.E. (1997). *Images of the Mind*. Scientific American Library. New York: W.H. Freeman.

Posner, M.I., & Raichle, M.E. (1998). The neuroimaging of human brain function. *Proceedings of the National Acadamy of Sciences USA, 95*, 763–764.

Posner, M.I., & Rothbart, M.K. (1998). Attention, self-regualtion and consciousness. *Philosophical Transactions of the Royal Society London Series B, 353*, 1915–1927.

Posner, M.I., Walker, J.A., Friedrich, F.J., & Rafal, R.D. (1984). Effects of parietal injury on covert orienting of visual attention. *Journal of Neuroscience, 4*, 1863–1874.

Postle, B.R., Berger, J.S., and D'Esposito, M. (1999). Functional neuroanatomical double dissociation of mnemonic and executive control processes contributing to working memory performance. *Proceedings of the National Academy of Sciences USA, 96*, 12959–12964.

Potter, M.C. (1993). Very short-term conceptual memory. *Memory and Cognition, 21*, 156–161.

Powell, G.E. (1979). *Brain and Personality*. Farnborough, UK: Saxon House.

Powell, G.E., Polkey, C.E., & McMillan, T. (1985). The Maudsley series of temporal lobectomy. I. Short-term cognitive effects. *British Journal of Clinical Psychology, 24*, 109–124.

Pratt, M.W., Luszcz, M.A., MacKenzie-Keating, S., & Manning, A. (1982). Thinking about stories: The story schema in metacognition. *Journal of Verbal Learning and Verbal Behavior, 21*, 493–505.

Pratt, R.T.C., & Warrington, E.K. (1972). The assessment of unilateral dominance with unilateral ECT. *British Journal of Psychiatry, 121*, 327–328.

Prigatano, G.P. (1986). *Neuropsychological rehabilitation after brain injury*. Baltimore: Johns Hopkins University Press.

Prigatano, G.P. (1991). Awareness following brain injury. In H. Levin, H. Eisenberg, & A. Benton (Eds.), *Frontal lobe function and dysfunction* (pp. 381–397). New York: Oxford University Press.

Prisko, L. (1963). *Short-term memory in focal cerebral damage*. Unpublished doctoral dissertation, McGill University, Montreal.

Ptito, A., Zatorre, R.J., Larson, W.L., & Tosoni, C. (1991). Stereopsis after unilateral anterior temporal lobectomy. *Brain, 114*, 1323–1333.

Ptito, A., Zatorre, R.J., Petrides, M., Frey, S., Alivisatos, B., & Evans, A.C. (1993). Localization and lateralization of stereoscopic processing in the human brain. *Neuroreport, 4*, 1155–1158.

Puce, A., Allison, T., Asgari, M., Gore, J.C., & McCarthy, G. (1996). Differential sensitivity of human visual cortex to faces, letter strings, and textures: A functional magnetic resonance imaging study. *Journal of Neuroscience, 16*, 5205–5215.

Puce, A., Smith, A., & Allison, T. (2000). ERP's evoked by viewing facial movements. *Cognitive Neuropsychology, 17*, 221–240.

Purcell, R., Maruff, P., Kyrios, M., & Pantelis, C. (1998). Neuropsychological deficits in obsessive-compulsive disorder: A comparison with unipolar depression, panic disorder, and normal controls. *Archives of General Psychiatry. 55*, 415–423.

Quinn, K.J., Didier, A.J., Baker, J.F., & Peterson, B.W. (1998). Modeling learning in brain stem and cerebellar sites responsible for VOR plasticity. *Brain Research Bulletin, 46*, 333–346.

Quinn, N.P. (1990). The clinical application of cell grafting techniques in patients with Parkinson's disease. *Progress in Brain Research, 82*, 619–625.

Quintana, J., & Fuster, J.M. (1999). From perception to action: Temporal integrative functions of prefrontal and parietal neurons. *Cerebral Cortex, 9*, 213–222.

Rafal, R.D., Posner, M.I., Friedman, J.H., Inhoff, A.W., & Bernstein, E. (1988). Orienting of visual attention in progressive supranuclear palsy. *Brain, 111* (2), 267–280.

Rafal, R., & Robertson, L. (1995). The neurology of visual attention. In M.S. Gazzaniga (Ed.), *The Cognitive Neurosciences* (Ch. 40, pp. 625–649). Cambridge, MA: Bradford Books.

Raichle, M.E., Fiez, T.O., Videen, A.K., MacLeod, J.V., & Pardo, P.T. (1994). Practice-related changes in human brain functional anatomy during non-motor learning. *Cerebral Cortex, 4*, 8–26.

Raij, T. (1999). Patterns of brain activity during visual imagery of letters. *Journal of Cognitive Neuroscience, 11*, 282–299.

Ramachandran, V.S. (1995). Ansosognosia in parietal lobe syndrome. *Conscious Cognition, 4*, 22–51.

Ramachandran, V.S. (1998). Consciousness and body image: Lessons from phantom limbs, Capgras syndrome and pain asymbolia. *Philosophical Transactions of the Royal Society London, Series B, 353*, 1851–1860.

Ramamurthi, B. (1988). Stereotactic operation in behaviour disorders: Amygdalotomy and hypothalotomy. *Acta Neurochirurgica Supplement* (Wien), *44*, 152–157.

Rapcsak, S.Z., Arthur, S.A., & Rubens, A.B. (1988). Lexical agraphia from a focal lesion in the left precentral gyrus. *Neurology, 38*, 1119–1123.

Rapcsak, S.Z., Polster, M.R., Glisky, M.L., & Comer, J.F. (1996). False recognition of unfamiliar faces following right hemisphere damage: Neuropsychological and anatomical observations. *Cortex, 32*, 593–611.

Rapcsak, S.Z., Reminger, S.L., Glisky, E.L., Kaszniak, A.W., & Comer, J.F. (1999). Neuropsychological mechanisms of false facial recognition following frontal lobe damage. *Cognitive Neuropsychology, 16*, 267–292.

Rapcsak, S.Z., & Rubens, A.B. (1994) Localization of lesions in transcortical aphasia. In A. Kertescz (Ed.), *Localization and neuroimaging in neuropsychology* (Ch. 10, pp. 297–323). San Diego, Academic Press.

Rapoport, J.L., Buchsbaum, M.S., Zahn, T.P., Weingartner, H., Ludlow, C., & Mikkelson, E.J. (1978). Dextroamphetamine: Cognitive and behavioural effects in normal prepubertal boys. *Science, 199,* 560–563.

Rasmussen, T., & Milner, B. (1977). The role of early left brain injury in determining lateralization of cerebral speech function. *Annals of the New York Academy of Sciences, 229,* 355–369.

Rasmussen, T., & Milner, B. (1976). Clinical and surgical studies of the cerebral speech areas in man. In K.J. Zulch, O. Creutzfeldt, & G. Galbraith (Eds.), *Otfrid Foerster symposium on cerebral localisation.* (pp. 238–254). Heidelberg: Springer.

Ratcliff, R. (1979). Spatial thought, mental rotation, and the right cerebral hemisphere. *Neuropsychologia, 17,* 49–54.

Rauch, H.-G. (1974). *En masse.* Collier Books. New York: Macmillan.

Rauch, S.L., Whalen, P.J., Shin, L.M., McInerney, S.C., Macklin, M.L., Lasko, N.B., Orr S.P., & Pitman, R.K. (2000). Exaggerated amygdala response to masked facial stimuli in posttraumatic stress disorder: A functional MRI study. *Biological Psychiatry, 47,* 769–776.

Raymer, A.M., Foundas, A.L., Maher, L.M., Greenwald, M.L., Morris, M., Rothi, L.J., & Heilman, K.M. (1997). Cognitive neuropsychological analysis and neuroanatomic correlates in a case of acute anomia. *Brain Language, 58,* 137–156.

Reason, J.T. (1992). Cognitive underspecification: Its varieties and consequences. In B.J. Baars (Ed.), *Exploring the architecture of volition* (pp. 71–91). Plenum: New York.

Rees, G., & Frith, C.D. (1998). How do we select perceptions and actions? Human brain imaging studies. *Philosophical Transactions of the Royal Society London, Series B, 353.* 1283–1293.

Rees, G., Frith, C.D., & Lavie, N. (1997). Modulating irrelevant motion perception by varying attentional load in an unlearned task. *Science, 278,* 1616–1619.

Reeves, A.G., & Hagamen, W.D. (1971). Behavioral and EEG asymmetry following unilateral lesions of the forebrain and midbrain in cats. *Electroencephalography and Clinical Neurophysiology, 30,* 83–86.

Reid, S.N.M., & Juraska, J.N. (1992). Sex differences in the gross size of the rat neocortex. *Journal of Comparative Neurology, 321,* 448–455.

Reitan, R.M. (1972a). Studies of interference in serial verbal reactions. *Journal of Experimental Psychology, 18,* 643–662.

Reitan, R.M. (1972b). Verbal problem-solving as related to cerebral damage. *Perceptual and Motor Skills, 34,* 515–524.

Reitan, R.M., & Wolfson, D. (1997). Emotional disturbances and their interaction with neuropsychological deficits. *Neuropsychology Review, 7,* 3–20.

Rey, A. (1941). Psychological examination of traumatic encephalopathy. *Archives de Psychologie, 28,* 286–340 (sections translated by J. Corwin & F.W. Bylsma, *The Clinical Neuropsychologists, 7,* 3–15.

Rey, A. (1964). *L'examen clinique en psychologie.* Paris: Presses. Universitaires de France.

Rey, G.J., Bonnie, L.E., Rodas, R., Bowen, B.C., & Nedd, K. (1994). A longitudinal examination of crossed aphasia. *Archives of Neurology, 51,* 95–100.

Reynolds, J.H., Chelazzi, L., & Desimone, R. (1999). Competitive mechanisms subserve attention in macaque areas V2 and V4. *Journal of Neuroscience, 19,* 1736–1753.

Rhodes, G. (1993). Configural coding, expertise, and right hemisphere advantage for face recognition. *Brain and Cognition, 22,* 19–41.

Rhodes, G., & Wooding, R. (1989). Laterality effects in identification of caricatures and photographs of famous faces. *Brain and Cognition, 9,* 201–209.

Richardson, J.T.E., & Barry, C. (1985). *Cognitive Neuropsychology, 2,* 149–168.

Richer, F., Decary, A., LaPierre, M.P., Rouleau, I., Bouvier, G., & Saint-Hilaire, J.M. (1993). Target detection deficits in frontal lobectomy. *Brain and Cognition, 21,* 203–211.

Riddoch, M.J., & Humphreys, G.W. (1987a). A case of integrative visual agnosia. *Cognitive Neuropsychology, 4,* 131–185.

Riddoch, M.J., & Humphreys, G.W. (1987b). Visual object processing in optic aphasia: A case of semantic access agnosia. *Cognitive Neuropsychology, 4,* 131–185.

Riddoch, M.J., & Humphreys, G.W. (1995). 17 + 14 =41? Three cases of working memory impairment. In R. Campbell & M.R. Conway (Eds.). *Broken memories: Case studies in memory impairment* (Ch. 18, pp. 253–266). Oxford: Blackwell.

Riddoch, M.J., Humphreys, G.W., Cleton, P., & Fery, P. (1990). Interaction of attentional and lexical processes in neglect dyslexia. *Cognitive Neuropsychology, 7,* 479–518.

Riddoch, M.J., Humphreys, G.W., Coltheart, M., & Funnell, M. (1988). Semantic systems or system? Neuropsychological evidence re-examined. *Cognitive Neuropsychology, 5,* 3–25.

Riddoch, M.J., Humphreys, G.W., & Price, C.J. (1997). Top-down processes in object identification: Evidence from experimental psychology, neuropsychology and functional anatomy. *Philosophical Transactions of the Royal Society London, Series B, 352* (1358), 1275–1282.

Rilling, J.K., & Insel, T.R. (1999). The primate neocortex: A comparative perspective using magnetic resonance imaging. *Journal of Human Evolution, 37,* 191–223.

Rizzolatti, G., & Arbib, M.A. (1998). Language within our grasp. *Trends in Neuroscience, 21,* 188–194.

Rizzolatti, G., & Berti, A. (1993). Neural mechanisms of spatial neglect. In I.H. Robertson & J.C. Marshall (Eds.), *Unilateral neglect: Clinical and experimental studies* (pp. 87–106). Hove, UK: Lawrence Erlbaum Associates Ltd.

Rizzolatti, G., Fadiga, L., Gallese, V., & Fogassi L. (1996). Premotor cortex and the recognition of motor actions. *Brain Research and Cognition Brain Research, 3,* 131–141.

Robbins, T.W. (1990) The case for frontostriatal dysfunction in schizophrenia. *Schizophrenia Bulletin, 16,* 391–402.

Robbins, T.W. (1998). Dissociating executive functions of the prefrontal cortex. In A.C. Roberts, T.W. Robbins, & L.Weiskrantz (Eds.), *The prefrontal cortex and cognitive functions* (Ch. 9, pp. 117–131). New York: Oxford University Press.

Robbins, T.W. (2000). Chemical neuromodulation of frontal-executive functions in humans and other animals. *Experimental Brain Research, 133,* 130–138.

Robbins, T.W., Anderson, E.J., Barker, D.R., Bradley, A.C., Fearnyhough, C., Henson, R., & Hudson, S.R. (1996). Working memory in chess. *Memory and Cognition, 24,* 83–93.

Robbins, T.W., & Everitt, B.J. (1995). Arousal systems and attention. In M.S. Gazzaniga (Ed.), *The cognitive neurosciences* (pp. 703–720). Cambridge, MA: The MIT Press.

Roberts, A.C., Robbins, T.W., Everitt, B.J., & Muir, J.L. (1992). A specific form of cognitive rigidity following excitotoxic lesions of the basal forebrain in the monkey. *Neuroscience, 47,* 251–264.

Robertson, I.H. (1993). The relationship between later-

alised and non-lateralised attentional deficits in unilateral neglect. In I.H. Robertson & J.C. Marshall (Eds.) *Unilateral neglect: clinical and experimental studies* (pp. 257–273). Hove, UK: Lawrence Erlbaum Associates Ltd.

Robertson, I.H. (1995). Sustained attention training for unilateral neglect: Theoretical and rehabilitation implications. *Journal of Clinical and Experimental Neuropsychology, 17,* 416–430.

Robertson, I.H. (1999). Theory-driven neuropsychological rehabilitation: The role of attention and competition in recovery of function after brain damage. In D. Gopher, & A. Koriat (Eds.). *Attention and performance,* Vol 17 (pp. 677–696). Cambridge, MA: MIT Press.

Robertson, I.H., Halligan, P.W., Bergego, C., Hômberg, V., Pizzamiglio, L., Weber, E., & Wilson, B.A. (1994). Right neglect after right brain damage? *Cortex, 30,* 199–214.

Robertson, I.H., Mattingley, J.B., Rorden, C., & Driver, J. (1998). Phasic alerting of neglect patients overcomes their spatial deficit in visual awareness *Nature, 395,* 169–172.

Robertson, I.H., & Murre, J.M.J. (1999). Rehabilitation of brain damage: Brain plasticity and principles of guided recovery. *Psychological Bulletin 125,* 544–575.

Robertson, I.H., Tegner, R., Tham, K., Lo, A., & Nimmo-Smith, I. (1995). Sustained attention training for unilateral neglect: Theoretical and rehabilitation implications. *Journal of Clinical and Experimental Psychology, 17,* 416–430.

Robertson, I.H., Ward, T., Ridgeway, V., & Nimmo-Smith I. (1996). The structure of normal human attention: The Test of Everyday Attention. *Journal of the International Neuropsychology Society, 2,* 525–534.

Robertson, L.C., & Eglin, M. (1993). Attentional search in unilateral neglect. In I.H. Robertson & J.C. Marshall (Eds.), *Unilateral neglect: Clinical and experimental studies.* Hove, UK: Lawrence Erlbaum Associates Ltd.

Robertson, L.C., & Lamb, M.R. (1991). Neuropsychological contributions to theories of part/whole organisation. *Cognitive Psychology, 23,* 299–330.

Robertson, L.C., Lamb, M.R., & Zaidel, E. (1993). Interhemispheric relations in processing hierarchical patterns: Evidence from normal and commissurotomized subjects. *Neuropsychology, 7,* 325–342.

Robins, A.H. (1976). Depression in patients with

Parkinsonism. *British Journal of Psychiatry, 128,* 141–145.

Robinson, F.B. (1970). *Effective study.* New York: Harper & Row.

Robinson, R.G. (1985). Lateralized behavioral and neurochemical consequences of unilateral brain damage in rats. In S.G. Glick (Ed.), *Cerebral lateralisation in non-human species* (pp. 138–156). Orlando, FL: Academic Press.

Robinson, R.G., & Benson, D.F. (1981). Depression in aphasic patients: Frequency, severity and clinical pathological correlations. *Brain and Language, 14,* 610–614.

Robinson, R.G., Kubos, K.L., Starr, L.B., Rao, K., & Price, T.R. (1984). Mood disorders in stroke patients. *Brain, 107,* 81–93.

Robinson, R.G., Starr, L.B., & Price, T.R. (1984). A two year longitudinal study of mood disorders following stroke: Prevalence and duration at six months follow-up. *British Journal of Psychiatry, 144,* 256–262.

Roediger, H.L., & McDermott, K.B. (1999). False alarms and false memories. *Psychological Review, 106,* 406–410.

Roeltgen, D. (1994). Localization of lesions in agraphia. In A. Kertescz (Ed.), *Localization and neuroimaging in neuropsychology* (Ch. 12, pp. 377–402). San Diego: Academic Press.

Roeltgen, D., & Heilman, K.M. (1984). Lexical agraphia: Further support for the two strategy hypothesis of linguistic agraphia. *Brain, 107,* 811–827.

Roesler, A., Lanquillon, S., Dippel, O., & Braune, H.J. (1997). Impairment of facial recognition in patients with right cerebral infarcts quantified by computer aided "morphing". *Journal of Neurology, Neurosurgery and Psychiatry, 62,* 261–264

Rogers, R.D., Sahakian, B.J., Hodges, J.R., Polkey, C.E., Kenard, C., & Robbins, T.W. (1998). Dissociating executive mechanisms of task control following frontal lobe damage and Parkinson's disease. *Brain, 121,* 815–842.

Roland, P.E., & Gulyas, B. (1994). Visual imagery and visual representation. *Trends in Neurosciences, 17,* 281–287.

Roland, P.E., Larsen, B., Lassen, N.A., & Skinhoj, E. (1980). Supplementary motor area and other cortical areas in organisation of voluntary movements in man. *Journal of Neurophysiology, 43,* 118–136.

Roland, P.E., & Zilles, K. (1996). Functions and structures of the motor cortices in humans. *Current Opinion in Neurobiology, 6,* 773–781.

Rolls, E.T. (1994). Brain mechanisms for invariant visual recognition and learning behaviour. *Behavioural Proceedings, 33,* 113–138.

Rolls, E.T. (2000). The orbitofrontal cortex and reward. *Cerebral Cortex, 10,* 284–294.

Rolls, E.T. (1995). A theory of emotion and consciousness, and its application to the understanding the neural basis of emotion. In M.S. Gazzaniga (Ed.), *The cognitive neurosciences* (pp. 1091–1117). Cambridge MA: MIT Press.

Rolls, E.T., Hornak, J., Wade, D., & McGrath, J. (1994). Emotion-related learning in patients with social and emotional changes associated with frontal damage. *Journal of Neurology, Neurosurgery and Psychiatry, 57,* 1518–1524.

Romanski, L.M., Bates, J.F., & Goldman-Rakic, P.S. (1999). Auditory belt and parabelt projections to the prefrontal cortex in the rhesus monkey. *Journal of Comparative Neurology, 403,* 141–157.

Rosenkilde, C.E. (1979). Functional heterogeneity of the prefrontal cortex in the monkey: A review. *Behavioral and Neural Biology, 25,* 301–345.

Rosenzweig, M.R. (1984). Experience, memory and the brain. *American Psychologist, 4,* 365–376.

Ross, E.D. (1981). The asprosodias: Functional–anatomical organisation of affective components of language in the right hemisphere. *Archives of Neurology, 38,* 561–569.

Ross, E.D., & Rush, A.J. (1981). Diagnosis and neuroanatomical correlates of depression in brain damaged patients. *Archives of General Psychiatry, 38,* 1344–1354.

Ross, E.D., Thompson, R.D., & Yenkosky, J. (1997). Lateralization of affective prosody in brain and the callosal integration of hemispheric language functions. *Brain and Language, 56,* 27–54.

Rosselli, M., & Ardila, A. (1989). Calculation deficits in patients with right and left hemisphere damage. *Neuropsychologia, 27,* 607–617.

Rossi, G.F., & Rosadini, G. (1967). Experimental analysis of cerebral dominance in man. In C. Millikan & F.L. Darley (Eds.), *Brain mechanisms underlying speech and language* (pp. 167–184). New York: Grune & Stratton.

Rossor, M.N., Warrington, E.K., & Cipolotti, L. (1995). The isolation of calculation skills. *Journal of Neurology, 242,* 78–81.

Rousseaux, M., Cabaret, M., Lesoin, F., Devos, P., & Petit, H. (1986). L'Amnésie des infarctus thalamiques. *Encephale, 12,* 19–26.

Roy, E.A., & Square, P.A. (1985). Common considerations in the study of limb, verbal and oral apraxia.

In E.A. Roy (Ed.), *Advances in psychology: Vol. 23. Neuropsychological studies of apraxia and related disorders* (pp. 111–159). Amsterdam: North-Holland.

Roy, E.A., & Square, P.A. (1994). Neuropsychology of movement sequencing disorders and apraxia. In D.W. Zaidel (Ed.), *Neuropsychology* (pp. 185–214). San Diego: Academic Press.

Rubens, A.B. (1975). Aphasia with infarction in the region of the anterior cerebral territory. *Cortex, 11,* 239–250.

Rubia, K., Overmeyer, Russell, T., Brammer, M., Bullmore, E., Williams, S., Simmons, A., Andrew, C., & Sharma, T. (2000). *The functional localization of response inhibition: A cross-task conjunction approach.* Abstract, Cognitive Neuroscience Society annual meeting programme 2000: A supplement of the *Journal of Cognitive Neuroscience* (p. 113). Dartmouth College, Hanover, USA.

Rubin, D.C., & Wallace, W.T. (1989). Rhyme and reason: Analyses of dual retrieval cues. *Journal of Experimental Psychology: Learning, Memory and Cognition, 15,* 698–709.

Rueckert, L., & Grafman, J. (1998). Sustained attention deficits in patients with lesions of posterior cortex. *Neuropsychologia, 36,* 653–660.

Ruff, C.B., Trinkaus, E., & Holliday, T.W. (1997). Body mass and encephalization in pleistocene *Homo. Nature, 387,* 173–176.

Rugg, M.D., Fletcher, P.C., Chua, P.M., & Dolan, R.J. (1999). The role of the prefrontal cortex in recognition memory and memory for source: An fMRI study. *Neuroimage, 10,* 520–529.

Rutherford, W.H. (1989). Post concussion symptoms: Relationship to acute neurological indices, individual differences, and circumstance of injury. In H.S. Levin, H.M. Eisenberg, & A.L. Benton (Eds.), *Mild head injury* (Ch. 14, pp. 217–229). New York: Oxford University Press.

Rypma, B., & D'Esposito, M. (1999). The roles of prefrontal brain regions in components of working memory: Effects of memory load and individual differences. *Proceedings of the National Academy of Sciences USA, 96,* 6558–6563.

Sacks, O. (1985). The man who tilted: Jurgensen sees what must be done. *Science, 25* (3), 16–19.

Sacks, O. (1986). *The man who mistook his wife for a hat.* London: Pan Books.

Sacks, O., & Wasserman, R. (1987). The painter who became colour blind. *New York Review of Books, 34,* 25–33.

Safer, D.J. (2000). Are stimulants overprescribed for youths with ADHD? *Annals of Clinical Psychiatry, 12,* 55–62.

Saffran, E.M., Berndt, R.S., & Schwartz, M.F. (1989). The quantitative analysis of agrammatic production: Procedure and data. *Brain and Language, 37,* 440–479.

Saffran, E.M., & Martin, N. (1990). Neuropsychological evidence for lexical involvement in short-term memory. In G. Vallar & T. Shallice (Eds.), *Neuropsychological impairments of short-term memory.* Cambridge UK: Cambridge University Press.

Saffran, E.M., Schwartz, M.F., & Marin, O.S.M. (1980a). Evidence from aphasia: Isolating the components of a production model. In B. Butterworth (Ed.), *Language production,* Vol 1 (pp. 145–166). London: Academic Press.

Saffran, E.M., Schwartz, M.F., & Marin, O.S.M. (1980b). The word order problem in agrammatism. II. Production. *Brain and Language, 10.* 249–262.

Sahakian, B.J., Owen, A.M., Morant, N.J., Eagger, S.A., Boddington, S., Crayton, L., Crockford, H.A., Crooks, M., Hill, K., & Levy, R. (1993) Further analysis of the cognitive effects of tetrahydroaminoacridine (THA) in Alzheimer's disease: Assessment of attentional and mnemonic function using CANTAB. *Psychopharmacology* (Berlin), *110* (4), 395–401.

Sakata, H., Shibutani, H., Ito, Y., & Tsurugai, K. (1986). Parietal cortical neurons responding to rotary movements in space. *Experimental Brain Research, 61,* 658–663.

Salamé, P., & Baddeley, A.D. (1982). Disruption of memory by unattended speech: Implications for the structure of working memory. *Journal of Verbal Learning and Verbal Behaviour, 21,* 150–164.

Sanders, S.K., & Shekhar, A. (1995). Regulation of anxiety by GABAA receptors in the rat amygdala. *Pharmacology, Biochemistry and Behavior, 52,* 701–706.

Sandson, J., & Albert, M. (1984). Varieties of perseveration. *Neuropsychologia, 22,* 715–732.

Sandstom, N.J., Kaufman, J., & Huettal, S.A. (1998). Males and females use different distal cues in a virtual environment navigation task. *Brain Research and Cognitive Brain Research, 6,* 351–360.

Sartori, G., & Job, R. (1988). The oyster with four legs: A neuropsychological study on the interaction of visual and semantic information. *Cognitive Neuropsychology, 5,* 105–132.

Sartori, G., Miozzo, M., & Job, R. (1993). Category specific naming impairments? Yes. *Quarterly Journal of Experimental Psychology, 46* (A), 489–504.

Sass, K.J., Sass, A., Westerveld, M., et al. (1992). Specificity in the correlation of verbal memory and hippocampal neuron loss: Dissociation of memory, language and verbal intellectual ability. *Journal of Clinical and Experimental Neuropsychology, 14,* 662–672.

Saver, J.L., & Damasio, A.R. (1991). Preserved access and processing of social knowledge in a patient with acquired sociopathy due to ventromedial damage frontal damage. *Neuropsychologia, 29,* 1241–1249.

Sawaguchi, T., & Goldman-Rakic, P.S. (1991). D1 dopamine receptors in prefrontal cortex: Involvement in working memory. *Science, 22* (251), 947–950.

Sax, D.S., O'Donnell, B., Butter, N., Nenzer, L., Montgomery, K., & Kayne, H. (1983). Computed tomographic, neurologic, and neuropsychological correlates of Huntington's disease. *International Journal of Neuroscience, 18,* 21–36.

Sbordone, R.J. (1987). A conceptual model of neuropsychologically-based cognitive rehabilitation. In J.M. Williams & C.J. Long (Eds.), *The rehabilitation of cognitive disabilities* (pp. 3–27). New York: Plenum Press.

Scalaidhe, S.P., Rodman, H.R., Albright, T.D., & Gross, C.G. (1997). The effects of combined superior temporal polysensory area and frontal eye field lesions on eye movements in the macaque monkey. *Behavioural Brain Research, 84,* 31–46.

Schachter, S., & Singer, J.E. (1962) Cognitive, social and physiological determinants of emotional state. *Psychological Review, 69,* 379–399.

Schacter, D.L. (1987). Implicit memory: History and current status. *Journal of Experimental Psychology: Learning, Memory and Cognition, 13,* 501–518.

Schacter, D.L. (1995). Implicit memory: A new frontier for cognitive neuroscience. In M.S. Gazzaniga (Ed.), *The cognitive neurosciences* (pp. 815–824). Cambridge, MA: MIT Press.

Schacter, D.L. (1997). The cognitive neuroscience of memory: Perspectives from neuroimaging research. *Philosophical Transactions of the Royal Society London, Series B, 352,* 1689–1697.

Schacter, D.L., Buckner, R.L., & Koutstaal, W. (1998). Memory, consciousness and neuroimaging. *Philosophical Transactions of the Royal Society London, Series B, 353,*1861–1878.

Schacter, D.L., Buckner, R.L., Koutstaal, W., Dale, A.M., & Rosen, B.R. (1997). Late onset of anterior prefrontal activity during true and false recognition: An event related fMRI study. *Neuroimage, 6* (4), 259–269.

Schacter, D.L., & Church, B. (1992). Auditory priming: Implicit and explicit memory for words and voices. *Journal of Experimental Psychology: Learning Memory and Cognition, 18,* 915–936.

Schacter, D.L., & Crovitz, H.F. (1977). Memory functioning after closed head injury: A review of quantitative research. *Cortex, 13,* 150–176.

Schacter, D.L., & Graf, P. (1986). Effects of elaborative processing on implicit and explicit memory for new associations. *Journal of Experimental Psychology: Learning, Memory and Cognition, 12,* 432–444.

Schacter, D.L., McGlynn, S.M., Milberg, W.P., & Church, B.A. (1993). Spared priming despite impaired comprehension: Implicit memory in a case of word-meaning deafness. *Neuropsychology, 7,* 107–118.

Schacter, D.L., Rich, S.A., & Stampp, M.S. (1985). Remediation of memory disorders: Evaluation of the spaced-retrieval technique. *Journal of Clinical and Experimental Neuropsychology, 7,* 79–96.

Schaffer, C.E., Davidson, R.J., & Saron, C. (1983). Frontal and parietal EEG asymmetries in depressed and non-depressed subjects. *Biological Psychiatry, 18,* 753–762.

Schall, J.D., Hanes, D.P., Thompson, K.G., & King, D.J. (1995). Saccade target selection in frontal eye field of macaque. I. Visual and premovement activation. *Journal of Neuroscience, 15* (10), 6905–6918.

Schaltenbrand, G. (1965). The effects of stereotactic surgery electrical stimulation in the depth of the brain. *Brain, 88,* 835–840.

Schaltenbrand, G. (1975). The effects of speech and language of stereotactical stimulation in the thalamus and corpus callosum. *Brain and Language, 2,* 70–77.

Scheibel, A.B., Fried, I., Paul, L., Forsythe, A., Tomiyasu, U. et al. (1985). Differentiating aspects of the human speech cortex: A quantitative Golgi study. In D.F. Benson & E. Zaidel (Eds.), *The dual brain.* New York: Guilford Press.

Schneider, S.J. (1976). Selective attention in schizophrenia. *Journal of Abnormal Psychology, 89,* 109–114.

Schneider, W. (1993). Varieties of working memory as seen in biology and in connectionist/control architectures. *Memory and Cognition, 21,* 184–192.

Schneider, W., & Detweiler, M. (1988). The role of practice in dual-task performance towards workload modelling in a convectional/control architecture. *Human Factors, 30,* 539–566.

Schneider, W., & Shiffrin, R.M. (1977). Controlled and automatic human information processing. 1.

Detection, search, and attention. *Psychological Review, 84,* 1–66.

Schultz, G., & Melzack, R. (1991). The Charles Bonnet syndrome: "Phantom visual images". *Perception, 20,* 809–825.

Schwab, R.S., Chafetz, M.E., & Walker, S. (1954). Control of two simultaneous voluntary motor acts in normals and in Parkinsonism. *Archives of Neurology and Psychiatry, Chicago, 72,* 591–598.

Schwartz, M.F. (1995). Re-examining the role of the executive functions in routine actions. *Annals of the New York Academy of Sciences, 769,* 321–336.

Schwartz, M.F., Fink, R.B., & Saffran, E.M. (1995). The modular treatment of agrammatism. In R.S. Berndt & C.C. Mitchum (Eds.), *Cognitive neuropsychological approaches to the treatment of language disorders* (pp. 93–127). Hove, UK: Lawrence Erlbaum Associates Ltd.

Schwartz, M.F., Lineberger, M.C., Saffran, E.M., & Pate (1987). *Language and Cognitive Processing, 2,* 85–113.

Schwartz, M.F., Reed, E.S., Montgomery, C., Palmer, C., & Mayer, M.H. (1991). The quantitive description of of action disorganisation after brain damage. *Cognitive Neuropsychology, 8,* 381–414.

Schwartz, M.F., Saffran, E.M., & Marin, O.S.M. (1980a). Fractionating the reading process in dementia: Evidence for word specific print-to-sound associations. In M. Coltheart, K.E. Patterson, & J.C. Marshall (Eds.), *Deep dyslexia.* London: Routledge & Kegan Paul.

Schwartz, M.F., Saffran, E.M., & Marin, O.S.M. (1980b). The word order problem in agrammatism. I. Comprehension. *Brain and Language, 10,* 249–262.

Seitz, D., Widmann, U., Seeger, U., Nagele, T., Klose, U., Mann K., & Grodd, W. (1999). Localized proton magnetic resonance spectroscopy of the cerebellum in detoxifying alcoholics. *Alcoholism, Clinical and Experimental Research, 23,* 158–163.

Selemon, L.D., & Goldman-Rakic, P.S. (1988). Common cortical and subcortical target areas of the dorsolateral prefrontal and posterior parietal cortices in the rhesus monkeys: evidence for distributed neural networks subserving spatially guided behaviour. *Journal of Neuroscience, 8,* 4049–4068.

Semendeferi, K., & Damasio, H. (2000). The brain and its main anatomical subdivisions in living hominids using MRI. *Journal of Human Evolution, 38,* 317–332.

Semendeferi, K., Damasio, H., Frank, R., & Van Hoesen, G.W. (1997). The evolution of the frontal lobes:

A volumetric analysis based on three-dimensional reconstructions of magnetic resonance scans of human and ape brains. *Journal of Human Evolution, 32,* 375–388.

Semmes, J. (1965). A non-tactual factor in astereognosis. *Neuropsychologia, 3,* 295–315.

Semmes, J. (1968). Hemispheric specialization: A possible clue to mechanism. *Neuropsychologia, 6,* 11–26.

Semmes, J., Weinstein S., Ghent, L., & Teuber, H.L. (1955). Spatial orientation after brain injury in man following analysis by location of lesion. *Journal of Psychology, 39,* 227–244.

Semmes, J., Weinstein S., Ghent, L., & Teuber, H.L. (1963). Correlates of impaired orientation in personal and extrapersonal space. *Brain, 86,* 747–772.

Sengpiel, F. (2000). An alternative view of perceptual rivalry. *Current Biology, 29* (10), R482–485.

Serle, J.R. (1998). How to study consciousness scientifically. *Philosophical Transactions of the Royal Society London, Series B, 353,* 1935–1942.

Shah, P., & Miyake, A. (1996). The separability of working memory resources for spatial thinking and language processing: An indiviual differences approach. *Journal of Experimental Psychology: General, 125,* 4–27.

Shaikh, M.B., Lu, C.L., MacGregor, M., & Siegel, A. (1991). Dopaminergic regulation of quiet biting attack behaviour in the cat. *Brain Research Bulletin, 27,* 725–730.

Shallice, T. (1981). Phonological agraphia and the lexical route in writing. *Brain, 104,* 413–429.

Shallice, T. (1982). Specific impairments of planning. *Philosophical Transactions of the Royal Society of London, Series B, 298,* 199–209.

Shallice, T. (1988a). *From neuropsychology to mental structure.* Cambridge, UK: Cambridge University Press.

Shallice, T. (1988b). Specialisation within the semantic system. *Cognitive Neuropsychology, 5,* 133–142.

Shallice, T., & Burgess, P.W. (1991a). Deficits in strategy application following frontal lobe damage in man. *Brain, 114* (2) 727–740.

Shallice, T., & Burgess, P.W. (1991b). Higher order cognitive impairments in man. In H.S. Levin, H.M. Eisenberg, & A.L. Benton (Eds.), *Frontal lobe function and dysfunction* (pp. 125–139). Oxford: Oxford University Press.

Shallice, T., & Burgess, P.W. (1996). The domain of supervisory processes and temporal organisation of behaviour. *Philosophical Transaction of the Royal Society London, Series B, 351,* 1405–1412.

Shallice, T., & Burgess, P.W. (1998). In A.C. Roberts, T.W. Robbins, & L. Weiskrantz (Eds.), The prefrontal cortex and cognitive functions (Ch. 8, 100–117). New York: Oxford University Press.

Shallice, T., & Evans, M.E. (1978). The involvement of the frontal lobes in cognitive estimation. *Cortex, 14,* 294–303.

Shallice, T., Fletcher, P., Frith, C.D., Grasby, P., Frackowiak, R.S., & Dolan, R.J. (1994). Brain regions associated with acquisition and retrieval of verbal episodic memory. *Nature, 14* (368), 633–635.

Shallice, T., & Warrington, E.K. (1977). Auditory verbal short-term memory impairment and spontaneous speech. *Brain and Language, 4,* 479–491.

Sharpe, M., Hawton, K., House, A., Molyneux, A., Sandercock, P., Bamford, J., & Warlow, C. (1990). Mood disorders in long-term survivors of stroke: Associations with brain lesion location and volume. *Psychological Medicine, 20,* 815–828.

Sheinberg, D.L., & Logothetis, N.K. (1997). The role of temporal cortical areas in perceptual organization. *Proceedings of the National Academy of Sciences USA, 94,* 3408–3413.

Shelton, P.A., Bowers, D., Duara, R., & Heilman, K.M. (1994). Apperceptive visual agnosia: A case study. *Brain and Cognition, 25,* 1–23.

Shepard, R.N. (1967). Recognition memory for words, sentences and pictures. *Journal of Verbal Learning and Verbal Behaviour, 6,* 156–163.

Shergill, S.S., Murray, R.M., & McGuire, P.K. (1998). Auditory hallucinations: A review of psychological treatments. *Schizophrenia Research, 32,* 137–150.

Sheridan, J., & Humphreys, G.W. (1993). A verbal–semantic category-specific recognition impairment. *Cognitive Neuropsychology, 10,* 143–184.

Sherman, A.G., Shaw, T.G., & Gliddon, H. (1994). Emotional behaviour as an agenda in neuropsychological evaluation. *Neuropsychology Review, 4,* 45–69.

Shiel, A., Wilson, B., Horn, S., Watson, M., & McLellan, L. (1993). Can patients in coma following traumatic head injury learn simple tasks? *Neuropsychological Rehabilitation, 3,* 161–175.

Shiffrin, R.M., & Schneider, W. (1977). Controlled and automatic human information processing. II. Perceptual learning, automatic attending, and a general theory. *Psychological Review, 84,* 127–190.

Shimamura, A.P., Berry, J.M., Mangels, J.A., Rusting, C.L., et al. (1995). Memory and cognitive abilities in university professors: Evidence for successful aging. *Psychological Science, 6,* 271–277.

Shimamura, A.P., Janowsky, J.S., & Squire, L.R. (1991). Memory for the temporal order of events in patients with frontal lobe lesions and amnesic patients. *Neuropsychologia, 28,* 803–813.

Shimamura, A.P., Jernigan, T.L., & Squire, L.R. (1988). Korsakoff syndrome with radiological (CT) findings and neuropsychological correlation. *Journal of Neuroscience, 8,* 4400–4410.

Shipp, S., de Jong, B.M., Zihl, J. et al. (1994). The brain activity related to residual motion of vision in a patient with bilateral lesions of V5. *Brain. 117,* 1023–1038.

Shipp, S., & Zeki, S. (1995). Segregation and convergence of specialised pathways in the macaque monkey visual cortex. *Journal of Anatomy, 187,* 547–562.

Shulman, H.G. (1971). Similarity effects in short-term memory. *Psychological Bulletin, 75,* 399–415.

Sidtis, J., Volpe, B., Holtzman, J., Wilson,D., & Gazzaniga, M. (1981). Cognitive interaction and staged callosal section: Evidence of transfer of semantic activation. *Science, 212,* 344–346.

Siegal, A., & Edinger, H.M. (1983). Role of the limbic system in hypothalamically elicited attack behaviour. *Neuroscience and Biobehavioral Reviews, 7,* 395–407.

Signoret, J.L.P., Castaigne, F., L'hermitte, R., Abelanet, R., & Lavorel, P. (1984). Rediscovery of Lebirgne's brain: Anatomical description with CT scan. *Brain and Language, 22,* 303–319.

Silbersweig, D.A., & Stern, E. (1998). Towards a functional neuroanatomy of conscious perception and its modulation by volition: Implications of human auditory neuroimaging studies. *Philosophical Transactions of the Royal Society London, Series B, 353,* 1883–1888.

Silverman, I.E., Grossman, M., Galetta, S.L., Liu, G.T., Rosenquist, A.C., & Alavi, A. (1995). Understanding human visual cortex: The role of functional imaging. *Neuropsychiatry, Neurology and Behavioural Neurology, 1,* 241–254.

Simmons, N.N. (1990). Conduction aphasia. In L.L. La Pointe (Ed.), *Aphasia and related neurogenic language disorders* (Ch. 3, 54–77). New York. Thieme.

Simon, H.A. (1974). How big is a chunk? *Science, 183,* 482–488.

Singer, W. (1977). Control of thalamic transmission by corticofugal and ascending reticular pathways in the visual system. *Physiological Review, 57,* 386–420.

Sinyor, D., Jacques, P., Kaloupek, Becker, R., Goldenberg, M., & Coopersmith, H. (1986). Poststroke depression and lesion location: An attempted replication, *Brain, 109*, 537–546.

Sirigu, A., Cohen, L., Zalla, T., Pradat-Diehl, P., Van Eeckhout, P., Grafman, J., & Agid, Y. (1998). Distinct frontal regions for processing sentence syntax and story grammar. *Cortex, 34*, 771–778.

Sirigu, A., Zalla, T., Pillon, B., Graffman, J., Dubois, B., & Agid, Y. (1995). Planning and script analysis following prefrontal lobe lesions. *Annals of the New York Academy of Sciences, 769*, 277–288.

Small, M., Cowey, A., & Ellis, S. (1994). How lateralised is visuo-spatial neglect? *Neuropsychologia, 32*, 449–464.

Smith, A. (1973). Symbol Digit Modalities Test. Los Angeles: Western Psychological Services.

Smith, E.E., & Jonides, J. (1997). Working memory: A view from neuroimaging. *Cognitive Psychology, 33*, 5–42.

Smith, M.L., & Milner, B. (1984). Differential effects of frontal lobe lesions on cognitive stimulation and spatial memory. *Neuropsychologia, 22*, 697–705.

Snowden, J.S., Crauford, D., & Neary, D. (1995). Loss of awareness of involuntary movements in Huntington's disease. (Abstract). *Journal of the International Neuropsychological Society, 1*, 211.

Snowden, J.S., Goulding, P.J., & Neary, D. (1989). Semantic dementia: A form of circumscribed cerebral atrophy. *Behavioural Neurology, 2*, 167–182.

Snowden, J.S., Griffiths, H., & Neary, D. (1994). Semantic dementia: Autobiographical contribution to preservation of meaning. *Cognitive Neuropsychology, 11*, 265–288.

Snowden, J.S., Griffiths, H.L., & Neary, D. (1999). The impact of autobiographical experience on meaning: Reply to Graham, Lambon Ralph, and Hodges. *Cognitive Neuropsychology, 16*, 673–687.

Sohlberg, M.M., White, O., Evans, E., & Mateer, C. (1992). Background and initial case studies into the effects of prospective memory training. *Brain Injury, 11*, 129–138.

Solms, M., Turnbull, O.H., Kaplan-Solms, K., & Miller, P. (1998). Rotated drawing: The range of performance and anatomical correlates in a series of 16 patients. *Brain and Cognition, 38*, 358–368.

Spearman,C. (1927). *The abilities of man*. New York: Macmillan.

Sperry, R.W. (1964). The great cerebral commissure. *Scientific American, 210*, 45–52.

Sperry, R.W. (1974). Lateral specialization in the surgically separated hemispheres. In F.O. Schmitt & F.G. Worden (Eds.), *The neurosciences: 3rd study program* (pp.5–19). Cambridge, MA: MIT Press.

Sperry, R.W. (1984a). Consciousness, personal identity and the divided brain. *Neuropsychologia, 22*, 661–673.

Sperry, R.W. (1984b). Corpus section for seizure control: Rationale and review of experimental and clinical data. *Cleveland Clinic, 51*, 319–332.

Sperry, R.W., Zaidel, E., & Zaidel, D. (1979). Self recognition and social awareness in the deconnected minor hemisphere. *Neuropsychologia, 17*, 153–166.

Spikman, J.M., Van Zomeran, A.H., & Deelman, B.G. (1996). Deficits of attention after closed-head injury: Slowness only? *Journal of Clinical and Experimental Neuropsychology, 18*, 755–767.

Spillane, J.D. (1947). *Nutritional disorders of the nervous system*. Edinburgh: Livingstone.

Spitzer, M., Kwong, K.K., Kennedy, W., Rosen, B.R., & Belliveau, J.W. (1995). Category specific brain activation in fMRI during picture naming. *NeuroReport, 6*, 2109–2112.

Squire, L. (1992). Memory and the hippocampus: A synthesis from findings with rats, monkeys, and humans. *Psychological Review, 99*, 195–231.

Squire, L.R., Amaral, D.G., Zola-Morgan, S., Kritchevsky, M., & Press, G. (1989). Description of brain injury in the amnesic patient NA based on magnetic resonance imaging. *Experimental Neurology, 105*, 23–35.

Squire, L.R., & Frambach, M. (1990). Cognitive skill learning in amnesia. *Psychobiology, 18*, 109–117.

Squire, L.R., Slater, P.C., & Chace, P.M. (1975). Retrograde amnesia: Temporal gradient in very long term memory following electroconvulsive therapy. *Science, 187*, 77–79.

Squire, L.R., & Zola, S.M. (1997). Amnesia, memory and brain systems. *Philosophical Transactions of the Royal Society London, Series B, 352*, 1663–1675.

Stanhope, N., Guinram, E., & Kopelman, M.D. (1998). Frequency judgements of abstract designs by patients with diencephalic, temporal lobe and frontal lesions. *Neuropsychologia, 36*, 1367–1385.

Starkstein, S.E., Boston, J.D., & Robinson, R.G. (1988). Mechanisms of mania after brain injury. *Journal of Nervous and Mental Disease, 176*, 87–99.

Starkstein, S.E., Cohen, B.S., Federoff, P., Parikh, R.M. et al. (1990). Relationship between anxiety disorders and depressive disorders in patients with cerebrovascular injury. *Archives of General Psychiatry, 47*, 246–251.

Starkstein, S.E., Federoff, J.P., Price, T.R., Leiguarda, R., & Robinson, R.G. (1991). Apathy following cerebrovascular lesions. *Stroke, 24*, 1625–1630.

Starkstein, S.E., Federoff, J.-P., Price, T.R., & Leiguarda, R.C. et al. (1994). Neuropsychological and neuroradiologic correlates of emotional prosody comprehension. *Neurology, 44*, 515–522

Starkstein, S.E., Migliorelli, R., Teson, A., Petracca, G., Chemerinsky, E., Manes, F., & Leiguarda, R. (1995). Prevalence and clinical correlates of pathological affective display in Alzheimer's disease. *Journal of Neurology, Neurosurgery and Psychiatry, 59*, 55–60.

Starkstein, S.E., & Robinson, R.G. (1991). The role of the frontal lobes in affective disorders following stroke. In H.S. Levin, H.M. Eisenberg, & A. Benton (Eds.), *Frontal lobe function and dysfunction* (Ch. 15). Oxford: Oxford University Press.

Starkstein, S.E., Robinson, R.G., Berthier, M.L., Parikh, R.M., & Price, T.R. (1988a). Differential mood changes following basal ganglia vs. thalamic lesions. *Archives of Neurology, 45*, 725–730.

Starkstein, S.E., Robinson, R.G., & Price, T.R. (1987). Comparison of cortical and subcortical lesions in the production of post-stroke mood disorders. *Brain, 110*, 1045–1059.

Stein BE. (1998). Neural mechanisms for synthesizing sensory information and producing adaptive behaviors. Experiemntal Brain Research. 1998, 123, 124–35..

Stein, D.G., & Glasier, M.M. (1992). An overview of developments in research on recovery from brain injury. In F.D. Rose & D.A. Johnson (Eds.), *Recovery from brain damage. Advances in Experimental Medicine and Biology, No. 325* (pp. 1–23). New York: Plenum Press.

Stelmach, G.E., Worringham, C.J., & Strand, E.A. (1986). Movement preparation in Parkinson's disease: The use of advance information. *Brain, 109*, 1179–1194.

Stemmer, B., Giroux, F., & Joanette, Y. (1994). Production and evaluation of requests by right hemisphere brain-damaged individuals. *Brain and Language, 47*, 1–31.

Stenhouse, L.M., Knight, R.G., Longmore, B.E., & Bishara, S.N. (1991). Long-term cognitive deficits in patients after surgery on aneurysms of the anterior communicating artery. *Journal of Neurology, Neurosurgery and Psychiatry, 54*, 909–914.

Stephan, H., & Andy, O.J. (1969). Quantitative comparative neuroanatomy of primates: An attempt at phylogenic interpretation. *Annals of the New York Academy of Sciences, 167*, 370–387.

Stern, C.E., Owen, A.M., Tracey, I., Look, R.B., & Rosen, B.R. (2000). Activity in ventrolateral and mid-dorsolateral prefrontal cortex during nonspatial visual working memory processing: evidence from functional magnetic resonance imaging. *Neuroimage, 11* (5), 392–399.

Sternberg, S. (1966). High-speed scanning in human memory. *Science, 153*, 652–654.

Stevens, J.R. (1999). Epilepsy, schizophrenia, and the extended amygdala. *Annals of the New York Academy of Sciences, 877*, 548–561.

Stewart, F., Parkin, A.J., & Hunkin, N.M. (1992). Naming impairments following recovery from herpes simplex encephalitis: Category specific? *Quarterly Journal of Experimental Psychology, 44* (A), 261–284.

Stewart, J., & Kolb, B. (1988). The effects of neonatal gonadectomy and prenatal stress on cortical thickness and asymmetry in rats. *Behavioral and Neural Biology, 49*, 344–360.

Stoerig, P., & Cowey, A. (1997). Blindsight in man and monkey. *Brain, 120* (3), 535–559.

Stone, S.P., Wilson, B., Wroot, A., Halligan, P.W., Lange, L.S., Marshall, J.C., & Greenwood, R.J. (1991). The assessment of visuo-spatial neglect after stroke. *Journal of Neurology, Neurosurgery and Psychiatry, 54*, 345–350.

Stone, V.E., Nisenson, L., Eliassen, J.C., & Gazzaniga, M.S. (1996). Left hemisphere representations of emotional facial expressions. *Neuropsychologia, 34*, 23–26.

Strauss, E., Risser, A., & Jones, M.W. (1982). Fear responses in patients with epilepsy. *Neurology, 39*, 626–630.

Stroop, J.R. (1935). Studies of interference in serial verbal reactions. *Journal of Experimental Psychology, 18*, 643–662.

Stuss, D.T. (1991). Disturbance of self-awareness of deficit after frontal system damage. In G.P. Prigatano & D.L. Schacter (Eds.), *Awareness of deficit after brain injury* (pp. 63–83). Oxford: Oxford University Press.

Stuss, D.T., Alexander, M.P., Palumbo, C.L., Buckle, L., Sayer, L., & Pogue, J. (1994). Organizational strategies of patients with unilateral or bilateral frontal lobe injury in word list learning tasks. *Neuropsychology, 8*, 355–373.

Stuss, D.T., & Benson, F.D. (1984). Neuropsychological studies of the frontal lobes. *Psychological Bulletin, 95*, 3–28.

Stuss, D.T., & Benson, F.D. (1986). Control of cognition and memory. In E. Perecman (Ed.), *The frontal lobes revisited* (pp. 141–154). Hillsdale, NJ: Lawrence Erlbaum Associates Ltd.

Stuss, D.T., Eskes, G.A., & Foster, J.K. (1994). Experimental neuropsychological studies of frontal lobe functions. In F. Biller & J. Graman (Eds.), *Handbook of neuropsychology* (Vol. 9, pp. 149–185). New York: Elsevier Science.

Stuss, D.T., Gow, C.A., & Hetherington, C.R. (1992). No longer Gage: Frontal lobe dysfunction and emotional changes. *Journal of Consulting and Clinical Psychology, 60,* 349–359.

Stuss, D.T., Kaplan, E.D., Benson, D.F., Weir, W.S., Chiulli, S., & Sarazin, F.F. (1982). Evidence of the involvement of the orbito frontal cortex in memory functions: An interference effect. *Journal of Comparative and Physiological Psychology, 96,* 913–925.

Stuss, D.T., Levine, B., Alexander, M.P., Hong, J., Palumbo, C., Hamer, L., Murphy, K.J., & Izukawa, D. (2000). Wisconsin card sorting test performance in patients with focal frontal and posterior brain damage: Effects of lesion location and test structure on separable cognitive processes. *Neuropsychologia, 38,* 388–402.

Stuss, D.T., Shallice, T, Alexander, M.P., & Picton, T.W. (1995). A multidisciplinary approach to anterior attentional function. *Annals of the New York Academy of Sciences, 769,* 191–211.

Suberi, M., & McKeever, W. (1977). Differential right hemisphere memory storage of emotional and nonemotional faces. *Neuropsychologia, 15,* 757–768.

Sunderland, A., Harris, J.E., & Gleave, J. (1984). Memory failures in everyday life following severe head injury. *Journal of Clinical Neuropsychology, 6* (2), 127–142.

Suresh P.A., & Sebastian, S. (2000). Developmental Gerstmann's syndrome: A distinct clinical entity of learning disabilities. *Pediatric Neurology, 22,* 267–278.

Szeszko, P.R., Robinson, D., Alvir, J.M., Bilder, R.M., Lencz T. et al. (1999). Orbital frontal and amygdala volume reductions in obsessive-compulsive disorder. *Archives of General Psychiatry, 56,* 913–919.

Takahashi, N., Kawamura, M., Hirayama, K., Shiota, J., & Isono, O. (1995). Prosopagnosia: A clinical and anatomical study of four patients. *Cortex, 31,* 317–329.

Takamatsu, K., Yamamoto, M., Yamano, T., & Ohno, F. (1990). A case of amnestic syndrome due to right thalamic infarction. *Japanese Journal of Medicine, 29,* 301–304.

Takayama, Y., Sugishita, M., Akiguchi, I., & Kimura, J. (1994). Isolated acalculia due to left parietal lesion. *Archives of Neurology, 51,* 286–291.

Talland, G.A. (1965). *Deranged memory.* New York: Academic Press.

Tanaka, Y. (1997). Amnesia following damage to the mammillary bodies. *Neurology, 48,* 160–165.

Tanji, J. (1996). New concepts of the supplementary motor area. *Current Opinion in Neurobiology, 6,* 782–787.

Taylor, D.C., & Marsh, S. (1979). The influence of sex and side of operation on personality questionnaire responses after temporal lobectomy. In J. Gruzelier & P. Flor-Henry (Eds.), *Hemisphere asymmetry's of function in psychopathology.* New York: Elsevier.

Taylor, J. (Ed.) (1933). *Selected writings of John Hughlings Jackson,* (Vols. 1 and 2), London: Hodder.

Teasdale, G., & Jennett, B. (1976). Assessment and prognosis of coma after head injury. *Acta Neurochirurgica (Wien), 34,* 45–55.

Teicher, M.H., Anderson, C.M., Polcari, A., Glod, C.A., Maas, L.C., & Renshaw, P.F. (2000). Functional deficits in basal ganglia of children with attention-deficit/hyperactivity disorder shown with functional magnetic resonance imaging relaxometry. *National Medicine, 6,* 470–473.

Tempini, M.L., Price, C.J., Josephs, O., Vandenberghe, R., Cappa, S.F., Kapur, N., & Frackowiak, R.S. (1998). The neural systems sustaining face and proper-name processing. *Brain, 121,* 2103–2118.

Tenenbaum, G., Tehan, G., Stewart, G., & Christensen, S. (1999). Recalling a floor routine: The effects of skill and age on memory for order. *Applied Cognitive Psychology, 13,* 101–123.

Teuber, H.L. (1964). The riddle of the frontal lobe function in man. In J.M. Warren & K. Akert (Eds.), *The frontal granular cortex and behaviour.* New York: McGraw-Hill.

Teuber, H.L. (1968). Alteration of perception and memory in man. In L. Weiskrantz (Ed.), *Analysis of behavioural change.* New York: Harper & Row.

Teuber, H.L. (1975). Effects of focal brain injury on human behaviour. In D.B. Tower (Ed.), *The nervous system: Vol. 2. The clinical neurosciences.* New York: Raven Press.

Teuber, H.L., & Mishkin, M. (1954). Judgement of visual and postural vertical orientation after brain injury. *Journal of Psychology, 38,* 161–175.

Thach, W.T. (1998). Combination, complementarity and automatic control: A role for the cerebellum in learning and movement coordination. In G.R. Block & J.A. Goode (Eds.), *Sensory guidance of movements: Novartis symposium foundation* (Vol. 218, pp. 219–232). Chichester, UK: Wiley.

Thoene, A.I.T., & Glisky, E.L. (1995). Learning of

name–face associations in memory impaired patients: A comparison of different training procedures. *Journal of the International Neuropsychological Society, 1,* 29–38.

Thompson, P.D., Berardelli, A., Rothwell, J.C., Day, B.L., Dick, J.P., Benecke, R., & Marsden, C.D. (1988). The coexistence of bradykinesia and chorea in Huntington's disease and its implications for theories of basal ganglia control of movement. *Brain, 111* (2), 223–244 .

Thompson. R. (1985). *The brain: An introduction to neural science.* New York: W.H. Freeman.

Tissot, R., Mounin, G., & L'hermitte, F. (1973). *L'Agrammatisme.* Paris: Dessart.

Tobias, P.V. (1995). The brain of the first hominids. In J.-P. Changeux & J. Chavaillon (Eds.), *Origins of the human brain.* Oxford: Clarendon Press.

Tonkonogy, J.M. (1986). *Vascular aphasia.* Cambridge, MA: Bradford Books.

Tranel, D. (1994). "Acquired sociopathy": The development of sociopathic behaviour following brain damage. *Progress in Experimental Personality and Psychopathology Research, 17,* 285–311.

Tranel, D., Anderson, S.W., & Benton, A.L. (1994). Development of the concept of "executive function" and its relationship to the frontal lobes. *Handbook of Neuropsychology, 9,* 125–148.

Tranel, D., & Damasio, A.R. (1985). Knowledge without awareness: An automatic index of facial recognition by prosopagnosics. *Science, 228,* 1453–1454.

Tranel, D., & Hyman, B.T. (1990). Neuropsychological correlates of bilateral amygdala damage. *Archives of Neurology, 47,* 349–355.

Treisman, A.M. (1964). Monitoring and storage of irrelevant messages in selective attention. *Journal of Verbal Learning and Verbal Behaviour, 3,* 449–459.

Treisman, A.M. (1998). Feature binding, attention and object perception. *Philosophical Transactions of the Royal Society London, Series B, 353,* 1295–1306.

Treisman, A.M., & Gelade, G. (1980). A feature-integration theory of attention. *Cognitive Psychology, 12,* 97–136.

Trenerry, M.R., Jack Jr, C.R., Ivnik, R.J. et al. (1993). MRI hippocampal volumes and memory function before and after temporal lobectomy. *Neurology, 43,* 1800–1805.

Troyer, A.K., Moscovitch, M., & Winocur, G. (1997). Clustering and switching as two components of verbal fluency: Evidence from younger and older healthy adults. *Neuropsychology, 11,* 138–146.

Troyer, A.K., Moscovitch, M., Winocur, G., Alexander,

M.P., & Stuss, D. (1998). Clustering and switching on verbal fluency: The effects of focal frontal- and temporal-lobe lesions. *Neuropsychologia, 36,* 499–504.

Tsal, Y. (1983). Movement of attention across the visual field. *Journal of Experimental Psychology: Human Perception and Performance, 9,* 523–530.

Tulving, E. (1972). Episodic and semantic memory. In E. Tulving & W. Donaldson (Eds.), *Organisation of memory* (pp. 37–74). New York: Wiley.

Tulving, E. (1983). *Elements of episodic memory.* Oxford: Clarendon Press.

Tulving, E., Kapur, S., & Craik, F.I.M. et al. (1994). Hemispheric encoding/retrieval asymmetry in episodic memory: Positron emission tomography findings. *Proceedings of the National Academy of Sciences USA, 91,* 2012–2015.

Turnbull, O.H, Beschin, N., & Della Sala, S. (1996). Agnosia for objects orientation: Implications for theories of object recognition. *Neuropsychologia, 35,* 153–163.

Turnbull, O.H., Carey, D.P., & McCarthy, R.A. (1997). The neuropsychology of object constancy. *Journal of the International Neuropsychological Society, 3,* 288–298.

Turvey, M.T., Brick, P., & Osborn, J. (1970). Proactive interference in short-term memory as a function of prior-item retention interval. *Quarterly Journal of Experimental Psychology, 22,* 142–147.

Tzeng, O.J.L. (1973). Positive recency effects in delayed free recall. *Journal of Verbal Learning and Verbal Behaviour, 12,* 436–439.

Ullman, S. (1998). Three-dimensional object recognition based on a combination of views. *Cognition, 67,* 21–44.

Vacanti, F.X., & Ames A., III (1984). Mild hypothermia and Mg^{++} protect against irreversible damage during CNS ischemia. *Stroke, 15,* 695–698.

Vaernet, K., & Marsden, A. (1970). Stereotaxic amygdalectomy and basofrontal tractotomy in psychotics with aggressive behaviour. *Journal of Neurosurgery and Psychiatry, 33,* 858–867.

Vaidya, C.J., Austin, G., Kirkorian, G., Ridlehuber, H.W., Desmond, J.E., Glover, G.H., & Gabrieli, J.D. (1998). Selective effects of methylphenidate in attention deficit hyperactivity disorder: A functional magnetic resonance study. *Proceedings of the National Academy of Sciences USA, 95,* 14494–14499.

Vakil, E., Hyphen, D., & Blackstone, H. (1992). Total amount learned versus learning rate of verbal and non-verbal information in differentiating left from right brain injured patients. *Archives of Clinical Neuropsychology, 7,* 111–120.

Valenstein, E.S. (1986). Therapeutic exuberance: A double-edged sword. In A. Harrington (Ed.), *So human a brain: Knowledge and values in the neurosciences* (pp. 159–178). Boston: Birkhauser.

Valenstein, E.S. (1990). The prefrontal area and psychosurgery. *Progress in Brain Research, 85,* 539–554.

Valenstein, E.S., Cox, V.C., & Kakolewski, J.W. (1970). Reexamination of the role of the hypothalamus in motivation. *Psychology Review, 77,* 16–31.

Vallar, G. (1993). The anatomical basis of spatial hemineglect in humans. In I.H. Robertson & J.C. Marshall (Eds.), *Unilateral neglect: clinical and experimental studies* (pp. 27–53). Hove, U.K.: Lawrence Erlbaum Associates Ltd.

Vallar, G., & Baddeley, A.D. (1984). Phonological short-term store, phonological processing and sentence comprehension: A neuropsychological case study. *Cognitive Neuropsychology, 4,* 417–438

Vallar, G., & Papagno, C. (1995a). Neuropsychological impairments of short-term memory. In A.D. Baddeley, B.A. Wilson, & F.N. Watts (Eds.), *Handbook of memory disorders* (pp. 135–166). Chichester, UK: Wiley.

Vallar, G., & Papagno, C. (1995b). To learn or not to learn: Vocabulary in foreign languages and the problem with phonological memory. In R. Campbell & M.A. Conway (Eds.), *Broken memories: Case studies in memory impairment* (Ch. 20, pp. 285–301). Oxford: Blackwell.

Vallar, G., Papagno, C., & Baddeley, A.D. (1991). Long-term recency effects and phonological short-term memory: A neuropsychological case study. *Cortex, 27,* 323–326.

Vallar, G., & Perani, D. (1986). The anatomy of unilateral neglect after right hemisphere stroke lesions: A clinical CT/scan correlation study in man. *Neuropsychologia, 24,* 609–622.

Van Buren, J.M., Li, C.L., & Ojemann, G.A. (1966). The fronto-striatal arrest response in man. *Electroencephalography and Clinical Neurophysiology, 21,* 114–130.

Van Buren, J.M. (1966). Evidence regarding the more precise localization of the frontal–caudate arrest response in man. *Journal of Neurosurgery, 20,* 416–417.

Van Hoesen, G.W., Augustinack, J.C., & Redman, S.J. (1999). Ventromedial temporal lobe pathology in dementia, brain trauma, and schizophrenia. *Annals of the New York Academy of Sciences, 877,* 575–594.

Vanier, M., & Caplan, D. (1985). CT correlates of surface dyslexia. In K.E. Patterson, Coltheart M. & J.C. Marshall (Eds.), *Surface dyslexia* (pp. 93–127). Hillsdale, NJ: Lawrence Erlbaum Associates Ltd.

Vanier, M., & Caplan, D. (1990). CT scan correlates of agrammatism. In L. Menn & L. Obler (Eds.), *Agrammatic aphasia* (pp. 97–114). Amsterdam: Benjamins.

Van Lancker, D. (1997). Rags to riches: Our increasing appreciation of cognitive and communicative abilities of the human right cerebral hemisphere. *Brain and Language, 57,* 1–11.

Van Lawick-Goodall, J. (1971). *In the shadow of man.* Glasgow: William Collins.

Vargha-Khadem, F., Carr, L.J., Isaacs, E. Brett, E. Adamas, C., Mishkin, M. (1997). Onset of speech after left hemispherectomy in a nine-year old boy. *Brain, 120,* 159–162.

Vargha-Khadem, F., Gadian, D.G., Watkins, K.E. et al. (1997). Differential effects of early hippocampal pathology on episodic and semantic memory. *Science, 277,* 376–380.

Vargha-Khadem, F., & Polkey, C.E. (1992). A review of cognitive outcome after hemidecortication in humans. *Advances in Experimental Medicine and Biology, 325,* 137–151.

Vendrell, P., Junque, C., Pujol, J., Jurado, M.A., Molet, J., & Graman, J. (1995). The role of prefrontal regions in the Stroop task. *Neuropsychologia, 33,* 341–352.

Verfaellie, M., Reiss, L., & Roth, H.L. (1995). Knowledge of new English vocabulary in amnesia: An examination of premorbidly acquired semantic memory. *Journal of the International Neuropsychological Society, 1,* 443–454.

Vicente, K.J., & Wang, J.H. (1998). An ecological theory of expertise effects in memory recall. *Psychological Review, 105,* 33–57.

Victor, M., Adams, R.D., & Collins, G.H. (1971). *The Wernicke–Korsakoff syndrome.* Philadelphia: F.A. Davis.

Victor, M., & Yakovlev, P.I. (1955). SS Korsakoff's psychic disorder in conjunction with peripheral neuritis: A translation of Korsakoff's original article with brief comments. *Neurology, 5,* 394–406.

Vidal, F., Bonnet, M., & Macar, F. (1995). Programming the duration of a motor sequence: Role of the primary supplementary motor areas in man. *Experimental Brain Research, 106.* 339–350.

Vilkki, J. (1992). Cognitive flexibility and mental programming after closed head injuries and anterior or posterior cerebral excisions. *Neuropsychologia, 30*, 807–814.

Vilkki, J., Ahola, K., Holst, P., Ohman, J., Servo, A., & Heiskanen, O. (1994). Prediction of psychosocial recovery after head injury with cognitive tests and neurobehavioural ratings. *Journal of Clinical and Experimental Neuropsychology, 16*, 325–338.

Visser, P.J., Krabbendam, L., Verhey, F.R.J., Hofman, P.A.M., Verhoeven, W.M.A., Tuinier, S., Wester, A., Van Den Berg, Y.W.M.M., Goessens, L.F.M., Van Der Werf, Y.D., & Jolles, J. (1999). Brain correlates of memory dysfunction in alcoholic Korsakoff's syndrome. *Journal of Neurology, Neurosurgery and Psychiatry, 67*, 774–778.

Von Cramon, D.Y. & Mathes-von Cramon, G. (1990). Frontal lobe dysfunctions in patients: Therapeutical approaches. In R.Ll. Wood & I. Fussey (Eds.), *Cognitive rehabilitation in perspective* (pp. 164–179). London: Taylor & Francis.

Von Cramon, D.Y., & Matthes-Von Cramon, G. (1994). Back to work with a chronic dysexecutive syndrome. *Neuropsychological Rehabilitation, 4*, 399–417.

Von Monakow, C. (1914). *Die Lokalisation in Grosshirn und der Abbau der Funktion durch Kortikale Herde.* Wiesbaden: J.F. Bergmann.

Wada, J.A., Clarke, R., & Hamm, A. (1975). Cerebral hemispheric asymmetry in humans. *Archives of Neurology, 32*, 239–246.

Wade, D.T., Wood, V.A., & Hewer, R.L. (1988). Recovery of cognitive function soon after stroke: A study of visual neglect, attention span and verbal recall. *Journal of Neurology, Neurosurgery and Psychiatry, 51*, 10–13.

Walker, D.F., Diforio, D., & Baum, K. (1999). Developmental neuropathology and the precursors of schizophrenia. *Acta Psychiatrica Scandinavica, 99* (Suppl. 395), 12–19.

Wall, P.D. (1980). Mechanisms of plasticity of connection following damage in the adult mammalian nervous systems. In P. Bach-Y-Rita (Ed.), *Recovery of function: Theoretical considerations for brain injury rehabilitation* (pp. 99–105). Bern: Hans Huber.

Wallace, M.T., Meredith, M.A., & Stein, B.E. (1998). Multisensory integration in the superior colliculus of the alert cat. *Journal of Neurophysiology, 80*, 1006–1010.

Walsh, K.W. (1985). Understanding brain damage. London: Churchill Livingstone.

Walsh, K.W. (1987). *Neuropsychology: A clinical approach.* Edinburgh: Churchill Livingstone.

Walsh, K.W. (1991). *Understanding brain damage* (2nd ed.). Edinburgh: Churchill Livingstone.

Wapner, W., Judd, T., & Gardner, H., (1978). Visual agnosia in an artist. *Cortex, 14*, 343–364.

Warrington, E.K., (1975). The selective impairment of semantic memory. *Quarterly Journal of Experimental Psychology, 27*, 187–199.

Warrington, E.K. (1982). The fractionation of arithmetical skills: A single case study. *Quarterly Journal of Experimental Psychology, 34A*, 31–51.

Warrington, E.K. (1984). The recognition memory test. Windsor, UK: NFER-Nelson.

Warrington, E.K. (1985). Agnosia: The impairment of object recognition. In P.J. Vinken, G.W. Bruyn, & H.L. Klawans (Eds.), *Handbook of clinical neurology* (pp. 333–349). Amsterdam: Elsevier Science.

Warrington, E.K. (1991). Right neglect dyslexia: A single case study. *Cognitive Neuropsychology, 8*, 193–212.

Warrington, E.K., Cipolotti, L., & McNeil, J. (1993). Attention dyslexia: A single case study. *Neuropsychologia, 31*, 871–886.

Warrington, E.K., & McCarthy, R.A. (1983). Category specific access dysphasia. *Brain, 106*, 859–878.

Warrington, E.K., & McCarthy, R.A. (1987). Categories of knowledge: Further fractionation and an attempted integration. *Brain, 110*, 1273–1296.

Warrington, E.K., & Rabin, P. (1971). Visual span of apprehension in patients with unilateral cerebral lesions. *Quarterly Journal of Experimental Psychology, 23*, 423–431.

Warrington, E.K., & Shallice, T. (1969). The selective impairment of auditory–verbal short-term memory. *Brain, 92*, 885–896.

Warrington, E.K., & Shallice, T. (1979). Semantic access dyslexia. *Brain, 102*, 43–69.

Warrington, E.K., & Shallice, T. (1984). Category-specific semantic impairments. *Brain, 107*, 829–854.

Warrington, E.K., & Taylor, A.M. (1973). The contribution of the right parietal lobe to visual object recognition. *Cortex, 9*, 152–164.

Warrington, E.K., & Weiskrantz, L. (1968). New method of testing long-term retention with special reference to amnesic patients. *Nature, 228*, 628–630.

Warrington, E.K., & Weiskrantz, L. (1970). Amnesic syndrome: Consolidation or retrieval? *Nature, 228*, 628–630.

Warrington, E.K., & Weiskrantz, L. (1978). Further analysis of the prior learning effect in amnesic patients. *Neuropsychologia, 16*, 169–176.

Watson, D.G., & Humphreys, G.W. (1997). Visual marking: Prioritizing selection for new objects by top-down attentional inhibition of old objects. *Psychological Review, 104*, 90–122.

Watson, R.T., Fleet, W.S., Gonzalez-Rothi, L., & Heilman, K.M. (1986). Apraxia and the supplementary motor area. *Archives of Neurology, 43*, 787–792.

Watson, R.T., Miller, B.D., & Heilman, K.M. (1977). Evoked potential in neglect. *Archives of Neurology, 34*, 224–227.

Watt, S., Jokel, R., & Behrmann, M. (1997). Surface dyslexia in nonfluent progressive aphasia. *Brain and Language, 56*, 211–233.

Waugh, N.C., & Norman, D.A. (1965). Primary memory. *Psychological Review, 72*, 89–104.

Wechsler, D. (1981). *Wechsler Adult Intelligence Scale—Revised manual.* New York: Psychological Corporation/Harcourt Brace Jovanovich.

Wechsler, D. (1987). *Wechsler Memory Scale—Revised manual.* Cleveland, OH: Psychological Corporation/Harcourt Brace Jovanovich.

Weekes, B. & Coltheart, M. (1996). Surface dyslexia and surface dysgraphia: Treatment studies and their theoretical implications. *Cognitive Neuropsychology, 13*, 277–315.

Weiler, M.A., Buchsbaum, M.S., Gillin, J.C., Tafalla, R., & Bunney, W.E. Jr (1990). Explorations in the relationship of dream sleep to schizophrenia using positron emission tomography. *Neuropsychobiology, 91* (23), 109–118.

Weinberger, D.R., Berman, K.F., & Zec, R.F. (1986). Physiologic dysfunction of dorsolateral prefrontal cortex in schizophrenia. *Archives of General Psychiatry, 43*, 114–124.

Weinstein, E.A. (1994). Hemineglect and extinction. *Neuropsychological Rehabilitation, 75*, 221–224.

Weintraub, S., & Mesulam, M.M. (1987). Right cerebral dominance in spatial attention: Further evidence based on ipsilateral neglect. *Archives of Neurology, 44*, 621–625.

Weiskrantz, L. (1956). Behavioural changes related to the destruction of the amygdaloid complex. *Journal of Comparative and Physiological Psychology, 49*, 381–391.

Weiskrantz, L. (1986). *Blindsight: A case study and implications.* Oxford: Oxford University Press.

Welsh, M.C., Pennington, B.F., Ozonoff, S., Rouse, B., & McCabe, E.R. (1990). Neuropsychology of early-treated phenylketonuria: Specific executive function deficits. *Child Development, 61*, 1697–1713.

Welt, L. (1888). Uber Charakterveranderungen des Menschen infolge von Lasionen des Stirnhirns. *Deutsche Archiv fur Klinische Medizin 42*, 339–390.

Wernicke, C. (1876). *Der Aphasiche Symptomenkomplex.* Breslau: Frank & Wegart.

Wernicke, C. (1881). *Lehrbuch der Gehirnkrankheiten.* Berlin: Theodor Fischer.

Wernicke, C. (1908). The symptom complex of aphasia. In E.D. Church (Ed.), *Modern clinical medicine: Diseases of the nervous system* (pp. 265–324). New York: Appleton-Century-Crofts.

West, R., & Craik, F.I.M. (1999). Age-related decline in prospective memory: The roles of cue accessibility and cue sensitivity. *Psychology and Aging, 14*, 264–272.

Wheeler, M.A., Stuss, D.T., & Tulving E. (1995). Frontal damage produces episodic memory impairment. *Journal of the International Society, 1*, 525–536.

Wheeler, M.A., Stuss, D.T., & Tulving, E. (1997), Toward a theory of episodic memory: The frontal lobes and autoenoetic consciousness. *Psychological Bulletin, 121*, 331–354.

Whitty, C.W.M., & Zangwill, O.L. (1977). *Traumatic amnesia.* In C.W.M. Whitty & O.L. Zangwill (Eds.), (pp. 118–136). *Amnesia.* London: Butterworths.

Wichman, T., & DeLong, M.R. (1996). Functional and pathophysiological models of the basal ganglia. *Current Opinion in Neurobiology, 6*, 751–758.

Wilkins, A.J., & Baddeley, A.D. (1978). Remembering to recall in everyday life: An approach to absent-mindedness. In M.M. Gruneberg, P.E. Morris, & R.N. Skyes (Eds.), *Practical aspects of memory* (pp. 27–34). London: Academic Press.

Wilkins, A.J., Shallice, T., & McCarthy, R. (1987). Frontal lesions and sustained attention. *Neuropsychologia, 25*, 359–365.

Will, B., & Kelche, C. (1992). Environmental approaches to recovery of function from brain damage: A review of animal studies (1981 to 1991). In F.D. Rose & D.A. Johnson (Eds.), *Recovery from brain damage* (pp. 79–103). New York: Plenum Press.

Willmes, K., & Poeck, K. (1993). To what extent can aphasic syndromes be localized? *Brain, 116*, 1527–1540.

Wilson, B.A. (1987). *Rehabilitation of memory.* New York: Guilford Press.

Wilson, B.A. (1989). Models of cognitive rehabilitation. In R.L. Wood & P. Eames (Eds.), *Models of brain injury rehabilitation* (pp. 117–141). London: Chapman & Hall.

Wilson, B.A. (1992a). Recovery and compensatory strategies in head injured memory impaired people several years after insult. *Journal of Neurology, Neurosurgery and Psychiatry, 55*, 177–180.

Wilson, B.A. (1992b). Rehabilitation and memory

Author index

Note: Page references in **bold** indicate a citation in boxed text or in the text accompanying a figure.

Subject index

Note: Page references in **bold** type refer to boxed text or to the text accompanying a figure.